13 JUN 88

TO   JESSIE ♡ ROSE
      OUR UP AND COMING
ACTRESS !! WE'RE VERY PROUD.
WE KNOW THAT YOU'LL BE
INCLUDED IN THE 1999 OR
2005 EDITION !!
      CONGRATS !!!.

WE LOVE AND ADMIRE YOU,
      DAD + PAM

The Illustrated Who's Who of the Cinema

The Illustrated Who's Who of the Cinema

Edited by Ann Lloyd and Graham Fuller
Consultant Editor: Arnold Desser

PORTLAND HOUSE
NEW YORK

Facing title-page: The filming of Beyond the Blue Horizon *(1942),
with Dorothy Lamour and Richard Denning, Alfred Fantell directing*

First published in Great Britain in 1983
by Orbis Publishing Limited, London

This 1987 edition published by Portland House, distributed by
Crown Publishers, Inc., 225 Park Avenue South, New York,
New York 10003. By arrangement with Macdonald & Co.
(Publishers) Ltd, London & Sydney.

A member of BPCC plc

Library of Congress Cataloging in Publication Data

The Illustrated who's who in cinema.

   Updated edition of: The Illustrated who's who of the cinema,
1983.
   1. Moving-pictures—Biography—Dictionaries.
I. Lloyd, Ann, 1945-   . II. Fuller, Graham.
III. Desser, Arnold.   IV. Illustrated who's who of the
cinema.   1983.
PN1998.A2148   1987   791.43'092'2 [B]   87–11701
ISBN 0-517-64419-3

Printed and bound in Hong Kong by Dai Nippon Printing
Company

h g f e d c b a

Many of the illustrations come from stills issued to publicize films made or
distributed by the following companies: Allied Artists, American
International Pictures, American Zoetrope, Amicus, Anglo Amalgamated,
The Archers, Artcraft, Associated British, Associated British Pictures/
Hammer, Avco Embassy, Boulting Brothers, British and Dominion, British
Lion, Samuel Bronston, CBS Television, Les Films du Carosse, Charles
Chaplin Corporation, Cineguild, Cinema Center, Cineriz, Columbia,
Cosmopolitan, Daiei; Defa, Dino De Laurentiis, Cecil B. DeMille, EMI, EON,
Ealing, Famous Players-Lasky, Film Polski, Film Trust, Films Jean Renoir,
Filmverlag der Autoren, Filmways, First National, Franco-London/Film
Indus-Rizzoli, Gainsborough Pictures, Gaumont, Gaumont British, Samuel
Goldwyn, Grand National, D. W. Griffith, Alberto Grimaldi, Hammer,
Hepworth Picture Plays, Werner Herzog/Munich/ZDF, Debra Hill/Avco
Embassy, Alfred Hitchcock, Howard Hughes, ITC, Jury, Stanley Kramer,
Alexander Korda, Lenfilm, Lira Films, London Films, Lucasfilm Ltd, Lux,
MCA, MGM, MTM(TV), Memorial, Mirisch, Monogram, Mosfilm, Mutual,
Nero Film, New South Wales Film Corporation, Nouvelle Editions/Artistes
Associés/Vidas, Orion, PEA/Artistes Associés/Artemis, Paramount, Gabriel
Pascal, Pathé, André Paulvé, Phalanx, Carlo Ponti, Producers Releasing
Corporation, RKO, Rank, Rastar, Readers Digest, Renown, Republic, Hal
Roach, Alexander Salkind, Sandrews, Sedif, David O. Selznick, Seven Arts,
Solax, Svensk Filmindustri/Svenska Filminstitutet, Titanus, Tobis, Toho,
Triangle, 20th Century-Fox, Two Cities Films, Ufa, United Artists, United
States Pictures, Universal, Vitagraph, Vitaphone, Hal B. Wallis, Walter
Wanger, Warner Brothers, Winkfast, Woodfall, Darryl F. Zanuck.

Acknowledgments: Arnold Desser, Greg Edwards/Flashbacks Archive, Joel
Finler Collection, Graham Fuller, Ronald Grant Archive, The Kobal
Collection, National Film Archive, Asta Nielsen Film Museum, Rex
Features, David Robinson, Bob Willoughby.

We apologize in advance for any unintentional omission or neglect and will
be pleased to insert the appropriate acknowledgments to companies or
individuals in any subsequent edition of this publication.

The editors would like to acknowledge the valuable contributions of Dan
Millar, David Kent, Lindsey Lowe, Susan Leonard, Liz Heasman, Jack
Lodge, David Robinson, Sally Hibbin, Patricia Coward, Alastair Dougall,
and also of Annette Brown, Beverley Byrne, Joel Finler, Ian J. Knight,
Marie-Jaqueline Lancaster, Elizabeth Lodge, Robert Murphy and Jennifer
Samson.
Designer: Ray Kirkpatrick

Introduction

The *Illustrated Who's Who of the Cinema* is both generous and critical. Selective it has to be. From the host of names that fill the history of the cinema some have had to be left on the cutting-room floor. Certain guidelines, however, have been followed. There has been the fullest treatment of the great decades, the Twenties and the Thirties, with the Forties not far behind. From those periods every significant name, we feel, is here. But one of the most exciting developments of recent years has been the growing realization that the earliest years of American cinema were not exclusively the Griffith years, and with the gradual emergence of long-forgotten films it has become clear that other notable talents were at work. So we find room for Lois Weber and John Collins, Albert Capellani and Sidney Olcott.

The Fifties and the Sixties are more straightforward. Time enough has passed for some kind of critical consensus. The films are well known and fresh in the mind, and in that area we remind the reader of delights he knows. Perhaps the hardest selection has been from the latest cinema. No one can yet say whose work will last. When it has seemed likely to us that a name will still be known in twenty or thirty years' time, that name is here.

It may seem that avant-garde and Underground cinema has been scurvily treated. So in a way it has, but this is an encyclopedia of mainstream cinema. The discoveries and the innovations of the early avant-garde have to a large degree entered that mainstream. To see whether that happens to their successors we have to wait. So Louis Delluc and Germaine Dulac are here, and Jean Vigo and Viking Eggeling with them, but Malcolm Le Grice and Stephen Dwoskin, Chantal Akerman and Curt McDowell are not.

These biographies are based upon facts compiled by a team of researchers but even within that framework it is possible to introduce an element of considered evaluation of the films and personalities. Although the balance of fact and opinion varies considerably, in general the more important the artist the more space has been given to critical comment. Considering that even the longest entries are relatively brief, a writer cannot argue a case; in dealing with a major talent, an Eisenstein or a Griffith, a Murnau or a Welles, he can only indicate what seems to him the essential man.

This work has also been a celebration of cinema. As a celebration, it is inevitably generous. An encyclopedia is no place for merciless dissection. The dull, the meretricious, the frankly dreadful, can be left on one side. Every

Buster Keaton co-directed and starred in Sherlock, Jr *(1924), said to be one of his best feature comedies, in which he played a movie projectionist who dreams of being a detective. The film is full of great gags, displays technical ingenuities when Keaton walks* into *the picture he is showing, and ends with a classic chase sequence with Keaton doing his own stunts on a motor cycle – and beating the train*

hard-working professional director or actor has toiled through his share of routine, but in almost every case there are one or two films that are better, sometimes a lot better, than routine; those are the moments which we have sought to bring to your attention.

A similar principle governs the filmographies. Complete lists would clearly be preferable, but would require perhaps three times the space. In most cases, therefore, we mark the beginning and end, if there is an end, of a career, and in between we cite the films that seem characteristic of the artist's best work. In the body of the work we use original titles for English-speaking films; *The Enforcer* (USA) and not *Murder Inc.* (GB); *A Matter of Life and Death* (GB) and not *Stairway to Heaven* (USA). With foreign-language films we use the title by which a film is generally known in the United States or Britain; *Hiroshima, Mon Amour*, therefore, but *Battleship Potemkin* (not *Bronenosets Potemkin*). The filmographies provide the alternatives.

The assiduous reader will find some seeming contradictions. One writer says of Ben Hecht, for example, that his excursions into direction were usually failures; but the entry on Charles MacArthur, who was Hecht's co-director, allows for warm praise of two of their films. With a work by many hands, there is the advantage of wider and more provocative interpretations.

At this time more than at any other, there is room for such a work as this. For although cinema audiences are tiny now, yet paradoxically more people see old films than they ever did. Until a generation or so ago, it was a long and painful, and often vain, struggle to fill the gaps and to recapture the past. Then came repertory cinemas, films on television and, later, video. In a year the viewer can manage what once took twenty. Perhaps some of the new ways of looking at films are a feeble imitation of the cinema experience, but they are here and fulfil a need. If a film survives, then somewhere, sometime, it will come our way. For audiences – and equally for single viewers – rediscovering old films and old directors, actors and actresses of perhaps half a century ago, this book may also fulfil a need. And its excellence of illustration and design speak for themselves.

For the film enthusiast this volume should prove a lasting delight. All the beloved character actors are here . . . Thomas Mitchell and Elisha Cook, John Carradine and Isabel Jewell and scores more. There is a wealth too of esoteric information in which the true enthusiast revels. What does the 'Q' stand for in Anna Q. Nilsson? Who is Herbert Schluderpacheru? Who was (five times) the World Champion All-round Cowboy? The answers are within. JACK LODGE

Left: Paul Newman relishing his role as director on Harry and Son *(1984)*

Abbreviations used in filmographies

add: additional; **anim:** animation; **art dir:** art direction; **ass:** assistant; **assoc:** associate; **chor:** choreography; **comm:** commentary; **cost:** costume; **dec:** decoration; **des:** design; **dial:** dialogue; **dial dir:** dialogue direction; **dir:** direction; **doc:** documentary; **ed:** film editing; **ep:** episode; **exec:** executive; **lyr:** lyrics; **mus:** music; **narr:** narration; **photo:** photography; **prod:** production; **prod co:** production company; **prod sup:** production supervision; **sc:** scenario/screenplay/script; **sd:** sound; **sp eff:** special effects; **sup:** supervision.

Standard abbreviations for countries are used. Most are self-evident but note: A = Austria; AUS = Australia; GER = Germany and West Germany after 1945; E.GER = East Germany.

Film dates

The dating of many films presents problems because production, completion and release may be separated by months or even years. We give here the date of the earliest known showing – whether private, trade or public – of the *completed* film.

A

ABBAS, Khwaja Ahmed

(b.1914). Director/screenwriter/producer. Born: Panipat, India

A fierce social critic of Indian society, Abbas was one of the first Indian directors to have his work screened internationally. His debut feature film, *Dharti Ke Lal*, dealt with the effects of the Bengal famine; his second major film, *Munna*, made by his own production company, broke with the traditions of Indian cinema by using neither songs nor stars in its story of an orphan – and was acclaimed internationally. He won the President's Gold Medal for his incisive *Shehar aur Sapna*. Also an active left-wing journalist and novelist, he has consistently campaigned for the nationalization of the Indian film industry.

Films include: 1949 Dharti Ke Lal (dir. only). '52 Awara (USA/GB: The Vagabond) (sc. only). '54 Munna (GB: The Lost Child). '57 Pardesi/Khozhdeniye za Tri Morya (prod; + co-dir) (IND-USSR). '59 Char Dil Char Rahen (GB: Four Faces of India). '64 Shehar aur Sapna (GB/USA: The City and the Dream). '70 Saat Hindustani. '72 Do Boond Pani. '81 The Naxalites.

ABBOTT & COSTELLO

Abbott, Bud (1895–1974). Actor. Born: William Abbott; Asbury Park, New Jersey, USA

Costello, Lou (1906–1959). Actor. Born: Louis Francis Cristillo; Paterson, New Jersey, USA

Costello, short and pudgy with a squeaky voice, and Abbott, the thin and smooth-talking straight man of the act, joined forces in 1931. By 1938 they were a powerful radio team; a year later they hit Broadway and, in 1940, their first film, *One Night in the Tropics*, was produced by Universal. The comic duo, famed for their backchat and slapstick, worked mainly at that studio and made numerous films before they split acrimoniously in 1957. For a time Abbott tried to go it alone without his partner but met with little success.

Films include: 1940 One Night in the Tropics/Caribbean Holiday. '41 Buck Privates (GB: Rookies); In the Navy; Keep 'em Flying. '42 Ride 'em Cowboy; Rio Rita; Pardon My Sarong; Who Done It? '43 It Ain't Hay (GB: Money for Jam). '44 In Society. '45 The Naughty Nineties. '46 The Time of Their Lives. '48 Abbott & Costello Meet Frankenstein (GB: Abbott & Costello Meet the Ghosts). '54 Abbott & Costello Meet the Keystone Kops.

ABEL, Walter

(b.1898). Actor. Born: St Paul, Minnesota, USA

After earning a reputation as a comedian at school, Abel entered the American Academy of Dramatic Arts and changed direction to become a straight stage actor in 1924. After a few very minor roles he signed with Paramount in 1932 and was subsequently cast as D'Artagnan in *The Three Musketeers*. He then built a lengthy career as a reliable and versatile character actor.

Films include: 1934 Liliom. '35 The Three Musketeers. '36 Fury. '38 Men With Wings. '40 Arise My Love. '42 Holiday Inn. '43 Star Spangled Rhythm; So Proudly We Hail. '44 Mr Skeffington; Follow the Boys. '46 The Kid From Brooklyn; 13 Rue Madeleine. '48 That Lady in Ermine. '53 Island in the Sky. '57 Raintree County. '74 Silent Night, Bloody Night.

ACRES, Birt

(1854–1918). Inventor. Born: Richmond, Virginia, USA

The son of English parents who were killed in the American Civil War, Acres returned to England where he worked in a photographic factory. In 1893 he demonstrated to the Royal Photographic Society his rapid-exposure plate camera which he used to produce a series of pictures of clouds lazily crossing the sky. A year later he devised a projector and movie camera and in 1895 patented the Kineopticon camera with which he photographed the *Oxford and Cambridge University Boat Race*, *The Derby* and the *Opening of the Kiel Canal* in Germany. He continued his experiments with film and sound techniques until the end of his life.

Films include: 1895 Hay-cart Crossing Hadley Green; Oxford and Cambridge University Boat Race; The Derby; Opening of the Kiel Canal; The Arrest of a Pickpocket; Charge of the Uhlans in the Tempelhof Feldt-Berlin. '96 Henley Regatta; The Opening of the Cardiff Exhibition by HRH the Prince of Wales; The Royal Wedding.

ADAMS, Edie

(b.1927). Actress. Born: Elizabeth Edith Enke; Kingston, Pennsylvania, USA

Trained as an opera singer at the Juilliard School of Music, Adams made her impact on the stage and in films as a comedienne. After winning a Miss US TV competition and singing in nightclubs, she made her first stage appearance on Broadway in *Wonderful Town*, and as a result she won the Donaldson Award for Best Debut. She was married to comedian Ernie Kovacs for seven years and made frequent guest appearances on his television show. Her first major film role was in the Doris Day – Rock Hudson comedy *Lover Come Back*. Adams appeared in many other films but remains best known for her role as Daisy Mae in *Li'l Abner* on Broadway.

Films: 1960 The Apartment. '61 Lover Come Back. '63 Call Me Bwana; It's a Mad, Mad, Mad, Mad World; Under the Yum Yum Tree; Love With the Proper Stranger. '64 The Best Man. '66 Made in Paris; The Oscar. '67 The Honey Pot. '79 Racquet.

Below, far left: Bud (left) and Lou in Bud Abbott and Lou Costello in Hollywood *(1945). Below left: Walter Abel in* Mr Skeffington. *Below: Edie Adams in* Love With the Proper Stranger, *with Steve McQueen*

ADAMS, Nick

(1931–1968). Actor. Born: Nick Adamschock; Nanticoke, Pennsylvania, USA

After hitch-hiking to California in 1950, Adams worked as a soda-jerk, cab driver and odd-job man. An appearance in a commercial with James Dean led to his screen debut in *Somebody Loves Me*. When he returned from fighting in Korea in 1953, he resumed his career and became part of the Fifties Hollywood set that included Dean, Natalie Wood and Robert Wagner. His major starring role was not, however, in films, but on television as the hero of *The Rebel* series. He died from a drug overdose.

Films: 1952 Somebody Loves Me. '55 Picnic; Mister Roberts; Rebel Without a Cause; Strange Lady in Town; I Died a Thousand Times. '56 A Strange Adventure; Our Miss Brooks; The Last Wagon. '57 Fury at Showdown. '58 No Time for Sergeants; Teacher's Pet. '59 Pillow Talk; The FBI Story. '62 Hell Is for Heroes; The Hook. '63 Twilight of Honor (GB: The Charge Is Murder). '64 The Young Lovers (GB: Chance Meeting). '65 Young Dillinger.

ADDAMS, Dawn

(1930–1985), Actress. Born: Felixstowe, Suffolk, England

Dawn Addams spent her childhood in India, where her serviceman father was stationed. On her return to England she studied acting at the Royal Academy of Dramatic Art (RADA) in London, and began her career in repertory theatre, touring round England and Europe. In 1950 she left for Hollywood and a screen test at MGM – which resulted in her first movie role, *Night Into Morning*, the following year. A glamorous actress, Addams was known in the Fifties more for her love life than for her films (although she was the leading lady in Charles Chaplin's *A King in New York*). She preceded Grace Kelly into the realm of actress-princesses by marrying Italian aristocrat Prince Vittorio Massimo in 1954. The remainder of her career was spent alternating between Hollywood and Europe.

Films include: 1951 Night Into Morning. '52 Hour of Thirteen; Plymouth Adventure. '53 The Moon Is Blue. '54 Khyber Patrol. '56 Il Tesoro di Rommell (IT) (GB/USA: Rommel's Treasure). '57 A King in New York. '60 The Two Faces of Dr Jekyll. '61 Die tausend Augen des Dr Mabuse (GER) (GB: Thousand Eyes of Dr Mabuse). '66 Where the Bullets Fly (GB).

ADDISON, John

(b.1920). Composer. Born: West Chobham, Surrey, England

Addison was educated at Wellington College and the Royal Academy of Music where he studied composition, oboe, clarinet and piano. During the Fifties he scored the music for several stage productions of new British playwrights, like John Osborne and others at the Royal Court Theatre. He began composing for film in the same period and he went on to score over fifty films including dramas, adventures and comedies. He has composed a musical revue (*Cranks*) and also a ballet (*Carte Blanche*).

Films include: 1948 The Guinea Pig. '50 Seven Days to Noon. '56 Private's Progress. '57 Lucky Jim. '59 Look Back in Anger. '60 The Entertainer. '61 A Taste of Honey. '62 The Loneliness of the Long-Distance Runner. '63 Tom Jones. '65 The Loved One (USA). '66 Torn Curtain (USA). '67 Smashing Time. '68 Charge of the Light Brigade. '77 A Bridge Too Far (USA).

ADJANI, Isabelle

(b.1955). Actress. Born: Paris, France

Born of a German mother and Turkish father, Isabelle Adjani made her first screen appearance, aged only 14, in *Le Petit Bougnat*. She has also worked in the theatre, acting in the Comédie Française in 1972. Adjani is renowned for her pale ethereal beauty, a quality *Time* magazine recognized when it granted her the accolade of a cover story in 1977. Her work for François Truffaut and other directors has received much critical acclaim, and in 1981 she was named Best Actress at the Cannes Film Festival for her performance in James Ivory's *Quartet*. The role with which she is probably most memorably identified is that of the besotted Adèle Hugo in Truffaut's *The Story of Adèle H.*

Films: 1970 Le Petit Bougnat. '72 Faustine et le Bel Eté (GB: Growing Up). '74 Le Gifle (FR-IT). '75 L'Histoire d'Adèle H. (USA/GB: The Story of Adèle H.). '76 Le Locataire (GB: The Tenant); Barocco. '77 Violette et François. '78 The Driver (USA). '79 Nosferatu: Phantom der Nacht (FR-GER) (USA/GB: Nosferatu, the Vampyre); Les Soeurs Brontë. '81 Possession (FR-GER); Clara et les Chics Types; Quartet (FR-GB). '82 C'Est Bien Parce Que Je T'Aime; Antonieta (FR-MEX-SP).

Right: Isabelle Adjani in Roman Polanski's The Tenant. *Below right: Dawn Addams. Below: Nick Adams –*

ADLER, Buddy

(1909–1960). Producer. Born: E. Maurice Adler; New York City, USA

Previously a short-story writer under the name Bradley Allen, Adler became a writer for MGM in 1936. He won an Academy Award for his story *Quicker 'n a Wink* (1940). After the war he went to Columbia as a producer and his production of *From Here to Eternity* won several Oscars. Adler shortly moved to 20th Century-Fox where, in 1956, he succeeded Darryl F. Zanuck as head of production. He steered the company through the next few difficult years in Hollywood, winning the Cecil B. DeMille Award in 1957 for outstanding contribution to the industry.

Films include: 1953 From Here to Eternity. '55 House of Bamboo; Love Is a Many Splendored Thing. '56 Anastasia (GB); Bus Stop; The Revolt of Mamie Stover. '57 Heaven Knows, Mr Allison; A Hatful of Rain. '58 Inn of the Sixth Happiness (GB); South Pacific.

ADLER, Luther

(1903–1984). Actor. Born: New York City, USA

Adler's acting was often better than the films he appeared in, a testament perhaps to his own extensive experience as a stage actor (he made his debut at the age of five) and to the nurturing influence of his well-known acting family. Being thick-lipped and heavy-set did not, however, invite

Below left: Luther Adler in Hoodlum Empire *(1952). Below, far left: John Agar (centre), Harry Carey Jr and Joanne Dru in* She Wore a Yellow Ribbon. *Left: Renée Adorée during the making of* Eternal Struggle *(1923)*

AGAR, John

(b.1921). Actor. Born: Chicago, Illinois, USA

Home on leave from the armed services in 1945, Agar met producer David O. Selznick who saw his potential as a screen actor and signed him to a long-term contract. He appeared in John Ford's *Fort Apache* with his wife, Shirley Temple (they were married in 1946), from whom he parted the following year. Agar was also in Ford's next cavalry Western, *She Wore a Yellow Ribbon*, and seemed set for a big career but instead drifted into routine action pictures. He retired from acting to become an insurance salesman but later returned to work in films and television.

Films include: 1948 Fort Apache. '49 She Wore a Yellow Ribbon; The Sands of Iwo Jima; The Woman on Pier Thirteen. '53 Man of Conflict. '55 The Lonesome Trail. '59 Invisible Invaders. '67 The St Valentine's Day Massacre. '76 King Kong.

AGEE, James

(1909–1955). Film critic/ screenwriter/novelist/poet. Born: Knoxville, Tennessee, USA

One of America's foremost film critics in the Forties, Agee was able to write for – as well as about – the movies. He was also a poet (he won a prize at Harvard), a novelist (*A Death in the Family* was awarded a Pulitzer Prize in 1958), and a non-fiction writer of the first order (*Let Us Now Praise Famous Men*). His scripts for *The African Queen* and *The Night of the Hunter* were both outstanding.

Films include: 1950 The Quiet One. '51 The African Queen (USA-GB). '55 The Night of the Hunter. '63 All the Way Home (novel basis only).

AGOSTINI, Philippe

(b.1910). Cinematographer/ director. Born: Paris, France

A technically excellent cinematographer renowned for his stark lighting, Agostini began his career in 1934 working as an assistant photographer, learning his craft from such experts as Georges Périnal and Armand Thirard. Having interrupted his career in order to be an army photographer during World War II, he made his first film as director of photography, *Homage à Bizet*, in 1943. He subsequently became a leader in his field – collaborating with such respected directors as Robert Bresson and Max Ophuls. Since 1953 he himself has worked as a director, but with only limited success.

Films include: 1939 Le Jour se Lève (ass. photo) (USA: Daybreak). '43 Les Anges du Péché. '45 Les Dames du Bois de Boulogne; Sylvie et le Fantôme (USA: Sylvie and the Phantom; GB: Sylvia and the Ghost). '46 Les Portes de la Nuit (USA/GB: Gates of the Night). '52 Le Plaisir. '55 Du Rififi Chez les Hommes (GB: Rififi). '61 Rencontres (dir).

film-directors to cast him as a nice guy – and so they didn't. Adler may have played Hitler more times than any other American actor. He was married to the actress Sylvia Sidney from 1938 to 1948.

Films include: 1949 Wake of the Red Witch; D.O.A. '51 The Desert Fox (GB: Rommel – Desert Fox). '54 The Miami Story. '59 The Last Angry Man. '66 Cast a Giant Shadow. '68 The Brotherhood.

ADORÉE, Renée

(1898–1933). Actress. Born: Jeanne de la Fonte; Lille, France

A trouper from infancy, Adorée spent her formative years touring Europe with circus performers and pantomime artistes. After World War I she developed her own dance act and travelled throughout France and England. In 1919 she left for America where, having caught the eye of a casting director, she was signed by Fox and made her first film a year later. Fame was by no means instant, and it was only after her performance in *The Big Parade* that she achieved stardom. A heavy work-load and a hectic personal life left her ill with tuberculosis in 1930. She was undeterred, however, and after coming out of hospital resumed her former life style. Three years later she was dead.

Films include: 1920 The Strongest. '24 A Man's Mate. '25 The Big Parade. '26 The Black Bird; La Bohème; The Exquisite Sinner. '28 Show People. '29 Tide of Empire; The Pagan. '30 Call of the Flesh.

ADRIAN, Gilbert

(1903–1959). Costume designer. Born: Adrian Adolph Greenberg; Naugatuck, Connecticut, USA

Appointed MGM's chief costume designer in 1927, Adrian was instrumental in the glamorizing of Greta Garbo, Norma Shearer and Jean Harlow. His biggest success, though, was the coat-hanger silhouette – the padded-shoulder look favoured by Joan Crawford in the Forties. He excelled in his use of light and dark tones and in creating elegantly designed evening dresses. Earlier in his career, after he came to Hollywood from the New York School for Applied and Fine Arts, he also created fashions for male stars, including Valentino. In 1942 Adrian left MGM and opened his own salon to service most of the major studios. He was married to Janet Gaynor.

Films include: 1930 Anna Christie; Madame Satan. '32 Grand Hotel. '33 Queen Christina. '36 Camille. '40 The Philadelphia Story. '41 Ziegfeld Girl. '42 Woman of the Year.

AGUTTER, Jenny

(b.1952). Actress. Born: Taunton, Somerset, England

Best known for her roles as young girls in films such as *The Railway Children* and *Walkabout*, Jenny Agutter made her first screen appearance aged 11 in *East of Sudan*. Unfortunately, as she has matured, she seems to have been cast more for her attractiveness than for the acting capabilities she showed in her earlier roles. In addition she has worked successfully in television and theatre – in 1971 she received an Emmy award for Best Supporting Actress in *The Snow Goose*, and in 1974 appeared on stage at the National Theatre.

Films include: 1964 East of Sudan. '68 Star! (USA). '70 The Railway Children. '71 Walkabout (AUS). '76 Logan's Run (USA); The Eagle Has Landed. '77 Equus. '79 The Riddle of the Sands. '81 An American Werewolf in London (USA).

AHERNE, Brian

(1902–1986). Actor. Born: Kings Norton, Worcestershire, England

A child actor in the theatre from the age of nine, Aherne achieved wider popularity in British silent films and went to the USA in 1931 to appear on Broadway. He moved on to Hollywood in 1933, playing romantic leads and becoming typecast as an upper-class English gentleman. He married Joan Fontaine in 1939, but they were divorced five years later. He then returned briefly to the stage, and eventually retired to Vevey in Switzerland, publishing his ironically-titled autobiography, *A Proper Job*, in 1969.

Films include: 1924 The Eleventh Commandment (GB). '28 Underground (GB). '33 The Constant Nymph (GB). '36 Sylvia Scarlett; Beloved Enemy. '37 The Great Garrick. '39 Juarez. '40 The Lady in Question. '46 The Locket. '52 I Confess.

AIMÉE, Anouk

(b.1932). Actress. Born: Françoise Sorya; Paris, France

A haughtily beautiful brunette. Anouk Aimée attended dancing lessons at the Opera of Marseilles followed by drama classes in Paris, thus making the contacts that enabled her to appear in her first film *La Maison Sous la Mer* (1947). Success came two years later when she was offered contracts in Britain and the USA as a result of her acting in *Les Amants de Vérone* (1949). She has made relatively few films, showing little interest in stardom during a career that possibly reached its peak when she worked with the director Claude Lelouch on *A Man and a Woman*. She was married to the actor Albert Finney from 1970 to 1978.

Films include: 1953 Le Rideau Cramoisi Short (GB: The Crimson Curtain). '58 Montparnasse 19 (FR-IT). '59 La Dolce Vita (IT). '61 Lola (FR-IT). '62 Sodoma e Gomorra (IT-USA) (USA/GB: Sodom and Gomorrah). '63 Otto e Mezzo (IT-FR) (USA/GB: 8½). '66 Un Homme et une Femme (GB: A Man and a Woman). '69 Justine (USA). '81 La Tragedia di un Uomo Ridicolo (IT) (USA: A Man's Tragedy; GB: Tragedy of a Ridiculous Man).

AKINS, Claude

(b.1918). Actor. Born: Nelson, Georgia, USA

Akins is tall and menacing, and often plays his parts with a pronounced and threatening Southern red-neck drawl – clearly not a man whose enemies would turn their backs on in a Western or a crime melodrama. Educated at Northwestern University near Chicago, Akins toured with various theatrical companies, making his Broadway debut in 1951. The next year he was in Hollywood for his first film *From Here to Eternity* – the beginning of a long and moderately successful career in film and television.

Films include: 1953 From Here to Eternity. '54 The Caine Mutiny. '58 The Defiant Ones. '59 Rio Bravo; Porgy and Bess. '60 Inherit the Wind. '62 Merrill's Marauders; How the West Was Won. '64 The Killers. '73 Battle for the Planet of the Apes.

ALBERINI, Filoteo

(1865–1937). Showman/inventor/director/producer. Born: Turin, Italy

In 1895, while working as an engineer at the Istituto Geografico Militare, Alberini patented a device for shooting, printing and developing films. He opened a cinema in Florence in 1901 and another in Rome in 1904, and also co-founded a production company which in 1906 became Cinès. While producing and sometimes directing, he continued his research, developing the Autostereoscopio, a steroscopic process, in 1911, and the Panoramica Alberini, one of the earliest attempts at creating a wide-screen film, in 1914. He was basically a showman – his inventions were technically crude, and filmmakers generally preferred French or German equivalents. In 1928 he continued his wide-screen experiments with Roy Hill, the British film engineer.

Films as producer include: 1905 La Presa di Roma (+dir); Terremoto in Calabria (doc). '06 La Malia dell'Oro; Viaggio di una Stella; L'Armonica Misterioso; La Pila Elettrica. '10 Lucrezia Borgia. '11 La Gerusalemme Liberata. '12 Quo Vadis? '22 Cirano di Bergerac.

ALBERS, Hans

(1892–1960). Actor. Born: Hamburg, Germany

After a few years with touring companies, Albers joined the Thalia Theatre in Hamburg. During World War I he served on both Eastern and Western fronts and was twice wounded. On several of his leaves he took bit parts in films. After the war he became active on the Berlin stage, and also appeared in a variety of film roles, making over a hundred movies before *The Blue Angel* really launched his screen career. Though much in demand in the cinema, he also continued in the theatre. He worked throughout the Nazi period but, since his wife Hansi Burg was Jewish, he avoided political involvement. In the postwar era his film appearances were few and unmemorable.

Films include: 1918 Der Mut zur Sünde. '20 Die Marquise von O; Der Falschspieler. '30 Der blaue Engel (English-language version: The Blue Angel, USA-GB, 1931); Der Greifer. '31 Bomben auf Monte Carlo (USA: The Bombardment of Monte Carlo). '32 Quick; FP 1 Antwortet nicht (GB: No Answer from FP 1). '34 Peer Gynt; Gold. '35 Varieté (GB: Vaudeville). '43 Münchhausen. '60 Kein Engel ist so rein.

Far left: Jenny Agutter in The Railway Children. Left: Anouk Aimée and Omar Sharif in The Appointment (1969). Below, far left: Brian Aherne in Sylvia Scarlett, with Katharine Hepburn. Below left: Claude Akins. Below: Hans Albers. Below right: Eddie Albert in The Heartbreak Kid. Bottom right: television M*A*S*H star Alan Alda. Bottom left: Lola Albright

ALBERT, Eddie

(b.1908). Actor. Born: Eddie Albert Heimberger; Rock Island, Illinois, USA

With the snuffly cheerfulness of a big bear slightly unsure of his welcome, and an occasional alternative line in creepy villains, Eddie Albert has been a useful supporting actor since the late Thirties. Before that he was a singer, at first to pay his way through college, and then on NBC radio. Joining the navy in 1942, he served in the South Pacific during the war. He married the actress Margo in 1945, starred with Eva Gabor in the television series Green Acres in the late Sixties, and won Oscar nominations as Best Supporting Actor for Roman Holiday and The Heartbreak Kid. He runs his own production company, making educational and industrial films.

Films include: 1938 Brother Rat. '40 A Dispatch From Reuters (GB: This Man

Reuter). '46 Strange Voyage. '47 Time Out of Mind. '51 You're in the Navy Now. '53 Roman Holiday. '55 Oklahoma!; I'll Cry Tomorrow. '56 The Teahouse of the August Moon. '57 The Sun Also Rises. '59 Beloved Infidel. '61 Madison Avenue. '62 The Longest Day. '65 Seven Women. '72 The Heartbreak Kid. '75 Hustle.

ALBRIGHT, Lola

(b.1925). Actress. Born: Akron, Ohio, USA

Following a dead-end job at a radio station, Lola Albright took up modelling in Chicago for the photographer Paul Hesse, which led to a contract with MGM and Warners. After a few small parts with MGM and Warners, she was given a leading role in Champion by the producer Stanley Kramer, which should have launched her to stardom. But her combination of blonde beauty and lively intelligence had strangely little appeal to other producers (except of Westerns) and she appeared in only a few worthwhile films, though she

won critical praise as a mature stripper in love with a teenager in A Cold Wind in August. Active in television since the late Fifties, she virtually retired from the big screen after 1968. She was married to the actor Jack Carson in the Fifties.

Films include: 1948 The Pirate. '49 Champion. '50 The Good Humor Man; Sierra Passage. '55 The Magnificent Matador (GB: The Brave and the Beautiful). '58 Oregon Passage. '61 A Cold Wind in August. '62 Kid Galahad. '66 Lord Love a Duck. '67 The Way West. '68 Where Were You When the Lights Went Out?

ALCOTT, John

(1931–1986). Cinematographer. Born: London, England

After studying photography at a Bournemouth college in the Forties, John Alcott joined Gainsborough at the Lime Grove studios in London's Shepherds Bush. Following National Service in the Royal Navy Film Unit, he became an assistant cameraman at Pinewood Studios, travelling to many foreign locations for such films as The Purple Plain (1955), A Town Like Alice and The Battle of the River Plate (both 1956). He freelanced in Germany and England, and worked on a few documentaries, before graduating to lighting cameraman for the model and exterior shots and the 'Dawn of Man' sequence in Stanley Kubrick's 2001: A Space Odyssey. He won an Oscar for another Kubrick production, Barry Lyndon.

Films include: 1968 2001: A Space Odyssey (add. photo. only). '71 A Clockwork Orange. '74 Little Malcolm and His Struggle Against the Eunuchs. '75 Overlord; Barry Lyndon. '77 The Disappearance (GB-CAN); March or Die. '78 Who Is Killing the Great Chefs of Europe? (USA-GER) (GB: Too Many Chefs). '80 The Shining. '81 Fort Apache, the Bronx (USA).

ALDA, Alan

(b.1936). Actor/writer/director. Born: New York City, USA

His father, Robert Alda, wanted him to be a doctor but he graduated from Fordham College, meanwhile getting acting experience, sometimes with his father, during college vacations. His work with an improvisational troupe led to television and Broadway. From 1972 Alda starred in the television comedy series M*A*S*H, for which he also occasionally wrote and directed. He won Emmys as Best Actor (Comedy Series) in 1974 and Best Writer (Comedy Series) in 1979. After the success of his political film The Seduction of Joe Tynan, Universal gave him a three-picture contract as writer-director and star, and in 1981 he made The Four Seasons.

Films include: 1963 Gone Are the Days (reissued as: The Man from COTTON). '68 The Extraordinary Seaman; Paper Lion. '69 Jenny. '70 The Moonshine War. '71 The Mephisto Waltz. '72 To Kill a Clown (GB) (USA: Choke Cherry Bay). '78 California Suite; Same Time Next Year. '79 The Seduction of Joe Tynan (+sc). '81 The Four Seasons (+dir;+sc).

ALDA, Robert

(1914–1986). Actor. Born: Alfonso Giuseppe Giovanni Roberto d'Abruzzo; New York City, USA

Robert Alda began his career as a singer on radio and in nightclubs, went into vaudeville in 1935 and in 1942 joined a touring unit putting on shows for the troops. He made his screen debut as George Gershwin in *Rhapsody in Blue*; but in general his screen career has been indifferent, his greater success being on the stage where he won the Antoinette Perry Theatrical Award and the Drama Critics' Award. He lived in Rome from the early Sixties, frequently appearing in Italian and European movies. He was also seen in many of the major American television series.

Films include: 1945 Rhapsody in Blue. '46 Cloak and Dagger; Cinderella Jones. '47 Nora Prentiss. '49 Homicide. '55 La Donna più Bella del Mondo (IT) (GB: Beautiful But Dangerous). '62 I Moschettieri del Mare (IT-FR). '67 The Devil's Hand. '69 The Girl Who Knew Too Much. '73 Le Serpent (FR-IT-GER) (GB: The Serpent; USA TV: Night Flight From Moscow). '76 La Casa dell'Esorcismo (IT) (GB: The House of Exorcism; I Will I Will . . . for Now.

ALDO, G.R.

(1902–1953). Cinematographer. Born: Aldo Graziati; Treviso, Italy

Aldo moved to France while still in his teens, becoming a stage actor and then a still photographer, in which capacity he worked on Jean Cocteau's *La Belle et la Bête*. He became a lighting cameraman and returned to Italy, working with such distinguished directors as Luchino Visconti, Orson Welles and Vittorio De Sica. His technical and artistic abilities were devoted to bringing out the specific qualities of real locations, without drawing attention to the cinematography itself. He had already demonstrated the same virtues in his use of colour before he was killed in a car crash while shooting Visconti's *Senso*, which Robert Krasker completed.

Films include: '45 La Belle et la Bête (still photo. only) (FR) (USA/GB: Beauty and the Beast). '48 La Terra Trema. '49 Les Derniers Jours de Pompéi/Gli Ultimi Giorni di Pompei (FR-IT) (USA: Sins of Pompeii); Cielo Sulla Palude (GB: Heaven Over the Marshes). '51 Miracolo a Milano (USA/GB: Miracle in Milan); Umberto D. '52 Othello (co-photo. only) '53 La Provinciale (GB: Wayward Wife); Stazione Termini (USA: Indiscretion of an American Wife; GB: Indiscretion). '54 Senso (co-photo) (GB: The Wanton Countess).

ALDRICH, Robert

(1918–1983). Director. Born: Cranston, Rhode Island, USA

Robert Aldrich was born into an illustrious family of politicians and businessmen. He started his career as a production clerk at RKO and rose to assistant director on films by Jean Renoir, Charles Chaplin, William Wellman, Lewis Milestone, Robert Rossen, Abraham Polonsky and Joseph Losey. He directed briefly in television before making his first

cinema film in 1953. Aldrich was frequently his own producer, but his output was uneven. He owned his own studio until four box-office flops in a row deprived him of it. His forceful talent found a niche in macho action movies, sometimes verging on self-parody, though he was evidently reluctant to be confined to this genre, as witness the Hollywood Gothic of *What Ever Happened to Baby Jane?*, for example.

Films include: 1953 Big Leaguer. '54 Vera Cruz. '55 Kiss Me Deadly. '56 Attack! '62 What Ever Happened to Baby Jane? '64 Hush . . . Hush, Sweet Charlotte. '67 The Dirty Dozen (USA-GB). '68 The Legend of Lylah Clare; The Killing of Sister George. '70 Too Late the Hero. '71 The Grissom Gang. '72 Ulzana's Raid. '73 The Emperor of the North Pole (GB: Emperor of the North). '74 The Longest Yard (GB: The Mean Machine). '75 Hustle. '77 Twilight's Last Gleaming (USA-GER) (reissued in GB as: Nuclear Countdown). '81 . . . All the Marbles (GB: The California Dolls).

ALEXANDROV, Grigori

(1903–1983). Director. Born: Grigori Mormonenko; Ekaterinburg, Russia

As a youth he wrote, directed and acted for theatres at the front in the Russian Civil War. He met Sergei M. Eisenstein in 1922 and he was his regular collaborator, in the Proletkult experimental theatre and then in films, for a decade, until the fiasco of the unfinished *Que Viva Mexico!* (which in his old age Alexandrov re-edited). As a solo director he began to make successful musical comedies, usually starring Lyubov Orlova, whom he married, and won international acclaim. He gained several honours and awards in the USSR and abroad, though his work in the post-war period was more conformist than in his adventurous youth when with Eisenstein and cameraman Eduard Tisse he formed a great creative triumvirate.

Films include: 1925 Stachka (ass. dir; + act) (GB: Strike); Bronenosets Potemkin (ass. dir; + act) (USA/GB: Battleship Potemkin). '27 Oktyabr (co-dir; + co-sc) (USA: Ten Days That Shook the World; GB: October). '28 Generalnaya Liniya/Staroye i Novoye (co-dir; + co-sc) (GB: The General Line/The Old and the New). '30 Romance Sentimentale (short) (dir. credited as co-dir). '31 Que Viva Mexico! (unfinished) (co-dir; + co-sc) (USA). '34 Vesolye Rebyata (+ co-sc) (USA: Jolly Fellows; GB: Jazz Comedy). '37 Volga-Volga (+ sc). '49 Vstrecha na Elbe (GB: Meeting on the Elbe). '52 Kompozitor Glinka (GB: Glinka – Man of Music). '60 Russkii Suvenir (Russian Souvenir).

ALEXEIEFF, Alexandre

(1901–1982). Animator. Born: Kazan, Russia

During the Twenties, Alexeieff studied painting in Paris, where he also developed an interest in theatre-set design, book illustration and engraving. In the Thirties he became involved in animated films, developing the 'pin screen' process by which thousands of pinheads are illuminated to produce shadowy images. From 1931 he and his wife, the animator Claire Parker, collaborated on many films. His major achievement was an animated interpretation of the composer Mussorgsky's 'Une Nuit Sur le Mont Chauve'. He has since become almost exclusively involved in advertising work, although he was widely praised for his animated prologue to Orson Welles' *Le Procès* (1962, *The Trial*).

Films include: 1933 Une Nuit Sur le Mont Chauve (USA/GB: Night on a Bare Mountain). '35 La Belle au Bois Dormant. '36 Ligner Werke (GER); Opta Empfangt (GER); Parade de Chapeaux; Le Trône de France; Franck Aroma (GER); La Crème Simon. '38 Les Vêtements Sigrand; Huilor; Eau d'Evian; Balatum; Les Fonderies Martin; Les Cigarettes Davro. '39 Cenpa; Le Gaz. '43 En Passant. '52 Masques. '54 Nocturne; Pure Beauté. '56 Bain D'x. '57 Cocinor; Anonyme. '62 Divertissement. '63 Le Nez.

ALLAN, Elizabeth

(b.1910). Actress. Born: Skegness, Lincolnshire, England

As the youngest of five children, Elizabeth Allan had to overcome parental disapproval of her decision to become an actress before taking up a scholarship at the Old Vic training school. After two years on the road with various repertory companies, she made her West End debut in *Michael and Mary*. Her aristocratic good looks and 'Englishness' set her aside to play pretty, genteel young women in the movies, and with the aid of her agent husband Bill O'Bryen, she signed for MGM and left for Hollywood in 1933. There she found immediate success in costume dramas such as *David Copperfield* and *Camille*, but after a few lean years in the mid-Thirties she returned to Britain. In 1951 she became a regular panellist on the BBC's *What's My Line?*

Films include: 1931 Alibi; Black Coffee; Michael and Mary. '32 Service for Ladies; Nine Till Six; The Lodger (USA: The Phantom Fiend); Down Our Street; Insult. '33 The Shadow; No Marriage Ties (USA); Ace of Aces (USA). '34 Java Head; Men in White (USA). '35 David Copperfield (USA); Mark of the Vampire (USA); A Tale of Two Cities (USA). '36 Camille (USA). '37 Michael Strogoff (USA) (GB: The Soldier and the Lady); Slave Ship (USA). '39 The Girl Who Forgot. '42 Went the Day Well? '51 No Highway. '52 Folly to be Wise. '53 Front Page Story.

ALLÉGRET, Marc

(1900–1973). Director. Born: Basle, Switzerland

Marc Allégret's movie career was launched after his film of his uncle André Gide's trip to the Congo was warmly received by public and critics alike. He then became assistant to the director Robert Florey, while continuing to produce his own shorts. After taking over from Florey on Le Blanc et Noir (1931), he became a director in his own right, concentrating on stylish melodramas – of which Fanny is his shining example. He worked with his artistes and was partially responsible for the discovery of such talents as Simone Simon, Jeanne Moreau and Brigitte Bardot.

Films include: 1926 Voyage au Congo. '31 La Petite Chocolatière. '32 Fanny. '34 Lac aux Dames. '35 Les Beaux Jours. '36 Les Amants Terribles. '37 La Dame de Malacca; Orage. '41 Parade en Sept Nuits. '48 Blanche Fury. '51 Blackmailed (GB). '52 Avec André Gide (GB: André Gide). '55 L'Amant de Lady Chatterley (USA/GB: Lady Chatterley's Lover). '56 En Effeuillant la Marguerite (GB: Mam'zelle Striptease).

ALLÉGRET, Yves

(b.1907). Director. Born: Paris, France

The younger brother of director Marc Allégret, Yves began his career by assisting his brother and Jean Renoir on several projects. But throughout the Thirties he confined his solo talents to the direction of shorts and work as an art director. For the duration of World War II, Yves Allégret took refuge in Nice where he came into his own as the director Yves Champlain. On his return to Paris he reverted to his real name and set about making sophisticated gangster-thrillers that were grounded in the American films noirs of the Forties, but which achieved a poetic quality and French atmosphere all of their own. Although still involved in the business, and up until the early Sixties averaging a film per year, he perhaps reached a creative peak in those films made with his short-time wife Simone Signoret between 1946 and 1949.

Films include: 1936 Vous N'Avez Rien à Déclarer? '42 Les Deux Timides (under pseudonym). '43 La Boîte aux Rêves. '48 Dédée d'Anvers; Une si Jolie Petite Plage (GB: Such a Pretty Little Beach). '50 Manèges (GB: The Wanton). '53 Les Orgueilleux (FR-MEX) (USA/GB: The Proud Ones). '54 Oasis (FR-GER). '62 Germinal (FR-IT). '66 Johnny Banco (FR-IT-GER).

ALLEN, Dede

(b.1925). Film editor. Born: Dorothea Carothers Allen; Cleveland, Ohio, USA

After being denied an entrée into the film business as a director – prejudice being rife against women film-makers – Dede Allen worked her way through the cutting room at Columbia, editing her first feature, Terror From the Year 5000, in 1958. Since then she has worked with such revered directors as Robert Wise, Arthur Penn, Elia Kazan and Robert Rossen.

Films include: 1958 Terror From the Year 5000 (GB: Cage of Doom). '59 Odds Against Tomorrow. '61 The Hustler. '63 America, America (GB: The Anatolian Smile). '67 Bonnie and Clyde. '68 Rachel, Rachel. '69 Alice's Restaurant. '70 Little Big Man. '72 Slaughterhouse 5. '73 Visions of Eight; Serpico. '75 Dog Day Afternoon; Night Moves. '76 The Missouri Breaks. '81 Reds.

Opposite page. Top: Robert Alda in Rhapsody in Blue. Bottom: Elizabeth Allan (centre) with Freddie Bartholomew and Jessie Ralph in David Copperfield. Below: How Green Was My Valley – Sarah Allgood and Roddy McDowall. Bottom: Woody Allen looking paranoid, obsessed and inept

ALLEN, Irwin

(b.1915). Producer/director/writer. Born: New York City, USA

After majoring in journalism and advertising at Columbia University, Irwin Allen went to Hollywood as the editor of Key magazine in 1938. The following year he began a one-hour radio show, and its success resulted in a Hollywood newspaper column. Determined to exhaust all media sources, he created the first television celebrity panel-show and then opened a literary agency. Eventually motion-picture packaging attracted his attention and became his overriding interest. All other commitments were forgotten with the setting up of his own Windsor Productions, and as a film-maker solely concerned with commercial viability – The Towering Inferno, The Poseidon Adventure – he has become a much sought-after producer-director. Other succesful ventures have been the television series Voyage to the Bottom of the Sea, Lost in Space, Swiss Family Robinson and The Time Tunnel.

Films include: 1951 A Girl in Every Port (prod. only). '53 The Sea Around Us. '54 Dangerous Mission (prod. only). '56 The Animal World. '57 The Story of Mankind. '59 The Big Circus (prod; +sc. only). '60 The Lost World. '72 The Poseidon Adventure (prod. only). '74 The Towering Inferno (co-dir; +prod. only). '78 The Swarm (dir; +prod. only). '79 Beyond the Poseidon Adventure (dir; +prod). '80 When Time Ran Out . . . (prod. only).

ALLEN, Woody

(b.1935). Screenwriter/director/actor. Born: Allen Stewart Konigsberg; New York City, USA

Allen began writing comedy material for New York newspapers while still at school. After graduating, he progressed to writing gags for TV comics, nightclub acts and Broadway revues. It wasn't until 1961 that he decided to use the material himself, and became a stand-up comic. Allen was working at the Blue Angel club in Manhattan when the movies 'found' him. He was asked to write the script for and feature in What's New, Pussycat? The film was a great success, and launched Allen as an actor. Four years later he made his directorial debut with Take the Money and Run. Since then he has continued to write, direct and star in his own films, which are usually comedies with a growing emphasis on paranoia, obsession, ineptitude and imagined inadequacy. In 1978 he won the Best Director Oscar for Annie Hall, which was also voted Best Picture and Best Original Screenplay. Interiors was an attempt at serious drama and bore similarities to the films of Ingmar Bergman, a director Allen much admires.

Films include: 1965 What's New. Pussycat? (sc; +act. only). '69 Take the Money and Run. '72 Play It Again Sam (sc. from own play; +act. only); Everything You Always Wanted to Know About Sex, But Were Afraid to Ask. '73 Sleeper. '75 Love and Death. '76 The Front (actor only). '77 Annie Hall. '78 Interiors (dir; +sc. only). '79 Manhattan. '80 Stardust Memories. '82 A Midsummer Night's Sex Comedy.

ALLGOOD, Sarah

(1883–1950). Actress. Born: Dublin, Eire

Considered by some to be Ireland's greatest actress, Allgood learned her art on the Dublin and London stage, where she received accolades from the poet W.B. Yeats and others. She moved to Hollywood in 1940, and became a naturalized American citizen in 1945. In her film work she is mainly remembered for her Irish character parts, such as the long-suffering wife and mother in Juno and the Paycock, and matronly roles like the Welsh Mrs Morgan in How Green Was My Valley.

Films include: 1926 The Lodger (GB). '29 Blackmail (GB). '30 Juno and the Paycock (GB). '38 Londonderry Air (GB). '41 How Green Was My Valley (USA); That Hamilton Woman! (USA) (GB: Lady Hamilton). '42 Roxie Hart (USA). '43 Jane Eyre (USA). '45 The Spiral Staircase (USA). '46 Cluny Brown (USA). '50 Sierra (USA).

ALLYSON, June

(b.1918). Actress. Born: Ella Geisman; New York City, USA

Injured in a childhood accident, Allyson decided to put her strict exercises to practical use after seeing a Fred Astaire film. Following a successful period on Broadway, she made several shorts, and was taken up by MGM. Her clean-cut, apple-pie charm and looks and friendly demeanour made her a natural light-romantic heroine in films like *Little Women*. Then she progressed to playing doting, supportive wives in *The Stratton Story* and *The Glenn Miller Story*. *The Shrike* was a bold but largely unsuccesful attempt to break this mould and cast her as a nag. Though her saccharine sweetness went out of fashion in the Sixties, she continued to work and had her own TV show for a period. She is the widow of actor Dick Powell.

Films include: 1943 Best Foot Forward. '44 Music for Millions. '46 Till the Clouds Roll By. '47 Good News. '49 Little Women; The Stratton Story. '50 The Reformer and the Redhead. '53 The Glenn Miller Story. '54 The Shrike; Executive Suite; Woman's World. '55 Strategic Air Command. '57 Interlude. '73 They Only Kill Their Masters.

ALMENDROS, Nestor

(b.1930). Cinematographer. Born: Barcelona, Spain

Taken to Cuba by his Loyalist father in his teens, Almendros studied literature and philosophy at Havana and then film at Centro Sperimentale in Rome. His first work was on shorts in Cuba and the USA, followed by an educational TV series in Paris where he met the French critic and film-maker Eric Rohmer. This led to highly regarded work with Rohmer, Barbet Schroeder and François Truffaut. Despite Almendros' disclaimer that he only undertakes such work for the money, he has become one of the most outstanding cameramen working today. In 1970 he won the National Society of Film Critics Best Photography Award, for *Ma Nuit Chez Maud* and *L'Enfant Sauvage*. He is particularly renowned for his stunning use of natural light in films like *Days of Heaven*.

Films include: 1967 La Collectionneuse (FR) (USA/GB: The Collector). '69 Ma Nuit Chez Maud (FR) (GB: My Night With Maud). '70 L'Enfant Sauvage (FR) (USA/GB: The Wild Child); Domicile Conjugal (FR-IT) (USA/GB: Bed and Board); Le Genou de Claire (FR) (GB: Claire's Knee). '71 Les Deux Anglaises et le Continent (FR) (USA: Two English Girls; GB Anne and Muriel). '72 La Vallée (USA/GB: The Valley – Obscured by Clouds); L'Amour, l'Après-midi (FR) (USA/GB: Love in the Afternoon). '74 Cockfighter/Born to Kill (USA). '75 L'Histoire d'Adèle H. (FR) (USA/GB: The Story of Adèle H.). '76 Maîtresse (FR); Die Marquise von O (GER-FR) (USA/GB: The Marquise of O). '77 L'Homme Qui Aimait les Femmes (USA: The Man Who Loved Love; GB: The Man Who Loved Women). '78 Days of Heaven (USA). '80 The Blue Lagoon (USA).

Below: June Allyson. Below right: Eddie Anderson in I Love a Bandleader *(1945). Below, far right: Broncho Billy Anderson (right). Far right: Leon Ames has* A Date With Judy *(1948) – and a youthful Elizabeth Taylor. Right: Don Ameche*

ALTMAN, Robert

(b.1925). Director/writer/producer. Born: Kansas City, Missouri, USA

Now one of the few American directors regarded as a genuine *auteur*, Altman was 45 with a history of minor features and TV work behind him when *M*A*S*H* brought him to the public eye and established his controversial reputation. It revealed his satirical eye for American ways of life, in this case in war, and a stylistic naturalism – a shift away from plot and an overlapping of dialogue. These preoccupations and methods are most obvious in *Nashville*, a rambling, multi-layered, humorous and almost plotless study of over twenty characters staying in or visiting the home of country-and-western music. His subsequent work has continued to divide critics, though *Buffalo Bill and the Indians . . . or Sitting Bull's History Lesson* was almost universally panned as being self-indulgent, over-long and pretentious. *Popeye* eccentrically – and expensively – re-created the character in a live-action format.

Films as director include: 1957 The James Dean Story (doc) (co-dir). '67 Countdown. '70 M*A*S*H; Brewster McCloud. '71 McCabe and Mrs Miller. '73 The Long Goodbye. '74 Thieves Like Us; California Split. '75 Nashville. '76 Buffalo Bill and the Indians . . . or Sitting Bull's History Lesson; Three Women. '78 A Wedding. '79 Quintet; A Perfect Couple. '80 Popeye. '82 Come Back to the Five and Dime, Jimmy Dean, Jimmy Dean.

ALWYN, William

(1905–1985). Composer. Born: Northampton, England

William Alwyn was a prolific English composer who had a distinguished career prior to his entry into films. A graduate of the Royal Academy of Music, he held the prestigious Collard Fellowship of Music from 1937 to 1940. *The Future's in the Air*, made in 1936, was the forerunner of over sixty films which he has scored. Initially he worked on documentaries, like Humphrey Jennings' *Fires Were Started*,

but he later progressed to drama and thrillers, such as *The Fallen Idol*. In 1940 he was elected an Honorary Freeman of the Musicians Company. Alwyn was awarded the CBE in 1978.

Films include: 1936 The Future's in the Air. **'43** Fires Were Started; Welcome to Britain. **'44** The Way Ahead. **'45** The Rake's Progress. **'47** Odd Man Out. **'48** The Fallen Idol. **'49** The History of Mr Polly. **'52** Mandy (USA: Crash of Silence). **'54** The Million Pound Note (USA: Man With a Million). **'58** A Night to Remember. **'62** Life for Ruth (USA: Walk in the Shadow).

AMBROSIO, Arturo

(1869–1960). Producer. Born: Turin, Italy

Arturo Ambrosio could be described as the father of the Italian film industry. His chosen career was that of an optician specializing in photographic equipment, but in 1904 he founded a film company with Roberto Omegna and produced the first Italian features in his Turin studios during the early years of the twentieth century. In 1911 the Tsar invited him to Russia, where Ambrosio set about the organization of Russian cinema. By 1912 he was back in Italy and had signed a contract for the exclusive screen rights to the poet Gabriele D'Annunzio's writings. After World War I he temporarily abandoned the cinema, returning as a major producer in 1939 and continuing to work after World War II. His legacy was Italian supremacy in epics during the silent era and the discovery of such talents as Duse and Novelli.

Films include: 1908 Cavalleria Infernale Gli Ultimi Giorni di Pompei/The Last Days of Pompeii. **'09** Tor di Quinti. **'19** Theodora. **'20** La Nave/The Ship.

AMECHE, Don

(b.1908). Actor. Born: Dominic Felix Amici; Kenosha, Wisconsin, USA

Don Ameche's pencil-thin moustache and slick good looks made him a natural romantic lead in the Thirties. After abandoning a career as a lawyer, Ameche established a reputation as a radio actor and a star of Broadway musicals before Hollywood took an interest and 20th Century-Fox signed him up. He specialized in light-hearted heroic characters in films like *The Three Musketeers*, or the leads in historical biographies such as *The Story of Alexander Graham Bell*, following which telephones were for a while known as 'Ameches' in America. After World War II his career in films declined, aggravated by miscasting, though he found some work in television, and still occasionally makes cameo appearances, also acting on stage.

Films include: 1936 Sins of Man; Ramona. **'38** In Old Chicago; Alexander's Ragtime Band. **'39** The Three Musketeers (GB: The Singing Musketeer); The Story of Alexander Graham Bell; Hollywood Cavalcade; Swanee River. **'40** Lillian Russell; Down Argentine Way. **'41** That Night in Rio. **'43** Heaven Can Wait. **'44** Greenwich Village. **'45** It's in the Bag (GB: The Fifth Chair).

AMES, Leon

(b.1903). Actor. Born: Leon Waycoff; Portland, Indiana, USA

Ames entered films after a long apprenticeship in amateur theatricals and broadway, making his screen debut in *The Murders in the Rue Morgue*. In Hollywood he played a wide variety of character parts, but is particularly remembered as a dapper man-about-town who always had money but seldom any apparent means of making it. Later in his career he extended this role into middle age, and played a series of harassed fathers, most notably in the television series *Life With Father* and *Father of the Bride*. He cut short his retirement in 1970 and is still active.

Films include: 1932 Murders in the Rue Morgue. **'34** The Count of Monte Cristo. **'38** Walking Down Broadway. **'44** Thirty Seconds Over Tokyo; Meet Me in St Louis. **'45** Yolanda and the Thief. **'46** The Postman Always Rings Twice. **'47** Song of the Thin Man. **'49** Little Women. **'51** On Moonlight Bay. **'52** Angel Face. **'57** Peyton Place. **'60** From the Terrace. **'70** Tora! Tora! Tora! (USA-JAP).

AMIDEI, Sergio

(1904–1981). Scriptwriter. Born: Trieste, Italy

Amidei has been called the 'father of neo-realism'. He first entered the film industry doing a variety of jobs for the FERT company in 1925. After the war, he became actively involved in the flourishing Italian neo-realist cinema. The films it produced were in stark contrast to the propaganda gloss of the Mussolini era, boasting simple and dramatic plots, a raw visual sense and a concern for ordinary people. Amidei co-scripted some of the more notable of these movies including Roberto Rossellini's *Roma, Città Aperta* and *Paisà* and Vittorio De Sica's *Sciuscià*. He also founded his own production company, Colonna-Film, in 1949 and continued to write scripts until the late Seventies.

Films include: 1945 Roma, Città Aperta (co-sc) (USA: Rome, Open City; GB: Open City). **'46** Paisà (co-sc) (USA/GB: Paisan); Sciuscià (co-sc) (USA/GB: Shoeshine). **'48** Sotto il Sole di Roma (co-sc) (GB: Sunday in August); Stromboli/Stromboli, Terra di Dio (co-sc) (USA: God's Land). **'54** Cronache di Poveri Amanti (co-sc); Angst/La Paura (co-sc) (GER-IT) (GB: Fear). **'59** Il Generale Della Rovere (co-sc) (IT-FR). **'60** Era Notte a Roma (co-sc) (USA/GB: It Was Night in Rome).

ANDERSON, Eddie 'Rochester'

(1905–1977). Actor. Born: Oakland, California, USA

Eddie Anderson was an old trouper, the son of showbusiness parents, who went on the stage at an early age and learned the comedian's art in vaudeville. His first speaking part was in *What Price Hollywood?*, when he played a valet, a role he was to specialize in. In 1937 he appeared on Jack Benny's radio show, and was to become a firm favourite on this and Benny's subsequent television show. Gradually, however, his wide-eyed, gravel-voiced image became a racially unacceptable stereotype, and he retired from movies in 1946, returning only for a brief appearance in *It's a Mad, Mad, Mad, Mad World*.

Films include: 1927 No Place to Go/Her Primitive Mate. **'32** What Price Hollywood? **'36** The Green Pastures. **'38** Jezebel. **'39** You Can't Cheat an Honest Man. **'40** Buck Benny Rides Again. **'41** Topper Returns; The Birth of the Blues. **'42** Tales of Manhattan. **'43** Cabin in the Sky. **'45** Brewster's Millions. **'63** It's a Mad, Mad, Mad, Mad World.

ANDERSON, G.M. ('Broncho Billy')

(1883–1971). Actor/producer/ director. Born: Max Aronson; Pine Bluff, Arkansas, USA

Anderson was working in vaudeville when he first met the director Edwin S. Porter and drifted into films. He had a small part in *The Great Train Robbery*, an early and cinematically inventive Western. Inspired by this, Anderson went into partnership with George K. Spoor and formed the Essanay production company, which made a stream of one-reel cowboy pictures depicting the adventures of Broncho Billy. The company also made films for some of the great silent stars, including Charles Chaplin, Gloria Swanson and Wallace Beery. In the early Twenties, however, rival cowboy star William S. Hart was dominating the market, and Anderson retired from the business in 1926.

Films include: 1903 The Great Train Robbery (actor only). **'05** Raffles, the American Cracksman. **'08** The Bandit Makes Good. **'10** Broncho Billy's Redemption. **'12** Broncho Billy's Love Affair; Broncho Billy's Mexican Wife; Alkali Ike's Boarding House (dir. only). **'13** Alkali Ike's Misfortunes (dir. only); The Making of Broncho Billy. **'15** Broncho Billy and the Posse; Broncho Billy and the Sisters; Broncho Billy and the Vigilante; Broncho Billy Begins Life Anew. **'22** Ashes (dir. only).

ANDERSON, Judith

(b.1898). Actress. Born: Frances Anderson; Adelaide, Australia

It took considerable effort – and a certain amount of shuffling between her native Australia and Hollywood – before Judith Anderson was able to transfer her impressive stage reputation to the screen. She first visited the USA in 1918, but it was not until 1930 that she made her film debut. Although the theatre continued to dominate her career, her occasional film work included some excellent character roles, most notably in *Rebecca*, which cast her as the housekeeper Mrs Danvers and, typically, made use of her dark-haired, sinister looks. She was made a Dame of the British Empire in 1960.

Films include: 1940 Rebecca. '41 Kings Row. '42 All Through the Night. '43 Edge of Darkness; Stage Door Canteen. '44 Laura. '46 Diary of a Chambermaid; The Strange Love of Martha Ivers. '47 Pursued. '50 The Furies. '53 Salome. '56 The Ten Commandments. '58 Cat on a Hot Tin Roof. '60 Cinderfella. '70 A Man Called Horse.

ANDERSON, Lindsay

(b.1923). Director/writer. Born: Bangalore, India

From the first, Lindsay Anderson's career has displayed a passionate concern for the art of the film. In 1947 he was a founder of the British film magazine *Sequence*, and in the Fifties he was an initiator of Free Cinema, an independent documentary movement, which included his own *Every Day Except Christmas*. Social concern dominated his first feature, *This Sporting Life*, an earthy tale of a working-class rugby player. In *If. . . .*, which drew on his own background as the public-school-educated son of an army Major-General, his ideals emerged in a passionate and visionary attack on established authority. Critics remain wary of Anderson's approach, and his subsequent limited output has been received with mixed feelings, particularly *O Lucky Man!*, the film that brought *If. . . .* into the Seventies. His wry comedy *Britannia Hospital* was one of Britain's entries at the Cannes Film Festival in 1982.

Films as director include: 1948 Meet the Pioneers (doc. short). '53 O Dreamland (doc. short). '54 Thursday's Children (doc. short). '55 Green and Pleasant Land (doc. short); A Hundred Thousand Children (doc. short). '57 Every Day Except Christmas (doc. short). '59 March to Aldermaston (doc. short). '63 This Sporting Life. '68 The White Bus (short); If. . . . '73 O Lucky Man. '75 In Celebration. '82 Britannia Hospital.

ANDERSON, Michael

(b.1920). Director. Born: London, England

Anderson began his career as an office boy at Elstree studios, and graduated to working with directors like Anthony Asquith, Noel Coward and David Lean. His first major success in his own right was *The Dam Busters*, a patriotic World War II story about a British raid on Germany. Following *Around the World in 80 Days* he moved

to Hollywood, and has since specialized in action films and thrillers starring 'name' actors. Most recently he has moved into science-fiction films with *Logan's Run* and, on television, *The Martian Chronicles*. In 1957 he won the Silver Medallion for outstanding work from the Screen Directors Guild of America. His son, Michael Anderson Jr, is a film actor.

Films include: 1949 Private Angelo (co-dir). '55 The Dam Busters. '56 Around the World in 80 Days; 1984. '57 Yangtse Incident. '59 Shake Hands With the Devil; The Wreck of the Mary Deare (USA). '65 Operation Crossbow (GB-IT). '66 The Quiller Memorandum (GB-USA). '68 The Shoes of the Fisherman. '72 Pope Joan. '76 Logan's Run (USA). '77 Orca (GB: Orca . . . Killer Whale).

ANDERSSON, Bibi

(b.1935). Actress. Born: Birgitta Andersson; Stockholm, Sweden

Andersson is best known for her work with Ingmar Bergman; she was a 17-year-old drama student when she first worked for him on a soap commercial. Bergman later made the most of her child-like good looks as a symbol of hope in *The Seventh Seal* and *Wild Strawberries*. Her later work shows considerable maturity, especially as one of the complex and anguished characters in *Persona*. She has also appeared in American films, working with John Huston (*The Kremlin Letter*) and Robert Altman (*Quintet*), as well as in commercial movies like *Airport '79 – Concorde* (1979), where she often takes ruthless or sensual parts. In 1958 shared the Best Actress Award at Cannes for *So Close to Life*.

Films include: 1953 Dum-Bom. '55 Sommarnattens Leende (USA/GB: Smiles of a Summer Night). '57 Det Sjunde Inseglet (USA/GB: The Seventh Seal); Smultronstället (USA/GB: Wild Strawberries). '58 Nära Livet (USA: Brink of Life; GB: So Close to Life); Ansiktet (USA: The Magician; GB: The Face). '61 Lustgården (USA: The Pleasure Garden). '66 Syskonbädd (USA/GB: My Sister, My Love); Persona. '69 En Passion (USA: The Passion of Anna; GB: A Passion). '70 The Kremlin Letter (USA). '71 Beröringen (USA-SWED) (USA/GB: The Touch). '77 I Never Promised You a Rose Garden (USA). '79 Quintet (USA).

ANDERSSON, Harriet

(b.1932). Actress. Born: Stockholm, Sweden

Born in a poor part of Stockholm, Andersson left school at 15 and studied acting in her spare time while working as a lift operator. She began her show business career as a dancer, graduating to films and 'straight' theatre. She has worked extensively with Ingmar Bergman, notably in *Summer With Monika*, *Through a Glass Darkly* and *Cries and Whispers*. Bergman cast her in sultry, sexy but down-to-earth roles. She has continued to work for Swedish 'new wave' directors such as her husband Jörn Donner, Vilgot Sjöman and Mai Zetterling. She won the Best Actress Award at the Venice Film Festival in 1964 for her performance in Donner's *To Love*.

Films include: 1953 Sommaren Med Monika (USA: Monika; GB: Summer with Monika); Gycklarnas Afton (USA: The Naked Night; GB: Sawdust and Tinsel). '54 En Lektion i Kärlek (USA/GB: A Lesson in Love). '55 Sommarnattens Leende (USA/GB: Smiles of a Summer Night). '61 Såsom i en Spegel (USA/GB: Through a Glass Darkly). '64 För att inte Tala om Alla Dessa Kvinnor (USA: All These Women; GB: Now About These Women); Älskande Par (USA/GB: Loving Couples); Att Älska (USA/GB: To Love). '67 The Deadly Affair (GB); Stimulantia. '72 Viskningar och Rop (USA/GB: Cries and Whispers).

ANDRESS, Ursula

(b.1936). Actress. Born: Berne, Switzerland

The most striking image of Ursula Andress is of her first appearance in *Dr No* – she arises, statuesque, from the pounding surf, clad in a white bikini and clutching a harpoon gun. The daughter of a German diplomat, she played various small roles in Italy, but her career remained static until the James Bond film brought her to stardom. Her best work since has made the most of her cold, classical beauty, such as *She*, which cast her as H. Rider Haggard's vulnerable goddess. During Andress' marriage to actor-director John Derek from 1957–66 she emerged as one of the great sex symbols of the decade, but her more recent films have failed to fulfil her promise.

Films include: 1962 Dr No (GB). '63 Four for Texas (USA). '65 She (GB); Fun in Acapulco (USA); What's New, Pussycat? (USA-FR); La Decima Vittima (IT-FR) (GB: The Tenth Victim). '66 The Blue Max (GB). '71 Soleil Rouge (FR-SP-IT) (USA/GB: Red Sun). '77 Spogliamoci Così Senza Pudor .`. . (IT) (GB: Love in Four Easy Lessons). '81 Clash of the Titans (USA).

ANDREWS, Dana

(b.1912). Actor. Born: Carver Dana Andrews; Collins, Mississippi, USA

The son of a minister, Andrews had ambitions to be a singer when he left his job in accountancy and hitch-hiked to Hollywood. Instead he ended up in the movies and his early parts were mostly supporting roles in Westerns. He was acclaimed for his portrayal of the victim of a lynch-mob in *The Ox-Bow Incident*, and since then his dark good looks and gravel voice have brought him a steady stream of all-American male roles. Sometimes, as with *The Best Years of Our Lives*, in which he played a war veteran returning to an unfaithful wife, he was able to suggest subtle unvoiced unease behind the handsome façade. His decision to work outside the studio system in 1952 meant that good parts became fewer. In later years he suffered a drink problem, but continued to make occasional appearances on screen.

Films include: 1940 The Westerner. '43 The Ox-Bow Incident. '44 Laura. '45 A Walk in the Sun; Fallen Angel. '46 The Best Years of Our Lives. '47 Daisy Kenyon. '50 Where the Sidewalk Ends. '55 Strange Lady in Town; While the City Sleeps. '56 Beyond a Reasonable Doubt. '65 In Harm's Way; Battle of the Bulge. '76 The Last Tycoon.

ANDREWS, Harry

(b.1911). Actor. Born: Tonbridge, Kent, England

Harry Andrews' first choice of career was as a sailor; when this failed to materialize, he applied to join the police, but entered the theatre instead – and achieved an enviable reputation as a Shakespearian actor. After war service he moved into films and since the Fifties has been much in demand in supporting character roles. His

Above, far left: Judith Anderson as Lady Scarface (1941). Above left: Bibi Andersson. Above: Harriet Andersson in Flickorna *(1968, The Girls)*

height, bearing and lantern-jawed appearance have made him perfect for strong, stiff-upper-lip military types, most notably in *The Hill* and *Charge of the Light Brigade*. He has been awarded the CBE.

Films include: 1953 The Red Beret (USA: Paratrooper). '56 Moby Dick; A Hill in Korea (USA: Hell in Korea). '58 Ice Cold in Alex. '63 Cleopatra (USA); 55 Days at Peking (USA). '65 The Hill (USA-IT). '66 Modesty Blaise. '67 The Deadly Affair. '68 A Dandy in Aspic; Charge of the Light Brigade. '69 Battle of Britain. '70 Entertaining Mr Sloane. '78 Death on the Nile.

ANDREWS, Julie

(b.1935). Actress. Born: Julia Elizabeth Wells; Walton-on-Thames, Surrey, England

Fate had Julie Andrews marked out for great things at an early age; before she was 10 she had appeared on stage with her showbusiness parents, and at 13 she was the youngest soloist ever to appear in the Royal Variety Performance. At 19 she crossed the Atlantic and sang in two hit shows on Broadway, subsequently starring in two of the most successful musical

films ever made: *Mary Poppins* and *The Sound of Music*, for which she won the Best Actress Oscar. Much of that film's immense popularity is no doubt due to Andrews' charm, a very English mix of innocence and briskness. Her films since, especially *Star!*, have been disappointing, and recently she has moved towards a change of image and more knowing roles with *10*, *S.O.B.*, and *Victor/Victoria*, all directed by her husband Blake Edwards.

Films include: 1964 Mary Poppins (USA). '65 The Sound of Music (USA). '66 Torn Curtain (USA); Hawaii (USA). '67 Thoroughly Modern Millie (USA). '68 Star! (USA). '70 Darling Lili (USA). '74 The Tamarind Seed (GB). '79 '10' (USA). '81 S.O.B. (USA). '82 Victor/Victoria (GB).

ANGELI, Pier

(1932–1971). Actress. Born: Anna Maria Pierangeli; Cagliari, Sardinia, Italy

While studying in Rome, Angeli was spotted by French director Léonide Moguy, who cast her in his *Domani è Troppo Tardi*. It was an auspicious start – it won the Venice Film Festival Best Italian Film Award. She moved to

Hollywood, and made an impact with *Teresa*, but her subsequent roles, often as quiet or fragile girlfriends, were routine until she played opposite Paul Newman in *Somebody Up There Likes Me*. Later in her career the calibre of her roles declined, and her private life became traumatic; she was married twice, and at one time linked romantically with James Dean. She died from a drug overdose in 1971.

Films include: 1950 Domani è Troppo Tardi (USA/GB: Tomorrow Is Too Late). '51 Domani è un Altro Giorno; Teresa (USA). '53 The Story of Three Loves (USA). '55 The Silver Chalice (USA). '56 Somebody Up There Likes Me (USA). '58 Merry Andrew (USA). '60 The Angry Silence (GB). '62 I Moschettieri del Mare (IT-FR). '65 Battle of the Bulge (USA). '68 Rose Rosse per il Führer (IT). '71 Nelle Pieghe Della Carne/Las Endemoniadas (SP-IT).

Top centre: intrigue for Dana Andrews in Assignment Paris *(1952). Above left: Harry Andrews in Sidney Lumet's thriller* The Deadly Affair. *Above centre: Julie Andrews relaxing during the filming of* Hawaii. *Above right: what a welcome to the oasis – Ursula Andress. Right: MGM portrait of their young Italian star Pier Angeli taken during the Fifties*

*Left: Annabella. Above: Susan Anspach.
Below left: Ann-Margret. Below: Fatty
Arbuckle. Below right: Francesca
Annis in* Macbeth. *Bottom right:
Michelangelo Antonioni*

ANGER, Kenneth

(b.1930). Film-maker/writer. Born:
Santa Monica, California, USA

Born in a time and place much influenced by the movies, it was perhaps
inevitable that Anger should find his
way into films; he did so at the age of
four, playing the Indian princeling in
A Midsummer Night's Dream. He
began making films at an early age,
too, and has become a major exponent of underground and avant-
garde films, experimenting with montage and the use of contemporary
music on soundtracks. He made his
first major impact with *Scorpio Rising,*
a swirling study of a motorcycle gang,
awash with homosexual and black
magic imagery. His other films, like
Invocation of My Demon Brother, continue his fascination with 'magick'. In
1975 his best-known book, *Hollywood
Babylon,* a seedy study of scandals in
the movie world, was first published
in English.

Films include: 1935 A Midsummer Night's
Dream (actor only). **'47** Fireworks. **'49** Puce
Moment. **'53** Eaux d'Artifice. **'54** Inauguration of the Pleasure Dome (2nd version,
1959; 3rd version, 1966). **'61** The Story of O.
'63 Scorpio Rising. **'65** Kustom Kar Kommandos. **'69** Invocation of My Demon Brother. **'70** Rabbit's Moon. **'66–'81** Lucifer
Rising (unfinished).

ANHALT, Edward

(b.1914). Screenwriter. Born: New
York City, USA

After an early career in journalism,
Anhalt graduated to making documentaries, working variously for
Pathé and CBS-TV. During the war he
wrote pulp fiction with his wife, Edna
J. Richards, and soon they began
writing screenplays for thrillers, beginning with *Bulldog Drummond
Strikes Back.* Since then, Anhalt has
established an enviable reputation for
swiftly and professionally written
scripts. He has worked mainly in
quality commercial films, and has
won two Oscars – for *Panic in the
Streets* and *Becket.* He continues to
write in addition to lecturing.

Films include: 1947 Bulldog Drummond
Strikes Back (co-sc). **'50** Panic in the Streets
(co-sc). **'52** The Member of the Wedding
(co-sc). **'55** Not as a Stranger (co-sc). **'57**
The Pride and the Passion (co-sc). **'58** The
Young Lions. **'61** The Young Savages (co-
sc). **'64** Becket (GB). **'68** The Boston Strangler. **'69** The Madwoman of Chaillot (GB).
'72 Jeremiah Johnson (co-sc). **'75** The Man
in the Glass Booth.

ANNABELLA

(b.1909). Actress. Born: Suzanne
Georgette Charpentier; Paris, France

When Annabella was a child, her
father had her photographed and sent
the results to a producer friend who
managed to get her a part in Abel
Gance's *Napoléon.* A couple of years
later René Clair cast her in his *Le
Million,* the first of a series of films they
made together. As a result, Annabella
became a top European star. In the
Thirties she made several films in
England, including *Wings of the Morning,* before moving to Hollywood and
20th Century-Fox. She married
Tyrone Power, her second husband,
in 1939, and became an American

citizen in 1942, but returned to
France shortly after the marriage collapsed in 1948.

Films include: 1927 Napoléon (GB: Napoleon). **'31** Le Million (USA: The Million).
'32 Quatorze Juillet (USA: July 14th). **'37**
Wings of the Morning (GB); Under the Red
Robe (GB); Dinner at the Ritz (GB). **'38** Suez
(USA). **'43** Tonight We Raid Calais (USA).
'46 13 Rue Madeleine (USA). **'49** Dernier
Amour.

ANNAKIN, Ken

(b.1914). Director, Born: Beverley,
Yorkshire, England

Annakin's early career was varied; he
worked as a civil servant, sold advertising space and became a journalist before joining Verity Films after
being invalided out of the RAF in
1942. He worked up from camera
assistant to director of documentaries,
and in 1946 went to work for Gainsborough. His first feature followed a
year later. Since then he has made
many successful commercial films,
specializing in spectacular mad-cap
comedies, like *Monte Carlo or Bust!* and

*Those Magnificent Men in Their Flying
Machines,* and war dramas such as
Battle of the Bulge and *The Longest Day.*

Films include: 1943 London 1942 (doc) (co-
dir). **'47** Holiday Camp. **'48** Miranda; Here
Come the Huggetts; Quartet (co-dir). **'49**
Vote for Huggett. **'60** Swiss Family Robinson. **'62** The Longest Day (co-dir) (USA). **'65**
Those Magnificent Men in Their Flying
Machines; Battle of the Bulge (USA). **'69**
Quei Temerari Sulle Loro Pazze Acatenate
Scalcinate (IT-FR) (USA: Those Daring
Young Men in Their Jaunty Jalopies; GB:
Monte Carlo or Bust!). **'72** The Call of the
Wild (GB-GER-SP-IT-FR). **'82** The Pirate
Movie.

ANNIS, Francesca

(b.1944). Actress. Born: London,
England

Annis' initial ambitions to be a dancer
changed when she was offered a television role at the age of 15. Several
small films and a part in *Cleopatra*
followed, and she has worked extensively on stage, screen and television
since. Her early roles were mainly as
teenagers in 'Swinging Sixties'

movies, until Roman Polanski cast her as Lady Macbeth in his adaptation of Shakespeare's play. This enabled her to take on more dramatic roles on the small screen playing in such prestigious series as *Madame Bovary* and *Lillie*. She also acts for the Royal Shakespeare Company at Stratford-on-Avon.

Films include: 1959 The Cat Gang. '60 No Kidding (USA: Beware of Children). '63 Cleopatra (USA); Crooks in Cloisters; The Eyes of Annie Jones. '64 Flipper's New Adventures (USA) (GB: Flipper and the Pirates); Saturday Night Out. '65 The Pleasure Girls. '70 The Walking Stick. '71 Macbeth.

ANN-MARGRET

(b.1941). Actress. Born: Ann-Margaret Olsson; Stockholm, Sweden

After leaving Northwestern University, Illinois, Ann-Margret sang with a jazz group. They toured the USA but split, and Ann-Margret went solo,

working with comedian George Burns and appearing on the Jack Benny television show. This led to a role in *Pocketful of Miracles* and started her movie career. Her full-blown glamour and vital personality led to her being cast in a series of 'sex kitten' parts. She married actor Roger Smith in 1967, and his subsequent work as her manager ensured better roles, notably in *Carnal Knowledge*, in which she was able to add depth and subtlety to the part of a disillusioned mistress. She continues to work in song-and-dance shows, and has had her own stage and TV spectaculars. In films, she was superb as the old flame in *Magic* (1978).

Films include: 1961 Pocketful of Miracles. '63 Bye, Bye Birdie. '64 Viva Las Vegas (GB: Love in Las Vegas). '65 Bus Riley's Back in Town; The Cincinnati Kid. '66 Stagecoach; The Swinger. '70 R.P.M. '71 Carnal Knowledge. '75 Tommy (GB). '77 The Last Remake of Beau Geste. '78 The Cheap Detective. '80 Middle Age Crazy (CAN).

ANSPACH, Susan

(b.1944). Actress. Born: New York City, USA

After acting at college, Anspach was accepted at the New York Actors' Studio, and subsequently acted in many off-Broadway productions. She had a leading role in the stage version of *Hair*, and went to Hollywood to appear opposite Jack Nicholson in Bob Rafelson's *Five Easy Pieces*, a study of American rootlessness. This, and parts in *The Landlord* and *Play it Again Sam*, established her reputation. She now divides her time between film, television and stage work, and also teaches acting. The actress was acclaimed for her performance in the droll sex comedy *Montenegro*.

Films include: 1970 Five Easy Pieces; The Landlord. '72 Play it Again Sam. '73 Blume in Love. '78 The Big Fix. '79 Running (CAN). '81 The Devil and Max Devlin; Montenegro or Pigs and Pearls (SWED-GB).

ANSTEY, Edgar

(b.1907). Producer/director. Born: Watford, Hertfordshire, England

Edgar Anstey was one of the founders of the British documentary movement. In 1930 he joined John Grierson at the Empire Marketing Board, and later worked as an assistant to Grierson and Robert Flaherty on their famous *Industrial Britain* (1933). His own contributions in this fertile period include the socially aware *Enough to Eat?* and *Housing Problems*. After World War II, Anstey founded British Transport Films for the British Railway Board and continued to make a variety of documentary films on industrial subjects. From 1941 to 1946 he was film critic for *The Spectator*, and was for a while President of the British Film Academy. In 1967 he won an Oscar for *Wild Wings*, a holiday travel film.

Films include: 1933 Eskimo Village; Uncharted Waters. '35 Housing Problems (co-dir). '36 Enough to Eat? '40 A Day in a Factory. '42 Keeping Rabbits for Extra Meat (assoc. prod); Fruit Spraying; National Fire Service Mobilizing Procedure. '43 Summer on the Farm (assoc. prod); Radio in Battle. '44 The Grassy Shires. '66 Wild Wings.

ANTONIONI, Michelangelo

(b.1912). Director. Born: Ferrara, Tuscany, Italy

After graduating from the University of Bologna, Antonioni went to the Centro Sperimentale in Rome, then a lively centre of anti-fascist resistance. He was a film critic for a while and, after World War II, began to direct probing documentaries – though he was critical of the flourishing neo-realist movement. His career as a features director was given a boost by the support of critics in the Fifties. His films are obsessed with the human condition, with alienation and emptiness, whether in Italy, Swinging London (*Blow-Up*) or in Californian universities (*Zabriskie Point*). Reaction to them is mixed. In 1955 he won the Silver Lion at Venice for *Le Amiche*.

Films include: 1947 Gente del Po (doc. short). '50 Cronaca di un Amore. '53 I Vinti (IT-FR); La Signora Senza Camelie (USA: Woman Without Camellias); Amore in Città *ep* Tentato Suicidio). '55 Le Amiche (GB: The Girl Friends). '57 Il Grido (IT-USA) (GB: The Cry). '60 L'Avventura (IT-FR) (USA/GB: The Adventure). 61 La Notte (IT-FR) (GB: The Night). '62 L'Eclisse (FR-IT) (USA/GB: The Eclipse). '64 Deserto Rosso (IT-FR) (USA/GB: Red Desert). '66 Blow-Up (GB). '70 Zabriskie Point (USA). '75 Professione: Reporter (IT-FR-SP) (USA/GB: The Passenger). '80 Il Mistero di Oberwald (GB: The Oberwald Mystery). '82 Identificazione di una Donna (IT) (GB: Identification of a Woman).

APTED, Michael

(b.1941). Director. Born: Aylesbury, Buckinghamshire, England

After studying law at Cambridge, Apted was trained by Granada television. He first worked as a researcher for the current-affairs programme *World in Action*, and later directed episodes of *All Our Yesterdays* and *Coronation Street*. He has directed over fifty TV plays by authors such as Colin Welland and Alun Owen. Apted's first feature film was *The Triple Echo*, a tense drama starring Glenda Jackson and Oliver Reed. He has since worked with producer David Puttnam on *Stardust* and *Agatha*, and specializes in strong, polished stories using well-known actors. His recent work in Hollywood includes *Coal Miner's Daughter*, about singer Loretta Lynn.

Films include: 1972 The Triple Echo. '74 Stardust. '77 The Squeeze. '79 Agatha. '80 Coal Miner's Daughter. '81 Continental Divide.

ARBUCKLE, Roscoe ('Fatty')

(1887–1933). Actor/director. Born: Smith Center, Kansas, USA

The story of Fatty Arbuckle remains a monument to the fickleness of fame. After extensive stage experience, he worked in films as an extra until spotted by comedy producer Mack Sennett. He subsequently became one of the great slapstick comedians of the silent era, always willing to poke riotous fun at his own appearance. At one stage in his career he was earning over $1000 a day, and running his own company. In 1921, however, he was the centre of a scandal in which a young starlet, Virginia Rappe, died at a wild party. Although Arbuckle was finally cleared by a jury, the mud stuck and his career was ruined. No-one wanted to see his films and he was banned from the screen for 11 years. He attempted to make a career as a director, using a pseudonym, but was broken by his experience. He died of a heart attack at the age of 46, one of the cinema's first tragic victims.

Films include: 1913 Mabel's New Hero; Mother's Boy; A Quiet Little Wedding; Fatty's Day Off. '14 The Rounders. '15 Mabel and Fatty's Wash Day; Mabel and Fatty's Married Life. '16 Fatty and Mabel Adrift. '20 The Garage. '31 The Last of Hollywood (short) (dir. under pseydonym); Honeymoon Trio (short) (dir. under pseudonym). '32 Anybody's Goat (short) (dir. under pseudonym).

ARDEN, Eve

(b.1912). Actress. Born: Eunice Quedens; Mill Valley, California, USA

Arden joined a stock company in San Francisco on leaving school and soon found herself in minor stage roles, including one in *The Ziegfeld Follies*. An early part in the film *Oh Doctor!* (1937) attracted favourable attention, and she then worked steadily in supporting roles, where her fast-talking snappy quips – whether hunting man or mink – were much cherished. She was at her best as Joan Crawford's wisecracking friend in *Mildred Pierce*, a role for which she received an Oscar nomination. She worked increasingly in television, and won an Emmy in 1954 as television's top comedienne. She has also received awards for her performance on stage as *Mame*, as well as the Sarah Siddons Award.

Films include: 1937 Stage Door. **'41** Ziegfeld Girl; That Uncertain Feeling. **'44** Cover Girl. **'45** Mildred Pierce. **'46** Night and Day. **'59** Anatomy of a Murder. **'60** Dark at the Top of the Stairs. **'65** Sergeant Deadhead. **'78** Grease.

ARGENTO, Dario

(b.1940). Director/scriptwriter/critic. Born: Rome, Italy

The son of Salvatore Argento, a veteran of the Italian cinema, Dario Argento began his career as a critic for

the journal *Paese Sera* before becoming a director. He has his own production company, Seda Productions, which employs the talents of both his father and younger brother Claudio. Argento's work has mostly been commercial and Americanized – for example, he co-scripted the celebrated 'spaghetti' Western *C'Era una Volta il West*. His other films show a great capacity for suspense and horror, notably *Suspiria*, a tale concerning black magic.

Films include: 1968 C'Era una Volta il West (co-sc. only) (USA/GB: Once Upon a Time in the West); Himmelfahrtskommando El Alamein (IT-GER) (USA/GB: Commandos); Oggi a me . . . Domani a te! (co-sc. only) (USA/GB: Today It's Me, Tomorrow You). **'69** Un Eserato di 5 Uomini (co-sc. only) (USA/GB: The Five Man Army); Metti, una Sera a Cana (USA: One Night, at Dinner; GB: The Love Circle); Probabilità Zero (co-dir. only); La Rivoluzione Sessuale (co-sc. only). **'71** Il Gatto a Nove Code (+ co-sc) (FR-IT-GER) (USA/GB: Cat o' Nine Tails); 4 Mosche di Velluto Grigio (+ sc) (IT-FR) (USA/GB: Four Flies in Grey Velvet). **'77** Suspiria. **'80** Inferno.

ARKIN, Alan

(b.1934). Actor. Born: New York City, USA

The son of Russian-German-Jewish parents, Arkin always wanted to be an actor, although in the mid-Fifties he gave up acting in order to sing with a folk group called The Tarriers. He

returned to the stage to work in St Louis, Chicago and New York, and was involved in several hits on and off Broadway. His first film role, as a Russian submarine officer washed up on the coast of America in *The Russians are Coming, the Russians are Coming*, brought him an Oscar nomination, and set the scene for his subsequent work in comedy – whether as the zany cop in *Freebie and the Bean* (1974) or as the subtly anarchic Yossarian in *Catch 22*. Folksinging and Hollywood comedy aside, Arkin is an author of children's books, a director, a photographer and composer. He is also a talented serious actor, and has won the New York Film Critics Award for *The Heart Is a Lonely Hunter* and *Hearts of the West*.

Films include: 1966 The Russians Are Coming, the Russians Are Coming. **'67** Wait Until Dark. **'68** The Heart Is a Lonely Hunter. **'70** Catch 22. **'71** Little Murders (+ dir). **'72** The Last of the Red Hot Lovers. **'75** Hearts of the West. **'77** Fire Sale (+ dir).

ARKOFF, Samuel Z.

(b.1918). Executive producer. Born: Fort Dodge, Iowa, USA

Abandoning an early career in law, Arkoff began working as a producer for NBC television in the Fifties. In 1954 he set up American International Pictures, in partnership with James Nicholson, for just $3000. The company was subsequently instrumental in launching the careers of

Roger Corman, Francis Ford Coppola, Martin Scorsese and other 'new' Hollywood directors. Arkoff's own films were usually cheap, speedily shot exploitation movies with horror, motorbike, beach-party or other youth-orientated themes. He seldom lost money with an AIP film. Recently, he has moved towards more lavish blockbusters such as *Force 10 From Navarone*. In 1981 he established Arkoff International Pictures.

Films include: 1954 Monster From the Ocean Floor. **'55** The Day the World Ended. **'57** I Was a Teenage Frankenstein. **'58** The Bonnie Parker Story. **'61** The Pit and the Pendulum. **'65** How to Stuff a Wild Bikini (GB: How to Fill a Wild Bikini); Beach Blanket Bingo. **'70** Bloody Mama. **'72** Blacula. **'76** Futureworld. **'78** Force 10 From Navarone.

ARLEN, Harold

(1905–1986). Songwriter. Born: Hyman Arlock; Buffalo, New York, USA

The son of a cantor, Arlen served his apprenticeship in vaudeville. In 1933 he went to Hollywood and made an impact with his song 'Stormy Weather' written with Ted Koehler for Harlem's Cotton Club. He contributed to over thirty Hollywood musicals, winning an Academy Award for 'Over the Rainbow' from *The Wizard of Oz*. His other best known songs include 'That Old Black Magic' and 'Accentuate the Positive'. He also worked in

partnership with Johnny Mercer and Ira Gershwin and wrote scores for Broadway.

Films include: 1936 Gold Diggers of 1937; Stage Struck. '39 The Wizard of Oz. '43 Cabin in the Sky; Star Spangled-Rhythm. '44 Here Come the Waves; Kismet; Up in Arms. '53 Down Among the Sheltering Palms. '54 A Star Is Born. '62 Gay Purr-ee.

ARLEN, Richard

(1899–1976). Actor. Born: Cornelius Van Mattimore; Charlottesville, Virginia, USA

Arlen drifted to Los Angeles after World War I and first worked as a messenger for a film laboratory. A minor road accident in a vehicle owned by Paramount Pictures brought him to the studio's attention and won him a job as an extra. He progressed through parts in films like *Old Ironsides* (1926) and his wartime experience in the air force won him the lead in *Wings*, a tale about air-aces. His athletic looks ensured that he was always in demand for tough, cynical American-hero parts. At the end of the Forties his popularity waned, and he moved increasingly into theatre and television.

Films include: 1923 Vengeance of the Deep. '27 Wings. '28 Beggars of Life. '29 The Four Feathers; The Virginian. '33 College Humor. '43 Aerial Gunner. '64 The Best Man. '66 Apache Uprising.

ARLETTY

(b.1898). Actress. Born: Arlette-Léonie Bathiat; Courbevoie, France

Arletty was the dark-haired, husky-voiced middle-aged beauty who brought an elegance and wit, and sometimes a sadness, to the poetic realism of the films of Marcel Carné and other French directors. Her most famous role was that of Garance, the heartbroken courtesan left watching her former lover performing in the theatre at the end of Carné's *Les Enfants du Paradis*. On leaving school, Arletty had been a factory-worker, a secretary and a model before her music-hall debut in 1918. She continued to act in stage comedy and drama after her 1931 screen debut in *Chien Qui Rapporte*. Though briefly imprisoned after the Liberation owing to her affair with a German officer, she returned to the screen in the late Forties. Since an accident in 1957 she has fought a partially successful battle against blindness. Few French actresses have been so missed.

Top, from left to right: Eve Arden; Alan Arkin; Richard Arlen at his home in the Thirties; Arletty suffers the attentions of an admirer in Hôtel du Nord. Above, from left to right: the 'first gentleman of the screen' – George Arliss in The House of Rothschild; Edward Arnold in Diamond Jim; Françoise Arnoul; Jean Arthur in The Whole Town's Talking

Films include: 1931 Un Chien Qui Rapporte. '34 La Guerre des Valses (GB: The Court Waltzes). '38 Hôtel du Nord. '39 Le Jour se Lève (USA: Daybreak); Fric-Frac; Circonstances Atténuantes (USA: Extenuating Circumstances). '40 Tempête/Tempête sur Paris. '41 Madame Sans Gêne. '42 Les Visiteurs du Soir (USA: The Devil's Own Envoy). '45 Les Enfants du Paradis (USA: Children of Paradise). '49 Portrait d'un Assassin. '51 L'Amour, Madame. '54 Le Grand Jeu (FR-IT) (GB: The Card of Fate); Huis Clos (GB: Vicious Circle). '62 La Gamberge; The Longest Day (USA).

ARLISS, George

(1868–1946). Actor. Born: George Augustus Andrews; London, England

George Arliss' first experience in acting came on the stage of the Elephant and Castle Theatre in South London. In 1901 he went to America with Mrs Patrick Campbell's Company, and was a great success on Broadway. He established a notable reputation as a character actor and carried this into films, playing, in a mannered, rococo style, the likes of *Disraeli*, the Duke of Wellington in *The Iron Duke*, and *Alexander Hamilton*. His distinctive voice and elegant appearance, often with a monocle, earned him the nickname 'First Gentleman of the Screen'. He returned to the London stage in 1923, and continued working until his retirement in 1937.

Films include: 1921 The Devil. '29 Disraeli. '31 The Millionaire; Alexander Hamilton. '32 The Man Who Played God (GB: The Silent Voice). '33 Voltaire. '34 The House of Rothschild. '35 The Iron Duke; Cardinal Richelieu. '37 Doctor Syn (GB).

ARNOLD, Edward

(1890–1956). Actor. Born: Guenther Edward Schneider; New York City, USA

Born to a German immigrant family, Arnold worked as a bellhop, butcher's boy and stoker before his stage debut at the age of seventeen in *A Midsummer Night's Dream*. He was eight years on the stage before getting a job in 1915 with Essanay, a company with whom he was to make more than fifty silent one-reelers. He became famous as a character actor during the Thirties, specializing in genial gaudy rogues (*Diamond Jim*), blustering tycoons, crooked politicians, millionaires and detectives like *Nero Wolfe*. He was married three times, and was a President of the Screen Actors' Guild.

Films include: 1932 Rasputin and the Empress. '35 Diamond Jim; Remember Last Night? '36 Sutter's Gold; Meet Nero Wolfe. '37 Toast of New York. '38 You Can't Take it With You. '39 Mr Smith Goes to Washington. '40 Lillian Russell. '41 All That Money Can Buy.

ARNOLD, Jack

(b.1916). Director. Born: New Haven, Connecticut, USA

The son of a construction engineer, Arnold attended Ohio State University and then the American Academy of Dramatic Arts. After service in the US air force and a spell with documen-

tary maker Robert Flaherty, he began directing features in 1953. Although prolific and versatile, his films ranging from thrillers to light comedy, he is best remembered for a string of sensational, cheaply-made science-fiction films, including *The Incredible Shrinking Man* and *Creature From the Black Lagoon*.

Films include: 1953 Girls in the Night (GB: Life After Dark); It Came From Outer Space. '54 Creature From the Black Lagoon. '55 The Man From Bitter Ridge; Revenge of the Creature; Tarantula. '57 The Incredible Shrinking Man; The Tattered Dress; The Lady Takes a Flyer. '58 High School Confidential; The Space Children. '59 The Mouse That Roared. '61 Bachelor in Paradise. '75 The Swiss Conspiracy (USA-GER).

ARNOUL, Françoise

(b.1931). Actress. Born: Françoise Annette Marie Mathilde Gautsch; Constantine, Algeria

Arnoul's father, a General in the French Army, was serving in North Africa when she was born. She went to Paris in the hope of getting into films, and when the director Willy Rozier saw a photograph of her he got her a part in *L'Epave*. Most of her subsequent parts made good use of her slight figure and pretty face; Roger Vadim cast her, brooding and moody, in *When the Devil Drives* and established her in provocative 'bad girl' parts. Some of her films were banned from America, and in Britain she was billed as 'The X Girl'. Her career waned with the emergence of Brigitte Bardot.

Films include: 1949 L'Epave. '51 La Plus Belle Fille du Monde. '53 Les Compagnes de la Nuit; La Rage au Corps. '55 French Can-Can. '56 Sait-On Jamais (FR-IT) (USA: No Sun in Venice; GB: When the Devil Drives). '58 La Chatte. '62 Le Diable et les Dix Commandements. '65 Compartiment Tueurs (GB: The Sleeping Car Murders). '66 Le Dimanche de la Vie (FR-IT-GER) (GB/USA: The Sunday of Life). '77 Violette et François; Dernière Sortie Avant Roissy (USA: Last Exit Before Roissy).

ARTHUR, Jean

(b.1908). Actress. Born: Gladys Greene; New York City, USA

A photographer's daughter, Jean Arthur did modelling which brought her to Hollywood's notice. She made over twenty silent films, mostly comedies and Westerns for small companies, but her first feature success was with Columbia in *The Whole Town's Talking*. This assured her of a steady stream of lead roles, mostly in screwball comedies, playing honest, resourceful, down-to-earth all-American girls, notably in Frank Capra's *Mr Deeds Goes to Town* and *You Can't Take It With You*. She was never really happy with Hollywood, however, and retired from the screen in 1944. Apart from a couple of returns to movies, her subsequent work has been in the theatre.

Films include: 1923 Cameo Kirby. '28 Sins of the Fathers. '30 Young Eagles. '34 Whirlpool. '35 The Whole Town's Talking. '36 Mr Deeds Goes to Town; The Plainsman. '37 Easy Living. '38 You Can't Take It With You. '39 Only Angels Have Wings; Mr Smith Goes to Washington. '42 Talk of the Town. '48 A Foreign Affair. '53 Shane.

ARZNER, Dorothy

(1900–1979). Director/editor. Born: San Francisco, California, USA

Dorothy Arzner worked her way up from the bottom to become one of Hollywood's first women directors. Her father ran a restaurant in Los Angeles, which gave her contacts in films; Arzner dropped out of university to take up a typist's job at Paramount. She progressed to the editing room and, as a cutter, worked on the Rudolph Valentino film *Blood and Sand* (1922), and *The Covered Wagon* (1923). Her early films as a director were conventional comedies and dramas about male/female relationships and some, like *Working Girls*, were mildly feminist in their celebration of independent women. Arzner retired from the film industry when she suffered a bout of pneumonia in 1943, emerging only to teach at UCLA for a time and to make some television commercials. In 1975 she was honoured by the Director's Guild of America.

Films include: 1927 Fashions for Women; Ten Modern Commandments; Get Your Man. '29 The Wild Party. '30 Anybody's Woman. '31 Honor Among Lovers; Working Girls. '32 Merrily We Go to Hell. '33 Christopher Strong. '34 Nana (GB: Lady of the Boulevards). '36 Craig's Wife. '37 The Bride Wore Red. '40 Dance, Girl, Dance. '43 First Comes Courage.

ASHBY, Hal

(b.1930). Director/editor. Born: Ogden, Utah, USA

Ashby's early career was varied and his private life painful. An unhappy child, he was later divorced twice before he was 21. After graduating at Utah State University, he worked in the theatre before moving on to involve himself in almost every aspect of film making. He excelled as an editor, and worked frequently with director Norman Jewison, winning an Academy Award for editing *In The Heat of the Night*. His own films as director have earned Ashby a reputation as a radical, though some critics consider him to be merely a smug liberal. *Harold and Maude*, about a love affair between an 80-year-old woman and a 20-year-old man has achieved cult status, while *Coming Home* looks at the Vietnam War through its effects on emotionally and physically disabled veterans.

Films as editor include: 1965 The Loved One; The Cincinnati Kid. '67 In the Heat of the Night. '68 The Thomas Crown Affair. '69 Gaily, Gaily (+ assoc. prod) (GB: Chicago, Chicago). As director: '70 The Landlord. '71 Harold and Maude. '73 The Last Detail. '75 Shampoo. '76 Bound for Glory. '78 Coming Home. '79 Being There.

ASHER, Jane

(b.1946). Actress. Born: London, England

Jane Asher's first role was in *Mandy* when she was only seven; since then this daughter of a Wimpole Street doctor has been continuously in work in films, television or on stage. She emerged as a face of the Sixties through her part as one of Casanova Michael Caine's conquests in *Alfie*,

and her small-screen work in popular series like *Robin Hood* and *The Saint*. More prestigious television work has included *Brideshead Revisited* (as the neglected Mrs Ryder) and an important role in the BBC drama *Love Is Old, Love Is New*. She was also prominent in the London stage production of *Whose Life Is It Anyway?*

Films include: 1952 Mandy (USA: Crash of Silence). '55 The Quatermass Experiment (USA: The Creeping Unknown). '64 The Masque of the Red Death. '66 Alfie; The Winter's Tale. '70 Deep End.

ASHERSON, Renée

(b.1920). Actress. Born: Renée Ascherson; London, England

Originally a stage actress, Asherson joined Birmingham Repertory Company before graduating to the Old Vic and the West End play *Lottie Dundas*. This led to a starring part in Laurence Olivier's famous movie version of *Henry V*. In 1950 she played opposite Robert Donat (d.1958) in *The Cure for Love*, which led to their marriage. Asherson's later film work included several science-fiction and horror films, including the Hammer melodrama *Rasputin the Mad Monk*.

Films include: 1944 The Way Ahead; Henry V. '45 The Way to the Stars (USA: Johnny in the Clouds). '51 Pool of London. '61 The Day the Earth Caught Fire. '66 Rasputin the Mad Monk.

ASHLEY, Elizabeth

(b.1939). Actress. Born: Elizabeth Cole; Ocala, Florida, USA

Originally a model, Elizabeth Ashley made her stage reputation opposite Robert Redford in the Broadway version of *Barefoot in the Park*. This led to a part in the film *The Carpetbaggers*, and a traumatic marriage, her second, to George Peppard. After a period of retirement, she returned to work occasionally in films and television. In 1961 she won a Tony award for her part as Art Carney's daughter in *Take Her, She's Mine*.

Films include: 1964 The Carpetbaggers. '65 Ship of Fools. '71 The Marriage of a Young Stockbroker. '78 Coma. '81 Paternity.

ASNER, Edward

(b.1925). Actor. Born: Kansas City, Kansas, USA

After college, Asner worked in a steel mill and as a door-to-door salesman before being drafted. After military service, he joined a Chicago theatre group, progressing to New York and Broadway. Since the late Sixties the actor has established a solid reputation in supporting roles, chiefly playing tough, hard characters, sometimes with a heart of gold, as in *Fort Apache, the Bronx*. He has also worked extensively on television, notably in *The Mary Tyler Moore Show*, *Roots* and as *Lou Grant*. He has been awarded two Emmys, and in 1981 became a controversial President of the Screen Actors' Guild.

Films include: 1967 Gunn. '70 They Call Me Mister Tibbs! '81 Fort Apache, the Bronx.

Right, from left to right: Jane Asher in Deep End; *Renee Asherson in* Malta Story *(1953); Elizabeth Ashley; Fred Astaire in* Three Little Words *(1950). Below right, from left to right: Edward Asner as TV's Lou Grant; Nils Asther; Mary Astor. Bottom: William Atherton in* Day of the Locust

ASQUITH, Anthony

(1902–1968). Director. Born: London, England

As might be expected from the son of a famous Liberal Prime Minister, a man educated at Winchester and Balliol, Anthony Asquith's films were very English, technically proficient, well-acted, tasteful and often stiff-upper-lip in tone. He specialized in light comedy and social satire, and was at his best translating British stage classics to the screen, notably Oscar Wilde's *The Importance of Being Earnest* and Terence Rattigan's *The Winslow Boy*. His later films, such as *The Yellow Rolls-Royce*, were all-star vehicles exploiting the appeal of glamour and wealth.

Films include: 1927 Shooting Stars. '28 Underground. '29 A Cottage on Dartmoor (USA: Escaped From Dartmoor). '31 Tell England (USA: Battle of Gallipoli). '38 Pygmalion. '39 French Without Tears. '44 Fanny By Gaslight (USA: Man of Evil). '45 The Way to the Stars (USA: Johnny in the Clouds). '48 The Winslow Boy. '51 The Browning Version. '52 The Importance of Being Earnest. '54 Carrington VC (USA: Court Martial). '58 Orders to Kill. '60 The Millionairess. '64 The Yellow Rolls Royce.

ASTAIRE, Fred

(b.1899). Actor. Born: Frederick Austerlitz; Omaha, Nebraska, USA

Perhaps the most famous of all cinema song-and-dance men, Astaire owes some part of his success to his ambitious mother who enrolled him in a dance school at the age of four. His first partner was his sister Adele, with whom he danced in several Broadway shows. Following Adele's retirement to get married, Astaire moved into films, and a casual partnering with Ginger Rogers in *Flying Down to Rio* led to a series of hugely popular films together. The secret of their success was the romantic pairing of his sophisticated man-about-town style and her girl-next-door appeal, and their remarkable dancing. *Top Hat* epitomizes the extraordinary grace, elegance and stylishness of Astaire. After the demise of the partnership with Rogers, he continued to dance with a variety of actresses. In the Sixties he shifted to television spectaculars, and has since made several straight acting appearances in cameo roles. In 1949 he won a special Academy Award and in 1979 an Emmy Award for *A Family Upside Down*.

Films include: 1933 Flying Down to Rio. '34 The Gay Divorcee (GB: The Gay Divorce). '35 Roberta; Top Hat. '36 Follow the Fleet; Swing Time. '37 Shall We Dance. '39 The Story of Irene and Vernon Castle. '40 Broadway Melody of 1940. '41 You'll Never Get Rich. '42 You Were Never Lovelier. '45 Yolanda and the Thief. '48 Easter Parade. '53 The Band Wagon. '57 Silk Stockings. '67 Finian's Rainbow. '81 Ghost Story.

ASTHER, Nils

(1897–1981). Actor. Born: Hellerup, Copenhagen, Denmark

Raised by wealthy Swedish parents in Malmö, he studied in Stockholm and then began a stage career in Copenhagen. Mauritz Stiller gave him his first chance in films. Asther subsequently acted for Victor Sjöström in Sweden and Michael Curtiz in Germany, before going in 1927 to Hollywood, where he played exotic, romantic roles opposite such stars as Greta Garbo, Pola Negri and Joan Crawford. His foreign accent was no asset after the coming of sound, and in 1934 he went to Britain, having been blacklisted for breaking a contract. He returned in 1938 but his career waned, and by 1949 he was broke and driving a truck. In 1958 he went back to Sweden, playing small parts in television and the theatre.

Films include: 1916 Vingarne. '22 Vem Dömer? (USA: Mortal Clay; GB: Love's Crucible). '28 Laugh, Clown, Laugh (USA); Loves of an Actress (USA); Our Dancing Daughters (USA); Dream of Love (USA). '29 Wild Orchids (USA). '32 The Bitter Tea of General Yen. '63 Gudrun (DEN).

16

ASTOR, Mary

(b.1906). Actress. Born: Lucille Langhanke; Quincy, Illinois, USA

A beauty queen at 15, Astor was pushed into films by her father. Her major silent roles were as innocent heroines in costume dramas, notably opposite John Barrymore in *Don Juan*. She remained a leading lady in talkies – surviving a scandalous divorce case in 1936 – and in 1941 played her archetypal role as the prim villainess Brigid O'Shaughnessy in *The Maltese Falcon*, also winning that year's Best Supporting Actress Oscar for her bitch in *The Great Lie*. Maternal parts at MGM followed but her career dwindled in the Fifties after a breakdown. Four times married, she has written two autobiographies (*My Story*, 1951; *A Life on Film*, 1967) and five novels.

Films include: '24 Beau Brummell. '25 Don Q, Son of Zorro. '26 Don Juan. '27 Two Arabian Knights. '30 Holiday. '32 Red Dust. '36 Dodsworth. '37 The Prisoner of Zenda. '41 The Great Lie; The Maltese Falcon; The Palm Beach Story. '42 Across the Pacific. '44 Meet Me in St Louis. '49 Little Women. '64 Hush . . . Hush, Sweet Charlotte.

ASTRUC, Alexandre

(b.1923). Director/critic. Born: Paris, France

The young Astruc studied law and literature and completed a novel, *Les Vacances* (1945), before assisting Marc Allégret on *Blanche Fury* (1948). Ostensibly a literary and film critic, in 1948 he wrote an influential article, 'The Birth of a New Avant-Garde: Le Camera-Stylo', stressing the importance of style and film language beyond the commercial demands of mere narrative. His theory, developed by other critics and directors, was central to the *nouvelle vague* and has been demonstrated by Astruc himself in his own formalistic, coldly beautiful films, notably *Une Vie*. He has also directed for television.

Films include: 1953 Le Rideau Cramoisi (GB: The Crimson Curtain). '55 Les Mauvaises Rencontres. '58 Une Vie (USA: End of Desire; GB: One Life). '61 La Proie Pour l'Ombre (USA/GB: Shadow of Adultery); L'Education Sentimentale. '63 Le Puits et le Pendule (USA/GB: The Pit and the Pendulum). '65 Evariste Galois. '66 La Longue Marche. '68 Flammes sur l'Adriatique. '76 Sartre par lui-même (doc) (co-dir).

ATHERTON, William

(b.1947). Actor. Born: William Knight; New Haven, Connecticut, USA

Raised on a farm, Atherton became the youngest member of the Long Wharf Theatre company in New Haven while still at high school. He won a scholarship to the Pasadena Playhouse and studied drama at Carnegie Tech. He gained early stage experience on tour in *Little Murders* and off-Broadway, winning several awards. A slim, red-haired, sometimes nervous-looking leading man, he made his film debut in *The New Centurions*. His best-known role was as an escaped convict in *The Sugarland Express*, though he gave a good performance as the Hollywood set designer he played in *Day of the Locust*.

Films include: 1972 The New Centurions (GB: Precinct 45 – Los Angeles Police). '73 Class of '44. '74 The Sugarland Express. '75 Day of the Locust; The Hindenburg. '77 Looking for Mr Goodbar.

ATTENBOROUGH, Richard

(b.1923). Actor/director. Born: Cambridge, England

He won a scholarship to RADA and made his stage debut in 1941. A meeting with Noel Coward led to his first appearance in a film, *In Which We Serve*; and he specialized for a while in other-ranks military roles, usually as a snivelling cockney or a coward. Playing a successful general in Satyajit Ray's *The Chess Players* must have been a late consolation. After serving in the army, he married actress Sheila Sim in 1945. He formed a production company with Bryan Forbes in the late Fifties; and he won the BAFTA Best Actor award in 1964 for his performances in *Guns at Batasi* and *Seance on a Wet Afternoon*. He took up directing with *Oh! What a Lovely War* and followed this with other large-budget, star-studded epics. He was knighted in 1976.

Films include: 1942 In Which We Serve (actor only). '46 A Matter of Life and Death (actor only) (USA: Stairway to Heaven). '47 Brighton Rock (actor only). '59 I'm All Right Jack (actor only). '60 The Angry Silence (actor only); League of Gentlemen (actor only). '63 The Great Escape (USA) (actor only). '64 Seance on a Wet Afternoon (actor only); Guns at Batasi (actor only). '67 Doctor Dolittle (USA) (actor only). '69 Oh! What a Lovely War (dir. only). '71 10, Rillington Place (actor only). '72 Young Winston (dir. only). '77 A Bridge Too Far (USA) (dir. only); Shatranj ke Khilari (IND) (actor only) (USA/GB: The Chess Players). '78 Magic (USA) (dir. only). '82 Gandhi (GB-IND) (dir. only).

ATWILL, Lionel

(1885–1946). Actor. Born: Croydon, Surrey, England

Well-known as a dark and menacing doctor or villain in Hollywood horror and adventure films of the Thirties and Forties, Atwill began his career on the English stage in *Walls of Jericho* (1904). In 1916 he came to America and soon gained a reputation as Broadway's 'perfect lover' opposite such leading ladies as Alla Nazimova and Helen Hayes. Suavely handsome, he soon found his way into films and made his debut in *For Sale* (1918). Though he won greater acclaim as a stage actor and director, he was, at his peak, one of the screen's most reliable and prolific character actors. Atwill died of pneumonia.

Films include: 1932 Doctor X. '33 The Mystery of the Wax Museum; Song of Songs. '34 Nana (GB: Lady of the Boulevards); Stamboul Quest. '35 Mark of the Vampire; The Devil Is a Woman; Captain Blood. '39 Son of Frankenstein; The Three Musketeers (GB: The Singing Musketeer). '40 Boom Town. '42 Sherlock Holmes and the Secret Weapon. '44 House of Dracula.

AUBERJONOIS, Rene

(b.1940). Actor. Born: New York City, USA

One of director Robert Altman's stock company, Auberjonois seems to fall between two stools. He's never really typecast, nor is he anonymous,

although his roles have him playing characters who are slightly odd or displaced. He was most memorable in Altman's *Brewster McCloud* as an ornithology lecturer who slowly and magnificently metamorphoses into a giant, filthy, wing-flapping bird.

Films include: 1964 Lilith. '68 Petulia. '70 M*A*S*H; Brewster McCloud. '71 McCabe and Mrs Miller. '72 Images; Pete 'n' Tillie. '75 The Hindenburg. '76 The Big Bus; King Kong. '78 The Eyes of Laura Mars. '80 Where the Buffalo Roam.

AUDRAN, Stéphane

(b.1932). Actress. Born: Colette Suzanne Dacheville; Versailles, France

Stéphane Audran brings a glossy beauty, elegance and an air of hauteur to the chic wives she generally plays in the satires and murder melodramas of Claude Chabrol, her husband since 1964. Her career is inseparable from his since she has worked for Chabrol over 15 times since her first appearance for him in *Les Cousins* (1959). Her most successful performances were as the sophisticated lesbian in *Les Biches* and as a cold Dordogne schoolteacher, passionate under the surface, in *Le Boucher*; while for Luis Buñuel she

perfectly embodied *The Discreet Charm of the Bourgeoisie*. As a young woman Audran studied acting and worked mainly in classical drama on provincial tours. She was previously married to the film actor Jean-Louis Trintignant.

Films include: 1960 Les Bonnes Femmes (FR-IT). '67 Le Scandale/The Champagne Murders. '68 Les Biches (FR-IT) (GB: The Does); La Femme Infidèle (FR-IT). '70 Le Boucher (FR-IT); La Rupture (FR-IT-BELG). '71 Juste Avant la Nuit (FR-IT) (GB: Just Before Nightfall). '72 Le Charme Discret de la Bourgeoisie (FR-SP-IT) (USA/GB: The Discreet Charm of the Bourgeoisie). '73 Les Noces Rouges (USA: Wedding in Blood; GB: Red Wedding). 77 Blood Relatives/Les Liens de Sang (CAN-FR). '78 Violette Nozière (FR-CAN) (USA: Violette). '80 The Big Red One (USA). '81 Coup de Torchon (GB: Clean Slate).

AUER, Mischa

(1905–1967). Actor. Born: Mischa Ounskowski; St Petersburg, Russia

Bulging eyes, a lean and drooping physique, broken English and zany behaviour characterize Mischa Auer, one of the cinema's most popular and enduring supporting actors. The story goes that he escaped Russia after the Revolution and made his way to New York, joining up with his uncle,

violinist Leopold Auer. From 1925 he was on stage and from 1928 in films. At first he was mostly cast as a villain, but soon began to make his name as an eccentric or exotic. He is best remembered for his impersonation of an ape in *My Man Godfrey*, a performance that earned him an Oscar nomination. After the war he worked mainly in Europe.

Films include: 1928 Something Always Happens. '35 The Lives of a Bengal Lancer; Clive of India. '36 My Man Godfrey; Winterset. '37 Three Smart Girls; One Hundred Men and a Girl. '38 You Can't Take It With You. '39 Destry Rides Again. '40 The Flame of New Orleans. '42 Hellzapoppin'. '45 A Royal Scandal (GB: Czarina). '54 Mr Arkadin/Confidential Report (SP-FR). '62 Drop Dead Darling (GB) (USA: Arrivederci Baby).

AUGUST, Joseph H.

(1890–1947). Cinematographer. Born: Idaho Springs, Colorado, USA

One of the most admired cameramen in America's silent cinema, August joined pioneer producer-director Thomas H. Ince as assistant cameraman in 1911 and quickly worked his way up to first cameraman. He worked on Ince's epic *Civilization* and became director of photography on W.S. Hart's Westerns, later moving to

AURIC, Georges

(1899–1983). Composer. Born: Lodéve, France

Auric studied music at the Paris Conservatoire and then at the Scuola Cantorum. His first material was published at 15, he wrote ballets and in the late Twenties became the youngest member of the avant-garde group of musicians known as 'Les Six'. He was also one of the intellectuals featured in René Clair's *Entr'acte* (1924), and he would later score Clair's *A Nous la Liberté*. His first film music was for Jean Cocteau's *Le Sang d'un Poète*. He also scored Cocteau's *La Belle et la Bête* and *Orphée*. France's pre-eminent composer of film music, he also worked in Britain, mainly on Ealing comedies, and for Hollywood, providing music for *Roman Holiday* and a popular waltz theme for *Moulin Rouge* (both made in Europe).

Films include: 1930 *Le Sang d'un Poète* (USA/GB: The Blood of a Poet). '31 *A Nous la Liberté*. '43 *L'Eternel Retour* (USA/GB: Love Eternal). '45 *La Belle et la Bête* (USA/GB: Beauty and the Beast); *Dead of Night* (GB). '47 *It Always Rains on Sunday* (GB). '49 *Passport to Pimlico* (GB). '50 *Orphée* (FR) (USA: Orpheus). '52 *Moulin Rouge* (USA). '53 *Roman Holiday* (USA). '58 *Bonjour Tristesse* (USA). '61 *Goodbye Again/Aimez-Vous Brahms?* (USA-FR). '68 *Thérèse and Isabelle* (USA-GER). '69 *L'Arbre de Noel* (USA/GB: The Christmas Tree).

AUTANT-LARA, Claude

(b.1903). Director. Born: Luzarches, France

Claude Autant-Lara commenced his career as an art director and designer in the theatre. In 1919 he began working as assistant director to the film-maker Marcel L'Herbier, and during the Twenties he also assisted Réne Clair and Jean Renoir. His debut as a director was *Faits Divers*, an avant-garde short made in 1923 for L'Herbier's Cinagraphie studio. In 1930 he signed a short contract with MGM to make French versions of Hollywood productions, but by 1932 he was back in France, where he produced many films with predominantly leftist and atheist viewpoints – later to be decried by the *nouvelle vague*. However, he is still much respected for his social and political satires, such as his award-winning *Le Diable au Corps* and *Occupe-toi d'Amélie*.

Films include: 1942 *Le Mariage de Chiffon*. '47 *Le Diable au Corps* (GB: Devil in the Flesh). '49 *Occupe-toi d'Amélie* (GB: Keep an Eye on Amelia). '54 *Le Blé en Herbe* (GB: Ripening Seed); *Le Rouge et le Noir* (GB: Scarlet and Black). '56 *La Traversée de Paris* (GB: Pig Across Paris). '58 *Le Joueur* (FR-IT) (USA: The Gambler). '62 *Le Meurtrier* (FR-IT-GER) (USA: Enough Rope). '64 *Le Journal d'une Femme en Blanc* (GB: Woman in White).

Fox, Metro and RKO. In 1919 he co-founded the ASC (American Society of Cinematographers). August's skilful shooting of landscape and ability to endow the mundane with mystery brought him work with Hollywood's top directors, including Howard Hawks, William Wellman, Frank Borzage, William Dieterle and most notably John Ford, for whom he shot *Lightnin'*, *The Whole Town's Talking*, *The Informer*, *Mary of Scotland* and others. August served as a naval commander during World War II and then returned to Hollywood. He died on the set of *Portrait of Jennie*.

Films include: 1916 *Civilization* (co-photo). '20 *The Toll Gate*. '25 *Tumbleweeds; Lightnin'*. '26 *The Road to Glory*. '32 *No More Orchids; Man's Castle*. '34 *Twentieth Century*. '35 *The Whole Town's Talking; The Informer*. '36 *Mary of Scotland*. '39 *The Hunchback of Notre Dame*. '48 *Portrait of Jennie* (GB: Jennie).

AUMONT, Jean-Pierre

(b.1909). Actor. Born: Jean-Pierre Salomons; Paris, France

In the Thirties, he appeared in many notable stage productions and in films with such stars as Annabella, Simone Simon and Jean Gabin. In 1939 he joined the French Tank Corps and won the Croix de Guerre. Medically discharged in 1941, he went to the USA and appeared on stage and in films. Aumont returned to France to serve with the Free French Army, was wounded and earned the Legion of Honour. He went back to Hollywood in 1946 and has continued to act, dividing his time between American and French productions. His most notable later role was as an ageing homosexual matinée idol in *Day for Night*. His second wife (1943–51) was Maria Montez, and he married the actress Marisa Pavan in 1956.

Films include: 1936 *Le Chemin de Rio* (USA: Traffic in Souls). '37 *Drôle de Drame* (USA: Bizarre, Bizarre). '38 *Hotel du Nord*. '43 *The Cross of Lorraine* (USA). '47 *Song of Scheherazade* (USA). '48 *Siren of Atlantis* (USA). '61 *The Devil at 4 O'Clock* (USA). '62 *Le Couteau dans la Plaie* (FR-IT) (GB: Five Miles to Midnight). '69 *Castle Keep* (USA). '73 *La Nuit Américaine* (FR-IT) (USA/GB: Day for Night).

AURENCHE, Jean

(b.1904). Screenwriter. Born: Pierrelatte, France

Educated by the Jesuits, he went into advertising and then into films in the early Thirties. He became a screenwriter in the late Thirties, and began his long collaboration with Pierre Bost in 1943. They concentrated on adaptations of literary novels which claimed to be faithful to the spirit of the originals while inventing cinematic equivalents to the details, and they frequently wrote bitterly satirical scripts for the director Claude Autant-Lara. Aurenche was mainly responsible for the outline of the scenes while Bost worked on dialogue. They were vigorously attacked as representatives of the so-called 'tradition of quality' by François Truffaut in *Cahiers du Cinéma* (January 1954), and they went out of fashion with the coming of the *nouvelle vague*, but made an effective comeback with Bertrand Tavernier's *L'Horloger de Saint-Paul*.

Films include: 1943 *Douce* (co-sc). '46 *La Symphonie Pastorale* (co-sc). '47 *Le Diable au Corps* (co-sc) (USA: Devil in the Flesh). '49 *Au Delà des Grilles* (co-sc) (FR-IT) (GB: Beyond the Gates). '50 *Dieu a Besoin des Hommes* (co-sc) (USA/GB: Isle of Sinners). '51 *L'Auberge Rouge* (co-sc) (USA/GB: The Red Inn). '52 *Jeux Interdits* (co-sc) (USA: Forbidden Games; GB: Secret Games). '54 *Le Blé en Herbe* (co-sc) (GB: Ripening Seed); *Le Rouge et le Noir* (co-sc) (FR-IT) (GB: Scarlet and Black). '56 *Gervaise* (co-sc); *La Traversée de Paris* (co-sc) (FR-IT) (GB: Pig Across Paris). '73 *L'Horloger de Saint-Paul* (co-sc) (GB: Watchmaker of Saint-Paul). '75 *Que la Fête Commence...* (co-sc) (USA: Let Joy Reign Supreme). '81 *Coup de Torchon* (co-sc) (GB: Clean Slate).

AUTRY, Gene

(b.1907). Singer/actor. Born: Orvion Autry; Tioga, Texas, USA

The son of an impoverished tenant farmer, Gene Autry learned to ride as a boy and by the age of 15 was travelling the West with a patent medicine show. While working in Chelsea, Oklahoma, he bought his first guitar to accompany his own singing. His break came when he appeared on a radio show called The Oklahoma Yodeling Cowboy. His first record sold a million. In 1934 Autry was signed by Republic, and within a year was starring in his own movies. By 1938 he was the top Western star in Hollywood and the only cowboy in the box-office top ten. With his smooth, chubby-faced appearance he was the true romantic cowboy hero – who always had time for a song or two. He served in the Army Air Corps during World War II. Afterwards he returned to Hollywood (often producing his own films) and made radio and television appearances. In the mid-Fifties he retired from the screen to pursue his business interests.

Films include: 1936 The Singing Vagabond. **'39** South of the Border. **'41** Ridin' on a Rainbow. **'42** Serenade of the West; Bells of Capistrano. **'46** Sioux City Sue. **'47** The Last Round-Up. **'50** Riders of the Whistling Pines. **'52** The Old West.

AVALON, Frankie

(b.1939). Singer/actor. Born: Francis Thomas Avallone; Philadelphia, Pennsylvania, USA

Avalon was a musical child – his first love was the trumpet, but in his teens he opted for singing. Chancellor Records signed him up while he was still a youth, and his first record, 'De De Durrah', was an enormous hit. Television and radio were quick to cash in on the new teenage idol and the movies – in search of another Frank Sinatra – soon had the same idea. His 'lean and handsome' appearance won him initial admiration, but it quickly became apparent that, despite his willingness, Avalon sadly lacked the necessary ability.

Films include: 1960 The Alamo. **'61** Voyage to the Bottom of the Sea. **'62** Panic in Year Zero. **'63** The Castilian (SP); Beach Party. **'64** Bikini Beach. **'65** Beach Blanket Bingo. **'78** Grease.

AVERBACK, Hy

(b.1925). Director/producer/actor. Born: Minneapolis, Minnesota, USA

While still a teenager, Hy Averback joined the KMPC radio station as an announcer and scriptwriter. During World War II he became a well-known radio personality and presented shows for the American troops. After the war he became involved in acting and appeared in various light-entertainment films such as *The Benny Goodman Story*. But working behind the camera was what really attracted Averback, and he turned his attention to direction. He spent four years as a director-producer at Four Star Productions, producing over three hundred programmes – mainly comedies for television – including the successful series *Burke's Law, The Rogues* and *Pearl*.

Films include: 1951 Cry Danger (actor only). **'55** The Benny Goodman Story (actor only). **'56** Four Girls in Town (actor only). **'67** How to Succeed in Business Without Really Trying (actor only). **'68** Where Were You When the Lights Went Out?; I Love You, Alice B. Toklas! **'70** Suppose They Gave a War and Nobody Came?

AVERY, Tex

(1907–1980). Animator. Born: Fred Bean Avery; Dallas, Texas, USA

A graduate of North Dallas High School in 1927, Avery intended to be a newspaper-strip cartoonist but in 1930 was sidetracked into Walter Lantz's animation studio as a way of earning money while he developed his art. There he fell in love with movie cartoons and stayed on in the business to become one of the greatest of all screen animators. Anarchic, free-wheeling, violent and surreal are just some of the adjectives used to describe his undoubtedly frenzied films featuring such famous characters as Bugs Bunny, Elmer Fudd, Porky Pig, Egghead, Daffy Duck, Lucky Ducky and the lugubrious hound Droopy. Avery exerted a great influence on colleagues and contemporaries like Friz Freleng and Chuck Jones during his sojourns with Warner Brothers and, later, MGM. From the late Fifties he concentrated on making animated commercials.

Films include: 1936 Golddiggers of 49. **'40** A Wild Hare. **'42** The Early Bird Dood It. **'43** One Ham's Family. **'45** The Shooting of Dan McGoo; Swing Shift Cinderella. **'46** Lonesome Lenny. **'47** Slap Happy Lion. **'49** Bad Luck Blackie; Señor Droopy; Outfoxed. **'51** Cock-A-Doodle Dog. **'54** Drag-A-Long Droopy. **'57** Cat's Meow.

AVILDSEN, John G.

(b.1936). Director. Born: Chicago, Illinois, USA

On leaving the army, he was involved in making an independent feature film with a friend, and became interested in a career in films. Meanwhile he worked in an advertising agency, writing and directing commercials. He worked in various production capacities on such films as *Mickey One* (1965) and *Hurry Sundown* (1967), and learned enough about cinematography to act as both photographer and director on his first features, including *Joe*, an incisive study of a working-class right-winger. His success with several low-budget features allowed him to move to larger productions; and for *Rocky* he won the Oscar and Directors Guild Award as Best Director. His view of the fringes of American society varies from acerbic realism to sentimental fantasy.

Films include: 1969 Turn on to Love. **'70** Sweet Dreams; Guess What We Learned in School Today?; Joe. **'71** Cry Uncle (GB: Super Dick). **'72** The Stoolie. **'73** Save the Tiger. **'75** WW and the Dixie Dancekings. **'76** Rocky. **'78** Slow Dancing in the Big City. **'80** The Formula.

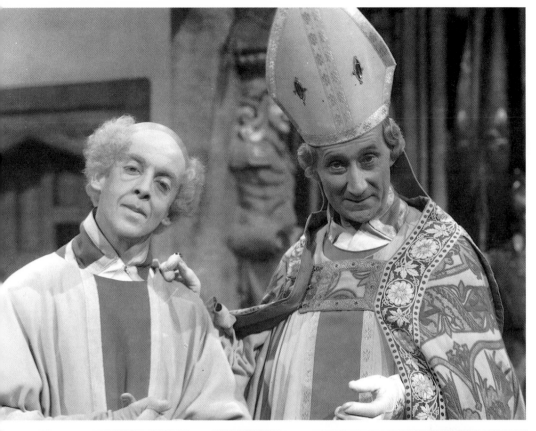

Above: Lew Ayres conveys the misery of war in All Quiet on the Western Front. *Top: Felix Aylmer (right) as the Archbishop of Canterbury in* Henry V. *with his partner in persuasion (Robert Helpmann). Above right: Charles Aznavour*

AXELROD, George

(b. 1922). Screenwriter/director. Born: New York City, USA

Axelrod had an unremarkable early career as a stage actor and manager, and opted for radio instead. Though interrupted by wartime service, by 1952 he had completed scripts for some four hundred radio and television shows. Following the Broadway success of *The Seven Year Itch*, the first of his several hit plays, in 1954 he came to Hollywood and turned both it and William Inge's *Bus Stop* into vehicles for Marilyn Monroe as a girl unaware of her devastating sex appeal. Though his true milieu is slyly witty sex comedy, Axelrod scripted the spy thriller *The Manchurian Candidate*. In the Sixties he proved himself an able director and producer of his own screen material. He is famed as a raconteur.

Films as screenwriter: 1954 Phffft!. '55 The Seven Year Itch (co-sc; + play basis). '56 Bus Stop. '57 Will Success Spoil Rock Hunter? (play basis only). '61 Breakfast at Tiffany's. '62 The Manchurian Candidate. '64 Paris When It Sizzles. '65 How to Murder Your Wife. '66 Lord Love a Duck (+ dir). '68 The Secret Life of an American Wife (+ dir). '79 The Lady Vanishes.

AYLMER, Felix

(1889–1979). Actor. Born: Felix Edward Aylmer-Jones; Corsham, Wiltshire, England

Felix Aylmer was educated at Oxford and went on to study drama, making his professional debut at the London Coliseum in 1911. He served with the RNVR during World War I, but returned to the stage to resume a career that lasted well into the Sixties. Involved in films from the early Thirties, he became typecast in elderly, benevolent or doddery roles – mainly as clerics and schoolteachers: for example, he was the vicar in charge of a wartime children's party in *The Way to the Stars*. He is perhaps best remembered for his portrayals of the wily Archbishop of Laurence Olivier's *Henry V* and Father Anselm in the television series *Oh, Brother*. This enduring English actor was awarded the OBE in 1950 and was knighted in 1965.

Films include: 1930 Escape (GB). '37 The Rat. '38 The Citadel; Sixty Glorious Years. '42 The Young Mr Pitt. '43 The Life and Death of Colonel Blimp. '44 Henry V. '45 The Way to the Stars. '48 Hamlet; Macbeth. '52 Ivanhoe. '64 Becket

AYRES, Lew

(b. 1908). Actor. Born: Lewis Ayres; Minneapolis, Minnesota, USA

There is a certain irony to be drawn between Ayres' private life and screen career. He studied medicine at the University of Arizona but, with a musical background, he decided to join the Henry Halstead Orchestra. While playing in a Hollywood nightclub in 1928, a Pathé talent-scout spotted him and producer Paul Bern subsequently signed him to play opposite Greta Garbo in *The Kiss*. He then gained international fame as the pacifist soldier in *All Quiet on the Western Front*, a role that was not to sit so easily upon his shoulders in real life when he turned conscientous objector in 1941. After a year and a half as a non-combatant medic he returned to the screen and became Dr Kildare. However, his stand during the war desroyed his popularity and he now devotes his time to studying philosophy and comparative religion. He has been twice married and divorced: Lola Lane (from 1931 to 1933); Ginger Rogers (1934 to 1940).

Films include: 1929 The Kiss. '30 All Quiet on the Western Front. '34 Let's Be Ritzy (GB: Millionaire for a Day). '38 Holiday (GB: Free to Live); Young Dr Kildare. '39 The Secret of Dr Kildare. '46 The Dark Mirror. '48 Johnny Belinda. '64 The Carpetbaggers.

AZNAVOUR, Charles

(b. 1924). Singer/actor/songwriter. Born: Shahnour Varenagh Aznavourian; Paris, France

The son of Armenian parents, Aznavour studied dance and drama as a child and by the age of ten was a seasoned performer who made an early film debut. During World War II he supported his family from the proceeds of his stage appearances and began writing songs and singing for extra income. Encouraged by Edith Piaf, he continued to sing, and by the mid-Fifties was France's leading performer. Diminutive and rugged looking, he has appeared as the archetypal Frenchman in many movies, but has shown little real interest in the medium. Perhaps his most memorable screen role is as the café entertainer in François Truffaut's *Tirez sur le Pianiste*. He has also written music for the cinema.

Films include: 1960 Tirez sur le Pianiste (GB: Shoot the Pianist). '62 Les Quatres Vérités (FR-SP-IT) (GB: The Three Fables of Love). '63 Le Rat d'Amérique (FR-IT). '64 Pourquoi Paris? (FR-IT). '66 Paris au Mois d'Août (USA/GB: Paris in August). '68 Candy (USA-IT-FR). '70 The Adventurers (GB). '75 And Then There Were None (GER-FR-SP). '79 Die Blechtrommel (GER-FR) (GB: The Tin Drum). '82 Les Fantômes du Chapelier (GB: The Hatter's Ghosts).

B

BACALL, Lauren

(b. 1924). Actress. Born: Betty Perske; New York City, USA

She was 19, tall, skinny, almost gawky and a model in the women's magazine *Harper's Bazaar*, where she was spotted by Howard Hawks' wife. Hawks gave her the lead opposite Humphrey Bogart in *To Have and Have Not*, and a romantic involvement between the two stars added spice and sparks to the film. They were married from 1945 until Bogart's death in 1957. She was subsequently married to Jason Robards from 1961 to 1973. Bacall's deep, sexy voice, warm personality and air of sophisticated toughness were assets in *films noirs* and melodramas, and also carried her through more conventional romances and occasional comedies. In 1970 she won a Tony for her leading role in *Applause* (a musical version of *All About Eve*) on Broadway.

Films include: **1944** To Have and Have Not. **'46** The Big Sleep. **'47** Dark Passage. **'48** Key Largo. **'50** Young Man With a Horn. **'53** How to Marry a Millionaire. **'55** The Cobweb. **'56** Written on the Wind. **'57** Designing Woman. **'59** North West Frontier (GB) (USA: Flame Over India). **'66** Harper (GB: The Moving Target). **'74** Murder on the Orient Express (GB). **'76** The Shootist. **'80** Health.

BACHARACH, Burt

(b. 1929). Composer. Born: Kansas City, Missouri, USA

During the mid-Fifties Bacharach was a piano accompanist for singers Vic Damone and Steve Lawrence. In 1958 he was engaged as conductor and accompanist by Marlene Dietrich. He teamed up with the lyricist Hal David to form a highly successful songwriting team, collaborating closely with the singer Dionne Warwick on such hits as 'Walk On By' and 'Do You Know the Way to San Jose?' Bacharach's songs are melodically inventive and emotional, but with a sentimental tendency not always held in check. In 1969 he won Oscars for Best Song ('Raindrops Keep Fallin' on My Head') and Best Original Score for *Butch Cassidy and the Sundance Kid*. He has been married to the actress Angie Dickinson and the singer/composer Carol Bayer Sager.

Films include: **1965** What's New, Pussycat? (USA-FR). **'66** Alfie (GB); Caccia alla Volpe (IT) (USA/GB: After the Fox). **'67** Casino Royale (GB). **'69** Butch Cassidy and the Sundance Kid. **'73** Lost Horizon.

BACKUS, Jim

(b. 1913). Actor. Born: Cleveland, Ohio, USA

After graduating from the American Academy of Dramatic Arts, Backus found work in a stock company, in vaudeville and then in radio. In 1936 he went to New York to act in the theatre and on radio, eventually getting his own radio show. He moved to Hollywood in the late Forties, concentrating on films and television. His best-known film role was as the confused father of Jim (James Dean) in *Rebel Without a Cause*; but his voice was even more familiar in the UPA Mr Magoo cartoon series as that of the short-sighted but intrepid hero. He starred with Joan Davis in the television series *I Married Joan*. His square-built figure and characterful, expressive face have lent sturdy support to over seventy films.

Films include: **1942** The Pied Piper. **'50** The Killer That Stalked New York (GB: Frightened City). **'51** His Kind of Woman. **'52** Pat and Mike; Don't Bother to Knock. **'55** Rebel Without a Cause. **'62** Boys' Night Out. **'63** Johnny Cool; It's a Mad, Mad, Mad, Mad World; The Wheeler Dealers (GB: Separate Beds). **'67** Hurry Sundown; Don't Make Waves.

BACLANOVA, Olga

(1896–1974). Actress. Born: Olga Baklanova; Moscow, USSR

She acted from the age of 16 at the Moscow Art Theatre, where Constantin Stanislavsky refused to speak to her for six months after she began working concurrently in films. She visited the USA with a Russian stage production in 1923 and stayed. Her American film career was brief, beginning in 1928 and virtually over after 1932, but she remained in the USA. Her outstanding roles were as a cast-off street girl in Mauritz Stiller's *The Street of Sin*; as a sailor's wife who kills her faithless husband in Josef von Sternberg's *The Docks of New York*; as the seductive Duchess in Paul Leni's *The Man Who Laughs*; and as the glamorous but evil trapeze-artist in Tod Browning's *Freaks*.

Films include: **1914** Kogda Zvuchat Struni Serdtza; Simfoniya Lyubvi i Smerti. **'15** Veliky Magaraz. **'17** Tsveti Zapozdaliye. **'27** The Dove (USA). **'28** The Street of Sin (USA); The Docks of New York (USA); The Man Who Laughs (USA). **'32** Freaks (USA). **'43** Claudia (USA)

BACON, Lloyd

(1889–1955). Director. Born: San Jose, California, USA

From a background in vaudeville, he joined Essanay as an actor, appearing with Charlie Chaplin in such comedies as *The Champion* and *The Tramp* (both 1915). He moved to Mutual with Chaplin in 1916 and made several more films with him, including *The Floorwalker* and *The Vagabond* (both 1916), before going off to war service in the navy. In 1921 he became a director for the comedian Lloyd Hamilton, and then turned out two-reelers for Mack Sennett before moving to Warner Brothers to direct features.

There he specialized in musicals, including *The Singing Fool* and *42nd Street*, and also in comedies and tough crime melodramas such as *Marked Woman*. His career was long and prolific though with few high points after the Thirties – apart from some censorship scandal over Jane Russell's costumes in *The French Line*.

Films include: 1928 The Singing Fool. '33 42nd Street. '37 Marked Woman; San Quentin. '40 Brother Orchid. '47 I Wonder Who's Kissing Her Now. '48 Give My Regards to Broadway. '50 The Good Humor Man. '52 The I Don't Care Girl. '54 She Couldn't Say No; The French Line.

BADDELEY, Hermione

(1906–1986). Actress. Born: Hermione Clinton-Baddeley; Broseley, Shropshire, England

Plump, pretty and funny, she was on the stage at 16, appeared in revues with Noel Coward in the Twenties, and made her film debut in 1927. A fashionable marriage to David Tennant (1928–37) kept her away from the theatre for four years. She established herself as a comedienne and in character parts, appearing in British films of the Forties and Fifties – *Room at the Top* brought her a Best Supporting Actress Oscar nomination – and then in American films of the Sixties. She also had a five-year run on American television as the housekeeper in *Maud*. She kept in touch with the London theatre, performing in a revue with Hermione Gingold and starring in *The Killing of Sister George* in 1966 and *The Threepenny Opera* in 1972. The stage and TV actress Angela Baddeley (1904–76) was her sister.

Films include: 1927 A Daughter in Revolt. '41 Kipps. '47 Brighton Rock. '48 Quartet. '49 Passport to Pimlico. '51 Scrooge; Tom Brown's Schooldays. '52 The Pickwick Papers. '59 Room at the Top; Expresso Bongo. '64 Mary Poppins (USA); The Un-

sinkable Molly Brown (USA). '65 Marriage on the Rocks (USA). '74 The Black Windmill.

BADEL, Alan

(1923–1982). Actor. Born: Manchester, England

After winning a Gold Medal at RADA, Badel took a variety of classical and modern parts in repertory theatre, notably as Romeo to Claire Bloom's Juliet at the Old Vic in 1953. His fine, impressive presence and rich, distinctive voice appeared to advantage not only on stage but in a long list of film and television credits. Though he sometimes took lead roles in the theatre (*Kean*, 1971) and television (*The Count of Monte Cristo*, 1964) he was mainly a character actor in films – for instance, as a wealthy and faintly corrupt director of a Rugby League club in *This Sporting Life*. His relatively early death was a considerable loss. He was the father of actress Sarah Badel.

Films include: 1942 The Young Mr Pitt. '53 Salome (USA). '54 Three Cases of Murder. '63 This Sporting Life. '64 The Yellow Rolls Royce. '69 Otley. '73 The Day of the Jackal. '77 Telefon. '79 The Riddle of the Sands; Agatha. '80 Nijinsky.

BADGER, Clarence

(1880–1964). Director. Born: San Francisco, California, USA

Educated at the Boston Polytechnic Institute, Badger was working as a journalist when he was engaged as a writer for Mack Sennett at Triangle-Keystone in 1915. Almost immediately he moved on to directing two-reelers. Through 1916–17 he directed numerous Gloria Swanson–Bobby Vernon comedies which gave Swanson an excellent introduction to stardom. Characteristic films of his include: *Jubilo*, an attractive small-town Will Rogers vehicle; *Hands Up!*, a very funny

Civil War comedy with Raymond Griffith; and *It!*, a charming Clara Bow comedy. Badger Also directed Bow in two other features. *Red Hair* and *Three Week-Ends*. His films have a gentle, relaxed charm. His American directorial career ended in 1933, though he emigrated to Australia and later made two final films there.

Films include: 1919 Jubilo. '26 Hands Up! '27 It!; Señorita; She's a Sheik; A Kiss in a Taxi. '28 Hot News; Red Hair; Three Week-Ends. '30 No. No, Nanette.

BADHAM, John

Director. Born: England

After studying philosophy at Yale, he went on to its drama school. A job in the mailroom at Universal led to his becoming a guide on the famous studio tour. He was an associate producer for Steven Spielberg and made trailers. He became a television director for *Streets of San Francisco*, *Night Gallery*, *The Bold Ones* and other series in the early Seventies, and also directed seven television films including an entertaining drama, *The Law* (1974), which won Emmy awards. Moving to feature films, Badham applied an all-out frantic style to a variety of subject-matter: baseball's race problems, disco-dancing, vampirism and euthanasia. His box-office breakthrough, *Saturday Night Fever*, made a star of John Travolta.

Films: 1976 The Bingo Long Traveling All-Stars and Motor Kings. '77 Saturday Night Fever. '79 Dracula. '81 Whose Life Is It Anyway?

Below, from left to right: Lauren Bacall; Jim Backus (left) in Hurry Sundown, *with Michael Caine; Olga Baclanova; Hermione Baddeley as Mrs Bardell in* The Pickwick Papers. *Right: Alan Badel as a sadistic security chief in* The Adventurers *(1970)*

BAGGOT, King

(1874–1948). Actor/director. Born: St Louis, Missouri, USA

A former stage actor, Baggot made his film acting debut in 1910 and was a star from 1911. He was tall, burly, handsome and immensely popular. *Ivanhoe* was typical of his upstanding heroes; his Hyde in *Dr Jekyll and Mr Hyde* was a marvellously evil characterization. As an actor he loved disguise and in *Shadows* he played all ten parts, ranging from the young hero to an elderly Chinese. He took up directing in 1915 but, apart from the William S. Hart Western *Tumbleweeds*, with its superb land-rush sequence, most of his films were routine. He gave up directing after the late Twenties, and returned to acting with occasional character parts in sound films.

Films include: 1912 Camille (actor only). '13 Ivanhoe (actor only); Dr Jekyll and Mr Hyde (actor only). '14 Shadows (actor only). '21 Cheated Love (dir. only). '22 Human Hearts (dir. only). '25 Raffles, the Amateur Cracksman (dir. only); Tumbleweeds (dir. only). '26 Lovey Mary (dir, only). '28 Across the Atlantic (actor only); Romance of a Rogue.

BAILEY, Pearl

(b. 1918). Singer/actress. Born: Washington DC, USA

Renowned for her unique singing style, with asides and comments, Pearl Bailey has been only an occasional visitor to films. The daughter of a small-town preacher, she was in vaudeville and was a big-band singer. She made her Broadway debut in 1946 in *St Louis Woman* and her film debut a year later. She was in both the stage and film versions of *Porgy and Bess*, and won a Tony for her leading role in a stage version of *Hello, Dolly!* with an all-black cast. In 1975 she was appointed special adviser to the United States Mission to the United Nations. She has published five books including an autobiography, *The Raw Pearl*.

Films: 1947 Variety Girl. '48 Isn't It Romantic? '54 Carmen Jones. '56 That Certain Feeling. '58 St Louis Blues. '59 Porgy and Bess. '60 All the Fine Young Cannibals. '70 The Landlord. '81 The Fox and the Hound (voice only).

BAINTER, Fay

(1892–1968). Actress. Born: Los Angeles, California, USA

Fay Bainter made her Broadway debut in 1912 with *The Rose of Panama*, and entertained the troops in Europe during World War I. She continued to star on Broadway and was already 41 when she made her screen debut. She won a Best Supporting Actress Oscar in 1938 for her role as the aunt of the wayward girl played by Bette Davis in *Jezebel*. In the same year she was also nominated as Best Actress for her part in *White Banners*, but Davis won – for *Jezebel*. This was the high point of a career spent playing understanding friends or relatives – aunts, mothers and, latterly, grandmothers. Fay Bainter was married to Admiral Reginald Venable from 1921 to 1964.

Films include: 1932 A Bill of Divorcement. '38 Jezebel; White Banners. '39 Daughters Courageous. '40 Our Town. '41 Babes on Broadway. '42 Woman of the Year; Mrs Wiggs of the Cabbage Patch. '45 State Fair. '46 The Kid From Brooklyn. '47 The Secret Life of Walter Mitty. '48 Give My Regards to Broadway.

BAKER, Carroll

(b. 1931). Actress. Born: Johnstown, Pennsylvania, USA

Following an unhappy childhood, Carroll Baker moved to Florida with her mother, who had divorced and remarried. After working in a magic act and as a dancer Baker moved to New York where she appeared in a chorus line and in television commercials for Coca-Cola. She then joined the Actors' Studio and through the recommendations of its influential director, Lee Strasberg, she gained her first major movie role as Liz Benedict in *Giant*. Then came her most notorious performance, as the sexy, mentally retarded teenager in Elia Kazan's *Baby Doll*. As a result of that film, Baker was typecast in the Sixties as a leggy, brassy blonde – hence she was

ideal for *The Carpetbaggers* and *Harlow* – but tired of such roles and moved to Rome to appear in Italian films. In 1969 she was divorced from her second husband, the director Jack Garfein. Her particular brand of vulgar sex appeal may now prove too dated for a successful return to Hollywood.

Films include: 1953 Easy to Love. '56 Giant; Baby Doll. '58 The Big Country. '62 How the West Was Won. '63 Station Six Sahara (GB-GER). '64 The Carpetbaggers; Cheyenne Autumn. '65 The Greatest Story Ever Told; Harlow. '68 Il Dolce Corpo di Deborah (IT-FR) (USA/GB: The Sweet Body of Deborah). '79 The World Is Full of Married Men (GB).

BAKER, Joe Don

(b. 1936). Actor. Born: Groesbeck, Texas, USA

Texas-born, Baker lives up to the rugged, tough, macho image associated with his native state. Raised in Houston, he studied at the Actors' Studio in New York. In 1967 he went to Hollywood and made his screen debut with a bit part in *Cool Hand Luke* the same year. He has appeared in several TV series, such as *Gunsmoke* and *Bonanza* and in television films. His characteristic roles on the big screen have been such villains as Molly, the Mafia hitman, in *Charley Varrick*, who claims: 'Ah don't sleep with whores – at least, not knowin'ly'. But his biggest success was as the hard-hitting Tennessee Sheriff Buford Pusser in *Walking Tall*, though he relinquished the role in the two sequels.

Films include: 1969 Guns of the Magnificent Seven. '70 Adam at 6 AM. '71 Wild Rovers. '72 Junior Bonner; Welcome Home, Soldier Boys. '73 Charley Varrick; The Outfit; Walking Tall. '74 Golden Needles. '75 Framed; Mitchell. '76 Checkered Flag or Crash (GB: Crash). '78 Speedtrap.

BAKER, Roy Ward

(b. 1916). Director. Born: London, England

On leaving school Roy Ward Baker entered the glamorous world of film as teaboy at the Gainsborough Studios, and within three years was working as an assistant director. During World War II he worked in the Army Kinematograph Unit under the writer Eric Ambler who gave him the opportunity to direct his first film, *The October Man*, after the war. Despite a seven-year spell in Hollywood during the Fifties, he has made his best films in England, particularly *A Night to Remember*, which was voted one of the ten best films of the year in 1959 by New York critics. During the Sixties he directed a number of Hammer horror films as well as segments of several British television series. He continues to work successfully in both media.

Films include: 1947 The October Man. '48 The Weaker Sex. '49 Paper Orchid. '50 Morning Departure (USA: Operation Disaster); Highly Dangerous. '52 Don't Bother to Knock (USA). '58 A Night to Remember. '60 The Singer Not the Song. '67 Quatermass and the Pit. '72 Asylum.

Left: Pearl Bailey in The Landlord.
Above: Fay Bainter. Right: Joe Don
Baker in Walking Tall. Below:
Stanley Baker in Zulu. Below left:
Carroll Baker in The Carpetbaggers

BAKER, Stanley

(1927–1976). Actor. Born: Ferndale,
Glamorgan, Wales

A miner's son, Baker made his screen
debut as a Yugoslav schoolboy in
Sergei Nolbandov's war-time Ealing
film *Undercover* (1943). After two
years at Birmingham Repertory
Theatre, he went to London. *The Cruel
Sea* established him as a screen actor
and he won a long-term contract with
Rank. He frequently played tough
guys and villains, but his four films
with the director Joseph Losey (*Blind
Date*, *The Criminal*, *Eva* and *Accident*)
brought out a wider range – not only
a policeman and a thief but a
plagiarizing Welsh novelist and an
adulterous Oxford television don. He
co-produced several of his own films,
including *Zulu*, *Robbery* and *Where's
Jack?* Baker was knighted in 1976,
shortly before his death.

Films include: 1951 Captain Horatio
Hornblower (USA) (GB: Captain Horatio
Hornblower RN). '53 The Cruel Sea. '54 The
Good Die Young. '55 Helen of Troy (USA).
'56 A Hill in Korea; Alexander the Great
(USA). '57 Hell Drivers. '59 Blind Date. '60
The Criminal (USA: The Concrete Jungle).
'61 The Guns of Navarone. '62 Eva (FR-IT)
(GB: Eve). '63 Zulu. '67 Accident; Robbery.
'69 Where's Jack?

BAKSHI, Ralph

(b. 1939). Animation director. Born:
New York City, USA

The son of Russian Jewish immigrants, Bakshi grew up in a ghetto
neighbourhood of New York City,
then found a job inking cartoons for
Terrytoons. He worked for several
years at Paramount's animation
studio until it closed down, whereupon he formed his own production
company with the producer Steve

Krantz. The violently satirical (and
popular) *Fritz the Cat* caused controversy with its crude depiction of
race and sex, and the furore increased
with his subsequent films, especially
Coon Skin, which was criticized by the
Congress of Racial Equality (CORE).
As a result, Paramount halted its
distribution and withdrew finance
from *Hey Good Looking* in mid-
production. With *Wizards* and *The
Lord of the Rings*, Bakshi turned to
fantasy but kept a realistic element in
his use of rotoscoping – animating by
tracing live-action characters. His
American Pop returned to a satirical
treatment.

Films: 1972 Fritz the Cat. '73 Heavy Traffic.
'75 Coon Skin. '74–'76 Hey Good Looking
(unfinished). '77 Wizards. '79 The Lord of
the Rings. '81 American Pop.

BALÁZS, Béla

(1884–1949). Theorist/screenwriter/
novelist. Born: Herbert Bauer;
Szeged, Hungary

Driven out of Hungary in 1919 as a
Marxist, Balázs settled in Vienna with
other exiles, including Alexander
Korda, Michael Curtiz and Bela
Lugosi. In 1924 he published his first
book of film theory, *Der Sichtbare
Mensch*, emphasizing close-ups and
montage. In 1926 he moved to Berlin,
where he became involved in left-
wing film and theatre projects with
the director G. W. Pabst, the producer
Erwin Piscator and the writer Bertolt
Brecht. He co-scripted films and published *Der Geist des Films* in 1930,
warning against the changes in film
form brought about by talkies. In
1931 he moved to the USSR as a
professor and in 1945 returned to
Hungary, helping to rebuild its film
industry. He continued to be an influential film theorist and teacher and a
selection of his writings was published
in English as *Theory of the Film* in 1952.
After his death, the Béla Balázs studio
for young experimental film-makers
was opened in Budapest.

Films include: 1924 Moderne Ehen (co-sc)
(GER). '26 Madame wünscht keine Kinder
(GER); Die Abenteuer eines Zehn-
markscheines (GER) (GB: Adventures of a
Ten Mark Note). '27 1 + 1 = 3/Eins plus Eins
gleich Drei (co-sc) (GER); Doña Juana (co-
sc) (GER). '29 Fräulein Else (co-sc) (GER);
Narkose (co-sc) (GER). '31 Die Dreigroschenoper (co-sc) (GER/USA) (USA/GB: The
Threepenny Opera). '32 Das blaue Licht
(co-dir; + sc) (GER) (GB: The Blue Light). '47
Valahol Európában (co-sc) (GB: Somewhere
in Europe/Kuksi); Ének a Búzamezokröl
(artistic consultant only) (GB: Song of the
Wheatfields).

BALCHIN, Nigel

(1908–70). Novelist/screenwriter.
Born: Potterne, Wiltshire, England

Balchin read Natural Sciences at
Cambridge and then worked as an
industrial scientist in the Thirties.
During World War II he rose to the
rank of Brigadier and Deputy Scientific Adviser to the Army, an experience he drew on in his most
famous novel *The Small Back Room*.
After the war he combined scientific
research with writing. Several of
Balchin's novels were filmed, and he
wrote the scripts for a couple of these.
He became a screenwriter for British
films and later in Hollywood. His
novels were characterized by strong
narratives, fast pace, vitality of
characters and psychological analysis; and he brought similar qualities
to his better screenplays. He won a
British Film Academy Award in 1956
for *The Man Who Never Was*, a war
film based partly on fact.

Films include: 1947 Fame Is the Spur; Mine
Own Executioner (from own novel). '49 The
Small Back Room (novel basis only) (USA:
Hour of Glory). '52 Mandy (co-sc) (USA:
Crash of Silence). '53 Malta Story (co-sc).
'55 The Man Who Never Was; Josephine
and Men. '56 23 Paces to Baker Street
(USA). '59 The Blue Angel (USA). '60 The
Singer Not the Song; Circle of Deception;
Suspect (from own novel) (USA: The Risk).
'61 Barabba (co-sc) (IT) (USA/GB:
Barabbas).

25

BALCON, Michael

(1896–1978). Producer. Born: Birmingham, England

After World War I, Balcon began film production at Islington studios, which he later acquired for his Gainsborough company, and in 1931 he also took over production for Gaumont-British, with considerable success until 1936. Following a brief, unsatisfactory co-production deal with MGM, he moved to Ealing Studios as head of production in 1938. Ealing's principal contribution at first was war films and traditional comedies. After the war, Balcon led his talented team into a new area of mildly anarchic comedy, typified by *Passport to Pimlico*, and pioneered production of dramas in Commonwealth locations. Forced to sell the studio to the BBC in 1955, Ealing soon ran out of steam. Balcon later helped to set up Bryanston, which backed many of the British 'New Wave' films, and headed the group that revived British Lion distributors. He was knighted in 1948 for his crucial contribution to the development of British films.

Films include: 1922 Woman to Woman. '27 Easy Virtue. '28 The Constant Nymph. '30 Journey's End. '31 The Ghost Train. '32 Rome Express. '34 Man of Aran (doc). '35 The Thirty-Nine Steps. '36 Sabotage. '39 The Proud Valley. '40 Convoy. '42 The Foreman Went to France. '47 Hue and Cry. '49 Passport to Pimlico; Whisky Galore! (USA: Tight Little Island). '53 The Cruel Sea (exec. prod).

BALFOUR, Betty

(1903–1979). Actress. Born: Elizabeth Balfour; London, England

Betty Balfour made her stage debut at the Empire Theatre, Wood Green, London, at the age of 11. Six years later she appeared in her first film, *Nothing Else Matters*. Blue-eyed and blonde, she was a lively heroine of many British silent comedies, and made four in the 'Squibs' series about a cockney flower-seller. She also made a few talkies, but concentrated on her own Betty Balfour Pictures productions. In 1924 she won the Daily News contest for the most popular actress in British films.

Films include: 1920 Nothing Else Matters. '21 Squibs. '22 Squibs Wins the Calcutta Sweep. '23 Love, Life and Laughter. '26 Cinders. '28 Champagne. '30 The Vagabond Queen; The Brat/The Nipper. '34 Evergreen. '35 Forever England (USA: Born for Glory). '45 29, Acacia Avenue (USA: Facts of Love).

BALL, Lucille

(b. 1911). Actress. Born: Jamestown, New York, USA *Died April 89*

After training at drama school in New York City, Lucille Ball became a successful fashion model under the name Diane Belmont. In the early Thirties, an MGM talent scout took her to Hollywood, supposedly for six weeks' work, but the weeks became months, and the fiery redhead found herself as a glamorous bit player in B movies. She eventually signed for RKO, and

after several years as a semi-serious actress established herself as one of America's foremost comediennes. In 1950 she and her first husband, Cuban bandleader Desi Arnaz, started their incredibly successful television comedy series *I Love Lucy*, a pioneer situation comedy. Their company, Desilu, later bought the RKO studio and turned it into a lucrative television studio. Arnaz sold his share to Ball after their divorce. In 1961 she married nightclub comedian Gary Morton. She continues to make appearances in films and on television.

Films include: 1933 Roman Scandals. '36 Follow the Fleet. '37 Stage Door. '40 Dance Girl, Dance. '42 The Big Street. '43 Du Barry Was a Lady. '46 Ziegfeld Follies. '47 Lured (GB: Personal Column). '49 Sorrowful Jones. '73 Mame.

BALLARD, Lucien

(b. 1908). Cinematographer. Born: Miami, Oklahoma, USA

Ballard first found employment in movies as an editor and assistant cameraman in 1929. In the latter capacity he worked with cinematographer Lee Garmes on *Morocco* (1930) and thereby gained his entrée into feature films. Josef von Sternberg employed him as his co-cinematographer on *The Devil Is a Woman*, after which he was regarded as a fully-fledged director of photography. Already a specialist in black and white interior shooting, his use of colour in Westerns (often for Sam Peckinpah) came to be highly respected. He worked on many films with actress Merle Oberon, whom he married and divorced in the late Forties.

Films include: 1935 The Devil Is a Woman. '44 Laura. '51 The House on Telegraph Hill. '56 The Killing. '62 Ride the High Country. '65 The Sons of Katie Elder. '67 Will Penny. '69 The Wild Bunch; True Grit. '70 The Ballad of Cable Hogue. '72 Junior Bonner.

BALSAM, Martin

(b. 1919). Actor. Born: New York City, USA

Balsam, a kindly though pugnacious-looking character actor, studied drama under Erwin Piscator (and later at the Actor's Studio). After a few stage appearances he joined up for the duration of World War II and on his return found his niche in television. His Method training stood him in good stead with the arrival of live television drama. His success on the small screen brought him some substantial movie roles in such films as *On the Waterfront* and *Psycho*. He won an Oscar for Best Supporting Actor for his part in *A Thousand Clowns*.

Films include: 1954 On the Waterfront. '57 Twelve Angry Men. '60 Psycho. '61 Breakfast at Tiffany's. '65 The Bedford Incident; A Thousand Clowns. '67 Hombre. '70 Little Big Man; Tora! Tora! Tora! '71 The Anderson Tapes. '73 Summer Wishes, Winter Dreams. '74 The Taking of Pelham 1, 2, 3. '76 All the Presidents Men.

Right: Betty Balfour. Far right: Anne Bancroft in The Graduate. *Above, far right: Martin Balsam in* All the President's Men

BANCROFT, Anne

(b. 1931). Actress. Born: Anna Maria Italiano; New York City, USA

Anne Bancroft trained at the American Academy of Dramatic Arts and while still at college was offered a job in television. She made her debut in 1950 using the name Anne Marno. In 1951 she did a screen test for 20th Century-Fox and made her debut for them in *Don't Bother to Knock*. A handful of minor roles followed and she became a 'starlet'. After 1954 she freelanced, appearing on the stage and television. Having appeared in the play 'The Miracle Worker', she then made the film and won herself an Oscar. Intense and emotionally charged, she also has great capacity for comedy, as excellently exploited by her husband, the comedian and director Mel Brooks, in *Silent Movie*.

Films include: 1952 Don't Bother to Knock. '62 The Miracle Worker. '64 The Pumpkin Eater. '65 Seven Women. '67 The Graduate. '72 Young Winston. '74 The Prisoner of Second Avenue. '76 Silent Movie. '77 The Turning Point. '80 The Elephant Man.

BANCROFT, George

(1882–1956). Actor. Born: Philadelphia, Pennsylvania, USA

George Bancroft was educated at the Annapolis Naval Academy and while serving in the forces organized entertainments for his fellow-servicemen. On leaving the Navy he took up a theatrical career in earnest, making his first appearance as a black-faced minstrel in a song-and-dance revue. He then progressed to Broadway dramas and in 1921 made his screen debut in *The Journey's End*. A 'heavy' character projecting tough masculinity, he had, nevertheless, a kindly face and was used by Josef von Sternberg as a 'good guy' gangster and smiling villain. He retired to run a ranch in 1942.

Films include: 1921 The Journey's End. '26 Old Ironsides. '27 Underworld. '28 The Docks of New York. '29 Thunderbolt. '31 Scandal Sheet. '36 Mr Deeds Goes to Town. '38 Angels With Dirty Faces. '39 Stagecoach. '40 When the Daltons Rode; North West Mounted Police.

BANKHEAD, Tallulah

(1902–1968). Actress. Born: Huntsville, Alabama, USA

Born into a very wealthy and politically influential family (her father and uncle were congressmen, her grandfather a senator), Bankhead won a film-magazine competition when only 15 years old. Part of the prize was a trip to New York, where she stayed on to begin a distinguished stage career. In 1923 she went to London and quickly became celebrated for her husky voice, outrageous behaviour and quick wit. Whisked off to play sophisticated bitch roles by the star-makers of Hollywood, she unhappily never found the roles to exploit her full potential.

Films include: 1919 The Virtuous Vamp. '28 His House in Order (GB); A Woman's Law (GB); My Sin; The Cheat. '32 Faithless. '43 Stage Door Canteen. '44 Lifeboat. '45 A Royal Scandal (GB: Czarina). '65 Fanatic/Die! Die! My Darling (GB).

26

BANKY, Vilma

(b. 1898). Actress. Born: Vilma Lonchit; Budapest, Hungary

Little is known of Vilma Banky's early films, but while on a European tour in 1924 Samuel Goldwyn was so impressed by one of them that he signed her up and took her to Hollywood. Blonde, petite, blue-grey-eyed and billed as 'The Hungarian Rhapsody', she found fame as a romantic heroine, often opposite Ronald Colman. With the coming of sound she retired to concentrate on her marriage to fellow actor Rod La Rocque (which lasted from 1927 until his death in 1969). A golf fanatic, she still remains active in her eighties.

Films include: 1920 Im Letzten Augenblick (AUS-HUN). '21 Galathea (HUN). '24 Das Verbotene Land (AUS). '25 The Eagle (USA). '26 The Son of the Sheik (USA); The Winning of Barbara Worth (USA). '27 The Night of Love (USA); The Magic Flame (USA). '29 This Is Heaven (USA). '30 A Lady to Love. '32 Der Rebell (GER).

BARA, Theda

(1890–1955). Actress. Born: Theodosia Goodman; Cincinnati, Ohio, USA

The word 'vamp' was probably invented for Theda Bara. Dark-haired, deathly pale and with large staring eyes, she was the pre-Twenties idea of the *femme fatale* – a depraved, merciless enslaver of men in such films as *A Fool There Was, Carmen, Cleopatra* and *Salome*. Her publicity-minded studio, Fox, spread the word that this poisonous, exotic creature was the love-child of a European artist and an Arab princess. In fact, she was the shy, good-humoured and short-sighted daughter of a Cincinnati tailor, an actress who graduated to films via Broadway and became a major star. But despite film roles as sweet costume-drama heroines, she could not escape the vamp label, and her career quickly waned with the advent of the Jazz Age. A comeback in the Twenties failed. She was married to director Charles Brabin.

Films include: 1915 A Fool There Was; The Clemenceau Case (GB: Infidelity); The Two Orphans; Sin; Carmen. '16 The Serpent (GB: Fires of Hate); Under Two Flags; Romeo and Juliet; The Vixen (GB: The Love Pirate). '17 The Darling of Paris; Camille; Cleopatra; Madame Dubarry. '18 Salome. '19 Kathleen Mavourneen. '25 The Unchastened Woman.

BARBERA, Joseph

see HANNA & BARBERA

BARDEM, Juan Antonio

(b. 1922). Director/screenwriter/producer. Born: Madrid, Spain

A talented and outspoken critic of Spain under Franco, Bardem had his career blighted by censorship when he was at his most potent as a realist film-maker in the Fifties. He first worked for the Film Department of the Ministry of Agriculture. In 1947 he entered the Spanish cinema institute but, perhaps because he was already airing his political views, failed to win his diploma. He supported himself as a critic and in 1951 broke into films in collaboration with Luis Garcia Berlanga, his one noteworthy contemporary in the slumbering Spanish cinema. *Death of a Cyclist*, the story of illicit lovers who run down a cyclist, has remained his most biting and effective work, and was the 1956 winner of the International Critics Award at Cannes. During the making of his next film, *Calle Mayor*, Bardem was arrested by the authorities but released after an international uproar. Bardem's recent work as director lacks his former bite.

Films include: 1951 Esa Pareja Feliz (co-dir). '52 Bienvenido, Mr Marshall! (co-sc. only) (USA/GB: Welcome Mr Marshall). '54 Felices Pascuas!; Comicos. '55 Muerte de un Ciclista (USA/GB: Death of a Cyclist). '56 Calle Mayor (SP-FR) (GB: Grand' Rue). '57 La Venganza (USA: The Vengeance). '59 Sonatas (SP-MEX). '60 A Los Cinco de la Tarde. '63 Nunca Pasa Nada (SP-FR) (USA: Nothing Ever Happens).

Left: Lucille Ball in Ziegfeld Follies. Above: George Bancroft. Above right: Tallulah Bankhead in Lifeboat. Right: Theda Bara. Below: Vilma Banky in The Awakening *(1928)*

BARDOT, Brigitte

(b. 1934). Actress. Born: Camille Javal; Paris, France

Once unveiled in full CinemaScope glory in Roger Vadim's *Et Dieu Créa la Femme* in 1956, the body, the dishevelled blonde mane and the sex-kitten pout quickly became legend, but Brigitte Bardot had already been working for years as a model, cover girl and bit-part actress. The daughter of a French industrialist, she studied ballet and in 1950 was discovered by director Marc Allégret. His assistant, Vadim, married her and sent her to acting school. In the late Fifties and early Sixties her promiscuous heroines – mostly in arty films like *Vie Privée*, *Le Mépris* and *Viva Maria!* – made BB Europe's biggest sex symbol and also showed she could act. Twice married and divorced since splitting from Vadim in 1957, she has now retired and devoted herself to caring for endangered animals.

Films include: 1955 Les Grandes Manoeuvres (FT-IT) (USA: The Grand Maneuver); Doctor at Sea (GB). '56 Et Dieu Créa la Femme (USA/GB: And Woman . . . Was Created/And God Created Woman). '58 La Femme et le Pantin (FR-IT) (GB: A Woman Like Satan). '59 Babette s'en va-t'en Guerre (FR) (USA/GB: Babette Goes to War). '62 Vie Privée (FR-IT) (GB: A Very Private Affair); Le Repos du Guerrier (FR-IT) (GB: Warrior's Rest/Love on a Pillow). '63 Le Mépris (FR-IT) (USA/GB: Contempt). '65 Viva Maria! (FR-IT). '67 A Coeur Joie (FR-GB) (GB: Two Weeks in September). '68 Shalako (GB). '69 Les Femmes (FR-IT) (USA: The Women). '73 Don Juan 1973, ou Si Don Juan Etait une Femme (FR-IT) (USA/GB: Don Juan or, If Don Juan Were a Woman).

BARKER, Lex

(1919–1973). Actor. Born: Alexander Crichlow Barker; Rye, New York, USA

Handsome, muscular, six-foot-four Lex was an obvious choice to play Tarzan after Johnny Weissmuller left the role in 1948, and he did so five times – becoming, perhaps, the screen's second most famous 'King of

the Jungle'. In 1953 he moved on to Westerns and action films, many of them made in Germany – where he became a popular star – and Italy, where he also appeared in Fellini's *La Dolce Vita*. Somewhat stately looking, as befits the son of eminent New Yorkers, he had left Princeton University to go on the stage as a young man, and during the war served as a major in the infantry. His five wives included stars Arlene Dahl and Lana Turner.

Films include: 1945 Doll Face. '46 The Farmer's Daughter. '47 Crossfire. '48 Mr Blandings Builds His Dream House. '49 Tarzan's Magic Fountain. '50 Tarzan and the Slave Girl. '51 Tarzan's Peril. '52 Tarzan's Savage Fury. '53 Tarzan and the She-Devil. '57 Girl in the Kremlin. '59 La Dolce Vita (IT); Mission en Narruecos (SP) (GB: Mission in Morocco). '67 Woman Times Seven (FR-USA).

BARKER, Will

(1867–1951). Pioneer/producer. Born: London, England

A commercial traveller for 26 years, Will Barker first entered the film world as a cameraman on such early newsreels as *Queen Victoria's Diamond Jubilee* in 1897. By the turn of the century he was deeply involved in cinema and within a few years had founded the Autoscope Company and set up the very first studios at Ealing. His were by far the most lavish productions of the time and his melodramas were famous for their use of authentic locations such as railway stations and dock areas. In addition he placed great emphasis on acting and this, in conjunction with the high wages he paid, meant that many notables, such as Sir Herbert Tree and George Formby Sr, could be seen on the screen. He retired from the cinema after World War I.

Films include: 1897 Queen Victoria's Diamond Jubilee. 1911 Henry VIII. '13 East Lynne; The Road to Ruin; London by Night; Humanity; Younita – From Gutter to Footlights; Sixty Years a Queen; The Great Bullion Robbery. '14 As a Man Sows, or, An

Angel of the Slums. '15 Brigadier Gerard; Jane Shore.

BARNES, Binnie

(b. 1908). Actress. Born: Gertrude Maude Barnes; London, England

The daughter of a policeman, Binnie Barnes had many diverse jobs – including milkmaid, asylum nurse and ballroom dancer – before she started working in films in 1929. After making numerous shorts, she had her first feature role in *A Night in Montmartre* (1931). After this she made a brief visit to America in 1932 to work for the Fox studios but soon returned to England where she played Catherine Howard in *The Private Life of Henry VIII*. By 1934 she was back in America. She appeared in many more films, particularly in comic-villain roles. In 1940 she married Mike Frankovich, a production executive at Columbia Pictures.

Films include: 1933 The Private Life of Henry VIII (GB). '34 The Private Life of Don Juan (GB). '35 Diamond Jim (USA). '37 Three Smart Girls (USA); Broadway Melody of 1938 (USA). '38 Holiday (USA) (GB: Free to Live/Unconventional Linda). '39 The Three Musketeers (USA) (GB: The Singing Musketeer). '41 Skylark (USA). '52 Decameron Nights (GB). '54 Malaga (GB) (USA: Fire Over Africa). '66 The Trouble With Angels (USA). '73 40 Carats (USA).

BARNET, Boris

(1902–1965). Director/actor. Born: Moscow, Russia

A member of the medical services during the Revolution, Boris Barnet trained at the State Film School before becoming a member of Lev Kuleshov's collective. His first chance came when he collaborated with the director Fedor Ozep on the script and direction of the serial thriller *Miss Mend* in 1926. It was during the Twenties and Thirties that Barnet directed, and occasionally acted in, his best known films including *Okraina* – with its imaginative use of the new medium of sound – and *Devushka s Korobkoi* and

Above, left to right: Brigitte Bardot in Viva Maria; Lex Barker as Tarzan; Binnie Barnes; Jean-Louis Barrault in Drôle de Drame; Wendy Barrie as

Dom na Trubnoi, with their warm, beautifully observed view of human eccentricities. He continued making movies until 1963, although his later work was hardly seen outside the USSR. He committed suicide in 1965.

Films include: 1926 Miss Mend (co-dir). '27 Devushka s Korobkoi (GB: Girl With the Hat-Box); Moskva v Oktyabre (GB: Moscow That Weeps and Laughs). '28 Dom na Trubnoi (GB: The House on Trubnaya Square). '31 Lyodolom (GB: Thaw). '33 Okraina (USA: Patriots; GB: Outskirts). '36 U Samovo Sinyevo Morya (GB: By the Bluest of Seas). '40 Stari Nayezdnik (GB: The Old Jockey). '45 Odnazhdii Noch. '57 Boryets i Kloun (co-dir) (GB: The Wrestler and the Clown). '63 Polustanok.

BARRAULT, Jean-Louis

(b. 1910). Actor. Born: Vésinet, Paris, France

Having worked his way through college, where he studied History of Art, Jean-Louis Barrault went to Charles Dullin's Theatre School in 1931. He was so poor he had to sleep in the

Jane Seymour; Gene Barry in The War of the Worlds. *Below left: Ethel Barrymore. Below right: John Barrymore as* Don Juan

theatre but, after working his way up through minor roles, he directed his first play in 1935. He then moved into films, acting frequently for the director Marc Allégret. While continuing his film work, in 1940 he joined the Comédie Française as an actor and director, leaving six years later to establish an independent repertory company with his wife, Madeleine Renaud. This accomplished performer, unforgettable in his role as Baptiste, the mime-artist in Carné's *Les Enfants du Paradis*, has, in addition, been consistently honoured by his first home – the French theatre.

Films include: 1935 Les Beaux Jours. '**36** Jenny. '**37** Les Perles de la Couronne (USA/GB: Pearls of the Crown); Drôle de Drame (USA: Bizarre, Bizarre); Mademoiselle Docteur (USA: Street of Shadows). '**42** La Symphonie Fantastique. '**44** L'Ange de la Nuit. '**45** Les Enfants du Paradis (USA: Children of Paradise). '**50** La Ronde. '**61** Le Testament du Dr Cordelier (GB: Experiment in Evil). '**62** The Longest Day (USA). '**66** Chappaqua (USA). '**82** La Nuit de Varennes (FR-IT).

BARRIE, Wendy

(1912–1978). Actress. Born: Marguerite Wendy Jenkins; Hong Kong

Marguerite Jenkins was the daughter of a well-to-do British lawyer, and was educated at a convent school in England before attending a finishing school in Switzerland. She then worked in a beauty parlour and took a secretarial course before going on the English stage as Wendy Barrie – a name taken from her godfather, novelist and playwright J. M. Barrie – in 1930. From there she progressed to the screen and, following her success as Jane Seymour in Alexander Korda's *The Private Life of Henry VIII*, was snapped up by Hollywood. She stopped making films in the Sixties, but hosted television chat-shows and appeared on numerous radio programmes. Her name was at one time linked with that of gangster Bugsy Siegel.

Films include: 1932 Collision (GB); Wedding Rehearsal (GB). '**33** The Private Life of Henry VIII (GB). '**35** The Big Broadcast of 1936 (USA). '**37** Dead End (USA). '**39** The Hound of the Baskervilles (USA). '**43** Forever and a Day (USA); Follies Girl (USA). '**63** The Moving Finger (USA).

BARRY, Gene

(b. 1921). Actor. Born: Eugene Klass; New York City, USA

Gene Barry was interested in acting from an early age and followed the well-trodden path through school and college dramatics to a music scholarship. Well-dressed and smooth-looking, he soon found himself much in demand for routine Hollywood films made during the Fifties, but it was in television that he excelled, becoming a household name as the hero in the series *Burke's Law* (1963–65) and *The Name of the Game* (1968–70). He has since moved into the sphere of production, forming a company with his son Michael.

Films include: 1952 The Atomic City. '**53** The War of the Worlds; The Girls of Pleasure Island. '**54** Red Garters; Naked Alibi. '**55** Soldier of Fortune. '**57** China Gate. '**58** Thunder Road. '**68** Maroc 7. '**70** Subterfuge. '**77** The Second Coming of Suzanne (+exec. prod).

BARRY, John

(b. 1933). Composer. Born: John Barry Prendergast; York, England

Barry discovered his gift for music at an early age and studied under Dr Francis Jackson, Master of Music at York Minster. He was called up for National Service at the age of 19 and while in the army took a correspondence course in harmony, orchestration and composition. After his release from service he became an arranger for band leaders Johnny Dankworth, Jack Parnell and Ted Heath. By the mid-Fifties he was further establishing his reputation with the John Barry Seven. As a composer and arranger he quickly progressed to writing scores for films and his James Bond themes gained him international recognition. His first major score was for *Zulu*, but it was for his work on *The Lion in Winter* that he won an Oscar in 1969. In 1975 he became resident in Los Angeles.

Films include: 1962 The L-Shaped Room. '**63** From Russia With Love; Zulu. '**64** Goldfinger. '**65** The Knack. '**66** The Chase. '**68** The Lion in Winter. '**69** Midnight Cowboy. '**71** Walkabout (AUS). '**75** Day of the Locust. '**81** Body Heat.

BARRYMORE, Ethel

(1879–1959). Actress. Born: Ethel Mae Blythe; Philadelphia, Pennsylvania, USA

One of the 'Fabulous Barrymores' – daughter of artistes Maurice Barrymore (Herbert Blythe) and Georgina Drew, sister to Lionel and John – the young Ethel quickly established herself as the first lady of the American stage. Handsome rather than beautiful, she made her screen debut in *The Nightingale* in 1914, but despite many excellent subsequent performances she was never totally happy away from the stage. In 1944, after a prolonged absence from the screen, she made an appearance in *None But the Lonely Heart*, for which she won an Academy Award. She then played character roles until her death.

Films include: 1914 The Nightingale. '**19** The Divorcee (GB: Lady Frederick). '**32** Rasputin and the Empress (GB: Rasputin, the Mad Monk). '**44** None But the Lonely Heart. '**45** The Spiral Staircase. '**46** The Farmer's Daughter. '**47** The Paradine Case. '**48** Portrait of Jennie (GB: Jennie). '**50** It's a Big Country. '**52** Just for You.

BARRYMORE, John

(1882–1942). Actor. Born: John Blythe; Philadelphia, Pennsylvania, USA

John, the youngest Barrymore and possessor of 'the Great Profile', started his working life as a cartoonist on a New York newspaper. Acting was in his blood, however, and in 1903 he made his stage debut. His magnificent presence – tall, upright and very handsome, with a flamboyant theatrical manner and marvellous voice – soon made him the leading matinée idol of the day. His speciality was Shakespeare, and he is regarded as one of the greatest Hamlets of all time. In films he played many romantic heroes (*Don Juan, Beau Brummell*) but preferred bizarre, demoniac roles (*Dr Jekyll and Mr Hyde, Svengali*). His ever-increasing alcohol consumption took its toll, and by the late Twenties Barrymore was past his prime. He was married four times, and two of his wives, Dolores Costello and Diane Barry, were actresses. Daughter Diana (1921–60) and son John (b. 1932) both had abortive film careers and inherited their father's self-destructive habits. Barrymore Sr was played by his old drinking companion Errol Flynn in *Too Much, Too Soon* (1958).

Films include: 1913 An American Citizen. '**20** Dr Jekyll and Mr Hyde. '**22** Sherlock Holmes (GB: Moriarty). '**24** Beau Brummell. '**25** The Sea Beast. '**26** Don Juan. '**27** The Beloved Rogue. '**31** Svengali; The Mad Genius. '**32** Grand Hotel; A Bill of Divorcement. '**34** Twentieth Century. '**36** Romeo and Juliet.

BARRYMORE, Lionel

(1878–1954). Actor. Born: Lionel Blythe; Philadelphia, Pennsylvania, USA

The eldest of the famous Barrymores, Lionel Barrymore made his stage debut as part of his parents' act while still an infant. By 1900 he had become a leading Broadway actor and after a brief sojourn among the moneyed and artistic 'bohemian' circles of Paris he returned to acting and made his screen debut in 1911. Over the next forty years he built up a reputation for being – unlike brother John – professional, hard-working and ambitious. His roles were, however, on the dull side and featured him largely as friendly 'elder-statesman' types. For the last 15 years of his life he was confined to a wheelchair, crippled by arthritis and an incapacitating leg injury. Nevertheless, he continued to perform until his death.

Films include: 1911 The Battle. '12 The New York Hat. '14 The Battle of Elderbush Gulch. '19 The Copperhead. '26 The Temptress. '28 Sadie Thompson. '29 Madame X (dir. only); His Glorious Night (dir; + mus). '32 Mata Hari. '36 The Road to Glory; The Devil Doll; Camille. '37 Captains Courageous. '38 You Can't Take It With You; Young Dr Kildare. '46 It's a Wonderful Life; Duel in the Sun.

BARSACQ, Léon

(1906–1969). Art director. Born: Crimea, Russia

Having studied at the School of Decorative Arts in Paris, Barsacq became involved in the French film industry during the early Thirties, working under fellow Russian set designer André Andrejew and others. By 1937 he was a qualified art director in charge of Jean Renoir's La Marseillaise and from then on built up a solid reputation as a creator of atmosphere. He worked on many René Clair films and endeavoured to explain his craft in the book Le Décor de Film, published posthumously in 1970.

Films include: 1937 La Marseillaise (USA: Marseillaise). '45 Les Enfants du Paradis (USA: Children of Paradise); Boule de Suif. '47 Le Silence Est d'Or (USA: Man About Town). '49 La Beauté du Diable (FR-IT) (USA: Beauty and the Devil; GB: Beauty and the Beast). '55 Les Grandes Manoeuvres (FR-IT) (USA: The Grand Maneuver); Les Diaboliques (GB: The Fiends). '57 Porte des Lilas (FR-IT) (USA: Gates of Paris). '62 The Longest Day (USA). '68 Phèdre.

BARTHELMESS, Richard

(1895–1963). Actor. Born: New York City, USA

Barthelmess was on vacation from Trinity College, Connecticut, when Alla Nazimova – the famous actress and a friend of his mother – offered him a part in War Brides. He never returned to college. Barthelmess' ability to enter completely into the skin of his characters made him a great 'natural' actor, and this, combined with his good looks, marked him as star material. By 1919 he was very popular, and remained so throughout the rest of the silent era. Although the talkies were not to be the bugbear for Barthelmess that they were for so many others, his roles began to diminish in stature and in 1942, the year he joined the Naval Reserve, he was playing character parts that usually called on him to act the heavy. After World War II he retired from the screen to live in style on Long Island until his death from cancer.

Films include: 1916 War Brides. '19 Broken Blossoms. '20 Way Down East. '21 Tol'able David. '27 The Patent Leather Kid. '30 The Dawn Patrol (GB: The Flight Commander). '35 Four Hours to Kill. '39 Only Angels Have Wings. '40 The Man Who Talked Too Much. '42 The Spoilers.

BARTHOLOMEW, Freddie

(b. 1924). Actor. Born: Frederick Llewellyn; London, England

Frederick Llewellyn's parents were so often absent that his aunt, Millicent Bartholomew, brought him up and managed his career. On the stage from the age of three, he was taken by his aunt to the Italia Conti stage school in London, where he met George Cukor and David O. Selznick who were casting MGM's David Copperfield. He was offered the role and to escape government regulations forbidding his 'exportation', his aunt took him for a 'holiday' in Hollywood. Once there he stayed, becoming the toff among child stars of the Thirties. He played the boy-hero in many adaptations of adventure classics until his career began to decline in the Forties, aided by long drawn-out legal battles between his relations over his custody and earnings. He was a fighter pilot in World War II and later became an advertising executive.

Films include: 1935 David Copperfield; Anna Karenina. '36 Little Lord Fauntleroy; Lloyds of London. '37 Captains Courageous. '38 Swiss Family Robinson; Tom Brown's Schooldays. '47 Sepia Cinderella. '51 St Benny the Dip.

BARTLETT, Sy

(1909–1978). Screenwriter/producer. Born: Sacha Baraniev; Nikolaiev, Russia

Bartlett was raised in Chicago from the age of four and studied at the Medill School of Journalism before becoming a reporter. In the Twenties he went to Hollywood and soon began working for the major studios as a screenwriter. Bartlett was an outspoken anti-Nazi who once punched the German consular attaché for repeatedly shouting 'Heil Hitler' in a San Francisco nightclub in 1940. He was also proud of being the first US air force officer to be involved in a bombing mission over Berlin with the RAF. In 1956 he formed Melville Productions with Gregory Peck and, a few years afterwards, Bartlett Productions with Chico Day.

Films include: 1938 Cocoanut Grove (co-sc. only). '41 The Road to Zanzibar (sc. only). '42 Two Yanks in Trinidad (sc. only). '46 13 Rue Madeleine (sc. only). '49 12 O'Clock High (sc. only). '58 The Big Country (co-sc. only). '59 Beloved Infidel (sc; + prod); Pork Chop Hill (prod. only). '63 A Gathering of Eagles (prod. only).

BASEHART, Richard

(1919–1984). Actor. Born: Zanesville, Ohio, USA

The son of a newspaper editor, Basehart became a reporter and radio announcer on leaving college. After a controversy over one of his stories he was forced to leave his paper and decided to follow up his childhood love – the theatre. His gravelly voice and strong face won him many interesting roles in his five years with the Philadelphia Hedgerow Theatre. In 1938 he made his Broadway debut, and seven years later won the New York Critics' Best Newcomer Award for his lead role in The Hasty Heart. The result of this success was a film contract. A strong leading man more at home in psychological roles involving decisions and mental anguish than in all-action vehicles, he always avoided typecasting and proved his versatility in both films and in television series such as A Voyage to the Bottom of the Sea. His twenty-year marriage to the actress Valentina Cortese ended in divorce in 1971.

Films include: 1948 He Walked by Night. '51 Fourteen Hours. '54 La Strada (IT). '55 Il Bidone (IT) (GB: The Swindlers). '56 Moby Dick. '57 Time Limit. '58 The Brothers Karamazov. '72 Chato's Land. '77 The Island of Dr Moreau. '79 Being There.

BASEVI, James

(b. 1890). Art director. Born: Plymouth, Devon, England

After World War I, Basevi immigrated to America and went to work for the newly-formed MGM in 1924. There he was in charge of set design and also became a director of special effects responsible for, among other things, the marvellous earthquake sequence in San Francisco. In the early Forties he joined 20th Century-Fox where he won an Oscar in 1943 for his work in The Song of Bernadette. He also designed a number of John Ford films.

Films include: 1925 The Big Parade. '39 Wuthering Heights. '43 The Ox-Bow Incident; The Song of Bernadette; Stormy Weather. '44 Lifeboat. '45 Spellbound. '46 Duel in the Sun; My Darling Clementine. '56 The Searchers.

Above: Richard Basehart in Moby Dick. Top: Lionel Barrymore in Washington Masquerade (1932)

BASS, Saul

(b. 1920). Designer/animator/director. Born: New York City, USA

The design of the title sequence in Carmen Jones heralded the arrival of a new talent in Hollywood. Saul Bass' bold and inventive use of graphics has since added to – and has often been more impressive than – every film he has worked on. His first job after studying at Brooklyn College was with an advertising agency, but he soon quit and went to Hollywood where he began designing movie posters. Success quickly followed and eventually he started making his own award-winning shorts. But Bass continues to design for film and television advertising and also lectures on film-making and design.

Films include: 1954 Carmen Jones. '56 Around the World in 80 Days. '58 Vertigo. '59 North by Northwest. '60 Spartacus; Psycho; Exodus. '61 West Side Story. '62 Walk on the Wild Side. '63 It's a Mad, Mad, Mad, Mad World. '79 The Solar Film (short) (dir).

BASSERMAN, Albert

(1867–1952). Actor. Born: Albert Bassermann; Mannheim, Germany

Even had he made terrible films, Basserman would deserve considerable admiration. How many actors

BATES, Alan

(b. 1934). Born: Allestree, Derbyshire, England

Dark-eyed, dishevelled, unpredictable – the images projected by Bates later in his film career accord with those characterizations of angry young men he created first on the stage. He achieved international success with *Zorba the Greek*, although in Britain he had already established himself at the Royal Court Theatre and in 'kitchen-sink' drama, notably *A Kind of Loving*, so typical of films made in Britain in the early Sixties. His biggest successes have been as English literary heroes – Gabriel Oak in *Far From the Madding Crowd*, Rupert Birkin in *Women in Love* – and it was as a similar provider of sympathy and romance for *An Unmarried Woman* that Bates achieved major Hollywood stardom.

Films include: 1962 A Kind of Loving. '64 Zorba the Greek (GR-USA). '66 Georgy Girl. '67 Far From the Madding Crowd. '69 Women in Love. '71 The Go-Between. '74 Butley. '78 An Unmarried Woman (USA). '80 Nijinsky (USA). '81 Quartet (FR-GB).

BAUR, Harry

(1880–1943). Actor. Born: Paris, France

One of the most popular leads in French films before World War II, Baur was generally starred in costume dramas. In 1942 he was arrested by the Gestapo on charges of forging papers to prove his Aryan origins in order to fool the German authorities into allowing him to star in a 2-million mark production. He was tortured and imprisoned, but released in 1943. He died mysteriously days later.

Films include: 1913 Shylock. '32 Poil de Carotte. '34 Nuits Moscovites. '35 Crime et Châtiment (GB: Crime and Punishment). '36 Samson; Tarass Boulba; Un Grand Amour de Beethoven (GB: Beethoven). '37 Un Carnet de Bal (USA: Life Dances On; GB: Christine). '40 Volpone. '42 Symphonie eines Lebens (GER).

could, at the age of 66, flee their native country where they had an established career, end up in America via Switzerland and embark, at 72, on a Hollywood career? A German stage and silent-screen star, Basserman was forced to leave in 1933. For the remainder of his acting life he continued to convey the image he created in Hitchcock's *Foreign Correspondent* – that of a civilized, cultured, upright and indomitable gentleman.

Films include: 1940 Dr Ehrlich's Magic Bullet; Foreign Correspondent; A Dispatch From Reuters (GB: This Man Reuter). '41 The Shanghai Gesture. '42 Once Upon a Honeymoon. '44 Madame Curie; Since You Went Away. '45 Rhapsody in Blue. '47 Escape Me Never. '48 The Red Shoes (GB).

BATCHELOR, Joy

see HALAS & BATCHELOR

BAVA, Mario

(1914–1980).
Director/cinematographer. Born:
San Remo, Italy

Also known variously as John Foam and John M. Old, Bava is most appreciated by cultist followers in Europe who admire his tongue-in-cheek horror and science-fiction movies. He entered the film industry at the age of 19 and, during the period between 1943 and 1963, worked as a lighting cameraman. He directed his first feature in 1961 and through the rest of the Sixties became noted not because of his direction or choice of subject, but rather for his use of dazzling sets, costumes and colour. In later years he directed special effects sequences for Franco Rossi and Federico Fellini.

Films include: 1960 Seddok, l'Erede di Satana (photo. only) (GB: Seddok). '61 La Maschera del Demonico (USA: Black Sunday; GB: Revenge of the Vampire); Gli Invasori (IT-FR) (USA: Erik the Conqueror; GB: Fury of the Vikings); Ercole al Centro della Terra (+photo). '62 La Ragazza che Sapeva Troppo (IT-US) (USA/GB: The Evil Eye). '63 La Frusta e il Corpo (IT-FR) (GB: Night Is the Phantom); I Tre Volti della Paura (IT-FR) (USA/GB: Black Sabbath). '64 Sei Donne per l'Assassino (Six Femmes pour l'Assassin) (IT-FR-MON) (USA/GB: Blood and Black Lace). '65 Terrore nello Spazio (IT-SP) (USA/GB: Planet of the Vampires). '66 Operazione Paura (USA: Kill, Baby, Kill; GB: Curse of the Dead). '68 Diabolik (IT-FR) (USA/GB: Danger: Diabolik).

BAXTER, Anne

(1923–1985). Actress. Born:
Michigan City, Indiana, USA

Dark and attractive, an experienced stage actress from her teens, and Academy Award winner in 1946 for her role in *The Razor's Edge* – a recipe for stardom, but somehow Anne Baxter never quite reached the expected heights. She was tested for Hitchcock's *Rebecca* (1940) at the age of 16 but was considered too young. Another test, however, led to her being offered a long-term contract with 20th Century-Fox. Soon she was appearing in films made by some of Hollywood's best-known directors –

Billy Wilder, Hitchcock, Orson Welles and Joseph Mankiewicz, to name a few. In 1966 she married a rancher and went to live on a huge sheep farm in Australia. But she came out of retirement four years later to resume her career on television and the stage.

Films include: 1942 The Magnificent Ambersons. '43 Five Graves to Cairo; The North Star. '46 Angel On My Shoulder; The Razor's Edge. '50 All About Eve. '52 I Confess. '53 The Blue Gardenia. '56 The Ten Commandments. '71 Fool's Parade (GB: Dynamite Man From Glory Jail).

BAXTER, Warner

(1891–1951). Actor. Born:
Columbus, Ohio, USA

At the end of the Thirties, Warner Baxter was reputed to be the highest paid actor in Hollywood, second only to Bette Davis. Yet by that time he was well past his prime and his career as a tall, dark and handsome leading man was declining rapidly to B thrillers. During the late Twenties and Thirties, though, he was very popular, winning an Academy Award for his performance as a sympathetic Mexican, Cisco Kid, in *In Old Arizona*, and excellent as the harried, hard-driving show-biz producer in *42nd Street*. Whatever the role, Baxter was one of Hollywood's great reliable performers and gave his best even in the most routine films.

Films include: 1918 All Woman. '19 Daddy Long Legs. '22 If I Were Queen. '28 Craig's Wife; In Old Arizona. '31 Cisco Kid. '33 42nd Street. '36 The Prisoner of Shark Island; The Road to Glory. '38 Kidnapped. '43 Crime Doctor.

BAZIN, André

(1918–1958). Critic. Born: Angers, France

Probably the most significant film critic and theorist in the post-war period, Bazin wrote prolifically for a number of French journals and newspapers. In 1951 he co-founded *Cahiers du Cinéma*, perhaps the most influential of all film magazines. Bazin is primarily remembered for his consideration of realism, its relationship to Sergei M. Eisenstein's theory of montage (of which he was highly critical) and its visual manifestation in the work of Orson Welles and the Italian neo-realists among others. His influence on the French *nouvelle vague* directors, many of whom were regular contributors to *Cahiers* before they began making films, was considerable, partly because he took mainstream Hollywood films so seriously. But Bazin disagreed with many of his younger colleagues, especially François Truffaut, for subscribing so rigidly to the *auteur* theory. His writings were collected in four volumes entitled *Qu'est-ce que le cinema?* (*What Is Cinema?*). Tuberculosis led to Bazin's untimely death at 40.

THE BEATLES

John Lennon (1940–1980). Born: Liverpool, England
Ringo Starr (b. 1940). Born: Richard Starkey; Liverpool, England
Paul McCartney (b. 1942). Born: James Paul McCartney; Liverpool, England
George Harrison (b. 1943). Born: Liverpool, England

After the Beatles' phenomenal success in the pop world, their manager Brian

Above from left to right: Anne Baxter, George Sanders in All About Eve; *Warner Baxter in* In Old Arizona; *Ned Beatty in* Deliverance; *Robert Beatty in* Albert RN (1953). *Left: The Beatles. Below: Warren Beatty in* Heaven Can Wait

Epstein and record company decided to cash in on movies starring them and especially geared to the youth market. This resulted in *A Hard Day's Night*, a documentary-style comedy of the Fab Four at large in London, and *Help!*, a much more lavish thriller spoof. Both were immensely successful anarchic comedies directed by Richard Lester and featuring the Beatles' lacerating Liverpudlian wit – and, of course, the songs. Later came *Yellow Submarine*, an adventurous animated feature, and *Let It Be*, a documentary of the Beatles at work just before they split. Lennon acted in *How I Won the War* and later made some minimalist shorts before he was tragically murdered; Starr has appeared in a number of movies as actor, most notably *That'll Be the Day*; and Harrison has moved into production with his company HandMade Films.

Films include: 1964 A Hard Day's Night. '65 Help! '68 Yellow Submarine. '70 Let It Be. *John Lennon only:* '67 How I Won the War. *Ringo Starr only:* '68 Candy (USA-FR-IT). '72 Blindman (USA-IT). '73 That'll Be the Day. '75 Lisztomania. '81 Caveman (USA). *Paul McCartney only:* '79 Wings Over the World (doc). *George Harrison only:* '79 Monty Python's Life of Brian (exec. prod; + act). '81 Time Bandits (exec. prod. only). '82 The Missionary (exec. prod. only).

BEATON, Cecil

(1904–1980). Costume and set designer. Born: London, England

Cecil Beaton's interest in photography began during his teens, and by the time he went to Cambridge University he was already renting his own studio. After university he continued to build up a clientele for his photographic portraits while working for the family business. He soon became a renowned society photographer. During his career he photographed some of the most famous and glamorous people in the world. His work as a scenery and costume designer in theatre, opera and ballet began in 1930, and he subsequently moved into films. He provided lavish, breathtaking designs for such costume dramas as *Anna Karenina*, *Gigi* and *My Fair Lady*.

Films as costume designer include: 1941 Kipps; Major Barbara; Dangerous Moonlight. '42 The Young Mr Pitt. '47 An Ideal Husband. '48 Anna Karenina. '57 The Truth About Women. '58 Gigi (+sets; +prod. des) (USA); The Doctor's Dilemma. '64 My Fair Lady (+prod. des) (USA). '70 On a Clear Day You Can See Forever (co-cost) (USA).

BEATTY, Ned

(b. 1937). Actor. Born: Lexington, Kentucky, USA

Ned Beatty gained his acting experience by working in regional stock companies for seven years, and was finally recruited by the director John Boorman for a major role in his excellent film *Deliverance*. Since then Beatty has put his powerful build (though oddly vulnerable appearance) and deep voice to good acting use in many notable supporting roles. He was particularly effective in his portrayal of the stupid sidekick to Gene Hackman's Lex Luther in *Superman, The Movie*. He received an Academy Award nomination for his rendering of the fiery chairman of the board in *Network*.

Films include: 1972 Deliverance. '73 The Thief Who Came to Dinner; White Lightning. '75 WW and the Dixie Dance Kings; Nashville. '76 Network; All the President's Men; Silver Streak. '77 Exorcist II: The Heretic. '78 Gray Lady Down; Superman, The Movie. '79 1941. '81 The Incredible Shrinking Woman.

BEATTY, Robert

(b. 1909). Actor. Born: Hamilton, Ontario, Canada

Having studied at university in Toronto, Robert Beatty travelled to London to attend the Royal Academy of Dramatic Art. After making some minor stage appearances he became a newsreader for the BBC, working for the Overseas News Service during the war. He then continued his acting career, this time on film, with his tough masculine appearance making him a favourite for leading roles in the British crime movies of the Fifties. At this time his voice also became very familiar on radio as the detective Philip O'Dell, and since then he has been heard narrating numerous documentaries.

Films include: 1943 San Demetrio, London. '47 Odd Man Out. '50 Her Favourite Husband. '51 Captain Horatio Hornblower (USA) (GB: Captain Horatio Hornblower RN); Calling Bulldog Drummond. '53 Man on a Tightrope (USA). '57 Something of Value (USA). '68 2001: A Space Odyssey; Where Eagles Dare. '72 Pope Joan. '76 The Pink Panther Strikes Again.

BEATTY, Warren

(b. 1937). Actor. Born: Warren Beaty; Richmond, Virginia, USA

Warren Beatty, younger brother of the actress Shirley MacLaine, quit college and left behind a football scholarship in order to work his way through acting school – a task which included spells as bricklayer, ratcatcher and piano player. Having appeared in repertory seasons and minor television roles, he finally broke into the Hollywood set and was proclaimed the new James Dean. Sometimes better known for his Casanova image than for his acting ability, Beatty has always been careful about the roles he has accepted – a philosophy that has worked to his advantage in such films as *Bonnie and Clyde* and *McCabe and Mrs Miller*. In addition he has turned his hand to direction and production and proved very successful at both – in 1982 he received an Academy Award as Best Director for *Reds*, a film he also produced, co-scripted and starred in.

Films include: 1961 Splendor in the Grass; The Roman Spring of Mrs Stone (GB). '62 All Fall Down. '64 Lilith. '65 Mickey One. '66 Kaleidoscope (GB); Promise Her Anything (GB). '67 Bonnie and Clyde (+prod). '70 The Only Game in Town. '71 McCabe and Mrs Miller; Dollars/$ (GB: The Heist).

'74 The Parallax View. '75 Shampoo (+prod); The Fortune. '78 Heaven Can Wait (+prod; +dir; +co-sc). '81 Reds (+prod; +dir; +co-sc).

BEAUDINE, William

(1892–1970). Director. Born: New York City, USA

As a young man William Beaudine became a hired hand at the Biograph studios, graduating from this lowly position to work as an actor, assistant props manager and assistant photographer. He then began directing shorts and, in 1922, began his long career as a director of features. He worked with such famous stars as Mary Pickford and W. C. Fields during the Twenties, and his later output was prodigious – he produced hundreds of films with great speed and competence. He also worked busily in England for three years during the mid-Thirties, often on comedies like the Will Hay vehicle *Windbag the Sailor*. He continued directing, for film and television, well into the Sixties – making movies with such dubious titles as *Jesse James Meets Frankenstein's Daughter*.

Films include: 1922 Catch My Smoke. '23 Her Fatal Millions. '25 Little Annie Rooney. '26 Sparrows. '28 The Cohens and the Kellys in Paris. '29 The Girl From Woolworths. '34 The Old Fashioned Way. '36 Windbag the Sailor (GB). '43 Clancy Street Boys. '48 The Feathered Serpent; Kidnapped. '53 Murder Without Tears; Roar of the Crowd. '66 Billy the Kid vs Dracula; Jesse James Meets Frankenstein's Daughter.

BECKER, Jacques

(1906–1960). Director. Born: Paris, France

Becker was born into a family connected with the world of *haute couture*, but his future career was signposted when he became assistant to the American director King Vidor while he was in Paris. Vidor gave Becker the opportunity to return to Hollywood with him, but he refused, becoming instead assistant to the French director Jean Renoir in 1932. Within ten years Becker was directing his own films through which he displayed a fascination for the diverse lifestyles of those living around him. The most internationally famous of his films is the underworld love story *Casque d'Or*. Unfortunately, his later work suffered due to financial difficulties and his ill-health – he finally died of lung cancer. His son, Jean Becker, is also a director.

Films include: 1940 L'Or du Cristobal. '42 Le Dernier Atout. '43 Goupi Mains Rouges (USA: It Happened at the Inn). '45 Falbalas (USA: Paris Frills). '47 Antoine et Antoinette. '49 Rendez-vous de Juillet. '51 Edouard et Caroline (GB: Edward and Caroline); Casque d'Or (USA: Golden Helmet; GB: Golden Marie). '54 Touchez Pas au Grisbi (GB: Honour Among Thieves); Ali Baba et les 40 Voleurs (GB: Ali-Baba). '57 Les Aventures d'Arsène Lupin (FR-IT) (GB: The Adventures of Arsène Lupin). '58 Montparnasse 19 (FR-IT) (GB: The Lovers of Montparnasse). '60 Le Trou (FR-IT) (GB: The Hole).

BEERY, Noah

(1884–1946). Actor. Born: Kansas City, Missouri, USA

As a young man Noah Beery, brother of the actor Wallace Beery, went to New York to seek fame and fortune. There he was persuaded to become a singer and his career as a performer began. He worked primarily as a stage actor for 19 years but made his screen debut in 1912. During the silent period he was best known for his portrayals of moustachioed blackguards and lecherous villains – giving his most memorable performance as the brutal Sergeant Lejaune in *Beau Geste*. With the coming of sound he continued to work regularly as a stock heavy in Westerns and serials.

Films include: 1920 The Mark of Zorro. '21 Tol'able David. '25 The Thundering Herd. '26 Beau Geste. '28 Noah's Ark. '29 Four Feathers; Isle of Lost Ships. '30 Under a Texas Moon. '33 She Done Him Wrong. '45 This Man's Navy.

BEERY Jr, Noah

Actor. Born: New York City, USA

Noah Beery Jr was born in New York where his father was working as a stage and screen actor (his birthdate remains something of a mystery, and could easily be anywhere between 1912 and 1917). The family then moved to California where he led an outdoor life on a ranch. He entered movies as a child, appearing with his father in *The Mark of Zorro*. His natural athleticism meant that he was ideal for Westerns, and it was in cowboy films that he ultimately made his mark, after having worked extensively in serials. Since then he has proved a very reliable supporting actor, often playing characters considerably older than himself, and is now most recognizable as Rocky, the benevolent father to James Garner's Rockford in the popular American television series *The Rockford Files*.

Films include: 1939 Of Mice and Men; Only Angels Have Wings. '41 Sergeant York. '43 Gung Ho! '48 Red River. '60 Inherit the Wind; Guns of the Timberland. '70 Little Fauss and Big Halsey. '73 Walking Tall.

BEERY, Wallace

(1885–1949). Actor. Born: Kansas City, Missouri, USA

Wallace Beery was an elephant trainer's assistant at the Ringling Brothers Circus, but left when a leopard clawed his arm. Prompted by a letter from his brother, Noah Beery, he then went to New York where he appeared in musical variety. Having alternated between Broadway and road shows he travelled to Hollywood, working as a comedian in silent shorts before becoming a notable actor in sound films, generally playing boozy, sly, grubby but essentially lovable characters. He received an Academy Award as Best Actor for his portrayal of a drunken prizefighter in *The Champ*, and was briefly married to the actress Gloria Swanson between 1916 and 1918.

Films include: 1919 The Last of the Mohicans. '21 The Four Horsemen of the Apocalypse. '23 Robin Hood. '30 Big House; Min and Bill. '31 The Champ. '32 Grand Hotel; Flesh. '33 Dinner at Eight. '35 China Seas; Ah, Wilderness!

BEGLEY, Ed

(1901–1970). Actor. Born: Hartford, Connecticut, USA

Born of Irish immigrant parents, Ed Begley ran away from home at the age of 11 to work in fairs, carnivals and circuses. In 1931, after appearing in vaudeville, he began working in all areas of show business – and on radio his voice was heard in over twelve thousand programmes. He commenced a successful career on Broadway in 1943 and went to Hollywood in 1947, where he proved equally at home in the movies. Begley was a notable character actor and is particularly well remembered for his part as Boss Finley in *Sweet Bird of Youth*, a role for which he won the Oscar for Best Supporting Actor.

Films include: 1957 Twelve Angry Men. '62 Sweet Bird of Youth. '64 The Unsinkable Molly Brown. '67 Warning Shot. '68 Hang 'em High; Wild in the Streets.

BELAFONTE, Harry

(b. 1927). Singer/actor. Born: Harold George Belafonte; New York City, USA

Harry Belafonte spent the early part of his impoverished childhood in the West Indies. His family then returned to New York, and on leaving school Belafonte joined the Navy as a maintenance man. Once out of the services he continued to do manual jobs while attending the Dramatic Workshop in New York along with the likes of Marlon Brando and Tony Curtis. In 1952 he began his singing career, and a year later – at the same time as his career on Broadway was taking off – he made his film debut in *Bright Road*. A member of the American Negro Theatre and a campaigner for civil rights, Belafonte continues to appear regularly in cabaret and makes occasional movies. Since the Fifties he and Sidney Poitier have worked together to encourage the making of films with all-black casts.

Films include: 1953 Bright Road. '54 Carmen Jones. '57 Island in the Sun. '59 The World, the Flesh and the Devil; Odds Against Tomorrow. '70 The Angel Levine. '72 Buck and the Preacher (+prod). '74 Uptown Saturday Night.

BELL, Tom

(b. 1933). Actor. Born: Liverpool, England

Coming from a large working-class family, Tom Bell won a free place at the Bradford Civic Theatre School. On graduation he spent eight years in repertory and, with the advent of realist drama in the early Sixties, became much in demand, rising to prominence in Joan Littlewood's

Left: Ed Begley. Above left: Noah Beery Jr in Little Fauss and Big Halsy. *Above: Noah Beery in* She Done Him Wrong. *Below: Wallace Beery in* Viva Villa *(1934)*

Theatre Workshop. He then moved into television, giving some memorable performances and making a name for himself with the critics – Kenneth Tynan called him 'one of the six best young actors' of that time. He appeared in many British productions, eventually achieving fame on both sides of the Atlantic in *The L-Shaped Room*. Unfortunately his clashes with the establishment have meant that he may not have been offered the roles he merits, and he now works mainly on television.

Films include: 1960 The Criminal. '61 Payroll. '62 HMS Defiant; The L-Shaped Room. '65 Ballad in Blue. '68 The Long Day's Dying. '69 Lock Up Your Daughters!; The Violent Enemy. '78 The Sailor's Return.

BELLAMY, Ralph

(b. 1904). Actor. Born: Ralph Rexford Bellamy; Chicago, Illinois, USA

The son of an advertising executive, Ralph Bellamy showed acting promise at school. Having organized the North Shore Players in 1922, he then joined the Madison, Wisconsin Stock Company. After nine years of touring with various companies he made his first Broadway appearance in *Town Boy* in 1929. The following year he was signed by Fox and as a result he made over eighty films in twelve years, often as the second leading man who doesn't get the girl. In 1943 he returned to the New York stage, winning a Tony award that same year for his portrayal of Franklin D. Roosevelt in *Sunrise at Campobello* (a role he later recreated on the screen). He continued to work well into his late Sixties in both theatre and television.

Films include: 1931 The Magnificent Lie. '31 Surrender. '32 Forbidden. '37 The Awful Truth. '38 Carefree. '40 His Girl Friday; Ellery Queen, Master Detective. '41 Ellery Queen's Penthouse Mystery. '44 Guest in the House. '55 The Court-Martial of Billy Mitchell. '60 Sunrise at Campobello. '68 Rosemary's Baby.

Above: Tom Bell in All the Right Noises (1969). *Top: Harry Belafonte in* Buck and the Preacher. *Below: Ralph Bellamy in* Rosemary's Baby. *Right: Jean-Paul Belmondo*

BELLOCCHIO, Marco

(b. 1939). Director. Born: Piacenza, Italy

Marco Bellocchio first studied at the Centro Sperimentale di Cinematografia in Rome before three of his short films earned him a scholarship to the Slade School of Art in London in 1964. On finishing his course he made his first feature – the award-winning black comedy *Pugni in Tasca*, a drama about an epileptic. The majority of his following films have tended to be studies of rebellion, such as *Nel Nome del Padre*, about life in a Catholic school, and *La Cine e'Vicina*, a satire on Italian politics. And in fact his outspoken political views have hampered financial backing for his films. He has also acted and directed for television, in addition to directing stage plays.

Films as director: 1961 La Colpa e la Pena (short). '62 Abbasso Lo Zio! (doc. short). '64 Ginepro Fatto Uomo (short). '65 Pugni in Tasca (GB: Fists in the Pocket). '67 La Cine e'Vicina (USA/GB: China is Near). '69 Amore e Rabbia *ep* Discutiamo, discutiamo (FR-IT) (USA/GB: Love and Anger). '71 Nel Nome del Padre (USA: In the Name of the Father). '72 Sbatti il Mostro in Prima Pagina! (FR-IT) (USA: The Monster on Page One). '76 Matti da Slegare (USA: Fit to Be Untied); Marcia Trionfale (FR-IT-GER) (USA: Victory March). '77 Il Gabbiano (USA: The Sea Gull). '78 La Macchina Cinema (USA: The Cinema Machine). '80 Salta nel Vuoto (GB: Leap Into the Vow). '82 Gli Occhi, La Bocca (IT-FR).

BELMONDO, Jean-Paul

(b. 1933). Actor. Born: Neuilly-sur-Seine, France

Jean-Paul Belmondo was educated in Paris and became interested in boxing and the theatre at an early age. He was thought to have little acting ability but persevered in his studies at the Conservatoire National d'Art Dramatique, after which he joined a small touring theatre group. Breaking into films, he appeared in Marc Allégret's *Sois Belle et Tais-toi* (1957) and Marcel Carné's *Les Tricheurs* (1958). He was spotted by Jean-Luc Godard and cast in *A Bout de Souffle*. The film was an overnight success, and Belmondo's performance led to his being heralded as the cinema's new anti-hero. This was aided by his ugly-handsome features – sloping eyes and broken-nose – and gruff sex appeal. He went on to make films for all the leading French directors, mainly semi-serious adventures as a good-humoured petty criminal or carefree blackguard.

Films include: 1959 Paris Brule-t-il? (USA/GB: Is Paris Burning?); A Double Tour (USA: Leda; GB: Web of Passion). '60 Moderato Cantabile (FR-IT) (GB: Seven Days . . . Seven Nights); A Bout de Souffle (USA/GB: Breathless). '61 Une Femme est Une Femme (USA: A Woman Is a Woman); La Viacca (IT-FR) (GB: The Love Makers); La Ciociara (FR-IT) (GB: Two Women); Leon Morin Pretre (GB: Leon Morin, Priest). '65 Pierrot le Fou (FR-IT). '67 Le Voleur (FR-IT) (USA: The Thief of Paris; GB: The Thief). '69 La Sirène du Mississippi (FR-IT). '70 Borsalino (FR-IT). '74 Stavisky (FR-IT). '80 Le Guignolo (FR-IT). '81 Le Professionnel (USA: The Professional). '82 L'As des As (FR-GER).

BELUSHI, John

(1949–1982). Comedian/actor. Born: Chicago, Illinois, USA

The son of Albanian parents, Belushi spent his youth playing in Chicago rock bands and in 1967 opened the Universal Life Church Coffee House with a group of friends, the aim of which was to have somewhere to put on their own theatrical productions. In the early Seventies he joined an improvisational troupe called Second City, and here developed his gift for mimicry. The National Lampoon satire team invited him to join their Broadway musical *Lemmings* in 1973, and Belushi came into his own with his imitation of the singer Joe Cocker and also his original 'announcer' character. National Lampoon then did *Saturday Night Live* for NBC, and Belushi featured as a grunting Samurai, a Greek laundrette owner, a rambling weather-forecaster and a killer bee. He made his film debut in 1978, and his outrageous, manic and anarchic behaviour soon made him a cult figure. He died at the age of 33 from a drug overdose.

Films include: 1978 National Lampoon's Animal House; Goin' South. '79 1941; Old Boyfriends. '80 The Blues Brothers. '81 Continental Divide; Neighbors.

BENCHLEY, Robert

(1889–1945). Screenwriter/actor/critic. Born: Worcester, Massachusetts, USA

In 1912 Robert Benchley graduated from Harvard University with a degree in philosophy. He then took up publicity and advertising before becoming a journalist on the *New York Tribune* – and eventually its editor. During the late Twenties and early Thirties he edited *Vanity Fair* and was a columnist on the *New York World* as well as being drama critic for *Life* and *The New Yorker*. Additionally he was writing dialogue, and in 1928 was asked to script the film *The Treasurer's Report*. All his creations were in a dry, humorous style and his talents as both writer and actor translated well to the screen. Some essays written between 1920 and 1935 on the tribulations of 'The Normal Bumbler' provided the basis for his award-winning series of shorts on 'how to' do things – *How to Sleep, How to Start the Day* – which Benchley narrated as if they were scientific lectures. His film appearances also played on his understated world-weary style and sense of comic timing.

Films include: 1935 How to Sleep (sc; + narr; + act); China Seas (actor only). '36 How to Be a Detective (sc; + narr; + act). '37 How to Start the Day (sc; + narr; + act). '40 Foreign Correspondent (co-sc; + act); That Inferior Feeling (sc; + narr; + act). '42 The Major and the Minor (actor only); Take a Letter Darling (actor only). '45 It's in the Bag (actor only) (GB: The Fifth Chair).

Top: John Belushi in National Lampoon's Animal House. *Above centre: Robert Benchley. Right: William Bendix in* The Blue Dahlia. *Far right: Richard Benjamin*

BENDIX, William

(1906–1964). Actor. Born: New York City, USA

Bendix was born into a musical family but favoured sports, becoming adept at football and baseball. However, he decided to make 'business' his career and bought a wholesale grocery store. By way of creative diversion he acted as a master of ceremonies in clubs and cabarets and when the Depression hit his business he turned to acting, joining the New York Theatre Guild. In 1941 he signed with MGM and appeared in his only starring vehicle, *Brooklyn Orchid*, which was not a success. However, his large, thick frame, broken nose, square jaw, rasping voice and Brooklyn accent made him an obvious tough-guy character actor for thrillers such as *The Glass Key* and *The Blue Dahlia*, and a dim-witted, clumsy heavy in comedies like *The Hairy Ape*. He has also worked on the stage and appeared in the very popular Fifties television series *The Life of Riley*.

Films include: 1942 The Glass Key. '44 Lifeboat; The Hairy Ape. '46 The Blue Dahlia. '48 The Babe Ruth Story. '49 The Big Steal; A Connecticut Yankee in King Arthur's Court (GB: A Yankee in King Arthur's Court); The Life of Riley. '51 Detective Story. '52 Macao. '61 Johnny Nobody (GB).

BENEDEK, Laslo

(b. 1907). Director. Born: László Benedek; Budapest, Hungary

After studying drama and psychiatry at the University of Vienna, Benedek went to Berlin. There he met the producer Joe Pasternak and became his assistant cameraman at Ufa. He worked his way up to producer's assistant, and after the rise of the Nazis returned to Vienna with Pasternak in 1933. Travelling to Paris as an editor and to England as a screenwriter, he finally ended up in America in 1937. He signed with MGM and a few years later resumed his association with Pasternak, helping to direct some sequences in the latter's later musicals. In 1948 Benedek directed his first film, the musical *The Kissing Bandit*, starring Frank Sinatra. His two most successful films have been for the producer Stanley Kramer: *Death of a Salesman* and *The Wild One*. He has also worked on the television series *Naked City, The Outer Limits* and *Rawhide*.

Films include: 1948 The Kissing Bandit. '49 Port of New York. '51 Death of a Salesman. '53 The Wild One. '57 Affair in Havana. '59 Moments of Danger. '66 Namu the Killer Whale (doc). '71 The Night Visitor.

BENJAMIN, Richard

(b. 1938). Actor. Born: New York City, USA

Educated at the High School of Performing Arts and Northwestern University drama school, Benjamin played teenage walk-on roles in Hollywood movies of the Fifties before making his mark on Broadway in successful plays such as *Barefoot in the Park* with Myrna Loy, and *The Odd Couple* with Dan Dailey. He came back into movies as a star, but retained his boyish image – enhanced by his dark curly hair and 'nice Jewish boy' manner – in *Goodbye Columbus*. The early Seventies saw him racing to fame in a series of black comedies featuring him as a clean-cut wierdo. He has been married to actress Paula Prentiss since 1961.

Films include: 1969 Goodbye Columbus. '70 Catch 22; The Diary of a Mad Housewife. '71 The Marriage of a Young Stockbroker. '72 Portnoy's Complaint. '73 Westworld; The Last of Sheila. '75 The Sunshine Boys. '78 House Calls. '79 Love at First Bite. '80 The Last Married Couple in America. '82 My Favorite Year (dir. only).

BENNETT, Constance

(1906–1965). Actress. Born: New York City, USA

Born into a theatrical family and the eldest of three beautiful sisters (Joan was the youngest), Constance Bennett appeared in over a dozen silent films before marriage to a millionaire took her away to Paris and a busy social life. After her divorce in 1929, she returned to Hollywood as talkies were coming in, and rapidly became one of the highest-paid stars. Her willowy blonde beauty and husky voice were a great success in *What Price Hollywood?* – an appropriate title, since she soon acquired a reputation for shrewd business sense, investing in the cosmetic and fashion industries. In 1944 she also formed her own film company. Having made her stage debut in 1940 in Noel Coward's *Easy Virtue*, she combined a theatrical career with film appearances in later years.

Films include: 1925 The Goose Hangs High; Code of the West; Sally, Irene and Mary. '29 This Thing Called Love. '30 Three Faces East. '31 Born to Love. '32 What Price Hollywood? '34 Moulin Rouge. '39 Tail Spin. '41 Two-Faced Woman. '74 The Unsuspected. '66 Madame X.

BENNETT, Hywel

(b. 1944). Actor. Born: Garnant, Dyfed, Wales

Hywel Bennett's look of baby-faced innocence has sometimes been played straight and sometimes used for twisted, neurotic or mentally unstable characters. After five years at the National Youth Theatre and a scholarship to RADA, he stayed in films only a few years, perhaps limited by typecasting. His debut was as the bridegroom temporarily unable to consummate his marriage in *The Family Way*, opposite Hayley Mills. He was sinister in *Twisted Nerve*, but had more fun with the anarchic comedy of *Loot*, based on Joe Orton's play. For most of the Seventies he devoted himself to the theatre (including directing) and television, notably as the layabout hero of the comedy series *Shelley*. He was divorced from the ex-television presenter Cathy McGowan in 1978.

Films include: 1966 The Family Way. '68 Il Marito è Mio a l'Amazzo Quando Mi Pare (IT) (USA: Drop Dead, My Love); Twisted

Nerve. '69 The Virgin Soldiers. '70 Loot; The Buttercup Chain. '72 Endless Night; Alice's Adventure in Wonderland. '73 It's a 2 Ft 6 Ins Above the Ground World/The Love Ban. '80 Towards the Morning (short).

BENNETT, Jill

(b. 1930). Actress. Born: Penang, Malaysia

Jill Bennett's *jolie-laide* style of upper-crust beauty with a neurotic edge is not easy to cast in the conventional film-star mode; her best work has been in the theatre and in such prestigious television plays as David Mercer's *The Parachute* (1968). She made her name in a season at Stratford-on-Avon with Laurence Olivier, who subsequently brought her to London. She was later associated with the Royal Court Theatre, particularly in the plays of John Osborne, to whom she was married from 1968 to 1977. Her first major screen role was as a Norwegian girl devoted to harpooning whales in *Hell Below Zero*; and she made some impact in the fuzzily-written role of a villain's mistress in *The Criminal*.

Films include: 1953 Moulin Rouge; Hell Below Zero. '56 Lust for Life. '60 The Criminal (USA: The Concrete Jungle). '65 The Nanny. '68 Charge of the Light Brigade; Inadmissible Evidence. '70 Julius Caesar. '72 I Want What I Want. '75 Mister Quilp/The Old Curiosity Shop. '77 Full circle (GB-CAN).

BENNETT, Joan

(b. 1910). Actress. Born: Palisades, New Jersey, USA

Constance's youngest sister, Joan Bennett made her stage debut with their actor father Richard Bennett, and then entered films in 1929. She worked with several major directors (George Cukor, Frank Borzage) in *ingénue* roles in the Thirties but was eclipsed by Constance. Then in 1940 she met the producer Walter Wanger. He became her third husband and introduced her to Fritz Lang, who starred her in several *films noirs* and changed her blonde image to the brunette *femme fatale* of *The Woman in the Window* and *Scarlet Street* (produced by Wanger). She moved on to play the mother of teenage girls in Max Ophuls' melodrama *The Reckless Moment* and Vincente Minnelli's comedy *Father of the Bride*. Her career was damaged by a scandal when Wanger was imprisoned for shooting Jennings Lang, her press agent. She later turned to television films and series, though still makes occasional movies.

Films include: 1929 Disraeli. '32 Me and My Gal (GB: Pier 13). '33 Little Women. '39 The Man in the Iron Mask. '44 The Woman in the Window. '45 Scarlet Street. '46 The Woman on the Beach. '48 Secret Beyond the Door. '49 The Reckless Moment. '50 Father of the Bride. '55 We're No Angels. '77 Suspiria (IT).

Top: Constance Bennett in The Affairs of Cellini *(1934). Above centre: Hywel Bennett in* The Virgin Soldiers. *Left: Joan Bennett in* The Woman in the Window. *Far left: Jill Bennett in* The Nanny

BENNETT, Richard Rodney

(b. 1936). Composer. Born:
Broadstairs, Kent, England

Richard Rodney Bennett wrote his first
musical work at the age of 6. When he
was 15 he completed a major string
quartet and since then he has composed prolifically. After attending the
Royal Academy of Music, Bennett
studied in Paris under the respected
French composer Pierre Boulez. When
he was 19 he wrote some music for a
documentary film (about insurance)
and discovered that not only did it pay
well but that his musical timing and
technique was augmented by his
ability to make the music match an
image. There followed a stream of B
movie scores, but as his reputation and
experience grew he found himself in
demand for more distinguished productions. He restricts his film work to
Britain, composing for such directors
as John Schlesinger and Joseph Losey.
Bennett has received three Oscar
nominations. In 1977 he was awarded
the CBE.

Films include: 1958 Indiscreet. '63 Billy
Liar. '65 The Nanny; Darling . . . '67 Far
From the Madding Crowd; Billion Dollar
Brain. '70 Figures in a Landscape. '71
Nicholas & Alexandra. '77 Equus. '79
Yanks.

BENNY, Jack

(1894–1974). Actor. Born: Benjamin
Kubelsky; Waukegan, Illinois, USA

Originally a child prodigy on the
violin, Benny served his apprenticeship in vaudeville and on Broadway,
but made his breakthrough in radio as
a guest on the Ed Sullivan show in
1932. In his own famous radio
comedy show through the Thirties
and Forties, he developed his persona
as a stingy miser, perpetually
threatening to play the violin, and
acting as fall guy to his own supporting cast which included his wife
Mary Livingston. He was then in
television for 24 years, winning 8
Emmys. Benny incidentally appeared
in over thirty films. The most famous of
these was Ernst Lubitsch's To Be or Not
to Be, in which he played a Polish ham
actor who uses his theatrical skills to
fool the Nazis.

Films include: 1929 The Hollywood Revue
of 1929. '35 Broadway Melody of 1936. '36
Big Broadcast of 1937. '37 Artists and
Models. '39 Man About Town. '41 Love Thy
Neighbour. '42 To Be or Not to Be. '44
Hollywood Canteen. '45 It's in the Bag (GB:
The Fifth Chair); The Horn Blows at Mid-
night. '52 Somebody Loves Me. '63 It's a
Mad, Mad, Mad, Mad World.

BENTON, Robert

(b. 1932). Screenwriter/director.
Born: Waxahachie, Texas, USA

He studied art at the University of
Texas and in the Fifties worked his
way up to art director of Esquire. That
magazine's sophisticated satire must
have inspired Benton, who turned
to writing screenplays – mostly in
collaboration with David Newman –

in the early Sixties, quickly proving
himself a sharp, witty and cogent
observer of American life. Arthur
Penn's Bonnie and Clyde is the team's
masterpiece, a biting rejection of the
establishment that in 1967 caught the
prevailing counter-culture winds.
Benton, who made his directorial
debut with Bad Company, has continued to examine wryly such American institutions as the comic-strip
hero (Superman, The Movie) and the
movies themselves (The Late Show,
What's Up Doc?), but it was the considerably less barbed Kramer vs
Kramer that earned him Oscars for
Best Film and Best Screenplay in 1981.

Films: 1964 A Texas Romance (short) (co-
dir). '67 Bonnie and Clyde (co-sc. only). '70
There Was a Crooked Man . . . (co-sc. only).
'71 Bad Company (dir; +co-sc). '72 What's
Up Doc? (co-sc. only); Oh! Calcutta! (co-sc).
'77 The Late Show (dir; +sc). '78 Superman, The Movie (co-sc. only). '79 Kramer vs
Kramer (dir; +sc). '81 Stab.

BERENSON, Marisa

(b. 1947). Actress. Born: New York
City, USA

Marisa Berenson is a dark-haired,
ethereal, though sometimes vacant
beauty. She is also highly born – the
daughter of a diplomat and a Mar-
chesa, the grandniece of art historian
Bernard Berenson and the grand-
daughter of couturier Elsa Schiapar-
elli. She was studying interior design
when a friend photographed her for
Vogue and launched her into a career
as an international fashion model and
famed jet-setter. In 1971 Luchino Visconti cast her (without a test) as the
ineffectual wife in Death in Venice, and
her best roles since have been as a rich
Jewish girl in Cabaret (a moving performance) and as the love of Barry
Lyndon. She also appeared in the
controversial television drama series
Holocaust. She was the favourite to
play the star Vivien Leigh in an un-
realized biopic in the mid-Seventies.

Films include: 1971 Morte a Venezia (IT)
(USA/GB: Death in Venice). '72 Cabaret. '75
Barry Lyndon (USA-GB). '80 La Città delle
Donne (IT-FR (USA/GB: The City of
Women). '81 S.O.B.

BERESFORD, Bruce

(b. 1940). Director. Born: Sydney,
Australia

He graduated from Sydney University
in 1962 and, after working as a film
editor in Nigeria, came to England
where he headed the British Film
Institute Production Board for five
years. During this time he began to
make his own shorts, mostly documentaries on artists. In 1971 Beresford returned to Australia and directed The Adventures of Barry McKenzie, a ribald satire with Australian
comic archetypes – including Dame
Edna Everage, played by Beresford's
friend Barry Humphries who co-
scripted the film with him. Its international success helped establish the
Australian 'New Wave' and Beresford
has remained at the forefront of that
movement. Though principally concerned with Australian subject-

matter, he is versatile: Don's Party is a
broad male comedy; The Getting of
Wisdom sensitively deals with life in a
Victorian boarding school for girls;
Breaker Morant is about a tense court-
martial set during the Boer War.

Films include: 1972 The Adventures of
Barry McKenzie. '74 Barry McKenzie Holds
his Own (GB). '75 Side by Side (GB). '76
Don's Party. '77 The Getting of Wisdom. '78
The Money Movers. '80 Breaker Morant;
The Club. '82 Puberty Blues; Tender
Mercies.

BERGEN, Candice

(b. 1946). Actress. Born: Beverly
Hills, California, USA

Blonde, all-American co-ed type with
a forceful, abrasive manner, Candice
Bergen was ideal for rebellious, independent roles in the late Sixties and
early Seventies. thus she appeared to
good advantage as a rioting student in
Getting Straight and as a white renegade living with Indians in Soldier
Blue. Before that the daughter of
ventriloquist Edgar Bergen attended
a finishing school in Switzerland,
the University of Pennsylvania, and
worked as a model and photo-
journalist. She made her film debut in
The Group in 1965 and afterwards
went straight into The Sand Pebbles.
The good parts in good movies have
been scarce since the mid-Seventies,

though George Cukor's Rich and
Famous, co-starring her with Jacqueline Bisset, thrust her back into the
public eye in 1981. The previous year
she married the French director Louis
Malle. Bergen, an ardent feminist, has
written for television and completed a
play, The Freezer.

Films include: 1965 The Group. '66 The
Sand Pebbles. '70 The Adventurers; Getting
Straight; Soldier Blue. '71 Carnal Know-
ledge. '74 11 Harrowhouse. '75 Bite the
Bullet. '79 Starting Over. '81 Rich and
Famous. '82 Gandhi (GB-IND).

BERGER, Helmut

(b. 1944). Actor. Born: Helmut Steinberger; Salzburg, Austria

At 19 Helmut Berger turned his back on the family restaurant business and determined to become an actor. He gained experience in Paris and London and then took a drama course at the University of Perugia in Italy. In 1967 Luchino Visconti gave him a small part in the episode he directed in *Le Streghe*. Visconti took a great interest in the young actor's career and cast him as the neurotic Martin in *The Damned*. Blond, wiry and boyishly handsome, Berger was perfectly attuned to the decadence of that film and he has since brought his talent to many important European movies, often in similar roles. Off screen he is a hell-raiser of some repute, and in 1977 he nearly died of a drug overdose.

Films include: 1967 Le Streghe (GB: The Witches). '69 La Caduta degli Dei (IT-GER) (USA/GB: The Damned). '70 Das Bildnis des Dorian Gray (GER-IT-LICH) (USA/GB: Dorian Gray). '71 Il Giardino dei Finzi-Contini (IT) (USA/GB: The Garden of the Finzi-Continis); Un Beau Monstre (FR-IT) (GB: A Strange Love Affair); La Farfalla con le Ali Insanguinate (IT). '73 Ash Wednesday (USA); Ludwig (IT-FR-GER). '75 The Romantic Englishwoman (GB-FR).

BERGER, Senta

(b. 1941). Actress. Born: Vienna, Austria

A model whose face appeared on magazine covers throughout Europe in the late Fifties, Berger soon became dissatisfied with playing cover girl and took up acting. She appeared in several minor films until actor Richard Widmark signed her for *The Secret Ways*, a violent thriller he was producing. A rather shapeless Hollywood career followed which never allowed much scope for her talents. But she achieved some success in Carl Foreman's overblown war film *The Victors*. She returned to Europe and resides in Munich, appearing infrequently in films.

Films include: 1960 Der Brave Soldat Schwejk (GER) (USA: The Good Soldier Schweik). '61 The Secret Ways. '63 The Victors. '65 Major Dundee. '66 Cast a Giant Shadow; The Quiller Memorandum. '67 The Ambushers. '71 Der Graben (GER). '77 Cross of Iron.

BERGMAN, Ingmar

(b. 1918). Director. Born: Uppsala, Sweden

Bergman and 'art-house' became synonymous in the Sixties, especially in America, where cultist audiences who grew up on a steady diet of Hollywood were enthralled with the discovery that not all films had to cater to the lowest common denominator. For Bergman spun them a web of symbolic dreams and dream-like symbols and enmeshed his select audiences in the harsh visions of his themes – the search for belief, the nature of good and evil, the artist and society – and the endless, bitter and solitary suffering endured by his troubled characters. Laughter is something rarely heard in, or at, a Bergman film. He worked in the theatre in the late Thirties and from 1944 onwards divided his time between stage and film. In the Sixties he was head of the Royal Dramatic Theatre in Stockholm. Bergman's life has been as angst-ridden as his films, marked by emotional entanglements with his actresses and a forced exile from Sweden because of tax difficulties.

Films include: 1951 Sommarlek (USA: Illicit Interlude; GB: Summer Interlude). '53 Gycklarnas Afton (USA: The Naked Night; GB: Sawdust and Tinsel). '55 Sommarnattens Leende (USA/GB: Smiles of a Summer Night). '57 Det Sjunde Inseglet (USA/GB: The Seventh Seal); Smultronstället (USA/GB: Wild Strawberries). '61 Sasom i en Spegel (USA/GB: Through a Glass, Darkly). '62 Nattvardsgästerna (USA/GB: Winter Light). '63 Tystnaden (USA/GB: The Silence). '66 Persona. '68 Skammen (USA: The Shame; GB: Shame). '69 En Passion (USA: The Passion of Anna; GB: A Passion). '71 Beröringen (USA-SWED) (USA/GB: The Touch). '72 Viskningar och Rop (USA/GB: Cries and Whispers). '73 Scener ur ett Äktenskap (USA/GB: Scenes From a Marriage) (orig. TV). '77 Das Schlangenei (GER/USA) (USA/GB: The Serpent's Egg). '78 Herbstsonate (GER) (USA/GB: Autumn Sonata). '81 Fanny och Alexander (SWED-GER-FR) (USA/GB: Fanny and Alexander).

Below left: Helmut Berger. Left: Candice Bergen in 11 Harrowhouse. *Above left: Jack Benny (left) in* The Horn Blows at Midnight, *with*

Allyn Joslin. Above: Marisa Berenson in Cabaret. *Below: Senta Berger. Below right: Ingmar Bergman (right) with cameraman Sven Nykvist*

BERGMAN, Ingrid

(1915–1982). Actress. Born: Stockholm, Sweden

As a teenager, Bergman enrolled in Sweden's Royal Dramatic Theatre Drama School and in the same year began her film career, becoming in a few years a star. In 1939 producer David O. Selznick brought her to Hollywood and cast her alongside Leslie Howard in *Intermezzo: a Love Story*. America took to this tall, big-boned, healthy-looking Swede. But, recognizing the dangers that lay in being typecast, she took on more ambivalent roles as duplicitous heroines. In the early Fifties she scandalized Hollywood because of her adulterous relationship with the Italian neo-realist director Roberto Rossellini, whom she married and made several films with. They split up in 1957 and she returned to Hollywood. Bergman has won Academy Awards as Best Actress for her appearances in *Gaslight* and *Anastasia*, and as Best Supporting Actress in *Murder on the Orient Express*. In 1978 she managed for the first time to work with her namesake, fellow Swede Ingmar Bergman, in *Autumn Sonata*.

Films include: 1936 På Solsidan (SWED). '39 Intermezzo: a Love Story (USA) (GB: Escape to Happiness). '41 Dr Jekyll and Mr Hyde (USA). '42 Casablanca (USA). '43 For Whom the Bell Tolls (USA). '44 Gaslight (USA) (GB: The Murder in Thornton Square). '45 The Bells of St Mary's (USA). '46 Notorious (USA). '48 Joan of Arc (USA). '49 Under Capricorn (GB). '50 Stromboli, Terra di Dio (IT) (USA: God's Land). '51 Europa '51 (IT) (USA: The Greatest Love). '56 Anastasia (GB). '58 The Inn of the Sixth Happiness (GB). '74 Murder on the Orient Express (GB). '78 Herbstsonate (GER) (USA/GB: Autumn Sonata).

BERGNER, Elisabeth

(1900–1986). Actress. Born: Drohobycz, Poland

Educated at the Vienna Conservatory, Bergner made her stage debut in Switzerland in 1919 and shortly afterward appeared on Broadway. Most of her early film successes were directed by her husband Paul Czinner. They were forced to leave Germany in 1933, whereupon she worked in Britain and Hollywood, but her fair, frail little-boy appearance made her especially popular with British cinemagoers. Remarkably active, Bergner continued appearing in films into her late seventies.

Films include: 1923 Der Evangelimann. '24 Nju Eine Unverstandene Frau (GB: Husbands or Lovers?). '26 Der Geiger von Florenz (USA: Impetuous Youth; GB: The Violinist of Florence); Liebe/ Der Herzogen von Langeais. '28 Königin Luise. '29 Fräulein Else. '31 Ariane. '32 Der Träumende Mund. '34 Catherine the Great (GB). '35 Escape Me Never (GB). '36 As You Like It (GB). '37 Dreaming Lips (GB). '39 A Stolen Life (GB). '41 Paris Calling (USA). '70 Cry of the Banshee (GB). '79 Pringstrausflug.

BERKELEY, Busby

(1895–1976). Choreographer/ director. Born: William Berkeley Enos; Los Angeles, California, USA

Although his parents were stage people Berkeley's first show business experience was not in the theatre but in the army during World War I when he trained men to do skilfully devised precision drills. From the army he went to the theatre and then to Broadway. In 1930 he arrived in Hollywood, staging the dance numbers for Samuel Goldwyn productions, and started showing his form two years later in Warner Brothers' *42nd Street* with its extravagantly staged setpieces. Surprising camera angles, vast sets, dozens of dancers (mostly scantily-clad girls) and inventively bizarre choreography came to be the hallmarks of a Berkeley musical in the Thirties. He also directed films – thrillers as well as musicals.

Films include: 1930 Whoopee! (chor). '33 42nd Street (chor); Gold Diggers of 1933 (chor;+act); Footlight Parade (chor); Roman Scandals (chor). '34 Dames (chor). '35 Gold Diggers of 1935 (dir; +chor). '39 They Made Me a Criminal (dir); Babes in Arms. '40 Strike Up the Band. '41 Ziegfeld Girl (chor); Babes on Broadway. '43 The Gang's All Here (GB: The Girls He Left Behind). '49 Take Me Out to the Ball Game (GB: Everybody's Cheering). '52 Million Dollar Mermaid (chor) (GB: The One-Piece Bathing Suit).

BERLANGA, Luis Garcia

(b. 1921). Director. Born: Valencia, Spain

During the Franco regime there was only a handful of film-makers whose work was screened outside Spain. One director whose films were seen periodically was Berlanga, who somehow managed to survive the heavy hands of church and state censors. After studying literature at the University of Valencia he enrolled in film school in Madrid. His first film to receive international notice was *Bienvenido, Mr Marshall!* made with his colleague Juan Antonio Bardem, and, throughout the Fifties and Sixties Berlanga was awarded prizes at Cannes, Venice and other film festivals. His films tend to be satirical treatments of off-beat subjects and have been compared to those of his American contemporary, Billy Wilder.

Films include: 1951 Esa Pareja Feliz (co-dir). '53 Bienvenido, Mr Marshall! (USA/GB: Welcome Mr Marshall). '54 Novio a la Vista. '56 Calabuch (SP-IT) (IT: Clalbiug). '58 Los Jeuves Milagro (SP-IT). '62 Plácido; Les Quatre Vérités (FR-SP-IT) (GB: The Three Fables of Love). '63 El Verdugo (SP-IT) (USA/GB: The Executioner). '67 Las Piraños (ARG-SP) (USA: The Piranhas); Vivan los Novios! (USA: Long Live the Bride and Groom).

BERLIN, Irving

(b. 1888). Composer. Born: Israel Baline; Temum, Russia

It could be the plot of a Hollywood musical. Born in Tsarist Russia, the hero is welcomed to the bosom of America as an infant. His father dies a few years later and the hero helps support his family by singing on street corners for pennies. Soon he's appearing in Bowery dives where he learns to play piano (in one key only). He composes his first song and earns the princely sum of 37 cents from its publication. From then on the streets were increasingly paved with gold for Irving Berlin, especially after he wrote 'Alexander's Ragtime Band' in 1911 and became an international celebrity. Hit after hit followed, but it wasn't till 1935 that he wrote his first musical expressly for the movies. Some of Berlin's songs, like 'White Christmas' were more than hits, or even classics. They became firmly embedded in the cultural history of a nation.

Films include: 1935 Top Hat. '36 Follow the Fleet. '38 Alexander's Ragtime Band. '41 Louisiana Purcase. '42 Holiday Inn. '43 This Is the Army (+act). '46 Blue Skies. '48 Easter Parade. '50 Annie Get Your Gun. '54 There's No Business Like Show Business; White Christmas.

BERMAN, Pandro S.

(b. 1905). Producer. Born:
Pittsburgh. Pennsylvania, USA

His father, Harry M. Berman, was a
distributor and exhibitor of films, and
Pandro S. Berman led a nomadic
childhood before finally settling in
New York City. In 1923 he went to
Hollywood as a script clerk, and by
1931 had risen to produce his first film
at RKO, where he helped to establish
the famous dancing partnership of
Fred Astaire and Ginger Rogers. He
specialized in light comedies and musicals, but on moving to MGM in 1940
he began to extend his range, and
contributed to the prestige of the
company at a time when it was
beginning to lose the premier position
it had held in the Thirties. His name
has been regularly associated with
films of taste, intelligence and a
certain 'chocolate box' charm.

Films include: 1932 What Price Hollywood?
'34 The Gay Divorcee (GB: The Gay Div-
orce). '35 Top Hat. '41 Ziegfeld Girl. '44
National Velvet. '48 The Three Musketeers.
'50 Father of the Bride. '52 The Prisoner of
Zenda; Ivanhoe (GB). '55 The Blackboard
Jungle. '56 Bhowani Junction. '58 The
Brothers Karamazov. '62 Sweet Bird of
Youth. '69 Justine.

BERNHARDT, Curtis

(1899–1981). Director. Born: Kurt
Bernhardt; Worms. Germany

Bernhardt studied drama in Frankfurt
and established a reputation as a
stage actor in Berlin before moving to
film direction, mainly war movies.
He directed Ufa's first all-talking picture, *Die letzte Kompanie*. After being
arrested and released by the Gestapo,
he went to France in 1934 and then to
England where, in 1937, he founded
British Unity Pictures, though continuing to make films in France. In
1940 he went to the USA on a Warner
Brothers contract, later working for
MGM and RKO. He made sound commercial studio productions in a
variety of genres, getting good performances from his actors, who included Marlene Dietrich and Conrad
Veidt in Germany, and Joan Crawford,
Robert Taylor and Ronald Reagan in
the USA.

Films include: 1929 Die Frau. nach der Man
Sich Sehnt (USA: Three Loves). '30 Die
letzte Kompanie (USA: 13 Men and a Girl;
GB: The Last Company). '33 Der Tunnel.
'36 The Beloved Vagabond (GB). '46 A
Stolen Life (USA). '47 Possessed (USA);
High Wall (USA). '51 Sirocco (USA); The
Blue Veil (USA). '53 Miss Sadie Thompson
(USA). '54 Beau Brummel (USA). '64 Kisses
for My President (USA).

BERNHARDT, Sarah

(1844–1923). Actress. Born:
Henriette-Rosine Bernard; Paris
France

The most famous stage actress of her
time, Sarah Bernhardt made her first
film appearance – as Hamlet – when
she was in her mid-fifties. Moviegoers

at that time, therefore, were deprived
of seeing her at her peak when she
was a dark-haired, imposing beauty.
Today a few unflattering fragments of
her work survive, and they are of
historical interest only.

Films: 1900 Hamlet – Duel Scene. '08 La
Tosca (unreleased). '11 La Dame aux
Camélias. '12 La Reine Elisabeth. '13
Adrienne Lecouvreur. '16 Jeanne Doré. '17
Mères Françaises. '23 La Voyante
(unfinished).

BERNSTEIN, Elmer

(b. 1922). Composer. Born: New
York City. USA

After graduating from New York University. Bernstein attempted many
branches of the artistic tree. He was a
dancer, actor and painter before settling for the concert platform as a
pianist in the Forties. He had previously studied composition and
began to write scores during World
War II while working in the service

radio unit and arranging numbers for
Glenn Miller and the Army Air Force
Band. Gradually jazz became more
appealing to him, and Bernstein was
soon associated with 'modern' me-
lodic music. He was awarded an
Emmy for his television score, *The
Making of a President*, and an Oscar for
Thoroughly Modern Millie. From
1963–1969 he was the vice-president
of the Academy of Motion Picture Arts
and Sciences. His scores are generally
loud, noisy and gutsy.

Films include: 1956 The Ten Command-
ments. '60 The Magnificent Seven. '61
Summer and Smoke. '62 The Coman-
cheros; To Kill a Mockingbird; Walk on the
Wild Side; Birdman of Alcatraz. '63 The
Great Escape. '65 The Hallelujah Trail; The
Sons of Katie Elder. '67 Thoroughly Modern
Millie. '69 True Grit. '78 National
Lampoon's Animal House. '81 An Amer-
ican Werewolf in London.

BERNSTEIN, Leonard

(b. 1918). Composer. Born:
Lawrence. Massachusetts, USA

Bernstein majored in music at Harvard and the Curtis Institute of Music.
By 1942 he had become assistant
conductor of the New York Philharmonic Orchestra and in 1957 took up
the post of principal conductor, a
position he was to hold for the next 13
years. He has written primarily
classical works and was the first
native American to be invited to conduct at La Scala in Milan. On his
return to America he was asked to
write the music for *On the Waterfront*.
His Broadway musicals include *On the
Town. Wonderful Town. Candide* and
West Side Story. As well as composing
and conducting, he writes and lectures extensively on music.

Films: 1949 On the Town. '54 On the
Waterfront. '61 West Side Story.

BERRY, Jules

(1889–1951). Actor. Born: Jules
Paufichet; Poitiers, France

After a long and distinguished stage
career in Paris and Brussels. Jules
Berry, tall. lean-faced and vulpine.
took to the screen in two silent films –
Cromwell and *L'Argent*. Their success
ensured him a long and distinguished
career. even with the arrival of sound.
He could be the oiliest of villains (a
crooked publisher in *Le Crime de M.
Lange*, a young girl's seducer in *Le Jour
se Lève*) and yet still extract reluctant
sympathy from his audience. The directors Jean Renoir and Marcel Carné
recognized this appeal and it was as
the Devil in Carné's *Les Visiteurs du
Soir* that Berry gave his most memorable – and malevolent – performance, dominating a superbly acted
film.

Films include: 1911 Cromwell. '28
L'Argent. '35 Le Crime de M. Lange (GB:
The Crime of Monsieur Lange). '37 Le
Voleur de Femmes. '39 Derrière la Façade;
Le Jour se Lève (USA: Daybreak). '42 La
Symphonie Fantastique; Les Visiteurs du
Soir (USA: The Devil's Own Enemy). '43 Le
Voyageur de la Toussaint. '50 Les Maitres
Nageurs.

BERTOLUCCI, Bernardo

(b. 1941). Director. Born: Parma, Italy

Attilio Bertolucci, a well-known poet and film critic, encouraged his son Bernardo to write poetry from an early age. By the time he was 12, the younger Bertolucci was being published. Later, at Rome University, he won a national poetry prize. While still in his teens, Bernardo also developed an interest in films. After making several 16mm shorts, he became Pier Paolo Pasolini's assistant director on *Accatone*, and the following year he directed his debut feature, *La Commare Secca*, from a script by Pasolini. His first major success was *La Strategia del Ragno*, which interwove psychoanalysis, politics, history, literary criticism and sexuality, themes he has continued to explore throughout his career. He is one of the most important directors from the 'young' generation of Italian filmmakers and although his films are so deeply concerned with provocative ideas, they remain popular and accessible.

Films include: 1961 Accattone (ass. dir. only). '62 La Commare Secca (GB: The Grim Reaper). '64 Prima della Rivoluzione (IT-FR) (USA/GB: Before the Revolution). '68 C'Era una Volta il West (co-sc. only) (USA/GB: Once Upon a Time in the West). '70 La Strategia del Ragno (GB: The Spider's Strategem); Il Conformista (IT-FR-GER) (USA/GB: The Conformist). '72 Ultimo Tango a Parigi (IT-FR) (USA/GB: Last Tango in Paris). '76 Novecento/1900. '79 La Luna (USA: Luna). '81 Tragedia di un Uomo Ridicolo (USA/GB: Tragedy of a Ridiculous Man).

BESSIE, Alvah

(1904–1985). Scriptwriter/ Journalist/ novelist. Born: New York City, USA

As a member of the International Brigade, Alvah Bessie fought in the Spanish Civil War in 1938 and on returning to America wrote 'Men in Battle', a book about his wartime experiences. At Warner Brothers he

worked as a screenwriter in the mid-Forties, but in 1947 he was summoned before the House Un-American Activities Committee where he refused to affirm or deny his membership of the Communist Party. One of the 'Hollywood Ten' who preferred to be imprisoned rather than betray his beliefs, he was sentenced to one year in gaol in 1950. After that his work was blacklisted. He wrote a book about this period of his life, *Inquisition in Eden*, in 1965 and ten years later *Spain Again*, an account of his collaboration as screenwriter and actor on the Spanish film *España Otra Vez*, was published.

BETTGER, Lyle

(b. 1915). Actor. Born: Philadelphia, Pennsylvania, USA

After studying at the American Academy of Dramatic Arts in New York, Lyle Bettger worked in summer stock and on Broadway before entering the film business in the Fifties. Heavily built, with the sullen look of a villain,

Films include: 1943 Northern Pursuit. '44 The Very Thought of You. '45 Objective Burma! (original sc. only); Hotel Berlin. '48 Smart Woman. '69 España Otra Vez (+ act) (USA: Spain Again).

Bettger became typecast as a bad guy in many Westerns. He was, for example, an obvious choice to play Ike Clanton in *Gunfight at the OK Corral*. He has continued to work steadily throughout his career and in the Seventies began appearing in television series such as *Hawaii Five-O* and *Police Story*, as well as making a sizeable income from commercials.

Films include: 1951 The Greatest Show on Earth. '53 The Vanquished. '54 Drums Across the River; Destiny. '57 Gunfight at the OK Corral. '66 Nevada Smith. '70 The Hawaiians (GB: Master of the Islands). '71 The Seven Minutes.

BEVAN, Billy

(1887–1957). Actor. Born: William Bevan Harris; Orange, Australia

Billy Bevan was educated at the University of Sydney and learnt much of his stage-craft as a member of the Pollard Opera Company. He left for America and during the Twenties became one of Mack Sennett's leading clowns. A gutsy, resilient little man with a large, bushy moustache, he made a steady living as a character actor after 1929, appearing for many distinguished directors. Perhaps his triumph in his depiction of the cockney Lt Trotter in *Journey's End*.

Films include: 1920 Let 'er Go (short); The Quack Doctor (short). **'24** Lizzies of the Field (short). **'27** The Golf Nut (short). **'28** The Bicycle Flirt (short). **'30** Journey's End (GB). **'33** Cavalcade. **'34** The Lost Patrol. **'40** The Long Voyage Home. **'44** National Velvet. **'46** Cluny Brown.

BIBERMAN, Herbert J.

(1900–1971). Director. Born: Philadelphia, Pennsylvania, USA

Herbert J. Biberman graduated in economics from the University of Pennsylvania and went straight into the family textile business. He soon returned to college, however, to study drama in a course that took him to Europe for a year. Back in New York he joined the Theater Guild, becoming an actor, stage manager and then a director. In 1935 Columbia took him to Hollywood, where he quickly found his way around other studios like RKO and United Artists. In 1950 he became one of the 'Hollywood Ten' who refused to confirm or deny their apparent affiliation with the Communist Party in front of the House Un-American Activities Committee and so was jailed. This resulted in the dramatic curtailment of his career, and his name appeared on the official blacklist. Apart from *Salt of the Earth*, a film about striking New Mexico

miners that only really received a decent showing in Europe, Biberman did not make another film until his last, *Slaves*, in 1969.

Films include: 1935 One Way Ticket. **'36** Meet Nero Wolfe. **'39** King of Chinatown (sc. only). **'44** The Master Race; Action in Arabia (co-sc. only); Together Again (co-sc. only). **'47** New Orleans (co-sc; + ass. prod. only). **'52** The Hollywood Ten (short) (co-sc; + appearance as himself only). **'54** Salt of the Earth. **'69** Slaves.

BICKFORD, Charles

(1889–1967). Actor. Born: Cambridge, Massachusetts, USA

With his hard, craggy face, crinkled hair and gruff voice, it seems hardly surprising that Charles Bickford began his career by training to be a construction engineer at the Massachusetts Institute before becoming a stoker and lieutenant in the American navy in World War I. After the war he turned to acting, and for the next ten years appeared in vaudeville and New York stage productions. His film debut came for Cecil B. DeMille in *Dynamite* (1929), and although his contribution was small he made enough of an impression to establish a Hollywood career for himself. He became infamous for his outspoken views on fellow artists, as well as about the companies he worked for. Appearing regularly over the next thirty years, Bickford received Oscar nominations for three films – *The Song of Bernadette*, *The Farmer's Daughter*, *Johnny Belinda* – but was unsuccessful each time. He became a household face, if not name, through his portrayal of the fierce ranch-boss in *The Virginian* television series.

Films include: 1930 Anna Christie; Hell's Heroes. **'36** The Plainsman. **'43** Song of Bernadette. **'46** The Farmer's Daughter; Duel in the Sun. **'48** Johnny Belinda. **'54** A Star Is Born. **'58** The Big Country. **'62** Days of Wine and Roses.

BING, Herman

(1889–1947). Actor. Born: Frankfurt, Germany

As F. W. Murnau's assistant director, Herman Bing – former vaudeville clown – travelled with him to the United States where they made *Sunrise* (1927). Afterward he reverted to being a character comedian. Short, plump, dark-haired and in an almost permanent fluster, Herman Bing was a delight in his brief Hollywood screen appearances of the Thirties. His put-upon Middle-Europeans are always memorable, whether in romantic musicals – where he acts as an antidote to the saccharine – or in sophisticated dramas. He committed suicide in 1947.

Films include: 1929 Married in Hollywood; A Song of Kentucky. **'33** Dinner at Eight; The Bowery. **'34** Twentieth Century. **'36** Rose Marie; The Great Ziegfeld. **'37** Maytime. **'38** The Great Waltz; Bluebeard's Eighth Wife. **'40** Bitter Sweet. **'46** Night and Day; Rendezvous 24.

BIRKIN, Jane

(b. 1947). Actress. Born: London, England

The daughter of actress Judy Campbell, Birkin left school and with no formal training went straight onto the stage. Her debut play was *Carving a Statue*, starring Ralph Richardson. Her stage-craft left more than a little to be desired, but she again had luck on her side and landed a part in *The Knack*, followed by a role as one of the nude models in Michelangelo Antonioni's *Blow-Up*. Long-legged with straight hair, a fringe and a very 'English' appearance, Jane Birkin epitomized London's Swinging Sixties. Her marriage to composer John Barry was unsuccessful, and she moved to France. There – aided by her liaison with composer-director Serge Gainsbourg – she worked steadily through the Seventies and emerged an international star in such films as Agatha Christie's *Evil Under the Sun*.

Films include: 1966 Blow-Up. **'69** La Piscine (FR-IT) (USA: The Swimming Pool; GB: The Sinners). **'71** Romance of a Horse Thief (USA-YUG). **'73** Don Juan 73, ou si Don Juan Etait une Femme (USA/GB: Don Juan, or if Don Juan Were a Woman). **'74** Le Mouton Énragé (FR-IT) (USA: The Enraged Sheep; GB: The French Way). **'75** La Course a l'Echalotte (FR) (USA: The Wild Goose Chase). **'76** Je T'Aime Moi Non Plus (FR-GER) (USA: I Love You, Me No Longer; GB: I Love You, I Don't); Le Diable au Coeur (FR) (USA: The Devil in the Heart). **'81** La Fille Prodigue (FR) (USA: The Prodigal Daughter); Evil Under the Sun (GB). **'82** Nestor Burma, Detective de Choc (FR-IT) (USA: Nestor Burma, Schlock Detective).

BIROC, Joseph

(b. 1903). Cinematographer. Born: New York City, USA

Starting out as a studio office boy, Joseph Biroc worked his way up to become cinematographer George Folsey's assistant. During World War II he was a Captain in the Signal Corps and was the first American cameraman to film the Liberation of Paris. After the war he found himself a cameraman in his own right and in 1952 filmed the first-ever 3-D movie, *Bwana Devil*. During the Sixties and Seventies he shot a number of films for the director Robert Aldrich, including *The Killing of Sister George* and *The Grissom Gang*. He has also worked in television, notably on the series *Washington Behind Closed Doors*.

Films include: 1946 It's a Wonderful Life. **'57** Forty Guns. **'59** The FBI Story. **'64** Hush… Hush, Sweet Charlotte. **'66** The Flight of the Phoenix; The Russians Are Coming, the Russians Are Coming. **'67** Tony Rome. **'68** The Killing of Sister George. **'70** Too Late the Hero. **'71** Escape From the Planet of the Apes; The Grissom Gang.

Below: Herman Bing (centre) with William Gargan and horse in Rendezvous 24. *Below left: Sixties sex-kitten Jane Birkin*

BISSET, Jacqueline

(b. 1944). Actress. Born: Weybridge, Surrey, England

Jacqueline Bisset was the daughter of an English doctor and his French wife and was brought up in a comfortable middle-class home, taking dancing lessons and attending a public school. At 16 she was sent to the French Lycée in London and at 18 embarked on a career as a photographic model. She was encouraged to take up acting, and her good looks won her a tiny part in the film *The Knack* (1965). She then appeared in Roman Polanski's *Cul-de-Sac*, and after her success in *Two For the Road* (1966) was offered a seven-year contract by 20th Century-Fox. Her pretty but somewhat characterless features lent themselves to many roles as the romantic interest for her leading men, and she was seen as something of a sex-symbol. Since making such films as *The Detective* and *Bullit* she has become a European 'star', working for directors like François Truffaut. Bisset recently turned her cool business head towards production with *Rich and Famous*.

Films include: 1966 Cul-de-Sac. '68 The Detective; Bullitt. '69 La Promesse (FR) (USA: Secret World). '71 The Mephisto Waltz (USA). '72 The Life and Times of Judge Roy Bean (USA). '73 La Nuit Américaine (FR-IT) (USA/GB: Day for Night). '78 The Greek Tycoon (USA). '81 Rich and Famous (+co-prod) (USA).

BITZER, G. W. ('Billy')

(1872–1944). Cinematographer. Born: Johann Gottlob Willhelm Bitzer; Roxbury, Massachusetts, USA

An apprentice silversmith, Bitzer joined the Magic Introduction Company in 1894. When it became the American Mutoscope and Biograph Company, Bitzer turned his newfound talents as a cameraman towards shooting 'story-films'. By 1909 the company had become known as Biograph. When the great pioneer director D. W. Griffith arrived there he and Bitzer worked so closely together – until 1920 when Griffith began to use other cameramen – that it became impossible to distinguish between their respective innovations. What Griffith asked for, Bitzer provided. Between them they introduced the use of firelight and candlelight, backlighting, soft-focus, fades, travelling-shots, and so on. Others may have attempted to use some of these techniques earlier, but Bitzer and his director made them work. He retired at the end of the Twenties.

Films include: 1909 Edgar Allen Poe. '11 The Battle. '12 The Mender of Nets; The New York Hat. '13 Judith of Bethulia. '15 The Birth of a Nation. '16 Intolerance. '18 Hearts of the World. '19 True Heart Susie; Broken Blossoms. '20 Way Down East (co-photo. only). '21 Orphans of the Storm (co-photo. only).

BJÖRNSTRAND, Gunnar

(1909–1986). Actor. Born: Stockholm, Sweden

Gunnar Björnstrand was the son of an actor and studied at the Royal Dramatic Theatre Drama School (in the same class as Ingrid Bergman). After a variety of jobs, including several as a film extra, he took to the stage and continued to build his reputation there until in 1941 he met the film director Ingmar Bergman, became a member of his repertory company, and appeared in over a dozen Bergman films. A stately, mature actor with a weathered face, he was best in tragi-comic roles and gave powerful performances even when not the centre of attention. Björnstrand undoubtedly numbered among Sweden's greatest players.

Films include: 1953 Gycklarnas Afton (USA: The Naked Night; GB: Sawdust and Tinsel). '54 En Lektion i Kärlek (USA/GB: A Lesson in Love). '55 Kvinnodröm (USA: Dreams;

Above, from left to right: Jacqueline Bisset; Karen Black in Day of the Locust; *Honor Blackman in* Goldfinger; *Colin Blakeley in the* Private Life of Sherlock Holmes. *Left: Gunnar Björnstrand (centre) in* A Lesson in Love. *Below: Linda Blair in* Exorcist II. *Below right: Ronee Blakley*

GB: Journey Into Autumn). '56 Sjunde Himlen. '57 Det Sjunde Inseglet (USA/GB: The Seventh Seal); Smultronstallet (USA/GB: Wild Strawberries). '58 Ansiktet (USA: The Magician; GB: The Face). '61 Såsom i en Spegel (USA/GB: Through a Glass Darkly). '62 Nattvardsgästerna (USA/GB: Winter Light). '66 Persona. '67 Den Røde Kappe (DEN-SWED-ICE) (USA/GB: The Red Mantle). '78 Herbstsonate (USA/GB: Autumn Sonata).

BLACK, Karen

(b. 1943). Actress. Born: Karen Ziegler; Park Ridge, Illinois, USA

A hard-driving talent and a disturbingly cross-eyed gaze distinguish Karen Black among Hollywood's top actresses of the Seventies. She entered Northwestern University at 15 but she left at 17, deciding to concentrate on drama. Slogging through off-Broadway and a New York Shakespeare festival, she made it to Broadway and was nominated for the New York Drama Critics Award as Best

Actress. After her film role in Francis Ford Coppola's *You're a Big Boy Now*, she starred on Broadway and on television. *Easy Rider* and, especially, *Five Easy Pieces*, for which she won the New York Film Critics' Award as Best Supporting Actress, really launched her screen career. She has composed music for films, as well as the songs she sung herself in *Nashville*.

Films include: 1966 You're a Big Boy Now. '69 Easy Rider. '70 Five Easy Pieces. '71 Drive, He Said; Cisco Pike. '72 Portnoy's Complaint. '74 The Great Gatsby. '75 The Day of the Locust; Nashville. '81 The Grass Is Singing (GB-SWED-ZAMBIA). '82 Come Back to the Five and Dime, Jimmy Dean, Jimmy Dean.

BLACKMAN, Honor

(b. 1926). Actress. Born: London, England

Honor Blackman has had several successive careers in films, interspersed with television and stage work. She

was still an understudy in the West End theatre when she was picked by Rank for grooming as a starlet in the late Forties. Her blonde good looks doomed her at first to conventional roles. She married and went to Canada for several years, and on her return was in minor films for some time. Her leather-clad Cathy Gale in the early series of television's *The Avengers* gave her a fresh image and led to the role of Pussy Galore in *Goldfinger*. After a stint of playing glamorous 'liberated' women, and some Hollywood parts, she returned to the stage and television, with only occasional character roles in films.

Films include: 1947 Fame Is the Spur. '50 So Long at the Fair. '54 The Delavine Affair. '55 The Glass Cage. '57 Suspended Alibi. '58 A Night to Remember. '64 Goldfinger. '65 Life at the Top. '68 Shalako. '70 The Virgin and the Gypsy.

BLACKTON, James Stuart

(1875–1946). Producer/director. Born: Sheffield, Yorkshire, England

Blackton emigrated to America as a youth and became a journalist. With a friend, Albert E. Smith, he bought some projecting machines from Edison and soon began to make his own movies, at first in an improvised studio. In 1897, with Smith and William T. Rock, he founded Vitagraph, the first organization specifically for the production of photoplays. His list of achievements is remarkable: he pioneered war and news films (some faked), directed some of the earliest American story films, and developed single-frame animation. Vitagraph built America's first glass-enclosed studio in Brooklyn and was a leader in making films longer than one reel. Blackton made several films in England after World War I and took a keen interest in the growth of the British film industry.

Films include: 1898 Tearing Down the Spanish Flag. 1905 Raffles, the Amateur Cracksman. '06 The Automobile Thieves (+act); The Haunted Hotel; Humorous Phases of a Funny Face. '07 The Magic Fountain Pen. '09 Napoleon: The Man of Destiny. '11 A Tale of Two Cities. '14 My Official Wife (prod. only); The Christian (prod. only). '15 The Battle Cry of Peace. '19 The Vengeance of Durand (prod. only).

BLAIR, Linda

(b. 1959). Actress. Born: Westport, Connecticut, USA

A child model, Linda Blair landed the part of the demonically possessed little girl in *The Exorcist* after a nationwide search launched by writer-producer William Peter Blatty and director William Friedkin. She received an Academy Award nomination for Best Supporting Actress (only to be defeated by the even younger Tatum O'Neal). She became a regular actress in cinema and television films, and plunged into the Hollywood life-style, experimenting with sex and drugs. In 1979 she was put on probation for three years after being found guilty on drugs charges. Since then her personal life has quietened down, but she has been unable to equal the impact

she made in *The Exorcist* and *Exorcist II: The Heretic*. A more than capable actress, Linda Blair seems unable to break away from playing hysterical heroines in horror potboilers.

Films: 1970 The Way We Live Now. '71 The Sporting Club. '73 The Exorcist. '74 Airport 1975. '76 Victory at Entebbe. '77 Exorcist II: The Heretic. '78 Stranger in Our House (GB: Summer of Fear). '79 Roller Boogie. '81 Hell Night.

BLAKELY, Colin

(b. 1930). Actor. Born: Bangor, Co. Down, Northern Ireland

As a management trainee, Blakely played rugby and football for Northern Ireland. His interest in amateur dramatics led to his first professional role, replacing another actor, at the Group Theatre, Belfast. In 1959 he was at London's Royal Court and Arts Theatre Club, and then got his first film role in *Saturday Night and Sunday Morning*. In 1961 he joined the Royal Shakespeare Company for a season and then returned to the Royal Court. After a bigger screen role in *This Sporting Life*, he joined the National Theatre at the Old Vic. Since then he has been a versatile character actor in such roles as the hero's best friend in Albert Finney's *Charlie Bubbles* and as an amusing and red-blooded Dr Watson – a much stronger character than the melancholy Holmes (Robert Stephens) – in Billy Wilder's *The Private Life of Sherlock Holmes*. Blakely is married to the actress Margaret Whiting.

Films include: 1960 Saturday Night and Sunday Morning. '63 This Sporting Life. '66 A Man for All Seasons. '68 Charlie Bubbles. '70 The Private Life of Sherlock Holmes. '72 Young Winston. '73 The National Health. '74 Murder on the Orient Express; Galileo (GB-CAN). '76 The Pink Panther Strikes Again. '77 Equus. '80 Nijinsky. '81 Little Lord Fauntleroy.

BLAKLEY, Ronee

(b. 1946). Singer/actress/composer. Born: Stanley, Idaho, USA

Ronee Blakley is a tall, slim, attractive brunette whose film performances seem to be as yet a sideline to her main career as a singer and composer. After studies at Stanford University and the Juilliard School of Music, she spent a year acting in Boston. In 1969 she gave a recital at Carnegie Hall. Blakley wrote her first film score, *Welcome Home, Soldier Boys*, and issued her first album in 1972. She was asked by the director Robert Altman to appear in *Nashville* when she showed him some songs she had written for it, and her first screen role, as Barbara Jean, the neurotic country-and-western singer who is finally assassinated, was also her best to date. She played a non-singing part in *The Driver*, but the character again came to a violent end

Films: 1972 Welcome Home, Soldier Boys (mus. only). '75 Nashville (act;+some songs). '78 Renaldo and Clara (act;+own song); The Driver (act. only); The Private Files of J. Edgar Hoover (act. only); China 9, Liberty 37/Amore, Piombo e Furore (mus. only) (IT). '80 The Baltimore Bullet (act;+own song); Lightning Over Water (act;+own song) (USA-GER-SWED).

BLASETTI, Alessandro

(b. 1900). Director. Born: Rome, Italy

A law student turned film critic, Blasetti started an early film journal calling for a new Italian cinema. In 1928 he formed a film cooperative, Augustus, to produce his first film, *Sole*, which marked a decisive experimental step forward. He also helped to found Italy's influential film school, the Centro Sperimentale di Cinematografia. Blasetti was the leading Italian director during much of the Fascist period. Many of his films, such as *1860*, were historical reconstructions of Italy's past; but he also dealt with contemporary life, as in *Quattro Passi fra le Nuvole*, in a style prefiguring neo-realism. His postwar work was somewhat overblown, but the important influence of his early films is incontestable.

Films include: 1928 Sole. '30 Nerone. '33 1860. '35 Vecchia Guardia. '37 La Contessa di Parma. '39 Un'Avventura di Salvator Rosa. '41 La Corona di Ferro; La Cena delle Beffe. '42 Quattro Passi fra le Nuvole (GB: Four Steps in the Clouds). '49 Fabiola (IT-FR). '51 Bellissima (appearance as himself). '52 Altri Tempi! (GB: Infidelity). '54 Peccato Che Sia una Canaglia (GB: Too Bad She's Bad). '56 La Fortuna di Essere Donna (IT-FR) (GB: Lucky to Be a Woman). '59 Europa di Notti (IT-FR) (GB: European Nights).

BLIER, Bertrand

(b. 1939). Director. Born: Paris, France

The son of actor Bernard Blier, Bertrand Blier served as an assistant director to Georges Lautner, John Berry, Christian-Jaque, Denys de la Patellière and Jean Delannoy for two years before directing his own first film, *Hitler Connais Pas*, a portrait of French youth that featured non-professionals. Later films were invariably provocative: *Les Valseuses* was considered shocking in its depiction of the sexual escapades of two worthless young villains, and *Calmos* was denounced, not only by feminists, for its misogyny. *Préparez Vos Mouchoirs*, an amiable sex comedy, was an international hit and won the Oscar for Foreign-Language Film, though against remarkably weak opposition. The bizarre humour of Blier's films continues to meet with a mixed critical reception.

Films: 1963 Hitler Connais Pas. '66 La Grimace (short). '67 Si J'Etais un Espion (USA: If I Were a Spy/Breakdown). '71 Laisse Aller, C'Est une Valse (sc. only) (FR-IT) (USA: Take It Easy It's a Waltz; GB: Troubleshooters). '74 Les Valseuses (USA: Making It). '76 Calmos (USA: Femmes Fatales). '77 Préparez Vos Mouchoirs (FR-BELG) (USA/GB: Get Out Your Handerkerchiefs). '79 Buffet Froid (USA/GB: Cold Cuts). '81 Beau-Père.

BLONDELL, Joan

(1909–1979). Actress. Born: New York City, USA

A bubbly blonde with large eyes and a big smile, Joan Blondell was typically cast in the Thirties as a wisecracking chorus girl, the heroine's best friend,

or a cheerful floozie. She was born into a vaudeville family and appeared on stage at the age of three. After years of touring, she made her New York debut in the Ziegfeld Follies, where she was later joined by James Cagney. Both of them starred on Broadway in *Penny Arcade* and were brought out to Hollywood by Warners to make the film version, *Sinner's Holiday* (1930). She appeared in many Warner musicals and some early gangster films, but switched in the Forties to straight comedy and dramatic roles, and from the Fifties onwards concentrated on character parts. She was nominated for an Oscar as Best Supporting Actress in *The Blue Veil*. Her best late role was as a poker dealer in *The Cincinnati Kid*.

Films include: 1931 The Crowd Roars; The Public Enemy (GB: Enemies of the Public). '33 Footlight Parade; Gold Diggers of 1933. '36 Bullets or Ballots; Gold Diggers of 1937. '45 A Tree Grows in Brooklyn. '47 Nightmare Alley. '51 The Blue Veil. '57 Desk Set (GB: His Other Woman). '61 Angel Baby. '65 The Cincinnati Kid. '78 Grease.

BLOOM, Claire

(b. 1931). Actress. Born: Claire Blume; London, England

Claire Bloom's cool, dark-eyed beauty and abundant acting talent should have made her a major screen star instead of a top-flight character actress, which is what she developed into after a promising start. She was already a stage success, after a season at Stratford-on-Avon, with a lead role in Jean Anouilh's *Ring Round the Moon* in 1950 when she was recommended to Charles Chaplin for the part of the young ballet dancer in *Limelight*, her big break. More films followed, including several in America, where she settled for some years while married to actor Rod Steiger (1959–69); but she was too English for the Hollywood mould and her projects with Steiger were indifferent. Her later successes were in the London theatre (*A Streetcar Named Desire*) and on television (*Brideshead Revisited*).

Films include: 1948 The Blind Goddess. '52 Limelight (USA). '53 The Man Between. '56 Richard III; Alexander the Great (USA). '59 Look Back in Anger. '62 The Chapman Report (USA). '64 The Outrage (USA). '65 The Spy Who Came in From the Cold. '68 Charly (USA). '69 The Illustrated Man (USA); Three Into Two Won't Go. '71 A Severed Head. '73 A Doll's House. '81 Clash of the Titans.

BLORE, Eric

(1887–1959). Actor. Born: London, England

Eric Blore was an insurance agent before going on the stage. After working in England and Australia, he reached the USA in 1923, played on Broadway and then embarked on a successful screen career. Blore was pre-eminent among the great Hollywood butlers. He was completely unflappable, his look could kill across a crowded room and he wrapped his tongue with zest around every word he uttered. The Astaire-Rogers musicals were his happiest home, but the writer-director Preston Sturges also used his peculiar talents to good purpose in *The Lady Eve* and *Sullivan's Travels*.

Films include: 1926 The Great Gatsby. '30 Laughter. '34 The Gay Divorcee (GB: The Gay Divorce). '35 Top Hat. '36 Swing Time. '37 Shall We Dance? '41 The Lady Eve; Sullivan's Travels; The Shanghai Gesture. '45 Kitty.

BLUE, Monte

(1890–1963). Actor. Born: Indianapolis, Indiana, USA

Monte Blue was a very tall, tough, dour hero of the silent period. Orphaned as a child – he was part-Cherokee Indian – he worked at many jobs (cowboy, railway porter, gravedigger) before being hired by D. W. Griffith as a jack-of-all-trades. He became a stunt man and then eventually an actor, and after a couple of smaller roles he played Danton in

Orphans of the Storm. His career was briefly transformed by Ernst Lubitsch, who discovered the deprecating humour and slightly bewildered charm behind Blue's rather lugubrious countenance, and put these qualities to good use in *The Marriage Circle*, *Kiss Me Again* and *So This Is Paris*. Afterwards he played gradually smaller and smaller parts, usually for Warner Brothers. He is almost invisible as the alcoholic father of the Mary Astor character in the closing scenes of *Across the Pacific* (1942).

Films include: 1915 The Birth of a Nation. '16 Intolerance. '21 Orphans of the Storm. '22 Peacock Alley. '23 Main Street. '24 The Marriage Circle. '25 Kiss Me Again. '26 So This Is Paris; Across the Pacific. '28 White Shadows in the South Seas. '36 Mary of Scotland. '42 Across the Pacific.

BLYTH, Ann

(b. 1928). Actress. Born: Mount Kisco, New York, USA

A wide-mouthed, large-eyed Irish beauty with an operatic voice, Ann Blyth made her radio debut at five, and sang three seasons with the San Carlos Opera Company while attending the Children's Professional School in New York. Touring with a Broadway show, she was seen in Los Angeles and started in films. Initially she played adolescents and was nominated for an Oscar as Best Supporting Actress for her role as the wayward daughter in *Mildred Pierce*. In 1945 she broke her back and was bedridden for a year but she resumed her career, taking dramatic roles, notably the innocent girl condemned to death for murder in *Thunder on the Hill*. Her performance as Dorothy Caruso in *The Great Caruso* earned her a contract with MGM and a string of musical parts. Then, after a couple of biopics – *The Helen Morgan Story* in which she played the great torch singer, and *The Buster Keaton Story*, as the silent comic's true love – she suddenly retired to domestic life at the age of 29.

Films include: 1944 Chip Off the Old Block. '45 Mildred Pierce. '47 Brute Force. '48 Another Part of the Forest. '51 Thunder on the Hill (GB: Bonaventure); The Great Caruso. '52 The World in His Arms. '54 Rose Marie; The Student Prince. '55 Kismet. '57 The Helen Morgan Story (GB: Both Ends of the Candle); The Buster Keaton Story.

Above, from left to right: Joan Blondell; Claire Bloom in Three Into Two Won't Go; *Eric Blore (right) in* I Live My Life *(1936), with Frank Morgan; Ann Blyth in* The Student Prince, *with Edmund Purdom. Right: Betty Blythe as* The Queen of Sheba. *Below: Monte Blue*

BLYTHE, Betty

(1893–1972). Actress. Born: Elizabeth Blythe Slaughter; Los Angeles, California, USA

Having studied art in Paris and worked on the stage in both Europe and New York, Betty Blythe made her first films in 1918 for the Vitagraph studios. She reached the peak of her career in the early Twenties, notably in the title role in *The Queen of Sheba* – a lavish production in which her exotic costumes enhanced her vamp-like image. After this she never really fulfilled her early promise, and her career suffered, particularly when her director J. Gordon Edwards quarrelled with Fox Studios and left. She continued to play leading roles for small companies as well as doing some stage and film work in England. A durable lady, she pursued her career well into the Forties and cropped up again in 1964 in *My Fair Lady*.

Films include: 1921 The Queen of Sheba. '22 Fair Lady; How Women Love. '23 The Truth About Wives; Chu Chin Chow (GB). '24 The Folly of Vanity; The Spitfire. '25 She (GB). '27 Eager Lips; The Girl From Gay Paree. '28 Glorious Betsy.

BODEEN, DeWitt

(b. 1908). Screenwriter. Born: Fresno, California, USA

DeWitt Bodeen was a stage actor for two years before becoming a playwright with works like *Thing for Beauty* and *Escape to Autumn*. He then made the transition to film, and has received many Writer's Guild Nominations throughout his lengthy

career for such films as *Cat People* and *The Enchanted Cottage*. He also contributes regularly to film magazines and has written several books, including *The Films of Cecil B. DeMille*.

Films include: 1942 Cat People (sc + dial. dir). '43 The Seventh Victim (co-sc); Yellow Canary (co-sc) (GB). '44 The Curse of the Cat People (sc). '45 The Enchanted Cottage (co-sc). '48 I Remember Mama (sc). '49 Mrs Mike (co-sc). '57 The Girl in the Kremlin (co-sc. only). '60 12 to the Moon (sc). '62 Billy Budd (co-sc).

BOETTICHER, Budd

(b. 1916). Director. Born: Oscar Boetticher Jr; Chicago, Illinois, USA

At 20, having gone to university and military academy, Budd Boetticher made an unusual decision – he went to Mexico to become a professional matador. On his return to California, he was hired by Fox to be technical advisor on the bullfights in Rouben Mamoulian's *Blood and Sand* (1941).

He continued to work in films as an assistant director and, after serving as a marine in World War II, he began to direct his own films, achieving his first notable success with *The Bullfighter and the Lady*. This led to his teaming-up with producer Joe Brown, scriptwriter Burt Kennedy and actor Randolph Scott to make the series of psychological Westerns that became known as the Ranown Cycle. In 1960 he went back to Mexico to make *Arruza*, a documentary about bull-

fighters, and there he stayed for a further eight years until the film's completion. Back in Hollywood again he returned to work as a director for both cinema and television.

Films include: 1951 The Bullfighter and the Lady. '53 The Man From the Alamo. '56 Seven Men From Now. '57 The Tall T; Decision at Sundown. '58 Buchanan Rides Alone. '59 Ride Lonesome. '60 Comanche Station; The Rise and Fall of Legs Diamond. '68 Arruza (doc). '69 A Time for Dying.

BOGARDE, Dirk

(b. 1921). Actor. Born: Derek van den Bogaerde; London, England

Dirk Bogarde was brought up in an artistic environment – his father was art editor of *The Times*, his mother an actress. On leaving school he took up a scholarship at the Royal College of Art in London. Before the war he worked his way up in the world of theatre, and when he came out of the Army in 1946 – with the rank of major – he returned to the stage. He was spotted by a Rank producer in *Power Without Glory* and subsequently signed with them. During his early career the studio took over his destiny, seeing him as a matinée idol, and casting him as such in films like *A Tale of Two Cities* and *Doctor at Sea*. He finally broke away from typecasting by taking the part of the homosexual barrister, Melvyn Farr, in *The Victim*. More varied and challenging films followed in which Bogarde proved himself worthy of roles he had previously been denied – including Joseph Losey's *The Servant* and arthouse pictures such as Luchino Visconti's *The Damned* and *Death in Venice*. He now lives in France and still works in movies – but in those of his own choosing. He also writes novels.

Films include: 1947 Dancing With Crime. '50 The Blue Lamp. '54 The Sleeping Tiger. '55 Doctor at Sea. '58 A Tale of Two Cities. '61 The Victim. '63 The Servant. '64 King and Country. '66 Modesty Blaise. '67 Accident. '69 La Caduta degli Dei (IT-GER) (USA/GB: The Damned). '71 Morte a Venezia (IT) (USA/GB: Death in Venice). '74 Il Portiere di Notte (IT) (USA/GB: The Night Porter). '77 Providence (FR-SWITZ). '78 Despair (GER-FR).

BOGART, Humphrey

(1899–1957). Actor. Born: New York City, USA

As time goes by so Humphrey Bogart continues to be elevated in the most extraordinary way to the highest levels of cult status. Born into a New York society family, he was not a dedicated student and on expulsion from the prestigious Phillips Military Academy he joined the US Marines and served for several months. Once back in the civilian world he started to work as a road manager for the theatrical producer William A. Brady and then progressed to acting. It would have been hard for Broadway audiences who saw him as a handsome, fresh-faced young actor in the late Twenties to envisage the sardonic, tough, haggard and world-weary characters he would eventually come to portray. The first glimpse of this came in 1935 when he played Duke Mantee, wild-eyed and unshaven, in the stage version of *The Petrified Forest*, a role he recreated on film the following year. Most of the movies that followed were not classics, but some were – like *The Maltese Falcon, Casablanca, The Big Sleep* and *The African Queen*. To all of them Bogart brought a certain something that makes them unforgettable. His greatest screen persona is irresistible, morally and ethically centred in a crowd of duplicitous villains, but not without a few rough edges himself – someone who knew bad times, bad women, bad booze but hadn't been embittered by cynicism. The off-screen Bogart was pretty irresistible, too. His wisecracks, his drinking, his need for privacy, his love of the sea, his courage during his fatal illness, and most of all his fairytale romance with Lauren Bacall (his fourth wife) – these things show that his personality was not manufactured by the studios. That's why Bogie became a legend.

Films include: 1931 Bad Sister. '36 The Petrified Forest. '37 Marked Woman. '40 They Drive by Night (GB: The Road to Frisco); Brother Orchid. '41 High Sierra; The Maltese Falcon. '42 Casablanca. '44 To Have and Have Not. '45 Conflict; The Two Mrs Carrolls. '46 The Big Sleep. '48 Key Largo; The Treasure of the Sierra Madre. '49 Knock on Any Door. '50 In a Lonely Place. '51 The Enforcer; Sirocco; The African Queen. '53 Beat the Devil. '54 The Caine Mutiny; The Barefoot Contessa. '55 We're No Angels; The Desperate Hours.

BOGART, Paul

(b. 1919). Director. Born: New York City, USA

Paul Bogart began his career in the entertainment business as a puppeteer with the Berkely Marionettes. On entering television he worked on an early puppet series, *Fearless Fosdick*, while pursuing his ambition to direct television pilot shows and series. This he did very successfully, and throughout his time as a television director he has worked on many of America's most popular shows. He ventured into the world of the big screen in the late Sixties, directing fairly lightweight, often humorous films such as *Marlowe* and *The Skin Game*, but his movies never really fulfilled the promise shown by his television work. He won an Emmy Award for the series *The Defenders*, and continues to work in both television and video.

Films include: 1969 Marlowe. '70 Halls of Anger. '71 The Skin Game. '72 Cancel My Reservation. '73 Class of '44 (+prod). '75 Mr Ricco.

Far left: Dirk Bogarde in Death in Venice. Centre left: Mary Boland in Ruggles of Red Gap. Left John Boles. in She Married an Artist (1938). Below, far left: Humphrey Bogart in The Maltese Falcon. Below left: Ray Bolger in The Great Ziegfeld

BOGDANOVICH, Peter

(b. 1939). Director. Born: Kingston, New York, USA

Bogdanovich is the prime case of the film buff turned film director. Though he began acting, directing and producing on the off-Broadway stage, his heart was in film history and criticism – later on, he published book-length interviews with John Ford, Fritz Lang and Allan Dwan. After an apprenticeship with Roger Corman in the mid-Sixties, he started his directing career with a bang – *Targets* was Boris Karloff's best film for years and a chilling study of a quietly psychopathic young sniper, while Bogdanovich himself gave a respectable performance as a budding film-maker. Since then his films have paid elaborate tribute to his favourite directors and genres and to Hollywood itself. Three hits were followed by three flops, and latterly Bogdanovich has been struggling to regain the success that came rather early and easily.

Films include: 1966 The Wild Angels (ass. dir; + act). '67 The Trip (actor only); Targets. '71 The Last Picture Show. '72 What's Up, Doc? '73 Paper Moon. '74 Daisy Miller. '75 At Long Last Love. '76 Nickelodeon (USA-GB). '79 Saint Jack. '81 They All Laughed.

BOLAND, Mary

(1880–1965). Actress. Born: Philadelphia, Pennsylvania, USA

The daughter of William A. Boland, a travelling actor, she had a late stage debut at the age of 21 but soon became a leading lady, playing in *Strongheart* on Broadway. By 1915 she was in films, beginning with Thomas H. Ince's *The Edge of the Abyss*, and carving a niche for herself typically in roles as a social-climbing wife. She concentrated on the stage, but with the talkies was signed by Paramount and there developed her talent as a comic actress playing blonde, buxom, though henpecking or dotty spouses and mothers, notably opposite Charles Ruggles in *If I Had a Million*, *The Pursuit of Happiness* and *Ruggles of Red Gap*. From 1936 Mary Boland acted for all the major studios, maturing into a fine character player.

Films include: 1915 The Edge of the Abyss. '20 His Temporary Wife. '32 If I Had a Million; Trouble in Paradise. '34 The Pursuit of Happiness. '35 Ruggles of Red Gap. '39 The Women. '40 Pride and Prejudice. '44 In Our Time; Nothing But Trouble.

BOLES, John

(1900–1969). Actor/singer. Born: Greenville, Texas, USA

Dark and handsome, with a neat moustache and a song on his lips and in his heart, romantic and unfailingly attentive to such leading ladies as Bebe Daniels, Rosalind Russell, Irene Dunne and Shirley Temple – these are the qualities that made John Boles a screen heart-throb in the Thirties. Early musicals – especially *Rio Rita* and *The Desert Song* – and weepies such as *Back Street* were his forte, though interestingly he was to be found in *Frankenstein*, too. He was the son of a banker and studied medicine at the University of Texas before World War I took him to France as an interpreter. He remained there to train as a singer after the war and in the Twenties appeared in light operas and stage musicals in Hollywood. Gloria Swanson gave him his break in films – casting him opposite herself in the silent *The Love of Sunya*. But talkies – and musicals – enabled him to become a star. He returned to the stage in 1943, but then switched careers and finally ended up in the oil business.

Films include: 1925 The Love of Sunya. '29 Rio Rita; The Desert Song. '30 King of Jazz. '31 Frankenstein. '32 Back Street. '34 Music in the Air. '35 The Littlest Rebel. '36 Craig's Wife. '37 Stella Dallas. '43 Thousands Cheer.

BOLESLAVSKY, Richard

(1889–1937). Director. Born: Ryszard Srzednicki Boleslawsky; Warsaw, Poland

A stage actor from the age of 16, Boleslavsky became director of the second studio of the Moscow Art Theatre, performing under Stanislavsky. He acted in Russian films from 1914, directing from 1915. He fought in the White Polish Army against the Bolsheviks in the Civil War, and was in charge of film coverage of the Polish campaigns. After acting in Germany, he went to New York and became director of the Laboratory Theatre. Then he went to Hollywood as a dialogue director, becoming a feature director at several studios, notably MGM, where he made large-scale elaborate melodramas. He died suddenly while filming *The Last of Mrs Cheyney*, which was completed by George Fitzmaurice.

Films include: 1918 Khleb (co-dir; + act) (USSR). '22 Die Gezeichneten (actor only) (GER). '31 Woman Pursued. '32 Rasputin and the Empress. '34 The Painted Veil. '35 Metropolitan; Les Misérables. '36 Theodora Goes Wild; The Garden of Allah. '37 The Last of Mrs Cheyney (co-dir).

BOLGER, Ray

(1904–1987). Actor/dancer. Born: Boston, Massachusetts, USA

Ray Bolger is best remembered as the Scarecrow in *The Wizard of Oz*. Though he made plenty of other screen appearances, his considerable musical and comic gifts were largely wasted in very mundane dancing roles with the occasional touch of comedy. He began in vaudeville as half of a double act that failed to take Broadway by storm and broke up. Bolger then produced some two-reelers with himself as star. He went back into the theatre and eventually starred in *Life Begins at 8:40*. This led to his first feature, *The Great Ziegfeld* and an MGM contract. During World War II he made world-wide appearances for the USO, entertaining the troops. Afterwards he continued in films and theatre as well as doing nightclub and television shows.

Films include: 1936 The Great Ziegfeld. '37 Rosalie. '39 The Wizard of Oz. '41 Sunny; Four Jacks and a Jill. '43 Stage Door Canteen. '46 The Harvey Girls. '49 Make Mine Laughs. '52 April in Paris; Where's Charley? (GB).

BOLOGNINI, Mauro

(b. 1922). Director. Born: Pistoia, Italy

Bolognini studied architecture at the University of Florence and then trained in set design and directing at the Italian film school, Centro Sperimentale di Cinematografia. Between 1948 and 1952 he served his apprenticeship as assistant director under the neo-realist film-maker Luigi Zampa and then went to France where he worked as assistant to Yves Allégret and Jean Delannoy. His most effective films are from scripts by Pier-Paolo Pasolini (such as *La Notte Brava*) and from literary sources, such as the writing of Alberto Moravia, to which he adds his special skill at recreating period atmosphere.

Films include: 1953 Ci Troviamo in Galeria. '56 Gli Innamorata (IT-FR). '58 Giovani Mariti (IT-FR) (USA/GB: Young Husbands). '59 La Notte Brava. '60 Il Bell'Antonio (IT-FR); La Giornata Balorda (IT-FR) (GB: A Day of Sin). '61 La Viaccia (IT-FR) (GB: The Love Makers). '62 Senilita (IT-FR); Agostino. '64 La Corruzione (IT-FR) (USA: Corruption).

BOLT, Robert

(b. 1924). Writer/director. Born: Robert Oxon Bolt; Manchester, England

Writer of some of the biggest and most successful film and stage hits of the Sixties, Bolt tended to favour large-scale figures, real (Thomas More, Lawrence of Arabia, Lord Byron) or otherwise (Doctor Zhivago), whom he examined through the perspective of history. Between grammar school and university in Manchester, he worked as an office boy, but then came the war and service in the RAF. Afterwards he taught at Millfield public school and it was here that he began to write plays for radio and television. His first real success was in 1957 with *Flowering Cherry*. *A Man for All Seasons* was written shortly afterwards and was a great triumph in the West End and on Broadway. The rest, as they say, is history. In 1979 he suffered a severe stroke and incurred some loss of speech and paralysis as a result. But he recovered sufficiently to resume work in the early Eighties. Bolt was married for a time to the actress Sarah Miles, who starred in his *Ryan's Daughter* and *Lady Caroline Lamb*.

Films: 1962 Lawrence of Arabia. '65 Doctor Zhivago (USA). '66 A Man For All Seasons. '70 Ryan's Daughter. '72 Lady Caroline Lamb (+ dir) (GB-IT).

BONANOVA, Fortunio

(1895–1969). Actor/singer. Born: Luis Moll; Palma de Mallorca, Spain

There are two roles of Bonanova's that remain in the memory, both drawing on his Mediterranean temperament and opera-training. The first is in *Citizen Kane* where he plays the excitable singing teacher whose patience is stretched to breaking point by Kane's talentless wife. She cannot sing nor will she ever be able to. The hapless teacher is expected to do the impossible and all he can do is tear out his hair. The second quintessential role is in *Kiss Me Deadly* where the Bonanova character watches in frozen horror as his priceless collection of opera records is broken by a sadistic seeker after information. In real life Bonanova was an opera singer, a protegé of the great Russian bass, Chaliapin. He made his opera debut in Paris in 1922 and the following year toured Europe and South America and ran his own rep company. When he finally went to Hollywood it was as an actor frequently called upon to play Italians or Spaniards in a very large number of films.

Films include: 1940 Citizen Kane. '41 Blood and Sand. '43 Five Graves to Cairo; For Whom the Bell Tolls. '44 Going My Way; Double Indemnity. '49 Whirlpool '53 The Moon Is Blue. '55 New York Confidential; Kiss Me Deadly. '57 An Affair to Remember.

BOND, Ward

(1903–1960). Actor. Born: Denver, Colorado, USA

Ward Bond appeared in so many films that he was almost as recognizable as the MGM lion. And yet he never really became a genuine leading actor until he made his television series, *Wagon Train*, in the late Fifties. A long-time favourite of John Ford, he appeared in many of his films, notably as a blustering crook in *Young Mr Lincoln* and the parson-cum-Texas Ranger in *The Searchers*. Other directors also noted his special hard-on-the-outside, soft-on-the-inside qualities. John Huston, for example, cast him as the gruff police detective who seems to be the only decent person around in *The Maltese Falcon*. In *The Wings of Eagles*, Ford has Bond play film-director John Dodge (*viz* Ford). It seemed fitting somehow that it was Bond to whom Ford entrusted his personal hallmarks of hat, pipe and eye-patch.

Films include: 1929 Salute. '34 It Happenened One Night. '39 Young Mr Lincoln. '41 The Maltese Falcon. '46 It's a Wonderful Life; My Darling Clementine. '50 Wagonmaster. '52 The Quiet Man. '54 Johnny Guitar. '56 The Searchers. '57 The Wings of Eagles. '59 Rio Bravo.

BONDARCHUK, Sergei

(b. 1920). Actor/director. Born: Belozersk, Ukraine, USSR

Bondarchuk studied drama in Rostov and was a front-line entertainer with the Red Army during World War II. He was taught by the director Sergei

Gerasimov at the Moscow film school, and cast by him as a resistance fighter in *The Young Guard*. He went on to play the revolutionary poet *Taras Shevchenko* and Shakespeare's hero *Othello* and, as a result, became a screen idol. He moved to directing as well as acting in *Destiny of a Man* as a Russian POW, for which he won a Lenin Prize in 1960. He was entrusted with the mammoth epic *War and Peace* which won an Oscar, and then with the East-West co-production *Waterloo*, starring Rod Steiger as Napoleon. These pretentious and inflated works won him a seat in the Supreme Soviet. His later films have made little international impact.

Films include: 1948 Molodaya Guardya (actor only) (USA/GB: The Young Guard). '51 Taras Shevchenko (actor only). '56 Othello (actor only). '55 Poprigunya (actor only) (USA/GB: The Grasshopper). '59 Sudba Cheloveka (dir; +act) (USA/GB: Destiny of a Man). '60 Era Notte a Roma (actor only) (IT-FR) (USA: It Was Night in Rome); Seryozha (actor only) (GB: The Splendid Days). '65–'67 Voina i Mir (four parts) (dir; +act) (USA/GB: War and Peace). '70 Waterloo (dir; +co-sc. only) (IT-USSR). '75 Oni Srajalis za Rodinou (dir; +act) (USA: They Fought for the Motherland). '76 Urhovi Zelengore (actor only) (YUG) (USA: The Peaks of Zelengore). '78 Step (dir; +sc. only) (USA: The Steppe).

BONDI, Beulah

(1892–1981). Actress. Born: Beulah Bondy; Chicago, Illinois, USA

In 1901 Beulah Bondi made her stage debut in *Little Lord Fauntleroy* – she was nine. At 21, having completed a university education, she began her acting career proper by studying at the Chicago Little Theatre. Six years later she had progressed to mid-western stock theatre companies and she finally acted on Broadway in 1925 in *One of the Family*. She went to Hollywood in 1931 to recreate a role she had already made famous on stage – that of the gossipy, hard-bitten woman in *Street Scene*. This type of character was obviously her forte, or so the studios thought, and for the rest of her acting life she was relied upon to play mothers and elderly women – as she did in her only major film, *Make Way For Tomorrow*. She also did some television work and received an Emmy for her guest appearance in *The Waltons*.

Films include: 1931 Street Scene; Arrowsmith. '32 Rain. '36 The Trail of the Lonesome Pine; The Gorgeous Hussy. '37 Make Way For Tomorrow. '38 Of Human Hearts. '39 Mr Smith Goes to Washington. '40 Our Town. '43 Watch on the Rhine. '46 It's a Wonderful Life. '48 The Snake Pit. '54 Track of the Cat.

BOONE, Pat

(b. 1934). Singer/actor. Born: Charles Eugene Boone; Jacksonville, Florida, USA

A descendant of the American frontiersman Daniel Boone, Pat Boone helped to widen the horizons of the American music scene by becoming the first teen-idol that moms also

approved of, thus providing the acceptable face of rock and roll. He made his singing debut at the age of 10 in Nashville and by the time he was 17 had his own radio show. The following year he won a talent contest and appeared on television in Ted Mack's *Amateur Hour*. He soon gained a recording contract, and had his own television programme by the mid-Fifties. But this clean-cut, healthy-living star still found time to study and graduated in 1958 – the same year that he signed a $1 million film contract with 20th Century-Fox. The resulting films, like his songs and his image, were tame, respectable and suitable for all the family. He now restricts himself to gospel singing with his wife and four daughters.

Films: 1957 Bernardine; April Love. '58 Mardi Gras. '59 Journey to the Center of the Earth. '61 All Hands on Deck. '62 State Fair; The Main Attraction. '63 The Yellow Canary. '64 Never Put It in Writing (GB); The Horror of It All (GB); Goodbye Charlie. '65 The Greatest Story Ever Told. '67 The Perils of Pauline. '70 The Cross and the Switchblade.

BOONE, Richard

(1917–1981). Actor. Born: Los Angeles, California, USA

Boone studied at Stanford University and learned drama at the Neighborhood Playhouse school, served in the navy during World War II and then joined the Actors' Studio in New York. He was in *Medea* and other plays on Broadway and, though unsuccessfully tested for a part in the film of *A Streetcar Named Desire* (1951), was cast in the war film *Halls of Montezuma*. Tall, craggy (he had done his share of prizefighting), no-nonsense heroes – or vicious killers – were Boone's specialty, and he seldom escaped action films. Typical roles included the bandit Cicero Grimes in *Hombre* and Pontius Pilate in *The Robe*, but he is, perhaps, best remembered as Paladin, the cultured, hired-gun hero of the television Western series *Have Gun Will Travel*. On TV he also hosted, naturally, *The*

Richard Boone Show. In his mid-sixties he eased himself out of films, spending most of his time painting in Florida.

Films include: 1950 Halls of Montezuma. '51 The Desert Fox (GB: Rommel – Desert Fox). '53 The Robe. '55 Man Without a Star. '57 The Tall T. '60 The Alamo. '67 Hombre. '68 The Night of the Following Day. '69 The Arrangement. '70 The Kremlin Letter. '72 The War Lord. '76 The Shootist.

BOORMAN, John

(b. 1933). Director. Born: London, England

At 17 Boorman was already writing film criticism for a girls' magazine and broadcasting about films. He joined Independent Television News as a film editor and then worked in documentaries for Southern Television. He went to the BBC and was involved in documentary drama, eventually taking over the documentary film unit at Bristol where he made *The Newcomers* (1964), a six-part series about a couple in Bristol. His first feature film, *Catch Us If You Can*, evolved out of documentary drama. Then he had the chance to direct a gangster film in

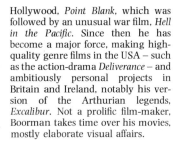

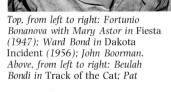

Hollywood, *Point Blank*, which was followed by an unusual war film, *Hell in the Pacific*. Since then he has become a major force, making high-quality genre films in the USA – such as the action-drama *Deliverance* – and ambitiously personal projects in Britain and Ireland, notably his version of the Arthurian legends, *Excalibur*. Not a prolific film-maker, Boorman takes time over his movies, mostly elaborate visual affairs.

Films: 1965 Catch Us If You Can (USA: Having a Wild Weekend). '67 Point Blank (USA). '68 Hell in the Pacific (USA). '70 Leo the Last. '72 Deliverance (USA). '74 Zardoz. '77 Exorcist II: The Heretic (USA). '81 Excalibur (EIRE-USA).

BOOTH, James

(b. 1930). Actor. Born: David Greeves-Booth; Croydon, Surrey, England

Tall and dark, Booth has the rude grin of a cockney spiv, but disenchantment is never far away. So it is not surprising to find him as the most bitter of the British soldiers trapped in the Natal in *Zulu*, or as the husband who walks out on his wife and son in *That'll Be the Day*. After army service he went into business in Southend and joined an amateur theatre there. A scholarship with RADA was followed by the Old Vic and a star part in *Fings Ain't Wot They Used t'Be* in the West End before he became a member of the Royal Shakespeare Company. His first film was *Jazzboat* (1960), and, under the direction of Joan Littlewood, he was outstanding as the cockney seaman in both the stage and screen versions of *Sparrows Can't Sing*. The collapse of his property company caused bankruptcy, and since 1976 Booth has lived in Los Angeles where he rewrites film scripts and makes occasional appearances.

Films include: 1960 The Trials of Oscar Wilde (USA: The Man With the Green Carnation). '63 Sparrows Can't Sing; Zulu. '64 French Dressing. '67 Robbery. '68 The Bliss of Mrs Blossom. '70 The Man Who Had Power Over Women. '73 That'll Be the Day. '75 Brannigan. '76 I'm Not Feeling Myself Tonight! '77 Airport '77 (USA). '80 The Jazz Singer (USA).

BORGNINE, Ernest

(b. 1917). Actor. Born: Ermès B. Borgnino; Hamden, Connecticut, USA

Of Italian origin, Borgnine spent six years in the navy, including four years' war service. In 1945 he enrolled at the Randall School of Dramatic Art in Hartford, Connecticut. After experience in a summer stock company, he made his Broadway debut in *Harvey* in 1950, and in the same year had a couple of small film parts. His first major role was as the sadistic Sergeant 'Fatso' Judson in *From Here to Eternity*. *Marty* gave him an unusually sympathetic role, sensitively played, as the lonely butcher and brought him an Academy Award as Best Actor. He then had access to a better range of parts; but his heavy stature and broad, squat face with large, protruding eyes ensured that he often gravitated back to villainous roles. On television he played Commander McHale in the comedy series *McHale's Navy*, for which he won an Emmy. Borgnine remains one of Hollywood's most polished rough diamonds.

Films include: 1951 Whistle at Eaton Falls (GB: Richer Than the Earth). '53 From Here to Eternity. '54 Johnny Guitar; Vera Cruz. '55 Marty; Bad Day at Black Rock. '67 The Dirty Dozen. '68 The Legend of Lylah Clare; Ice Station Zebra. '69 The Wild Bunch. '71 Willard. '73 The Emperor of the North Pole (GB: Emperor of the North). '75 Hustle. '81 Escape From New York.

BOROWCZYK, Walerian

(b. 1923). Director/animator. Born: Kwilcz, Poland

Borowczyk studied painting at the Academy of Fine Arts in Cracow and also made some experimental films. He worked afterwards as a painter and lithographer, designing movie posters. In the late Fifties he made animated and live-action shorts, at first in collaboration with the animator Jan Lenica. In 1958 Borowczyk moved to Paris and spent ten years making animated shorts which won many international awards. He then put together an animated feature – essentially a series of loosely connected episodes – before moving on to live-action features, some starring his wife Ligia Branice. His early features were harsh but delicately detailed allegorical period pieces; since then he has drifted towards the area of classy, subversive pornography.

Films include: 1958 Dom (short) (co-dir) (POL) (GB: The House). '62 Le Concert de Monsieur et Madame Kabal (short) (GB: The Concert of Monsieur and Madame Kabal). '64 Les Jeux des Anges (short). '67 Diptyque (short) (GB: Diptych); Le Théâtre de Monsieur et Madame Kabal (USA: Mr and Mrs Kabal's Theatre; GB: The Theatre of Mr and Mrs Kabal). '68 Goto, l'Ile d'Amour (USA/GB: Goto, Island of Love). '69 Le Phonographe (short). '71 Blanche. '74 Contes Immoraux (USA/GB: Immoral Tales). '75 'L'Armoire', sketch in Collections Privées (FR-JAP) (USA/GB: Private Collections); Dzieje Grzechu (POL) (USA: Story of a Sin; GB: The Story of Sin); La Bête (USA/GB: The Beast). '81 Dr Jekyll et les Femmes.

Top, from left to right: Fortunio Bonanova with Mary Astor in Fiesta *(1947); Ward Bond in* Dakota Incident *(1956); John Boorman. Above, from left to right: Beulah Bondi in* Track of the Cat; *Pat*

Boone in Journey to the Center of the Earth; *James Booth in* Sparrows Can't Sing. *Below: Richard Boone in* The Shootist. *Below right: Ernest Borgnine in* McHale's Navy *TV series*

BORZAGE, Frank

(1893–1962). Director/actor. Born: Salt Lake City, Utah, USA

As a youth Borzage worked with a touring company and graduated to acting. *When Lee Surrenders* (1912) was the first of countless Western and comedy shorts he would act in, including those he directed himself from 1916. By the mid-Twenties he was a major Hollywood director and would remain so for 25 years. Borzage is now one of those film-makers whose career is undergoing critical reassessment. The films of his greatest period – the late Twenties and early Thirties – are filled with his unique blend of romanticism and spirituality, and feature pairs of lovers living out their charmed lives against backgrounds like the Great War (*Seventh Heaven*), the Depression (*Man's Castle*) and the rise of fascism in Europe (*Little Man, What Now?*). He was a supreme technician, especially adept at rendering mysticism with adventurous camerawork and lighting. At the climax of *Seventh Heaven* the living and the dead are on one plane: Borzage's world can contain both. In 1962 he won the D. W. Griffith Award for 'outstanding contributions in the field of film direction'; he had earlier won Best Director Academy Awards for *Seventh Heaven* and *Bad Girl*.

Films as director include: 1920 Humoresque. **'24** Secrets. **'27** Seventh Heaven. **'28** Street Angel; The River. **'31** Bad Girl. **'32** A Farewell to Arms; Man's Castle. **'33** Secrets. **'34** No Greater Glory; Little Man, What Now? **'36** Desire. **'37** Mannequin. **'38** Three Comrades. **'40** The Mortal Storm. **'48** Moonrise. **'59** The Big Fisherman.

BOST, Pierre

(1901–1975). Screenwriter. Born: Lasalle, France

Bost entered the civil service in the Twenties and in his spare time wrote novels; his first stage play was produced in 1923. He had a solo screenplay credit on *L'Héritier de Mondésir* (1939), but in 1943 joined up with Jean Aurenche to form one of the most successful writing partnerships in French film history. The pair became famous for their literary adaptations, especially those they wrote for

Above: Michael Bouquet. Below: Timothy Bottoms in Rollercoaster. *Right: Clara Bow. Far right: David Bowie in* The Man Who Fell to Earth. *Bottom, far right: Stephen Boyd in* The Fall of the Roman Empire

the director Claude Autant-Lara, including *Douce*, a cruel tale about two fortune-seekers in love with each other, and the highly acclaimed *Le Diable au Corps*, the story of an ill-fated love affair. For René Clément they wrote the melodrama *Au Delà des Grilles*, and *Jeux Interdits* which expressed their nonconformist views in its depiction of two children who build a war-time cemetery for animals. Though initially reviled by the *nouvelle vague*, Aurenche and Bost continued to write screenplays, and set the seal on their joint career with the 1973 thriller *L'Horloger de Saint-Paul*. Bost was the editor of several French magazines and also wrote for television.

Films include: 1939 L'Héritier de Mondésir. **'43** Douce (co-sc). **'46** La Symphonie Pastorale (co-sc). **'47** Le Diable au Corps (co-sc) (USA: Devil in the Flesh). **'49** Au Delà des Grilles (co-sc) (FR-IT) (GB: Beyond the Gates). **'50** Dieu à Besoin des Hommes (co-sc) (USA/GB: Isle of Sinners). **'51** L'Auberge Rouge (co-sc) (USA/GB: The Red Inn). **'52** Jeux Interdits (co-sc) (USA: Forbidden Games; GB: Secret Games). **'54** Le Blé en Herbe (co-sc) (GB: Ripening Seed); Le Rouge et le Noir (co-sc) (FR-IT) (GB: Scarlet and Black). **'56** Gervaise (co-sc); La Traversée de Paris (co-sc) (FR-IT) (GB: Pig Across Paris). **'73** L'Horloger de Saint-Paul (co-sc) (GB: Watchmaker of Saint-Paul).

BOTTOMS, Timothy

(b. 1949). Actor. Born: Santa Barbara, California, USA

Fair-haired, kind-featured and engagingly awkward Timothy Bottoms is best-known for his role as Sonny, a teenager in the early Fifties who leaves his adolescence behind after an affair with a married woman and the death of his friend Sam in *The Last Picture Show*. He became a member of the Youth Theater Productions while still at school and toured Europe with the Santa Barbara Madrigal Society in 1967. Universal spotted him while he was acting in *Romeo and Juliet* and he made his first movie appearance as a young soldier in *Johnny Got His Gun*. He has divided his subsequent career between films and television, but may have lost his opportunity to become a major star. One of his three younger actor brothers Sam played the mute Billy in *The Last Picture Show* and was the gunner Lance going upriver to Cambodia in *Apocalypse Now* (1979).

Films include: 1971 Johnny Got His Gun; The Last Picture Show. **'73** Love and Pain and the Whole Damn Thing (GB); The Paper Chase. **'74** The White Dawn; The Crazy World of Julius Vrooder. **'76** Operation Daybreak (USA-CZECH); A Small Town in Texas. **'77** Rollercoaster. **'79** Hurricane.

BOULTING, John and Roy

John (1913–1985); Roy (b.1913). Directors/producers. Born: Bray, Buckinghamshire, England

Generally alternating the tasks of directing and producing, identical twins John and Roy Boulting worked closely together in the British film industry from 1937, when they formed Charter Films. Before that John worked in film distribution and drove an ambulance in the Spanish Civil War; Roy went to Canada and returned as a crewman of a cattle ship before becoming a film salesman and then an assistant director. As feature-film makers they were at their creative peak in the Forties with the lighthouse drama *Thunder Rock* and the gangster thriller *Brighton Rock*. However seedy, the latter exudes a proud 'Britishness' that is also central to the Boultings' Fifties comedy satires on such institutions as the army (*Private's Progress*) and shop-floor politics (*I'm All Right Jack*). Accordingly, the brothers consistently used actors like Peter Sellers, Ian Carmichael and Hayley Mills, to whom Roy was briefly married during the Seventies.

Films include: 1940 Pastor Hall (dir. Roy; prod. John). **'42** Thunder Rock (dir. Roy; prod. John). **'43** Desert Victory (doc) (dir.

Roy). '45 Burma Victory (doc) (dir. Roy); Journey Together (dir. John). '47 Brighton Rock (dir. John; prod. Roy); Fame Is the Spur (dir. Roy; prod. John). '50 Seven Days to Noon (dir. John; prod. Roy). '56 Private's Progress (dir. John; prod. Roy). '57 Lucky Jim (dir. John; prod. Roy). '59 I'm All Right Jack (dir. John; prod. Roy). '63 Heavens Above (dir. John; prod. John). '67 The Family Way (dir. Roy; prod. John). '68 Twisted Nerve (dir. Roy; exec. prod. John). '70 There's a Girl in My Soup (dir. Roy; prod. John). '74 Soft Beds – Hard Battles (dir. Roy; prod. John).

BOUQUET, Michel

(b. 1926). Actor. Born: Paris, France

Michel Bouquet is not exactly handsome but he has the sort of world-weary, middle-aged charm that a woman seeking an extra-marital affair might fall for . . . or a wife stray from. So he was ideal as the married man who murders his mistress and as the cuckold who kills his wife's lover in two Claude Chabrol films, *Juste Avant la Nuit* and *La Femme Infidèle* respectively. An outstanding actor in all sorts of roles, he learned his craft as a student of Maurice Escande and Mme Dussane and at the Paris Conservatoire. On stage from 1943, he broke into films with *Monsieur Vincent* four years later but had little screen success until the Sixties when he worked with Chabrol, Nelly Kaplan,

and François Truffaut. Bouquet's finest performances have been in the theatre (especially in the plays of Jean Anouilh with whom he has worked closely). He has also acted in television.

Films include: 1947 Monsieur Vincent. '49 Pattes Blanches (GB: White Legs). '52 Trois Femmes (USA/GB: Three Women). '64 Les Amitiés Particulières (USA: This Special Friendship). '67 Lamiel (FR-IT); La Route de Corinthe (FR-IT-GREECE) (USA/GB: The Road to Corinth). '68 La Mariée Etait en Noir (FR-IT) (GB: The Bride Wore Black); La Femme Infidèle (FR-IT). '69 La Sirène du Mississippi (FR-IT) (USA/GB: Mississippi Mermaid). '70 Le Dernier Saut (USA: The Last Leap); La Rupture (FR-IT-BELG) (USA: The Breakup). '71 Juste Avant la Nuit (FR-GB) (GB: Just Before Nightfall).

BOW, Clara

(1907–1965). Actress. Born: New York City, USA

At the time she was the sexiest woman in films, and the 'It' girl's teasing appeal – gaily amoral, exuberant to the point of being uncontrollable, pouting and winking under the mop of red hair – has not dated. The time in question was the Jazz Age and certainly few stars have been so clearly of their period: 'Clara Bow *was* the Twenties' said another sexy actress, Louise Brooks. At 16 Clara won a beauty contest and then came to

Hollywood where, after a few cheap pictures, Paramount snapped her up for her finest films. She was inevitably cast as a flapper (*Dancing Mothers, It!, Mantrap*) but was equally convincing – and as vivaciously pretty – as a good girl, especially as the ambulance driver in the war film *Wings*. But the ravages of a dreadful childhood, a string of affairs and scandals (leading to a lawsuit against her slanderous secretary) wrecked her career and her health in the early Thirties. She suffered chronic breakdowns and was in and out of sanatoriums for the rest of her life. The sheer joy she radiated in all her films, good and bad alike, remains. In 1932 Clara was married to Rex Bell, a cowboy actor and later Lieutenant Governor of Nevada. She appeared in the *Mrs Hush* television series in 1947.

Films include: 1922 Beyond the Rainbow. '23 The Daring Years. '24 Black Oxen. '25 Kiss Me Again; The Plastic Age. '26 Dancing Mothers; Mantrap; Kid Boots. '27 It!; Children of Divorce; Rough House Rosie; Wings. '28 The Fleet's In. '29 The Wild Party. '32 Call Her Savage.

BOWIE, David

(b. 1947). Rock performer/actor. Born: David Jones; Brixton, London, England

Arguably the most creative and influential rock artist since the Beatles, Bowie was always likely to move into films. He first appeared on screen in a short, *The Image*, and in a bit part in *The Virgin Soldiers* in 1969 – also the year of his most famous hit single, 'Space Oddity'. In the early Seventies the visionary, futuristic quality of his songs and stage shows – accommodating his (variable) pale-skinned, delicate, androgynous image – made him a superstar, and he kept that aura intact for his first major film role as the alien in Nicolas Roeg's *The Man Who Fell to Earth*. *Just a Gigolo*, co-starring Marlene Dietrich, did him little credit at all, but Bowie is now in a position to command top parts in top films. He has been acclaimed for his performances as *The Elephant Man* on Broadway and as *Baal* on television, and continues to make vital and challenging records.

Films: 1969 The Image (short); The Virgin Soldiers. '76 The Man Who Fell to Earth. '78 Schöner Gigolo – Armer Gigolo (GER) (USA/GB: Just a Gigolo). '81 Christiane F. Wir Kinder vom Bahnhof Zoo (GER) (USA: We Children from Bahnhof Zoo; GB: Christiane F.). '82 The Hunger.

BOX, Muriel and Sydney

Box, Muriel (b. 1905). Screenwriter/director. Born: Muriel Baker; Tolworth, Surrey, England

Box, Sydney (1907–1983). Screenwriter/producer. Born: Beckenham, Kent, England

Muriel started out as a typist in the scenario department of British Instructional Films. In 1933 she married Sydney Box, a former journalist working in the theatre, and together they produced nearly a hundred one-act

plays. In 1940 Sydney became a director of Verity Films, producing over 120 shorts in two years, mostly for the war effort. Among his first features was the romantic melodrama *The Seventh Veil*, a colossal hit that won the husband-and-wife team the 1946 Oscar for Best Screenplay. Sydney continued his success at Rank and then Pinewood where he was put in charge of production in 1949. He retired from films in 1959 and became a television executive, but with Muriel founded London Independent Producers. She had continued to write, and in the Fifties began to direct comedies and dramas (often centred around female characters), such as *The Beachcomber, The Truth About Women* and *Rattle of a Simple Man*. The Boxes divorced in 1969 and Muriel subsequently married Lord Gardiner. Betty Box (b. 1920) assisted her brother during the Forties and became a top producer herself, notably at the Islington Studios.

Films include: 1945 The Seventh Veil (prod. Sydney; sc. Muriel, Sydney). '48 The Blind Goddess (sc. Muriel, Sydney). '52 The Happy Family (dir. Muriel; prod. Sydney; sc. Muriel, Sydney) (USA: Mr Lord Says No). '53 Street Corner (dir. Muriel; sc. Muriel, Sydney) (USA: Both Sides of the Law). '54 The Beachcomber (dir. Muriel; sc. Sydney; To Dorothy, a Son (dir. Muriel). '55 The Prisoner (exec. prod. Sydney). '56 Eye Witness (dir. Muriel; prod. Sydney). '57 The Passionate Stranger (dir. Muriel; prod. Sydney; sc. Muriel, Sydney) (USA: A Novel Affair). '58 The Truth About Women (dir. Muriel; prod. Sydney; sc. Muriel, Sydney). '64 Rattle of a Simple Man (dir. Muriel; prod. co. Sydney Box Production). '67 Accident (prod. co. London Independent Producers).

BOYD, Stephen

(1928–1977). Actor. Born: William Miller; Belfast, Northern Ireland

Boyd was a swaggering but intelligent he-man – and America in the Fifties asked for little more. He started as a child actor and radio performer with the Ulster Theatre Group and made his professional stage debut at 16. After trying his luck in Canada and the USA he returned to Britain for television work and eventually a screen debut in *An Alligator Named Daisy* (1955), followed by *A Hill in Korea* and *Island in the Sun*. In Hollywood he became a star as the villain Messala in *Ben-Hur*, but the role typecast him for the better part of his career as a good-looking beefcake. Perhaps his most telling (and bravura) performance was as the actor whose rapid rise is followed by an equally rapid decline in *The Oscar*. Though working increasingly in television, Boyd formed his own film production company in 1973. He died, aged 48, of a heart attack while playing golf.

Films include: 1956 A Hill in Korea (GB). '57 Island in the Sun (USA). '58 The Bravados (USA). '59 Ben-Hur (USA). '62 The Inspector (GB) (USA: Lisa). '64 The Fall of the Roman Empire (USA). '66 The Oscar (USA); La Bibbia (IT) (USA/GB: The Bible . . . In the Beginning). '68 Shalako (GB). '71 Hannie Caulder (GB). '77 The Squeeze (GB).

BOYD, William

(1898–1972). Actor. Born: Cambridge, Ohio, USA

The son of a labourer, Boyd drifted West following the early death of his parents. Working in California, he got a job as an extra on Cecil B. DeMille's *Why Change Your Wife* (1920), and his rugged good looks and prematurely grey hair made him a well-liked star.

In 1935 he made *Hop-a-long Cassidy*, the first of 66 hugely successful films which cast him as the black-clad, clean-living, non-violent Western hero. With the advent of television, Boyd astutely established the character as a small-screen favourite, and went on to make a fortune selling Hopalong souvenirs to young fans. His popularity survived a scandal involving an actor of the same name for whom he was mistaken. He was married four times, and died a millionaire.

Films include: 1923 The Temple of Venus. '24 Changing Husbands. '26 The Volga Boatman. '27 The King of Kings; Two Arabian Knights. '28 Skyscraper. '30 The Spoilers. '31 The Painted Desert; Murder by the Clock. '33 Lucky Devils. '35 Port of Lost Dreams; Hop-a-long Cassidy. '44 Riders of the Deadline.

BOYER, Charles

(1899–1978). Actor. Born: Figeac, France

Amateur theatricals during his youth gave Boyer his taste for acting and, after studying philosophy at the Sorbonne and drama at the Paris Conservatoire, he went on to become one of France's leading matinee-idols. His early attempts to break into Hollywood were unsuccessful, but when he settled there in 1934 he soon earned a reputation as a romantic lead, with his velvet voice, deep brown eyes and suave style making him the personification of Gallic charm. Popularly associated with the inviting catchphrase 'Come with me to the Casbah', he never actually said it on screen. Boyer was much respected for his attempts to foster Franco-American cultural ties. He died of an overdose of barbiturates shortly after the death of his wife. Boyer – whose leading ladies included Greta Garbo, Marlene Dietrich and Hedy Lamarr – has been described as the last of the cinema's great lovers.

Films include: 1936 The Garden of Allah; Mayerling. '37 Conquest/Marie Walewska. '38 Algiers. '41 Hold Back the Dawn. '44 Gaslight. '53 Madame de . . . (FR-IT). '55 Nana (FR-IT). '61 Fanny. '67 Barefoot in the Park. '69 The Madwoman of Chaillot. '73 Lost Horizon. '74 Stavisky (FR).

BOYLE, Peter

(b. 1933). Actor. born: Philadelphia, Pennsylvania, USA

From an Irish family, Peter Boyle entered the Christian brotherhood as a monk, but left in the Sixties and began acting in small roles in off-Broadway stage productions. He soon graduated to Broadway and then the New York Shakespeare Festival. After a period touring with *The Odd Couple*, he moved into films via commercials. He is a character actor whose best screen roles, notably the campaign organizer in *The Candidate* and the hitman in *The Friends of Eddie Coyle*, have made the most of his unnerving appearance; tall, bald with a massive brow hovering over close-set eyes, sweaty and slightly overweight.

Films include: **1970** Joe. **'71** T. R. Baskin (GB: A Date With a Lonely Girl). **'72** The Candidate. **'73** Steelyard Blues; Slither; The Friends of Eddie Coyle. **'74** Young Frankenstein. **'78** F.I.S.T.; The Brink's Job. **'79** Beyond the Poseidon Adventure. **'80** Where the Buffalo Roam.

BRACKEN, Eddie

(b. 1920). Actor. Born: Astoria, New York, USA

Victory in a 'cute babies' contest at the age of four set the pattern for Bracken's early career. Educated at the New York Professional Actors' School, he went on to become a child star, appearing regularly on stage and in vaudeville before he was ten. His first screen appearances were in the Our Gang comedy shorts. In Hollywood his shy, bumbling onscreen character made him a popular juvenile lead in comedies, especially those made by Preston Sturges, and musicals. As he got older his popularity waned, and in 1953 he retired from films to make occasional appearances on television and the stage, and to concentrate on producing plays.

Films include: **1941** Caught in the Draft; Reaching for the Sun. **'42** The Fleet's In. **'43** The Miracle of Morgan's Creek; Star-Spangled Rhythm; Young and Willing; Happy Go Lucky (FR). **'44** Hail the Conquering Hero. **'50** Summer Stock (GB: If You Feel Like Singing). **'52** We're Not Married.

BRACKETT, Charles

(1892–1969). Producer/writer. Born: Saratoga Springs, New York, USA

Brackett's first novel, Council of the Ungodly, published in 1923, led him away from his earlier career in law. From 1925 to 1929 he was drama critic for The New Yorker magazine, and in 1932 he went to Hollywood to write scripts. Several years later he established a very successful partnership with Billy Wilder – Brackett producing, Wilder directing, and the two writing the witty, sardonic scripts together. The partnership won them two Academy Awards, for The Lost Weekend in 1945 and Sunset Boulevard in 1950. Brackett went on to produce many other successful films in collaboration with other directors, and in 1953 won a third Oscar for Titanic. In the Thirties he was President of the Screenwriters' Guild, and in 1949 he became president of the Academy of Motion Picture Arts and Sciences.

Films as scriptwriter include: **1938** Bluebeard's Eighth Wife. **'39** Ninotchka. **'41** Hold Back the Dawn; Ball of Fire. **'42** The Major and the Minor. **'43** Five Graves to Cairo. **'45** The Lost Weekend. **'48** A Foreign Affair. **'50** Sunset Boulevard. **'53** Titanic. **'56** The King and I (prod. only). **'57** Silk Stockings. **'62** State Fair (prod. only).

BRAHM, John

(1893–1982). Director. Born: Hans Brahm; Hamburg, Germany

The son of a German theatre director, Brahm worked on the stage until 1934 when he went to England and directed his first film. Three years later he moved to Hollywood. He specialized in suspense films, heavy with atmosphere and often concerned with madness; The Lodger was a moody tale of Jack the Ripper, and Hangover Square a study of a mad, murderous composer. His 1954 film The Mad Magician included the experimental use of 3-D effects. Since the Fifties Brahm has worked prolifically for television, directing episodes of Thriller and Alfred Hitchcock Presents.

Films include: **1936** Broken Blossoms (GB). **'39** Let Us Live. **'41** The Locket; Submarine Zone (GB: Escape to Glory). **'43** Tonight We Raid Calais; Wintertime. **'44** The Lodger. **'45** Hangover Square. **'47** The Brasher Doubloon (GB: The High Window). **'54** The Mad Magician. **'55** Die Goldene Pest (GER). **'67** Hot Rods to Hell.

BRAKHAGE, Stan

(b. 1933). Director. Born: Kansas City, Missouri, USA

One of the more influential of American avant-garde directors, Brakhage made his first film at the age of 18, after dropping out from college with a nervous breakdown. Most of his films have been shorts, and many have been made on 8 mm or 16 mm film. His approach is experimental, and he views his subjects through a swirl of movement or colour, distorting images through superimposition and scratching onto negatives. By shooting out of focus and off-centre, Brakhage attempts to stress the subjectivity of vision and the camera. The subject of his films, though less important than the technique, is often his own personal life.

Films include: **1954** Desist. **'55** Wonder Ring. **'59** Sirius Remembered; Window Water Baby Moving. **'62**–**'64** Dog Star Man (four parts). **'63** Mothlight. **'64**–**'69** Songs (series of 30 films). **'65** Fire of Water; The Art of Vision. **'67**–**'70** Scenes From Under Childhood (four films). **'71** Eyes. **'72** The Riddle of Lumen.

BRAND, Neville

(b. 1921). Actor. Born: Kewanee, Illinois, USA

After high school Neville Brand entered the American army. By 1945 he had emerged as the fourth most-decorated GI of World War II. He then studied drama in New York, and made his screen debut in 1949. Blessed with a thick-set frame and a cruel but intelligent face, Brand has found constant work as a heavy, notably as the mad killer in Starlight Slaughter and as the leader of the prison revolt in Don Siegel's Riot in Cell Block 11. He has played gangster Al Capone twice, in The Scarface Mob and The George Raft Story. He has also worked extensively on television, notably in the popular Sixties Western series Laredo.

Films include: **1950** Halls of Montezuma. **'51** Only the Valiant; The Mob (GB: Remember That Face). **'53** Stalag 17; Gun Fury. **'54** Riot in Cell Block 11. **'55** The Prodigal **'59** The Scarface Mob. **'61** The George Raft Story (GB: Spin of a Coin). **'62** Birdman of Alcatraz. **'73** Scalawag (USA-IT); Cahill, United States Marshal (GB: Cahill). **'77** Starlight Slaughter (re-released as: Eaten Alive) (GB: Death Trap).

Opposite page. Above, from left to right: William Boyd; Charles Boyer; Neville Brand. Far left: Peter Boyle in Young Frankenstein. *Centre left: Eddie Bracken in* Ladies' Man *(1947). Left: Marlon Brando in* The Godfather. *Above: Pierre Brasseur in* Lumière d'Eté

BRANDO, Marlon

(b. 1924). Actor. Born: Omaha, Nebraska, USA

Acclaimed by some as the most exciting actor of his generation, Brando has somehow failed to live up to his promise. Educated at a military academy and a New York drama school, he first made an impact with his electric, brooding, Method acting approach in the Broadway version of A Streetcar Named Desire, a role he was to repeat on film. His early movies, like On the Waterfront and The Wild One, capitalized on his extraordinary power. But they also earned him a reputation for mumbling rebellion which he came to resent and tried to shake off in a variety of films; these did little for him other than prove his versatility. His one effort at directing was with One-Eyed Jacks – an extraordinary Western in which he also starred. Outside the Hollywood scene, he worked sporadically until his return to form in the Seventies with The Godfather and Last Tango in Paris. His appearances since have been short, hugely expensive, and tinged with self-parody. He has won two Academy Awards – the first for On the Waterfront, the second (which he refused to collect himself as a protest against the persecution of Indians) for The Godfather. Brando, who has been married three times, retains his brutal, unsmiling charisma but now acts infrequently.

Films include: **1950** The Men. **'51** A Streetcar Named Desire. **'53** Julius Caesar; The Wild One. **'54** On the Waterfront. **'55** Guys and Dolls. **'58** The Young Lions. **'61** One-Eyed Jacks (+dir; +prod). **'62** Mutiny on the Bounty. **'66** The Chase. **'67** A Countess From Hong Kong (GB). **'69** Queimada! (IT-FR) (USA: Burn!). **'72** The Godfather; Ultimo Tango a Parigi (IT-FR) (USA/GB: Last Tango in Paris). **'76** The Missouri Breaks. **'78** Superman, The Movie. **'79** Apocalypse Now. **'80** The Formula.

BRASSEUR, Pierre

(1905–1972). Actor. Born: Pierre-Albert Espinasse; Paris, France

The son of acting parents, Brasseur began his career early, studying with Harry Baur, and making his stage debut at 15 and his first film five years later. In 1938 he established himself as a leading force in French films with Marcel Carné's Quai des Brumes. Perhaps his greatest part was as the nineteenth-century stage actor, Fernand Lemâitre, in Les Enfants du Paradis. In all, his wit and ironic manner won him a great variety of roles in over 80 films. He was also a poet and playwright.

Films include: **1925** Madame Sans-Gêne. **'38** Quai des Brumes (USA: Port of Shadows). **'43** Lumière d'Eté; Adieu Léonard. **'45** Les Enfants du Paradis (USA: Children of Paradise). **'46** Les Portes de la Nuit (USA: Gates of the Night). **'49** Les Amants de Vérone. **'51** Les Mains Sales (GB: Dirty Hands). **'52** Le Plaisir. **'54** La Tour de Nesle (USA: The Tower of Nesle; GB: The Tower of Lust). **'57** Porte des Lilas (FR-IT) (USA: Gates of Paris). **'59** La Tête Contre les Murs (GB: The Keepers); Les Yeux Sans Visage (FR-IT) (GB: Eyes Without a Face). **'61** Pleins Feux sur l'Assassin. **'68** Goto, l'Ile d'Amour (USA/GB: Goto, Island of Love).

BRAZZI, Rossano

(b. 1917). Actor. Born: Bologna, Italy

A one-time featherweight boxing champion, Brazzi studied law at the University of San Marco in Florence before turning to acting. An established star of the Italian cinema – he made over 70 films there – Brazzi found it difficult to break into Hollywood, but finally established himself in the Fifties, playing a series of Latin lovers and escorts, roles which made the most of his distinguished features and athletic physique. He continued to be involved with the Italian film industry, and in the Sixties he gained the title 'Commendatore' for his efforts to establish a new studio. Brazzi returned to Italy in 1969, but occasionally makes small appearances in American films.

Films include: 1940 Ritorno (IT). '54 Three Coins in the Fountain; The Barefoot Contessa (USA-IT). '55 Summer Madness (GB-USA) (USA: Summertime). '56 Loser Takes All (GB). '57 Interlude; The Story of Esther Costello (GB); Legend of the Lost (USA-IT). '58 South Pacific. '59 Count Your Blessings. '62 The Light in the Piazza. '69 The Italian Job. '72 The Great Waltz. '81 The Final Conflict.

BRDEČKA, Jiří

(1917–1982). Animator. Born: Jiří Brnečka; Hranice, Czechoslovakia

Brdečka was studying art history at Prague University when, in 1939, the Germans closed it down. He then became a writer and illustrator, and published a series of stories about Limonadovy Joe, an affectionate parody of the American Western. His film work displays the same interest in folklore, many of his subjects being animated fairy-tales. He worked in varying capacities with leading Czech animators, including Jiří Trnka. He was also a novelist and playwright.

Films include: 1947 Vzducholoď a láska (Love and the Zeppelin). '52 Staré pověsti české (Old Czech Legends). '58 Jak se člověk naučil létat (A Comic History of Aviation).

'60 Naše Karkulka (Our Little Red Riding Hood). '61 Člověk pod vodou (Man Under the Sea). '62 Rozum a cit (Reason and Emotion). '63 Špatně namalovaná slepice (The Grotesque Chicken); Až přijde kocour (That Cat). '64 Slóvce (Minstrel's Song); Limonádový Joe (Lemonade Joe). '66 Dezertér (GB: The Deserter); Proč se usmíváš, Mono Liso? (Why Do You Smile, Mona Lisa?). '68 Moc Osudu (Power of Destiny).

BRECHT, Bertolt

(1898–1956). Author/playwright/lyricist/critic. Born: Augsburg, Austria

Brecht is without doubt one of the most influential playwrights of this century. After serving in World War I, he became involved in the post-war German theatre which at the time, under the leadership of such people as the producer Erwin Piscator, was revolutionizing stage drama. Soon Brecht had established himself as the leading exponent of 'Expressionist' theatre and then 'narrative realism'. He achieved international acclaim with such works as Die Dreigroschenoper and The Rise and Fall of the Town of Mahogany. But Brecht, an ardent communist, soon aroused the displeasure of the Nazis and was forced to flee abroad. He arrived in the USA in 1941 and went to Hollywood, but produced very little in the nature of film work, his most successful project being the co-scenario of Fritz Lang's Hangmen Also Die! The politics that were his inspiration also became his stumbling block and Brecht inevitably fell foul of the House Un-American Activities Committee. He returned to Germany in 1948. The tragedy is that so little of his greatness ever found its way onto celluloid. Brecht attacked the 1931 screen version of Die Dreigroscheroper (The Threepenny Opera), but that is arguably the greatest adaptation from his work.

Films include: 1932 Kuhle Wampe oder Wem gehört die Welt? (GER) (co-sc). '42 Hangmen Also Die! (co-sc) (USA). '51 Das Leben unseres Prasidenten (lyr) (E. GER). '52 Frauenschicksale (lyr) (E. GER). '54 Lide der Strome.

BREMER, Lucille

(b. 1923). Actress/dancer. Born: Amsterdam, New York, USA

Lucille Bremer began dancing at the age of seven, and soon became a ballet dancer with the Philadelphia Opera. At 16 she was a chorus-girl with the Radio City Rockettes, and this brought her to the notice of MGM producer Arthur Freed. She made her film debut in 1944, and her tall, slender, red-haired charms seemed cut out for stardom. Although she partnered Fred Astaire in two films, her career oddly failed to take off, and MGM dropped her in 1947. She retired from films to marry Abelardo Rodriguez, the son of a Mexican president, and now runs a children's dress shop in California.

Films include: 1944 Meet Me in St Louis; Ziegfeld Follies. '45 Yolanda and the Thief. '46 Till the Clouds Roll By. '47 Dark Delusion (GB: Cynthia's Secret). '48 Adventures of Casanova; Ruthless; Behind Locked Doors.

BRENNAN, Walter

(1894–1974). Actor. Born: Swampscott, Massachusetts, USA

Brennan's early career was varied; he abandoned engineering in favour of vaudeville, and supported himself with a series of jobs ranging from bank clerk to lumberjack. After service in World War I he went to Hollywood where he found work as an extra and stuntman, and graduated to major supporting roles for such directors as Howard Hawks, King Vidor, Frank Capra, John Ford and Fritz Lang. Although he played a wide range of very different characters, he is best remembered for his portrayal of old men, most typically as the cantankerous, garrulous, grizzled old-timer in Rio Bravo, employing his false teeth to good comic effect. The popular Brennan won Academy Awards as Best Supporting Actor for three films, Come and Get It, Kentucky and The Westerner, in which he was superb as Judge Roy Bean.

Films include: 1927 Tearin' Into Trouble. '35 The Wedding Night. '36 Come and Get It. '38 Kentucky. '40 Northwest Passage; The Westerner. '41 Meet John Doe; Sergeant York. '43 Hangmen Also Die! '44 To Have and Have Not. '46 My Darling Clementine. '48 Red River. '54 The Far Country. '55 Bad Day at Black Rock. '59 Rio Bravo. '69 Support Your Local Sheriff.

BRENON, Herbert

(1880–1958). Director/actor/scenarist. Born: Alexander Herbert Reginald St John Brenon; Dún Laoghaire, Dublin, Eire

Herbert Brenon's parents emigrated to America when he was young. He began working as a menial in a New York theatre, and later became a stage actor and manager. In 1909 he opened a small picture house in Pennsylvania, and in 1911 was hired as a writer by Carle Laemmle. Three years later he directed his first feature and was an instant success. His films were mostly spectaculars laced with

Seventh Cross. '48 A Song Is Born; Portrait of Jennie (GB: Jennie).

BRESSON, Robert

(b. 1907). Director. Born: Bromont-Lamothe, Auvergne, France

Initially a painter and photographer, Bresson gained some film experience in the Thirties, which included his directing a medium-length comedy. After a year in a German POW camp, he made his feature debut in 1943 with an austere melodrama about nuns and murder, Les Anges du Péché. Most of his films since then have been literary adaptations, made in his own unique style, pared-down and restrained, with carefully planned soundtracks carrying information not directly shown in the images. Since 1950 he has used non-professional actors, who can better subordinate themselves to his intentions and give something of their own inner being. His obsessive concentration on themes of grace, innocence and guilt, death (especially suicide), spiritual regeneration and decay, together with his pessimistically unorthodox Catholic viewpoint, have made him a deeply respected but never popular film-maker.

Films include: 1934 Les Affaires Publiques. '43 Les Anges du Péché. '51 Le Journal d'un Curé de Campagne. (USA: Diary of a Country Priest). '56 Un Condamné à Mort S'Est Echappé ou Le Vent Souffle Où Il Veut (USA: A Man Escaped). '59 Pickpocket. '62 Le Procès de Jeanne d'Arc (USA/GB: The Trial of Joan of Arc). '66 Au Hasard, Balthazar (USA/GB: Balthazar). '67 Mouchette. '69 Une Femme Douce (USA/GB: A Gentle Creature). '74 Lancelot du Lac (FR-IT). '77 Le Diable, Probablement (USA/GB: The Devil, Probably).

BRIALY, Jean-Claude

(b. 1933). Actor. Born: Aumale, Algeria

The son of a high-ranking Army officer, Brialy was educated in Algeria, France and Germany. While studying philosophy at Strasbourg University he also attended drama classes at the Strasbourg Conservatoire and appeared in a wide variety of plays. He made several short films with Jacques Rivette and Jean-Luc Godard. However, it was Claude Chabrol's Les Cousins that established his reputation, and made him a favourite with the French nouvelle vague directors. Those he has worked with include François Truffaut, Louis Malle, Luis Buñuel and Roger Vadim. He continues to divide his time between film and the theatre.

Films include: 1958 Ascenseur par l'Echafaud (USA: Frantic; GB: Lift to the Scaffold). '59 Les Cousins. '61 Une Femme Est Une Femme (USA: A Woman Is a Woman). '64 La Ronde (USA: Circle of Love). '67 Lamiel (FR-IT). '68 La Mariée Etait en Noir (FR-IT) (GB: The Bride Wore Black). '70 Le Genou de Claire (GB: Claire's Knee). '72 Un Meurtre Est un Meurtre (FR-IT) (GB: A Murder Is a Murder). '74 Le Fantôme de la Liberté (GB: The Phantom of Liberty). '76 Le Juge et l'Assassin. '81 Les Uns et les Autres. '82 La Nuit de Varennes (FR-IT).

Above, from left to right: Rossano Brazzi; Lucille Bremer in Adventures of Casanova; *Evelyn Brent in* Underworld; *George Brent. Far left: Walter Brennan in* Rio Bravo. *Left: Felix Bressart in* Greenwich Village *(1944). Below: Jean-Claude Brialy in* Claire's Knee

charm and wit. Brenon often acted in his own films, and was injured while making Neptune's Daughter (1914) when a water tank exploded. He regarded the coming of sound with suspicion and his career waned in the Thirties. He retired in 1940.

Films as director include: 1913 Ivanhoe. '15 The Kreutzer Sonata; The Two Orphans. '16 War Bride. '17 The Eternal Sin. '18 The Passing of the Third Floor Back. '24 Peter Pan. '26 Dancing Mothers; Beau Geste; The Great Gatsby; A Kiss for Cinderella. '28 Laugh, Clown, Laugh. '38 Yellow Sands (GB).

BRENT, Evelyn

(1899–1975). Actress. Born: Mary Elizabeth Riggs; Tampa, Florida, USA

A visit to Fort Lee Studios as a schoolgirl led to Evelyn Brent's first job as an extra. Small acting parts followed, and by 1916 she was playing leads. She acted in several British films in the

Twenties, but had her real success back in America as the star of Josef von Sternberg's Underworld. Her best work made good use of her sultry looks to emphasize her roles as vamps or slightly crooked but sympathetic heroines. She survived the transition to sound easily enough, but the quality of her films gradually declined to B Westerns and thrillers. She made one excellent return to form as the satanist in Val Lewton's The Seventh Victim in 1943, but retired at the end of the decade.

Films include: 1917 Raffles the Amateur Cracksman. '24 Loving Lies; Silk Stocking Sal. '25 Midnight Molly; Forbidden Cargo; Smooth as Satin. '27 Love 'em and Leave 'em; Underworld. '28 The Last Command; The Drag Net. '29 Broadway. '30 Framed. '43 The Seventh Victim.

BRENT, George

(1904–1979). Actor. Born: George Nolan; Shannonsbridge, nr Dublin, Eire

Orphaned at the age of 11, Brent went to live with relatives in America. He returned to start a career on the stage, but had to flee because of his involvement in the Irish Rebellion. In New York he worked with various stock companies, finally graduating to Broadway and films. He worked steadily, often playing suave, gentlemanly roles opposite strong leading ladies like Greta Garbo, Barbara Stanwyck and especially Bette Davis. Good parts were few and far between in the Forties, and he eventually retired from the screen to breed race-horses, though he returned for a cameo appearance in 1978 in Born Again. Brent was married five times.

Films include: 1933 Baby Face. '34 The Painted Veil. '38 Jezebel. '39 Dark Victory; The Old Maid; The Rains Came. '40 The Fighting 69th; The Man Who Talked Too Much; 'Til We Meet Again. '45 The Affairs of Susan; The Spiral Staircase; My Reputation. '46 Lover Come Back.

BRESSART, Felix

(1892–1949). Actor. Born: Eydtkunen, East Prussia, Germany

Felix Bressart was one of many distinguished German actors forced to pursue their careers abroad by the rise of the Nazi regime. A stage and film comedy character actor, he fled to Switzerland in 1933. After a period in France, he settled in Hollywood in 1937. His first major success there was as one of the Commissars in Ernst Lubitsch's Ninotchka. He worked regularly until his death ten years later, often playing amiable, wistful Europeans in light romantic comedies.

Films include: 1930 Die Drei von der Tankstelle (GER). '39 Three Smart Girls Grow Up; Ninotchka. '40 The Shop Around the Corner; Edison the Man; Bitter Sweet. '41 Ziegfeld Girl. '42 To Be or Not to Be. '43 Above Suspicion; Song of Russia. '44 The

BRICE, Fanny

(1891–1951). Actress. Born: Fanny Borach; New York City, USA

Fanny Brice's spectacular success as a stage and nightclub comedienne did not carry over into movies. She started her career in Brooklyn shows and progressed to Manhattan burlesque, where her singing and dancing was spotted by Florenz Ziegfeld. She subsequently became a *Follies* star, and her Brooklyn-style comedy won her a substantial following. She was given her own radio show, *Baby Snooks*, but only worked sporadically in films where she made little impact. Her life story was the subject of *Funny Girl* (1968) and its sequel *Funny Lady* (1975), both of which starred Barbra Streisand.

Films include: 1928 My Man. '30 Be Yourself; The Man From Blankley's. '36 The Great Ziegfeld. '38 Everybody Sing. '46 Ziegfeld Follies.

BRIDGES, Beau

(b. 1941). Actor. Born: Hollywood, Los Angeles, USA

Eldest son of Lloyd and brother of Jeff, Beau Bridges made his screen debut at the age of seven. Later he abandoned acting in favour of his studies at UCLA and the University of Hawaii, and for a while toyed with the idea of becoming an athlete. Instead he returned to acting. His innocent expression and bronzed Californian looks have served him well in films where he has been called upon to suggest naiveté, notably in *The Landlord*. He has also appeared regularly on television and works with the Los Angeles Theater West stage company.

Films include: 1949 The Red Pony. '67 The Incident. '69 Gaily, Gaily (GB: Chicago, Chicago). '70 The Landlord. '73 Child's Play. '74 Lovin' Molly. '79 Norma Rae; The Runner Stumbles. '81 Honky Tonk Freeway.

BRIDGES, Jeff

(b. 1949). Actor. Born: Hollywood, Los Angeles, USA

Jeff Bridges gained his first experience acting for television and appearing on stage with his father Lloyd. After high school he studied in New York with former actress Uta Hagen. It was his third movie, Peter Bogdanovich's *The Last Picture Show*, that won him recognition and an Oscar nomination. His performances in *Fat City* and *Bad Company* have established him as one of America's most talented contemporary actors, particularly strong when portraying troubled youths.

Films include: 1971 The Last Picture Show; Bad Company. '72 Fat City. '73 The Iceman Cometh; The Last American Hero. '74 Thunderbolt and Lightfoot. '76 Stay Hungry. '80 Heaven's Gate. '81 Cutter's Way.

BRIDGES, Lloyd

(b. 1913). Actor. Born: San Leandro, California, USA

Lloyd Bridges studied political science at UCLA and appeared in university stage productions. Going on stage professionally, he toured, reached New York and formed an off-Broadway company. Offered a contract with Columbia, he gained critical and public approval in *Home of the Brave*, and went on to play many roles, usually as a character actor in parts involving physical action. A well-built, hard-faced man, Bridges seldom seems stretched in his acting, although the odd, more demanding film, like *A Walk in the Sun*, indicated what he might have done with better chances. He has done much television work, starring in the *Sea Hunt* series.

Films include: 1944 The Master Race. '45 A Walk in the Sun. '49 Home of the Brave. '50 The Sound of Fury. '52 High Noon; Plymouth Adventure. '53 The Limping Man (GB). '56 The Rainmaker. '58 The Goddess. '80 Airplane!

BROCKA, Lino

(b. 1939). Director. Born: San Jose Nueva Ecija, Philippines

Lino Brocka worked in the theatre while still a university student, and after graduation acted in a travelling group. Later, he founded, and still runs, the PEDA theatre group, many members of which appear in his films. After some television work, he directed his first feature in 1970. His best known film, *Manila*, tells of a young man's search for his childhood love, and is characteristic of Third World productions in its harsh, documentary view of the sordid side of city life. Brocka continues to work in film, theatre and television.

Films include: 1970 Wanted: Perfect Brother. '71 Rubog Sa Gunto. '72 Cherry Blossoms. '74 Human Imperfections/Ye Have Been Weighed in the Balance and Found Wanting. '75 Manila, Sa Mga Kuko Ng Liwanag (USA: The Nail of Brightness; GB: Manila). '77 Tahan Na Empy, Tahan; Inay. '78 Insiang. '79 Ina Ka Ng Anak Mo. '80 Jaguar.

BROCCOLI, Albert R.

(b. 1909). Producer. Born: New York City, USA

'Cubby' Broccoli entered films in 1938 as a messenger, rising to publicist and to assistant director. A successful agent after the war, he came to London to set up Warwick Films, and stayed on to produce action movies with American stars. With Harry Saltzman, a producer who was trying to set up a 'James Bond' picture, he formed Eon films, and since then has made a string of Bond movies. Very expensive, and very successful financially, they have proved the greatest money-making series in film history. Broccoli received a special award at the Oscars ceremony in 1982.

Films include: '55 The Cockleshell Heroes. '57 Fire Down Below. '60 The Trials of Oscar Wilde (USA: The Man With the Green Carnation). '62 Dr No. '63 From Russia With Love. '64 Goldfinger. '65 Thunderball. '68 Chitty Chitty Bang Bang. '71 Diamonds Are Forever. '79 Moonraker (GB-FR). '81 For Your Eyes Only.

Above: Jeff Bridges in Bad Company. *Above right: Lloyd Bridges. Above, far right: Clive Brook. Right: Louise Brooks. Below: Charles Bronson*

Films include: 1953 House of Wax. '58 Machine Gun Kelly. '60 The Magnificent Seven. '63 The Great Escape; Four for Texas. '65 The Sandpiper. '67 The Dirty Dozen. '68 C'Era Una Volta il West (IT) (USA/GB: Once Upon a Time in the West). '72 Chato's Land (GB). '72 The Mechanic (re-released in GB as: Killer of Killers). '74 Death Wish. '75 Hard Times (GB: The Streetfighter); Breakout. '77 Telefon. '82 Death Wish II.

BROOK, Clive

(1887–1974). Actor. Born: Clifford Hardman Brook; London, England

Educated at Dulwich College, Clive Brook worked in insurance and journalism before World War I service in the Artists' Rifles. Afterwards he went on stage, making his London debut in 1920 and his first films the same year. From 1924–1935 he worked in American films, from 1935–1943 in British studios, but thereafter concentrated on the theatre. Many of his film parts made him the honest, brave, stiff-necked Englishman, but he could play elegant variations, as in his two great films for Sternberg: in *Underworld* his seedy lawyer retained enough flair and polish to fascinate the gangster and the girl; in *Shanghai Express* he was one of Dietrich's few leading men not to be swamped. His one shot at direction, *On Approval*, had pace and a nice comic sense.

Films include: 1920 Trent's Last Case. '25 Seven Sinners. '27 Barbed Wire (USA); Underworld. '32 Shanghai Express (USA); Sherlock Holmes (USA). '33 Cavalcade. '37 Action for Slander. '38 The Ware Case. '44 On Approval (+ dir). '63 The List of Adrian Messenger (USA).

BROOKS, Louise

(1906–1985). Actress. Born: Cherryvale, Kansas, USA

Louise Brooks was a dancer with the Ruth St Denis company. She then appeared in George White's Scandals and the Ziegfeld Follies, and from 1925 made films for Paramount in New York and later in Hollywood. Her role in *A Girl in Every Port* induced the German director G. W. Pabst to sign her for *Pandora's Box* and two more European films followed. Her career collapsed when she returned to the USA, but after years of obscurity she re-emerged late in life as a vividly intelligent writer on cinema. Brooks began as a Jazz-era flapper, and foil for W. C. Fields. In *Beggars of Life* her boy-hobo is spirited and touching; then, in her films for Pabst, she transcended mere acting. In *Pandora's Box* player and character fused totally in one of the screen's sublime experiences. She is now regarded as one of the cinema's greatest actresses – and perhaps its most sensual.

Films include: 1925 The Street of Forgotten Men. '26 A Social Celebrity; It's the Old Army Game. '27 Love 'em and Leave 'em; Rolled Stockings; The City Gone Wild. '28 A Girl in Every Port; Beggars of Life. '29 The Canary Murder Case; Die Büchse der Pandora (USA/GB: Pandora's Box); Das Tagebuch einer Verlorenen (GB: Diary of a Lost Girl/Diary of a Lost One). '30 Prix de Beauté (GB: Miss Europe).

BROLIN, James

(b. 1940). Actor. Born: Los Angeles, California, USA

James Brolin studied theatre arts at UCLA, leaving to work under Robert Paris, an old-time studio coach. Director Henry King helped him to a contract at 20th Century-Fox, and he also did television work, co-starring with Robert Young from 1969 in the popular series *Marcus Welby, MD*. For this Brolin gained an Emmy award, and was able to land better parts in better movies. In *Gable and Lombard* he played Clark Gable, but could not suggest the charisma of the original. Recently he has set up his own production company, and acting may play a smaller part in his career.

Films include: 1963 Take Her She's Mine. '65 Von Ryan's Express; Our Man Flint. '66 Fantastic Voyage. '67 The Capetown Affair (USA-S. AFRICA). '68 The Boston Strangler. '72 Skyjacked. '73 Westworld. '76 Gable and Lombard. '77 The Car. '78 Capricorn One. '79 The Amityville Horror. '80 Night of the Juggler.

BRONSON, Betty

(1906–1971). Actress. Born: Elizabeth Ada Bronson; Trenton, New Jersey, USA

After two years with Famous Players–Lasky, Betty Bronson was catapulted to fame in 1924 as Peter Pan. She was boyish, witty, energetic, and slightly wistful – the perfect Peter. Although good parts for this tiny comedienne were not easy to find, she was excellent as the clever schoolgirl of *Are Parents People?* and her casting in the cameo role of the Madonna in *Ben-Hur* shows the prestige she had attained. *A Kiss for Cinderella* was probably her finest performance, and in it she was directed by Herbert Brenon, who had guided her in *Peter Pan*. In 1932 she retired, though she later returned in character roles.

Films include: 1924 Peter Pan. '25 Are Parents People?; Ben-Hur. '26 The Cat's Pyjamas; A Kiss For Cinderella. '28 The Singing Fool. '29 The Bellamy Trial; One Stolen Night. '31 Lover Come Back. '64 The Naked Kiss. '71 Evil Knievel.

BRONSON, Charles

(b. 1921). Actor. Born: Charles Buchinsky; Ehrenfeld, Pennsylvania, USA

Charles Bronson's father died when he was 13, and he went to work in the mines with his two elder brothers before being drafted into the army in World War II. After the war he became interested in acting, working on stage in Philadelphia and New York. Moving on to the Pasadena Playhouse, he was spotted in 1951 by Henry Hathaway and signed for his first film role. By the late Fifties he was playing leads in B movies, and in the Sixties – after being one of *The Magnificent Seven* – advanced to lead heavy in big-budget films. European thrillers and Westerns made him a big draw, and he returned to the USA as a star, his roles now sympathetic or at worst ambivalent (as witness his vigilante in the *Death Wish* films); his craggy physique and his inscrutable expression, however, always retain a touch of menace. He is married to actress and co-star Jill Ireland.

Above: Jim Brown in 100 Rifles. *Top: Mel Brooks in* Silent Movie. *Right: Joe E. Brown with Thelma Todd in* Son of a Sailor *(1933)*

BROOKS, Mel

(b. 1926). Director/actor. Born: Melvin Kaminsky; New York, USA

Mel Brooks began as an impressionist, an amateur drummer and a pianist. For ten years he was a gag-writer for Sid Caesar's television shows. Then came comedy albums with Carl Reiner and Dick Cavett, the *Get Smart* television series of spy parodies, and an entry into feature films with *The Producers*. (He had previously written and narrated one cartoon, *The Critic*, which won an Academy Award). In the features he has directed Brooks has scored by turning the techniques of genre movies upside down. For *Blazing Saddles* he built the set of the Western town as a decoy; he had mime-artist Marcel Marceau speak in *Silent Movie*; and he staged a Nazi musical in *The Producers*. His work is in bad taste, irreverent and funny, and highly knowledgeable about the characteristics of the movies he satirizes. Brooks generally scripts and acts in his movies. He is married to actress Anne Bancroft.

Films include: 1963 The Critic (anim. short) (sc; +narr. only). **'69** Putney Swope (actor only). **'70** The Twelve Chairs. **'74** Blazing Saddles; Young Frankenstein. **'76** Silent Movie. **'77** High Anxiety. **'81** History of the World – Part One.

BROOKS, Richard

(b. 1912). Writer/director. Born: Philadelphia, Pennsylvania, USA

In the Thirties Richard Brooks was a sports writer who also wrote for and broadcasted on radio. After service with the marines during World War II, he moved into films, working on scripts such as *The Killers* (1946) and *Key Largo* (1948). In 1950 he began a prolific career as writer-director with *Crisis*. His best films combine hard-hitting social comment with an acute sense of entertainment value; in his less successful work the didactic element has tended to get out of hand. Brooks has also written novels, one of which, *The Brick Foxhole*, was filmed as *Crossfire* (1947). In 1960 Brooks married actress Jean Simmons.

Films include: 1952 Deadline USA (GB: Deadline). **'54** The Last Time I Saw Paris; Flame and the Flesh. **'55** The Blackboard Jungle. **'58** Cat on a Hot Tin Roof. **'60** Elmer Gantry. **'62** Sweet Bird of Youth. **'65** Lord Jim. **'66** The Professionals. **'67** In Cold Blood. **'75** Bite the Bullet. **'77** Looking for Mr Goodbar.

BROWN, Clarence

(b. 1890). Director. Born: Clinton, Massachusetts, USA

After gaining degrees in engineering at the University of Tennessee, Clarence Brown worked in the motor industry until 1915. He then entered films as assistant to Maurice Tourneur and for seven years remained with

him, editing, title-writing and shooting exteriors. His first solo attempt at direction was in 1920, and he made 52 features between then and 1952. Brown was a great pictorialist; he was also a marvellous director of actors (seven films with Garbo), and his films were rich in human qualities. In 1971 Brown helped to set up the Clarence Brown Theater for the Performing Arts at his old university. He married and divorced actresses Mona Maris and Alice Joyce.

Films include: 1919 The Last of the Mohicans (co-dir). **'25** The Goose Woman; The Eagle. **'27** Flesh and the Devil. **'30** Anna Christie. **'35** Anna Karenina. **'36** Wife Versus Secretary. **'37** Conquest (GB: Marie Walewska). **'44** National Velvet. **'46** The Yearling. **'49** Intruder in the Dust.

BROWN, Jim

(b. 1935). Actor. Born: James Nathaniel Brown; St Simons Island, Georgia, USA

Educated at Syracuse University, Jim Brown played professional football for the Cleveland Browns. In 1964 he won the Hickok Belt, awarded to the athlete of the year. His first film appearance was in the same year, and in 1967 he retired from football to become a movie star. Good-looking and virile, he was well suited to heroic roles, and made sufficient impact to be reckoned a genuine symbol of black manhood. What he did need – and still does – was a good movie to be symbolic in. He formed his own film company, Nathaniel Productions to promote the image of blacks in the industry.

Films include: 1964 Rio Conchos. **'67** The Dirty Dozen (USA-GB). **'68** Ice Station Zebra; The Mercenaries (GB) (USA: Dark of the Sun). **'69** 100 Rifles. **'70** Tick . . . Tick . . . Tick. **'72** Black Gunn; Slaughter. **'73** I Escaped From Devil's Island. **'74** Three the Hard Way. **'78** Fingers. **'82** One Down Two to Go.

BROWN, Joe E.

(1892–1973). Actor. Born: Joe Evans Brown; Holgate, Ohio, USA

Joe E. Brown was a circus acrobat (at 9), baseball player, star of vaudeville and burlesque, and (by 1918) Broadway comedian. Entering the movies in 1928, he normally starred in second-feature comedies – good-natured slapstick exploiting his wide-mouthed grin and country-innocent character. He was, however, splendid as Flute in Max Reinhardt's *A Midsummer Night's Dream*, and later, when semi-retired, memorable as Captain Andy in the 1951 *Show Boat* and as the millionaire who falls for Jack Lemmon, a musician in drag, in *Some Like It Hot*. *The Tender Years* gave Brown a rare dramatic part and showed he was a fine actor.

Films include: 1928 The Circus Kid. **'32** Fireman, Save My Child; You Said a Mouthful. **'33** Elmer the Great. **'34** The Circus Clown. **'35** Alibi Ike; A Midsummer Night's Dream. **'40** So You Won't Talk. **'47** The Tender Years. **'51** Show Boat. **'56** Around the World in 80 Days. **'59** Some Like It Hot. **'63** It's a Mad, Mad, Mad, Mad World; The Comedy of Terrors.

BROWN, Johnny Mack

(1904–1974). Actor. Born; Dothan, Alabama, USA

An All-American half-back, Johnny Mack Brown scored the winning touchdown for the University of Alabama in the Rose Bowl game of 1926. Choosing the movies rather than football, he was signed to an MGM contract, and for a few years (1928–1931) played leads opposite some of the greatest stars (Greta Garbo, Mary Pickford, Norma Shearer). Though never a great actor, Brown had muscular good looks, and developed into a highly competent leading man. When his vogue waned, he used his riding ability and moved over into B Westerns, remaining popular in this field for many years, working steadily until 1953 and occasionally thereafter.

Top: Johnny Mack Brown in The Oregon Trail *(1939). Above: Bruno S in Werner Herzog's* The Enigma of Kaspar Hauser. *Below: Nigel Bruce as Watson and Basil Rathbone as Holmes in* Sherlock Holmes and the Secret Weapon *(1942), fourth of their 14 films as the famous duo*

Films include: **1928** Our Dancing Daughters. **'29** Coquette. **'30** Montana Moon; Billy the Kid. **'33** Fighting With Kit Carson (serial). **'35** Rustlers of Red Dog (serial). **'40** West of Carson City. **'43** Lone Star Trail. **'47** Raiders of the South. **'49** Law of the West.

'65 Requiem for a Gunfighter. '66 Apache Uprising.

BROWN, Nacio Herb

(1896–1964). Composer. Born: Ignacio Herb Brown; Deming, New Mexico, USA

Music was originally Nacio Herb Brown's hobby. He opened a clothing shop in Los Angeles, but made big money from land investment in Beverly Hills. After the 1929 Crash, he joined MGM, and began a long collaboration with Arthur Freed on the studio's first musical, *The Broadway Melody*, for which he composed the classic 'You Were Meant for Me'. 'Singin' in the Rain' (from *Hollywood Revue of 1929*) soon followed, and the partnership continued successfully into the Forties. The film *Singin' in the Rain* gave a new lease of life to many of the old Brown-Freed numbers in 1952, but two years previously Brown had retired. He married one of the stars of *The Broadway Melody*, Anita Page, but the marriage did not endure.

Films include: **1929** The Broadway Melody; The Pagan. **'30** Montana Moon. **'35** Broadway Melody of 1936. **'37** Thoroughbreds Don't Cry. **'39** Babes in Arms. **'41** Ziegfeld Girl. **'43** Wintertime. **'50** Pagan Love Song. **'52** Singin' in the Rain.

BROWNING, Tod

(1880–1962). Director. Born: Louisville, Kentucky, USA

Tod Browning knocked about the USA in carnivals, circuses and vaudeville before entering films as an actor in 1913. He wrote scripts. directed shorts, and made his first features in 1917. In the Twenties he became famous as a director of macabre subjects, often with Lon Chaney as star. Chaney was perfectly suited to realize Browning's fantasies, but the world

they created was durable enough to survive the actor's death. *Freaks* is the most extraordinary film ever to emerge from MGM: set in an almost unbearable, nightmare world, filled with misshapen beings, it reaches a climax as frightening as any in cinema. In Britain the film was banned for thirty years. Beside it, *Dracula* (the Bela Lugosi original) and *The Devil Doll* are amiable diversions. From 1939 Browning lived quietly in retirement.

Films include: **1920** The Virgin of Stamboul. **'21** Outside the Law. **'23** White Tiger. **'25** The Unholy Three. **'26** The Road to Mandalay. **'27** The Unknown; London After Midnight. **'28** West of Zanzibar. **'30** Outside the Law. **'31** Dracula. **'32** Freaks. **'35** Mark of the Vampire. **'36** The Devil Doll.

BRUCE, Nigel

(1895–1953). Actor. Born: William Nigel Bruce; Ensenada, Mexico

The son of a baronet, Nigel Bruce was born in Mexico while his parents were touring there. After being seriously wounded in World War I, he went on the stage in 1920 and into British films in 1930. In 1934 he moved to Hollywood, and played substantial supporting parts there for the rest of his life. Plump, greying, bumbling, Bruce will always be remembered as the perfect Dr Watson. He was slower-witted than the original, but his extraordinary sympathy with Basil Rathbone's Holmes compensated. Re-reading the stories now, one sees Watson as Bruce. He had a narrow range, essentially playing himself, but within those limits he had no better.

Films include: **1932** Lord Camber's Ladies (GB). **'35** The Scarlet Pimpernel (GB); Becky Sharp. **'36** The Charge of the Light Brigade. **'37** The Hound of the Baskervilles; The Adventures of Sherlock Holmes (GB: Sherlock Holmes). **'40** Rebecca. **'41** Suspicion. **'44** The Scarlet Claw. **'45** The House of Fear. **'52** Limelight.

BRUNO S

(b. 1932). Actor. Born: Berlin, Germany

Abandoned by his mother, Bruno S, an illegitimate child, grew up in mental homes and children's homes. After running away several times, he was put in a closed institution for ten years and then discharged to earn a living as a warehouseman and busker. A short documentary about him, made in 1970 by Lutz Eisholz, brought him to director Werner Herzog's attention. This led to his being cast as Kaspar Hauser, who in 1828 was found forsaken at the age of 16 in the town square of Nuremberg after having spent his whole life chained in a cellar. Bruno S effectively portrayed the young man's painfully bewildering encounter with civilized society, and Herzog employed him again in *Stroszek*, as a Berlin jailbird trying to make a new life in Wisconsin.

Films: **1970** Bruno – der Schwarze, es blies ein Jäger wohl in sein Horn (doc). **'75** Jeder für sich und Gott gegen alle (USA: The Mystery of Kaspar Hauser; GB: The Enigma of Kaspar Hauser). **'77** Stroszek.

BRYAN, Dora

(b. 1924). Actress. Born: Southport, Lancashire, England

Dora Bryan never gets the glamorous parts but she is usually ready to play for laughs or a touch of sentiment – her mobile face looks always ready to break into a smile or collapse in tears. She started out in repertory theatres at the age of 16 and toured with ENSA during the war. She reached the West End stage in *Private Lives* and played in revues at the Lyric and Globe Theatres. A small part in *Odd Man Out* led to a ten-minute bit as a prostitute in *The Fallen Idol*. Her best role was as the tarty mother in *A Taste of Honey*, striking sparks in her encounters with Rita Tushingham. She has been in many films and stage plays – and she was once an improbable Lorelei Lee in *Gentlemen Prefer Blondes* at the Princes Theatre.

Films include: 1947 Odd Man Out. '48 The Fallen Idol. '50 The Cure for Love; The Blue Lamp. '52 Miss Robin Hood; The Ringer. '54 You Know What Sailors Are. '58 Carry On Sergeant; The Man Who Wouldn't Talk. '61 A Taste of Honey. '66 The Great St Trinian's Train Robbery.

BRYNNER, Yul

(1915–1985). Actor. Born: Youl Bryner; Cape Yelizavety, Sakhalin Island, Russia

Bald, oriental-looking, Yul Brynner was a genuine exotic, and it is odd that in gravitating towards Westerns he played gunfighters rather than Indians. He was raised in Peking and educated in Paris, where he played the guitar in nightclubs at the age of 13. He joined the Cirque d'Hiver as an acrobat and fell from the high trapeze. In 1941 he went to the USA, broadcasting for The Voice of America in Russian and French. He then worked in television and on Broadway, where his biggest success was as the King of Siam in *The King and I*, for which he won a Tony and other awards. The film version won him a Best Actor Oscar. In 1979 he again played the role on the stage.

Films include: 1949 Port of New York. '56 The King and I; The Ten Commandments. '58 The Buccaneer. '59 The Sound and the Fury; Solomon and Sheba. '60 The Magnificent Seven. '62 Taras Bulba. '64 Invitation to a Gunfighter. '66 Cast a Giant Shadow. '68 Villa Rides. '72 Fuzz. '73 Westworld. '76 Futureworld.

BUCHANAN, Edgar

(1903–1979). Actor. Born: Humansville, Missouri, USA

Raised in Oregon, Edgar Buchanan was a successful dentist, heading the oral surgery department at Eugene Hospital, Oregon, from 1929 to 1937. Then he moved to California and joined the Pasadena Community Playhouse. Bitten by the film bug, he became a character actor in supporting roles, usually in Westerns as an old-timer, unshaven and cynical. He also appeared in television series, such as *Hopalong Cassidy*, *Judge Roy Bean* and as Uncle Joe in *Petticoat Junction*, as well as in television films, including

The Over-the-Hill Gang (1969). He made over ninety cinema films in a career that lasted 35 years. Hollywood movies would not be the same without recurrent faces like his.

Films include: 1940 My Son Is Guilty (GB: Crime's End); Arizona. '44 Buffalo Bill. '46 Abilene Town. '50 The Great Missouri Raid; Cheaper by the Dozen. '58 The Sheepman. '62 The Comancheros; Ride the High Country (GB: Guns in the Afternoon). '63 Move Over, Darling. '67 Welcome to Hard Times (GB: Killer on a Horse).

BUCHANAN, Jack

(1891–1957). Actor. Born: Helensburgh, Dunbarton, Scotland

Jack Buchanan was primarily a song-and-dance man and light comedian on the London stage, immaculate in white tie and tails, seeming to sing and dance casually and effortlessly. He was in *The Grass Widow* at the Apollo Theatre in 1912, and from 1922 he began to produce as well as act in plays, musical comedies and revues. His movie career fell into three phases: he was a silent star in the Twenties; he specialized mainly in British musicals in the Thirties, running a production company with Herbert Wilcox; and he made a brilliant comeback in Hollywood in the Fifties playing the over-enthusiastic Broadway producer in *The Band Wagon* (in which he co-starred with Fred Astaire), following this with a few last British comedies. His idiosyncratic singing style also made him a successful recording artist.

Films include: 1925 The Happy Ending. '27 Confetti. '30 Monte Carlo (USA). '32 Goodnight Vienna. '33 That's a Good Girl (+ dir). '35 Brewster's Millions. '36 When Knights Were Bold. '37 The Sky's the Limit. '39 The Gang's All Here. '53 The Band Wagon (USA). '55 As Long as They're Happy.

BUCHHOLZ, Horst

(b. 1933). Actor. Born: Horst Buchholtz; Berlin, Germany

In his teens Buchholz was acting in the theatre and on radio as well as dubbing films. In 1951 he took up acting professionally, appearing at the Schloss and Schiller Theatres in Berlin. Then Julien Duvivier cast him in the French film *Marianne de Ma Jeunesse*. Buchholz won acting prizes in Germany and at Cannes for his third film, *Himmel ohne Sterne*. He was soon a top box-office star in Germany and began to do English-language films such as *Tiger Bay* and *The Magnificent Seven*. After appearing on the Broadway stage he was signed by Warners for *Fanny*, an ambitious remake of Marcel Pagnol's Thirties films of life on the Marseilles waterfront. Although he has continued to work regularly, Buchholz's international success did not outlast the early Sixties.

Films include: 1955 Marianne de Ma Jeunesse (FR-GER); Himmel ohne Sterne. '57 Die Bekenntnisse des Hochstaplers Felix Krull (USA; The Confessions of Felix Krull); Monpti. '59 Tiger Bay (GB). '60 The

Magnificent Seven (USA). '61 One, Two, Three (USA); Fanny (USA). '63 Nine Hours to Rama (GB). '65 La Fabuleuse Aventure de Marco Polo (FR-IT-YUG-AFGHAN) (GB: The Fabulous Adventures of Marco Polo). '72 The Great Waltz (USA). '78 The Savage Bees (USA).

BUCHMAN, Sidney

(1902–1975). Screenwriter/producer. Born: Duluth, Minnesota, USA

After studies at Minnesota, Columbia and Oxford universities, Buchman was an assistant stage director for a year at London's Old Vic Theatre. Back in New York he wrote plays and won a screenwriting contract with Paramount. He then switched to Columbia, becoming a producer in 1937. From 1942 to 1951 he was assistant to Harry Cohn, head of Columbia, and had his own production company within the studio. Then in 1952, as a former member of the Communist Party, he refused to testify before the House Un-American Activities Committee. Found guilty of contempt, he was blacklisted until 1960. His best comedy scripts, in the Thirties and Forties, had explored the oppositions between innocent and honest country life and the sophisticated, corrupt city.

He shared an Academy Award for the screenplay of *Here Comes Mr Jordan*, but he wrote nothing better than the magnificent script for Capra's *Mr Smith Goes to Washington*.

Films include: 1932 The Sign of the Cross (co-sc). '35 She Married Her Boss (sc). '36 Theodora Goes Wild (sc). '38 Holiday (co-sc) (GB: Free to Live). '39 Mr Smith Goes to Washington (sc). '41 Here Comes Mr Jordan (co-sc). '42 The Talk of the Town (co-sc). '45 A Song to Remember (prod; + sc). '46 The Jolson Story (co-sc). '49 Jolson Sings Again (prod; + sc). '63 Cleopatra (co-sc). '65 The Group (prod; + sc).

BUJOLD, Geneviève

(b. 1942). Actress. Born: Montreal, Quebec, Canada

From a French-Canadian working-class background, Bujold started as an actress in French-language theatre. For the first ten years of her career she made more films in Canada than abroad, including three directed by her then husband Paul Almond (married 1967–73). But they were never seen anywhere else, and she has had to concentrate on working in America, Britain and France to follow up her early success in *La Guerre Est*

Finie and, especially, *Anne of the Thousand Days*, in which her performance as Anne Boleyn brought her an Academy Award nomination. Her kittenish face and fragile figure make her look younger than her years, but she has struggled long and hard for international stardom which she has only precariously achieved, despite her undoubted talent.

Films include: 1966 La Guerre Est Finie (FR-SWED) (GB: The War Is Over); Le Roi de Coeur (IT-FR) (USA/GB: King of Hearts). '68 Isabel (CAN). '69 Anne of the Thousand Days (GB). '70 Act of the Heart (CAN). '71 The Trojan Women (USA). '74 Earthquake (USA). '76 Obsession (USA). '77 Un Autre Homme une Autre Chance (FR) (USA: Another Man, Another Woman; GB: Another Man, Another Chance). '78 Coma (USA). '79 Murder by Decree (GB-CAN) (USA: Sherlock Holmes: Murder by Decree).

Above, far left: Dora Bryan. Above left: Edgar Buchanan in The Swordsman *(1947). Below, from left to right: Yul Brynner in* Taras Bulba; *Horst Buchholz in* The Magnificent Seven; *Geneviève Bujold in* Anne of the Thousand Days. *Bottom, from left to right: Jack Buchanan in* Brewster's Millions; *John Bunny in* Bunny's Suicide *(1912); Luis Buñuel*

BUNNY, John

(1863–1915). Actor. Born: New York City, USA

The son of an English naval officer, John Bunny was on the stage at 20 in vaudeville. In 1910 he was engaged to act in comedy films by Vitagraph and by 1912 he was earning $1000 a week. In that year he made some films in England for Vitagraph, and he continued working until he fell ill and died in 1915. He was a very large, fat man, finally weighing 300 pounds. For most of his four years in films he was the most famous comedian in the world. He played some classic roles in Dickens and Thackeray adaptations, but his usual character was that of a selfish, rather raffish husband much beset by women and henpecked, generally by his regular foil Flora Finch. Bunny had grace and elegance in spite of his enormous bulk, and he went beyond slapstick to a comedy of manners and character.

Films include: 1911 A Tale of Two Cities; Vanity Fair. '12 Cure for Pokeritis; Stenographer Wanted; Bunny All at Sea; Bunny at the Derby. '13 Bunny Blarneyed, or the Blarney Stone; The Feudists; Pickwick Papers; Bunny for the Cause.

BUNUEL, Luis

(1900–1983). Director. Born: Calanda, Spain

Buñuel was the great iconoclast of cinema, with an untiring capacity to shock and surprise. Born into the Spanish middle class and educated by the Jesuits, he never ceased to denounce with biting humour the repressive bonds of religion and the bourgeoisie. Spain's greatest director, he rarely worked in his native country after the Thirties, spending long periods in the USA, Mexico and France. His film career began among the Surrealists in Paris, and this strand was constant in his work, convincingly combined with a down-to-earth stylistic realism and a brisk way with telling a story. His best films combine passion and intellectual force with anarchic and frequently absurdist comedy, an element that became more marked with the passing of time. His own adaptability to awkward working circumstances that did not ease till his later years was remarkable and exemplary. He won major prizes for several films.

Films include: 1928 Un Chien Andalou (co-dir) (FR). '30 L'Age d'Or (FR). '32 Las Hurdes – Tierra Sin Pan (doc) (SP) (USA/GB: Land Without Bread). '50 Los Olvidados (MEX) (USA/GB: The Young and the Damned). '53 Él (MEX) (USA: This Strange Passion). '54 Robinsón Crusoe/ Adventures of Robinson Crusoe (MEX-USA). '58 Nazarín (MEX). '61 Viridiana (SP-MEX). '62 El Ángel Exterminador (MEX) (USA/GB: The Exterminating Angel). '64 Le Journal d'une Femme de Chambre (FR-IT) (USA/GB: The Diary of a Chambermaid). '67 Belle de Jour (FR-IT). '70 Tristana (FR-IT-SP). '72 Le Charme Discret de la Bourgeoisie (FR-SP-IT) (USA/GB: The Discreet Charm of the Bourgeoisie). '74 Le Fantôme de la Liberté (FR) (USA/GB: The Phantom of Liberty). '77 Cet Obscur Objet du Désir (FR-SP) (USA/GB: That Obscure Object of Desire).

BUREL, Léonce-Henry

(1892–1977). Cinematographer.
Born: Indret, France

Burel's career began in 1913 when he photographed some comedy shorts; but it was his work with the director Abel Gance, particularly from *Mater Dolorosa* onwards, that established his reputation as a leading cameraman. Their most interesting experimental work together was on *La Roue* – Burel was not mainly responsible for the great *Napoleon*, only supervising the second-unit cameramen. He also worked with Jacques Feyder and Rex Ingram, among many others. His most notable later contribution was to the Fifties films of Robert Bresson, where his harsh greys and sooty matt blacks perfectly matched the director's abstract realism. Burel continued to work until 1966, notching up some one hundred and twenty credits, including three as director or co-director.

Films include: 1917 Mater Dolorosa. '18 J'Accuse. '23 La Roue (co-photo). '25 Visages d'Enfants (co-photo) (SWITZ) (USA: Faces of Children). '27 Napoléon (co-photo) (GB: Napoleon). '28 The Three Passions (GB). '32 Baroud (co-photo) (FR-GB) (USA: Love in Morocco). '37 La Mort du Cygne. '41 La Vénus Aveugle. '51 Le Journal d'un Curé de Campagne (USA/GB: Diary of a Country Priest). '56 Un Condamné à Mort S'Est Echappé ou Le Vent Souffle Où Il Veut (USA/GB: A Man Escaped). '59 Pickpocket. '62 Le Procès de Jeanne d'Arc (USA/GB: The Trial of Joan of Arc).

BURKE, Billie

(1885–1970). Actress. Born: Mary William Ethelbert Appleton Burke; Washington DC, USA

Billie Burke's father was a famous clown (Billy Burke) and for the first few years of her life she toured much of Europe with both parents, ending up in England. In 1902 she appeared on the stage in her own right at the London Pavilion. Five years later the impresario Charles Frohman took her to Broadway to star opposite John Drew in *My Wife*. A red-haired beauty with a tremulous voice, she became the toast of New York society. While at a party she met Florenz Ziegfeld and they were married in 1914. The following year she signed a film contract with Thomas Ince but, not yet at home in pictures, she returned to the stage. When Ziegfeld was ruined by the Wall Street Crash in 1929, Billie Burke returned to Hollywood in order to support him until his death in 1932. This time she enjoyed herself and went on to appear as a fluffy, feather-brained comedienne in films such as *Dinner at Eight*, *The Wizard of Oz* and *The Man Who Came to Dinner*. In 1949 her autobiography, *With a Feather on My Nose*, was published.

Films include: 1933 Dinner at Eight; Christopher Strong; Only Yesterday. '34 Forsaking All Others. '35 After Office Hours; Doubting Thomas. '37 Topper. '38 Merrily We Live. '39 The Wizard of Oz. '41 The Man Who Came to Dinner. '50 Father of the Bride.

BURKS, Robert

(1910–1968). Cinematographer.
Born: Newport Beach, California, USA

Between 1944 and 1949 Robert Burks was a special-effects technician at Warner Brothers. He then became a director of photography and moved on to Paramount in the same capacity. During the Fifties and Sixties he was primarily involved on Alfred Hitchcock's movies, providing the broodingly threatening and tense atmospheres for Hitchcock's famous thrillers. Because Burks was always ready to provide exactly what was requested of him, his work varied in range and standard.

Films include: 1944 Arsenic and Old Lace (sp. eff. only). '46 Night and Day (sp. eff. only). '47 The Unsuspected (sp. eff. only). '48 Key Largo (sp. eff. only). '50 The Glass Menagerie. '51 Strangers on a Train. '54 Dial M For Murder; Rear Window. '57 The Spirit of St Louis. '58 Vertigo. '59 North by Northwest. '63 The Birds.

BURNETT, Carol

(b. 1933). Comedienne/actress.
Born: San Antonio, Texas, USA

While at the University of California at Los Angeles (UCLA), Carol Burnett began acting and on graduation went to drama school. Her first professional assignment was as the girlfriend of a ventriloquist's dummy on a television show. She then set about establishing herself as a brash comedienne and eventually was given *The Carol Burnett Show* on television, part of her act being spoofs on movies – *Mildred Fierce*, *From There to Eternity* and the famous 'dress-from-old-curtain' scene from *Gone With the Wind* (1939) which, in Burnett's version, included curtain rods and hooks. Despite her success on stage, radio and television, she has found it hard to break into films, but was superb both as the

tight-lipped, moral mother of the bride in *A Wedding*, and as the alcoholic, nymphomaniac matron of the orphanage in *Annie*.

Films: 1963 Who's Been Sleeping in My Bed? '72 Pete 'n' Tillie. '74 The Front Page. '78 A Wedding. '80 Health. '82 Annie.

BURNS, George

(b. 1896). Comedian/actor. Born: Nathan Birnbaum; New York City, USA

When he was 12 years old George Burns formed the Peewee Quartet with three friends, and for a year or so they toured the saloons around Staten Island. A few years later he formed a vaudeville act 'Brown and Williams, Singers and Dancers and Roller Skaters', before going it alone as a song-and-dance comedian. In the Twenties he teamed up with (and married) Gracie Allen, and together they became incredibly successful, appearing on the radio and making a handful of comedy films. Their act consisted of comic banter calling

for Burns to be the straightman, a role he excelled in with his impeccable sense of timing. Having made what he thought was his last film in 1939, Burns was brought out of retirement to replace Jack Benny (after Benny's sudden death) in *The Sunshine Boys*. Since then, from the age of 79, he has found a new, enthusiastic audience among those who missed him the first time around.

Films include: 1932 The Big Broadcast. '33 College Humor. '35 The Big Broadcast of 1936. '37 A Damsel in Distress. '38 College Swing (GB: Swing, Teacher, Swing). '75 The Sunshine Boys. '77 Oh, God! '78 Sergeant Pepper's Lonely Hearts Club Band (USA-GER). '79 Just You and Me Kid; Going in Style.

BURR, Raymond

(b. 1917). Actor. Born: New Westminster, British Columbia, Canada

Raymond Burr made his acting debut with his local stock company in Vancouver when only 12 years old. After graduating he became a director of and lecturer at the Pasadena Community Playhouse, near Los Angeles, before starting his career as a screen actor. Over six foot, with a large frame and square jaw, he was unsurprisingly cast as a supporting heavy in most of his films. However, once he moved into television his image went to the opposite extreme and he became the ever-triumphant lawyer *Perry Mason* and, later, the wheelchair-ridden detective *Ironside* with enormous success. Seventeen years on television resulted in his becoming a multi-millionaire and in 1979 – perhaps to compensate for a tragic private life (two wives died, a third divorced him and a son died of leukaemia at the age of 10) – he bought a South Pacific island in order to give a home to over sixty deprived children.

Films include: 1946 Without Reservations. '48 Walk a Crooked Mile. '49 Criss Cross. '50 Key to the City. '51 A Place in the Sun. '52 Horizons West. '53 The Blue Gardenia. '54 Casanova's Big Night; Rear Window; Gorilla at Large. '56 Great Day in the Morning. '57 Crime of Passion. '78 Tomorrow Never Comes. '80 Out of the Blue.

BURSTYN, Ellen

(b. 1932). Actress. Born: Edna Rae Gillooly; Detroit, Michigan, USA

Ellen Burstyn is an actress who excels in roles calling for the eventual triumph of a downtrodden but determined woman, and perhaps this is the direct result of her own hard struggle to establish herself as an actress. She was an art student, a fashion model, waitress, shop assistant and dancer before going into television commercials under the name Keri Flynn. She then appeared on television as a Gleason Girl in Jackie Gleason's comedy show (this time under the name Edna Rae) until given her chance to appear in *Fair Game* on Broadway. After attending the Actors' Studio, she made an impression in *Tropic of Cancer* under her married name of Burstyn, and then appeared in a string of films prior to her Tony Award-winning performance in *Same Time, Next Year* on Broadway (a role she re-created on screen). She received an Oscar for her portrayal of Alice Hyatt in *Alice Doesn't Live Here Anymore* and has been nominated for Academy Awards for *The Last Picture Show*, *The Exorcist*

and *Same Time, Next Year*, in which she played an adulteress who sees her lover once every 12 months.

Films include: 1964 Goodbye Charlie. '69 Tropic of Cancer. '70 Alex in Wonderland. '71 The Last Picture Show. '72 The King of Marvin Gardens. '73 The Exorcist. '74 Alice Doesn't Live Here Anymore; Harry and Tonto. '77 Providence. '78 A Dream of Passion (SWITZ-GREECE); Same Time, Next Year. '80 Resurrection.

BURTON, Richard

(1925–1984). Actor. Born: Richard Jenkins; Pontrhydyfen, South Wales

The twelfth of a coal-miner's thirteen children, the young Richard Jenkins was most influenced by his school drama and English teacher Philip Burton. In 1943 Richard became Philip Burton's ward and took his surname. Encouraged by his mentor, he read Classics at Oxford and became the mainstay of the Oxford University Drama Society. After national service he established himself as a distinguished performer. His film career took off at around the same time and his good looks, very distinctive

voice and generally fiery screen persona – perhaps best exemplified in *Look Back in Anger* – should have won him better roles. As it was he became rather too embroiled in costume drama and an over-emphatic style. Additionally, he had begun his stormy relationship with Elizabeth Taylor. He alternated between stage and screen and was nominated for Oscars for his performances in *Anne of the Thousand Days* (1969), *The Robe*, *My Cousin Rachel* (1952), *The Spy Who Came in From the Cold*, *Who's Afraid of Virginia Woolf?* and *Becket*. Burton was married four times: Sybil Williams (1949–63); Elizabeth Taylor (1964–74 and 1975–76); Suzy Hunt (1976). He was a CBE.

Films include: 1953 The Robe (USA). '54 Prince of Players (USA). '55 The Rains of Ranchipur (USA). '59 Look Back in Anger. '63 Cleopatra (USA); The VIPs (USA; International Hotel). '64 The Night of the Iguana (USA); Becket. '65 The Spy Who Came in From the Cold. '66 Who's Afraid of Virginia Woolf? (USA). '67 The Taming of the Shrew (USA-IT). '68 Where Eagles Dare. '71 Under Milk Wood. '72 Hammersmith Is Out. '77 Equus; Exorcist II: The Heretic (USA). '78 The Wild Geese.

Top, far left: Billie Burke in Topper. *Top left: George Burns in* The Sunshine Boys. *Above left: Ellen Burstyn in* The King of Marvin Gardens. *Above: Carol Burnett in* Pete 'n' Tillie. *Right: Richard Burton in* Where Eagles Dare. *Below: Raymond Burr in* Rear Window

in 1927. His was a lengthy but undistinguished career, but *Sunny Side Up* stands out as an imaginatively handled and zestful film. His work is that of a competent studio director specializing in comedies and musicals featuring the likes of Bing Crosby, Shirley Temple and Doris Day. His career as an actor in silent days was quite similar; he worked with such illustrious directors as John Ford, Frank Borzage and D. W. Griffith, and his performances were reliable and unassuming.

Films as director include: 1929 Sunny Side Up. '31 A Connecticut Yankee at King Arthur's Court (GB: A Yankee at King Arthur's Court). '35 The Little Colonel. '36 White Fang. '37 Ali Baba Goes to Town. '42 Road to Morocco. '43 Thank Your Lucky Stars. '44 The Princess and the Pirate. '53 Calamity Jane. '54 The Command.

BUTTONS, Red

(b. 1918). Actor/comedian.
Born: Aaron Chwatt; New York City, USA

At the age of 16, immigrant-milliner's son Aaron Chwatt was a singing bellhop at Dinty Moore's City Island Tavern in the Bronx. For the job he had to wear a uniform with prominent, shiny buttons and thus became known as Red Buttons. After working as a vaudeville comedian and appearing in a few films he was given his own show on television in 1952. In 1957 he was offered the role of Sergeant Joe Kelly in *Sayonara*, and his sensitive tragi-comic portrayal led to his being awarded an Oscar for Best Supporting Actor. This in turn led to many more film appearances (notably as the sailor dance contestant in *They Shoot Horses, Don't They?*), although he still works mostly in nightclubs and on television.

Films include: 1944 Winged Victory. '57 Sayonara. '62 The Longest Day. '66 Stagecoach. '69 They Shoot Horses, Don't They? '72 The Poseidon Adventure. '76 Gable and Lombard. '77 Pete's Dragon. '78 Movie Movie. '80 When Time Ran Out . . . .

BYINGTON, Spring

(1893–1971). Actress. Born: Colorado Springs, Colorado, USA

While still in her teens Spring Byington began touring America with a Denver stock company and by 1924 was appearing on Broadway. By 1933 she was in films, often playing good-hearted, slightly dotty mothers or aunts (she was Marmee in *Little Women*, for example), and she was nominated for an Oscar for her performance as the distracted lady of the house in *You Can't Take It With You*. Between 1936 and 1940 she was a regular in the film series that followed the fortunes of the 'Jones Family' and in the Fifties appeared on television in the *December Bride* and *Laramie* series.

Films include: 1933 Little Women. '35 Ah, Wilderness!; Mutiny on the Bounty; Way Down East. '36 The Charge of the Light Brigade. '38 You Can't Take It With You. '41 Meet John Doe. '42 Roxie Hart. '46 Dragonwyck. '60 Please Don't Eat the Daisies.

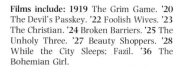

Left: Spring Byington with the corn in Down on the Farm *(1938). Above left: Francis X. Bushman. Above: Red Buttons in uniform for* Sayonara. *Top: Mae Busch with Laurel and Hardy up in* Them Thar Hills *(1934)*

BUSCH, Mae

(1897–1946). Actress. Born: Melbourne, Australia

Mae Busch was taken to America as a child and educated at a convent in New Jersey. By 1912 she had joined the Keystone studio and rose steadily to leading roles, specializing in vamps and shady ladies. In Erich von Stroheim's *Foolish Wives* she epitomized phony glamour, while in Tod Browning's *The Unholy Three* she was a bad penny who redeemed herself in the end. During the Thirties Busch became perhaps better known as the sharp-tongued virago in Laurel and Hardy films. She continued to work in shorts, B pictures and on the stage until her death.

Films include: 1919 The Grim Game. '20 The Devil's Passkey. '22 Foolish Wives. '23 The Christian. '24 Broken Barriers. '25 The Unholy Three. '27 Beauty Shoppers. '28 While the City Sleeps; Fazil. '36 The Bohemian Girl.

BUSHMAN, Francis X.

(1883–1966). Actor. Born: Norfolk, Virginia, USA

Francis X. Bushman had always wanted to act and took to the stage at an early age. By 1911 he was also appearing in films and, aided by his good looks and physique, quickly became an extremely popular romantic star. *Romeo and Juliet* provided him with an early success, but it was as Messala in *Ben-Hur* that he really came to prominence. Although his early acting style was extremely rhetorical and – particularly in *Ben-Hur* – frequently over the top, his technique mellowed with age and his later appearances as a character actor show much sensitivity.

Films include: 1912 The Magic Wand; The Fall of Montezuma. '13 The Spy's Defeat. '16 In the Diplomatic Service. '25 The Masked Bride; Ben-Hur. '27 The Thirteenth Juror. '44 Wilson. '51 David and Bathsheba. '54 Sabrina (GB: Sabrina Fair).

BUTLER, David

(1894–1979). Director/actor. Born: David Wyngate Butler; San Francisco, California, USA

David Butler's father was a theatre director who encouraged his son to appear on the stage from an early age. Educated at the Lowell High School, Hitchcock Military Academy and Stanford University, he followed family tradition on graduation and directed his first film, *High School Hero*,

CAAN, James

(b. 1939). Actor. Born: New York City, USA

Educated at Michigan State University and Hofstra College, Long Island, Caan studied acting for two years at the Neighborhood Playhouse before his off-Broadway debut in *La Ronde* in 1961. Broadway and television work preceded his first film appearances in 1963. This large, muscular man soon showed himself capable of surprising gentleness and subtlety, two notable performances for Howard Hawks being followed by his touching portrayal of a mentally retarded footballer in Francis Ford Coppola's *The Rain People* (1969). Caan's breakthrough came with his Sonny Corleone in *The Godfather*. Since then he has been a big box-office name, notably in *Rollerball*. He has also directed himself in *Hide in Plain Sight*.

Films include: 1963 Lady in a Cage. **'65** Red Line 7000. **'66** El Dorado. **'67** Games. **'69** The Rain People. **'72** The Godfather. **'73** Slither. **'74** The Gambler. **'75** Funny Lady; Rollerball. **'77** A Bridge Too Far (GB). **'78** Comes a Horseman. **'80** Hide in Plain Sight (+dir). **'81** Thief (GB: Violent Streets); Les Uns et les Autres (FR) (USA: The Ins and the Outs).

CABANNE, Christy

(1888–1950). Director. Born: William Christy Cabanne; St Louis, Missouri, USA

Christy Cabanne was one of the many assistants of D.W. Griffith who developed into fully-fledged directors. Entering movies in 1910 after naval service, he joined Griffith as actor, assistant director, and (from 1913) director. He soon rose high, directing Douglas Fairbanks in early action-comedies, and the Gish sisters. Later, his simple, swift style condemned him to programme pictures, although he had a spell at MGM in the Twenties with more generous budgets and big stars. This period included his uncredited direction of the Madonna scenes in *Ben-Hur* (1925). In the Thirties and Forties Cabanne was down to B Westerns, Spanish versions, and the cheapest of action pictures.

Films include: 1914 The Hunchback; The Sisters; The Life of General Villa (co-dir). **'15** The Lamb. **'16** Diane of the Follies; Reggie Mixes In. **'25** The Masked Bride (co-dir). **'26** Monte Carlo. **'30** Conspiracy. **'34** Jane Eyre. **'36** We Who Are About to Die. **'41** Scattergood Baines.

CABOT, Bruce

(1905–1972). Actor. Born: Etienne Jacques de Bujac; Carlsbad, New Mexico, USA

A hard-working heavy for forty years, Bruce Cabot was of Franco-Irish and Cherokee descent, the son of a wealthy lawyer, and educated at the University of the South at Sewanee, Tennessee. He had a varied early life, with spells as prize-fighter and stage actor, and dabbled in bonds and real estate. He got his film break in 1932 while running a Hollywood nightclub, and the following year he was the human hero of *King Kong*, one of his rare sympathetic roles. He was memorable, too, as the local rabble-rouser in Fritz Lang's *Fury*, but by and large he had few chances to exercise his gifts as a brutal if handsome villain in other than routine action movies. When his career faded, his friendship with John Wayne helped to keep it alive in such films as *Hatari!* and *The Comancheros*. He married four times, one of his wives being actress Adrienne Ames.

Films include: 1933 King Kong. **'36** Robin Hood of El Dorado; Fury. **'40** Flame of New Orleans. **'43** The Desert Song. **'45** Fallen Angel. **'47** The Angel and the Badman. **'58** The Quiet American; The Sheriff of Fractured Jaw (GB). **'62** Hatari!; The Comancheros. **'65** Cat Ballou. **'66** The Chase. **'67** The War Wagon. **'68** The Green Berets. **'69** The Undefeated. **'70** Chisum. **'71** Big Jake; Diamonds Are Forever (GB).

CACOYANNIS, Michael

(b. 1922). Director/writer. Born: Mikhalis Kakogiannis; Cyprus

Michael Cacoyannis came to England to study law, and during World War II was a producer for the Greek Service of the BBC. He studied acting at the Central School of Dramatic Art in London, and direction at the Old Vic, making his stage debut in 1946 as Herod in Oscar Wilde's *Salome*. He began writing in 1950, returned to Greece in 1953, and wrote and directed his first film that year. His early films gained international success. They were fresh, lively and charming, and they introduced vivid new players like Melina Mercouri. *Stella*, starring Mercouri, won the Critics' Prize at Cannes, and the Golden Globe from Hollywood's foreign press. In the Sixties Cacoyannis went to the USA, directing Greek tragedy and opera in the theatre, and making his most famous film, *Zorba the Greek*. He writes the scripts for all of his films.

Films include: 1954 Kyriakatiko Xypnima (GB: Windfall in Athens). **'55** Stella; To Koritsi Me Ta Mavra (GB: The Girl in Black). **'57** To Telefteo Psema (GB: A Matter of Dignity). **'60** Eroica (GB: Our Last Spring). **'61** Il Relitto (IT) (GB: The Wastrel). **'62** Electra. **'64** Zorba the Greek (USA). **'67** The Day the Fish Came Out (GB). **'71** The Trojan Women (USA). **'75** Attila 74 (doc). **'77** Iphigenia.

Left: James Caan in The Godfather.
Below: Bruce Cabot with Fay Wray in King Kong

CAGNEY, James

(1899–1986). Actor. Born: James Francis Cagney Jr; New York City, USA

James Cagney was educated at Columbia University, by 1920 was a Broadway chorus boy, and spent the next ten years in vaudeville, plays and revues. He made his film debut in 1930, and the following year his startling performance as the gangster Tom Powers in *The Public Enemy* made him a star. For three decades he played leads, and was active off screen as well. He was an early organizer of the Screen Actors' Guild, and President in 1942–43. For long under contract to Warner Brothers, he frequently fought them over salary and parts, and briefly, in 1936, left them for Grand National. In 1942 Cagney won an Academy Award as Best Actor for *Yankee Doodle Dandy*, while in 1974 he won the American Film Institute's Life Achievement Award. Cagney retired after making *One, Two, Three* in 1961, but surprised and delighted his fans by returning in 1981 in *Ragtime*. One of the great screen actors of all time, Cagney exemplified the truth that, for cinema, the role must be a projection of the actor's essential self. As times changed, so his roles shifted from sympathetic heavies to heroes, and back again (as in *White Heat*) to monstrous egoists. He enjoyed the odd departure from type, too, using his vaudeville background for *Footlight Parade* and *Yankee Doodle Dandy*, and turning in a marvellously vulnerable and moving Bottom in Max Reinhardt's *A Midsummer Night's Dream*. But whatever he played, there was always the electric energy, rapid delivery and undaunted cock-sparrow charm that spelt Cagney.

Films include: 1931 The Public Enemy (GB: Enemies of the Public); Blonde Crazy (GB: Larceny Lane). '32 The Crowd Roars. '33 Hard to Handle; Footlight Parade. '35 G-Men; A Midsummer Night's Dream; Ceiling Zero. '38 Angels with Dirty Faces. '39 Each Dawn I Die. '41 The Strawberry Blonde. '42 Yankee Doodle Dandy. '48 The Time of Your Life. '49 White Heat. '53 A Lion Is in the Streets. '55 Mister Roberts. '61 One, Two, Three. '81 Ragtime.

CAHN, Sammy

(b. 1913). Lyricist. Born: Samuel Cohen; New York City, USA

Sammy Cahn's family were Polish immigrants, living on the Lower East Side of Manhattan. In his early days, Sammy played the violin for strip acts in burlesque houses. His first songwriting partner, around 1935, was Saul Chaplin. Later he worked with Jules Styne. His songs have been heard in films from 1940 onwards, and four of them, the best known being 'Three Coins in the Fountain', won Academy Awards. In 1974 Cahn gave his first stage performance, singing his own songs in *Words and Music* at the Golden Theatre. Words and music was the story of Cahn's life.

Films include: 1940 Argentine Nights. '45 Anchors Aweigh. '46 The Kid from Brooklyn; Cinderella Jones. '48 Romance on the High Seas. '54 Three Coins in the Fountain. '56 Anything Goes; Meet Me in Las Vegas. '57 Pal Joey; The Joker Is Wild. '59 A Hole in the Head. '62 Road to Hong Kong. '67 Thoroughly Modern Millie.

CAINE, Michael

(b. 1933). Actor. Born: Maurice Joseph Micklewhite; Bermondsey, London, England

Michael Caine was raised in London's East End, his father a fish-market porter, his mother a charlady. The young Caine worked as a cement-mixer, a building labourer, and in Smithfield meat market. He took part in amateur dramatics, joined a repertory company as assistant stage manager, and got a part when a cockney accent was needed. He acted with Joan Littlewood's Theatre Workshop, and spent five years touring and in television before his first large film part in *Zulu*, where, ironically, he played an upper-class English officer. He consolidated his position with his portrayal of the anti-heroic secret agent Harry Palmer in three films drawn from Len Deighton novels, and has continued playing leading roles in Britain, and latterly in the USA, with much success. Tough, sympathetic, and with a great sense of fun, Michael Caine comes nearer than anyone to being a true working-class hero of British movies, carrying with him into every role a bit of *Alfie*'s charmingly conniving cockney cheekiness.

Films include: 1963 Zulu. '65 The Ipcress File. '66 Alfie; Funeral in Berlin. '67 Billion Dollar Brain. '70 Get Carter. '73 Sleuth. '75 The Man Who Would Be King. '76 The Eagle Has Landed; Harry and Walter Go to New York (USA). '78 California Suite (USA). '80 Dressed to Kill (USA).

CALAMAI, Clara

(b. 1915). Actress. Born: Prato, Italy

Clara Calamai was taken to Rome as a child, played her first film part in 1938 and rapidly became the biggest star of Italian cinema. In 1941 alone she had leading parts in 14 films. She possessed talent and charm, and specialized in playing troublesome women. Her most famous role was in Luchino Visconti's *Ossessione*, in which she played the unfaithful and murderous wife. Calamai's career waned after the war, her only important appearance being in another Visconti film, *White Nights*.

Films include 1939 Ettore Fieramosca. '40 Boccaccio. '41 Regina di Navarra. '42 Ossessione. '45 Adultera; La Resa di Titi (GB: The Merry Chase). '46 Ultimo Amore. '57 Le Notti Bianche (FR-IT) (USA/GB: White Nights). '58 Aphrodite. '67 Le Streghe (IT-FR) (GB: The Witches).

CALHERN, Louis

(1895–1956). Actor. Born: Carl Vogt; New York City, USA

Louis Calhern was on the New York stage at 14. Thereafter he played in repertory, vaudeville, burlesque, in drama, Shakespeare and musicals. He had a long and distinguished Broadway career, acted in a few silent films in the early Twenties, and came back for steady employment as a character player from 1931 until his death. Tall, hawk-nosed, suave and imposing, Calhern went through various phases in his movie career. An arrogant college-boy in *The Blot*, Calhern got his comeuppance, and the girl as well; his Thirties villains had to settle for the former. But he gained in solidity and dignity in his last decade, usually at MGM. He played *Julius Caesar* alongside Marlon Brando and John Gielgud; he was Oliver Wendell Holmes in *The Magnificent Yankee*; he was curiously touching in *The Asphalt Jungle*, as a crooked lawyer absurdly snared by love. And he died on the job, in Tokyo, filming *The Teahouse of the August Moon*.

Films include: 1921 The Blot. '33 Duck Soup. '34 The Count of Monte Cristo. '35 The Last Days of Pompeii. '37 The Life of Emile Zola. '46 Notorious. '50 Annie Get Your Gun; The Asphalt Jungle; The Magnificent Yankee (GB: The Man With Thirty Sons). '53 Julius Caesar. '54 Executive Suite. '56 High Society.

CALHOUN, Rory,

(b. 1922). Actor. Born: Francis Timothy McGown; Hollywood, California, USA

Francis Durgin, as he became on adoption when his father was lost at sea, won the Golden Gloves title as a young boxer, and then wandered the West doing lumberjacking and cowpunching. He served a three-year sentence in Springfield State Prison for car-stealing, but then his life changed overnight when he was spotted by Alan Ladd, whose wife, an agent, found work for him at 20th Century-Fox. Tall, athletic, ruggedly handsome, he played small parts until his appearance as Jim Corbett in *The Great John L.* led to stardom in Westerns and other action pictures. Calhoun also appeared in two films with Marilyn Monroe. He was married for 21 years to actress Lita Baron before they were divorced in 1970.

Films include: 1945 The Great John L. '51 I'd Climb the Highest Mountain. '53 Powder River; How to Marry a Millionaire.

'54 River of No Return; Four Guns to the Border; A Bullet Is Waiting. '55 The Treasure of Pancho Villa; Ain't Misbehavin'; The Spoilers. '62 Requiem for a Heavyweight. '72 Night of the Lepus.

CALLEIA, Joseph

(1887–1975). Actor. Born: Joseph Alexander Herstall Vincent Calleja; Rebat, Malta

Sent to London by his parents to study engineering, young Calleja preferred the music-hall stage, where he did impressions of Harry Lauder, no easy feat for a Maltese. Voice training led to a singing career in Italy and New York, and modest success. Composing followed; then the stage, with much acclaim in New York and London. From the early Thirties he played numerous character parts in Hollywood films, usually as an oily Latinate heavy, but all his roles had a distinctive flavour. He enjoyed the occasional performance with tongue in cheek, such as his masked bandit in Mae West's *My Little Chickadee*, as a change from racketeers and night-club owners, but was best of all when, as it seldom did, his part had a little depth and complexity. His loyal and agonized cop in *Touch of Evil* is perhaps Calleia's most memorable performance.

Films include: 1936 After the Thin Man. '38 Algiers; Marie Antoinette. '39 Juarez; Golden Boy. '40 My Little Chickadee. '42 The Glass Key. '43 For Whom the Bell Tolls; The Cross of Lorraine. '46 Gilda. '47 The Beginning or the End. '58 Touch of Evil.

CALMETTES, André

(1861–1942). Director/actor. Born: Paris, France

André Calmettes was a famous stage actor who in 1908, together with his colleague Charles Le Bargy, founded the Film d'Art company, which engaged established dramatists and actors from the Comédie Française in an attempt to give respectability to the cinema. The first result was *L'Assassinat du Duc de Guise*, starring Le Bargy (who may also have co-

directed with Calmettes) and featuring original music by Saint-Saëns. Film d'Art soon abandoned original scenarios in favour of adapted novels and plays, but at least it stressed the importance of the writer, and it played a vital role in making the cinema seem as worthy of attention as the theatre. Its products were, however, stagy in decors and acting style, with the director regarding himself simply as a stage producer. In 1913 Calmettes retired from the cinema, returning thereafter for occasional acting appearances.

Films include: 1908 L'Assassinat du Duc de Guise; Le Retour d'Ulysse. '10 La Grande Bretèche (+act); Macbeth; L'Avare; Werther. '11 Madame Sans-Gêne (co-dir). '12 Les Trois Mousquetaires. '25 La Closerie des Genêts (actor only)

CALVERT, Phyllis

(b. 1915). Actress. Born: Phyllis Bickle; London, England

From the age of six she trained as a dancer and at ten she was playing opposite Ellen Terry on stage. Later she appeared in a show specially written for her, *She Shall Have Music*. After this she gave up dancing to concentrate on acting and worked in several provincial repertory companies before reaching the London stage and winning a lead role in a Gainsborough film. Phyllis Calvert's genteel ladylike manner made her a star in the Forties, usually with Rank. In 1946 she went to Hollywood and made a couple of pictures, but she did not establish herself there. Later in her career she concentrated mainly on the stage and on a long-running television series, *Kate*, making only occasional appearances in films, generally in cameo roles. She was excellent as the mother of the deaf girl in *Mandy*.

Films include: 1941 Kipps (USA: The Remarkable Mr Kipps). '42 The Young Mr Pitt. '44 Fanny by Gaslight (USA: Man of Evil). '46 The Magic Bow. '51 Mr Denning Drives North. '52 Mandy (USA: Crash of Silence). '53 The Net (USA: Project M.7). '58 Indiscreet. '68 Twisted Nerve. '69 Oh! What a Lovely War.

Above: Louis Calhern with Marilyn Monroe in The Asphalt Jungle. *Below: Rory Calhoun in* Big Caper *(1957). Right: Joseph Calleia in* The Silk Noose *(1948). Far right: Phyllis Calvert in* The Young Mr Pitt

CAMBRIDGE, Godfrey

(1933–76). Actor. Born: New York City, USA

Cambridge won a four-year scholarship to study medicine but decided instead to become an actor, leaving college in his third year. He acted in many off-Broadway productions, winning the *Village Voice*'s Obie Award in Jean Genet's *The Blacks*; and on Broadway he gained a Tony Award nomination in *Purlie Victorious*. It was as a comedian that he broke into television, initially in *The Jack Paar Show*. Having previously had occasional parts, he established himself in films in the late Sixties. He played both straight and comic roles, but is likely to be best remembered for such portrayals as that of the white bigot who wakes up one morning to find himself turned black in *The Watermelon Man*. Cambridge's compulsive eating probably contributed to his untimely death on the set of the television film *Victory at Entebbe* (1977), in which he was to have played General Idi Amin.

Films include: 1966 A Funny Thing Happened on the Way to the Forum. '67 The Busy Body; The President's Analyst. '68 Bye, Bye, Braverman; The Biggest Bundle of Them All. '70 The Watermelon Man; Cotton Comes to Harlem. '72 Come Back Charleston Blue. '77 Scott Joplin.

CAMUS, Marcel

(1912–1982). Director. Born: Chappes, France

Trained as an artist, Camus was a drawing teacher until he was captured in World War II and held as a prisoner of war for four years. During this time he designed sets and directed plays at camps in Germany. After the war he became an assistant director in films, working with Henri Decoin, Jacques Feyder and others. In the late Fifties he turned to directing and his second film, *Black Orpheus*, a mysterious fable set in the carnival of Rio de Janeiro, won both the Foreign-Language Film Oscar and the Golden Palm at Cannes. Camus became briefly connected with the *nouvelle vague*, though he was a generation older than most of its youthful directors. His later films aroused little interest and after the Sixties he worked mostly in television.

Films include: 1957 Mort en Fraude (USA/GB: Fugitive in Saigon). '59 Orfeu Negro (FR-IT) (USA/GB: Black Orpheus). '60 Os Bandeirantes (FR-IT). '62 L'Oiseau de Paradis (FR-IT) (USA: Dragon Sky). '65 Le Chant du Monde. '68 Vivre la Nuit (FR-IT). '70 Une Eté Sauvage; Le Mur de l'Atlantique. '76 Otalia de Bahia (FR-BRAZ).

CANNON, Dyan

(b. 1937). Actress. Born: Samille Diane Friesen; Tacoma, Washington, USA

Cannon studied anthropology at the University of Washington before going to Los Angeles to work as a model. Producer Jerry Wald arranged a screen test for her and she made her debut on television in *Playhouse 90*.

After a couple of film roles, she acted on Broadway with Jane Fonda in *The Fun Couple*. Having lived with Cary Grant for several years, she married him in 1965 (divorced 1968). She resumed her film career with *Bob & Carol & Ted & Alice*, which decisively established her as a leading actress. Five years later she stopped acting for a few years and directed her first short film *Number One*. When she returned to acting, she carefully chose varied and interesting roles. Blonde and curvy, Dyan Cannon has a world-weary look that goes well with her stop-start career and her evident ambition.

Films include: 1960 The Rise and Fall of Legs Diamond. '69 Bob & Carol & Ted & Alice. '71 The Anderson Tapes; Doctors' Wives; The Love Machine; Such Good Friends. '73 The Last of Sheila. '74 Child Under a Leaf (CAN) (GB: Love Child). '76 Number One (short) (dir. only). '78 Heaven Can Wait; The Revenge of the Pink Panther. '80 Honeysuckle Rose.

CANTINFLAS

(b. 1918). Actor. Born: Mario Moreno; Mexico City, Mexico

Coming from a poor family, he had to leave medical school before qualifying and worked in a tent-show doing bit-parts. Eventually he took over a principal part and was soon the star of the show. This led to the theatre and to some short advertising films. The advertising-film company decided to switch to features, with Cantinflas as vice president and exclusive star. He made a film a year and was more successful in Mexico and South America than Chaplin or *Gone With the Wind* (1939). Cantinflas' success in Hollywood was more equivocal. He did well as the valet Passepartout in *Around the World in 80 Days*. But the attempted follow-up, *Pepe*, was a total flop and he returned to Mexican films, where he continued to play the sad-faced, bright-eyed little man who comes out, against all odds, on top in the end.

Films include: 1937 No te Engañes Corazón. '43 El Circo. '44 Gran Hotel. '52 El Mago. '52 El Bombero Atómico. '55 Arriba el Telón. '56 Around the World in 80 Days (USA). '60 Pepe (USA). '76 El Ministro y Yo. '77 Patrullero 777.

CANTOR, Eddie

(1892–1964). Actor. Born: Edward Israel Iskowitz; New York City, USA

Born of Russian immigrant parents, Cantor was in show business from childhood, rising from singing waiter through burlesque and vaudeville to the Ziegfeld shows. He entered films in 1926 but did not appear regularly until the sound era. In such lively and spectacular Goldwyn musicals as *The Kid From Spain* and *Roman Scandals* Cantor exploited his stage character – he was always the perky, resilient innocent, always ready with a song. He was around forty by then, but still tremendously energetic and youthful, and he put over his songs with the punch of the great vaudeville clown he was. He continued to make films

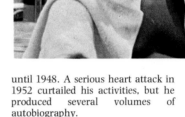

until 1948. A serious heart attack in 1952 curtailed his activities, but he produced several volumes of autobiography.

Films include: 1926 Kid Boots. '29 Glorifying the American Girl. '30 Whoopee! '31 Palmy Days. '32 The Kid From Spain. '33 Roman Scandals. '34 Kid Millions. '36 Strike Me Pink. '43 Thank Your Lucky Stars. '48 If You Knew Susie.

CANUTT, Yakima

(1895–1986). Stunt man/actor/director. Born: Enos Edward Canutt; Colfax, Washington, USA

Of Scots-Irish, Dutch and German (not Red Indian) origins, Canutt won the title of World's Champion All-Round Cowboy five times between 1917 and 1923, and was a leading player in minor Westerns by the mid-Twenties. With the coming of sound he switched mainly to stunting, doubling for John Wayne, Errol Flynn, Clark Gable, Tyrone Power, Randolph Scott and others. In 1939 he took up second-unit directing, co-ordinating the action sequences, and from 1945 also directed a few films. His reputation was made by the stunts he did himself, as in *Stagecoach*, but now mainly rests on the spectacular stunts he staged in such films as *Ben-Hur* and *Spartacus*. He received an Honorary Oscar in 1967 for achievement as a stunt man and for developing safety devices to protect stunt men.

Films include: 1925 Romance and Rustlers (actor). '26 Fighting Stallion (actor). '36 San Francisco (stunt man). '37 Riders of the Dawn (stunt man). '39 Gone With the Wind (stunt man); Stagecoach (2nd unit dir; +stunt man). '42 They Died With Their Boots On (2nd unit dir; +stunt man). '43 In Old Oklahoma/War of the Wildcats (2nd unit dir; +stunt man). '45 Sheriff of Cimarron (dir). '48 Oklahoma Badlands (dir). '54 The Lawless Rider (dir). '59 Ben-Hur (2nd unit dir). '60 Spartacus (2nd unit dir). '64 The Fall of the Roman Empire (2nd unit dir).

CAPELLANI, Albert

(1870–1931). Director. Born: Paris, France

Capellani entered films in 1905 with Pathé and within a few years became the leading director of its art-film subsidiary company, Société Cinématographique des Auteurs et Gens de Lettres (SCAGL). His films, mostly adapted from well-known novels, were thoroughly cinematic, often notable for their sets, lighting and acting. Capellani went to the USA in 1914 and worked there until 1922, directing such stars as Alla Nazimova and Clara Kimball Young, and helping to make the Metro company a force to be respected. Then he became seriously ill, suffering from paralysis. He returned to France but was unable to work again, a tragic loss to the silent cinema. Possibly his most remarkable achievement was the two-part *Les Misérables*, which ran for around five hours.

Films include: 1909 L'Assommoir; L'Arlésienne. '11 Notre Dame de Paris. '12 Les Misérables (part one). '13 Les Misérables (part two); Germinal; La Vie de Bohème. '15 Camille. '19 Out of the Fog; The Red Lantern. '22 Sisters.

CAPRA, Frank

(b. 1897). Director. Born: Palermo, Sicily, Italy

Taken to America at six, Capra later qualified as a chemical engineer at the California Institute of Technology and then served during World War I in the Coast Artillery. He made his way into films by way of comedies; he was a gagman for Mack Sennett and wrote and then also directed for the silent comedian Harry Langdon. On moving to Columbia, Capra developed a line in populist comedy, championing the ordinary American and small-town virtues, that was enormously successful in the Thirties but did not really survive the Forties. During World War II, Capra helped to make the Why We Fight documentary series. After

Above, left to right: Godfrey Cambridge with Estelle Parsons in The Watermelon Man; *Dyan Cannon; Frank Capra. Below, left to right: Cantinflas; Eddie Cantor in* Show Business *(1944); Capucine*

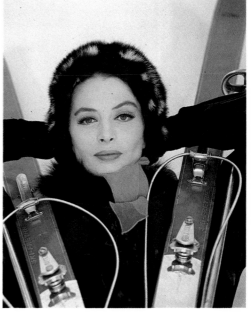

the war, he made one film as an independent producer-director and was then forced to sell the company, Liberty Films, to Paramount, virtually ending his career as an innovative and personal director. He won Best Director Oscars for *It Happened One Night*, *Mr Deeds Goes to Town* and *You Can't Take It With You*, screwball comedies that made the average cinemagoer feel less unimportant in the face of impersonal economic forces while laughing at the rich and rooting for the ordinary guy.

Films include: 1926 Tramp, Tramp, Tramp (co-dir. uncredited); The Strong Man. **'27** Long Pants. **'31** Platinum Blonde. **'32** The Bitter Tea of General Yen. **'34** It Happened One Night. **'36** Mr Deeds Goes to Town. **'37** Lost Horizon. **'38** You Can't Take It With You. **'39** Mr Smith Goes to Washington. **'41** Meet John Doe. **'42** Prelude to War (doc). **'44** Arsenic and Old Lace. **'46** It's a Wonderful Life. **'48** State of the Union (GB: The World and His Wife). **'59** A Hole in the Head. **'61** Pocketful of Miracles.

CAPUCINE

(b. 1935). Actress. Born: Germaine Lefebvre; Toulon, France

Though Capucine's family wanted her to be a schoolteacher, her looks ensured that she became a top fashion model – she was tall, slim and elegant, with a classically structured face, heavy-lidded eyes and a remote, far-away look. Although she could at first speak no English, producer Charles Feldman flew her to Hollywood for a screen test and she was cast as a Russian princess in *Song Without End*. Her career as an international star lasted only a few years. Her best roles were those in which she self-parodyingly played neurotic versions of her own cool, poised persona in such comedies as *The Pink Panther* (Inspector Clouseau's treacherous wife) and *What's New, Pussycat?* (a nymphomaniac treated by a philandering psychiatrist, again played by Peter Sellers).

Films include: 1960 Song Without End (USA). **'62** The Lion (GB); Walk on the Wild Side (USA). **'63** The Pink Panther (USA). **'64** The Seventh Dawn (USA). **'65** What's New, Pussycat? (USA–FR). **'67** The Honey Pot (USA–IT). **'69** Fellini – Satyricon (IT–FR) (USA: Fellini's Satyricon; Fraülein Doktor (IT–YUG). **'71** Soleil Rouge (FR–IT–SP) (USA/GB: Red Sun).

CARDIFF, Jack

(b. 1914). Cinematographer/director. Born: Great Yarmouth, Norfolk, England

Cardiff was a good colour cinematographer whose ambitions took him into directing in the late Fifties. After making 13 films in 17 years, with only moderate success, he returned mainly to his original trade in the mid-Seventies. He began as a child actor, playing with Dorothy Gish, Will Rogers, Pola Negri, Ivor Novello and other stars. Then he became a camera operator and a lighting cameraman for a Technicolor travelogue series. This led on to his work in feature films, especially for Michael Powell and Emeric Pressburger, which culminated in a Best Colour Cinematography Academy Award for *Black Narcissus*. Soon Cardiff was shooting films for such directors as Alfred Hitchcock, John Huston and King Vidor. Cardiff's own best films as a director are probably *Sons and Lovers*, *Young Cassidy* and *Girl on a Motorcycle*.

Films include: 1943 The Life and Death of Colonel Blimp (add. photo). **'46** A Matter of Life and Death (photo). **'47** Black Narcissus (photo). **'48** The Red Shoes (photo). **'50** The Black Rose (photo). **'51** The Magic Box (photo); The African Queen (photo) (USA–GB). **'56** War and Peace (co-photo) (IT–USA). **'60** Sons and Lovers (dir). **'62** The Lion (dir). **'65** Young Cassidy (dir). **'68** Girl on a Motorcycle (dir) (GB–FR). **'78** Death on the Nile (photo). **'80** The Dogs of War (photo).

CARDINALE, Claudia

(b. 1939). Actress. Born: Tunis, Tunisia

Born in Tunisia of Italian parents, Claudia Cardinale grew up to be a dark-haired, dark-eyed, voluptuous Mediterranean beauty, tall enough to play for the Tunisian national basketball team. In 1957 she won a beauty-queen competition, earning a trip to the Venice Film Festival, followed by a movie contract with Franco Cristaldi, who later married her and tried to build her up as the successor to the international Italian stars of the Fifties. Her Italian debut film, *I Soliti Ignoti*, was a smash comedy hit, notably in the USA; but her subsequent career took her only intermittently to Hollywood. Fellini used her emblematically in *8½*; but her most ambitious work has been with Luchino Visconti – she was excellently cast as the ambitious heiress Angelica in *The Leopard*, her raucous voice suggesting her non-aristocratic origins, but out of her depth with the incestuous undertones in *Of a Thousand Delights*. She is versatile enough to have appeared also in several Westerns, including *Once Upon a Time in the West*.

Films include: 1958 I Soliti Ignoti (USA: Big Deal on Madonna Street; GB: Persons Unknown). '60 Il Bell 'Antonio; Rocco e i Suoi Fratelli (IT-FR) (USA/GB: Rocco and His Brothers). '61 La Ragazza con la Valigia (IT-FR) (USA/GB: The Girl With a Suitcase). '63 Il Gattopardo (IT-FR) (USA/GB: The Leopard); Otto e Mezzo (IT-FR) (USA/GB: 8½); The Pink Panther (USA). '64 Circus World (USA) (GB: The Magnificent Showman). '65 Vaghe Stelle dell'Orsa (USA: Sandra; GB: Of a Thousand Delights). '66 The Professionals (USA). '68 C'Era una Volta il West (USA/GB: Once Upon a Time in the West). '70 Krasnaya Palatka/La Tenda Rossa (USSR-IT) (USA/GB: The Red Tent). '78 Corleone. '82 Le Cadeau (FR-IT).

CARETTE, Julien

(1897–1966). Actor. Born: Paris, France

During the late Thirties and early Forties Carette (as he was billed) seemed to be in every French film of any stature. This short, swarthy, cheerful actor, who came to films via theatre and music-hall, became a very familiar figure, normally playing tough, no-nonsense little men, who gave a touch of reality to all the doomed romances and poetic fantasies of the time. And it was the director Jean Renoir who probably used his talents to best effect – Carette's portrayal of the poacher in *La Règle du Jeu* is a marvellous creation, a wily shiftless character, who because he knows so well his own strengths is able to play on his opponent's weakness. He died tragically from the burns suffered in a fire that started when he fell asleep smoking a cigarette.

Films include: 1933 L'Affaire Est dans le Sac (GB: It's in the Bag). '37 La Grande Illusion (USA: Grand Illusion; GB: The Great Illusion). '38 Entrée des Artistes; La Bête Humaine (USA: The Human Beast; GB: Judas Was a Woman). '39 La Règle du Jeu (USA: The Rules of the Game). '43 Adieu Léonard. '46 Les Portes de la Nuit (USA:

Left: Claudia Cardinale. Above: Julien Carette in La Règle du Jeu. *Right: Harry Carey in* Tiger Thompson *(1924); Below, left to right: Harry Carey Jr (centre) in* She Wore a Yellow Ribbon; *Ian Carmichael (left) with Peter Sellers in* I'm All Right Jack *(1959); Richard Carlson. Bottom right: Macdonald Carey in* The Damned. *Far right: Hoagy Carmichael with Fredric March and Myrna Loy in* The Best Years of Our Lives.

Gates of the Night). '48 Une Si Jolie Petite Plage (GB: Such a Pretty Little Beach). '50 La Marie du Port. '56 Eléna et les Hommes (USA: Paris Does Strange Things; GB: The Night Does Strange Things).

CAREY, Harry

(1878–1947). Actor. Born: Henry DeWitt Carey II; New York City, USA

'To the memory of Harry Carey – bright star of the early Western sky' – so ran the dedication of John Ford's *Three Godfathers* (1948). Cinematically Ford and Carey had grown up together, collaborating on the scripts and direction of the Cheyenne Harry movies – two Easterners in love with the West. Carey was the son of a judge and graduated in law before trying his hand as a playwright. In 1909 he joined D.W. Griffith at the Biograph studios – eight years later he was a Western star. During the Twenties his career waned somewhat but revived when he was given the lead role in *Trader Horn*. Later he became the most reliable of supporting players – tough, rugged and totally relaxed.

Films include: 1912 The Musketeers of Pig Alley. '17 Cheyenne's Pal; Straight Shooting. '19 The Outcasts of Poker Flat. '28 The Trail of '98. '31 Trader Horn. '36 The Prisoner of Shark Island. '37 Kid Galahad. '39 Mr Smith Goes to Washington. '43 Air Force. '48 Red River.

CAREY Jr, Harry

(b. 1921). Actor. Born: Saugus, California, USA

Harry Carey Jr, although completely unlike his father in appearance, has spent much of his acting career following in Harry Carey Sr's footsteps. He spent his childhood on a ranch, and on leaving a military academy in 1938 joined his father working in summer repertory. After three years in the US Navy he signed a long-term contract with John Ford and made his first major film appearance in *Three Godfathers* in a role played by his father in an earlier version of the same film. His career then took a different course; he began to play hard-bitten characters and he eventually found himself working primarily in Italian Westerns. He will be best remembered as the blond trooper in Ford's *She Wore a Yellow Ribbon* and *Rio Grande*.

Films include: 1947 Pursued. '48 Red River; Three Godfathers. '49 She Wore a Yellow Ribbon. '50 Wagonmaster; Rio Grande. '56 The Searchers. '67 The Way West. '68 Bandolero! '70 Dirty Dingus Magee. '71 Big Jake. '72 E Poi Lo Chiamarono il Magnifico (IT-FR) (GB: Man of the East). '80 The Long Riders.

CAREY, MacDonald

(b. 1913). Actor. Born: Edward MacDonald Carey; Sioux City, Iowa, USA

MacDonald Carey had a Celtic background – an Irish father and a Scots mother. He first considered singing for his living; he had been a bass baritone while at school and was the lead in Gilbert and Sullivan operettas performed at the University of Iowa.

On graduation, however, he joined the Globe Players, a group primarily involved in performing Shakespeare. From this illustrious beginning he found himself descending into radio soap opera. He made his Broadway debut in *Lady in the Dark* in 1941 and then found work in Hollywood. His career was interrupted by service in the marines, and by the time he returned his chance for stardom had passed. He was not a distinctive enough personality and became typecast in bland supporting roles as doctors, lawyers, detectives and insurance agents. He now concentrates on television movies and soap operas.

Films include: 1942 Wake Island; Take a Letter, Darling. '43 Shadow of a Doubt. '49 The Great Gatsby. '50 The Lawless (GB: The Dividing Line); The Great Missouri Raid. '51 Let's Make It Legal. '62 The Damned (GB) (USA: These Are the Damned).

CARLSON, Richard

(1914–1977). Actor/director. Born: Albert Lea; Minnesota, USA

Tall and rather solemn, Richard Carlson looked like an academic rather than an actor, and could easily have been one. He was the son of an attorney, and taught briefly at the University of Minnesota, but then opened his own theatre, starred in his own plays, and at 23 was playing opposite Ethel Barrymore on Broadway. His play, *Western Waters*, reached Broadway too, and flopped. David O. Selznick then signed him on a writer/director/actor contract. He made his movie acting debut in *The Young in Heart*, with Janet Gaynor, and for the next 20 years played leads

in lesser films and supporting parts in major ones. But in spite of that contract, he didn't direct until 1954, when he made *Riders to the Stars*, an off-beat sci-fi movie that was well reviewed but little seen.

Films as actor include: 1938 The Young in Heart. '39 Winter Carnival. '40 The Howards of Virginia (GB: Tree of Liberty). '41 No No Nanette; The Little Foxes; Back Street. '50 King Solomon's Mines. '53 It Came From Outer Space. '54 Creature From the Black Lagoon; Riders to the Stars (dir. only); Four Guns to the Border (dir. only). '69 The Valley of Gwangi.

CARMICHAEL, Hoagy

(1899–1981). Composer/actor. Born: Hoagland Howard Carmichael; Bloomington, Indiana, USA

A boy from Bloomington who found little difficulty in breaking away, Hoagy Carmichael graduated in and briefly flirted with law before settling to his long career as jazz-composer, songwriter, and eventually actor. He was a self-taught musician; his songs were usually plaintive and nostalgic, his voice gravelly, his manner worldweary, casually unconcerned. When he acted in movies, he made no attempt to be other than himself, and in the right setting that worked superbly. As Bogart and Bacall strike sparks off each other in *To Have and Have Not*, Carmichael's wry pianist comments on, underlines, and joyfully celebrates their discovery of one another. 'Stardust' and 'Georgia' were his finest songs, and 'In the Cool, Cool, Cool of the Evening' won an Academy Award.

Films as composer include: 1936 Anything Goes. '38 College Swing (GB: Swing, Teacher, Swing); Thanks for the Memory. '44 To Have and Have Not (+act). '46 The Best Years of Our Lives (+act); Canyon Passage (+act). '47 Night Song (+act). '50 Young Man with a Horn (GB: Young Man of Music) (act. only). '51 Here Comes the Groom. '53 Gentlemen Prefer Blondes.

CARMICHAEL, Ian

(b. 1920). Actor. Born: Hull, Yorkshire, England

A popular light comedian too seldom given respectable material to work on, Ian Carmichael first made a mark in theatrical revue in the early Fifties, and soon moved into films with the Boulting brothers. Usually playing a pleasant, none-too-clever, upperclass type, he has combined British films with long West End runs in revues and farces. His lead in *Private's Progress* (right down his street – he had been to Sandhurst) boosted his career, but the film looks sadly dated today. His television work includes the Dorothy L. Sayers detective series, in which he was a very light-weight Lord Peter Wimsey.

Films include: 1955 Storm over the Nile. '56 Private's Progress. '57 Lucky Jim; Brothers in Law. '59 I'm All Right, Jack. '60 School for Scoundrels. '62 The Amorous Prawn. '63 Heavens Above. '67 Smashing Time. '71 The Magnificent Seven Deadly Sins. '79 The Lady Vanishes.

CARNÉ, Marcel

(b. 1909). Director. Born: Paris, France

Marcel Carné wrote for various film magazines from 1929, entered the industry as assistant to Jacques Feyder and René Clair, and in 1936 formed a famous partnership with the poet Jacques Prévert. In eleven years Carné directed seven films from scripts by Prévert. In the main they shared a dark, urban poetry and a sense of fatality, but there were variations too – the surrealist comedy of *Drôle de Drame*, the bright, enchanted myth of *Les Visiteurs du Soir*, the teeming life of a whole epoch in *Les Enfants du Paradis*. How much of it all was due to Carné? He had a superb writer, and in Gabin, Jouvet, Arletty, Morgan and the rest he had the finest acting team which any director has been privileged to use. Certainly, too, Carné's work deteriorated badly when those collaborators left. If he was, in the last analysis, gifted largely in channelling the genius of others, then that alone is a praiseworthy epitaph.

Films include: **1936** Jenny. **'37** Drôle de Drame (USA: Bizarre, Bizarre). **'38** Le Quai des Brumes; Hôtel du Nord. **'39** Le Jour se Lève (USA: Daybreak). **'42** Les Visiteurs du Soir (USA: The Devil's Own Envoy). **'45** Les Enfants du Paradis (USA: Children of Paradise). **'46** Les Portes de la Nuit (USA: Gates of the Night). **'49** La Marie du Port. **'53** Thérèse Raquin. **'58** Les Tricheurs. **'65** Trois Chambres à Manhattan.

CARNEY, Art

(b. 1918). Actor. Born: Arthur Carney; Mount Vernon, New York, USA

Art Carney won the Best Actor Oscar in 1974 for his performance in *Harry and Tonto*, the odyssey of an eccentric old gentleman and his cat. At that time he had made very few films, but had a reputation on the Broadway stage as a notable character actor; he had scored a great success in the role later played by Jack Lemmon in *The Odd Couple*. Originally a radio comic, he was wounded in World War II (hence his limp), and gradually made his way, through television (where he supported comedian Jackie Gleason in a long-running series) to Broadway and, when nearing fifty, to the movies. After *Harry and Tonto* he was much in demand for cantankerous old chaps with soft hearts – the Lionel Barrymore of the Sentimental Seventies.

Films include: **1964** The Yellow Rolls Royce (GB). **'67** A Guide for the Married Man. **'74** Harry and Tonto. **'75** W.W. and the Dixie Dance Kings. **'76** Won Ton Ton, the Dog That Saved Hollywood. **'77** The Late Show. **'78** House Calls; Movie Movie. **'79** Steel; Sunburn. **'80** Roadie.

CAROL, Martine

(1922–1967). Actress. Born: Maryse Mourer; Biarritz, France

Martine Carol had a brief stage career and a few film parts in the Forties, but it was *Caroline Chérie* in 1951 which established her as the reigning sex-symbol of French cinema in the days

before Bardot. Her movies were innocent enough – usually tastefully decorated period romps, often directed by her then husband Christian-Jaque, in which her beauty, her *déshabillé* and her bubble baths provided gentle titillation. Her one great part showed what might have been. Max Ophuls cast her as *Lola Montès*, and transformed her. For Ophuls, Carol showed that she could act well enough. As Lola, she had to be the object of all men's dreams, and she was. But there were no more parts like that. She had a serious accident, retired for a while, and died from a heart attack while planning a comeback.

Films include: **1942** Les Inconnus dans la Maison. **'49** Les Amants de Vérone. **'51** Caroline Chérie. **'52** Les Belles de Nuits (USA: Beauties of the Night); Adorables Créatures (FR) (USA/GB: Adorable Creatures). **'53** Lucrèce Borgia (USA/GB: Lucretia Borgia). **'54** Madame Du Barry (FR-IT) (GB: Mistress Du Barry). **'55** Nana (FR-IT); Lola Montès (FR-GER) (GB: The Fall of Lola Montes). **'57** Action of the Tiger (GB). **'60** Austerlitz. **'61** Vanina Vanini (USA: The Betrayer).

CARON, Leslie

(b. 1931). Actress/dancer. Born: Boulogne-Billancourt, Paris, France

The daughter of a dancer, Leslie Caron at 16 was a member of Roland Petit's Ballet des Champs-Elysées, and soon was dancing leading roles in works like Cocteau's *Le Jeune Homme et la Mort!* Gene Kelly saw her in Paris, and this led to her film debut opposite him in *An American in Paris*. Her witty, elfin charm, allied to her dancing, made her an immediate success. The following year *Lili* won her a British Film Academy Award, as did *The L-Shaped Room* when she moved on to more serious roles. From the mid-Fifties Leslie Caron has worked in theatre and cinema, her marriage to producer Peter Hall leading to work in some British films. Her films have been a patchy lot, never quite giving her the chance to recapture that early vivacity, but her emergence recently as a character actress has been interesting, and promises a new start.

Films include: **1951** An American in Paris (USA). **'53** Lili (USA). **'56** Gaby (USA). **'58** Gigi (USA). **'61** Fanny (USA). **'62** The L-Shaped Room (GB). **'66** Paris Brûle-t-Il? (USA/GB: Is Paris Burning?). **'70** Madron (ISRAEL). **'76** Serail. **'77** L'Homme Qui Aimait les Femmes (USA: The Man Who Loved Love; GB: The Man Who Loved Women); Valentino (GB). **'80** Kontrakt (POL)(GB:The Contract). **'82** Die Unerreichbare (GER) (GB: The Unapproachable).

CARPENTER, John

(b. 1948). Director. Born: Bowling Green, Kentucky, USA

Crazy about movies from early childhood, John Carpenter studied film at the University of Southern California, made a number of student films there, and with one of them, *The Resurrection of Bronco Billy*, won the 1970 Oscar for best live-action short. This enabled him to expand *Dark Star* from 16mm to a 35mm feature; at first unsuccessful, it has become a favourite cult-movie. This film and Carpenter's next,

Top left: Art Carney in Harry and Tonto. *Above left: Martine Carol in* Lola Montes. *Left: Leslie Caron with Fred Astaire in* Daddy Long Legs *(1954). This page: the Carradines – David (top) in* Bound for Glory, *John (above) in* The Grapes of Wrath, *and Keith in* The Duellists, *Robert (below) in* The Cowboys

Assault on Precinct 13, *remain by far his best. The work of a man steeped in cinema, they communicate the delight with which they were made, and in their different moods – the first romantic, nostalgic, and funny, the second tense and frightening – they show an original mind bending the rules of genre to its own purposes. Then came* Halloween, *with its brilliant opening never quite fulfilled, and the flood of movie references failing to cover up the squalid plot. And almost any horror-director could have made his later films. Carpenter is a director,*

writer, editor, composer. He is obviously enormously talented, but he could easily become lost in schlock-horror. He himself has spoken wistfully of RKO circa 1950, but all that is gone forever.

Films: 1970 The Resurrection of Bronco Billy (short) (co-dir. only). '74 Dark Star. '76 Assault on Precinct 13. '78 Hallowe'en. '79 Elvis (GB: Elvis – The Movie). '80 The Fog. '81 Escape From New York. '82 The Thing.

CARRADINE, David

(b. 1936). Actor/director. Born: Hollywood, California, USA

The eldest son of John Carradine, David studied music in San Francisco, joined a Shakespearian repertory company there, and eventually (after an abortive attempt at Hollywood and a spell in the army) reached the New York stage. Some success there led to television roles (the series *Kung Fu* made him a star) and a return, this time more auspicious, to Hollywood. He has worked steadily in films since then, has directed two features, and written music for some of his films. His career is hard to pin down, with cheap exploitation pictures side by side with weightier efforts from Scorsese and Bergman. For a while he cultivated an unfettered life-style, reflected in his portrayal of folk-singer Woody Guthrie in *Bound for Glory* and in his frequent casting in anti-hero parts. But good films have been rare, and his future could lie as a director. His long-time companion is actress Barbara Hershey, co-star of his *Americana*.

Films include: 1964 Taggart. '67 The Violent Ones. '69 Young Billy Young. '72 Boxcar Bertha. '73 Mean Streets. '74 You and Me (+dir). '75 Death Race 2000. '76 Bound for Glory. '77 Das Schlangenei (GER-USA) (USA/GB: The Serpent's Egg). '78 Gray Lady Down. '80 The Long Riders. '81 Americana (+dir). '82 The Winged Serpent.

CARRADINE, John

(b. 1906). Actor. Born: Richmond Reed Carradine; New York City, USA

In the early Thirties there was a promising young character actor named Peter Richmond. Frequently uncredited, he still made his mark in telling little bits, such as the informer in *The Invisible Man*. He had been a marine artist and a portrait painter, and was engaged as a designer by Cecil B. DeMille. But acting took over. He changed his name to John Carradine (the 'Carradine' really was his name), and began a career, as yet unfinished, which made him one of the finest of Hollywood's great array of supporting players. Most people recall him as a villain, and his lean, dark looks often had him cast that way, but some of his most memorable parts were very different. With that quiet voice and piercing eyes he could radiate spirituality; his Bartolomeo Romagna (*viz* Vanzetti) in *Winterset* is an utterly convincing picture of sheer goodness. His ebullient unfrocked preacher, Casy, in *The Grapes of Wrath* had an energy that burst from the screen, while in contrast his gambler, Hatfield, in *Stagecoach* was cool, charming, and contained. And so one could go on. The man's credits are a roll of honour of the American cinema.

Films include: 1935 The Bride of Frankenstein. '36 The Prisoner of Shark Island; Mary of Scotland; Winterset. '38 Of Human Hearts. '39 Stagecoach. '40 The Return of Frank James; The Grapes of Wrath. '41 Manhunt. '54 Johnny Guitar. '58 The Last Hurrah. '76 The Shootist.

CARRADINE, Keith

(b. 1951). Actor. Born: San Mateo, California, USA

Son of John Carradine and half-brother of David, Keith Carradine had an early success in a stage production of *Hair*, leading to film parts from 1971. Keith had his father's knack of being in good films by good directors, with Robert Altman a particular influence. Carradine's performance in *Nashville* as the country-singer Tom Frank made him a big name. He also composed the songs which he sang, and one of them, 'I'm Easy' won an Academy Award. This prestige enabled him to continue a career largely outside mainstream American cinema, and to develop a range not unworthy of his father as, for example, a Napoleonic officer in *The Duellists*, a French photographer in *Pretty Baby*, a mentally unstable teenager in *Old Boyfriends*.

Films include: 1971 A Gunfight; McCabe and Mrs Miller. '73 The Emperor of the North Pole (GB: Emperor of the North). '74 Thieves Like Us; You and Me. '75 Nashville (+songs). '76 Welcome to LA. '77 The Duellists (GB). '78 Pretty Baby. '79 Old Boyfriends. '80 The Long Riders. '82 Southern Comfort.

CARRADINE, Robert

(b. 1954). Actor. Born: San Mateo, California, USA

The youngest Carradine – there were seven brothers – was the last to enter the film profession, having begun an acting career while still at Hollywood High. Robert appeared with brother David in *Mean Streets*, but then he had little interesting to do until *Coming Home* gave him a better chance as a tragic veteran of Vietnam. After that, he played the novelist-narrator of Samuel Fuller's *The Big Red One*, a film from the old Hollywood that would have fitted snugly into his father John's career.

Films include: 1972 The Cowboys. '73 Mean Streets. '74 You and Me. '76 Jackson County Jail; Cannonball (GB: Carquake). '77 Joyride; Orca (GB: Orca . . . Killer Whale). '78 Coming Home. '80 The Long Riders; The Big Red One. '81 Heartaches (CAN). '82 TAG-The Assassination Game.

CARRIÈRE, Jean-Claude

(b. 1931). Screenwriter. Born: Colombières, France

During *Belle de Jour*, the blonde Séverine (Catherine Deneuve), a beautiful provincial wife who satisfies her lust working as a whore in the afternoons, is tied to a post and her face and bare arms pelted with mud. Was it the director Luis Buñuel or the screenwriter Jean-Claude Carrière who invented that fantasy sequence? The former had been the cinema's master of the surreal for decades, but Séverine's degradation may have been thought up by the witty, anarchic Carrière, who became Buñuel's major collaborator in the Sixties and Seventies in a joint assault on bourgeois manners and morals. He had originally intended to teach, but tried cartoons, short stories, novels and plays before a meeting with the comedy actor-director Jacques Tati led to his first collaboration on scripts with Tati's assistant, Pierre Etaix. Carrière has since written for Miloš Forman, Louis Malle and also Volker Schlöndorff, whose *The Tin Drum*, a bizarre chronicle of the outbreak of World War II in Poland, greatly benefitted from the writer's outlandish comic vision. A prolific screenwriter, Carrière has also acted in films and directed several shorts.

Films include: 1965 Viva Maria! (co-sc) (FR-IT). '67 Belle de Jour (co-sc) (FR-IT). '70 Borsalino (co-sc) (FR-IT). '71 Taking Off (co-sc) (USA). '72 Le Charme Discret de la Bourgeoisie (co-sc) (FR-SP-IT) (USA/GB: The Discreet Charm of the Bourgeoisie). '74 Le Fantôme de la Liberté (USA/GB: The Phantom of Liberty). '76 Les Oeufs Brouillés (co-sc). '77 Cet Obscur Objet du Désir (FR-SP) (USA/GB: That Obscure Object of Desire); Julie Pot de Colle (co-sc). '78 Un Papillon sur l'Epaule (co-sc). '79 Die Blechtrommel (co-sc) (GER-FR) (GB: The Tin Drum).

Right: Leo G. Carroll in The Spy in a Green Hat *(1966). Far right: Madeleine Carroll in* It's All Yours *(1937). Bottom: Maria Casarès in* Bagarres

CARROLL, Leo G.

(1892-1972). Actor. Born: Weedon, Northamptonshire, England

If Leo G. Carroll's lived-in face and grave air of officialdom is best remembered from his perfect performances as the spy-boss Mr Waverly in the Sixties television series *The Man From UNCLE*, it should be noted that fifty years of acting experience preceded that final, quiet apotheosis. He began in school productions of Gilbert and Sullivan, and made his professional stage debut in *The Prisoner of Zenda* in London in 1911. After serving as an infantryman during World War I, he left for America and embarked on a long and distinguished career on Broadway and in Hollywood, where his soft-spoken manner usually cast him as a doctor, gent or suave and particularly sinister villain, most notably in films by Alfred Hitchcock – including *Rebecca*, *Suspicion* and *Spellbound*.

Films include: 1934 The Barretts of Wimpole Street. '39 Wuthering Heights; The Private Lives of Elizabeth and Essex. '40 Rebecca. '41 Suspicion. '45 Spellbound; The House on 92nd Street. '47 Forever Amber; The Paradine Case. '50 Father of the Bride. '59 North by Northwest.

CARROLL, Madeleine

(b. 1906). Actress. Born: Marie-Madeleine Bernadette O'Carroll; West Bromwich, Staffordshire, England

Madeleine Carroll was one of Hitchcock's prototype ice-blondes: as Pamela in *The Thirty-Nine Steps* she finds herself painfully handcuffed to the fugitive Richard Hannay (Robert Donat) and dragged complainingly over the moor – but does she mind too much? Hitchcock was always quick to see that a cool, ladylike demeanour might be a façade for depravity, and Carroll fitted the bill perfectly. After gaining a BA from Birmingham University, she relinquished a teaching career for the stage in 1927 and a film debut the following year. Stardom was immediate; she went to Hollywood in the mid-Thirties and remained an aristocratic leading lady, though it needed a Hitchcock to bring out more than just her beauty. She distinguished herself working for the Red Cross during World War II, and afterwards worked mainly in theatre, radio and television. Two of her four husbands (all divorced) were actor Sterling Hayden and producer Henri Lavorel.

Films include: 1928 The Guns of Loos. '29 Atlantic. '35 The Thirty-Nine Steps. '36 The Secret Agent; The General Died at Dawn (USA). '37 The Prisoner of Zenda (USA); On the Avenue (USA). '39 Café Society (USA). '40 North West Mounted Police (USA); My Son, My Son (USA). '41 Virginia (USA). '42 My Favorite Blonde (USA). '48 Don't Trust Your Husband (USA). '49 The Fan (USA) (GB: Lady Windermere's Fan).

CARSON, Jack

(1910–1963). Actor. Born: John Elmer Carson; Carmen, Manitoba, Canada

Raised in Milwaukee, Carson slogged it in insurance, in vaudeville, on stage, radio and as a Hollywood extra before he emerged in the mid-Thirties as a popular, dependable character actor in countless comedies, musicals and Westerns. Tall, bulky, bluff and with pliable features, he was reserved for the unheroic – the amiable man most likely to lose the girl (*Mildred Pierce*), the pal with a heart of gold and a line in double-takes (*The Male Animal*), the egregious son and brother-in-law in *Cat on a Hot Tin Roof*. Carson packed four marriages into his 53 years – his third wife was actress Lola Albright.

Films include: 1937 You Only Live Once. '38 The Saint in New York; Vivacious Lady; Carefree. '39 Destry Rides Again. '41 The Strawberry Blonde; The Bride Came COD. '42 The Male Animal. '44 Arsenic and Old Lace. '45 Mildred Pierce; Roughly Speaking. '54 A Star Is Born. '58 Cat on a Hot Tin Roof; Rally 'Round the Flag, Boys! '61 King of the Roaring '20s.

CARSTAIRS, John Paddy

(1910–1970). Director/screenwriter. Born: John Keys; London, England

The son of stage comedian Nelson 'Bunch' Keys, Carstairs showed his early interest in film by forming a school cinema club at Repton. In 1927 he joined the camera staff of the Stoll studio and then worked as a script clerk, editor, assistant cameraman, assistant director and scenarist for Herbert Wilcox. He had a couple of spells in Hollywood – his jobs ranging from gateman at Paramount to writer at MGM – before establishing himself as a British director with the war film *Incident in Shanghai* and the George Formby comedy *Spare a Copper*. *The Chiltern Hundreds*, about a butler standing against his employer's son in an election, was his best post-war film, though it was Carstairs who was at the helm of the first six Norman Wisdom comedies that established the bungling 'little man' as Britain's top box-office star in the Fifties. Carstairs also directed for television, wrote film scripts, novels and children's stories and held exhibitions of his paintings.

Films include: 1937 Night Ride. '38 Incident in Shanghai; Lassie From Lancashire. '39 The Saint in London. '40 Spare a Copper. '48 Sleeping Car to Trieste. '49 The Chiltern Hundreds (USA: The Amazing Mr Beecham). '53 Trouble in Store. '57 Just My Luck. '58 The Square Peg. '59 Tommy the Toreador. '60 Sands of the Desert.

CASARÈS, Maria

(b. 1922). Actress. Born: La Coruña, Spain

A dark Spanish beauty capable of great heights of emotion, Casarès has enjoyed her major successes on the Paris stage. Indeed, she claims she dislikes acting in films because of its impersonal nature, but she has privileged the cinema with several remarkable performances. As a teenager she studied in Madrid and worked as a nurse during the Spanish Civil War before being exiled along with her Loyalist father. She learned drama at the Paris Conservatoire and soon made her name as a classical actress. In 1945 Casarès was cast as Nathalie, the jilted wife in Marcel Carné's *Les Enfants du Paradis*, and brought calculating spite to the spurned mistress in Robert Bresson's *Les Dames du Bois de Boulogne*. In Jean Cocteau's *Orphée*, she was cold and mysterious as an agent of death who falls in love with the mortal hero – fate itself catching up with the ultimate *femme fatale*. The actress then concentrated on the theatre but made a welcome return to films in *Flavia la Monaca Musulmana* in 1974.

Films include: 1945 Les Enfants du Paradis (USA: Children of Paradise); Les Dames du Bois de Boulogne. '46 Roger-la-Honte. '47 L'Amour autour de la Maison. '48 La Chartreuse de Parme; Bagarres. '50 Orphée (USA: Orpheus). '51 Ombre et Lumière. '59 Le Testament d'Orphée (USA: Testament of Orpheus). '74 Flavia la Monaca Musulmana (IT-FR) (GB: The Rebel Nun).

CASERINI, Mario

(1874–1920). Director. Born: Rome, Italy

Caserini's beginnings as an artist are evident in the wider canvas of the lavish and spectacular costume dramas he directed in Italy, mostly in the years before World War I. Working at the Cinès studio, he was a prolific film-maker, a contemporary of Giovanni Pastrone, Giuseppe De Liguoro and Enrico Guazzoni, whose epics were then the best and biggest in world cinema. Caserini's pictures include historical biopics such as *Messalina* and *Lucrezia Borgia*, versions of *Macbeth* and *The Last Days of Pompeii*, comedies and, latterly,

passionate dramas like *Ma l'Amore Mio Non Muore*. His wife Maria was one of his stars.

Films include: 1908 Romeo e Giulietta. '09 Beatrice Cenci; Macbeth; I Tre Moschettieri (GB: The Three Musketeers). '10 Catilina; Messalina; Lucrezia Borgia; Il Cid. '12 Dante e Beatrice. '13 Gli Ultimi Giorni di Pompei (GB: The Last Days of Pompeii); Ma l'Amore Mio Non Amore. '20 La Modella.

CASSAVETES, John

(b. 1929). Actor/director/ screenwriter. Born: New York City, USA

Cassavetes began his career playing young toughs in the early Fifties, but he made his first real impression as the jazz-pianist/private eye in the excellent *Johnny Staccato* series on television in 1959. Then he directed the first of his several independently produced films, *Shadows*, about a black New York family. He returned to acting, appearing in such Sixties hits as *The Dirty Dozen* and *Rosemary's Baby* and ploughing the money he earned from them into his next film, *Faces*. And so it continues with Cassavetes alternating between acting in other people's films and directing (and sometimes appearing) in his own, surrounding himself with family and friends, including his wife Gena Rowlands and pals like Peter Falk, Ben Gazzara and Seymour Cassel and assorted in-laws and children. All of his films depend more or less on the inter-relationships of the actors rather than on intricate plot structures. They are, at the very least, interesting. At their best they are intensely excoriating experiences.

Films include: 1951 Fourteen Hours (extra only). '56 Crime in the Streets (actor only). '60 Shadows. '64 The Killers (actor only). '67 The Dirty Dozen (actor only). '68 Rosemary's Baby (actor only); Faces (dir; + sc. only). '70 Husbands. '74 A Woman Under the Influence (dir; + sc. only). '76 The Killing of a Chinese Bookie (dir; + sc. only). '77 Opening Night. '78 The Fury (actor only). '80 Gloria (dir; + sc. only).

CASSEL, Jean-Pierre

(b. 1932). Actor. Born: Jean-Pierre Crochon; Paris, France

A tall, engagingly offhand Gallic charmer, Jean-Pierre Cassel was ideal as the dinner-host in Luis Buñuel's *The Discreet Charm of the Bourgeoisie* – so discreet that he and his wife (Stéphane Audran) sneak out to make love in the garden while their guests wait indoors. A doctor's son, Cassel was originally a dancer spotted by Gene Kelly in a Paris nightclub. He had several small parts in French movies before comic roles in Philippe De Broca's *Les Jeux de l'Amour, Le Farceur* and *L'Amant de Cinq Jours* established him as a star and brought him work with directors such as Claude Chabrol, Jean Renoir and Buñuel. He has also added a Parisian touch to *Those Magnificent Men in Their Flying Machines, Oh! What a Lovely War* and *Murder on the Orient Express*, toured in Michael Cacoyannis' *Hamlet* (performed in halls and gymnasiums) and appeared on stage in London in *A Chorus Line*.

Films include: 1960 Les Jeux de l'Amour (GB: Playing at Love); Le Farceur (GB: The Joker). '61 L'Amant de Cinq Jours (FR-IT) (USA: Five Day Lover; GB: Infidelity). '62 Le Caporal Epinglé (USA: The Elusive Corporal; GB: The Vanishing Corporal). '65 Those Magnificent Men in Their Flying Machines (GB). '66 Paris Brûle-t'il? (USA/GB: Is Paris Burning?). '67 Jeu de Massacre (USA: The Killing Game; GB: Comic Strip Hero). '69 Oh! What a Lovely War (GB). '70 La Rupture (FR-IT-BELG). '71 Le Bateau sur l'Herbe. '72 Le Charme Discret de la Bourgeoisie (FR-SP-IT) (USA/GB: The Discreet Charm of the Bourgeoisie). '73 Baxter! (GB). '74 Murder on the Orient Express (GB). '78 Who Is Killing the Great Chefs of Europe? (USA-GER) (GB: Too Many Chefs). '82 La Truite (FR).

CASTELLANI, Renato

(1913–1985). Director. Born: Finale Ligure, Italy

Castellani's films of the late Forties introduced a little laughter into the often grey world of Italian neorealism. The tone of movies like *Sotto il Sole di Roma* and *Due Soldi di Speranza* – in which social and moral problems are overcome by love and

the quest for happiness – is essentially optimistic and summed up by the title of the latter, released in Britain as *Two Pennyworth of Hope*. Castellani, brought up in Argentina, studied architecture in Milan and in the Thirties wrote scripts for such directors as Mario Soldati and Alessandro Blasetti. The cold elegance of his first film as director *Un Colpo di Pistola* – about two soldiers in love with the same girl – was repeated in his 1954 version of *Romeo and Juliet* and his works since, mostly star vehicles, lacked the warmth and charm of that brief postwar flourish. His television work after the late Sixties included a life of Leonardo da Vinci.

Films include: 1941 Un Colpo di Pistola. '43 La Donna della Montagna. '46 Mio Figlio Professore (GB: My Son, the Professor). '48 Sotto il Sole di Roma. '52 Due Soldi di Speranza (GB: Two Pennyworth of Hope). '54 Romeo and Juliet (GB-IT). '57 I Sogni nel Cassetto (IT-FR). '59 Nella Città l'Inferno (IT-FR) (GB: Caged). '61 Il Brigante. '69 Una Breve Stagione.

CASTLE, William

(1914–1977). Producer/director. Born: New York City, USA

Step Right Up! I'm Gonna Scare the Pants Off America – the title of William Castle's autobiography sums up his career as a producer and director of sensationally promoted, low-budget exploitation horror films (most of them made before the term 'exploitation' was used for movies). He started as an actor with a Broadway debut at 15, and three years later became New York's youngest director with his version of *Dracula*. Castle then worked his way through most jobs in the movie industry, graduating to direct Westerns and crime films in the Forties. In 1957 he became an independent producer specializing in cheap and chilling titles like *The Tingler, Macabre* and *House on Haunted Hill* – which respectively lured big audiences with cinema seats wired up to give electric shocks, $1000 insurance against death by fright, and plastic skeletons flying across the auditorium (on a suspended trolley). These were all tongue-in-cheek comedies of terror, expertly devised by a master showman. Of a much higher quality was his production of Roman Polanski's occult movie *Rosemary's Baby*. Castle died of a heart attack, but not before signing off with acting roles as Hollywood film-makers in *Shampoo* and *Day of the Locust*.

Films include: 1944 The Whistler (dir. only). '49 Johnny Stool Pigeon (dir. only). '51 Hollywood Story (dir. only). '55 The Gun That Won the West (dir. only). '58 Macabre; House on Haunted Hill. '59 The Tingler. '61 Homicidal. '64 The Night Walker. '65 I Saw What You Did. '66 Let's Kill Uncle. '68 Project X; Rosemary's Baby (prod. only). '75 Day of the Locust (actor only); Shampoo (actor only).

Top: John Cassavetes working on Gloria. *Far left: Jack Carson in* The Time, the Place and the Girl *(1946)*. *Left: Jean-Pierre Cassel in* Oh! What a Lovely War

CAULFIELD, Joan

(b. 1922). Actress. Born: Beatrice
Joan Caulfield; Orange, New Jersey,
USA

Joan Caulfield's career in front of
cameras began when she took modelling jobs while still at university. After
a spell in the chorus of the stage
musical *Beat the Band*, she graduated
to the lead in *Kiss and Tell* on Broadway which led to a contract at Paramount. She won the New York Drama
Critics' Award for Most Promising
Newcomer in 1943, and for several
years was one of Paramount's main
stars, playing demure, well-bred
glamour girls. Her contract was not
renewed in 1949, however, and after
appearing in a couple of films produced by her then husband, Frank
Ross, she moved into television, starring in *My Favourite Husband*. After
her divorce in 1959 she made several
comebacks, but with little success. In
the late Sixties and early Seventies
Caulfield appeared in several low-
budget Westerns.

Films include: 1946 Monsieur Beaucaire;
Blue Skies. '47 Dear Ruth; Variety Girl;
Unsuspected. '48 The Sainted Sisters; Lar-
ceny. '50 The Petty Girl (GB: Girl of the
Year). '51 The Lady Says No. '55 The Rains
of Ranchipur. '68 Buckskin.

CAVALCANTI, Alberto

(1897–1982). Director/producer/
screenwriter. Born: Alberto de
Almeida Cavalcanti; Rio de Janeiro,
Brazil

The son of a famous mathematician,
Cavalcanti abandoned his law studies
in Geneva in favour of architecture
and interior design in Paris. This led to
work as a set designer with French
avant-garde film-makers. In 1926 he
began directing his own films. He
came to Britain in the Thirties and
became part of the British documentary movement. In the Forties he went
to Ealing Studios as a feature director,
but in the Fifties returned to his native
Brazil. His career there was cut short

for political reasons and, once again,
he returned to Europe to work mainly
in East Germany and Austria. His
documentaries – including *Coal Face*
(1935) and *North Sea* (1938) – are
landmarks in screen realism; his features are polished but atmospheric.
Cavalcanti will perhaps be best remembered for the chilling
'Ventriloquist's Dummy' episode in
Dead of Night.

Films include: 1926 Rien que les Heures
(FR). '27 La P'tite Lili (FR). 28 En Rache
(FR). '34 Pett and Pott. '42 Went the Day
Well? (USA: 48 Hours). '44 Champagne
Charlie. '45 Dead of Night *eps* The
Ventriloquist's Dummy and The Christmas
Party. '47 They Made Me a Fugitive (USA: I
Became a Criminal); Nicholas Nickleby. '53
O Canto do Mar (prod; +co-sc. only)
(BRAZ).

CAVANI, Liliana

(b. 1937). Director. Born: Carpi,
Italy

Educated in classical literature at the
University of Bologna, Cavani then
studied film at the Centro Sperimentale di Cinematografia in Rome.
She made dramas and documentaries
for Italian television and won the
Golden Lion Award for the Best Television Programme in 1965 with an
hour-long film about why Marshal
Pétain, the Premier of Vichy France,
should not be 'rehabilitated' in the
history books. Much of her work is
characterized by hard-hitting political
content, often looking at Italian fascism and confronting the issues facing
Italy's intellectual radicals. The resulting censorship problems encouraged her to move into films in the
late Sixties. Her most successful is
The Night Porter, a controversial
study of sado-masochism and fascism.

Films include: 1968 Galileo (IT-BULG). '70 I
Cannibali (GB: The Cannibals). '71 L'Ospite.
'74 Il Portiere di Notte (USA/GB: The Night
Porter); Milarepa. '77 Al di là del Bene e del
Male (IT-FR-GER) (GB: Beyond Good and
Evil). '81 La Pelle (IT-FR).

Above left: Joan Caulfield in
Unsuspected. *Above: John Cazale in*
The Godfather, Part II. *Above right:*
Adolfo Celi in Diabolik *(1968)*

Below: George Chakiris in West Side
Story. *Right: Richard Chamberlain in*
The Music Lovers. *Bottom right: Jeff*
Chandler in Return to Peyton Place

CAYATTE, André

(b. 1909). Director/screenwriter. Born: Carcassonne, France

Cayatte abandoned his early career in law and journalism in favour of films in 1938, but his training left its mark, for many of Cayatte's films reveal a preoccupation with the moral questions posed by the French judicial system. He has also made a number of romantic films like *Les Amants de Vérone*, and in 1963 completed a two-part study of the break-up of a marriage – *La Vie Conjugale*. Cayatte has scripted or co-scripted all his films, and several have won awards, including *Nous Somme Tous des Assassins* (Special Jury Prize at Cannes) and a POW escape story *Le Passage du Rhin* (winner of the Golden Lion at Venice).

Films include: 1949 Les Amants de Vérone. '50 Justice Est Faite (GB: Let Justice Be Done/Justice Is Done). '52 Nous Sommes Tous des Assassins (USA: We Are All Murderers; GB: Are We All Murderers?). '54 Avant le Deluge. '58 Le Miroir a Deux Faces (FR-IT) (GB: The Mirror Has Two Faces). '60 Le Passage du Rhin (FR-GER) (GB: The Crossing of the Rhine). '63 Le Glaive et la Balance (FR-IT) (USA: Two Are Guilty). '71 Mourir d'Aimer (FR-IT) (USA: To Die of Love). '77 A Chacun Son Enfer (FR-GER). '78 La Raison d'Etat (FR-IT).

CAZALE, John

(1936–1978). Actor. Born: Boston, Massachusetts, USA

John Cazale's promising career was cut short by his tragic death from cancer in 1978. Educated at Oberlin College, he then studied drama at Boston University. He gained considerable experience in regional theatre and later won several awards for his off-Broadway work. In films he often played supporting character roles as weak and ineffectual young men. His part as one of the bank-robbers in *Dog Day Afternoon* won him a Golden Globe Award.

Films include: 1972 The Godfather. '74 The Godfather, Part II: The Conversation. '75 Dog Day Afternoon. '78 The Deer Hunter.

CECCHI D'AMICO, Suso

(b. 1914). Screenwriter. Born: Giovanna Susanna Cecchi; Rome, Italy

The daughter of well-known critic, scenarist and producer Emilio Cecchi, Suso was educated in Rome, working first as a journalist and as a translator of English plays in the theatre. In 1945 she collaborated on a film with scriptwriter and director Renato Castellani, which led to similar work with leading neo-realist directors like Vittorio De Sica. She has since collaborated on scripts for most of the leading Italian directors, including Michelangelo Antonioni, Franco Zeffirelli and Luchino Visconti and has won many Italian awards.

Films include: 1946 Roma Città Libera. '47 Vivere in Pace (GB: To Live in Peace). '48 Ladri di Biciclette (co-sc) (USA: Bicycle Thief; GB: Bicycle Thieves). '51 Miracolo a Milano (co-sc) (USA/GB: Miracle in Milan); Bellissima (co-sc). '55 Le Amiche (co-sc) (GB: The Girl Friends). '60 Rocco e i Suoi Fratelli (co-sc) (USA/GB: Rocco and His Brothers). '63 Il Gattopardo (co-sc) (USA/GB: The Leopard). '67 The Taming of the Shrew (co-sc) (IT-USA). '73 Ludwig (co-sc) (IT-FR-GER).

CELI, Adolfo

(1922–1986). Actor. Born: Messina, Sicily

Educated at Messina University and the Rome Academy of Dramatic Arts, Celi began work as an actor and director in the Italian theatre, then played a few parts in Italian films. In 1948 he went to Brazil where he stayed for 15 years, becoming director of the Brazilian Theatre in São Paulo, and director of the Rio Opera House. He also directed some Brazilian films. In 1963 he returned to acting in Philippe De Broca's *L'Homme de Rio*, which initiated a busy career in international films. Tall, burly, with a prominently hooked nose and greying hair, he often played villains, notably Largo in *Thunderball*, and Pope Alexander VI in the BBC's television series *The Borgias*.

Films include: 1964 L'Homme de Rio (FR-IT) (GB: That Man From Rio). '65 Von Ryan's Express (USA); The Agony and the Ecstasy (USA-IT); Thunderball (GB); E Venne un Uomo (USA: And There Came a Man; GB: A Man Called John). '72 Fratello Sole, Sorella Luna (IT-GB) (USA/GB: Brother Sun, Sister Moon). '73 Hitler: The Last Ten Days (GB-IT). '74 Le Fantôme de la Liberté (FR) (USA/GB: The Phantom of Liberty); The Tempter/Il Sorriso del Grande Tentatore (IT-GB) (USA: The Devil Is a Woman). '75 And Then There Were None (GER-FR-SP-IT).

CHABROL, Claude

(b. 1930). Director. Born: Paris, France

Many of the themes which were to emerge in Chabrol's work were the result of his middle-class upbringing. The son of a chemist, Chabrol himself trained initially in pharmacy, but after military service got a job with the Paris department of 20th Century-Fox. He became a critic for the influential *Cahiers du Cinéma*, and subsequently, with Eric Rohmer, wrote an analytical book on Hitchcock, whose style was to influence his own. An inheritance from his first wife Agnès enabled him to finance his first film, *Le Beau Serge*, a milestone in the development of the French *nouvelle vague*. His output since has been prolific and varied, from straightforward murder thrillers to studies of the foibles and follies of the bourgeoisie. His marriage and working relationship with actress Stéphane Audran has clearly inspired his later films. Chabrol has appeared in several of his friends' films, and in small parts in his own. He won the Golden Bear Award at the Berlin Film Festival for *Les Cousins*.

Films include: 1958 Le Beau Serge (GB: Handsome Serge). '59 Les Cousins. '60 Les Bonnes Femmes. '63 Landru (FR-IT) (GB: Bluebeard). '67 Le Scandale/The Champagne Murders. '68 Les Biches (FR-IT) (GB: The Does); La Femme Infidèle (FR-IT). '69 Que la Bête Meure (FR-IT) (USA: This Man Must Die; GB: Killer!). '70 Le Boucher (FR-IT). '71 Juste Avant la Nuit (FR-IT) (GB: Just Before Nightfall). '73 Les Noces Rouges (USA: Wedding in Blood; GB: Red Wedding). '76 Folies Bourgeoises/The Twist (FR-IT-GER). '78 Violette Nozière (FR-CAN) (USA: Violette). '80 Le Cheval d'Orgeuil (GB: The Proud Ones). '82 Les Fantômes du Chapelier (GB: The Hatter's Ghosts).

CHAKIRIS, George

(b. 1933). Actor/dancer/singer. Born: Norwood, Ohio, USA

The son of Greek immigrants, Chakiris was educated at Tucson and Long Beach, California. He then worked in a store, training as a dancer in the evenings. He made his film debut singing in the chorus of *Song of Love* (1947), studied dance and appeared in several musicals, including *Gentlemen Prefer Blondes* and *White Christmas*. His most successful role, and one in which he was able to utilize all his talents, was as Bernardo in *West Side Story*, a performance which won him both an Academy Award as Best Supporting Actor and a Golden Globe Award. He has worked since, both as a straight actor and a dancer, in a variety of films and stage productions, but few beyond Jacques Demy's *Les Demoiselles de Rochefort* have made much impact.

Films include: 1953 Gentlemen Prefer Blondes. '54 White Christmas. '61 West Side Story. '62 Diamond Head. '64 Flight From Ashiya (USA-JAP). '65 The High Bright Sun (GB) (USA: McGuire, Go Home!). '66 Paris Brûle-t-il? (FR) (USA/GB: Is Paris Burning?). '67 Les Demoiselles de Rochefort (FR) (GB: The Young Girls of Rochefort). '68 Le Rouble à Deux Faces (FR-SP-USA) (USA: The Day the Hot Line Got Hot). '69 The Big Cube (MEX-USA). '79 Why Not Stay for Breakfast? (GB).

CHAMBERLAIN, Richard

(b. 1935). Actor. Born: Beverly Hills, California, USA

The role as the good-looking, clean-cut, antiseptic hero of the long-running television series *Dr Kildare* spelt stardom for Chamberlain. Educated at Beverly Hills High School and Pomona College, he served in the army for two years and this meant a tour of Korea. His early acting work consisted of small roles in television series but the success of *Dr Kildare* established his reputation as a heart throb – an image from which he has tried to escape by acting in Shakespeare on the English stage and in difficult film parts in *The Music Lovers* and the Australian *The Last Wave*. More recently he has returned to American television with *Shogun*, issued as a much-edited film in Britain. He has also made several recordings as a pop ballad singer.

Films include: 1960 The Secret of the Purple Reef. '63 Petulia. '69 The Madwoman of Chaillot (GB). '70 Julius Caesar (GB). '71 The Music Lovers (GB). '72 Lady Caroline Lamb (GB-IT). '73 The Three Musketeers: The Queen's Diamonds (PAN). '75 The Four Musketeers: The Revenge of Milady (PAN-SP); The Slipper and the Rose (GB). '77 The Last Wave (AUS). '80 Shogun (USA-JAP).

CHANDLER, Jeff

(1918–1961). Actor. Born: Ira Grossel; New York, USA

The son of a Jewish silk-merchant, Chandler took a drama course after high school, and then worked for theatrical stock companies. After his military service in World War II he acted in radio dramas until discovered by Universal International. Tall, well-built and with distinctive silver-grey curly hair, he soon became a popular hero in Western and action pictures, twice playing the Apache chief Cochise. He was nominated for an Oscar for his performance in *Broken Arrow*. Tragically, his career was cut short when he died aged 42 from blood poisoning after an operation for a slipped disc.

Films include: 1949 Sword in the Desert. '50 Broken Arrow. '52 Red Ball Express. '53 East of Sumatra. '54 Sign of the Pagan. '56 Away All Boats. '57 Jeanne Eagels. '59 Thunder in the Sun. '61 Return to Peyton Place. '62 Merrill's Marauders.

Above: Lon Chaney in The Road to Mandalay *(1926). Right: Lon Chaney Jr in* Son of Dracula. *Far right: Carol Channing in* Skidoo! *Below right: Stockard Channing in* The Big Bus

CHANDLER, Raymond

(1888–1959). Writer. Born: Chicago, Illinois, USA

Chandler's parents moved to England when he was young, and he was educated first at Dulwich College and then in France and Germany. After service in World War I, he tried a variety of jobs – including journalism – and finally found a niche writing pulp thriller fiction. His private-eye character Philip Marlowe soon became a favourite in Hollywood *film noir*. Marlowe's world was traversed by sleazy streets where dialogue and violence exploded in equal amounts. Chandler summarized his style as 'When in doubt, have a man come through the door with a gun in his hand'. He also worked as a scriptwriter, and won an Oscar nomination for *The Blue Dahlia*.

Films of Chandler's novels include: 1944 Double Indemnity (co-sc. only); Murder My Sweet (GB: Farewell My Lovely). '46 The Blue Dahlia (sc. only); The Big Sleep; Lady In the Lake. '51 Strangers on a Train (co-sc. only). 73 The Long Goodbye. '75 Farewell My Lovely (USA-GB).

CHANEY, Lon

(1883-1930). Actor. Born: Alonso Chaney; Colorado Springs, USA

Chaney's parents were deaf and dumb, and he became adept at communicating using mime and facial expressions, a skill that was to stand him in good stead. He left school early to look after his parents, working in many jobs before touring in a play he wrote with his brother. In Hollywood he started as an extra and worked his way up, achieving a spectacular success in the Twenties with a variety of extraordinary performances in horror films. Dubbed 'The Man of a Thousand Faces', he was justly re-nowned for his remarkable make-up, the tortuous lengths he went to in order to create a character and the sensitivity of his acting. He also directed six films for Universal. Reluctantly but successfully he made the transition to sound, but died of throat cancer after making his first talkie. The supreme technician among horror actors, Chaney would have

doubtless played many of the parts taken in the Thirties by Boris Karloff and Bela Lugosi. As it was, he proved their greatest influence.

Films include: 1917 Hell Morgan's Girl; A Doll's House. '18 Riddle Gawne. '19 The Miracle Man. '23 The Hunchback of Notre Dame. '24 He Who Gets Slapped. '25 The Unholy Three; The Phantom of the Opera; The Tower of Lies. '27 The Unknown; Mockery; London After Midnight (GB: The Hypnotist). '28 Laugh, Clown, Laugh; West of Zanzibar. '30 The Unholy Three.

CHANEY Jr, Lon

(1906–1973). Actor. Born: Creighton Chaney, Oklahoma City, USA

The son of silent star Lon Chaney and his first wife Cleva Creighton, Chaney began his career under his real name but changed it in 1935. He first gained attention with his superb portrayal of the gentle half-wit Lennie in *Of Mice and Men*, but soon moved into the horror genre, where his burly frame, rugged face, famous name and willingness to ham were always in demand. He was impressive in *The Wolf Man*, but most of his films were uninspired sequels or remakes of earlier Karloff and Lugosi successes. He

continued working in movies for 38 years and appeared in over one hundred and fifty.

Films include: 1939 Of Mice and Men. '40 One Million BC. '41 The Wolf Man. '42 The Ghost of Frankenstein. '43 Son of Dracula; Frankenstein Meets the Wolf Man. '44 House of Frankenstein. '52 High Noon. '55 I Died a Thousand Times. '63 The Haunted Palace. '65 Witchcraft (GB).

CHANNING, Carol

(b. 1921). Actress/singer. Born: Seattle, Washington, USA

The daughter of a Christian Scientist lecturer and journalist, Channing left Bennington College in 1941 to work as a comedy actress. Blonde, dynamic and raucous, she became a favourite stage and nightclub entertainer. She scored an early success in the Broadway version of *Gentlemen Prefer Blondes* singing 'Diamonds are a Girl's Best Friend', a song which became her trademark. Her film performances have been few, but she won an Oscar nomination as Best Supporting Actress in the musical comedy *Thoroughly Modern Millie* in a characteristically charming, exuberant and eccentric role.

Films include: 1956 The First Travelling Saleslady. '67 Thoroughly Modern Millie. '68 Skidoo! '71 Shinbone Alley (voice only).

CHANNING, Stockard

(b. 1944). Actress. Born: Susan Williams Antonia Stockard; New York City, USA

Channing was raised on Park Avenue and educated at private schools. After graduating from Radcliffe College where she became interested in drama, she worked with several theatrical repertory companies. Several small television and cinema roles followed her appearances on stage on the West Coast. Her big break came with Mike Nichols' offbeat comedy *The Fortune*, in which she played opposite Warren Beatty and Jack Nicholson. She has worked steadily since. Channing has been married three times, and her current husband is screenwriter David Debin. Dark and diminutive, as Betty Rizzo in *Grease* Channing strikingly resembled Elizabeth Taylor in her twenties.

Films include: 1975 The Fortune. '76 The Big Bus; Sweet Revenge. '78 Grease; The Cheap Detective. '79 The Fish That Saved Pittsburgh.

CHAPLIN, Charles

(1889–1977). Actor/director/screenwriter/producer/composer. Born: Charles Spencer Chaplin; Walworth, London, England

An impoverished music-hall background forced Chaplin onto the stage at the age of five. He acted with juvenile troupes and in the legitimate theatre (including the West End) before joining his brother Sydney in Fred Karno's comedy companies. On tour with them in America in 1913, Chaplin signed for Mack Sennett's Keystone film company and made his screen debut as an English dandy in *Making a Living*. He was immediately successful and after a dozen pictures began to write and direct his own material based on the Tramp character whose slapstick antics combined with romance, pathos and tragedy to make Charlie Chaplin the most recognizable figure in the history of movies. Moving from Keystone to Essanay and then to Mutual, Chaplin commanded huge fees for his films and became an international celebrity, scoring major hits with *Easy Street*, *The Immigrant*, *The Kid* and others. In 1919 he cofounded United Artists, for which he made *A Woman of Paris*, a sophisticated and influential drama, and more familiar comedy features like *The Gold Rush* and *The Circus*. His films became sporadic but no less inventive. Resisting sound, Chaplin filmed *City Lights* and then *Modern Times*, the last appearance of the Tramp and a spoof on mechanization which was followed by his satire on fascism, *The Great Dictator*, in which he first spoke dialogue. The Bluebeard-murder comedy *Monsieur Verdoux* was not popular, however, and lawsuits and scandals over Chaplin's alleged communism and his private life led to his exile from America in 1953. Chaplin's tempestuous romantic involvements included affairs with actresses Edna Purviance (his most memorable leading lady) and Pola Negri, and four marriages, the third to another leading lady, Paulette Goddard, and the last and happiest to playwright Eugene O'Neill's daughter Oona. His last American film, *Limelight*, told the story of a fading clown; *A King in New York* glared at the McCarthy era in the USA; and *A Countess From Hong Kong* saw him instructing Marlon Brando and Sophia Loren in the art of screen comedy. Chaplin was finally acknowledged for his work with a special Oscar in 1971 and a knighthood in 1975. The cinema has produced no greater clown and no greater rags-to-riches story than Chaplin. But his message is twofold: it resides in the expression of hope in the face of *The Immigrant* arriving in New York harbour, mirroring the universal expectations of the underprivileged; and in the resignation of the Tramp – with ill-fitting suit, cane and bowler – wandering away down a dusty road, his dreams mislaid.

Films include: 1914 Making a Living (actor only); Mabel at the Wheel (actor only); Dough and Dynamite; His Musical Career; Tillie's Punctured Romance (actor only). '15 His New Job; The Tramp '16 The Floorwalker; The Vagabond. '17 Easy Street; The Immigrant. '18 Shoulder Arms.
'21 The Kid. '23 The Pilgrim; A Woman of Paris (dir; +prod; +sc. only). '25 The Gold Rush. '28 The Circus. '31 City Lights. '36 Modern Times. '40 The Great Dictator. '47 Monsieur Verdoux. '52 Limelight. '57 A King in New York (GB). '67 A Countess From Hong Kong (GB).

CHAPLIN, Geraldine

(b. 1944). Actress. Born: Santa Monica, California, USA

The daughter of Charles Chaplin and his fourth wife, Oona O'Neill, Geraldine was educated in Swiss schools, and began her career as a dancer with the Royal Ballet in England. Her first main screen role, the hero's wife in *Doctor Zhivago*, established her reputation, and led to further film and stage work, including the 1967 Broadway production of *The Little Foxes*. She has made several films with Spanish director Carlos Saura, with whom she lives, and with Robert Altman, including *A Wedding* and *Buffalo Bill and the Indians . . . or Sitting Bull's History Lesson*. Her characteristic roles are as superficially assured but internally neurotic heroines, such as the garrulous BBC reporter Opal in Altman's *Nashville*.

Films include: 1965 Doctor Zhivago. '67 Stranger in the House (GB); Peppermint Frappé (SP); J'ai Tué Raspoutine (FR-IT) (GB: I Killed Rasputin). '70 The Hawaiians (GB: Master of the Islands). '73 The Three Musketeers: The Queen's Diamonds (PAN). '75 Nashville. '76 Criá Cuervos (SP) (USA: Cria!; GB: Raise Ravens); Buffalo Bill and the Indians . . . or Sitting Bull's History Lesson. '77 Roseland. '78 Remember My Name; A Wedding. '81 Les Uns et les Autres (FR).

CHAPLIN, Saul

(b. 1921). Composer/conductor/arranger/producer. Born: Saul Kaplan; New York, USA

The son of a clothing manufacturer, Chaplin studied accounting at New York University, playing piano at dances in his spare time. He teamed up with Sammy Cahn to write songs for the stage and vaudeville, eventually working with the likes of Phil Silvers, Betty Hutton, Bing Crosby and the Andrews Sisters. At the end of the Thirties the pair made a series of musical shorts for Vitaphone before moving to Columbia. Although Chaplin and Cahn split up, both continued to work in films, Chaplin winning Academy Awards for his work in the musicals *An American in Paris*, *Seven Brides for Seven Brothers* and *West Side Story*. Since 1957 Chaplin has been increasingly involved in production.

Films include: 1951 An American in Paris (co-mus. arr). '53 High Society (co-mus. supervisor); Kiss Me Kate (co-mus. dir). '54 Seven Brides for Seven Brothers (mus. supervisor). '56 Tea House of the August Moon (mus. supervisor). '61 West Side Story (assoc. prod). '63 I Could Go on Singing (mus. supervisor) (GB). '65 The Sound of Music (assoc. prod). '68 Star! (prod). '76 That's Entertainment Part 2 (co-prod).

Above: Charles Chaplin in A Dog's Life *(1918). Below: Geraldine Chaplin in* The Three Musketeers: The Queen's Diamonds

CHARISSE, Cyd

(b. 1921). Actress. Born: Tula Ellice
Finklea; Amarillo, Texas, USA

Cyd Charisse, owner of one of the
finest pair of legs ever to grace the
silver screen, began dancing at the
age of eight. Her early film work for
MGM, like *Ziegfeld Follies* (1946), was
largely uncredited, but she soon emerged as one of the most popular dancing
stars of the Forties, working with Gene
Kelly, and as the last – but perfectly
matched – partner for Fred Astaire.
With the decline of the musical in the
Fifties she turned to straight acting,
but with little success. In 1948 she
married singer Tony Martin, and the
two produced a joint autobiography,
The Two of Us, in 1976.

Films include: **1946** Till the Clouds Roll By;
The Harvey Girls. **'48** Words and Music. **'52**
Singin' in the Rain. **'53** The Band Wagon.
'54 Brigadoon; Deep in My Heart. **'55** It's
Always Fair Weather. **'56** Meet Me in Las
Vegas (GB: Viva Las Vegas). **'57** Silk Stock-
ings. **'58** Party Girl.

CHARTOFF, Robert

(b. 1934). Producer. Born: New
York City, USA

Chartoff's introduction to drama
came when he began working for a
theatrical agent in an effort to pay his
way through medical school. He abandoned medicine in favour of law at
the Columbia Law School, and after
graduation he started his own law
firm, specializing in artiste management. Through this he met Irwin
Winkler, and the two formed Chartoff-
Winkler Productions in 1965. Since
then they have produced over twenty
films, and revealed a talent for spot-
ting a good script. Their films have
been commercial but good quality,
notably *Point Blank*, *They Shoot
Horses, Don't They?* and *Raging Bull*.

Films include: **1967** Point Blank. **'69** They
Shoot Horses, Don't They? **'70** The Straw-
berry Statement. **'72** The New Centurions
(GB: Precinct 45 – Los Angeles Police). **'74**
The Gambler. **'76** Rocky. **'77** New York,
New York; Valentino. **'80** Raging Bull. **'81**
True Confessions.

CHASE, Borden

(1900–1971). Screenwriter. Born:
Frank Fowler; Chicago, Illinois, USA

Chase's early career was colourful. He
left school at 14 and worked in a
variety of jobs before becoming chauffeur to gangster Frankie Yale. When
Yale was murdered, possibly by Al
Capone, Chase turned to more mundane work as a tunnel digger in New
York. The accidental death of a colleague there gave him the idea for a
story, and he turned to writing. Hollywood invited him to script his novel
Sandbag, which emerged as *Under

Pressure. After that, Chase produced
many original screenplays which
were turned into competent action
films, often Westerns. He wrote the
scripts for the pilots for the television
series *Laredo* and *Daniel Boone*.

Films include: **1935** Under Pressure (co-sc).
'44 Fighting Seabees (co-sc). **'45** This Man's
Navy. **'48** Red River (co-sc). **'50** Winchester
'73 (co-sc). **'52** Lone Star; Bend of the River
(GB: Where the River Bends). **'54** Vera Cruz
(co-sc); The Far Country. **'56** Backlash.

CHASE, Charlie

(1893–1940). Actor/director. Born:
Charles Parrott; Baltimore,
Maryland, USA

Chase left school early for financial
reasons, working instead as a singer
in a Baltimore penny arcade. He
graduated to musical comedy and
vaudeville, but moved to Hollywood
to avoid the pace. By 1914 he was
with Keystone, playing in Arbuckle
and Chaplin vehicles. His major successes came when he moved to Hal
Roach's studios and directed a series
of comedy shorts. He later returned to
acting, creating a hero who was
smart and dapper but naive and

accident-prone, in a series of films
directed initially by Leo McCarey and
later by himself and his brother.
When Roach stopped making shorts in
1936, he moved to Columbia, where
he continued to work until his death
from a heart attack in 1940.

Films include: **1923** Sold at Auction (dir).
'24 All Wet. **'26** Mighty Like a Moose; Dog
Shy. **'27** Never the Dames Shall Meet. **'28**
Limousine Love. **'33** Nature in the Wrong;
Fallen Arches. **'39** Rattling Romeo. **'40** The
Heckler.

CHATTERJEE, Soumitra

(b. 1935). Actor. Born: Calcutta,
India

Soumitra Chatterjee's first appearance in a film shot him to stardom. In
1958 he was spotted by the director
Satyajit Ray who immediately cast
him in the lead in *Apur Sansar*, the
final part of his tremendously successful Apu trilogy. Prior to this he had
been a poet, a journalist and a stage
actor. Since his appearance in *Apur
Sansar* this tall, distinguished actor
with his classic Indian features has
worked with some of India's greatest
directors, and has maintained his

popularity through a series of finely
acted roles, mostly in Indian contemporary 'realist' dramas. He has
received the West Bengal Government's Award for Best Actor.

Films include: **1959** Apur Sansar (GB: The
World of Apu). **'60** Devi (GB: The Goddess).
'61 Teen Kanya (GB: Two Daughters). **'62**
Abhijaan (GB: The Expedition). **'64** Char-
ulata (GB: The Lonely Wife). **'65** Akash
Kusum; Kaparush-o-Mahapurish. **'73**
Ashani Sanket (GB: Distant Thunder). **'75**
Sonar Kella (GB: The Golden Fortress).

CHATTERTON, Ruth

(1893–1961). Actress. Born: New
York City, USA

During the late Twenties Hollywood
talent scouts were scouring the New
York stage for performers to appear in
the new sound films. At this time Ruth
Chatterton had been working on
Broadway for over ten years, having
achieved her first major success in
Daddy Long Legs in 1914. She soon
succumbed to the studios' offers, and
abandoned the stage to work exclusively in film. Over the next few years
she became one of the movies' most
popular stars, but her roles were not

good. By the mid-Thirties her career was slipping badly and was only saved by her excellent performance in *Dodsworth* in 1936. After this she returned to the stage – working in London and on Broadway, but by the Forties she was appearing almost exclusively in summer stock. She made her last performance on stage in *The Chalk Garden* in St Louis.

Films include: 1928 Sins of the Fathers. '29 Madame X; The Doctor's Secret; The Laughing Lady. '30 Sarah and Son; Anybody's Woman. '31 Once a Lady. '33 Female. '36 Dodsworth. '37 The Rat (GB).

CHAUVEL, Charles

(1897–1959). Director/producer. Born: Warwick, Queensland, Australia

The young Charles Chauvel studied art and kept fit by attending a gym run by sportsman Snowy Baker. Baker began making silent films and Chauvel became Baker's general dogsbody, giving up the idea of being an artist. He eventually took some acting lessons and appeared in the films himself. When Baker left for America and vaudeville, Chauvel

went with him, but he was set on working in movies and went to Hollywood, where he progressed from electrician, to actor, to publicity writer and finally to becoming assistant director to Fred Niblo. In 1923 he returned to Australia, and, after a financial struggle, started his own production company, making two films in 1926. He went to Hollywood to promote them but found he had been caught out by the coming of sound. He returned to Australia in 1930 and made *In the Wake of the Bounty* in 1933. The film was a great success and allowed him to continue making films set in the rugged Australian outback, often re-creating melodramatically episodes from history or folklore, and put him on the road to becoming one of the greatest Australian directors of all time. During the war he made documentaries and a couple of combat features, one of which, *Forty Thousand Horsemen*, was his biggest hit.

Films include: 1926 Moth of Moonbi; Greenhide. '33 In the Wake of the Bounty. '35 Heritage. '36 Uncivilised. '40 Forty Thousand Horsemen. '44 Rats of Tobruk (doc). '49 Sons of Matthew. '54 Jedda (USA: Jedda the Uncivilised).

CHAYEFSKY, Paddy

(1923–1981). Screenwriter. Born: New York City, USA

While recovering from wounds received fighting in Germany during World War II Paddy Chayefsky wrote a musical comedy that was performed to GIs throughout Europe. He then came to the notice of the writer Garson Kanin who invited him to contribute to *The True Glory* (1945), an award-winning documentary. Some time later Kanin again remembered Chayefsky's writing promise and gave him $500 to write a play but this, in addition to much of his early film work, proved unfruitful. He eventually made his breakthrough in television where he established himself with many hour-length plays. One of these, *Marty*, became his first major movie success. As a result of this he was able to turn out a number of screenplays that were mostly biting satirical views of contemporary American life. He won many prizes for his plays and films, receiving Oscars for *Marty* and *The Hospital*.

Films include: 1951 As Young As You Feel. '55 Marty. '56 The Catered Affair (GB: Wedding Breakfast). '57 The Bachelor

Party. '58 The Goddess. '59 Middle of the Night. '64 The Americanization of Emily. '69 Paint Your Wagon. '71 The Hospital. '76 Network. '80 Altered States.

CHERKASSOV, Nikolai

(1903–1966). Actor. Born: St Petersburg, Russia

As a young man Cherkassov was an avid theatre-goer and at the age of 16 he started working at the Marinsky Theatre. He first made his name in music-hall, and toured Central Asia in 1926. But he was soon bored with being a comic actor and became involved in serious theatre, which in turn led to leading roles in films such as *Baltic Deputy* and *Peter the First*. The director Sergei Eisenstein then cast him in the lead in *Alexander Nevsky*, and although the two seemed to have disagreements they continued to work together on both parts of *Ivan the Terrible*. Cherkassov also did much work in the theatre. This powerful actor with his strong features and deep resounding voice was greatly loved in the Soviet Union – and he received both the Order of Lenin and the Order of the Red Banner.

Films include: 1937 Deputat Baltiki (Baltic Deputy); Pyotr Pervyi I (GB: Peter the First, Part I). '38 Aleksandr Nevskii (GB: Alexander Nevsky). '39 Pyotr Pervyi II (GB: Peter the First, Part II). '44 Ivan Grosny I (GB: Ivan the Terrible, Part I). '46 Ivan Grosny II: Boyarskii Zagovar (GB: Ivan the Terrible: The Boyars' Plot). '47 Pirogov; Vo Imya Zhizni (In the Name of Life). '57 Don Kikhot (Don Quixote).

CHEVALIER, Maurice

(1888–1972). Singer/actor. Born: Menilmontant, Paris, France

Maurice Chevalier had his first taste of show business when, encouraged by his elder brother, he ran away from his poor family to become an acrobat. He then moved on to music-hall, and the turning point in his career arrived when he formed a partnership with the dancer Mistinguett. They performed at the Folies Bergère, became the toast of Paris and worked together intermittently for ten years. Having served in the French Army during World War I Chevalier continued his career in 1918 and ten years later went to Hollywood. Before long he was starring in his own vehicles, mostly playing crooning international romantic leads, often with comic touches. He returned to France in 1935 and continued in films and on stage. He stayed in France during World War II. There was some suspicion of his collaborating with the Nazis. As a result his career suffered and he concentrated mainly on one-man shows and French movies. He returned to America during the Fifties and Sixties.

Films include: 1929 The Love Parade. '31 The Smiling Lieutenant. '32 One Hour With You; Love Me Tonight. '33 The Way to Love. '34 The Merry Widow. '37 Break the News (GB). '47 Le Silence Est d'Or (FR) (USA: Man About Town). '58 Gigi. '62 In Search of the Castaways (GB: The Castaways).

CHIARI, Mario

(b. 1900). Art director. Born: Florence, Italy

Mario Chiari had been involved with the world of design during boyhood when he helped with the annual Maggio Musicale opera and various Florentine plays. In 1940 he went to Rome and began working as an assistant director on documentaries. Five years later he was working with Luchino Visconti, helping with the design for plays he was staging. In 1952 Chiari began designing for films and gradually developed his lush, ornate, finely observed style. Since then he has worked on a number of good productions, especially those of Visconti, with whom he seems to have a great affinity. He has also designed for theatre and opera, mainly in Italy, but occasionally in America.

Films include: 1951 Miracolo a Milano (cost. only). '53 I Vitelloni (IT-FR) (GB: The Spivs). '56 War and Peace (co-art dir) (IT-USA). '57 Le Notti Bianche (co-art dir) (FR-it) (GB: White Nights). '60 Five Branded Women (IT-USA). '66 La Bibbia/The Bible – In the Beginning (IT). '67 Doctor Dolittle (GB). '73 Ludwig (co-art dir) (IT-FR-GER). '76 King Kong (co-art dir) (USA).

CHRISTENSEN, Benjamin

(1879–1959). Director/actor. Born: Viborg, Denmark

Christensen began performing as an opera singer in 1902, and from there he moved to stage acting and directing – four years later he was also acting in films. He began to direct movies in 1913 and his early Danish films are thrillers, beautifully set and lit and with macabre undertones. But his career was a thing of fits and starts and there was a long gap before his next film, Häxan, appeared in 1922. This film, made in Sweden, is a masterly survey of medieval horrors. He then made three films in Germany for Ufa before going to America in 1925. From this period Mockery is a glum but powerful vehicle for the actor Lon Chaney, while Seven Footprints to Satan, an 'old-dark-house' send up, is a sheer delight – inventive, funny and striking to look at. He returned to Denmark in the early Thirties and made some minor films there between 1939 and 1943.

Films include: 1913 Det Hemmelighedsfulde X (+act) (DEN). '16 Haevnens Nat (DEN). '22 Häxan (+act) (SWED) (GB: Witchcraft Through the Ages). '24 Michael (actor only) (GER). '26 The Devil's Circus (USA). '27 Mockery (USA). '28 The Hawk's Nest (USA); The Haunted House (USA). '29 Seven Footprints to Satan (USA); The House of Horror (USA).

CHRISTIE, Julie

(b. 1941). Actress. Born: Assam, India

Mini-skirted and insouciantly swinging her handbag in Billy Liar and, later, a soft-lipped, hard-edged seductress in Darling . . ., Julie Christie was emblematic of the Sixties-generation young women in British films. But wider horizons were soon hers as she became much in demand as an international star, sought after by directors like David Lean, Joseph Losey, Nicolas Roeg and Robert Altman. The daughter of a tea planter, educated in England, she studied art in France before attending the Central School of Speech and Drama in London. After a spell in repertory in the late Fifties she eventually made her name in the title role of the television series A for Andromeda, which led to minor film roles and then Billy Liar. She continued to act on stage and eventually joined the Royal Shakespeare Company, touring America with Paul Scofield in A Comedy of Errors. It was soon after this that John Schlesinger's Darling . . . was written specifically for her, the film for which she won an Academy Award. She now lives on a farm and is an ardent campaigner for nuclear disarmament.

Films include: 1963 Billy Liar. '65 Doctor Zhivago (USA); Darling. . . . '66 Fahrenheit 451. '67 Far From the Madding Crowd. '68 Petulia (USA). '70 In Search of Gregory (GB-IT). '71 McCabe and Mrs Miller (USA); The Go-Between. '73 Don't Look Now (GB-IT). '75 Shampoo (USA). '81 Memoirs of a Survivor.

CHUKHRAI, Grigori

(b. 1921). Director. Born: Melitopol, Ukraine, USSR

Raised in Moscow, Chukhrai enrolled at the film school VGIK in 1939 but his studies were interrupted by the war. He became a paratrooper and was wounded five times. He completed his studies with the directors Mikhail Romm and Sergei Yutkevich, and worked as an assistant director with Romm. As a director, he remade a silent classic, The Forty-First, about a Red girl sniper in love with a White Russian soldier whom she eventually kills during the Civil War. Ballad of a Soldier, which won a prize at Cannes, continued to view the human aspect of war in its tale of a young hero briefly on leave. Clear Skies, an attack on Stalinism, confirmed Chukhrai's importance in the reaction against the restrictions of socialist realism. He went out of favour with the fall of Khruschev in 1964 but continued to make films intermittently, though with little international notice.

Films include: 1956 Sorok Pervyi (GB: The Forty-First). '60 Ballada o Soldate (USA/GB: Ballad of a Soldier). '61 Chisto'e Nebo (USA/GB: Clear Skies). '65 Zhili-Byli Starik So Starukhoi (USA: The Couple). '72 Pamyat (Remembrance). '78 Netepichnaja Istoria (An Untypical Story).

CHYTILOVÁ, Věra

(b. 1929). Director. Born: Ostrava, Czechoslovakia

Having abandoned her studies and done various odd jobs, Věra Chytilová worked her way up to assignments as assistant director at the Barrandov studios before attending the Prague film school (FAMU). Here she met most of the bright young talents who soon formed the Czech 'New Wave' of

Above: Julie Christie as the 'passionate, tender Lara' in Doctor Zhivago.
Below: Dane Clark in Deep Valley, *a thriller about an escaped gangster*

Above right: Diane Cilento in the suspense thriller The Naked Edge.
Right: Fred Clark in Don't Go Near the Water

the mid-Sixties. Like them she was strongly influenced by *cinéma-vérité*, preferring to use non-professional actors and improvisation; but, in collaboration with her husband and cameraman Jaroslav Kučera, she also aimed at an experimental and visually exciting look to her films. Her feminist viewpoint has been expressed in protest, sometimes astringently comic, against the boredom, disillusion and alienation in the lives of women. After the Russian invasion of 1968, she was unable to work again in Czechoslovakia until 1976.

Films include: 1962 Strop (short) (GB: The Ceiling); Pytel blech (short) (GB: A Bag of Fleas); O něčem jiném (GB: Something Different). '65 Perličky na dně *ep* Automat svět (GB: Pearls of the Deep *ep* The World of Self-Service). '66 Sedmikrásky (GB: Daisies). '70 Ovoce stromů rajských jíme (CZ-BELG) (We May Eat of the Fruit of the Trees of the Garden/The Fruits of Paradise). '77 Hra o jablko (GB: The Apple Game). '80 Kalamita (Calamity); Panelstory (Story From a Housing Estate).

CILENTO, Diane

(b. 1933). Actress. Born: New Guinea

Diane Cilento never really found the characteristic role that she deserved, and possibly gained more notoriety from the fact that she was married to Sean Connery than anything else. She was educated in Queensland and New York, studied at the American Academy of Dramatic Arts and went to RADA in London in 1950. It was her excellent stage performances at the Mercury Theatre in London and particularly at the Library Theatre in Manchester that earned her the critical acclaim that allowed her to break into films.

Films include: 1954 The Angel Who Pawned Her Harp. '57 The Admirable Crichton (USA: Paradise Lagoon). '59 Jet Storm. '61 The Naked Edge. '62 I Thank a Fool. '63 Tom Jones. '64 The Rattle of a Simple Man. '67 Hombre (USA). '73 Hitler: the Last Ten Days (GB-IT). '76 The Tiger Lily.

CIMINO, Michael

(b. 1943). Director/writer. Born: New York City, USA

Before actually working in film Cimino spent a short time with the directors' unit of the Actors' Studio in New York. He then became linked with the 'superbrats' generation of film-makers – Coppola, Spielberg, Scorsese and others – and became a protégé of Clint Eastwood with the films *Magnum Force* and *Thunderbolt and Lightfoot*. After the stunning box-office and critical success of *The Deer Hunter* he was given large amounts of money to make the epic *Heaven's Gate*. The film, hailed as the revival of the Western, in fact totally reverses certain genre characteristics of a Western: the cavalry arrives, but to rescue the baddies. The film was considered a failure by United Artists who produced it and it was severely edited before being released to critics and audiences, who seemed more than willing to damn it because of the publicity that surrounded its enormous budget.

Films: 1972 Silent Running (co-sc. only). '73 Magnum Force (co-sc. only). '74 Thunderbolt and Lightfoot. '78 The Deer Hunter. '80 Heaven's Gate.

CLAIR, René

(1898–1981). Director. Born: Paris, France

After service as a volunteer ambulanceman in World War I, Clair began acting in films but soon turned to writing and directing, showing a flair for fantasy and comedy. His association with the Surrealists is commemorated in *Entr'acte*; but he made his international reputation with a traditional farce, *The Italian Straw Hat*, which he enriched with elaborate visual comedy. His early sound films, *Sous les Toits de Paris* and *Le Million*, showed ordinary Parisians as they wished to see themselves, with humour and a touch of sentiment. *A Nous la Liberté* came close to political statement in its tale of a boss who gives his factory to the workers. *Le Dernier Milliardaire* ridiculed dictatorship and was his first failure. He went to work in England and, during the war years, in Hollywood. He was glad to return to France in 1945, but found it changed. His later comedies became gradually darker in tone, though he had a run of lively successes starring the actor Gérard Philippe. With the coming of the *nouvelle vague*, he seemed increasingly out of date and made no more films after 1965. In his heyday he had been ranked among the greatest French directors; and in 1960 he became the first film-maker as such to be elected to the prestigious French Academy.

Films include: 1923 Paris Qui Dort (GB: The Crazy Ray). '24 Entr'acte (short). '27 Un Chapeau de Paille d'Italie (USA: The Horse Ate the Hat; GB: The Italian Straw Hat). '30 Sous les Toits de Paris (USA: Under the Roofs of Paris). '31 Le Million (USA: The Million); A Nous la Liberté. '34 Le Dernier Milliardaire. '35 The Ghost Goes West (GB). '42 I Married a Witch (USA). '47 Le Silence

Est d'Or (USA: Man About Town). '49 La Beauté du Diable (FR-IT) (USA: Beauty and the Devil; GB: Beauty and the Beast). '52 Les Belles de Nuit (FR-IT) (USA: Beauties of the Night). '55 Les Grandes Manoeuvres (FR-IT) (USA: The Grand Maneuver). '61 Tout l'Or du Monde (FR-IT) (USA/GB: All the Gold in the World). '65 Les Fêtes Galantes (FR-RUM).

CLARK, Dane

(b. 1913). Actor. Born: Bernard Zaneville; New York City, USA

On the advice of his friend John Garfield, Dane Clark began acting when his studies at law school ended after the death of his sponsor. He worked in radio and theatre and then starred in several off-Broadway productions. After serving in the army in World War II he went to Hollywood where he managed to get some bit-parts. He then signed a one-picture deal with Warner Brothers for *Action in the North Atlantic* (1943). The film's star Humphrey Bogart, liked Clark and helped him to get another movie and a firm start in the business. During the Forties he tended to be cast as the first or second lead, often verging on the criminal. He was a fine actor, but due to continual bad casting his career waned and in 1950 Warners no longer wanted him. His work in Hollywood diminished and he concentrated mainly on Broadway and television. More recently Dane Clark has graduated to directing his own documentaries.

Films include: 1942 The Glass Key. '43 Destination Tokyo. '45 Pride of the Marines (GB: Forever in Love); God is My Co-Pilot. '46 A Stolen Life. '47 Deep Valley. '48 Moonrise. '50 Backfire; Highly Dangerous (GB). '55 The Toughest Man Alive. '70 The McMasters (GB: The McMasters . . . Tougher Than the West Itself).

CLARK, Fred

(1914-1968). Comedian/actor. Born: Lincoln, California, USA

Fred Clark had only previously appeared in college theatricals during his pre-med course at Stanford University when he decided to make acting his career. He won a two-year scholarship to the American Academy of Dramatic Arts in New York, and after graduating went on to the stage before making it to Hollywood where he tried to work as a heavy. Later on he established himself as a comic actor, and master of the 'slow burn'; his bald head, large face, cigar and authoritative-looking moustache made him the ideal witty and/or irascible businessman. In the later half of his career he appeared on television in shows such as the *Burns and Allen Show* and Milton Berle's comedy series, as well as making commercials for a dog-food company.

Films include: 1947 Unsuspected. '49 Flamingo Road. '50 Sunset Boulevard. '51 A Place in the Sun. '53 How to Marry a Millionaire. '54 Daddy Long Legs. '56 The Solid Gold Cadillac. '57 Don't Go Near the Water. '58 Auntie Mame. '68 Skidoo!

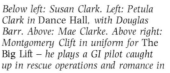

Below left: Susan Clark. Left: Petula Clark in Dance Hall, *with Douglas Barr. Above: Mae Clarke. Above right: Montgomery Clift in uniform for* The Big Lift – *he plays a GI pilot caught up in rescue operations and romance in post-World War II Germany. Above right: Jill Clayburgh as a nursery-school teacher nervously* Starting Over *in romance. Below: Pierre Clementi, an actor who has worked for some of Europe's best directors*

CLARK, Petula

(b. 1932). Actress/singer. Born: West Ewell, Surrey, England

When only nine years old, Petula Clark sang a song for her uncle on the BBC programme broadcasting to the forces during World War II. She was an outstanding success with the listeners and was taken on as a regular performer. By the age of 12 she had made over five thousand appearances broadcasting to a war-weary population, and was soon taken up by the British movie industry. At first she appeared as the 'cute kid' with an angelic voice, but as she began to mature rapidly, so it became harder to find the right roles for her. She made her television debut in the Fifties, but shortly afterwards moved to France with her husband. It wasn't until the Sixties that Clark began to make successful pop records, and since then she has become a popular club and show singer, as well as featuring in films such as *Finian's Rainbow* and *Goodbye Mr Chips*. In 1982 she appeared on stage in the lead role of *The Sound of Music* in London's West End.

Films include: 1945 I Know Where I'm Going. '48 Here Come the Huggetts; Vice Versa. '49 Don't Ever Leave Me; Vote for Huggett. '50 Dance Hall. '52 Made in Heaven. '67 Finian's Rainbow. '69 Goodbye Mr Chips. '80 Second Star to the Right (USA).

CLARK, Susan

(b. 1940). Actress. Born: Sarnia, Ontario, Canada

Susan Clark was born into a wealthy family and as a child studied ballet, piano and singing. When she was 12 years old her parents enrolled her with the Toronto Children's Players. On leaving school she took up modelling before landing herself a part in the stage show *Silk Stockings*. After a short period of travelling with various stock companies, Clark decided to leave Canada and sign on at RADA in London, where she stayed after the completion of her course, finding work on the stage and in television. In 1964 she returned to Canada but Universal were attracted by her talent and signed her for a long-term contract. Since then this dark-haired,

elegant yet tough actress has found work in film and theatre and has scored many successes, notably in *Tell Them Willie Boy Is Here* and *Babe*.

Films include: 1968 Madigan; Coogan's Bluff. **'69** Tell Them Willie Boy Is Here. **'71** Valdez Is Coming; The Skin Game. **'74** The Midnight Man; Airport 1975. **'75** Night Moves; Babe. **'79** Murder By Decree.

CLARKE, Mae

(b. 1910). Actress. Born: Philadelphia, Pennsylvania, USA

Having grown up in Atlantic City and studied dancing as a child, Mae Clarke began her career in vaudeville and night-clubs. Her big break came while she was appearing in a musical comedy, *Manhattan Mary*, on Broadway; Fox decided to sign her up and in 1929 she made her film debut in *Big Time*. Offers of work then followed in quick succession, but Clarke never achieved the same star status as Barbara Stanwyck, her great friend from chorus-line days. Nevertheless, her roles were varied and interesting – hers was the face that received the grapefruit from James Cagney's hand in *The Public Enemy*. Blonde and very pretty, she was mainly favoured for character roles and second leads, and worked continuously throughout the Thirties, Forties and Fifties. In the Sixties she began doing a lot of work for television, but in the Seventies decided to retire and teach drama in California.

Films include: 1931 Reckless Living; Waterloo Bridge; The Public Enemy (GB: Enemies of the Public). **'32** Breach of Promise. **'33** Turn Back the Clock. **'34** This Side of Heaven; The Man With Two Faces. **'55** I Died a Thousand Times.

CLARKE, Shirley

(b. 1925). Director. Born: New York City, USA

On leaving school, Shirley Clarke took up modern dance under Martha Graham and started to perform her own works at the Dance Theatre in New York. From there she progressed

to Carnegie Hall and began to tour. It was while she was serving on the board of the National Dance Association that she became aware of the potential existing for dance on film, and in 1953 gave up her dancing career for movie-making. Initially her films were dance-orientated – very low-budget and always independently financed – but in the late Fifties she introduced other subject-matter and received special critical attention for *A Moment in Love*. In recent years, and perhaps because of her previous difficulty in finding finance for her work, Shirley Clarke has turned her attentions toward video.

Films include: 1954 Dance in the Sun (short). **'55** In Paris Parks (short); Bullfight (short). **'57** A Moment in Love (short). **'60** A Scary Time (short) (United Nations). **'61** The Connection. **'63** The Cool World/ Harlem Story/Echoes of the Jungle. **'67** Portrait of Jason. **'69** Lions Love (actor only).

CLARKE, T.E.B.

(b. 1907). Screenwriter. Born: Watford, Hertfordshire, England

Despite studying law at Cambridge, 'Tibby' Clarke was more interested in writing, and after graduation went to Australia where he found a job on a magazine. Back in London he worked as a staff writer in Fleet Street and after being a correspondent in Argentina for some years he wrote a book, *Go South – Go West*, in which he related his experiences. He continued to work as a freelance journalist and produced five novels. In 1943 he met the scenario editor for Ealing Studios and was taken on as a collaborator until his solo effort on *Hue and Cry* proved his own ability. This led to a fruitful partnership between Clarke and Ealing which lasted until the late Fifties. By 1970 he seemed to have tired of the screen, having worked from 1966 on several unfilmed Hollywood projects.

Films include: 1954 Dead of Night (golfing sequence only). **'47** Hue and Cry. **'49** Passport to Pimlico. **'50** The Blue Lamp; The Magnet. **'51** The Lavender Hill Mob. **'53** The Titfield Thunderbolt. **'54** The Rainbow Jacket. **'58** A Tale of Two Cities. **'60** Sons and Lovers (co-sc).

CLAYBURGH, Jill

(b. 1944). Actress. Born: New York City, USA

Jill Clayburgh studied philosophy and drama at the Sarah Lawrence College in Boston before joining the children's theatre at the city's Charles Playhouse. After several years in off-Broadway productions she made it to Broadway in the successful musicals *Pippin* and *The Rothschilds*, and during the Seventies became a sought-after Shakespearian actress. It wasn't until her appearance as Carole Lombard in *Gable and Lombard* that film companies really showed interest. International fame came to her through her role as an independent woman in *An Unmarried Woman*, for which she received an Academy Award nomination and the Best Actress prize at Cannes. Since then she has starred in several well-

received films as the woman struggling to choose between her man and her career.

Films include: 1972 Portnoy's Complaint. **'73** The Thief Who Came to Dinner. **'74** The Terminal Man. **'76** Silver Streak; Gable and Lombard. **'77** Semi-Tough. **'78** An Unmarried Woman. **'79** La Luna (IT) (USA: Luna); Starting Over. **'80** It's My Turn. **'82** I'm Dancing as Fast as I Can.

CLAYTON, Jack

(b. 1921). Director. Born: Brighton, Sussex, England

Jack Clayton wrote to the producer Alexander Korda while still in his teens and was taken on as a tea boy at Denham Studios. He worked hard and eventually graduated to the post of assistant director, after which he spent a short time in the cutting room at Warner Brothers. During World War II he served in the RAF and was transferred to the documentary film unit. After the war he worked with the director Anthony Asquith for a while before going back to Denham as an associate producer. The films he was then involved in included *The Queen of Spades* (1949), *I Am A Camera* (1955) and *The Story of Esther Costello* (1957). In 1956 he directed the short *The Bespoke Overcoat* which won awards at Edinburgh and Venice, as well as being honoured with an Oscar. This success brought him many offers of work as a director, and his international standing was secured with *Room At the Top*.

Films: 1944 Naples Is a Battlefield (doc). **'55** The Bespoke Overcoat (short). **'59** Room At the Top. **'61** The Innocents. **'64** The Pumpkin Eater. **'67** Our Mother's House. **'74** The Great Gatsby (USA).

CLÉMENT, René

(b. 1913). Director. Born: Bordeaux, France

René Clément studied architecture at the Ecole des Beaux Arts before deciding that his overriding interest lay in cameras and photography. He became a camera operator on short films and from 1936 made shorts by himself. During World War II he was at the Artistic and Technical Centre for young film-makers in Nice, where he made his propagandist movie *Chefs de Demain*. In 1945 he made *La Bataille du Rail* in Paris and this success was followed by his becoming the technical director for Jean Cocteau's *La Belle et la Bête* (1946). His most memorable film is *Jeux Interdits* with its heart-rending portrayals of children in war-torn France. After 1956 Clément specialized in large-budget international productions, but their quality has sadly declined.

Films include: 1936 Soigne Ton Gauche (short). **'43** Chefs de Demain (short). **'46** La Bataille du Rail. **'47** Les Maudits (GB: The Damned). **'49** Au Delà des Grilles (FR-IT) (GB: Beyond the Gates). **'50** Le Chateau de Verre. **'52** Jeux Interdits (USA: Forbidden Games; GB: Secret Games). **'54** Knave of Hearts (GB) (USA: Lovers, Happy Lovers). **'56** Gervaise. **'60** Plein Soleil (FR-IT) (GB: Blazing Sun). **'66** Paris Brule-t-il? (USA/GB:

Is Paris Burning?). **'71** La Maison Sous les Arbres (FR-IT) (USA/GB: The Deadly Trap).

CLEMENTI, Pierre

(b. 1942). Actor. Born: Paris, France

Born in Paris, Pierre Clementi studied acting at the Théâtre National Populaire and after a variety of non-acting jobs – telegraphist, messenger – he went onto the stage. His film debut was *Chien de Pique* (1960), directed by Yves Allégret, but it took him a further seven years to achieve stardom, which came with his appearances in Luis Buñuel's *Belle de Jour* and *La Voie Lactée*. His dark good looks and thin exotic features were then increasingly put to use by the young avant-garde film-makers such as Bernardo Bertolucci, Philippe Garrel, Liliana Cavani and Pier-Paolo Pasolini. In 1972 Clementi was arrested in Italy for drug possession. After 17 months' imprisonment he was released unconvicted and wrote a book, about his experiences.

Films include: 1961 Adorable Menteuse. **'62** Il Gattopardo (IT) (USA/GB: The Leopard). **'67** Belle de Jour (FR-IT). **'68** La Voie Lactée (FR-IT) (USA/GB: The Milky Way); Partner (IT); Benjamin ou Les Mémoires d'un Puceau. **'69** Le Lit de la Vierge; Porcile (IT-FR) (USA/GB: Pigsty). **'70** Il Conformista (IT-FR-GER) (USA/GB: The Conformist); I Cannibali (IT) (GB: The Cannibals). **'74** Steppenwolf (SWITZ).

CLIFT, Montgomery

(1920–1966). Actor. Born: Omaha, Nebraska, USA

Educated in Chicago, New York and St Moritz, Clift was on the amateur stage by the age of 13 and by the time he was 15 he was appearing in small professional roles. As he notched up Broadway successes, so he became critically recognized and Hollywood soon snapped him up to appear in *Red River* and *The Search*. Of slight build, with gaunt features and expressive eyes, Clift quickly became a romantic figure, especially when rumours of an affair with Elizabeth Taylor were rife. He appeared in three films with her – *A Place in the Sun*, *Raintree County* and *Suddenly, Last Summer* – but refused all her offers of marriage. In 1957, while making *Raintree County*, he was seriously injured in a car accident which affected him facially and emotionally. His looks deteriorated and his concentration on the set sadly declined. A sensitive, moody, introspective actor, he had great screen presence but was always hypercritical of his own performances. He died – ostensibly from a heart attack – while about to commence his fourth film with Elizabeth Taylor.

Films include: 1948 The Search (SWITZ-USA); Red River. **'49** The Heiress. **'50** The Big Lift. **'51** A Place in the Sun. **'52** I Confess. **'53** From Here to Eternity. **'57** Raintree County. **'58** The Young Lions; Lonely Hearts. **'59** Suddenly, Last Summer (GB). **'60** Wild River. **'61** Judgement at Nuremberg; The Misfits. **'62** Freud (GB: Freud – The Secret Passion). **'66** L'Espion (GER-FR) (USA/GB: The Defector).

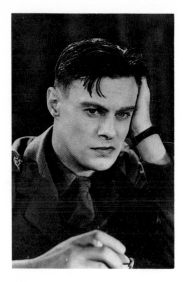

Above: Colin Clive as Captain Stanhope in Journey's End, *set in the trenches in France during World War I. The familiar faces of Lee J. Cobb (above right) and Charles Coburn (above, far right)*

CLIFTON, Elmer

(1892–1949). Director/actor. Born: Chicago, Illinois, USA

A stage actor from 1907, Elmer Clifton worked in films with D.W. Griffith from 1913 to 1922, rising to director by 1917. He was well-respected in the early Twenties, but was making cheap pictures by the end of the silent period. He worked mainly on B Westerns until 1949. Clifton will probably remain little more than a name. He acted splendidly in *The Birth of a Nation* (1915) and *Intolerance* (1916), and the rediscovery of *Down to the Sea in Ships*, remembered primarily for introducing Clara Bow, although it was also an exciting epic of old whaling ships, meant that his work as a director was not entirely lost.

Films as director include: 1917 Flame of Youth. '18 Battling Jane. '19 Peppy Polly. '22 Down to the Sea in Ships. '23 Six Cylinder Love. '24 The Warrens of Virginia; Daughters of the Night. '27 The Wreck of the Hesperus; Let 'er Go Gallegher (GB: Gallegher). '28 Virgin Lips. '38 The Stranger From Arizona. '49 Not Wanted.

CLIVE, Colin

(1898–1937). Actor. Born Colin Clive-Greig; St Malo, France

Colin Clive was educated at Sandhurst, but a riding accident ended his military career. On the stage from 1919 in London, his great success came in 1928 as the doomed Captain Stanhope in *Journey's End*. He went to Hollywood for James Whale's screen version, and until his early death commuted between the American studios and the London stage. With his dark, brooding appearance and English accent, he tended to be cast as the jealous, and sometimes even cruel suitor/husband, but broke away effectively at times, especially in roles where he could live on the edge of hysteria. He was perfect as Frankenstein in the first two films of the

series, a natural for Mr Rochester in *Jane Eyre*, and horribly tormented as the pianist with, he believes, a murderer's hands in *Mad Love*.

Films include: 1930 Journey's End (USA-GB). '31 Frankenstein (USA). '33 Christopher Strong (USA). '34 The Key (USA); One More River (USA) (GB: Over the River); Jane Eyre (USA). '35 Clive of India (USA); The Bride of Frankenstein (USA); Mad Love (USA) (GB: Hands of Orlac); The Girl from 10th Avenue (USA) (GB: Men on Her Mind); The Man Who Broke the Bank at Monte Carlo (USA). '37 History Is Made at Night (USA).

CLOUZOT, Henri-Georges

(1907–1977). Director. Born: Niort, France

A former journalist, Clouzot entered films in 1931 as a writer, worked on French versions of German films, suffered a long illness, and came back to direct his first feature in 1941. His next film, *Le Corbeau*, an account of the havoc wrought by a poison-pen writer in a small French town, was a superbly executed *noir* thriller, but it was made for a German-controlled company and presented an unlovely view of French character. Accordingly, Clouzot was charged after the war with collaboration, and received a suspended sentence. The film was banned for two years. He returned after a four-year break with *Quai des Orfèvres*, his best film – a marvellously atmospheric study of a Paris murder-hunt, dominated by the great actor Louis Jouvet. *Les Diaboliques*, massacred by English distributors' cuts, was his last outstanding film, a suspense thriller which gave full scope for the director's pessimistic outlook, his penchant for shock editing, and his ability to make a complicated narrative smooth and clear.

Films as director: 1942 L'Assassin Habite au 21. '43 Le Corbeau (GB: The Raven). '47 Quai des Orfèvres (USA: Jenny Lamour). '49 Manon; Retour à la Vie *ep* Le Retour de Jean (GB: Return to Life). '50 Miquette et sa Mère. '53 Le Salaire de la Peur (FR-IT) (GB: Wages of Fear). '55 Les Diaboliques (GB: The Fiends). '56 Le Mystère Picasso. '57 Les Espions. '60 La Vérité (FR-IT) (GB: The Truth). '68 La Prisonnière (GB: Woman in Chains).

COBB, Lee J.

(1911–1976). Actor. Born: Leo Jacoby; New York City, USA

One of the most striking American character actors of the Forties and Fifties, Lee Cobb made his stage debut at the Pasadena Playhouse in 1931. By 1935 he was a member of New York's famous Group Theater, appearing notably in *Golden Boy* and other plays by Clifford Odets. Later on, he scored an enormous success in the leading role of Arthur Miller's *Death of a Salesman*. His film career began in 1937, and this thickset, powerful, heavy-faced actor soon made his way as a supporting actor, also playing occasional leads. He could be a snarling tough, a benign patriarch, a cynical editor or cop; as any of them, he swept the opposition aside. Cobb has one of the cinema's most privileged moments in *Coogan's Bluff*: as the worldweary New York cop, he looks at Clint Eastwood with ineffable pity, and delivers the immortal putdown, 'I know – a man's gotta do what a man's gotta do.'

Films include: 1939 Golden Boy. '47 Boomerang. '48 Call Northside 777; The Dark Past. '54 On the Waterfront. '57 Twelve Angry Men. '58 Man of the West; Party Girl; The Brothers Karamazov. '60 Exodus. '68 Coogan's Bluff.

COBURN, Charles

(1877–1961). Actor. Born: Macon, Georgia, USA

When Charles Coburn made his first movie in 1935 he had already been in the theatre for some forty years. He and his wife, the actress Ivah Wills, formed their own repertory company and until she died in 1937 he refused to settle down in Hollywood as a character player. From the very first he looked as though he had spent his life there. The rich voice, the monocle, the impeccable timing, all made him perfect for high comedy. He could also summon up a self-doubting shiftiness, hinting that the dignity was something of a façade. All those years on the road never really left him. Whatever he played, he was always acting the part of an actor. An Oscar came his way in 1943 for Best Supporting Actor in *The More the Merrier*.

Films include: 1938 Of Human Hearts. '39 Idiot's Delight. '41 The Lady Eve; The Devil and Miss Jones; King's Row. '43 Heaven Can Wait; The More the Merrier. '44 Wilson. '46 The Green Years. '47 The Paradine Case. '52 Monkey Business. '53 Gentlemen Prefer Blondes.

COBURN, James

(b. 1928). Actor. Born: Laurel, Nebraska, USA

James Coburn studied acting at the University of Southern California and at Stella Adler's school in New York. After theatre and television work, he made his film debut in Budd Boetticher's *Ride Lonesome*, and a year later attracted attention as the knife-throwing cowboy in *The Magnificent Seven*. The lean, lazily relaxed Coburn played a variety of character roles, moved over to the spy-spoofs of the Flint films, and then, in a successful attempt to get away from a none too attractive image, both financed and played the lead in the satirical comedy-thriller *The President's Analyst*. His Pat Garrett, too, in Sam Peckinpah's *Pat Garrett and Billy the Kid* revealed an actor happily matured. As he gets older comedies may provide his best opportunities.

Films include: 1959 Ride Lonesome. '60 The Magnificent Seven. '62 The Great Escape (USA-GER). '64 The Americanization of Emily. '65 Major Dundee; A High Wind in Jamaica (GB); Our Man Flint. '67 The President's Analyst. '73 The Last of Sheila; Pat Garrett and Billy the Kid. '77 Cross of Iron (USA-GER). '80 The Baltimore Bullet.

COCHRAN, Steve.

(1917–1965). Actor. Born: Robert Alexander Cochran; Eureka, California, USA

Steve Cochran went from the University of Wyoming to ranching jobs to touring companies. He played in Shakespeare at Carmel, California, and appeared with Mae West in the revival of *Diamond Lil* on Broadway. He started in films in 1945, but good roles were scarce. He was usually cast as a selfish tough guy or an insensitive lover, but he was striking as a gangster in *White Heat*. His best parts

Above: James Coburn in Hard Contract *(1969). Above right: Steve Cochran in* Highway 301 *(1950). Below: James Coco in* A New Leaf. *Right: Jean Cocteau in* Le Testament d'Orphée. *Far right: Bill Cody Sr*

came in the middle Fifties. In *Come Next Spring*, an atmospheric rustic drama, he was excellent as a farmer fighting his way back after years as an alcoholic, while for Michelangelo Antonioni's *Il Grido* he went to Italy to play a sad wanderer who can never find a safe place in which to settle. In 1965 Cochran wrote, directed, produced and starred in *Tell Me in the Sunlight*, which was released posthumously in 1967.

Films include: 1945 Wonder Man. '46 The Chase; The Kid From Brooklyn; The Best Years of Our Lives. '49 White Heat. '50 The Damned Don't Cry; Storm Warning. '54 Carnival Story; Private Hell 36. '55 Come Next Spring. '57 Il Grido (IT-USA) (USA/GB: The Cry). '67 Tell Me in the Sunlight (+dir; +sc; +prod).

COCO, James

(b. 1929). Actor. Born: New York City, USA

James Coco spent years in summer stock, and television commercials before the break came. He appeared in the play *Next*, which was directed by Elaine May, was seen in it by playwright Neil Simon, and cast in

Simon's *Last of the Red Hot Lovers*. This was a Broadway hit, and led to a steady run of character roles and occasional leads in the movies. May and Simon continued to serve him well. His tightwad uncle in May's *A New Leaf* was perhaps his best film part, and he also scored in several movies written by Simon, winning an Oscar nomination for Best Supporting Actor in *Only When I Laugh*. But modern films aren't a good field for character actors; Coco's bald, chubby malevolence would have been perfect for the Thirties.

Films include: 1964 Ensign Pulver. '70 The Strawberry Statement; Tell Me That You Love Me, Junie Moon. '71 A New Leaf; Such Good Friends. '72 Man of La Mancha (IT). '75 The Wild Party. '76 Murder by Death. '77 Charleston (IT). '78 The Cheap Detective. '80 Wholly Moses! '81 Only When I Laugh (GB: It Hurts Only When I Laugh).

COCTEAU, Jean

(1889–1963). Poet/painter/screenwriter/director. Born: Maisons Lafitte, France

Jean Cocteau published his first book of poems at the age of 20; thereafter he

moved from one art form to another, illuminating them all. In his first film, *Le Sang d'un Poète*, he was director, writer, editor and designer, and he dubbed the voices of all the cast bar the leading lady. Fifteen years passed before he directed again, but in the interim there were scripts for films such as Jean Delannoy's *L'Eternel Retour*, which was essentially a Cocteau film. Between 1945 and 1959 he directed his five major films. They form, in a sense, one long work – the autobiography of a poet. The films are pervaded by magic, by myth, by dream, and they work supremely well because Cocteau grounded them in unmistakeable reality.

Films include: 1930 Le Sang d'un Poète (USA: The Blood of a Poet). '40 La Comédie du Bonheur (sc. only). '43 Le Baron Fantôme (co-sc. only) (GB: The Phantom Baron); L'Eternel Retour (sc. only) (GB: Love Eternal). '45 La Belle et la Bête (USA/GB: Beauty and the Beast); Les Dames du Bois de Boulogne (co-sc. only). '47 L'Aigle à Deux Têtes (USA: The Eagle With Two Heads). '48 Les Parents Terribles (USA: Intimate Relations). '50 Les Enfants Terribles (co-sc. only); Orphée (USA: Orpheus). '59 Le Testament d'Orphée ou Ne Me Demandez Pas Pourquoi (USA: Testament of Orpheus). '64 Thomas l'Imposteur (co-sc. only).

CODY Sr, Bill

(1891–1948). Actor. Born: William Joseph Cody; Winnipeg, Manitoba, Canada

After touring with a stock company, Bill Cody ended up in Los Angeles in 1924 and made his movie debut in Pathé Westerns. He soon became a popular cowboy hero, after the William S. Hart pattern of the silent, strong man of action with little time for romance. From 1927 he had his own production company. When this folded, Cody worked for Universal. He continued to star through the Thirties under the Monogram banner, but by the end of the decade had retired from the screen. He made occasional appearances, however, in travelling shows with the Cole Brothers Circus. One Cody film is of outstanding interest. In 1927 he made *Gold from Weepah* in that boom town in Nevada while the gold rush was still on, and a Klondike old-timer directed it.

Films include: 1925 Border Justice; Cold Nerve. '27 Gold From Weepah. '28 Laddie Be Good. '31 Under Texas Skies. '32 Ghost City; Mason of the Mounted. '34 Frontier Days. '35 Cyclone Ranger. '39 The Fighting Gringo.

CODY, Lew

(1888–1934). Actor. Born: Louis Joseph Coté; Waterville, Maine, USA

Of French descent, Lew Cody abandoned a medical career to go on the stage. Vaudeville and stock were followed by films, at first with Thomas Ince, from 1915. By the early Twenties his career was flourishing. Debonair and handsome, but a shade exotic in appearance, he usually played villains in his early years, but moved over to light comedy, marital dramas and such, at times for prestigious directors like Cecil B. DeMille and Ernst Lubitsch. Cody was married to actresses Dorothy Dalton and Mabel Normand. He was a noted wit, and in considerable demand as an after-dinner speaker. He died young at a time when the suave comedies of the later Thirties could have revived a flagging career.

Films include: 1915 The Mating. '17 A Branded Soul. '19 Don't Change Your Husband. '22 The Secrets of Paris. '23 Rupert of Hentzau. '24 The Shooting of Dan McGrew; Three Women. '25 Time, the Comedian. '27 Tea for Three. '30 What a Widow!. '31 Dishonored. '33 Sitting Pretty.

COHN, Harry

(1891–1958). Production executive. Born: New York City, USA

Harry Cohn was the son of an immigrant tailor. He left school early, and was successively chorus-boy, song-plugger, singer in cinemas and vaudevillian. In 1919 Harry, his brother Jack and a former Universal employee, Joe Brandt, formed CBC Film Sales Company. In 1924 the little studio became Columbia Pictures. By the end of the Twenties Columbia, with one outstanding director in Frank Capra, was advancing. By the mid-Thirties, helped by the phenomenal success of Capra's It Happened One Night, the studio could be reckoned a major, a position it retained until Harry Cohn's death in 1958. Cohn was single-minded, overbearing, bullying, foul-mouthed and unscrupulous. He was also capable of extreme personal kindness. He had a passion for movies, and was a superb judge of material, paying huge sums for a property he trusted. He developed countless stars (Rita Hayworth, Jean Arthur, William Holden, Jack Lemmon, Kim Novak), and suspended them ruthlessly if they resisted his bidding. They called this man 'Harry the Horror' and 'White Fang', and worse no doubt, but his drive and his belief in his studio created some of the best movies of Hollywood's Golden Age, and if he judged films, as they said, by the reaction of his posterior, there were a lot worse guides than that.

Columbia films in Cohn's time include: 1934 It Happened One Night. '35 The Whole Town's Talking (GB: Passport to Fame). '36 Mr Deeds Goes to Town. '37 The Awful Truth. '38 You Can't Take It with You. '39 Mr Smith Goes to Washington; Only Angels Have Wings. '40 His Girl Friday. '44 Cover Girl. '49 All the King's Men. '50 Born Yesterday. '54 On the Waterfront.

COLBERT, Claudette

(b. 1905). Actress. Born: Claudette Cauchoin; Saint-Mandé, Paris, France

Claudette Colbert came to New York as a child, and was appearing on the stage by the early Twenties. She had some success, but her one silent film, For the Love of Mike, directed by Frank Capra, was a failure. Her film career proper began with sound. At first she played a wide variety of roles, from sophisticated comedy with Ernst Lubitsch (The Smiling Lieutenant) to sexy frolics for DeMille (The Sign of the Cross). Then in 1934, It Happened One Night, in which she played a runaway heiress with enormous charm and spirit, not only made her a big star – it showed how skilful she was at light romantic comedy with cutting lines for her to deliver. For ten years or so she had scarcely a failure, and directors like Mitchell Leisen, Preston Sturges, and Lubitsch drew from her a succession of perfectly timed, devastatingly witty performances.

Films include: 1927 For the Love of Mike. '31 The Smiling Lieutenant. '32 The Sign of the Cross. '33 Three-Cornered Moon. '34 It Happened One Night; Cleopatra; Imitation of Life. '36 She Married Her Boss. '37 Tovarich. '38 Bluebeard's Eight Wife. '39 Midnight; Drums Along the Mohawk. '40 Arise My Love. '42 The Palm Beach Story.

COLE, George

(b. 1925). Actor. Born: Tooting, London, England

Hard-working character actor of British films, radio and television, George Cole left school at the age of 14, and the same year landed himself a stage part as the cockney evacuee in Cottage to Let, a role he was to repeat in Anthony Asquith's screen version. Coaching from the distinguished actor Alastair Sim led to better stage and film parts, and when Cole returned to stage and cinema after war service he settled into a long series of comedy portrayals, usually as a well-meaning, bullied, mild little chap, and later on as spiv or con-man, notably as 'Flash Harry' in the St Trinian's series. He enjoyed further success as a small-time racketeer in the television series Minder, and in the West End version of The Pirates of Penzance.

Films include: 1941 Cottage to Let (USA: Bombsight Stolen). '44 Henry V. '51 Laughter in Paradise. '52 Top Secret (USA: Mr Potts Goes to Moscow). '53 The Intruder. '54 The Belles of St Trinian's. '57 Blue Murder at St Trinian's. '59 Too Many Crooks. '61 The Anatomist. '65 One Way Pendulum. '76 The Blue Bird (USA-USSR).

COLE, Nat 'King'

(1919–1965). Singer/pianist/actor. Born: Nathaniel Adams Coles; Montgomery, Alabama, USA

One of four brothers, all professional musicians, Nat 'King' Cole grew up in Chicago, and by 1934 was leader of his own band. He toured in the road show Shuffle Along, was a piano soloist in Los Angeles clubs, and (not yet a

Left: George Cole in The Belles of St Trinian's. Above left: Lew Cody. Above: Claudette Colbert. Below: Joan Collins in Game for Vultures (1979). Right: Bonar Colleano in Pool of London. Below right: Ronald Colman in The Man Who Broke the Bank at Monte Carlo

lead singer) formed a popular group, the King Cole Trio. In the late Forties Cole's solo singing became more prominent, and the trio disbanded. His film appearances were usually as a singer, but he did play one starring role, as W.C. Handy in St Louis Blues.

Films include: 1943 Here Comes Elmer. '44 Pin-Up Girl. '49 Make-Believe Ballroom. '53 The Blue Gardenia; Small Town Girl. '55 Kiss Me Deadly. '56 Istanbul. '57 China Gate. '58 St Louis Blues. '65 Cat Ballou.

COLLEANO, Bonar

(1924–1958). Actor. Born: Bonar William Sullivan; New York City, USA

From the age of five Bonar Colleano was a member of his family's acrobatic circus act. He graduated, via music hall and radio, to the stage, where in 1949 he played opposite Vivien Leigh in A Streetcar Named Desire. On the British screen from 1944, he gave many fine, sinewy performances, usually as a brash American on the loose in England but occasionally playing a crook. He always enlivened what were frequently rather dull movies. He was killed in a car crash at the age of 34.

Films include: 1945 The Way to the Stars (USA: Johnny in the Clouds). '46 A Matter of Life and Death (USA: Stairway to Heaven). '48 Sleeping Car to Trieste. '49 Give Us This Day (USA: Salt to the Devil). '51 Pool of London. '54 Flame and the Flesh; The Sea Shall Not Have Them. '55 Joe Macbeth. '56 Zarak. '57 Fire Down Below. '58 The Man Inside.

COLLINS, Alf

(1866–?). Director. Born: Walworth, London, England

A small part player in the London theatre towards the end of the nineteenth century, and for thirty years stage manager for music-hall star Kate Carney, Alf Collins found himself drawn to early motion pictures, and in 1903 the pioneer R.W. Paul gave him the chance to make his first film. Collins went on to make animated shorts for the music hall, and other shorts for Gaumont, including, up to 1910, a series of chase movies, often shot on location. His 1903 film *Welshed, A Derby Day Incident* opened with a panning shot, highly unusual for that time, and later chase films contained point-of-view shots from pursued and pursuing cars. Some of Collins' work survives, notably *Raid on a Coiner's Den*, a nice little suspense film, influenced by Edwin S. Porter's *The Great Train Robbery* (1903) and by no

means inferior to it. It is not known when Collins died.

Films include: 1903 Welshed, A Derby Day Incident; Rip Van Winkle; The Pickpocket – a Chase Through London; The Runaway Match/Marriage by Motor. '04 Raid on a Coiner's Den. '08 Black-Eyed Susan/The Lass Who Loved a Sailor. '09 The Quicksilver Pudding. '10 Winning a Widow.

COLLINS, John H.

(1892–1918). Director. Born: New York City, USA

Soon after leaving school, John Collins joined the Edison Company in New York, and worked there as a casting director and special-effects technician. In 1913 he began directing. In the six years left to him (he died, tragically young, in the great epidemic of Spanish influenza in 1918) he directed over forty films. In 1916 he and his wife, the actress Viola Dana, joined the new Metro company, and Collins made films for them – mostly starring Dana – in New York and in Hollywood. Collins is the great rediscovery of early American cinema. Some half dozen of the films survive, including the magnificent *Blue Jeans*. Collins turned this old stage melodrama into a classic piece of Americana that is amusing, moving and exciting, and beautifully shot by the great cameraman, John Arnold, who worked on all Collins' later films.

Films include: 1915 On Dangerous Paths; The Children of Eve. '16 The Cossack Whip; The Flower of No Man's Land. '17 A Wife by Proxy; The Girl Without a Soul; Blue Jeans. '18 A Weaver of Dreams; Riders of the Night; Flower of the Dusk.

COLLINS, Joan

(b. 1933). Actress. Born: Bayswater, London, England

Joan Collins appeared in four films before graduating from the Royal Academy of Dramatic Art. Originally tending to be cast as a juvenile delinquent, she moved on to glamorous brunette leads, and from 1955 starred in a number of Hollywood films. She was married to Maxwell Reed and then to Anthony Newley, for a time submerging her career in his. Latterly she has appeared in horror films, or lavish soft-core movies like *The Stud* (from a novel by her sister, Jackie Collins). Her forty-odd films do include one Henry Hathaway and one Howard Hawks (from which the director wanted his name removed), but are otherwise a pretty depressing lot. She remains, however, a popular and ageless sex symbol.

Films include: 1952 I Believe in You. '55 Land of the Pharaohs (USA). '58 Rally 'Round the Flag Boys (USA). '60 Seven Thieves (USA). '62 The Road to Hong Kong (GB-USA). '69 Can Hieronymous Merkin Ever Forget Mercy Humppe and Find True Happiness? '72 Tales From the Crypt. '78 The Stud. '79 The Bitch; Sunburn (USA). '82 Nutcracker.

COLLINSON, Peter

(1939–1980). Director. Born: Cleethorpes, Lincolnshire, England

When still very young, Peter Collinson had a one-man variety act. He moved into commercial television, and began directing in Ireland. After a number of well-written, low-budget films, Collinson directed *The Italian Job*, a competent and successful crime thriller. His later films tended to the stylishly superficial but, in all fairness, he did find himself landed with some numbingly awful scripts, for example *Ten Little Indians*, and to go all out for a flashy impact was probably all he could do.

Films include: 1967 The Penthouse. '68 The Long Day's Dying. '69 The Italian Job. '70 You Can't Win Them All. '72 Innocent Bystanders. '73 A Man Called Noon (GB-SP-IT). '74 Los Cazadores (SP-SWITZ) (GB/USA: Open Season). '75 Ten Little Indians (USA: And Then There Were None). '76 The Sell Out. '78 Tomorrow Never Comes. '79 The House on Garibaldi Street (USA).

COLMAN, Ronald

(1891–1958). Actor. Born: Richmond, Surrey, England

Ronald Colman was invalided out of the Army in 1916, went on the stage and into British films, and emigrated to the USA in 1920. A stage performance brought him to Lillian Gish's attention, and Colman was given the lead opposite her in Henry King's *The White Sister*. His urbane, romantic air, distinguished appearance, allied to his acting ability, made him a great star in the last years of the silents, his partnership with Vilma Banky being especially notable. Sound enabled him to use his cultured, very English and very expressive voice, and for another twenty years he played leading roles. He was usually the idealistic hero of adventure epics or swashbucklers, but he was never typed, being highly effective in parts as different from his accepted line as the doctor in John Ford's *Arrowsmith* or the actor in George Cukor's *A Double Life*, for which in 1947 he won the Oscar for Best Actor. Above all, Ronald Colman never took himself too seriously. There was always a suspicion of irony, and rather more than a flicker of humour, behind that supremely gentlemanly manner and that sympathetic smile. His second wife was actress Benita Hume.

Films include: 1923 The White Sister. '24 Romola. '25 Stella Dallas; Lady Windermere's Fan. '26 Beau Geste; The Winning of Barbara Worth. '29 Bulldog Drummond. '30 Raffles. '31 Arrowsmith. '35 Clive of India; The Man Who Broke the Bank at Monte Carlo; A Tale of Two Cities. '37 Lost Horizon; The Prisoner of Zenda. '42 The Talk of the Town; Random Harvest. '47 A Double Life.

COMDEN, Betty

(b. 1916). Lyricist/scriptwriter. Born: Betty Cohen; New York, USA

Betty Comden was educated at New York University. In 1939 she joined Judy Holliday and Adolph Green in a cabaret act. She went on to collaborate with Green on the book and lyrics of *On the Town* and other Broadway musicals. In 1947 the partnership went into films with Arthur Freed's unit at MGM, producing ten musicals. All were intensely enjoyable: *On the Town* and *Singin' in the Rain* are acknowledged masterpieces, and the underrated *Take Me Out to the Ball Game* falls little short. The Comden-Green musicals integrate plot, character and song, but they tend to do so by reducing the storyline to a minimum, substituting a lavish helping of gags, and gaining a great deal of character development in the lyrics.

Films: 1947 Good News (co-sc; +co-lyr). '49 Take Me Out to the Ball Game (co-lyr. only); The Barkleys of Broadway (co-sc. only); On the Town (co-sc; +co-lyr). '52 Singin' in the Rain (co-sc; +co-lyr). '53 The Band Wagon (co-sc. only). '55 It's Always Fair Weather (co-sc; +co-lyr). '58 Auntie Marie (co-sc. only). '60 Bells Are Ringing (co-sc; +co-lyr). '64 What a Way to Go! (co-sc; +co-lyr).

Above: Betty Compson in She Got What She Wanted *(1930). Right: Chester Conklin. Far right: Jimmy Conlin. Below: Fay Compton as the grandmother in* The Virgin and the Gypsy, *directed by Christopher Miles*

COMENCINI, Luigi

(b. 1916). Director. Born: Salò, Italy

After living in France during his adolescence, Comencini returned to Italy to study architecture in Milan. There he met another future director, Alberto Lattuada, and with him organized a private film club, collecting old films and laying the foundations for the Cineteca Italiana, the national film archive. He also worked for a while as an assistant director and film critic. After the war he wrote for the Socialist paper *Avanti* and started to direct with a short, socially critical documentary about young people living in Naples, *Bambini in Città*. Once in features, he soon became more commercial, setting aside his original sympathies with neo-realism and using poverty as a picturesque background for successful comedies. His *Bread, Love and Dreams* helped to establish Vittorio De Sica and Gina Lollobrigida as international stars.

Films include: 1946 Bambini in Città (doc. short). '54 Pane, Amore e Fantasia (GB: Bread, Love and Dreams); Pane, Amore e Gelosia (GB: Bread, Love and Jealousy). '61 Tutti a Casa (IT-FR) (USA: Everybody Go Home). '62 A Cavallo della Tigre (GB: Jail Break). '64 La Ragazza di Bube (GB: Bebo's Girl); La Mia Signora ep Eritrea; Tre Notti d'Amore ep Fate Bene Fratelli (IT-FR). '65

La Bugiarda (IT-FR-SP); Il Compagno Don Camillo (IT-FR-GER); Le Bambole *ep* Il Trattato di Eugenetica (IT-FR) (GB: Four Kinds of Love *ep* A Treatise on Eugenics). '78 Il Gatto (USA: The Cat).

COMPSON, Betty

(1897–1974). Actress. Born: Eleanor Luicime Compson; Beaver, Utah, USA

Betty Compson started in show business as a vaudeville violinist, entering films in 1915 in Al Christie comedies. After several years of slapstick and Westerns, she was cast by the director George Loane Tucker as the girl member of a gang of confidence tricksters in *The Miracle Man*. She was enormously successful and soon had her own production company. Her other famous silent performance was in *The Docks of New York*, as the touching waif rescued from attempted suicide by the hero (George Bancroft). She was also notable as the unhappy assistant to a crazed ventriloquist (Erich von Stroheim) in *The Great Gabbo*, directed by her then husband James Cruze. She declined from lead to character roles in the Thirties, but continued to work sporadically through the Forties until her last film in 1948.

Films include: 1919 The Miracle Man. '21 Prisoners of Love; Ladies Must Live; The Little Minister. '22 Always the Woman; To Have and to Hold. '25 The Pony Express. '28 The Big City; The Docks of New York. '29 The Great Gabbo.

COMPTON, Fay

(1894–1978). Actress. Born: Virginia Lilian Emmiline Compton; London, England

Primarily a theatre actress, and familiar on radio (her voice was distinctive and beautiful) and on television, Fay Compton also had a long and distinguished career in films, mainly as a character actress. Born into a theatrical family, she went on the stage early, working her way through farce and revue to drama, including the title role of *Mary Rose*, written especially for her by J.M. Barrie. During the Twenties she made silent films and also appeared on the West End stage. In the late Twenties she went to America, but a Broadway play and an early talkie with Adolphe Menjou both failed. She returned to London and regained her star status in the play *Autumn Crocus*. The most notable role of her later career was Emilia in Orson Welles' *Othello*, though she also made her presence felt as the obnoxious Grandma in *The Virgin and the Gypsy*. She was awarded the CBE in 1975.

Films include: 1921 A Woman of No Importance. '22 The Old Wives' Tale. '47 Odd Man Out; Nicholas Nickleby. '48 London Belongs to Me. '51 Laughter in Paradise. '52 Othello (MOR). '57 The Story of Esther Costello. '63 The Haunting. '69 I Start Counting. '70 The Virgin and the Gypsy.

CONKLIN, Chester

(1888–1971). Actor. Born: Oskaloosa, Iowa, USA

Small in stature and with bulging, myopic eyes, Conklin sported a walrus moustache and an engaging personal line in lunacy. From a road-show and circus background, he joined Mack

Sennett just before World War I and was at first chiefly associated with the Keystone Kops. After several hundred comedies for Sennett, he essayed his first straight role as the father of the unhappy Trina (ZaSu Pitts) in Erich von Stroheim's *Greed*. He was badly hit by the Wall Street Crash and the coming of sound, but he went on acting occasionally, even after the Forties. For a while, he worked as a Santa Claus in a Los Angeles department store. In 1965 he eloped to Las Vegas, at the age of 77, with 65-year-old June Gunther, his fourth wife. Conklin is familiar to everyone who has seen one of those silent-comedy compilation features.

Films include: 1914 Dough and Dynamite; The Face on the Bar Room Floor; Tillie's Punctured Romance. '17 A Pullman Bride. '25 Greed. '26 We're in the Navy Now. '36 Modern Times. '39 Hollywood Cavalcade. '40 The Great Dictator. '49 The Beautiful Blonde From Bashful Bend.

CONLIN, Jimmy

(1885–1962). Actor. Born: James Conlin; Camden, New Jersey, USA

Small and as fragile-looking as a sparrow, Jimmy Conlin came through the tough training of vaudeville, where he had formed a team with his wife Myrtle Glass, to appear in Warners' first all-talkie short, *Sharps and Flats*, and in their first all-talkie feature, *Lights of New York* (both 1928). He settled in Hollywood in 1932 and made many films there over a thirty-year period, sometimes using the name James Conlon. He was a favourite of the director Preston Sturges, who cast him in several films. He also appeared in a television series, *Duffy's Tavern*.

Films include: 1933 College Humor. '34 City Limits. '38 Crashing Hollywood. '41 The Lady Eve; Sullivan's Travels. '42 The Remarkable Andrew. '43 The Miracle of Morgan's Creek. '45 An Angel Comes to Brooklyn. '46 Mad Wednesday (orig. title: The Sin of Harold Diddlebock). '47 Mourning Becomes Electra. '50 The Great Rupert. '59 Anatomy of a Murder.

CONNERY, Sean

(b. 1930). Actor. Born: Thomas Connery; Edinburgh, Scotland

Sean Connery took some time to throw off the James Bond image that he had made his own in the Sixties and to establish himself in other interesting roles as a middle-aged and gradually balding, but still tough hero. Before Bond he was a slow starter working his way up, after a spell in the Royal Navy, through male modelling and the West End chorus of *South Pacific* to repertory and film extra jobs. He got bigger parts in action movies of the late Fifties and early Sixties until *Dr No* transformed his career. He made five Bond films in six years and his last, *Diamonds Are Forever*, after a four-year gap. Then he finally discarded the toupée and the slick image, going his own way in such varied parts as the murderously self-righteous policeman in *The Offence*, the romantic Arab chieftain in *The Wind and the Lion*, the Kiplingesque soldier in *The Man Who Would Be King*, and the ageing Robin Hood in *Robin and Marian*. These were distinguished developments of the talent he had already shown in *Marnie*, *The Hill*, *A Fine Madness* and *The Molly Maguires*. He was married to actress Diane Cilento from 1962 to 1972.

Films include: 1957 No Road Back. '61 The Frightened City. '62 The Longest Day (USA); Dr No. '63 From Russia With Love. '64 Marnie (USA); Goldfinger. '65 The Hill; Thunderball. '66 A Fine Madness. '67 You Only Live Twice. '68 Shalako. '70 The Molly Maguires (USA). '71 Diamonds Are Forever. '72 The Offence. '74 Murder on the Orient Express. '75 The Wind and the Lion (USA); The Man Who Would Be King. '76 Robin and Marian (USA). '79 The First Great Train Robbery (USA: The Great Train Robbery). '81 Outland. '82 Five Days One Summer (USA); Wrong is Right (USA) (GB: The Man with the Deadly Lens). '83 Never Say Never Again.

CONNOLLY, Walter

(1887–1940). Actor. Born: Cincinnati, Ohio, USA

A Broadway actor before moving to Hollywood, Walter Connolly was heavily built with a black moustache and large jowls. He had a talent for playing older men with dangerously high blood pressure, always in a panic, such as the father of the heiress (Claudette Colbert) in *It Happened One Night*. But he also acted straight dramatic roles with some expertise. His career was cut short by his untimely death at 53 from a stroke.

Films include: 1932 The Bitter Tea of General Yen. '33 Lady for a Day. '34 It Happened One Night; Twentieth Century. '36 Soak the Rich; Libeled Lady. '37 The Good Earth. '38 Too Hot to Handle. '39 The Adventures of Huckleberry Finn; The Great Victor Herbert.

CONNORS, Chuck

(b. 1921). Actor. Born: Kevin Joseph Connors; New York City, USA

As a professional baseball player, Chuck Connors appeared for the Los Angeles Angels and was noticed by movie people for his comic antics on the field, which led to bit parts. William Wyler gave him a bigger role as the brutish, cowardly son in *The Big Country*, and he decided to concentrate on acting. He started to work in television and was eventually cast in the lead in *Rifleman*, the series that made him a star of the small screen. He never achieved the same success in movies, though he appeared in quite a number, particularly Westerns; perhaps his macho style and looks came to seem a little dated.

Films include: 1952 Pat and Mike. '55 Target Zero. '57 The Hired Gun; Death in Small Doses. '58 The Big Country. '62 Geronimo (USA-MEX). '63 Move Over, Darling. '69 Captain Nemo and the Underwater City (GB). '72 Pancho Villa (SP). '73 Soylent Green.

CONSTANTINE, Eddie

(b. 1917). Actor. Born: Los Angeles, California, USA

Eddie Constantine came from a family of opera-singers and he himself had trained in Los Angeles, London and Vienna; but this led only to work in a radio choir in Los Angeles and a few chorus parts in MGM musicals. So he went with his wife to France when she found work as a dancer there. He became a successful singer in cabarets and music halls in Paris, and started to play Peter Cheyney's tough hero Lemmy Caution in French films. He was soon identified with this role – even in Jean-Luc Godard's eccentric variant *Alphaville* – and with the private-eye Nick Carter. Though he made considerable efforts to broaden his range, including appearing in a couple of films by the German director Rainer Werner Fassbinder, his craggy face and American tough-guy looks tend to stereotype him for European audiences.

Films include: 1953 La Môme Vert de Gris. '56 Les Truands (GB: Lock Up Your Spoons). '58 Incognito. '59 Du Rififi Chez les Femmes (FR-IT) (GB: Rififi and the Women); Passport to Shame (GB) (USA: Room 43). '62 L'Empire de la Nuit. '65 Alphaville, une Etrange Aventure de Lemmy Caution (FR-IT). '69 Lions Love (USA). '71 Warnung vor einer heiligen Nutte (GER-IT) (USA/GB: Beware of a Holy Whore). '76 Le Couple Témoin (FR-SWITZ). '79 Die dritte Generation (GER) (USA/GB: The Third Generation). '80 The Long Good Friday (GB).

CONTE, Richard

(1914–1975). Actor. Born: Nicholas Conte; Jersey City, New Jersey, USA

Born to Italian immigrant parents, Conte did odd jobs until he was spotted doing an act at a resort hotel by Elia Kazan and John Garfield, and offered a scholarship at the Neighborhood Playhouse in New York. His stage career was a success and he was named by the drama critic George Jean Nathan as the most outstanding actor of 1942 for his performance in the play *Jason*. After brief army service he was signed by 20th Century-Fox, and appeared at first mainly in war films like *A Walk in the Sun*. But his dark, strong, Italian looks led him during the late Forties and Fifties to *film noir*, frequently as a criminal on the run or a loner fighting the system. His career became less prominent with the decline of the genre, but he appeared regularly in films and television in the Sixties and early Seventies. His increasingly lined and life-worn face seemed to reflect a whole movie world of strains, tensions and sudden violence.

Films include: 1944 The Purple Heart. '45 A Walk in the Sun. '46 Somewhere in the Night. '48 Call Northside 777; Cry of the City. '49 Thieves' Highway; Whirlpool. '50 The Sleeping City; Under the Gun. '53 The Blue Gardenia. '55 New York Confidential. '67 Tony Rome. '68 Lady in Cement. '72 The Godfather.

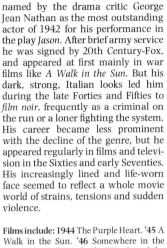

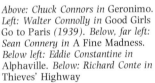
Above: Chuck Connors in Geronimo. *Left: Walter Connolly in* Good Girls Go to Paris *(1939). Below, far left: Sean Connery in* A Fine Madness. *Below left: Eddie Constantine in* Alphaville. *Below: Richard Conte in* Thieves' Highway

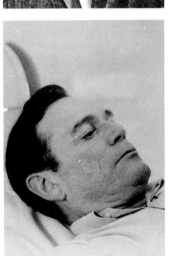

CONWAY, Jack

(1887–1952). Director. Born: Graceville, Minnesota, USA

Of Irish descent, Conway joined a stock company after high school. He then began acting in films, mostly Westerns, from 1911 and is reputed to have played over a hundred roles. He started to direct in 1915 and worked continuously until the late Forties, mostly for MGM, where he was a typical journeyman director with little personal touch or style but considerable competence. Conway will probably be best remembered for *A Tale of Two Cities*, with Ronald Colman, and *Boom Town*, with Spencer Tracy and Clark Gable.

Films include: 1915 The Old High Chair. '16 The Silent Battle. '17 Her Soul's Inspiration. '25 The Hunted Woman. '32 Arsene Lupin; Red-Headed Woman. '34 A Tale of Two Cities. '36 Libeled Lady. '38 A Yank at Oxford (GB). '40 Boom Town. '41 Honky Tonk. '47 The Hucksters.

CONWAY, Tom

(1904–1967). Actor. Born: Thomas Charles Sanders; St Petersburg, Russia

Tom Sanders and his brother, actor George Sanders, were of British descent, though living in Russia until just before the Revolution. Tom was educated at Bedales (which expelled him) and Brighton College with his brother, who later encouraged him to try the stage. He changed his name to Conway and, after some repertory and radio work, went to Hollywood and got a contract with MGM, playing supporting roles. He moved to RKO in 1942 and co-starred with George in *The Falcon's Brother*; shortly afterwards he took over from George the part of Tom Lawrence, ex-jewel thief turned private eye, known as The Falcon. He made nine more Falcon films and three horror films with producer Val Lewton at RKO. Later his career declined, though he worked regularly till about 1960, and he became destitute before his death in 1967. He had always been overshadowed by his brother, whom he resembled in being an upper-crust English type, tall, suave and handsome in a tweedy, conventional way, but with much less personal style, wit or charm.

Films include: 1940 Sky Murder. '41 Free and Easy. '42 Rio Rita; Mrs Miniver; The Falcon's Brother; Cat People. '43 I Walked With a Zombie; The Falcon Strikes Back. '46 Whistle Stop. '47 Lost Honeymoon. '48 One Touch of Venus. '51 Bride of the Gorilla. '53 Park Plaza 605 (GB) (USA: Norman Conquest).

COOGAN, Jackie

(1914–1984). Actor. Born: John Leslie Coogan; Los Angeles, California, USA

His father was an eccentric dancer in vaudeville and his mother had been a child star, Baby Lillian. Jackie Coogan's first screen appearance was in *Skinner's Baby* for Essanay. He toured with his parents as a child and was seen in Los Angeles by Charles Chaplin, who chose him for *The Kid*, first trying him out in *A Day's Pleasure*. The huge success of *The Kid* led to many other child roles and worldwide vaudeville tours with his father, who died in 1935. His mother then married his business manager, Arthur Bernstein, and in 1938 Coogan sued them for a share of his earnings as a child. The suit was settled in 1939 and he was awarded $126,000; the case led to Californian legislation, popularly known as the Coogan Act, which provided for the setting up of trust funds to safeguard the earnings of young actors. Coogan's waning career was interrupted by war service as a glider pilot. Unable to make a success of leading roles, he became a character actor in the Fifties. Having been fair-haired, wistful and appealing as a child, he had grown burly, beefy and bald, and frequently played heavies. A new generation probably knew him best as Uncle Fester in *The Addams Family* on television. Betty Grable was the first (1936–39) of his four wives.

Films include: 1917 Skinner's Baby. '19 A Day's Pleasure. '21 The Kid; Peck's Bad Boy. '22 Trouble; Oliver Twist. '30 Tom Sawyer. '56 The Proud Ones. '57 The Joker Is Wild. '58 High School Confidential. '66 A Fine Madness. '73 Cahill, United States Marshal (GB: Cahill).

COOK, Donald

(1901–1961). Actor. Born: Portland, Oregon, USA

Educated at the University of Oregon, Donald Cook went into vaudeville and straight theatre, making his Broadway debut in 1925. He entered films in 1930, playing many supporting roles, such as the self-righteous brother of the gangster (James Cagney) in *The Public Enemy*. He looked good, being tall, dark, smooth-haired and with even features, but he was rather stiff and expressionless, projecting little personality. In later years he worked mostly in the theatre, specializing in middle-aged roués, but occasionally returned to films – for instance, as the father of the heroine (Ann Blyth) in *Our Very Own*.

Films include: 1931 The Public Enemy (GB: Enemies of the Public). '32 The Conquerors (reissued as The Pioneer Builders). '33 Jennie Gerhardt; Baby Face; Brief Moment. '34 Viva Villa!; Jealousy. '35 The Casino Murder Case. '36 Showboat. '44 Bowery to Broadway. '45 Here Come the Co-eds. '50 Our Very Own.

COOK Jr, Elisha

(b. 1906). Actor. Born: San Francisco, California, USA

Everybody feels sorry for him. He always gets the fuzzy end of the lollipop and usually he half-deserves it. A small man with a gentle, nervous face and wild eyes, topped by a shock of brown hair, he cannot keep a whine out of his voice while trying to act tough. He is quite likely to pull a gun and wave it around but he usu-

ally ends up violently dead. Elisha Cook Jr was a stage actor from the age of 14 and signed with Paramount in 1936. He achieved notice and established a recognizable image as Wilmer, the inefficient gunman, in *The Maltese Falcon*, perpetually being humiliated and disarmed by Sam Spade (Humphrey Bogart). He encountered Bogart again (who this time was playing Philip Marlowe) as Harry Jones, the gallant but doomed loser, in *The Big Sleep*. Cook has continued to make a virtue of vulnerability right into the Eighties, taking time out to appear in the theatre, where he played Arturo Ui, the Hitler figure of Bertolt Brecht's play *The Resistible Rise of Arturo Ui* in 1963.

Films include: 1940 Stranger on the Third Floor. '41 I Wake Up Screaming; The Maltese Falcon; Hellzapoppin'. '44 Phantom Lady. '45 Dillinger. '46 The Big Sleep. '53 Shane. '56 The Killing. '57 Baby Face Nelson. '68 Rosemary's Baby. '75 The Black Bird.

COOPER, Gary

(1901–1961). Actor. Born: Frank Cooper; Helena, Montana, USA

His parents were immigrants and he was educated in England, but in films 'Coop' was the truest son of the American soil. He espoused the smalltown or backwoods virtues of simplicity, honour, gallantry and integrity. He was a tall, lean, laconic loner faced by corruption, deceit and sophisticated women, and in that role – through *Mr Deeds Goes to Town*, *The Fountainhead* and *High Noon* – he became one of the great stars, though by the Fifties his handsomeness and the dark voice were cracking under the strain. Perhaps, in his movies, Cooper had carried the burden of America's troubles for too long. He originally came to Los Angeles looking for a job as a newspaper cartoonist but found his way into films as a $10-a-day extra. The silents enabled him to be taciturn, and after *The Winning of Barbara Worth* Paramount snapped him up and at first cast him as a shy lover for Clara Bow. Few can match Cooper's record for excellence. He was a major Western star for over thirty years – *The Virginian* (still strong and silent in his first talkie), *The Westerner*, *Man of the*

West and as the lonest of all marshals in *High Noon*, which brought him his second Oscar. He appeared in some of the best screwball comedies – *Design for Living*, *Bluebeard's Eighth Wife*, *Ball of Fire*. He was the archetypal populist hero for Frank Capra in *Mr Deeds Goes to Town* and *Meet John Doe* and a troubled but ideal war hero in *Sergeant York* (the first Oscar). And, as the star of *A Farewell to Arms* and *For Whom the Bell Tolls*, he was the perfect Hemingway hero, the prettiness of movies never obscuring his essential masculinity, solitariness, or naturalness. Gary Cooper was at various times romantically involved with co-stars Clara Bow, Evelyn Brent, Fay Wray and Patricia Neal. In 1933 he married New York socialite Veronica Balfe, whom he widowed when he died in 1961, still an American but one who had never played a bad guy.

Above, far left: Tom Conway in The Falcon Strikes Back. *Left: Jackie Coogan in* Little Robinson Crusoe *(1924). Above: Elisha Cook Jr. Below left: Donald Cook*

Below: Gary Cooper in Garden of Evil *(1954). Below right: Jackie Cooper in* The Bowery, *set during the Gay Nineties. Right: Gladys Cooper, madeup for* Now, Voyager

Films include: 1926 The Winning of Barbara Worth. **'27** Wings. **'29** The Virginian. **'30** Morocco. **'32** A Farewell to Arms. **'33** Design for Living. **'35** The Lives of a Bengal Lancer. **'36** Mr Deeds Goes to Town; The Plainsman. **'38** Bluebeard's Eighth Wife. **'40** The Westerner. **'41** Meet John Doe; Sergeant York; Ball of Fire. **'43** For Whom the Bell Tolls. **'49** The Fountainhead. **'52** High Noon. **'54** Vera Cruz. **'57** Love in the Afternoon. **'58** Man of the West. **'59** The Wreck of the Mary Deare. **'61** The Naked Edge.

COOPER, Gladys

(1888–1971). Actress. Born: Lewisham, London, England

Her father, prominent publisher Charles Frederick Cooper, hated the idea of her going on the stage but in 1905 Gladys made her debut. During World War I, following a film debut in *The Eleventh Commandment* in 1913, she became a famous pin-up girl for the troops, also entertaining them at the front. She disliked films at first and worked mainly in the theatre, establishing herself critically in the Twenties when she starred in and presented Somerset Maugham plays. Pretty, gracious, ageless, one of the first ladies of the English stage, she went to Hollywood as a character actress to appear in Alfred Hitchcock's *Rebecca* and stayed there for thirty years, working in many classic melodramas and earning Oscar nominations for her performances in *Now, Voyager*, *The Song of Bernadette* and *My Fair Lady*. She took in Broadway, *The Rogues* television series and ended up playing dignified but impish old ladies. She was a Dame of the British Empire.

Films include: 1923 Bonnie Prince Charlie (GB). **'35** The Iron Duke (GB). **'40** Rebecca (USA). **'41** That Hamilton Woman! (USA) (GB: Lady Hamilton); The Black Cat (USA). **'42** Now, Voyager (USA). **'43** The Song of Bernadette (USA); Forever and a Day (USA). **'49** The Secret Garden (USA). **'58** Separate Tables (USA). **'64** My Fair Lady (USA).

COOPER, Jackie

(b. 1923). Actor. Born: Richard Cooper; Los Angeles, California, USA

His father was a comedian, his mother a pianist and his uncle film director Norman Taurog, so it was only natural that from the age of three Jackie Cooper should start acting on screen and radio. He became one of the main stars of the Our Gang series of comedy shorts and then Taurog gave him the lead in *Skippy*, for which Jackie was nominated for an Oscar. He worked hard in the next few years and became one of the most popular of juvenile stars. Snub-nosed, fair-haired, tough and defiant or kindly and weeping, he may have been America's idea of perfect little boyhood. His best films – *The Champ* and *Treasure Island* – cast him as the half-pint pal of burly Wallace Beery, but then Cooper grew up. His film appearances became infrequent and he gravitated towards the stage and television as actor, producer and director. But he can be seen in *Superman, The Movie* and *Superman II*, now a man – but still in a boy's world.

Films include: 1929 Sunny Side Up. **'31** Skippy; The Champ. **'32** When a Feller Needs a Friend. **'33** The Bowery. **'34** Treasure Island. **'36** The Devil Is a Sissy. **'37** Boy of the Streets. **'38** That Certain Age. **'39** What a Life. **'40** The Return of Frank James. **'47** Kilroy Was Here. **'72** Stand Up and Be Counted (dir. only). **'78** Superman, The Movie. **'80** Superman II.

COOPER, Merian C.

(1894–1973). Producer/director. Born: Jacksonville, Florida, USA

Cooper was the model for Carl Denham, the producer in *King Kong* who brings Kong to New York – and that more or less summarizes his greatest achievement. A graduate from Annapolis, he served as a captain in World War I and afterwards became an expeditionary reporter. He then joined up with wartime friend Ernest B. Schoedsack and together they produced and directed for their own company two influential travelogue documentaries, *Grass* and *Chang*, shot respectively in Persia and Siam, and an adventure feature, *The Four Feathers*. Cooper then joined David O. Selznick at RKO, dreamed up *King Kong* and sent for Schoedsack to help him make it in a studio-built jungle. As an adventure-fantasy movie, the story of the giant ape who grapples with dinosaurs, rampages through Manhattan and finally topples from the Empire State Building is simply unsurpassed. In the Thirties Cooper took over from Selznick as head of production at RKO and later joined him at his independent company. He was a much-decorated Chief of Staff of the China Air Task Force during World War II, after which he co-produced with John Ford some of the latter's finest Westerns – including *Wagonmaster*, *The Searchers* and the Cavalry trilogy. In the Fifties Cooper also helped to develop Cinerama.

Films include: 1926 Grass (co-dir; +co-prod). **'27** Chang (co-dir; +co-prod). **'29** The Four Feathers (co-dir; +co-prod). **'32** The Most Dangerous Game (assoc. prod) (GB: Hounds of Zaroff). **'33** King Kong (co-dir; +co-prod); Little Women (exec. prod); Flying Down to Rio (exec. prod). **'35** The Last Days of Pompeii (co-prod). **'48** Fort Apache (co-prod). **'49** She Wore a Yellow Ribbon (co-prod); Mighty Joe Young (co-prod). **'50** Wagonmaster (co-prod); Rio Grande (co-prod). **'52** The Quiet Man (co-prod). **'56** The Searchers (exec. prod).

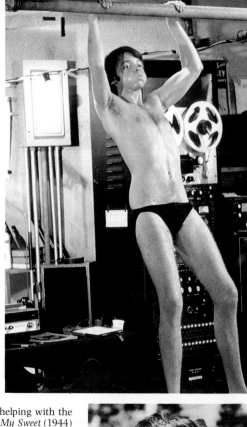

COOTE, Robert

(1909–1982). Actor. Born: London, England.

Coote played the 'Tally Ho!' RAF pilot Bob who is killed in action and cheerfully registers himself in heaven while his squadron leader (David Niven) faces a divine tribunal in *A Matter of Life and Death*. Impeccably English, with a plump face, round eyes and a big moustache, the actor made a career out of such roles, playing a series of officers and eccentrics. The son of comedian Bert Coote and from a long line of actors, he began in stock after public school and made his film debut along with Gracie Fields in *Sally in Our Alley*. Before and after the war – in which he served in the Royal Canadian Air Force – he worked in Hollywood as well as Britain, but in the Fifties concentrated, very successfully, on the stage. His film appearances since then were sporadic.

Films include: 1931 Sally in Our Alley. **'38** A Yank at Oxford. **'39** Gunga Din (USA); Nurse Edith Cavell (USA). **'46** A Matter of Life and Death (USA: Stairway to Heaven). **'47** Forever Amber (USA); The Ghost and Mrs Muir (USA). **'50** The Elusive Pimpernel (USA: The Fighting Pimpernel). **'52** The Prisoner of Zenda (USA). **'60** The League of Gentlemen. **'68** Prudence and the Pill. **'73** Theatre of Blood.

COPPOLA, Francis Ford

(b. 1939). Director/producer/screenwriter. Born: Detroit, Michigan, USA

The giant of Hollywood's 'movie brat' generation, Francis Coppola has unremittingly ploughed his money and his talent – is it genius? – into making massive personal movies that have, with the exception of the universally acclaimed *The Godfather*, divided both critics and cinemagoers. *The Godfather* and *The Godfather, Part II* comprise a sprawling ballad of organized crime in America. *The Conversation* is a comparatively modest study of surveillance and paranoia, introducing Watergate into the American home. *Apocalypse Now* is an awesome voyage movie that goes far deeper than any other film on the Vietnam War. If there is an underlying theme in these

pictures, then it is obsession – chiefly Coppola's. He studied theatre arts in New York and then film-making at UCLA; while there he got a job as a production assistant with Roger Corman and directed his first film, *Dementia 13*. He moved to Warner Brothers as a scriptwriter and, after directing the Fred Astaire musical *Finian's Rainbow* and a 'feminist' road movie, *The Rain People*, went independent in 1969 with his own studio American Zoetrope – which the failure of *One From the Heart* forced him to sell in 1982. Like Corman, Coppola has financially encouraged young film-makers, and has even found time to immerse himself in distribution, publishing (with *City* magazine), and radio-station and theatre ownership. Like a latterday Charles Foster Kane or Don Vito Corleone, Coppola does nothing by halves.

Films include: 1963 Dementia 13 (USA-EIRE) (GB: The Haunted and the Hunted). **'66** You're a Big Boy Now. **'67** Finian's Rainbow. **'69** The Rain People. **'72** The Godfather. **'73** American Graffiti (co-prod. only). **'74** The Great Gatsby (sc. only); The Conversation; The Godfather, Part II. **'79** Apocalypse Now. **'81** One From the Heart. **'82** Hammett (exec. prod. only); The Outsiders.

CORBY, Ellen

(b. 1913). Actress. Born: Ellen Hansen; Racine, Wisconsin, USA

She started as an amateur stage actress in Philadelphia, worked on the chorus line in an Atlantic City nightclub and went to try her luck in Hollywood. After a couple of bit parts she settled for being a script girl for 12 years – writing a couple of Hopalong

Cassidy movies and helping with the dialogue on *Murder, My Sweet* (1944) – before going back in front of the cameras in *Cornered*. Corby quickly became typecast as a domestic servant or town busybody, too nosey for her own good, and as such she was indispensable to several movies. She was nominated for the Best Supporting Actress Oscar for her Norwegian maid in *I Remember Mama* and won an Emmy in 1973 for her portrayal of the much-loved Grandma in television's *The Waltons*, a series to which she also contributed scripts.

Films include: 1945 Cornered; The Spiral Staircase. **'46** It's a Wonderful Life. **'47** Forever Amber. **'48** I Remember Mama. **'49** Little Women. **'50** The Gunfighter. **'53** Shane. **'58** Vertigo. **'64** Hush. . .Hush, Sweet Charlotte. **'68** The Legend of Lylah Clare.

COREY, Jeff

(b. 1914). Actor/dramatic coach. Born: New York City, USA

Corey is gaunt, often bearded, with large, dark eyebrows and the apprehensive look of a man used to life's troubles. He first acted on the New York stage and on tour during the Thirties. He went to Hollywood in 1937 and soon found work in supporting roles. Profoundly interested in his craft, he helped found the Actors' Laboratory and between 1951 and 1963, when he was blacklisted and unable to make films, taught drama. In the Sixties he returned to character roles – playing the sheriff in *Butch Cassidy and the Sundance Kid* and Wild Bill Hickok in *Little Big Man* – but continues to teach, running the Jeff

Corey Acting Studio. He is regarded a leading dramatic coach in Hollywood. Corey has also directed for television.

Films include: 1946 The Killers. **'47** Brute Force. **'49** Home of the Brave. **'64** Lady in a Cage. **'65** Mickey One. **'67** In Cold Blood. **'68** The Boston Strangler. **'69** Butch Cassidy and the Sundance Kid. **'70** Little Big Man. **'77** Oh, God! **'78** Jennifer.

COREY, Wendell

(1914–1968). Actor. Born: Dracut, Massachusetts, USA

Cynical-looking Wendell Corey gave solid, understated support to more celebrated stars in many post-war thrillers and dramas, whether playing a cop (*Rear Window*) or a murderer (*The Killer Is Loose*, 1956). Before 1945,

Far left: Robert Coote in Prudence and the Pill. *Centre left: Francis Ford Coppola. Left: Bud Cort in* Brewster McCloud. *Above, left to right: Allen Corby in* The Family Jewels; *Adrienne Corri in* The Vampire Lovers *(1970). Valentina Cortese in* Day For Night. *Below: Wendell Corey. Below, left: Jeff Corey in* True Grit

when his performances in the play *Dream Girl* first brought him to Hollywood's attention, he had been a salesman, a war hero (awarded the Legion of Honour by Czechoslovakia) and a hardworking but not immediately successful actor. In the Sixties this former president of the Academy of Motion Picture Arts and Sciences became a member of the Santa Monica, California, City Council, holding the post until his death from a liver complaint caused by alcoholism. He appeared in the television series *Climax* and *11th Hour*.

Films include: 1947 Desert Fury. **'48** The Accused; Sorry, Wrong Number; The Search. **'49** Any Number Can Play; The File on Thelma Jordan. **'53** Laughing Anne. **'54** Rear Window. **'55** The Big Knife. **'56** The Rainmaker. **'68** Buckskin.

CORMAN, Roger

(b. 1926). Producer/director. Born: Detroit, Michigan, USA

Corman's record is enviable. Though his films have been modest and sometimes lacking in quality, he has proved himself – with innumerable hits and not one major failure among the 150-odd films he has directed, supervised and produced – the most successful film-maker in America since the early Sixties. He spent three years in the navy after studying engineering at Stanford University and then worked his way up from messenger boy to story analyst at 20th Century-Fox. He studied English at Oxford University in England before returning to Hollywood as a literary agent and breaking into films again. Since the early Fifties he has striven to put the excellence into exploitation movies chiefly for the teen market, completing dozens of monster, science-fiction, horror (notably his personal series of Edgar Allan Poe adaptations starring Vincent Price), hot-rod, drug, 'nurse' and gangster movies – most of them for American International Pictures and his own company New World. All were quickly made on non-existent budgets. He has commendably given vital chances to such directors as Francis Ford Coppola, Martin Scorsese, Peter Bogdanovich and Monte Hellman, and actors Jack Nicholson, Peter Fonda, Ellen Burstyn and David Carradine. In the Seventies he extended his scope to the distribution of European 'art' movies. As a director he has yet to astound the critics, but *The Intruder* is an incisive social-conscience drama, and the Poe films are imaginative, colourful and creepy.

Films include: 1954 The Monster From the Ocean Floor (prod. only). **'55** The Beast With 1,000,000 Eyes (prod. only); Swamp Women. **'58** Viking Women and the Sea Serpent (GB: Viking Women); Machine Gun Kelly. **'60** Fall of the House of Usher/House of Usher; The Little Shop of Horrors (+ act). **'61** The Pit and the Pendulum. **'62** The Premature Burial; The Intruder/I Hate Your Guts. **'63** The Raven; The Man With the X-Ray Eyes. **'64** The Masque of the Red Death (GB-USA); The Tomb of Ligeia (GB-USA). **'66** The Wild Angels. **'67** The St Valentine's Day Massacre; The Trip; Targets (prod. only).

'70 Bloody Mama. **'72** Boxcar Bertha (prod. only). **'75** Death Race 2000 (prod. only). **'79** Saint Jack (prod. only). **'80** Battle Beyond the Stars (exec. prod. only).

CORRI, Adrienne

(b. 1930). Actress. Born: Adrienne Riccoboni; Glasgow, Scotland

The Glaswegian, red-haired daughter of an Italian, Adrienne Corri has, not surprisingly, a fiery, flamboyant temperament that won her a number of roles as sexy, headstrong girls in horror films in the early Sixties. After RADA (where she was the youngest pupil), she achieved some stage success in England and the USA and made her film debut in *The Romantic Age*, soon afterwards appearing in Jean Renoir's Indian film *The River*. Her theatrical style perhaps prevented her becoming a leading star, and she has worked mainly on stage and in television. But she appeared advantageously in *A Clockwork Orange*, the victim of a bizarre gang-rape. She is married to actor Daniel Massey.

Films include: 1949 The Romantic Age (USA: Naughty Arlette). **'51** The River (IND); Quo Vadis? (USA). **'54** Lease of Life. **'60** The Tell-Tale Heart. **'61** The Hellfire Club. **'65** Doctor Zhivago (USA); A Study in Terror (USA: Fog); Bunny Lake Is Missing. **'67** The Viking Queen. **'71** A Clockwork Orange. **'75** Rosebud (USA). **'78** Revenge of the Pink Panther. **'79** The Human Factor (GB-USA).

CORT, Bud

(b. 1949). Actor. Born: Walter Cox; New Rochelle, New York, USA

Cort is not conventional movie-star material. Slight, baby-faced, with big, innocent eyes sometimes hiding behind glasses and threatened by a dark fringe, he has the appearance of an awkward, screwed-up adolescent and that is the role he has mostly played. Two films stand out – *Brewster McCloud*, in which he plays a youth aspiring to be a bird, and *Harold and Maude*, in which he is a teenager forming a bizarre relationship with an old lady. The son of bandleader Joe

Cox, Cort studied art but worked in New York fringe theatre and revue where he was noticed by Robert Altman who launched his eccentric film career by giving him a small part in *M*A*S*H*.

Films include: 1967 Up the Down Staircase. **'69** Sweet Charity. **'70** M*A*S*H; Brewster McCloud; The Traveling Executioner; The Strawberry Statement; Gas-s-s-s, or It May Be Necessary To Destroy the World in Order To Save It. **'71** Harold and Maude. **'76** Bernice Bobs Her Hair (orig. TV). **'77** Why Shoot the Teacher? (CAN). **'78** Hitler's Son (GER). **'81** She Dances Alone (A-USA).

CORTESE, Valentina

(b. 1925). Actress. Born: Milan, Italy

At 15 she enrolled at the Academy of Dramatic Arts in Rome and was almost immediately chosen by one of her teachers for a role in a theatrical film, *Orizzonte Dipinto*. Cortese, dark and sensual, then worked steadily in Italian films and plays until she achieved international fame as the remote beauty – an Englishman's dream girl – in the British *The Glass Mountain*, more legendary even than its theme music. After that, her name changed to Cortesa, she played a series of exotic broads for 20th Century-Fox – notably in *Thieves' Highway* and *The House on Telegraph Hill* – during her brief Hollywood sojourn. Back in Europe, she has worked for Federico Fellini, François Truffaut (an excellent performance in *Day for Night*) and other leading directors, and also acted in Brecht and Pirandello in the Italian theatre. Her first of two husbands was actor Richard Basehart.

Films include: 1940 Orizzonte Dipinto (IT). **'49** The Glass Mountain (GB); Thieves' Highway (USA). **'51** The House on Telegraph Hill (USA). **'54** The Barefoot Contessa (USA-IT). **'55** Le Amiche (IT) (GB: The Girl Friends). **'65** Giulietta Degli Spiriti (IT-FR) (GB: Juliet of the Spirits). **'68** The Legend of Lylah Clare (USA). **'69** The Secret of Santa Vittorio (USA). **'72** Fratello Sole, Sorella Luna (IT-GB) (USA/GB: Brother Sun, Sister Moon); L'Assassinat de Trotsky (GB-FR-IT). **'73** La Nuit Américaine (FR-IT) (USA/GB: Day for Night). **'80** When Time Ran Out . . . .

CORTEZ, Stanley

(b. 1908). Cinematographer. Born: Stanley Krantz; New York City, USA

Cortez's camerawork on Orson Welles' *The Magnificent Ambersons* is as beautiful as any in cinema. His expert use of angles, close-ups, lighting effects and other techniques were fused by Welles into a sublime pictorial experience. Cortez's only other masterpiece was Charles Laughton's *The Night of the Hunter* – memorable for the shot of the drowned Shelley Winters' hair flowing on the 'breeze' of an underwater current. Educated at New York University, Cortez assisted portrait photographers until he got a chance to join Gloria Swanson Productions. He learned his craft under such cinematographers as Lee Garmes and Hal Mohr at Warner Brothers and shot his first feature, *Four Days' Wonder*, in 1937. He continued to shoot films until the early Seventies but worked mostly on B pictures, a sad waste of an undoubted talent. His brother was Ricardo Cortez (1899–1977), a romantic lead in Latin lover roles in the Twenties and Thirties who played opposite Garbo in her American debut *The Torrent* (1926) and later directed a few films.

Films include: 1932 Scherzo (short) (+dir; +sc). '41 The Black Cat. '42 The Magnificent Ambersons. '44 Since You Went Away (co-photo). '48 Secret Beyond the Door. '55 The Night of the Hunter. '57 The Three Faces of Eve. '63 Shock Corridor. '64 The Naked Kiss; Madmen of Mandoras. '68 Blue.

COSTA-GAVRAS

(b. 1933). Director. Born: Konstantinos Gavras; Athens, Greece

Costa-Gavras left Greece for France at 19, studied at the Sorbonne and then at IDHEC, the Paris film school. His apprenticeship was illustrious – he worked as assistant for such noted directors as René Clément, René Clair, Jacques Demy, Marcel Ophuls and Henry Verneuil. In 1965 he directed his first feature, a police thriller called *The Sleeping Car Murders*. Z, made four years later, was his breakthrough – the first in a string of powerful and controversial political thrillers that has made Costa-Gavras a force to be reckoned with. Z deals with the neofascist assassination of a left-wing political figure in Greece. It was followed by *L'Aveu*, a fierce view of the Stalinist show trials in Czechoslovakia, and *State of Siege*, based on the abduction by the Tupamaros of an American 'advisor' to the Uruguayan government. All of Costa-Gavras' films appeal to audiences more for their superb use of the thriller framework than for their ideological statements, and the director would rather be associated with their humanist than their radically political angle, as *Missing*, his American debut showed. This prizewinner at Cannes and critical and commercial hit harrowingly describes an American businessman's search for his son during the military coup in Chile in 1973, and, though pointing the finger at the CIA's in-

volvement in South America, is most effective in its depiction of Jack Lemmon as the father, a man confronted with the possibility that his son is dead.

Films include: 1961 Tout l'Or du Monde (ass. dir) (FR-IT) (USA/GB: All the Gold in the World). '65 Compartiment Tueurs (FR) (USA/GB: The Sleeping Car Murders). '67 Un Homme de Trop (FR-IT) (USA: Shock Troops). '69 Z (FR-ALG). '70 L'Aveu (USA/GB: The Confession). '73 Etat de Siège (FR-IT-GER) (USA/GB: State of Siege). '75 Section Spéciale (FR-IT-GER) (USA: Special Section). '79 Clair de Femme (FR-IT-GER). '82 Missing (USA).

COSTELLO, Dolores

(1905–1979). Actress. Born: Pittsburgh, Pennsylvania, USA

Dolores Costello was a slender, delicate blonde beauty with patrician poise and bearing, the heroine of melodramas (*Tenderloin*), costume dramas (*When a Man Loves*) and epics (*Noah's Ark*) in the late Twenties. She and her sister Helene (1903–1957) were child actresses for Vitagraph, whose star was their father Maurice. Stage and occasional film parts, as well as modelling, occupied them until 1924 when they joined Warner Brothers. There Dolores met John Barrymore who demanded her for his leading lady in *The Sea Beast* – launching her as a major star – and subsequently married her. She retired in 1930 to have a daughter and son, (later the actor John Barrymore Jr), divorced Barrymore in 1935 and returned to the screen as Dearest in *Little Lord Fauntleroy*. She then played Isabel in *The Magnificent Ambersons*. This performance was screen acting at its best, combining beauty, gentleness and strength – Costello's permanent retirement shortly afterwards deprived the cinema of a charming and talented star.

Films include: 1911 A Geranium. '25 The Sea Beast. '26 Mannequin; The Third Degree. '27 When a Man Loves (GB: His Lady); Old San Francisco; The Heart of Maryland. '26 Glorious Betsy; Tenderloin. '29 Noah's Ark. '36 Little Lord Fauntleroy. '42 The Magnificent Ambersons.

COSTELLO, Lou

see ABBOTT & COSTELLO

COSTELLO, Maurice

(1877–1950). Actor. Born: Pittsburgh, Pennsylvania, USA

A handsome, dark-haired matinée idol, Costello became one of the cinema's first stars at a time when mature masculinity was the vogue. He was also among the earliest Broadway stars to turn to films, first in Edison shorts from 1906, and then for Vitagraph. His Shakespeare films gave him little chance to do anything but pose in a series of stage pictures, but in light comedy (like *The Romance of an Umbrella*) he was effortlessly charming. He also starred in costume dramas, playing, for example, Sydney Carton in an early *A Tale of Two Cities*. He not only starred in, but directed a

Above left: Dolores Costello as Dearest in Little Lord Fauntleroy. *Above right: Maurice Costello. Below: Joseph Cotten as Holly Martins in search of Harry Lime in* The Third Man. *Below right: George Coulouris in* Tarzan and

the Lost Safari *(1957). Right: Cicely Courtneidge in* The Perfect Gentleman, *her MGM screen debut. Bottom right: Tom Courtenay in* The Day the Fish Came Out, *a comedy about two atom bombs that go missing*

few of his own films, too, and remained in lead parts until 1920, also playing a few character parts in talkies. His daughters were actresses Helene and Dolores Costello, whose marriage to John Barrymore he bitterly opposed.

Films include: 1908 Richard III; Julius Caesar. '09 The Romance of an Umbrella. '11 A Tale of Two Cities. '13 Extremities. '14 Mr Barnes of New York. '15 The Man Who Couldn't Beat God; Tried for His Own Murder; The Crown Prince's Double. '19 The Cambric Mask. '39 Mr Smith Goes to Washington.

COTTAFAVI, Vittorio

(b. 1914). Director. Born: Modena, Italy

Vittorio Cottafavi made his first film as director in 1943 and up until the mid-Sixties, when he began to work solely in television, his films achieved cult status, particularly in France. He began working in the movie industry as a clapper boy, having attended the Centro Sperimentale di Cinematografia. He soon graduated to screenwriter and then became an assistant to directors Alessandro Blasetti and Vittorio De Sica. His own films are mostly tongue-in-cheek, lavish spectacles with an historic – often Roman – basis.

Films include: 1952 Una Donna Ha Ucciso. '53 Traviata 53 (IT-FR); Il Boia di Lilla (GB: Milady and the Musketeers). '55 Nel Gorgo del Peccato. '58 La Rivolta dei Gladiatori (IT-SP) (USA/GB: The Warriors and the Slave Girl). '60 Le Legioni di Cleopatra (FR-SP-IT) (GB: Legions of the Nile); Messalina, Venere Imperatrice; La Vendetta di Ercole (IT-FR) (GB: Goliath and the Dragon). '61 Ercole alla Conquesta di Atlantide (IT-FR) (GB: Hercules Conquers Atlantis/Hercules and the Captive Women). '65 I Cento Cavalieri (IT-SP-GER).

COTTEN, Joseph

(b. 1905). Actor. Born: Petersburg, Virginia, USA

It was after meeting and working with Orson Welles at the Mercury Theatre Project in New York that Joseph Cotten went to Hollywood to appear in *Citizen Kane*. Indeed, if Welles' original plan to make a film about Howard Hughes had come to fruition, Cotten would have played the lead. Even so, after his appearance in *Citizen Kane* Cotten did become an established star and went on to give excellent performances in many fine films, particularly for Welles and Alfred Hitchcock. He often played naive, sincere men who have their illusions shattered, as in *The Third Man*. His acting experience was initially gained working with a small theatre company in Miami, before he went to New York where he got a job as understudy and assistant stage manager at the Belasco Theatre. In later years he has continued to do some stage work with his wife, Patricia Medina, and he now runs his own television production company, Fordyce Productions.

Films include: 1940 Citizen Kane. '42 The Magnificent Ambersons; Journey Into Fear. '43 Shadow of a Doubt. '44 Gaslight. '46 Duel in the Sun. '48 Portrait of Jennie (GB: Jennie). '49 The Third Man (GB); Under Capricorn. '64 Hush. . .Hush, Sweet Charlotte.

COULOURIS, George

(b. 1903). Actor. Born: Manchester, England

When George Coulouris went to New York to try his luck on the Broadway stage he passed himself off as a well-known Shakespearian actor and as a result he worked regularly for ten years. The truth was far less glamorous; having attended the Central School of Speech and Drama in London, he had some minor roles at the Old Vic and his leading parts were at the Festival Theatre in Cambridge. In New York he eventually joined Orson Welles' Mercury Theatre Project and went to Hollywood with the rest of the company for the making of

Citizen Kane. His appearance in this film was the making of his screen career and he spent many years playing immaculate villains. He soon found this typecasting boring, and returned to England in the late Forties to pursue his stage career, while still managing to appear in an occasional film.

Films include: 1940 Citizen Kane. '43 For Whom the Bell Tolls. '44 None But the Lonely Heart. '45 Lady on a Train; Confidential Agent. '46 Nobody Lives Forever. '48 Joan of Arc. '51 Outcast of the Islands (GB). '58 I Accuse! (GB). '65 The Skull (GB).

COURTENAY, Tom

(b. 1937). Actor. Born: Hull, Yorkshire, England

At a time when films were becoming anti-establishment, the director Tony Richardson was looking for someone to play the rebellious Borstal boy in *The Loneliness of the Long Distance Runner*. The actor he chose was Tom Courtenay, whom he had spotted playing Konstantin in Chekhov's *The Seagull* at the Old Vic. Prior to this Courtenay had attended RADA, having become interested in the theatre while studying English at the University of London. After *The Loneliness of the Long Distance Runner* his film career was further established by his performance as the ineffectual, fantasizing Northerner *Billy Liar*. By the end of the Sixties Courtenay was spending more time in the theatre and made fewer and fewer appearances in films. He was outstanding in *The Dresser* in the West End and on Broadway.

Films include: 1962 The Loneliness of the Long Distance Runner; Private Potter. '63 Billy Liar. '64 King and Country. '65 Operation Crossbow (GB-IT) (USA: The Great Spy Mission); King Rat; Doctor Zhivago (USA). '67 The Night of the Generals (GB-FR); The Day the Fish Came Out (GB). '68 A Dandy in Aspic. '69 Otley. '71 Catch Me a Spy (GB-FR-US); One Day in the Life of Ivan Denisovitch (GB-NOR).

COURTNEIDGE, Cicely

(1893–1980). Actress. Born: Sydney, Australia

Cicely Courtneidge and her husband Jack Hulbert were among the most successful musical-comedy teams to appear in British films. They first met in 1913 when they were in a play together, and three years later they were married and starring in a show put on by her father, the actor and producer Robert Courtneidge. During World War I Cicely continued the slow haul through music-hall and theatre, and after the war she and Hulbert joined up as an act in movies, reaching their peak in the Thirties. After World War II she continued her career alone as a straight actress, at first playing benevolent aunties and then grandmothers or maiden ladies, and she gave one of her best performances as an ageing lesbian in *The L-Shaped Room*. She continued to act until the time of her death.

Films include: 1931 The Ghost Train. '32 Jack's the Boy (USA: Night and Day). '33

Aunt Sally (USA: Along Came Sally); Soldiers of the King. '35 The Perfect Gentleman (USA) (GB: The Imperfect Lady); Things Are Looking Up. '37 Take My Tip. '40 Under Your Hat. '62 The L-Shaped Room. '66 The Wrong Box.

COUSTEAU, Jacques-Yves

(b. 1910). Oceanographer/documentarist. Born: St André de Cubzac, France

Jacques Cousteau is probably best known for his ABC television series *The Undersea World of Jacques Cousteau*. What is not commonly known is that his oceanographic innovations and inventions – he invented the aqualung in 1943 with Emile Gagnan – are second to none. Since 1953 he has been making films to record life under the sea. During World War II, while seemingly making underwater films, he was also involved in covert intelligence work. After the war he founded the Group for Undersea Research in the French navy, and on leaving the navy in 1957 he was elected director of the Musée Oceanographique of Monaco. He has received both the Legion of Honour and the Croix de Guerre.

Films include: 1943 Par Dix-Huit Mètres de Fond. '46 Espaves. '47 Paysages Sous-Marins/Paysages du Silence. '49 Les Phoques du Rio de Oro. '50 Carnet de Plongée; Une Sortie du Rubis. '55 La Mer Rouge. '56 Le Monde du Silence (GB: The Silent World). '64 Le Monde Sans Soleil (FR-IT) (GB: World Without Sun). '76 Le Voyage au Bout du Monde (USA: Voyage to the Edge of the World).

COUTARD, Raoul

(b. 1924). Cinematographer. Born: Paris, France

Coutard spent five years in Vietnam working for the French Military Information Service, and later as a civilian photographer employed by such magazines as *Time* and *Paris-Match*. Originally he had wanted to be a chemist but abandoned this idea during World War II, and found employment in photo laboratories. On returning to France he formed a production company with a fellow ex-military photographer. Having made a number of documentaries, Coutard contacted the director Jean-Luc Godard through their mutual producer Georges de Beauregard, and as a result became cinematographer on Godard's first feature *A Bout de Souffle*. The film was an international success and established Coutard as the seminal *nouvelle vague* cinematographer. His style of shooting, using natural light and hand-held cameras, came to be used by other key directors like François Truffaut and Costa-Gavras.

Films include: 1960 A Bout de Souffle (USA/GB: Breathless); Tirez Sur le Pianiste (GB: Shoot the Pianist). '62 Jules et Jim (GB: Jules and Jim). '63 Les Carabiniers (FR-IT) (GB: The Soldiers). '65 Alphaville, une Etrange Aventure de Lemmy Caution (FR-IT); Pierrot le Fou (FR-IT); La 317eme Section/Trois Cent Dixseptième (FR-SP). '67 Weekend (FR-IT). '69 Z (FR-ALG). '70 L'Aveu (FR-IT) (USA: The Confession).

College. '38 Flash Gordon's Trip to Mars (serial). '39 Buck Rogers (serial). '40 Flash Gordon Conquers the Universe (serial). '41 Jungle Man. '46 Swamp Fire. '47 Last of the Redmen (GB: Last of the Redskins). '48 Caged Fury.

CRAIN, Jeanne

(b. 1925). Actress. Born: Barstow, California, USA

After winning beauty contests and working as a model, Jeanne Crain was spotted by a 20th Century-Fox talent scout while modelling in a bread advertisement and signed for the studio. Fresh-faced and auburn-haired, she was soon established as the ideal girl-next-door type and played the role in many movies over the next few years, becoming America's teenage sweetheart, as in *Margie*, where she perpetually but innocently loses her knickers. She began to outgrow this image in the Fifties and tried stronger dramatic roles but generally with little success. For various reasons – a tempestuous private life, changing fashions, age – she made fewer movies in the Sixties, though she remained active in television, and virtually retired from the big screen in the Seventies. She was nominated for an Academy Award in 1949 for her untypical role as a black girl passing for white in *Pinky*.

Films include: 1945 State Fair; Leave Her to Heaven. '46 Margie. '48 A Letter to Three Wives. '49 The Fan (GB: Lady Windermere's Fan); Pinky. '50 Cheaper by the Dozen. '51 Take Care of My Little Girl; People Will Talk. '52 O. Henry's Full House (GB: Full House). '55 Gentlemen Marry Brunettes. '72 Skyjacked.

CRAWFORD, Broderick

(1911–1986). Actor. Born: Philadelphia, Pennsylvania, USA

Crawford had an inimitable machine-gun-fire manner of speaking, spitting out his words in short bursts of anger or impatience. Because of this and his heavy-set appearance, he was quickly typecast as a gangster or villain. After high-school he became a seaman, but soon decided it was not the life for him and became a radio actor. He then followed his parents onto the stage where his performance in the lead role in *Punches and Judy* won him a film contract with Samuel Goldwyn. However, he left Hollywood in 1938, a decision that paradoxically secured his later stardom there, for he played Lennie in the Broadway production of *Of Mice and Men* and its phenomenal success won him many film offers. After fighting in World War II he resumed his career, winning an Oscar for his performance in *All the King's Men*. He continued to work in films and on stage and television.

Films include: 1939 The Real Glory. '40 Seven Sinners. '46 The Black Angel. '48 The Time of Your Life. '49 All the King's Men. '50 Born Yesterday. '54 Night People/ Counterspy. '55 Il Bidone (IT-FR) (GB: The Swindlers); New York Confidential. '78 The Private Files of J. Edgar Hoover.

Above: Noel Coward as the Witch of Capri in Joseph Losey's Boom. *Below: Buster Crabbe in the familiar guise of Flash Gordon. Bottom: Broderick Crawford (right) in his Academy*

Award-winning role of a Southern state governor in Robert Rossen's All the King's Men, *with Walter Bunke. Above right: Jeanne Crain in one of her later sophisticated roles*

COWARD, Noel

(1899–1973). Dramatist/composer/ actor/screenwriter/director/producer. Born: Teddington, London, England

A man of the theatre and the cinema, a man of words, music, elegance, wit and style – that was Noel Coward. After a limited formal education, he made his first stage appearance at the age of ten in a children's play. Before long he was appearing in his own works, and in 1925 he had his first major success with *The Vortex*. He began to pour out light musical dramas and with them seemed to capture the very essence of 'high' society between the wars. In addition many of his plays, such as *Private Lives*, *Blithe Spirit* and *Brief Encounter*, were later adapted for the screen. Coward himself began his film career aged 18 opposite Dorothy Gish in *Hearts of the World*, but surprisingly

only acted in a further seven films, finishing with a flourish as the inmate controller of *The Italian Job* in 1969. But he proved himself much more than a playwright or an actor. Even very early in his career he had established himself as a celebrity – and it was this position that he continued to occupy, with great dignity, throughout his life. He was knighted in 1970.

Films include: 1918 Hearts of the World (actor) (USA). '27 The Vortex (play basis). '31 Private Lives (play basis) (USA). '35 The Scoundrel (actor). '42 In Which We Serve (co-dir; +prod; +sc; +act; +mus). '45 Blithe Spirit (prod; +play basis); Brief Encounter (prod; +play basis; +co-sc). '59 Our Man in Havana (actor). '60 Surprise Package (actor). '65 Bunny Lake Is Missing (actor). '68 Boom (actor). '69 The Italian Job (actor).

CRABBE, Larry ('Buster')

(1907–1983). Actor. Born: Clarence Linton Crabbe; Oakland, California, USA

Crabbe went to Hawaii as a child and later attended its university, where he excelled in sports, especially swimming. He returned to California and in 1932, the year of his graduation from the University of California, won an Olympic gold medal for swimming. He briefly rivalled another swimming star, Johnny Weissmuller, in playing the screen role of Tarzan before finding his own niche as the embodiment of popular comic-strip heroes of the sci-fi future in such serials as *Flash Gordon* (which had two sequels) and *Buck Rogers*, which showed off his blond clean-cut Californian looks and athletic build to advantage. After that he appeared mostly in B Westerns, especially in the Forties and more intermittently in the Fifties and Sixties. He continued to promote health and fitness, wrote *The Arthritis Exercise Book* and sold Buster Crabbe swimming pools.

Films include: 1933 King of the Jungle. '36 Flash Gordon (serial). '37 Murder Goes to

CRAWFORD, Joan

(1904–1977). Actress. Born: Lucille Fay LeSueur; San Antonio, Texas, USA

From childhood – which was marred by her parents' divorce and an accident that kept her in bed for a year when she was only seven – Lucille LeSueur wanted to be a dancer. After a somewhat scrappy education she began her chosen career on the nightclub circuit and in 1924 was given her chance in the chorus of *Innocent Eyes* on Broadway. An MGM contract followed when a talent scout spotted her and chose her for Norma Shearer's anonymous double. From there she worked her way up to lead roles and in 1928 established herself playing a dark and pretty 'jazz-baby' in *Our Dancing Daughters*. Her image kept on changing, settling down in the Forties to the 'classic' Crawford whose heavy lipstick emphasized an already broad mouth, and whose eye make-up further enlarged her dominant eyes. Her dresses and jackets had shoulders broad enough to rival any man's and lent her the appearance of one who was determined to succeed whatever the cost. She went from strength to strength, picking her projects with care; period costume dramas soon revealed themselves as entirely unsuitable because of her particularly 'modern' personality. When she approached middle-age, MGM decided to let Crawford go and she was snapped up by Warner Brothers, where her career was revitalized by her Oscar-winning performance in *Mildred Pierce*. Ups and downs followed, but she continued to appear regularly in films until 1970. Her last great roles were as Vienna in the Western *Johnny Guitar* and as the crippled sister in *What Ever Happened to Baby Jane?*, co-starring her with long-time rival Bette Davis. The ultimate professional star, she was married to two others, Douglas Fairbanks Jr and Franchot Tone, then to B-film actor Philip Terry and finally to Pepsi-Cola tycoon Alfred Steele. She was posthumously attacked in a book by her adopted daughter Christina called *Mommie Dearest*, filmed in 1981 with Faye Dunaway playing a bitch-goddess Crawford.

Films include: 1925 Lady of the Night. '26 Tramp, Tramp, Tramp. '28 Our Dancing Daughters. '32 Grand Hotel. '34 Chained; Forsaking All Others. '37 The Last of Mrs Cheyney; Mannequin. '40 Strange Cargo; Susan and God (GB: The Gay Mrs Trexel). '41 A Woman's Face. '45 Mildred Pierce. '46 Humoresque. '47 Possessed; Daisy Kenyon. '50 The Damned Don't Cry. '52 Sudden Fear. '53 Torch Song. '54 Johnny Guitar. '62 What Ever Happened to Baby Jane? '67 Berserk (GB). '70 Trog (GB).

CRAWFORD, Michael

(b. 1942). Actor. Born: Salisbury, Wiltshire, England

Michael Crawford is the son of an RAF pilot who was killed six months before the birth of his child during World War II. While still at school Michael began appearing in plays, as well as in the 1958 films *Soap-Box Derby* and *Blow Your Own Trumpet*, both made by the Children's Film Foundation. At the age of 16 he began singing, and toured with the musical *Let's Make an Opera*. In 1963 Crawford made his mark on the adult acting world as a cack-handed would-be lover in *Two Left Feet*. From there he went on to star in similar vein in *The Knack*, his slight build, squeaky voice and naive manner securing him a prominent place in British cinema at a time when 'cool' was in vogue. He appeared in *Hello Dolly!* in Hollywood and then became the accident-prone hero of the smash-hit television situation comedy *Some Mothers Do 'Ave 'Em*, later starring in the amazingly successful West End stage show *Barnum*. Crawford returned to films with *Condorman*.

Films include: 1960 A French Mistress. '62 The War Lover. '65 The Knack. '66 A Funny Thing Happened On the Way to the Forum (USA). '67 The Jokers; How I Won the War. '69 Hello Dolly! (USA). '70 Hello Goodbye (USA); The Games. '81 Condorman (USA).

CREGAR, Laird

(1916–1944). Actor. Born: Philadelphia, Pennsylvania, USA

Cregar was twice the weight he should have been and looked twice his age, but for a while it was his fortune. At the age of eight he was sent to England to study at Winchester School, and while there played child roles with the Stratford-on-Avon Players. He returned to America, and eventually won a scholarship to the Pasadena Community Playhouse drama school, coming to prominence in the Los Angeles stage production of *Oscar Wilde*. Film work as a corpulent villain or sinister cop followed – his most celebrated performance was as Jack the Ripper in *The Lodger* – but his career was short-lived. He went on a severe diet which strained his heart, and died while undergoing an operation at the age of 28.

Films include: 1940 Hudson's Bay. '41 Charley's Aunt (GB: Charley's American Aunt); Blood and Sand; I Wake Up Screaming/Hot Spot. '42 This Gun for Hire; The Black Swan. '43 Hello, Frisco, Hello; Heaven Can Wait. '44 The Lodger. '45 Hangover Square.

CRENNA, Richard

(b. 1926). Actor. Born: Los Angeles, California, USA

A graduate of the University of Southern California, Richard Crenna began his career on the radio, starring in the popular series *Our Miss Brooks*, followed by a six-year run in *The Real McCoys* and parts in radio serials. Tall, auburn-haired and mellow-voiced, he then became a well-known actor in films. Robert Wise cast him in the *The Sand Pebbles* and this dramatic success led to many other offers. Nonetheless, his unassuming good looks and quiet manner have rather relegated Crenna to supporting roles and television.

Films include: 1952 Red Skies of Montana. '64 John Goldfarb Please Come Home. '66 The Sand Pebbles. '67 Wait Until Dark. '68 Star! '69 Marooned; Midas Run (GB: A Run on Gold). '71 Catlow (GB); Doctors' Wives; Red Sky at Morning. '76 Breakheart Pass. '81 Body Heat.

Above: Joan Crawford solemnly shows A Woman's Face. *Below: Michael Crawford in* The Jokers. *Bottom: Richard Crenna. Bottom left: Laird Cregar expires in* Hangover Square

CRICHTON, Charles

(b. 1910). Director. Born: Wallasey, Cheshire, England

Charles Crichton worked in the cutting room at Denham studio during the Thirties, editing such films as *Sanders of the River* (1935), *Things to Come* (1936) and *Elephant Boy* (1937). In 1940 he went to Ealing where he became one of the studio's foremost directors, specializing in light comedy. His major successes – including *The Lavender Hill Mob* and *The Titfield Thunderbolt* – were founded on excellent scripts by T.E.B. Clarke. Crichton was one of the architects of the eccentric style which became the cornerstone of Ealing comedy in the late Forties and Fifties. He tried his luck in Hollywood, but withdrew from his first film there, *Birdman of Alcatraz* (1961), soon after shooting began because of a disagreement. He has since worked on successful television series such as *The Avengers* and *Danger Man*.

Films include: 1944 For Those In Peril. '47 Hue and Cry. '51 The Lavender Hill Mob. '53 The Titfield Thunderbolt. '54 The Divided Heart. '58 Law and Disorder; Floods of Fear. '59 The Battle of the Sexes.

CRISP, Donald

(1881–1974). Actor/director. Born: Aberfeldy, Scotland

After Eton and Oxford, Donald Crisp fought at Kimberley and Ladysmith during the Boer War. When peace was declared he went to the USA intent on becoming an actor. He made a name for himself in the theatre, met the great director D.W. Griffith and began to assist the master. His credits as assistant or associate director in this period include *Birth of a Nation* (in which he also acted), *Broken Blossoms* and *Intolerance*. Breaking away from Griffith, Crisp worked steadily as a director through the Twenties, making over a hundred well-thought-of movies, some starring top names like Douglas Fairbanks and Buster Keaton. Before the advent of sound he had already started to concentrate on acting, and soon became one of Hollywood's mainstay character players. He was memorable as crusty, white-haired patriarchs with hearts of gold, for example Velvet's disapproving father (surreptitiously slipping a bet on her Grand National horse The Pie) in *National Velvet*. In 1941 he won the Best Supporting Actor Academy Award for his sentimental performance as the Welsh paterfamilias of a coal-mining family in *How Green Was My Valley*.

Films include: 1915 Birth of a Nation (ass. dir). '16 Intolerance (ass. dir). '17 Ramona (dir. only). '19 Broken Blossoms (actor only). '24 The Navigator (co-sc; +co-dir). '25 Don Q, Son of Zorro (dir. only). '26 Man Bait (dir. only). '27 The Black Pirate (actor only). '32 Red Dust (actor only). '33 Mutiny on the Bounty (actor only). '36 Charge of the Light Brigade (actor only). '39 Wuthering Heights (actor only). '41 How Green Was My Valley (actor only). '44 National Velvet (actor only). '55 The Man From Laramie (actor only). '60 Pollyanna (actor only).

CRISTALDI, Franco

(b. 1924). Producer. Born: Turin, Italy

During the Forties Franco Cristaldi put aside his training in law in favour of film-making. After his first tentative feature his career really took off and he became a major producer of Italian post-neo-realist cinema for directors such as Luchino Visconti and Francesco Rosi. Cristaldi has also encouraged young directors, and stars such as Vittorio Gassman and Claudia Cardinale, whom he married. In 1966 he acted as president of the National Association of Film Producers, and in 1977 became president of the International Federation of the Film Producers Association.

Films include: 1957 Notti Bianche (IT-FR) (USA/GB: The White Nights). '58 Il Soliti Ignoti (USA: Big Deal on Madonna Street; GB: Persons Unknown). '59 I Magliari. '62 Divorzio all'Italiana (USA/GB: Divorce Italian Style); Salvatore Giuliano (GB: The Dreaded Mafia). '63 I Compagni (IT-FR) (USA/GB: The Organizer). '64 La Ragazza di Bube (USA/GB: Bebo's Girl). '65 Vaghe Stelle dell'Orsa (USA: Sandra; GB: Of a Thousand Delights); Le Tenda Rossa (IT-USSR) (GB: The Red Tent). '72 Il Caso Mattei (USA/GB: The Mattei Affair). '74 Amarcord (IT-FR). '81 Sharky's Machine (USA).

CROMBIE, Donald

(b. 1942). Director. Born: Brisbane, Australia

Donald Crombie began directing for the Commonwealth Film Unit (later known as Film Australia) in 1966. Returning in 1971 after a spell at the BBC, he teamed with producer Anthony Buckley to make a number of television films and, eventually, features. Crombie has become one of the major 'New Wave' Australian directors. His films have shown a sensitive approach to the lives of ordinary people, especially those who are powerless in society, and a marked interest in the problems of women fighting for their basic existence.

Films include: 1976 Caddie. '78 The Irishman. '79 Cathy's Child. '81 The Killing of Angel Street.

CROMWELL, John

(1887–1979). Director/actor. Born: Elwood Dager Cromwell; Toledo, Ohio, USA

On the stage from around 1906, John Cromwell was a successful producer and director of plays throughout the Twenties. He went to Hollywood in 1928, and rapidly established himself as a reliable studio contract director and, thanks perhaps to his stage work, as a remarkable director of actors. Players as different as Bette Davis, Raymond Massey, Robert Mitchum and Irene Dunne did some of their best work for Cromwell, a man who, when in his eighties, was still a magnetic personality brimming with enthusiasm. Cromwell had been one of the founders of the Screen Directors' Guild, and in the early Fifties, after a quarrel with RKO chief Howard Hughes over his supposed

leftist views, he left Hollywood to return, as director and occasional actor, to the more liberal atmosphere of the Broadway stage. Later on, he directed three more films and acted, at the age of 89, in Robert Altman's *A Wedding* (1978).

Films include: 1930 Street of Chance. '34 Spitfire; Of Human Bondage. '35 Village Tale. '36 Little Lord Fauntleroy. '37 The Prisoner of Zenda. '38 Algiers. '40 Abe Lincoln in Illinois (GB: Spirit of the People). '44 Since You Went Away. '46 Anna and the King of Siam. '47 Dead Reckoning. '51 The Racket. '58 The Goddess.

CRONYN, Hume

(b. 1911). Actor. Born: London, Ontario, Canada

Hume Cronyn appeared with the Montreal Repertory company while still a student at McGill. He went on to professional theatre in the USA, and made his film debut in 1943 in Hitchcock's *Shadow of a Doubt*. The next year he gave a most moving performance as an anti-Nazi in *The Seventh Cross* which gained him an Oscar nomination. Films have been subordinate to Cronyn's long and distinguished career as actor and director in the theatre, but he has contributed many a notable character to the cinema, specializing in cool, intelligent portrayals of ruthless villains. The sadistic warden in *Brute Force* is Cronyn at his most frightening. He is married to the actress Jessica Tandy.

Films include: 1943 Shadow of a Doubt. '44 Lifeboat; The Seventh Cross. '46 The Postman Always Rings Twice. '47 Brute Force. '60 Sunrise at Campobello. '63 Cleopatra. '64 Hamlet. '81 Honky Tonk Freeway.

CROSBY, Bing

(1901–1977). Actor/singer. Born: Harry Lillis Crosby; Tacoma, Washington, USA

A drummer and vocalist while still at college, Bing Crosby later formed a singing trio called The Rhythm Boys. Next he joined Paul Whiteman's band, and appeared as its singer in the film *The King of Jazz* (1930). Shorts for Mack Sennett and fame on radio led to his Paramount contract and to some twenty-five years as one of the most popular Hollywood stars. He played the casual, decent, homely guy, sang with deceptive ease, made plenty of bad movies bearable, and a few good ones the more attractive for his friendly, civilized presence. In the 'Road' series he perfectly balanced Bob Hope's pushiness and Dorothy Lamour's sophistication. His Oscar for *Going My Way* may have reflected Hollywood's vulnerability to misty sentiment rather than its discrimination, but when *The Country Girl* came along, Crosby rose splendidly to a harsher challenge.

Films include: 1932 The Big Broadcast. '35 Mississippi. '36 Pennies From Heaven; Anything Goes. '40 Road to Singapore. '42 Holiday Inn. '44 Going My Way. '48 The Emperor Waltz. '54 White Christmas; The Country Girl. '56 High Society. '66 Stagecoach.

CROSBY, Floyd D.

(1899–1985). Cinematographer. Born: New York City, USA

Floyd Crosby's career began in the early Thirties with documentary work. He photographed films for Joris Ivens, Pare Lorentz and Robert Flaherty, winning an Academy Award for his camerawork on the Flaherty-Murnau semi-documentary *Tabu*. In the Fifties Crosby moved into features. He worked largely on low-budget films for Roger Corman, with the odd exception like *High Noon* in 1952. Crosby's elegant, highly atmospheric camerawork made such Corman movies as *The Fall of the House of Usher* look a great deal more expensive than they really were.

Films include: 1931 Tabu. '37 The River (co-photo). '40 Power and the Land (co-photo). '51 The Brave Bulls. '52 High Noon. '58 Machine Gun Kelly. '59 Crime and Punishment USA. '60 The Fall of the House of Usher. '61 The Pit and the Pendulum; A Cold Wind in August. '63 The Raven. '64 Bikini Beach.

CROSLAND, Alan

(1894–1936). Director. Born: New York City, USA

Alan Crosland is remembered now as the director of *The Jazz Singer*, but he had been in films for a long time before that. He joined Edison in 1909 as an actor, moving on to publicity and casting. By 1916 he was directing for Famous Players. In the Army Photo Service in World War I, he came back to earn a reputation for dealing with difficult actors like John Barrymore and Al Jolson, and was successful in injecting movement and action into lavish spectacles like *Don Juan*. *The Jazz Singer* doomed Crosland to a spell on uninspired musicals, but before his early death in a motor accident he had moved on to low-budget but well-crafted thrillers like *The Case of the Howling Dog* and *The White Cockatoo*, which are still recalled with affection.

Films include: 1917 Kidnapped. '21 Worlds Apart. '24 Three Weeks (GB: The Romance of a Queen). '26 Don Juan. '27 The Beloved Rogue; The Jazz Singer. '28 Glorious Betsy.

'29 General Crack. '33 Massacre. '34 The Case of the Howling Dog. '35 The White Cockatoo; Mister Dynamite.

CRUZE, James

(1884–1942). Director/actor. Born: Jens Cruz Bosen; Five Points, near Ogden, Utah, USA

James Cruze was the son of Danish immigrants: his father, a Mormon, had 19 children (some say 24). Cruze ran away from home at 15, worked in Alaska to pay for drama school, played in stock, vaudeville and New York rep, and by 1911 was in films with the Thanhouser company as an actor, playing the lead in a celebrated early version of *Dr Jekyll and Mr Hyde* (1912). He moved to Lasky, and was directing by 1918. Cruze worked fast and reliably, and had great success in the Twenties with a wide range of subjects. Little of his work survives. His major fantasy films (*Beggar on Horseback, Hollywood*) are missing, so that he stands or falls on his two epic Westerns, *The Covered Wagon* and *The Pony Express*. The former still works superbly, with a raw immediacy in sequences like the river crossing, and visual majesty in the great panoramic shots of the wagon train. Yet he made the movie reluctantly, disliking the idea of 'demotion' to Westerns.

Films as director include: 1921 Leap Year. **'23** The Covered Wagon; Hollywood;

Ruggles of Red Gap. **'24** Merton of the Movies. **'25** Beggar on Horseback; The Pony Express. **'26** Old Ironsides (GB: Sons of the Sea). **'29** The Great Gabbo. **'32** If I Had a Million (co-dir). **'36** Sutter's Gold.

CUKOR, George

(1899–1983). Director. Born: New York City, USA

George Cukor worked in the theatre throughout the Twenties, and in the latter half of the decade he directed Broadway productions starring such names as Ethel Barrymore and Dorothy Gish. Arriving in Hollywood in 1929, he was dialogue director on *All Quiet on the Western Front* (1930), co-directed a few films, and made his first solo movie in 1931. He was still directing precisely 50 years later. Cukor's early work for RKO, especially films like *Girls About Town* and *What Price Hollywood?*, showed a talent for sardonic comedy which surfaced only occasionally in his later MGM period, but through all those fifty years he was an unsurpassed director of actors. Cukor's nine films with Katharine Hepburn show a great actress at her finest; he brought out an intense tenderness which could elude other directors. He falls short at times when civilized style is not quite enough. But when it comes to the sheer joy of being with wonderful people that a film like *Pat and Mike* communicates, Cukor could contrive miracles.

Films include: 1931 Girls About Town. **'32** What Price Hollywood? **'33** Dinner at Eight; Little Women. **'35** David Copperfield. **'36** Romeo and Juliet; Sylvia Scarlett; Camille. **'38** Holiday (GB: Free and Easy/ Unconventional Linda). **'42** Keeper of the Flame. **'44** Gaslight (GB: The Murder in Thornton Square). **'48** A Double Life. **'50** Born Yesterday. **'52** Pat and Mike. **'54** A Star Is Born. **'60** Heller in Pink Tights. **'64** My Fair Lady. **'81** Rich and Famous.

CULP, Robert

(b. 1930). Actor. Born: Oakland, California, USA

A University of Washington athlete, Robert Culp went into the theatre, and after years of small success gained an award for Best Actor of the Year in an Off-Broadway Play for his performance in *He Who Gets Slapped*. Television work followed, the series *I Spy* causing him to be typecast as the cool young executive, secret agent or troubleshooter always emerging from tight spots without a hair out of place. This image has dogged Culp through a sporadic film career in which it is difficult to find a movie worth seeing with the exception of *Bob & Carol & Ted & Alice* where he and his co-stars play ageing trendies. He has directed two films, neither of which attracted much attention.

Films include: 1963 PT-109; Sunday in New York; Rhino! **'69** Bob & Carol & Ted &

Alice. **'71** Hannie Caulder (GB). **'72** Hickey and Boggs (+dir). **'75** Inside Out (GB-GER). **'76** Breaking Point (CAN); The Great Scout and Cathouse Thursday. **'79** Goldengirl.

CUMMINGS, Constance

(b. 1910). Actress. Born: Constance Cummings Halverstadt; Seattle, Washington, USA

On the New York stage at 16, Constance Cummings was in Hollywood by 1931 and played in over twenty films in four years. In the mid-Thirties she came to England for a stage appearance, and remained. She married the playwright and producer Benn Levy and thereafter concentrated on the stage, where she had a distinguished career. She found time, however, for occasional films. A cool, attractive, quietly spoken blonde, Constance Cummings was equally at home in light comedy and serious drama. In her Hollywood days she acted for Howard Hawks, Frank Capra and James Whale, and was Harold Lloyd's heart-throb in *Movie Crazy*; British films gave her *Blithe Spirit*, but little else that was worth remembering.

Films include: 1931 The Criminal Code; The Last Parade. **'32** Movie Crazy; American Madness. **'35** Remember Last Night? **'36** Seven Sinners (GB) (USA: Doomed Cargo). **'41** This England (GB). **'45** Blithe Spirit (GB). **'56** The Intimate Stranger (GB) (USA: Finger of Guilt). **'70** Jane Eyre (GB).

CUMMINGS, Irving

(1888–1959). Director/actor. Born: New York City, USA

Irving Cummings was acting on Broadway by 1908, alongside great names of the period – Lillian Russell, Ethel Barrymore, Alice Brady. He entered films in 1910, and became a popular leading man. In 1922 he turned to direction, still acting from time to time, and for almost thirty years turned out well-crafted if unoriginal movies. Essentially a studio pro, he handled a number of Shirley Temple pictures, musicals with Bob Hope and Betty Grable, and biopics like *Lillian Russell*, a tribute to the lady with whom he had acted thirty years before.

Films include: 1922 The Man from Hell's River (+ act). '24 The Rose of Paris. '26 The Johnstown Flood. '31 The Cisco Kid. '35 Curly Top. '36 The Poor Little Rich Girl. '40 Down Argentine Way; Lillian Russell. '41 Louisiana Purchase. '42 Springtime in the Rockies. '51 Double Dynamite.

CUMMINGS, Robert

(b. 1910). Actor. Born: Charles Clarence Robert Cummings; Joplin, Missouri, USA

Finding it hard to get jobs on the Broadway stage, Robert Cummings visited England to acquire the accent, passed himself off as one Blade Stanhope Conway, actor-manager-director of the Harrogate Rep, and landed a part in Galsworthy's *The Roof*. Five years later he is said to have posed as a Texan to clinch his Paramount contract. These were precisely the kind of ploys which the Cummings screen character would carry off with a disarming smile and a likeable naivety. He seemed to be a lightweight actor, but the parts were to blame for that. When films like *Kings Row* and *The Lost Moment* made greater demands, he could add strength to the unfailing charm. Cummings' television work includes *Twelve Angry Men* (1954), for which he won an Emmy Award.

Films include: 1935 So Red the Rose. '37 Souls at Sea. '39 Three Smart Girls Grow Up. '41 Kings Row; The Devil and Miss Jones. '42 Saboteur. '43 Flesh and Fantasy. '47 The Lost Moment. '48 Sleep, My Love. '54 Dial M for Murder. '64 The Carpetbaggers. '66 Stagecoach.

CUNY, Alain

(b. 1908). Actor. Born: St Malo, France

Alain Cuny studied painting and drawing at the Ecole des Beaux Arts in Paris, became a poster and theatre designer, and entered the cinema as set and costume designer for Alberto Cavalcanti, Jacques Feyder and Jean Renoir. He then turned to acting on stage and screen, his first notable film part being in Marcel Carné's *Les Visiteurs du Soir*. A statuesque figure with harsh, sculptured features, Cuny played romantic solitaires and tortured intellectuals, his brooding presence making many a supporting role distinctive. After a lull in his career, he returned in 1950 in Curzio Malaparte's *Il Cristo Proibito*, and this led to numerous successes in Italian as well as French cinema.

Films include: 1940 Remorques. '42 Les Visiteurs du Soir (USA: The Devil's Own Envoy). '50 Il Cristo Proibito (IT) (USA: Strange Deception; GB: The Forbidden Christ). '53 La Signora Senza Camelie (IT) (USA: Woman Without Camellias). '56 Notre Dame de Paris (FR-IT) (GB: The Hunchback of Notre Dame). '58 Les Amants (GB: The Lovers). '59 La Dolce Vita (IT). '64 La Corruzione (IT-FR). '69 La Voie Lacteé (FR-IT) (GB: The Milky Way); Fellini Satyricon (IT-FR). '70 Uomini Contro (IT-YUG). '76 Cadaveri Eccellenti (IT-FR) (GB: Illustrious Corpses). '79 Cristo si è Fermato a Eboli (IT-FR) (USA: Eboli; GB: Christ Stopped at Eboli).

CURRIE, Finlay

(1878–1968). Actor. Born: Edinburgh, Scotland

The Scottish character actor Finlay Currie made his stage debut in Edinburgh in 1898. He appeared in London and New York, and spent ten years in Australia. He was a vocalist and a comedian, and formed a songs-and-patter team with his wife, the American musical comedy star Maude Courtney. Currie entered films in 1932, and thereafter appeared regularly. His thick white hair and resonant voice with its Scottish burr made him a striking figure. Notable roles included the convict Magwitch in David Lean's version of *Great Expectations* and Queen Victoria's servant John Brown in *The Mudlark*. He ended his long career at the age of 87 by playing the old doll-maker in Otto Preminger's *Bunny Lake Is Missing*.

Films include: 1908 The War in the Air. '32 Rome Express. '45 I Know Where I'm Going. '46 Great Expectations. '48 Bonnie Prince Charlie. '49 The History of Mr Polly. '50 The Mudlark; Treasure Island. '51 Quo Vadis? (USA). '52 Ivanhoe. '53 Rob Roy, the Highland Rogue. '59 Ben-Hur (USA). '65 Bunny Lake Is Missing.

Top left: Robert Cummings. Top centre: Alain Cuny comes the old soldier in Uomini Contro. *Top right: Finlay Currie as Queen Victoria's John Brown with Andrew Ray in* The Mudlark

Top, far right: Tony Curtis guest-stars as himself in Pepe *(1960). Right: Cyril Cusack in* The Taming of the Shrew. *Below: Tim Curry in* The Rocky Horror Picture Show

CURRY, Tim

(b. 1946). Actor. Born: Cheshire, England

Essentially a stage actor and singer, Tim Curry appeared in London in the original cast of *Hair*, worked with the Royal Shakespeare Company, and spent five years in the USA, where he acted on Broadway in Tom Stoppard's *Travesties* and Peter Shaffer's *Amadeus*. His few films include *The Rocky Horror Picture Show*, in which he played the transvestite Frank N. Furter. This was a repetition of the stage role which had made him an overnight star. The film has become the subject of an inexplicable late-night cult, notably in New York, where it is regularly submerged by audience participation.

Films: 1975 The Rocky Horror Picture Show. '78 The Shout. '80 Times Square (USA). '82 Annie (USA).

CURTIS, Tony

(b. 1925). Actor. Born: Bernard Schwartz; New York City, USA

The child of Hungarian immigrants, Tony Curtis grew up in the Bronx, saw naval service in World War II, and embarked on a theatrical career in various off-Broadway companies. A performance in *Golden Boy* caught the eye of a Universal scout, and Curtis was signed for the movies. He was made for *film noir* (first appearing in Robert Siodmak's *Criss Cross*), but Universal preferred to cast him in costume spectaculars, and not until he finally shook free in *Sweet Smell of Success* was a fine actor fully revealed. As the ambitious press-agent Sidney Falco, Curtis created a marvellous picture of unscrupulous, corrupted charm, a small-time predator barely surviving in a big-time jungle. He went on to his shrewd female impersonation in *Some Like It Hot*, delicately steering clear of coarseness, and wickedly parodying Cary Grant. Other good comedy roles followed, until in the mid-Sixties Hollywood comedy became more forced and frenetic, and Curtis' career declined with it. One good serious role, as the deranged killer in *The Boston Strangler*, remained. The first of Curtis' three wives was actress Janet Leigh, their daughter actress Jamie Lee Curtis.

Films include: 1949 Criss Cross. '51 The Prince Who Was a Thief. '54 The Black Shield of Falworth. '56 Trapeze. '57 Sweet Smell of Success. '58 The Defiant Ones. '59 Some Like It Hot. '60 Spartacus. '62 Taras Bulba. '63 The Great Race. '64 Goodbye Charlie; Sex and the Single Girl. '68 The Boston Strangler.

CURTIZ, Michael

(1888–1962). Director. Born: Mihály Kertész; Budapest, Hungary

Michael Curtiz directed Hungarian films from 1912 to 1919 (with brief service in the infantry in World War I). In 1919, after the Hungarian studios were nationalized, Curtiz left for a seven-year stint in Austria. A superb costume spectacular, *Moon of Israel*, appealed to Harry Warner, and in 1926 Curtiz was brought to Hollywood to make his first American movie, *The Third Degree*. Not until 1954 did he make a film away from Warners. Over the years he was that studio's finest director. Prolific, dedicated and versatile, he could move confidently from Errol Flynn swashbucklers to the quiet charm of a film like *Daughters Courageous*; to *Casablanca* and *Mildred Pierce* he brought the supreme professionalism which could combine with great actors and great scripts to create classic movies. Of course it could not go on for ever. He worked until 1961, but his last genuine Curtiz film (in 1947) was the extraordinary *noir* thriller, *The Unsuspected*; after that, he went through the motions. It would be a pity if Curtiz were remembered only for *Casablanca*. The early Thirties, especially, was a marvellous period for him. Making four or five films a year, he produced superb low-budget horror movies (*Doctor X*, 1932; *The Walking Dead*, 1936), crime thrillers (*The Kennel Murder Case*, 1933), and cynical low-life studies (*The Strange Love of Molly Louvain*, 1932). *Casablanca* won Curtiz his only Academy Award, but those forgotten films of the previous decade were not inferior.

Films include: 1912 Az Utolsó Bohem (HUN). '20 Boccaccio (A). '24 Die Sklavenkönigin (A) (USA: Moon of Israel). '26 The Third Degree. '28 Noah's Ark. '35 Captain Blood. '36 The Charge of the Light Brigade. '38 The Adventures of Robin Hood (co-dir); Angels With Dirty Faces. '39 Daughters Courageous; Dodge City; The Private Lives of Elizabeth and Essex. '40 The Sea Hawk. '42 Yankee Doodle Dandy; Casablanca. '45 Mildred Pierce. '54 White Christmas. '62 The Comancheros.

CUSACK, Cyril

(b. 1910). Actor. Born: Durban, Natal, South Africa

Cyril Cusack has given memorable performances on film, but his roots are firmly established in the theatre. In 1932 he joined the Abbey Theatre in Dublin, soon became one of the leading Irish actors, and in 1945 was abla to form his own company. In later years he has appeared with the Royal Shakespeare Company, and often on television. In 1918 Cusack acted in *Knocknagow*, an early Irish silent, but his feature debut was in Carol Reed's *Odd Man Out* in 1947. A versatile character actor whose gentle manner is tinged with a resigned melancholy, Cusack has been outstanding in films like *The Spy Who Came in From the Cold* (as the Secret Service chief) and *Fahrenheit 451* (playing against the grain as the book-burning fire-brigade captain).

Films include: 1947 Odd Man Out. '49 The Small Back Room (USA: Hour of Glory). '50 The Elusive Pimpernel (USA: The Fighting Pimpernel). '57 Ill Met by Moonlight (USA: Night Ambush). '62 The Waltz of the Toreadors. '65 The Spy Who Came in From the Cold. '66 I Was Happy Here; Fahrenheit 451. '67 The Taming of the Shrew (IT-USA). '68 Galileo (IT-BULG). '69 David Copperfield. '73 The Homecoming (GB-USA); The Day of the Jackal (GB-FR). '81 True Confessions.

CUSHING, Peter

(b. 1913). Actor. Born: Kenley, Surrey, England

Peter Cushing spent four years in repertory in England before going to Hollywood in 1939. There he did little beyond doubling for Louis Hayward and supporting Laurel and Hardy, but he managed a New York stage debut before his return to England. More stage work led to a part in Laurence Olivier's film of *Hamlet* in 1948, but not until 1953 did regular film work come his way. Four years later he played Frankenstein in Hammer's *The Curse of Frankenstein*. This brought him international fame – and caused him to be typed thereafter in countless routine horror movies. His quietly authoritative, yet sinister, manner made him superb in such parts, but it was a dreadful waste of a fine actor. He was an excellent Sherlock Holmes in *The Hound of the Baskervilles*, when for once he escaped from the treadmill.

Films include: 1940 A Chump at Oxford (USA). **'48** Hamlet. **'56** Alexander the Great (USA). **'57** The Curse of Frankenstein. **'58** The Revenge of Frankenstein. **'59** The Hound of the Baskervilles; The Mummy. **'60** The Brides of Dracula; Sword of Sherwood Forest. **'62** Captain Clegg (USA: Night Creatures). **'64** The Evil of Frankenstein. **'71** The House That Dripped Blood. **'77** Star Wars (USA).

CUTTS, Graham

(1885–1958). Director. Born: Brighton, Sussex, England

Graham Cutts was trained as an engineer, but abandoned that career for film exhibition in Newcastle. In 1922 he produced and directed a film called *While London Sleeps*, on the tricky subject of drug addiction. Soon afterwards Cutts, Michael Balcon and Victor Saville founded Gainsborough Pictures. As a director Cutts had many virtues. He told his tales simply and well, had a marked visual sense, and was good with actors. When sound came, he gradually slipped to second features and shorts; if his Twenties reputation is restored, it will be through *The Rat* and its two sequels, in which Cutts steered Ivor Novello through some lurid adventures in Paris.

Films include: 1922 While London Sleeps; Flames of Passion. **'23** Paddy the Next Best Thing; Woman to Woman. **'24** The White Shadow (USA: White Shadows); The Passionate Adventure. **'25** The Blackguard; The Rat. **'26** The Triumph of the Rat. **'27** Confetti. **'29** The Return of the Rat. **'32** The Sign of Four (co-dir). **'33** Three Men in a Boat. **'39** Just William.

CYBULSKI, Zbigniew

(1927–1967). Actor. Born: Kniaze, Ukraine, USSR

Zbigniew Cybulski studied at the Theatre School in Cracow. He co-founded both the student theatre, Bim-Bom, in Gdansk in 1954 and two years later the Theatre of Talks. His film career began in 1954, and in 1958 he achieved international fame with his performance in Andrzej Wajda's *Ashes and Diamonds*. Playing a disillusioned idealist caught up in Poland's post-war troubles, he filled the part with a passionate intensity which seemed to speak for a whole bewildered generation. Cybulski became an idolized cult-figure, but to see him as a Polish James Dean is to underrate an actor of considerable range. He was excellent in lighter vein, as in the charming *See You Tomorrow*, and convincing, too, as the bemused Guardsman in *The Saragossa Manuscript*. His early death resulted from a fall as he tried to board a moving train.

Films include: 1955 Pokolenie (USA/GB: A Generation/Light in the Darkness). **'57** Ósmi Dzienń Tygodnia (USA: The Eighth Day of the Week). **'58** Popioł i Diament (USA/GB: Ashes and Diamonds). **'59** Pociag (USA/GB: Night Train). **'60** Do Widzenia do Jutra (+co-sc) (USA/GB: See You Tomorrow); Niewinni Czarodzieje (USA/GB: Innocent Sorcerers). **'62** La Poupée (FR) (USA/GB: He, She or It; Jak być Kochana (USA/GB: How to Be Loved). **'63** Milczenie (USA/GB: Silence). **'64** Rekopis Znaleziony w Saragossie (USA/GB: The Saragossa Manuscript); Att Älska (SWED) (USA/GB: To Love). **'67** Jowita (USA/GB: Yovita).

CZINNER, Paul

(1890–1972). Director. Born: Budapest, Hungary

An infant prodigy on the violin, Paul Czinner emigrated to Austria where he became a drama critic at 16, then to Germany. Before he was 30 he had established himself in films as writer, director and producer, his first big success coming with *Nju* in 1924. This psychological drama starred the actress Elisabeth Bergner, who appeared in almost all Czinner's later films. They came to England in 1930, married in 1933 and became British citizens. Czinner's British films with Bergher are careful, stiff and literary, the plodding direction ill-matched to the idiosyncrasies of the actress. The Czinners moved to the USA in 1940 and concentrated on the theatre. Later on, back in England, Czinner made films of ballet and opera, interesting as historical record but of small account as cinema.

Films include: 1924 Nju (GER) **'26** Der Geiger von Florenz (GER) (GB: Impetuous Youth/The Violinist of Florence). **'31** Ariane. **'34** Catherine the Great. **'35** Escape Me Never. **'36** As You Like It. **'39** Stolen Life. **'55** Don Giovanni. **'57** The Bolshoi Ballet. **'60** The Royal Ballet. **'62** Der Rosenkavalier. **'66** Romeo and Juliet.

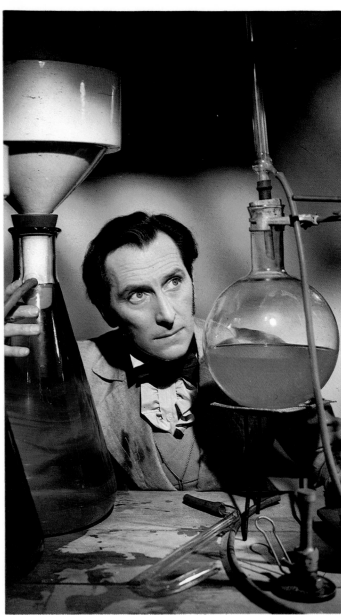

Above: Peter Cushing plays Baron Frankenstein in The Curse of Frankenstein, *a role he was to repeat in several Hammer films to the company's considerable profit*

Right: Zbigniew Cybulski as a right-wing activist in Ashes and Diamonds, *fatally wounded after having murdered an important Communist Party official*

D

DAGOVER, Lil

(1897–1980). Actress. Born: Marta
Maria Lilitts; Madiven, Java

At the very start of her film career, Lil
Dagover was immortalized in one of
the most legendary and haunting of
all film roles – the beautiful and
ethereal Jane, heroine of *The Cabinet of
Dr Caligari*, abducted and carried off
over the rooftops by the somnambulist Cesar (Conrad Veidt). She was
brought to Germany by her father, a
forestry inspector, at ten, after the
death of her mother. A brief marriage
to the dramatist Fritz Daghofer suggested her professional name. After
The Cabinet of Dr Caligari, Dagover's
beauty and strong screen presence
were much in demand; and she appeared in a whole series of classic
silents. In *Congress Dances* she revealed a rich wit, but there were few
important parts left to her in talkies,
though she continued to work in films
till the early Seventies. Dagover
worked briefly in France (1928–29)
and Hollywood (*The Woman From
Monte Carlo*).

Films include: 1919 Hara-Kiri; Das Kabinett
des Dr Caligari (GB: The Cabinet of Dr
Caligari); Die Spinnen (GB: The Spiders).
'21 Der Müde Tod (GB: Destiny). **'22** Dr
Mabuse der Spieler (GB: Dr Mabuse, the
Gambler); Phantom. **'25** Tartüff (GB: Tar-
tuffe); Die Chronik von Grieshuus (GB:
Chronicles of the Grey House). **'31** Der
Kongress Tanzt (GB: Congress Dances). **'32**
The Woman From Monte Carlo (USA). **'36**
Schlussakkord (GB: Final Accord).

DAHL, Arlene

(b. 1925). Actress. Born:
Minneapolis, Minnesota, USA

While only 15 and still at high school,
Arlene Dahl was given a part in a
weekly radio serial. She later became
a model and then a dancer on Broadway, where she was spotted by Jack
Warner and given a screen test. Her
looks were greater than her talent,
but she was taken to Hollywood
anyway. Her red hair and piercing
blue eyes were ideally suited to Technicolor and for a decade she enjoyed
steady success in undemanding roles.
Then, as her screen appearances
became fewer, she started to write a
beauty column and began to sell
clothes under the Arlene Dahl Enterprises label, as well as taking occasional parts in the theatre. Having
been thought one of the richest
women in New York (probably on
account of her lavish life-style), she
declared herself bankrupt in 1981.

Films include: 1947 My Wild Irish Rose. **'48**
The Bride Goes Wild. **'50** Three Little
Words. **'51** Inside Straight; No Questions
Asked. **'53** Jamaica Run. **'54** Bengal Brigade
(GB: Bengal Rifles); A Woman's World. **'56**
Wicked As They Come. **'59** Journey to the
Center of the Earth.

DAHLBECK, Eva

(b. 1920). Actress. Born: Stockholm,
Sweden

Eva Dahlbeck trained at the Royal
Dramatic Theatre Drama School in
Stockholm and made her film debut in
Gustaf Molander's *Rid i Natt* (1942),
having played the same part on the
stage. She had a considerable screen
career before first working with
Ingmar Bergman in 1952. In his films
she showed herself a subtle and
glamorous comedienne, as in *Smiles of
a Summer Night*. But it was in a
dramatic role, as a happily pregnant
mother who loses her baby, that she
shared the Cannes Best Actress prize
with her colleagues in *So Close to Life*.
She has played in segments of an
American television series, *Foreign
Intrigue* (1952–55), and in an American film, *The Counterfeit Traitor*
(1962). She has written several
novels.

Films include: 1948 Eva. **'49** Kvinna i Vitt;
Bara en Mor (GB: Only a Mother). **'52** Trots;
Kvinnors Vantan (USA: Secrets of Women;
GB: Waiting Women). **'54** En Lektion i
Kärlek (USA/GB: A Lesson in Love). **'55**
Kvinnodröm (USA: Dreams; GB: Journey
Into Autumn); Sommarnattens Leende
(USA/GB: Smiles of a Summer Night). **'58**
Nära Livet (USA: Brink of Life; GB: So Close
to Life). **'64** För att inte Tala om Alla Dessa
Kvinnor (USA: All These Women; GB: Now
About These Women); Älskande Par
(USA/GB: Loving Couples). **'66** Les Créa-
tures (FR-SWED); Yngsjömordet (sc. only)
(GB: Woman of Darkness). **'70** Tintomara
(DEN).

*Far left: Lil Dagover. Left: Arlene Dahl
as a scheming wife who tries to get
her husband a new top job in* A
Woman's World. *Below: Eva
Dahlbeck in her only American film to
date,* The Counterfeit Traitor

DAILEY, Dan

(1917–1978). Actor/dancer. Born: New York City, USA

Dan Dailey was stagestruck at an early age and began as an amateur before getting into vaudeville and the chorus at the Roxy, which led to larger parts in musical comedy. Tall and rangy, with an engaging personality and big smile, he was basically a song-and-dance man. Though he was given a contract by MGM in 1939, he did not dance on screen until he moved to 20th Century-Fox and was cast opposite Betty Grable in *Mother Wore Tights*. He was nominated for an Oscar in *When My Baby Smiles at Me*, and was also outstanding as one of the trio of ex-servicemen in *It's Always Fair Weather*, with Gene Kelly and Michael Kidd. As he grew older he danced less and concentrated more on straight roles in the theatre and television. In 1970 Dailey won a Golden Globe Award for his television role in *The Governor and J.J.*

Films include: 1940 The Mortal Storm. '41 Ziegfeld Girl; Lady Be Good. '42 Panama Hattie. '47 Mother Wore Tights. '48 When My Baby Smiles at Me. '50 When Willie Comes Marching Home. '52 Meet Me at the Fair. '54 There's No Business Like Show Business. '55 It's Always Fair Weather. '56 Meet Me in Las Vegas (GB: Viva Las Vegas); The Best Things in Life Are Free. '62 Hemingway's Adventures of a Young Man. '78 The Private Files of J. Edgar Hoover.

DALI, Salvador

(b. 1904). Artist. Born: Figueras, Spain

The famous Spanish Surrealist painter has had a hit-and-miss relationship with the cinema since his early and stormy collaboration with Luis Buñuel on *Un Chien Andalou* and *L'Age d'Or*. In 1932 he published a screenplay, *Babaouo*, followed in 1935 by *The Super-Realist Mysteries of New York*; but neither was filmed. In 1935 Dali went to Hollywood, taking a harp strung with barbed wire, and stayed with Harpo Marx, whom he greatly admired; he developed a screenplay, *Giraffes on Hunchback Salad*, which was never made. In 1945 he designed the dream sequence in Hitchcock's *Spellbound*. He was then invited by Walt Disney to create a six-minute animated sequence, *Destino*; but only one section was finished, since it proved too expensive.

Films include: 1928 Un Chien Andalou (co-sc; + act) (FR). '30 L'Age d'Or (co-sc) (FR). '45 Spellbound (designs for dream sequence) (USA). '54 The Prodigious Adventure of the Lace-Maker and the Rhinoceros (unfinished work in progress).

DALIO, Marcel

(1901–1983). Actor. Born: Paris, France

Marcel Dalio's enforced exile during World War II resulted in his becoming one of the best-known Hollywood character players of the period, specializing in smooth and generally shifty foreigners (in *The Shanghai Gesture* and *Casablanca*, for example). It nevertheless interrupted a singularly promising career in his native France where he had created two of his most memorable roles for Jean Renoir – the little Jewish prisoner of war in *La Grande Illusion* and the Marquis de la Chesnaye in *La Règle du Jeu*. The latter, an incomparable portrait of aristocracy, was created by a man who had been born the child of Romanian Jewish immigrants. Dalio's career started in revue and music hall; and he was 32 when he made his first film appearance in *Pépé-le-Moko*. Clearly the conditions of his exile were not unsympathetic to him, and after the war he regularly returned to work in Hollywood pictures.

Films include: 1936 Pépé-le-Moko. '37 La Grande Illusion (USA: Grand Illusion; GB: The Great Illusion). '38 Entrée des Artistes. '39 La Règle du Jeu (USA: The Rules of the Game). '41 The Shanghai Gesture (USA). '42 Casablanca (USA). '44 To Have and Have Not (USA). '49 Les Amants de Vérone. '54 Sabrina (USA) (GB: Sabrina Fair). '63 Donovan's Reef (USA).

DALLESANDRO, Joe

(b. 1949). Actor. Born: New York City, USA

Joe Dallesandro was initially associated with the movies directed or produced by the American artist Andy Warhol during the period when Warhol was making eccentric but quite commerical features rather than his earlier Underground experiments. Dallesandro fitted into the stereotype of the well-built handsome all-American boy, frequently appearing nude; but the stories of the films immersed him in the seamier side of American life – homosexual prostitution, drug addiction, the flesh-peddling of Hollywood. Dallesandro insists that he never wanted to make soft-porn films but intended to pursue a straight acting career. He came to Europe and appeared in films by some of the leading French directors – Jacques Rivette, for example – as the result of moving in avant-garde film circles. But it cannot be said that his acting has improved much over the years.

Films include: 1967 Four Stars. '68 Lonesome Cowboys; Flesh; The Loves of Ondine. '70 Trash. '72 Heat. '73 Andy Warhol's Frankenstein; Dracula Vuole Vivere: Cerca Sangue di Vergine (IT-FR) (USA: Andy Warhol's Dracula; GB: Blood for Dracula).

Above left: Dan Dailey in Chicken Every Sunday *(1948)*. *Above: Marcel Dalio as a rich Jewish prisoner of war in* La Grande Illusion. *Below: Roger Daltrey as Franz Liszt in* Lisztomania

Top right: Dorothy Dandridge. Top, far right: Timothy Dalton in Flash Gordon. *Right: Joe Dallesandro in* Flesh. *Far right: Viola Dana in* Don't Doubt Your Husband *(1924)*

'75 Black Moon (FR-GER). '76 La Marge (FR) (GB: Streetwalker). '79 Merry-Go-Round (FR).

DALRYMPLE, Ian

(b. 1903). Producer/screenwriter/director/editor. Born: Johannesburg, South Africa

The son of Sir William Dalrymple, Ian Dalrymple was educated at Rugby and Cambridge. He became an assistant film editor with Michael Balcon at Gainsborough, helping on the silent version of *The Constant Nymph* (1928). He worked his way up to supervising editor on such films as *Rome Express* (1932) and *The Good Companions* (1933). He also co-scripted the second of these and concentrated on screenwriting in the second half of the Thirties. From 1940 to 1943 he was executive producer with the Crown Film Unit, making wartime documentaries. He then became a producer for Alexander Korda, and in 1946 he formed his own Wessex company, which was quite successful for several years. After that Dalrymple produced and wrote for various companies, and in the late Sixties advised record companies about film projects.

Films include: 1938 The Citadel (co-sc); South Riding (co-sc); Pygmalion (co-sc). '40 Old Bill and Son (dir; + co-sc). '41 Target for Tonight (prod). '42 Coastal Command (prod); Listen to Britain (prod). '47 The Woman in the Hall (prod; + co-sc). '48 Esther Waters (co-dir; + prod). '50 The Wooden Horse (prod). '53 The Heart of the Matter (prod; + co-sc). '57 The Admirable Crichton (prod)(USA: Paradise Lagoon). '67 Calamity the Cow (prod).

DALTON, Timothy

(b. 1946). Actor. Born: Colwyn Bay, Denbigh, Wales

With his curly black hair, aristocratic looks and classically theatrical voice, Timothy Dalton was clearly destined to play royalty and romantic lovers in period dramas. He is a product of the National Youth Theatre and two years of RADA. In 1966 he took the lead in the stage version of *Little Malcolm and His Struggle Against the*

Commissioner to the District Attorney). '72 L'Istruttoria è Chiusa: Dimentichi! '75 The Tempter/Il Sorriso del Grande Tentatore (GB-IT) (USA: The Devil Is a Woman); Perchè si Uccide un Magistrato. '76 Un Genio, Due Compari, un Pollo (IT-FR-GER).

DANA, Viola

(b. 1898). Actress. Born: Viola Flugrath; Brooklyn, New York City, USA

With her sisters Shirley Mason and Edna Flugrath, Viola went on the stage as a small child and starred in *The Model* on Broadway. She made her screen debut in 1910 for Edison with Shirley. After having a big hit on the stage in *Poor Little Rich Girl*, she returned to Edison where Edna was already a top star. The director John Collins cast her as the lead in *The Stone Heart* and married her the same year, 1915. Almost at once *The Stoning* made her a star, and she appeared in all of Collins' films until his death in 1918. She moved to Metro, staying eight years, and then on to Paramount. Her fashionable well-bred look – dark hair in ringlets, big sad eyes, bee-stung lips – kept her a star in romantic melodramas and comedies throughout the silent era, but her career came to a total halt in 1929 with *The Show of Shows* for Warners. She later commented: 'We were not casualties of sound because we couldn't talk; we were just ignored, put on the shelf.'

Films include: 1915 The Stone Heart; The Stoning. **'17** Blue Jeans. **'20** The Willow Tree. **'24** Merton of the Movies; Open All Night. **'25** The Necessary Evil; As Man Desires. **'28** That Certain Thing. **'29** The Show of Shows.

DANDRIDGE, Dorothy

(1923–1965). Actress. Born: Cleveland, Ohio, USA

The daughter of a minister, Dorothy Dandridge learned singing and dancing from her mother. Taken to Hollywood at four, she got bit parts, including one in *A Day at the Races*, in her teens. She dropped out of high school and formed a trio that sang with Jimmy Lunceford's band in the Thirties. Dandridge established herself internationally as a nightclub singer and big-band vocalist before attempting to resume her film career, at first in minor roles. After a struggle, largely because of her colour, she was given a lead role in *Bright Road*, a minor MGM movie, but it was *Carmen Jones* that finally gave her a chance to display her talent (though her singing voice was dubbed) and win an Oscar nomination. But she had to wait three years for her next part in *Island in the Sun*; and when she was cast as Bess in *Porgy and Bess* she was again dubbed. After a couple of minor movies, she died suddenly of an embolism.

Films include: 1937 A Day at the Races. **'43** Hit Parade of 1943. **'51** Tarzan's Peril (GB: Tarzan and the Jungle Queen). **'53** Bright Road; Remains to Be Seen. **'54** Carmen Jones. **'57** Island in the Sun. **'58** Tamango; The Decks Ran Red. **'59** Porgy and Bess. **'60** Moment of Danger (GB) (USA: Malaga).

Eunuchs, which resulted in a contract with Birmingham Repertory Theatre and the lead in a television series. His small but effective part as the charming, boyish strategist King Philip of France in *The Lion in Winter* brought him other roles including Heathcliff in *Wuthering Heights*. He has continued to alternate between stage and film work.

Films include: 1968 The Lion in Winter. **'70** Cromwell. **'71** Wuthering Heights; Le Voyeur (IT-FR). **'72** Mary, Queen of Scots. **'75** Permission to Kill (USA-A). **'78** Sextette. **'79** Agatha. **'80** Flash Gordon. **'82** Chanel Solitaire (FR-GB).

DALTREY, Roger

(b. 1945). Singer/actor. Born: London, England

Roger Daltrey first met his future colleagues Pete Townshend and John Entwistle at Acton Grammar School before being expelled. Along with Keith Moon, they formed the rock band The Who in the early Sixties, with Daltrey as lead vocalist. With his mane of curly hair and his attacking style, he became one of the icons of the period. His film career came later, when he played the deaf, dumb and blind pinball player in Townshend's rock opera *Tommy*, filmed by Ken Russell, who also cast Daltrey as Liszt in *Lisztomania*. *The Kids Are Alright* was a documentary about the history of The Who. The group formed a film subsidiary and acquired part ownership of Shepperton studios to make *Quadrophenia* and other films. Daltrey's main straight role was as *McVicar*, an East End crook who goes straight after imprisonment.

Films: 1970 Woodstock (USA). **'75** Tommy; Lisztomania. **'78** The Legacy. **'79** The Kids Are Alright (doc); Quadrophenia (co-prod. only). **'80** McVicar.

DAMIANI, Damiano

(b. 1922). Director/screenwriter. Born: Pasiano, Italy

Having studied at the Brera Academy of Fine Arts in Milan, Damiani entered feature films as an art director. He also directed 17 documentaries between 1946 and 1955, and collaborated on ten scripts, mostly in the Fifties. He worked with Cesare Zavattini, who co-scripted his first film as director, *Red Lips*, a study of the problems of female adolescence in the form of á detective story, which won a prize at San Sebastian. His best-known film abroad, *Confessions of a Police Commissioner to the District Attorney*, a political thriller about the violent clash between two building speculators, was based on real events in Palermo in 1969. Although Damiani has won much critical acclaim at film festivals, he has not had as much recognition abroad as he undoubtedly deserves.

Films include: 1960 Il Rossetto (FR-IT) (GB: Red Lips). **'62** L'Isola di Arturo (USA/GB: Arthur's Island). **'64** La Noia (IT-FR) (USA/GB: The Empty Canvas). **'66** La Strega in Amore (GB: The Witch in Love). **'67** Quien Sabe? (dir. only) (GB: A Bullet for the General). **'69** Una Ragazza Piuttosto Complicata (GB: Complicated Girl). **'70** La Moglie Più Bella. **'71** Confessione di un Commissario di Polizia al Procuratore della Repubblica (GB: Confessions of a Police

D'ANGELO, Beverly

(b. 1952). Actress. Born: Columbus, Ohio, USA

After studying art, D'Angelo worked for a while as a cartoonist with the Hanna Barbera animation studio. She also sang in coffee houses and made her Broadway debut in *Rockabye Hamlet* as Ophelia. In the late Seventies she began what promised to be a successful career in film, especially well-suited to off-beat characterizations like the nymphomaniac waitress in *Honky Tonk Freeway*.

Films: 1977 Annie Hall; The Sentinel; First Love. '78 Every Which Way But Loose. '79 Hair. '80 Highpoint (CAN); Coal Miner's Daughter. '81 Paternity; Honky Tonk Freeway.

DANIELL, Henry

(1894–1963). Actor. Born: London, England

Stone-faced, frigidly reptilian, intelligent – most of the time when Daniell appeared in a film, audiences could sense he was up to no good, even if he did appear to be neatly turned out and spoke English with the proper accent. Daniell's first big break came when he was chosen to star in a stage play in 1914. Unfortunately it opened the day the war broke out. Perhaps this accounted for the fact that, thereafter, Daniell looked like someone who had been done some incalculable injustice which had rendered him cold and mean. Not for nothing was he perfectly cast as the arch-villain and criminal mastermind, Professor Moriarty, the unvanquishable enemy of Sherlock Holmes.

Films include: 1929 Jealousy. '36 Camille. '39 The Private Lives of Elizabeth and Essex. '40 All This and Heaven Too; The Philadelphia Story; The Sea Hawk; The Great Dictator. '41 Four Jacks and a Jill. '42 Sherlock Holmes and the Voice of Terror. '43 Jane Eyre. '56 Lust for Life. '57 Witness for the Prosecution. '62 The Comancheros.

DANIELS, Bebe

(1901–1971). Actress. Born: Dallas, Texas, USA

Bebe Daniel was a true trouper. Her parents were respectively manager and star of a stock company, and Bebe

Top, left to right: Beverely D'Angelo with John Savage in Hair *(1979); Henry Daniell (right) in* The Sea Hawk; *Bebe Daniels in* Singed Wings *(1922); Roy Danton in* The Rise and Fall of Legs Diamond. *Centre, left to right: Bobby Darin; Kim Darby; Danielle Darrieux as Madame de . . . Bottom left: Linda Darnell in* Forever Amber

was acting by the time she was four. At six she made her first screen appearance in a Selig short, and in 1914 signed with Hal Roach who was then producing for Pathé. During the next five years she made some 200 shorts, most notably as Harold Lloyd's heroine. Her feature career began with a Paramount contract in 1919. She could be a sophisticated woman of the world in Cecil B. DeMille's *Male and Female, Why Change Your Wife?* and *The Affairs of Anatol*; a romantic partner to Rudolph Valentino in *Monsieur Beaucaire*; or a madcap flapper in Edward Sutherland's *Wild, Wild Susan* or Gregory La Cava's *Feel My Pulse*. With sound, her good singing voice revived her career in *Rio Rita*, but despite such admirable performances as the bitchy star in *42nd Street* her Hollywood career was slipping. She had no more luck in British films; but in the Forties and Fifties she, her husband Ben Lyon and their children became great BBC radio favourites.

Films include: 1917 Luke's Movie Muddle. '19 Male and Female (GB: The Admirable Crichton). '20 Bumping Into Broadway; Why Change Your Wife? '21 The Affairs of Anatol. '24 Monsieur Beaucaire. '25 Wild, Wild Susan. '28 Feel My Pulse. '29 Rio Rita. '31 The Maltese Falcon; Counsellor-at-Law. '54 Life With the Lyons (GB) (USA: Family Affair).

DANIELS, William

(1895–1970). Cinematographer. Born: Cleveland, Ohio, USA

Daniels will always be remembered as 'Garbo's cameraman': his tact in dealing with the shy star and his ability to capture on film her luminosity and interior quality made an incalculable contribution to the enduring Garbo myth. There were many other aspects, though, to Daniels' 54-year career in films. Leaving the University of Southern California in 1917, he became an assistant cameraman at Triangle. In 1919 he was signed by Universal, and it was here that he first worked with Erich von Stroheim with whom he collaborated on six films, including *Foolish Wives* and *Greed*. At MGM between 1924 and 1943 he contributed much to the legendary visual gloss which was the company's hallmark; but later showed a versatility which could embrace the harsh realism of *Brute Force* or *The Naked City* and an imaginative use of colour.

Films include: 1922 Foolish Wives (co-photo). '25 Greed (co-photo). '27 Flesh and the Devil; Love (GB: Anna Karenina). '28 A Woman of Affairs. '29 Wild Orchids. '32 Mata Hari; Grand Hotel. '33 Queen Christina. '35 Anna Karenina. '39 Ninotchka. '40 The Mortal Storm. '42 Keeper of the Flame. '47 Brute Force. '48 The Naked City. '50 Winchester '73. '65 Von Ryan's Express.

DANTON, Ray

(b. 1931). Actor. Born: Raymond Danton; New York City, USA

Slender, suave, smooth and deadly, Danton looked as if he could be trusted only as far as he could be thrown. More should have happened with his career and he deserved better than his long run of B-film appearances, playing cheap, flashy hoods like Legs Diamond. In the Seventies he directed some low-budget horror films. He married actress Julie Adams in 1955.

Films include: 1955 I'll Cry Tomorrow. '58 Onionhead. '60 The Rise and Fall of Legs Diamond. '61 Portrait of a Mobster; The George Raft Story (GB: Spin of a Coin). '62 The Chapman Report; The Longest Day. '72 Crypt of the Living Dead (dir. only) (GB: Vampire Woman); The Deathmaster (dir. only). '75 Psychic Killer (dir. only).

DARBY, Kim

(b. 1948). Actress. Born: Deborah Zerby; Hollywood, California, USA

Darby is an actress who, having appeared in only a handful of films, made a substantial impression on audiences. In *True Grit* she played opposite John Wayne and showed herself fully capable of holding her own as Mattie Ross, the determined ball of fire bent on avenging her father's murder. She made her debut at the age of 16 in a segment of the intelligent Sixties television series *Mr Novak*, as a blind student who falls in love with the high-school-teacher hero. This led to regular television work and eventually to movies.

Films: 1965 Bus Riley's Back in Town. '67 The Karate Killers. '69 Generation (GB: A Time for Giving); True Grit. '70 The Strawberry Statement; Norwood. '71 The Grissom Gang. '78 The One and Only.

DARIN, Bobby

(1936–1973). Singer/actor. Born: Walden Robert Cassotto; Bronx, New York City, USA

A drop-out from music and drama studies, Darin wrote radio jingles until, in 1958, he recorded one of his own songs, *Splish Splash*, and became an overnight sensation. He rapidly moved into the nightclub circuit and established himself as a polished performer and a likely and able successor to the older generation of American crooners like Perry Como and Frank Sinatra. The first film he appeared in – and wrote the title song for – was *Come September*. A few years later he received an Oscar nomination for his supporting role in *Captain Newman MD*. In the late Sixties his career declined somewhat but he began making a comeback with his own television show and with Las Vegas nightclub acts. In 1971 Darin underwent open-heart surgery: two years and two operations later he was dead at the age of 37. Actress Sandra Dee was his wife from 1960 to 1967.

Films include: 1961 Come September; Too Late Blues. '62 Hell Is for Heroes; If a Man Answers; Pressure Point; State Fair. '63 Captain Newman MD. '67 Gunfight in Abilene. '69 The Happy Ending. '73 Happy Mother's Day, Love George.

DARNELL, Linda

(1923–1965). Actress. Born: Monetta Eloyse Darnell; Dallas, Texas, USA

She was publicized by 20th Century-Fox as 'the girl with the perfect face' and, for once, it wasn't studio hype. Darnell entered movies at the age of 15 and was groomed for stardom, usually playing demure young girls, often opposite Tyrone Power. In the Forties she began to shed her innocent screen image by playing seductresses and tarty waitresses, culminating in her roles as Chihuahua the wildcat saloon girl in *My Darling Clementine* and as Amber St Clare in *Forever Amber*. In later life she shifted gear and tried, unsuccessfully, to become a cabaret star. She died of burns as the result of a fire started while she was watching one of her own films on television.

Films include: 1940 Brigham Young; The Mark of Zorro. '41 Blood and Sand. '44 It Happened Tomorrow. '45 Hangover Square; Fallen Angel. '46 My Darling Clementine. '47 Forever Amber. '48 A Letter to Three Wives; Unfaithfully Yours.

d'ARRAST, Harry d'Abbadie

(1893–1968). Director. Born: Henri d'Abbadie d'Arrast; Argentina

D'Arrast had a brief, sparkling and stormy career as a director of witty social comedy. He was brought to Hollywood by the director George Fitzmaurice and employed by Chaplin as an assistant on *A Woman of Paris* (1923). Embarking as a director in his own right at Paramount, d'Arrast directed Adolphe Menjou, star of *A Woman of Paris*, in three bright and caustic comedies: *Service for Ladies, A Gentleman of Paris* and *Serenade*. A handful of subsequent features, passing on into the talkie era, showed the same sophisticated and cynical wit – his masterpiece in this line was *Laughter* – but d'Arrast's career was handicapped and eventually ended by his irascibility, which caused fallings-out with Goldwyn over *Raffles* and Selznick over *Topaze* (adapted from Pagnol and starring John Barrymore). D'Arrast retired to Europe and was reputed to have earned a living at the gambling tables of Monte Carlo.

Films: 1927 Service for Ladies; A Gentleman of Paris; Serenade. '28 The Magnificent Flirt; Dry Martini. '30 Raffles (uncredited); Laughter. '33 Topaze. '34 La Traviesa Molinera (SP) (USA/GB: It Happened in Spain).

DARRIEUX, Danielle

(b. 1917). Actress. Born: Bordeaux, France

One of the beauties of pre-war French cinema, Darrieux became much-beloved for her roles as innocent sophisticates. She acted in her first film, *Le Bal*, when only 14; five years later she was an international star after her appearance with Charles Boyer in *Mayerling*. In the Fifties she appeared in three Max Ophuls films: as the sympathetic mistress-to-be, Emilie Breitkopf, in *La Ronde*; as Rosa in *Le Plaisir*; and as the tormented Countess Louise de . . . in *Madame de . . .* In 1971 she took over the lead from Katharine Hepburn in the Broadway musical *Coco*. During the Thirties Darrieux was married to the film-maker Henri Decoin who directed her in several comedies.

Films include: 1931 Le Bal. '36 Mayerling. '38 Retour a l'Aube. '49 Occupe-toi d'Amelie (GB: Keep an Eye on Amelia). '50 La Ronde. '51 Rich, Young and Pretty (USA). '52 Le Plaisir. '53 Madame de . . . (FR-IT). '55 L'Amant de Lady Chatterly. '61 The Greengage Summer (GB) (USA: Loss of Innocence). '63 Landru (FR-IT) (GB: Bluebeard). '82 Une Chambre en Ville (GB: A Room in Town).

DARWELL, Jane

(1880–1967). Actress. Born: Patti Woodward; Palmyra, Missouri, USA

Jane Darwell's Oscar-winning performance as Ma Joad in John Ford's *The Grapes of Wrath* is one of Hollywood's sacred monuments. But it wasn't the first time stalwart sentiment had been provided by this durable character player, who could readily turn from the emotional roles she did for Ford to feather-brained old biddies, or a garrulous busybody like Mrs Merriwether in *Gone With the Wind*. Trained in music and acting, she worked on stage in London, Paris and Berlin. She made sporadic appearances in silent films from 1914 (such as Cecil B. DeMille's *Rose of the Rancho*); but her film career proper began with sound and *Tom Sawyer* (1930). After that she worked in Hollywood fairly constantly almost to her death. Her final appearance was in *Mary Poppins*.

Films include: 1914 Rose of the Rancho. '33 Only Yesterday. '34 The Scarlet Empress. '35 One More Spring. '36 Craig's Wife. '39 Gone With the Wind; Jesse James. '40 The Grapes of Wrath. '41 All That Money Can Buy/The Devil and Daniel Webster. '43 The Ox-Bow Incident (GB: Strange Incident). '46 My Darling Clementine. '50 Wagonmaster. '58 The Last Hurrah. '64 Mary Poppins.

DA SILVA, Howard

(1909–1978). Actor. Born: Harold Silverblatt; Cleveland, Ohio, USA

Pleading the Fifth Amendment in 1951, Da Silva became another victim of the Hollywood blacklist and disappeared from the movies for a decade. His theatrical background stood him in good stead, however, and he returned to acting, producing and directing on Broadway. In the Forties he established himself as a more than competent character actor playing heavies, notably as one of the escaped convicts who go on a murderous spree of robbery in *They Live by Night*, the prototype for *Bonnie and Clyde* (1967).

Films include: 1940 Abe Lincoln in Illinois (GB: Spirit of the People). '45 The Lost Weekend. '46 Two Years Before the Mast; The Blue Dahlia. '47 Unconquered. '48 They Live by Night. '49 Border Incident; The Great Gatsby. '51 Fourteen Hours. '78 The Private Files of J. Edgar Hoover.

DASSIN, Jules

(b. 1911). Director. Born: Middletown, Connecticut, USA

Born of Russian immigrant parents, raised in Harlem, an actor in the Yiddish Theater Company, blacklisted in the Fifties, winner of the Grand Prix at Cannes for *Rififi* (the film he made in exile in France), husband of the Greek firebrand Melina Mercouri, whom he directed in the international hit *Never on Sunday* – not many people have a *curriculum vitae* as varied or interesting as Dassin. Yet, since the mid-Sixties, he has failed to produce anything as exciting as his Forties location-shot crime films like *The*

Naked City, or as innovative as *Rififi*, one of the first 'heist' films, or, indeed, as pleasurable as *Never on Sunday*.

Films include: 1942 Nazi Agent. '47 Brute Force. '48 The Naked City. '49 Thieves' Highway. '50 Night and the City (GB). '55 Du Rififi Chez les Hommes (FR) (GB: Rififi). '59 Pote Tin Kyriaki (GREECE) (GB/USA: Never on Sunday). '62 Phaedra (USA-GREECE). '64 Topkapi (USA-FR). '68 Up Tight. '78 A Dream of Passion (SWITZ-GREECE).

DAVENPORT, Harry

(1866–1949). Actor. Born: New York City, USA

Frail, white-haired and bright-eyed, Davenport specialized in playing judges, old soldiers or any other role that might conceivably require the services of an elderly character actor. The son of one of the leading tragedians of his day, Davenport began his stage career at the age of five. By the time he entered the film business, in 1912, he had firmly established himself as a stage actor. Initially he worked as a director for Vitagraph, but he soon returned to acting. He died with his boots on, preparing, at the age of 83, for a part in a comedy.

Films include: 1938 The Cowboy and the Lady. '39 The Hunchback of Notre Dame; Gone With the Wind. '40 Lucky Partners. '41 The Bride Came COD. '43 The Amazing Mrs Holliday; The Ox-Bow Incident (GB: Strange Incident). '45 The Enchanted Forest. '47 Sport of Kings. '49 That Forsyte Woman (GB: The Forsyte Saga).

DAVENPORT, Nigel

(b. 1928). Actor. Born: Shelford, Cambridge, England

A man of great physical stature, Nigel Davenport also adds emotional

weight to a film. A prime example of this is his superb portrayal of the bewildered, forceful Duke of Norfolk who is unable to understand why his friend Sir Thomas More (Paul Scofield) refuses to renounce his religion in *A Man for All Seasons*. It was only with middle age that Davenport became suitable for such roles – he had previously been restricted to minor parts in run-of-the-mill British films of the Sixties. Prior to this he gained his acting experience as an understudy in the West End and as an early member of the English Stage Company at the Royal Court Theatre. He had his first major stage success in Joan Littlewood's *A Taste of Honey*, initially at Stratford East, and then during its runs in London and on Broadway.

Films include: 1965 A High Wind in Jamaica; Life at the Top; The Sands of the Kalahari; Where the Spies Are. '66 A Man for All Seasons. '69 The Virgin Soldiers. '72 Mary, Queen of Scots. '78 Nighthawks. '79 Zulu Dawn (USA-HOLL). '81 Chariots of Fire.

DAVES, Delmer

(1904–1977). Director. Born: San Francisco, California, USA

During his writing and directing career Delmer Daves made just about every kind of film with nearly every major studio. He wrote both musicals and dramas, and the topics of films he directed were just as diverse. But he most liked to direct action dramas and he was particularly eager to obtain a high degree of precision in them – accordingly the westerns *Broken Arrow* and *3.10 to Yuma* are outstanding genre films. Daves began in Hollywood as a props boy, initially for James Cruze Productions and later with MGM. He then began acting and writing and, in 1934, joined Warner

Brothers as a scenarist. After some time as a freelancer he returned to Warners as a director and a writer, before eventually signing with 20th Century-Fox in 1949.

Films include: 1943 Destination Tokyo. '44 Hollywood Canteen. '45 Pride of the Marines (GB: Forever in Love). '47 Dark Passage. '50 Broken Arrow. '57 3.10 to Yuma. '58 Kings Go Forth; Cowboy; The Badlanders. '61 Susan Slade.

DAVIES, Marion

(1893–1961). Actress. Born: Marion Cecilia Douras; New York, USA

Orson Welles' thinly veiled and unflattering portrait of Marion Davies in Susan Alexander, the mistress of *Citizen Kane* whom the newspaper magnate tries to make into an operatic star despite her evident lack of talent, should not be taken too seriously. True, Davies was for many years openly the mistress of William Randolph Hearst, and Hearst spent many millions of dollars and used all his influence to promote her as a star. But Davies had real talent; she was a charming and gifted comedienne as King Vidor amply demonstrated in *The Patsy* and *Show People*. The problem was that the doting Hearst did not want to see his idol hit in the face with custard pies and instead pushed her into romantic costume roles (*When Knighthood Was in Flower*, *Quality Street*) which did not show her real gifts. Davies was a Ziegfeld chorus girl when Hearst spotted her. Their love affair was touching (in the Thirties

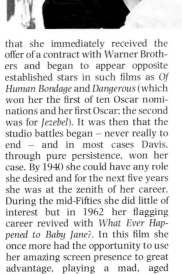

she sold her jewelry to help him out of a money crisis) and lasted till his death in 1951. Later Davies married quite happily, but was a long and permanent victim of alcoholism.

Films include: 1922 The Young Diana; When Knighthood Was in Flower. '23 Little Old New York. '26 Beverly of Graustark. '27 Quality Street. '28 The Patsy (GB: The Politic Flapper); Show People. '29 Marianne. '30 The Floradora Girl (GB: The Gay Nineties). '32 Blondie of the Follies. '36 Cain and Mabel.

DAVIS, Bette

(b. 1903). Actress. Born: Ruth Elizabeth Davis; Lowell, Massachusetts, USA

Bette Davis endured continual battles with the studios before she was able to prove to them that she was more than a clotheshorse and was entirely capable of using her flashing eyes, her vital and expressive face and her strong personality in intelligent and demanding roles. Those were the qualities she then brought to costume pictures like *Elizabeth and Essex*, melodramas like *Dark Victory, Now, Voyager* and *A Stolen Life*, and caustic dramas like *All About Eve* (as Margo Channing – her archetypal bitch). Davis gained her first acting experience in stock and then on Broadway before going to Hollywood in 1930 to work for Universal. But they quickly decided that her appeal was minimal and began to loan her out to other studios. Then in 1932 she appeared in *The Man Who Played God*. Her performance was so impressive

that she immediately received the offer of a contract with Warner Brothers and began to appear opposite established stars in such films as *Of Human Bondage* and *Dangerous* (which won her the first of ten Oscar nominations and her first Oscar; the second was for *Jezebel*). It was then that the studio battles began – never really to end – and in most cases Davis, through pure persistence, won her case. By 1940 she could have any role she desired and for the next five years she was at the zenith of her career. During the mid-Fifties she did little of interest but in 1962 her flagging career revived with *What Ever Happened to Baby Jane?*. In this film she once more had the opportunity to use her amazing screen presence to great advantage, playing a mad, aged former child star who cruelly torments her crippled sister (Joan Crawford). Since then she has been seen intermittently in some unfortunate horror movies and star-studded spectaculars. Despite this she still brings atmosphere and energy to any film she appears in – and she still has that mischievous twinkle in those large, wilful eyes.

Films include: 1931 Bad Sister. '33 20,000 Years in Sing Sing. '34 Of Human Bondage. '35 Dangerous. '36 The Petrified Forest. '38 Jezebel. '39 Dark Victory; The Private Lives of Elizabeth and Essex. '42 Now, Voyager. '44 Mr Skeffington. '46 A Stolen Life. '50 All About Eve. '62 What Ever Happened to Baby Jane?. '64 Hush . . . Hush, Sweet Charlotte. '78 Death on the Nile (GB).

DAVIS, Brad

Actor. Born: Tallahassee, Florida, USA

Davis is said to have had one of the most impressive film debuts ever – in the television movie *Sybil*, with Sally Field. He earned this chance after

working his way up in the early Seventies through local theatre in Atlanta, Georgia, then the American Academy of Dramatic Art in New York and finally off-Broadway productions. His most famous and demanding role has probably been as the young American caught smuggling drugs in *Midnight Express*. He seems to have struck up a good working relationship with the producer of this film, David Puttnam, with whom he worked again on *Chariots of Fire*. Davis has also acted in *Querelle*, which was finished shortly before the death of its director Rainer Werner Fassbinder.

Films include: 1978 Midnight Express. '80 A Small Circle of Friends. '81 Chariots of Fire. '82 Querelle (GER).

DAVIS, Judy

(b. 1955). Actress. Born: Perth, Western Australia

While still a student, Judy Davis appeared in Tim Burstall's *High Rolling*. Then, on graduation from the National Institute of Dramatic Art in Sydney, she landed the part of Sybilla in *My Brilliant Career*. Her excellent portrayal of the strong, independent literary woman who has to choose between her man and her writing in a time and a place where it was totally unacceptable for a woman even to contemplate having such a vocation, was internationally acclaimed. The British Academy's award for Best Actress was just one prize she won for her performance. Thus, this intelligent actress, who began by performing with jazz and pop bands, embarked on a promising, possibly brilliant, career in theatre, film and television.

Films: '77 High Rolling. '79 My Brilliant Career. '81 Winter of Our Dreams; Heatwave; Hoodwink. '82 Who Dares Wins (GB).

Top, left to right: Jane Darwell and Henry Fonda in Jesse James; *Howard Da Silva in* Border Incident; Nigel Davenport in Play Dirty (1969); *Marion Davies; Bette Davis in* The Little Foxes (1941). *Above, left to right: Harry Davenport in* The Man From Texas (1948); *Brad Davis; Judy Davis with Sam Neill in* My Brilliant Career; Sammy Davis Jr in Robin and the Seven Hoods, *a typical 'rat-pack' movie, spoofing caper thrillers*

DAVIS JR, Sammy

(b. 1926). Singer/actor. Born: New York City, USA

By the age of four Sammy Davis Jr was a fully-fledged professional dancer and a veteran of the stage – having begun his show business career at the age of 18 months. He remained with his family act until 1943. During the war he worked for Special Services entertaining the troops, and afterwards rejoined his father and uncle in the Will Mastin Trio. Eventually Davis, dapper and nimble, went it alone and soon began appearing on Broadway and releasing records. In 1954 he was involved in a serious car crash that resulted in the loss of his left eye. But he recovered, and by 1958 he was fulfilling his ambition to appear in movies. His films tend to be musicals and light comedies that also usually involve other members of the Las Vegas 'rat pack' – Frank Sinatra, Dean Martin and Peter Lawford. Above all Davis is not just an actor, singer, dancer or comedian – he is a skilful all-round entertainer.

Films include: 1958 Anna Lucasta. '59 Porgy and Bess. '60 Ocean's 11. '62 Sergeants 3. '64 Robin and the Seven Hoods. '66 A Man Called Adam. '68 Salt and Pepper (GB). '69 Sweet Charity. '70 One More Time (GB). '78 Sammy Stops the World.

DAWLEY, J. Searle

(d. 1950). Director. Born: Del Norte, Colorado, USA

Dawley has at least two major claims to fame. In 1907 he directed a young actor in his first film role *Rescued From an Eagle's Nest*: the debutant, destined to greater fame in other fields, was D.W. Griffith. And, in 1910, Dawley made the first screen *Frankenstein*. Dawley (date of birth unknown) started his career as a stage actor, but was writing and directing short skits for the Spooner Stock Company when the Edison Company recruited him as a writer. He quickly became assistant to Edwin S. Porter in his role as principal director and (though Porter generally assigned him the 'sentimental' subjects) made a lively *The Charge of the Light Brigade* (1912). Dawley's stage connections enabled him to lure theatre players like Maurice Costello and John Barrymore into films. It was then natural that he moved in 1912 along with Porter to Famous Players where he made many features, including some with Mary Pickford.

Films include: 1907 Rescued From an Eagle's Nest (co-dir). '10 Frankenstein. '11 The Battle of Bunker Hill. '13 Tess of the d'Urbervilles; In the Bishop's Carriage (co-dir); An American Citizen. '14 One of Millions. '15 A Daughter of the People. '22 Who Are My Parents? '23 Broadway Broke.

DAY, Doris

(b. 1924). Actress/singer. Born: Doris Kappelhoff; Cincinnati, Ohio, USA

Had it not been for a car accident during her childhood, Doris Day might have continued on the road to becoming a dancer instead of settling for being an actress in the movies. Nor would she ever have earned the title 'the professional virgin' as a result of the puritanical, morally upright (but blonde, freckled and attractive) ladies she usually portrayed. This reputation was assured particularly with the run of sophisticated but wholesome sex comedies she made with such symbols of all-American manhood as Rock Hudson and James Garner. In real life her lot was not such a happy one and, according to her autobiography, her first three husbands variously beat her, deserted her and cheated her. No wonder, then, that she now lives as a recluse in the Carmel Valley in California. The loss is a particularly sad one.

Films include: 1948 Romance on the High Seas (GB: It's Magic). '53 Young Man With Horn (GB: Young Man of Music). '53 Calamity Jane. '55 Love Me or Leave Me. '56 The Man Who Knew Too Much. '57 The Pajama Game. '59 Pillow Talk. '60 Please Don't Eat the Daisies. '61 Lover Come Back. '62 That Touch of Mink. '63 The Thrill of It All; Move Over, Darling. '64 Send Me No Flowers.

DAY, Laraine

(b. 1920). Actress. Born: Loraine Johnson; Roosevelt, Utah, USA

Having spent much of her childhood with the Utes Indians – for whom her father was an interpreter – Laraine Day must have found things very different when she moved with her family to Long Beach, California. Once there she studied drama while still at school and then became a member of the Long Beach Little Theatre Guild. She continued to act there for some time, as film contracts with both Samuel Goldwyn and Paramount proved very unproductive. She had a brief spell as leading lady opposite George O'Brien in some Westerns but again returned to the theatre. Finally MGM saw her on stage in *Lost Horizon* and signed her to appear as Nurse Mary Lamont in the Dr Kildare series. Misguidedly, she was eventually killed-off in the series so that she could expand her career. But apart from some mediocre films in the late Fifties and a few more in the early Seventies she gradually went out of circulation to concentrate her energies on the Mormon church.

Films include: 1939 Scandal Sheet; Sergeant Madden; The Secret of Dr Kildare. '40 Dr Kildare's Strange Case; Foreign Correspondent. '43 Mr Lucky. '44 The Story of Dr Wassell. '49 I Married a Communist (GB: The Woman on Pier 13). '54 The High and the Mighty. '60 The Third Voice.

DAY, Richard

(1896–1972). Art director. Born: Victoria, British Columbia, Canada

Seven Oscars for Art Direction – *The Dark Angel, Dodsworth, How Green Was My Valley, This Above All, My Gal Sal, A Streetcar Named Desire, On the Waterfront* – indicate Richard Day's skill and range as a supreme technician, but probably tell less than half the story. His greatest work was done for Erich von Stroheim who notoriously had Day build some of the most splendid and costly sets in Hollywood's history, the most famous of which was the magnificent recreation of Monte Carlo at Universal City for *Foolish Wives*. For Stroheim, too, Day constructed the squalid slums for *Greed*, and also the high altar for *The Wedding March*, so realistic that the cameraman Hal Mohr was actually married in front of it. Captain Richard Day arrived in Hollywood in 1918 and first worked as a set decorator for Stroheim and MGM, before joining Samuel Goldwyn in the Thirties and, in 1939, 20th Century-Fox where he was head of the art department until 1943. He then freelanced until his retirement in 1970. Of his later contributions the best-known were to *A Streetcar Named Desire* and *On the Waterfront* – creating shabby, squalid worlds for the young Marlon Brando to contend in – and the John Ford Western *Cheyenne Autumn*.

Films include: 1919 Blind Husbands (set dec). '20 The Devil's Passkey (set dec). '22 Foolish Wives (co-art dir). '25 Greed (co-art dir). '28 The Wedding March (co-art dir). '32 Rain. '33 Roman Scandals. '35 The Dark Angel. '36 Dodsworth. '37 Dead End. '41 How Green Was My Valley (co-art dir). '42 This Above All (co-art dir); My Gal Sal. '49 Force of Evil. '51 A Streetcar Named Desire. '54 On the Waterfront. '64 Cheyenne Autumn.

DEAN, Basil

(1888–1978). Producer/director. Born: Croydon, Surrey, England

Essentially an organizer and a man of the theatre, Basil Dean almost incidentally devoted some of his abundant energy to the cinema in the Thirties. He had been an actor in repertory for years before he became assistant to the actor-manager Sir Herbert Beerbohm Tree and eventually himself one of the best-known producer-directors in the British theatre. The coming of talkies sparked his serious interest in films, though some of his theatre productions had become silent films. He felt there was a great future for British talkies because 'we have the best voices in the world'. In 1929 he formed Associated Talking Pictures (ATP) and in 1931 he built Ealing Studios, which he ran until 1938, producing literary and theatrical adaptations as well as the Gracie Fields and George Formby comedies. He was in charge of forces' entertainments in both World Wars, founding ENSA in World War II. After the war he concentrated on the theatre, his first love and a considerable influence in his films.

Films include: 1929 The Return of Sherlock Holmes (dir; + co-sc. only) (USA). '32 The Water Gipsies (prod; + co-sc. only). '33 Loyalties; The Constant Nymph (dir; + co-sc. only); Three Men in a Boat (prod. only). '34 Sing As We Go!; Lorna Doone; Autumn Crocus (+ co-sc); Java Head (prod. only). '35 No Limit (prod. only). '36 Laburnum Grove (prod. only). '38 I See Ice (prod. only).

DEAN, James

(1931–1955). Actor. Born: Marion, Indiana, USA

Books have been written and films made about Dean, dissecting the man behind the legend, his sexual proclivities, his supposed death-wish and his role as symbol of disenchanted youth (invoking words like 'angst', 'lonesome', 'despair', 'beat' and, most frequently, 'rebel'). Clear away the mystique and you are left with an actor – a brilliant, natural, Method actor who filled the screen with tortured emotion – who had his moments of truculence and rebellion but who was probably a good deal more in control than either Cal Trask or Jim Stark. Those were the two confused adolescents Dean played in, respectively, *East of Eden* and *Rebel Without a Cause*, the roles that, along with the embittered oil tycoon Jett Rink in *Giant*, made him a figurehead for malcontent Fifties teenagers, especially after he died at 24 in a car crash. It must never be forgotten that Dean was *acting* and that he was a supreme manipulator of the mantle that was thrust upon him. He had a disrupted childhood – the classic grounding for an unhappy adolescence – but won a recitation contest and eventually got to UCLA. Dropping out of university, Dean got extra parts in movies and did a Pepsi-Cola commercial. He went to

New York and mostly played truant from the Actors' Studio before his part in a play, *The Jaguar*, earned him television work. He was successful enough to be able to choose his film parts and picked *East of Eden* for his first star role. He developed a close relationship with that other rebel, director Nicholas Ray, while filming *Rebel Without a Cause* and it is likely that they would have again worked together and that Dean would later have directed his own movies.

Films: 1951 Fixed Bayonets; Sailor Beware. '52 Has Anybody Seen My Gal? '53 Trouble Along the Way. '55 East of Eden; Rebel Without a Cause. '56 Giant.

DEARDEN, Basil

(1911–1971). Director/producer. Born: Westcliff-on-Sea, Essex, England

After acting in repertory and on tour in the USA, Dearden stage-managed for Basil Dean for five years and went to work at Ealing in 1937. He helped on several George Formby vehicles, co-directed with Will Hay the last of his comedies and in 1943 made *The Bells Go Down*, about the fire service in wartime. In the Fifties, working mostly in collaboration with Michael Relph, he turned his mind to social-problem films – tackling such issues as race-relations (*Sapphire*) and homo-

sexuality (*Victim*) – but his approach, though liberal, was timid and sober. Dearden was altogether happier with a crime drama like *The Blue Lamp* or a gentle comedy like *The Smallest Show on Earth*, while *Khartoum* is a worthy adventure film. He was killed in a car crash.

Films include: 1941 The Black Sheep of Whitehall (co-dir). '42 The Goose Steps Out (co-dir). '43 The Bells Go Down. '45 Dead of Night (co-dir). '46 The Captive Heart. '48 Saraband for Dead Lovers (co-dir). '50 The Blue Lamp. '57 The Smallest Show on Earth. '58 Violent Playground. '59 Sapphire. '60 League of Gentlemen. '61 Victim. '66 Khartoum. '70 The Man Who Haunted Himself (co-dir).

DE BANZIE, Brenda

(1915–1981). Actress. Born: Manchester, Lancashire, England

After a variety of theatrical experience (including *Venus Observed* with Laurence Olivier in the West End) and some minor film parts, Brenda de Banzie was cast in the lead role of David Lean's *Hobson's Choice* as Maggie Hobson, a strong-minded 30-year-old spinster set on marriage to her father's employee. Her theatrical breakthrough came later at the Royal Court Theatre in 1957, as the long-suffering wife of Archie Rice (Olivier again) in John Osborne's *The Entertainer*, a performance she repeated in New York and in the film version.

Films include: 1952 I Believe in You. '54 Hobson's Choice. '55 A Kid for Two Farthings; Doctor at Sea. '56 The Man Who Knew Too Much (USA). '59 The 39 Steps; Too Many Crooks. '60 The Entertainer. '63 The Pink Panther (USA). '67 Pretty Polly (USA: A Matter of Innocence).

DE BROCA, Philippe

(b. 1933). Director. Born: Paris, France

His first three films, *Les Jeux de l'Amour*, *Le Farceur* and *L'Amant de Cinq Jours* – tender, naughty and charming comedies starring Jean-Pierre Cassel – established de Broca as a popular director at the onset of the French *nouvelle vague*. The spy-spoof *L'Homme de Rio* and the World War I farce *Le Roi de Coeur* were just as

hilarious, but de Broca has not lasted the course, his films becoming increasingly laboured. After studying photographic techniques, he worked as a cameraman on a Sahara expedition and stayed on to make documentaries. He served with the Army Film Service in Algeria and returned to France to assist such directors as Henri Decoin, Georges Lacombe, François Truffaut and Claude Chabrol, whose production company gave de Broca his first opportunities to direct.

Films include: 1960 Les Jeux de l'Amour (GB: Playing at Love); Le Farceur (GB: The Joker). '61 L'Amant de Cinq Jours (USA: Five Day Lover; GB: Infidelity). '62 Cartouche (FR-IT) (GB: Swords of Blood). '64 Un Monsieur de Compagnie (FR-IT) (USA/GB: Male Companion); L'Homme de Rio (FR-IT) (GB: That Man From Rio). '66 Le Roi de Coeur (FR-IT) (USA/GB: King of Hearts). '69 Le Diable par la Queue (FR-IT) (USA: The Devil by the Tail). '70 Les Caprices de Marie (FR-IT) (USA: Give Her the Moon). '71 La Poudre d'Escampette. '72 Chère Louise (FR-IT) (USA: Louise). '75 L'Incorrigible (FR). '77 Tendre Poulet (USA: Dear Detective; GB: Dear Inspector).

DE CARLO, Yvonne

(b. 1922). Actress. Born: Peggy Yvonne Middleton; Vancouver, British Columbia, Canada

Despite poverty, her mother scraped enough money together to send her to the Vancouver School of Dance when she was six. She then danced her way through playhouses and nightclubs, became 'Miss Venice Beach' of 1941 and signed for Paramount. There she made shorts, followed by a feature debut in *Harvard Here I Come* while on loan to Columbia. Her best chances were *The Deerslayer* and *Salome, Where She Danced* – an ideal showcase for her dark, exotic beauty – but neither did her credit. Raoul Walsh cast her several times as the romantic interest (often with a temper or tart sense of humour) for action heroes in the Fifties and she was Sephora in *The Ten Commandments*. In the Sixties de Carlo was memorable as a Western cook falling downstairs with John Wayne in *McLintock!* and as Lily Munster in the television horror-spoof series, *The Munsters*. She still makes the odd screen appearance and in 1971 turned up in Russ Meyer's *The Seven Minutes*.

Films include: 1941 Harvard Here I Come (GB: Here I Come). '43 Deerslayer. '45 Salome, Where She Danced. '47 Song of Scheherazade; Brute Force. '49 Criss Cross. '53 Sea Devils (GB); The Captain's Paradise (GB); Sombrero. '56 The Ten Commandments. '57 Band of Angels. '63 McLintock! '75 Won, Ton Ton, the Dog That Saved Hollywood. '80 Sam Marlowe, Private Eye.

DEE, Frances

(b. 1907). Actress. Born: Jean Dee, Pasadena, Los Angeles, USA

A graduate of the University of Chicago, Dee gained her first acting experience at the Pasadena Playhouse and made her film debut as an extra at Fox. She then moved to Paramount and Maurice Chevalier chose her as his leading lady for *Playboy of Paris*. Dark-haired and strikingly pretty, she remained a star through the Thirties – mostly in ingénue roles, like Meg in *Little Women*, for example – but collapsed on the set of *My Son, My Son* in 1940 and thereafter restricted her film appearances. In 1945 she returned to the stage in *Patrick the Great*. Frances Dee and Joel McCrea, her husband (and occasional co-star) since 1933, are one of Hollywood's best-loved couples.

Films include: 1930 Playboy in Paris. '31 An American Tragedy. '33 One Man's Journey; Little Women. '34 Of Human Bondage. '35 Becky Sharp. '36 Come and Get It. '37 Souls at Sea; Wells Fargo. '43 I Walked With a Zombie. '48 Four Faces West (GB: They Passed This Way). '53 Mr Scoutmaster.

Far left: James Dean in his most famous role as a high-school misfit, spoiled but not understood by his parents, in Rebel Without a Cause. *Left: Brenda de Banzie as Madame Ballu, a Parisian lady involved in a hunt for a gang of forgers in* House of Secrets *(1956). Below, left to right: Doris Day as a housewife who discovers* The Thrill of It All *(1963) when she becomes a star of television soap commercials; Laraine Day as the girlfriend of a reformed gambler in* Mr Lucky *(1943); Yvonne de Carlo inspires the Russian composer Rimsky-Korsakov in* Song of Scheherazade; *Frances Dee taken by surprise in* The Gay Deception *(1935)*

DEE, Sandra

(b. 1942). Actress. Born: Alexandra Zuck; Bayonne, New Jersey, USA

Sandra Dee was a younger version of Doris Day – a clean-scrubbed, pony-tailed blonde, every boy's dream date for the high-school prom, every girl's best friend. It comes as no surprise to learn that she was first spotted modelling in a girl-scout charity show. At 12 she turned professional and quickly became a top model and cover girl. Universal producer Ross Hunter signed her and at 14 she starred in *Until They Sail*. She became a teen idol after playing a good girl lusted after by beach bums in *Gidget*, was a daughter with mother-trouble in *Imitation of Life* and starred opposite her male counterpart Troy Donahue in *A Summer Place*. She remained very popular in the early Sixties in the 'Tammy' films but that was about it – high-school ended and, after working out her Universal contract in routine thrillers and comedies, Sandra Dee went freelance in 1967. She has since worked mostly in television and on stage. From 1960 to 1967 she was married to actor-singer Bobby Darin.

Films include: 1957 Until They Sail. '58 The Reluctant Debutante; The Restless Years (GB: The Wonderful Years). '59 Imitation of Life; Gidget; A Summer Place. '61 Romanoff and Juliet; Come September; Tammy, Tell Me True. '63 Tammy and the Doctor; Take Her She's Mine. '65 That Funny Feeling. '66 A Man Could Get Killed. '70 The Dunwich Horror.

DEED, André

(1884–1938). Actor. Born: André Chapuis; Le Havre, France

Deed was the first true comic star of the movies. A music-hall singer and acrobat, he had occasionally worked in films with Georges Méliès; but his film career proper began when Charles Pathé saw him on stage and engaged him for a chase film, *La Course à la Perruque* (1905). Within months he was famous throughout Europe for his magnificently destructive idiocy, with each nation giving him its own name: Boireau in France, Beoncelli in Italy, Sanchez in Spain and so on. When Deed transferred his talents to the Itala Company of Turin, he acquired a whole new set of names: Cretinetti (Italy), Gribouille (France), Toribio (Spain), Glupishkin (Russia), Foolshead (England). His last years were spent as a menial at the Pathé studios where he had once reigned.

Films include: 1905 La Course à la Perruque. '07 Boireau Lutteur. '08 De l'Homme Singe; L'Apprenti-Architecte; Boireau Fait la Noce. '09 Cretinetti e il Matrimonio. '11 Cretinetti Mannequin. '13 Boireau Domestique. '19 Il Documento Umano (+dir). '24 Phi-Phi. '28 Graine au Vent.

DE FILIPPO, Eduardo

(1900–1984). Actor/playwright/director. Born: Eduardo Passarelli; Naples, Italy

An outstanding all-rounder, De Filippo was the son of the great actor-playwright Eduardo Scarpetta and acted on stage as a child. Soon, with his brother Peppino and sister Titina, he was putting on variety shows for his own company, writing and acting in his own plays, and enjoying big success in the comic theatre. The De Filippos continued as popular film comedians in the Thirties, and in 1939 Eduardo – a handsome charmer on screen – made his directorial debut with *In Campagna è Caduta una Stella*. De Filippo's films are mostly Neapolitan comedies, strongly influenced by the traditions of *commedia dell'arte* and also by neo-realism. The three most famous – *Napoli Milionaria, Filumena Marturano* and *Questi Fantasmi* – were all adapted from his own plays and respectively concern the comic doings of a poor family in Naples dehumanized by the black market, a rich Neapolitan's increasingly desperate attempts to get rid of his mistress of 25 years' standing, and a husband who believes his wife's lover is a ghost.

Films include: 1932 Tre Uomini in Frak (actor only). '39 In Campagna è Caduta una Stella (dir;+sc;+act). '43 Ti Conosco, Mascherina! (dir;+sc). '48 Campane a Martello (actor only). '50 Napoli Milionaria (dir;+sc;+act;+play basis). '51 Filumena Marturano (dir; +sc; +act +play basis); Le Ragazze di Piazza di Spagna (act) (dir;+co-sc). '52 I Sette Peccati Capitali (dir. *eps* only) (FR-IT) (USA/GB: Seven Deadly Sins); Marito e Moglie (dir;+sc;+act); Ragazze da Marito (dir;+sc;+act). '53 Napoletani a Milano (dir;+sc;+act); Traviata '53 (actor only) (IT-FR). '54 Questi Fantasmi (dir; +co-sc;+play basis); L'Oro di Napoli (actor only) (GB: Gold of Naples); Tempi Nostri (actor only) (IT-FR) (GB: A Slice of Life). '58 Fortunella. '59 Il Sogno di una Notte di Mezza Sbornia (dir;+act). '64 Ieri, Oggi, Domani (co-sc. only) (IT-FR) (USA/GB: Yesterday, Today and Tomorrow).

DE FOREST, Lee

(1873–1961). Inventor. Born: Council Bluffs, Iowa, USA

The sound of silence would probably still be greeting cinema audiences were it not for the pioneering work in electronics done by Lee de Forest. By 1906 he had perfected the 'audion' amplifying valve and pointed the way towards the future sophistication of radio broadcasting, radar and electronics techniques. He was the first to broadcast the voice of the great singer Caruso, and in 1916 he was responsible for relaying the first radio news bulletin. Three years later he developed the Phonofilm system whereby sound waves were actually photographed, and thus paved the path that led to talking pictures.

DE FUNÈS, Louis

(1914–1983). Actor. Born: Louis de Funès de Gallarza; Courbevoie, France

Before World War II, Louis de Funès made his living decorating and designing car bodies. During the war he took an acting course at the René Simon School, but until the mid-Forties worked as a cocktail pianist and odd-job man before making his stage debut (at the late age of 40), which then led him into cabaret, more theatre work, radio and television. From 1945 he appeared in films, taking supporting roles as the archetypal eccentric Frenchman, described by one critic as being a middle-aged Groucho Marx. A heart attack in 1975 seriously curtailed his activities, but he still took the occasional less physically demanding character roles.

Films include: 1945 Les Hommes ne Pensent qu'á Ça; Papa, Maman, la Bonne et Moi (GB: Papa, Mama, the Maid and I). '56 La Traversée de Paris (FR-IT) (GB: A Pig Across Paris). '58 Ni Vu ni Connu (GB: Vive Monsieur Blaireau). '61 La Belle Américaine. '63 Pouic-Pouic. '64 Fantômas; Le Gendarme de Saint Tropez (FR-IT) (GB: The Gendarme of Saint Tropez). '66 La Grand Vadrouille (FR-GB) (GB: Don't Look Now . . . We're Being Shot At!). '67 Oscar

DE GRUNWALD, Anatole

(1910–1967). Producer/writer. Born: St. Petersburg, Russia

De Grunwald received the best of a European education, attending Cambridge and the Sorbonne. Just before the outbreak of World War II, he began working with playwright Terence Rattigan and director Ian Dalrymple on a screen adaptation of the play *French Without Tears*. He went on to adapt many theatrical works for the screen. By 1943 he was an established producer/writer, and he was able to produce what was to become his favourite movie, *The Way to the Stars*, a picture combining patriotism, poetry and humour. Anatole de Grunwald has always been associated with the best British films of the war years; indeed he was 'more British than the British' (as was also the case with other foreign-born British producers Alexander Korda and Filippo Del Giudice). In 1959 he became a producer for MGM, and oversaw such films as *The VIPs* and *The Yellow Rolls Royce*.

Above: Sandra Dee and Bobby Darin (real-life husband and wife) have That Funny Feeling. Above right: Louis de Funès in La Folie des Grandeurs (1972). Bottom, left to right: Gloria de Haven in The Penalty (1941); Olivia de Havilland as the screen's most famous Maid Marian in The Adventures of Robin Hood; Albert Dekker in the courtroom drama Illegal (1955)

Films include: 1939 French Without Tears. '40 Quiet Wedding. '41 Pimpernel Smith (USA: Mister V). '42 The First of the Few (USA: Spitfire). '43 The Demi-Paradise (USA: Adventure For Two). '45 The Way to the Stars (USA: Johnny in the Clouds). '48 The Winslow Boy. '49 Queen of Spades. '58 The Doctor's Dilemma. '63 The VIPs (USA: International Hotel). '64 The Yellow Rolls Royce.

DE HAVEN, Gloria

(b. 1924). Actress/singer. Born: Los Angeles, California, USA

Carter and Flora de Haven were vaudeville stars who also appeared in a few films during the early Twenties. When their daughter was born they decided to give her the best education they could afford and Gloria was packed off to private schools before being enrolled at stage school. Her first (uncredited) part was in Charles Chaplin's *Modern Times*, a film on which her father assisted, but her first named role came in George Cukor's *Susan and God*. She then concentrated on singing and began to make quite a name for herself as a solo artist with big bands such as Bob Crosby's. This success led to a contract at MGM and a part in their musical *Best Foot Forward*. She then appeared regularly in extravaganzas such as *Summer Holiday*, *Three Little Words* and *Summer Stock* before the decline in the popularity of musicals led to a parallel decline in de Haven's career. She now makes occasional appearances on television and Broadway.

Films include: 1936 Modern Times (uncredited). '40 Susan and God. '43 Best Foot Forward. '44 Two Girls and a Sailor; Step Lively. '47 Summer Holiday. '50 Three Little Words; Summer Stock (GB: If You Feel Like Singing). '54 So This Is Paris. '55 The Girl Rush.

DE HAVILLAND, Olivia

(b. 1916). Actress. Born: Tokyo, Japan

After their parents' divorce Olivia de Havilland and her younger sister Joan Fontaine were brought up by their mother in California. While at college Olivia was chosen as second understudy for Hermia in Max Reinhardt's Hollywood Bowl production of A Midsummer Night's Dream and was subsequently cast in the role in his film version. A seven-year contract with Warners followed, but she was not entirely happy there because of the pretty, furrow-browed and insipid costume-drama heroines she was forced to play – mostly opposite Errol Flynn. Her most successful pictures were those she made while on loan to other companies: MGM's Gone With the Wind (her Melanie as gracious as Scarlett is selfish), Paramount's Hold Back the Dawn and RKO's Government Girl. When de Havilland's contract with Warners expired, the studio tried to spin it out by six months; there followed a two-year legal battle which de Havilland won, and afterwards she freelanced. Her best work was to follow – she gave a remarkable performance as a mental patient in The Snake Pit, and won the 1946 and 1949 Best Actress Oscars for her performances in To Each His Own and The Heiress. In the mid-Fifties she moved to Paris to live with her second husband, Pierre Paul Galante, then editor of Paris Match, and only worked sporadically during the Sixties and Seventies, taking the occasional role in television and all-star efforts such as Airport '77. In 1982 she was chosen to play the Queen Mother in a TV film.

Films include: 1935 A Midsummer Night's Dream; Captain Blood. '36 The Charge of the Light Brigade. '38 The Adventures of Robin Hood. '39 Gone With the Wind; Raffles. '41 Hold Back the Dawn; The Strawberry Blonde. '42 They Died With Their Boots On. '43 Government Girl. '46 To Each His Own. '48 The Snake Pit. '49 The Heiress. '56 The Ambassador's Daughter. '58 The Proud Rebel. '59 Libel. '62 The Light in the Piazza (GB). '64 Hush . . . Hush, Sweet Charlotte. '77 Airport '77.

DEKKER, Albert

(1905–1968). Actor. Born: New York City, USA

While studying medicine and psychology at college, Dekker took an interest in amateur dramatics and on graduation was persuaded to go into the theatre. He went to Cincinnati and got work as fourth assistant stage manager but soon found himself in front of the lights and eventually made it to Broadway in the Theater Guild's production of Marco's Millions. He gave many memorable stage performances and his appearance – tall, barrel-chested and moustached – made him the perfect villain. He was eventually persuaded to go to Hollywood, where he served a term as Hollywood's representative in the Californian legislature. He is probably best remembered for his acting in Suddenly, Last Summer and East of Eden, and in the Broadway productions of Death of a Salesman and A Man for All Seasons. Dekker committed suicide in 1968, but not before completing his part in The Wild Bunch.

Films include: 1939 The Man in the Iron Mask. '40 Seven Sinners. '45 Salome, Where She Danced. '46 The Killers; Two Years Before the Mast. '49 Bride of Vengeance. '55 Kiss Me Deadly; East of Eden. '59 Suddenly, Last Summer. '69 The Wild Bunch.

DELANNOY, Jean

(b. 1908). Director/editor/screen writer. Born: Noisy-le-Sec, France

The brother of actress Henriette Delannoy, Jean Delannoy studied literature at Lille University. He himself appeared in a handful of films as an actor but decided that he preferred editing. After working for a time at Paramount Studios in Joinville, he became chief editor there in the mid-Thirties. By the end of the decade he had progressed to direction and his La Symphonie Pastorale and L'Eternel Retour were well-received, despite a tendency towards the sentimental. During the Occupation the Germans demanded that Erich von Stroheim's scenes be cut from Macao, l'Enfer du Jeu; Delannoy obliged but kept the footage and released the whole film after the war. As well as directing and supervising the editing, he also put his former literary training to good use, collaborating on most of his shooting scripts. With the coming of the nouvelle vague, Delannoy found himself much criticized for his rigid adherence to conventional techniques, but he rode out the storm. In 1975 he became president of IDHEC, the Paris film school.

Films include: 1934 Paris-Deauville. '39 Macao, l'Enfer du Jeu (USA: Mask of Korea; GB: Gambling Hell). '42 L'Assassin a Peur la Nuit. '43 L'Eternel Retour (GB: Love Eternal). '46 La Symphonie Pastorale. '47 Les Jeux Sont Faits (GB: The Die Is Cast). '50 Dieu a Besoin des Hommes (USA/GB: Isle of Sinners). '56 Notre Dame de Paris (FR-IT) (GB: The Hunchback of Notre Dame). '58 Maigret Tend un Piège (FR-IT) (GB: Maigret Sets a Trap).

DE LAURENTIIS, Dino

(b. 1919). Producer. Born: Torre Annunziata, Italy

By the age of 14 Dino De Laurentiis was making his living as a salesman in the family pasta business. However, two years later he left home to enrol at the Centro Sperimentale di Cinematografia in Rome with the idea of becoming an actor. Finding that this was not quite what he had in mind, he decided to become a producer. By the time he was 21 he had formed his own company in Turin but World War II put an end to his involvement there and he moved to Paris. After the war De Laurentiis became heavily involved in Italy's underground cinema and was a leader in the neo-realist movement, making several successful films with Silvana Mangano, whom he married in 1949. The following year De Laurentiis and Carlo Ponti became partners, producing the films of Fellini and Rossellini. Spreading his wings, De Laurentiis produced War and Peace, beginning his contradictory policy of making commercial films with one hand and European 'art' films with the other. A charge of receiving Mafia money was repudiated, but there is no doubt that sharp finance is one of De Laurentiis' fortes. He now works in America, mostly on big-budget spectaculars.

Films include: 1949 Riso Amaro (IT) (GB: Bitter Rice). '54 La Strada. '56 War and Peace (IT-USA). '57 Le Notti di Cabiria (GB: Nights of Cabiria). '66 La Bibbia (USA/GB: The Bible – In the Beginning). '68 Barbarella (FR-IT). '72 Joe Valachi, i Segreti di Cosa Nostra (IT-FR) (USA/GB: The Valachi Papers). '74 Death Wish. '76 King Kong (USA). '80 Flash Gordon (GB).

DELERUE, Georges

(b. 1925). Composer. Born: Roubaix, France

Delerue studied music under Darius Milhaud at the Paris Conservatoire while still a youth. Having won various prizes he became an orchestra leader on French television and began scoring for plays and films. During the Fifties his reputation grew and it seemed as though most French films featured Delerue's music. He has worked for many prominent directors and his credits include music for François Truffaut's *La Peau Douce* and *Jules et Jim*, Jean-Luc Godard's *Le Mépris*, Louis Malle's *Viva Maria!* and Bernardo Bertolucci's *The Conformist*. He has also worked in America and in Britain on *Women in Love* and *A Man for All Seasons*.

Films include: 1960 Les Jeux de l'Amour (GB: Playing At Love); Tirez sur le Pianiste (GB: Shoot the Pianist). '62 Jules et Jim (GB: Jules and Jim). '63 L'Immortelle (FR-IT-TURKEY); L'Aîné des Ferchaux (FR-IT); Le Mépris (USA/GB: Contempt). '64 The Pumpkin Eater (GB); La Peau Douce (USA/GB: Silken Skin). '65 Viva Maria! (FR-IT). '66 A Man for All Seasons (GB). '67 Our Mother's House (GB). '68 Interlude (GB). '69 Women in Love (GB); Anne of the Thousand Days (GB). '70 Il Conformista (IT-FR-GER) (USA/GB: The Conformist).

DEL GIUDICE, Filippo

(1892–1963). Production executive. Born: Trani, Italy

After studying law in Rome, Filippo Del Giudice became a refugee from Fascist Italy and arrived in London. For a while he taught Italian, but eventually set up a law practice and through this became involved in films. In 1937 he established the Two Cities film company in association with Rank. Ten years later he had a disagreement with Rank over the high cost of production versus low returns and broke away to form Pilgrim Films. In 1958 the British Home Office refused to renew Del Giudice's visa and he went to try his luck in America. Sadly he died penniless, but during his time in Britain he enjoyed a reputation for being a genius at gathering together money and people for attractive prospects.

Films include: 1942 In Which We Serve. '44 This Happy Breed; Henry V; The Way Ahead; Tawny Pipit. '45 Blithe Spirit; The Way to the Stars (USA: Johnny in the Clouds). '46 School for Secrets.

DELLUC, Louis

(1890–1924). Critic/director. Born: Cadouin, France

The slogan of Delluc's magazine *Cinéma* – 'The French cinema must be *cinema*: the French cinema must be *French*' – was a watchword that laid the foundations of the classic cinema of René Clair and Jean Renoir. Delluc arrived in Paris from his native Dordogne at 15 and instantly made a place for himself as a poet and journalist in the artistic world of the capital. He shared the prevalent snobbery towards the cinema until 1914, when Cecil B. DeMille's *The Squaw Man*

(1913) effected his conversion. From that time he became a prolific writer on films, establishing new standards of critical appreciation. His own films – generally starring his wife, Eve Francis – all vindicated Delluc's belief that a film should be an original, autonomous work, not an adaptation from another medium. Delluc was co-founder of the world's first film society. He died of tuberculosis at 34. Appropriately the highest award in French cinema is named the Prix Delluc.

Films include: 1919 La Fête Espagnole (sc. only). '20 Fumée Noire (co-dir); Le Silence. '21 Fièvre; Prométhée Banquier (actor only); Le Chemin d'Ernoa/L'Américain (short); Le Tonnerre. '22 La Femme de Nulle Part. '23 L'Inondation.

DELON, Alain

(b. 1935). Actor. Born: Sceaux, France

The son of a movie house manager, Delon knocked around in many different jobs, including a stint as a parachutist in Indo-china, before he made his film debut at the age of 22. His dark, Italian good looks meant that he was much in demand for gangster and action pictures. He worked with a number of leading Italian and French directors – including Luchino Visconti and René Clément – and tried his luck in American films for a brief period during the Sixties. In 1968 he was seriously involved in a national scandal in France when the corpse of his bodyguard was found under suspicious circumstances. But the subsequent notoriety appears to have benefited his career rather than to have hurt it. He was married for a time to the actress Nathalie Delon and during the Seventies extended his activities into film production and, most recently, direction.

Films include: 1960 Plein Soleil (FR-IT) (GB: Blazing Sun; reissued as Purple Noon); Rocco e i Suoi Fratelli (IT-FR) (USA/GB: Rocco and His Brothers). '62 L'Eclisse (IT-FR) (USA/GB: The Eclipse). '63 Il Gattopardo (IT-FR) (USA/GB: The Leopard). '64 The Yellow Rolls Royce (GB). '66 Paris Brûle-t-il? (USA/GB: Is Paris Burning?). '67 Le Samourai (FR-IT) (USA: The Godson; GB: The Samurai). '68 Girl on a Motorcycle (GB-FR). '70 Borsalino (FR-IT). '72 The Assassination of Trotsky (GB-FR-IT). '81 Pour la Peau d'un Flic (+dir).

DEL RIO, Dolores

(1905–1983). Actress. Born: Lolita Dolores Martinez Asunsolo Lopez Negrette; Durango, Mexico

Convent-educated, the daughter of a banker and second cousin of Ramon Navarro, she was married to a writer by the age of 16. Her 1925 debut in *Joanna* came about when she was discovered by director Edwin Carewe at a tea party in Mexico City. Her striking good looks led to parts in numerous silent films for Carewe and Raoul Walsh, but the advent of sound revealed her accent and restricted the range of her roles. After the death of her first husband she married leading art director Cedric Gibbons in 1930.

During later years she appeared in few Hollywood films, having returned to Mexico in 1943. But she was in two by John Ford – *The Fugitive*, and *Cheyenne Autumn*, in which she was still beautiful as an Indian squaw threatened with homelessness.

Films include: 1926 What Price Glory? '27 Loves of Carmen. '28 Ramona; The Trail of '98. '29 Evangeline. '33 Flying Down to Rio. '42 Journey Into Fear. '44 Maria Candelaria (MEX). '47 The Fugitive. '64 Cheyenne Autumn. '67 C'Era una Volta (IT) (USA: More Than a Miracle; GB: Cinderella – Italian Style); Rio Blanco (MEX). '78 The Children of Sanchez (USA-MEX).

DEL RUTH, Roy

(1895–1961). Director. Born: Philadelphia, Pennsylvania, USA

After early experience as a journalist, he entered films in 1915 as a gagman for Mack Sennett and soon graduated to directing two-reelers. He was signed up by Warner Brothers in 1925 and during the following years demonstrated his abilities as a workmanlike, if undistinguished craftsman. As a typical Hollywood all-

Top left: Dom DeLuise handles Hot Stuff as leader of the Miami Burglary Task Force and rounds up all the local thieves. Top right: Alain Delon. Above: Dolores Del Rio as a South Sea island beauty in Bird of Paradise (1932). Above right: William Demarest. Right: Cecil B. DeMille

rounder he shifted easily from gangsters to love stories and musicals. When he moved from Warner Brothers to 20th Century-Fox and then on to MGM in the Forties, his budgets got larger, but the pictures remained routine. And he ended up back at Warners in the early Fifties directing Doris Day musicals and a 3-D version of *Phantom of the Rue Morgue* followed by some work in television.

Films include: 1929 Gold Diggers of Broadway; The Desert Song. '31 The Maltese Falcon. '33 Lady Killer. '34 Kid Millions. '36 Born to Dance. '43 Du Barry Was a Lady. '44 Broadway Rhythm. '47 It Happened on Fifth Avenue. '54 Phantom of the Rue Morgue.

DeLUISE, Dom

(b. 1933). Actor. Born: New York City, USA

Dom DeLuise studied drama at New York's High School for the Performing Arts and then biology at Tufts University. After two seasons at the Cleveland Playhouse he travelled to New York to appear in off-Broadway productions, but he really came to notice when he created his Dominick the Great character on Garry Moore's television show. His chance to do a serious role came when the director Sidney Lumet cast him in *Fail Safe*. As a comic he has appeared in four films for Mel Brooks, establishing himself as one of the more inventive of 'new generation' comics. Fat, heavy-faced and balding, he is much in demand as a modern slapstick comedian 'Buddy Bizarre', his character's name in *Blazing Saddles*, perhaps sums up his appeal.

Films include: 1957 The Ordeal of Thomas Moon. **'64** Diary of a Bachelor. **'66** The Glass Bottom Boat. **'70** The Twelve Chairs. **'71** Who Is Harry Kellerman and Why Is He Saying Those Terrible Things About Me? **'74** Blazing Saddles. **'76** Silent Movie. **'79** Hot Stuff (+ dir). **'80** The Last Married Couple in America. **'81** History of the World – Part One.

DELVAUX, André

(b. 1926). Director. Born: Héverlé, Belgium

After completing his studies at the Free University of Brussels, he worked as a teacher for a number of years. Attracted to the cinema, he became interested in film education and aesthetics and made a number of programmes about film-makers for Belgian television before completing his first feature, *The Man Who Had His Hair Cut Short*, in 1966. This picture immediately demonstrated his own highly personal and economical style and talent for observing the world with fresh eyes, qualities he developed in later films as writer-director. His central preoccupation with the nature of illusion vs reality, strongly influenced by surrealism, follows in the tradition of such European masters as Buñuel and Bresson.

Films include: 1966 De Man Die Zijn Haar Kort Liet Knippen/L'Homme au Crâne Rasé (BELG) (GB: The Man Who Had His Hair Cut Short). **'68** Un Soir, un Train (FR-BELG). **'71** Rendez-vous à Bray (FR-BELG-GER) (GB: Rendezvous at Bray). **'73** Belle (FR-BELG). **'79** Een Vrouw Tussen Hond en Wolf/Une Femme Entre Chien et Loup (BELG-FR) (GB: Woman in a Twilight Garden). **'80** To Woody Allen, From Europe With Love (BELG).

DEMAREST, William

(1892–1985). Actor. Born: St Paul, Minnesota, USA

Heavy-featured and of stocky build, generally cast as a dry cop, a pushy businessman, or the opinionated friend of the hero, William Demarest was one of that army of invaluable Hollywood character players whose faces, if not their names, were as familiar as telephone kiosks. Demarest was in vaudeville, in an act with his two brothers, from 1905, and made his film debut, in *Fingerprints*, in 1927 – shortly afterwards appearing alongside Al Jolson in *The Jazz Singer*. After 1934 and William Dieterle's *Fog Over 'Frisco* Demarest was constantly busy, and continued to work until he was well over eighty (becoming well known on television as Bub in *My Three Sons*). The most memorable phase of his career, however, was the series of films by Preston Sturges, who was clearly amused by Demarest's personality and created a gallery of rich eccentric roles for him in *The Great McGinty*, *The Lady Eve*, *Sullivan's Travels*, *Hail the Conquering Hero* and *The Miracle of Morgan's Creek*. In 1946 Demarest revisited his past by appearing in *The Jolson Story*.

Films include: 1927 Fingerprints; The Jazz Singer. **'34** Fog Over 'Frisco. **'35** Diamond Jim. **'37** Easy Living. **'39** Mr Smith Goes to Washington. **'40** The Great McGinty (GB: Down Went McGinty). **'41** The Lady Eve; Sullivan's Travels. **'43** The Miracle of Morgan's Creek. **'44** Hail the Conquering Hero. **'46** The Jolson Story. **'49** Sorrowful Jones. **'63** It's a Mad, Mad, Mad, Mad World. **'75** Won Ton Ton, the Dog That Saved Hollywood.

DeMILLE, Cecil B.

(1881–1959). Director. Born: Cecil Blount De Mille; Ashfield, Massachusetts, USA

With his megaphone, his boots and his air of a general commanding a huge army, DeMille was the first 'star' director. He was from a family of playwrights – both his clergyman-father and mother wrote plays, while his older brother William became an established writer and director – and it was inevitable that he should develop an interest in the theatre. He studied at the American Academy of Dramatic Arts and after graduating in 1900 developed a moderately successful theatrical career combining acting with writing and directing. But he soon became dissatisfied with the theatre, and his friendship with Jesse Lasky and Sam Goldfish (later Goldwyn) led him to try movies instead. The three men set up the Jesse L. Lasky Feature Play Company based on DeMille's yet unproven talent to write and direct motion pictures. In 1913 he travelled west and produced as his first effort the highly successful picture, *The Squaw Man*. The subsequent rapid progress of his career paralleled the development of Hollywood as the world's movie capital, and DeMille remained a leading creative force within the newly formed Famous Players-Lasky/ Paramount film company headed by Adolph Zukor. He directed a wide range of pictures, including social comedies starring Gloria Swanson, and biblical epics such as *The Ten Commandments* and *The King of Kings*. An astute showman, he continued to produce and direct a large number of highly successful epics from the Twenties until the mid-Fifties, staying with his old company, Paramount, up to the end. Although he never received an Oscar for directing, he was awarded a special Oscar in 1949 and the Irving Thalberg Award in 1952, the year that his *The Greatest Show On Earth* won the Oscar for Best Picture.

Films include: 1913 The Squaw Man. **'15** The Cheat. **'16** The Golden Chance; Joan the Woman. **'17** The Woman God Forgot. **'18** The Whispering Chorus; Old Wives for New. **'19** Don't Change Your Husband; Male and Female (GB: The Admirable Crichton). **'20** Why Change Your Wife? **'21** The Affairs of Anatol (GB: A Prodigal Knight). **'23** The Ten Commandments. **'25** The Road to Yesterday. **'27** The King of Kings. **'32** The Sign of the Cross. **'34** Cleopatra. **'36** The Plainsman. **'39** Union Pacific. **'47** Unconquered. **'49** Samson and Delilah. **'51** The Greatest Show on Earth. **'56** The Ten Commandments.

DE MILLE, William C.

(1878–1955). Director/writer. Born: Washington, D.C., USA

Elder brother of Cecil B. and son of dramatist Henry Churchill de Mille, he was educated at Columbia University and an established writer by the time Cecil was first thinking of a theatrical career. Only reluctantly becoming involved in films – his first love remained the stage – he directed with some success, often writing his own scenarios and making adaptations of his own plays. William retained the family way of spelling the patronymic de Mille. Brother Cecil spelled his name DeMille.

Films include: 1920 Conrad in Quest of Youth. **'21** What Every Woman Knows. **'22** Peg o' My Heart; Miss Lulu Bett; Nice People; Clarence. **'23** Only 38; The Marriage Maker (GB: The Faun). **'25** Lost – a Wife. **'26** The Runaway.

DEMME, Jonathan

(b. 1944). Writer/director. Born: New York City, USA

Although trained as a veterinarian, Demme had a chance meeting with producer Joe Levine which led to a job as a writer in film publicity. Encouraged by Roger Corman, he tried his hand at writing a film script. Before long he had graduated to directing and often scripting his own features, with six films appearing in the space of only seven years. Although outside Hollywood's mainstream, his films are wry, often satirical in their observation of modern America and its culture, most notably in *Melvin and Howard*, his biggest critical success to date. Apparently based on a true incident, a bizarre desert encounter between a garage attendant and the eccentric billionaire Howard Hughes, the picture earned an Oscar nomination for Jason Robards with Oscars awarded to scriptwriter Bo Goldman and supporting actress Mary Steenburgen.

Films include: 1972 The Hot Box (sc. only). **'74** Caged Heat. **'75** Crazy Mama. **'76** Fighting Mad. **'77** Citizens Band. **'79** Last Embrace. **'80** Melvin and Howard.

DEMPSTER, Carol

(b. 1902). Actress. Born: Duluth, Minnesota, USA

Her parents sought to develop her natural talent for dancing, providing her with professional training. Chosen by D.W. Griffith for a dancing bit in *Intolerance* (1916), she did not become seriously interested in film acting until a number of years later. Small, attractive and graceful, she emerged as Griffith's leading actress during 1918–26 and reputedly turned down his offer of marriage. In 1926 she retired from films to marry an investment broker. Most of her performances had been intense and moving.

Films include: 1919 The Girl Who Stayed at Home. '20 The Love Flower. '21 Dream Street. '22 Sherlock Holmes (GB: Moriarty); One Exciting Night. '23 The White Rose. '24 Isn't Life Wonderful?; America (GB: Love and Sacrifice). '25 Sally of the Sawdust. '26 The Sorrows of Satan.

DEMY, Jacques

(b. 1931). Director/writer. Born: Pont-Château, France

After completing his studies in art and film, Demy worked as an assistant to Paul Grimault and Georges Rouquier, then made his mark during the late Fifties as the director of a number of shorts. Like many other new young directors, he got his first opportunity to direct a feature (*Lola*) at the height of the *nouvelle vague*, assisted by producer Georges de Beauregard. A sensitive and evocative work starring Amouk Aimée, the picture set the tone for his later works and reflected his preoccupation with the relationship between dreams and reality. In 1964 he won the Golden Palm at Cannes with his third feature, *Les Parapluies de Cherbourg*, a musical in colour in which all the dialogue is set to music, and one of several films he has made with Catherine Deneuve. In America, Demy and Aimée followed the progress of Lola in *Model Shop*. He

Top: Carol Dempster discovers showbiz as Sally of the Circus. *Above: Catherine Deneuve as a daytime whore in Luis Buñuel's* Belle de Jour. *Above right: Maurice Denham plays a clergyman with daughter problems in* The Virgin and the Gypsy *(1970). Right: Robert De Niro as a murderous* Taxi Driver *obsessed with ridding New York of its vice*

is married to the film director Agnès Varda.

Films include: 1961 Lola (IT-FR). '62 Les Sept Péchés Capitaux *ep* La Luxure (USA: Seven Capital Sins). '63 La Baie des Anges (GB: Bay of Angels). '64 Les Parapluies de Cherbourg (FR-GER) (GB: The Umbrellas of Cherbourg). '67 Les Demoiselles de Rochefort (GB: The Young Girls of Rochefort). '69 Model Shop (USA). '70 Peau d'Ane (GB: The Magic Donkey). '72 The Pied Piper (GB-GER). '73 L'Événement le Plus Important Depuis que l'Homme a Marché sur la Lune (FR-IT) (GB: The Slightly Pregnant Man). '79 Lady Oscar (FR-JAP). '82 Une Chambre en Ville (GB: A Room in Town).

DENEUVE, Catherine

(b. 1943). Actress. Born: Catherine Dorléac; Paris, France

Deneuve was a protégée of director Roger Vadim, although she remained relatively unknown until cast in Jacques Demy's popular musical *Les Parapluies de Cherbourg*. An exquisite, distinctively blonde beauty who is often cast in roles which require her to appear cool, calm and self-assured, she is equally capable of suggesting inner turmoil or even mental imbalance. Her most memorable parts have been designed for her by directors like Roman Polanski or Luis Buñuel, who delight in probing beneath the surface of that cool exterior as in *Repulsion* or *Belle de Jour*. She has been unlucky in her choice of English-language films like *Hustle*, for example, or *March or Die*, and has never aspired to international stardom. Similarly independent in her private life, she has had children by both Vadim and Marcello Mastronianni without bothering to marry them. The actress Françoise Dorléac was her sister.

Films include: 1964 Les Parapluies de Cherbourg (FR-GER) (GB: The Umbrellas of Cherbourg). '65 Repulsion (GB). '66 Les Creatures (FR-SWED). '67 Belle de Jour (FR-IT); Les Demoiselles de Rochefort (GB: The Young Girls of Rochefort). '68 Mayerling (GB-FR). '69 La Sirène du Mississippi (FR-IT) (USA: Mississippi Mermaid). '70 Tristana (FR-SP-IT); Peau d'Ane (GB: The Magic Donkey). '75 Hustle (USA). '77 March or Die (GB). '80 Le Dernier Métro (USA/GB: The Last Metro). '82 The Hunger (GB).

DENHAM, Maurice

(b. 1909). Actor. Born: Beckenham, Kent, England

Determined to become an actor after leaving school Denham spent a number of years in rep, then made his West End debut in 1936. He embarked on his film career in 1945 and soon developed into a solid, dependable character actor equally at ease in comedy – *Doctor at Sea*, *Two-Way Stretch* – or more serious roles, most notably as Blore, the disturbed officer in *The Purple Plain* who ends up committing suicide.

Films include: 1947 Fame is the Spur; Jassy; They Made Me a Fugitive (USA: I Became a Criminal). '48 London Belongs to Me. '51 No Highway (USA: No Highway in the Sky). '54 The Purple Plain. '55 Doctor at Sea. '59 Our Man in Havana. '60 Two-Way Stretch.

DE NIRO, Robert

(b. 1943). Actor. Born: New York City, USA

De Niro was born and raised in the 'Little Italy' section of the East Side. His rebellious temperament was evident from an early age when he dropped out of high school to devote himself entirely to acting and studying under Stella Adler and Lee Strasberg. This led to numerous off-Broadway parts and low-budget feature films. His career suddenly took off during 1973–74 when he appeared in *Bang the Drum Slowly*, followed by

Mean Streets, directed by his friend Martin Scorsese and drawing on their experiences growing up in 'Little Italy'. His portrayal of the young, ambitious Vito Corleone in *The Godfather, Part II* earned him the Best Supporting Actor Oscar. An intense and dedicated actor, De Niro selects his roles carefully and devotes incredible attention to each part. During recent years he has been nominated for Oscars for his performances in *Taxi Driver* and *The Deer Hunter* and won his second Oscar in 1980 for his remarkable portrayal of the boxer Jake LaMotta in *Raging Bull*.

Films: 1967 The Wedding Party. '68 Greetings. '70 Hi, Mom!; Bloody Mama. '71 Born to Win; Jennifer on My Mind; The Gang That Couldn't Shoot Straight. '73 Bang the Drum Slowly; Mean Streets. '74 The Godfather, Part II. '76 Taxi Driver; 1900/Novecento (IT): The Last Tycoon. '77 New York, New York. '78 The Deer Hunter. '80 Raging Bull. '81 True Confessions.

DENISON, Michael

(b. 1915). Actor. Born: Doncaster, Yorkshire, England

Educated at Harrow and Oxford, Denison came to London to study at the Webber-Douglas School of Drama and made his stage debut in 1938. He married actress Dulcie Gray in 1939 and appeared in his first film *Tilly of Bloomsbury* before his war service. Perfectly filling the role of the romantic and sophisticated Englishman, he easily resumed his stage and film career after the war, often appearing alongside his wife in such pictures as *My Brother Jonathan* and *The Glass Mountain*.

Films include: 1940 Tilly of Bloomsbury. '46 Hungry Hill. '48 My Brother Jonathan. '49 The Glass Mountain. '51 The Magic Box; The Franchise Affair. '52 Angels One Five; The Importance of Being Earnest. '55 Contraband Spain. '60 Faces in the Dark.

DENNIS, Sandy

(b. 1937). Actress. Born: Hastings, Nebraska, USA

Dennis gained her first acting experience in local theatre companies before moving to New York and making her mark on the off-Broadway theatre during the early Sixties. She won two Tony Awards in succession for *A Thousand Clowns* (1963) and *Any Wednesday* (1964). She followed this with an Oscar-winning performance in her first major movie role, as the mousy, introverted young wife in *Who's Afraid of Virginia Woolf?*, directed by Mike Nichols. Dennis is seen at her best in light comedy roles such as the put-upon new schoolteacher in *Up the Down Staircase* or as Jack Lemmon's wife in *The Out-of-Towners*. She is separated from jazzman Gerry Mulligan.

Films include: 1961 Splendor in the Grass. '66 Who's Afraid of Virginia Woolf? '67 Up the Down Staircase. '68 Sweet November. '69 That Cold Day in the Park (USA-CAN). '70 The Out-of-Towners. '76 Demon. '77 Nasty Habits (GB). '82 Come Back to the Five and Dime, Jimmy Dean, Jimmy Dean.

DE PALMA, Brian

(b. 1940). Director. Born: Newark, New Jersey, USA

Educated at Columbia University, he first became interested in the cinema and directed a number of short films while still an undergraduate. Moving quickly on to his first attempt at a feature-length picture, he made *The Wedding Party* while he was a postgraduate student. In 1968 he completed an inventive and topical movie, *Greetings*, which was filmed quickly and cheaply on the streets of New York. It represented something of a breakthrough, winning the Silver Bear at Berlin and achieving a full commercial release and box-office success. His next independent feature, *Sisters*, established De Palma as a leading exponent of gripping but often lurid psychological thrillers in the tradition of Alfred Hitchcock. *Carrie* in 1976 boasted a remarkable performance from Sissy Spacek. De Palma's

Above: Michael Denison in My Brother Jonathan. *Below: Sandy Dennis in* Who's Afraid of Virginia Woolf? *Bottom: Lya de Putti. Below right: Gérard Depardieu. Bottom right: Bo Derek in* Tarzan, the Ape Man

wife, Nancy Allen, has appeared in his subsequent shockers, *Dressed to Kill* and *Blow Out*. Most of De Palma's pictures have been extremely successful at the box-office.

Films include: 1967 The Wedding Party (co-dir). '68 Greetings. '70 Hi, Mom! '72 Sisters (GB: Blood Sisters). '74 Phantom of the Paradise. '76 Carrie; Obsession. '78 The Fury. '80 Dressed to Kill. '81 Blow Out.

DEPARDIEU, Gérard

(b. 1948). Actor. Born: Chateauroux, France

Turning to acting classes at the age of sixteen as an escape from a difficult home life, he soon established himself as one of the leading young actors in France both in television and movies. Heavily built and not very handsome, he proved himself a sensitive and intelligent performer on the screen and has established a solid world-wide reputation during recent years in a variety of roles – though most famously as an earthy, insolent lout – for such leading directors as Bernardo Bertolucci (*1900*), François Truffaut (*The Last Metro*), Alain Resnais (*My American Uncle*) along with three notable pictures for Bertrand Blier.

Films include: 1974 Vincent, François, Paul . . . et les Autres; Les Valseuses (USA: Making It); Stavisky . . . (FR-IT). '76 Maîtresse; 1900/Novecento (IT); Je T'Aime, Moi Non Plus (GB: I Love You, I Don't); L'Ultima Donna (IT-FR) (USA/GB: The Last Woman). '77 Préparez voz Mouchoirs (FR-BELG) (GB: Get Out Your Handkerchiefs). '79 Buffet Froid (USA/GB: Cold Cuts). '80 Le Dernier Métro (USA: The Last Metro); Loulou; Mon Oncle d'Amérique (GB: My American Uncle). '82 Danton (FR-POL).

DE PUTTI, Lya

(1901–1931). Actress. Born: Vesce, Hungary

Lya began her career as a popular dancer in Budapest, and moved on to classical ballet in Berlin, then into films during the early Twenties. A petite brunette with large and expressive brown eyes, she first made her mark in Fritz Lang's *Das indische Grabmal* followed by Murnau's *Phantom* and Dupont's *Varieté* in which she created one of the screen's most memorable temptresses. Like many of the other leading figures at the highly successful Ufa studio, she was offered, and accepted, an invitation to Hollywood. Her notable appearance as the exotic Princess Olga in D.W. Griffith's *The Sorrows of Satan* was followed by a number of undistinguished roles. She came to England to film the first version of *The Informer*, but died a couple of years later from pneumonia.

Films include: 1921 Das indische Grabmal (USA: Mysteries of India; GB: The Indian Tombstone). '22 Der brennende Acker; Phantom; Othello. '25 Varieté (GB: Vaudeville). '26 The Sorrows of Satan (USA); God Gave Me Twenty Cents (USA). '28 Midnight Rose (USA); The Scarlet Lady (USA). '29 The Informer (GB).

DEREK, Bo

(b. 1957). Actress. Born: Mary Cathleen Collins; Long Beach, California, USA

A typical tall, slender, sun-loving California glamour-girl, she first met actor-turned-director John Derek when he was planning to shoot a feature film in Greece. He married her and immediately took charge of her career and refused to let her appear in films until the right part came along. She played a tiny role in *Orca . . . Killer Whale*, but shot to stardom with her first substantial role as Dudley Moore's fantasy girl in *'10'*. followed by a similar 'dream girl' role in *A Change of Seasons*. Determined to prove that she was not just a pretty face, Bo served as producer on (and also starred in) Derek's inept version of *Tarzan, the Ape Man*. Although she was required to do little more than cavort in front of the camera in various stages of undress, this was apparently enough to turn the picture into a moderate box-office hit. Derek's chief aim must now be to avoid the characteristic decline of most beautiful celebrities of her type.

Films include: 1977 Orca . . . Killer Whale (GB). '79 '10'. '80 A Change of Seasons. '81 Fantasies; Tarzan, the Ape Man (+ prod).

121

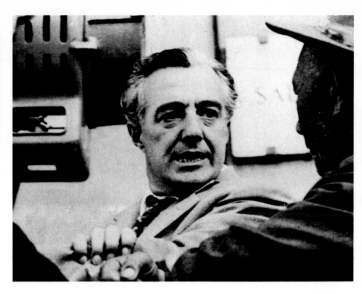

DEREK, John

(b. 1926). Actor/director. Born: Derek Harris; Hollywood, California, USA

Growing up in a Hollywood movie family (his father was a producer and his mother a former starlet), the dark, handsome young John Derek was naturally groomed for acting in movies before the war intervened. He got his big break shortly after the war when he won the role of the slum boy accused of murder in Nicholas Ray's *Knock on Any Door*. A small part in *All the King's Men* followed, but a succession of indifferent roles during the Fifties led him to turn his interests to photography and direction, taking advantage of the opportunity presented by his succession of attractive actresswives: second wife Ursula Andress starred with him in his first feature as director, *Once Before I Die*; third wife Linda Evans appeared in *Wildflowers* (1971), but most widely publicized of all was his remake of *Tarzan, the Ape Man* starring his fourth and youngest wife, Bo Derek.

Films include: 1944 I'll Be Seeing You. '49 Knock on Any Door; All the King's Men. '50 Rogues of Sherwood Forest. '52 Scandal Sheet (GB: The Dark Page); Thunderbirds. '55 Run For Cover. '56 The Ten Commandments. '59 I Battellieri del Volga (IT-FR) (USA/GB: The Boatmen). '67 Once Before I Die (+ dir). '81 Tarzan, the Ape Man (dir. only).

DERN, Bruce

(b. 1937). Actor. Born: Winnetka, Illinois, USA

Bruce Dern was born into a prominent American family connected with the law and politics. He attended prep school and went on to study at the University of Pennsylvania, but he soon gave up his studies in favour of acting. A stint at the Actors' Studio in New York led to many small roles in television and a bit part in Elia Kazan's *Wild River*. His gangly and slightly off-beat appearance along with his obvious talent led Roger Corman to cast him in a number of his violent action films – *The Wild Angels*, *The St Valentine's Day Massacre* and *Bloody Mama* – and Dern played in

numerous Westerns as well. Winner of the prestigious New York Critics' Award as supporting actor in *Drive, He Said*, he continued to develop throughout the Seventies in a variety of roles often featuring obsessive or demented characters, and received an Oscar nomination for his performance as the disturbed Vietnam veteran husband in *Coming Home*.

Films include: 1960 Wild River. '66 The Wild Angels. '67 The St Valentine's Day Massacre. '69 They Shoot Horses, Don't They? '70 Bloody Mama. '71 Drive, He Said. '72 The Cowboys; The King of Marvin Gardens. '74 The Great Gatsby. '76 Family Plot; Folies Bourgeoises (FR-IT-GER) (USA/GB: The Twist). '77 Black Sunday. '78 Coming Home; The Driver. '80 Middle-Age Crazy (CAN). '81 Tattoo.

DE ROCHEMONT, Louis

(1899–1978). Producer. Born: Chelsea, Massachusetts, USA

A New Englander by birth, he was educated at Harvard and the Massachusetts Institute of Technology. After working for various newsreel companies he had the idea of creating a new series of in-depth documentary shorts-cum-newsreels which emerged as the celebrated March of Time in 1935 and received a special Oscar the following year. Although the series continued for 16 years, he left to join 20th Century-Fox in 1943 where he produced the Oscar-winning documentary, *The Fighting Lady*. At the same studio he led the new trend toward filming on location for such thrillers as *The House on 92nd Street* and *Boomerang* which were based on true stories. He continued to make a major contribution to the cinema during the Fifties as the producer of the feature-length British cartoon *Animal Farm* and the highly successful *Cinerama Holiday*.

Films include: 1935–43 March of Time series. '44 The Fighting Lady. '45 The House on 92nd Street. '46 Boomerang. '49 Lost Boundaries. '53 Martin Luther. '54 Animal Farm (GB). '55 Cinerama Holiday. '58 Windjammer. '61 The Roman Spring of Mrs Stone (GB).

DE SANTIS, Giuseppe

(b. 1917) Director/writer. Born: Fondi, Italy

After studying literature, philosophy and film during the late Thirties, De Santis made a major contribution as a film critic, drawing attention to the shortcomings of the pictures being churned out by the Italian studios under the Fascist regime. He seized the opportunity to work with Luchino Visconti on *Ossessione* in 1942, the picture which anticipated the postwar neo-realist movement. After a number of years working as an assistant director and scriptwriter, he got his first opportunity to direct in 1947 with *Caccia Tragica*, which drew attention to the depressed conditions that still existed in post-war Italy. But while he dealt with social themes, De Santis was often forced to use stars and dilute his message. Thus, *Bitter Rice* is remembered more for the stunning Silvana Mangano than for its depiction of the appalling conditions experienced by the rice workers. (His original scenario for this picture was nominated for an Oscar.)

Films include: 1947 Caccia Tragica (GB: Tragic Pursuit). '48 Riso Amaro (GB: Bitter Rice). '50 Non C'è Pace tra gli Ulivi (GB: No Peace Among the Olives). '53 Roma Ore 11 (FR–IT) (USA: It Happened in Rome; GB: Rome 11 O'Clock). '55 Giorni d'Amore (IT–FR). '57 Uomini e Lupi (FR–IT). '60 La Garçonnière. '72 Un Apprezzato Professionista di Sicuro Avvenire.

DE SANTIS, Pasqualino

(b. 1927). Cinematographer. Born: Fondi, Italy

De Santis completed his studies at the Centro Sperimentale di Cinematografia in 1948, and immediately began to take part in the post-war renaissance of the Italian cinema. Following in the steps of his older brother, director Giuseppe, he worked as a camera assistant for Luchino Visconti on *Bellissima* (1951) and *Senso* (1954, *The Wanton Countess*). During the early Sixties he served as camera operator for the outstanding cinematographer, Gianni Di Venanzo, before graduating to full lighting cameraman status on such pictures as

The Damned and *Death in Venice*, again directed by Visconti. He won an Oscar for his soft and atmospheric photography of Franco Zeffirelli's *Romeo and Juliet* in 1968. But he was equally at home with the simpler and more direct style of Francesco Rosi, with whom he collaborated throughout the Seventies.

Films include: 1967 C'Era una Volta (IT-FR) (GB: Cinderella – Italian Style). '68 Romeo and Juliet (GB-IT); Amanti (IT-FR) (USA/GB: A Place for Lovers). '69 La Caduta degli Dei (IT-GER) (USA/GB: The Damned). '71 Morte a Venezia (USA/GB: Death in Venice). '72 The Assassination of Trotsky (GB-FR-IT); Il Caso Mattei (USA/GB: The Mattei Affair). '73 Lucky Luciano. '76 L'Innocente (IT-FR) (GB: The Innocent). '79 Cristo si è Fermato a Eboli (IT-FR) (USA: Eboli; GB: Christ Stopped at Eboli).

DE SICA, Vittorio

(1901–1974). Director/actor. Born: Sera, Italy

De Sica grew up in Naples and Rome and did his first acting while working as a clerk. In 1923 he joined a Russian acting troupe and by the late Twenties had established himself as a romantic lead in Italian films and on the stage. Tall, good-looking and sophisticated, he was always much in demand as an actor throughout his life and continued to act regularly in movies even after he began directing in 1940. The first sign of his exceptional talent as a director can be seen in his one outstanding film of the war period and the first of his pictures to be scripted by Cesare Zavattini, *The Children Are Watching Us*. He had a special ability and pleasure in working with children and with non-professional actors within natural settings and locations, and contributed to the development of the so-called Italian neo-realist style of filming after the war along with Roberto Rossellini, Luchino Visconti, and his own scriptwriter, Zavattini. They maintained a close working relationship over a period of thirty years with Zavattini providing virtually all his scripts from 1943 on, and focussing his interest on the difficult social and economic conditions in Italy during

Above, from left to right: John Derek as Robin Hood in Rogues of Sherwood Forest; *Bruce Dern in* Posse (1975); *the distinguished actor-director Vittorio De Sica; William Devane in* Marathon Man (1976); *Andy Devine as dependable as ever in* Montana Belle (1952). *Below: production shot of Brandon de Wilde as the young boy who worships* Shane *in George Stevens' classic Western about a nomadic gunman come to stay*

the post-war years. De Sica quickly won wide international recognition for his achievement during this period and was awarded special Oscars for *Shoeshine* and *Bicycle Thieves*, perhaps the most celebrated of the neo-realist films, while Zavattini received Oscar nominations for his screenplays. During later years De Sica won Foreign-Language Film Oscars for *Yesterday, Today and Tomorrow* and *The Garden of the Finzi-Continis*. His later works have tended to be glossy, sometimes superficial affairs.

Films include: 1940 Rose Scarlatte (co-dir; + act). '43 I Bambini ci Guardano (USA/GB: The Children Are Watching Us). '46 Sciuscià (USA/GB: Shoeshine). '48 Ladri di Biciclette (USA/GB: Bicycle Thieves). '51 Miracolo a Milano (USA/GB: Miracle in Milan); Umberto D. '53 Stazione Termini (IT-USA) (USA: Indiscretion of an American Wife; GB: Indiscretion). '61 La Ciociara (IT-FR) (USA/GB: Two Women). '64 Ieri, Oggi, Domani (IT-FR) (USA/GB: Yesterday, Today and Tomorrow); Matrimonio all'Italiana (IT-FR) (USA/GB: Marriage Italian Style). '70 Il Giardino dei Finzi-Contini (USA/GB: The Garden of the Finzi-Continis). '74 Il Viaggio (USA/GB: The Journey).

DE TOTH, André

(b. 1913). Director/scriptwriter/producer. Born: Sásvrái Farkasfawi Tóthfalusi Toth Endre Antai Mihály; Mako, Hungary

De Toth studied law at the Royal University, Budapest and, after a brief foray into the theatre, began to work in films in the Thirties. He directed his first features in Hungary just before the war, then moved to England and on to Hollywood as an assistant to Alexander Korda. He emerged as an interesting director in his own right during the middle and late Forties, specializing in action pictures and Westerns including a pair starring his wife, Veronica Lake. At Warners during the early Fifties he directed a number of the first films shot in the new Warnercolor (Eastman) process and the most successful 3-D feature, *House of Wax*. He remained active throughout the following years, first in the USA and then in Europe, and was second-unit director on *Superman, The Movie* (1978) and *Superman II* (1980) and on Mustapha Akkad's epic, *Lion of the Desert* (1981).

Films include: 1943 Passport to Suez. '47 Ramrod. '50 The Gunfighter (co-sc. only). '53 House of Wax; Thunder Over the Plains.

'54 The Bounty Hunters. '67 Billion Dollar Brain (exec. prod. only) (GB). '68 Play Dirty (GB).

DEUTSCH, Adolph

(1897–1980). Composer/conductor/arranger. Born: London, England

Deutsch emigrated to the USA while still a teenager after studying at the Royal Academy of Music. He built a career as a freelance arranger and music director in New York City during the Twenties and Thirties, and worked at Paul Whiteman's Music Hall. He moved to California in 1937 when he was signed by Warner Brothers and spent the following years scoring many of the studio's most characteristically low-keyed pictures like *The Maltese Falcon* and *The Mask of Dimitrios*. After ten years with Warners, he was hired by MGM and suddenly found himself in the light and colourful world of comedies – *Little Women, Father of the Bride* – and musicals. Between 1950 and 1955 Deutsch received five Oscar nominations and won three Oscars – for his scoring of *Annie Get Your Gun, Seven Brides for Seven Brothers*, and *Oklahoma!*. He was a founder member of the Screen Composers' Association and served as its president.

Films include: 1941 The Maltese Falcon. '44 The Mask of Dimitrios. '49 Take Me Out to the Ball Game (GB: Everybody's Cheering); Little Women. '50 Father of the Bride; Annie Get Your Gun. '51 Show Boat. '53 The Band Wagon. '54 Seven Brides for Seven Brothers. '55 Oklahoma!

DEVANE, William

(b. 1939). Actor. Born: Albany, New York, USA

William Devane gained his first acting experience with the New York Shakespeare Festival and appeared in numerous plays off-Broadway, making use of his training at the American Academy of Dramatic Arts. Starring roles on television followed soon after, including one in *Fear on Trial* and a portrayal of John F. Kennedy in *The Missiles of October*, for which he re-

ceived an Emmy nomination. A solid and dependable performer, he was given his first big break by Alfred Hitchcock who cast him as a stylish crook in *Family Plot*. His three pictures with British director John Schlesinger all failed to make any impact at the box office, but Devane continues to work regularly on television.

Films include: 1971 McCabe and Mrs Miller. '76 Marathon Man; Family Plot. '77 Bad News Bears in Breaking Training; Rolling Thunder. '79 Yanks (GB). '81 Honky Tonk Freeway.

DEVINE, Andy

(1905–1977). Actor. Born: Jeremiah Schwartz; Flagstaff, Arizona, USA

As a young man Devine travelled to Hollywood where he succeeded in breaking into silent pictures. There he established himself as a bit-part and supporting player, though the arrival of sound threatened to finish his career. However, his rasping, high-pitched voice and bulky shape proved an ideal combination for comedy relief, especially in Westerns and adventure movies. He played the dependable and sympathetic friend of the actress (Janet Gaynor) in the 1937 version of *A Star Is Born* and was cast in numerous John Ford pictures including *Doctor Bull* (1933), as the stage driver in *Stagecoach* and as the cowardly sheriff in *The Man Who Shot Liberty Valance*. He also worked on television during the Fifties.

Films include: 1932 Spirit of Notre Dame (GB: Vigour of Youth). '36 Romeo and Juliet. '37 A Star Is Born. '38 In Old Chicago. '39 Stagecoach; Destry Rides Again. '51 The Red Badge of Courage. '62 The Man Who Shot Liberty Valance; How the West Was Won. '63 It's a Mad, Mad, Mad, Mad World.

DE WILDE, Brandon

(1942–1972). Actor. Born: André Brandon de Wilde; New York City, USA

Born into a theatrical family, he made a much-acclaimed Broadway debut at the age of nine in *The Member of the Wedding*. He was the first child actor to win the Donaldson Award and went on to repeat his role in the film version directed by Fred Zinnemann in 1952. As the blonde, blue-eyed Joey who idolizes the strange gunman (Alan Ladd) in *Shane*, he all but stole the picture and was rewarded with an Oscar nomination the following year. He starred in his own television series, *Jamie*, during 1953–54 and made his mark as a screen adolescent during the early Sixties playing younger brothers in *All Fall Down* and *Hud*. But he had failed to establish himself as an adult star at the time of his premature death in a car accident.

Films include: 1952 The Member of the Wedding. '53 Shane. '56 Goodbye My Lady. '57 Night Passage. '59 Blue Denim (GB: Blue Jeans). '62 All Fall Down. '63 Hud. '64 Those Callaways. '65 In Harm's Way. '71 The Deserter. '72 Black Jack (GB: Wild in the Sky).

123

DEXTER, Brad

(b. 1922). Actor/producer. Born: Goldfield, Nevada, USA

Square-jawed, smooth-talking, generally appearing in the role of a cool customer it is advisable to keep an eye on, Dexter played the heavy in a number of Fifties gangster films – one who usually came to a bad end. Born in Nevada, Dexter studied at the University of Southern California and acted at the Pasadena Playhouse before the war. After serving in the air force for four-and-a-half years he toured with *Winged Victory* and acted on Broadway before being offered his first film roles. Best known for his performances in *The Asphalt Jungle*, *The George Raft Story* and as the easily forgettable seventh of *The Magnificent Seven*, he has turned to producing.

Films include: 1950 The Asphalt Jungle. '52 Macao. '58 Run Silent, Run Deep. '60 The Magnificent Seven. '61 The George Raft Story (GB: Spin of a Coin). '62 Taras Bulba. '65 None But the Brave (USA-JAP); Von Ryan's Express. '67 The Naked Runner (prod. only) (GB). '70 Little Fauss and Big Halsy (prod. only). '75 Shampoo.

DIAMOND, I.A.L.

(b. 1920). Screenwriter. Born: Itec Domnici; Ungeny, Romania

Diamond came to America with his family at the age of nine and found time while at Columbia University to edit *The Daily Spectator* and write four varsity shows. He went to Hollywood in 1941 and, graduating from a junior to contract writer, worked at Paramount (until 1945), Warner Brothers (1945–48) and 20th Century-Fox (1950–55). Since 1957 and *Love in the Afternoon* he has supplied the scripts – pungent, anarchic and biting – for Billy Wilder's best comedies, and acted as associate producer on several of them. They include *Some Like It Hot*, which mercilessly parodies its female star – Marilyn Monroe – and the gangster genre; *The Apartment*, a savagely funny look at office politics (and Oscar-winner for Best Film and Best Screenplay); and *Fedora*, a baleful view of stardom – *Sunset Boulevard* (1950) revisited. In Diamond, Wilder gained his most important collaborator since Charles Brackett, his co-writer up to 1950.

Films include: 1946 Two Guys From Milwaukee (GB: Royal Flush). '52 Monkey Business (co-sc). '56 That Certain Feeling (co-sc). '57 Love in the Afternoon (co-sc). '58 Merry Andrew (co-sc). '59 Some Like It Hot (co-sc). '60 The Apartment (co-sc). '61 One, Two, Three (co-sc). '63 Irma La Douce (co-sc). '66 The Fortune Cookie (co-sc) (GB: Meet Whiplash Willie). '70 The Private Life of Sherlock Holmes (co-sc) (GB). '72 Avanti! (co-sc). '74 The Front Page (co-sc). '78 Fedora (co-sc) (GER). '82 Buddy Buddy (co-sc).

DICKINSON, Angie

(b. 1931). Actress. Born: Kulm, North Dakota, USA

A hard-edged, glamorous blonde with a superb figure, Dickinson has generally played tarts with hearts and sexy, self-possessed broads. Her finest performance was as Feathers, the tough, good-natured saloon girl who helps out the sheriff (John Wayne) and his boys in *Rio Bravo* – an inspired piece of casting by Howard Hawks. She started out by winning a television beauty contest, and gave up her secretarial job for further television work while training at a drama workshop in Hollywood. Then came a film debut in *Lucky Me*, the role as the half-caste in Samuel Fuller's *China Gate*, *Rio Bravo*, stardom and a short-lived marriage to songwriter Burt Bacharach. Her best films since are probably *The Killers*, *Point Blank* and *Dressed to Kill*. Dickinson seems to get more popular as she gets older, enjoying big success as the heroines of television's *Police Woman* and *Pearl*, a war-time drama serial in which she was at her sultry best as a discontented wife.

Films include: 1955 Lucky Me. '57 China Gate. '59 Rio Bravo. '61 The Sins of Rachel Cade. '62 La Sage-Femme, le Curé et le Bon Dieu (FR-IT) (USA/GB: Jessica). '64 The Killers. '66 The Chase; Cast a Giant Shadow. '67 Point Blank. '69 Sam Whiskey. '79 Jigsaw/L'Homme en Colère (FR-CAN). '80 Dressed to Kill.

DICKINSON, Thorold

(b. 1903). Director. Born: Bristol, England

Dickinson directed a number of plays as a student at Keble College, Oxford and entered the film industry in 1925. He worked his way up to film editor before embarking on a successful career as a director during 1937–55. Although rarely provided with adequate budgets, he was adept at creating a period atmosphere on the screen, working quickly and efficiently and drawing on his experience as an editor. Best known for his psychological thrillers *Gaslight* and *The Queen of Spades* in black-and-white, he also made *Men of Two Worlds*, an ambitious African venture in Technicolor. From 1956 to 1960 he headed the UN's Film Services, and his life-long interest in film education and the film society movement led him to take up the post of senior lecturer in (from 1967, professor of) film at University College, London from 1960 through 1971.

Films include: 1937 The High Command. '39 The Arsenal Stadium Mystery. '40 Gaslight (USA: Angel Street). '41 The Prime Minister. '42 The Next of Kin. '46 Men· of Two Worlds. '49 The Queen of Spades. '52 Secret People. '55 Hill 24 Doesn't Answer (ISRAEL).

DIETERLE, William

(1893–1972). Director. Born: Wilhelm Dieterle; Ludwigshafen, Germany

Establishing himself as a leading actor in Germany at an early age, Dieterle appeared in numerous plays and films. Although he directed his first film in 1923, his career as a director did not develop until the late Twenties, and he continued to act in such films as *Das Wachsfigurenkabinett* (1924, *Waxworks*) and Murnau's

Faust (1926). He arrived in Hollywood in 1930 and was soon established as one of the leading contract directors at Warners where he took charge of many of their prestige productions like *A Midsummer Night's Dream*, co-directed with his old theatre associate, Max Reinhardt, and the Oscar-winning *The Life of Emile Zola*. Moving to RKO in 1939 he directed a successful remake of *The Hunchback of Notre Dame* starring Charles Laughton. Although he continued active on a wide range of pictures throughout the Forties and Fifties, the results were rarely noteworthy and he retired in 1960.

Films include: 1923 Der Mensch am Wege (sc; +act) (GER). '31 The Last Flight. '32 Jewel Robbery. '34 Fog Over Frisco. '35 A Midsummer Night's Dream (co-dir). '37 The Life of Emile Zola. '39 Juarez; The Hunchback of Notre Dame. '40 Dr Ehrlich's Magic Bullet; A Dispatch From Reuters (GB: This Man Reuter). '41 All That Money Can Buy/The Devil and Daniel Webster. '42 Tennessee Johnson (GB: The Man on America's Conscience). '48 Portrait of Jennie (GB: Jennie). '53 Salome. '60 Die Fastnachtsbeichte (GER).

DIETRICH, Marlene

(b. 1901). Actress. Born: Maria Magdalene Dietrich; Berlin, Germany

The haunting, illuminated face; the mocking eyes drowsy with the thought of sin; the suspendered thighs and the unobtainable body sheathed in furs, silks and sequins – Dietrich was a screen goddess worshipped by everyone from her director down. That was the general idea, even if by the late Thirties – and following the departure of Josef von Sternberg, her mentor and creator of her greatest films – she was no longer big box-office. It hardly mattered; those movies have become masterpieces of romantic nostalgia, incarnating her like an old and perfect love now out of reach. The daughter of a Prussian police officer, she was trained in music and acted in the theatre and was the veteran of over a dozen movies when Sternberg 'discovered' her and starred her as the *femme fatale* Lola-Lola in *The Blue Angel*. Its success led immediately to a contract at Paramount in Hol-

lywood (she brought with her a husband, former production assistant Rudolf Sieber, and baby daughter), and there Sternberg and Dietrich filmed six more fables of exotica and sexual longing – *Morocco*, *Dishonored*, *Shanghai Express*, *Blonde Venus*, *The Scarlet Empress* and *The Devil Is a Woman* – before they went their separate ways. Dietrich's subsequent films were less enticing but the spoof Western *Destry Rides Again* cast her in a frontier version of her habitual nightclub-singer role and kept her a star. She tirelessly entertained the Allied troops during World War II and afterwards gave some excellent dramatic performances for Alfred Hitchcock (*Stage Fright*), Fritz Lang (*Rancho Notorious*), Billy Wilder (*Witness for the Prosecution*) and Orson Welles (*Touch of Evil* – her last great role, as the brothel-keeper). Still beautiful and glamorous as she ap-

O'Neill's *The Iceman Cometh* (1973) showed that he still had much to offer when given a chance.

Films include: 1958 A Certain Smile; In Love and War. '59 Compulsion. '60 Crack in the Mirror; Circle of Deception (GB). '61 Francis of Assisi; Sanctuary. '68 The Helicopter Spies. '71 The Mephisto Waltz. '74 Gold (GB).

DISNEY, Walt

(1901–1966). Producer/animator. Born: Chicago, Illinois, USA

The dominating world figure in animated films originally wanted to be a newspaper cartoonist. He served as an ambulance driver after the end of World War I and returned to Kansas City, where he had grown up, getting a job as an apprentice in a commercial art studio. He met Ub Iwerks and together they joined an animation studio. In 1922 Disney formed Laugh-O-Gram Films, producing cartoon fairy tales. When this went bankrupt in 1923, Disney went to Hollywood where he embarked on the Alice series of cartoons, on which he was joined in 1924 by Iwerks. In 1927 he began the Oswald the Lucky Rabbit series and in 1928 he started making sound cartoons starring Mickey Mouse, to whom he gave his own voice, and the Silly Symphony series. Walt Disney Productions rapidly emerged as the world's leading animation studio. Donald Duck first appeared in 1934 and in 1937 *Snow White and the Seven Dwarfs* became Disney's first animated feature, to be followed by many more in the Forties and three or four a decade thereafter. Production of shorts, plentiful until then, fell off after the mid-Fifties; but the first live-action feature, *Treasure Island*, came out in 1950 and this aspect of the studio's production became increasingly important, aiming like the cartoons at children and the family market. A series of documentary nature films beginning in the late Forties was the prelude to the first feature of this type, *The Living Desert*, produced in 1953. Diversification also involved training films in World War II, much television and the opening in 1955 of the amusement park Disneyland in Anaheim, California, to be followed after Disney's death by Walt Disney World at Orlando, Florida, opened in 1971. Despite his multitude of activities, Disney's claim to fame lies in his professionalization of cartoon animation, which in his studios reached a level unrivalled elsewhere. Even so some of his more elaborate methods were too expensive for regular or continued use, even in his own films.

Films include: 1928 Steamboat Willie. '28–53 Mickey Mouse series. '29 Skeleton Dance. '32 Flowers and Trees. '33 Three Little Pigs. '37 Snow White and the Seven Dwarfs. '40 Pinocchio; Fantasia. '41 The Reluctant Dragon; Dumbo. '42 Bambi. '43 Victory Through Air Power; Saludos Amigos. '44 The Three Caballeros. '50 Cinderella; Treasure Island (GB). '51 Alice in Wonderland. '53 Peter Pan; The Living Desert. '55 Lady and the Tramp. '59 Sleeping Beauty. '61 101 Dalmations. '63 The Sword in the Stone. '64 Mary Poppins. '67 The Jungle Book.

DIFFRING, Anton

(b. 1920). Actor. Born: Koblenz, Germany

Tall, fair-haired, aristocratic, with piercing eyes, Diffring was for many years British cinema's favourite German officer, playing variations of that role many times. He was born into one of Europe's oldest theatrical families and studied drama in Vienna and Berlin before fleeing Germany in 1939. Interned in Canada during the war, he afterwards worked extensively in theatre there and in the USA. Visiting England in 1950, Diffring was offered his first film part in *State Secret*. He stayed on for dozens of movies plus stage and television work, but moved to Rome in 1968 to try to escape being typecast as a cruel and supercilious Nazi.

Films include: 1951 Hotel Sahara. '53 Albert RN. '54 Betrayed (USA). '55 I Am a Camera. '57 The Crooked Sky. '59 The Man Who Could Cheat Death. '66 Fahrenheit 451. '71 Zeppelin. '72 Dead Pigeon on Beethoven Street (USA). '76 Operation Daybreak (USA-CZECH). '77 Valentino. '81 Victory (USA) (GB: Escape to Victory).

DILLMAN, Bradford

(b. 1930). Actor. Born: San Francisco, California, USA

Yale-educated Bradford Dillman started acting off-Broadway in 1951, appearing with James Dean, Eli Wallach and Patricia Neal. Soon he was on Broadway and won a Tony Award for his role in Eugene O'Neill's *Long Day's Journey Into Night*. He then went to 20th Century-Fox for several years, playing character parts and leads, notably as one of the two upper-class young murderers in *Compulsion*. He worked in television, starring as a military lawyer in the series *Court Martial*, as well as continuing a film career in which he has tended to become typecast as a cool villain, usually with psychotic tendencies. But his performance in the American Film Theatre version of Eugene

Above, far left: Brad Dexter in The Magnificent Seven. *Left: Angie Dickinson in* Rome Adventure *(1962). Above: Marlene Dietrich in* Destry Rides Again. *Below: Anton Diffring in* Fahrenheit 451. *Above right: Bradford Dillman as one of the toffish murderers in* Compulsion

proached 60, she began a series of famous live concert tours that turned the Dietrich myth into a phenomenon. She retired from films after her disappointment with *Just a Gigolo*, made when she was 78. Marlene Dietrich is the movies' greatest symbol of unfulfilled desire, a woman safe in the knowledge that the men *always* come back for more.

Films include: 1922 So sind die Männer (GER). '29 Die Frau, nach der Man sich sehnt (GER) (USA/GB: Three Loves). '30 Der blaue Engel (GER) (English-language version: The Blue Angel); Morocco. '31 Dishonored. '32 Shanghai Express; Blonde Venus. '33 The Song of Songs. '34 The Scarlet Empress. '35 The Devil Is a Woman. '36 Desire. '39 Destry Rides Again. '40 The Flame of New Orleans. '48 A Foreign Affair. '49 Stage Fright (GB). '52 Rancho Notorious. '57 Witness for the Prosecution. '58 Touch of Evil. '61 Judgement at Nuremberg. '79 Schöner Gigolo – Armer Gigolo (GER) (GB: Just a Gigolo).

DIX, Richard

(1894–1949). Actor. Born: Ernest Brimmer; St Paul, Minnesota, USA

After toying with various career possibilities – as a surgeon, a banker, an architect – Richard Dix went into repertory theatre and quickly became a leading man. He was signed by Sam Goldwyn for *Not Guilty* and played upright cowboys and clean-cut American heroes in the silent era. He was the idealist Yancey Cravat in the 1931 version of *Cimarron* and concentrated for a time on historical and pioneer roles. Towards the end of his career he played mainly alcholics and other neurotics. Charles Chaplin is reputed to have told him that he would never make a star.

Films include: 1921 Not Guilty. '22 The Bonded Woman. '23 The Christian; The Ten Commandments. '24 Sinners in Heaven. '25 The Vanishing American. '26 Let's Get Married. '31 Cimarron. '32 The Lost Squadron. '39 Blind Alley. '43 The Ghost Ship. '44 The Whistler.

DMYTRYK, Edward

(b. 1908). Director. Born: Grand Forks, British Columbia, Canada

Dmytryk was the Canadian son of Ukrainian immigrants. He entered movies at 14, working as an office boy at Paramount and eventually moving into the cutting room. After directing some cheap and interesting horror movies, Dmytryk established himself with *Murder, My Sweet*, a skilfully made film noir with Dick Powell cast out of type as detective Philip Marlowe. Director and actor repeated their success with *Cornered*. *Crossfire* was Dmytryk's third fine thriller in three years, and boasted an outstanding performance by Robert Ryan as an anti-semitic psychopath. In 1947 Dmytryk was investigated by HUAC and became one of the Hollywood Ten found guilty of contempt of Congress. After imprisonment, he worked briefly in England but returned to the USA, was cleared after offering evidence and freed from the blacklist to direct *The Sniper*, *The Caine Mutiny* and *Broken Lance*. His budgets have since expanded, but the glossiness of star vehicles like *Walk on the Wild Side*, *The Carpetbaggers* and *Shalako* wears pale and thin beside Dmytryk's Forties thrillers.

Films include: 1935 The Hawk. '42 Hitler's Children. '44 Murder, My Sweet (GB: Farewell My Lovely). '45 Cornered. '47 Crossfire. '49 Give Us This Day (GB) (USA: Salt to the Devil). '52 The Sniper. '54 The Caine Mutiny; Broken Lance. '58 The Young Lions. '62 Walk on the Wild Side. '64 The Carpetbaggers. '68 Shalako (GB).

DONAHUE, Troy

(b. 1937) Actor. Born: Merle Johnson; New York City, USA

Troy Donahue's blond boyish good looks, vaguely sulky and immature, suited a certain stereotype popular in the late Fifties and early Sixties but were curiously dated by the advent of hippiedom. He started his career by playing bit parts in films and television for Universal – he was the bigot who beat up his black girlfriend passing for white (Susan Kohner) in *Imitation of Life* (1959). In 1959 he signed a contract with Warners, rapidly becoming a screen idol in beach movies and tales of young love, starring opposite Sandra Dee and Connie Stevens. He also had a television series, *Surfside 6*. Warners dropped him in 1966 and he sank to B movies, with an occasional role in bigger films. He also moved into production.

Films include: 1957 The Tarnished Angels. '58 Live Fast Die Young. '59 A Summer Place. '61 Parrish; Susan Slade. '62 Rome Adventure (GB: Lovers Must Learn). '63 Palm Springs Weekend. '64 A Distant Trumpet. '67 Come Spy With Me. '74 The Godfather, Part II; Cockfighter/Born to Kill.

DONAT, Robert

(1905–1958). Actor. Born: Manchester, Lancashire, England

Given elocution lessons at an early age, young Donat developed a fine stage voice and presence. He played a variety of classical roles on the stage from the age of 16. Tall and distinguished-looking, he received his first film offers during 1932–34 when he appeared in Korda's *The Private Life of Henry VIII* followed by *The Count of Monte Cristo* in Hollywood. He turned down the offer of a Hollywood contract and returned to Britain to continue his stage and film career as a very popular leading man. He was perfectly cast as Richard Hannay in Alfred Hitchcock's superb version of *The Thirty-Nine Steps* and won an Oscar for his delightful performance as the beloved schoolmaster in *Goodbye, Mr Chips* a few years later. Dogged by ill-health and indecision for many years, he worked only infrequently during the last decade of his life, but directed a comedy, *The Cure for Love* (and married its leading lady Renée Asherson), and gave a memorable farewell performance as the mandarin in *The Inn of the Sixth Happiness*.

Films include: 1933 Men of Tomorrow; The Private Life of Henry VIII. '34 The Count of Monte Cristo (USA). '35 The Thirty-Nine Steps; The Ghost Goes West. '37 Knight Without Armour. '38 The Citadel. '39 Goodbye, Mr Chips. '42 The Young Mr Pitt. '43 Adventures of Tartu. '45 Perfect Stranger (USA: Vacation From Marriage). '48 The Winslow Boy. '49 The Cure for Love (+ dir; + prod; + co-sc). '51 The Magic Box. '54 Lease of Life. '58 The Inn of the Sixth Happiness.

DONEN, Stanley

(b. 1924). Director. Born: Columbia, South Carolina, USA

Stanley Donen first teamed up with the dancer-actor Gene Kelly as an aspiring young hoofer and assistant choreographer on Broadway in 1941. They met again in Hollywood in 1944 and worked for over a decade as choreographers and then as co-directors. Together they made a vital contribution to the brief flowering of the MGM musical as an integrated art-form which culminated in *Singin' in the Rain*. Each kept a separate career going – Donen directed *Seven Brides for Seven Brothers* on his own and moved to Paramount for *Funny Face* before going on to Warners for *The Pajama Game* and *Damn Yankees*. By the late Fifties he was diversifying into sophisticated romantic comedies, varied by comedy-thrillers in the Sixties. Then his career began to falter, with a five-year gap between the laboured homosexual study *Staircase* (1969) and the odd musical fantasy *The Little Prince* (1974). Donen has not been able to find other genres that suited him as well as the classic musical; but his achievement there is enough to establish for him a distinguished place in film history.

Films include: 1974 Cover Girl (co-chor. only). '45 Anchors Aweigh (co-chor. only). '49 Take Me Out to the Ball Game (co-chor. only); On the Town (co-dir; + co-chor). '52 Singin' in the Rain (co-dir; + co-chor). '54 Seven Brides for Seven Brothers. '55 It's Always Fair Weather (co-dir; + co-chor). '57 Funny Face; The Pajama Game (co-dir; + co-prod). '58 Indiscreet (+ prod) (GB); Damn Yankees (co-dir; + co-prod) (GB: What Lola Wants). '60 The Grass Is Greener (+ prod) (GB). '63 Charade (+ prod). '66 Arabesque (+ prod); Two for the Road (+ prod) (GB). '67 Bedazzled (+ prod) (GB). '75 Lucky Lady. '78 Movie Movie.

DONLEVY, Brian

(1901–1972). Actor. Born: Portadown, Armagh, Ireland

Square-jawed and broad-shouldered, with a dour and heavy look, Brian Donlevy was originally one of Hollywood's archetypal villains, but writer-director Preston Sturges partially redeemed him with a comic role in *The Great McGinty* and thereafter he often played aggressive heroes as well. Brought up in Cleveland, Ohio, he was a genuine fighting man – or rather adolescent – having served with General Pershing in Mexico and flown with the French Lafayette Squadron in World War I. After considerable stage experience he went to Hollywood in 1929. He made his name as the black-cloaked villain in *Barbary Coast* and broke into major roles with his sadistic Foreign Legion sergeant in *Beau Geste*. But by the late Forties his career was starting to go downhill. He had his own television series, *Dangerous Assignment*, for a while; but by the Sixties his film parts were marginal and he was seen only sporadically on television. Even heavies don't last forever.

Films include: 1935 Barbary Coast. '36 High Tension. '39 Jesse James; Beau Geste; Destry Rides Again. '40 The Great McGinty (GB: Down Went McGinty). '42 The Glass Key. '43 Hangmen Also Die!; The Miracle of Morgan's Creek. '46 The Virginian. '55 The Quatermass Experiment (GB) (USA: The Creeping Unknown). '65 How to Stuff a Wild Bikini (GB: How to Fill a Wild Bikini). '68 Rogue's Gallery.

Above: Richard Dix in Cimarron. *Top right: Troy Donahue in* My Blood Runs Cold *(1965). Above right: Robert Donat in* The Winslow Boy

DONNER, Clive

(b. 1926). Director. Born: London, England

The Sixties was Donner's period. Before that he was a film editor, graduating to direction via television episodes and commercials and Edgar Wallace quickies. Then, after winning critical respect with the youth-oriented *Some People* and an atmospheric version of Harold Pinter's *The Caretaker*, he caught the mood of the time with the social-climbing black comedy of *Nothing But the Best* and the fashionable erotic antics of *What's New, Pussycat?* Another youth picture, *Here We Go Round the Mulberry Bush*, tried rather too hard to make Stevenage New Town trendy and *Alfred the Great* was an epic flop. Donner's film career seemed to lose its way in the Seventies, when he was probably doing his best work for television and the theatre. *Vampira* was a weak if elegantly staged spoof, while *Rogue Male* (for television) was a tensely intelligent action adventure.

Films include: 1957 The Secret Place. '60 Marriage of Convenience. '61 The Sinister Man. '62 Some People. '63 The Caretaker (USA: The Guest). '64 Nothing But the Best. '65 What's New, Pussycat? (USA-FR). '68 Here We Go Round the Mulberry Bush. '69 Alfred the Great. '74 Vampira (USA: Old Dracula). '80 The Nude Bomb (USA).

DORLÉAC, Françoise

(1942–1967). Actress. Born: Paris, France

From a theatrical family, Françoise Dorléac was the elder sister of the actress Catherine Deneuve, who was already the better-known of the two when Françoise met her untimely death in a car accident. Françoise had made her first stage appearance at the age of ten, and continued in the theatre as well as modelling for Christian Dior. From 1959 to 1961 she studied at the Conservatoire d'Art Dramatique while playing her first film roles. She shot to stardom as the cool air hostess in La Peau Douce, which precipitated her brief international career, notably as the sluttish wife in Cul-de-Sac. She and Catherine made a stunning team in the lavish musical Les Demoiselles de Rochefort shortly before her abrupt end. She was a pale, delicate, dark-haired beauty, more versatile if less striking than her talented blonde sister.

Films include: 1957 Mensonges (short). '61 Tout l'Or du Monde (FR-IT) (USA/GB: All the Gold in the world). '62 Arsène Lupin Contre Arsène Lupin (FR-IT). '64 L'Homme de Rio (FR-IT) (GB: That Man From Rio); La Peau Douce (USA: The Soft Skin; GB: Silken Skin). '65 Genghis Khan (USA-GER-YUG); Where the Spies Are (GB). '66 Cul-de-Sac (GB). '67 Les Demoiselles de Rochefort (GB: The Young Girls of Rochefort); Billion Dollar Brain (GB).

DONNER, Jörn

(b. 1933). Director/producer/writer/critic/actor. Born: Helsinki, Finland

Donner seems already to have packed several careers into one lifetime. Born in Finland of Swedish-speaking parents who were German by descent, he had written 11 books by the age of 30, including novels and reportage as well as film criticism; he had also directed five shorts. Having moved to Sweden as a film critic, he began to make feature films there, usually starring Harriet Andersson. From the late Sixties he did much to revive the Finnish film industry, both in his own films (in which he also acted) and by supporting young directors. Then he returned to Sweden to work for the Swedish Film Institute, of which he became managing director in 1978. He also served as chairman of the Finnish Film Foundation. His films are generally arguments rather than entertainments, ironical in tone, mainly concerned with problems of love and sex, set against carefully delimited social backgrounds and tempered with a dry wit.

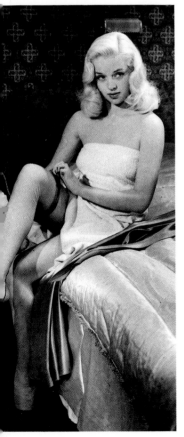

Below: Diana Dors in The Saint's Girl Friday/The Saint's Return *(1953). Above right: Brian Donlevy. Above, far right: Françoise Dorléac*

Films include: 1963 En Söndag i September (SWED) (GB: A Sunday in September). '64 Att Älska (SWED) (USA/GB: To Love). '67 Stimulantia ep Han – Hon (He – She) (SWED); Tvärbalk (SWED) (Rooftree). '68 Mustaa Volkoisella (FIN) (GB: Black and White). '70 Naisenkuvia (FIN) (GB: Portraits of Women); Anna. '71 Perkele! Kuvia Suomesta (FIN) (Fuck Off! Images From Finland). '72 Hellyys (FIN) (Tenderness) – remade as Ömhet (SWED, 1972) (Tenderness). '73 Baksmälla (SWED) (Hangover). '78 Män Kan inte Valdtas (SWED-FIN) (GB: Men Can't Be Raped).

DONNER, Richard

(b. 1930). Director. Born: New York City, USA

Richard Donner directed episodes of television series before making his first feature film in 1962. After more television he made a couple of film flops in Britain, and then worked mainly on *Kojak* and television movies until the unexpected success of *The Omen*, a

Satanic thriller rather than a horror film, launched him into the big time. *Superman, The Movie*, with its remarkable special effects and fine acting, confirmed his success; but a legal row over the sequel led to another director, Richard Lester, being assigned to *Superman II* (1980).

Films: 1961 X-15. '68 Salt and Pepper (GB). '70 Twinky (GB) (USA: Lola). '76 The Omen. '78 Superman, The Movie. '80 Inside Moves.

DONSKOI, Mark

(1901–1981). Director. Born: Odessa, Ukraine, Russia

After serving with the Red Army in the Civil War, Donskoi studied medicine and then law, becoming a police prosecutor in the Ukraine. In 1926 he enrolled as a pupil of Eisenstein's at the State Film Institute, and from 1927 he worked as a director, achieving international fame for the Maxim Gorki trilogy. *The Childhood of Maxim Gorki*, with its passionate humanism, struck a new note in the Soviet cinema and, together with the rest of the trilogy, showed that a Russian director could be reflective and generous as well as combative. Continuing the educational theme, *Children of the Soviet Arctic* and *The Village Teacher* were both about the bringing of learning to remote parts of the Soviet Union. *Mother* was a remake of Gorki's play, but less overwhelming than Pudovkin's silent version. The two Lenin films, *Heart of a Mother* and *A Mother's Devotion*, were typically gentle and loving treatments of their subject, never losing a human scale. Donskoi received the Order of Lenin in 1944 for his work on war films.

Films include: 1928 V Bolshom Gorode (In a Big City). '31 Ogon (The Fire). '38 Dyetstvo Gorkovo (GB: The Childhood of Maxim Gorki). '39 V Lyudyakh (GB: My Apprenticeship/Out in the World). '40 Moi Universiteti (GB: My Universities). '41 Romantiki (GB: Children of the Soviet Arctic). '47 Selskaya Uchitelnitsa (GB: The Village Teacher). '56 Mat' (GB: Mother). '66 Serdtze Materi (GB: Heart of a Mother). '67 Vernost Materi (GB: A Mother's Devotion).

DORS, Diana

(1931–1984). Actress. Born: Diana Fluck; Swindon, Wiltshire, England

Diana Dors was Britain's pneumatic blonde sex symbol of the Fifties, a gift to press gossip and at one time boosted as a home-grown rival to Marilyn Monroe. She started off at 15 playing teenagers, and after a few years was publicized as a glamour girl, with newspapers featuring the vicissitudes of her private life rather than her screen roles. When she had proved she could act by playing the condemned murderess in *Yield to the Night* she went to Hollywood but her studio contract was suspended after two pictures while the press concentrated on her alleged affair with co-star Rod Steiger. She had another try at Hollywood in the early Sixties but again with little success. By the early Seventies she had matured into a character actress, fat, dark and cheerful, scoring a television hit with *Queenie's Castle* and emphasizing her new maternal image by playing the stage role of Jocasta in *Oedipus* at Chichester. Other television work included appearances in *Shoestring*, an Adam and the Ants pop video and as a witch in a horror drama. She was married three times, subdued cancer and remained a British national monument.

Films include: 1951 Lady Godiva Rides Again. '54 The Weak and the Wicked. '55 A Kid for Two Farthings. '56 Yield to the Night. '57 The Unholy Wife (USA). '58 I Married a Woman (USA). '70 There's a Girl in My Soup; Deep End (USA-GER). '72 The Amazing Mr Blunden. '74 From Beyond the Grave. '76 Adventures of a Taxi Driver. '79 Confessions From the David Galaxy Affair.

Right: Kirk Douglas as the ruthless producer who gets the right result at an unacceptable cost in The Bad and the Beautiful. *Far right: a moment of moody reflection for Melvyn Douglas, usually the centre of light romance*

DOUGLAS, Gordon

(b. 1909). Director. Born: New York City, USA

As a boy extra at the Vitagraph studios in New York, Gordon Douglas acted in the matinée idol Maurice Costello's films. He returned to films on completing his studies, going to Hollywood in 1929 to work for Hal Roach in various capacities including actor. He rose to be director of the Our Gang shorts, one of which, *Bored of Education*, won a 1936 Academy Award, his last to date. He directed a Laurel and Hardy feature and then launched into a variety of genres, mainly comedy at first but soon taking on war pictures, thrillers, period pieces, Westerns and even musicals, not to mention such propagandist efforts as *I Was a Communist for the FBI*, his first assignment at Warners after a period of freelancing. He has worked for several other studios including 20th Century-Fox, where he made his notable trio of films with Frank Sinatra – *Tony Rome, The Detective* and *Lady in Cement*.

Films include: 1940 Saps at Sea. '50 Kiss Tomorrow Goodbye. '51 I Was a Communist for the FBI. '52 The Iron Mistress. '61 The Sins of Rachel Cade. '64 Rio Conchos. '67 Chuka; Tony Rome. '68 The Detective; Lady in Cement. '70 They Call Me Mister Tibbs! '77 Viva Knievel!

DOUGLAS, Kirk

(b. 1916). Actor/producer. Born: Issur Danielovitch Demsky; Amsterdam, New York, USA

Young Demsky's parents were Russian immigrants who settled in America before the birth of their son. Having 'Americanized' his name, Kirk Douglas attended the American Academy of Dramatic Arts. He graduated in 1941 and made his New York debut in *Spring Again*, but World War II then interrupted his progress. After naval service, he returned to the stage and was spotted by the producer Hal Wallis. In 1945 he went to Hollywood to star in *The Strange Love of Martha Ivers*, the film that established him in his intense tough-guy image. He was then cast in thrillers (*Out of the Past*), Westerns (*Gunfight at the OK Corral*) and costume epics (*Spartacus*), bringing more than mere strength to each role he played. His characters are usually the victims of their own aggression, as best seen in the roles he plays in *Detective Story, Champion* and *Ace in the Hole*. His anguished portrayal of Vincent Van Gogh in *Lust for Life* may be his greatest performance. In 1955 Douglas formed a production company that produced many outstanding movies such as *Paths Of Glory, Spartacus* and *Lonely Are the Brave*. Since then he has moved into other areas of film-making and is now regarded as a director of some considerable skill.

Films include: 1946 The Strange Love of Martha Ivers. '47 Out of the Past (GB: Build My Gallows High). '48 A Letter to Three Wives. '49 Champion. '50 Young Man With a Horn (GB: Young Man of Music). '51 Ace in the Hole; Detective Story. '52 The Bad and the Beautiful. '56 Lust for Life. '57 Gunfight at the OK Corral; Paths of Glory. '59 The Last Train From Gun Hill. '60 Spartacus. '62 Lonely Are the Brave; Two Weeks in Another Town. '64 Seven Days in May. '69 The Arrangement. '71 A Gunfight. '73 Scalawag (+dir) (USA-IT). '75 Posse (+dir). '80 Saturn 3.

DOUGLAS, Melvyn

(1901–1981). Actor. Born: Melvyn Hesselberg; Macon, Georgia, USA

His father was a concert pianist and consequently Melvyn Douglas spent his formative years travelling the world, also gaining experience as a child actor. At 17 he joined the army and after World War I returned to the stage and a Broadway debut in *A Free Soul*. Gloria Swanson spotted him in *Tonight or Never* and asked for him as her leading man in the screen adaptation. During the Thirties, Douglas – smooth, elegant, witty and charming – played opposite the most famous leading ladies of the day, including Greta Garbo (making her laugh in *Ninotchka*), Marlene Dietrich (*Angel*) and Joan Crawford (*A Woman's Face*), and excelled mainly in romantic, light-hearted roles. After service in World War II he became a revered character actor, often playing distinguished elderly gentlemen. Late in his career he received Best Supporting Actor Oscars for his performances in such parts in *Hud* and *Being There*.

Films include: 1931 Tonight or Never. '32 The Old Dark House. '33 Counsellor-at-Law. '36 The Gorgeous Hussy. '37 Angel. '39 Ninotchka. '41 A Woman's Face; That Uncertain Feeling; Two-Faced Woman. '62 Billy Budd. '63 Hud. '70 I Never Sang for My Father. '72 The Candidate. '79 The Seduction of Joe Tynan; Being There. '80 Tell Me a Riddle.

Below: Michael Douglas as the doctor after allegations of malpractice in Coma. *Below right: Paul Douglas. Below, far right: Brad Dourif in*

DOUGLAS, Michael

(b. 1944). Actor/producer. Born: New Brunswick, New Jersey, USA

Son of Kirk Douglas, Michael had movies in his blood; by the age of 17 he was assisting the cutter on *Lonely Are the Brave* (1962). He majored in drama at the University of California, and on graduation auditioned for parts in the television series *The Experiment* and the film *Hail, Hero*. He did well, winning both roles, and subsequently made his name as a regular in the long-running *The Streets of San Francisco*. Douglas then discovered a talent for production, carefully choosing his films. His first effort, *One Flew Over the Cuckoo's Nest*, won five Academy Awards. Five years later he co-starred in and produced another big hit, *The China Syndrome*.

Films: 1969 Hail, Hero (actor). '70 Adam at 6 am (actor). '71 Summertree (actor). '72

Group Portrait with a Lady. *Bottom right: Lesley-Anne Down in* Hanover Street. *Bottom, far right: Marie Dressler in* Min and Bill

Napoleon and Samantha (actor). '75 One Flew Over the Cuckoo's Nest (co-prod). '76 Gator (actor). '78 Coma (actor). '79 The China Syndrome (prod; + co-sc; + act). '80 It's My Turn (actor).

DOUGLAS, Paul

(1908–1959). Actor. Born: Philadelphia, Pennsylvania, USA

A burly hulk of a man with a lived-in face, Douglas usually played cynical, middle-aged aggressive types in both comedies and melodramas. He also was involved in his own sports series for Fox-Movietone News – *Paul Douglas' Sports Review*. He died of a heart attack only ten years into his movie career.

Films include: 1949 Twelve O'Clock High. '50 Panic in the Streets. '51 Fourteen Hours. '52 Clash by Night. '54 Executive Suite; The Maggie (GB) (USA: High and Dry). '55 Joe Macbeth (GB). '56 The Solid Gold Cadillac; The Gamma People.

DOURIF, Brad

(b. 1950). Actor. Born: Huntington, West Virginia, USA

After university, Brad Dourif appeared in various roles with the Greenbrier Repertory Theater in West Virginia. He then moved to New York, where he joined the Circle Repertory Company and acted at the East Side Playhouse. His appearance in the play *When You Comin' Back, Red Ryder?* excited great critical interest, and Dourif was subsequently offered a role in *One Flew Over the Cuckoo's Nest*. His performance as a stuttering asylum inmate won him a Best Supporting Actor Oscar nomination. Much television work followed, and Dourif's emaciated, wild-looking appearance has led to parts as strange, enigmatic young men in films such as *Wise Blood*. His casting in such prestigious movies as *Heaven's Gate* (as Mr Eggleston) and *Ragtime* (as Younger Brother) suggests he is now among the Hollywood elite.

Films include: 1975 One Flew Over the Cuckoo's Nest; W.W. and the Dixie Dancekings. '77 Gruppenbild mit Dame (GER-FR) (USA/GB: Group Portrait With a Lady). '78 The Eyes of Laura Mars. '79 Wise Blood (USA-GER). '80 Heaven's Gate. '81 Ragtime.

DOUY, Max

(b. 1914). Art director. Born: Issy-les-Mouliniaux, France

In 1930 Max Douy joined the Pathé-Natan studios, having been introduced to them by Francoeur Studios' art director Eugène Carrè. Douy became assistant draftsman to the resident designers at Pathé and he drew and built sets for Jean Vigo's film *L'Atalante* (1934) from Francis Jourdain's sketches. During 1944 he came into his own as an art director for Robert Bresson, and after World War II began his 30-year-long association with director Claude Autant-Lara. In 1969 he designed the interiors for *Castle Keep*, creating remarkable Gothic and Renaissance structures. More recently he has worked on the James Bond extravaganzas *Thunderball* and *Moonraker*, for which he constructed the sets from Ken Adam's drawings. His brother Jacques, ten years his junior, has also worked successfully as an art director.

Films include: 1943 Lumière d'Eté. '45 Les Dames du Bois de Boulogne. '47 Quai des Orfèvres (USA: Jenny Lamour); Le Diable au Corps (GB: Devil in the Flesh). '55 French Cancan (FR-IT) (USA: Only the French Can). '56 Marguerite de la Nuit (FR-IT). '58 Tamango. '61 Non Uccidere (IT-YUG-GER).

'62 Phaedra (USA-GREECE). '65 Thunderball (GB). '69 Castle Keep (USA). '75 Section Spéciale (FR-IT-GER) (USA: Special Section). '79 Moonraker (GB-FR).

DOVZHENKO, Alexander

(1894–1956). Director. Born: Sosnitsa, Ukraine, Russia

Born into a farming family, Dovzhenko spent his youth in the Ukraine before attending the Teachers' Institute for four years followed by eighteen months of university and three years in the Commercial Institute. After World War I and the Russian Revolution, he worked at Soviet embassies in Warsaw and Berlin. At this time he studied painting, and submitted work to newspapers and periodicals until, in 1926, he concluded that painting was a dying art and decided, like his contemporaries Eisenstein, Kuleshov, Pudovkin and Vertov, to turn his talents to film. He went to Odessa and joined the All-Ukrainian Photo-Cinema Administration (VUFKU). After writing a couple of scenarios he directed and acted in a political thriller, *The Diplomatic Pouch*. Dovzhenko's films usually centre around lyrical treatments of death – *Arsenal*, for example, is about work and revolutionary struggle, while *Earth* concerns the murderous rivalry between different factions in an idyllic Ukrainian village. After his own death his wife, the actress Yulia Solntseva, dedicated herself to the completion of his unfinished projects.

Films include: 1926 Vasya Reformator (co-dir) (GB: Vasya the Reformer). '27 Sumka Dipkurera (GB: The Diplomatic Pouch). '29 Arsenal (GB: January Uprising in Kiev in 1918). '30 Zemlya (USA: Soil; GB: Earth/Song of New Life). '32 Ivan. '35 Aerograd (USA: Frontier). '39 Shchors (co-dir). '40 Osvobozhdenie (co-dir) (GB: Liberation). '43 Bitza za Nashu Sovietskayu Ukrainu (GB: The Fight for Our Soviet Ukraine/Ukraine in Flames). '48 Michurin.

DOWN, Lesley-Anne

(b. 1954). Actress. Born: London, England

Dark-haired Lesley-Anne Down became a model for commercials while still only 10. She was voted Britain's 'Most Beautiful Teenager', and her face was much sought-after; at 15 she left school to work in provincial theatres and as a film extra. Her big chance came when she played the young Lady Georgina in *Upstairs, Downstairs*, the award-winning television series about an aristocratic Edwardian family in London. She became a star in Britain and America on the strength of the show's success, and has since featured as a cool, feminine romantic lead in a number of films. On television she also appeared in a blonde wig and little else as stripper Phyllis Dixey. Her second husband is director William Friedkin.

Films include: 1972 Pope Joan. '73 Scalawag (USA-IT). '75 Brannigan. '76 The Pink Panther Strikes Again. '77 A Little Night Music (USA-A-GER). '78 The Betsy (USA);

The First Great Train Robbery (USA: The Great Train Robbery). '79 Hanover Street. '80 Rough Cut (USA). '81 Sphinx (USA).

DREIER, Hans

(1885–1966). Art Director. Born: Bremen, Germany

Each Hollywood studio in the Thirties had its characteristic 'look': the continental elegance and sophistication that typified Paramount productions was very largely due to its supervising art director, Hans Dreier. Trained as an architect, he became an assistant designer at the Ufa studios after World War I. Alongside Ernst Lubitsch, he was an early recruit to Hollywood, where he designed his first film, *The Hunchback of Notre Dame*. Working regularly with Lubitsch and later Billy Wilder, Dreier himself was so eclectic that he has left no distinctive signature. He was, however, significant for the overall level of taste and integrity he brought to film design.

Films include: 1923 The Hunchback of Notre Dame. '24 Forbidden Paradise. '27 Underworld. '28 The Docks of New York; The Street of Sin. '29 The Love Parade; The Case of Lena Smith. '31 Dr Jekyll and Mr Hyde. '32 A Farewell to Arms (co-art dir); Trouble in Paradise. '33 Duck Soup (co-art dir); I'm No Angel (co-art dir). '34 The Scarlet Empress (co-art dir); Cleopatra (co-art dir). '35 The Crusades; The Lives of a Bengal Lancer (co-art dir). '36 The Plainsman (co-art dir). '38 Bluebeard's Eighth Wife. '39 The Cat and the Canary. '44 Frenchman's Creek. '49 Samson and Delilah. '50 Sunset Boulevard (co-art dir). '51 A Place in the Sun (co-art dir).

DRESSLER, Marie

(1869–1934). Actress. Born: Leila Koerber; Coburg, Ontario, Canada

Grey-haired, leather-faced, 60 years old and weighing 200 pounds, Marie Dressler was not the ordinary stuff of Hollywood top box-office stars of the early Thirties. She reached the peak of her popularity in her final years after a bumpy career. Romantically she ran away to join the circus at six, and by 14 was a chorus girl. By the early years of the century she was a star comedienne in vaudeville; and when Mack Sennett adapted her stage success *Tillie's Nightmare* as the first comedy feature, *Tillie's Punctured Romance*, Dressler, of right, took billing over the young Charlie Chaplin. Thirteen years later she was jobless, broke and about to take a domestic job when the writer Frances Marion, for old times' sake, persuaded MGM to give her a small film part. Within three years, *Anna Christie*, Garbo's first talkie, restored Dressler's fame. The following year *Min and Bill* won her an Oscar; and when she died of cancer in 1934 this large-built and (on and offscreen alike) large-hearted woman was mourned as America's best-loved star.

Films include: 1914 Tillie's Punctured Romance. '27 The Joy Girl. '29 The Hollywood Revue of 1929. '30 Anna Christie; Caught Short; Min and Bill; One Romantic Night. '31 Reducing; Politics. '33 Tugboat Annie; Dinner at Eight; Christopher Bean.

DREYER, Carl Theodor

(1889–1968). Director. Born: Copenhagen, Denmark

Dreyer, in half a century of work, never compromised his art, his talent or his ability to depict themes of an interior and spiritual quality. Starting his career as a journalist, he joined the Nordisk film company as a writer and editor. His first film as director, *Praesidenten*, made in 1919, already dealt with the theme of a man's conscience. After four more films in Denmark, he went to Germany where he made a remarkable study of homosexuality, *Michael*. In France he created his masterwork *La Passion de Jeanne d'Arc*, but its commercial failure discouraged both Dreyer and his patrons. After the mesmeric horror story *Vampyr*, he was inactive for more than a decade. In 1955 he won the Golden Lion of the Venice Festival with *Ordet*, and, at 75, he created a last masterpiece, *Gertrud*, a majestic reflection upon love.

Films include: 1919 Praesidenten. '20 Blade af Satans Bog; Prästänkan (USA/GB: The Parson's Widow). '22 Die Gezeichneten (GER). '24 Michael (GER) (USA: Chained; GB: Heart's Desire). '25 Du Skal Aere Din Hustru (GB: Master of the House). '28 La Passion of Joan of Arc) (FR) (USA/GB: The Passion of Joan of Arc). '32 Vampyr: Der Traum des Allan Gray (GER) (USA: Vampire; GB: Vampyr: The Strange Adventures of David Gray). '43 Vredens Dag (USA/GB: Day of Wrath). '55 Ordet (GB: The Word). '64 Gertrud.

DREYFUSS, Richard

(b. 1947). Actor. Born: New York City, USA

One of the few new American leading men to emerge in the Seventies, Richard Dreyfuss is far from the matinée idol ideal. Short and not notably good-looking, he tends to play characters whose objectionable aggression almost defies the audience to like them. His Russian-Jewish family moved to Los Angeles when he was a child; and he began his career as a stage actor in California. He had made several film appearances (including an uncredited part in *The Graduate*) when George Lucas cast him in *American Graffiti*, the film that really got his career off the ground. *Jaws* and *Close Encounters of the Third Kind* confirmed Dreyfuss as a major star. He won an Oscar for *The Goodbye Girl*.

Films: 1967 The Graduate; Valley of the Dolls. '68 The Young Runaways. '69 Hello Down There. '73 Dillinger; American Graffiti. '74 The Apprenticeship of Duddy Kravitz (CAN); The Second Coming of Suzanne. '75 Jaws; Inserts (GB). '77 Close Encounters of the Third Kind; The Goodbye Girl. '78 The Big Fix (+ co-prod). '80 The Competition; The Special Edition (of) Close Encounters of the Third Kind. '81 Whose Life Is It Anyway?

DRISCOLL, Bobby

(1936–1968). Actor. Born: Cedar Rapids, Iowa, USA

Few Hollywood child stars won through to happy adulthood. Bobby Driscoll summed up his own life: 'I

was carried on a satin cushion and then dropped into the garbage can'. He was picked out at a mass audition at MGM, and cast in a small role in a Margaret O'Brien picture, *Lost Angel*. Quickly he was earning $800 a week and being kept busy on hire to other studios. At nine he was signed for Disney's *Song of the South*; in 1947 and 1949 he won special Juvenile Academy Awards for *So Dear to My Heart* and his highly dramatic role in *The Window*; and he was a memorable Jim Hawkins in *Treasure Island*. As a teenager he found himself no longer in demand in Hollywood, and the lurid 'youth' picture *Party Crashers* failed to effect a comeback for him. He was in the news in 1961, with a jail sentence as a drug addict. Driscoll died broke and neglected in New York, at 31.

Films include: 1943 Lost Angel. '46 Song of the South; From This Day Forward; So Goes My Love (GB: Genius in the Family); OSS. '48 So Dear to My Heart. '49 The Window. '50 Treasure Island. '51 When I Grow Up. '58 Party Crashers.

DRU, Joanne

(b. 1923). Actress. Born: Joanne Letitia LaCock; Logan, West Virginia, USA

Petite and extremely pretty, Joanne Dru began as a model and made her stage debut as a showgirl in *Hold on to Your Hats*. She joined a theatrical group in Hollywood and was spotted by a studio scout, leading to her star role as an Irish girl who troublesomely marries a Jewish boy in *Abie's Irish Rose*. Dru then made her name in three of the best post-war Westerns: as Tess Millay, reconciling Dunson (John Wayne) and Matt (Montgomery Clift) in Howard Hawks' *Red River*; fetching in uniform as a cavalryman's daughter in John Ford's *She Wore a Yellow Ribbon*; and as the gypsyish, bewitching Denver, flashing her eyes at and spurning Travis (Ben Johnson) in *Wagonmaster*, also for Ford. She appeared in a less light-hearted role in Robert Rossen's *All the King's Men*, and then a series of Westerns and adventure films that failed to reward her bright start. She was married to actor-singer Dick Haymes from 1941 to 1949 and to her occasional co-star John Ireland from 1949 to 1958.

Films include: 1946 Abie's Irish Rose. '48 Red River. '49 She Wore a Yellow Ribbon;

All the King's Men. '50 Wagonmaster. '52 Return of the Texan; The Pride of St Louis. '53 Thunder Bay; Forbidden. '54 Duffy of San Quentin (GB: Men Behind Bars). '55 The Dark Avenger (GB) (USA: The Warriors). '57 Drango. '60 September Storm. '65 Sylvia.

DUFF, Howard

(b. 1917). Actor. Born: Bremerton, Washington, USA

Duff's so obviously honest good looks always gave a certain piquancy when he was cast in the more dubious roles in late Forties and Fifties thrillers. A rather bitty start to his career, as a rep and radio actor, was interrupted by the war, during which he was attached to the Armed Forces Radio Service. After the war he had a major break when he was picked to play Sam Spade in a Dashiell Hammett radio series. After directing him on stage, Jules Dassin cast him in *Brute Force*, Duff's movie debut. The producer Mark Hellinger promoted the actor's early career; after Hellinger's death Duff moved to Universal as a useful character player. Married to Ida Lupino, he played in a number of films with her, including Fritz Lang's *While the City Sleeps*.

Films include: 1947 Brute Force. '48 The Naked City. '49 Johnny Stool Pigeon; Red Canyon; Woman in Hiding. '50 Shakedown. '52 Steel Town. '54 Jennifer. '55 While the City Sleeps. '56 The Broken Star. '62 Boys' Night Out. '78 A Wedding. '79 Kramer vs Kramer.

Top, left to right: Richard Dreyfuss in Close Encounters of the Third Kind; *Bobby Driscoll in* The Window; *Joanne Dru in* She Wore a Yellow Ribbon. *Above, left to right: Howard Duff in* Johnny Stool Pigeon; *Keir Dullea in* Welcome to Blood City *(1977). Faye Dunaway in* Chinatown. *Below: Margaret Dumont and Groucho Marx in* The Big Stop. *Right: James Dunn in* A Tree Grows in Brooklyn. *Below right: Irene Dunne*

DULAC, Germaine

(1882–1942). Director/writer. Born: Charlotte Elisabeth Germaine Saisset-Schneider; Asnières, France

Germaine Dulac was one of the rare women directors of the silent period, though her claim to fame is rather as a

member of the avant-garde surrounding Louis Delluc and battling for a concept of 'pure cinema' with its own aesthetic, independent of literature and the stage. Born into a middle-class family and starting her career as a journalist with feminist inclinations, she formed a company with Marie-Louis Albert Dulac, whom she married. Her earlier films tended to be conventional and commercial. Later she was infected with the urge to make art films, which resulted in flirtations with current art '-isms' as seen in the pseudo-surrealist *La Coquille et le Clergyman* and in her best film *La Souriante Madame Beudet* with its objective visualisation of psychological states. Dulac's career effectively ended with the coming of sound; during the Thirties she worked for French newsreel companies.

Films include: 1917 Les Soeurs Ennemies; Vénus Victrix; Ames de Fous. '19 La Fête Espagnole. '20 Malencontre. '22 La Souriante Madame Beudet. '24 Le Diable dans la Ville. '27 La Coquille et le Clergyman (GB: Seashell and the Clergyman); L'Invitation au Voyage.

DULLEA, Keir

(b. 1936). Actor. Born: Cleveland, Ohio, USA

An attractive, intelligent and off-beat leading man, Keir Dullea (pronounced 'dew-lay') enjoyed gratifying success in his first two roles – as a neurotic young criminal in *The Hoodlum Priest*, and a mental hospital patient in *David and Lisa* – and inevitably found himself typecast thereafter as a brooding neurotic. Efforts to escape the mould included the leading role in *2001: A Space Odyssey* and a period of retirement, after which he re-emerged with distinction as the lead in a television film *Brave New World*. Educated at Rutgers University and San Francisco State College, he worked with Stanford Meisner, a notable Method exponent at the New York Neighborhood Playhouse, and has continued to work on stage between his screen appearances.

Films include: 1961 The Hoodlum Priest. '62 David and Lisa. '64 The Thin Red Line; Mail Order Bride (GB: West of Montana). '65 Bunny Lake Is Missing (GB). '66 Madame X. '67 The Fox. '68 2001: A Space Odyssey (GB). '69 De Sade (USA-GER). '73 The Paperback Hero. '74 Paul and Michelle (FR-GB).

DUMONT, Margaret

(1889–1965). Actress. Born: Daisy Baker; Atlanta, Georgia, USA

Although she had a stage career that stretched back to 1907, was trained for the opera and worked as a show-girl in Europe, Margaret Dumont will always be remembered as the stately socialite pursued and humiliated through seven films (from *The Cocoanuts* to *The Big Store*) by a merciless Groucho Marx. The name of the character might change: sometimes she was a widow; sometimes she was the wife of an outraged tycoon; but

always she was rich and wide open to Groucho's insults and undisguised efforts to divest her of her fortune. Groucho said that privately she could never see what was funny about it all – which enriched the joke immeasurably. A notable piece of Americana in her own right, she was the goddaughter of Joel Chandler Harris, creator of Uncle Remus, who raised her in a decorous Southern atmosphere. Aside from the Marx Brothers, she did odd stints as the butt for W. C. Fields, Jack Benny and Laurel and Hardy.

Films include: 1917 A Tale of Two Cities. '29 The Cocoanuts. '30 Animal Crackers. '33 Duck Soup. '35 A Night at the Opera; Rendezvous. '36 Anything Goes. '37 A Day at the Races. '39 The Women; At the Circus. '41 The Big Store; Never Give a Sucker an Even Break (GB: What a Man). '42 Rhythm Parade; Dancing Masters. '44 Up in Arms. '45 The Horn Blows at Midnight. '64 What a Way to Go!

DUNAWAY, Faye

(b. 1941). Actress. Born: Bascom, Florida, USA

The daughter of an army officer, Faye Dunaway studied theatre arts at the University of Boston. She successfully auditioned for the Lincoln Center Repertory Company where she stayed for three years, and was directed in *After the Fall* by Elia Kazan. She entered films in 1966 and her third movie, *Bonnie and Clyde*, made her famous overnight. Whatever is said about the film, there is no doubt about Dunaway's performance. In that bizarre ambience she beautifully conveys an essential innocence. Since then her films have been mixed. She was superb as the enigmatic, incestuous lady in *Chinatown*, enjoyed her broad Western comedy in *Little Big Man*, and vigorously impersonated Joan Crawford in *Mommie Dearest*. But there have been too many roles that anyone could play. Alfred Hitchcock might have been able to do wonders with her.

Films include: 1967 Hurry Sundown; The Happening; Bonnie and Clyde. '68 The Thomas Crown Affair; Amanti (IT-FR) (USA/GB: A Place for Lovers). '69 The Arrangement. '70 Little Big Man. '71 Doc. '73 Oklahoma Crude; The Three Musketeers; The Queen's Diamonds (PAN). '74 Chinatown; The Towering Inferno. '75 The Four Musketeers: The Revenge of Milady (PAN-SP); Three Days of the Condor. '76 Network. '78 The Eyes of Laura Mars. '79 The Champ. '81 Mommie Dearest.

DUNING, George

(b. 1908). Composer. Born: Richmond, Indiana, USA

George Duning came from a musical family. His mother taught organ and piano; his father conducted and lectured. Duning studied at the Cincinnati Conservatory of Music, played trumpet professionally, and was musical director of radio shows. In 1947 he was appointed as a composer and conductor by Columbia Pictures. He stayed until 1962, then freelanced, and worked also in television. Duning was responsible for the scores of over

one hundred films, and gained five nominations for Academy Awards for scoring dramatic pictures. Among the most notable are those for *The Dark Past*, *Jolson Sings Again*, *From Here to Eternity* and *3:10 to Yuma*.

Films include: 1947 The Corpse Came COD. '48 The Dark Past. '49 Jolson Sings Again. '50 No Sad Songs for Me. '53 From Here to Eternity. '55 The Man From Laramie; Picnic. '56 The Eddy Duchin Story. '57 3:10 to Yuma. '59 1,001 Arabian Nights. '60 Strangers When We Meet; The World of Suzie Wong (GB). '63 Toys in the Attic. '65 Dear Brigitte.

DUNN, James

(1905–1967). Actor. Born: New York City, USA

James Dunn worked on the New York stage and as an extra in the movies until he was signed up by Fox in 1931. He made an impressive start in a good film, *Bad Girl*, but his career never really took off. Dunn's pleasant, bluff, boy-next-door personality simply wasn't positive enough to impose itself on a bad movie. All too soon he was reduced to supporting Shirley Temple, and, to his credit, he did it charmingly. But he lapsed into alcoholism, emerged briefly in 1945 to win a Best Supporting Actor Oscar for *A Tree Grows in Brooklyn*, and by 1951 was unemployed and bankrupt.

Films include: 1931 Bad Girl; Over the Hill. '32 Dance Team. '33 Jimmy and Sally; Hold Me Tight; Hello Sister; Take a Chance. '34 Stand Up and Cheer; Baby Take a Bow; 365 Nights in Hollywood; Bright Eyes. '35 Bad Boy. '38 Shadows Over Shanghai. '45 A Tree Grows in Brooklyn. '57 Revolt at Fort Laramie.

DUNNE, Irene

(b. 1904). Actress. Born: Louisville, Kentucky, USA

Irene Dunne trained as an opera singer, narrowly failed a crucial audition for the New York Metropolitan, and found consolation in the musical comedy theatre, notably in the leading role of Florenz Ziegfeld's roadshow production of *Show Boat*. This brought a contract with RKO. She remained immensely popular throughout the Thirties and Forties in a wide variety of parts – in musicals like *Roberta*, and in sentimental dramas like *Back Street* and *Magnificent Obsession*. But she was best of all in screwball comedy. She gained two of her five Oscar nominations in this genre – for *Theodora Goes Wild* and *The Awful Truth*. Retiring from the movies in 1952, she was appointed by President Eisenhower as a United Nations delegate in 1957–58.

Films include: 1930 Leathernecking (GB: Present Arms). '31 Cimarron. '32 Back Street. '33 Ann Vickers; The Silver Cord. '34 Stingaree. '35 Sweet Adeline; Roberta; Magnificent Obsession. '36 Show Boat; Theodora Goes Wild. '37 The Awful Truth. '39 Love Affair; When Tomorrow Comes. '43 A Guy Named Joe. '44 The White Cliffs of Dover. '46 Anna and the King of Siam. '47 Life With Father. '48 I Remember Mama. '50 The Mudlark (GB).

Far left: Jimmy Durante in Beau James *(1957). Left: Dan Duryea in* Johnny Stool Pigeon *(1949). Above, from left to right: Deanna Durbin in* Three Smart Girls Grow Up *(1939); Shelley Duvall; Robert Duvall with Kim Darby in* True Grit; *Anna Dvorak in* Scarface

DURAS, Marguerite

(b. 1914). Writer/director. Born: Marguerite Donnadieu; Giadinh, French Indo-China

After a childhood spent in Saigon, Marguerite Duras came to France at 17, studied at the Sorbonne, worked in publishing, and was an active member of the Resistance. Her first novel appeared in 1943. She soon enjoyed international esteem. In 1959 she wrote the magnificent script for Alain Resnais' *Hiroshima Mon Amour;* her skilful playing with narrative is perfect for Resnais' delicate cinematic sensibility. Duras worked on scripts for Peter Brook and Henri Colpi, and in 1966 began to direct her own films. Rapidly and cheaply made, experimental in form and highly literary, the films have met a mixed reception. Some have found *India Song* compellingly beautiful; others think it pretentious rubbish. It may well depend on if one is interested in Art or the cinema.

Films include: 1959 Hiroshima Mon Amour (sc. only) (FR-JAP). '67 La Musica (co-dir). '69 Détruire Dit-Elle (GB: Destroy She Said). '71 Jaune le Soleil. '72 Nathalie Granger. '74 La Femme du Gange (USA: Woman of the Ganges). '75 India Song. '76 Son Nom de Venise dans Calcutta Desert; Des Journées Entières dans les Arbres (GB: Entire Days in the Trees). '77 Le Camion (GB: The Lorry; USA: The Truck).

DURBIN, Deanna

(b. 1921). Actress. Born: Edna Mae Durbin; Winnipeg, Manitoba, Canada

At 15, Deanna Durbin appeared in an MGM short with Judy Garland. The company kept Judy and let Deanna go. Universal made no such error. In film after film, beginning with *Three Smart Girls,* she sang sweetly, looked radiant, and sorted out the tangled affairs of parents and friends with an indefatigable niceness. The directors were good, the Cinderella plots more

DUNNING, George

(1920–1979). Animator. Born: Toronto, Ontario, Canada

George Dunning learned animation under Norman McLaren at the National Film Board of Canada. In 1955 he began work for UPA in New York and agreed to run their London offshoot. When this folded, Dunning stayed in England and formed his own company. His approach was eclectic, with a marked divide between his personal and commercial work. Best of the former, perhaps, was *Damon the Mower,* based on a poem by Andrew Marvell, while the great success of the full-length *Yellow Submarine,* a psychedelic adventure 'featuring' the Beatles, was crucial in keeping the British animation industry afloat. But in whatever line he worked, Dunning's films used a wide array of techniques. He was adept in glass work, cut-outs, pencil animation, and he had an engaging humour, beautifully displayed in tiny gems like *The Flying Man* and *The Apple.*

Films include: 1944 Chants Populaires No. 2: Auprès de Ma Blonde. '45 The Three Blind Mice. '48 Family Tree (co-dir). '62 The Apple (GB); The Flying Man (GB). '67 The Chair (GB). '68 Yellow Submarine (GB). '71 Moon Rock (co-dir) (GB). '73 Damon the Mower (GB).

DUPONT, E. A.

(1891–1956). Director. Born: Ewald Andreas Dupont; Zeitz, Germany

Dupont was a film critic at 20. He wrote a number of scripts, and by 1917 was directing. Of his 25 German silents, only the last, *Varieté,* is remembered now, but that film, with its dazzling lighting effects, is a classic of Expressionist cinema. Dupont made one American film, and then had a spell in England, where he began with two stylish silents, *Moulin Rouge* and *Piccadilly,* and then made an awkward transition to sound with *Atlantic.* The vivid images were still there, but the handling of dialogue laborious and the acting crude. Dupont never really came to terms with sound. He worked in the USA from 1933, with little success. A modest comeback in the Fifties saw two fine B movies, *The Scarf* and *The Steel Lady.*

Films include: 1917 Das Geheimnis des Amerika-Docks. '23 Die grüne Manuela (GB: The Green Manuela); Das alte Gesetz (GB: The Ancient Law). '25 Varieté (GB: Vaudeville). '28 Moulin Rouge (GB). '29 Piccadilly (GB). '30 Atlantic (GB); Cape Forlorn (GB); Two Worlds (GB). '31 Salto Mortale (GB: The Circus of Sin). '35 The Bishop Misbehaves (USA) (GB: The Bishop's Misadventures). '51 The Scarf (USA). '53 The Steel Lady (GB: The Treasure of Kalifa).

DURANTE, Jimmy

(1893–1980). Actor. Born: New York City, USA

Jimmy Durante began his career in show business as a Coney Island pianist. In the Twenties, teamed with Lou Clayton (dancer) and Eddie Jackson (singer), he had great success in vaudeville and night clubs, and by 1929 the trio were appearing for Ziegfeld on Broadway. With the beginning of sound Durante went into movies as a solo comedian. His was a vehement, effervescent humour, but films hardly capture the warmth and intimacy he was able to create with a live audience. However, his unflagging energy, hoarse voice and imposing nose enlivened a lot of bad films, and enhanced the joys of his few good ones. *Blondie of the Follies* and *The Man Who Came to Dinner* were worthy of Durante; in the latter he gave a superb impersonation of Harpo Marx.

Films include: 1930 Roadhouse Nights. '31 New Adventures of Get-Rich-Quick Wallingford. '32 Blondie of the Follies. '34 Palooka (GB: The Great Schnozzle). '41 The Man Who Came to Dinner. '44 Two Girls and a Sailor; Music for Millions. '48 On an Island with You. '50 The Milkman. '62 Jumbo. '63 It's a Mad, Mad, Mad, Mad World.

DVORAK, Ann

(1912–1979). Actress. Born: Anna McKim; New York City, USA

Back in 1916 Ann Dvorak was in Donald Crisp's *Ramona*. She was three years old, and billed as 'Baby Anna Lehr'. Her mother, Anna Lehr, was an actress, her father, Samuel McKim, became a film director. Ann herself returned to the studios in 1929, played bits for a while at MGM, was noticed by Howard Hughes, and given leads in *Sky Devils* and *Scarface*. Moving to Warner Brothers, she had four very successful years, but her career was hindered by clashes with the studio. She was an actress of great individuality who cannot have been easy to cast, and therein perhaps lay the trouble. Although she worked on until 1951 her later films gave her little chance.

Films include: 1916 Ramona. '30 Bright Lights; Free and Easy. '31 The Guardsman; Just a Gigolo (GB: The Dancing Partner); The Crowd Roars. '32 Sky Devils; Scarface; Three on a Match; The Strange Love of Molly Louvain. '34 Massacre. '35 G-Men. '50 A Life of Her Own.

than serviceable, and the girl irresistible. Scenes like the opening of *Mad About Music*, with Deanna carolling away at the head of her parade of schoolgirl cyclists, were among the era's cherished moments.

Films include: 1937 Three Smart Girls. '38 Mad About Music; That Certain Age. '39 First Love. '41 Nice Girl?; It Started With Eve. '43 Hers to Hold; His Butler's Sister. '44 Christmas Holiday. '45 Lady on a Train.

DURYEA, Dan

(1907–1968). Actor. Born: White Plains, New York, USA

Amateur drama at Cornell University, advertising, bit parts in the theatre, and eventually the part of Leo in *The Little Foxes* on Broadway, brought Dan Duryea in the end to Hollywood to repeat that role in the film of the play. Duryea was superb as a weak and ineffectual sadist, and went on to project a more spirited and malicious brand of villainy in three Fritz Lang movies, notably *Scarlet Street*, in Westerns like *Winchester '73*, and in sixty-odd films in all in a quarter century as a well-loved heavy. There was an occasional change of pace, like the stodgy accountant he played in *Flight of the Phoenix*, but most of the time it was villains, and it was the wry amusement with which Duryea viewed his own misdeeds that made him so enjoyable.

Films include: 1941 The Little Foxes. '43 Sahara. '44 Ministry of Fear; The Woman in the Window. '45 Scarlet Street; Along Came Jones; Valley of Decision. '49 Criss Cross. '50 Winchester '73. '51 Chicago Calling. '53 Thunder Bay. '55 Fox Fire. '64 He Rides Tall. '66 Flight of the Phoenix.

DUSE, Eleanora

(1859–1924). Actress. Born: Venice, Italy

Duse made only one movie, but no cinema history should overlook her. Sarah Bernhardt's rival as the greatest actress of her time, she was enthusiastic about the potential of the cinema, but believed that she was too old to adapt to it. In her one film, *Cenere* (Ashes) in 1916, she enters

totally into the part, is restrained and natural, and seems instinctively to understand the medium. It is said that she wanted the film withdrawn. Happily, it survives as a triumphant record of her art.

DUVALL, Robert

(b. 1931). Actor. Born: San Diego, California, USA

The son of a rear-admiral, Robert Duvall graduated in drama, served in Korea, and after demob joined the Neighborhood Players in New York. His work in an off-Broadway production of *A View from the Bridge* led to Broadway and to a film debut as the strange, kind simpleton in *To Kill a Mockingbird*. After playing heavies through the Sixties, he received an Oscar nomination for *The Godfather*, and after that he had many more varied and attractive parts. Of stocky build, balding, tough and pugnacious, Duvall has become one of the few genuinely distinguished and regularly employed character actors in Hollywood today, tending possibly to excess, but versatile enough to exude menace, authority or unease with the slightest of opportunities. His Kilgore – the gung-ho officer of the 'air cav' – in *Apocalypse Now* is an awesome study of misguided, Satanic enthusiasm and won him another Oscar nomination.

Films include: 1962 To Kill a Mockingbird. '69 True Grit; The Rain People. '70 THX 1138. '72 The Great Northfield Minnesota Raid; The Godfather. '74 The Conversation; The Godfather, Part II. '75 The Killer Elite. '76 The Eagle Has Landed (GB). '79 Apocalypse Now. '81 True Confessions.

DUVALL, Shelley

(b. 1949). Actress. Born: Houston, Texas, USA

Shelley Duvall caught Robert Altman's eye when he came to Houston to film *Brewster McCloud*. Altman tested her, put her in the film, and she stayed to become a leading member of his stock company. Tall and thin, with large eyes and an air of sad surprise, she became an expert portrayer of lost, vacuous ladies whose lives are in

a dreadful tangle. Her best work has been for Altman. In *Thieves Like Us* she was wonderfully touching and vulnerable, and *Three Women* deservedly gained her the Best Actress Award at Cannes. She was seemingly made for the part of Olive Oyl, the gangling girlfriend of *Popeye*, in Altman's flesh-and-blood film about the famous cartoon characters.

Films include: 1970 Brewster McCloud. '71 McCabe and Mrs Miller. '74 Thieves Like Us. '75 Nashville. '76 Buffalo Bill and the Indians . . . or Sitting Bull's History Lesson. '77 Three Women; Annie Hall. '80 The Shining (GB); Popeye. '81 Time Bandits.

DUVIVIER, Julien

(1896–1967). Director. Born: Lille, France

Julien Duvivier was directing from 1919 until his death, in a car accident, in 1967. As a young assistant at Gaumont he worked with Louis Feuillade and Marcel L'Herbier, wrote scripts, and directed some twenty silents, all of which await rediscovery. By the later Thirties Duvivier was reckoned to be a great director. This is the period in which, with the actor Jean Gabin usually starring, he made films like *La Bandéra* and *Pépé-le-Moko*, atmospheric, beautifully scripted and photographed, and played by a collection of perhaps the finest screen actors of all time. His wartime stay in America also yielded treasures, especially the Expressionist *Flesh and Fantasy*. His later work was openly commercial, and modern critics tend to find him lacking in individuality. But at the very least, he was a superb co-ordinator of the talents of others.

Films include: 1919 Haceldama/Le Prix du Sang. '32 Poil de Carotte; La Tête d'un Homme. '35 La Bandéra (USA: Escape From Yesterday). '36 La Belle Equipe (USA: They Were Five); Le Golem (USA: The Golem; GB: The Legend of Prague); Pépé-le-Moko. '37 Un Carnet de Bal (USA: Christine). '43 Flesh and Fantasy (USA). '48 Anna Karenina (GB). '50 Black Jack (FR-USA) (USA: Captain Blackjack). '52 Il Piccolo Mondo di Don Camillo (IT-FR) (USA/GB: The Little World of Don Camillo). '58 La Femme et le Pantin (FR-IT) (USA: The Female; GB: A Woman Like Satan). '60 Boulevard.

DWAN, Allan

(1885–1981). Director. Born: Joseph Aloysius Dwan; Toronto, Ontario, Canada

Allan Dwan was 'The Last Pioneer', the title of Peter Bogdanovich's affectionate study of his career. Between 1911 and 1958 he directed over 400 films, and never lost his visual sense, his humour and his love of action. In 1909 he was working for a Chicago illumination company, was sent to talk business with Essanay, and found that his life was changed. He stayed, sold a few stories, and edited. In 1911 he was pitchforked into direction (now for the American Film Company), learned the basics from his actors, and never looked back. His technical wizardry was outstanding – it was Dwan, not D. W. Griffith, who devised the breathtaking crane shot in *Intolerance* (1916). By then Dwan was with Triangle, where he began the association with Douglas Fairbanks which produced his most famous films, like *Robin Hood* and *The Iron Mask*. He directed Mary Pickford, too, and made two of the best Gloria Swanson movies in *Zaza* and *Manhandled*. Dwan wasn't much impressed by sound, but carried on, often with poor material. His later career had its moments – *Suez* in the Thirties, a fine war film in *The Sands of Iwo Jima*, and some excellent Fifties Westerns. Dwan simply couldn't stop. As he said, 'Directing movies – I'd do it free, I like it that well'.

Films include: 1916 Manhattan Madness; The Half-Breed. '17 A Modern Musketeer. '18 Bound in Morocco. '19 The Luck of the Irish. '20 The Forbidden Thing. '21 A Perfect Crime. '23 Zaza; Robin Hood; While Paris Sleeps. '24 A Society Scandal; Manhandled. '29 The Iron Mask. '37 One Mile From Heaven; Heidi. '38 Suez. '39 The Three Musketeers. '47 Calendar Girl. '49 The Sands of Iwo Jima. '52 I Dream of Jeannie. '57 The Restless Breed.

Below right: a man named Clint Eastwood in Two Mules for Sister Sara. Bottom, from left to right: Buddy Ebsen with Lois Nettleton in Mail Order Bride (1963); Nelson Eddy in Maytime; Richard Egan in the war film The Hunters; Samantha Eggar was kidnapped by a butterfly enthusiast in The Collector

EASTMAN, George

(1854–1932). Industrialist. Born: Waterville, New York, USA

Eastman brought photography to the masses. In 1879 he devised a way of commercially manufacturing a dry photographic plate. But for ordinary people who wanted to take pictures with a minimum of fuss and mess, he really made life simpler by sensitizing a flexible roll of paper, loading it into a hand-holdable camera and providing a developing and printing service. He called the device the Kodak camera. In 1889 he was able to go one step further by introducing emulsion-coated celluloid roll film, the concept on which every frame of every movie ever made is based. Eastman gave much of his money away, but the Eastman Kodak Company went on to become, and remains, a major international force in the development and marketing of film and photographic equipment.

EASTWOOD, Clint

(b. 1930). Actor/director/producer. Born: San Francisco, California, USA

Clint Eastwood achieved megastar status in the Sixties after appearing in Sergio Leone's Italian 'Dollars' trilogy – A Fistful of Dollars, For a Few Dollars More, The Good, the Bad and the Ugly – in which he played the Man With No Name, an inscrutable, monosyllabic, poncho-clad, cheroot-smoking bounty hunter and a violent new anti-hero. From a poor family hit by the Depression, Eastwood joined the army after struggling to earn a living in various manual jobs. He became an army swimming instructor and on leaving the services took a course in business administration – a discipline that has stood him in good stead throughout his career. He entered films by chance, having been offered a screen test by Universal on the strength of an introduction from a friend working at the studio. His looks carried him through it – tall, lean, blue-eyed, with a resolute jawline – and he appeared as an extra in over a dozen Universal films. His break came when he was cast in the CBS television series Rawhide. But in 1961 he was weary of his stereotyped fresh-faced cowboy role of Rowdy Yates and made his feelings known, demanding to direct episodes of the series. He soon left for Europe where he and Leone began their legendary partnership. More Westerns followed and in 1968 Eastwood teamed up with director Don Siegel for Coogan's Bluff, the first in a controversial pair of crime thrillers they made together featuring the star as a vicious, Waspish cop. As the soft-spoken Harry Callahan in Dirty Harry, Magnum Force and The Enforcer, Eastwood reached new levels of screen violence – and became the biggest star in America. He had already begun to direct, successfully following the pattern of Leone and Siegel with his own 'spaghetti' Western-spoof (High Plains Drifter) and action thriller (The Gauntlet), produced by his own company Malpaso. Bronco Billy is his one (unaccountable) failure to date. Eastwood's acting roles have taken a step towards maturer characterizations and a softening of the famous steely gaze in comedies like Every Which Way But Loose. His separation from his wife coincided with a romance with his leading lady Sondra Locke. Clint is the greatest of modern superstars, and peerless in the field of actor-director-producer.

Films include: 1955 Revenge of the Creature: Francis in the Navy. '64 Per un Pugno di Dollari (IT-GER-SP) (USA/GB: A Fistful of Dollars). '66 Per Qualche Dollaro in Più (IT-GER-SP) (USA/GB: For a Few Dollars More). '67 Il Buono, il Brutto, il Cattivo (IT-GER-SP) (USA/GB: The Good, the Bad and the Ugly). '68 Hang 'em High; Coogan's Bluff; Where Eagles Dare (GB). '69 Paint Your Wagon. '70 Two Mules for Sister Sara; Kelly's Heroes (USA-YUG). '71 The Beguiled; Play Misty For Me (+dir); Dirty Harry. '73 High Plains Drifter (+dir); Breezy (dir. only); Magnum Force. '75 The Eiger Sanction (+dir). '76 The Outlaw Josey Wales (+dir); The Enforcer. '77 The Gauntlet (+dir). '78 Every Which Way But Loose. '79 Escape From Alcatraz. '80 Bronco Billy (+dir); Any Which Way You Can. '82 Firefox (+dir).

EBSEN, Buddy

(b. 1908). Actor. Born: Christian Rudolph Ebsen; Belleville, Illinois, USA

Tall and gangling, with the face of a backwoodsman from Tennessee, Buddy Ebsen was a soda jerk at Penn Station in New York (and a trained dancer) when somehow he caught the eye of Florenz Ziegfeld. From

chorus boy he worked up to vaudeville and Broadway success, often in a double-act with his sister Vilma. They appeared together in *Broadway Melody of 1936*, and Buddy's eccentric dancing and easygoing rustic good nature were seen in a number of Thirties films and occasionally thereafter. He was a great hit in the *Beverly Hillbillies* television series, and was still hard at work in his Seventies.

Films include: 1935 Broadway Melody of 1936. '36 Captain January; Banjo on My Knee. '38 The Girl of the Golden West; Yellow Jack; My Lucky Star. '39 Four Girls in White. '55 Davy Crockett, King of the Wild Frontier. '56 Attack! '61 Breakfast at Tiffany's.

EDDY, Nelson

(1901–1967). Singer/actor. Born: Providence, Rhode Island, USA

Nelson Eddy sang with the Philadelphia Civic Opera, went to New York for Berg's *Wozzeck*, and was promptly whisked off to Hollywood. From 1935 to 1942 he and Jeanette MacDonald starred in a series of MGM operettas which were sensationally successful at the box-office. They made few demands on Eddy's acting ability. Changing fashions after the war took away the team's audience, and Eddy went back, with some success, to the stage and the concert platform.

Films include: 1933 Broadway to Hollywood (GB: Ring Up the Curtain). '35 Naughty Marietta. '36 Rose Marie. '37 Maytime; Rosalie. '40 New Moon; Bitter Sweet. '41 The Chocolate Soldier. '42 I Married an Angel. '43 The Phantom of the Opera.

EDENS, Roger

(1906–1970). Composer/producer. Born: Hillsboro, Texas, USA

In the early Thirties Roger Edens was working as accompanist and vocal arranger for singer Ethel Merman. He went to Hollywood in 1933 to supervise her material for *Kid Millions*, and went on to MGM. From 1936 to 1953, in association with Arthur Freed, he was composer, arranger, and eventually producer on a number of the company's musicals, winning Academy Awards for his part in scoring *Easter Parade*, *On the Town*, and *Annie Get Your Gun*. Edens produced other musicals after his MGM days. The last was *Hello, Dolly!* in 1969. He then went to New York to coach Katharine Hepburn for her songs in *Coco*, but died the following year.

Films include: 1937 Broadway Melody of 1938 (mus. arr). '38 Listen Darling (orchestrator). '46 Ziegfeld Follies (mus. assoc). '48 Easter Parade (assoc. prod; + co-orchestrator/mus. arr). '49 Take Me Out to the Ball Game (assoc. prod; + co-mus; + co-lyr); On the Town (assoc. prod; + co-orchestrator/mus. arr). '50 Annie Get Your Gun (assoc. prod; + co-orchestrator/mus. arr). '54 Deep in My Heart (prod). '57 Funny Face (prod; + add. co-mus; + add. co-lyr). '69 Hello, Dolly! (assoc. prod).

EDESON, Arthur

(1891–1970). Cinematographer. Born: New York City, USA

Arthur Edeson entered the film industry with the Eclair Company in 1911, working his way up from actor to photographer. He then joined Douglas Fairbanks, for whom in such films as *The Thief of Bagdad* he created wonderful fantastic images in the camera. Before that, in 1918, he had been a founder of the American Society of Cinematographers. When sound came, Edeson was among the first to work on location with the new equipment (on *In Old Arizona*, 1928). In the Thirties, first at Universal, Edeson did his finest work. The atmospheric gloom of *Frankenstein*, the sad greys of *All Quiet on the Western Front*, and a little later the harsh black and white of *The Maltese Falcon*, were all Edeson. Think of a good-looking movie of the period, and it's even money that Arthur Edeson was around.

Films include: 1914 The Dollar Mark. '21 The Three Musketeers. '24 The Thief of Bagdad. '25 The Lost World (co-photo). '30 All Quiet on the Western Front (co-photo). '31 Frankenstein. '35 Mutiny on the Bounty. '40 They Drive by Night. '41 Sergeant York (battle sequences only); The Maltese Falcon. '42 Casablanca.

EDISON, Thomas Alva

(1847–1931). Inventor. Born: Milan, Ohio, USA

The man who invented the incandescent electric light bulb in 1879 made it possible for the cinema to exist today. He developed the motion picture camera, improved on the designs for the first projectors, built the first movie studio (the 'Black Maria' at Orange, New Jersey), and experimented with the synchronization of phonograph records with film. Much of the practical work in these developments was done by Edison's gifted assistant, W. K. L. Dickson. In 1894 the first Kinetoscope (peepshow) parlours opened. The first public showing in America of moving pictures on a screen – the Vitascope – came on April 23, 1896. Edison retained patents on all his machines until in 1917 antitrust action dissolved his monopoly. In the meantime, independent companies had begun filming in the West to escape the clutches of the Motion Picture Patents Company, the group licensed by Edison to use his equipment. These restrictions imposed by Edison hence led directly to the birth of Hollywood as the film centre. The Edison Company itself, which in 1903 had made *The Great Train Robbery*, the first significant story-film, abandoned film-making in 1917.

EDWARDS, Blake

(b. 1922). Director/producer/writer. Born: William Blake McEdwards; Tulsa, Oklahoma, USA

The grandson of silent director J. Gordon Edwards, and son of production manager Jack McEdwards, Blake Edwards grew up in Hollywood. In the Forties he was a minor actor. From 1952 on he flourished as a writer with a series of excellent scripts for director Richard Quine, and in 1955 turned to direction himself. For a while Edwards showed enormous promise, with a lively and varied output; his films included a taut thriller in *Experiment in Terror*, and a bleak study of alcoholism in *Days of Wine and Roses*. With *The Pink Panther* and its offspring the rot set in, with Edwards providing a broad cartoon setting for the antics of Peter Sellers. In fairness to Edwards, he has complained much and bitterly of studio interference with his projects. That may be so, but his later work, with the possible exception of *Victor/Victoria*, has not been kindly noticed. He is married to actress Julie Andrews.

Films as director include: 1948 Panhandle (co-prod; + co-sc; + act. only). '53 All Ashore (co-sc. only). '59 Operation Petticoat. '61 Breakfast at Tiffany's. '62 Experiment in Terror (GB: The Grip of Fear); Days of Wine and Roses. '63 The Pink Panther. '64 A Shot in the Dark (USA-GB). '65 The Great Race. '70 Darling Lili. '79 '10'. '81 S.O.B. '82 Victor/Victoria (GB).

EGAN, Richard

(b. 1921). Actor. Born: San Francisco, California, USA

A product of university theatre, Richard Egan studied and taught drama at various Western colleges, and moved on to Hollywood in 1949. Dark and rugged in appearance, he gradually worked up from bits to significant parts, mainly in action pictures, and some leads, notably in *The 300 Spartans*. But Egan lacked range, and his career petered out. Since the late Sixties he has concentrated on television and the stage.

Films include: 1950 The Damned Don't Cry. '51 Up Front. '52 The Devil Makes Three; One Minute to Zero. '53 Split Second; The Glory Brigade. '55 The View From Pompey's Head (GB: Secret Interlude). '57 Slaughter on 10th Avenue. '58 The Hunters. '62 The 300 Spartans.

EGGAR, Samantha

(b. 1939). Actress. Born: Victoria Eggar; Hampstead, London, England

Samantha Eggar was playing Olivia in *Twelfth Night* at the Royal Court Theatre in London when she was spotted by film-producer Betty Box and cast in the film *The Wild and the Willing*. Four years later, in William Wyler's *The Collector*, she attracted international attention, and, inevitably, moved to America. Fair and attractive, and very much a product of the Sixties, she appeared in fewer movies as the years went by, and their quality dropped (with *The Molly Maguires* a notable exception). She has lately tended to work in multinational productions of dubious merit.

Films include: 1962 The Wild and the Willing. '64 Psyche 59. '65 The Collector (GB-USA). '66 Walk, Don't Run (USA). '67 Doctor Dolittle. '70 The Molly Maguires (USA); The Walking Stick. '71 Light at the Edge of the World (USA-SP-LICHTENSTEIN). '77 Why Shoot the Teacher? (CAN); Welcome to Blood City (GB-CAN). '79 The Brood (CAN). '80 The Exterminator (USA).

EGGELING, Viking

(1880–1925). Director. Born: Lund, Sweden

Viking Eggeling left Sweden at 17 for the artistic circles of Paris and Zürich. In 1918 he began a collaboration with the German painter Hans Richter. They used abstract picture strips to study the essence of rhythm in painting, and this led them to experiment with abstract film. Eggeling went on alone to Berlin to work on his *Horizontal-Vertical Orchestra*, based on scroll paintings. Eggeling never showed this film, which he and a new partner, Erna Niemayer, had finished by 1923, but they then made *Diagonal Symphonie*, shown in 1925 a few days after Eggeling's death. This was a key work in abstract cinema.

Films: 1923 Horizontal-Vertical Orchestra. '25 Diagonal Symphonie.

EISENSTEIN, Sergei Mikhailovich

(1898–1948). Director. Born: Riga, Latvia

From 1915 to 1917 Sergei Eisenstein studied engineering and architecture at the Petrograd Institute of Civil Engineering. On the outbreak of the Civil War he joined, and fought with, the Red Army, and helped to produce posters for the agit-prop military trains. After the war, he joined the Moscow Proletkult Theatre as a designer, and moved into stage direction. Eisenstein left to study theatre under Meyerhold, and returned to the Proletkult to direct a stage production which included a film insert, *Glumov's Diary*, his first film work. Proletkult then assisted him with his first feature, *Strike*. Later that year came *Battleship Potemkin*, enthusiastically welcomed at home and abroad, but even as early as this Eisenstein was not popular with the Soviet authorities, the rhythmical montage and the unfamiliar imagery incurring the charge of formalism, a charge which was to haunt the director's whole career. In the 23 years he directed, Eisenstein was able to complete only seven films. His American journey to work for Paramount produced nothing; a film project in Mexico was aborted, leaving only some inspired fragments to be assembled by other hands. Back in the USSR, film after film was abandoned or suppressed, and the director was forced publicly to confess his errors. In the years of inactivity he wrote theoretical works on film, and taught. In the West he was always honoured, and frequently *Battleship Potemkin* was voted the best film of all time. But in his own country only *Alexander Nevsky* and the first part of *Ivan the Terrible* were welcomed, their patriotic themes being acceptable to the politics of the day. He died at his desk, from a heart attack, aged just 50.

Films include: 1923 Kinodnevik Glumova (short) (Glumov's Diary). '25 Stachka (+co-sc;+ed) (GB: Strike); Bronenosets Potemkin (+co-sc;+ed) (USA/GB: Battleship Potemkin). '27 Oktyabr (co-dir;+co-sc;+ed) (USA: Ten Days That Shook the World; GB: October). '28 Staroye i Novoye/Generalnaya Liniya (co-dir;+co-sc;+co-ed) (GB: The Old and the New/The General Line). '31 Que Viva Mexico! (unfinished) (co-dir; +co-sc) (USA). '37 Bezhin Lug (unfinished) (+co-sc) (GB: Bezhin Meadow). '38 Aleksandr Nevskii (co-dir; +co-sc; +ed; +set des; +cost) (GB: Alexander Nevsky). '44 Ivan Grozny (+sc;+ed;+set des;+cost) (GB: Ivan the Terrible). '46 Ivan Grozny II: Boyarskii Zagovar (+sc;+ed;+set des;+cost) (GB: Ivan the Terrible, Part II: The Boyars' Plot).

EISLER, Hanns

(1898–1962). Composer. Born: Leipzig, Germany

Eisler studied in Vienna under the Austrian modernist composer Arnold Schönberg and in the Twenties began to compose music for films and plays, working with other left-wing artists like Bertolt Brecht on propaganda pieces and anti-fascist songs. He fled from the Nazis in 1933 and worked in Holland, England, France and the USSR, eventually settling for a while in the USA. There he inevitably fell foul of HUAC and returned to East Germany, whose national anthem he composed. Eisler believed music should serve a social – not to say socialist – function, and to this end experimented in his film work with matching sound and vision in a number of innovative ways, cleverly using strings, woodwind and jazz styles. Among the films he scored were Joris Ivens' silent *Rain* (adding music to it in 1940), Fritz Lang's *Hangmen Also Die!* (reteaming him with its co-scriptwriter, Brecht) and Alain Resnais' film on the Nazi concentration camps, *Night and Fog*.

Films include: 1931 Niemandsland (GER) (GB: War Is Hell/No Man's Land); Kühle Wampe (GER) (GB: Whither Germany?). '33 Le Grand Jeu (FR) (GB: The Great Game). '36 La Vie Est à Nous (song only) (FR) (USA: People of France). '40 Regen (short made in 1929) (HOLL) (USA/GB: Rain). '43 Hangmen Also Die! (USA). '45 The Spanish Main (USA). '46 The Woman on the Beach (USA). '49 Unser täglich Brot (E. GER) (USA/GB: Our Daily Bread). '55 Nuit et Brouillard (short) (USA/GB: Night and Fog). '63 Unbändiges Spanien (E. GER).

EKBERG, Anita

(b. 1931). Actress. Born: Malmö, Sweden

Her most vital statistics were a 39-23-37 figure, a goddess-like face and a stream of blonde hair. But Ekberg was also a capable actress with a lively sense of humour, one willing to parody the manufactured sex-symbol image she quickly attained in the Fifties. She did so most effectively as Sylvia – an empty-headed Hollywood bombshell arriving in Rome – in Federico Fellini's *La Dolce Vita*; her wild dance in that film is the stuff that erotic dreams are made of. As Miss Sweden she came to America in 1951 to take part in the Miss Universe contest. Modelling – usually in provocative poses – and nightclub work followed, and Bob Hope took 'the Iceberg' to Greenland to entertain the troops. Early movies included a couple of Jerry Lewis–Dean Martin comedies and *War and Peace*, the latter made in Italy where she became a star. Her career seems to have dwindled as her weight has grown. She has been married to two actors, Anthony Steel and Friedrich Van Nutter.

Films include: 1953 The Golden Blade (USA). '55 Artists and Models (USA). '56 War and Peace (USA). '57 Interpol (GB). '59 La Dolce Vita (IT). '62 Boccaccio '70 (IT-FR). '63 Four for Texas (USA). '66 The Alphabet Murders (GB). '67 Woman Times Seven (USA-FR). '69 If It's Tuesday, This Must Be Belgium (USA). '79 Suor Omicidi (IT) (GB: Killer Nun).

EKLAND, Britt

(b. 1942). Actress. Born: Britt-Marie Eklund; Stockholm, Sweden

A sharp-eyed, glamorous Scandinavian, Britt Ekland was enticingly naive as the first girl to do a striptease in *The Night They Raided Minsky's* and tantalizingly sexy on the phone to Michael Caine in *Get Carter*, but her intermittent film career has failed to sustain as much public interest as her private life. Drama school in Sweden was followed by work with a travelling theatre company and then films. She became a star first in Italy and was famously married to Peter Sellers from 1964 to 1968 (a later affair with rock star Rod Stewart ended acrimoniously in 1977 and she sued him for £15 million). Within the conventional blonde stereotype she ranges from spiteful to appealing and, though good roles have been scarce, she was a popular 'Bond girl' in *The Man With the Golden Gun* in 1974. Britt made her stage debut in *Mate* in 1978 and has done much television work.

Left: a portrait of the great Russian director Sergei M. Eisenstein. Bottom left: Jack Elam. Bottom: Denholm Elliott. Below: Anita Ekberg with Ursula Andress in Four for Texas, *a Western comedy about rival saloon owners. Right: Britt Ekland as the local belle whom an unsuccessful bullfighter must seduce to get work in* The Bobo

Films include: 1963 Kort är Sommaren (SWED); Il Commandante (IT). **'66** Caccia alla Volpe (IT) (USA/GB: After the Fox). **'67** The Bobo (GB). **'68** The Night They Raided Minsky's (USA) (GB: The Night They Invented Striptease). **'70** I Cannibali (IT) (GB: The Cannibals). **'71** Get Carter (GB). **'72** Asylum (GB). **'74** The Wicker Man (GB); The Man With the Golden Gun (GB). **'75** Royal Flash (GB). **'78** Casanova and Co (A-IT-FR-GER) (GB: The Rise and Rise of Casanova); King Solomon's Treasure (CAN). **'80** The Monster Club (GB).

ELAM, Jack

(b. 1916). Actor. Born: Phoenix, Arizona, USA

Few Westerns of the Fifties and Sixties could survive without giving a role to Jack Elam as a particularly vicious thug. Gaunt, cruel-looking, with an evil, disfigured (and sightless) left eye, Elam cornered the market in sadistic sidekicks and stupid killers, and as such became one of Hollywood's most popular character actors. He was originally an accountant with Stan-

dard Oil of California and did auditing for hotels and film companies. Breaking into movies in 1950 with a part in the violent *One Way Street*, he followed it with seventy-odd films in seven years, most of them top-notch Westerns and crime dramas. In the Sixties he played more sympathetic roles in television series like *Cheyenne, 77 Sunset Strip* and *Temple Houston*, and began to send up his old image in 'spaghetti' and comedy Westerns. He continues to arrange money for independent film companies as well as act.

Films include: 1950 One Way Street. **'52** Rancho Notorious. **'54** The Far Country; Vera Cruz. **'55** Artists and Models; Kiss Me Deadly; The Man From Laramie. **'57** Gunfight at the OK Corral. **'63** Four for Texas. **'68** C'Era una Volta il West (IT) (USA/GB: Once Upon a Time in the West). **'69** Support Your Local Sheriff. **'70** Rio Lobo. **'73** Pat Garrett and Billy the Kid.

ELLIOTT, Denholm

(b. 1922. Actor. Born: London, England

Round-faced, plummy-voiced and exuding a boozy, supercilious charm, Denholm Elliott excels as seedy, tweedy upper-class professionals or scoundrels. Thus he was superb as the Oxbridge conman selecting a public-school tie for his working-class protégé (Alan Bates) in *Nothing But the Best*. He generally brings a satirical bite to such roles, but can play them straight (as an academic in *Raiders of the Lost Ark*) or with rancour (as the 'other man' in *Bad Timing*); consequently he is one of Britain's busiest and most distinguished actors. Educated at Malvern College, he was studying at RADA when war broke out. He joined the RAF, was captured in action and held as a POW in

Germany until 1945. Resuming his stage career, he made his debut in repertory and quickly graduated to the West End, Broadway and a 15-year film contract with Alexander Korda. His most notable early role was as one of the corvette lieutenants in *The Cruel Sea*.

Films include: 1949 Dear Mr Prohack. **'53** The Cruel Sea; The Heart of the Matter. **'64** Nothing But the Best. **'65** King Rat (USA). **'66** Alfie. **'68** Here We Go Round the Mulberry Bush. **'74** The Apprenticeship of Duddy Kravitz (CAN). **'77** A Bridge Too Far (USA). **'79** Saint Jack (USA). **'80** Bad Timing. **'81** Raiders of the Lost Ark (USA). **'82** The Missionary.

ELTON, Arthur

(1906–1972). Documentary producer/director. Born: London, England

A leading light of the British documentary movement in the Thirties and Forties, Elton began as a scriptwriter on features at Gainsborough in 1927 after graduating from Cambridge. The following year he went to Berlin as the company's German representative, and in 1929 joined John Grierson's Empire Marketing Board Film Unit, subsequently directing his first film, *Shadow of the Mountain*, in 1931. His *Housing Problems*, co-directed with Edgar Anstey, was one of the most powerful documentaries of this era, adventurous in its use of interviews with slum-dwellers and brave in its condemnation of their plight. It was Grierson's favourite among the films made by his recruits. During the war Elton was film-production supervisor at the Ministry of Information, and later film consultant for oil-companies and the Danish government. He was additionally a governor of the British Film Institute and a president of the

Scientific Film Association. He was knighted in 1960.

Films include: 1931 Shadow of the Mountain. **'32** Upstream. **'33** Industrial Britain (co-dir). **'35** Housing Problems (co-dir). **'38** Dawn of Iran (prod. only). **'40** Protection of Fruit (prod. only); Air Screw (prod. only). **'44** Two Fathers (prod. only).

ELVEY, Maurice

(1887–1967). Director. Born: William Seward Folkard; Darlington, Co. Durham, England

Elvey made over 300 features and many shorts and, though they reveal little ambition or personal style, that is a daunting feat unsurpassed in British film history. He was a hotel pageboy at the age of nine, and in 1905 made his stage debut playing the king in *Dick Whittington*. He quickly became a director in the theatre and in 1913 began to film documentaries and historical biopics. With short spells in Europe and Hollywood, he continued to direct until 1957. His silent work consisted mostly of popular adaptations – *Dombey and Son, The Elusive Pimpernel, The Hound of the Baskervilles*. His 1927 version of *Hindle Wakes* enlivened the old favourite about a mill-girl's romance; *Sally in Our Alley* set Gracie Fields on the road to stardom; and *The Gentle Sex*, co-directed with Leslie Howard, was a moving study of women soldiers during World War II. Elvey was at one time married to actress Isobel Elsom.

Films include: 1917 Dombey and Son. **'20** At the Villa Rose; The Elusive Pimpernel. **'21** The Hound of the Baskervilles. **'23** The Wandering Jew. **'27** Hindle Wakes. **'29** High Treason. **'31** Sally in Our Alley. **'32** The Lodger (USA: The Phantom Fiend). **'43** The Gentle Sex (co-dir). **'46** Beware of Pity. **'56** Dry Rot.

EMERSON, John

(1874–1956). Director/
screenwriter/producer/actor. Born:
Sandusky, Ohio, USA

John Emerson was the husband of
Anita Loos. If that sounds like a
feminist backlash then it is probably
justified, because Emerson took the
lion's share of the financial rewards
and at least half the credit for many of
the sharp and witty screen satires
written by his devoted and more talented wife. The son of an Episcopalian
minister, he was educated at the universities of Heidelberg and Chicago
and began his acting career in New
York in 1904, subsequently managing
and directing for the theatre. In 1912
he began writing screenplays and
appearing in films, directing from
1915 under D. W. Griffith at Triangle.
He was not one of Griffith's more
notable protégés, but he was responsible for elevating Loos from a one-
reeler scenarist to pre-eminent
screenwriter, giving her the vital
chance to write a feature script on a
Douglas Fairbanks film, *His Picture in
the Papers*. Emerson and Loos were
married in 1919. They collaborated
on many scripts together, Emerson
eventually giving up directing to write
and produce. He spent the last 18
years of his life confined to a hospital
bed.

Films include: 1915 Ghosts (co-dir); In Old
Heidelberg (dir; + sc). '16 His Picture in the
Papers (dir); Macbeth (dir); The Americano
(dir; + sc). '17 Wild and Woolly (dir). '22
Polly of the Follies (dir; + co-sc). '28 Gentle-
men Prefer Blondes (co-sc). '31 The
Struggle (co-sc). '36 San Francisco (prod.
only).

ENDFIELD, Cy

(b. 1914). Director/screenwriter.
Born: Cyril Raker Endfield;
Scranton, Pennsylvania, USA

Yale-educated Cy Endfield quickly
found his way into the New York
theatre as a director and choreographer of musicals. He also taught
drama. In 1946, following some documentary shorts for MGM, he directed
his first movie, *Gentleman Joe Palooka*.

But his liberal views got him onto the
Hollywood blacklist and in 1950 he
came to Britain to continue his career,
at first working under a pseudonym.
Since then he has proved himself one
of those eclectic, highly cultured directors who seem content with a stop-
go film career. *The Sound of Fury* is a
powerful, socially concerned indictment of mob-rule. *Hell Drivers* is a
tough and unusual British thriller
about lorry drivers starring Stanley
Baker, with whom Endfield formed a
production company in the Sixties. Its
finest achievement was *Zulu*, which
shows Endfield's social concern transposed into an interest in imperialism
and African history.

Films include: 1946 Gentleman Joe Palooka
(USA). '50 The Underworld Story (USA);
The Sound of Fury (USA). '57 Hell Drivers
(GB). '58 Sea Fury (GB). '63 Zulu (GB). '64
Hide and Seek (GB). '65 Sands of the
Kalahari (GB). '69 De Sade (co-dir) (USA-
GER). '72 Universal Soldier (GB). '79 Zulu
Dawn (USA-HOLL).

ENRIGHT, Ray

(1896–1965). Director. Born:
Anderson, Indiana, USA

Ray Enright decided to give up his job
on the *Los Angeles Times* and move
over to the up-and-coming movie
industry. He began by working for
Mack Sennett, initially as a cutter and
gagman and eventually as supervising editor, with an interval between
while he fought with the American
Expeditionary Force in France in
World War I. In 1927 he signed for
Warner Brothers as a director,
making many wisecracking comedies
for them during the Thirties. He
stayed with them until 1941 and
spent the remainder of his career
working on Westerns for various
studios, including films like the interesting *Return of the Bad Men* with
Randolph Scott and Robert Ryan
which he made for RKO.

Films include: 1927 Tracked by the Police;
Jaws of Steel. '30 Dancing Sweeties. '33 The
Silk Express. '36 Miss Pacific Fleet. '38 Gold
Diggers in Paris (GB: The Gay Impostors).
'39 Naughty But Nice. '41 Bad Men of
Missouri. '47 Trail Street. '48 Return of the
Bad Men.

EPSTEIN, Jean

(1897–1953). Director/theorist/
pioneer. Born: Warsaw, Poland

He began by studying to be a doctor,
but Epstein soon realized that he was
far more interested in movies than
medicine. The son of a French father
and Polish mother, he had already
had books of his poetry published by
the early Twenties. He went on to
become one of the giants of the French
avant-garde and a leading film theorist.
In the mid-Twenties he was experimenting in fantasy and narrative
films – frequently collaborating on the
scripts with his sister Marie. He eventually devoted himself to directing
documentaries and realistic films
and these became known collectively
as 'Seascapes' because they mainly
centred around the sea and coast of
Brittany.

Films include: 1922 Pasteur. '23 La Mon-
tagne Infidèle (doc); L'Auberge Rouge. '25
Les Aventures de Robert Macaire. '26 Au
Pays de George Sand (short). '27 La Glace à
Trois Faces. '28 La Chute de la Maison
Usher (GB: The Fall of the House of Usher).
'32 L'Or des Mers. '34 Chanson d'Armor.
'37 Vive la Vie.

*Top left: David Essex as an ill-fated
rock performer in Stardust. Above:
Edith Evans puts her mark on Tom
Jones. Top right: the popular Pimple –
Fred Evans. Right: Tom Ewell and
Rita Moreno get to know each other in
The Lieutenant Wore Skirts, a story
about a scriptwriter who tries to enlist
but is rejected on medical grounds*

ESSEX, David

(b. 1947). Singer/actor/composer.
Born: David Albert Cook; Plaistow,
London, England

In *That'll Be the Day* and *Stardust*
David Essex plays a singer who climbs
his way up from near-poverty to
superstardom, only to suffer eventual
disintegration from the pressures of
such adulation. In reality, only the
beginning of this story is true. After a
childhood spent in council institutions, Essex found an outlet for his
energies when he learned to play the
drums and began to appear with a trio
in pubs on Saturday nights. He then
joined a band, The Everons, before
going solo. A spell in rep followed
before he landed the role of Jesus
Christ in the West End production of
Godspell, and it was his two years in

this musical that led to his being cast as the lead in *That'll Be the Day*. He continues to work as a recording artist while still pursuing his stage and film careers. He was the original Che Guevara in the musical *Evita*, and he has also starred in *Silver Dream Racer* as a motorbike fanatic – a film in which he tackled some of his own stunts as well as composing the score.

Films: 1971 Assault. '72 All Coppers Are. . . . '73 That'll Be the Day. '74 Stardust. '80 Silver Dream Racer (+mus).

ETAIX, Pierre

(b. 1928). Director/actor. Born: Roanne, France

'Don't laugh at me 'cos I'm a fool' – so the song goes, but in the case of Pierre Etaix that is precisely why he does want people to laugh. Because of his very visual sense of the comic he has often been likened to such master comedians as Max Linder and Buster Keaton; he has also been greatly influenced by the work of Jacques Tati. Etaix himself had always longed to be a clown – and this fascination is obvious in his acting and directing. He produced his own clown shows shortly after leaving school. In 1949, after a year's military service, he began working as an assistant director, and nine years later he was working as a designer on Tati's *Mon Oncle*. The following year he played a thief in Bresson's *Pickpocket*. In 1961 he directed his first film, the short *Rupture*, and in 1962 he directed his first feature *Le Soupirant*. The highlight of his comic career, however, may well have been in the early Sixties when he was, for a short time, partner to Nino the Clown.

Films include: 1961 Rupture (short) (co-dir). '62 Heureux Anniversaire (short) (co-dir; +act). '63 Le Soupirant (GB: The Suitor); Nous N'Irons Plus au Bois (short) (+act); Insomnie (short) (+act) (GB: Insomnia). '65 Yoyo. '66 Tant qu'On a la Santé (GB: As Long as You're Healthy). '69 Le Grand Amour (GB: The Great Love). '71 Pays de Cocagne (doc).

EUSTACHE, Jean

(1938–1981). Director. Born: Pessac, France

Jean Eustache had very definite ideas about the purpose and the style of his films. He believed that, above all, dialogue was far more important than action and that cinema should be used as a tool for self-exploration. As a result of his ideas and ideals he became a mentor to many young French film-makers. He began as an amateur film-maker and then worked for French television before moving over to films. He made his directorial debut – *Les Mauvaises Frequentations* – in 1964, and soon gained a reputation as á director of realist films outside the commercial cinema. He is thought to have had both psychological and professional difficulties in his life, and he committed suicide a year after he sustained serious injuries in a fall.

Films include: 1964 Les Mauvaises Fréquentations. '65 Du Côté de Robinson (short). '66 Le Père Noël a les Yeux Bleus. '73 La Maman et la Putain - (+act) (USA/GB: The Mother and the Whore). '75 Mes Petites Amoureuses. '77 Une Sále Histoire.

EVANS, Edith

(1888–1976). Actress. Born: London, England

Edith Evans is inextricably linked to Lady Bracknell in *The Importance of Being Earnest*. She made this part her own, on stage, film and radio, before she grew tired of such repetition and refused to play her again. For many years she was also well known purely as a tremendous stage actress, in Shakespeare and Restoration comedy. In fact she did not make her sound film debut until she was 60 (although she did make two silent films very early in her acting career). This first major film was *The Queen of Spades*, and although she does not speak throughout, her use of facial expression makes dialogue superfluous. She soon became renowned for her great timing and delivery. Even at the age of 79 she gave a superb performance as a lonely old woman living in an illusionary world in *The Whisperers*. In 1946 she was created Dame of the British Empire for her services to the theatre.

Films include: 1949 The Queen of Spades; The Last Days of Dolwyn (USA: Woman of Dolwyn). '52 The Importance of Being Earnest. '59 Look Back in Anger; The Nun's Story (USA). '63 Tom Jones. '64 The Chalk Garden. '67 The Whisperers. '69 The Madwoman of Chaillot; Crooks and Coronets (USA: Sophie's Place); David Copperfield. '70 Scrooge.

EVANS, Fred

(1889–1915). Actor. Born: London, England

The one comedy star in Britain who could rival the popularity of Chaplin during the silent era was Fred Evans. His famous character Pimple, with his little cricket cap, long hair, baggy trousers and big boots made British audiences roar with laughter in films such as *Pimple's Ivanhoe* and *Sexton Pimple*. Evans was born into a large family of music hall and circus performers and his skill as a knockabout acrobat made him a natural for films. He joined the Cricks and Martin studios and soon had his own Charley Smiler series in which he played a dapper Max Linder-type toff. Then he left to start his own company with his brother and his uncle, and this was when the Pimple character was born. After a disagreement Evans and his brother broke away and continued to produce Pimple films at their own studios on an island in the Thames.

Films include: 1910 The Last of the Dandy. '11 Charley Smiler Joins the Boy Scouts. '12 Pimple Does the Turkey Trot. '13 Pimple's Battle of Waterloo; Pimple's Ivanhoe. '14 Pimple's Proposal (+co-dir; +co-sc); How Lieutenant Pimple Captured the Kaiser (+co-dir; +co-sc). '15 Sexton Pimple (+co-dir; +co-sc); Pimple's Royal Divorce. '18 Pimple's Better 'Ole (+co-dir; +co-sc). '22 Pimple's Three Musketeers (+prod; +co-dir; +co-sc).

EWELL, Tom

(b. 1909). Actor. Born: Yewell Tomkins; Owensboro, Kentucky, USA

It took Tom Ewell many years of hard work in unsuccessful Broadway plays before he received a modicum of the recognition he deserved. After 14 years of supporting himself with additional jobs and the odd movie part he finally appeared in two highly acclaimed plays in one year – *John Loves Mary* and *Small Wonder* – and won various awards for both. Originally he had intended to be a lawyer, but he caught the acting bug and gave up his studies to appear with a stock company. That was in 1928. Two decades later he had his first important film role as a nervous philanderer in *Adam's Rib*. He soon became recognized as a useful comedy actor and was excellent in such films as *The Seven Year Itch* and *The Girl Can't Help It*. Although his allegiance is mainly to the theatre he continues to appear in movies occasionally.

Films include: 1949 Adam's Rib. '51 Finders Keepers. '55 The Seven Year Itch; The Lieutenant Wore Skirts. '56 The Girl Can't Help It; The Great American Pastime. '62 Tender Is the Night; State Fair. '70 Suppose They Gave a War and Nobody Came. '74 The Great Gatsby.

FÁBRI, Zoltán

(b. 1917). Director. Born: Budapest, Hungary

One of the principal film-makers in the post-war Hungarian cinema, Zoltán Fábri was instrumental in the total reorganization of the film industry. His films deal with anti-fascist themes, and often feature the difficulties of living during times of social and historical crisis. *Életjel*, for example, deals with the trauma of a group of miners who are trapped underground, while *Hannibál Tanár Úr* is a tragi-comedy about a schoolmaster turned hero in the fight against fascism. Fábri's films are also highly influenced by his background as a painter – he had studied fine art before moving into the world of drama, and also worked as a set designer.

Films include: 1952 Vihar (The Storm). '54 Életjel (Fourteen Lives Saved). '55 Körhinta (GB: Merry Go Round). '57 Hannibál Tanár Úr (GB: Professor Hannibal). '59 Édes Anna (Anna). '62 Két Félidö a Pokolban (GB: The Last Goal/Eleven Men). '65 Húsz Óra (GB: Twenty Hours). '69 A Pál Utcai Fiuk (HUN-USA) (USA: The Boys of Paul Street). '75 141 Perc a Befejezetlen Mondatbol (The Unfinished Sentence in 141 Minutes). '76 Az ö Tödik Pecsét (The Fifth Seal). '78 Magyarok (GB: Hungarians).

FAIRBANKS Sr, Douglas

(1883–1939). Actor/producer. Born: Douglas Elton Ulman; Denver, Colorado, USA

Fairbanks was the first and the ultimate Hollywood hero. With a flash of his dazzling, daring smile and a ripple of his bronzed muscles he could take a ship single-handed, swinging on ropes and sliding down sails like greased lightning. Audiences adored him and his 15-year marriage to Mary Pickford completed the storybook picture. His childhood also has a theatrical air about it. He was son of a Southern belle and an upper-middle class Jewish lawyer. His acting career began on stage at the age of 12, but his path to stardom was temporarily halted in 1907 by a respectable marriage to Anna Beth Sully (mother of Fairbanks Jr) and an equally respectable career in a soap factory. But with the collapse of his job he returned to

the theatre, and by 1915 he had signed a $2000-a-week contract with Triangle Pictures. A year later he was released from his contract to form the Douglas Fairbanks Pictures Company. And finally in 1919 he joined in the formation of United Artists. Often producing and writing his Twenties costume epics, he was the model for all creative actor-producers.

Films include: 1915 The Lamb. '16 The Half-Breed. '20 The Mark of Zorro (+prod;+co-sc). '21 The Three Musketeers (+prod). '22 Robin Hood (+prod;+co-sc). '24 The Thief of Bagdad (+prod;+co-sc). '27 The Black Pirate (+prod;+co-sc); The Gaucho (+prod;+co-sc). '29 The Iron Mask (+prod;+sc). '34 The Private Life of Don Juan (GB).

FAIRBANKS Jr, Douglas

(b. 1909). Actor. Born: Douglas Elton Ulman Fairbanks; New York City, USA

Douglas Fairbanks Jr had a daunting act to follow. His father, after all, was a swashbuckling star adored by millions and the first king of Hollywood. Fairbanks Jr entered the movie business at the age of 14. The career that followed never matched that of his father, but he handled himself admirably, becoming a smooth matinée idol by the Thirties, and making numerous successful films with a debonair charm that has remained with him throughout his life. He occasionally followed in his father's swashbuckling footsteps in films like *The Prisoner of Zenda*, and proved himself to be quite equal to the task. He also had a distinguished war record, receiving many decorations for gallantry, as well as the OBE in 1949 for services to Anglo-American relations. He retired from films in 1951 to work as a television producer, only making intermittent appearances on stage and film since then. He was married to Joan Crawford from 1929 to 1933, during which time the couple was under threat by Mary Pickford not to make her a grandmother.

Films include: 1926 Stella Dallas. '28 A Woman of Affairs. '30 Party Girl; Little Caesar. '32 Scarlet Dawn; Love Is a Racket. '33 Morning Glory. '37 The Prisoner of Zenda. '39 Gunga Din; '47 The Exile.

Left: Douglas Fairbanks as The Gaucho, *the swaggering outlaw of the pampas who is eventually converted from his roguish ways. Below: Douglas Fairbanks Jr following family tradition as the swashbuckling Rupert of Hentzau in the classic Hollywood version of* The Prisoner of Zenda

FALCONETTI

(1893–1944). Actress. Born: Renée Jeanne Falconetti; Paris, France

She made only one film and gained an enormous reputation as a result of it. The film was *La Passion de Jeanne d'Arc* (1928, *The Passion of Joan of Arc*), and the director Carl Dreyer offered her the part of Joan after seeing her act on stage. Falconetti agreed to appear without makeup and with her hair shorn and she studied the role intently. As a result the extraordinary persona of Joan that she created has never been equalled for sheer power. After the film she returned to the stage, buying her own theatre, L'Avenue, in Paris. But the venture flopped within a year, leaving her financially ruined. During the Occupation she moved to Switzerland, then Brazil and finally to Argentina, living by small acting, singing or teaching jobs. At the end of the war she hoped to return to Paris and the stage, but having become overweight she went on a crash diet and died within a few days in Buenos Aires – a sadly degrading death for such a fine actress.

FALK, Peter

(b. 1927). Actor. Born: Peter Michael Falk; New York City, USA

Peter Falk is perhaps best known for his part as the television detective Columbo – the scruffy, bumbling, apparently idiotic policeman who always, irritatingly, manages to outsmart the villain. The soggy cigar that the character always carries is an affectation but the lopsided expression is not – he lost his right eye when he was three as the result of a tumour. His early career also seems to have something of the planned disorganization that the Columbo character uses to such good effect. Between gaining a BA in political science and an MA in public administration Falk also found time to be a cook in the Merchant Navy and to complete a tour of Europe. The interest in acting that had started at college finally took over. He made for New York and the off-Broadway stage, studying at the Actors' Studio before making his Broadway debut opposite Siobhan McKenna in *Saint Joan*. Film roles followed, and he established his career with an excellent performance as the killer in *Murder Inc*. He worked successfully in television, film and theatre, and has had a particularly good working relationship with the director John Cassavetes, with whom he has made *Husbands* and *A Woman Under the Influence*.

Films include: 1951 Murder Inc. (GB: The Enforcer). '58 Wind Across the Everglades. '61 Pocketful of Miracles. '65 The Great Race. '68 Lo Sbarco di Anzio (IT) (USA: Anzio; GB: The Battle for Anzio). '69 Castle Keep. '70 Husbands. '74 A Woman Under the Influence. '76 Murder by Death. '78 The Cheap Detective.

FARMER, Frances

(1914–1970). Actress. Born: Seattle, Washington, USA

In the Hollywood environment where odd characters and opinions are supposedly the norm it seems strange that Frances Farmer had her career and, eventually, her life, ruined for those very reasons. As a student she was interested in drama, politics and writing, eventually being branded a communist when she won a trip to the USSR sponsored by a communist newspaper. Once back in America she went to New York, met a talent scout and made her screen debut in 1936 in *Too Many Parents*. Dubbed 'the new Garbo', she had a few successful years at the end of the Thirties, playing leading roles opposite the likes of Bing Crosby and Tyrone Power. From that time onwards her career declined – a return to Broadway failed and she was reduced to second billing in Hollywood, where she was branded as rebellious and difficult when she resisted the one-dimensional, glamorous roles assigned to her. As a result she began drinking heavily, had a nervous breakdown and in 1944 she was committed as insane for five years, with several of them spent in hellish asylums. She fought back, however, and briefly returned to work on television. She died of cancer of the esophagus. But her life had been ruined years before. Frances Farmer's first of three husbands was Hollywood actor Leif Erickson (b. 1911), who in the late Sixties became well known on television as the rancher John Cannon in *The High Chaparral*.

Films include: 1936 Too Many Parents; Come and Get It; Rhythm On the Range. '37 The Toast of New York; Exclusive; Ebb Tide. '38 Ride a Crooked Mile (GB: Escape From Yesterday). '40 Flowing Gold; South of Pago Pago. '41 Badlands of Dakota. '42 Sun of Fury.

FARNUM, Dustin

(1874–1929). Actor. Born: Hampton Beach, New Hampshire, USA

When Dustin Farnum transferred his tall, adventurous, romantic cowboy characters from stage hits to tremendously successful films like *The Squaw Man* and *The Virginian* he became one of the earliest Western movie stars. He came from an acting family and, when he left the Lasky Corporation in 1914, he made his way via Triangle to the Fox Film Corporation where his younger brother William was already a star. Dustin continued to appear in popular Westerns until 1926, when he retired from films in order to return to the stage. But the following year he had a nervous breakdown and two years later he died.

Films include: 1913 The Squaw Man. '14 The Virginian. '15 Cameo Kirby. '16 Davy Crockett. '17 The Scarlet Pimpernel; Durand of the Bad Lands. '19 The Corsican Brothers; A Man's Flight. '21 The Devil Within. '26 Flaming Frontier.

FARNUM, William

(1876–1953). Actor. Born: Boston, Massachusetts, USA

One of the first screen idols, William Farnum was among the highest paid actors in Hollywood. He began as a popular stage actor, appearing with stock companies and on Broadway. He was also a great showman – in the final scene of his first film *The Spoilers*, he staged a real fight that hospitalized him. His career continued to blossom until the late Twenties when the death of his brother, the Wall Street Crash and an accident caused a brief retirement from the screen. But he returned a few years later and, until his death, occupied himself as a reliable character actor, becoming particularly renowned for playing kindly old gentlemen.

Films include: 1914 The Spoilers. '16 A Man of Sorrow. '17 A Tale of Two Cities. '18 Les Miserables. '20 If I Were King. '22 A Stage Romance. '24 The Man Who Fights Alone. '31 A Connecticut Yankee; The Painted Desert. '40 Kit Carson. '52 Lone Star.

Above: Falconetti as Joan in La Passion de Jeanne d'Arc. *Above right: the tragic Frances Farmer. Right: Dustin Farnum – early hero of the West on stage and on film. Far right: his heart-throb brother William in* A Stage Romance. *Below: Peter Falk using his skill at portraying Humphrey Bogart in* The Cheap Detective

FARR, Felicia

(b. 1932). Actress. Born: Westchester County, New York, USA

The daughter of a New York attorney, Farr moved with her family to Los Angeles owing to her mother's ill-health. She had already been involved with the theatre in a minor way, but once on the West Coast she won the lead role in the play *Picnic* for the Players Ring Theatre. A Columbia executive saw her and gave her a screen test. Since then she has been mostly seen as a witty, talented leading lady in Westerns, with intermittent substantial roles in such films as *Charley Varrick*, and *Kotch*, which was directed by her husband Jack Lemmon. She excelled as the lovingly unfaithful wife in *Kiss Me, Stupid*.

Films include: 1955 Big House, USA. '56 The First Texan; Jubal; Timetable. '57 3:10 to Yuma. '60 Hell Bent for Leather. '64 Kiss Me, Stupid/It Happened In Climax, Nevada. '67 The Venetian Affair. '71 Kotch. '73 Charley Varrick.

FARRAR, David

(b. 1908). Actor. Born: Forest Gate, London, England

During his life David Farrar has managed to work his way to the top of two professions – journalism and acting. Several successful West End shows gained him recognition as an actor as well as a few minor film roles, and he eventually secured a contract with Warner Brothers at Teddington Studios. This rugged, swarthy actor, was tougher than previous leading men and he became a favourite with English audiences during the Forties, usually in films by Michael Powell. In the early Fifties he decided, unwisely, to look for wider fame in Hollywood and his career faded.

Films include: 1937 Return of a Stranger. '42 Went the Day Well? '43 The Dark Tower; They Met in the Dark; Headline. '44 Meet Sexton Blake. '45 The World Owes Me a Living. '47 Black Narcissus. '49 The Small Back Room. '54 Lilacs in the Spring. '58 I Accuse! '62 The 300 Spartans (USA).

FARRAR, Geraldine

(1882–1967). Singer/actress. Born: Melrose, Massachusetts, USA

Geraldine Farrar was encouraged to sing by her parents, and by the age of 12 she was showing considerable talent. She studied in Boston and New York, until she was spotted by Mrs Bertram Webb, a wealthy socialite, who paid for her to study in Europe. She made her debut in 1901 at the Royal Opera in Berlin. She continued to study in Paris while at the same time singing throughout Europe, and eventually forming her famous partnership with Caruso. She also began to work in Hollywood, primarily for Cecil B. DeMille; her first film with him was *Carmen*, her most celebrated *Joan the Woman*. Unfortunately in 1922 at the age of 40 she began to believe that her voice was failing, and retired permanently.

Films include: 1915 Carmen; Temptation. '16 Joan the Woman; Maria Rosa. '17 The Devil Stone. '18 The Hell Cat; The Turn of the Wheel. '19 Shadows; The Stronger Vow; The Flame of the Desert.

FARRELL, Charles

(b. 1905). Actor. Born: East Walpole, Massachusetts, USA

As a child Charles Farrell was constantly haunting his father's theatres, longing to become a performer himself. But his parents did not approve and he went to Boston University instead. He then became business manager to a vaudeville act and followed it across America. They disbanded in Los Angeles, so he decided to take up acting. He soon became friends with the actor Richard Arlen, and found himself getting work as an extra. He was young, good-looking, athletic and very photogenic and within a short time he landed the lead in *Wings of Youth* opposite Madge Bellamy. Initially with Fox, his big breaks came in *Old Ironsides* and *The Rough Riders* for Paramount. He soon became top box-office and during the last years of the silents he and Janet Gaynor were the leading romantic team in Hollywood. The arrival of sound nearly ended his career, but he managed to survive and went on to play leads and character parts until his retirement in 1941. He then moved to Palm Springs where he served as mayor for seven years.

Films include: 1923 The Cheat. '25 Wings of Youth. '26 Old Ironsides. '27 Seventh

Heaven; The Rough Riders (GB: The Trumpet Call). '28 Street Angel. '29 Lucky Star. '30 City Girl; Liliom. '31 Body and Soul. '32 Wild Girl (GB: Salomy Jane). '32 After Tomorrow; Tess of the Storm Country.

FARRELL, Glenda

(1904–1971). Actress. Born: Enid, Oklahoma, USA

A small, grey-eyed blonde, Glenda Farrell was self-reliant and vivacious in her typical Thirties roles; by the Fifties she had diversified to become a popular character actress, also taking on television and stage roles. She began in the theatre, playing a 17-year-old Little Eva in *Uncle Tom's Cabin*, and graduated by way of much provincial experience to Broadway. Warners talent scouts signed her on to start a prolific career – as a gangster's moll in *Little Caesar*, as a fast-talking chiseller with Joan Blondell in several films (including *Gold Diggers of 1937*) and as the enterprising girl reporter Torchy Blane in a series of B pictures (she made seven of these, starting with *Smart Blonde*). According to writer-director Garson Kanin: 'She invented and developed that made-tough, uncompromising, knowing, wisecracking, undefeatable blonde.'

Films include: 1930 Little Caesar. '32 I Am a Fugitive From a Chain Gang (GB: I Am a Fugitive From the Chain Gang). '33 The Mystery of the Wax Museum. '34 Hi, Nellie. '35 Miss Pacific Fleet. '36 Gold Diggers of 1937; Smart Blonde. '38 Torchy Blane in Panama. '41 Johnny Eager. '54 Susan Slept Here. '59 Middle of the Night.

Far left: Felicia Farr in Kiss Me, Stupid. *Left: David Farrar in* Duel in the Jungle *(1954). Below: Geraldine Farrar in* The Devil Stone. *Below left: Glenda Farrell in* Havana Widows *(1933). Below, far left: Charles Farrell*

Above right: an acting role for director Rainer Werner Fassbinder. Right: Mia Farrow in Rosemary's Baby. *Below right: Farrah Fawcett in* Sunburn. *Below, far right: Alice Faye In* Old Chicago

FARROW, Mia

(b. 1945). Actress. Born: Maria de Lourdes Villiers Farrow; Los Angeles, California, USA

The daughter of actress Maureen O'Sullivan and film director John Farrow, Mia Farrow contracted polio at the age of nine, which left her with the elfin fragile look that is part of her appeal and her acting repertoire. In 1962 she won the National Forensic League Drama Award for dramatic monologues, leading to a Broadway appearance in *The Importance of Being Earnest*, and national fame as Allison MacKenzie in the television soap opera *Peyton Place*, a role she played from 1963 to 1965. It was as the mother of a demonic infant that she won international stardom in *Rosemary's Baby*, and established the frail child-woman image in which she has since become somewhat typecast. She has been married to Frank Sinatra (from 1966 to 1968) and André Previn (from 1971 to 1979), and romantically linked with Woody Allen.

Films include: 1964 Guns at Batasi (GB). '68 A Dandy in Aspic (GB); Secret Ceremony (GB); Rosemary's Baby. '69 John and Mary. '71 Blind Terror (GB) (USA: See No Evil). '74 The Great Gatsby. '77 Full Circle (GB-CAN). '78 A Wedding; Death on the Nile (GB); Avalanche. '79 Hurricane.

FASSBINDER, Rainer Werner

(1946–1982). Director/screenwriter/actor. Born: Bad Wörishofen, Germany

Brought up in the chaos of postwar Germany, Fassbinder had family problems from an early age; sent to the cinema each day by a busy divorced mother, he became obsessed with films, particularly the American melodramas of Douglas Sirk. He studied drama in Munich and acted with a couple of experimental theatre groups, the members of which formed the basis of his film repertory company. He made two shorts and acted in one by Jean-Marie Straub before launching into features in 1969 with *Love Is Colder Than Death*. He soon became the most prolific writer-director (and frequently actor) of the New German Cinema, and also worked in television and the theatre. Many of his films are angst-ridden studies of despair, filmed in a detached and alienating though increasingly lush style. He was building up a wide and incisively critical panorama of German life during the postwar period in his latest films when he died of a mixture of drink and drugs at the age of 36. He was briefly married to the actress Ingrid Caven, but in more than one of his films he proclaimed and discussed his homosexuality.

Films include: 1965 Der Stadtstreicher (short). '69 Liebe ist kälter als der Tod (GB: Love Is Colder Than Death). '70 Der amerikanische Soldat (USA/GB: The American Soldier). '72 Die bitteren Tränen der Petra von Kant. '74 Angst essen Seele auf (USA: Ali: Fear Eats the Soul; GB: Fear Eats the Soul); Fontane Effi Briest (USA/GB: Effi Briest). '75 Faustrecht der Freiheit (USA/GB: Fox/Fox and His Friends); Mutter Küsters Fahrt zum Himmel (USA: Mother Kuster Goes to Heaven; GB: Mother Kuster's Trip to Heaven). '78 Despair/Eine Reise in Lichts (GER-FR). '79 Die Ehe der Maria Braun (USA/GB: The Marriage of Maria Braun); Die dritte Generation. '81 Lili Marleen; Lola. '82 Die Sehnsucht der Veronika Voss; Querelle. '82 Theater in Trance (doc).

FAULKNER, William

(1897–1962). Novelist/screenwriter. Born: New Albany, Mississippi, USA

In the late Twenties and the Thirties Faulkner, Southerner by birth and conviction, wrote many of the books that would establish him as one of America's finest novelists. But recognition was slow in coming and he made the first of many trips to Hollywood in 1932, purely to earn a living and support his elaborate lifestyle in Oxford, Mississippi, the centre of his fictional universe as well as his home. He had little flair for screenwriting and most of his projects came to nothing but he obtained a few credits in partnership with a kindred spirit, Howard Hawks, with whom he shared a flying background in World War I. He took no part in the adaptations of his novels, of which only *Intruder in the Dust* and *The Tarnished Angels* (based on *Pylon*) captured some of the qualities of their originals.

Films include: 1933 Today We Live (story basis); The Story of Temple Drake (novel basis). '36 The Road to Glory (co-sc). '44 To Have and Have Not (co-sc). '46 The Big Sleep (co-sc). '49 Intruder in the Dust (novel basis). '55 Land of the Pharaohs (co-sc). '57 The Tarnished Angels (novel basis). '58 The Long, Hot Summer (novel basis). '61 Sanctuary (novel and play basis).

FAWCETT, Farrah

(b. 1947). Actress. Born: Corpus Christi, Texas, USA

A classic Texan suntanned toothy blonde, Farrah Fawcett won a beauty contest, took up modelling and television commercials and played a bit part in a Claude Lelouch film. She was cast as one of the original trio of girl detectives in the television series *Charlie's Angels*, instantly achieving worldwide fame, though she left after one season (1976–77) to make feature films – none successful – and television movies. Her lack of any distinctive qualities except conventional good looks severely limits her future. She was married to the television actor Lee Majors for a time and was then generally known as Farrah Fawcett-Majors.

Films include: 1969 Un Homme Qui Me Plaît (FR) (GB: Love Is a Funny Thing). '70 Myra Breckinridge. '76 Logan's Run. '78 Somebody Killed Her Husband. '79 Sunburn (GB-USA). '80 Saturn 3. '81 The Cannonball Run.

FAYE, Alice

(b. 1912). Actress. Born: Alice Leppert; New York City, USA

From a working-class New York background, Alice Faye showed an early aptitude for dancing and took it up professionally in cabaret and vaudeville. She danced in *George White's Scandals* on Broadway and sang on the radio before becoming a crooner with Rudy Vallee's band. Her first movie appearance was with Vallee in the film version of *George White's Scandals*, after which she became a mainstay of 20th Century-Fox musicals during the Thirties and early Forties, capitalizing on her cute blonde prettiness and usually playing the hard-done-by heroine not appreciated by the romantic lead (probably Tyrone Power, Don Ameche or John Payne) until the last reel. She retired in 1945 and has made only a few screen appearances since then, though she occasionally played in the theatre. After a brief marriage (1936–40) with singer Tony Martin, she wed bandleader Phil Harris in 1941. She remains a cult figure among musicals fans.

Films include: 1934 George White's Scandals. '37 On the Avenue. '38 Alexander's Ragtime Band; In Old Chicago. '39 Rose of Washington Square; Hollywood Cavalcade. '40 Tin Pan Alley. '41 That Night in Rio; Weekend in Havana. '43 Hello, Frisco, Hello. '45 Fallen Angel.

FAZENDA, Louise

(1895–1962). Actress. Born: Lafayette, Indiana, USA

Louise Fazenda was one of Mack Sennett's original bathing beauties, but her looks were average and her real talent was for comedy. She became one of the most popular comediennes of the silent period, concentrating at first on Sennett two-reelers and features, and then branching out into dramas as well as comedies for Warners. She married the producer Hal B. Wallis in 1927. With the coming of sound she continued to work, usually in small comic-relief parts, though she did star in the occasional two-reeler. She retired from the screen in 1939 after appearing in the Bette Davis vehicle *The Old Maid*.

Films include: 1918 The Kitchen Lady (short); Her First Mistake. '24 Galloping Fish. '25 Bobbed Hair; Hogan's Alley. '27 Babe Comes Home. '28 Tillie's Punctured Romance. '29 The House of Horror. '33 Alice in Wonderland. '39 The Old Maid.

FEJOS, Paul

(1897–1963). Director. Born: Pál Fejös; Budapest, Hungary

His medical studies interrupted by World War I, Fejos became a producer of army theatricals, a set designer for films and, in 1920, a director of thrillers. In 1923 he went to the USA to complete his medical education, becoming a research assistant at the Rockefeller Institute in New York (1924–26). Then the lure of Hollywood drew him to try his hand at films again, and on a tiny budget he made *The Last Moment*, an experimental film about the visions of a suicidal drowning man. This opened the doors of Universal and *Lonesome*, a touching study of two young New Yorkers falling in love, sealed his reputation. His first sound film, *Broadway*, was a mammoth musical spectacular, full of dazzling crane shots but unconvincing in its tale of a male dancer trying to escape the gangster-ridden environment of a flashy nightclub. It failed and his career at Universal faltered. After briefly working for MGM, Fejos returned to Europe, making films in France, Hungary, Austria and Denmark before abandoning features for ethnographic documentaries about Madagascar, Siam and Central America. Unable to complete his study of the Yagua, an Amerindian tribe, he made no more films after 1941, but devoted himself to scientific studies. In 1954 he was appointed director of New York's Wenner-Gren Foundation for anthropological research.

Films include: 1920 Pán (HUN). '28 The Last Moment (USA); Lonesome (USA). '29 Broadway (USA); The Last Performance (USA) (GB: Erik the Great Illusionist). '30 Menschen hinter Gittern (USA) (German-language version of The Big House). '31 Fantômas (FR). '32 Tavaszi Zápor (HUN) (+French-language version: Marie, Légende Hongroise, HUN; GB: Marie). '33 Sonnenstrahl (A) (GB: Together We Too). '39 Man och Kvinna/En Handfull Ris (doc) (co-dir) (SWED).

FELDMAN, Marty

(1933–1982). Actor/writer/director. Born: London, England

After touring with a comedy act, Marty Feldman joined radio's comedy show *Educating Archy*. He formed a successful comedy-writing team with Barry Took, eventually moving from radio to television with *At Last the 1948 Show*. He then established himself as a performer, helped by his zany appearance and manner, and was given his own television show, *Marty*. Parts in British movies were a stepping-stone to America, where he became very popular making guest appearances, notably in the Mel Brooks–Gene Wilder movies. He turned writer-director with *The Last Remake of Beau Geste*, a Foreign Legion spoof.

Films include: 1969 The Bed Sitting Room. '70 Every Home Should Have One (USA: Think Dirty). '74 Young Frankenstein (USA). '75 The Adventure of Sherlock Holmes' Smarter Brother. '76 Silent Movie (USA). '77 The Last Remake of Beau Geste (+dir) (USA). '80 In God We Trust (Or Gimme That Prime Time Religion) (+dir;+co-sc) (USA).

FELLINI, Federico

(b. 1920). Director. Born: Rimini, Italy

The son of a grocery salesman in Rimini, on the Adriatic, Fellini left an undistinguished career at school in 1938 to go to Florence and then Rome, where he enrolled at the University but, instead of attending classes, he wrote and drew cartoons for a satirical magazine. He began to collaborate on film scripts until the Germans closed down production in 1943, the year he married the actress Giulietta Masina. His big chance came after the Liberation, when he collaborated with the director Roberto Rossellini on the script of *Open City* and then *Paisà* and other films. He co-directed his first film in 1950 and went solo in 1952; but it was the autobiographical *I Vitelloni*, about a gang of young layabouts in a provincial town, that established him, while *La Strada*, starring Giulietta Masina as a pathetically retarded waif whose love and death almost redeem a brutal showman, brought him international fame and the first of four Best Foreign-Language Film Oscars. His next big success was *La Dolce Vita*, a panoramic study of modern Roman corruption, which was followed by two personal films, *8½*, the story of a film director whose life and work are collapsing about him, and *Juliet of the Spirits*, in which Giulietta Masina played a middle-aged wife coping with a breakdown. Working on a larger canvas, he then explored the past in *Fellini Satyricon*, a literary adaptation, and *Fellini's Roma*, which examined the prewar Fascist period as well as a fantasized present. *Amarcord* represented a charming return to Rimini and childhood. Since then Fellini has made more ambitious attempts to explore ideas – male sexuality, feminism – with mixed success. His big films have tended to divide critics and the

Below: Louise Fazenda – an actress who proved her talent for comedy in silent shorts and features. Bottom: the zany features of Marty Feldman in

public more than his small-scale personal works; but they attest to his seriousness as a modern artist, while his flair for inventive film imagery has never been in doubt.

Films include: 1945 Roma, Città Aperta (co-sc. only) (USA: Rome, Open City; GB: Open City). '46 Paisà (co-sc. only) (USA/GB: Paisan). '50 Luci del Varietà (co-dir) (USA/GB: Lights of Variety/Variety Lights). '52 Lo Sceicco Bianco (USA/GB: The White Sheik). '53 I Vitelloni (USA/GB: The Spivs/The Wastrels/The Young and the Passionate). '54 La Strada. '55 Il Bidone (GB: The Swindlers). '57 Le Notti di Cabiria (IT-FR) (USA/GB: Nights of Cabiria). '59 La Dolce Vita. '63 Otto e Mezzo (IT-FR) (USA/GB: 8½). '65 Giulietta degli Spiriti (USA/GB: Juliet of the Spirits). '69 Fellini Satyricon. '70 I Clowns (IT-FR-GER) (orig. TV). '72 Fellini's Roma. '73 Amarcord. '76 Il Casanova di Federico Fellini (USA/GB: Casanova/Fellini's Casanova). '78 Prova d'Orchestra (IT-MONACO) (orig. TV) (USA/GB: Orchestra Rehearsal). '80 La Città delle Donne (USA/GB: City of Women).

FERNANDEL

(1903–1971). Actor. Born: Fernand Joseph Désiré Contandin; Marseilles, France

For decades the horsy jaw, tombstone teeth and huge grin of Fernandel summed up French humour, and he was rewarded with membership of the Legion of Honour for his work as 'marchand de bonheur' (trader in happiness). He apparently got his stage name from being called 'Fernand d'elle' (her Fernand) by his future mother-in-law. His father was a music-hall singer and Fernandel followed the same trade, making his Paris debut in 1928 in a revue at the Concert Mayol as a comedy singer. The writer-director-actor Sacha Guitry offered him a small part in *Le Blanc et le Noir*, which led on to several comedy farces and his first notable success in a more serious role as the idiot son of a grocer in *Le Rosier de Madame Husson*. Though used in films

The Adventure of Sherlock Holmes' Smarter Brother. *Right: French comic Fernandel seems oddly confused when faced with a fortune*

mainly as a comedian, he also showed his versatility in character roles, as in Marcel Pagnol's *Angèle* and Claude Autant-Lara's *Fric-Frac*. He became internationally famous as Don Camillo in the series of comedies about an Italian village priest in continual conflict with the local communist mayor. TV viewers in Britain probably remember him best for his Dubonnet commercials.

Films include: 1931 Le Blanc et le Noir; Le Rosier de Madame Husson. '34 Angèle. '37 Regain (GB: Harvest); Un Carnet de Bal (USA: Life Dances On; GB: Christine). '39 Fric-Frac. '40 La Fille du Puisatier (GB: The Welldigger's Daughter). '48 L'Armoire Volante (GB: The Cupboard Was Bare). '51 L'Auberge Rouge. '52 Il Piccolo Mondo di Don Camillo (IT-FR) (GB: The Little World of Don Camillo). '54 Le Mouton à Cinq Pattes (GB: The Sheep Has Five Legs).

FERNANDEZ, Emilio

(1904–1986). Director/actor. Born: El Seco, Coahuila, Mexico

Known as 'El Indio' from his part-Indian family background, Fernandez had an adventurous life – as a boy he shot a man who attempted to rape

his mother and in his seventies he served a year in prison for homicide. In between he fought on both sides in the Mexican Revolution, and skipped over the border to become an extra in Westerns. Through an encounter with a jealous husband he was deported to Mexico, where he became a leading actor and then turned director, particularly of the later films of Dolores Del Rio – *María Candelaria* won a prize at the first Cannes Film Festival in 1946. Like many of his films it concerned the Mexican revolution. Fernandez did more than anyone else to create a Mexican national cinema, though by the Fifties his work was regarded as dated and too melodramatic. He continued to act, appearing late in his career in Sam Peckinpah's *The Wild Bunch, Pat Garrett and Billy the Kid* and *Bring Me the Head of Alfredo Garcia*.

Films include: 1942 La Isla de la Pasión (+ act). '43 Flor Silvestre (+ act). '44 María Candelaria. '45 Las Abandonadas. '46 Enamorada. '47 La Perla. '48 Río Escondido; Maclovia. '49 Pueblerina; Salón México. '53 La Red. '69 The Wild Bunch (actor only) (USA). '73 Pat Garrett and Billy the Kid (actor only) (USA). '74 Bring Me the Head of Alfredo Garcia (actor only) (USA-MEX).

FERRER, José

(b. 1909). Actor/director. Born: José Vincente Ferrer Otero y Cintron; Santurce, Puerto Rico

Excellent in larger-than-life roles, José Ferrer seems more suited to the theatre than to the cinema; but he has made his mark in movies not only as an actor but, to a lesser extent, as a director. The son of a lawyer, he came to the United States at six and passed the entrance examinations for Princeton University at fourteen. He made his Broadway debut in 1935, and in 1940 directed as well as acted in *Charley's Aunt*. In 1946 he was directed by Mel Ferrer (no relation) in the Broadway production of *Cyrano de Bergerac*, which led to his first film role as the Dauphin in *Joan of Arc* and an Academy Award nomination. He actually won the Best Actor Academy Award as the long-nosed romantic poet in the film version of *Cyrano de Bergerac* and was nominated again as Toulouse-Lautrec in *Moulin Rouge*. He won four Tony Awards for directing plays, including *The Shrike*, with which he also made his debut as a film director. The films he directed were not on the whole successful and he returned to the stage, but continued to make fairly frequent acting appearances in films. He married the actress Uta Hagen in 1938, Phyllis Hill in 1948 and the singer-actress Rosemary Clooney in 1953.

Films include: 1948 Joan of Arc (actor only). '50 Cyrano de Bergerac (actor only). '52 Moulin Rouge (actor only) (GB). '53 Miss Sadie Thompson (actor only). '54 The Caine Mutiny (actor only); Deep in My Heart (actor only). '55 The Shrike; Cockleshell Heroes (GB). '56 The Great Man. '58 I Accuse (GB); The High Cost of Loving. '61 Return to Peyton Place (dir. only). '62 Lawrence of Arabia (actor only) (GB); State Fair (dir. only). '63 Nine Hours to Rama (actor only). '65 Ship of Fools (actor only). '78 The Swarm (actor only); Fedora (actor only) (GER). '79 The Fifth Musketeer (actor only) (GB-A).

FERRER, Mel

(b. 1917). Actor/director/producer. Born: Melchior Gaston Ferrer; Elberon, New Jersey, USA

While at Princeton University, Mel Ferrer won a playwrights' award and left after two years to pursue a writing career. He published a children's book, *Tito's Hats*, and was an editor for a year before going on the Broadway stage as a dancer in Cole Porter's *You Never Know* and then becoming a radio producer for NBC. In 1945 he was working in Hollywood and made his directorial debut with *Girl of the Limberlost*. In 1947 he assisted John Ford on *The Fugitive* and helped to found the La Jolla Playhouse Company. In 1949 he made his screen debut as an actor in *Lost Boundaries*, playing a black doctor who passed as white for 20 years. Though he directed and later produced a few more films, acting became the mainstay of his career with such roles as the gunfighter in *Rancho Notorious*, the crippled puppet-master in *Lili*, Prince Andrei in *War and Peace* and the frustrated lover Robert Cohn in *The Sun Also Rises*. He directed Audrey Hepburn, his third wife (1954–68), in *Green Mansions*. In the Seventies he worked mostly in Europe.

Films include: 1945 Girl of the Limberlost (dir). '49 Lost Boundaries (act). '52 Rancho Notorious (act); Scaramouche (act). '53 Lili (act). '55 Oh, Rosalinda!! (act) (GB). '56 War and Peace (act) (IT-USA); Elena et les Hommes (act) (FR) (USA: Paris Does Strange Things; GB: The Night Does Strange Things). '57 The Sun Also Rises (act). '59 The World, the Flesh and the Devil (act); Green Mansions (dir). '64 Sex and the Single Girl (act). '65 El Greco (prod; + act) (IT-FR). '66 Cabriola (dir; + prod; + sc) (SP). '67 Wait Until Dark (prod). '81 Lili Marleen (act) (GER).

Above: Mel Ferrer as El Greco. *Left: José Ferrer as Toulouse-Lautrec in* Moulin Rouge. *Above, centre right: Emilio Fernandez in* A Covenant With Death *(1967). Above, centre left: Federico Fellini directing*

FERRERI, Marco

(b. 1928). Director. Born: Milan,
Italy

Initially a student of medicine, Ferreri
made a few advertising shorts and
helped to promote a cine-magazine,
Documento Mensile, a series of compilation films made by De Sica, Visconti,
Antonioni and others, which folded
after only two months. In 1953 he
worked as co-producer on an om-
nibus film *Amore in Città*, partly directed by Antonioni and Fellini. In 1957
he went to Spain and worked with
Rafael Azcona on several scripts, leading to his directorial debut with *El
Pisito*. He made three black comedies
in Spain and the success at the Venice
Film Festival of the last of these, *El
Cochecito*, about an unscrupulous old
man in a wheelchair, enabled him to
launch his career. His depiction of an
obsession with food as representing
the consumer society is apparent in
Dillinger Is Dead and *Blow-Out*, a satirical tale in bad taste of four men
eating themselves to death. His films
also examine the sexual mores of the
middle class, which he sees as leading
to self-mutilation (as in *The Last
Woman*) and death.

Films include: 1958 El Pisito (SP). '59 El
Cochecito (SP) (GB: The Wheelchair). '63
Una Storia Moderna: L'Ape Regina (IT-FR)
(USA: The Conjugal Bed). '64 La Donna
Scimmia (IT-FR) (USA: The Ape Woman).
'68 L'Uomo dai Palloncini (IT-FR) (USA:
The Man With the Balloons). '69 Dillinger
è Morto (GB: Dillinger Is Dead). '73 La
Grande Bouffe (FR-IT) (GB: Blow-Out). '76
L'Ultima Donna (IT-FR) (USA/GB: The Last
Woman). '78 Ciao Maschio. '81 Storie di
Ordinaria Follia (IT-FR).

FERZETTI, Gabriele

(b. 1925). Actor. Born: Pasquale
Ferzetti; Rome, Italy

An actor in university plays, Ferzetti
won a scholarship to the Rome Academy of Dramatic Art, from which
he was expelled for working in a
professional company. He joined the
National Theatre but left after a year
to star in Vivi Gioi's theatrical company. After supporting parts in several movies, he played his first lead
opposite Gina Lollobrigida in *La Provinciale*, establishing himself as a top
romantic player. Having been in
Antonioni's *Le Amiche*, he took the
lead as the failed architect and vacil-
lating lover in *L'Avventura*. He then
went on to more varied roles, often
playing a man who conceals weaknesses behind a suave exterior. But his
career as an international actor never
really got off the ground, despite occasional parts in foreign films.

Films include: 1953 La Provinciale (GB:
Wayward Wife). '55 Le Amiche (GB: The
Girl Friends). '60 L'Avventura (USA: The
Adventure); Annibale (IT-USA) (GB: Han-
nibal). '65 Trois Chambres à Manhattan
(FR) (USA: Three Rooms in Manhattan).
'66 La Bibbia (IT) (USA/GB: The Bible – In
the Beginning). '67 A Ciascuno il Suo (USA:
We Still Kill the Old Way). '68 C'Era una
Volta il West (USA/GB: Once Upon a Time
in the West). '69 On Her Majesty's Secret
Service (GB). '70 L'Aveu (FR-IT) (USA: The
Confession). '74 Il Portiere di Notte
(USA/GB: The Night Porter).

FETCHIT, Stepin

(1892–1985). Actor. Born: Lincoln
Theodore Monroe Andrew Perry;
Key West, Florida, USA

Stepin Fetchit was the recurrent
grossly stereotyped Negro figure in
Thirties film, nervously cringing, con-
genitally lazy and almost cretinously
stupid. He was of West Indian descent
– his father was a cigar-maker in
Florida. As a child he toured with
minstrel shows, taking his stage name
from a winning racehorse. He moved
into vaudeville and then, almost by
accident, into films. He was teamed by
20th Century-Fox with Will Rogers
until Rogers died in a plane crash in
1935. Fetchit made few films after the
Thirties and was bankrupt by 1945.
He was given a few bit parts, for
instance by John Ford, and then came
a twenty-year gap in his career. In the
Seventies he re-emerged as a stand-up
comedian and sued for damages, unsuccessfully, when described as a
'white man's Negro' in a documentary. In 1976 an illness caused him to
lose the power of speech.

Films include: 1927 In Old Kentucky. '29
Hearts of Dixie. '34 Carolina; Stand Up and
Cheer; Judge Priest. '35 The County Chairman; Steamboat Round the Bend. '48 Miracle in Harlem. '53 The Sun Shines Bright.
'75 Won Ton Ton, the Dog That Saved
Hollywood.

FEUILLADE, Louis

(1873–1925). Director. Born: Lunel,
France

After four years in the cavalry, Feuillade became a provincial journalist,
writing bullfight reviews. He went to
Paris and started a satirical magazine,
La Tomate, that lasted three months.
He joined Gaumont as a scenarist in
1905 and rose at the start of 1907 to be
head of production. In 1911, forced to
make economies, he launched a series
of cheap location-made films, *La Vie
Telle Qu'Elle Est*, which made a virtue
of their realistic backgrounds. The
crime series and serials that made
Feuillade's lasting reputation similarly had convincing Parisian settings
as backdrops to their fantastic events,
often invented on location. *Fantômas*
and *Les Vampires* dealt with the adventures of larger-than-life master
criminals; *Judex* was a mysterious
avenger on the side of good. For
suspense and excitement as well as
atmosphere, these films far surpassed
the contemporary American serials.
After the war Feuillade was considered old-fashioned but he continued to work prolifically until his
death. The Surrealists admired his
great serials and did much to restore
his reputation.

Films include: 1910–13 Bébé series (75
shorts). '11–13 La Vie Telle Qu'Elle Est
series (18 shorts). '12–16 Bout-de-Zan
series (52 shorts). '13 Fantômas (3-part
feature); Juve Contre Fantômas (4-part feature). '14 Fantômas Contre Fantômas (4-
part feature). '15 Les Vampires (10-ep.
serial). '16 Judex (12-ep. serial). '17 La
Nouvelle Mission de Judex (12-ep. serial).
'18 Tih Minh (12-ep. serial). '19 Barrabas
(12-ep. serial).

*Top left: Gabriele Ferzetti starring in
L'Avventura. Top: Stepin Fetchit in
The Sun Shines Bright. Left: Edwige
Feuillère in Sans Lendemain. Above:
Sally Field as Norma Rae, her most
challenging and successful role.*

FEUILLÈRE, Edwige

(b. 1907). Actress. Born: Edwige Cunatti-Koenig; Vesoul, France

The grand old lady of the French theatre has made many films and worked with such directors as Max Ophuls and Jean Cocteau, whose artificiality of style showed off her dramatic qualities; but she has always been more at home on the stage than on the screen. On graduating from the Paris Conservatoire in 1931, she joined the Comédie Française and married Pierre Feuillère; but both commitments proved short-lived. She also started her film career around the same time, usually playing elegant women of the world. She was hailed as the new Sarah Bernhardt and had a fruitful collaboration with Jean-Louis Barrault on the stage – she came to London with him in 1951 in Paul

Above: Shirley Ann Field in The Damned. *Below left: Britain's own – the much-loved Gracie Fields. Below: W.C. Fields – cynical, suspicious, rude, but still charismatic – in one of his celebrated golfing sketches*

Claudel's *Partage de Midi*. She appeared in films regularly until the late Fifties and occasionally thereafter. The best-remembered of her later roles is as the older woman who teaches a teenage boy about sexual love in *Le Blé en Herbe*, adapted from a Colette novel. Edwige Feuillère was made a member of the Legion of Honour in 1980.

Films include: 1933 Topaze. **'35** Golgotha; Lucrèce Borgia. **'40** Sans Lendemain; De Mayerling à Sarajevo. **'48** L'Aigle à Deux Têtes (USA: The Eagle With Two Heads; GB: The Eagle Has Two Heads). **'51** Olivia. **'54** Le Blé en Herbe (GB: Ripening Seed). **'58** En Cas de Malheur (FR-IT) (GB: Love Is My Profession). **'64** Aimez-Vous les Femmes? (FR-IT) (GB: Do You Like Women?).

FEYDER, Jacques

(1888–1948). Director. Born: Jacques Frederix; Ixelles, Belgium

Jacques Feyder began his career as a theatre actor in 1912, and started to write and direct short films for Gaumont in 1916. He married the actress Françoise Rosay in 1917 and she later appeared in many of his films. After service at the front and in an army theatrical troupe, he made his first major film *L'Atlantide* in 1921, shooting it on location in the Sahara. After establishing his reputation with *Crainquebille* and other films, Feyder was signed by MGM in 1928 and worked with Greta Garbo on *The Kiss* and the German and Swedish versions of *Anna Christie* (1930); but otherwise he did not enjoy American production-line methods and returned to Paris in 1933. In 1935 he made his most famous film, *La Kermesse Héroïque*, an erotic comedy set in seventeenth-century Flanders and starring Françoise Rosay. Soon afterwards he was invited by Alexander Korda to make his only English film, *Knight Without Armour*, set in the Russian Revolution. During World War II he took refuge in Switzerland,

making one film and teaching at the Conservatoire in Geneva. After the war he returned to Paris but, apart from supervising *Macadam* (1946), he was unable to resume his career. He is generally considered Belgium's greatest director although, unlike his countryman André Delvaux, he made no Belgian films.

Films include: 1921 L'Atlantide (USA: Missing Husbands; GB: Atlantide). **'22** Crainquebille (GB: Ole Bill of Paris). **'25** Visages d'Enfants (SWITZ) (USA: Faces of Children); Gribiche. **'28** Thérèse Raquin/Du sollst nicht ehebrechen! (GER-FR) (USA: Shadows of Fear; GB: Thou Shalt Not). **'29** The Kiss (USA). **'31** Daybreak (USA). **'34** Pension Mimosas. **'35** La Kermesse Héroïque (USA/GB: Carnival in Flanders). **'37** Knight Without Armour (GB).

FIELD, Sally

(b. 1946). Actress. Born: Pasadena, California, USA

A talented and likeable actress, Sally Field battled to escape from roles as Gidget-style ingénue, only to find herself again typed as gutsy little campaigners in *Norma Rae* and *Absence of Malice*. Having landed the lead in the TV *Gidget* series at the age of 19, she spent much of the next eight years in television – another leading role was in the *Flying Nun* series. Her film debut came in *The Way West*; *Stay Hungry* gave her more chance to show what she could do. Her private liaison with Burt Reynolds led to one or two film appearances together. The title role of the young labour organizer in *Norma Rae*, however, remains the big showpiece of Field's career. It won her the 1979 Academy Award for Best Actress.

Films include: 1967 The Way West. **'76** Stay Hungry. **'77** Smokey and the Bandit; Heroes. **'78** The End; Hooper. **'79** Norma Rae; Beyond the Poseidon Adventure. **'80** Smokey and the Bandit II (GB: Smokey and the Bandit Ride Again). **'81** Backroads; Absence of Malice.

FIELD, Shirley Ann

(b. 1938). Actress. Born: London, England

With her red hair and slightly pinched prettiness, Shirley Ann Field was a favourite face in British cinema during the early Sixties. She was also a child of the times. At five, her East End home was blitzed. She was subsequently reared in a Lancashire orphanage, and only found her mother again in 1978. As a 15-year-old office worker, she saved up for drama lessons. Modelling led to television where she attracted notice in a quiz show and won bit parts in both theatre and films. A leading role came with *Horrors of the Black Museum*, though her most memorable films remain *The Entertainer, Saturday Night and Sunday Morning* and *Alfie*. She continues to appear regularly on television, usually as the sexually bored or sharp-tongued wife of an executive.

Films include: 1959 Horrors of the Black Museum. **'60** The Entertainer; Saturday Night and Sunday Morning. **'62** The Damned (USA: These Are the Damned). **'66** Alfie.

FIELDS, Gracie

(1898–1979). Actress. Born: Grace Stansfield; Rochdale, Lancashire, England

Gracie Fields was the best-loved British comedienne of her times. Doggedly asserting her working class and regional origins at a time when these qualities were less in fashion, her films (the best of them directed by Basil Dean) spoke of and to the British people of the Depression era. Born over a chip shop, she was already entertaining audiences by the time she was 13. After World War I she conquered London in the revue *Mr Tower of London*, which ran for seven years. Her robust character comedy and intrepid coloratura singing translated well into films: the eleven she made, from *Sally in Our Alley* to *Shipyard Sally* have lost none of their spirit while they have gained a rich quality of nostalgia.

Films: 1931 Sally in Our Alley. **'32** Looking on the Bright Side. **'33** This Week of Grace. **'34** Love, Life and Laughter; Sing As We Go! **'35** Look Up and Laugh. **'36** Queen of Hearts. **'37** The Show Goes On. **'38** We're Going to Be Rich; Keep Smiling (USA: Smiling Along). **'39** Shipyard Sally. **'43** Stage Door Canteen (USA); Holy Matrimony (USA). **'45** Paris Underground (USA) (GB: Madame Pimpernel).

FIELDS, W. C.

(1879–1946). Actor. Born: William Claude Dukinfield; Philadelphia, Pennsylvania, USA

Perhaps the secret of Fields' indestructible fascination is that his comedy was so close to tragedy. He is the only comedian whose stock-in-trade is a convinced misanthropy born of hard experience that the rest of mankind is made up of knaves, fools, thieves, liars, doctors, dogs, babies, nagging wives, mothers-in-law, policemen, bankers and lesser menaces; and that the only defences available to an honest man are wariness, larceny and deception or, when they don't work, the bottle. In his youth Fields drove himself to become the best juggler of his day. A vaudeville star by 1900, he featured regularly in the Ziegfeld Follies, and first-committed one of his stage sketches to film in 1915, *Pool Sharks*. A major contribution to the development of the ultimate Fields character was his role in the stage play *Poppy*, which was twice filmed (first as *Sally of the Sawdust*). A dedicated Dickensian, Fields made a memorable Micawber in Cukor's *David Copperfield*. Fields wrote most of his later films, under such discreet *noms de plume* as Otis Criblecoblis and Mahatma Kane Jeeves. His ultimate jest was to die on Christmas Day, a festival which, above all others, he claimed to despise.

Films include: 1915 Pool Sharks. **'25** Sally of the Sawdust. **'28** Tillie's Punctured Romance. **'30** The Golf Specialist (short). **'33** Alice in Wonderland. **'34** Mrs Wiggs of the Cabbage Patch. **'35** David Copperfield. **'36** Poppy. **'40** My Little Chickadee (+co-sc); The Bank Dick (+sc) (GB: The Bank Detective). **'41** Never Give a Sucker an Even Break (GB: What a Man).

Above: Jon Finch in Macbeth. *Above right: Peter Finch in* Judith *(1966). Above, far right: Frank Finlay in* Othello. *Right: James Finlayson and Laurel and Hardy in* Big Business

FINCH, Jon

(b. 1942). Actor. Born: Surrey, England

A dark, handsome and virile Seventies actor, Finch never managed to equal his peak year of 1971 when, from a cameo part in *Sunday, Bloody Sunday*, he leapt to major roles in Roman Polanski's *Macbeth* and Alfred Hitchcock's *Frenzy*. After school, Finch spent 18 months with the SAS then drifted into the theatre, doing stints in rep and appearing in television series (*Z-Cars*; *Coronation Street*). A lead role in another series, *Counterstrike*, and parts in Hammer horrors eventually ·launched his modest stardom.

Films include: 1970 The Vampire Lovers. '71 Macbeth; Sunday, Bloody Sunday. '72 Frenzy; Lady Caroline Lamb (GB-IT). '78 Death on the Nile. '80 Breaking Glass; Gary Cooper Que Estos en Los Culos (SP). '81 Doktor Faustus (GER); La Amenaza (USA-SP) (USA: The Threat).

FINCH, Peter

(1916–1977). Actor. Born: William Mitchell; London, England

One of the most versatile and sensitive actors in English films from the Fifties to the Seventies, Finch was able to play a tough Australian soldier (*A Town Like Alice*) or the hurt homosexuals of *The Trials of Oscar Wilde* or *Sunday, Bloody Sunday*. As a child Finch was taken from London to his father's native Australia. Among a variety of jobs, including sheep farming, he appeared in one or two Australian films (*Dad and Dave Come to Town, Mr Chedworth Steps Out*, both 1938) though his acting career only began seriously after his service in World War II. Encouraged by Laurence Olivier he came to work in England where he was as much in demand for American films as British. The Seventies brought him unrewarding blockbuster roles, though his last appearance, in *Network*, won him a posthumous Oscar.

Films include: 1949 Eureka Stockade (+2nd ass. dir; + cast. dir) (USA: Massacre Hill). '53 The Heart of the Matter. '54 Elephant Walk. '56 A Town Like Alice (USA: The Rape of Malaya); The Battle of the River Plate (USA: Pursuit of the Graf Spee). '57 Robbery Under Arms; Windom's Way. '60 The Trials of Oscar Wilde (USA: The Man With the Green Carnation/The Green Carnation). '61 No Love for Johnnie. '67 Far From the Madding Crowd. '68 The Legend of Lylah Clare (USA). '71 Sunday, Bloody Sunday. '73 England Made Me; Bequest to the Nation (USA: The Nelson Affair). '76 Network.

FINLAY, Frank

(b. 1926). Actor. Born: Farnworth, near Bolton, Lancashire, England

Frank Finlay's regular casting in the roles of rather plodding villains and very average husbands tends to obscure the fact that he is a useful and, on occasion, excellent character actor. Leaving school at 14, he worked in a variety of jobs, but maintained an interest in amateur theatre and eventually made his professional debut in Scotland in 1951. After a period of work in bit parts and as assistant stage manager, he made his way to RADA and thence to bigger roles in Guildford Rep. London success came with his performances in Wesker plays at the Royal Court Theatre; and he made his film debut in *The Longest Day* (1962). His most substantial film appearance was as Iago to Olivier's *Othello* in a film adaptation of the notable stage production. In 1970 Finlay formed a film company in a partnership that included the director Alan Bridges.

Films include: 1962 Life for Ruth (USA: Walk in the Shadow). '65 A Study in Terror (USA: Fog); Othello. '67 Robbery. '68 Twisted Nerve. '70 The Molly Maguires (USA); Cromwell. '71 Assault; Gumshoe. '72 Sitting Target. '73 The Three Musketeers: The Queen's Diamonds (PAN). '75 The Four Musketeers: The Revenge of Milady (PAN-SP).

FINLAYSON, James

(1887–1953). Actor. Born: Falkirk, Scotland

After doing an apprenticeship in his father's iron foundry, Finlayson studied at Edinburgh University where he became friendly with actor John Clyde. He then took up acting himself and became a professional stage comedian and character actor.

In 1912 he went to America to appear in *Bunty Pulls the Strings* on Broadway and also toured in vaudeville. In 1916 he took to films. A three-year stint with Mack Sennett, co-starring in the Keystone Kops with Ben Turpin, was followed by a four-year stretch with Hal Roach in Culver City. He is best remembered for his appearances as the bald-headed, exasperated comic foil to Laurel and Hardy. Illness eventually forced him to retire.

Films include: 1929 Big Business. '30 Another Fine Mess. '35 Bonnie Scotland. '36 The Bohemian Girl. '37 Way Out West. '38 Block-heads. '40 Saps at Sea; A Chump at Oxford. '42 To Be or Not to Be. '51 Royal Wedding.

FINNEY, Albert

(b. 1936). Actor/producer/director. Born: Salford, Lancashire, England

The son of a Lancashire bookmaker, Finney won a scholarship to RADA in 1956 – his fellow students included Alan Bates and Peter O'Toole – before appearing at Birmingham Repertory and understudying Laurence Olivier at Stratford. After appearing in the

148

Above: Peter Firth in Equus. *Above left: Albert Finney as* Tom Jones. *Left: Carrie Fisher as Princess Leia in* The Empire Strikes Back. *Below: Barry Fitzgerald in* The Catered Affair *(1956, Wedding Breakfast)*

stage hit *Billy Liar*, Finney was offered his first major screen role, in *Saturday Night and Sunday Morning*. This established him as a brooding working-class Lancashire lad – a role he varyingly repeated several times in the next few years. He then returned to the stage, working closely with the playwright John Osborne and director Tony Richardson. In 1963 came his most famous screen role, as *Tom Jones*. By 1965 he had become involved in film production and formed Memorial Enterprises – the company responsible for *Gumshoe, If . . .* (1968) and other successful ventures. He then tried his hand at direction with *Charlie Bubbles*, the story of a well-known author going back to the north to find his roots, and topped this by becoming the artistic director at the Royal Court Theatre. Twenty years on, Finney had refined his accent and smoothed away the 'rough' edges to become a wealthy international star with the versatility to excel in lightweight musicals (*Annie*) or emotional dramas (*Shoot the Moon*). He was married for a time to the French actress Anouk Aimée.

Films include: 1960 Saturday Night and Sunday Morning. '63 Tom Jones. '64 Night Must Fall. '68 Charlie Bubbles (+ dir). '70

Scrooge. '71 Gumshoe. '74 Murder on the Orient Express. '77 The Duellists. '81 Annie; Shoot the Moon.

FIRTH, Peter

(b. 1953). Actor. Born: Bradford, Yorkshire, England

While still at school Peter Firth attended Saturday morning drama lessons at the Bradford Civic Theatre Drama Club. Various walk-on parts for Yorkshire Television led to a major role in the children's series *The Flaxton Boys*. On leaving school he moved to London and was able to further establish himself in children's television. He was Friar Elia in Franco Zefferelli's film *Brother Sun, Sister Moon* and, staying in Italy appeared as Daniel in *Daniel e Maria*. He also worked in Disney's *Diamonds on Wheels*. Firth has since won major roles as worried young men: Armand in the BBC's *Lady of the Camellias*; a psychologically disturbed boy in *Equus*; and the baby-faced, sanctimonious Angel Clare in *Tess*.

Films include: 1972 Diamonds on Wheels. '73 Daniel e Maria (IT); Fratello Sole, Sorella Luna (IT) (USA/GB: Brother Sun, Sister

Moon. '76 Aces High (GB-FR). '77 Joseph Andrews; Equus. '79 When You Comin' Back, Red Ryder? (USA); Tess (FR-GB).

FISHER, Carrie

(b. 1956). Actress. Born: Los Angeles, California, USA

The daughter of Debbie Reynolds and Eddie Fisher, Carrie Fisher appeared on her mother's television shows at the age of 13 and was performing on the New York stage by the time she was 17. After a minor role in Warren Beatty's *Shampoo*, she was voted Newcomer of the Year by Photoplay magazine. In 1974 she played the London Palladium – in a variety act – and successfully auditioned for the Central School of Speech and Drama where she studied for two years. She then appeared as Princess Leia Organa in *Star Wars* and has since made a TV spectacular, *Come Back Little Sheba*.

Films include: 1975 Shampoo. '77 Star Wars. '78 I Want to Hold Your Hand. '79 Wise Blood (USA-GER); Mr Mike's Mondo Video. '80 The Empire Strikes back; The Blues Brothers. '81 Under the Rainbow.

FISHER, Gerry

(b. 1926). Cinematographer. Born: London, England

On leaving school Gerry Fisher was employed by Kodak as a draughtsman. After service with the Royal Navy during World War II he became clapperboy and focus-puller with Alliance Riverside Studios. When they closed he joined Wessex Films, assisting in the shooting of documentaries. At the British Lion Studios in Shepperton he rose to assistant cameraman and was eventually promoted to camera-operator on David Lean's *The Bridge On the River Kwai* (1957). Ten years later he became a fully-fledged lighting-cameraman when Joseph Losey hired him to shoot *Accident*. Thereafter Fisher worked as cinematographer with Losey and also Billy Wilder on many successful films.

Films include: 1967 Accident. '68 Secret Ceremony. '70 Ned Kelly. '71 The Go-Between. '73 Bequest to a Nation; A Doll's House. '76 Aces High (GB-FR); Mr Klein (FR-IT). '78 Fedora (GER).

FISHER, Terence

(1940–1980). Director. Born: London, England

Terence Fisher was educated at Christ's Hospital School in Sussex and spent seven years as a merchant seaman. He then worked as a window-dresser in Chelsea and became a member of the London Film Society. He joined Gaumont British as a trainee under Michael Balcon and rose to the post of supervising editor at Teddington Studios. While there he co-directed two Rank 'quickies' – *The Astonished Heart* with Noel Coward and *So Long at the Fair* with Dirk Bogarde. In 1957 Hammer offered him the directorship of *The Curse of Frankenstein*. Many other horror movies led to his being described as an 'international cult *auteur*'.

Films include: 1950 The Astonished Heart; So Long at the Fair. '57 The Curse of Frankenstein. '58 Dracula (USA: Horror of Dracula). '59 The Hound of the Baskervilles. '60 The Brides of Dracula; Two Faces of Dr Jekyll. '62 The Phantom of the Opera. '64 The Gorgon. '66 Island of Terror. '68 The Devil Rides Out (USA: The Devil's Bride).

FITZGERALD, Barry

(1888–1961). Actor. Born: William Joseph Shields; Dublin, Ireland

William Shields attended the Merchant Taylor's school in Dublin before doing a book-keeping course and becoming a clerk with the Board of Trade in 1911. He loved acting and made the Abbey Theatre his second home until, in 1916, he won his first walk-on part and took a suitably Irish sounding stage name. In 1929 Sean O'Casey wrote *The Silver Tassle* for him and its success led Fitzgerald into his most famous stage role as the alcoholic in *Juno and the Paycock*. In 1944 he found himself in America with a Paramount contract. He became their resident Irish character actor, and in this capacity he appeared in *Going My Way, Naked City, The Quiet Man* and many other films. His best work was, inevitably, for John Ford, but it was as the grumpy old priest in *Going My Way* that he won his Oscar.

Films include: 1936 The Plough and the Stars. '41 How Green Was My Valley. '44 Going My Way; None But the Lonely Heart. '45 Incendiary Blonde; And Then There Were None (GB: Ten Little Niggers). '46 Two Years Before the Mast. '48 Naked City. '49 Top o' the Morning. '52 The Quiet Man.

FITZGERALD, F. Scott

(1896–1940). Writer. Born: Francis Scott Key Fitzgerald; St Paul, Minnesota, USA

Following the success of his first novel in 1920, F. Scott Fitzgerald was able to sell three of his stories to Hollywood and his second novel, *The Beautiful and the Damned*, was filmed in 1922. His first confident trip to Hollywood in 1924 was a jaunt that produced no useable scripts; a longer visit in 1927 resulted in an original screen story, *Lipstick*, but it was not filmed. In 1931, pushed for money after his wife Zelda's mental breakdown, he co-scripted *Red-Headed Woman* (1932) but his version was not used for the film. In 1937 he settled permanently in Hollywood but 18 months at MGM produced only one credit, *Three Comrades*, and the producer drastically altered the script. Then he freelanced, hampered by his heavy drinking, and also created potentially the finest of Hollywood novels, *The Last Tycoon*, an idealized portrait of Irving Thalberg, left unfinished at Fitzgerald's premature death. Both his writings and his life story have since provided abundant material for films and television.

Films based on Fitzgerald's stories include: 1920 The Chorus Girl's Romance; The Husband Hunter. '21 The Off-Shore Pirate. '26 The Great Gatsby. '28 Pusher-in-the-Face. '38 Three Comrades (co-sc. only). '49 The Great Gatsby. '54 The Last Time I Saw Paris. '62 Tender Is the Night. '74 The Great Gatsby. '76 The Last Tycoon.

FITZMAURICE, George

(1885–1940). Director. Born: Paris, France

Of Irish parentage, George Fitzmaurice found himself heading for the diplomatic service but opted for the more glamorous life of an artist. After a few years his itchy feet took him to India where he lived for nine years working as a cotton, jute and hemp salesman. On his return to France he began his career in films as a scriptwriter for Pathé and, after emigrating to America, eventually became a director. His artistic bent soon surfaced in films such as *The Son of the Sheik* and *As You Desire Me*, and he quickly established a reputation for meticulous accuracy and a pronounced visual style.

Films include: 1918 The Naulahka. '20 On With the Dance (USA). '26 The Son of the Sheik. '27 The Night of Love. '31 One Heavenly Night (USA); Strangers May Kiss (USA). '32 As You Desire Me. '38 Arsène Lupin Returns (USA); Vacation From Love (USA).

FLAHERTY, Robert J.

(1884–1951). Documentarist/explorer. Born: Iron Mountain, Michigan, USA

The son of an iron-ore miner, Robert Flaherty studied at the Michigan College of Mines before accompanying his father on prospecting expeditions that taught him survival and a respect for wild terrain. He then began to record his travels on film and took a particular interest in the peoples of the Arctic wastes. *Nanook of the North* was his first full-length documentary and charted the life of an Eskimo and his family. He went on to make similar films in the South Seas, Ireland, America and India. As well as being authentic records of 'the noble savage' and his environment, his films are strikingly beautiful to look at.

Films include: 1922 Nanook of the North. '24 Moana (A Romance of the Golden Age)/The Sea. '30 Tabu (uncredited co-dir). '33 Industrial Britain (short) (GB). '34 Man of Aran (GB). '37 Elephant Boy (co-dir) (GB). '42 The Land. '48 Louisiana Story.

FLAIANO, Ennio

(1910–1972). Screenwriter. Born: Pescara, Italy

Flaiano trained as an architect before turning to journalism. In 1939 he became a critic for *Film* magazine and during World War II he began to write scripts. At first he collaborated with Alberto Moravia and Suso Cecchi d'Amico on films for the director Alessandro Blasetti, then he formed a long, close-working relationship with Federico Fellini. He also wrote *Time to Kill*, a novel about a soldier in post-World War II Africa, and several volumes of satirical short stories.

Films include: 1946 Roma Città Libera (co-sc). '51 Dov'è la Libertà? (co-sc). '53 I Vitelloni (co-sc) (GB: The Spivs). '54 La Strada (co-sc); Totò e Carolina (co-sc). '59 La Dolce Vita (co-sc). '61 La Notte (co-sc)

(IT-FR) (GB: The Night). '63 Otto e Mezzo (co-sc) (IT-FR) (USA/GB: 8½). '65 Giulietta degli Spiriti (co-sc) (IT-FR) (GB: Juliet of the Spirits); La Decima Vittima (co-sc) (IT-FR) (GB: The Tenth Victim). '71 Liza (co-sc) (GB: Love to Eternity).

FLEISCHER, Max and Dave

Fleischer, Max (1883–1972). Animator. Born: Vienna, Austria

Fleischer, Dave (1894–1979). Animator. Born: New York City, USA

Max studied art in New York and was a commercial artist before inventing the rotoscope, which traced live-action film to create cartoons, in 1915. He took nearly a year to make his first film, *Out of the Inkwell*, and then went to Paramount, where his brother Dave, already an experienced film editor, joined him as assistant and Rotoscope model. Both worked for the army in World War I and in 1919 formed Out of the Inkwell Inc to make comic cartoons. Soon they were turning out masses of Koko the Clown films, with Max as producer and Dave as director. In 1929 they founded Fleischer Studios Inc, releasing through Paramount. In 1930 they invented the sexy little cutie Betty Boop, who continued to give scandal until 1939; and in 1933 they began the Popeye the Sailor series that continued in their charge until 1942, by which time their studio, moved from New York to Miami in 1939, had been closed down by Paramount, following the failure of two feature films, *Gulliver's Travels* and *Mr Bug Goes to Town*. Max produced training films for a while and in 1962 formed a production company for television cartoons before retiring in 1963. Dave headed Columbia's animation unit from 1942 to 1944, when he went to Universal until his retirement in 1967. Max was the father of director Richard Fleischer.

Films include: 1915 Out of the Inkwell. '19 The Clown's Pup. '24 Ko-Ko in 1999. '26 My Old Kentucky Home. '30 Dizzy Dishes. '31 Betty Co-ed. '32 Boop-Oop-a-Doop. '33 Popeye the Sailor. '34 Betty Boop's Rise to Fame (compilation). '35 Adventures of Popeye (compilation). '36 Popeye the Sailor Meets Sinbad the Sailor (two-reeler). '37 Popeye the Sailor Meets Ali Baba's Forty Thieves (two-reeler). '39 Aladdin and His Wonderful Lamp (two-reeler); Gulliver's Travels (feature). '41 Mr Bug Goes to Town (feature) (GB: Hoppity Goes to Town); Superman in The Mechanical Monsters. '42 Olive Oyl and Water Don't Mix; Superman in Terror on the Midway.

FLEISCHER, Richard

(b. 1916). Director. Born: New York City, USA

The son of animator Max Fleischer, Richard gave up his medical studies in favour of a drama course at Yale. While there he formed the Arena Players drama group, becoming producer and director of all the plays they put on. In 1940 he joined RKO, and for the next three years edited and co-wrote the Pathé newsreel series *This Is America*. He followed this with a series

of silent-film compilations written and produced by himself – the *Flicker Flashbacks*. From 1946 he has directed features, mainly suspense and drama thrillers such as *Violent Saturday* and *Compulsion*, with varying degrees of success.

Films include: 1946 Child of Divorce. '52 The Narrow Margin. '54 20,000 Leagues Under the Sea. '55 Violent Saturday; The Girl in the Red Velvet Swing. '58 The Vikings. '59 Compulsion. '62 Barabba/Barabbas (IT). '66 Fantastic Voyage. '67 Doctor Dolittle. '68 The Boston Strangler. '70 Tora! Tora! Tora! (co-dir) (USA-JAP). '71 10 Rillington Place (GB). '72 The New Centurions. '73 Soylent Green. '76 The Incredible Sarah (GB). '79 Ashanti.

FLEMING, Rhonda

(b. 1923). Actress. Born: Marilyn Louis; Los Angeles, California, USA

Marilyn Louis' parents were in show business. While still at Beverly Hills High School she reached the finals of a radio talent contest and found herself on the cover of a magazine. This early fame brought her to the attention of 20th Century-Fox, but it was for David O. Selznick that she first appeared in a role of any note – that of one of the inmates in a psychiatric hospital in *Spellbound*. With auburn hair and dazzlingly green eyes, Fleming was at her best in her Technicolor films such as *A Connecticut Yankee in King Arthur's Court*. She also excelled in *femme fatale* roles, playing brittle, nervous women – the secretary framing a private detective for murder in *Out of the Past*; the adulterous wife of a newspaper tycoon in *While the City Sleeps*. Married four times, she divorced her last husband, director Hall Bartlett, in 1971.

Films include: 1945 Spellbound; The Spiral Staircase. '47 Out of the Past (GB: Build My Gallows High). '49 A Connecticut Yankee in King Arthur's Court. '50 Cry Danger. '53 Inferno. '54 Yankee Pasha. '56 While the City Sleeps. '57 Gunfight at the OK Corral.

FLEMING, Victor

(1883–1949). Director. Born: Pasadena, California, USA

Victor Fleming entered the film industry in 1910 as a cameraman, and went on to work in that capacity for D.W. Griffith and Douglas Fairbanks. He turned to direction in 1920. Usually reckoned an action specialist, Fleming was in fact remarkably versatile. A tough character himself, he got the best from tough ladies like Clara Bow and Jean Harlow; he handled sentiment capably in *Captains Courageous*; and in 1939 he brought off the astonishing double of *The Wizard of Oz* and *Gone With the Wind*. Neither of these films is entirely Fleming's work (King Vidor, George Cukor and Sam Wood were also involved), but *The Wizard of Oz* has the innocence of the silents in which Fleming grew up, and a very hard, tough core, while Fleming's sympathy with Gable at least partially rescued *Gone With the Wind* from simpering prettiness.

Above: Rhonda Fleming in A Connecticut Yankee in King Arthur's Court. *Above right: Jay C. Flippen with John Wayne in* Flying Leathernecks *(1951). Right: Errol Flynn at the peak of his career in* The Sea Hawk. *Below: Louise Fletcher in* One Flew Over the Cuckoo's Nest

Films include: **1919** When the Clouds Roll By (co-dir). **'20** The Mollycoddle. **'25** Lord Jim. **'29** Abie's Irish Rose; The Virginian. **'32** Red Dust. **'35** Reckless. **'37** Captains Courageous. **'39** The Wizard of Oz; Gone With the Wind. **'41** Dr Jekyll and Mr Hyde. **'42** Tortilla Flat. **'43** A Guy Named Joe. **'48** Joan of Arc.

FLETCHER, Louise

(b. 1934). Actress. Born: Birmingham, Alabama, USA

To win a Best Actress Oscar in your second year in the movies is no small feat. Louise Fletcher managed it in *One Flew Over the Cuckoo's Nest* for her performance as the long-suffering, invincibly correct and entirely misguided Nurse Ratched. After some television work she had retired for family reasons in 1964. Ten years later came her first film, Robert Altman's doom-laden *Thieves Like Us*, in which she first impressed as a much put-upon lady. Her sense of humour, till then unsuspected, was nicely in evidence in *The Cheap Detective*, a *Casablanca* parody with Miss Fletcher devastating in the Ingrid Bergman role.

Films include: **1974** Thieves Like Us. **'75** Russian Roulette; One Flew Over the Cuckoo's Nest. **'77** Exorcist II: The Heretic. **'78** The Cheap Detective. **'79** The Magician of Lublin (ISRAEL-GER); Lady in Red; Natural Enemies. **'80** Mama Dracula (FR-BELG); The Lucky Star (CAN).

FLIPPEN, Jay C.

(1900–1971). Actor. Born: Little Rock, Arkansas, USA

After thirty years on the stage, Jay C. Flippen began a Hollywood career in 1947 (a brief flirtation with the medium in around 1934 hardly counts). A slow-moving, slow-talking, hard-bitten veteran, he was a splendid supporting player in Westerns for Anthony Mann and Samuel Fuller, and outstanding too in Stanley Kubrick's *The Killing*. In 1965 Flippen suffered the amputation of a leg, and after that acted from a wheelchair.

Films include: **1934** Marie Galante. **'47** Brute Force. **'48** They Live by Night. **'50** Winchester '73. **'52** Bend of the River (GB: Where the River Bends). **'53** The Wild One. **'55** The Far Country; Oklahoma! **'56** The Killing. **'57** Run of the Arrow. **'60** Wild River. **'62** How the West Was Won. **'65** Cat Ballou. **'68** Firecreek. **'71** The Seven Minutes.

FLOREY, Robert.

(1900–1979). Director. Born: Paris, France

Robert Florey was a Frenchman who fell in love with Hollywood. He had written on film, directed a few shorts, and been assistant to Louis Feuillade before sailing to America as correspondent for a French film magazine. Once there, he learned his craft thoroughly as assistant to, among others, King Vidor, Josef von Sternberg and Henry King, and made more shorts, including the famous Expressionist fantasy, *Life and Death of 9413, a Hollywood Extra*. From 1927 to 1950 Florey directed features. Most were small scale crime films, but *The Beast With Five Fingers* is a horror classic, while *Murders in the Rue Morgue* deserves to be. Florey also wrote two of the most fascinating books on Hollywood history, and in 1950, newly decorated by the French government with the Legion of Honour for his contribution to cinema, slipped off to television, where his output was prodigious.

Films include: **1927** Life and Death of 9413, a Hollywood Extra (short) (co-dir); One Hour of Love. **'29** The Cocoanuts (co-dir). **'31** Le Blanc et le noir (co-dir) (FR); Frankenstein (co-sc. only). **'32** Murders in the Rue Morgue. **'35** The Woman in Red. **'41** Meet Boston Blackie. **'43** The Desert Song. **'46** The Beast With Five Fingers. **'47** Monsieur Verdoux (assoc. dir). **'50** Johnny OneEye.

FLYNN, Errol

(1909–1959). Actor. Born: Hobart, Tasmania, Australia

When Errol Flynn came to England in 1933 he had worked at a variety of jobs, mainly outdoors, in Australia and New Guinea, and made one Australian film. He acted for 18 months with the Northampton Rep, and made a film for Warners' British company. The parent studio promptly carried him off to Hollywood, and within two years he was a top star. The rest is a bizarre mixture of legend, notoriety, accusation, and slow physical decay. In his early years in America he was a splendidly athletic and sympathetic hero in action pictures – especially the swashbucklers *Captain Blood*, *The Adventures of Robin Hood* and *The Sea Hawk* – but without the heroics to bolster it, Flynn's own personality on screen was demure, even self-effacing. Warners gave him two great action directors in Michael Curtiz and Raoul Walsh, and he needed them. When his youth went, he did little of note until his last few movies, in which he played a series of sad middle-aged drunks. By now his own life was in ruins. Always a heavy drinker, he came to have problems with drugs also, and his three marriages (two of them to actresses Lili Damita and Patrice Wymore) were never stable enough to help him. There was, too, the famous trial in 1942 for statutory rape, and though Flynn was acquitted he could never escape his reputation as a lecher. Whether he had been a Nazi agent, as charged in Charles Higham's well-documented book *Errol Flynn: The Untold Story*, will perhaps never be known. Flynn's greatest ambition was to be taken seriously as an actor – if, ultimately, he didn't make it, he remains the screen's greatest Robin Hood and General Custer.

Films include: **1935** The Case of the Curious Bride; Captain Blood; The Charge of the Light Brigade. **'37** The Prince and the Pauper. **'38** The Adventures of Robin Hood. **'40** The Sea Hawk. **'41** They Died With Their Boots On. **'42** Gentleman Jim. **'45** Objective, Burma! **'53** The Master of Ballantrae (GB); William Tell (+ co-prod) (unfinished). **'58** The Roots of Heaven. **'59** Cuban Rebel Girls.

FOCH, Nina

(b. 1924). Actress. Born: Nina Fock; Leyden, Holland

Daughter of a Dutch musician and an American actress, Nina Foch went to live in America at the age of ten, and switched her ambitions from music to the stage. Before she was 20 she was signed by Columbia, who used her in lesser, but often good pictures. She was versatile. Tough and smouldering in *The Dark Past*, she was a demure wife in *The Undercover Man*, and when MGM put her in bigger movies she was effective as a spoiled rich girl in *An American in Paris* and as the supremely efficient secretary of *Executive Suite*. But she didn't fit studio patterns, went back frequently to the stage, and by 1980 was teaching acting at the University of Southern California and running her own drama school.

Films include: 1944 Return of the Vampire. '45 My Name Is Julia Ross; Prison Ship. '48 Dark Past. '49 The Undercover Man. '51 An American in Paris. '52 Scaramouche. '53 Sombrero; Fast Company. '54 Executive Suite.

FOLSEY, George

(b. 1898). Cinematographer. Born: New York City, USA

George Folsey was a lighting cameraman in 1919, and still working in 1976. His first job was as office-boy for the Lasky Feature Play Company in New York. He was 14. Five years later, after being camera assistant and second cameraman, his career proper as one of Hollywood's most enduring professionals began. In a long stay at MGM, from the Thirties into the Fifties, Folsey brought originality into the studio look. He preferred soft lighting to harsh contrasts, and his work in black and white for Frank Borzage in particular was outstanding. Going on to musicals and to a fruitful partnership with Vincente Minnelli, he helped to make films like *Meet Me in St Louis* so ravishing to look at.

Films include: 1919 His Bridal Night. '22 Slim Shoulders. '29 The Cocoanuts; Applause. '30 Animal Crackers. '36 Hearts Divided. '37 The Bride Wore Red. '44 Meet Me in St Louis. '49 Adam's Rib. '54 Seven Brides for Seven Brothers. '55 The Cobweb.

FONDA, Henry

(1905–1982). Actor. Born: Grand Island, Nebraska, USA

Local theatre and summer stock took Henry Fonda eastwards to the University Players. Here he played leads opposite Margaret Sullavan, who was to be the first of his five wives. Fonda reached Broadway by 1934 and was making a name for himself, but went to Hollywood the next year. He began as a shy juvenile lead, with traces of the country boy he was. In 1939 John Ford cast him as *Young Mr Lincoln*, and created an enduring image of the American hero. Next year, in *The Grapes of Wrath*, Fonda embodied the common man's anger at oppression. These roles set the pattern for his career. As cowhand and sheriff, juryman and presidential candidate, Fonda stood for integrity, and a stormy private life never marred this magnificent actor's playing of that life-long part. The one pity is that he had so few shots at comedy. *The Lady Eve* had him as a studious snake-expert dazzled by Barbara Stanwyck. He was marvellously funny, and still a man to look up to. As if to show that he could do it, he played a vicious killer in *Once Upon a Time in the West*; having done it, he returned to orthodox Fonda roles, and in 1981 he won the Best Actor Oscar, at last, for his crusty octogenarian in *On Golden Pond*.

Films include: 1935 The Farmer Takes a Wife. '36 The Trail of the Lonesome Pine. '37 You Only Live Once. '38 Jezebel. '39 Young Mr Lincoln; Drums Along the Mohawk. '40 The Grapes of Wrath. '41 The Lady Eve. '43 The Ox-Bow Incident (GB: Strange Incident). '46 My Darling Clementine. '56 War and Peace. '57 The Wrong Man. '62 Advise and Consent. '68 Madigan; C'Era una Volta il West (IT) (USA/GB: Once Upon a Time in the West). '70 The Cheyenne Social Club; There Was a Crooked Man. . . . '76 Midway (GB: Battle of Midway). '78 Fedora (GER). '81 On Golden Pond.

FONDA, Jane

(b. 1937). Actress/producer. Born: New York City, USA

Henry Fonda's daughter Jane appeared with her father in summer stock productions of *The Country Girl* and *The Male Animal*. After studying at Lee Strasberg's Actors' studio, she reached Broadway and also played her first film roles. The second phase of her career involved marriage to French director Roger Vadim and her transition from an ingénue to a sex-symbol in his movies. With the Seventies came political commitment, opposition to the Vietnam war, emergence as a serious actress, and her first Oscar for *Klute*. Now married to political activist Tom Hayden, she has contrived to combine stardom with her political career in such films as *Coming Home* (on the aftermath of Vietnam), which won her a second Oscar, and *The China Syndrome* (an attack on nuclear power). And at last she learned to relax, playing in *On Golden Pond* the most graceful of tributes to her father's very different career.

Films include: 1960 Tall Story. '62 Walk on the Wild Side. '64 La Ronde (FR-IT) (USA: Circle of Love). '65 Cat Ballou. '67 Barefoot In the Park. '68 Barbarella (FR-IT). '69 They Shoot Horses, Don't They?. '71 Klute. '73 Steelyard Blues/Final Crash. '77 Julia. '78 Coming Home. '79 The China Syndrome. '80 9 to 5. '81 On Golden Pond. '82 Rollover.

FONDA, Peter

(b. 1939). Actor/director. Born: New York City, USA

In 1960 Peter Fonda won the New York Drama Critics' Most Promising Newcomer Award for his acting in *Blood, Sweat and Stanley Poole*. His film career began three years later. He gave an interesting and touching performance in *Lilith*, as a young schizophrenic hopelessly in love. Fonda then found a niche with Roger Corman and Jack Nicholson in bike movies, had a history-making success in *Easy Rider*, and came to symbolize the rebel youth of his time, with its drugs, bikes, long hair and anarchy. He hasn't really found another niche since. In 1971 Fonda directed *The Hired Hand*; highly praised by some, it was held up by others as an example of what an 'overbudgeted and undisciplined director' can do.

Films include: 1964 Lilith. '66 The Wild Angels. '67 The Trip. '68 Histoire Extraordinaires (FR-IT) (USA/GB: Tales of Mystery. '69 Easy Rider (+ prod; + co-sc). '71 The Last Movie; The Hired Hand (+ dir). '74 Dirty Mary. Crazy Larry. '75 Race With the Devil. '76 Futureworld.

FONTAINE, Joan

(b. 1917). Actress. Born: Joan de Beauvoir de Havilland; Tokyo, Japan

Born in Japan of English parents, Joan Fontaine came to the USA with her mother at the age of two. She made a stage debut in San Francisco in 1934, was in one movie the next year (as Joan Burfield) and signed with RKO in 1937. Two films for Alfred Hitchcock, *Rebecca* and *Suspicion*, brought her acclaim and (for the latter) an Oscar. Before that, she had been a sweet little thing. Hitchcock let her grow up, and discovered the backbone and pride in

her. They were still there in her greatest film, Max Ophuls' *Letter From an Unknown Woman*. She had occasional fun, too, playing really nasty ladies, as in *Ivy*, but the Fifties wasted her, and she has done little since. Actor Brian Aherne was the first of her four husbands, and Olivia de Havilland is her sister.

Films include: 1937 Quality Street. '38 Maid's Night Out. '39 Gunga Din; The Women. '40 Rebecca. '41 Suspicion. '42 This Above All. '43 The Constant Nymph; Jane Eyre. '47 Ivy. '48 Letter From an Unknown Woman. '50 September Affair. '56 Beyond a Reasonable Doubt. '62 Tender Is the Night. '66 The Witches (GB) (USA: The Devil's Own).

FORBES, Bryan

(b. 1926). Director/writer/actor/production chief. Born: John Theobald Clarke; Stratford, London, England

In 1942 Bryan Forbes was question master in the BBC's Junior Brains Trust. In 1969 he was – temporarily – head of production for Associated British at Elstree. In between he had acted in 25 movies, directed 8 and written all or part of another 17: As a short, dark-haired actor stuck with other-ranks roles, he had few possibilities of being promoted to leading man. Writing – especially his neat scripts for *The Angry Silence* and *League of Gentlemen* (both 1960) – brought him more distinction and led to direction. At his best with realist settings and everyday emotions, he has nevertheless branched out with varied success. *Whistle Down the Wind* is a worthy attempt at religious allegory; *The L-Shaped Room* is a sad look at London bedsitterland; *The Raging Moon* treats an affair between paraplegics with sensitive candour; and *The Slipper and the Rose* is a charming musical version of Cinderella. Forbes is married to the actress Nanette Newman.

Films include: 1949 The Small Back Room (actor only). '50 The Wooden Horse (actor only). '54 An Inspector Calls (actor only). '55 The Colditz Story (actor only). '61 Whistle Down the Wind. '62 The L-Shaped Room. '64 Seance on a Wet Afternoon. '65 King Rat. '66 The Wrong Box. '67 The Whisperers. '68 Deadfall. '71 The Raging Moon (USA: Long Ago, Tomorrow). '75 The Stepford Wives; The Slipper and the Rose – The Story of Cinderella. '78 International Velvet.

FORBES-ROBERTSON, Johnstone

(1853–1937). Actor. Born: London, England

A great actor-manager noted for his flawless elocution, Sir Johnstone Forbes-Robertson was in his sixtieth year when his famous Hamlet was transferred to the screen in 1913. But he had been notable for his restraint and his departure from Victorian exaggeration, and he showed himself a natural film actor. This was clearer still when in 1918 he played the stranger in Herbert Brenon's film of *The Passing of the Third Floor Back*. A quiet, calm portrait of spiritual

strength, this was, like Eleonora Duse's *Cenere* (1916), a superb record of a legendary actor. The film survives, a textbook of the actor's art.

Films: 1913 Hamlet. '18 The Passing of the Third Floor Back.

FORD, Aleksander

(1908–1980). Director. Born: Lodz, Poland

Aleksander Ford spans much of the history of Polish cinema. He began in the late Twenties with documentaries, and by the outbreak of war had completed half a dozen features. In the USSR during the war, Ford organized and headed the Polish Army film unit. Back in Poland after the war, he became director of the state-run Film Polski company, continued to direct on his own account, and spent much time teaching the new generation of film-makers who were to shine so brightly. Ford left Poland for Israel in 1960, and moved on to Denmark. Although Ford's films have never been widely shown in the West, *Five Boys from Barska Street* was praised for its warm human sympathies, while *Knights of the Teutonic Order* showed him equally at home with a spectacular historical piece.

Films include: 1930 Mascotte. '32 Legion Ulicy (GB: The Legion of the Streets). '35 Sabra. '48 Ulica Graniczna (GB: Border Street/That Others May Live). '51 Mlodosc Chopina (GB: Young Chopin). '54 Piatka z Ulicy Barskiej (GB: Five Boys From Barska Street). '60 Krzyzacy (GB: Knights of the Teutonic Order). '66 Angeklagt Nach Paragraph 218 (SWITZ–GER) (GB: The Doctor Speaks).

FORD, Francis

(1882–1953). Director/actor/screenwriter. Born: Francis O'Fearna; Portland, Maine, USA

The grizzled, amiable, almost wordless drunk in most of John Ford's later movies was his elder brother Francis. But there had been a time when Francis was the bigger name. An actor with Edison in the early days, by 1913 Francis was the star of action movies at Universal, and wrote and directed them, and made serials, with Grace Cunard, his co-star. Francis Ford went on directing until the end of the silents. With sound he became a character actor, a lovable old ruffian dreaming of the past. And it was Francis who first suggested to John that he, too, should work in the movies.

Films include: 1913 From Railsplitter to President (dir; + act). '14 Lucille Love, the Girl of Mystery (serial) (dir; + act). '15 The Broken Coin (serial) (dir; + act). '16 Chicken-Hearted Jim (dir; + sc; + act); Peg o' the Ring (serial) (dir; + act); '16–17 The Purple Mask (serial) (dir; + co-sc; + act). '32 Destry Rides Again (actor only). '33 Charlie Chan's Greatest Case (actor only). '35 The Informer (actor only). '39 Young Mr Lincoln (actor only); Drums Along the Mohawk (actor only). '41 Tobacco Road (actor only). '46 My Darling Clementine (actor only). '52 The Quiet Man (actor only). '54 The Sun Shines Bright (actor only).

Opposite page. Top left: Nina Foch in the kidnap thriller My Name is Julia Ross. *Top centre: Henry Fonda's Oscar-winning performance in* On Golden Pond. *Above left: Jane Fonda in her sex-symbol days in Roger Vadim's* Barbarella. *Above, far left: Peter Fonda has never matched the success of his father and sister and* Easy Rider *remains his best-known film. Left: Joan Fontaine. This page. Top: Bryan Forbes in* The League of Gentlemen. *Above: Johnstone Forbes-Robertson. Below: Francis Ford, elder brother of director John*

Left: Harrison Ford as Indiana Jones in Raiders of the Lost Ark. Above: Glenn Ford plays the step-father of a super-hero in Superman, The Movie

Above right: Paul Ford in The Music Man. Above, far right: one of the greatest directors of all time – master of the Western, John Ford

Below left: not looking too impoverished, George Formby sings Spare a Copper. Below: Willi Forst in Der Herr auf Bestellung (1930)

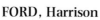

FORD, Glenn

(b. 1916). Actor. Born: Gwyllyn Newton; Quebec, Canada

Glenn Ford's family moved to California when he was eight. He went on the stage, worked his way up to leads with various little theatre groups, and landed a Hollywood contract in 1939. In the next 40 years he appeared in around 90 films, usually playing leads and becoming a popular star. A solid, thoughtful actor, with a knack of combining determination with worry, he made his first real mark opposite Rita Hayworth in *Gilda*. But his best period came in the mid-Fifties, with *Human Desire, Blackboard Jungle* and, above all, *The Big Heat*. As the dogged cop who takes on a corrupt city single-handed, Ford acted with an intensity which made one regret the lightness of so many of his roles. He was married to actress Eleanor Powell from 1943 to 1959.

Films include: 1946 Gilda. '53 The Big Heat. '54 Human Desire. '55 Blackboard Jungle. '56 Jubal; The Teahouse of the August Moon. '57 3:10 to Yuma. '58 The Sheepman. '60 Cimarron. '61 Cry for Happy. '62 The Four Horsemen of the Apocalypse. '63 The Courtship of Eddie's Father. '68 Day of the Evil Gun. '78 Superman, The Movie.

FORD, Harrison

(b. 1942). Actor. Born: Chicago, Illinois, USA

In 1964 Columbia signed Harrison Ford to a seven-year contract as part of a new-talent programme. Ford got nowhere, and moved to Universal, where things were little better, although he had his chance in an excellent Civil War movie, *Journey to Shiloh*. He gave up films for a while, then met George Lucas, was in *American Graffiti* and Coppola's *The Conversation*, and never looked back. His Han Solo in *Star Wars* and his Indiana Jones in *Raiders of the Lost Ark* might well have typecast him as a hero of comic-strip adventure, but in several of his later films he seems to have avoided that. At any rate the one-time Columbia failure has starred in three of the four top box-office successes of all time. He seems set to continue in an unabated run of Lucas-Spielberg successes.

Films include: 1967 Journey to Shiloh. '70 Getting Straight. '73 American Graffiti. '74 The Conversation. '77 Star Wars; Heroes. '79 Apocalypse Now. '80 The Empire Strikes Back. '81 Raiders of the Lost Ark. '82 Blade Runner. '83 The Revenge of the Jedi.

FORD, John

(1895–1973). Director. Born: Sean Aloysius O'Fearna; Cape Elizabeth, Maine, USA

Some years ago, Orson Welles was asked which American directors most appealed to him. Welles replied, ' . . . the old masters. By which I mean John Ford, John Ford and John Ford . . . With Ford at his best, you feel that the movie has lived and breathed in a real world . . .' The world of John Ford is made up of some 110 features, shot between 1917 and 1965. He was the thirteenth and last child of Irish immigrants, and in 1913 went to join his brother Francis in Hollywood. Until 1917 he was stunt man, prop man, assistant director and actor, and he rode with the Klan in *The Birth of a Nation*. He directed for Universal until 1921, for Fox until 1931. Thereafter he was his own master, and if he accepted routine assignments, it was to gain freedom to make the films he wanted to make. With Ford it is important to think of the great Westerns first, as he did: *Stagecoach, My Darling Clementine, She Wore a Yellow Ribbon, Wagonmaster, The Searchers, The Man Who Shot Liberty Valance*. In his old age he lectured from time to time to young men at universities, and he would introduce himself by saying, 'My name is John Ford. I make Westerns.' He made them better than anyone else, bringing gentleness and sympathy to the rugged world of the traditional Western, but wherever in American history he ranged, he painted an entire and convincing picture of that place and that moment,

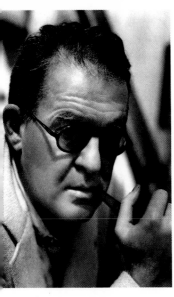

and he lightened dark times with his humour and his courage. With Ford an emotional commitment cannot be avoided. He has had detractors, objecting to his politics, his sentimentality, his misty idealism. Perhaps it is necessary to go some way to meet him, but unless temperament debars, Ford can give more joy than any other film-maker, from the great silents like *The Iron Horse*, *Three Bad Men* and *Four Sons*, through that forgotten period of the early Thirties, with *Pilgrimage*, *Arrowsmith* and *The Lost Patrol*, to the familiar masterpieces of the final years.

Films include: 1915 The Birth of a Nation (actor only). '17 The Tornado; Straight Shooting. '19 The Outcasts of Poker Flats. '20 Just Pals. '23 Cameo Kirby. '24 The Iron Horse. '25 Lightnin'. '26 Three Bad Men. '28 Four Sons. '31 Arrowsmith. '33 Pilgrimage. '34 The Lost Patrol; Judge Priest. '35 The Whole Town's Talking (GB: Passport to Fame); The Informer. '39 Stagecoach; Young Mr Lincoln; Drums Along the Mohawk. '40 The Grapes of Wrath; The Long Voyage Home. '41 How Green Was My Valley. '42 The Battle of Midway (doc). '45 They Were Expendable. '46 My Darling Clementine. '48 Fort Apache. '49 She Wore a Yellow Ribbon. '50 Wagonmaster; Rio Grande. '52 The Quiet Man. '53 The Sun Shines Bright. '56 The Searchers. '59 The Horse Soldiers. '62 The Man Who Shot Liberty Valance. '64 Cheyenne Autumn. '65 Seven Women.

FORD, Paul

(1901–1976). Actor. Born: Paul Ford Weaver; Baltimore, Maryland, USA

Paul Ford was 40 when his acting career began, but he then moved fast. He was on Broadway by 1944, and in the cinema a year later. Tall, large-bellied, balding and lugubrious, eternally harassed and eternally soft-hearted, Ford had his moments on the big screen – most memorably in *A Big Hand for the Little Lady*, as the crooked bank manager waving an inquisitive teller away with that sublime command, 'Back to the cage, Freeson'. But his real glory was on television. In the *Sergeant Bilko* series Ford played Colonel John D. Hall, a good man outrageously misused, and played

him with a baffled dignity that still touches as much as it delights.

Films include: 1945 The House on 92nd Street. '48 The Naked City. '49 All the King's Men. '56 The Teahouse of the August Moon. '58 The Matchmaker. '62 Advise and Consent; The Music Man. '63 It's a Mad, Mad, Mad, Mad World. '65 Never Too Late. '66 The Russians Are Coming, the Russians Are Coming; A Big Hand for the Little Lady. '67 The Comedians (USA-BERM-FR).

FORDE, Walter

(1896–1984). Director. Born: Thomas Seymour; Bradford, Yorkshire, England

Walter Forde was a popular slapstick comedian in British silent shorts, some of which he directed. Turning to features in the late Twenties, he directed over forty films in the next twenty years, mainly thrillers and comedies. Too often saddled with dubious talents like Jack Hulbert and Arthur Askey (who, whatever else they were, were not film actors), Forde always did a workmanlike job. And when he did get a break, as in *Rome Express*, with actors like Conrad Veidt and Cedric Hardwicke, he could turn out as neat and stylish a movie as almost anyone in British studios.

Films include: 1928 Wait and See (+ act). '31 The Ghost Train. '32 Rome Express. '34 Chu Chin Chow. '35 Bulldog Jack (USA: Alias Bulldog Drummond). '36 King of the Damned. '38 The Gaunt Stranger (USA: The Phantom Strikes). '39 Cheer, Boys, Cheer. '41 The Ghost Train. '47 The Master of Bankdam. '49 Cardboard Cavalier.

FOREMAN, Carl

(1914–1984). Screenwriter/producer/director. Born: Chicago, Illinois, USA

The son of Russian immigrant parents, Carl Foreman studied at several universities before becoming a newspaper reporter and then working around little theatres. He went to Hollywood in the late Thirties as a reader and story analyst, then a laboratory assistant. He began writing for Bob Hope and Eddie Cantor radio shows and then joined Frank Capra's army documentary unit during World War II. After the war he collaborated with Stanley Kramer in setting up production companies and established himself as a successful scriptwriter, gaining Oscar nominations in 1949, 1950 and 1952. But in 1952 he refused to testify before the House Un-American Activities Committee and was blacklisted. He came to England and worked for Alexander Korda as a script consultant (1954–56) before co-scriptwriting *The Bridge on the River Kwai* with Michael Wilson, also blacklisted, and winning a pseudonymous Oscar. He then came out of the darkness, forming the first of several production companies and winning two more Oscar nominations for *The Guns of Navarone* and *Young Winston*. His only attempt at direction, *The Victors*, was a simplistic anti-war fable, and he was more successful at exploiting the thrills of war. In 1981–82 he planned projects on a

test-tube baby and on Sun Yat-Sen, father of the Chinese revolution, as well as a television series *To Gallipoli and Beyond*.

Films include: 1948 So This Is New York (co-sc). '49 Champion (sc); Home of the Brave (sc). '50 Young Man With a Horn (co-sc) (GB: Young Man of Music); The Men (sc). '52 High Noon (sc). '57 The Bridge on the River Kwai (co-sc. uncred) (GB). '58 The Key (exec. prod; + sc) (GB). '59 The Mouse That Roared (prod) (GB). '61 The Guns of Navarone (prod. co; + sc) (GB). '63 The Victors (dir; + prod; + sc) (GB). '66 Born Free (exec. prod) (GB). '69 Otley (exec. prod) (GB); The Virgin Soldiers (exec. prod) (GB); MacKenna's Gold (co-prod; + sc) (USA). '72 Young Winston (prod; + sc). '78 Force 10 From Navarone (exec. prod; + co-sc).

FORMAN, Miloš

(b. 1932). Director. Born: Cáslav, Czechoslovakia

Forman is the only director from the briefly flowering Czech 'New Wave' to establish himself in big-time American film-making. He has said that every European has two homelands, his own and America, an attitude that may have helped him to adjust to the expatriate life after a beginning deeply immersed in the minutiae of the Czech scene. After studying at FAMU, the Prague film school, he was involved with the Laterna Magika presentations, mixing film with live actors, and made his directorial debut as a semi-documentarist, filming an audition – a situation he repeated to hilarious effect in the opening sequence of *Taking Off* in New York. His Czech features, especially *A Blonde in Love* and *The Firemen's Ball*, brought him worldwide fame and Oscar nominations for his ironic but humane observation of human frailties and self-deceptions, often using non-actors and an air of improvisation. The satirical overtones of *The Firemen's Ball*, widely seen as a comment on incompetent bureaucracy, presaged the 'Prague Spring' of 1968, repressed by Russian tanks. Forman was in Paris at the time of the invasion and remained abroad, going to New York in 1969. His first American feature, *Taking Off*, combined his previous wit and sympathy with a lively new-world zip, but it was surprisingly a box-office failure. But *One Flew Over the Cuckoo's Nest*, a tragi-comedy set in a madhouse, won five Oscars, including Best Director. Forman became an American citizen and was on the road to recapitulating the traditional triumphs of European directors in the USA.

Films as director: 1963 Konkurs (USA: The Competition/Talent Competition) comprising two shorts: Konkurs (USA: The Audition) and Kdyby ty muziky nebyly (+ co-sc) (USA: Why Do We Need All Those Brass Bands?/If There Was No Music); Cerný Petr (USA: Black Peter; GB: Peter and Pavla). '65 Lasky jedné plavovlásky (USA: Loves of a Blonde; GB: A Blonde in Love). '67 Hoři, má panenko (USA/GB: The Firemen's Ball). '71 Taking Off (USA). '73 Visions of Eight ep The Decathlon (USA). '75 One Flew Over the Cuckoo's Nest (USA). '79 Hair (USA). '81 Ragtime (USA).

FORMBY, George

(1904–1961). Actor. Born: Wigan, Lancashire, England

Flashing his flat-faced toothy grin and twanging his ukelele, George Formby was the epitome of gormless Lancashire comedians. He had the bonus of his innocently suggestive little songs, naughty as seaside postcards and sung in an inimitable style which was actually imitated from his father, a successful music-hall performer. His own daft but good-natured music-hall persona was ideal for slapstick comedies and Basil Dean signed him to work at Ealing from 1935 to 1941, where he rivalled and eventually surpassed Gracie Fields as top box-office star. He continued to be successful for several years when he moved to Columbia, still playing the underdog who manages by chance to win out in the end; but his film career declined rapidly in the postwar era, which also saw the fading away of the music-hall tradition from which he had sprung. Formby was guided through his greatest years by a domineering wife who forbade him to kiss his leading ladies.

Films include: 1934 Boots! Boots! '35 Off the Dole; No Limit. '36 Keep Your Seats Please. '38 It's in the Air (USA: George Takes the Air). '39 Trouble Brewing; Come On George. '40 Spare a Copper; Let George Do It. '41 Turned Out Nice Again. '43 Bell Bottom George.

FORST, Willi

(1903–1980). Actor/director. Born: Wilhelm Anton Frohs; Vienna, Austria

Forst started his career as an actor in operettas and light musicals in the Viennese and Berlin theatres. He made his film debut as an actor in 1920 but did not start directing films until 1933. As an actor he played the charming, romantic hero, an effect enhanced when his singing voice was heard, as in the early German sound film *Atlantik*. He became a stylish director, frequently scripting and acting in his own films, which often evoked turn-of-the-century Vienna or Paris as a setting for amorous intrigues in fastidiously detailed decors. He angered the propaganda minister Joseph Goebbels by refusing to play in an anti-semitic film; but he continued to work under the Nazis, taking an apolitical stance. In 1951 a nude long-shot of Hildegard Knef in *Die Sünderin* caused a storm in a teacup. In the mid-Fifties Forst returned to Austria to make his last few films and run a short-lived film magazine.

Films include: 1930 Atlantik (actor only). '32 Ein blonder Traum (actor only) (USA: A Blonde Dream/A Blonde's Dream). '34 Maskerade (dir; + sc. only) (A) (USA: Masquerade in Vienna). '35 Mazurka (dir. only). '36 Allotria (dir; + co-sc. only) (USA: The Private Life of Louis XIV). '39 Bel Ami/Der Liebling schöner Frauen (dir; + co-sc; + act); Ich bin Sebastian Ott (co-dir; + act) (GB: I Am Sebastian Ott). '40 Operette (dir; + prod; + co-sc; + act) (GB: Operetta). '49 Wiener Mädeln (dir; + co-sc; + act; filmed in 1945) (USA: Viennese Maidens). '51 Die Sünderin (dir; + co-sc. only).

FORSYTH, Bill

(b. 1949). Director. Born: Glasgow, Scotland

Bill Forsyth went to the National Film School in Beaconsfield but left after a couple of months. He founded Tree Films with others, making sponsored documentaries, and decided to try a feature film, using a cast from the Glasgow Youth Theatre with whom he had been working. Unable to get funds from the British Film Institute for *Gregory's Girl*, a school comedy of love and football, he put together a small budget from various sources to fund *That Sinking Feeling*, about a gang of unemployed Glasgow teenagers who steal a batch of stainless-steel sinks, to considerable comic effect. A hit at film festivals, *That Sinking Feeling* opened the way for *Gregory's Girl*, which was a big success in both Britain and the USA. Turning from comedy, Forsyth then made a delicate ghost story, *Andrina*, for television in 1981, and moved on to an ambitious film about oil rigs in northern Scotland, *Local Hero*, in 1982.

Films: 1979 That Sinking Feeling. '80 Gregory's Girl.

FOSSE, Bob

(b. 1927). Dancer/choreographer/director. Born: Robert Louis Fosse; Chicago, Illinois, USA

Bob Fosse made his stage debut at 13 and has consistently kept his links with the theatre through a long but intermittent film career. After war service and touring he teamed with dancer Mary Ann Niles, his first wife, and developed an original choreographic style mixing ballet and tap. Spotted in the Broadway show *Pal Joey* he went to Hollywood and appeared in some musicals but soon returned to Broadway, choreographing *The Pajama Game*, for which he won a 1955 Tony Award. The lead dancer was Gwen Verdon, later to become his third wife (subsequently divorced), and she starred for him in *Sweet Charity* and *Damn Yankees*, shows that were eventually filmed with Fosse as choreographer and, for *Sweet Charity*, director. This debut was a flop but *Cabaret* compensated, bringing him the Best Director Oscar for his stylishly decadent evocation of prewar Berlin. In the same year he won two Tony Awards for the stage musical *Pippin* and an Emmy Award for the television show *Liza With a Z*. After directing the non-musical *Lenny*, Fosse suffered a serious heart attack, providing the basis for his semi-autobiographical *All That Jazz*, an ambitious fantasy musical that won four minor Oscars and exemplified his aim to use music and dance in expressing large themes – sexuality, art, death. His theatre work has meanwhile remained less pretentious, stressing American energy rather than the European-style sophistication of his movies.

Films: 1953 The Affairs of Dobie Gillis (actor); Kiss Me Kate (actor); Give a Girl a Break (actor). '55 My Sister Eileen (chor; + act). '57 The Pajama Game (chor).

'58 Damn Yankees (chor; + act) (GB: What Lola Wants). '67 How to Succeed in Business Without Really Trying (co-chor). '69 Sweet Charity (dir; + chor). '72 Cabaret (dir; + chor). '74 The Little Prince (co-chor; + act) (GB); Lenny (dir). '77 Thieves (actor). '79 All That Jazz (dir; + co-sc; + chor).

FOSSEY, Brigitte

(b. 1947). Actress. Born: Tourcoing, France

Brigitte Fossey did not become a child star, despite her remarkable performance at 5 in *Jeux Interdits* as the little refugee girl obsessed with creating an animal graveyard in wartime France. After one other role in a Gene Kelly movie, she went on to study philosophy and gain a qualification in translation work. She was rediscovered by director Jean-Gabriel Albicocco for his version of Alain-Fournier's novel *Le Grand Meaulnes*; in it she played the idealized girl Yvonne de Galais, for which her romantic looks (fair hair, pale blue eyes) well suited her. She studied acting with Andréas Voutsinas, Jane Fonda's mentor, and tried to vary her roles as her professional career developed, mainly in France, though director Robert Altman cast her in his sci-fi movie *Quintet*. She has also worked in the French theatre and television.

Films include: 1952 Jeux Interdits (USA: Forbidden Games; GB: Secret Games). '57 The Happy Road (USA). '67 Le Grand Meaulnes (GB: The Wanderer). '68 Adieu l'Ami (FR-IT) (USA/GB: Farewell Friend). '71 M Comme Mathieu. '74 Les Valseuses (USA: Making It). '77 Le Pays Bleu (USA: The Blue Country); L'Homme Qui Aimait les Femmes (USA: The Man Who Loved Love; GB: The Man Who Loved Women); Les Enfants du Placard (GB: The Closet Children). '79 Quintet (USA). '80 Un Mauvais Fils.

FOSTER, Jodie

(b. 1963). Actress. Born: New York City, USA

An actress in television commercials from the age of three, Jodie Foster had a career in television series, such as *My Three Sons, Gunsmoke, Ironside*

Bottom left: Edward Fox in Force 10 From Navarone. *Left: Jodie Foster as a sleazy singer in the juvenile underworld of* Bugsy Malone. *Above left: Bob Fosse brings his sophisticated style of dance to the world of* The Little Prince. *Above: Brigitte Fossey in* Adieu l'Ami. *Below: Anthony Franciosa in* The Sweet Ride. *Below left: James Fox plays an inmate of a Singapore POW camp during World War II in* King Rat

and *The Partridge Family*. Later she took film roles in Disney films and a small part in *Alice Doesn't Live Here Anymore* as a worldly-wise kid, the recurrent type that seemed to go with her androgynous blonde looks and deep voice. In *Freaky Friday* she played a 13-year-old girl whose body is inhabited by her mother, an appropriate image of her precocity; but she became better known as the child prostitute in *Taxi Driver* and the slinky nightclub singer in *Bugsy Malone*. After that she continued in Disney films while also appearing in European films with marked sexual overtones. She gained unwelcome extra-cinematic publicity when a frustrated long-distance admirer of hers, John Hinckley, attempted to assassinate President Ronald Reagan.

Films include: 1972 Napoleon and Samantha. '73 One Little Indian. '74 Alice Doesn't Live Here Anymore. '76 Taxi Driver; Bugsy Malone (GB): Freaky Friday. '77 The Little Girl Who Lives Down the Lane (USA-CAN-FR); Il Casotto (IT); Candleshoe. '80 Foxes.

FOX, Edward

(b. 1937). Actor. Born: London, England

The son of an actors' agent, Edward Fox is a product of Harrow, The Coldstream Guards and the Royal Academy of Dramatic Art. This background and his clean-cut classic good looks ideally suited him for upper-class, very English roles, such as Viscount Trimingham in *The Go-Between*, though he has managed to avoid total typecasting. His early career was overshadowed by that of his younger brother, James Fox, but he came into his own in the Seventies, partly through aristocratic roles on television including Edward VIII in *Edward and Mrs Simpson*. He also made a considerable impression as the

ruthless professional assassin who nearly kills President de Gaulle in *The Day of the Jackal*.

Films include: 1966 Morgan, a Suitable Case for Treatment. '69 Oh! What a Lovely War; The Battle of Britain. '71 The Go-Between. '73 The Day of the Jackal (GB-FR); A Doll's House. '74 Galileo (GB-CAN). '77 The Duellists; A Bridge Too Far (USA). '78 Force 10 From Navarone. '80 The Mirror Crack'd. '82 Gandhi (GB-IND).

FOX, James

(b. 1939). Actor. Born: William Fox; London, England

The younger brother of Edward Fox, William (who became James in 1963) went through Harrow, the Central School of Speech and Drama and the Coldstream Guards, besides a stint as a child actor, to emerge as the slim blond English-gentleman type, polite, wealthy and a bit daft. This was given a sinister twist in *The Servant*, which shows the downfall of the type. But in *Performance* he played an East End gangster, role-swapping with a jaded rock star (Mick Jagger). Then he abandoned acting to become an evangelist and was out of films for nearly a decade. His main comeback was on television, in such roles as Waldorf Astor in the series *Nancy Astor*.

Films include: 1962 The Loneliness of the Long Distance Runner. '63 The Servant. '65 Those Magnificent Men in Their Flying Machines (or How I Flew From London to Paris in 11 Hours 25 Minutes); King Rat (USA). '66 The Chase (USA). '67 Thoroughly Modern Millie (USA). '68 Isadora; Duffy. '70 Performance. '78 No Longer Alone (USA).

FOX, William

(1879–1952). Production executive. Born: Wilhelm Fried; Tulchva, Hungary

Brought to the USA at the age of nine months, Fox had an early career in the clothing business before joining in the nickelodeon boom and then expanding into distribution. From 1908 he defied the would-be monopoly of the Motion Picture Patents Company and after years of legal battling finally destroyed their claims in court. Meanwhile, in 1912, he set up his own production company, which introduced Theda Bara, Dolores Del Rio and Annette Kellerman to the screen. By the late Twenties the Fox Film Corporation was one of the biggest American production companies and also owned nearly a thousand cinemas. Fox was quick to realize the importance of sound and his attempt to take over MGM In 1929 was foiled only by an unlucky combination of circumstances and timing. He was forced to sell his shares in his company in 1930. Without him the company did disastrously until it was forced to merge with 20th Century in 1935. Fox meanwhile was involved in prolonged litigation, ending in bankruptcy and then in 1942 a six-month prison sentence for bribing a federal judge. Finally he paid off his debts and still had something to live on besides the memories of Fox's great days over which he had presided.

Fox films include: 1915 A Fool There Was. '17 Cleopatra. '22 A Fool There Was (remake). '24 The Iron Horse. '25 East Lynne. '26 What Price Glory? '27 Sunrise; Seventh Heaven. '28 Street Angel; Four Sons. '29 Sunny Side Up; In Old Arizona. '30 The Big Trail.

FRANCIOSA, Anthony

(b. 1928). Actor. Born: Anthony George Papaleo; New York City, USA

After a variety of jobs, Franciosa took up acting at 18 and won a four-year scholarship at the Dramatic Workshop of the New School for Social Research, under the direction of Erwin Piscator. After considerable theatrical experience, he enjoyed critical success in 1955 playing Polo, the drug addict's friend, in the play *A Hatful of Rain*. Elia Kazan chose him to play the ruthless Joey in *A Face in the Crowd*, his film debut, and Franciosa also re-created his stage role in the film version of *A Hatful of Rain*, gaining an Academy Award nomination. He appeared in many films during the Sixties, bringing a macho Italian forcefulness to his roles; but since then he has concentrated more on television, where his best-known part was as a fearless reporter in *The Name of the Game* (1968–71). He was briefly married (1957–60) to actress Shelley Winters.

Films include: 1957 A Face in the Crowd; A Hatful of Rain; Wild Is the Wind. '58 The Long Hot Summer. '59 The Naked Maja (USA-IT). '62 Period of Adjustment. '68 The Sweet Ride; In Enemy Country. '69 A Man Called Gannon. '72 Across 110th Street.

FRANCIS, Freddie

(b. 1917). Director/cinematographer. Born: London, England

Freddie Francis studied engineering and entered the film industry as a clapper/loader in 1935. He rose to camera assistant at Pinewood before serving in the Army Kinematograph Unit during the war. As a camera operator for London Films he was particularly associated with the later films of Michael Powell and Emeric Pressburger, including *The Small Back Room* (1949). He became a lighting cameraman in 1956 and was a key figure in the British 'New Wave', photographing *Room at the Top* (1959), *Sons and Lovers* – for which he won an Oscar – and *Saturday Night and Sunday Morning* (both 1960). In 1962 he turned director, specializing to such an extent in horror films that a dozen years later he apparently rebelled against being so rigidly typecast – he would prefer to do light sophisticated comedy – and set up his own production company, from which nothing emerged for the big screen. However, he has been active since 1966 in television.

Films as director include: 1963 Paranoiac; Nightmare. '64 The Evil of Frankenstein; Dr Terror's House of Horrors; Traitor's Gate. '65 The Skull. '67 Torture Garden. '68 Dracula Has Risen From the Grave. '72 Tales From the Crypt. '75 Legend of the Werewolf. '80 The Elephant Man (photo. only).

FRANCIS, Kay

(1905–1968). Actress. Born: Katharine Edwina Gibbs; Oklahoma City, Oklahoma, USA

The daughter of stage actress Katherine Clinton, Kay Francis (who took her stage name from her first husband Dwight Francis) was in the theatre herself from the early Twenties, notably in a modern-dress version of *Hamlet* in 1925. She acted in films from 1929, in which year she had a small part with the Marx Brothers in *The Cocoanuts*. After a brief period with Paramount, she went to Warners until 1939, emerging as a stylish and beautifully dressed star of light comedies and strong romantic weepies such as *One Way Passage*, in which she was smitten both by an incurable disease and by a convict (William Powell) under sentence of death. Her slight lisp added to her dark-haired, grey-eyed charm and she was reputed to be the highest-paid woman in pictures. But Bette Davis began to eclipse her at Warners, and by the mid-Forties her screen career declined to co-producing her own pictures at Monogram and then nothing. She returned to the stage and retired in 1952.

Films include: 1930 Raffles. '32 One Way Passage; Trouble in Paradise; Cynara. '33 I Loved a Woman. '34 British Agent. '35 I Found Stella Parrish. '37 First Lady. '39 In Name Only. '40 It's a Date. '44 Four Jills in a Jeep.

FRANJU, Georges

(b. 1912). Director. Born: Fourgères, France

Georges Franju studied stage design and did sets for the Folies Bergère. He met Henri Langlois and collaborated with him on a film *Le Métro* (1935), in founding a film society and a short-lived film magazine and in 1936 in establishing the Cinémathèque Française, then the only French national film archive. From 1949 to 1957 Franju made unique documentaries, expressing an outlook both left-wing and surrealist in images at once direct and powerfully expressive – the slaughtered animals in *Le Sang des Bêtes*, the maimed veterans in *Hôtel des Invalides*. His feature films, mostly made in the first half of the Sixties, likewise combine realism with shocking or beautiful effects, as in *Les Yeux Sans Visage*, a complex horror story about a scientist who tries to replace

his daughter's ruined face with those of girls he murders for the purpose. *Judex* was a graceful and marvellously evocative tribute to the pioneer Louis Feuillade. Most of Franju's later work has been for television, both documentaries and features, and has been little seen outside France. He has collaborated frequently with the cameraman Marcel Fradetal.

Films include: 1949 Le Sang des Bêtes (doc. short). '51 En Passant par la Lorraine (doc. short). '52 Hôtel des Invalides (doc. short). '59 La Tête Contre les Murs (GB: The Keepers); Les Yeux Sans Visage (FR-IT) (GB: Eyes Without a Face). '61 Pleins Feux sur l'Assassin. '62 Thérèse Desqueyroux (GB: Therese). '63 Judex (FR-IT). '65 Thomas l'Imposteur (GB: Thomas the Imposter); Les Rideaux Blancs (short). '70 La Faute de l'Abbé Mouret (FR-IT) (GB: The Sin of Father Mouret). '74 Nuits Rouges (FR-IT) (GB: Showdown).

FRANK, Melvin

(b. 1913). Screenwriter/director/producer. Born: Chicago, Illinois, USA

Melvin Frank switched from engineering to English at the University of Chicago and began a writing collaboration with fellow-student Norman Panama that was to last until the early Sixties. By the late Thirties they were writing radio scripts for Bob Hope and moved into films by devising the original story for his comedy *My Favorite Blonde* (1942). Establishing themselves as writers, they began co-producing in 1948 and co-directing in 1949, an arrangement that lasted until 1956. Frank then turned solo director but continued to collaborate in writing and took up producing again in 1965, nearly always in the field of comedy, and working with such stars as Hope, Danny Kaye and, more recently, George Segal, Glenda Jackson and Jack Lemmon. *A Touch of Class* was nominated for an Academy Award as Best Picture and won Glenda Jackson the Best Actress Award.

Films include: 1950 The Reformer and the Redhead (co-dir; + co-prod; + co-sc). '54 Knock on Wood (co-dir; + co-prod; + co-sc). '59 The Jaywalkers (dir; + co-prod; + co-sc); Li'l Abner (dir; + co-sc). '60 The Facts of Life (dir; + co-sc). '68 Buona Sera, Mrs Campbell (dir; + prod; + co-sc; + lyr). '73 A Touch of Class (dir; + prod; + co-sc) (GB). '74 the Prisoner of Second Avenue (dir; + prod). '76

The Duchess and the Dirtwater Fox (dir; +prod; +co-sc; +lyr). '79 Lost and Found (dir; +prod; +co-sc) (GB).

FRANKENHEIMER, John

(b. 1930). Director. Born: Malba, Long Island, New York, USA

Of mixed Catholic and Jewish parentage, John Frankenheimer began making films as a conscript in the US air force and joined CBS when discharged in 1953, becoming a director of live-television drama in 1954. He moved from New York to Hollywood in 1955 and made most of his television shows there. His film debut in 1957 was a version of a two-year-old television play; but his film career began in earnest in 1961, after live-television drama had given way to videotape and film. He made five pictures in association with actor-producer Burt Lancaster; but the best-

remembered of his early films was his first independent production, *The Manchurian Candidate*, about an attempted Communist take-over of the US Presidency, a wittily satirical story punctuated by a series of ingeniously staged assassinations. In the mid-Sixties Frankenheimer's reputation for thoughtful action series and psychological studies was slightly damaged by the self-indulgent spectacular *Grand Prix*; but then his career took a nose-dive as he made five box-office flops in a row and an unreleased film in France. His American Film Theatre version of Eugene O'Neill's alcohol-soaked play *The Iceman Cometh* showed that he could still direct actors and hold together a long film. He came back to big-time filmmaking with *French Connection II* and *Black Sunday*, both thrillers and box-office successes. But these and the ecological horror film *Prophecy* were hardly sufficient to re-establish him in the career position he had enjoyed in the early Sixties.

Films include: 1956 The Young Stranger. '62 All Fall Down; Birdman of Alcatraz; The Manchurian Candidate. '64 Seven Days in May; The Train (USA-FR-IT). '66 Seconds; Grand Prix. '68 The Fixer. '73 The Iceman Cometh. '75 French Connection II. '77 Black Sunday (+act). '79 Prophecy.

FRANKLIN, Pamela

(b. 1950). Actress. Born: Yokohama, Japan

Pamela Franklin came to England at the age of eight to attend ballet school. At eleven she was cast in Jack Clayton's *The Innocents*, and went on to a spate of animal films. A self-contained, brooding child, she played a schizophrenic in *The Third Secret*, a delinquent in *The Nanny*, and then, growing up, the juvenile lead in *Our Mother's House*. *The Prime of Miss Jean Brodie* was her best critical success; in the Seventies she found it hard to escape from routine American horror.

Films include: 1961 The Innocents. '64 The Third Secret. '65 The Nanny. '67 Our Mother's House. '68 The Night of the Following Day. '69 The Prime of Miss Jean Brodie; David Copperfield. '70 And Soon the Darkness. '73 The Legend of Hell House. '76 The Food of the Gods (USA).

FRANKLIN, Sidney A.

(1893–1972). Director/producer. Born: San Francisco, California, USA

In 1914 Sidney Franklin and his brother Chester made a split-reel comedy, *The Sheriff*, for $400. D.W. Griffith liked it, and set them to making children's movies for Triangle. From 1918 the brothers worked separately. Sidney directed Norma and Constance Talmadge, Pickford, and Garbo. *Smilin' Through*, in 1922, put him in the front rank, and there, until he became a producer in the late Thirties, he stayed. In 1926 he had moved from Schenck to MGM, where he worked for 32 years. As a director, he was stylish and sentimental. Films like *Reunion in Vienna* and *Private Lives* had pace and wit, and were handsome to look at; and *Wild Orchids*, although Franklin disliked it, is among Garbo's most beautiful films.

Films include: 1918 Bride of Fear; The Safety Curtain. '22 Smilin' Through. '24 Her Night of Romance. '27 Quality Street. '29 Wild Orchids. '31 Private Lives. '32 The Guardsman. '33 Reunion in Vienna. '34 The Barretts of Wimpole Street. '37 The Good Earth. '40 Waterloo Bridge (prod. only). '42 Mrs Miniver (prod. only); Random Harvest (prod. only). '46 The Yearling (prod. only). '57 The Barretts of Wimpole Street.

FRASER, Ronald

(b. 1929). Actor. Born: Ashton-under-Lyne, Lancashire, England

Stocky, battered Ronald Fraser has been playing good-hearted toughs in British films (and the odd American one) since 1960. In a varied early career, he had been in the army, ADC to the Governor of Cyprus, Donald Wolfit's dresser, and a stage actor of quality. Although his directors have included Aldrich and Huston, his film roles have on the whole tended to be less interesting than those he has played on television.

Films include: 1961 The Long, the Short and the Tall. '62 The Pot Carriers; The Punch and Judy Man. '66 The Flight of the Phoenix (USA). '67 The Whisperers. '68 The Killing of Sister George (USA). '70 The Rise and Rise of Michael Rimmer. '72 Rentadick. '78 The Wild Geese.

FRAZER, Liz

(b. 1933). Actress. Born: Elizabeth Winch; London, England

After repertory and television work Liz Frazer began playing small parts in films, first gaining notice as Peter Sellers' daughter in *I'm All Right Jack*. Larger parts in comedy, with a number of *Carry On* roles, followed. She was typed as the dumb, bosomy blonde, or a scatterbrained young cockney, an image which she tried to leave behind her when she played the mother in *Up the Junction*. If that effort failed in films, on the stage she has played straight dramatic roles with greater success.

Films include: 1959 I'm All Right Jack. '60 Two Way Stretch; Doctor in Love. '61 The Rebel; Double Bunk; Carry on Regardless. '63 Carry on Cabby. '64 The Americanization of Emily (USA). '66 The Family Way. '68 Up the Junction. '71 Dad's Army. '80 The Great Rock 'n' Roll Swindle.

FRAWLEY, William

(1887–1966). Actor. Born: Burlington, Iowa, USA

William Frawley's vaudeville double act with his brother was broken up by their respectable, middle-class mother who didn't approve. William persevered, and reached Broadway in 1927 in a musical, *The Gingham Girl*. He entered films four years later, and for twenty-odd years worked steadily as a character actor. Frawley played tough, cheerful urban types, cops and petty crooks, agents and hustlers, chewing on his cigar and ever ready with a cutting wisecrack.

Films include: 1933 Moonlight and Pretzels. '34 The Witching Hour. '36 The General Dies at Dawn. '37 High, Wide and Handsome. '40 The Farmer's Daughter. '41 The Bride Came COD. '42 Roxie Hart. '46 Rendezvous With Annie. '51 Abbott and Costello Meet the Invisible Man. '52 Rancho Notorious.

FREDERICK, Pauline

(1883–1938). Actress. Born: Beatrice Pauline Libbey; Boston, Massachusetts, USA

Pauline Frederick was one of Broadway's greatest names when she made her first films in 1915. Her fame endured for most of the silent period. In the Twenties she turned to middle-aged character leads, and two of her performances in this line survive. She was one of Lubitsch's *Three Women*, painfully losing her lover to her own daughter; and in Clarence Brown's *Smouldering Fires* she played a rich businesswoman similarly defeated by youth. These are deeply felt, splendidly restrained performances, which make one infinitely regret that so many of her films seem lost.

Films: 1915 The Eternal City; Bella Donna. '20 Madame X. '24 Three Women; Married Flirts. '25 Smouldering Fires. '26 Her Honour the Governor. '29 The Sacred Flame. '31 This Modern Age. '37 Thank You, Mr Moto.

Above, far left: Kay Francis in Mandalay *(1934). Top left: Pamela Franklin in* The Legend of Hell House. *Above left: Ronald Fraser in* Swallows and Amazons *(1974). Above: Liz Fraser in* Carry on Cruising *(1962). Below: William Frawley. Below right: Pauline Frederick in* On Trial *(1928)*

FREED, Arthur

(1894–1973). Producer/lyricist.
Born: Arthur Grossman; Charleston,
South Carolina, USA

Arthur Freed as producer was the
man ultimately responsible for the
MGM musical in its golden Forties and
Fifties. Freed had been a song-plugger
in Chicago, appeared in vaudeville
with the Marx Brothers and written
lyrics for composer Nacio Herb
Brown. When sound came, MGM
signed him as a lyricist, and his songs
adorned many a Thirties musical. *The
Wizard of Oz* marked his translation to
producer in 1939. The surest judge of
talent, Freed built his musicals round
directors like Minnelli and Berkeley,
stars like Garland and Kelly, and
choreographers and art directors of
vivid originality. For twenty years,
until the film musical withered at the
end of the Fifties, and the great studios
disintegrated, Freed and his unit gave
infinite joy, and collected 21 Oscars in
the process.

Films include: 1939 The Wizard of Oz
(assoc. prod); Babes in Arms. **'40** Strike Up
the Band. **'43** Cabin in the Sky; Du Barry
Was a Lady. **'44** Meet Me in St Louis. **'48**
Easter Parade. **'49** On the Town. **'50** Annie
Get Your Gun. **'51** Show Boat; An Amer-
ican in Paris. **'52** Singin' in the Rain. **'53**
The Band Wagon. **'57** Silk Stockings. **'58**
Gigi. **'60** Bells Are Ringing.

FREGONESE, Hugo

(b. 1908). Director. Born: Mendoza,
Argentina

In the USA from 1935 to 1938, studying at Columbia University and then
technical adviser in Hollywood, Hugo
Fregonese returned to Argentina and
worked his way up to director. He
made four features before a second
stay in Hollywood. In five years he
directed the ten films on which his
reputation rests. Fregonese had a feel
for atmosphere, an eye for landscape
and a liking for the bizarre. *Black
Tuesday* is a frightening crime film,
and *Apache Drums* a startling Western
made for Val Lewton. The death of
Lewton soon afterwards ended the
prospect of a happy alliance between
two parties adept in making a small
film into something special. Fregonese
went to Europe in the mid-Fifties, and
ended his career back home in
Argentina.

Films include: 1950 One Way Street. **'51**
Apache Drums. **'52** Decameron Nights
(GB); Untamed Frontier. **'53** Blowing Wild.
'54 Black Tuesday; The Raid. **'58** Harry
Black (GB) (USA: Harry Black and the
Tiger).

FRELENG, Friz

(b. *c*1900). Animator. Born: Isadore
Freleng; Kansas City, Missouri, USA

In the animation business from 1924,
Friz Freleng worked briefly for Disney
in 1927, and in 1930 joined the new
animation unit at Warner Brothers.
Apart from a fleeting visit to MGM, he
stayed until 1963, forming his own

production company after that.
Freleng's cartoons for Warners in the
Forties and Fifties have been described
as '20 years of pure gold'. Certainly, as
one of the creators of Bugs Bunny,
Daffy Duck and the rest, he has given
a great deal of innocent fun, but
compared with almost anything from
UPA (or Eastern Europe) Freleng's is
bang-bang, slaphappy stuff.

Films include: 1935 I Haven't Got a Hat. **'36**
Coo Coo Nut Grove. **'37** Plenty of Money
and You. **'43** Yankee Doodle Daffy. **'47**
Tweetie Pie; A Hare Grows in Manhattan.
'52 A Streetcar Named Sylvester. **'55**
Speedy Gonzales. **'58** Knightly Knight Bugs.
'63 Nuts and Volts. **'63** The Pink Panther
(title sequence only).

FREND, Charles

(1909–1977). Director. Born:
Pulborough, Sussex, England

Educated at Trinity College, Oxford,
and film critic for 'Isis', Charles Frend
entered the industry in 1931, worked
in the Elstree cutting rooms, and by
1933 was an editor for Gaumont
British. He followed Michael Balcon to
MGM-British and to Ealing, where
Balcon set him to direct. Frend edited
four Hitchcock films, Vidor's *The Citadel* (1938), and *Major Barbara* (1941)
– an excellent record. His best-known
film as director, *San Demetrio, London*,
was in fact completed by Robert
Hamer when Frend fell ill, but seems
characteristic Frend nonetheless. His
was a low-keyed, modest approach,
averse from the heroic and the spectacular, and unsuited to comedy. He
found a congenial home with Balcon,
but after Ealing did little of
consequence.

Films include: 1942 The Foreman Went to
France (USA: Somewhere in France). **'43**
San Demetrio, London. **'47** The Loves of
Joanna Godden. **'48** Scott of the Antarctic.
'49 A Run for Your Money. **'50** The Magnet.
'53 The Cruel Sea. **'54** Lease of Life. **'57**
Barnacle Bill. **'62** Girl on Approval.

FRESNAY, Pierre

(1897–1975). Actor. Born: Pierre-
Jules Laudenbach; Paris, France

Pierre Fresnay made his film debut in
1915, but until the early Thirties he
was best known as a stage actor, at
the Comédie Française and elsewhere.
He made his first impact in the cinema
playing Marius in Marcel Pagnol's
Marseilles trilogy, came to England for
Hitchcock's *The Man Who Knew Too
Much*, and went on to appear in many
distinguished French films of that
period. His notable roles included the
aristocratic officer, de Boëldieu, in
Renoir's *La Grande Illusion*; the tormented doctor in Clouzot's *Le Corbeau*;
and the title role of the priest and
philanthropist in *Monsieur Vincent*. He
continued his stage work, usually
with his third wife, the actress Yvonne
Printemps, interspersing it with films
until 1960. But the great period of
French films was ending, and he had
few good roles in later years.

Films include: 1931 Marius. **'32** Fanny. **'34**
La Dame au Camélias. **'35** The Man Who
Knew Too Much; Königsmark (GB: Koenig-
smark). **'36** César. **'37** La Grande Illusion
(USA: Grand Illusion). **'42** L'Assassin
Habite au 21 (USA: The Murderer Lives at
Number 21). **'43** Le Corbeau (USA: The
Raven). **'44** Le Voyager Sans Bagages. **'47**
Monsieur Vincent. **'50** Le Valse de Paris
(USA: The Paris Waltz).

FREUND, Karl

(1890–1969). Cinematographer/
director. Born: Koeniginhof,
Bohemia

Karl Freund was a newsreel cameraman for Pathé in 1908, and then
worked in Vienna and Berlin, becoming director of photography by 1912.
After a brilliant career in Germany, he
emigrated to the USA in 1929, and
worked there with distinction until
1950, when he moved to television.
From 1932–35 he directed eight Hollywood films. Few cameramen can
have worked on more outstanding
films than Freund. In Germany there
were seven films for Murnau, as well
as *Metropolis* and *Varieté*. Freund's
contribution was enormous. He was a
master of light and shadow, a virtuoso
of camera movement. He was also
fertile in innovation, and it was Technicolor who invited him to America.
His American work was less startling,
but covered an enormous range, with
Dracula, *The Good Earth* (which won
him an Oscar), and *Key Largo* giving
him perhaps the best chances to
regain old glories.

Films include: 1920 Der Golem: Wide er in
die Welt kam (GER) (GB: The Golem). **'22**
Die Brennende Acker (co-photo. only)
(GER). **'24** Mikael (GER). **'25** Der letzte
Mann (GER) (GB: The Last Laugh); Varieté
(GER) (GB: Vaudeville); Tartüff (GER) (GB:
Tartuffe). **'27** Metropolis (co-photo. only)
(GER). **'31** Dracula (USA). **'32** The Mummy
(dir. only). **'36** Camille (co-photo. only)
(USA). **'37** The Good Earth (USA). **'42**
Tortilla Flat (USA). **'43** Du Barry Was a
Lady (USA); A Guy Named Joe (co-photo.
only) (USA). **'44** The Seventh Cross (USA).
'48 Key Largo (USA).

160

FRIEDHOFER, Hugo

(1902–1981). Composer. Born: San Francisco, California, USA

The son of a cellist, Hugo Friedhofer was invited to Hollywood with the advent of sound to work as an arranger for Fox. He had spent two years with the People's Orchestra in San Francisco, and had been an arranger for stage bands. Five years later, he was an orchestrator at Warner Brothers, working with Erich Korngold and Max Steiner. In the mid Forties, the composer Alfred Newman invited him to 20th Century-Fox as composer. Goldwyn also employed him. He wrote the music for over seventy films, with the score for *The Best Years of Our Lives* being perhaps his most notable.

Films include: 1938 The Adventures of Marco Polo. '44 The Lodger; The Woman in the Window. '46 The Best Years of Our Lives. '48 Joan of Arc. '51 Ace in the Hole. '54 Vera Cruz. '55 The Rains of Ranchipur. '58 The Young Lions. '61 One-Eyed Jacks.

FRIEDKIN, William

(b. 1939). Director. Born: Chicago, Illinois, USA

A television director at 17, Friedkin was responsible, it is said, for more than two thousand shows. Entering the cinema in 1967, he made four modest films, among them a pleasant piece of theatrical nostalgia in *The Night They Raided Minsky's*, followed by two enormous box-office successes, *The French Connection* and *The Exorcist*. These two made Friedkin a desirable acquisition, but they are flashy, vulgar films, contemptuous in their exploitation of the easy shock. Friedkin's later work, which has included a remake of Clouzot's *Le Salaire de la Peur* (1953, *The Wages of Fear*), has done little to recover critical esteem.

Films include: 1967 Good Times. '68 The Night They Raided Minsky's; The Birthday Party (GB). '70 The Boys in the Band. '71 The French Connection. '73 The Exorcist. '77 Sorcerer (GB: Wages of Fear). '78 The Brink's Job. '80 Cruising.

FRIESE-GREENE, William

(1855–1921). Inventor. Born: William Edward Green: Bristol, Gloucestershire, England

In the 1880s Friese-Greene owned a prosperous photographic business with branches in Bristol, Bath, London, Plymouth and Brighton. From 1880 he devoted his time and profits to inventing a camera capable of filming motion. In 1888 he presented to the London Photographic Society a camera that would expose a strip of photosensitive paper at a very slow speed. Unhappily his imagination tended to run away with him, and his advances were never integrated into a workable camera or projector. He also experimented with colour film, stereoscopy, and the combination of phonograph sound with pictures. He died unrecognized and almost penniless. In 1951 the film *The Magic Box* paid a somewhat exaggerated homage to his achievements.

FRITSCH, Willy

(1901–1973). Actor. Born: Kattowitz, Germany

Fritsch studied drama at the Max Reinhardt School in Berlin before entering German films in the early Twenties. He played leading parts with success in two Fritz Lang silents, *Spione* and *Die Frau im Mond*, but it was with sound that he achieved genuine stardom. He had a pleasant voice, and appeared with singing stars like Lilian Harvey in numerous operettas and musical romances. He survived the Nazi period, and was still acting in his sixties.

Films include: 1921 Razzia. '23 Seine Frau, die Unbekkante/Wilbur Crawfords wundersame Abenteuer. '26 Der Prinz und die Tänzerin/Der Prinz und die Kokotte. '28 Spione (USA: Spies). '29 Die Frau im Mond (USA: By Rocket to the Moon; GB: The Girl in the Moon); Melodie des Herzens (USA: Melody of the Heart). '30 Liebeswalzer; Die Drei von Tankstelle (GB: Three Men and Lilian). '31 Der Kongress Tanzt (USA: The Congress Dances; GB: Congress Dances). '36 Boccaccio. '45 Die Fledermaus (USA: The Bat). '55 Der fröhliche Wanderer (USA: The Happy Wanderer). '64 Verliebt in Heidelberg.

FRÖBE, Gert

(b. 1912). Actor. Born: Gert Frober; Zwickau, Germany

Gert Fröbe was an apprentice in theatre design at the Dresden Staatstheater, and acting on the Austrian and German stages, usually in character roles, from 1937. Entering German films with *Berliner Ballade* in 1948, he built up a great reputation as a heavy, and was even thought of as Emil Jannings' natural successor. A large, heavy man with thinning hair, he could be genuinely menacing; his child-murderer in *Es geschah am hellichten Tag* was a notable example. Unhappily Fröbe prospered to such an extent that he moved into British and international films as an all-purpose Teutonic villain (the eponymous villain in *Goldfinger* for example), usually played for comedy.

Films include: 1955 Les Héros Sont Fatigués (FR-IT) (GB: The Heroes Are Tired). '57 Celui Qui Doit Mourir (FR-IT) (GB: He Who Must Die). '58 Es geschah am hellichten Tag (SWITZ) (USA: It Happened in Broad Daylight; GB: Assault in Broad Daylight). '60 Die 1000 Augen des Dr Mabuse (GER-IT-FR) (GB: The 1000 Eyes of Dr Mabuse). '63 Die Dreigroschenoper (GER-FR); Peau de Banane (FR-IT). '64 Goldfinger (GB). '65 A High Wind in Jamaica (GB); Those Magnificent Men in Their Flying Machines (or How I Flew From London to Paris in 11 Hours 25 Minutes) (GB). '66 Paris Brûle-t-il? (FR) (USA/GB: Is Paris Burning?). '68 Chitty Chitty Bang Bang (GB). '73 Ludwig (IT-FR-GER). '79 Bloodling (USA-GER).

FRYE, Dwight

(1899–1943). Actor. Born: Salina, Kansas, USA

Dwight Frye was one of the stage actors called up by Hollywood in the early days of sound, and for a few years was a notable performer in macabre or neurotic parts. After a first major role as a felonious bank clerk in Allan Dwan's *Man to Man*, he went on to play the crazy gunsel (the Elisha Cook part) in the first *Maltese Falcon*, the vampire's devoted aide Renfield in *Dracula*, and various twisted creatures in the Frankenstein series. But the horror cycle faded away, and Frye's career with it.

Films include: **1930** Man to Man; The Doorway to Hell. **'31** The Maltese Falcon; Dracula; Frankenstein; Black Camel. **'33** The Vampire Bat; The Western Code; The Circus Queen Murder. **'35** The Bride of Frankenstein; The Crime of Dr Crespi. **'43** Dangerous Blondes.

FULLER, Samuel

(b. 1911). Director/writer/producer. Born: Worcester, Massachusetts, USA

Samuel Fuller was a crime reporter at 17, a B-movie scriptwriter from 1936, a novelist, a much-decorated infantryman in World War II and, from 1949, a director. For ten years or so Fuller's work was ignored; he had no press shows, no critical attention. Around the time of *Underworld USA*, he was taken up by *auteur* critics and a cult developed, first in France, then elsewhere. His films are filled with startling images, and complex and beautiful camera movements; they are deeply pessimistic, presenting a world in which there is a hysterical struggle for survival. This is the world of Fuller's own pulp novels, but on screen it is redeemed by the director's sheer delight in the medium, and at times suffused with a lyrical intensity.

Films include: **1948** I Shot Jesse James. **'51** The Steel Helmet; Fixed Bayonets. **'52** Park Row; Pickup on South Street. **'54** Hell and High Water. **'55** House of Bamboo. **'57** Run of the Arrow; China Gate; Forty Guns. **'60** Underworld USA. **'62** Merrill's Marauders. **'63** Shock Corridor; The Naked Kiss. **'80** The Big Red One.

FURIE, Sidney J.

(b. 1933). Director. Born: Toronto, Ontario, Canada.

A writer-director from Canadian television, Sidney Furie made two features in Canada before coming to England in 1960. The Canadian films had an attractive freshness that Furie found hard to recapture. He had a modest success with his Sixties 'youth' films, and *The Ipcress File* was a lively spy-movie that probably owed more to its cast and script than to its director, who gave it an irritatingly flashy surface. Furie went off to Hollywood in 1966, directed Brando and Sinatra in indifferent films, and has provided little of interest since.

Films include: **1958** A Dangerous Age (CAN). **'61** The Young Ones (GB) (USA: It's Wonderful to Be Young). **'63** The Leather Boys (GB). **'64** Wonderful Life (GB). **'65** The Ipcress File (GB). **'66** The Appaloosa (USA) (GB: South West to Sonora). **'67** The Naked Runner (GB). **'69** The Lawyer (USA). **'70** Little Fauss and Big Halsy (USA). **'72** Lady Sings the Blues (USA). **'76** Gable and Lombard (USA).

FURSE, Roger

(1903–1972). Designer. Born: Ightham, Kent, England

A product of Eton and the Slade School of Fine Art, Roger Furse worked in Paris and the USA as a commercial or portrait artist before turning to stage design in 1936. He designed Laurence Olivier's *Hamlet* at the Old Vic, and afterwards rejoined Olivier as art director of his Shakespearian films. Furse's austere and spacious sets for the film of *Hamlet* won an Academy Award for art direction. Other outstanding designs included those for Carol Reed's *Odd Man Out*. Furse's wife Margaret (1911–1974), a costume designer who had been one of the Motley group of stage designers, assisted her husband on many of his films, and also designed costumes for some forty films.

Films include: **1944** Henry V (cost. des. Roger). **'47** Odd Man Out (prod. des. Roger). **'48** Hamlet (prod. des. Roger); Oliver Twist (cost. des. Margaret). **'49** Under Capricorn (cost. des. Roger). **'50** The Mudlark (cost. des. Margaret). **'52** Ivanhoe (cost. des. Roger). **'56** Richard III (prod. des. Roger). **'57** Saint Joan (prod. des. Roger). **'58** The Inn of the Sixth Happiness (cost. des. Margaret). **'64** Becket (cost. des. Margaret). **'75** Love Among the Ruins (cost. des. Margaret) (USA).

FURTHMAN, Jules

(1888–1960). Screenwriter. Born: Julius Furthmann; Chicago, Illinois, USA

Jules Furthman's career as a Hollywood screenwriter ran from 1917 to 1958, and 'Stephen Fox' who provided scripts for Henry King and Maurice Tourneur from 1918 to 1920 was Furthman in disguise, fearing to disclose a Germanic name. Much of his best work was done for Paramount from 1925 on: *Hotel Imperial*, *Barbed Wire*, and a fruitful collaboration (seven films) with Josef von Sternberg. Furthman used larger-than-life characters, colourful settings and a salty wit; his contribution to the Sternberg/ Dietrich saga shouldn't be undervalued. Later on, Furthman wrote or co-wrote four of Howard Hawks' finest films; the heroic comedy of *Only Angels Have Wings* is quintessential Furthman.

Films include: **1920** Treasure Island. **'27** Hotel Imperial; Barbed Wire. **'28** The Docks of New York. **'30** Morocco. **'32** Shanghai Express; Blonde Venus (co-sc). **'33** Blonde Bombshell (co-sc). **'35** China Seas (co-sc); Mutiny on the Bounty (co-sc). **'39** Only Angels Have Wings (co-sc). **'44** To Have and Have Not (co-sc). **'59** Rio Bravo (co-sc).

Left: Dwight Frye in The Bride of Frankenstein. *Below: Samuel Fuller*

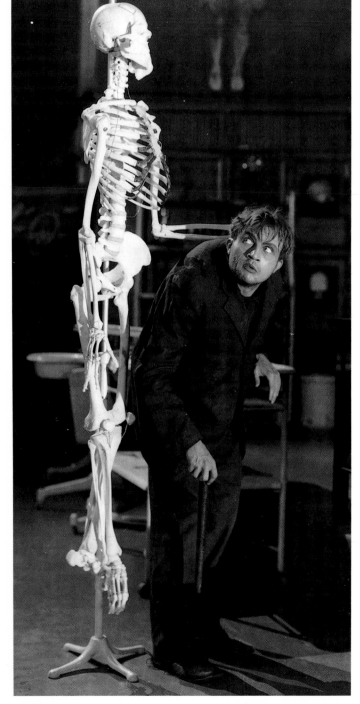

G

GAÁL, István

(b. 1933). Director. Born: Salgótarján, Hungary

If Andrzej Wajda, Miloš Forman and Miklós Jancsó are the outstanding directors to have emerged from Eastern Europe since the mid-Fifties, then István Gaál, with his probing and intelligent films about Hungarian youth and society (*Sodrásban, Zöldár, Keresztelő*), is not very far behind. Gaál originally intended to be an electrotechnician but studied film-making at the Academy of Dramatic and Cinematic Arts and in 1959 won a state scholarship to the Centro Sperimentale di Cinematografia in Rome. His first films were shorts and documentaries made in collaboration with cameraman Sándor Sára. *Sodrásban* was Gaál's first (award-winning) feature. Later successes included *Magasiskola*, a political allegory about a boy horrified at the 'brainwashing' treatment of birds in a falconry, and *Holt Vidék*, which portrayed the alienation of three people left in an abandoned community.

Films: 1959 Pálymunkások (short) (Surfacemen). '61 Etude (short). '62 Oda-Vissza (short) (To and Fro). '63 Tisza – Öszi Vázlatok (short) (Tisza – Autumn Sketches). '64 Sodrasban (GB: Current). '65 Zöldár (Green Years). '68 Keresztelő (Baptism); Kronika (short) (Chronicle). '69 Tiz Éves Kuba (short) (Cuba's Ten Years). '70 Magasiskola (The Falcons). '71 Bartók Béla: Az Éjszaka Zenéje (short) (Béla Bartók: The Music of the Night). '72 Holt Vidék (Dead Landscape). '78 Legato. '81 Cserepek (Potteries).

GABIN, Jean

(1904–1976). Actor. Born: Jean-Alexis Moncorgé; Paris, France

Following, at first reluctantly, in his parents' footsteps, Jean Gabin was a singer and dancer in music-hall and operetta during the Twenties. He was in films from 1930, at first in frothy comedies, but the five films he made for Julien Duvivier between 1934 and 1936 created the Gabin who was so essential a part of the French cinema of those days. In the films of Marcel Carné and Jean Renoir that character gained in complexity and achieved a wonderful humanity, with a touching gentleness behind the rugged ex-

terior. The Gabin hero was a dreamer. As thief or soldier, exile or plain Parisian worker, he longed for peace, for a return home, for a better life, and he seldom found them. The alleys of the Casbah, the attic room of *Le Jour se Lève*, the witchery of Simone Simon . . . none of them would let him go. He played himself, with nothing laid on from outside, and did it with the inner conviction that marks all great screen acting. After the war he turned to middle-aged character roles. Dominant as ever, he ran to fat and a touch of complacency, and had no liking for the new young directors who took over. His impresario in *French Cancan*, back to Renoir and the scenes of his own beginning, is the last real Gabin part.

Films include: 1930 Chacun sa Chance. '31 Coeur de Lilas. '34 Maria Chapdeleine. '35 La Bandera (USA: Escape From Yesterday). '36 La Belle Equipe (USA: They Were Five); Pépé-le-Moko. '37 Les Bas-Fonds (USA: The Lower Depths); La Grande Illusion (USA: Grand Illusion). '38 Quai des Brumes (USA: Port of Shadows); La Bête Humaine (USA: The Human Beast). '39 Le Jour se Lève

(USA: Daybreak). '55 French Cancan (FR-IT) (USA: Only the French Can). '71 Le Chat (FR-IT). '76 L'Anneé Saint (USA: The Holy Saint).

GABLE, Clark

(1901–1960). Actor. Born: William Clark Gable; Cadiz, Ohio, USA

It seems that there are two birth certificates and Gable may have been born in Meadville, Pennsylvania. Curious that the origins of so straightforward an actor should be so mysterious. He was of Dutch descent, had odd jobs around Ohio, moved from amateur acting to stock, and joined Josephine Dillon's company. She taught him acting, and they married. There was a failed attempt at Hollywood in the Twenties, a slow progress to Broadway, the odd lead, and, after a hit with the LA production of *The Last Mile*, the movies for keeps. He made one Western; then spent 23 years at MGM. His first years, when he often played heavies with insolent charm, were by far the most interesting, and there was still a freshness and

attack about his heroes in films like *Red Dust* and *It Happened One Night*. But his enormous popularity – he was styled 'The King of Hollywood' – meant the end of him as an actor. MGM played safe with their biggest asset, and produced a succession of anodyne movies in which Gable treated his ladies with the offhand roughness they were supposed to love. But it all came together beautifully in *Gone With the Wind* – the book could have been written for him, and probably was. The third of Gable's five marriages was to the actress Carole Lombard.

Films include: 1931 The Painted Desert; Night Nurse; Susan Lenox: Her Fall and Rise (GB: The Rise of Helga). '32 Red Dust; No Man of Her Own. '34 It Happened One Night. '35 China Seas; Mutiny on the Bounty. '36 San Francisco. '37 Saratoga. '39 Idiot's Delight; Gone With the Wind. '41 Honky Tonk. '48 Command Decision. '51 Across the Wide Missouri. '53 Mogambo. '61 The Misfits.

Below left: Jean Gabin in La Grande Illusion. *Below: Clark Gable in* Strange Cargo *(1935)*

163

GABOR, Zsa Zsa

(b. 1923). Actress. Born: Sari Gábor; Budapest, Hungary

Despite some interesting roles in films like Orson Welles' *Touch of Evil*, Zsa Zsa Gabor's screen career is largely irrelevant. What really counts is the self-possessed, glamorous woman-of-the-world clad in diamonds and furs (and sometimes that's all), the ever-increasing list of ex-husbands (eight to date, including millionaire Conrad Hilton and actor George Sanders) and the readiness with a biting quip for reporters and chat-show hosts, each and every one of whom is 'Darlink!' Against the wishes of a domineering father, she was a 15-year-old Miss Hungary and a bride and society hostess at 16. Then came theatre, Hollywood and international stardom in the Fifties with her success in *Moulin Rouge*. Her lookalike sister Eva (b. 1924) made her Hollywood debut earlier in *Forced Landing* (1941) but achieved her biggest success as the beautiful but hopeless city girl married to a wealthy farmer in the Sixties television comedy series *Green Acres*. Both sisters have worked on Broadway.

Films include: 1952 Lovely to Look At; We're Not Married; Moulin Rouge (GB). '53 The Story of Three Loves. '54 Three Ring Circus. '56 Death of a Scoundrel. '57 Girl in the Kremlin. '58 Touch of Evil. '59 Serenade einer grossen Liebe (GER) (USA/GB: For the First Time). '62 Boy's Night Out. '66 Picture Mommy Dead. '67 Jack of Diamonds (USA-GER). '72 Up the Front (GB). '75 Won Ton Ton, the Dog That Saved Hollywood.

GAD, Urban

(1879–1947). Director. Born: Copenhagen, Denmark

A pioneer director in the Danish cinema from 1910, Gad discovered Asta Nielsen and directed her in Denmark and in Germany until 1917. It was a time when Danish films were highly advanced and imaginative, with directors like Gad and Benjamin Christensen making films of real quality. Nielsen went on to become the greatest European star of the day. She and Gad married in 1912, were divorced in 1926. Gad worked in Germany, with other actresses and less success, until 1922.

Films include: 1910 Afgrunden. '11 Sydens Born. '12 Nina; Der Totentanz (DEN-GER); Das Mädchen ohne Vaterland (GER-DEN). '13 Komödianten (DEN-GER); Engelein (GER). '14 Zapatas Bande (GER); Das Feuer (GER). '18 Die Kleptomanin (GER). '19 Das Spiel von Liebe und Tod (GER). '22 Hanneles Himmelfahrt (GER). '27 Likkehjulet (DEN).

GALEEN, Henrik

(1882–1949). Director/screenwriter. Born: Henryk Galeen; Denmark

No figure in all cinema is as mysterious as Galeen. It is not even certain that he was a Dane. By 1906 he was assisting Max Reinhardt, trying to obtain German citizenship, and preparing for an acting career. He acted in films from 1910, collaborated with Paul Wegener on the first *Golem* in 1913, and after the War was a leading director and writer in the great period of German silents. Galeen wrote the later, classic *Golem* (1920) for Paul Wegener, *Nosferatu, the Vampire* (1922) for F.W. Murnau and *Waxworks* (1924) for Paul Leni. His direction included a famous version of *The Student of Prague*, and a masterpiece of fantasy, the first *Alraune*. He left Germany in 1933 for the USA, and the darkness descends once more. There is no trace of his being in America. Until very recently, it was even thought that he might still be living, but it now seems that he died in 1949. Those lost years could be the subject of a movie as darkly foreboding as any of Galeen's own fevered creations.

Films as director include: 1913 Der Golem (GB: The Golem). '20 Der verbotene Weg; Judith Trachtenberg. '23 Stadt in Sicht. '24 Die Liebesbriefe der Baronin von S. '26 Der Student von Prag (GB: The Student of Prague). '28 Alraune. '29 After the Verdict (GB). '33 Salon Dora Green.

GALLONE, Carmine

(1886–1973). Director. Born: Taggia, Italy

Gallone wrote his first play at the age of 15 and in 1911 won a national contest for verse tragedy. Two years later, after an apprenticeship writing screenplays, he began his fifty-year career as a director with *Il Bacio di Cirano*. His many films, mostly melodramas and costume epics, greatly contributed to the rebirth of Italian cinema between the wars, though from the mid-Twenties Gallone worked in England, Germany and France. In 1937 he returned to Italy to sing the praises of fascism in *Scipione l'Africano*, a famous epic of Ancient Roman history. His post-war films, however, like *Davanti a Lui Tremava Tutta Roma*, showed his support for the Partisans. Musicals and operatic films occupied him for the rest of his career, among them a version of *Madame Butterfly* made in Japan.

Films include: 1913 Il Bacio di Cirano. '14 Turbine d'Odio; La Donna Nuda. '15 Avatar. '19 Amleto e l Suo Clown. '26 Gli Ultimi Giorni di Pompei. '31 Un Soir de Rafle (FR). '32 Un Fils d'Amérique (FR). '34 Eine Nacht in Venedig (GER). '37 Scipione l'Africano. '46 Davanti a Lui Tremava Tutta Roma. '48 La Leggenda di Faust (GB: Faust and the Devil). '49 Il Trovatore. '55 Madama Butterfly (JAP-IT) (GB: Madame Butterfly). '56 Michel Strogoff (FR-IT). '60 Cartagina in Fiamme (IT-FR) (GB: Carthage in Flames).

GANCE, Abel

(1889–1981). Director. Born: Paris, France

Before the first World War, the young Gance wrote film scripts, acted on stage and in films, mixed with painters and poets, wrote a play (never produced) for Sarah Bernhardt, and

directed a few small films. In 1915 he made an unsuccessful experimental film, turned back to commercial safety, and waited for another chance. *Mater Dolorosa* in 1917 was the real beginning. *J'Accuse*, *La Roue* and *Napoléon* filled the rest of the silent period. He made some 20 sound films, the majority tasteful, mildly interesting and safe. But Gance's reputation rests on his three great silent films, and *J'Accuse* and *La Roue*, though far less often seen than *Napoléon*, fall little short of it in their technical audacity, their visionary fervour, their determination to give the new medium the intensity of the older arts. To the producers and financiers of the time, Gance seemed a madman. After they had mangled his first sound film, *La Fin du Monde*, he toed the line, rather than make no films at all. His heart was elsewhere – with his incessant reconstructions of *Napoléon*, with his experiments in both widescreen and sound. As his name came to mean only the travestied fragments of

Films include: 1942 Kid Glove Killer. '45 She Went to the Races. '46 The Killers. '47 The Hucksters. '49 The Bribe. '51 Show Boat; Pandora and the Flying Dutchman (GB). '53 Mogambo; Ride Vaquero!; The Snows of Kilimanjaro. '54 The Barefoot Contessa. '56 Bhowani Junction. '57 The Little Hut. '60 On the Beach. '63 55 Days at Peking. '64 The Night of the Iguana. '68 Mayerling (GB-FR). '74 Earthquake. '75 Permission to Kill (USA-A). '77 The Cassandra Crossing (GB-IT-GER). '79 City on Fire (USA-CAN).

GARDINER, Reginald

(1903–1980). Actor. Born: Wimbledon, London, England

When Reginald Gardiner appeared in *Born to Dance* on Broadway he played a crazy New York cop conducting an imaginary orchestra in moonlit Central Park. It was a strange beginning but it got him noticed. Soon he was acting regularly in Hollywood comedies, sporting his pencil-thin moustache and his natural ability for humour. Born in England, Gardiner trained initially to be an architect, but soon decided to attend RADA instead. And it was his numerous parts in West End stage shows as well as a few minor film roles that led to his seeking, and finding, success on Broadway. During the Fifties and Sixties he also did some television and stage work, appearing in the Broadway production of *My Fair Lady* as Alfred Doolittle in 1962. He died of pneumonia in Los Angeles.

Films include: 1936 Born to Dance. '37 A Damsel in Distress. '38 Marie Antoinette. '40 The Great Dictator. '41 A Yank in the RAF; The Man Who Came to Dinner. '45 The Dolly Sisters. '46 Cluny Brown. '50 Halls of Montezuma. '54 The Black Widow.

GARFIELD, John

(1913–1952). Actor. Born: Julius Garfinkel; New York City, USA

John Garfield played tough loners – outcasts of the Depression with chips on their shoulders, symbols of adolescent rebellion. He knew what he was portraying, for he had grown up in a difficult area, the son of Jewish immigrants from Russia, and he had attended a school for problem boys. Unlike many others, though, he had managed to get out by winning a drama scholarship. He subsequently acted with the American Laboratory Theater before being offered bit parts and small roles on the New York stage. By the late Thirties he was in Hollywood working for Warner Brothers and he spent 13 years as a major box-office attraction. Then the House Un-American Activities Committee sank their claws into him; suddenly he could not find work in Hollywood. He returned to the stage, but the strain of the HUAC investigations had taken its toll. He died at 39.

Films include: 1933 Footlight Parade (extra). '38 Four Daughters. '39 They Made Me a Criminal; Juarez. '41 The Sea Wolf. '42 Tortilla Flat. '43 Air Force; Destination Tokyo. '46 The Postman Always Rings Twice; Humoresque. '47 Body and Soul. '51 He Ran all the Way.

Far left: glamorous Zsa Zsa Gabor. Centre left: Garbo in The Single Standard *(1929). Left: Ava Gardner. Above: Reginald Gardiner (centre) spoofing Noel Coward in* The Man Who Came to Dinner. *Below left: Bruno Ganz in* Circle of Deceit. *Below: John Garfield suffering in the high society yarn* Humoresque, *directed by Jean Negulesco*

Napoléon that were seen, even historians came to belittle him for his empty rhetoric. But he had the last word, living to 92, and knowing that new, enraptured audiences were seeing his great work in its true form at last.

Films include: 1915 La Folie du Docteur Tube. '17 Mater Dolorosa. '18 La Dixième Symphonie; J'Accuse. '23 La Roue; Au Secours! (GB: The Haunted House). '27 Napoléon (vu par Abel Gance) (GB: Napoleon). '30 La Fin du Monde (co-dir). '32 Mater Dolorosa. '35 Lucrèce Borgia. '37 J'Accuse (USA: That They May Live; GB: I Accuse). '41 La Vénus Aveugle. '54 La Tour de Nesle (IT-FR) (USA: The Tower of Nesle; GB: The Tower of Lust). '60 Austerlitz (co-dir) (GB: The Battle of Austerlitz).

GANZ, Bruno

(b. 1941). Actor. Born: Zürich, Switzerland

Ganz is one of the leading actors of the New German Cinema of the Seventies and Eighties. Saturnine, intelligent, a saddened man forced to conceal the smile in his eyes, he gave outstanding performances as the tortured heroes of Wim Wenders' *The American Friend* (a terminally-ill picture-framer involved with gangsters) and Volker Schlöndorff's *Circle of Deceit* (a journalist with a conscience confronted with the war in the Lebanon). Away from the terrors of today, he was a numbed Jonathan Harker in *Nosferatu, the Vampyre*, finally taking the slain Dracula's place. After student theatre and drama school in Zürich, and then military service, Ganz became a leading stage actor in Germany in the early Seventies. His breakthrough in movies came in Eric Rohmer's *The Marquise of O*.

Films include: 1976 Die Marquise von O (GER-FR) (USA/GB): The Marquise of O); Sommergäste (GER) (GB: Summer Guests); Lumière (FR); Die Wildente (GER-A) (GB: The Wild Duck). '77 Der amerikanische Freund (GER-FR) (GB: The American Friend); Die linkshändige Frau (GB: The Left-Handed Woman). '78 The Boys From Brazil (USA). '79 Nosferatu: Phantom der Nacht (GER-FR) (GB: Nosferatu, the Vampyre). '81 Die Fälschung (GER-FR) (GB: Circle of Deceit).

GARBO, Greta

(b. 1905). Actress. Born: Greta Louisa Gustafsson; Stockholm, Sweden

A fashion model, and a student at the Royal School of Dramatic Art in Stockholm, Greta Garbo had appeared in advertising films and in one modest comedy when, in 1924, she was cast by director Mauritz Stiller in *The Atonement of Gösta Berling*. She played next in Pabst's *The Joyless Street*, came to Louis B. Mayer's attention, and sailed to America for 15 years and 24 films at MGM. Greta Garbo was, is, and will remain, the greatest and most famous of film stars. From the countless attempts to analyse her appeal, dissect her artistry, explain her retirement, little of value emerges. No word-spinning can describe the way Garbo's presence worked on the spectator. It was at once intimate and immediate, yet far away from the plain world outside. And a greater paradox is that while her art might be thought suited only to the surrendering dream that was silent cinema, and she, perhaps sensing this, resisted sound as long as she could, yet when she did speak, the miracle remained. MGM could reduce many an individual to pattern, yet for Garbo it was the right studio. She did not need great writers or directors (though, just once, Ernst Lubitsch revealed new facets of her); she needed the loving camera of a William Daniels, the sympathy of a modest director like Clarence Brown, freedom to make films where nothing detracted from that one film of a woman's life that her career represented.

Films include: 1920 En Lyckoriddare (SWED). '22 Luffar-Petter (SWED). (USA/GB: Peter the Tramp). '24 Gösta Berlings Saga (SWED) (USA/GB: The Atonement of Gösta Berling/The Legend of Gösta Berling). '25 Die freudlose Gasse (GER) (USA: Streets of Sorrow; GB: The Joyless Street). '26 The Torrent; The Temptress. '27 Flesh and the Devil; Love. '28 The Divine Woman; The Mysterious Lady. '29 Wild Orchids; The Kiss. '30 Anna Christie. '31 Susan Lenox: Her Fall and Rise (GB: The Rise of Helga). '32 Mata Hari; Grand Hotel. '33 Queen Christina. '34 The Painted Veil. '35 Anna Karenina. '36 Camille. '37 Conquest (GB: Marie Walewska). '39 Ninotchka. '41 Two-Faced Woman.

GARDNER, Ava

(b. 1922). Actress. Born: Smithfield, North Carolina, USA

Ava Gardner had had no acting experience whatever when photographs of her came to MGM's notice in 1941. Her looks were sufficient, and after some years of grooming, training and small parts she played her first major roles in 1946. Although her dramatic range remained narrow, she projected a unique combination of earthiness and glamour, and she had a sense of humour always noticeable in her delivery of cutting repartee. In 1955 she left Hollywood for Spain, but now lives in London, continuing to act in international productions. Her best roles, perhaps, were in *The Killers*, *Show Boat*, *Mogambo* (following Jean Harlow), and above all in *The Barefoot Contessa* where her Maria epitomized sultry beauty.

Right: Judy Garland in Meet Me in St Louis. *Far right: James Garner in* Support Your Local Sheriff. *Below right: Greer Garson in* Blossoms in the Dust

GARLAND, Judy

(1922–1969). Actress/singer. Born: Frances Gumm; Grand Rapids, Minnesota, USA

Judy Garland was brought up on a movie set, and she spent her adolescent years there, making films, while her private and public life became the property of the studios and eager fans. And when she put on weight or overslept or was insomniac, there was always a doctor at hand who could pump her with pills and keep her public image intact. Her entertainer parents had her on the stage as an infant; Baby Gumm sang 'Jingle Bells' at the age of three. In her early teens MGM put her under contract; they teamed her with Mickey Rooney, and sent her over the rainbow in *The Wizard of Oz*. By her twenties she was dependent on drugs, and although her films were successful, her life was a disaster. Before dying of an overdose in a London hotel she had been married five times (most famously to director Vincente Minnelli – their daughter is Liza), had witnessed tremendous success and suffered humiliating disappointments. Immensely talented, she was perhaps the best of all cinema song-and-dance ladies, a fine dramatic actress, and a great Hollywood star and casualty.

Films include: 1929 The Old Lady and the Shoe (short). **'36** Every Sunday (short). **'37** Broadway Melody of 1938. **'38** Love Finds Andy Hardy. **'39** The Wizard of Oz; Babes in Arms. **'42** For Me and My Gal (GB: For Me and My Girl). **'44** Meet Me in St Louis. **'45** The Clock (GB: Under the Clock). **'46** The Harvey Girls. **'48** The Pirate; Easter Parade; Words and Music. **'49** In the Good Old Summertime. **'50** Summer Stock (GB: If You Feel Like Singing). **'54** A Star Is Born. **'61** Judgement at Nuremberg. **'63** I Could Go on Singing (GB).

GARMES, Lee

(1898–1978). Cinematographer. Born: Peoria, Illinois, USA

Garmes was among the most innovative, versatile and adaptable of the early Hollywood cameramen. His work with the director Josef von Sternberg on such films as *Morocco* and *Shanghai Express* was inspired, and brought him numerous awards. Garmes started out in the movies in 1916 at the New York Motion Picture Company, but he was soon brought to the West Coast by Thomas Ince. He worked his way up from property boy to camera assistant on comedy shorts, and his camerawork soon gained him attention. One of the first cameramen to be given greater responsibility in production, he was greatly influenced by the paintings of Rembrandt as shown by his stunning use of light and shade in many of his films.

Films include: 1923 Fighting Blood. **'26** The Grand Duchess and the Waiter. **'27** The

Garden of Allah (co-photo). **'30** Morocco. **'31** Dishonored; An American Tragedy. **'32** Shanghai Express. **'33** Zoo in Budapest. **'34** Crime Without Passion. **'41** Lydia. **'51** Detective Story. **'55** Land of the Pharaohs. **'59** The Big Fisherman. **'64** Lady in a Cage. **'72** Lydia.

GARNER, James

(b. 1928). Actor. Born: James Baumgarner; Norman, Oklahoma, USA

To the viewing public James Garner is James Rockford, the amiable, human, often smart, often cool, but not infallible detective of the American television series *The Rockford Files*. It is that role above any others that has established him as one of the most popular film and television personalities in America. And indeed many of his film characters are variations of this street-wise, inventive, sometimes devious character, as shown in movies like *The Americanization of Emily*, *The Skin Game* and *Support Your Local Sheriff*. Garner had his first chance to act when he appeared in a minor role in *The Caine Mutiny Court Martial* on Broadway, having previously sampled various occupations, as well as serving in Korea (for which he received the Purple Heart). It was the original television series *Maverick* that initially brought him recognition. His film career then suffered in the early Sixties when, as Vice President of the Screen Actors Guild, he fought the studios over a contracts dispute. But, like Rockford, having endured some setbacks, Garner pulled through, beat the studios and went on to become a top star.

Films include: 1956 Toward the Unknown. **'57** Sayonara. **'58** Darby's Rangers (GB: The Young Invaders). **'59** Up Periscope!; Cash McCall. **'61** The Children's Hour (GB: The Loudest Whisper). **'62** Boys' Night out. **'63** The Great Escape (USA-GER); The Thrill of it All; Move Over Darling. **'64** The Americanization of Emily. **'66** Grand Prix. **'69**

Support Your Local Sheriff. **'71** The Skin Game. **'72** They Only Kill Their Masters. **'80** Health.

GARNETT, Tay

(1898–1977). Director. Born: William Taylor Garnett; Los Angeles, California, USA

Love stories, adventures, *films noirs*, screwball comedies, war films and documentaries – Tay Garnett was equally at home with any subject and also with any actor, having worked with nearly all of the top stars in Hollywood. Garnett entered the movie-industry in 1920 when Mack Sennett took him on as titler, scenarist and gag man. Prior to that he had appeared as a stunt flyer in a silent film. In 1927 he met Cecil B. DeMille who gave him his first opportunity to direct, and he subsequently worked as a scenarist, producer and director for DeMille at Pathé. In 1949 he formed his own production company, Thor Productions. Even after he stopped making films in the Fifties he continued to work regularly for television.

Films include: 1928 The Spieler. **'29** Oh, Yeah (GB: No Brakes). **'31** Bad Company. **'35** China Seas. **'37** Love Is News. **'38** Trade Winds; Joy of Living. **'40** Seven Sinners. **'46** The Postman Always Rings Twice. **'47** Wild Harvest. **'49** A Connecticut Yankee in King Arthur's Court (GB: A Yankee in King Arthur's Court). **'50** The Fireball. **'53** Main Street to Broadway.

GARNETT, Tony

(b. 1936). Producer. Born: Birmingham, England

Along with the director Ken Loach, Tony Garnett has proved himself one of the most influential documentary-drama film-makers in British television and cinema. He began his career as a stage manager and then, as a psychology student, took up acting in repertory and television. He met Ken Loach while working in the BBC drama department as script editor. The two of them worked together on the controversial *Cathy Come Home*, and soon became renowned for their use of location-shooting, unknown actors and local dialects, eventually setting up their own film company, Kestrel Films. Garnett continued to work for television, sparking off widespread discussion over the merits of dramatized documentaries. He also uses his films to analyze and investigate class structures. He made his first film as director, *Prostitute*, in 1980; he also wrote and produced it.

Films include: 1969 Kes. '70 The Body. '71 Family Life. '79 Black Jack. '80 Prostitute (+ dir; + sc).

GARSON, Greer

(b. 1908). Actress. Born: Co. Down, Ireland

Untiring wife, mother and pillar of society – that was the type of role with which Greer Garson became identified, through such films as *Mrs Miniver* and *Random Harvest*. Her films had a sense of security often lacking in the lives of many during and shortly after World War II. Her acting career began in England after she had given up a job in advertising. She appeared in repertory and finally moved to London to play opposite Laurence Olivier in *Golden Arrow*. She spent three years as a star in the West End, declining offers of films in favour of establishing herself in the theatre. But then MGM chief Louis B. Mayer spotted her warm, red-haired beauty and soon had her under contract. Before going to Hollywood she made a good start as the schoolmaster's wife in her first film *Goodbye, Mr Chips*. After a brief retirement in the Fifties she went back to the stage, and since then has only occasionally returned to the public eye on film and television.

Films include: 1939 Goodbye, Mr Chips (GB). '40 Pride and Prejudice. '41 Blossoms in the Dust. '42 Mrs Miniver; Random Harvest. '44 Madame Curie. '49 That Forsyte Woman (GB: The Forsyte Saga). '53 Julius Caesar. '55 Strange Lady in Town. '60 Sunrise at Campobello. '67 The Happiest Millionaire.

GASNIER, Louis J.

(1882–1963). Director. Born: Paris, France

Louis J. Gasnier spent ten years as an actor on the Paris stage before becoming a director and producer in the theatre. His obvious skills soon led to his moving to Pathé Films, and introducing the enormously successful comic Max Linder to cinema audiences. Having become Vice President of Pathé, Gasnier then travelled to America to set up a new studio in New Jersey. Soon he was turning out numerous comedy serials, again finding and creating new stars like Pearl White. By the Twenties he had turned to features, eventually working for Paramount. Despite a brief return to France to make three films, this pioneer French director was drawn to Hollywood, and although he retired in 1942 he remained there until his death.

Films include: 1905 La Première Sortie d'un Collégien (FR). '10 Max Fait du Ski. '14 The Perils of Pauline (serial). '15 The Exploits of Elaine (serial) (co-dir). '16 The Shielding Shadow (serial) (co-dir). '17 The Seven Pearls (serial). '20 The Corsican Brothers. '29 Darkened Rooms. '30 Shadow of the Lay (co-dir). '32 Topaze (FR). '33 Gambling Ship. '35 The Last Outpost. '42 Fight on Marines.

GASSMAN, Vittorio

(b. 1922). Actor. Born: Genoa, Italy

Had Vittorio Gassman's mother not discouraged him from studying law he might never have become one of Italy's leading actors. But she did, and by the late Forties Gassman was a respected stage actor. On the strength of his reputation he soon moved into films and became one of Italy's most popular stars. As a result he tried to widen his audience with an unhappy spell in Hollywood (during which time he was also briefly married to the actress Shelley Winters). Gassman soon returned to Italy where he found he could concentrate on both film and theatre, and where he also compounded his popularity by showing himself a natural for comedies.

Films include: 1946 Preludio d'Amore. '48 Riso Amaro (GB: Bitter Rice). '48 Il Cavaliere Misterioso. '53 Sombrero (USA). '54 Rhapsody (USA). '56 War and Peace (IT-USA). '57 Kean (+ dir; + co-sc). '67 Il Tigre (IT-USA) (USA/GB: The Tiger and The Pussycat). '67 Woman Times Seven (USA-FR). '78 A Wedding (USA). '79 Quintet (USA); La Terrazza (IT-FR).

GAUDIO, Tony

(1885–1951). Cinematographer. Born: Gaetano Antonio Gaudio; Cosenza, Italy

Gaudio's father and brother were portrait photographers and, on leaving art school, he joined them as an assistant. From 1903 he was cinematographer on hundreds of silent Italian shorts. Three years later he and his brother Eugene emigrated to America. Gaudio found himself a job at the Vitagraph laboratories in New York before becoming head of the positive and negative department at Carl Laemmle's laboratories. He stayed with Laemmle and was promoted to studio manager and chief cinematographer. By 1911 he was in Hollywood. After reorganizing the Universal camera department, he joined Warners where most of his best work was produced during the Thirties, especially *Little Caesar*, *Kid Galahad*, and *Anthony Adverse* for which he received an Academy Award. He was a major photographic innovator, and was one of the first cameramen to shoot 'day-for-night' sequences using filters to create the impression of darkness. In 1949, having worked on about a thousand films, he retired.

Films include: 1920 The Mark of Zorro. '26 The Gay Deceiver; The Temptress. '30 Little Caesar. '32 The Mask of Fu Manchu. '36 The White Angel; Anthony Adverse. '37 Kid Galahad; The Life of Emile Zola. '40 The Letter. '41 High Sierra. '49 The Red Pony.

GAUMONT, Léon

(1864–1946). Film executive. Born: Paris, France

Léon Gaumont was a manufacturer of photographic equipment who built himself an empire exploiting the possibilities of the camera. In 1895 he formed the Gaumont film production company with Alice Guy as his major director. The success of the Chronotographe – a camera-projector designed by Georges Demenÿ – enabled him to rebuild the studio in 1905, making it an arch rival of the Charles Pathé complex. He continued to improve his chronophone, introducing early colour and sound techniques, and expanded his interests throughout Europe. After World War I American competition proved too fierce and the American branch of Gaumont amalgamated with MGM, though the company continued to operate in Britain and France.

GAVIN, John

(b. 1928). Actor. Born: Jack Golenor; Los Angeles, California, USA

At his best (and it may be as the love-lorn photographer turned advertising executive in Douglas Sirk's histrionic *Imitation of Life*) Gavin looked, and acted, like a slimmer version of Rock Hudson. They have similar features and colouring, and both were absurdly 'handsome' in the context of Hollywood's notion of red-blooded American beefcake. As well as working on television and Broadway, Gavin has served a period as president of the Screen Actors' Guild.

Films include: 1959 Imitation of Life. '60 Spartacus; Psycho; A Breath of Scandal. '61 Romanoff and Juliet. '67 Thoroughly Modern Millie.

GAYNOR, Janet

(1906–1984). Actress. Born: Laura Gainer; Philadelphia, Pennsylvania, USA

After high school Laura Gainer moved to Los Angeles and enrolled at a Hollywood secretarial college. From 1924 she appeared as an extra in comedy shorts, and in 1925 made a successful screen test for the Fox studios. With her red hair, bright eyes and elfin appearance, she soon became 'the World's Sweetheart'. She was teamed with Charles Farrell in twelve films, and in 1928 was the first actress to receive the accolade of an Oscar for her performances in *Seventh Heaven*, *Sunrise* and *Street Angel*. By the early Thirties she was America's top box-office star, but then fell out of studio favour at the height of her career. Her popularity declined and she was given more and more unsuitable roles. She retired in the Fifties, but made a guest appearance in *Bernardine* in 1957. She had a successful run in *Harold and Maude* on the New York stage in 1980. Gaynor's performance in *Sunrise* suggests that she was a great screen actress – one whose intimations of despair (on the trolley ride into town) and joy (finally reunited with her husband) are totally believable.

Films include: 1927 Sunrise; Seventh Heaven. '28 Street Angel. '29 Sunny Side Up. '30 High Society Blues. '31 Delicious. '32 Tess of the Storm Country. '33 Adorable; State Fair; Paddy the Next Best Thing. '38 Three Loves Has Nancy; The Young in Heart. '57 Bernardine.

Above: Vittorio Gassman whose work in the theatre far surpasses his romantic film roles. Below left: John Gavin in Thoroughly Modern Millie *(1967). Below right: gamine star Janet Gaynor*

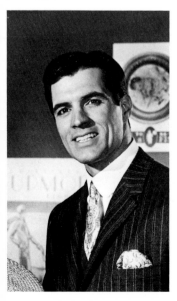

GAYNOR, Mitzi

(b. 1931). Actress. Born: Francesca Mitzi Marlene De Charney von Gerber; Chicago, Illinois, USA

Mitzi Gaynor's mother and aunt were dancers so it was only to be expected that Mitzi should follow in their footsteps. By the age of four she was on stage, and ten years later she appeared in the Los Angeles Light Opera Company's production of *Roberta*. While playing the lead role in *Naughty Marietta*, she was chosen by 20th Century-Fox to play a dancer in *My Blue Heaven*. A vivacious blonde, she went on to appear in many Fox musicals but never quite made it at the box-office and her option was dropped in 1954. That same year she married talent agent Jack Bean, and he rejuvenated her career. She proceeded to notch up successes opposite Bing Crosby, Frank Sinatra and Gene Kelly. She now performs in nightclubs and makes occasional guest appearances on television.

Films include: 1950 My Blue Heaven. '51 Golden Girl. '53 Down Among the Sheltering Palms. '54 There's No Business Like Show Business. '55 Anything Goes. '57 The Joker Is Wild; Les Girls. '58 South Pacific. '59 Happy Anniversary. '60 Surprise Package (GB).

GAZZARA, Ben

(b. 1930). Actor. Born: Biago Anthony Gazzara; New York, USA

In 1951 Gazzara was awarded a place at Lee Strasberg's Actors' Studio. His first major stage part was in *End as a Man*, and he repeated it in the screen version, re-named *The Strange One*. Since his auspicious Hollywood debut in *Convicts Four*, most of Gazzara's work has been for television but his teaming with director John Cassavetes has produced some interesting films, including *Husbands*, *The Killing of a Chinese Bookie* and *Opening Night*.

Films include: 1957 The Strange One (GB: End as a Man). '59 Anatomy of a Murder. '61 The Young Doctors. '62 Convicts Four (GB: Reprieve). '65 A Rage to Live. '70 Husbands. '76 The Killing of a Chinese Bookie; Voyage of the Damned (GB). '77 Opening Night. '79 Bloodline (USA-GER); Saint Jack. '81 They All Laughed; Inch On.

GEESON, Judy

(b. 1948). Actress. Born: Arundel, Sussex, England

Geeson studied at the Corona Stage School in London until she was 15 and while still at school did some minor work for television. Her face became better known when she appeared in the *Danger Man* series and *The Newcomers*. At the age of 17 she was chosen to play a sexy pupil in a tough East End school in *To Sir, With Love*, starring Sidney Poitier. Blonde-haired, blue-eyed, with full lips and a deceptively innocent manner, Geeson soon found herself cast as an English Bardot in a succession of British films fronted by American stars, notably *Three Into Two Won't Go*. Since the early Seventies she has concentrated

on television and stage work and in 1981 was back in London's West End for the first time in eight years.

Films include: 1967 To Sir. With Love; Berserk! '68 Here We Go Round the Mulberry Bush; Prudence and the Pill. '69 Three Into Two Won't Go. '70 The Executioner. '71 10, Rillington Place; Haendeligt Uhelp (DEN) (USA/GB: One of Those Things). '72 Doomwatch; Fear in the Night. '75 Brannigan. '76 The Eagle Has Landed.

GÉLIN, Daniel

(b. 1921). Actor. Born: Angers, France

Gélin studied drama at the Paris Conservatoire but never completed his course. Nevertheless, he gradually established himself as a leading player in French films after being given his chance in Jacques Becker's *Premier Rendez-Vous* (1941). Dark-haired and rugged-looking, Gélin invariably appears as a sad, romantic figure, nowhere better seen than as Albert, about to embark on his first affair with a married woman in *La Ronde*. He has directed one film – *Les Dents Longues* (1953) – and has also made a name for himself as a poet. His daughter is the actress Maria Schneider.

Films include: 1945 Les Cadets de l'Ocean. '46 Martin Roumagnac (FR). '50 La Ronde. '51 Edouard et Caroline. '52 Le Plaisir. '53 Le Maison du Silence (FR-IT). '55 Napoleon. '56 The Man Who Knew Too Much (USA). '59 Le Testament d'Orphée (USA/GB: Testament of Orpheus). '66 Paris Brûle-t-il? (USA/GB: Is Paris Burning?). '77 Nous Irons Tous au Paradis (GB: Pardon Mon Affaire, Too!). '82 La Nuit de Varennes (FR-IT).

GENN, Leo

(1905–1978). Actor. Born: London, England

Leo Genn studied law at Cambridge and was called to the Bar in 1928. After practising as a barrister until 1930, he began to take an interest in amateur dramatics and in turn critics became interested in him. Despite many tempting offers he refused to give up his career, but with the advent of World War II joined the Royal Artillery, rising to the rank of Lieutenant Colonel. After the war he served as one of the Nuremburg prosecutors, securing confessions from the Belsen concentration camp commanders. He never returned to law. He appeared on the London stage in *Green for Danger* and then Broadway beckoned. With a smooth manner, dark hair and eyes, he went down very well as 'the man with the black-velvet voice' in America. Genn's film career then took off, with constant offers of work from both sides of the Atlantic. In 1951 he was nominated for the Best Supporting Actor Oscar for his performance as Nero's adviser in *Quo Vadis?*.

Films include: 1940 Law and Disorder. '44 Henry V. '46 Green for Danger. '48 The Snake Pit. '47 Mourning Becomes Electra. '50 The Wooden Horse. '51 Quo Vadis?; A Streetcar Named Desire. '56 Moby Dick. '60 Too Hot to Handle.

GEORGE, Gladys

(1904–1954). Actress. Born: Gladys Anna Clare; Patten, Maine, USA

The daughter of Shakespearian actor Sir Arthur Evans Clare, Gladys Clare was plunged straight into the show business world. In 1918 she made her Broadway debut in *The Betrothed* starring Isadora Duncan, and until 1920 appeared in films for Thomas H. Ince. Unfortunately her screen career came to an abrupt halt when a domestic accident left her with severe facial burns. She returned to the stage and in the early Thirties was back on Broadway. MGM signed her up and for the rest of the decade she was the brassy blonde with a heart of gold in films such as *Valiant Is the Word for Carrie* and *The Lullaby of Broadway*, working also at Warner Brothers in gangster movies. She kept up her stage connections, turning to it when she felt in need of a challenging role: 'I'm a fugitive from playing the part of an old bag! In only one of the dozen pictures I've made have I been anything but a doddering momma or a harlot'. She was married and divorced four times.

Films include: 1934 Straight Is the Way. '36 Valiant Is the Word for Carrie. '38 Marie Antoinette. '39 The Roaring Twenties. '40 The Way of All Flesh. '41 The Maltese Falcon. '43 The Crystal Ball. '46 The Best Years of Our Lives. '51 The Lullaby of Broadway.

GEORGE, Susan

(b. 1950). Actress. Born: Surbiton, Surrey, England

As a child Susan George attended stage school and made her film debut at the age of four. Television commercials followed, and by the early Sixties she was appearing in major television productions. With her long

blonde hair, bee-stung pout and luminous blue eyes, she made an easy transition to movie nymphet, and after several sexy teenage roles played the provocative Amy who invokes rape and murder in *Straw Dogs*. In recent years her rather bland sex-symbol image has not been enough to get her very exciting parts, although she has worked consistently. Her publicity has been lively, and her name has been romantically linked with several pop and sports personalities, even, at one time, with Prince Charles. She still needs a good role in which to make the sexiness that remains her prime asset a sympathetic quality.

Films include: 1967 The Sorcerers. '68 Up the Junction; The Strange Affair. '69 All Neat in Black Stockings. '70 Twinky (USA: Lola); Spring and Port Wine. '71 Straw Dogs; Fright. '74 Dirty Mary, Crazy Larry. '75 Mandingo. '78 Tomorrow Never Comes. '82 Venom.

GERASIMOV, Sergei

(1906–1985). Director/actor. Born: Zlatoust, Urals, Russia

After leaving school at 14 to support his family, Sergei Gerasimov moved to Petrograd and as well as holding down a full-time job studied painting and theatre design. He became closely involved with an avant-garde group, Factory of the Eccentric Art (FEKS), and in 1930 began to direct. He also acted in such films as Vsevolod Pudovkin's *Dezerhr* (1933, *Deserter*). From 1936 to 1941 he taught in directors' seminars at the Lenfilm Studios, and again in Moscow from 1945. Gerasimov's aim was always to 'draw from life' in order to create starkly realistic atmospheres. In 1944 he joined the Communist Party and became head of the Central Newsreel and Documentary Studios in Moscow.

Left: Mitzi Gaynor (right) in There's No Business Like Show Business. *Above: Ben Gazzara. Right: Judy Geeson. Far right: Gladys George, cradling James Cagney, in* The Roaring Twenties. *Below, from left to right: Daniel Gélin in* La Ronde; *Leo Genn in* No Place for Jennifer *(1950); Susan George in* Fright; *Stephen Geray in* So Dark the Night. *Bottom: Richard Gere in* Days of Heaven

Films include: **1934** Liubliu Litebia? '**36** Semero Smelych. '**38** Komsomolsk (GB: The Frozen North). '**39** Uchitel. '**41** Maskarad (GB: Masquerade). '**47** Molodaya Guardiya (GB: The Young Guard). '**57** Tikhii Don (GB: Quiet Flows the Don). '**70** U Ozerza. '**75** Dochki Materi (+ act). '**80** Peters Jugend (USSR-GER).

GERAY, Stephen

(1899–1973). Actor. Born: Stefan Gyergyay; Uzhgorod, Czechoslovakia

From the Budapest University, Geray went to the National Theatre in Budapest and made his first stage appearance in 1924. In 1934 he arrived in Britain, where he began his career on radio and in films. Seven years later he was in Hollywood. He had a few minor starring roles but was at his best as a character actor. His pleasant, mild manner was used to greatest effect in *So Dark the Night*, a *film noir* in which he plays a French detective

methodically seeking out his lover's killer only to find that in a moment of insanity he had committed the crime himself.

Films include: **1935** Dance Band (GB). '**39** Inspector Hornleigh (GB). '**42** The Moon and Sixpence (USA). '**44** The Mask of Dimitrios (USA). '**46** So Dark the Night (USA); Gilda (USA). '**48** I Love Trouble (USA). '**52** The Big Sky (USA). '**56** The Birds and the Bees (USA). '**59** Count Your Blessings (USA).

GERE, Richard

(b. 1948). Actor. Born: Syracuse, New York, USA

Gere's first love was music. While at high school he learned several instruments and began to write scores for school productions. He then spent two years studying philosophy at the University of Massachusetts before doing

a short stint in repertory at the Princetown Playhouse and Seattle Repertory Theater. After unsuccessfully trying to launch a rock band, he seized his chance as replacement lead in the Broadway production of *Grease*. He moved to London with the show and by 1974 had established himself as an actor of note after his performance in Sam Shepherd's play *Killers Head*. Then came screen work and parts in *Looking for Mr Goodbar* and *Days of Heaven*. Dark-haired, sinewy and youthfully good looking, Gere has since, and perhaps unfortunately, found himself cast in John Travolta-type roles – *American Gigolo*, for example – that require little more than his obvious sex appeal.

Films include: **1975** Report to the Commissioner (GB: Operation Undercover). '**76** Baby Blue Marine. '**77** Looking for Mr Goodbar. '**78** Days of Heaven; Bloodbrothers. '**79** Yanks (GB). '**80** American Gigolo.

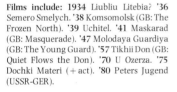

GERMI, Pietro

(1914–1974). Director/actor. Born: Colombo, Liguria, Italy

After three years at the Centro Sperimentale di Cinematografia in Rome, Germi tried his hand at almost every aspect of film production. He quickly established himself as one of Italy's leading neo-realist directors, and his early films centred on the social and political issues of the day. However, in the Sixties he found success with such comedies as *Divorce, Italian Style* – for which he won the Best Screenplay Oscar in 1962 – and *Seduced and Abandoned*. He continued to act until 1963 and direct until 1972. He was co-producing and writing a film when he died in 1974.

Films include: 1945 Il Testimone. '47 Gioventù Perduta (GB: Lost Youth). '49 In Nome della Legge (GB: In the Name of the Law). '51 Il Cammino della Speranza (GB: Road to Hope); Il Brigante di Tacca del Lupo. '56 Il Ferroviere (USA: The Railroad Man; GB: Man of Iron). '58 L'Uomo di Paglia (GB: The Seducer – Man of Straw). '59 Un Maledetto Imbroglio. '61 Divorzio all'Italiana (GB: Divorce – Italian Style). '64 Sedotta e Abbandonata (IT-FR) (USA-GB: Seduced and Abandoned).

GERSHWIN, George

(1898–1937). Composer. Born: Jacob Gershvin; New York City, USA

Composing for films did not play a large part in George Gershwin's career. He worked in Hollywood in the early Thirties and again, briefly, before his death from a brain tumour, in 1937. His finest film score, for *Shall We Dance?*, was composed at this time. Of the countless films using his music, *An American in Paris*, *Lady Be Good*, and *Manhattan*, with its ravishing linking of his 'Rhapsody in Blue' to the New York landscape, are perhaps the most memorable. His work for the theatre was extensive; he composed the full score for twenty-odd Broadway shows, as well as the opera *Porgy and Bess*.

Films include: 1923 The Sunshine Trail. '30 King of Jazz. '31 Delicious. '37 Shall We Dance?; A Damsel in Distress. '38 The Goldwyn Follies. '41 Lady Be Good. '43 Girl Crazy. '45 Rhapsody in Blue. '51 An American in Paris. '79 Manhattan.

GERSHWIN, Ira

(1896–1983). Lyricist. Born: Israel Gershvin, New York City, USA

Ira Gershwin first collaborated with his younger brother George in 1919, and worked regularly with him from 1924, writing lyrics for all George's film material. After his brother's death, Ira worked with other composers, notably with Kurt Weill on the show *Lady in the Dark* which was later filmed. The 'Arthur Francis' credited for songs written to accompany silent films is Ira Gershwin. He used that pseudonym until 1924. Ira's lyrics form an accurate guide to the popular excitements of the Thirties, and as such were used to evoke that era in films like *Chinatown*.

Films include: 1922 Fascination. '31 Delicious. '32 Girl Crazy. '33 That's a Good Girl (GB). '37 Shall We Dance?; A Damsel in Distress. '38 The Goldwyn Follies. '43 Princess O'Rourke; The North Star. '44 Cover Girl. '45 Where Do We Go From Here? '49 The Barkleys of Broadway. '53 Give a Girl a Break. '54 A Star Is Born. '54 The Country Girl. '74 Chinatown.

GHERARDI, Piero

(1909–1971). Art Director. Born: Florence, Italy

Gherardi entered films in 1945 as set decorator, becoming art director the following year. At first he worked mainly in neo-realist films, but in 1956 came the first of his four major films with Federico Fellini. Gherardi helped significantly in creating that expressionistic world between dream and reality that is characteristic of the director. He was a flamboyant and original art director, influenced certainly by such painters as Klimt and Moreau, but using an often macabre imagination in an individual and highly effective way. He also designed costumes, winning Academy Awards for *La Dolce Vita* and *8½*, and in 1969 created the settings for the National Theatre's *The White Devil* in London.

Films include: 1947 Senza Pietà. '48 Fuga in Francia (GB: Flight Into France). '52 Sensualità (GB: Enticement). '57 Le Notti di Cabiria (IT-FR) (USA/GB: Nights of Cabiria). '59 La Dolce Vita. '60 Kapò. '63 Otto e Mezzo (IT-FR) (USA/GB: 8½). '65 Giulietta degli Spiriti (IT-FR) (GB: Juliet of The Spirits). '69 The Appointment (USA). '70 Queimada! (USA: Burn!).

GIANNINI, Giancarlo

(b. 1942). Actor. Born: Spezia, Italy

Giancarlo Giannini appeared on stage for Franco Zeffirelli and Lina Wertmüller before entering films in 1966. He has since played leading parts in most of Miss Wertmuller's films. In *Swept Away* Giannini was a morose communist sailor whose arrogance was rendered acceptable by an underlying sensitivity; in *The Innocent*, Visconti's last film, his guileful and treacherous hero was oddly naive and charming in his corruption. Given the right roles, he could be the natural successor to Marcello Mastroianni.

Films include: 1966 Rita la Zanzara. '68 Lo Sbarco di Anzio (USA: Anzio; GB: The Battle for Anzio). '69 Fräulein Doktor (IT-YUG); The Secret of Santa Vittoria (USA). '72 Mimi Metallurgico Ferito nell'Onore (USA: The Seduction of Mimi). '73 Film d'Amore e d'Anarchia (USA: Love and Anarchy). '75 Travolti da un Insolito Destino nell'Azzurro Mare d'Agosto (GB: Swept Away). '76 Pasqualino Settebellezze (GB: Seven Beauties); L'Innocente (IT-FR) (GB: The Innocent).

GIBBONS, Cedric

(1893–1960). Art Director. Born: New York City, USA

The most celebrated production designer in film history, Cedric Gibbons entered the cinema in 1915 as assistant art director at Edison, where he made an early mark by banishing

painted backdrops. Moving to Goldwyn after the war, he went on to MGM as supervising art director when that company was formed in 1924. Gibbons' domain at MGM has been called a 'medieval fiefdom'. From 1924 until his retirement in 1956 he insisted on being credited as art director on all MGM films made in the US, whatever the degree of his involvement. This enabled him to win 11 Oscars – which was fair enough, for he had designed the statuette. Gibbons created the 'MGM look', bright but never harsh, with plush, polished, often white-walled sets, the acme of professionalism and a model for interior decorators everywhere in the Thirties. Only the occasional MGM director with clear ideas of his own needs (like Minnelli) could impose himself on Gibbons; the others happily accepted his decree. Gibbons was married to actresses Dolores del Rio and Hazel Brooks.

Films include: 1925 Ben Hur (co-art dir); The Big Parade (co-art. dir). '28 Our Dancing Daughters. '29 The Bridge of San Luis Rey. '34 The Merry Widow. '36 Romeo and Juliet (co-art. dir). '37 Conquest/Marie Walewska. '38 Marie Antoinette. '39 The Wizard of Oz. '51 Quo Vadis! (co-art dir).

GIBSON, Hoot

(1892–1960). Actor. Born: Edmund Richard Gibson; Tekemah, Nebraska, USA

Gibson acquired his nickname as a result of his boyhood passion for hunting owls. From the age of 13 he worked in the circus and in rodeo shows until 1914 when he went to Universal City as a stunt man and double. After fighting in the war, Gibson returned to supporting roles in John Ford Westerns. In 1921 he starred in his first feature films – Ford's five-reelers *Action* and *Sure Fire* and soon became Universal's most popular and well-paid star. Good looks and a flair for comedy ensured his popularity in his total of 211 films and titles such as *The Buckaroo Kid* (1926) and *Smiling Guns* (1929) indicated his character as an easy-going Western hero. Gibson's career faltered in 1931 when Universal failed to renew his

contract and he went from Allied Pictures to First Division Pictures. As the work diminished he faded into obscurity. Gibson suffered a series of tumultuous marriages, and alimony payments ensured that he died in poverty.

Films include: 1918 The Squaw Man. '21 Action; The Fire Eater; Sure Fire. '26 The Flaming Frontier. '31 Wild Horse. '33 The Dude Bandit. '35 Powdersmoke Range. '36 Swifty. '44 The Utah Kid. '53 The Marshal's Daughter. '59 The Horse Soldiers. '60 Ocean's Eleven.

GIELGUD, Sir John

(b. 1904). Actor. Born: Arthur John Gielgud; London, England

For almost half a century Gielgud has been regarded as one of the greatest English stage actors of his time. With the cinema, however, his involvement has been marginal. Until the Sixties he appeared seldom; his more frequent appearances since then, especially in the late Seventies and early Eighties, have usually offered little more than cameo roles in some very unsuitable films. Three performances, however, stand out: his Inigo Jollifant in *The Good Companions*, admirably light-hearted as the song-writing schoolmaster; his perplexed Ashenden in Hitchcock's *The Secret Agent*; and forty years later, the marvellous study of the old writer in Resnais' *Providence*.

Above left: Pietro Germi with his girl (Franca Bettoja) in L'Uomo di Paglia. *Left: John Gielgud in* Eleven Harrowhouse *(1974), a 'comedy' with twists. Above: Giancarlo Giannini in* Pasqualino Settebellezze, *a*

performance for which he received great critical praise. Above right: the cowboy with family appeal, Hoot Gibson. Below: John Gilbert, the great romantic idol of the late Twenties, in The Cossacks

Films include: 1924 Who Is The Man? **'33** The Good Companions. **'36** The Secret Agent. **'53** Julius Caesar (USA). **'56** Richard III; Saint Joan. **'64** Becket. **'65** The Loved One (USA). **'66** Campanadas a Medianoche (SP-SWITZ) (USA: Falstaff; GB: Chimes at Midnight). **'69** Oh! What a Lovely War. **'70** Julius Caesar. **'77** Providence (FR-SWITZ). **'80** The Elephant Man; Dyrygent (POL) (GB: The Conductor). **'81** Chariots of Fire; Arthur (USA). **'82** Gandhi (GB-IND).

GILBERT, John

(1895–1936: some sources give 1897). Actor. Born: John Pringle; Logan, Utah, USA

John Gilbert, who was to succeed Valentino as the greatest romantic male star of silent films, was an extra with Thomas Ince in 1915, and a lead player two years later. His ambitions were not confined to acting; in those days he wrote scripts, was assistant to Maurice Tourneur, and directed a film himself. But acting took over. At first with Fox, then with MGM, he gained enormous popularity. Gilbert was much more versatile and sensitive an actor than his reputation suggests. His GI in *The Big Parade* and his reporter up from the slums in *Man, Woman, and Sin* rank beside his romantic leads with Garbo. Then came sound, and the decline of his career. He was certainly not ruined by an inadequate voice; the films disprove that. Nor is it easy to believe that MGM deliberately destroyed him, or that his acting style would not carry over to sound. In 1932 he scripted, and acted in, the brilliant cynical comedy *Downstairs*; the next year he was excellent in *Queen Christina*. The studio had in fact given him every chance, but Gilbert was a deeply insecure and worried man, an alcoholic, and, sadly, increasingly unemployable. He was married to three actresses: Leatrice Joy, Ina Claire, and Virginia Bruce.

Films include: 1916 Hell's Hinges; Bullets and Brown Eyes. **'17** Princess of the Dark. **'19** Heart o' the Hills. **'20** The White Circle (+ co-sc); The Great Redeemer (+ co-sc); Deep Waters (+ co-sc). **'21** The Bait/The Bait, or Human Bait (sc. only). **'23** Cameo Kirby. **'25** The Merry Widow; The Big Parade. **'26** La Bohème; Bardelys the Magnificent. **'27** Flesh and the Devil; Love; Man,

Woman, and Sin. **'28** The Cossacks; A Woman of Affairs. **'32** Downstairs (+ co-sc). **'33** Queen Christina. **'34** The Captain Hates the Sea.

GILBERT, Lewis

(b. 1920). Director. Born: London, England

Gilbert was in films from childhood and began to take an interest in directing while still an actor before the war. Invalided out of the RAF in 1944, he joined British Instructional as a director of documentaries. His first feature, *The Little Ballerina*, was a children's picture, but his work from the Fifties reflects his documentary apprenticeship. *Reach for the Sky*, *Carve Her Name With Pride*, *Sink the Bismarck!* and *HMS Defiant* are all good solid war films, grey and realistic, with just a few moments of jolly euphoria interrupting the stiff-upper-lipped heroics. With *The Greengage Summer* and especially *Alfie*, Gilbert showed he understood the 'new morality' of the Sixties and, perhaps as a reward, he was given the prestigious job of directing some of the James Bond films where he must have at first wondered how to spend much bigger budgets than he was generally used to.

Films include: 1937 Over the Moon (actor only). **'47** The Little Ballerina. **'53** Albert RN. **'56** Reach for the Sky. **'58** Carve Her Name With Pride. **'60** Sink the Bismarck! **'61** The Greengage Summer (USA: Loss of Innocence). **'62** HMS Defiant. **'66** Alfie. **'67** You Only Live Twice. **'77** The Spy Who Loved Me. **'79** Moonraker (GB-FR).

GILLIAM, Terry

(b. 1940). Illustrator/animator/ designer/director/writer/actor. Born: Minneapolis, Minnesota, USA

Gilliam was responsible for the rude, surreal cartoons that linked together the immortal BBC television satire, *Monty Python's Flying Circus*, which was otherwise written and performed by John Cleese, Graham Chapman, Eric Idle, Terry Jones and Michael Palin. Though always considered the sixth Python, Gilliam has, since the team broke into movies, proved the most dedicated film-maker among them, with two solo efforts as director (aside from his work on the actual Python films). These are *Jabberwocky*, a medieval fantasy deep in mud and gore, and *The Time Bandits*, about a schoolboy's fantastic adventures with a gang of robber-dwarfs. The design on both films is excellent and testifies to Gilliam's outlandish artistic skills. After art college in Pasadena and work on Harvey Kurtzman's *Help* cartoon magazine in New York, Gilliam, an acquaintance of Cleese, came to England and worked with Idle, Jones and Palin on the children's television show *Do Not Adjust Your Set* before *Python* took off in 1969.

Films include: 1971 And Now for Something Completely Different (anim; + co-sc; + act). **'75** Monty Python and the Holy Grail (co-dir; + anim; + co-sc; + act). **'77** Jabberwocky (dir; + co-sc). **'79** Monty Python's Life of Brian (anim; + co-sc; + act). **'81** Time Bandits (dir; + prod; + co-sc).

Below right: Hermione Gingold in Promise Her Anything. *Right: Annie Girardot. Centre right: Massimo Girotti in* La Corona di Ferro. *Far right: Dorothy Gish in* Orphans of the Storm. *Below centre: Lillian Gish in* The Wind. *Below, far right: Jackie Gleason in* Skidoo! *Bottom right: James Gleason. Bottom, far right: Jean-Luc Godard*

GILLIAT, Sidney

see LAUNDER & GILLIAT

GINGOLD, Hermione

(b. 1897). Actress. Born: London, England

A much-loved comedy and character actress, Hermione Gingold – with her red hair, unique voice and endearing cartoon features – excelled as crazy aunts and witches in British and American films. At 11 she was on the stage and working in Shakespearian tragedies, later establishing herself as a talented comedienne in musicals (she won the Donaldson Award for Best Musical Comedy Debut when she first worked on Broadway). She made her entry into films in *Someone at the Door* in 1936, created the famous Mrs Doom character on radio and worked in revue during World War II. Her best movies came late in her career when she had settled in Hollywood. Twice married, she is an authoress and frequent and entertaining guest on chat shows.

Films include: 1936 Someone at the Door. '37 Merry Comes to Town. '38 Meet Mr Penny. '52 The Pickwick Papers. '54 Our Girl Friday (USA: The Adventures of Sadie). '56 Around the World in 80 Days (USA). '58 Bell, Book and Candle (USA); Gigi (USA). '61 The Naked Edge. '62 The Music Man (USA); Promise Her Anything. '67 Jules Verne's Rocket to the Moon (USA: Those Fantastic Flying Fools). '77 A Little Night Music (USA-AUS-GER).

GIRARDOT, Annie

(b. 1931). Actress. Born: Paris, France

Charming and attractive, with enticing green eyes, Annie Girardot abandoned her nursing career for the stage after the death of her father. Having won first prize for comedy at the Paris Conservatoire, she joined the Comédie Française and spent two years establishing herself in repertory. In 1955, she entered films, becoming one of France's best-loved actresses. With her wide diversity of roles – from her suffering heroine in Edouard Molinaro's comedy *La Mandarine* to the victim of male brutality in Luchino Visconti's *Rocco and His Brothers* – she continues to delight audiences with her talent and versatility. She is married to the Italian actor Renato Salvatori.

Films include: 1955 Treize à Table. '60 Rocco e i Suoi Fratelli (USA/GB: Rocco and His Brothers). '65 Trois Chambres à Manhattan (USA: Three Rooms in Manhattan). '67 Vivre Pour Vivre (GB: Live for Life); Le Streghe (USA: The Witches). '68 Les Anarchistes ou la Bande à Bonnot. '69 Un Homme qui Me Plait (USA: Love Is a Funny Thing); Erotissimo. '70 Les Novices (GB: The Novices); Storia di una Donna (USA/GB: Story of a Woman). '71 Mourir d'Aimer (USA: To Die of Love). '72 La Mandarine. '79 Le Calveur (USA: Practice Makes Perfect).

GIROTTI, Massimo

(b. 1918). Actor. Born: Mogliano, Italy

Massimo Girotti made his screen debut while still a law student and a year later won the lead in Alexander Blasetti's *La Corona di Ferro*. But it was as Gino, the passionate murderer of Luchino Visconti's *Ossessione*, that he established himself. In the Fifties, he had a short period of appearing in the Italian *peplum* films (to which his athletic build was ideally suited) before re-emerging as a dramatic actor working with such directors as Pier-Paolo Pasolini and Bernardo Bertolucci.

Films: 1940 Dora Nelson. '41 La Corona di Ferro. '42 Ossessione. '48 Molti Sogni per le Strade (GB: The Street Has Many Dreams). '50 Cronaco di un Amore. '53 Spartaco (USA: Sins of Rome; GB: Spartacus the Gladiator). '54 Senso (GB: The Wanton Countess); L'Amour d'une Femme (FR-IT). '61 Romolo e Remo (USA/GB: Duel of the Titans). '68 Teorema (GB: Theorem). '70 Medea. '72 Ultimo Tango a Parigi (USA/GB: Last Tango un Paris). '76 L'Innocente (USA/GB: The Innocent).

GISH, Dorothy

(1898–1968). Actress. Born: Dorothy de Guiche; Dayton, Ohio, USA

Like her older sister Lillian, Dorothy Gish was forced to act on stage from childhood. The girls began their film

careers in D. W. Griffith's *An Unseen Enemy* at Biograph. Dorothy starred in many of Griffith's two-reelers there, and her feature work for him included *Hearts of the World*, as a French girl (with a comic walk) in World War I, and *Orphans of the Storm*, as a French girl (this time blind) of the Revolution, both films also starring Lillian. A five-foot, blue-eyed blonde (who often wore a dark wig), Dorothy did not possess the elusive, ethereal qualities of her sister but was a more down-to-earth, mischievous beauty and this kept her in work in comedies. She starred in Lillian's directorial debut, *Remodelling Her Husband*, and in the mid-Twenties moved to England to take the lead roles in *Nell Gwyn* and *Madame Pompadour*. In 1928 she returned to the Broadway stage and made the occasional screen appearance thereafter.

Films include: 1912 An Unseen Enemy; The Musketeers of Pig Alley. '14 Home, Sweet Home. '15 An Old-Fashioned Girl; Out of Bondage; Old Heidelberg. '18 Hearts of the World; Battling Jane. '19 Nugget Nell. '20 Remodelling Her Husband (+ co-sc). '21 Orphans of the Storm. '23 Fury. '26 Nell Gwyn (GB). '27 London (GB). '28 Madame Pompadour (GB). '46 Centennial Summer. '63 The Cardinal.

GISH, Lillian

(b. 1896). Actress. Born: Lillian de Guiche; Springfield, Ohio, USA

She was the adorable, virginal waif at the heart of D. W. Griffith's threatened world of innocence, a sweet, good girl whose hope, conviction and defiance remains the shining light of early silent cinema. On his death her father left Lillian, her sister Dorothy and their mother destitute and, once the girls could walk, they made a living acting in stage melodramas. On tour they met Mary Pickford who introduced them to D. W. Griffith, and the sisters were paid $5 each to play a crowd scene in a 1912 two-reeler. (When Lillian signed for MGM in the Twenties it was for $1 million.) Working closely with Griffith over the next decade, Lillian graduated from his Biograph shorts to illuminate his greatest films: as Elsie Stoneman in *The Birth of a Nation*; the mother rocking the cradle of history in *Intolerance*; a war-bride frantic with grief in *Hearts of the World*; the wretched girl-woman forcing her lips into a smile with her finger in *Broken Blossoms*; radiant as Henrietta crying out to her blind sister in *Orphans of the Storm*. Her sensitive performances in these roles – and her Letty, forced to commit a murder in Victor Sjöstrom's *The Wind* – made Lillian Gish the greatest of all silent screen heroines. She had a stab at direction (*Remodelling Her Husband*) and survived the talkie revolution – but she became increasingly

bored with movies and limited her appearances. She gave marvellous interpretations of her roles as the guardian of the children in *Night of the Hunter* and as troubled Western mothers in *A Duel in the Sun* and *The Unforgiven*, however, and as late as 1978 appeared in Robert Altman's *A Wedding*. Gish had a long and distinguished career as a stage actress – often in classical parts – and was still busy on Broadway in her eighties. She also toured schools and colleges doing a one-woman show built around 'Mr Griffith's films – for she was undyingly devoted to them and his gift to the cinema. Hers, in its own way, was as important.

Films include: 1912 An Unseen Enemy; The Musketeers of Pig Alley; The New York Hat; Judith of Bethulia. '14 The Battle at Elderbush Gulch; The Battle of the Sexes; Home, Sweet Home. '15 The Birth of a Nation. '16 Intolerance. '18 Hearts of the World. '19 Broken Blossoms; True Heart Susie. '20 Remodelling Her Husband (dir; + co-sc. only); Way Down East. '21 Orphans of the Storm. '23 The White Sister. '24 Romola. '26 La Bohème; The Scarlet Letter. '28 The Wind. '46 Duel in the Sun. '48 Portrait of Jennie (GB: Jennie). '55 Night of the Hunter. '60 The Unforgiven. '67 The Comedians. '78 A Wedding.

GLEASON, Jackie

(b. 1916). Actor. Born: Herbert John Gleason; New York City, USA

Jackie Gleason – old trouper or superstar? From slogging it on the New York nightclub circuit to playing gangsters and Arabs in Forties movies, this popular comic actor battled and dabbled his way to the top, eventually to earn $100,000 a year for his own television show, which ran from 1957 to 1972. He is tall, stout, flamboyant, egotistical and immersed in showbiz – a Broadway star, a millionaire on his record sales as a composer alone – but it must be said that Gleason's talent as a screen actor in dramatic roles has been wasted. Only *The Hustler*, in which he played Minnesota Fats, gave him a chance to excel. It drew on his own poolhall experiences as a youth and won him an Oscar nomination for Best Supporting Actor.

Films include: 1941 Navy Blues. '42 Orchestra Wives; Springtime in the Rockies. '61 Breakfast at Tiffany's; The Hustler. '62 Gigot. '63 Soldier in the Rain; Papa's Delicate Condition. '68 Skidoo! '69 How to Commit Marriage. '77 Smokey and the Bandit.

GLEASON, James

(1886–1959). Actor. Born: New York City, USA

Small, long-faced, talking tough from the side of his mouth, James Gleason was once described as 'Irish dynamite' and inhabited the imaginary city of the Hollywood movie as if born there. He was in fact born to the theatre, acting practically from birth and establishing himself as a successful writer of Broadway comedies in the Twenties. Some of these were filmed and Gleason began appearing in films at the beginning of the sound era, also contributing to scripts at first. He took the lead in the movie version of his play *The Shannons of Broadway* in 1929 and was much in demand as a character actor and occasional lead until the late Fifties. His wife Lucille Gleason (1886–1947) and their son Russel Gleason (1908–45) also played in films, sometimes with him in the Higgins Family series of comedies. He was nominated for an Academy Award as Best Supporting Actor for his role in *Here Comes Mr Jordan*. His swan-song was fittingly in John Ford's *The Last Hurrah*.

Films include: 1931 A Free Soul. '38 Army Girl. '39 On Your Toes. '41 Meet John Doe; Here Comes Mr Jordan. '44 Arsenic and Old Lace. '45 A Tree Grows in Brooklyn. '47 The Bishop's Wife. '49 The Life of Riley. '52 What Price Glory? '55 Night of the Hunter. '58 The Last Hurrah.

GLENNON, Bert

(1893–1967). Cinematographer. Born: Anaconda, Montana, USA

Graduating from Stanford University in 1912, Bert Glennon worked for Keystone, Famous Players and then Clune, where he was laboratory superintendent. After photographing a couple of serials and working in Australia in 1920, he settled down to a long career as a cinematographer for such directors as Mauritz Stiller, James Cruze and particularly Josef von Sternberg, whose favourite cameraman he was, and John Ford. He tried his hand as a director from 1928 to 1932 but with little success. He then returned to his own métier, to which he brought an inventive and inquiring mind – he was one of the first cameramen to experiment with mercury vapour lamps as a way of improving lighting effects. His atmospheric work on Ford's *Stagecoach* was nominated for an Academy Award.

Films include: 1923 The Ten Commandments (co-photo). '27 Hotel Imperial; Underworld. '28 The Last Command. '32 Blonde Venus. '33 Christopher Strong. '34 The Scarlet Empress. '37 The Hurricane. '39 Stagecoach; Young Mr Lincoln. '42 They Died With Their Boots On. '43 This Is the Army. '50 Wagonmaster. '60 Sergeant Rutledge.

GODARD, Jean-Luc

(b. 1930). Director. Born: Paris, France

No director since Eisenstein has altered audiences' perceptions of movies to the extent that Godard has. The foremost of the *nouvelle vague* filmmakers, Godard had much the same professional beginnings as his colleagues (Truffaut, Chabrol and Rivette to name only a few); ostensibly he was a student at the Sorbonne studying ethnology while, in fact, he spent long hours transfixed in the cinemas of Paris. Like his friends he poured his feelings for the movies into the articles he wrote for *Cahiers du Cinéma*, articles which were full of admiration for the directors of cheap Hollywood action pictures and, at the same, expressed his disgust with commercial mainstream cinema. When he made his first feature, *A Bout de Souffle*, in 1960, no movie lover could have imagined what its effect on audiences was going to be. People never did rush to see Godard in the sense that they flocked to see, say, *The Sound of Music*. But word spread from Paris and it wasn't long before Godard was talked about as the most brilliant, fickle, influential, doctrinaire, hated and admired continental director of the Sixties and Seventies. People who loved his movies and the way he spat in the eye of conventional cinema swore by him. Others, who noted with increasing dismay from about 1966 onwards the gradual disappearance of plot and the foregrounding of technique, the elimination of characters with whom the audience could identify, the replacement of narrative with strident political rhetoric, and the substitution of pain for pleasure, swore at him. Godard was the guru of counter cinema, the Grand Inquisitor into the nature and meaning of movie images, their creation and their context, the traducer of the fallacy that cinema is an art that films life rather than being something that creates its own reality as it comes between art and life. For many he shattered the magic trance of going to the movies to experience other people's dreams washing over them; for others his films captured the social ferment of the times, not only because of what the films were about but for the way in which they were made.

Films include: 1954 Opération Béton (short) (SWITZ). '60 A Bout de Souffle (USA/GB: Breathless); Le Petit Soldat (released in 1963). '61 Une Femme Est une Femme (USA/GB: A Woman Is a Woman). '62 Vivre Sa Vie (USA: My Life To Live; GB: It's My Life). '63 Les Carabiniers (FR-IT) (GB: The Soldiers); Le Mépris (FR-IT) (USA/GB: Contempt). '64 Bande à Part (USA: Band of Outsiders; GB: The Outsiders); Une Femme Mariée (USA: The Married Woman; GB: A Married Woman). '65 Alphaville, une Étrange Aventure de Lemmy Caution (FR-IT); Pierrot le Fou (FR-IT). '66 Masculin-Féminin (FR-SWED). '67 Deux ou Trois Choses Que Je Sais d'Elle (USA/GB: Two or Three Things I Know About Her); La Chinoise, ou Plutôt à la Chinoise; Weekend (FR-IT). '68 One Plus One/Sympathy for the Devil (GB). '69 Le Gai Savoir (FR-GER). '72 Tout Va Bien (co-dir). '75 Numéro Deux. '80 Sauve Qui Peut (Le Vie) (co-dir) (FR-SWITZ) (USA: Every Man for Himself; GB: Slow Motion).

GODDARD, Paulette

(b. 1911). Actress. Born: Pauline Marion Goddard Levy; Whitestone Landings, Long Island, New York, USA

A child model, Paulette Goddard made her stage debut at 13 in a Ziegfeld show and contracted a wealthy marriage at 16 that soon ended in divorce. She went to Hollywood, getting small parts with Goldwyn and Hal Roach until she was spotted for her gamine personality by Charles Chaplin, who cast her in *Modern Times* and married her in 1935 (divorced 1942). She also played the Jewish girl in *The Great Dictator* for him. But it was probably her role as a predatory female in *The Women* that won her a contract at Paramount where she became a big star, notably in *The Cat and the Canary* and two other comedies with Bob Hope, and as a flirtatious wartime nurse in *So Proudly We Hail*, for which she was nominated for a Best Supporting Actress Academy Award. Possibly her best role was as a too-desirable servant in Jean Renoir's *The Diary of a Chambermaid*, which she made with Burgess Meredith, her third husband (1944–49). Her popularity declined in the Fifties and she made only one film after 1954. She lived in Europe with her fourth husband, novelist Erich Maria Remarque (1956–70) until his death and then returned to New York.

Films include: 1936 Modern Times. '39 The Women; The Cat and the Canary. '40 The Great Dictator; North West Mounted Police. '41 Hold Back the Dawn; Nothing But the Truth. '42 Reap the Wild Wind. '43 So Proudly We Hail. '45 Kitty. '46 The Diary of a Chambermaid. '47 Unconquered; An Ideal Husband (GB).

GODFREY, Bob

(b. 1921). Animator. Born: New South Wales, Australia

Bob Godfrey brought sex into cartoons for the first time since Betty Boop, looking at everyday sexual fantasies with a satirical yet sympathetic eye. In 1954 he co-founded Biographic, making hundreds of advertisements for television and the cinema and so financing his personal films with their gently anarchic brand of comedy. In 1964 he set up Bob Godfrey Productions. His *Henry 9 till 5* was given an X certificate and the even more outrageously inventive *Kama Sutra Rides Again* was nominated for an Academy Award. In 1974 Bob Godfrey's Movie Emporium made the *Roobarb* series for the BBC and the next year Godfrey actually won an Oscar for *Great*, which was not a sex comedy but a tribute to the great nineteenth-century engineer Isambard Kingdom Brunel in a dazzling variety of graphic styles. Godfrey's voice is familiar to British viewers in the Esso Blue commercials. Along with George Dunning and Richard Williams (who, like Godfrey, were not born in Britain) he made British animation a force on the world scene.

Films include: 1952 The Big Parade. '56 Watch the Birdie. '60 Polygamous Po-

lonius. '64 The Rise and Fall of Emily Sprod. '70 Henry 9 Till 5. '71 Kama Sutra Rides Again. '75 Great/Great Isambard Kingdom Brunel. '77 Dear Marjorie Boobs. '79 Dream Doll. '80 Instant Sex.

GOLAN, Menahem

(b. 1929). Director/producer. Born: Menahem Globus; Tiberias, Israel

After working at the Habimah Theatre in Tel Aviv, Golan studied stage direction in London and then returned to Israel, where the film industry was just starting. He was appointed head of the film, radio and television department at the Israeli consulate in New York, where he studied film-making at New York University. After a brief spell as assistant to Roger Corman, he produced and directed his first film *El Dorado* in Israel in 1963 – it was also the actor Topol's debut. Golan founded Noah Films, which later became the largest production and distribution company in Israel, and had a big success with another Topol film, *Sallah*. He branched out into international co-production while producing films in Israel for the international market, several of which have won Academy Award nominations. *Lemon Popsicle*

and its sequels, randy comedies aimed at the youth market, have been very popular in Israel and abroad.

Films include: 1964 Sallah (prod. only). '68 Tevye und seine sieben Töchter (GER-ISRAEL) (Tevye and His Seven Daughters). '69 What's Good for the Goose (GB). '72 Ani Oher Otach Rosa (prod. only) (USA/GB: I Love You Rosa). '73 Kazablan; The House on Chelouche Street (prod. only). '75 Lepke (LICHTENSTEIN-USA). '77 Operation Thunderbolt. '78 Eskimo Limon (co-prod. only) (USA/GB: Lemon Popsicle); Die Uranium-Verschwörung (ISRAEL-IT-GER) (USA/GB: The Uranium Conspiracy). '79 The Magician of Lublin (ISRAEL-GER); Yotz'im Kavina (co-prod. only) (USA/GB: Going Steady); Imi Hageneralit (co-prod. only) (My Mother the General). '81 Enter the Ninja (USA).

GOLD, Jack

(b. 1930). Director. Born: London, England

While studying law at University College London, Jack Gold made amateur films for the college film society. He went to the BBC in 1954 as a trainee and became a film editor and occasional director for the *Tonight* programme from 1955 to 1960. The British Film Institute backed his short

musical documentary *The Visit*, about a factory's annual outing – it made effective use of the hand-held camera and synchronized sound. Gold became one of the top documentary directors at the BBC before going freelance in 1965. His interests moved in the direction of feature films and television drama, usually shot on film, from the late Sixties onwards. His television work has won many awards including a Grand Prix at Monte Carlo, an Emmy Award in the USA and the Desmond Davis Award. Perhaps the most widely seen example was his witty and compassionate biography of the homosexual Quentin Crisp, *The Naked Civil Servant* (1975). His work for the cinema has been more uneven and sometimes poorly distributed, but he remains one of Britain's most formidable talents, with an active social and political conscience, conspicuous skill in directing actors and an experimental approach to film style.

Films include: 1960 The Visit (doc. short). '61 Living Jazz (doc). '68 The Bofors Gun. '69 The Reckoning. '73 The National Health; Who? (released in USA in 1975; unreleased in GB). '75 Man Friday. '76 Aces High (GB-FR). '78 The Medusa Touch (GB-FR); The Sailor's Return (orig. TV). '82 Praying Mantis (orig. TV).

Far left: Paulette Goddard with Ray Milland in Reap The Wild Wind. *Above left: Samuel Goldwyn. Left: Marius Goring in* Ill Met by Moonlight. *Above: Ruth Gordon in* Rosemary's Baby

GOLDMAN, William

(b. 1931). Novelist/screenwriter. Born: Chicago, Illinois, USA

William Goldman, younger brother of the writer James Goldman (who scripted *The Lion in Winter*, 1968), was educated at Oberlin College and Columbia University. His first novel, *The Temple of God*, was published in 1957 and he has produced a steady stream of novels since then, several of which have been filmed. He has pursued a parallel career as a screenwriter, winning an Academy Award for *Butch Cassidy and the Sundance Kid*, and adapting a couple of his own novels and other books as well as writing original screenplays. His scripts generally have strong, fast-moving narratives and lively dialogue. Some of his originals, such as *The Great Waldo Pepper*, have been published as books, since they are uncluttered with technical detail and readily illustrated from the films. His novel *Tinsel*, published in 1979, attempted to take the lid off Hollywood in a satirical tale of a projected film about the last hours of Marilyn Monroe.

Films include: 1963 Soldier in the Rain (novel basis only). '64 Masquerade (co-sc) (GB). '66 Harper (GB: The Moving Target). '68 No Way to Treat a Lady (novel basis only). '69 Butch Cassidy and the Sundance Kid. '72 The Hot Rock (GB: How to Steal a Diamond in Four Easy Lessons). '75 The Stepford Wives; The Great Waldo Pepper. '76 All the President's Men; Marathon Man (+ novel basis). '77 A Bridge Too Far. Magic (+ novel basis). '79 Butch and Sundance – The Early Days.

GOLDSMITH, Jerry

(b. 1929). Composer. Born: Jerrald Goldsmith; Los Angeles, California USA

Jerry Goldsmith studied film music with the veteran Miklós Rózsa before joining CBS to work in radio and then television, conducting and composing for such shows as *Gunsmoke*, *Dr Kildare* and *The Man From UNCLE*. His first big film success came with *Lonely Are the Brave*, with its subtle scoring of music under the dialogue, followed by *Freud*, which daringly introduced contemporary atonal music. He has continued to experiment in his many subsequent films, trying out a variety of styles from jazz to symphonic, usually stressing rhythm. He has been nominated for an Oscar nine times, winning with *The Omen*.

Films include: 1962 Lonely Are the Brave; Freud (GB: Freud – The Secret Passion). '63 Lilies of the Field. '65 A Patch of Blue. '66 The Sand Pebbles. '67 Planet of the Apes (GB). '70 Patton (GB: Patton – Lust for Glory). '73 Papillon. '74 Chinatown. '75 The Wind and the Lion. '76 The Omen. '78 Coma. '79 The First Great Train Robbery (USA: The Great Train Robbery); Star Trek – The Motion Picture.

GOLDWYN, Samuel

(1882–1974). Producer. Born: Samuel Goldfisch; Warsaw, Poland

No list of major film-makers can heed Goldwyn's saying, 'Include me out', one of his legendary distortions of the English language that became known as Goldwynisms. As Samuel Goldfish he made his way to England alone in 1893 and was apprenticed to a Birmingham blacksmith, which may help to account for his later aggressive fighting qualities. In 1895 he moved on to America and worked in the glove-making industry until he married Blanche Lasky in 1910 (divorced 1916) and persuaded her brother Jesse L. Lasky to enter the film industry with him and Cecil B. DeMille. *The Squaw Man* was a big success and in 1916 Lasky's company merged with Adolph Zukor's Famous Players to form the studio that eventually became Paramount. Goldfish was named chairman of the board but forced to resign after a few months. He then joined Edgar Selwyn to form Goldwyn, combining syllables from both names, and in 1918 Samuel adopted this as his surname. Pushed out of the company in 1922, before its merger with Metro and Mayer to form MGM, he founded Samuel Goldwyn Productions in 1923, determined to do without partners, though his second wife Frances Howard (1903–76), whom he married in 1925, later came to work closely with him on his productions. He aimed at family entertainment and quality pictures of some artistic merit, and was adept at putting together teams of talented personnel to create them. He used good writers, developed many stars including Gary Cooper and Danny Kaye, and worked well with the director William Wyler – both won Oscars for *The Best Years of Our Lives* and Goldwyn was given the Irving G. Thalberg Memorial Award the same year. He encouraged innovators like the cameraman Gregg Toland, who was experimenting with deep-focus photography. And he continued to quarrel – he had become a partner in his distributor, United Artists, in 1927 and after repeated attempts to buy out Charles Chaplin and Mary Pickford, he eventually left UA in 1941, distributing his films through RKO. His last films were big musicals, *Guys and Dolls* and *Porgy and Bess*.

Films include: 1913 The Squaw Man. '30 Whoopee! '31 Street Scene; Arrowsmith. '34 Nana. '36 Dodsworth; These Three. '37 Dead End. '38 The Goldwyn Follies. '39 Wuthering Heights. '44 Up in Arms. '46 The Best Years of Our Lives. '55 Guys and Dolls. '59 Porgy and Bess.

GORDON, Ruth

(1896–1985). Actress/screenwriter. Born: Wollaston, Massachusetts, USA

From a small-town, non-theatrical background (amusingly depicted in *The Actress*), Ruth Gordon persisted in her ambition to become an actress, despite her lack of success at the New York Academy of Dramatic Art, and won good reviews for her 1915 stage debut in *Peter Pan*. By the Thirties she was a leading stage actress not only on Broadway but as a visitor at the Old Vic in London. She acted in films in the early Forties and, having already begun to write plays, she later collaborated with writer-director Garson Kanin, whom she married in 1942, on several screenplays for George Cukor. It was not until the mid-Sixties that her regular career as a film actress began, when she was already 70. She specialized in playing eccentric old ladies, often with mysterious powers (*Rosemary's Baby*) or a spark of sexuality (*Harold and Maude*) and certainly with strong and positive personalities, which reflected her own character. At 80 she was still writing autobiographical books and new plays – and acting in them.

Films as actress include: 1940 Abe Lincoln in Illinois (GB: Spirit of the People). '41 Two-Faced Woman. '43 Edge of Darkness; Action in the North Atlantic. '48 A Double Life (co-sc. only). '49 Adam's Rib (co-sc. only). '52 The Marrying Kind (co-sc. only); Pat and Mike (co-sc. only). '53 The Actress (sc; + play basis). '65 Inside Daisy Clover.

'68 Rosemary's Baby. '70 Where's Poppa? '71 Harold and Maude. '76 The Big Bus. '78 Every Which Way But Loose. '79 Boardwalk.

GORETTA, Claude

(b. 1929). Director. Born: Geneva, Switzerland

After studying law at Geneva University, Claude Goretta came to London in 1955 with his friend Alain Tanner and worked briefly at the British Film Institute. They became involved with the Free Cinema group (Lindsay Anderson, Karel Reisz, Tony Richardson) and made a documentary about Piccadilly night life, *Nice Time*. Goretta returned to Geneva and directed television documentaries. In 1968 he helped to found the production company Groupe 5, and directed his first feature in 1970. Since then he has been less prominent than his former partner Tanner, whose films are more angry and attacking. Goretta's films allow final hope, as in *The Invitation*, or quietly understate disaster, as with the heroine's decline into passive madness in *The Lacemaker*. Goretta has a fine, small-scale talent that he has been careful not to overstrain. He tends to work chiefly in France.

Films: 1957 Nice Time (co-dir). '70 Le Fou (The Madman). '73 L'Invitation (SWITZ-FR) (GB: The Invitation). '75 Pas Si Méchant que Ça (FR-SWITZ) (USA: The Wonderful Crook). '77 La Dentellière (FR-SWITZ-GER) (GB: The Lacemaker). '78 Les Chemins de l'Exil, ou Les Dernières Années de Jean-Jacques Rousseau (FR) (GB: The Roads of Exile). '81 La Provinciale (FR-SWITZ) (GB: A Girl From Lorraine).

GORING, Marius

(b. 1912). Actor. Born: Newport, Isle of Wight, England

Educated at the Perse School, Cambridge, Marius Goring studied languages at various continental universities and acted with Harcourt Williams and at the Old Vic. He toured Europe as a stage actor and made his West End debut in 1934. He helped to found the London Theatre Studio in 1936 and entered films the same year. Most of his best roles were in the Powell-Pressburger films – he fitted peculiarly well into their conservative fantasy world as an excruciatingly camp heavenly messenger in *A Matter of Life and Death* and as a boyish composer unable to cope with his ballerina wife's problems in *The Red Shoes*. In recent years he has been less known for his films than for his role as a police pathologist in the television series *The Expert* and for leading the opposition to the more militant members (including Corin and Vanessa Redgrave) of the British actors' union Equity.

Films include: 1940 The Case of the Frightened Lady (USA: The Frightened Lady). '46 A Matter of Life and Death (USA: Stairway to Heaven). '47 Take My Life. '48 The Red Shoes; Mr Perrin and Mr Trail. '50 Odette. '51 The Magic Box. '57 Ill Met by Moonlight (USA: Night Ambush). '68 Girl on a Motorcycle (GB-FR). '71 Zeppelin.

GOSHO, Heinosuke

(1902–1981). Director. Born: Tokyo, Japan

The son of a geisha and a prosperous tobacco merchant whose business he inherited, Gosho first worked at the Shochiku studio as an assistant to Yasujiro Shimazu, the pioneer of *shomin-geki*, simple stories about the everyday life of ordinary people. From 1925 Gosho became a director, making films of this sort, often uniting pathos and humour within a naturalistic slice-of-life setting. His first box-office hit was *The Lonely Roughneck* in 1927, the story of a well-bred girl's love for a rough country horse-cart driver. He directed the first Japanese talkie, *The Neighbour's Wife and Mine*, in 1931, though he briefly went back to silent films later on. He preferred to work on location rather than in the studio, being much concerned with details of setting. Despite ill health he was immensely productive, making about a hundred films, of which only *Four Chimneys* is well-known in the West.

Films include: 1927 Sabishii Rambomono (The Lonely Roughneck). '31 Madamu to Nyobo (The Neighbour's Wife and Mine/Madame and Wife). '33 Hanayome no Negoto (The Bride Talks in Her Sleep); Izu no Odoriko (Dancing Girls of Izu); Aibu (Caress). '34 Ikitoshi Ikerumono (Everything That Lives). '35 Hanamuko no Negoto (The Bridegroom Talks in His Sleep). '36 Oboroyo no Onna (Woman of the Mist). '53 Entotsu no Mieru Basho (GB: Four Chimneys/Where Chimneys Are Seen). '54 Osaka no Yado (An Inn at Osaka/Hotel at Osaka). '58 Hotarubi (Fireflies). '59 Waga Ai (When a Woman Loves). '68 Meiji Haru Aki (A Girl of the Meiji Period).

GOUGH, Michael

(b. 1917). Actor. Born: Kuala Lumpur, Malaya

With his dark-brown voice and gravely melancholy appearance, Michael Gough gravitated towards horror films, particularly in the Sixties, but he has remained a versatile character actor. He was the sensible young officer of the bomb-disposal squad in *The Small Back Room* and the father of the headstrong girl (Julie Christie) in *The Go-Between*, as well as the sinister museum keeper conducting bizarre experiments in *Horrors of the Black Museum*. The son of a rubber planter, he dropped out of agricultural college to study acting at the Old Vic where his contemporaries were Laurence Olivier, Vivien Leigh and Edith Evans. He made his stage debut in 1936 but did not appear in films until 1948. Since then he has worked steadily in films, television and the theatre. He is also an amateur film-maker and his *Welcome to Washington*, a newsreel documentary of President Jimmy Carter and the Queen visiting Washington, Co. Durham, to honour George Washington's ancestors, was one of the *Movie Maker* ten best amateur films of 1978.

Films include: 1948 Blanche Fury; Saraband for Dead Lovers. '49 The Small Back Room (USA: Hour of Glory). '51 The Man in the White Suit. '56 Reach for the Sky. '57 Ill Met by Moonlight (USA: Night Ambush). '59 Horrors of the Black Museum; The Horse's Mouth. '67 Berserk! '71 The Go-Between.

GOULD, Elliott

(b. 1938). Actor. Born: Elliott Goldstein; New York City, USA

After drama lessons as a child and attendance at the Professional Children's School in Manhattan, as well as ballet studies, Gould adorned occasional Broadway chorus lines including that of *Irma la Douce*, which brought him the lead in *I Can Get It for You Wholesale*. His co-star was Barbra Streisand, whom he married in 1963 and divorced five years later. But her career flourished while his floundered. His ascent to Seventies stardom began after he made his first film, *The Night They Raided Minsky's*. Then, in quick succession, came *Bob & Carol & Ted & Alice*, for which he was nominated for an Oscar as Ted and *M*A*S*H*, where he was a smash hit as Hawkeye. Suddenly he was so much in demand that he was the top male box-office star in 1971 and acting for Ingmar Bergman in *The Touch*. His neurotic, wittily self-deprecating persona slipped over into his private life as a mental breakdown led to two years' unemployment, from which Robert Altman rescued him with the plum role of an updated Philip Marlowe in *The Long Goodbye* – he was also one of a pair of compulsive gamblers in *California Split* and made a guest appearance as himself in *Nashville*. He has remained active since then but the quality of his films has dropped sharply, and he is no longer an iconic figure summing up crucial aspects of the seventies.

Films include: 1968 The Night They Raided Minsky's (GB The Night They Invented Striptease). '69 Bob & Carol & Ted & Alice. '70 M*A*S*H; Getting Straight. '71 Beröringen (USA-SWED) (USA/GB: The Touch). '73 The Long Goodbye. '74 S*P*Y*S (GB); California Split. '75 Nashville (as himself). '76 Harry and Walter Go to New York. '78 The Silent Partner (CAN); Capricorn One; Matilda. '79 The Lady Vanishes (GB); Escape to Athena (GB). '81 The Devil and Max Devlin.

Above left: Michael Gough in Konga *(1961). Above right: Elliott Gould in* California Split *in which he and George Segal were a pair of happy gamblers. Below: Gibson Gowland in* Sea Bat *(1930). Below right: Betty Grable in* How to be Very Very Popular *(1955). Below right: Gloria Grahame in the thriller* The Big Heat *(1953). Bottom right: Farley Granger as the tennis-player drawn into a web of murderous intrigue in Hitchcock's* Strangers on a Train. *Bottom, far right: Stewart Granger*

GOULDING, Edmund

(1891–1959). Director/writer. Born: London, England

An actor in his youth, Edmund Goulding went to the USA in 1919 and entered films as a writer. His numerous scripts included that of the classic *Tol'able David* (1921). From 1925 he directed, writing his own scripts for many of his early films. Goulding was a sensitive director of emotional melodrama, and adept in handling actresses: Garbo in *Love*, Swanson in *The Trespasser*, Davis in *Dark Victory*. But he was a versatile man, turning out a song when required, adapting the delicacy of his style to the war film in his version of *The Dawn Patrol* (1938), and producing the extraordinary *Nightmare Alley* one of the bleakest pictures of human folly and cruelty in Hollywood cinema.

Films include: 1927 Love; Women Love Diamonds. '29 The Trespasser; The Broadway Melody (sc. only). '30 Paramount on Parade. '32 No Man of Her Own (sc. only). '39 Dark Victory. '40 Two Girls on Broadway (sc. only) (GB: Choose Your Partner). '43 Claudia. '45 Flight From Folly (sc. only).

(GB). '46 Of Human Bondage; The Razor's Edge. '47 Nightmare Alley. '49 Everybody Does It. '56 Teenage Rebel. '58 Mardi Gras.

GOWLAND, Gibson

(1882–1951). Actor. Born: Spennymoor, Durham, England

After a brief stage career Gibson Gowland entered films around 1916 and made a first mark as the mountain-guide, Silent Sieppe, in Stroheim's *Blind Husbands*. His most famous role was also for Stroheim, that of the rough, genial dentist, McTeague, in *Greed*. Gowland returned to England in the early Thirties and acted until 1937; he escaped notably from type-casting in *The Secret of the Loch*, where he played a superstitious Scottish gillie, but was offered little that was worthy of a man with his excellent Hollywood record.

Films include: 1919 Blind Husbands (USA). '21 Ladies Must Live (USA). '25 Greed (USA); The Phantom of the Opera. '28 Rose Marie. '32 Without Honours; Doomed Battalion. '33 SOS Eisberg (GER)

(USA: SOS Iceberg). '34 The Secret of the Loch; Private Life of Don Juan. '35 The Mystery of the Mary Celeste (GB) (USA: Phantom Ship). '37 Cotton Queen.

GRABLE, Betty

(1916–1973). Actress. Born: Elizabeth Ruth Grable; St Louis, Missouri, USA

In Hollywood from the early Thirties, Betty Grable (also known in those days as Frances Dean) made little impact with Goldwyn, RKO and Paramount, and seemed fated for nothing better than leads in B musicals. But Zanuck took her to Fox in 1940, she starred in a number of that studio's characteristic brassy musicals, and with World War II became an icon of the times, the GI's favourite pin-up. For a while she was Hollywood's highest-paid star (and possessed the world's most insured legs); for all her modest talents and strictly cover-girl looks, she had a longish run. Then, in the mid-Fifties, the musical declined, and her studio found Monroe. In 1955 Betty Grable went to the theatre. She was married

for over twenty years to the band-leader Harry James.

Films include: 1942 Song of the Islands. '43 Springtime in the Rockies; Coney Island; Sweet Rosie O'Grady. '44 Pin-Up Girl. '45 Diamond Horseshoe; The Dolly Sisters. '47 Mother Wore Tights. '53 How to Marry a Millionaire.

GRADE, Lew

(b. 1906). Producer. Born: Louis Winogradsky; Tokmak, Kirgiziya, Russia

The future Lord Grade came to London at the age of five, went into showbusiness as a dancer, and struck it rich as a theatrical agent. In 1955 he launched ATV, and made it into the largest of the ITV companies. He built up Associated Communications Corporation (turnover: £250 million) bought the Classic cinema circuit in 1977, and launched into film production. *The Muppet Movie* made a lot of money, squandered by his expensive disaster epics, and *Raise the Titanic!* finished him. In 1969 Grade had been knighted, in 1976 he became a life peer, and in 1982 he was eased out of his production company; ironically, it then had a winner in *On Golden Pond*.

Films as executive producer or distributor: 1978 Herbstsonate (GER) (GB: Autumn Sonata); The Big Sleep; The Medusa Touch (GB-FR); The Boys From Brazil (USA). '79 The Muppet Movie (USA); Escape to Athena. '80 All Quiet on the Western Front (USA); Raise the Titanic! (USA). '81 Hawk the Slayer; The Legend of the Lone Ranger (USA); On Golden Pond (USA).

GRAHAME, Gloria

(1925–1981). Actress. Born: Gloria Grahame Hallward; Los Angeles, California, USA

Only for a short while in the Fifties were Gloria Grahame's unique talents given full scope. She had been in films since 1944, but first caught the eye in 1950, in her then husband Nicholas Ray's *In a Lonely Place*. She won a Best

Supporting Actress Oscar for her Southern belle in *The Bad and the Beautiful*, but was infinitely better in two films for Fritz Lang. Her desperate, vulnerable Debbie in *The Big Heat* is unforgettable; her equivocal seductress in *Human Desire* (reworking a Simone Simon role) is less known, but just as good. But the neurotic wife in *The Cobweb* was her last real part, though against all odds she made bits of *Oklahoma!* watchable.

Films include: 1946 It's a Wonderful Life. '47 Crossfire. '50 In a Lonely Place. '52 Macao; The Bad and the Beautiful. '53 The Big Heat. '54 Human Desire. '55 The Cobweb; Oklahoma! '79 Head Over Heels. '80 Melvin and Howard.

GRANGER, Farley

(b. 1925). Actor. Born: San Jose, California, USA

For a while, in the early Fifties, Farley Granger was a very interesting actor. Starting as a juvenile lead with Goldwyn, he had come back after war service to play complex young criminals in Hitchcock's *Rope* and Nicholas Ray's *They Live by Night*. He was adept at conveying their charm, vulnerability and – in the Hitchcock film – slyness. His ambiguous hero in another of Hitchcock's films, *Strangers on a Train*, advanced his career further, but then, when he went to Italy for Visconti's *Senso*, a fine performance as the treacherous lover was ruined when distributors butchered the film. A year or so later Granger left film for stage and television, returning in the Seventies in dire continental movies.

Films include: 1943 The North Star (re-issued as: Armored Attack). '44 The Purple Heart. '48 Rope; Enchantment; They Live by Night. '49 Roseanna McCoy. '50 Our Very Own. '51 Strangers on a Train. '52 Hans Christian Andersen. '53 The Story of Three Loves. '54 Senso (IT) (GB cut and dubbed version: The Wanton Countess). '55 The Naked Street. '73 A Man Called Noon (GB-SP-IT); Le Serpent (FR-IT-GER) (USA/GB: The Serpent).

GRANGER, Stewart

(b. 1913). Actor. Born: James Stewart; London, England

A romantic leading man in British films of the Forties, Stewart Granger went to Hollywood in 1949 with his second wife, the actress Jean Simmons, and for seven years was an admirable swashbuckling hero. Though the films were little more than agreeable fun (with Lang's *Moonfleet* a notable exception), Granger's looks and his air of humorous irony carried him happily through. He was accustomed to disparage his own talents, but they were real enough, and it was sad to see his career linger on in Italian and German 'Westerns' and the like.

Films include: 1943 The Man in Grey. '44 Fanny By Gaslight; Love Story; Madonna of the Seven Moons. '45 Waterloo Road. '46 Caravan; The Magic Bow. '48 Saraband for Dead Lovers. '52 Scaramouche (USA). '56 Bhowani Junction (USA). '60 North to Alaska (USA). '78 The Wild Geese.

GRANT, Cary

(1904–1986). Actor. Born:
Archibald Leach; Bristol, England

The young Grant toured England and
the USA with an acrobatic troupe,
stayed in America, did a stint in
vaudeville, made it to Broadway, and
in 1932 signed a Paramount contract.
Such were the wayward beginnings of
the man whom critic David Thomson
has styled 'the best and most important actor in the history of the cinema'.
That large claim stands up to the
closest examination. Grant learned
the hard way, with 14 films in two
years, Mae West as partner twice, and
a taste of greatness with Sternberg.
Then he did *Sylvia Scarlett* for Cukor,
and thereafter was his own man. He
was a master of timing, not merely of
lines but of expression and gesture.
Like all great screen actors, Grant
never stooped to impersonation;
though always himself, he revealed a
character of inexhaustible complexity. His films for Cukor, *Holiday* and
The Philadelphia Story, show the light-
hearted Grant, but show, too, a man
whose sense of values is unerring.
Hitchcock in *Suspicion* and *Notorious*
made him a flawed hero, charming
still but potentially dangerous. And
finally, Grant's five films for Howard
Hawks (*Bringing Up Baby, Only Angels
Have Wings, His Girl Friday, I Was a
Male War Bride* and *Monkey Business*)
are films whose particular universe is
as much the creation of the actor as of
the director. Indeed, Hawks' world
would be incomplete without Grant.

Films include: 1932 Merrily We Go to Hell.
'33 She Done Him Wrong. '36 Sylvia Scar-
lett. '37 The Awful Truth. '38 Bringing Up
Baby; Holiday (GB: Free to Live/
Unconventional Linda). '39 Gunga
Din. '40 His Girl Friday; The Philadelphia
Story. '41 Suspicion. '44 Arsenic and Old
Lace. '46 Notorious. '48 Mr Blandings
Builds His Dream House. '49 I Was a Male
War Bride (GB: You Can't Sleep Here). '59
North By Northwest. '62 That Touch of
Mink (+ prod. co).

GRANT, Kathryn

(b. 1933). Actress. Born: Kathryn
Grandstaff; West Columbia, Texas,
USA

The daughter of a Texas State Government official, Kathryn Grant had achieved some success in pictures before
her marriage to Bing Crosby in 1957,
but two years after the marriage she
decided to retire. In the mid-Seventies,
however, she emerged as hostess of a
television interview programme in
San Francisco. Her brief film career
(seven years only) had included a few
good thrillers (*The Phenix City Story,
The Brothers Rico*) and an appearance
under her real name of Kathryn
Grandstaff in Hitchcock's *Rear
Window*.

Films include: 1953 Forever Female. '54
Casanova's Big Night; Rear Window. '55
Unchained; Cell 2455, Death Row; Five
against the House; The Phenix City Story.
'57 Guns of Fort Petticoat; Operation Mad
Ball; The Brothers Rico. '58 The Seventh
Voyage of Sinbad. '59 Anatomy of a Murder;
The Big Circus.

GRANT, Lee

(b. 1926). Actress. Born: Lyova
Rosenthal; New York City, USA

Lee Grant made a spectacular screen
debut as the shoplifter in *Detective
Story*. She had already played the part
on stage, winning a New York Critics'
Circle award, and the film brought her
an Oscar nomination and the best
actress award at Cannes. Her film
career was interrupted by the McCar-
thyite persecution – she had declined
to testify against her husband Arnold
Manhoff – but she returned in the
Sixties, played a wide variety of parts
ranging from the frivolous (*Plaza
Suite*) to the intensely dramatic (*In the
Heat of the Night*), won an Oscar for
Shampoo, and began a new career as
director with the feminist documentary, *The Stronger*.

Films include: 1951 Detective Story. '55
Storm Fear. '65 Terror in the City. '67 In the
Heat of the Night. '70 The Landlord. '71
Plaza Suite. '72 Portnoy's Complaint. '75
Shampoo. '76 The Stronger (doc) (dir.
only). '77 Airport '77. '78 Damien – Omen
II; The Swarm. '80 Little Miss Marker. '81
Tell Me A Riddle (dir. only).

GRAVES, Peter

(b. 1925). Actor. Born: Peter
Aurness; Minneapolis, Minnesota,
USA

Tall, handsome and muscular, but
with a calm commanding voice, Peter
Graves was ideal to play tough yet
understanding good guys. As a
teenager he excelled as an athlete and
as a saxophonist, and by the age of 16
he was a radio announcer at WMIN
Minnesota. Then, after two years in
the air force, he enrolled at the University of Minnesota to study drama.
From there he went to Hollywood
where he was spotted on a television
show and was offered his first film
part. Numerous roles followed, often
in Westerns, and as the years passed
expectations of becoming a major star
faded. But it was his television work
that gained him his greatest recognition, particularly as the leader in
Mission Impossible.

GRAY, Charles

(b. 1928). Actor. Born: Donald M.
Gray; Bournemouth, Hampshire,
England

With a curl of his lip and a sinister
sneer Charles Gray creates an aura of
cold, unfeeling superiority that he has
used to great advantage to portray
daunting characters on both film and
television. He believes that television
is the medium to which he is best
suited, and he has brought his air of
suave, unsympathetic confidence to
many a successful series. His first
acting experience was on the stage as
Charles the Wrestler in *As You Like It*.
He then joined the Royal Shakespeare
Company but tired of being incess-
antly cast as a military-clad heavy.
And it was when co-starring with
Paul Scofield in *Expresso Bongo* that
he was offered his first film parts. He
seems to be one of the few actors who
knows his limitations, and as a result

Above: Cary Grant in Suspicion.
*Left: Coleen Gray. Below: Lee Grant
in* Ransom for a Dead Man *(1971).
Bottom: Peter Graves. Opposite page,
right: Charles Gray in* The Devil
Rides Out. *Below right: Kathryn
Grant in* Operation Mad Ball. *Below,
far right: Sally Gray in* The Mark
of Cain. *Bottom: Dulcie Gray in*
My Brother Jonathan

Films include: 1951 Rogue River; Fort Defi-
ance. '53 Stalag 17. '54 The Raid; Black
Tuesday. '55 The Court Martial of Billy
Mitchell. '56 It Conquered the World. '65 A
Rage to Live. '66 Texas Across the River. '67
The Ballad of Josie. '70 Un Esercito di 5
Uomini (IT-SP) (USA/GB: The Five Man
Army).

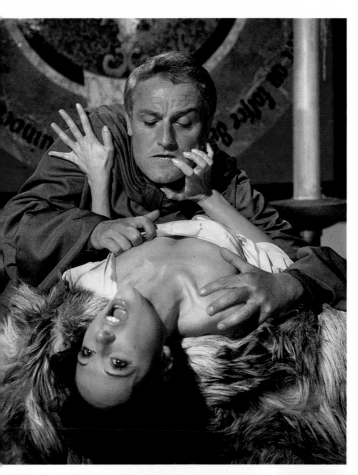

nearly always performs with great ease and satisfaction.

Films include: 1960 The Entertainer. '65 Masquerade. '67 The Night of the Generals (GB-FR). '68 The Secret War of Harry Frigg; The Devil Rides Out (USA: The Devil's Bride). '70 Cromwell. '71 Diamonds Are Forever. '74 The Beast Must Die. '75 The Rocky Horror Picture Show. '76 Seven Nights in Japan (GB-FR).

GRAY, Coleen

(b. 1922). Actress. Born: Doris Jensen; Staplehurst, Nebraska, USA

When male leads like Bing Crosby, Tyrone Power and George Raft appeared in the bread-and-butter movies of the Forties and Fifties, Coleen Gray was often the girl by their sides. Her pretty face and lively personality meant that she was ideal as a leading lady who could add a little sparkle to a film but never steal the show. Born of Danish parentage, she grew up in a small town farming community and began acting in amateur dramatics at school. She worked her way through college, then went to Los Angeles and began appearing in various small productions. Her big break came when she was spotted by the agent Jack Pomeroy and a 20th Century-Fox talent scout – she was signed by Fox, and appeared in her first film *Kiss of Death* at the age of 25. Never a big star she was nevertheless a vital performer in the numerous crime dramas, Westerns and action pictures in which she appeared.

Films include: 1947 Kiss of Death. '48 Red River. '50 Riding High. '51 I'll Get You for This (GB) (USA: Lucky Nick Cain); Apache Drums. '58 Johnny Rocco. '60 The Leech Woman. '65 Town Tamer. '71 The Late Liz.

GRAY, Dulcie

(b. 1919). Actress. Born: Kuala Lumpur, Malaya

In her early film appearances Dulcie Gray played rather helpless, scatty females, but as she developed she settled perfectly in the role of a homely, plucky, independent lady with an artistic streak, normally very much in love with and dedicated to her man. The role was so comfortable because it was very similar to her own character. Gray, on giving up a career in journalism in Malaysia, returned to England, where she had been educated, to attend drama school. And there she met and later married the actor Michael Denison, subsequently appearing with him on stage and then on film. During the Fifties she began to concentrate more on her role as a theatre actress and an author of murder mysteries. She continued successfully in both spheres, having a particularly good year in 1978 when she won the Times Educational Supplement Award for her book *Butterflies on My Mind* as well as receiving great critical acclaim for her stage role as Miss Marple in Agatha Christie's *A Murder is Announced*.

Films include: 1944 Madonna of the Seven Moons. '45 A Place of One's Own; They Were Sisters. '46 Wanted for Murder/Voice in the Night. '47 A Man About the House; Mine Own Executioner. '48 My Brother Jonathan. '49 The Glass Mountain. '51 The Franchise Affair. '66 A Man Could Get Killed (USA).

GRAY, Sally

(b. 1917). Actress. Born: Constance Vera Stevens; Holloway, London, England

Encouraged to dance by her ex-ballerina mother, Sally Gray was appearing on stage before she entered her teens. At the age of 18 she was snatched from the chorus line by the revue and film comedian Stanley Lupino who gave her leading roles in his films. Lupino died 11 years later and Gray had a nervous breakdown, but when she did return to the screen she turned away from her previous dumb blonde roles and put in some fine performances in Edward Dmytryk's *Obsession* as a faithless wife, and in Alberto Cavalcanti's *They Made Me a Fugitive* as a classy gangster's moll. Then in 1951 she left the cinema behind when she married a Lord and went to live with him in his castle in Ireland.

Films include: 1937 Over She Goes. '39 The Lambeth Walk. '41 Dangerous Moonlight. '46 Carnival; Green for Danger. '47 They Made Me a Fugitive (USA: I Became a Criminal). '48 The Mark of Cain. '49 Silent Dust; Obsession (USA: The Hidden Room). '53 Escape Route (USA: I'll Get You).

179

Above: Kathryn Grayson. Above right: Nigel Green in Fräulein Doktor *(1969). Below: Juliette Greco as Minna in Huston's* The Roots of Heaven, *an African melodrama*

GRAYSON, Kathryn

(b. 1922). Actress. Born: Zelma Hedrick; Winston-Salem, North Carolina, USA

Up until the mid-Fifties the operatic musical was extremely popular, and one of its leading ladies was Kathryn Grayson. Her colaratura soprano voice, endless energy and beauty charmed audiences as she teamed up with Howard Keel in films like *Show Boat, Kiss Me Kate*, and with Oreste in *The Vagabond King*. As a child she was encouraged to develop her voice and, when her family moved to Hollywood, MGM offered her a contract. But by 1955 audiences had changed their attitudes towards musicals and they wanted more relaxed singing styles as well as some energetic dancing. But Grayson couldn't dance – nor could she be anything but slightly stiff and operatic. She continued to perform on the stage though, and in 1960 took over from Julie Andrews in *Camelot*.

Films include: 1941 Andy Hardy's Private Secretary. '42 Rio Rita. '45 Anchors Aweigh. '46 Two Sisters From Boston. '47 It Happened in Brooklyn. '51 Show Boat. '52 Lovely to Look at. '53 The Desert Song; So This is Love (GB: The Grace Moore Story); Kiss Me, Kate. '56 The Vagabond King.

GRECO, Juliette

(b. 1927). Actress. Born: Montpelier, France

It is a shame that Juliette Greco's popularity in movies never matched her success as a singer among the clubs of the Left Bank of Paris. At fifteen she had been imprisoned, while her mother and sister were deported to Germany, and it was on her release at the end of the war that she settled in Paris. In the late-Forties and early-Fifties she became a cult figure, singing songs written by the existentialists, dressed all in black, with her sultry black hair and pale plaintive face. After a series of small film roles she starred in *Quand Tu Liras Cette Lettre* and thus attracted the attention of Darryl F. Zanuck who became her mentor and attempted to launch her as a star. But the majority of the roles given to her were appalling and by the Sixties she had sensibly returned to singing. With her sensual, melancholy voice, she is a fine interpreter of classic French street songs. She is married to the actor Michel Piccoli.

Films include: 1950 Orphée (USA: Orpheus). '52 The Green Glove (USA). '53 Quand Tu Liras Cette Lettre (FR-IT). '56 La Chatelaine du Liban (FR-IT) (GB: The Woman From Lebanon). '57 The Sun Also Rises (USA). '58 The Naked Earth (GB); Bonjour Tristesse (USA); The Roots of Heaven (USA). '59 Whirlpool (GB). '60 Crack in the Mirror (USA).

GREEN, Adolph

(b. 1918). Scriptwriter/lyricist. Born: New York City, USA

Adolph Green wanted to be an actor, and while looking for work in the theatre he met up with aspiring actresses Betty Comden and Judy Tuvim (later Holliday). They formed, with two others, a moderately successful five piece cabaret act called The Revuers. When the group split Comden and Green stayed together. They decided to expand the ballet *Fancy Free* into a musical, which they would write and star in. But after less than two days rehearsal the director of the Theatre Guild saw it and decided that it was destined for Broadway, where it became an instant hit as *On the Town*. During its subsequent adaptation to the screen Green and Comden met Gene Kelly and Stanley Donen and later collaborated with them on the classic *Singin' in the Rain*. They went on to become one of the most successful musical-writing duos in Hollywood, making numerous famous and delightful films, full of comedy and memorable tunes. Green

has also appeared as an actor in the film *Simon*.

Films include: 1947 Good News (co-sc). '49 Take Me Out to the Ball Game (co-lyr) (GB: Everybody's Cheering); The Barkleys of Broadway (co-sc); On the Town (co-lyr; + co-sc). '52 Singin' in the Rain (co-sc). '53 The Band Wagon (co-sc). '55 It's Always Fair Weather (co-sc; + co-lyr). '58 Auntie Mame (co-sc). '60 Bells Are Ringing (co-sc; + co-lyr). '64 What a Way to Go! (co-sc; + lyr).

GREEN, Guy

(b. 1913). Director/cinematographer. Born: Frome, Somerset, England

By the mid-Fifties, shortly before he turned to directing, Guy Green was one of the most respected cinematographers in British cinema. He began working with film at 16 as a projectionist on an Atlantic liner, and within a few years had formed a partnership to run a portrait photography studio. In 1933 he broke into the film industry proper with a job as an assistant cameraman at the Shepperton Studios. He soon established a reputation for reliability and ingenuity and the peak of his cinematographical career came when he won an Oscar for his photography on David Lean's *Great Expectations*. Unfortunately he has never really matched this success when directing, and despite some early successes with films dealing with social problems such as *The Mark* and *A Patch of Blue*, his later work has been disappointing.

Films as cinematographer include: 1944 The Way Ahead. '46 Carnival; Great Expectations. '48 Blanche Fury; Oliver Twist. '49 The Passionate Friends. '50 Madeleine. '55 I Am a Camera. As director: '60 The Angry Silence. '61 The Mark. '62 The Light in the Piazza; Diamond Head (USA). '65 A Patch of Blue (USA). '67 Pretty Polly (USA: A Matter of Innocence). '69 The Magus.

GREEN, Nigel

(1924–1972). Actor. Born: Pretoria, South Africa

Educated in England, Nigel Green studied chemical engineering before winning a scholarship to RADA. He began his career with a flourish, appearing at both the Old Vic and at Stratford when he was only 24. Despite receiving serious injuries in a fall in 1956 he recovered to become a familiar figure on both British film and television. Indeed he should have received greater recognition than he did, particularly after his splendid performances in both *Zulu* and *The Ipcress File*. From 1965 he worked increasingly in American films where he again proved himself a very capable actor. He was continuing to build on his career when he died of an accidental overdose of sleeping pills at the age of 48.

Films include: 1954 The Sea Shall Not Have Them. '56 Reach for the Sky. '57 Bitter Victory (FR-US). '60 The Criminal (USA: The Concrete Jungle); Tunes of Glory. '63 Jason and the Argonauts; Zulu. '65 The Ipcress File. '66 Deadlier Than the Male; Lets Kill Uncle (USA); Tobruk (USA); Khartoum. '72 The Ruling Class.

Right: Richard Greene as Robin Hood, his most famous role. Below right: Sydney Greenstreet in The Hucksters, *a piece of sharp post-war entertainment. Below, far right: Joan Greenwood in the historical romance* Bad Lord Byron. *Bottom: Jane Greer*

GREENE, David

(b. 1921). Actor/director. Born: Manchester, England

David Greene began his career as a junior reporter on the *Walthamstow Guardian* and then worked variously as furniture remover, deck-hand and hospital porter before joining the Merchant Navy at the outbreak of World War II. Invalided out in 1941, he became involved with the Everyman Theatre and enrolled at RADA. By the mid-Fifties he had joined the Canadian Broadcasting Corporation and proved his skill as a television director with the award-winning *Flight to Freedom*. In 1956 he went to New York where he earned himself a reputation as one of the top television directors. The Sixties were spent in Britain where he directed his first feature film, *The Shuttered Room*. He has a strong visual sense and the movies that followed show his sensitivity of feeling for locations as well as his penchant for sexual fantasy. He now lives in America.

Films include: 1948 Daughter of Darkness (actor only); The Small Voice (actor only) (USA: Hideout). '49 The Golden Madonna (actor only). '50 The Wooden Horse (actor only). '51 The Dark Light (actor only). '67 The Shuttered Room (dir. only). '68 Sebastian (dir. only); The Strange Affair (dir. only). '69 I Start Counting (dir. only). '72 Madame Sin (dir. only). '73 Godspell (dir. only) (USA). '76 The Count of Monte Cristo (dir. only) (USA). '78 Gray Lady Down (dir. only) (USA).

GREENE, Richard

(1918–1985). Actor. Born: Plymouth, Devonshire, England

A descendant of British film pioneer William Friese-Greene, he was educated in London before beginning repertory work while in his teens. He made a screen test for Alexander Korda and when Darryl Zanuck saw it he sent word for Greene to be rushed to Hollywood. There he was given a lead role opposite Loretta Young and signed a seven-year contract. He returned to England in 1940 and served as an officer in the 27th Lancers until December 1944. After the war he toured with a drama company entertaining the Allied troops. He then starred in a West End production of *Desert Rats* and freelanced in a handful of films. However, it was as the hero of the long-running series *Robin Hood* that he became a household name. On retiring from the screen he bred horses in Ireland.

Films include: 1938 My Lucky Star (USA); Submarine Patrol (USA). '39 The Hound of the Baskervilles (USA). '47 Forever Amber (USA). '49 The Fan (USA) (GB: Lady Windermere's Fan). '50 Shadow of the Eagle. '51 Lorna Doone (USA). '52 Captain Scarlett (USA). '60 Sword of Sherwood Forest. '68 The Blood of Fu Manchu.

GREENSTREET, Sydney

(1879–1954). Actor. Born: Sandwich, Kent, England

Grotesquely obese, purveyor of secrets for hard cash, habitué of exotic fleshpots, a man to whom swift physical action was denied because of his girth but who nevertheless compensated for it by his loquacity and quicksilver mind – Greenstreet was one of the great screen villains. The son of a tanner, he went to Ceylon in 1899 to start his career as a tea planter. However, he returned to England, studied acting and went on the stage. His screen debut as Gutman in *The Maltese Falcon* could not have been more auspicious even though it came when he was in his sixties. From then on he appeared in a number of films of varying quality, often with his physical alter ego, Peter Lorre. Together they formed a kind of Laurel and Hardy of crime melodrama. Greenstreet died four years after retiring from the screen.

Films include: 1941 The Maltese Falcon; They Died With Their Boots On. '42 Across the Pacific; Casablanca. '44 The Conspirators; The Mask of Dimitrios; Passage to Marseille. '45 Conflict. '47 The Hucksters. '50 Malaya.

GREENWOOD, Joan

(1921–1987). Actress. Born: London, England

Joan Greenwood was regarded as something of a celebrity from childhood as her father was the well-known artist Sydney Earnshaw Greenwood. After attending RADA she made her West End debut in 1938. She began appearing in films in 1940 and joined ENSA. Small, slim and with a seductively husky voice, she quickly became associated with sexy, kittenish roles in the successful Ealing productions of the Forties and Fifties. Her talents are shown to best advantage in *Kind Hearts and Coronets*, in which she plays the purring yet scheming Sibella opposite Dennis Price. Her charm was that she conveyed eroticism while remaining unmistakably English and 'correct'. She appeared on the stage and made a few television appearances into her sixties.

Films include: 1943 The Gentle Sex. '47 The Man Within (USA: The Smugglers); The October Man. '48 Saraband for Dead Lovers. '49 Kind Hearts and Coronets; Whisky Galore! (USA: Tight Little Island); The Bad Lord Byron. '51 The Man in the White Suit. '52 The Importance of Being Earnest. '55 Moonfleet (USA). '63 Tom Jones.

GREER, Jane

(b. 1924). Actress. Born: Bettejane Greer; Washington DC, USA

As a child Jane Greer suffered from facial paralysis, but learned to control her muscles so that it didn't disfigure her. She became president of her high school dramatic club and later received newsreel exposure while modelling WAC uniforms. She had been assured a contract with Paramount, but they then decided that she was too

ordinary and she took a job as a singer with a Latin-American orchestra at the Del Rio Club in Washington. In 1942 Howard Hughes decided to take a chance with her, but was unable to give her any suitable roles and she was released after only a year. This was a real disappointment, but by this time she was married to crooner Rudy Vallee (1943–45). He helped her secure a contract at RKO, where she was cast as villainous girls who usually came to a sticky end – most notably in *Out of the Past*. She graduated from B movies to more prestigious productions, but family concerns and general lack of ambition prevented her from becoming a star of any note.

Films include: 1937 Dick Tracy. '46 The Falcon's Alibi. '47 They Won't Believe Me; Out of the Past (GB: Build My Gallows High). '48 Station West. '49 The Big Steal. '50 The Company She Keeps. '52 You For Me; The Prisoner of Zenda. '65 Billie.

GREGSON, John

(1919–1975). Actor. Born: Liverpool, England

John Gregson began his career as a telephone engineer but was actively involved in amateur dramatics and after serving in the Royal Navy during World War II joined the Liverpool Old Vic. He made his London stage debut in *A Sleeping Clergyman* in 1948, and that same year appeared in the Ealing movie *Saraband for Dead Lovers*. Rank then offered him a long-term contract. Gregson's style of acting is down-to-earth and cheerful, a 'nice' guy who never gets to wear a decent suit. His best remembered role was in *Genevieve*, the vintage-car romp, co-starring Kenneth More, Dinah Sheridan and Kay Kendall.

Films include: 1948 Saraband for Dead Lovers; Scott of the Antarctic. '49 Whisky Galore! (USA: Tight Little Island). '51 The Lavender Hill Mob. '53 Genevieve. '56 The Battle of the River Plate (USA: Pursuit of the Graf Spee). '57 Miracle in Soho. '58 Roonie. '59 The Captain's Table. '61 The Frightened City. '62 Live Now, Pay Later.

GRÉMILLON, Jean

(1901–1959). Director. Born: Bayeux, Calvados, France

Jean Grémillon studied violin and composition at the Paris Schola Cantorum before becoming a musician in an orchestra accompanying silent films. From there his interest in movie-making grew and he began to direct short documentaries. By the time he was 25 he was making features but he had to wait another 14 years to make *Remorques* and be accepted as a director of note. He made some well-received films during World War II, but then found difficulty in securing backing for future projects – largely because he was too artistically ambitious. Little-known abroad, he has never quite achieved the success of his contemporaries René Clair and Marcel Carné.

Films include: 1929 Gardiens de Phare. '30 La Petite Lise. '37 L'Etrange M. Victor (FR-GER) (GB: The Strange Mr Victor). '40 Remorques. '43 Lumière d'Eté. '44 Le Ciel est à Vous. '45 Le Six Juin à l'Aube. '49 Pattes Blanches (GB: White Legs). '50 Les Charmes de l'Existence (short) (GB: The Charms of Life). '54 L'Amour d'une Femme (FR-IT). '55 La Maison aux Images (short).

GRENFELL, Joyce

(1910–1979). Actress. Born: Joyce Phipps; London, England

Grenfell's parents were both expatriate Americans; her father was an architect and her mother – Nora Langhorne – was Nancy Astor's sister and a former Gibson Girl. She studied for a while at RADA, but gave up her course in order to marry fellow student Reginald Grenfell. She soon found work as a radio critic for *The Observer* newspaper before going into broadcasting with character monologues. By 1939 she was appearing in revues at the Little Theatre. Tall, ungainly yet undeniably engaging, she described herself in somewhat unflattering terms: 'about eight feet tall with a face like a reflection in a spoon'. In view of her parentage it is ironic that she should have achieved such success in caricaturing the English gentlewoman. During the Forties she began appearing in films and was soon an internationally popular 'English eccentric' best known for her portrayal of eager policewoman Ruby Gates in the St Trinian's pictures.

Films include: 1949 Stage Fright. '50 The Happiest Days of Your Life. '51 Laughter in Paradise. '53 Genevieve. '54 The Million Pound Note (USA: Man With a Million); The Belles of St Trinian's. '57 Blue Murder at St Trinian's. '58 Happy Is the Bride. '64 The Yellow Rolls Royce; The Americanization of Emily.

GREY, Joel

(b. 1932). Actor. Born: Joel Katz; Cleveland, Ohio, USA

From the age of nine Joel appeared on stage singing, dancing and acting alongside his father, the comedian Mickey Katz. After high school he began working on radio comedy shows and in touring revues until he was discovered by Eddie Cantor on the *Colgate Comedy Hour* television show. He finally gained the recognition he deserved when he appeared as the MC in *Cabaret* and won the Academy Award for Best Supporting Actor. However, his film career has been sadly limited since then.

Films: 1952 About Face. '57 Calypso Heat Wave. '61 Come September. '72 Cabaret. '74 Man on a Swing. '76 Buffalo Bill and the Indians . . . or Sitting Bull's History Lesson; The Seven-Per-Cent Solution.

GREY, Virginia

(b. 1917). Actress. Born: Los Angeles, California, USA

As the daughter of Ray Grey, a Universal director and ex-Mack Sennett stock actor, Virginia was brought up in Hollywood. Her mother was also a cutter for Universal and from the age of nine Virginia was sent to various studio schools. Her classmates at MGM included Judy Garland, Mickey Rooney and Lana Turner. When she was ten, casting director Paul Kohner put her in *Uncle Tom's Cabin* as Little Eva, but her mother saw that she completed her schooling and it wasn't until the Thirties that Virginia Grey could really call herself an actress. From 1942 she freelanced, playing leads and supports until the Seventies. One of her most acclaimed performances was in *The Rose Tattoo*. She also appeared to good advantage in over a dozen Ross Hunter productions at Universal. Petite, blue-eyed and blonde-haired, she had a longstanding and well-publicized romance with Clark Gable.

Left: John Gregson in Hawks in the Sun. *Above: Joyce Grenfell, the archetypal eccentric Englishwoman. Below: Joel Grey and company at the Kit Kat Klub in* Cabaret, *a memorable performance*

Films include: **1927** Uncle Tom's Cabin. **'41** Back Street. **'42** Maisie Gets Her Man (GB: She Got Her Man). **'45** Men in Her Diary; Blonde Ransom; Flame of Barbary Coast. **'55** All That Heaven Allows; The Last Command; The Eternal Sea; The Rose Tattoo.

GRIERSON, John

(1898–1972). Documentarist. Born: Deanston, Perthshire, Scotland

The founder of the British documentary movement, and the first to use the term 'documentary' (in a review of Robert Flaherty's *Moana* in 1926), Grierson was a student at Glasgow University in the early Twenties. He went to the USA on a Rockefeller scholarship, wrote about art and film, and studied technique at Paramount. Back home in 1927, he persuaded the Empire Marketing Board to set up a film unit, and in 1929 made the key documentary *Drifters*, one of the few films he directed himself. In 1933 his unit moved to the GPO. This was Grierson's most creative period; great talents like Cavalcanti and Basil Wright were employed, and films of the quality of *Night Mail* and *Song of Ceylon* were made. In 1938 Grierson was invited by the Canadian government to set up the National Film Board; he was its commissioner until 1945. A varied later career included spells with UNESCO in Paris and the COI in London. He formed Group 3 to produce British features with social content, but little was achieved, and he moved on to Scottish Television, where he presented a series on documentary, *This Wonderful World*. His last years saw him back in Canada, lecturing.

Films as producer include: **1929** Drifters (+dir; +sc; +ed). **'30** Conquest (+co-dir). **'31** The Shadow on the Mountain. **'32** A Cattle Auction in the Hebrides. **'33** Industrial Britain. **'34** Hop Growers of Kent. **'35** Song of Ceylon; Coalface. **'36** Night Mail (exec. prod; +co-comm). **'37** Defence of Madrid. **'38** We Live in Two Worlds. **'52** The Brave Don't Cry (feature). **'62** The Heart of Scotland. **'63** The Big Mill.

GRIFFITH, Andy

(b. 1925). Actor. Born: Andrew Griffith; Mount Airy, North Carolina, USA

Andy Griffith's lazy personality and rustic drawl had made him famous on stage and television before the first of his half-dozen film appearances, in *A Face in the Crowd* in 1957. Griffith played a drunken down-and-out built up as a radio host, only to be smashed when he grew too powerful, and was an immediate success, but after a second hit repeating his stage role as a naive hillbilly in *No Time for Sergeants* his film career lapsed. Recently he was impressive as the President in the television serial *Washington: Behind Closed Doors* (1977).

Films include: **1957** A Face in the Crowd. **'58** Onionhead; No Time for Sergeants. **'61** The Second Time Around. **'68** Angel in My Pocket. **'75** Hearts of the West (GB: Hollywood Cowboy).

GRIFFITH, Corinne

(1899–1979). Actress. Born: Texarkana, Texas, USA

Known at the height of her stardom as 'the orchid lady of the screen', the lovely Corinne Griffith entered the movies in 1916 with Vitagraph, moved on to First National, and was one of the most glamorous of silent stars. Her most notable successes were in *Six Days*, from an Elinor Glyn novel; *Black Oxen*, in which she played a middle-aged lady mysteriously rejuvenated; and *The Divine Lady*, in which she was an Emma Hamilton far lovelier than the original. She retired in 1932, devoting herself to real estate, Christian Science, and campaigning for the abolition of income tax. In the mid-Sixties she claimed in a divorce court that the real Corinne had died in her thirties, and she, her stand-in, had replaced her in all her sound films.

Films include: **1918** Miss Ambition. **'19** A Girl at Bay. **'23** Six Days; The Common Law. **'24** Black Oxen; Lilies of the Field. **'25** The Marriage Whirl (GB: Modern Madness). **'27** Three Hours. **'28** The Garden of Eden; Outcast. **'29** The Divine Lady; Prisoners; Saturday's Children. **'30** Lilies of the Field; Back Pay. **'32** Lily Christine (GB).

GRIFFITH, D. W.

(1875–1948). Director. Born: Llewelyn Wark Griffith; Floydsfork (later known as Crestwood), Kentucky, USA

D. W. Griffith was the most important single figure in American cinema. He was a none-too-successful actor and playwright when in 1908 he approached the Edison studio to offer them scripts. He worked there as an actor, went on to Biograph and was given the chance to direct. By 1913 he had made some 450 short films, and in that time he laid down the ground rules of cinema. No-one can say who first used close-up, cross-cutting, camera movement and the rest of film's resources, but it was Griffith who fashioned them into a harmonious whole, abolishing for ever cinema's dependence on the stage. He moved to Hollywood, made his two

Above left: Virginia Grey in Blonde Inspiration. *Above: Andy Griffith in the melodramatic* A Face in the Crowd, *directed by Elia Kazan. Right: Corinne Griffith, hugely popular star of the silent screen, later an authoress. Below: the great director D.W. Griffith*

great epics, *The Birth of a Nation* and *Intolerance*, ruined himself financially, and caused cinema to be accepted as an art. He was not the only fine director in what was a very rich period, but he set the standard. In 1919 he helped to found United Artists; then he constructed his own studio on Long Island. *Broken Blossoms, True Heart Susie, Orphans of the Storm* showed his powers no whit lessened. *Isn't Life Wonderful?*, the study of poverty he made in Germany, could even be his finest film. But the world was changing round him, and he remained what he had always been, a courteous Southern gentleman, to whom film-making was as natural as breathing. He made one excellent sound film, *Abraham Lincoln*; its successor, *The Struggle*, failed, and he never directed again. In 1936 he received a special Academy citation for his life's work. In 1948 he died, alone, in a Hollywood hotel.

Films include: Shorts – **1907** Rescued From an Eagle's Nest (actor only). **'08** The Adventures of Dollie; Taming of the Shrew. **'09** The Curtain Pole; The Lonely Villa; Pippa Passes, or The Song of Conscience. **'10** Ramona; An Arcadian Maid; Two Little Waifs: a Modern Fairy Tale. **'11** The Lonedale Operator; The Battle. **'12** Lena and the Geese; Man's Genesis; The Musketeers of Pig Alley; The New York Hat. **'13** The Massacre. Features – **'13** Judith of Bethulia (re-released in longer version as: Her Condoned Sin, 1917). **'14** The Battle at Elderbush Gulch (short); Home, Sweet Home; The Escape; The Avenging Conscience (GB: Thou Shalt Not Kill). **'15** The Birth of a Nation. **'16** Intolerance. **'18** Hearts of the World. **'19** Broken Blossoms; True Heart Susie. **'20** Way Down East. **'21** Orphans of the Storm. **'23** The White Rose. **'24** America (GB: Love and Sacrifice); Isn't Life Wonderful?. **'25** Sally of the Sawdust; That Royle Girl. **'26** The Sorrows of Satan. **'28** Drums of Love; The Battle of the Sexes. **'29** Lady of the Pavements (GB: Lady of the Night). **'30** Abraham Lincoln. **'31** The Struggle.

GRIFFITH, Hugh

(1912–1980). Actor. Born: Marian Glas, Anglesey, Wales

After making his film debut in 1940, Hugh Griffith, a former bank clerk, spent six years with the Army in India. Returning to the screen in 1948, he enjoyed 30 successful years as a character actor in British and American films, playing forceful, exuberant, sometimes menacing roles. His raucous Squire Weston in *Tom Jones* was memorable, as was his Sheikh Ilderim in *Ben-Hur*; the latter won him a Best Supporting Actor Oscar. He also had a flourishing stage career, and was a notable Falstaff.

Films include: 1948 The Three Weird Sisters; London Belongs to Me. '49 A Run For Your Money; Kind Hearts and Coronets. '50 Gone to Earth (USA: The Wild Heart). '54 The Sleeping Tiger. '57 Lucky Jim. '59 Ben-Hur (USA). '60 Exodus (USA). '63 Tom Jones. '68 Oliver! '71 Wuthering Heights. '72 I Racconti di Canterbury (IT-FR) (GB: The Canterbury Tales).

GRIFFITH, Raymond

(1890–1957). Actor/producer. Born: Boston, Massachusetts, USA

Raymond Griffith entered films in 1914 and after years of supporting parts briefly flourished in the Twenties as a dapper, elegant comedian. His best work, notably the Civil War comedy *Hands Up!*, bears comparison with that of any of the better-remembered comedians of the period. But Griffith was at loggerheads with his studio, Paramount, and by 1927 his career was fading. He had a slight speech defect, but studio politics, not the coming of sound, were responsible for his eclipse. His last role was that of the dying French soldier in *All Quiet on the Western Front*. In the sound period Griffith worked as a producer, mainly at Fox.

Films include: 1915 Under New Management. '16 The Scoundrel's Tale. '17 False to

the Finish. '18 The Village Chestnut (+co-dir). '22 Fools First. '23 White Tiger. '24 Open All Night. '25 The Night Club. '26 Hands Up! '27 Time to Love. '29 Trent's Last Case. '30 All Quiet on the Western Front. '33 The Bowery (co-assoc. prod). '34 Looking for Trouble (assoc. prod). '38 Rebecca of Sunnybrook Farm (assoc. prod). '39 Drums Along the Mohawk (assoc. prod).

GRIFFITHS, Kenneth

(b. 1921). Actor/director. Born: Tenby, Pembrokeshire, Wales

Although leading roles have eluded him in over forty years as an actor in British films, Kenneth Griffiths has always been among the most reliable of supporting players, often cast unattractively as an envious little man. He has written and directed historical and political documentaries for television, and has frequently been in conflict with the authorities. A film on Irish patriots, made for ATV, was suppressed by Lew Grade as an incitement to disorder, and another on IRA veterans met the same fate. But Griffiths was luckier with *The Most Valuable Englishman Ever* (1981): Tom Paine had been dead long enough to be safe.

Films include: 1941 Love on the Dole. '46 The Shop at Sly Corner. '56 Private's Progress. '57 Lucky Jim. '59 Tiger Bay; I'm All Right Jack. '61 Only Two Can Play. '67 Casino Royale. '68 The Lion in Winter. '69 The Gamblers. '71 Jane Eyre; Revenge. '78 The Wild Geese. '80 The Sea Wolves.

GRIMALDI, Alberto

(b. 1926). Producer. Born: Naples, Italy

A lawyer specializing in the legal affairs of the film business, Grimaldi went into production in 1962 with costume romances and 'spaghetti' Westerns. Encouraged by financial success, he then worked with 'name' directors like Fellini, Pasolini and Bertolucci on a series of bizarre sexual curiosities alleviated by only one re-

markable film, Francesco Rosi's *Illustrious Corpses*.

Films include: 1963 Cavalca e Uccidi (IT-FR) (GB: Ride and Kill); Ombra di Zorro (IT-SP) (GB: Shadow of Sorrow). '65 Solo Contro Tutti (IT-SP). '66 Per Qualche Dollaro in Più (IT-GER-SP) (USA/GB: For a Few Dollars More). '67 Il Buono, il Brutto, il Cattivo (IT-GER-SP) (GB: The Good, the Bad and the Ugly); Requiem per un Agente Segreto (IT-SP-GER). '69 Fellini Satyricon (IT-FR); Ehi Amigo . . . C'è Sabata, Hai Chiuso. '71 Il Decameron (IT-FR-GER) (GB: The Decameron). '72 I Racconti di Canterbury (IT-FR) (GB: The Canterbury Tales); Ultimo Tango a Parigi (IT-FR) (USA/GB: Last Tango in Paris). '76 Cadaveri Eccellenti (IT-FR) (GB: Illustrious Corpses); 1900/ Novecento (IT-FR-GER).

GRODIN, Charles

(b. 1935). Actor. Born: Pittsburgh, Pennsylvania, USA

As a struggling actor in New York, Grodin studied for ten years at Lee Strasberg's Actors' Studio. His stage debut was in 1962; his first film came six years later, when he played the small part of the obstetrician in *Rosemary's Baby*. Grodin's best film part was in Elaine May's *The Heartbreak Kid*, where he manged to give some kind of charm to the unpleasant title-character. Grodin continued to act in films, to write, direct and act for the stage, and to write for television. As far as films go, he badly needs a good one.

Films include: 1922 Robin Hood (co-art dir). '24 The Thief of Bagdad (co-assoc. artist). '25 The Road to Yesterday (co-art dir). '27 White Gold; King of Kings (co-art dir). '30 No, No, Nanette; Little Caesar. '31 The Crowd Roars. '33 Gold Diggers of 1933; The Mystery of the Wax Museum. '35 Gold Diggers of 1935; Captain Blood. '36 Anthony Adverse. '39 Juarez (co-art dir). '41 The Sea Wolf. '45 Mildred Pierce. '50 Backfire.

GUARDINO, Harry

(b. 1925). Actor. Born: New York City, USA

The tough guy in numerous war movies and crime films since 1952. Harry Guardino had been a gunner's mate in the navy during the war in the Pacific, then a member of New York's Dramatic Workshop. He was then forced to alternate between the sea and occasional acting jobs, until a success in the play A Hatful of Rain led to a Paramount contract and a secure career on stage and screen. He will be best remembered for a vivid performance as Richard Widmark's partner in Madigan.

Films include: 1958 Houseboat. '59 Pork Chop Hill; The Five Pennies. '61 King of Kings. '62 Hell Is for Heroes; The Pigeon That Took Rome. '68 Madigan. '70 Lovers and Other Strangers. '71 Dirty Harry. '76 The Enforcer. '79 Goldengirl.

GUAZZONI, Enrico

(1876–1949). Director. Born: Rome, Italy

A pioneer Italian director and designer, Guazzoni specialized in lavish historical films, and in 1912 directed the first outstanding spectacular, Quo Vadis?, a film still extremely impressive to-day. Guazzoni had been a painter and designer, and as his own art director planned and constructed the enormous sets for his films. He continued directing well into the sound period, making his last film in 1943, but was never able to recapture those first glories, when 150 choral singers had accompanied Quo Vadis? and D. W. Griffith, who was to eclipse him, was still making two-reelers.

Films include: 1906 Un Invito a Pranzo. '10 Agrippina; Brutus. '12 Quo Vadis? '13 Marcantonio e Cleopatra. '14 Gaius Julius Caesar. '28 Myriam. '35 Il Re Burlone; Il Suo Destino. '41 Oro Nero.

GUFFEY, Burnett

(1905–1983). Cinematographer. Born: Del Rio, Tennessee, USA

Entering the industry in 1923, Burnett Guffey served a long apprenticeship, during which he was second-unit photographer on John Ford's The Iron Horse (1924), and camera operator for some 15 years, working with Ford and Alfred Hitchcock among others. Promoted in 1944 to cinematographer, he worked with distinction until 1970. Equally at home with black-and-white and colour, Guffey won two Academy Awards, for From Here to Eternity (black-and-white) and Bonnie and Clyde (colour). The latter

film belongs to Guffey as much as to anyone; his glowing camerawork perfectly caught its note of melancholy reminiscence.

Films include: 1944 Sailor's Holiday. '45 Eadie Was a Lady. '49 The Reckless Moment. '50 In A Lonely Place. '53 From Here to Eternity. '54 Human Desire. '62 Birdman of Alcatraz. '65 King Rat. '67 Bonnie and Clyde; The Ambushers. '69 Some Kind of a Nut. '70 The Great White Hope.

GUILLERMIN, John

(b. 1925). Director. Born: London, England

After war service with the RAF John Guillermin spent three years in France (he is of French parentage) learning his trade as assistant on documentaries and short films. From 1949 he directed low-budget features, until Town on Trial in 1957 won him something of a critical reputation; the film attacked English snobbery with frankness and realism. But Guillermin became more and more of a flashily clever director, and never developed a consistent style. Such anonymity made him the ideal director for later blockbusters like The Towering Inferno and the remake of King Kong, a far cry indeed from early days with John Grierson and Group 3.

Films include: 1957 Town on Trial. '58 I Was Monty's Double. '60 Never Let Go. '62 Waltz of the Toreadors. '64 Guns at Batasi. '65 Rapture (FR-USA). '69 The Bridge at Remagen (USA). '74 The Towering Inferno (USA). '76 King Kong (USA). '78 Death on the Nile.

GUINNESS, Alec

(b. 1914). Actor. Born: London, England

Before the war, Alec Guinness established a stage reputation and appeared in one film. Returning after naval service, he played Herbert Pocket in David Lean's film of Great Expectations (one of his stage roles), and followed with a tour de force as all eight members of the d'Ascoyne family in Kind Hearts and Coronets. In the succeeding years he has played a wide variety of parts, from Disraeli to Hitler, from master criminals to shabby sleuths. He won a Best Actor Oscar in 1957 for his portrayal of the stiff-backed British officer in The Bridge on the River Kwai, and two years later was knighted for his achievements on stage and screen.

Films include: 1946 Great Expectations. '48 Oliver Twist. '49 Kind Hearts and Coronets. '50 Last Holiday; The Mudlark. '51 The Lavender Hill Mob; The Man in the White Suit. '54 Father Brown (USA: The Detective). '55 The Prisoner; The Ladykillers. '57 The Bridge on the River Kwai; Barnacle Bill (USA: All at Sea). '59 Our Man in Havana. '60 Tunes of Glory. '62 Lawrence of Arabia. '65 Doctor Zhivago (USA). '67 The Comedians (GB-GER-FR). '70 Cromwell; Scrooge. '72 Fratello Sole, Sorella Luna (IT-GB) (GB: Brother Sun, Sister Moon). '63 Hitler: the Last Ten Days (GB-IT). '77 Star Wars (USA).

Top, from left to right: Hugh Griffith in Take Me High *(1973), a Cliff Richard musical; Raymond Griffith in* Hands Up! *; Charles Grodin, a protégé of Elaine May, with Jeannie Berlin in* The Heartbreak Kid. *Right: Alec Guinness in* Tunes of Glory, *a barracks melodrama. Below: Harry Guardino, tough character actor in* Dirty Harry, *a vehicle for Clint Eastwood that spawned two sequels. Left: Kenneth Griffiths in* Heavens Above! *(1963)*

Films include: 1968 Rosemary's Baby. '70 Catch-22. '72 The Heartbreak Kid. '74 11 Harrowhouse (GB). '76 King Kong. '78 Heaven Can Wait. '79 Sunburn (USA-GB); Real Life. '80 It's My Turn; Seems Like Old Times. '81 The Incredible Shrinking Woman; The Great Muppet Caper (GB).

GROT, Anton

(1884–1974). Art director. Born: Antocz Franziszek Grozewski; Kelbasin, Poland

Anton Grot came to the USA in 1909 after art studies in Cracow and Koenigsberg. By 1913 he was designing sets for the Lubin company, and went on to Paramount. In 1922 he

went to Los Angeles, worked for Fairbanks and DeMille, and in 1927 began the long association with Warners which lasted until his retirement in 1948. One of the greatest of art directors, Grot tried above all to echo in his sets the prevailing mood of a film. He excelled with the sinister, conjuring up menace through his intuitive, daring, always exquisitely finished sets, but was versatile enough to take musicals like Gold Diggers of 1933, fantasies and historical romances in his stride. As head of the art department, Grot at Warners, like Gibbons at MGM, was credited for many films on which his assistants may have been responsible for much of the creative work.

185

GUITRY, Sacha

(1885–1957). Director/playwright/ screenwriter/actor. Born: Alexandre Georges Pierre Guitry; St Petersburg, Russia

The son of a famous French actor, Lucien Guitry, Sacha was born in St Petersburg, the capital of Russia, while his parents were acting there. They returned to Paris when he was six. He left the last of nine schools when he was 16 to become a playwright – he had started acting at the age of five in St Petersburg. At 17 he joined the Renaissance Theatre in Paris, and in 1919 he became manager of his own theatre in Paris, the Mathurins. He wrote over a hundred plays, many of them grandiose historical works – he played many of

France's most famous historical figures, including Napoleon and several kings – but is better remembered for his bourgeois tragi-comedies. His involvement with the cinema was mainly to bring his inventive, witty plays to the screen. After the Liberation of Paris in 1944 he was accused of having acted for the Germans and spent two months in prison. His five wives were all actresses, the most famous being the second, Yvonne Printemps.

Films include: 1915 Ceux de Chez Nous (doc) (dir; + sc. only). **'35** Bonne Chance. **'36** Le Roman d'un Tricheur; Faisons un Rêve. **'37** Le Mot de Cambronne; Les Perles de la Couronne (co-dir) (USA/GB: The Pearls of the Crown). **'43** Donne-Moi Tes Yeux. **'48** Le Comédien. **'49** Tôa. **'51** Deburau; Le Poison. **'57** Assassins et Voleurs (dir; + sc. only). **'58** La Vie à Deux (sc. only).

GULPILIL, David

(b. 1954). Actor. Born: Maningrida, Arnhem Land, Northern Territory, Australia

An Aboriginal member of the Mandalbingu tribe, David Gulpilil was an assistant at a mission school teaching Aboriginal dances and culture when he was still only 12 or 13. In 1969 he was seen by the director Nicolas Roeg and cast as the Aboriginal boy who rescues a lost schoolgirl (Jenny Agutter) and her young brother from the outback in *Walkabout*. Gulpilil was featured as a dancer at Expo 70 in Japan and later led dance teams on overseas tours. After completing a film and television course in Sydney and picking up some English, he returned to films to play three important roles, including the friend of *Storm Boy*. He then appeared in four television series, and co-directed *Billy West*, the story of the whites' coming to the Northern Territory in 1898, told from the Aboriginal point of view.

Top: David Gulpilil in Walkabout, *a dazzling portrayal of human and cultural contrast. Above: Allen Gurevich in the black comedy* Mother,

Films: **1971** Walkabout. **'76** Mad Dog Morgan; Storm Boy. **'77** The Last Wave. **'82** Billy West (+ co-dir).

GUREVICH, Allen

(b. 1939). Actor. Born: Newark, New Jersey, USA

Known in most of his film credits as Allen Garfield, Gurevich zestfully plays sweaty, slobbish, disreputable types, occasionally with traces of fundamental decency showing underneath the layers of fatty tissue, but usually with few, if any, redeeming features. After studying at the Actors' Studio he established his persona by playing a porn merchant in Brian De Palma's early low-budget movie *Greetings*. He was a greasy wheeler-dealer as the political image-maker in *The Candidate* and as the husband-manager of the neurotic country singer (Ronee Blakley) in *Nashville*, and a treacherous villain in *Slither* and *The Conversation*. He is also interested in theatre directing, has written and directed an off-Broadway play and aims to form his own acting company. He is certainly one of the most talented and distinctive character actors to emerge in the modern American cinema.

Films include: 1968 Greetings. **'69** Putney Swope. **'70** The Owl and the Pussycat. **'71** Cry Uncle (GB: Super Dick); The Organisation. **'72** Get to Know Your Rabbit; The Candidate. **'73** Slither. **'74** The Conversation; The Front Page. **'75** Nashville. **'80** The Stunt Man.

GUTOWSKI, Gene

(b. 1925). Producer. Born: Eugene Gutowski; Poland

Leaving Poland for New York in 1954, Gutowski spent six years working in American television. In 1960 he came to Britain and set up his own production company. He persuaded fellow-countryman Roman Polanski to come to England to make a horror film which became the remarkable, hallucinatory *Repulsion*. Two more films followed, *Cul-de-Sac* and *Dance of the Vampires*, before Polanski left for Hollywood. Gutowski tried to repeat his success with another Polish director, Jerzy Skolimowski. But their one film together, *The Adventures of Gerard*, failed to fulfil expectations. Nor did Abraham Polonsky's *Romance of a Horsethief* break any box-office records.

Films include: 1963 Station Six Sahara (GB-GER). **'65** Repulsion. **'66** Cul-de-Sac. **'67** Dance of the Vampires (USA: The Fearless Vampire Killers, or Pardon Me, But Your Teeth Are in My Neck). **'70** The Adventures of Gerard (co-prod); A Day at the Beach. **'71** Romance of a Horsethief (USA-YUG).

GUY-BLACHÉ, Alice

(1875–1968). Director. Born: Alice Guy; Paris, France

Alice Guy was Léon Gaumont's secretary when the company turned to film production in 1896 and Gaumont

Jugs and Speed *(1976). Above: Edmund Gwenn, veteran of the West End stage in London and later of Hollywood in the Forties*

put her in charge of this new enterprise. She became the world's first woman director, directing over two hundred shorts and pioneering the early development of sound synchronization. In 1906 she married the English cameraman Herbert Blaché-Bolton and went with him to the USA where he became Gaumont's representative, dropping the latter part of his double-barrelled name. In 1910 Alice Guy-Blaché established her own production company, producing and directing about seventy films at her Fort Lee, New Jersey, studio. By the end of World War I she was no longer able to continue in independent production, though she directed occasionally for larger studios until 1920. On divorcing Blaché in 1922 she returned to France but was unable to continue her career. She was awarded the Legion of Honour in 1953.

Films include: 1896 La Fée aux Choux. **1903** Les Apaches pas Veinards. **'04** Rapt d'Enfants par les Romanichels. **'05** La Esmeralda. **'06** La Vie du Christ; La Fée Printemps. **'07** Carmen. **'11** The Violin Maker of Nuremberg (USA). **'12** Fallen Leaves (USA); Fra Diavolo (USA). **'13** Beasts of the Jungle (prod; + sc. only) (USA); The Pit and the Pendulum (USA). **'14** The Lure (USA); Shadows of the Moulin Rouge (USA). **'16** The Girl With the Green Eyes (USA). **'20** Tarnished Reputation (USA).

GWENN, Edmund

(1877–1959). Actor. Born: Edmund Kellaway; London, England

Educated at St Olave's and King's College, London, Edmund Gwenn made his West End stage debut in 1899, soon excelling in vulgar, rough, 'low' parts. From 1905 he established a reputation for his acting in George Bernard Shaw's plays and in 1916 he made his film debut. But his film career did not take off until the Thirties with his role as Jess Oakroyd in the film version of J. B. Priestley's popular novel *The Good Companions*. Then he went to Hollywood, intermittently from 1935 and permanently from 1939. He won an Oscar as Best Supporting Actor in 1947 for his department-store Santa Claus in *Miracle on 34th Street*, typical of the benevolent, irascible but endearing old men he usually played in America. But he was a good character actor, also capable of playing the villain, as a Nazi sympathizer in Ealing's *Cheer, Boys, Cheer* and a would-be killer who falls to his death from the tower of Westminster Cathedral in Alfred Hitchcock's *Foreign Correspondent*, or a dubious and finally pathetic conman, the father of the heroine (Katharine Hepburn), in *Sylvia Scarlett*.

Films include: 1920 The Skin Game. **'31** The Skin Game (sound remake). **'33** The Good Companions. **'34** Java Head. **'35** The Bishop Misbehaves (USA) (GB: The Bishop's Misadventures). **'36** Sylvia Scarlett (USA); Laburnum Grove. **'38** South Riding. **'39** Cheer, Boys, Cheer. **'40** Foreign Correspondent (USA). **'44** The Keys of the Kingdom (USA). **'47** The Miracle on 34th Street (USA) (GB: The Big Heart). **'50** Mr 880 (USA). **'56** The Trouble With Harry (USA).

HAANSTRA, Bert

(b. 1916). Director. Born: Holten Overijssel, Holland

Whereas the other famous Dutch documentarist Joris Ivens is essentially a citizen of the world, Haanstra has specialized in interpreting his own country to itself and other nations. He was interested in film-making from childhood but was a press photographer and painter in the Thirties before turning cameraman in 1948 and cameraman-director in 1949. His second documentary short, *Spiegel van Holland*, showing views of Holland reflected in the country's canals and waterways, won the Grand Prix for Documentary at Cannes in 1951, and *Glas* won the Documentary Short Oscar for 1959. Haanstra has worked for the Royal Dutch Shell Film Unit and has also made several feature films.

Films include: 1949 De Muiderkring Herleeft (doc. short) (GB: The Muyder Circle Lives Again). **'51** Spiegel van Holland (doc. short) (GB: Mirror of Holland). **'52** Panta Rhei (doc. short) (GB: All Things Flow);

Dijkbouw (doc. short) (Dike Builders). **'54** Ontstaan en Vergaan (doc. short) (The Changing Earth). **'55** The Rival World (GB). **'56** En de Zee Was Niet Meer (doc. short) (GB: And There Was No More Sea). **'57** Rembrandt, Schilder van de Mens (doc. short) (GB: Rembrandt, Painter of Man). **'58** Glas (doc. short) (GB: Glass); Fanfare. **'62** Delta Phase I (doc. short). **'64** Alleman (The Human Dutch). **'73** Bij de Beesten Af (USA-HOLL) (USA/GB: Ape and Superape). **'79** Een Pak Slaag (GB: Mr Slotter's Jubilee).

HACKETT, Buddy

(b. 1924). Actor/comedian. Born: Leonard Hacker; New York City, USA

While an apprentice upholsterer in his father's furniture shop, Buddy Hackett made his amateur stage debut with the WPA Federal Theater group. After serving in the army, he appeared in the Broadway show *Call Me Mister* in 1946–47 and toured the nightclubs as a stand-up comedian until he was signed by Universal for two years in 1952. Then television appearances made him a popular

comic and he returned to films as a Georgia country boy in *God's Little Acre*. One of his famous characterizations as a Chinese waiter led to the role of Chicasaw in *All Hands on Deck* and he was in a number of other films in the Sixties but since then he has returned to nightclubs and television.

Films: 1953 Walking My Baby Back Home. **'58** God's Little Acre. **'61** All Hands on Deck; Everything's Ducky. **'62** The Wonderful World of the Brothers Grimm; The Music Man. **'63** It's a Mad, Mad, Mad, Mad World. **'64** Muscle Beach Party. **'69** The Love Bug; The Good Guys and the Bad Guys.

HACKETT, Joan

(1939–1983). Actress. Born: New York City, USA

The offspring of an Irish father and Italian mother, Joan Hackett was initially a model. A cover-girl appearance on the magazine *Harper's Junior Bazaar* in 1952 led to a screen test for 20th Century-Fox but she turned

down a seven-year contract. She studied acting with Lee Strasberg from 1958 to 1963 at the Actors' Studio, and made her Broadway and television debuts in 1959. She played in John Gielgud's production of *Much Ado About Nothing* and had a big success in *Call Me by My Rightful Name* in 1961, winning a couple of stage awards. Her film debut was as the debutante Dottie in *The Group*. Her distinctive, rather deep voice and brisk gestures were effective in both dramatic films and comedies after that and she was nominated for an Oscar in *Only When I Laugh*. But she remained predominantly a stage and television actress, whose film career was marginal, even though she regularly played lead roles.

Films: 1965 The Group. **'67** Will Penny. **'68** Assignment to Kill. **'69** Support Your Local Sheriff. **'72** Rivals. **'73** The Last of Sheila. **'74** The Terminal Man. **'75** Mackintosh and T.J. **'76** Treasure of Matecumbe. **'79** Mr Mike's Mondo Video. **'80** One Trick Pony. **'81** Only When I Laugh (GB: It Hurts Only When I Laugh).

Left: multi-talented comedian Buddy Hackett (left) with Robert Preston in The Music Man, *adapted from Broadway. Above: Joan Hackett*

Right, from left to right: Gene Hackman; Jean Hagen in The Asphalt Jungle, *directed by John Huston; Alan Hale. Below: Jack Haley in* Danger – Love at Work *(1937)*

HACKMAN, Gene

(b. 1930). Actor. Born: Eugene Alden Hackman; San Bernardino, California, USA

Gene Hackman joined the marines at 16 and then studied radio technique at the University of Illinois, did odd jobs in television studios and learned acting at the Pasadena Playhouse. After summer stock, he landed the role of the young suitor in *Any Wednesday* on Broadway in 1964 and a small movie part as a racist unhappily married to the ex-girlfriend (Jessica Walter) of the hero (Warren Beatty) in *Lilith*. Beatty hired him to play Clyde's brother in *Bonnie and Clyde*, for which Hackman was nominated for an Academy Award as Best Supporting Actor. He was nominated again for *I Never Sang for My Father* and took the Best Actor Award in 1971 for his role as the tough New York drug-squad cop 'Popeye' Doyle in *The French Connection*. He moved on to playing confused loners such as the professional eavesdropper in *The Conversation* and the private eye in *Night Moves*, possibly his best roles. He has also played outright villains, sometimes with a comic edge, as in *Superman, The Movie* and *Superman II*. Hackman's versatility and force of personality have made him a star while playing essentially character parts rather than conventional heroes.

Films include: 1961 Mad Dog Coll. '64 Lilith. '66 Hawaii. '67 Bonnie and Clyde. '68 The Split. '69 Downhill Racer. '70 I Never Sang for My Father. '71 The French Connection; Cisco Pike. '72 The Poseidon Adventure. '73 Scarecrow. '74 The Conversation; Young Frankenstein. '75 Night Moves; French Connection II. '77 A Bridge Too Far. '78 Superman, The Movie. '80 Superman II. '81 All Night Long.

HAGEMAN, Richard

(1882–1966). Composer/conductor/pianist. Born: Leeuwarden, Holland

By the time he was a teenager Richard Hageman was a fully-fledged concert pianist. At 17 he became the conductor of Amsterdam's Royal Opera. In 1906 he emigrated to America and by 1915 was assistant conductor at the Metropolitan Opera in New York. He then freelanced with various companies until, in 1938, he arrived in Hollywood. There he composed scores for films, many for John Ford, as well as appearing as an actor in a handful of them, and also became principal conductor at the Hollywood Bowl. He shared an Oscar for the score of Ford's *Stagecoach*.

Films include: 1939 Stagecoach (co-mus. only); Hotel Imperial. '40 The Howards of Virginia (GB: The Tree of Liberty); The Long Voyage Home. '41 The Shanghai Gesture (USA); Paris Calling. '47 The Fugitive; Mourning Becomes Electra. '48 Fort Apache; The Three Godfathers. '49 She Wore a Yellow Ribbon. '50 Wagonmaster.

HAGEN, Jean

(1924–1977). Actress. Born: Jean Shirley ver Hagen; Chicago, Illinois, USA

Jean Hagen studied drama at Northwestern university, near Chicago, helping to pay her way through college by working in radio. She met writers Ben Hecht and Charles MacArthur who cast her in their play *Swan Song*. Other Broadway roles followed, until she was signed by MGM. She made an impression as a vulgar mistress in *Adam's Rib* and as a gangster's would-be moll in *The Asphalt Jungle*, but was overshadowed in these films by Judy Holliday and Marilyn Monroe respectively as a new discovery. Her best role was as Lina Lamont, the dumb-blonde film star with a high, nasal voice that has to be dubbed, in *Singin' in the Rain*, which brought her a nomination for an Academy Award as Best Supporting Actress. After a run of less good parts she left MGM in 1953 and became nationally known as the wife of Daddy (Danny Thomas) in the television series *Make Room for Daddy*, for which she won two Emmy nominations. Apart from a good cameo in *The Big Knife* her later film roles were undistinguished as well as intermittent and she retired from the screen in 1964, her proven ability in both drama and comedy having failed to ensure a satisfactory career.

Films include: 1949 Adam's Rib. '50 Side Street; Ambush; The Asphalt Jungle. '51 No Questions Asked. '52 Singin' in the Rain; Carbine Williams; Shadow in the Sky. '53 Arena; Latin Lovers; Half a Hero. '55 The Big Knife. '57 Spring Reunion. '62 Panic in Year Zero. '64 Dead Ringer (GB: Dead Image).

HAKIM, Robert

(b. 1907). Producer. Born: Alexandria, Egypt

Robert and his brother Raymond Hakim (1904–1980) were educated in France. Raymond joined Paramount Française as a salesman in 1931 and then went into distribution on his own. In 1934 Robert and Raymond Hakim founded Paris Film-Production and had their first big success with *Pépé-le-Moko*, starring Jean Gabin. In the Forties they moved for a while to the USA, where Robert co-produced Jean Renoir's *The Southerner* (1945) with David L. Loew and won the Golden Lion at Venice. They went back to France after a few years and became increasingly involved in Franco-Italian co-productions. They have worked with Michelangelo Antonioni, Luis Buñuel, Marcel Carné, Claude Chabrol, René Clément, Joseph Losey, Karel Reisz and Roger Vadim, among others. Their younger brother André (b. 1915) was also a producer, working for 20th Century-Fox in the Fifties. They all got together for Walerian Borowczyk's *La Marge* (1976, *Streetwalker*).

Films co-produced by Robert and Raymond Hakim include: 1936 Pépé-le-Moko. '38 La Bête Humaine (GB: Judas Was a Woman). '39 Le Jour se Lève (USA: Daybreak). '52 Casque d'Or (USA: Golden Helmet; GB: Golden Marie). '53 Thérèse Raquin (FR-IT) (reissued in GB as: The Adulteress). '62 L'Eclisse (IT-FR) (GB: The Eclipse). '66 Plein Soleil (FR-IT) (reissued in USA as: Purple Noon; in GB as: Blazing Sun). '67 Belle de Jour (FR-IT). '68 Isadora (GB) (USA: The Loves of Isadora).

HALAS & BATCHELOR

Halas, John (b. 1912). Animator. Born: Budapest, Hungary

Batchelor, Joy (b. 1914). Animator. Born: Watford, Hertfordshire, England

John Halas entered films as an assistant to George Pal in 1928. By 1934 he was producing his own cartoons and in 1936 arrived in England where he met Joy Batchelor. She had joined an animation studio after art school, but it flopped and she was looking for work when Halas appeared on the scene. They married and, in 1940, formed Halas and Batchelor Cartoon Films. During World War II they were mainly concerned with Government propaganda documentaries, but tried to inject a little attention-keeping humour into their figures. They went

on to make several notable artistic triumphs, one of them being the first feature-length British cartoon *Animal Farm*. They now concentrate largely on television work, and in 1972 relinquished their share of Halas and Batchelor Films in order to develop, produce and distribute material for schools and colleges through their company Educational Film Centre Ltd.

Films include: 1942 Dustbin Parade. '48 Robinson Charley. '51 The Poet and Painter (series). '53 The Owl and the Pussycat. '54 Animal Farm. '56 History of the Cinema. '59 The World of Little Ig. '60 Foo Foo (series). '63 Automania 2000. '82 Players (Halas only).

HALE, Alan

(1892–1950). Actor. Born: Rufus Alan McKahan; Washington DC, USA

Hale was the son of a Scottish patent medicine manufacturer. After attending the University of Pennsylvania he took up journalism and then tried to make it as an opera singer. Having no luck he went to the Lubin Company in 1911 and began a career in films.

Above: Georgia Hale in The Salvation Hunters, *directed by Josef von Sternberg. Above right: Mark Hamill in* Star Wars. *Below: character actor Charles Halton in* Dr Ehrlich's Magic Bullet *(1940)*

He met and married the actress Gretchen Hartman – and in the Twenties also directed several silent features for Cecil B. DeMille. With the coming of sound he became a well-known character actor in bluff, slow-witted but endearing roles. During the Thirties and Forties he played many an Errol Flynn sidekick. Tall, chubby blue-eyed, crinkly-haired and with a loud, raucous laugh, he could be either tough villain or put-upon softy. Perhaps his best role was in *The Adventures of Robin Hood* as Little John – a part he had played in the 1922 *Robin Hood*. His son, Alan Hale Jr, star of the the *Casey Jones* television series, looks absolutely identical to him.

Films include: 1914 Martin Chuzzlewit. '21 The Four Horsemen of the Apocalypse. '23 The Covered Wagon. '36 A Message to Garcia. '37 Stella Dallas. '38 The Adventures of Robin Hood. '39 Dodge City; The Man in the Iron Mask; The Private Lives of Elizabeth and Essex. '40 The Sea Hawk. '41 The Strawberry Blonde.

HALE, Georgia

(b. 1906). Actress. Born: St Joseph, Missouri, USA

Georgia Hale won a bathing beauty contest at the age of 17 and then took to the stage. After an undistinguished series of plays she made an uneventful film debut in New York and moved to Hollywood to appear in vaudeville and cabaret. However, Charles Chaplin liked her performance in *The Salvation Hunters* and cast her as his leading lady in *The Gold Rush*. She triumphed as the saloon girl who wins Charlie's heart and later shares his fortune, but her film career was short-lived and she retired with the advent of sound.

Films include: 1925 The Salvation Hunters; The Gold Rush. '26 The Great Gatsby; The Rainmaker; Man of the Forest. '27 Hills of Peril. '28 Wheel of Chance; The Rawhide Kid; The Last Moment; A Woman Against the World; Gypsy of the North; A Trick of Hearts; The Floating College.

HALEY, Jack

(1899–1979). Actor/singer. Born: John Joseph Haley; Boston, Massachusetts, USA

The son of an Irish ocean navigator, Jack Haley became an electrician's apprentice before deciding that he should be in show business. He began to do a musical comedy routine in vaudeville and by the late Twenties was appearing in Broadway musicals. He then broke into films, his most successful role being that of the Tin Man in *The Wizard of Oz*. After that he virtually retired from the screen, but in 1970 he had a cameo role in *Norwood*, a film directed by his son Jack Haley Jr, who was also the producer of *That's Entertainment* (1974). During his retirement Haley made himself a fortune dealing in real estate.

Films include: 1927 Broadway Madness. '30 Follow Thru. '33 Sitting Pretty. '35 Coronado. '36 Poor Little Rich Girl; Pigskin Parade (GB: Harmony Parade). '38 Rebecca of Sunnybrook Farm; Alexander's Ragtime Band. '39 The Wizard of Oz. '41 Moon Over Miami. '49 Make Mine Laughs.

HALLER, Ernest

(1896–1970). Cinematographer. Born: Los Angeles, California, USA

In 1914 Ernest Haller joined Biograph as an actor. The following year he made his debut as a cameraman and revealed his hitherto hidden gift. Between 1920 and 1964 he shot over one hundred and fifty films, all of them with style and imagination. *Jezebel, In This Our Life, Humoresque* and *Rebel Without a Cause* are all prime examples of his particular skills, creating moods verging on Expressionism without ever losing a grip on reality. From 1951 Haller freelanced until his death in a car accident. He shared an Academy Award with Ray Rennahan for his work on *Gone With the Wind*.

Films include: 1914 The Hazards of Helen. '24 Parisian Nights. '30 The Dawn Patrol (GB: The Flight Commander). '38 Jezebel. '39 Gone With the Wind; The Roaring Twenties. '40 Manpower. '42 In This Our Life. '46 Humoresque. '55 Rebel Without a Cause. '57 Men in War. '58 Man of the West.

HALTON, Charles

(1876–1959). Actor. Born: Washington DC, USA

Halton's father was an attorney and the family lived in the fashionable area of Georgetown. After his father's death, Charles was sent to live with his grandmother in Germany, but was homesick and returned to America three years later. He worked as a newspaper boy and under cover of the job frequently sneaked off to watch the famous actors and actresses of the day arriving at New York's theatres. His employer, on discovering Halton's passion for the stage, agreed to finance his studies at the New York Academy of Dramatic Arts, after which Halton joined the Lillian Russell touring group travelling America. Broadway and films followed. He was known for his beautiful speaking voice and flawless usage of the English language but his appearance – balding and stern (totally at odds with his essentially gentle

character) – was never striking enough for him to become a star.

Films include: 1937 The Prisoner of Zenda. '39 Jesse James; Young Mr Lincoln. '40 Dr Cyclops; They Drive by Night (GB: Road to Frisco). '41 Tobacco Road. '44 Up in Arms. '45 Rhapsody in Blue. '46 The Best Years of Our Lives. '52 Carrie. '53 The Moonlighter; How to Marry a Millionaire.

HAMER, Robert

(1911–1963). Director. Born: Kidderminster, Worcestershire, England

After school, Robert Hamer studied at Cambridge and in 1936 became a clapperboy for Gaumont. He moved to London Films as a cutting-room assistant and then worked for the producer Erich Pommer at Mayflower Films, a company set up by the latter with Alfred Hitchcock and Charles Laughton. There Hamer edited such films as *Vessel of Wrath* and *Jamaica Inn* before becoming a producer and director at Ealing Studios. A perfectionist, he was also the one Ealing director who never shied away from confronting questions of sex and class. However, his time there was stormy for he and Michael Balcon had a love-hate relationship resulting in major battles, the most notable being over *Kind Hearts and Coronets*. Balcon's view was that Hamer was 'self-destructive'. In fact he was not far wrong, for Hamer's alcoholism led to a decline in his career and ultimately to his death. His best remembered work after *Kind Hearts and Coronets* was the horrifying mirror episode from *Dead of Night*.

Films include: 1945 Dead of Night ep The Haunted Mirror; Pink String and Sealing Wax. '47 It Always Rains on Sunday. '49 Kind Hearts and Coronets; The Spider and the Fly. '52 His Excellency. '53 The Long Memory. '54 Father Brown. '55 To Paris With Love. '59 The Scapegoat. '60 School for Scoundrels.

HAMILL, Mark

(b. 1952). Actor. Born: Oakland, California, USA

One of seven children of a US navy captain, Hamill was drawn to acting after seeing *King Kong* (1933): 'It ignited my sense of wonder'. After travelling with the family and completing his high-school days in Japan, he spent two years as a theatre arts major and made his acting debut in the television series *The Bill Cosby Show*. After a succession of television assignments he shot to fame as Luke Skywalker in *Star Wars*, and, although taking the part for a negligible salary, was given (along with his three co-stars) one per cent of the profits. A clean-cut, blond, all-American hero, he is now enjoying enormous popularity and has appeared in two *Star Wars* sequels, *The Empire Strikes Back* and *The Revenge of the Jedi*.

Films include: 1977 Wizards (narr. only); Star Wars. '78 Corvette Summer (GB: The Hot One). '80 The Big Red One; The Empire Strikes Back. '83 The Revenge of the Jedi.

HAMILTON, George

(b. 1939). Actor. Born: George Stevens Hamilton; Memphis, Tennessee, USA

George Hamilton looks like an actor out of time. His suave good looks, his swept-back hair, and the cape he often affects give him the look of a romantic lead of the Thirties rather than a modern star of the Eighties. Obviously this is a role he enjoys and cultivates, for after his instant success in Hollywood as an effeminate young man in *Home From the Hill* he was quick to gain a flamboyant reputation, and was soon dismissed by the film community as a pampered playboy. But Hamilton refused to be swept aside and has subsequently found great popularity in spoof comedies such as *Love at First Bite* and *Zorro, the Gay Blade*.

Films include: 1959 Home From the Hill. '60 All the Fine Young Cannibals; Where the Boys Are. '62 Two Weeks in Another Town; The Light in the Piazza (GB). '63 The Victors. '65 Viva Maria! (FR-IT). '71 Evel Knievel. '75 Jacqueline Susann's Once Is Not Enough. '79 Love at First Bite. '81 Zorro, the Gay Blade.

HAMILTON, Guy

(b. 1922). Director. Born: Paris, France

In moments of great danger and stress the perfect Englishman is supposed to come up with a quip to ease the tension, and this sense of the stiff-upper-lip often crops up in Guy Hamilton's films. His love of sophisticated light comedy sometimes reveals itself at supposedly hair-raising moments – in a prisoner of war camp in *The Colditz Story*, *The Battle of Britain* and, of course, the Bond films. The son of a British diplomat, Hamilton's childhood dream was to become a director, and he set out to fulfil this ambition when, in 1939, he began working as a clapper boy at the Victorine Studio in Nice. He was soon working in England in the cutting rooms of British Paramount News. After his service in the navy during World War II he worked as assistant director on a number of interesting films, particularly with the director Carol Reed, by whom he and his work have been greatly influenced. He directed his first film *The Ringer*, in 1952, and since then has brought his particularly British style to many successful films.

Films include: 1952 The Ringer. '53 The Intruder. '55 The Colditz Story. '57 Manuela. '64 Goldfinger. '65 The Party's Over. '66 Funeral in Berlin. '69 Battle of Britain. '71 Diamonds Are Forever. '73 Live and Let Die. '74 The Man With the Golden Gun. '80 The Mirror Crack'd.

HAMLISCH, Marvin

(b. 1945). Composer/arranger. Born: New York City, USA

At the Academy Awards ceremony in Hollywood on April 2, 1974 Marvin Hamlisch became the first individual to win three Oscars in one night – two for *The Way We Were* and one for *The*

Sting. This is symbolic of his incredible success, for he has not had a failure since his initial big break as a result of playing the piano at a party thrown by the producer Sam Spiegel. It was obvious from very early on that Hamlisch was talented: at seven he was the youngest student to be admitted to the Juilliard School of Music; at seven and a half he wrote his first song; and at eight he played his first public recital. His great success must surely stem from his incredible versatility, for although he prefers emotional songs, he is capable of turning his hand to any style. As well as composing, conducting and performing he is also personal music consultant to Liza Minnelli, Joel Grey and Ann-Margret.

Films include: 1969 Take the Money and Run. '71 Bananas; Kotch. '73 The Way We Were; The Sting. '74 The Prisoner of Second Ave. '77 The Spy Who Loved Me (GB). '78 Same Time, Next Year. '79 Ice Castles.

HAMMERSTEIN II, Oscar

(1895–1960). Lyricist. Born: New York City, USA

In partnership with Richard Rodgers, Oscar Hammerstein has written some of the best-known and best-loved musicals of all time, with successes from *Oklahoma!* to *South Pacific*. He turned to the world of the theatre when his law career proved unrewarding, and it was his uncle, a Broadway producer, who helped him to learn the business. He soon began writing, and partnerships during the Twenties produced such musicals as *Rose Marie* and *Show Boat*. The Theatre Guild invited him to write the book and lyrics to a play called *Green Grow the Lilacs*, using a score by Richard Rodgers. The result was *Oklahoma!* and the winning partnership had been formed. Hammerstein has received Academy Awards for the songs 'The Last Time I Saw Paris' and 'It Might as Well Be Spring'.

Films include: 1929 The Desert Song; Show Boat. '30 New Moon. '41 Lady Be Good. '45 State Fair. '55 Oklahoma! '56 Carousel; The King and I. '58 South Pacific. '62 Flower Drum Song. '65 The Sound of Music.

HAMMETT, Dashiell

(1894–1961). Novelist. Born: St Mary's County, Maryland, USA

Dashiell Hammett was a pioneer of the tough-guy school of crime writing. He created earthy stories full of world-weary, hard-boiled detectives, notably Sam Spade – but also suaver types like Nick Charles. Hammett's stories were written from some personal experience, for among numerous other occupations he worked as a Pinkerton detective before he began writing pulp short stories. He was soon employed by Hollywood to brush up other people's scripts, while at the same time writing novels, three of which were later adapted for the screen. In the Thirties he began to write specifically (though not prolifically) for film, and among other work

completed an excellent screenplay for *Watch on the Rhine*. Then, in 1951, he was indicted by the House Un-American Activities Committee and shortly afterwards was sued for tax evasion. He never wrote again. He lived with the playwright Lillian Hellman for thirty years.

Films based on Hammett's novels and stories include: 1931 City Streets (co-sc. only). '34 The Thin Man; Woman in the Dark. '35 Mister Dynamite. '36 Satan Met a Lady; After the Thin Man. '39 Another Thin Man. '41 The Maltese Falcon. '42 The Glass Key. '43 Watch on the Rhine (sc. only). '75 The Black Bird.

HAMMOND, Kay

(1909–1980). Actress. Born: Dorothy Katherine Standing; London, England

Having come from a theatrical background (her father was the distinguished actor Sir Guy Standing), Kay Hammond was educated at RADA and she made her stage debut in repertory in London. During the Thirties she was much loved as a leading lady in British films, particularly in comedy roles. However, she then decided to make fewer films in order to concentrate on the stage, having particular success playing the ghostly Elvira in both the stage and screen versions of *Blithe Spirit*. During her last few years she was confined to a wheelchair because of her heart condition. Her second husband was the actor Sir John Clements.

Films include: 1930 Children of Chance. '31 Fascination; Carnival (USA: Venetian Nights). '32 Sally Bishop. '33 Bitter Sweet; Yes, Madam; Sleeping Car. '34 Bypass to Happiness. '36 Two on a Doorstep. '41 Jeannie. '45 Blithe Spirit. '61 Five Golden Hours.

HANCOCK, Tony

(1924–1968). Comedian/actor. Born: Birmingham, England

Tony Hancock could look glum, elated, innocent, guilty and melancholy in an instant. His wit was dry and resigned, and in his sketches and films there is always a sense of underlying doom. His characters always seem basically sad, bound never to triumph, and in the end this was also the story of his own life. Having toured with the RAF gang show, as a civilian he worked in straight plays, pantos and radio. By the mid-Fifties his radio show, Hancock's Half Hour, with Sid James, had become tremendously popular, and he also began to work in television and film. In the early Sixties, going it alone, he produced a new television series and a film, but both were poorly received. The film, *The Punch and Judy Man*, unlike the earlier and more successful *The Rebel*, was a depressing story of a struggling sea-side showman – the sort of theme expected from Hancock. In his personal life he was also struggling, he was plagued with drink and marriage problems, and he began a

relentless decline that culminated in his suicide in Sydney while working on an Australian television series.

Films: 1954 Orders are Orders. '61 The Rebel. '62 The Punch and Judy Man. '65 Those Magnificent Men in Their Flying Machines (or How I Flew From London to Paris in 11 Hours 25 Minutes). '66 The Wrong Box.

HANDL, Irene

(b. 1900). Actress. Born: London, England

Irene Handl did not start acting until her late thirties, but after a short course at drama school she found work immediately, and has been appearing in film, theatre and television ever since. Her performances, though invariably in small roles, are often scene-stealing – she was brilliant as

Left: much-loved comedienne of British cinema, Irene Handl. Above left: George Hamilton in Zorro, the Gay Blade. Above: Kay Hammond who appeared in many British films is here

seen in Britannia of Billingsgate (1933). Above right: Tony Hancock in The Rebel, the story of a businessman whose aspirations are to be an artist in Paris and live as a bohemian. Below:

Lars Hanson in The Scarlet Letter, directed by Victor Sjöström. Below: centre: former child star Jimmy Hanley in The Blue Lamp which also starred Jack Warner

HANSON, Lars

(1886–1965). Actor. Born: Gothenberg, Sweden

Lars Hanson entered the Stockholm Royal Dramatic Theatre in 1906 and within a few years had gained a reputation as a fine romantic actor, particularly in Shakespearian plays. As the Swedish cinema blossomed so did his career, and he attracted the attention of Swedens' premier directors Mauritz Stiller and Victor Sjöström. His screen career escalated until he became an international star opposite Greta Garbo in *Gösta Berlings Saga*. He soon followed Stiller and Garbo to Hollywood where, acting alongside stars like Lillian Gish and Garbo, and noted for his striking profile and piercing eyes, he proved a great success. He revealed a gift for comedy, but he was not content to stay in America and so returned to Europe. He continued to make a few films, but the Swedish film industry had stagnated. During the Thirties and Forties he only made the occasional film, preferring to work on the stage.

Films include: 1915 Dolken (The Dagger). '16 Thérèse. '20 Erotikon/Riddaren Av Igår (GB: Bonds That Chafe). '21 De Landsflyktige (The Exiles/The Emigrants). '24 Gösta Berlings Saga (USA/GB: The Legend of Gösta Berling/ The Atonement of Gösta Berling). '25 Ingmarsarvet (The Ingmar Inheritance). '26 The Scarlet Letter (USA). '27 Flesh and the Devil (USA). '28 The Divine Woman (USA); The Wind (USA). '29 The Informer (GB). '35 Abdul the Damned (GB).

the moaning wife of Peter Sellers' shop steward in *I'm All Right Jack*. Her stock role, however, is as the definitive cockney charwoman – dumpy, busybodyish and either cheery or indignant. A very familiar face in British comedies, she also writes novels.

Films include: 1940 The Girl in the News. '41 Pimpernel Smith (US: Mister V). '47 Temptation Harbour. '49 Silent Dust. '54 The Belles of St Trinians. '55 A Kid for Two Farthings. '59 I'm All Right Jack. '61 The Rebel. '70 The Private Life of Sherlock Holmes. '72 For the Love of Ada. '80 The Great Rock'n' Roll Swindle.

HANLEY, Jimmy

(1918–1970). Actor. Born: Norwich, Norfolk, England

Jimmy Hanley was most successful as a film actor during the Forties. His

jaunty, unsinkable, tough young working-class characters, often paired with the paternal figure of Jack Warner, remained popular until audiences began to demand a harsher authenticity. In 1952 he returned to the theatre, where he had originally made his debut as John Darling in *Peter Pan*, complaining that there was little work in British films. He subsequently became popular as a television presenter and disc jockey. He was married to actress Dinah Sheridan, and their daughter is television personality Jenny Hanley.

Films include: 1939 There Ain't No Justice. '44 The Way Ahead. '45 29 Acacia Avenue (USA: Facts of Love). '46 The Captive Heart. '47 Holiday Camp; The Master of Bankdam; It Always Rains on Sunday. '48 Here Come the Huggetts. '49 The Boys in Brown. '50 The Blue Lamp. '51 The Galloping Major. '55 The Deep Blue Sea.

HANNA & BARBERA

Hanna, William (b. 1910). Animator. Born: Melrose, New Mexico, USA

Barbera, Joseph (b. 1911). Animator. Born: New York City, USA

William Hanna and Joseph Barbera began working together in MGM's cartoon studio in 1940. Within 15 years they had taken over as heads of the department, and following its closure in 1957 they formed their own company, Hanna-Barbera Productions. Half the cartoonists in Hollywood work at their studio, including those sacked at the demise of MGM. And, through a computerized numbering system, they have turned out successes at an incredible rate. Together they have created such favourites as Tom and Jerry, Huckleberry Hound, The Flintstones and Yogi Bear. Of the two, Hanna had always worked in the film industry, but Barbera initially worked as an accountant in the New York world of banking. It was doodling and dreaming that prompted him to submit his cartoons to magazines, and when they started to be accepted he finally rejected banking in favour of cartooning. As a result of their incredible industry, he and his partner have received seven Academy Awards as well as an Emmy Award for 'outstanding achievements in children's programming'.

Films include: 1943 Yankee Doodle Mouse. '44 Mouse Trouble. '45 Quiet Please!; Mouse in Manhattan. '46 The Cat Concerto. '47 Dr Jekyll and Mr Mouse. '49 The Little Orphan. '50 Casanova Cat. '52 The Two Mouseketeers. '53 Johann Mouse. '54 Touché, Pussy Cat. '59 Life with Loopy. '62 Just a Wolf at Heart.

HARBOU, Thea von

(1888–1954). Screenwriter. Born: Taupeklitz, Bavaria

Thea von Harbou was already a successful novelist when she began collaborating with the director Fritz Lang in 1920. By 1924 the two were married and Harbou was working with many of the top names in German cinema. Her early work reflected the spirit of the nation at that time and she became a vital member of the Expressionist movement. By the Thirties she was directing, but with the coming of Nazism a rift began to develop between herself and Lang. Their last film, *Das Testament von Dr Mabuse*, marked their split. She took to elevating the Nazi party, while Lang feared its effects. Harbou was made an official screenwriter and stayed in Germany, never to match her previous form, and Lang left for the relative freedom of first France and then Hollywood.

Films include: 1922 Dr Mabuse der Spieler (USA: Dr Mabuse, the Gambler); Der brennende Acker (co-sc); Phantom. '24 Der Finanzien des Grossherzogs; Die Nibelungen (co-sc). '27 Metropolis (co-sc). '28 Spione (co-sc) (USA: Spies). '29 Frau im Mond (USA: By Rocket to the Moon; GB: The Girl in the Moon). '32 Das Testament von Dr Mabuse (co-sc) (USA: The Last Will of Dr Mabuse; GB: The Testament of Dr Mabuse). '33 Der Läufer von Marathon; Elisabeth und der Narr (dir. only). '34 Hanneles Himmelfahrt (+dir).

HARDING, Ann

(1902–1981). Actress. Born: Dorothy Walton Gatley; Houston, Texas, USA

During her childhood Ann Harding's family travelled around a great deal with her serviceman father, before finally settling in New York. She had appeared on the stage during a year spent at the prestigious Bryn Mawr College. In New York, though, she began as a clerk and a freelance script reader before she was finally given a small part in *The Inheritors*. She was soon on the move – from Greenwich Village to Broadway to Hollywood, where she signed with Pathé. She established herself as a leading lady of repute, but this willowy, poised, elegant actress never did fulfil her potential. Playing opposite the likes of Laurence Olivier, Leslie Howard and Ronald Colman, she was always in the same role: the honour-bound heroine, emotional and caring and always ready to sacrifice herself for the sake of goodness. She took the chance to retire in the late Thirties when she married her second husband, the conductor Werner Janssen. But she couldn't keep away and in the Forties she was back playing older, grander versions of the ladies she seemed unable to escape from.

Films include: 1929 Her Private Affair; Condemned. '30 Holiday. '31 Devotion. '32 Prestige; Westward Passage; The Animal Kingdom (GB: The Woman in His House). '33 The Right to Romance. '35 The Flame Within. '36 The Lady Consents (GB: The Lady Confesses). '44 Nine Girls. '56 The Man in the Gray Flannel Suit.

HARDWICKE, Cedric

(1893–1964). Actor. Born: Cedric Webotes Hardwicke; Stourbridge, Worcestershire, England

Cedric Hardwicke tended to play dignified, somewhat pompous, Victorian characters – but they were not necessarily gentlemen, and he could switch from kindly old fellows to blackhearted villains with the greatest of ease. The son of a country doctor, he was discouraged by his mother from following in his father's footsteps, and after a succession of amateur dramatics he went to RADA, making his London debut in 1912. After lengthy war service he returned to repertory where he developed a talent for playing men older than himself, and this led to his first major screen role in *Nelson* (1926). He reached the peak of his career in the early Thirties when he was knighted for his stage work. In 1935 he went to Hollywood, and proceeded to alternate between Britain and America. He gave fine performances in *Les Misérables*, as Bishop Bienvenu, and in John Cromwell's *Victory*, as the perverse, woman-hating Mr Jones. His last big role was as the father in *The Winslow Boy*. But he was hopeless with money and towards the end of his life admitted that he would take any role offered to him. He died virtually penniless in Hollywood.

Films include: 1932 Rome Express. '34 Nell Gwyn. '35 Les Misérables. '36 Laburnum Grove. '40 Victory (USA). '41 Suspicion (USA). '44 The Lodger (USA); The Keys of the Kingdom (USA). '48 The Winslow Boy. '56 Richard III.

HARDY, Oliver

see LAUREL & HARDY

HARLAN, Veit

(1899–1964). Director. Born: Berlin, Germany

The films of Veidt Harlan have a dominant strain of light comedy but there is also a darker streak running through them. The son of a playwright, he began his career as an actor in the Berlin theatre under Max Reinhardt, though he also had pretensions to becoming a sculptor and a photographer. He then moved into silent film acting and continued until he directed his first film in 1935. He began by specializing in kitsch comedies and soon became very popular. He was assigned by the Nazis to make *Der Herrscher*, a film about a Hitlerlike industrialist, and before long he was made the official director of the Nazi regime – Goebbels ordered him to

Above, from left to right: elegant Ann Harding; Cedric Hardwicke in Tom Brown's Schooldays (1940) from Thomas Hughes' novel; Jean Harlow in Blonde Bombshell. Below left: Jessica Harper in Inserts

make *Jud Süss*, a twisted version of an anti-fascist novel by a Jewish author. After the war, when he stood trial for this crime against humanity, he denied that he was anti-semitic, claiming he had had no choice in the matter and had tried to tone the film down. Despite a gruesome torture scene and a brutal rape in the film, he was acquitted. Having survived the trial he continued to work in the industry, but with little success.

Films include: 1936 Kater Lampe; Alles für Veronika. '37 Der Herrscher. '39 Die Reise nach Tilsit. '40 Jud Süss. '42 Die Goldene Stadt; Der grosse König. '43 Immensee. '44 Opfergang. '44 Kolberg

HARLOW, Jean

(1911–1937). Actress. Born: Harlean Carpenter; Kansas City, Missouri

In an age of great screen ladies at MGM, Harlow enjoyed the joke of playing a tarty society slattern, too lazy to bother with underwear beneath those silky, slinky, curve-caressing gowns. She was a broad in princess's clothing, a tarnished angel, the original art-deco or platinum

Above: Julie Harris. Above left: the appealing Barbara Harris in The War Between Men and Women *(1972), in which she stars with Jack Lemmon. Far left: Kathleen Harrison in* All For Mary *(1955), directed by Wendy Toye. Left: Richard Harris, enigmatic and unconventional both on and off screen, has nevertheless revelled in the popular image of a thirsty, brawling Irishman*

blonde. It was necessary to cast her opposite tough guys – the moll Cagney picks up off the street in *The Public Enemy*, cute and sexy but also caustic and loyal to Gable in *Red Dust*, a spoilt floozy married to Wallace Beery in *Dinner at Eight* – as only they wouldn't put up with her nonsense (even though she would pout, dissolve into baby-talk or throw a tantrum). She was primarily a comedienne whose gift to movies was not so much her skill with the common touch or her sexual frankness as her complete lack of concern – something the determinedly liberated heroines of today might envy. Underneath it all Harlow was a likeable, happy-go-lucky girl – a sensible enough professional and a dabbler in novel-writing – who suffered a traumatic private life. The product of a broken home, she was sent to private schools before she herself entered into a brief, unhappy marriage at 16. She moved into films the following year at Paramount – having her dress ripped off by Laurel and Hardy in *Double Whoopee* – and became a star with Howard Hughes' *Hell's Angels*. In 1932 she married MGM producer Paul Bern who shot himself two months later. A third marriage to cameraman Hal Rosson ended in divorce after six months. Harlow survived the scandals and the notoriety caused by her image of carnal indolence and remained a major star. But she was hurt by the end of her love affair with William Powell – her co-star in *Reckless* and *Libelled Lady*. She became ill and died of uremic poisoning. 'Baby' as Harlow was known to friends like Gable, was just 26. Carroll Baker played her in the biopic *Harlow* (1965) but without sufficient spark.

Films include: 1928 Moran of the Marines; Double Whoopee (short). '29 The Love Parade. '30 Hell's Angels. '31 The Public Enemy (GB: Enemies of the Public); City Lights; Goldie; Platinum Blonde. '32 Red-Headed Woman; Red Dust. '33 Bombshell (GB: Blonde Bombshell); Dinner at Eight. '34 The Girl From Missouri (GB: 100 Per Cent Pure). '35 Reckless; China Seas. '36 Riffraff; Wife vs Secretary; Libelled Lady. '37 Personal Property (GB: The Man in Possession); Saratoga.

HARPER, Jessica

(b. 1949). Actress. Born: Chicago, Illinois, USA

A pretty, dark-haired leading lady, Jessica Harper first attracted attention in the Broadway cast of *Hair*, which she joined after leaving Sarah Lawrence College. She won further parts in television and the theatre – bringing her talents as a singer and dancer to musicals especially – and made her screen bow in *Taking Off*. In the Seventies she moved towards stardom playing a rock singer in *Phantom of the Paradise* and appearing in Woody Allen's *Love and Death* and *Stardust Memories*, in which she was excellent as one of Woody's neurotic girlfriends. Sexier roles have come her way – the 'vamp' in *Shock Treatment* – while she was very impressive as the sad little wife in *Pennies From Heaven*, musicals obviously being her forte.

Films include: 1971 Taking Off. '74 Phantom of the the Paridise. '75 Love and Death; Inserts (GB). '77 Suspiria (IT). '80 Stardust Memories. '81 Shock Treatment (GB). '82 Pennies From Heaven; My Favorite Year (dir. only).

HARRIS, Barbara

(b. 1937). Actress. Born: Sandra Markowitz; Evanston, Illinois, USA

She specializes in losers – a struggling singer in *Who Is Harry Kellerman and Why Is He Saying Those Terrible Things About Me?*, the faithful wife of the straying senator in *The Seduction of Joe Tynan*. But she has had one supreme moment: as the blonde, mini-skirted Albuquerque she seizes the mike and her chance for stardom, leading the crowd in the singing of 'It Don't Worry Me' at the tragic ending of *Nashville*. From the Goodman School of the Theatre she joined a group of young actors (including Alan Arkin, Elaine May and Mike Nichols) in the famous Second City revue in Chicago, and went with them to New York in the early Sixties. She went from strength to strength on Broadway, directing as well as acting and picking up a Tony Award in 1967. Her mark on films has been small but effective and she had the distinction of being Hitchcock's last leading lady – in *Family Plot*.

Films include: 1965 A Thousand Clowns. '67 Oh Dad, Poor Dad, Mama's Hung You in the Closet and I'm Feeling So Sad. '71 Plaza Suite; Who Is Harry Kellerman and Why Is He Saying Those Terrible Things About Me? '75 Nashville. '76 Family Plot; Freaky Friday. '78 Movie Movie. '79 The Seduction of Joe Tynan.

HARRIS, Julie

(b. 1925). Actress. Born: Julie Ann Harris; Grosse Point, Michigan, USA

The daughter of an investment broker, Julie Harris studied for a year at the New York Drama School before becoming one of the first members of Lee Strasberg's Actors' Studio. After her success in *Member of the Wedding* on Broadway, she took the same role – as the tom-boy 12-year-old shattered by her brother's wedding – in the film version. She then went on to secure her right to success as Sally Bowles in *I Am a Camera*. Then came the part she is perhaps best known for, as the shy, hesitant, love-struck girl opposite James Dean in *East of Eden*, a role completely at odds with her previous forceful and extrovert portrayals. Afterwards she concentrated on Broadway, winning herself five Tony Awards in the process, and didn't really ever re-establish herself in films. Slight, with a sharp, anxious face and croaky voice, she was usually featured in those films she has made since the Sixties as a tragic or pathetic figure, calling on all her powers of intense emotional expression.

Films include: 1952 The Member of the Wedding (USA). '55 I Am a Camera (GB); East of Eden. '58 The Truth About Women (GB). '63 The Haunting (GB). '66 You're a Big Boy Now. '67 Reflections in a Golden Eye. '76 Voyage of the Damned (GB). '79 The Bell Jar.

HARRIS, Richard

(b. 1933). Actor. Born: Limerick, Eire

Having studied at the London Academy of Music and Dramatic Art, Harris joined Joan Littlewood's Theatre Workshop and was well-received in *View From the Bridge*. He then toured Russia with the group and was subsequently offered a film part in *Alive and Kicking*. It was as the brash, working-class rugby player in *This Sporting Life* that he made his name. He received an Academy Award nomination for that role, but has since failed to live up to his early promise. He moved on from boorish – often exaggeratedly Irish – parts in British 'New Wave' films to appear in international star-studded productions such as *Camelot*, in which it was discovered that he could sing. This led him off into other areas, and his recording of 'MacArthur Park' sold over five million copies. Ginger-haired, with a craggy face and a reputation for hard drinking and being difficult on set, 'Hellraiser' Harris has been likened to a second-rate Richard Burton by some, but nevertheless adds a certain excitement and prestige to many of the rather clichéd action-roles put his way. On television he was superb in an adaption of Paul Gallico's *The Snow Goose*.

Films include: 1958 Alive and Kicking. '61 The Long and the Short and the Tall. '63 This Sporting Life. '64 Deserto Rosso (IT-FR) (USA/GB: Red Desert). '65 The Heroes of Telemark; Major Dundee (USA). '66 Hawaii (USA). '67 Camelot (USA). '70 Cromwell; A Man Called Horse. '76 The Eagle Has Landed. '78 The Wild Geese. '81 Tarzan, the Ape Man (USA).

HARRISON, Kathleen

(b. 1898). Actress. Born: Blackburn, Lancashire, England

Clapham High School was followed by RADA, a film debut in *Our Boys* (1915), then eight years in Argentina where she and her husband raised a family. Back in England she worked on stage in Eastbourne and London, playing a maid in *The Cage* in 1927. Film parts as servants and working girls brought her eventually to the part of Ethel Huggett, the homely cockney missis (opposite Jack Warner) and mum in an immensely popular series about an English working-class family. This made her a star. Later she played an older version of the type in the *Mrs Thursday* television series: doleful, sometimes harassed, but always ready with a cup of tea and a sympathetic word. She has continued to work well into her eighties.

Films include: 1931 Hobson's Choice. '32 Happy Ever After. '41 Kipps (USA: The Remarkable Mr Kipps); Major Barbara. '43 In Which We Serve. '45 Caesar and Cleopatra. '47 Holiday Camp. '48 Here Come the Huggetts; Oliver Twist; The Winslow Boy. '49 Vote for Huggett; The Huggetts Abroad. '55 Cast a Dark Shadow. '61 On the Fiddle (USA: Operation Snafu). '69 Lock Up Your Daughters! '79 The London Connection (USA: The Omega Connection).

HARRISON, Rex

(b. 1908). Actor. Born: Reginald
Carey Harrison; Huyton,
Lancashire, England

At the age of 16 Harrison joined the
Liverpool Repertory Company and
subsequently made his London debut
at the Everyman Theatre in 1930. His
success in the 1935 production of
Heroes Don't Care led to a film contract
with Alexander Korda and his first
major screen role in *Storm in a Teacup*.
Lean, tall, charming and blasé, he was
excellently cast as the social parasite
and wastrel hero of *The Rake's Progress* and rose to the comedy in *Blithe
Spirit*, winning himself an accolade
from Noel Coward who said: 'After me
you're the best light comedian in the
world'. In 1964 Harrison was awarded an Oscar for his role as the aloof,
idiosyncratic Henry Higgins in *My
Fair Lady*, a role he had already made
his own on Broadway, but his Hollywood career has been largely disappointing: 'In Hollywood I played the
parts that I feel weren't right for me
. . . I did the best I could, but I was
often unhappy about the results'. He
continues to work on stage and
screen, and receives a fair amount of
coverage from the gossip columnists.
His formidable list of illustrious ex-
wives includes Lilli Palmer, Kay Kendall and Rachel Roberts.

Films include: 1937 Storm in a Teacup. '38
The Citadel (USA). '40 Night Train to
Munich. '41 Major Barbara. '45 Blithe
Spirit; The Rake's Progress. '47 The Foxes of
Harrow. '58 The Reluctant Debutante
(USA). '63 Cleopatra (USA). '64 My Fair
Lady (USA). '67 Doctor Dolittle.

HARRYHAUSEN, Ray

(b. 1920). Creator of special
effects/model animator. Born Los
Angeles, California, USA

A schoolboy passion for such special-
effects movies as *The Lost World* (1925)
and *King Kong* (1933) decided Ray
Harryhausen's future. At Los Angeles
City College he studied drama, photography and sculpture, and at the
University of California he took up art
direction and film editing. Willis
O'Brien, chief technician on *King
Kong*, encouraged him; and after military service in World War II and
work on such series as George Pal's
Puppetoons, he became O'Brien's assistant on *Mighty Joe Young* (1949),
another giant-ape story. From 1955
he began a partnership with the producer Charles H. Schneer which has
been successful for them both, and
Harryhausen has often acted as associate or co-producer as well as
taking charge of special effects. His
speciality, which he calls Dynam-
ation, is the animating of complex
models combined with live-action figures to create a fantasy world of
myth and legend. He now lives in
London and has his own special
studio in Slough.

Films include: 1953 The Beast From 20,000
Fathoms. '55 It Came From Beneath the
Sea. '57 Twenty Million Miles to Earth. '58
The Seventh Voyage of Sinbad. '60 The
Three Worlds of Gulliver (GB). '61 Myste-
rious Island (GB). '63 Jason and the Ar-

gonauts (GB). '66 One Million Years BC
(GB). '73 The Golden Voyage of Sinbad
(GB). '77 Sinbad and the Eye of the Tiger
(GB). '81 Clash of the Titans (GB).

HART, William S.

(1870–1946). Actor/director. Born:
William Surrey Hart; Newburgh,
New York, USA

Hart was the strong, silent knight of
the early Western. Middle-aged, dour,
saddleworn, he generally rode a
crooked trail until redeemed by the
love of a good woman whom he
would treat with the utmost chivalry.
He as much as anyone was responsible for turning the Western into a
beloved morality play and – despite
the authenticity of setting he achieved
– a myth with little basis in reality. His
father was a miller who moved West
when Hart was a boy, and he was
brought up beside an Indian reservation, later becoming a cowboy in
Kansas and learning to love the life he
would one day put on the screen. At
15 he moved back East and began
acting, mostly in Shakespeare, and
working his way up to the role of
Messala in *Ben-Hur* on Broadway by
1899. In 1914 he made his first Western shorts for Thomas H. Ince and
was soon directing his own features.
As he joined Ince at Triangle and then
switched to Famous Players Lasky
and United Artists as an independent,
his projects grew more expensive and
sentimental, but no less Victorian.
The stirring *Tumbleweeds* proved his
swansong, so poorly distributed by
United Artists that Hart's career was
ruined. He retired to his ranch – today
a public museum – and wrote his
memoirs.

Films include: 1915 The Disciple (+dir). '16
The Aryan (+dir); Hell's Hinges (+co-dir).
'17 The Narrow Trail (+co-sc); The Gunfighter (+dir). '18 Blue Blazes Rawden
(+dir). '19 Wagon Tracks. '20 The Toll
Gate (+co-sc). '23 Wild Bill Hickok (+co-
sc). '25 Tumbleweeds.

HARTNELL, William

(1908–1975). Actor. Born: Seaton,
Devon, England

William Hartnell trained to be a
jockey, but having gained too much
weight took to acting. He began touring the provinces with Frank
Benson's troupe in 1924, was appearing in films by 1931 and was successful on the London stage the following
year. World War II broke his progress
but on being invalided out of the
Royal Tank Corps he scored his first
major film triumph as the tough Sergeant Fletcher in *The Way Ahead*.
There followed a string of hard-nosed
characters – often crooks – in various
films and all of them were well-
received. They were a change from his
earlier roles before the war, when his
talents were largely wasted in light-
comedy, although his grim sergeant
in *Carry on Sergeant* helped launch
that popular series in 1958. He
became a household name and face
when he played the eccentric, white-
haired time traveller in the first series
of BBC television's *Dr Who*.

Films include: 1944 The Way Ahead. '47
Brighton Rock; Odd Man Out. '51 The
Magic Box. '52 The Pickwick Papers. '56
Private's Progress. '58 Carry On Sergeant.
'59 The Mouse That Roared. '63 This
Sporting Life; Heaven's Above.

194

Far left: Rex Harrison as Doctor Dolittle. Left: William S. Hart in Tumbleweeds. Above: William Hartnell in All On A Summers Day (1950). Above right: Laurence Harvey in Room at the Top. Below left: Henry Hathaway. Below: Lilian Harvey. Bottom: Hurd Hatfield

HARVEY, Anthony

(b. 1931). Director. Born: London, England

After a brief stay at RADA, Anthony Harvey went to work for the Crown Film Unit in 1949. He then became an assistant editor on *The Long Memory* (1953) amd was promoted to editor of films by the Boulting brothers (*I'm All Right Jack*, 1959), Bryan Forbes (*The L-Shaped Room*, 1962) and Stanley Kubrick (*Lolita*, 1962). His first film as director, *Dutchman*, was shot in six days with a cast of two and one set; based on LeRoi Jones' play, it parodied race relations in New York and won several festival awards. Harvey went on to make two films from scripts by James Goldman, *The Lion in Winter* (which brought Harvey an Oscar nomination) and *They Might Be Giants*. He then settled in New York and has mainly directed films made in and about America, though the 1980 television movie *Richard's Things*, made and set in England and scripted by Frederic Raphael, was a notable exception. Also for British television, he has made *On Giant's Shoulders* (1979), the dramatized true story of a thalidomide victim.

Films: 1967 Dutchman. '68 The Lion in Winter. '71 They Might Be Giants (USA). '73 The Glass Menagerie. '74 The Abdication. '79 Eagle's Wing; Players (USA).

HARVEY, Laurence

(1928–1973). Actor. Born: Hirsch Skikne; Joniskis, Lithuania

Brought up in South Africa, Harvey saw war service with the South African army before coming to England in 1946. After a brief spell at RADA he was on the stage by 1947 and in films the following year. His film career did not really take off until in 1958 he played the social-climber Joe Lampton in *Room at the Top*, a part which perfectly matched the cold arrogance of his screen personality. Leading parts in American films followed. Harvey was frequently cast as the callous opportunist, but when given the chance could show a gentler, more sympathetic side. His finest performance, as the brainwashed assassin in *The Manchurian Candidate*,

was most movingly done. He died of cancer at 45.

Films include: 1948 House of Darkness. '54 King Richard and the Crusaders (USA); Romeo and Juliet (GB-IT). '55 I Am a Camera; Storm Over the Nile. '59 Room at the Top; Expresso Bongo. '60 The Alamo (USA); Butterfield 8 (USA). '61 The Long and the Short and the Tall (USA: The Jungle Fighters). '62 Walk on the Wild Side (USA); The Manchurian Candidate (USA). '63 The Running Man; The Ceremony (+dir; +prod) (USA). '65 Darling .... '68 A Dandy in Aspic (+ add. dir, uncredited). '73 Welcome to Arrow Beach (+dir) (reissued as Tender Flesh) (USA).

HARVEY, Lilian

(1906–1968). Actress. Born: Lilian Pape; Edmonton, London, England

Educated in Berlin (she had a German father) and a trained dancer, Lilian Harvey was in the chorus of a Berlin revue when she was offered her first film part in 1925. She was immediately successful, and when sound came her singing voice and fluency in three languages made her an international star of light comedy and operetta. She worked in Hollywood and in England, but her real triumphs were in Germany, where she made her most famous film, *Congress Dances*, and a series of delightful musicals co-starring her husband, Willy Fritsch. She left Germany just before the war, and made two films in France, but after 1940 worked only on stage.

Films include: 1925 Der Fluch/Mein ist der Rache (A). '26 Prinzessin Tralala. '29 Adieu Mascotte/Die Modell von Montparnasse. '30 Liebeswalzer (GB version: Love Waltz); Die drei von der Tankstelle (GB: Three Men and Lilian). '31 Der Kongress tanzt (GB version: Congress Dances). '32 Ein blonder Traum (GB version: Happy Ever After). '33 My Weakness (USA); My Lips Betray (USA); I Am Suzanne (USA). '35 Invitation to the Waltz (GB). '40 Sérénade/Sérénade Eternelle (FR) (USA: Schubert's Serenade); Miquette (FR).

HAS, Wojciech Jerzy

(b. 1925). Director. Born: Cracow, Poland

Graduating in 1946 from the Film Institute in Cracow. Has worked as assistant director at the Łodz feature film studio, then at the Documentary Film Studio in Warsaw and the Educational Film Studio in Łodz. He directed shorts from 1948, features from 1957. Has is a quiet, observant director, not particularly Polish in his choice of subject matter, and at home with downbeat, nostalgic themes. His best known film, *The Saragossa Manuscript*, takes delight in the complexity of its interlocking stories, but *How to Be Loved*, in which an actress reminisces gently about past affairs, is the most characteristic of the director's work.

Films include: 1948 Harmoni (short) (Harmony). '57 Petla (The Noose). '58 Pozegnania (Farewell). '59 Wspólny Pokos (Shared Room). '60 Rozspanie (Partings). '62 Zloto (Gold); Jak Być Kochana (GB: How to Be Loved). '64 Rekopis Znaleziony w

Saragossie (GB: The Saragossa Manuscript). '66 Szy Fry (The Code). '68 Lalka (The Doll). '73 Sanatorium pod Klepsydra (The Hourglass Sanatorium).

HATFIELD, Hurd

(b. 1920). Actor. Born: William Ruckard Hurd Hatfield; New York City, USA

Educated at Columbia University, where he studied music, drama and art, Hatfield came to England for further training at the Chekhov Drama Studio in Devon. After repertory experience he returned to New York and was on the American stage before his first film in 1944. This was followed by the title role in *The Picture of Dorian Gray*, for which his almost unnaturally perfect looks made him ideal casting. He found it hard to shake off this image, and devoted more time to theatre and television than to movies, but after a longish absence he came back in the late Fifties for a number of interesting character roles. He was particularly impressive as the intrusive journalist Moultrie in *The Left-Handed Gun*, and as the mysterious tycoon in *Mickey One*, both films directed by Arthur Penn.

Films include: 1944 Dragon Seed. '45 The Picture of Dorian Gray. '46 Diary of a Chambermaid. '47 The Unsuspected. '48 Joan of Arc. '50 Tarzan and the Slave Girl. '58 The Left-Handed Gun. '61 King of Kings; El Cid (USA-IT). '65 Mickey One; Harlow. '68 The Boston Strangler. '71 Von Richtofen and Brown (GB: The Red Baron).

HATHAWAY, Henry

(1898–1985). Director. Born: Sacramento, California, USA

Hathaway spent 66 years in the film business – one of the longest careers on record. By 1908 he was a child actor with the American Film Company; by 1912 property boy and juvenile at Universal. In the Twenties he went on to Paramount, and rose to assistant director in 1923 (working regularly for Josef von Sternberg) and to director in 1932. Between then and 1973 he made sixty-odd films. A skilled and versatile craftsman, he made Westerns, crime and adventure films, with an impressive period in the Forties which included realistic crime dramas like *Call Northside 777* and a striking *film noir*, *Kiss of Death*. But the delicate fantasy *Peter Ibbetson* is unlike any other Hathaway film, and perhaps his most enduring work.

Films include: 1923 The Spoilers (ass. dir). '27 Underworld (ass. dir). '28 The Last Command (ass. dir). '29 Thunderbolt (ass. dir). '30 Morocco (ass. dir). '32 Shanghai Express (ass. dir); Heritage of the Desert. '35 The Lives of a Bengal Lancer; Peter Ibbetson. '36 Go West, Young Man; The Trail of the Lonesome Pine. '39 The Real Glory. '40 Brigham Young. '45 The House on 92nd Street. '46 The Dark Corner. '47 Kiss of Death. '48 Call Northside 777. '51 14 Hours; Rawhide. '53 Niagara. '64 Circus World (GB: The Magnificent Showman). '65 The Sons of Katie Elder. '66 Nevada Smith. '67 The Last Safari (GB). '69 True Grit. '73 Hangup.

HAVELOCK-ALLAN, Anthony

(b. 1905). Producer. Born: Blackwell Manor, Co. Durham, England

Entering the film industry in 1933 as a producer's assistant and casting director, Havelock-Allan became a producer three years later, making a string of 'quota quickies' for Paramount-British which introduced such players as Wendy Hiller, Margaret Rutherford and Wilfrid Hyde-White. His first big film, *This Man Is News*, was an excellent crime comedy with a very un-British pace to it. Havelock-Allan subsequently formed connections with Noel Coward and David Lean and produced *Blithe Spirit*, *Great Expectations* and other films much admired in their day. His later work included versions of some celebrated National Theatre productions. He was at one time married to actress Valerie Hobson.

Films include: 1938 This Man Is News. '42 In Which We Serve (assoc. prod. only). '44 This HappyBreed (assoc. prod. only). '45 Blithe Spirit (assoc. prod. only); Brief Encounter (co-assoc. prod. only). '46 Great Expectations (assoc. prod. only). '48 Blanche Fury. '58 Orders to Kill. '66 Romeo and Juliet (GB-IT). '68 Up the Junction (coprod). '70 Ryan's Daughter.

HAVER, June

(b. 1926). Actress. Born: June Stovenour; Rock Island, Illinois, USA

A former pianist and band-singer, blonde June Haver was signed by 20th Century-Fox in 1943 and groomed as a second Betty Grable for the studio's musicals. She played a number of leading roles without quite equalling Grable's popularity. She continued filming for Fox and Warners until 1953, when she retired and, briefly, entered a convent (she had hoped to marry a Catholic, but he had died before she could do so). When she emerged, she married Fred MacMurray, and apart from brief television appearances has lived in retirement since.

Films include: 1944 Home in Indiana. '45 Where Do We Go From Here?; The Dolly Sisters. '46 Wake Up and Dream. '47 I Wonder Who's Kissing Her Now. '49 Oh! You Beautiful Doll; Look For the Silver Lining. '50 The Daughter of Rosie O'Grady. '53 The Girl Next Door.

HAVOC, June

(b. 1916). Actress. Born: Ellen Evangeline Hovick; Seattle, Washington, USA

The younger sister of burlesque queen Gypsy Rose Lee, June Havoc was a stage child from the age of two, and also as a child acted in silent comedies. At 13 she eloped, and was forced during the Depression to work in dance marathons. She described this later in her autobiography, and wrote and directed a Broadway play about it, *Marathon '33*. In 1936 she ventured into straight theatre, and three years later a success in *Pal Joey* led to an RKO contract. But Hollywood seldom fully used her talent. Of her early comedies and musicals, only *My Sister Eileen* gave her much chance, and when she moved to more dramatic roles, playing a bigoted secretary in *Gentleman's Agreement*, this was one of the few worthwhile opportunities she had. Not surprisingly, she turned more and more to the stage.

Films include: 1941 Four Jacks and a Jill. '42 My Sister Eileen. '43 Hello, Frisco, Hello. '47 Gentleman's Agreement; Intrigue. '48 The Iron Curtain; When My Baby Smiles At Me. '49 Red Hot and Blue; Chicago Deadline. '78 The Private Files of J. Edgar Hoover. '80 Can't Stop the Music.

HAWKINS, Jack

(1910–1973). Actor. Born: John Edward Hawkins; Wood Green, London, England

Hawkins was a stage child, making his debut in 1923. Until the outbreak of war he acted regularly in the theatre in England and the USA, and made occasional British films without any great impact. Returning to the screen, in 1948, he had matured and was much more impressive, playing tough, determined, often ruthless characters. After 1951 he abandoned the stage, concentrating on films and working on occasion in America. In 1956 Hawkins contracted cancer of the larynx; in 1963 the larynx was removed, but he died in 1973 after a second, unsuccessful operation. His film roles were dubbed from *Great Catherine* onwards.

Films include: 1930 Birds of Prey (USA: The Perfect Alibi). '33 The Good Companions. '35 Peg of Old Drury. '48 The Fallen Idol. '49 The Small Back Room (USA: Hour of Glory). '50 The Elusive Pimpernel (USA: The Fighting Pimpernel). '52 Mandy (USA: Crash of Silence). '53 The Cruel Sea; Front Page Story. '55 Land of the Pharaohs (USA). '57 The Bridge on the River Kwai. '58 Gideon's Day (USA: Gideon of Scotland Yard). '59 Ben-Hur (USA). '62 Lawrence of Arabia. '63 Zulu. '64 Guns at Batasi. '65 Lord Jim (USA); Judith (USA). '67 Great Catherine. '70 Waterloo (IT-USSR). '72 Young Winston. '73 Theatre of Blood.

Films include: 1937 Good Morning, Boys. '39 Where's That Fire? '41 The Ghost of St Michael's. '44 A Canterbury Tale. '52 Brandy for the Parson; You're Only Young Twice. '58 Carry On Sergeant. '59 Carry On Nurse; Carry On Teacher. '60 Carry On Constable. '64 Carry On Jack. '66 Carry On Cowboy. '72 Carry On at Your Convenience; Carry On Abroad.

HAY, Will

(1888–1949). Actor. Born: William Thomson Hay; Stockton-on-Tees, Co. Durham, England

Before he was 20, Hay gave up an engineering apprenticeship to try his luck on the music halls, and after World War I established himself with the comedy sketch, *The Fourth Form at St Michael's*. He developed this act during his ten years in films (from 1933), portraying seedy incompetence as schoolmaster, stationmaster, sailor, policeman and so on. Hay's films were crude affairs, leaning heavily on the feeblest verbal humour, but were saved by the contrasting characters of their three leads, Hay himself, Graham Moffatt (1919–1965) as the insolent cockney fat boy, and Moore Marriott (1885–1949) as the shrill and toothless ancient. Their masterpiece is *Oh, Mr Porter!*, about a crumbling branch-line station.

Films include: 1933 Know Your Apples (short). '34 Radio Parade of 1935 (USA: Radio Follies). '35 Boys Will Be Boys. '36 Windbag the Sailor. '37 Good Morning, Boys (USA: Where There's a Will); Oh, Mr Porter! '38 Convict 99; Old Bones of the River. '39 Ask a Policeman; Where's That Fire? '41 The Ghost of St Michael's; The Black Sheep of Whitehall (+co-dir). '42 The Goose Steps Out. '43 My Learned Friend (+co-dir).

HAYAKAWA, Sessue

(1889–1973). Actor. Born: Kintaro Hayakawa; Chiba, Japan

Sessue Hayakawa studied political science and drama at the University of Chicago. He organized a Japanese touring company to put on a play, *The Typhoon*, which was seen by the film producer Thomas Ince. Ince signed him and his wife Tsura Aoki for the film version, which made Hayakawa a star. His first Hollywood career ended around 1923, after which he made films in Europe, usually France. He returned to Hollywood to act in *Tokyo Joe* with Humphrey Bogart and went on to play character roles, notably the prison-camp commandant in *The Bridge on the River Kwai*, which brought him a nomination for the Academy Award as Best Supporting Actor. Though his characters were sometimes heroes, he is best remembered as the archetypal smooth oriental villain which he had played in such early films as Cecil B. DeMille's *The Cheat*.

Films include: 1914 The Wrath of the Gods; The Typhoon. '15 The Cheat. '16 Alien Souls. '17 The Call of the East. '18 Hidden Pearls. '49 Tokyo Joe. '57 The Bridge on the River Kwai (GB). '59 Green Mansions. '60 Swiss Family Robinson (GB); Hell to Eternity. '61 The Big Wave.

HAWKS, Howard

(1896–1977). Director. Born: Goshen, Indiana, USA

On vacation from Cornell, where he graduated in mechanical engineering, Hawks drove racing cars and worked as a prop-boy for Famous Players-Lasky. At that point the great career began anonymously, with his direction of a couple of scenes in Mary Pickford's *The Little Princess* (1917). Later that year he joined the Army Air Corps. After the war he worked as a designer in an aircraft factory, but by 1922 was back in films, as cutter, story editor and casting director. Around 1924 he made one or two comedy shorts; in 1926 he sold a story to Fox on condition that he direct it. This was *The Road to Glory*, the first of 40 Hawks films in 45 years. Hawks was a practical man, active and witty and a famous raconteur. An expert in technique and in the total control of his material, he had a marvellous ability to sustain atmosphere and style through films in almost every genre. Although Hawks would probably have rejected the learned analyses of his work so fashionable now, two simple things do shine through all his films. One is the absolute clarity of his style, with its perfection of camera placement and its avoidance of every meretricious effect. The other is his genius for handling actors and raising the interplay of personality to a level scarcely touched by other filmmakers. Easy to say he was lucky in his actors (Grant, Hepburn, Russell, Arthur, Bogart, Bacall, Cooper), but Howard Hawks made his own luck.

Films include: 1926 The Road to Glory. '28 A Girl in Every Port. '30 The Dawn Patrol. '31 Scarface/Scarface, the Shame of a Nation. '33 Today We Live. '34 Twentieth Century. '36 The Road to Glory; Come and Get It (co-dir). '38 Bringing Up Baby. '39 Only Angels Have Wings. '40 His Girl Friday. '41 Sergeant York; Ball of Fire. '44 To Have and Have Not. '46 The Big Sleep. '48 Red River. '49 I Was a Male War Bride (GB: You Can't Sleep Here). '52 The Big Sky; Monkey Business. '53 Gentlemen Prefer Blondes. '55 Land of the Pharaohs. '59 Rio Bravo. '62 Hatari! '64 Man's Favorite Sport? '65 Red Line 7000. '67 El Dorado. '70 Rio Lobo.

HAWN, Goldie

(b. 1945). Actress. Born: Washington DC, USA

After a beginning as a teacher of dancing (at 18) and a dancer in musicals, Goldie Hawn gained fame on American television as a dumb blonde forever fluffing her lines. Her first major film, *Cactus Flower*, brought her an Academy Award as Best Supporting Actress, and she has sustained the character – a mixture of giggling blonde and calculating slyboots – in a dozen films since then. In 1980 she was also executive producer for her film *Private Benjamin*. Her first husband was director Gus Trikonis, who made a short film about her, *This Is My Wife*.

Films include: 1968 The One and Only Genuine, Original Family Band. '69 Cactus Flower. '70 There's a Girl in My Soup. '71 $/Dollars (GB: The Heist). '72 Butterflies Are Free. '74 The Sugarland Express; The Girl From Petrovka. '75 Shampoo. '76 The Duchess and the Dirtwater Fox. '78 Foul Play. '79 Viaggio con Anita (IT) (USA: Travels With Anita). '80 Private Benjamin (+exec. prod); Seems Like Old Times.

HAWTREY, Charles

(b. 1914). Actor. Born: Charles Hartree; Hounslow, Middlesex, England

Charles Hawtrey made gramophone records as a boy soprano, played in a musical, *Marry Me*, in 1932, trained at the Italia Conti school, and played bits on stage to support himself. His film career proper falls into three distinct phases. First, from 1937, he was a shrill and precocious ageing schoolboy in Will Hay comedies. Then he played more varied roles in better movies – the station-master in *A Canterbury Tale*, a temperance prig in *You're Only Young Twice*. And finally, he was swallowed alive by the monstrous Carry On series.

HAYDEN, Sterling

(1916–1986). Actor. Born: John Hamilton; Montclair, New Jersey, USA

Sterling Hayden ran away to sea at 15 and was a ship's captain at 22. Very tall, blond, and ruggedly handsome, he signed with Paramount and acted with Madeleine Carroll, whom he married in 1942 and divorced in 1946. After two films he left Hollywood to join the marines, returning to Paramount in 1947 and then freelancing. He won critical respect as the horse-loving robber in *The Asphalt Jungle*, But this was followed in 1951 by the traumatic experience of collaborating with the House Un-American Activities Committee (HUAC) and naming names of former communist comrades. He was very busy throughout most of the Fifties, but only a few good roles – as the preacher in *Take Me to Town*, the enigmatic gunfighter in *Johnny Guitar* and the stoic racetrack robber in *The Killing* – stood out from the general run of mediocre Westerns and action movies. He then embarked on a long sea voyage with his children and returned to films as an occasional character actor in the Sixties and Seventies. He evidently preferred the sea to Hollywood, but his tough reticence gave a detached quality to his performances that added to their strength.

Films include: 1941 Virginia, **'50** The Asphalt Jungle. **'53** Take Me to Town. **'54** Johnny Guitar; Naked Alibi. **'56** The Killing. **'57** Crime of Passion. **'64** Dr Strangelove, or How I learned to Stop Worrying and Love the Bomb (GB). **'70** Loving. **'73** The Godfather. **'73** The Long Goodbye; The Final Programme (GB) (USA: The Last Days of Man on Earth). **'76** 1900/Novecento (IT-FR-GER). **'80** 9 to 5.

HAYDN, Richard

(1905–1985). Actor. Born: London, England

Richard Haydn made his West End stage debut in the chorus of *Betty of Mayfair* in 1926, and evolved the character of Edwin Carp, the absent-minded professor, through several revues. Eventually he played on Broadway in Noel Coward's *Set to Music*, with Beatrice Lillie. He moved to Hollywood, making his screen debut in *Charley's Aunt*. His distinctive nasal voice, amusingly fussy mannerisms and talent for mimicry were ideally suited to comedy, but he also played serious character roles. He directed a few films in the late Forties, and wrote several Edwin Carp books.

Films include: 1941 Charley's Aunt (GB: Charley's American Aunt); Ball of Fire. **'45** And Then There Were None (GB: Ten Little Niggers). **'46** The Green Years. **'47** The Foxes of Harrow; Forever Amber. **'48** Miss Tatlock's Millions (+dir). **'53** The Merry Widow. **'58** Twilight for the Gods. **'62** Mutiny on the Bounty. **'65** The Sound of Music. **'74** Young Frankenstein.

HAYES, George ('Gabby')

(1885–1969). Actor. Born: George Hayes; Wellsville, New York, USA

After a successful vaudeville career, Hayes was wealthy enough to retire in 1928, but the stock market Crash of 1929 forced him back into show business. In numerous Westerns he played the grizzly, cantankerous sidekick to such heroes as Hopalong Cassidy (William Boyd) and Roy Rogers, and was in the top ten money-making Westerns of 1943 to 1952. He even had his own television show in the Fifties. The ultimate in typecasting, he played the same cowboy old-timer in some two hundred films.

Films include: 1923 Why Women Remarry. **'34** In Old Santa Fe. **'35** Hop-a-long Cassidy. **'36** Mr Deeds Goes to Town. **'38** Rose of the Rio Grande; The Frontiersman. **'40** Wagons Westward. **'42** The Man From Cheyenne. **'45** Don't Fence Me In. **'51** Pals of the Golden West.

HAYES, Helen

(b. 1900). Actress. Born: Helen Hayes Brown; Washington DC, USA

Often known as the 'First Lady of the American Theatre' with a Broadway theatre renamed after her, Helen Hayes, a stage actress from childhood, has had two widely separated careers in American films (not counting a couple of early silents). Having married the playwright and screenwriter Charles MacArthur in 1928, she went with him to Hollywood when he signed with MGM, and won a Best Actress Oscar for her role in *The Sin of Madelon Claudet*. She was also notable as the wartime nurse who falls in love with an American officer (Gary Cooper) in Frank Borzage's version of Ernest Hemingway's novel *A Farewell to Arms*. She returned to the theatre, with only intermittent film parts, until she scored success and won a Best Supporting Actress Oscar in *Airport*. Finding that her health was no longer equal to stage work, she acted in several undemanding Disney films and played Dora Bloch in *Victory at Entebbe*. The actor James MacArthur is her adopted son.

Films include: 1931 The Sin of Madelon Claudet; Arrowsmith. **'32** A Farewell to Arms; The Son-Daughter. **'56** Anastasia. **'70** Airport. **'74** Herbie Rides Again. **'75** One of Our Dinosaurs Is Missing (GB). **'77** Victory at Entebbe (orig. TV); Candleshoe.

HAYS, Will H.

(1879–1954). Censor. Born: Sullivan, Indiana, USA

Hays was a Mason, an elder of the Presbyterian church, a successful lawyer and an active politician who had been national chairman of the Republican Party and Postmaster General. He was a natural choice to act as figurehead and spokesman for the American film industry when it was under pressure, following the Arbuckle case and other scandals, to set up a system of self-censorship. He was appointed president of the newly-formed Motion Picture Producers and Distributors Association (MPPDA) in 1922 and held the post until 1945. He forbade the filming of over two hundred books and plays, and in 1930 the MPPDA, generally known as the Hays office, produced its production code, the Hays Code, a list of rules that had no legal standing but was accepted by the industry. It regulated sexual matters – a kiss must not be protracted, no love-making between people of different races and so on – crime, violence, religion, bad language and similar touchy subjects. It was strictly enforced from 1934, under the supervision of Joseph I. Breen, and remained unrevised until 1966.

HAYTER, James

(1907–1983). Actor. Born: Lonuvla, India

James Hayter was a squat, solid and round fellow, with kindly blue eyes and a rich, fruity voice. He excelled in all sorts of character roles, especially in comedy, though he also made a convincing villain. The son of a police superintendent in India, he was educated in Scotland and urged into acting by his headmaster. He studied at RADA for a year (1924–25) and then

joined a repertory company, eventually reaching the West End stage and the cinema screen in 1936. His stage successes included *1066 and All That* and *French Without Tears*. During the war he served with the Royal Armoured Corps and returned to take up a very active screen career. Characteristic roles included Friar Tuck in a couple of Robin Hood films and Mr Pickwick in *The Pickwick Papers*. He also appeared in several American productions and co-productions. His voice was familiar to British viewers in many television commercials, such as those for Mr Kipling cakes and Birds Eye frozen foods.

Films include: 1938 Marigold. **'39** Murder in Soho (USA: Murder in the Night). **'47** Nicholas Nickleby. **'48** Bonnie Prince Charlie; Once a Jolly Swagman (USA: Maniacs on Wheels). **'49** Passport to Pimlico. **'50** Night and the City. **'51** Flesh and Blood; Tom Brown's Schooldays. **'52** The Story of Robin Hood and His Merrie Men; The Crimson Pirate (USA); The Pickwick Papers. **'55** Land of the Pharoahs (USA). **'58** Gideon's Day (USA: Gideon of Scotland Yard). **'67** A Challenge for Robin Hood. **'68** Oliver!

HAYWARD, Susan

(1918–1975). Actress. Born: Edythe Marrener; New York City, USA

With her cute nose and her sharp tongue, Susan Hayward was the classic fighting redhead. The daughter of a Coney Island barker turned subway guard, she was eager to escape from her poverty-stricken environment and became a tough, ambitious model in her teens. Spotted by George Cukor on the cover of the *Saturday Evening Post*, she was tested unsuccessfully for the role of Scarlett O'Hara in *Gone With the Wind* (1939). But she used the screen test to get a six-month contract with Warners and was then taken up by Paramount. She gradually worked her way up to starring roles, particularly once she had teamed up with the independent producer Walter Wanger. It took her ten years to reach the first of her five Oscar nominations, for *Smash-Up*, in which she played the neglected, alcoholic wife of a popular singer. This set the pattern of her typical Oscar-nomination roles: she was the crippled singer Jane Froman in *With a Song in My Heart*, the alcoholic actress Lillian Roth in *I'll Cry Tomorrow* and a woman condemned to death for murder in *I Want to Live*, which finally brought her the Best Actress Award. She also excelled in less heavily emotional roles – for instance, as the innocently tempting wife of a rising rodeo star (Arthur Kennedy) who strikes sparks in her relationship with a fading one (Robert Mitchum) in *The Lusty Men*. Following the Oscar she appeared in a string of over-the-top melodramas that ended her regular career. After 1964 she played only occasional parts. She died of a brain tumour.

Films include: 1942 Reap the Wild Wind. '46 Canyon Passage. '47 Smash-Up/Smash-Up, the Story of a Woman (GB: A Woman Destroyed); The Lost Moment. '48 Tap Roots. '49 Tulsa; House of Strangers; My Foolish Heart. '52 With a Song in My Heart; The Lusty Men. '55 I'll Cry Tomorrow. '58 I Want to Live. '64 Where Love Has Gone. '67 The Valley of the Dolls.

HAYWORTH, Rita

(b. 1918). Actress. Born: Margarita Carmen Cansino; New York City, USA

With her hair dyed red, her voice softly caressing and her graceful body rhythmically moving, Rita Hayworth was the number one 'Love Goddess' of the Forties, until the third of her five relatively brief marriages, to Aly Khan (1949–51), broke the rhythm of her career and the fourth, to Dick Haymes (1953–55), made a second interruption that turned her from a glamorous star to a character lead. She had started off as a Spanish dancer in Mexican nightclubs at 13, and signed with Fox in 1935, only to be dropped when the company merged with 20th Century. In 1937 her first husband, Edward Judson, got her a contract with Columbia, where she was confined to B pictures until Howard Hawks cast her as a wife with a wandering eye in *Only Angels Have Wings*. She partnered James Cagney in *The Strawberry Blonde*, Fred Astaire in *You'll Never Get Rich* and *You Were Never Lovelier*, and Gene Kelly in *Cover Girl*. She was an innocent, misunderstood *femme fatale* in *Gilda*, her most famous role, and a guilty one in *The Lady from Shanghai*, directed by her second husband, Orson Welles (1943–47), who made her blonde for an ironic change. Then, in 1948, came the Aly Khan affair, a big scandal in its day, and the main part of Rita's career was over. She had further moments – as a wealthy ex-stripper in *Pal Joey*, as an ageing actress in *Separate Tables*, as an independent woman stranded in the Mexican desert in *They Came to Cordura*. But the mystique had faded, and the last part of her career was in low-budget films, several of them in Europe.

Films include: 1939 Only Angels Have Wings. '40 The Lady in Question; Angels Over Broadway. '41 The Strawberry Blonde; Blood and Sand; You'll Never Get Rich. '42 Tales of Manhattan; You Were Never Lovelier. '44 Cover Girl. '46 Gilda. '47 Down to Earth; The Lady From Shanghai. '48 The Loves of Carmen. '53 Salome; Miss Sadie Thompson. '57 Fire Down Below; Pal Joey. '58 Separate Tables. '59 They Came to Cordura. '64 Circus World. '65 The Money Trap. '70 Sur la Route de Salina (FR-IT) (USA/GB: Road to Salina).

HEAD, Edith

(1898–1981). Costume designer. Born: Los Angeles, California, USA

Hollywood's first lady of costume design taught languages before going to Paramount as a sketch artist in 1923. Fifteen years later she became the head of design at the same studio. During the course of a career which spanned sixty years and included over a thousand films, Edith Head has dressed almost every major star from Marlene Dietrich to Robert Redford. Her clothes, often glamorous, sometimes exotic (she is credited, for example, with putting Dorothy Lamour in a sarong), were individually designed to complement the character of the people she dressed.

Films include: 1933 She Done Him Wrong. '49 Samson and Delilah; The Heiress. '50 All About Eve; Sunset Boulevard. '51 A Place in the Sun. '53 Roman Holiday. '54 Sabrina (GB: Sabrina Fair). '60 The Facts of Life. '70 Myra Breckinridge. '73 The Sting.

Top left: a perfect Dickensian actor James Hayter as Mr Pickwick in The Pickwick Papers, *a loose adaptation directed by Noel Langley. Far left: beautiful, husky-voiced Susan Hayward who reached star stature despite a discouraging beginning. Left: Rita Hayworth as Gilda in the film of the same name, a story of a love triangle in classic Hollywood* film noir *style*

HEARD, John

Actor. Born: Washington DC, USA

John Heard first made his name on stage in the Chicago and New York productions of *WARP*, a space fantasy. He got his first good chance in films in Joan Micklin Silver's *Between the Lines*, and her *Head Over Heels* was written with him in mind. But he has made more public impact with his roles as the Fifties novelist Jack Kerouac in *Heart Beat* and as a one-eyed Vietnam veteran obsessed with solving a murder in *Cutter and Bone*. He is married to the actress Margot Kidder.

Films include: 1976 Marathon Man. '77 Between the Lines; Rush It; First Love. '79 Head Over Heels; Heart Beat. '81 Cutter and Bone (GB: Cutter's Way). '82 Cat People.

HECHT, Ben

(1893–1964). Screenwriter. Born: New York City, USA

After a colourful childhood in which he displayed talent as an acrobat and as a violinist, Ben Hecht worked on various newspapers and founded the Chicago *Literary Times*. In 1925, a telegram from Herman Mankiewicz took him to Hollywood where he began a successful career as a scriptwriter. His best films – often written in collaboration with Charles MacArthur – are stylish comedies, woven around strong stories, of which *The Front Page* and *Twentieth Century* were the most popular. His occasional excursions into directing were usually failures.

Films: 1928 The Big Noise. '29 The Great Gabbo. '31 The Front Page. '32 Scarface (co-sc). '33 Design for Living. '34 Twentieth Century (co-sc); Viva Villa. '35 The Scoundrel (co-dir; co-prod; co-sc). '40 His Girl Friday; Angels Over Broadway (co-dir). '45 Spellbound. '57 A Farewell to Arms.

HEDREN, Tippi

(b. 1935). Actress. Born: Nathalie Hedren; LaFayette, Minnesota, USA

Best-known for her role as Melanie, the terrorized heroine of *The Birds*, Tippi Hedren was spotted by Alfred Hitchcock in a television commercial. Petite and beautiful, she is a typical Hitchcock blonde in the style of Grace Kelly: she followed her successful debut with the title role in *Marnie*. Finding herself typecast, she earned a reputation for being difficult by turning down sex and horror films. Hedren appeared sporadically in the Seventies, but changed tack in 1981 with *Roar*, a film about a family of three children and 150 lions, tigers and other assorted four-legged creatures, which she had been preparing with her husband, producer Noel Marshall, for eleven years.

Films: 1963 The Birds. '64 Marnie. '65 Satan's Harvest. '67 A Countess From Hong Kong (GB). '69 The Man With the Albatross. '70 Tiger by the Tail. '73 The Harrad Experiment. '75 Adonde Muere el Viento (ARG). '81 Roar.

Below: John Heard in Cutter and Bone. *Right: Tippi Hedren, best known for her roles in Hitchcock films, here seen in* Marnie. *Far right: Van Heflin as Starrett, the farmer whose wife and son grow to love* Shane

HEFLIN, Van

(1910–71). Actor. Born: Emmett Evan Heflin Jr; Walters, Oklahoma, USA

Undecided between the sea and the stage, Van Heflin spent three years as a sailor in the Pacific after a disastrous acting debut. He returned to drama school and quickly landed a contract with first RKO, then MGM, generally cast as a romantic lead. After the war he established his lasting image of a rugged support player, alternating between thrillers and Westerns and both sides of the law. He won an Oscar for his portrayal of the gangster's drunken sidekick in Mervyn LeRoy's *Johnny Eager*, but he is best known as the stolid, brave homesteader whose family and livelihood are threatened but eventually rescued by *Shane*.

Films include: 1941 Johnny Eager. '47 Possessed. '48 The Three Musketeers. '49 Madame Bovary. '51 The Prowler. '53 Shane. '55 Battle Cry. '57 3:10 to Yuma. '65 The Greatest Story Ever Told; Once a Thief. '66 Stagecoach. '70 Airport.

HEIFITZ, Josif

(b. 1905). Director. Born: Minsk, Russia

Josif Heifitz joined Lenfilm as an apprentice and worked his way up to directing. He teamed up with Alexander Zarkhi in 1928, co-directing with him for over twenty years. Their most famous collaboration was *Baltic Deputy*, the story of a famous scientist who comes to accept the Revolution. Turning solo after 1950, Heifitz directed a variety of films but was particularly successful with his adaptations of Anton Chekhov's short stories: *Lady With a Little Dog*, a sad study of love between two people trapped by middle-class conventions, and *In the Town of 'S'*.

Films include: 1928 Pesnj o Metalle (co-dir) (A Song of Steel). '29 Luna Sleva (co-dir) (Facing the Wind/A Head Wind). '37 Deputat Baltiki (co-dir) (GB: Baltic Deputy). '40 Chlen Pravitelstva (co-dir) (GB: A Member of the Government). '54 Bolchaia Semia (GB: The Big Family). '56 Delo Rumyantseva (GB: The Rumiantsev Case). '59 Dama s Sobachkoi (GB: Lady With a Little Dog). '64 Den Stchastia (A Day of Happiness). '68 V Gorodye 'S' (GB: In the Town of 'S'). '78 Asya. '82 Vpervye Zamuzhem.

HELLER, Otto

(1896–1970). Cameraman. Born: Prague, Czechoslovakia

Whilst a soldier during World War I, Otto Heller was asked to film Emperor Franz Josef's funeral procession. He became a cameraman and after the war worked in Czechoslovakia, Germany and France, escaping the Nazis to join the Czech air force in Britain in 1940 where he eventually settled. His flexibility and imagination created some of the most visually interesting British films including the atmospheric *They Made Me a Fugitive* and the controversial *Peeping Tom*. He remained in demand as a competent technician until his death.

Films: 1942 Alibi. '47 They Made Me a Fugitive (USA: I Became a Criminal); Temptation Harbour. '49 The Queen of Spades. '52 The Crimson Pirate (USA). '55 The Ladykillers. '56 Richard III. '59 The Rough and the Smooth (USA: Portrait of a Sinner). '60 Peeping Tom. '61 Victim. '65 The Ipcress File. '66 Funeral in Berlin.

HELLINGER, Mark

(1903–1947). Producer. Born: New York City, USA

Raised in New York, Mark Hellinger was a successful journalist before turning to dramatic writing. He joined Warner Brothers as a producer in 1937. His films are mainly hard-hitting melodramas, with *Brute Force* and *The Killers* being central to the development of the *film noir* genre, and *The Naked City*, with its imaginative use of cityscapes pioneering the introduction of a new realism in gangster films. He became the model for Richard Brooks' novel *The Producer*.

Films: 1939 Hell's Kitchen; The Roaring Twenties. '40 They Drive by Night (GB: The Road to Freedom). '41 High Sierra; The Strawberry Blonde. '45 The Horn Blows at Midnight. '46 The Killers. '47 The Two Mrs Carrolls; Brute Force. '48 The Naked City.

HELLMAN, Lillian

(1905–1984). Playwright/screenwriter. Born: New Orleans, USA

A journalist and literary critic, Lillian Hellman shot to fame when her first play, *The Children's Hour* was produced on Broadway in 1934, although it was never allowed into the West End because of its lesbian undercurrents. One of America's leading female playwrights, she was working at the Goldwyn studios (where she wrote many successful films including *The Little Foxes*, adapted from her play) when she was blacklisted for refusing to name names to the House Un-American Activities Committee. She made a welcome return to Hollywood twenty years later to script Arthur Penn's *The Chase*. At the age of 62 she wrote a string of autobiographies about her life, her work and her association with writer Dashiell Hammett, one of which formed the basis for Zinnemann's film, *Julia* (1977).

Films: 1935 The Dark Angel (co-sc). '36 These Three (+play basis). '37 Dead End. '41 The Little Foxes (+play basis). '43 Watch on the Rhine (co-sc. +play basis); The North Star (reissued as Armoured Attack). '61 The Children's Hour (co-sc. +play basis). '66 The Chase.

Above: a German screen temptress – Brigitte Helm. Above right: David Hemmings in The Best House in London (1969), a historical comedy in which a plan is made to open a government-financed brothel. Below: Sonja Henie with a winning smile in Katina

HELLMAN, Monte

(b. 1932). Director. Born: New York City, USA

A product of Stanford University and UCLA, where he studied drama and film respectively, Hellman first directed under the guidance of the producer and director Roger Corman; the film was Beast From Haunted Cave. A shared interest in making A films on B budgets led to further collaborations, the highlights of which were the Westerns The Shooting and Ride the Whirlwind, made simultaneously for only $150,000 and featuring the then unknown Jack Nicholson. Frequently beset with distribution problems, most of Hellman's films are rarely seen, and this fact, coupled with their obsessive violence, quirky charm and at times apparently wilful obscurity, has made him something of a cult figure. Two-Lane Blacktop, featuring pop stars James Taylor and Dennis Wilson racing Warren Oates along American freeways, is perhaps the best known work of a director who has resolutely eschewed commercialism; this has led to directorial assignments being rather few and far between.

Films include: 1959 Beast From Haunted Cave. '64 Back Door to Hell (USA-PHIL). '65 Flight to Fury (USA-PHIL). '66 The Shooting; Ride in the Whirlwind. '71 Two-lane Blacktop. '74 Cockfighter/Born to Kill. '78 China 9, Liberty 37/Amore, Piombo e Furore (co-dir. only) (IT).

HELM, Brigitte

(b. 1908). Actress. Born: Gisela Eva Schittenhelm; Berlin, Germany

Helm scored a resounding success in her first film, Fritz Lang's Metropolis, playing the dual role of saint and robot. Her subsequent films gave her few chances to show the sensitivity she had displayed in that film; her remarkable physical beauty was exploited instead in a series of parts as a glacial femme fatale. Unwilling or unable to break out of this stereotype, which the coming of sound tended to render somewhat obsolete, she retired in 1936. An attempted comeback some years later proved unsuccessful.

Films include: 1927 Metropolis; Der Liebe der Jeanne Ney (GB: The Love of Jeanne Ney). '28 Abwege/Begierde (GB: Crisis); L'Argent (FR-GER). '29 Die wunderbare Lüge der Nina Petrowna. '30 Alraune. '32 The Blue Danube (GB); Die Herrin von Atlantis/L'Atlantide. '34 Gold. '37 Yoshiwara (FR).

HEMMINGS, David

(b. 1941). Actor/director. Born: Guildford, Surrey, England

Best remembered as the swinging fashion photographer given a (well-deserved) runaround by Vanessa Redgrave in Antonioni's Blow-Up, Hemmings started his showbiz career as a boy soprano with the English National Opera. He then turned to art and, though expelled from art school, held a successful exhibition of his paintings. He made his film debut with the Children's Film Foundation. Minor parts in film and television followed until Antonioni's movie made him a hot property. Several leading roles followed in which he displayed an attractive, boyish vulnerability, laced with the narcissism typical of male stars in the Sixties. With the formation of his own production company, Hemdale, he moved into directing, making his debut with Running Scared. He had a stormy, much publicized marriage with actress Gayle Hunnicut. They divorced in 1974 and he has since remarried. Perhaps his most notable recent success was persuading Marlene Dietrich out of retirement to play in Just a Gigolo. Hemmings' acting appearances have become less frequent and he works mainly as a producer and director, based in Australia.

Films include: 1966 Blow-Up. '67 Camelot (USA). '68 Charge of the Light Brigade; Barbarella (FR-IT); The Long Day's Dying. '70 Fragment of Fear. '71 Unman, Wittering and Zigo. '74 Juggernaut. '79 Schöner Gigolo – Armer Gigolo (+ dir) (GER) (GB: Just a Gigolo).

HENIE, Sonja

(1912–1969). Ice-skater/actress. Born: Oslo, Norway

The daughter of a fur wholesaler, Henie was Norwegian skating champion at 14, world champion a year later and an Olympic gold-medallist in 1928, 1932 and 1936. This success, coupled with her sunny personality and blonde good looks, both popularized the sport of ice-skating and attracted the attention of 20th Century-Fox, for whom she made a series of hugely successful light comedies (they grossed $36 million) in the late Thirties – all vehicles for her skating skills. She reaped further financial rewards as the producer and star of the Hollywood Ice Revues. Her apparently fragile five-foot-two-inch frame concealed an astute businesswoman, whose ability to drive a hard bargain led to the soubriquet 'The Iron Butterfly'. She was one of the ten wealthiest women in the world when she died (of leukemia).

Films include: 1936 One in a Million. '37 Thin Ice (GB: Lovely to Look At). '38 Happy Landing; My Lucky Star. '39 Everything Happens at Night. '41 Sun Valley Serenade. '42 Katina (GB: Iceland). '43 Wintertime. '45 It's a Pleasure. '48 Countess of Monte Cristo.

HENREID, Paul

(b. 1908). Actor. Born: Paul George Julius von Henreid; Trieste, Austria

An air of gentility pervades Henreid's acting. He was educated at the Maria Theresa Academy in Vienna and the Institute of Graphic Arts, subsequently working as a designer and translator for a publishing company managed by Otto Preminger. Preminger introduced him to Max Reinhardt, who invited Henreid to join his theatre. He arrived in England in 1935, appeared on stage and in films (including *Goodbye, Mr Chips*) and, from 1940 on, took up permanent residence in the USA. In *Now, Voyager*, opposite Bette Davis, he was the epitome of the cultured, sensitive, Continental lover, while in *Casablanca* he was cast as the idealistic freedom-fighter Victor Laszlo. Both roles appealed highly to American audiences. Henreid shook off his rather effete image by playing swashbuckling characters in such films as *The Spanish Main* and *Thief of Damascus*. In 1951 he made his directorial debut with *For Men Only*. His subsequent credits include *Dead Ringer* (1964), with Bette Davis, and he has also worked in television, directing episodes of the *Alfred Hitchcock Presents* series and *Bonanza*. He is still acting, generally in 'elder statesmen' roles, typified by his cardinal in *Exorcist II: The Heretic*.

Films include: 1939 Goodbye, Mr Chips (GB). '40 Night Train to Munich (GB). '42 Now, Voyager; Casablanca. '45 The Spanish Main. '47 Song of Love. '52 Thief of Damascus. '62 The Four Horsemen of the Apocalypse. '69 The Madwoman of Chaillot (GB). '77 Exorcist II: The Heretic.

HENRY, Buck

(b. 1930). Actor/screenwriter/director. Born: Buck Henry Zuckerman; New York City, USA

Henry was the son of an air-force general turned stockbroker and the actress Ruth Taylor, who had been part of Mack Sennett's stock company appearing in his comedies in the Twenties. After a spell at Harvard Military Academy, he decided to become an actor and appeared in bit parts on Broadway. Following military service in the Korean War, he moved to Hollywood and came to prominence in the Sixties as one of a new breed of satirists, that included Woody Allen, Elaine May and Alan Arkin, bringing new zest to television comedy, in particular the Steve Allen and Gary Moore shows. By the end of the decade he was working regularly in movies as a writer and/or actor, numbering among his script credits *The Graduate* (1967), *Candy* (1968), *Catch-22* (1970) and *What's Up, Doc?* (1972). He co-starred in Forman's *Taking Off* as a father searching for his runaway daughter, and played a mild-mannered patents lawyer in Roeg's *The Man Who Fell to Earth*. In 1978 he and Warren Beatty were nominated for the Best Director Oscar for *Heaven Can Wait*.

Films include: 1968 The Secret War of Harry Frigg. '71 Taking Off; Is There Sex

After Death? '76 The Man Who Fell to Earth. '78 Heaven Can Wait (+co-dir). '80 Gloria; First Family (+dir).

HEPBURN, Audrey

(b. 1929). Actress. Born: Edda Hepburn van Heemstra; Brussels, Belgium

Dark, slender, enchanting, sophisticated and aloof – Audrey Hepburn was the face of the Fifties. In 1964, still at the height of her profession, she played Eliza Doolittle in *My Fair Lady*, a flowergirl easily transformed into a well-spoken society piece. Yet, she is so prim and proper – a princess mingling with commoners in *Roman Holiday* (her Oscar role) – it is difficult to imagine her effecting the reverse operation so convincingly, despite her abandonment to sultriness as the half-breed in *The Unforgiven*. She lived in Holland during the war and after it studied ballet in London, returning for a Dutch film debut in 1948. Revue and chorus work led to a film contract with Associated British and she was promoted as a starlet. *Gigi* on Broadway followed and then Hollywood, where she became a very big star of romantic comedies (*Roman Holiday*, *Love in the Afternoon*), dramas (*The Nun's Story*) and musicals (*Funny Face*, *My Fair Lady*). She married and divorced actor Mel Ferrer and in 1968, after her fifth Academy Award nomination (for *Wait Until Dark*), retired to Rome with her second husband. Seven years later she re-emerged to play a middle-aged Maid Marian, leaving a nunnery surprisingly to make love to Robin Hood (Sean Connery) in a cornfield in *Robin and Marian*.

Films include: 1948 Nederland in 7 Lessen (HOLL). '51 The Lavender Hill Mob (GB). '53 Roman Holiday. '54 Sabrina (GB: Sabrina Fair). '56 War and Peace (IT-USA). '57 Funny Face; Love in the Afternoon. '59 The Nun's Story. '60 The Unforgiven. '61 Breakfast at Tiffany's; The Children's Hour (GB: The Loudest Whisper). '63 Charade. '64 My Fair Lady. '66 Two for the Road. '67 Wait Until Dark. '76 Robin and Marian. '79 Bloodline (USA-GER). '81 They All Laughed.

HEPBURN, Katharine

(b. 1907). Actress. Born: Hartford, Connecticut, USA

Among Hollywood's most talented actresses, Katharine Hepburn has never conformed to the conventional film-star image. Though her lower lip might tremble, she was not really vulnerable; she might show signs of weakness, but usually only to win her point. Brought up in New England in a very free environment by a feminist mother, she had private tutors, expensive schools and a first-class college education at Bryn Mawr, where she gained amateur acting experience. On graduation in 1928 she went straight into summer stock and reached Broadway with a minor part in *These Days*. By 1932 she was playing leads and David O. Selznick signed her for RKO, despite her demand for an improbably high salary. She soon won the first of her four Oscars for

Morning Glory, and established her image on and off-screen as an independent, strong-minded woman. In the late Thirties she demonstrated her skill in comedy, and in 1942 she made the first of nine films with Spencer Tracy, her partner also in a long love-affair that lasted until his death in 1967. Their films together, comedies and dramas, depicted a long-drawn-out battle of the sexes from which both emerged victorious. Always respected by the Hollywood community in which she played little public part, she was nominated for Oscars 11 more times, winning late in her career with *Guess Who's Coming to Dinner?*, *The Lion in Winter* and *On Golden Pond*. In recent years she has worked mainly in television films and the theatre, where she scored a Broadway success in 1969 as the French fashion designer Coco Chanel in *Coco*.

Films include: 1932 A Bill of Divorcement. '33 Christopher Strong; Morning Glory; Little Women. '35 Alice Adams. '36 Bringing Up Baby; Holiday (GB: Free to Live/Unconventional Linda). '40 The Philadelphia Story. '42 Woman of the Year; Keeper of the Flame. '48 State of the Union. '49 Adam's Rib. '51 The African Queen. '52 Pat and Mike. '55 Summer Madness (USA-GB) (USA: Summertime). '56 The Rainmaker. '59 Suddenly, Last Summer. '62 Guess Who's Coming to Dinner? '68 The Lion in Winter (GB). '75 Love Among the Ruins (orig. TV). '81 On Golden Pond.

HEPWORTH, Cecil

(1874–1953). Director. Born: London, England

The son of magic-lantern lecturer T.C. Hepworth, Cecil Hepworth was one of the British cinema's true pioneers. In addition to writing one of the first books on film, *Animated Photography*, in 1897, he invented a film developing and printing machine, setting up a processing company at Walton-on-Thames. Finding business slack, he made his own short films, notably *Rescued by Rover* – a revolutionary film in terms of narrative technique. He began selling films to the USA, set up his own stock company and created the first British movie stars,

such as Chrissie White, Alma Taylor and Violet Hopson. In 1913 his career reached a peak with his production of *Hamlet* starring the stage actor Sir Johnstone Forbes-Robertson. His fortunes were seriously affected by World War I and the subsequent economic recession and he went bankrupt in 1924. He later worked for National Screen Services, a company specializing in trailers. At the age of 77 he wrote his autobiography, *Come the Dawn.*

Films include: 1898 The Quarrelsome Anglers. **1900** How It Feels to Be Run Over. **'05** Rescued by Rover. **'13** Hamlet; Sally in Our Alley. **'16** Trelawny of the Wells; Coming Through the Rye. **'20** Alf's Button. **'21** Tansy. **'26** The House of Marney.

HERBERT, Hugh

(1887–1952). Actor. Born: Binghamton, New York, USA

A stage comic from the age of 16, Herbert also wrote playlets and variety sketches. He entered films in 1927 as actor and writer. In the Thirties acting took over, and he was one of the great array of character players at Warner Brothers. He

portrayed harmless, benevolent eccentrics, fluttering excitedly in the margin of countless comedies and musicals, with his hypochondriac moralist in *Dames* perhaps his richest creation. He played the odd lead in small movies, too. Hugh Herbert's early script credits are often confused with those of F. Hugh Herbert, a prolific Viennese author who wrote Hollywood scripts for thirty years.

Films include: 1930 Hook, Line and Sinker. **'32** Million Dollar Legs. **'33** Strictly Personal. **'34** Fashion Follies of 1934; Fog Over Frisco. **'35** We're In the Money; Gold Diggers of 1935. **'39** The Family Next Door. **'42** Hellzapoppin'. **'44** Kismet. **'48** A Song Is Born. **'49** The Beautiful Blond From Bashful Bend. **'51** Havana Rose.

HERLTH, Robert

(1893–1962). Art director. Born: Wriezen, Germany

The son of a brewer, Robert Herlth met the set designer Hermann Warm in 1916 while serving in the army, and spent the rest of the war working for an army theatre. After the war, and art studies, he began to collaborate with Walter Röhrig in designing for German films, creating brilliantly elaborate sets for Expressionist films and simpler, small-scale settings for *kammerspiel* (or intimate drama) films. Among the many directors they worked with were Fritz Lang and F.W. Murnau. The partnership broke up in 1936, after Herlth and Röhrig had written and directed *Hans im Glück* together. Then Herlth mostly worked solo for some years but he later collaborated with others, including Warm and his younger brother Kurt Herlth, who entered films in 1932.

Films include: 1921 Irrende Seelen (co-art dir); Der müde Tod (co-art dir) (USA: Between Two Worlds, re-ed. and shown as Beyond the Wall in 1927; GB: Destiny). **'25** Tartüff (co-art dir) (GB: Tartuffe). **'26** Faust (co-art dir). **'29** Die wunderbare Lüge der Nina Petrowna (co-art dir). **'32** Der schwarze Husar (co-art dir). **'36** Hans im Glück (co-dir; + co-sc; + co-art dir). **'37** Der Herrscher. **'38** Der Spieler. **'45** Die Fledermaus. **'61** Gustav Adolfs Page.

HERRMANN, Bernard

(1911–1975). Composer. Born: New York City, USA

Bernard Herrmann studied music at New York University and the Juilliard School. He founded the New Chamber Orchestra in New York and in 1933 joined CBS as a radio conductor. His best-known film work was for Orson Welles' early films and many of Alfred Hitchcock's later ones. He worked closely with Hitchcock for over a decade but their relationship was severed when Hitchcock wanted a more modern sound for *Torn Curtain*. But Herrmann continued to work with such admirers of Hitchcock as François Truffaut and Brian De Palma. He specialized in the classic symphonic style of film music with a direct, emotional sound, often evoking menace. He believed that, although music is the cement that binds a film together, it should not be noticed, though neither should it merely duplicate the action. He won an Oscar for *All That Money Can Buy.*

Films include: 1940 Citizen Kane. **'41** All That Money Can Buy. **'42** The Magnificent Ambersons. **'47** The Ghost and Mrs Muir. **'55** The Kentuckians. **'56** The Man Who Knew Too Much. **'58** Vertigo. **'59** North by Northwest. **'60** Psycho. **'63** The Birds (sd. consultant). **'64** La Mariée Etait en Noir (IT-FR) (GB: The Bride Wore Black). **'72** Sisters. **'76** Taxi Driver; Obsession.

HERSHOLT, Jean

(1886–1956). Actor. Born: Copenhagen, Denmark

From a Danish theatrical family, Jean Hersholt trained for the stage while also becoming national champion bicycle racer. In 1914 he was touring the USA in plays by Ibsen when he met Lon Chaney who introduced him to Hollywood. He began his screen career at Thomas H. Ince's studio in 1915 and became a naturalized American citizen in 1920. Stroheim's *Greed* brought him stardom as the rival of dentist McTeague, and he went on to portray both heavies and sympathetic characters. The coming of sound exposed his foreign accent, limiting his range; but he continued

in supporting parts and some leads, including the role of the Country Doctor in several films and a spin-off radio series. His humanitarian work brought him two Special Academy Awards, in 1939 as president of the Motion Picture Relief Fund, and again in 1949. He was also knighted by King Christian of Denmark in 1946 for his war-work as president of the US-Denmark Relief Organisation. After his death the Academy instituted the annual Jean Hersholt Humanitarian Award in his memory.

Films include: 1916 Hell's Hinges. **'21** The Four Horsemen of the Apocalypse. **'22** Tess of the Storm Country. **'23** Jazzmania. **'24** The Goldfish. **'25** Greed; Don Q, Son of Zorro. **'26** The Greater Glory. **'27** The Student Prince in Old Heidelberg (GB: The Student Prince). **'28** The Battle of the Sexes. **'31** Private Lives. **'36** The Country Doctor; One in a Million. **'37** Heidi. **'38** Alexander's Ragtime Band. **'49** Dancing in the Dark.

HERZOG, Werner

(b. 1942). Director/screenwriter/producer. Born: Werner H. Stipetic; Sachrang, Germany

Herzog is one of the leading and most unusual figures in world cinema. His films are set in timeless, far-flung never-never-lands – uncharted South American jungle (*Aguirre, Wrath of God* and *Fitzcarraldo*), a deserted Greek island (*Signs of Life*) or nineteenth century European villages out of the pages of Grimm (*The Enigma of Kaspar Hauser*). Place is as important as character to Herzog – one of his dominant themes is the metaphysical effect of the one upon the other. His main characters are either outside civilized society or fall victim to its cruelties. Their apartness is frequently made clear by some physical or mental deformity or abnormality. Herzog was obsessed by films at an early age, making his first when still at school. In the Sixties he travelled widely – film for him has remained something of an endurance test – making movies as he went. The critical acclaim that greeted these works encouraged the West German government to put money into his first feature, *Signs of Life*, but he remained and continues to remain resolutely independent in outlook. His romantic approach to his subjects owes something to the German Expressionists of the Twenties, to whom he paid homage in his *Nosferatu, the Vampyre*, a reworking of Murnau's 1922 film. The slow pace of Herzog's movies often makes them hard going, inviting accusations of artiness, while stories of his erratic behaviour towards his crew and actors are legion. He continues to amaze and offend, be adored or decried in equal measure.

Films include: 1968 Lebenszeichen (USA/GB: Signs of Life). **'70** Auch Zwerge Haben Klein Angefangen (USA/GB: Even Dwarfs Started Small). **'71** Fata Morgana. **'73** Aguirre, der Zorn Gottes (USA/GB: Aguirre, Wrath of God). **'75** Jeder für sich und Gott gegen Alles (USA: The Mystery of Kaspar Hauser; GB: The Enigma of Kaspar Hauser). **'77** Stroszek. **'79** Nosferatu: Phantom der Nacht (GER-FR) (USA/GB: Nosferatu, the Vampyre). **'82** Fitzcarraldo.

HESSLING, Catherine

(1899–1979). Actress. Born: Andrée Heuschling; Moronvilliers, France

Andrée Heuschling left her native village when it was bombarded during World War I, and went to Provence where in 1917 she became a model for the painter Auguste Renoir until his death in 1919. In 1920 she married his son Jean and went into films when he became a screenwriter and then a director. As Catherine Hessling she appeared in several of his early films as well as those of Alberto Cavalcanti, and acted in a stylized manner said to have been influenced by Charlie Chaplin – she was known in France as a female Charlot. She parted from Renoir in 1930 and turned her back on the cinema, though offered parts by G.W. Pabst and Carl Dreyer. She took up dancing and then returned briefly to films in the mid-Thirties, but never really established herself in the commercial cinema.

Films include: 1924 Une Vie Sans Joie (re-ed. and shown in France as Catherine in 1927); La Fille de l'Eau (GB: The Whirlpool of Fate). '26 Nana. '27 Yvette. '28 La Petite Marchande d'Allumettes (GB: The Little Match Girl); En Rade. '29 Le Petit Chaperon Rouge. '33 Du Haut en Bas. '35 Crime et Châtiment (GB: Crime and Punishment).

HESTON, Charlton

(b. 1923). Actor. Born: Charles Carter; Evanston, Illinois, USA

A commanding physical presence, handsome and rugged, with 'an eye like Mars to threaten and command' – Heston's appearance alone would have made him a likely candidate for stardom. An intelligent and dedicated approach to performance ensured it. He studied speech and drama at Northwestern University, playing major parts in college shows and gaining further experience in radio drama in Chicago. After a three-year spell in the air force, he made his Broadway debut in Katharine Cornell's production of Antony and Cleopatra. A series of meaty television parts in the late Forties – Antony in Julius Caesar, Heathcliff in Wuthering Heights among others – excited Hollywood's attention. His debut film was Dieterle's Dark City in 1950. Cecil B. DeMille first fully realized Heston's potential, casting him in The Greatest Show on Earth and The Ten Commandments. Heston brought a new integrity and truth to the epic heroes he frequently played, winning an Oscar in the title role of Ben-Hur. His single foray into direction was Antony and Cleopatra (1972), not a success despite Heston's diligence. He has served six terms as Chairman of the Trustees of the American Film Institute and is the author of The Actors Life: Journals 1956–1976. In 1977 he received the Jean Hersholt Humanitarian Award.

Film include: 1950 Dark City. '51 The Greatest Show on Earth. '53 Arrowhead. '56 The Ten Commandments. '58 Touch of Evil. '59 Ben-Hur. '61 El Cid (USA-IT). '65 The Agony and the Ecstasy (USA-IT). '66 Khartoum (GB). '67 Planet of the Apes. '73 Soylent Green. '74 Airport; Earthquake. '76 Two-Minute Warning.

HEYWOOD, Anne

(b. 1932). Actress. Born: Violet Pretty; Handsworth, Warwickshire, England

The daughter of a violinist, Anne Heywood had to look after the family when her mother died. She joined the Highbury Players in Birmingham and graduated from scene-painting to lead roles. She won a number of beauty-queen titles including Miss Great Britain, and became the hostess of Carol Levis' teenage discoveries programme on television. Playing Aladdin in a Christmas pantomime, she was spotted by a Rank casting director and given a seven-year contract, but played mostly routine nice-girl parts. When she married the producer Raymond Stross she began to attempt more ambitious and sexy roles, including the lesbian who falls in love with a man in The Fox and the young man who undergoes a sex-change operation in I Want What I Want. She is very popular in Italy, where she has been awarded the equivalent of an Oscar for her services to the cinema.

Films include: 1956 Checkpoint. '57 Doctor at Large; Dangerous Exile. '58 Violent Playground. '59 Upstairs and Downstairs. '63 The Very Edge. '67 The Fox (USA). '69 La Monaca di Monza (IT) (GB: The Awful Story of the Nun of Monza). '72 I Want What I Want. '73 Trader Horn. '75 La Prima Volta sull'Erba (IT).

HILL, Arthur

(b. 1922). Actor. Born: Melfort, Saskatchewan, Canada

The son of a lawyer, Hill supported his law studies at the University of British Columbia by working as a radio actor. He abandoned law in favour of acting and in 1948 flew with his actress wife Peggy to England, where both found work with the BBC. During the Fifties he became a regular performer on stage, radio and in low-budget films, his first being Miss Pilgrim's Progress (1950). When a play he was in, The Matchmaker, transferred to Broadway, Hill stayed on in the USA, winning a Tony Award in Who's Afraid of

Virginia Woolf? in 1962. He has since been frequently cast in Hollywood movies as a kindly, worried business-man.

Films include: 1952 Paul Temple Returns (GB). '54 Life With the Lyons (GB) (USA: Family Affair). '61 The Young Doctors. '66 Harper (GB: The Moving Target). '68 Petulia. '69 The Chairman (GB: The Most Dangerous Man in the World). '71 The Pursuit of Happiness; The Andromeda Strain. '77 A Bridge Too Far. '79 The Champ; A Little Romance (FR-USA).

HILL, George Roy

(b. 1923). Director. Born: Minneapolis, Minnesota, USA

The director of such popular hits as Butch Cassidy and the Sundance Kid and The Sting, for which he won an Oscar, Hill has not been a favourite with critics, one of whom has described his work as 'idiosyncratically odious oili-ness'; however, Hill's best films remain irresistible entertainment. He studied music at Yale and literature at Trinity College, Dublin. His first pro-fessional stage appearance was with Cyril Cusack's company in Dublin and he later acted in several off-Broadway shows. Following a notable career as a pilot with the US Marines during World War II and the Korean War, he became a television director. Period of Adjustment, starring a promising young actress called Jane Fonda, was Hill's first feature and he has worked consistently ever since, appearing most at ease with nostalgic subjects.

Films include: 1962 Period of Adjustment. '63 Toys in the Attic. '64 The World of Henry Orient. '66 Hawaii. '67 Thoroughly Modern Millie. '69 Butch Cassidy and the Sundance Kid. '72 Slaughterhouse-Five. '73 The Sting. '75 The Great Waldo Pepper. '79 A Little Romance (FR-USA). '82 The World According to Garp.

HILL, Terence

(b. 1941). Actor. Born: Mario Girotti; Venice, Italy

Blond, blue-eyed and good-looking, Hill is a huge box-office draw in Italy, Germany and South America, injecting beguiling touches of humour into the 'macho' heroes he usually plays. The son of a German mother and Italian father, Hill spent his early years in Dresden and Rome. He made his film debut at 12 and apart from three years spent studying classical literature at the University of Rome has hardly been out of the movie limelight. He changed his name in 1967 when he began to appear in the series of 'spaghetti' Westerns that made him a star. In these he was often teamed with the fat, surly Bud Spencer. The contrasting duo became very popular, especially in Europe. A more romantic side to Hill's personality came to the fore in *March or Die*; he plays a burglar who joins the French Foreign Legion to escape the police and, hardly surprisingly, falls in love with Catherine Deneuve.

Films include: 1958 Anna di Brooklyn (IT-USA) (GB: Anna of Brooklyn). '63 Il Gattopardo (IT-FR) (USA/GB: The Leopard). '67 Dio Persona. . .Io No! (IT-SP) (GB: God Forgives, I Don't/Blood River). '69 La Collina degli Stivali (IT) (USA: Boot Hill). '70 Lo Chiamavano Trinità (IT) (USA/GB: They Call Me Trinity). '71 Continuavamo a Chiamarlo Trinità (IT) (USA/GB: Trinity Is Still My Name). '73 Il Mio Nome e Nessumo (IT-FR-GER) (GB: My Name Is Nobody). '76 Un Genio, Due Comparie, Un Pollo (IT-FR-GER). '77 March or Die (GB); Mr Billion (USA). '79 Io Sto con gli Ippopotami (IT).

HILL, Walter

(b. 1942). Director. Born: Long Beach, California, USA

For Hill, the American South is easily the most fascinating part of America; three of his films bear witness to this preoccupation – *Hard Times*, *The Long Riders* and *Southern Comfort*. Hill's early ambition was to be a comic-book illustrator and the brevity and lurid immediacy of this type of literature is a feature of his work, particularly *The Warriors*, a gangland film spiced with equal parts of classical epic and wild fantasy. Asthma ruled him out of the Vietnam War and he began writing film scripts, supporting himself by doing odd jobs. Among his first screenplay credits were *The Getaway* (1972) and *The Mackintosh Man* (1973). Whatever his films' actual setting, they have at their centre the conventions and characters of the Western. Hill's style thus owes more to such masters of the action film as Walsh, Hawks and Ford than to contemporaries like Coppola and Scorsese.

Films include: 1975 Hard Times (GB: The Streetfighter). '78 The Driver. '79 The Warriors. '80 The Long Riders. '81 Southern Comfort. '82 48 Hrs.

HILLER, Arthur

(b. 1923). Director. Born: Edmonton, Alberta, Canada

Hiller became involved in amateur theatre while studying at the University of Toronto. He joined CBC Radio as a programmer, subsequently branching out into documentary and musical variety. In 1954 he broke into television drama, travelling to Hollywood to direct such series as *Matinée Theatre*, *Climax* and *Playhouse 90*. He made his feature film debut in 1957 with *The Careless Years*, worked steadily during the Sixties and then scored a smash hit with the most popular romance of the century, *Love Story* – for which many critics have never forgiven him. He has made a wide variety of films but his eclecticism has resulted in the lack of any discernible style. Hiller's best films have owed at least as much to the script as to his direction and *The Americanization of Emily* and *The Hospital*, witty and acerbic pieces written by Paddy Chayefsky, remain highlights of his career.

Films include: 1963 The Wheeler Dealers (GB: Separate Beds). '64 The Americanization of Emily. '66 The Tiger Makes Out. '70 Love Story. '71 Plaza Suite; The Hospital. '72 Man of La Mancha. '76 W.C. Fields and Me. '79 Nightwing (HOLL).

HILLER, Wendy

(b. 1912). Actress. Born: Bramhall, Cheshire, England

That Wendy Hiller, one of Britain's finest stage actresses (she was made a Dame of the British Empire in 1975), has had few chances to display her talent on film does not reflect particularly well on the British movie industry. She learned her craft in rep before making her West End debut as the lead in Ronald Gow's stage adaptation of *Love on the Dole*. In 1937 she made her film debut in the low-budget *Lancashire Luck*, also scripted by Gow, whom she married the same year. Other highlights of her sporadic film career include a superb portrayal of Eliza Doolittle in Asquith's version of Shaw's *Pygmalion* that makes subsequent 'Fair Ladies' look pale and insipid by comparison. She also showed typical charm and panache as a headstrong career girl coming to terms with Scottish rural life and finding love in the process in Powell and Pressburger's *I Know Where I'm Going*.

Films include: 1938 Pygmalion. '41 Major Barbara. '45 I Know Where I'm Going. '51 Outcast of the Islands. '58 Separate Tables. '60 Sons and Lovers. '63 Toys in the Attic (USA). '66 A Man for All Seasons. '69 David Copperfield. '74 Murder on the Orient Express. '80 The Elephant Man.

HINGLE, Pat

(b. 1923). Actor. Born: Martin Patterson Hingle; Denver, Colorado, USA

The son of a construction engineer, and himself a former construction worker, Pat Hingle joined the Actors' Studio in 1952 and spent 14 years on Broadway. In films from 1954, this burly character actor has been in much demand for redneck portrayals, notably as a hanging judge in *Hang 'em High*, as a right-wing fanatic in *WUSA*, and as a die-hard anti-unionist in *Norma Rae*.

Films include: 1954 On the Waterfront. '57 No Down Payment; The Strange One (GB: End as a Man). '62 Jigsaw (GB). '63 The Ugly American. '68 Hang 'em High. '77 The Gauntlet. '79 Norma Rae; When You Comin' Back, Red Ryder?

Top, far left: Catherine Hessling in Nana. *Top left: Charlton Heston as Ben-Hur, one of his great epic roles. Left: Anne Heywood in* Floods of Fear *(1958). Above: Arthur Hill in* The Andromeda Strain, *an allegorical tale about a village infected by a deadly germ. Above: Terence Hill. Below: Wendy Hiller in* Murder on the Orient Express – *is she the guilty party in this Agatha Christie mystery? Below right: Pat Hingle*

Right, from left to right: Valerie Hobson in Blanche Fury, *in which she starred with Stewart Granger; John Hodiak in* Lifeboat; *Dustin Hoffman in the tearjerker* Kramer vs Kramer; *Hal Holbrook in* Midway

Below, from left to right: Alfred Hitchcock on the set of Psycho; *William Holden in* Stalag 17; *Judy Holliday; Stanley Holloway in* The Titfield Thunderbolt, *one of the best and last of the famous Ealing comedies*

HITCHCOCK, Alfred

(1899–1980). Director. Born: Leytonstone, London, England

Hitchcock's first job in the film industry was as a designer of title cards at the Islington studios of Famous Players-Lasky. This was in 1919. Four years later he rose to scriptwriter for director Graham Cutts, and had a shot at art direction and editing. In 1926 he married the editor and continuity girl Alma Reville (1900–1982), who was to work closely with him throughout his life. That same year he directed, in Germany, the first two of his 53 features (52 of them, all save his second, *The Mountain Eagle*, survive). Until 1939 Hitchcock worked in England; he then went to Hollywood, where all but three of his remaining films were made. He became an American citizen in 1955, and shortly before his death in 1980 he was knighted. Library shelves groan under dissertations on the art of Hitchcock, from intricate Catholic theology to symbolic interpretations of the director's appearances in his films. Hitchcock himself never commented on this flourishing industry; when interviewed, his contributions were straightforward, even banal. Yet those 53 films are an astonishing body

of work. In his silent films he was a young man in love with the medium, eager to startle with innovations, far from committed to thrillers and happily accepting every kind of story that came along. Then came the famous British thrillers of the Thirties, ranging from the Germanic shadows of *Sabotage* to the pace and glitter of *The Lady Vanishes*. He went to Hollywood, where he had better technicians and better actors, and through the Forties and the Fifties perfected his skills, until in 1957 he could embark on the sequence of five masterpieces that crowned his career. These films, *Vertigo*, *North by Northwest*, *Psycho*, *The Birds* and *Marnie*, were not all well received, but time and repeated viewings have made evident all their richness and density, and their sympathetic understanding of human weakness. There were four more films, but they were the films of an old man relaxing, final sessions at a favourite game.

Films include: 1925 The Pleasure Garden. '26 The Mountain Eagle (USA: Fear o' God); The Lodger (USA: The Case of Jonathan Drew). '27 The Ring. '29 Blackmail (silent and sound versions). '34 The Man Who Knew Too Much. '35 The Thirty-Nine Steps. '36 Sabotage (USA: The Woman

Alone). '37 Young and Innocent (USA: The Girl Was Young). '38 The Lady Vanishes. '40 Rebecca (USA); Foreign Correspondent (USA). '41 Suspicion (USA). '42 Saboteur (USA). '43 Shadow of a Doubt (USA). '45 Spellbound (USA). '46 Notorious (USA). '49 Under Capricorn. '51 Strangers on a Train (USA). '52 I Confess (USA). '54 Rear Window (USA). '56 The Man Who Knew Too Much (USA). '57 The Wrong Man (USA). '58 Vertigo (USA). '59 North by Northwest (USA). '60 Psycho (USA). '63 The Birds (USA). '64 Marnie (USA). '66 Torn Curtain (USA). '69 Topaz (USA). '72 Frenzy. '76 Family Plot (USA).

HOBSON, Valerie

(b. 1917). Actress. Born: Larne, Northern Ireland

The stage exerted an early fascination for Valerie Hobson, the daughter of an army officer. She sandwiched a six-year spell at ballet school (she was deemed too tall) between stays at RADA, made her stage debut in *Two Hearts in Waltz Time* and rapidly graduated to movies, appearing in *Eyes of Fate* in 1934. Hollywood's Universal studio cast her in a series of horror films, but she became homesick and returned to become a stalwart of British films, specializing in

svelte, ladylike roles. She retired from showbusiness and married the politician John Profumo (her first husband had been the producer Anthony Havelock-Allan), coping well with the 1963 scandal that destroyed her husband's career and rocked the government. As an actress she was at her best as a cool, resourceful double-agent in Powell and Pressburger's *The Spy in Black* and as the frivolous mother unconsciously exploiting her son's devotion in *The Rocking Horse Winner* (1949).

Films include: 1935 The Werewolf in London (USA). '39 The Spy in Black. '40 Contraband. '46 The Years Between; Great Expectations. '48 Blanche Fury; The Small Voice (USA: Hideout). '49 Kind Hearts and Coronets. '52 The Card (USA: The Promoter).

HODIAK, John

(1914–1955). Actor. Born: Pittsburgh, Pennsylvania, USA

The son of Polish-Ukrainian parents, Hodiak was encouraged to act by his father who had had some amateur experience. Hodiak worked as a clerk for the Chevrolet automobile company before winning roles as a radio

Films include: 1967 The Graduate. '69 Midnight Cowboy; John and Mary. '70 Little Big Man. '71 Alfredo, Alfredo (IT-FR); Who Is Harry Kellerman and Why Is He Saying Those Terrible Things About Me?; Straw Dogs (GB). '73 Papillon. '74 Lenny. '76 All the President's Men; Marathon Man. '77 Straight Time. '79 Agatha (GB); Kramer vs Kramer. '82 Tootsie.

HOLBROOK, Hal

(b. 1925). Actor. Born: Harold Rowe Holbrook Jr; Cleveland, Ohio, USA

Holbrook's parents abandoned him when he was two; he was raised by relatives and educated at Culver Military Academy, Indiana, and Denison University, Ohio. He made his stage debut, aged 17, in *The Man Who Came to Dinner* and, following three years' war service, made it to Broadway. Further work on stage and in television attracted Hollywood and he has appeared in various character roles, notably Deep Throat in *All the President's Men*, Lillian Hellman's friend Alan Campbell in *Julia* and Father Malone in *The Fog*. His biggest stage success was *Mark Twain Tonight!*

Films include: 1965 The Group. '68 Wild in the Streets. '70 The Great White Hope; The People Next Door. '72 They Only Kill Their Masters. '73 Magnum Force. '74 The Girl From Petrovka. '76 Midway; All the President's Men. '77 Julia. '78 Capricorn One. '80 The Fog.

HOLDEN, William

(1918–1981). Actor. Born: William Franklin Beedle; O'Fallon, Illinois, USA

From his discovery by Paramount in 1938 – he was spotted at the Pasadena Playhouse – Holden rose to become one of Hollywood's best loved and most dependable leading men of the Fifties. Army service in World War II removed some of the gloss from the likeable boy-next door of *Golden Boy* and *Our Town*. Though he lost nothing of his mild-mannered charm, there was a wary light in his eyes, a touch of cynicism in his ready smile, that could be indicative of courageous integrity or double-dealing. These qualities invested his role as the writer-cum-gigolo in *Sunset Boulevard* with unsuspected depth and brought him an Oscar for his playing of a prisoner-of-war in *Stalag 17*. After a somewhat lean spell in the Sixties he added a manic streak of brutality to his acting repertoire for *The Wild Bunch*, while he showed that he had lost nothing of his subtlety in *Network*. A widely travelled businessman and fervent wildlife conservationist – he tried to spend six months a year at his Mount Kenya safari club – Holden tended to play down his performing skills; he certainly made acting look a deceptively easy business.

Films include: 1939 Golden Boy; Invisible Stripes. '40 Our Town. '50 Sunset Boulevard; Born Yesterday. '51 Boots Malone. '53 Stalag 17. '54 Executive Suite; Sabrina (GB: Sabrina Fair). '56 Picnic. '57 The Bridge on the River Kwai (GB). '69 The Wild Bunch. '76 Network. '78 Fedora (GER).

HOLLIDAY, Judy

(1923–1966). Actress/singer. Born: Judith Tuvim; New York City, USA

A not-at-all dumb blonde (whose nasal vowel sounds would have had Professor Higgins writhing in agony), Holliday delighted audiences in *Adam's Rib*, as the daffy defendant in an assault case, and *Born Yesterday*, for which she won an Oscar as an ex-chorus cutie who is a lot brighter than she seems. She began in the theatre as a backstage telephone operator for Orson Welles' Mercury Theatre, making her stage debut as part of the Revuers, a cabaret group formed with Betty Comden and Adolph Green. She appeared in small roles in three films in 1944 before being cast in the Broadway production of *Born Yesterday* by its author Garson Kanin. Her success in *Adam's Rib* added weight to Kanin's insistence that Columbia cast her in the movie version of his play. Her superb comic timing and quirky charm – an influence on later dizzy comediennes such as Goldie Hawn – was not especially well served by her subsequent films.

Films include: 1944 Greenwich Village; Something for the Boys; Winged Victory. '49 Adam's Rib. '50 Born Yesterday. '52 The Marrying Kind. '54 It Should Happen to You; Phffft! '56 The Solid Gold Cadillac; Full of Life. '60 Bells Are Ringing.

HOLLOWAY, Stanley

(1890–1982). Actor/singer. Born: Stanley Augustus Holloway; Walthamstow, London, England

For six decades Holloway epitomized the ebullient cockney spirit or the deadpan humour of Northern England on stage, screen, radio and record, becoming a massive favourite with British audiences. The son of a law clerk whose family had long-standing showbusiness connections, Holloway started out as a soloist in his local church choir. World War I cut short singing tuition in Italy and he served with the British army in France. He made his West End debut in 1919 in *Kissing Time*, joined a music-hall act called The Co-Optimists, and established himself as an outstanding comic entertainer. His world-famous monologues, some of which were filmed, many of which were recorded on disc, are an unforgettable part of Britain's comedy heritage. Holloway made his film debut in 1921 in *The Rotters* and appeared regularly in British features. He crowned a series of major comic roles with his performance as Alfred Doolittle in *My Fair Lady*, for which he received an Oscar nomination. A song from this musical furnished the title of his autobiography, *Wiv' a Little Bit of Luck*, published in 1969.

Films include: 1934 Sing As We Go! '37 The Vicar of Bray. '41 Major Barbara. '44 Champagne Charlie. '45 The Way to the Stars (USA: Johnny in the Clouds). '47 Nicholas Nickleby. '48 Another Shore. '49 Passport to Pimlico. '51 The Lavender Hill Mob. '53 The Titfield Thunderbolt; The Beggars' Opera. '64 My Fair Lady (USA).

actor. High blood pressure ruled him out of service in World War II and a sudden dearth of leading men owing to the war led to an MGM contract and good roles in movies such as Hitchcock's *Lifeboat* and *A Bell for Adano*. When war ended, Hodiak was relegated to supporting roles or leads in B features, though he maintained a successful stage career. Married to the actress Anne Baxter from 1946–1953, he died of a heart attack.

Films include: 1943 A Stranger in Town; Song of Russia. '44 Lifeboat. '45 A Bell for Adano. '47 Desert Fury. '48 Homecoming. '49 Battleground. '50 A Lady Without a Passport. '51 Night Into Morning; The Sellout.

HOFFMAN, Dustin

(b. 1937). Actor. Born: Los Angeles, California, USA

Stardom began at 30 for Dustin Hoffman. The son of a movie-struck mother and a father who worked as a props man, Hoffman trained at the Pasadena Playhouse and with Lee Strasberg in New York, but barely eked out a living in theatre and television until the director Mike Nichols saw his performance in *Eh?* and cast him in *The Graduate*. The years of struggle seem to have left their mark on Hoffman's screen persona. Despite their remarkable – but superficial – diversity, his characters are generally thinkers or observers rather than doers; he excites the kind of ready sympathy accorded to a little kid picked on by big boys in a school playground, until his humiliation goads him into action. In *The Graduate*, the bully came in the shapely form of Anne Bancroft, in *Marathon Man* as a loony Nazi war criminal and in *Straw Dogs* as a gruesome bunch of yokels. In *Midnight Cowboy* and *Little Big Man* he is victimized by society in general, while in *Who Is Harry Kellerman and Why Is He Saying Those Terrible Things About Me?* he falls foul of his own alter-ego. In certain movies (*Midnight Cowboy*, *Papillon*, *All the President's Men*) he is afforded the protection of an all-American type, a Jon Voight, Steve McQueen or Robert Redford. However, this is not to detract from Hoffman's achievement in elevating the character actor to star status and his acting remains scrupulously naturalistic. He has been nominated for an Oscar three times – for *The Graduate*, *Midnight Cowboy* and *Lenny*, finally winning one for *Kramer vs Kramer*.

HOLM, Celeste

(b. 1919). Actress. Born: New York City, USA

The only child of busy parents – her father was New York representative of Lloyds of London, her mother a well-known portrait painter – blonde, blue-eyed Celeste Holm studied acting at the Univeristy of Chicago, making her Broadway debut at 19. Following her success as Ado Annie, the girl who couldn't say 'No', in the stage version of *Oklahoma!*, she was signed up by 20th Century-Fox, winning a Best Supporting Actress Oscar for her third film, *Gentleman's Agreement*. This witty, intelligent actress has received Oscar nominations for her roles in *Come to the Stable* and *All About Eve* and scored a number of personal movie triumphs, especially memorable being her duet with Frank Sinatra, 'Who Wants to Be a Millionaire', in *High Society*.

Films include: 1947 Gentleman's Agreement. '48 Chicken Every Sunday; The Snake Pit. '49 Everybody Does It; Come to the Stable. '50 Champagne for Caesar; All About Eve. '55 The Tender Trap. '56 High Society. '78 The Private Files of J. Edgar Hoover.

HOLM, Ian

(b. 1931). Actor. Born: Ian Holm Cuthbert; Ilford, Essex, England

Holm has made few major film appearances and it is to be hoped that his fine, daring performance as athletics coach Sam Mussabini in *Chariots of Fire*, which won him a second British Film Academy Award (the first had been as Gunner Flynn in *The Bofors Gun*), brings more good roles his way. Holm studied at RADA and spent 13 years with the Royal Shakespeare Company which firmly established his reputation. His career diversified into films and television, and a nervous breakdown in 1980 has tended to reduce stage appearances. His small stature (five feet six inches), of which he seems acutely conscious, has led to him playing mainly character parts, but he manages to bring assurance and subtlety to everything he touches, even endowing the part of an android in *Alien* with a kind of gruesome pathos, stealing the movie from the monster in the process.

Films include: 1968 The Bofors Gun; The Fixer (USA-HUNG); A Midsummer Night's Dream. '69 Oh! What a Lovely War. '71 A Severed Head; Nicholas and Alexandra (USA). '72 Mary, Queen of Scots; Young Winston. '73 The Homecoming (GB-USA). '74 Juggernaut. '76 Shout at the Devil. '79 Alien. '81 Chariots of Fire; Time Bandits.

HOLT, Jack

(1881–1951). Actor. Born: Charles John Holt; Winchester, Virginia, USA

Tall, slim, raw-boned and an expert horseman, Holt, though a church minister's son, was a natural star of early Westerns. Indeed, cowpunching was one of his occupations before he drifted into movies as a stunt man and extra for Universal. His first major

screen credit was as a cad in *A Cigarette, That's All* and villainous roles were initially his speciality, until he graduated into a two-fisted hero in action adventures and a debonair man-about-town in society dramas. Among the highlights of his long career was the lead opposite Mary Pickford in *The Little American* and starring roles in the 13 Westerns based on Zane Grey stories distributed by Paramount. The first of these, *Wanderer of the Wasteland*, employed the then revolutionary two-strip Technicolor process. Holt also starred in Columbia's first talkie, *The Donovan Affair*. His son was actor Tim Holt.

Films include: 1914 Salomy Jane. '15 A Cigarette, That's All. '17 The Little American. '24 Wanderer of the Wasteland. '25 Light of Western Stars. '28 Avalanche. '29 The Donovan Affair. '40 Passport to Alcatraz. '42 Cat People. '45 They Were Expendable. '46 My Pal Trigger. '49 Brimstone. '50 The Return of the Frontiersman. '51 Across the Wide Missouri.

HOLT, Seth

(1923–1971). Director. Born: Palestine

The son of British parents, Holt worked as an actor before World War II. He joined Strand Films as an editor in 1942, moving to Ealing Studios at the invitation of his brother-in-law, the director Robert Hamer, where Holt worked on the former's *Kind Hearts and Coronets* (1949). He made his directing debut with *Nowhere to Go*, but this well-paced thriller about an escaped prisoner was not successful at the box-office. He subsequently combined directing with editing, also working in television and commercials. A drink problem resulted in several unfinished projects and robbed his career of its early promise. As a director he specialized in taut, psychological thrillers that were more American in style than British. His credits as an editor include some fine films, such as *The Lavender Hill Mob* (1951), *The Titfield Thunderbolt* (1953), and *Saturday Night and Sunday Morning* (1960).

Films include: 1958 Nowhere to Go. '61 Taste of Fear (USA: Scream of Fear). '63 Station Six Sahara (GB-GER). '65 The Nanny. '67 Danger Route. '71 Blood From the Mummy's Tomb.

HOLT, Tim

(1918–1973). Actor. Born: Charles John Holt; Beverly Hills, California, USA

The acting bug bit Tim Holt at an early age when he appeared in *The Vanishing Pioneer* with his father, the silent screen star Jack Holt. He attended Culver Military Academy and studied drama, and later joined the Westwood Theatre Guild in Hollywood. At the age of 16 Holt was put under a long-term contract by the producer Walter Wanger and began appearing in Westerns. After service in World War II he returned to films and in 1952 was named the favourite Western actor in a popularity poll. His was a prolific yet strangely typecast career. His non-Western parts showed him to be a very able actor, as was proved by his roles as the spoilt son in Orson Welles' *The Magnificent Ambersons* and as a greedy gold prospector in *The Treasure of the Sierra Madre*, yet he was rarely offered anything outside his niche. He retired from films in his mid-fifties and worked as a radio-station advertising chief.

Top, from left to right: Celeste Holm in Chicken Every Sunday; Ian Holm in Nicholas and Alexandra; Jack Holt in The Great Plane Robbery (1940). Above: Tim Holt in The Magnificent Ambersons, with Dolores Costello. Right: Skip Homeier in The Burning Hills (1956). Below, from left to right: Oscar Homolka; Bob Hope (right) in Road to Utopia, with Bing Crosby; Anthony Hopkins; Bo Hopkins

208

Films include: 1928 The Vanishing Pioneer. '37 Stella Dallas. '39 Stagecoach. '41 Back Street. '42 The Magnificent Ambersons. '46 My Darling Clementine. '48 The Treasure of the Sierra Madre. '50 Law of the Badlands. '57 The Monster That Challenged the World. '71 This Stuff'll Kill Ya!

HOMEIER, Skip

(b. 1930). Actor. Born: George Vincent Homeier; Chicago, Illinois, USA

Skip Homeier was already a child performer on New York radio shows when his mother took him to a Broadway audition for the part of a young Nazi in the play *Tomorrow the World*. Having won the role, he appeared on stage for a year before re-creating his performance for the big screen. He then followed a career playing juvenile delinquents before being cast in numerous Westerns, usually as a villain.

Films include: 1944 Tomorrow the World. '46 Boy's Ranch. '48 Mickey. '50 The Gunfighter; Halls of Montezuma. '51 Fixed Bayonets. '54 The Black Widow. '57 No Road Back (GB); The Tall T. '64 Bullet for a Badman. '68 Tiger by the Tail. '77 The Greatest (USA-GB).

HOMOLKA, Oscar

(1898–1978). Actor. Born: Vienna, Austria

On completion of his studies at the Royal Academy of Dramatic Arts in Vienna, Oscar Homolka became a stage actor in Vienna and from 1918 was based in Berlin as one of Max Reinhardt's leading men. On Hitler's rise to power he moved to London and was very well-received in *Close Quarters* opposite Flora Robson. His film career had begun during the Twenties, but his appearance – burly and heavily eyebrowed with the look of an amiable bloodhound – lent itself less readily to cinematic leading roles. He was usually cast in character parts as villains or heads of spy networks and was most impressive as the anarchist manufacturing bombs in the back room of his cinema in Alfred Hitchcock's *Sabotage*. He became a familiar evil face as the Russian spymaster in *Funeral in Berlin* and *Billion Dollar Brain* and played General Kutuzov in *War and Peace*. During the late Thirties he worked primarily in America, becoming a United States citizen in 1943 and winning himself an Oscar nomination for his benevolent Norwegian uncle in *I Remember Mama*.

Films include: 1936 Sabotage (GB); Rhodes of Africa (GB). '37 Ebb Tide. '41 Rage in Heaven; Ball of Fire. '43 Mission to Moscow. '48 I Remember Mama. '49 Anna Lucasta '55 The Seven Year Itch. '56 War and Peace (IT-USA). '57 A Farewell to Arms '66 Funeral in Berlin (GB). '67 Billion Dollar Brain (GB). '74 The Tamarind Seed (GB).

HOPE, Bob

(b. 1903). Actor/comedian. Born: Leslie Townes Hope; Eltham, London

Bob Hope's father was a stonemason who left England for Cleveland, Ohio, in 1907. One of seven sons, Hope did anything to get himself noticed and developed his natural aptitude for wisecracks. He had studied tap dancing at school and after a variety of jobs he made his show business debut as part of a dancing act in a Fatty Arbuckle stage show. After splitting up with his dancing partner, Hope became a stand-up comedian and soon received offers to do guest spots in shows such as *Roberta* and *Ziegfeld Follies*. As a comedian he has a relaxed manner and aims his breakneck wisecracks on semi-political issues at an American middle-class audience. His film debut, for Paramount, in *The Big Broadcast* was ecstatically greeted, and the song he sang in it – 'Thanks for the Memory' – became his theme tune. Hope was then cast opposite Paulette Goddard in *The Cat and the Canary*, and excelled in one of the best murder-mystery comedies ever made. There followed Paramount's popular Road series, which cast Hope as the shifty, conceited, cowardly half of a partnership – the other half was smooth, relaxed and crooning Bing Crosby – that went in pursuit of money and Dorothy Lamour in various exotic locations. Hope was equally cowardly as Paleface Potter, facing up to Red Indians and Jane Russell, in *The Paleface*. During World War II he entertained the troops, and continued to do so through the Korean and Vietnamese wars. He has his own radio show, performs as master of ceremonies at functions such as the Academy Awards and Miss World, does television specials and, until the early Seventies, made one film a year for Paramount in order to produce and finance his own pictures. He has won five Special Academy Awards for his contribution to the industry.

Films include: 1938 The Big Broadcast of 1938. '39 The Cat and the Canary. '40 Road to Singapore. '41 Road to Zanzibar. '42 Road to Morocco. '44 Road to Utopia. '46 Monsieur Beaucaire. '47 Road to Rio. '48 The Paleface. '52 Road to Bali. '54 Casanova's Big Night. '57 Beau James. '60 The Facts of Life. '62 The Road to Hong Kong (GB). '63 Call Me Bwana (GB). '69 How to Commit Marriage. '72 Cancel My Reservation.

HOPKINS, Anthony

(b. 1931). Actor. Born: Port Talbot, Glamorganshire, Wales

Intending to be a concert pianist, Anthony Hopkins went to the Welsh College of Music and Drama where he discovered a natural skill for acting.

RADA and repertory company work followed and in 1965 he joined the National Theatre at the Old Vic. His first major role was in *The Dance of Death*, understudying Laurence Olivier. A stocky figure with a lilting Welsh accent, he is perhaps best in historical roles; his first film (*The Lion in Winter*) featured him as Richard the Lionheart. He has since gone on to appear in many films adapted from original stage plays and has been reasonably successful on television.

Films include: 1968 The Lion in Winter. '69 Hamlet; The Looking Glass War. '71 When Eight Bells Toll. '72 Young Winston. '73 A Doll's House. '74 The Girl From Petrovka (USA); Juggernaut. '77 Audrey Rose (USA); A Bridge Too Far (USA). '78 International Velvet; Magic (USA). '80 The Elephant Man (USA).

HOPKINS, Bo

(b. 1942). Actor. Born: Greenwood, South Carolina, USA

Bo Hopkins had a troubled upbringing, but perhaps it is as a result of his experiences that he is able to portray the tough, streetwise characters that have become his speciality. He was sent to a reform school in his teens and at 16 joined the army, almost immediately being sent to fight in Korea. On his return he joined the Actors' Studio and appeared in television Westerns such as *Gunsmoke* and *The Virginian*. His film debut was in *The Wild Bunch* as 'Crazy Lee', and despite being killed-off early in the action he gave an impressive performance. He came to prominence in *American Graffiti*, and followed this with a fine performance as a psychopathic killer who nevertheless engages audience sympathy in *The Killer Elite*. He has since appeared in *Midnight Express* and seems likely to continue in tough, macho adventure movies.

Films include: 1969 The Wild Bunch; The Bridge at Remagen. '70 Macho Callahan; Monte Walsh. '72 The Culpepper Cattle Company. '73 The Man Who Loved Cat Dancing; White Lightning; American Graffiti. '75 The Day of the Locust; Posse; The Killer Elite. '78 Midnight Express. '80 Rodeo Girl.

Above, from left to right: Miriam Hopkins in Design for Living; *Dennis Hopper in* Easy Rider; *Michael Hordern in* I'll Never Forget What's-is-Name; *Lena Horne; Brigitte Horney in* Savoy Hotel 217 *(1936, GER); Edward Everett Horton in* The Gay Divorcee; *Robert Hossein in* La Longue Marche; *John Houseman in* Three Days of the Condor. *Opposite page, below: Ron Howard (left); Leslie Howard in* The Scarlet Pimpernel

HOPKINS, Miriam

(1902–1972). Actress. Born: Ellen Miriam Hopkins; Savannah, Georgia, USA

Hopkins became a chorus-girl and made her stage debut in *The Music Box Revue*. Many straight dramatic roles followed and she emerged as a leading Broadway actress in the Twenties. In 1930 she went to Hollywood. Five foot two inches tall and blonde, she was first featured in stereotype roles but she was no demure blonde-beauty, a fact recognized by Ernst Lubitsch who cast her as clever leading ladies with acid tongues in his *Design for Living*, *The Smiling Lieutenant* and *Trouble in Paradise*. In the late Thirties she starred with Bette Davis in *The Old Maid* and *Old Acquaintance*, and there then began rumours of a feud between the two actresses which supposedly led to Hopkins giving up films in favour of Broadway in 1943. She returned some years later to play supporting roles in films like *The Heiress* and *The Chase*.

Films include: 1931 The Smiling Lieutenant; Dr Jekyll and Mr Hyde. '32 Trouble in Paradise. '33 Design for Living; The Story of Temple Drake. '35 Becky Sharp. '36 These Three. '39 The Old Maid. '43 Old Acquaintance. '49 The Heiress. '52 Carrie. '66 The Chase.

HOPPER, Dennis

(b. 1936). Actor/director. Born: Dodge City, Kansas, USA

After an apprenticeship on the Californian stage and a few small parts in films, Hopper won better roles in *Rebel Without a Cause* and *Giant* through his friendship with James Dean. But Hopper was an uncompromising rep-

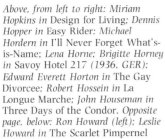

resentative of the hippie generation of the Sixties. Director Henry Hathaway (on *From Hell to Texas*) was among the first to brand him as uncontrollable, and the actor's career faltered until with Peter Fonda he was able to set up *Easy Rider*, which Hopper directed, acted in, and partly wrote. The film's phenomenal success helped him to form his own company, but the subsequent *The Last Movie*, although given the Best Picture award at Venice in 1971, proved too way-out for wide showing. He remains an influential movie-cult figure.

Films include: 1955 Rebel Without a Cause. '56 Giant. '58 From Hell to Texas (GB: Manhunt). '65 The Sons of Katie Elder. '67 Cool Hand Luke; The Trip. '69 Easy Rider (+dir). True Grit. '71 The Last Movie (+dir). '76 Mad Dog Morgan (AUS). '77 Der amerikanische Freund (GER-IT) (GB: The American Friend). '79 Apocalypse Now. '80 Out of the Blue (dir. only). '82 The Outsiders.

HORDERN, Michael

(b. 1911). Actor. Born: Berkhamstead, Hertfordshire, England

Michael Hordern was educated at Brighton College where he became interested in amateur dramatics. After a period as a schoolmaster and businessman he decided to turn professional in 1935. He made his stage debut in the West End production of *Night Sky*, joined Bristol Rep and then the Royal Shakespeare Company in Stratford. His film debut was in *The Girl in the News*, but with the onset of World War II he joined the Royal Navy. On resuming his career in 1945 he appeared in a succession of successful films – *School for Secrets*, *Passport to Pimlico*, *Train of Events* – including many with his great friend Richard Burton (*Cleopatra*, *The VIPs*, *The Spy Who Came in From the Cold*). However, Hordern is at his best in light comedy, where he has perfected a unique technique of hesitant delivery punctuated, with impeccable comic timing, by mannerisms such as grunts, sighs, winces, discreet coughs and nervous hand movements. His long, anxious face, like that of a

Bassett Hound, usually wears a world-weary or harrassed expression and he is generally cast as eccentrics or military leaders. Recently he has done work for television and his voice has brought Paddington Bear to life for numerous children.

Films include: 1940 The Girl in the News. '46 School for Secrets. '49 Passport to Pimlico; Train of Events. '63 Cleopatra; The VIPs. '65 The Spy Who Came in From the Cold. '56 The Spanish Gardener. '66 Khartoum; A Funny Thing Happened on the Way to the Forum (USA). '67 I'll Never Forget What's-'is-Name; How I Won the War; The Taming of the Shrew. '69 The Bed Sitting Room. '72 Alice's Adventures in Wonderland; England Made Me. '75 The Slipper and the Rose – the Story of Cinderella. '80 Shogun (USA-JAP).

HORNE, Lena

(b. 1917). Singer/actress. Born: New York City, USA

Dark, sultry and beautiful, Lena Horne began as a dancer at the Cotton Club in New York and toured as a singer with various bands. Her big breaks came with her appearances at Café Society in Greenwich Village and on stage in Los Angeles. She was signed by MGM and cast as the *femme fatale* in Vincente Minnelli's *Cabin in the Sky*, a duskyish member of an 'all-black' cast. On loan to Fox she was Selina in another all-black picture, *Stormy Weather*. But her career in movies was curtailed by protests from white audiences, resulting in several of her performances being edited out. She subsequently refused parts in *Showboat* (as a black girl passing for white) and *Pinky*. Then her association with singer-actor Paul Robeson led to further trouble and the blacklist in the Fifties. But singing success – with her gutsy voice (a Southern twang for speaking) and dynamic personality – could not be denied her, and she remains a popular celebrity, enjoying phenomenal success on Broadway and making occasional movie appearances. *Death of a Gunfighter* gave her a straight role in 1969.

Films include: 1942 Panama Hattie. '43 Stormy Weather; Thousands Cheer; Cabin

in the Sky. '44 Two Girls and a Sailor. '46 Ziegfeld Follies; Till the Clouds Roll By. '48 Words and Music. '69 Death of a Gunfighter. '78 The Wiz.

HORNEY, Brigitte

(b. 1911). Actress. Born: Berlin, Germany

Robert Siodmak's *Abschied* gave Brigitte Horney her first screen part. She played Hella, the girlfriend of a German youth who rebels against his sordid background and incurs the wrath of his father. A major German star through the Thirties and Forties, and dark-haired, deep-voiced and heavy lidded, she was generally cast as an especially seductive siren or a romantic heroine. In 1943 she was Catherine in the famous Ufa Nazi propaganda picture, *Munchhausen*. Before films she had attended the actors' school of the Deutsches Theatre in Berlin and first attracted attention at the Wurzburg State Theatre. German television has kept her name famous.

Films include: 1930 Abschied/So sind die Menschen. '32 Rasputin. '33 Heideschulmeister uwe Karsten. '38 Verklungene Melodie. '43 Munchhausen. '57 Der glaserne Turm (GB: The Glass Tower). '60 Nacht fiel uber Gotenhafen. '66 Ich suche einen Mann.

HORTON, Edward Everett

(1886–1970). Actor. Born: New York City, USA

While still a student at Columbia University, Horton made his stage debut and then began touring in stock companies. Arriving in California in 1918, he and his brother W.D. Horton set up their own theatrical production team and were moderately successful before film work lured Edward away. Tall and hawk-like, he excelled as a flustered, neurotic type, always apprehensive and given to bringing a clenched fist to his mouth while muttering 'Oh dear, oh dear!' at impending doom. Although good as a comedian in silents such as *Ruggles of Red Gap*, he really proved his talent in the talkies. He appeared in *The Hottentot*, one of Warners' first sound pictures, and then gave superb support to Fred Astaire and Ginger Rogers in several popular musicals of the Thirties. He had just the right touch for Ernst Lubitsch's sophisticated comedies, but in the latter stages of his career he concentrated on stage work.

Films include: 1923 Ruggles of Red Gap. '25 Beggar on Horse Back. '29 The Hottentot. '31 The Front Page. '32 Trouble in Paradise. '33 Design for Living; Alice in Wonderland. '34 The Gay Divorcee (GB: The Gay Divorce). '35 Top Hat. '37 Lost Horizon; Shall We Dance. '38 Bluebeard's Eighth Wife. '44 Arsenic and Old Lace. '57 The Story of Mankind. '64 Sex and the Single Girl.

HOSSEIN, Robert

(b. 1927). Actor/director. Born: Robert Hosseinoff; Paris, France

A stage actor and director, and the author of two successful plays, Hossein has written, directed and starred in his own films, and played leading roles for other directors (three times for Roger Vadim). The films he directed were violent melodramas; the Hossein character tends to be disturbing, unpredictable, and often villainous.

Films include: 1956 Crime et Chatiment (GB: Crime and Punishment). '63 Les Grands Chemins (FR-IT) (GB: Flesh and Blood); Chair de Poule (FR-IT) (GB: Highway Pick Up). '64 La Mort d'un Tueur (+dir) (FR-IT); Les Yeux Cernes (+dir) (FR-IT). '66 La Longue Marche. '67 J'ai Tué Raspoutine (+dir) (FR-IT) (GB: I Killed Rasputin). '69 Une Corde . . . un Colt (+dir) (FR-IT). '71 Le Casse (FR-IT) (USA/GB: The Burglars). '73 Don Juan 1973, ou Si Don Juan Etait une Femme (FR-IT) (USA/GB: Don Juan or, If Don Juan Were a Woman). '75 Le Faux-Cul. '78 L'Amant de Poche (GB: Lover Boy). '81 Les Uns et Les Autres (USA: The Ins and the Outs).

HOUSEMAN, John

(b. 1902). Producer/actor. Born: Jacques Haussmann; Bucharest, Romania

The son of an Alsatian father and an English mother, and educated at Clifton, Houseman went to America as a grain broker and stayed on as a stage producer and founder, with Orson Welles, of the Mercury Theatre. Going on with Welles to Hollywood, Houseman as producer played a crucial part in the fashioning of *Citizen Kane* (1940). His later career was split between films, TV and the theatre. As a creative producer, he worked on some of the best films of Nicholas Ray, Minnelli, Lang and Ophuls. He wrote a lucid and penetrating autobiography, and he turned to acting, first as the shifty admiral in *Seven Days in May* (1964), and then as the acid-tongued professor of law in *The Paper Chase* (1973), a performance which won him an Academy Award as Best Supporting Actor.

Films include: 1945 The Unseen; Tuesday in November. '46 The Blue Dahlia. '48 They Live by Night; Letter From an Unknown Woman. '52 The Bad and the Beautiful. '53 Julius Caesar. '54 Executive Suite. '55 The Cobweb. '56 Lust for Life. '62 Two Weeks in Another Town. '66 This Property Is Condemned. '75 Rollerball (act); Three Days of the Condor (act). '79 Old Boyfriends (act).

HOWARD, Leslie

(1893–1943). Actor. Born: Leslie Howard Stainer; London, England

Leslie Howard was born of Hungarian parents and worked in a bank until the outbreak of World War I. In 1917 he was sent home suffering from shell-shock and was advised to take up acting as therapy. He became moderately well-known on the London stage, but it was on Broadway that his career took off. Slim, fragile, blond-haired and of a somewhat fey appearance, Howard nonetheless became America's idea of the perfect English gent. During the Thirties he began to appear as the lead in films opposite some of the most glamorous leading ladies of the time. Roles that perhaps sum him up include the effete Sir Percy Blakeney in *The Scarlet Pimpernel*, the eccentric Professor Higgins in *Pygmalion* – which he also co-directed – and Ashley Wilkes, the honourbound Southern gentleman in *Gone With the Wind*. The mystique and sense of romantic tragedy inherent in all his characters finally took over his real life, for he was killed in 1943 while flying back to London after a secret wartime mission to Lisbon. Shortly before his death Howard had begun to take an increasing interest in film direction.

Films include: 1932 Service for Ladies (GB). '34 Of Human Bondage (USA). '35 The Scarlet Pimpernel (GB). '36 The Petrified Forest (USA). '38 Pygmalion (+co-dir) (GB). '39 Gone With the Wind (USA); Intermezzo (USA) (GB: Escape to Happiness). '41 Pimpernel Smith (GB) (USA: Mister V); 49th Parallel (GB). '42 The First of the Few (GB). '43 The Gentle Sex (co-dir. only).

HOWARD, Ron

(b. 1954). Actor. Born: Duncan, Oklahoma, USA

As a child, Ron Howard appeared on stage in *The Seven Year Itch* with his parents, and so began a continuous series of juvenile and adolescent roles. He played Andy Griffith's son for eight years in the television series *The Andy Griffith Show*; he co-starred with Henry Fonda in *The Smith Family*; and was sidekick to The Fonz (Henry Winkler) in the nostalgic world of *Happy Days*. Freckled and clean-cut, Howard was one of the Sixties teenagers in *American Graffiti*, later taking up with the Roger Corman stable of young, ambitious directors. In 1980 he refused to renew his contract as an actor in favour of directing Bette Davis in the television movie *Skyward*, thereby 'fulfilling a lifelong dream'. It seems likely that his future lies in direction.

Films include: 1959 The Journey. '62 The Music Man. '63 The Courtship of Eddie's Father. '71 The Wild Country. '73 American Graffiti. '74 The Spikes Gang. '76 Eat My Dust; The Shootist. '77 Grand Theft Auto. '79 More American Graffiti.

HOWARD, Trevor

(b. 1916). Actor. Born: Cliftonville, Kent, England

After travelling the world with his family as a boy, Trevor Howard studied at RADA and while there made his stage debut in *Revolt in the Reformatory* in 1934. He then had a successful stage career until he joined the army at the outbreak of World War II. Invalided out in 1944, he made his screen debut that year in *The Way Ahead* and leapt to stardom as the hesitant, worthy doctor stoically enduring his *Brief Encounter* with Celia Johnson. He went on to give some fine performances, including his sharp and bitter ex-airman in *They Made Me a Fugitive*, his stiff-upper-lip British officer in *The Third Man*, his weak, amoral and tragic figure in *Outcast of the Islands* and his mystical recluse in *Light Years Away*. As Howard worked his way through romantic, heroic and finally eccentric roles, so his appearance changed with them, his always interesting face becoming increasingly craggy and angst-ridden with the years. From the mid-Fifties he appeared in one or two Hollywood films but seems to have lacked the appeal necessary to make him as popular in America as he is in Britain. He is married to the actress Helen Cherry.

Films include: 1945 The Way to the Stars (USA: Johnny in the Clouds); Brief Encounter. **'47** So Well Remembered; They Made Me a Fugitive (USA: I Became a Criminal). **'49** The Third Man. **'51** Outcast of the Islands. **'53** The Heart of the Matter. **'57** Manuela (USA: Stowaway Girl). **'58** The Roots of Heaven. **'60** Sons and Lovers. **'68** The Charge of the Light Brigade. **'80** Light Years Away. **'82** Gandhi (GB-IND).

HOWARD, William K.

(1899–1954). Director. Born: William Kerrigan Howard; St Mary's, Ohio, USA

Having studied engineering and law, Howard drifted into film distribution, becoming the sales manager for the Vitagraph studio. He served in World War I, after which he decided to take on Hollywood. He began working as an assistant director at Universal before making his solo debut for Fox. His early films were primarily Westerns and featured beautiful shots of plains and sombre monoliths. *White Gold* is a strange, stylized exploration of passion and jealousy in a Western setting, and the influence of Howard's favourite director, F.W. Murnau, is apparent in the atmosphere. His later films saw him developing into a master of melodrama. In the late Thirties he went to England to make three films for Alexander Korda, including the costume spectacular *Fire Over England*, but on his return to America his career suffered an unexpected decline, linked perhaps to his excessive drinking. *Johnny Come Lately*, starring James Cagney, was Howard's last picture before he was virtually forced into retirement.

Films include: 1923 Let's Go. **'27** White Gold. **'30** Scotland Yard. **'31** Transatlantic. **'32** Sherlock Holmes. **'33** The Power and the

Glory. **'35** Mary Burns, Fugitive. **'36** The Princess Comes Across. **'37** Fire Over England (GB); The Squeaker (GB). **'43** Johnny Come Lately.

HOWE, James Wong

(1899–1976). Cinematographer. Born: Wong Tung Jim; Kwantung, Canton, China

James Wong Howe arrived in America with his parents when he was four. After completing his education he tried his hand as a boxer before pursuing his childhood interest in photography and entering films in 1917. He became Cecil B. DeMille's assistant cameraman and in 1922 graduated to chief cameraman at Paramount. During the Twenties and Thirties he became well-known for his realistic style. Refusing to accept the restrictions imposed on camera mobility owing to the bulk of the new sound equipment, he used hand-held cameras, put them on roller skates, in wheelchairs, anything to create a realistic image. He also used wide-angle lenses innovatively and in some films – such as *Transatlantic* – photographed sets with ceilings in order to create a claustrophobic environment. His eye for lighting enhanced all his other skills. In 1933 he went to MGM, where they credited him as James Wong Howe in order to make him sound more exotic on their publicity sheets – he had hitherto been known as James Howe. Unfortunately he didn't find the studio as inspiring as his name and while there merely conformed to their rather bland style. With his move to Warners in the Forties he entered his most prolific and creative period. He moulded the heavily atmospheric moods of the studio's grim melodramas, making himself a household name in the process. He was awarded Oscars for his work on *The Rose Tattoo* and *Hud* and nominated six other times.

Films include: 1924 Peter Pan. **'31** Transatlantic. **'33** The Power and the Glory. **'34** The Thin Man. **'38** The Adventures of Tom Sawyer; Algiers. **'40** Abe Lincoln in Illinois. **'41** Kings Row. **'45** Objective, Burma! **'47** Pursued; Body and Soul. **'57** Sweet Smell of Success. **'63** Hud. **'70** The Molly Maguires.

HOWERD, Frankie

(b. 1921). Actor/comedian. Born: Francis Howard; York, England

He was turned down by RADA and worked, discontentedly, in insurance while entering various talent contests without reward. He was next rejected by ENSA during the war but his break came shortly afterwards in the radio show *Variety Band Box*. Frankie Howerd specializes in risqué humour delivered with intimate ease, a camp flick of the wrist and roll of the eyes. His film debut was in *The Runaway Bus* in 1954, yet his screen career has always remained incidental to his variety performances. In *The Ladykillers* he played a barrow-boy persecuted by a little old lady, and he brought his

Above, far left: Frankie Howerd in Up Pompeii. *Above left: Trevor Howard in* The Charge of the Light Brigade. *Above: Jack Hulbert in* The Ghost Train. *Below, far left: Sally Ann Howes in* Pink String and Sealing Wax. *Below left: Rock Hudson in* Twilight for the Gods *(1958). Below: Benita Hume in* Lord Camber's Ladies

bawdy Roman slave of the television series *Up Pompeii* to the big screen with great aplomb. 'What I try to do is give the *impression* of being spontaneous. It's acting, and if I can claim to be an actor at all, that is what I do with it.'

Films include: 1954 The Runaway Bus. '55 The Ladykillers. '58 Further Up the Creek. '63 The Cool Mikado. '66 The Great St Trinian's Train Robbery. '67 Carry On Doctor. '71 Up Pompeii; Up the Chastity Belt. '73 The House in Nightmare Park. '78 Sergeant Pepper's Lonely Hearts Club Band (USA-GER).

HOWES, Sally Ann

(b. 1930). Actress. Born: St John's Wood, London, England

A starring role at the age of 12 in *Thursday's Child* cured Sally Ann Howes of wanting to be a vet and won her a contract with Ealing. Thus began a successful career as a child

actress which saw her in such roles as the plucky younger daughter of a Victorian patriarch in *Pink String and Sealing Wax*. As an adult she had more difficulty, only finding her stride when she turned to musicals. She took over from Julie Andrews in the Broadway production of *My Fair Lady* and returned to films as Truly Scrumptious in *Chitty Chitty Bang Bang*.

Films include: 1943 Thursday's Child. '44 The Halfway House. '45 Dead of Night; Pink String and Sealing Wax. '47 Nicholas Nickleby. '48 Anna Karenina. '49 The History of Mr Polly; Stop-Press Girl. '57 The Admirable Crichton (USA: Paradise Lagoon). '68 Chitty Chitty Bang Bang.

HUBLEY, John

(1914–1977). Animator. Born: Marinette, Wisconsin, USA

A graduate of the Art Center of Los Angeles, Hubley was apprenticed to the Disney Studio in 1935, working on *Fantasia* and other features. After the war Hubley helped to found United Productions of America (UPA), and for five years was a supervising director. UPA revolutionized American animation with its crisply economical style, sophisticated design and adroitness with human character. In 1955 Hubley and his wife Faith, a film and music editor and script supervisor, formed their own company, Storyboard Inc., and eventually the husband-and-wife team won over thirty national and international awards. *Moonbird* and *The Hole* won Oscars.

Films include: 1938 Snow White and the Seven Dwarfs (assoc. dir.) '40 Pinocchio (assoc. dir.) '41 Fantasia (assoc. dir); Dumbo (assoc. dir.) '42 Bambi (assoc. dir.) '50 Ragtime Bear (dir.) '52 Rooty Toot Toot. '57 Adventures of an Asterisk. '58 Tender Game. '59 Harlem Wednesday (co-dir); Moonbird. '61 Of Stars and Men. '63 The Hole (co-dir.) '64 The Hat (co-dir.)

HUDSON, Rock

(1925–1985). Actor. Born: Roy Scherer; Winnetka, Illinois, USA

Rock Hudson, a former truck-driver, had had no acting experience outside school plays when his agent persuaded Warners to give him a chance in 1948. Universal took over the contract and for some years subjected the handsome young man to intensive grooming. Hudson played numerous small parts and a few leads before his first real success in Douglas Sirk's *Magnificent Obsession* in 1954. Sirk saw the capacity for deep feeling behind the muscular façade, and used Hudson eight times, eliciting a superb performance from him as the drunken reporter in *The Tarnished Angels* (1957). The Sixties revealed a talent for comedy, in a series of Doris Day pictures, and especially in Hawks' *Man's Favorite Sport?*

Films include: 1948 Fighter Squadron. '50 Winchester '73. '54 Magnificent Obsession. '55 All That Heaven Allows. '56 Written on the Wind; Giant. '57 A Farewell to Arms. '58 Pillow Talk. '63 A Gathering of Eagles. '64 Man's Favorite Sport. '66 Seconds. '67 Tobruk. '71 Pretty Maids All in a Row. '80 The Mirror Crack'd (GB).

HUGHES, Howard

(1905–1976). Producer. Born: Houston, Texas, USA

Howard Hughes' father founded the family fortune three years after Howard's birth by setting up the Hughes Tool Company. Howard Hughes Sr died in 1924, leaving a sizeable inheritance to his son, who became involved in film production in 1926. Lewis Milestone won an Oscar as Best Comedy Director for his production of *Two Arabian Nights* and Hughes himself directed the flying epic *Hell's Angels*. In 1932 he left Hollywood to found the Hughes Aircraft Company. He returned to films in 1940 when, after sacking Howard Hawks, he began to direct a sultry Western, *The Outlaw*, completed in 1941 but only properly released, with a controversially vulgar breast-obsessed advertising campaign, in 1946. With his two films as director Hughes discovered two stars, Jean Harlow and Jane Russell. In 1948 he bought RKO and in 1951 he conducted a virulent anti-communist witch-hunt, virtually destroying the studio, though he still managed to sell it several years later at a profit, despite a horrendous loss-making record. After the mid-Fifties his interest in films was confined to marrying actress Jean Peters in 1957 – they separated in 1966 and divorced in 1970. He became a mystery man, seen by almost no-one in the last ten years of his life. He has inspired a television film drama and several movies, notably Jonathan Demme's *Melvin and Howard* (1980) and part of Orson Welles' *F for Fake* (1973).

Films include: 1927 Two Arabian Nights. '28 The Racket. '30 Hell's Angels (+dir). '31 The Front Page. '32 Scarface/Scarface, the Shame of a Nation; Sky Devils. '41 The Outlaw (+dir). '50 Vendetta. '51 His Kind of Woman (co-prod); Jet Pilot (exec. prod). '56 The Conqueror (exec. prod).

HUGHES, Ken

(b. 1922). Director/screenwriter. Born: Liverpool, England

At the age of 14 Ken Hughes made a film which won an award in an *Amateur Cine World* contest. He then worked in the projection room of a local cinema, as a sound boy, and eventually sound engineer, at the BBC, and as a maker of documentaries for World Wide Pictures. The first of his 25 or so features came in 1952. Hughes' fortunes have varied with the ups and downs of the British industry. *Joe Macbeth* was a taut gangster thriller, and *The Trials of Oscar Wilde* thoughtful if a little stolid, but too often Hughes has been reduced to giving banal material an American gloss. His *Cromwell* was described by one critic as 'a dreadfully forlorn piece of talking history', and its inaccuracies have outraged at least one expert on the period. *Alfie, Darling* was a misguided attempt to catch up with the adventures of the Sixties Casanova.

Films include: 1952 Wide Boy. '54 The House Across the Lake (USA: Heatwave). '55 Joe Macbeth; The Brain Machine; Little Red Monkey; Confession (USA: The

Deadliest Sin); Time Slip (USA: The Atomic Man). '60 In The Nick; Jazz Boat; The Trials of Oscar Wilde (sc. only) (USA: The Man With The Green Carnation). '66 Drop Dead Darling. '68 Chitty Chitty Bang Bang. '70 Cromwell. '75 Alfie, Darling (USA: Oh, Alfie).

HULBERT, Jack

(1896–1978). Actor. Born: Ely, Cambridgeshire, England

He was educated at Westminster School and Cambridge, where he spent most of his energy on acting and athletics. A play he was in transferred to London and he was spotted by theatre manager Robert Courtneidge who gave him his break as a professional actor in 1913 and – after army service during the war – his daughter's hand in marriage. Jack Hulbert and Cicely Courtneidge starred together in cheerful and popular musicals in the Twenties, repeating their success in films with the coming of sound, and back on the stage again after 1938. Tall, with a large, protuberant chin, Jack was a beaming, irrepressible incompetent always foiling the crooks and getting the girl, though his last couple of roles – for example, as plain-clothes policeman Mike Pemberton in *Kate Plus Ten* – were straighter. Brother Claude (1900–1964) excelled as absent-minded, upper-class buffoons. The pair are at their best together in *Bulldog Jack*, co-starring Fay Wray.

Films include: 1931 The Ghost Train; Sunshine Susie. '32 Jack's the Boy; Love on Wheels. '34 The Camels Are Coming. '35 Bulldog Jack. '36 Jack of All Trades (+co-dir) (USA: The Two of Us). '37 Take My Tip; Paradise for Two (USA: The Gaiety Girls). '38 Kate Plus Ten. '40 Under Your Hat. '60 The Spider's Web. '73 Not Now, Darling.

HUME, Benita

(1906–1967). Actress. Born: Egerton, Lancashire, England

Hume was educated at Clifton College in Bristol and RADA, and first appeared on stage at 17. Then came a film debut in the Jack Buchanan vehicle *The Happy Ending* in 1925. In 1933 she joined RKO in Hollywood, returning to Britain for lead roles in such films as *Jew Suss* and *The Private Life of Don Juan*. In 1938 she married Ronald Colman and retired. After Colman died she married another actor, George Sanders. Fetching, brown-haired and brown-eyed, she was not just reserved for colourless, upper-class ladies (though that's what she seems in films like *The Constant Nymph*). She was tough and appealing as an actress caught up in a web of intrigue and murder in *The Clue of the New Pin* and as the flower-girl mistress in *Lord Camber's Ladies* and other British dramas.

Films include: 1927 Easy Virtue. '28 The Constant Nymph. '29 The Clue of the New Pin. '32 Service for Ladies (USA: Reserved for Ladies); Lord Camber's Ladies '33 The Worst Woman in Paris (USA). '34 The Private Life of Don Juan; Jew Suss (USA: Power). '36 Moonlight Murder (USA) '37 The Last of Mrs Cheyney (USA).

Left: screen character actor and veteran of the stage, Arthur Hunnicutt. Below left: Gayle Hunnicutt in Eye of the Cat

Below: Martita Hunt as the mad Miss Havisham in Great Expectations, *a highly regarded adapation of the much loved novel*

HUNNICUTT, Arthur

(1911–1979). Actor. Born: Gravelly, Arkansas, USA

Forced by lack of funds to leave Arkansas State Teachers College, Arthur Hunnicutt worked in medicine shows and as a teacher during the Depression, raising money to attend the Phidela Rice School of Voice in Cleveland, Ohio. He went with Rice to the Massachusetts island of Martha's Vineyard, off Cape Cod, to appear in summer stock. His Broadway debut was in *Love's Old Sweet Song* in 1940. He entered films in 1942, playing character parts, frequently in Westerns. He was tall and lean with a slow country drawl that served him well in such roles through over three decades in the movies. Hunnicutt was nominated for an Oscar as Best Supporting Actor in *The Big Sky* and his most memorable later role was as the sidekick of John Wayne and Robert Mitchum in *El Dorado*, both films by Howard Hawks.

Films include: 1942 Wildcat. '49 Lust for Gold; Pinky. '51 Distant Drums; The Red Badge of Courage. '52 The Big Sky; The Lusty Men. '54 The French Line. '55 The Last Command. '63 The Cardinal. '65 Cat Ballou. '76 The Adventures of Bullwhip Griffin; El Dorado. '74 Harry and Tonto.

HUNNICUTT, Gayle

(b. 1943). Actress. Born: Fort Worth, Texas, USA

A luscious Texas rose with glorious red-brown hair, Gayle Hunnicutt is determined to be a serious actress rather than just a pretty starlet. After studying at Texas Christian University, she won a scholarship to major in theatre arts at the University of California at Los Angeles. A visiting lecturer, the director Jean Renoir, encouraged her ambition to become a professional actress. She worked in an advertising agency while acting at night in the Cahuenga Playhouse, meanwhile attending a speech clinic to get rid of her Texas accent (she can now virtually pass for English). She had already played a minor part in *The Wild Angels* and done some television work when actor George Peppard recommended her to the director John Guillermin for a *femme fatale* role in *P.J.* After a couple of Hollywood glamour parts, she went to England, having married actor-producer David Hemmings in 1968, a stormy union that ended in divorce in 1974, though not before he had directed her in *Running Scared*. She is still based in London and married to the political journalist Simon Jenkins. She has appeared in British and European as well as American films, mostly of little distinction. She does her best work in British television, notably in adaptations of Henry James' novels, and in the theatre.

Films include: 1966 The Wild Angels. '68 P.J. (GB: A New Face in Hell). '69 Eye of the Cat; Marlowe. '70 Fragment of Fear (GB). '72 Running Scared (GB). '73 The Legend of Hell House (GB); Scorpio; Voices (GB). '76 The Sell Out (GB-IT). '77 Blazing Magnum (IT-CAN) (USA: Strange Shadows in an Empty Room). '78 Once in Paris.

HUNT, Martita

(1900–1969). Actress. Born: Argentina

She was educated in Bournemouth, England, after living on a ranch in Argentina until she was ten. She then studied for the stage and made her professional debut with Liverpool Repertory Company, and went on to build up a fine reputation as a character actress, notably in Shakespeare, Wilde and Ibsen. Her triumph was 600 performances of *The Madwoman of Chaillot* in New York in 1948. Martita Hunt's film career, which began with a bit in *A Rank Outsider* in 1920, has been scattered with outstanding performances – most famous of all her Miss Havisham in *Great Expectations*, as broken, decrepit, sinister and daunting as Dickens' original. Eccentric, dominating *grandes dames*, in fact, gave the actress her best opportunities.

Films include: 1937 The Mill on the Floss. '45 The Wicked Lady. '46 Great Expectations. '48 Anna Karenina. '56 Anastasia. '57 The Admirable Crichton. '58 Bonjour Tristesse (USA). '62 The Wonderful World of the Brothers Grimm. '64 Becket. '65 Bunny Lake Is Missing.

HUNT, Marsha

(b. 1917). Actress. Born: Marcia Virginia Hunt; Chicago, Illinois, USA

A pretty, pleasing natural performer, Marsha Hunt has worked long and hard in films without ever winning the appreciation due to her. She studied at Theodore Irving School and modelled before signing with Paramount in 1935, later moving to MGM where her roles included Mary Bennett in *Pride and Prejudice*. Blacklisted in the early Fifties, she soon resumed her career, working increasingly in television. She is married to screenwriter Robert Presnell and now concentrates on civil rights and other humanitarian causes.

Films include: 1936 Hollywood Boulevard; The Accusing Finger. '39 These Glamour Girls. '40 Pride and Prejudice. '41 Blossoms in the Dust; Unholy Partners. '43 The Human Comedy. '44 Music for Millions. '56 No Place To Hide. '57 Bombers B 52 (GB: No Sleep Till Dawn). '71 Johnny Got His Gun.

HUNTE, Otto

(1881–1947). Art director. Born: Hamburg, Germany

Otto Hunte was the skilled, versatile art director who worked on Fritz Lang's films of the Twenties in Germany. The characteristically Gothic and menacing buildings and landscapes he contributed to *Destiny* and *Die Nibelungen* contrast dramatically with the stark modernity of the underground city in *Metropolis*. Like most German designers, Hunte worked in a team. He usually did the initial sketches with Erich Kettelhut and Karl Vollbrecht elaborating on them, and Lang adding his own personal visionary effects. During World War II, Hunte worked on Nazi propaganda films like *Jew Suss* and *Gold*, creating a laboratory for the latter that contained an atomic reactor so convincing that the film prints were seized by the Allies after the war. At the same time Hunte designed the anti-Nazi film *The Murderers Are Amongst Us*. Apart from *Metropolis*, his best-known set is the cinema's most decadent nightclub – *The Blue Angel*.

Films include: 1919 Die Spinnen (Part 1: Der goldene See) (USA/GB: The Spiders). '20 Die Spinnen (Part 2: Das brillianten Schiff) (USA/GB: The Spiders). '21 Der müde Tod (co-art dir) (USA: Between Two Worlds, re-ed. and shown as Beyond the Wall in 1927; GB: Destiny); Das indische

Grabmal (Part 1: Die Sendung des Yoghis; Part 2: Das indische Grabmal) (USA: Mysteries of India). '22 Dr Mabuse der Spieler (Part 1: Dr Mabuse der Spieler; Part 2: Inferno-Menschen der Zeit). '24 Die Nibelungen (Part 1: Siegfried; Part 2: Kriemhilds Rache) (USA: Part 1: Siegfried; Part 2: Kriemhild's Revenge). '27 Metropolis. '29 Frau im Mond (USA: By Rocket to the Moon; GB: The Girl in the Moon). '30 Der blaue Engel (USA/GB: The Blue Angel). '34 Gold. '40 Jüd Suss/Jew Suss. '46 Die Mörder sind unter uns (USA/GB: The Murderers Are Amongst Us). '47 Razzia (GB: Raid).

HUNTER, Ian

(1900–1975). Actor. Born: Kenilworth, near Cape Town, South Africa

A solid, grey-eyed six-footer best known for such kingly screen roles as Theseus in *A Midsummer Night's Dream* and Richard the Lionheart in *The Adventures of Robin Hood*, Hunter was, in fact, capable of a much wider range. He was the breezy, enterprising down-on-his-luck hero in Michael Powell's *Something Always Happens*; the mild, mystical Cambreau standing up to a bunch of desperados in *Strange Cargo*; and the ageing, gullible husband of a murderous *femme fatale* (Margaret Lockwood) in *Bedelia*. Educated in England, he joined the army in 1917 and fought in France. Afterwards he studied drama and made his stage debut in 1919, his screen debut in 1922. Then came a contract with Warner Brothers in Hollywood in 1934, and there followed a long, steady, unspectacular career in films, with much stage work in the Fifties.

Films include: 1930 Escape. '32 The Sign of Four '34 Something Always Happens. '35 The Phantom Light; A Midsummer Night's Dream (USA). '38 The Adventures of Robin Hood (USA). '40 Strange Cargo (USA). '41 Dr Jekyll and Mr Hyde (USA). '46 Bedelia. '49 Edward My Son. '56 The Battle of the River Plate (USA: Pursuit of the Graf Spee). '61 Dr Blood's Coffin.

HUNTER, Jeffrey

(1927–1969). Actor. Born: Henry H. McKinnies Jr; New Orleans, Louisiana, USA

Jeffrey Hunter was offered a screen test by 20th Century-Fox after playing in a university production of *All My Sons*. Cast in films like *The Searchers* (in which he was John Wayne's half-breed companion), the good-looking Hunter became something of a teenage idol – it caused a minor scandal when it was announced that he would play Christ in the biblical epic *King of Kings*. His career faltered when the critics attacked his acting ability, and he turned to drink. He died after a fall at his own home.

Films include: 1951 The Frogmen. '52 Red Skies of Montana; Belles on Their Toes; Lure of the Wilderness. '55 Seven Angry Men. '56 The Searchers. '57 The True Story of Jesse James; The Way to the Gold. '58 Count Five and Die (GB). '60 Sergeant Rutledge. '61 King of Kings. '68 Frau wirtin hat auch einen grafen (A-GER-IT) (GB: Sexy Susan Sins Again).

HUNTER, Kim

(b. 1922). Actress. Born: Janet Cole; Detroit, Michigan, USA

Hunter gave a very moving performance as the American radio operator, June, who falls in love with the doomed RAF pilot (David Niven) in the first blazing moments of Michael Powell's *A Matter of Life and Death*. Her reddish-haired, apple-pie good looks were equally well-used in the menacing occult world of Val Lewton's *Seventh Victim* – her debut, as a girl in search of her sister – and to the Southern malaise of Elia Kazan's *A Streetcar Named Desire*, in which she gave an Oscar-winning portrayal as Blanche's level-headed sister Stella Kowalski (having played the part successfully on Broadway). Hunter had worked in stock from the age of 17 and was spotted for films by David O. Selznick. The Red Scare of the early Fifties delayed her progress to stardom and she didn't get a decent chance again until the role of the liberal chimpanzee Dr Zira in *Planet of the Apes* came along, but this only mocked her loveliness. She has worked extensively in television and still makes the occasional film appearance.

HUNTER, Tab

(b. 1931). Actor. Born: Arthur Gelien; New York City, USA

With his athletic build, blond hair and blue eyes, Tab Hunter was rapidly snapped up by the film companies in the Fifties. He appeared in a series of sea and surf films as a glamorous all-American boy – his looks being more important to his career than his acting ability. Returning to the screen in the Eighties in films like *Polyester* and *Grease II*, he has capitalized on the modern taste for camp nostalgia.

Films include: 1954 Track of the Cat. '58 Lafayette Escadrille (GB: Hell Bent for Glory). '59 That Kind of Woman. '64 Ride the Wild Surf. '65 War Gods of the Deep (USA-GB) (GB: City Under the Sea). '72 The Life and Times of Judge Roy Bean; The Arousers/Sweet Kill. '81 Timber Tramps; Polyester; Grease II.

Films include: 1943 The Seventh Victim. '44 Tender Comrade. '46 A Matter of Life and Death (USA: Stairway to Heaven). '51 A Streetcar Named Desire. '52 Deadline USA (GB: Deadline). '56 Bermuda Affair (GB). '64 Lilith. '68 Planet of the Apes. '70 Beneath the Planet of the Apes. '71 Escape From the Planet of the Apes.

Above left: Marsha Hunt in None Shall Escape *(1944). Above: Ian Hunter in* Eight O'clock Walk *(1954). Above right: Jeffrey Hunter in* King of Kings. *Below left: Kim Hunter in A*

HUPPERT, Isabelle

(b. 1955). Actress. Born: Paris, France

Petite, freckled Isabelle Huppert is a quiet actress who often plays victims or failures, but she plays them with resolve and determination. After studying at the Conservatoire in Versailles, she landed her first film part in 1971, and in 1976 scored her first real success as the vulnerable protagonist of *The Lacemaker*. Two years later she won the Best Actress Award at Cannes for her study of a murderess in Chabrol's *Violette Nozière*. She went to America to play with great sensitivity in Michael Cimino's ill-fated *Heaven's Gate*.

Films include: 1976 Le Juge et l'Assassin. '77 La Dentellière (FR-SWITZ-GER) (USA/GB: The Lacemaker); Les Indiens Sont Encore Loin (SWITZ) (retitling for GB TV: The Indians Are Still Far Away). '78 Violette Nozière (FR-CAN) (USA: Violette). '79 Les Soeurs Brontë. '80 Sauve Qui Peut (La Vie) (SWITZ-FR) (USA: Every Man for Himself; GB: Slow Motion); Loulou; Heaven's Gate. '81 La Dame aux Camélias/La Vera Storia della Signora delle Camelie (FR-IT); Les Ailes de la Colombe (FR-IT). '82 Passion; La Truite (FR).

Matter of Life and Death, *as the American forces radio operator. Below left: Tab Hunter. Below: Isabelle Huppert as the girl driven to patricide in* Violette Nozière

HURT, John

(b. 1940). Actor. Born: Shirebrook, Derbyshire, England

Since his first film, *The Wild and the Willing* (1962), clergyman's son Hurt has moved falteringly towards major stardom, finally achieving it with a sequence of brilliant performances in bizarre roles. On TV he was widely acclaimed as the celebrated homosexual Quentin Crisp in *The Naked Civil Servant*; as a whining Caligula in *I, Claudius*; and in the cinema especially moving but totally unrecognizable beneath the grotesque deformities of *The Elephant Man*. There have been more weird, prestigious screen parts for him: in *10 Rillington Place*, *The Shout*, *Midnight Express* and as the first bloody victim of *The Alien*. Hurt – wiry, waspish, nervy, with freckles, shifty eyes and a voice that sounds as if it's permanently breaking – studied at RADA and worked rewardingly in plays by Osborne, Wesker and Pinter. Then came the part of the ambitious secretary in *A Man for All Seasons* and his long haul to the top, with one minor success, *Mr Forbush and the Penguins* (already hinting at eccentricity) along the way. He received Academy Award nominations for his work in *Midnight Express* and *The Elephant Man*.

Films include: 1966 A Man for All Seasons. '70 In Search of Gregory (GB-IT). '71 10 Rillington Place. '72 Mr Forbush and the Penguins. '78 The Shout; Midnight Express. '79 Alien. '80 The Elephant Man; Heaven's Gate (USA). '82 Partners (USA).

HURT, William

Actor. Born: Washington DC, USA

The stepson of Henry Luce III, founder of the Time-Life empire, Hurt has refused to release his birthdate, which was probably some time in the late Forties. He studied theology in Boston and London, and then acting at the Juilliard School in New York. Hurt's stage career has ranged from Shakespeare in New York to O'Neill in Oregon, and after his films he still returns to the prestigious Circle Rep, which has played a great part in his development as an actor. His film roles have been diverse: a scientist subjected to frightening experiments in *Altered States*, the mild janitor involved in murder in *Eyewitness*, and a swaggering, not-too-bright lawyer in *Body Heat*.

Films: 1980 Altered States. '81 Eyewitness (GB: The Janitor); Body Heat.

HUSSEY, Olivia

(b. 1951). Actress. Born: Buenos Aires, Argentina.

Hussey was her English mother's name. Her father was an Argentine opera singer named Andreas Osuna, who died when Olivia was two years old. Coming to England with her mother, she studied acting, and made her West End debut as a child in *The Prime of Miss Jean Brodie*. When she was 15, Franco Zeffirelli picked her to play Juliet in his film of *Romeo and Juliet*. She married and later divorced Dean Martin's son Dino, went to Hollywood for one or two fairly undistinguished films, and became a devotee of Eastern philosophy, dividing her time now between Hollywood and Japan.

Films include: 1965 The Battle of the Villa Fiorita; Cup Fever. '68 Romeo and Juliet (GB-IT). '69 All The Right Noises. '73 Lost Horizon (USA). '74 Black Christmas (CAN) (USA: Silent Night, Evil Night). '78 Death on the Nile; The Cat and the Canary. '80 Sam Marlowe, Private Eye (USA).

HUSSEY, Ruth

(b. 1914). Actress. Born: Ruth Carol O'Rourke; Providence, Rhode Island, USA

After following a drama course at the University of Michigan, Ruth Hussey began her professional acting career in stock companies and as a fashion commentator on the radio. Brought to Hollywood by MGM in the late Thirties, she had only a few worthwhile parts, like the cynical magazine photographer in George Cukor's *The Philadelphia Story*. She married radio executive Robert Longenecker in 1942 and made only occasional films in the Fifties, such as the suburban comedy, *The Facts of Life*.

Films include: 1938 Rich Man. Poor Girl. '39 Blackmail. '40 Northwest Passage; Susan and God (GB: The Gay Mrs Trexal); The Philadelphia Story; Flight Command. '44 The Uninvited. '49 The Great Gatsby. '53 The Lady Wants Mink. '60 The Facts of Life.

HUSTON, John

(b. 1906). Director. Born: Nevada, Missouri, USA

John Huston's image has in later years become well-known through his appearances in his own and other people's films – for instance, he was the sinisterly incestuous yet oddly sympathetic villain in *Chinatown* (1974). The battered, lived-in face and the casual drawl that seems to take the audience into his confidence are now part of the legend, like his early exploits as an amateur boxing champion and a Mexican cavalry officer or his fox-hunting days as an Irish squireen. He has been active as a faithful adapter of classic and popular novels; as a sympathetic director of actors ranging from his own father, Walter Huston to Humphrey Bogart to Marilyn Monroe, Katharine Hepburn and his own daughter, Anjelica Huston; and as a distinguished wartime documentarist and experimenter with colour effects and with 'difficult' topics (psychoanalysis, homosexuality). But all that has been less noticeable than his five marriages and his famous thrillers and action pictures, such as *The Maltese Falcon*, *The Asphalt Jungle* and *The African Queen*. The son of a famous film actor, he dabbled in screenwriting in the Thirties, gradually building up an impressive list of credits, before *The Maltese Falcon* made his name as a writer-director and set Bogart on the major phase of his career. By 1950 he was considered the finest contemporary American director by the critic James Agee, who co-wrote the script of *The African Queen* with him. But through much of the Fifties and Sixties his reputation wavered as routine or over-casual assignments and too-ambitious projects like adaptations of *Moby Dick* and the Bible alternated with intermittent returns to form. In the Seventies he earned new respect for his boxing picture *Fat City*, his impressively staged Kipling adaptation *The Man Who Would Be King* and his grim gothic tale of Southern religion *Wise Blood*, from Flannery O'Connor's novel. His decision to undertake his first full-scale musical – *Annie* – in his mid-seventies at least indicates that his vitality has in no way abated with the advent of artistic maturity.

Films include: 1941 The Maltese Falcon. '45 San Pietro/The Battle of San Pietro (doc). '46 Let There Be Light (doc). '48 The Treasure of the Sierra Madre (+ act); Key Largo. '50 The Asphalt Jungle. '51 The Red Badge of Courage; The African Queen. '52 Moulin Rouge. '56 Moby Dick. '58 The Roots of Heaven. '60 The Unforgiven. '61 The Misfits. '62 Freud (GB: Freud – The Secret Passion). '64 The Night of the Iguana. '66 La Bibbia (+ act) (IT) (USA/GB: The Bible – In the Beginning). '67 Reflections in a Golden Eye. '69 A Walk With Love and Death (+ act). '70 The Kremlin Letter (+ act). '72 Fat City; The Life and Times of Judge Roy Bean (+ act). '75 The Man Who Would Be King. '79 Wise Blood (+ act). '82 Annie.

HUSTON, Walter

(1884–1950). Actor. Born: Walter Houghston; Toronto, Canada

A versatile character actor, Walter Huston studied engineering before turning to vaudeville where he developed a song-and-dance act with his future wife, Bayonne Whipple. After the coming of sound, he entered movies, first as a lead, then a support. His roles have ranged from that of the great American president in D.W. Griffith's *Abraham Lincoln* to the sly

Top, from left to right: John Hurt plays a young Scotsman who wants to be a criminal in Sinful Davey *(1969); William Hurt in* Body Heat; *Olivia Hussey in* Romeo and Juliet; *Ruth Hussey in* The Philadelphia Story. *Above, from left to right: John Huston directing* The Mackintosh Man *(1973);*

Walter Huston in The Treasure of the Sierra Madre; *Betty Hutton in* Annie Get Your Gun; *Lauren Hutton in* The Gambler. *Below, from left to right: Timothy Hutton in* Ordinary People; *Wilfrid Hyde-White; Martha Hyer in* First Men in the Moon *(1964)*

Mr Scratch (the devil) in *All That Money Can Buy.* He won an Academy Award for his grizzled prospector in *The Treasure of the Sierra Madre,* directed by his son John.

Films include: 1914 The Virginian. **'30** Abraham Lincoln. **'32** A House Divided; Law and Order. **'33** Gabriel Over the White House. **'36** Dodsworth. **'41** All That Money Can Buy/The Devil and Daniel Webster. **'42** Yankee Doodle Dandy. **'43** Mission to Moscow. **'48** The Treasure of the Sierra Madre.

HUTTON, Betty

(b. 1921). Actress. Born: Elizabeth Jane Thornbury; Battle Creek, Michigan, USA

In 1939 at the age of 18, Betty Hutton had her first Broadway hit in *Panama Hattie* which led to a film contract: she had already performed in nightclubs and sung with the Vincent Lopez Band. For several years, this blonde song-and-dance star headed the cast of Paramount's successful musicals, reaching a peak as the tough cowgirl in *Annie Get Your Gun*. After a lengthy decline into obscurity and bankruptcy, she made a terrific comeback as Miss Hannigan, the mean, whisky-sodden harridan of the orphanage in the stage version of *Annie*.

Films include: 1942 The Fleet's In. **'43** Star Spangled Rhythm. **'44** And the Angels Sing; The Miracle of Morgan's Creek. **'45** Incendiary Blonde. **'47** The Perils of Pauline. **'50** Let's Dance; Annie Get Your Gun. **'51** Sailor Beware. **'52** The Greatest Show on Earth; Somebody Loves Me. **'57** Spring Reunion.

HUTTON, Lauren

(b. 1943). Actress. Born: Mary Lauren Hutton; Charleston, South Carolina, USA

Pretty but imperfect features (she has a gap between her two front teeth), enabled Lauren Hutton to become a top model before moving into films. She had a brief spell as a Playboy bunny, worked for Dior and posed for 24 covers of *Vogue*. She has yet to find her niche in cinema although she has had a measure of success playing strong, intelligent women from the zany photographer of *Welcome to LA* to the hippie heroine of *Little Fauss and Big Halsy*. She continues modelling occasionally for Revlon to ensure financial security.

Films include: 1968 Paper Lion. **'70** Little Fauss and Big Halsy; Pieces of Dreams. **'74** The Gambler. **'76** Gator; Welcome to LA. **'77** Viva Knievel! **'78** A Wedding. **'80** American Gigolo. **'81** Paternity. **'82** Hecate (SWITZ-FR).

HUTTON, Timothy

(b. 1960). Actor. Born: Malibu, California, USA

Coming from an acting family, Timothy Hutton grew up in the shadow of Hollywood. He left high school to play opposite his father in a stage production of *Harvey* and went straight from there into television. Hutton made his mark in films when Robert Redford chose him for the part of Conrad, the guilt-ridden son, in *Ordinary People*, a part which won him the Best Supporting Actor Academy Award. His first starring role was as the rebellious student leader of a military academy in *Taps* and he is rapidly becoming a thoughtful, sensitive leading man.

Films: 1980 Ordinary People. **'81** Taps.

HYDE-WHITE, Wilfrid

(b. 1903). Actor. Born: Bourton-on-the-Water, Gloucestershire, England

Everone knows him – he is the white-haired, crafty old rascal whose classy veneer does not hide his seedy intentions. The son of a canon, Wilfrid Hyde-White was educated at public school before going to RADA. After his stage debut in Tom Walls' *Tons of Money*, he served a long apprentice-ship playing bit parts in revues and farces. He entered films in 1934 and his range of dubious British authority figures – including the wily head-master of *The Browning Version* and the confused British Council organizer in *The Third Man* – turned him into a national institution. He has appeared in several Hollywood films and earned popularity amongst a younger generation with his humorous television roles.

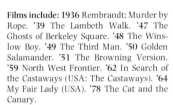

Films include: 1936 Rembrandt; Murder by Rope. **'39** The Lambeth Walk. **'47** The Ghosts of Berkeley Square. **'48** The Winslow Boy. **'49** The Third Man. **'50** Golden Salamander. **'51** The Browning Version. **'59** North West Frontier. **'62** In Search of the Castaways (USA: The Castaways). **'64** My Fair Lady (USA). **'78** The Cat and the Canary.

HYER, Martha

(b. 1924). Actress. Born: Fort Worth, Texas, USA

Martha Hyer took the traditional route into films when she was seen by a Paramount talent scout while appearing in the Pasadena Playhouse production of *The Women*. The next three years were spent playing a variety of daughters and schoolteachers in low-budget B movies. In the Fifties she dyed her hair to play a succession of icy blondes starting with the eponymous rich girl of Billy Wilder's *Sabrina*. She married producer Hal B. Wallis and has done little of note on the screen since.

Films include: 1947 Thunder Mountain. **'49** Roughshod. **'53** So Big. **'54** Sabrina (GB: Sabrina Fair). **'57** My Man Godfrey. **'58** Houseboat; Some Came Running. **'60** Desire in the Dust. **'63** Wives and Lovers. **'67** The Happening.

IBBETSON, Arthur

(b. 1921). Cinematographer. Born: England

A highly versatile cameraman, Arthur Ibbetson entered the film industry as a clapper-boy working on films like Alfred Hitchcock's *Jamaica Inn*. He graduated to director of photography in the late Fifties and shot a wide variety of films, from the colourful costume drama *Anne of the Thousand Days* (which led to an Oscar nomination) to the stark black and white of *The Angry Silence*. The cramped interiors of the barge in *The Inspector*, the scruffy bohemianism of *The Horse's Mouth* and the snowbound night scenes of *Where Eagles Dare* are among his memorable contributions to British cinema.

Films include: 1959 The Horse's Mouth. '60 The Angry Silence; Tunes of Glory. '62 The Inspector (USA: Lisa). '63 Nine Hours to Rama. '67 A Countess From Hong Kong. '68 Where Eagles Dare. '69 Anne of the Thousand Days. '71 The Railway Children. '73 A Doll's House. '77 A Little Night Music (USA-A-GER). '78 The Medusa Touch (GB-FR). '81 Little Lord Fauntleroy.

ICHIKAWA, Kon

(b. 1915). Director. Born: Ujiyamada, Japan

Kon Ichikawa's debut, the marionette movie *A Girl at Dojo Temple* based on a famous Kabuki dance, was banned by the American occupying forces, but his features met with greater success. Throughout the Fifties he made a series of satirical comedies whose black humour dealt with everything from sexual obsessions to home-made H-bombs. His later – bleaker – dramas are more well-known in the West, in particular *An Actor's Revenge*, a subtle story of identity based on the problems of a female impersonator. His films are often scripted by his wife, Natto Wada.

Films include: 1946 Musume Dojoji (USA/GB: A Girl at Dojo Temple). '54 Okuman Choja (A Millionaire). '55 Kokoro (USA/GB: The Heart) '56 Biruma no Tategoto (The Burmese Harp). '58 Enjo (USA/GB: The Conflagration). '59 Kagi (USA: The Key; GB: Odd Obsessions); Nobi (USA/GB: Fires on the Plain). '63 Yukinojo Henge (USA/GB: An Actor's Revenge); Taiheiyo Hitoribotchi (USA/GB: Alone on the Pacific). '65 Tokyo Orimpikku (USA/GB: Tokyo Olympiad). '73 Matatabi (GB: The Wanderers). '78 Joobachi (USA/GB: Queen Bee).

INCE, Ralph

(1887–1937). Actor/director. Born: Boston, Massachusetts, USA

In the early days of movie-making acting and directing were parallel activities, and Ralph Ince was involved with both functions in hundreds of silent shorts. Along with his two brothers he had turned to the entertainment business for a career, and it was after a spell as a commercial artist and a cartoonist that he returned to acting. Following his many successes he set up his own production company with his brother John, but unlike their other brother Thomas they did not do well. Then came the change to sound which severely restricted Ralph's directing career and he returned solely to character acting. He was to be seen mostly in tough-guy roles often verging on the sinister. In 1934 he travelled to England where he resumed acting and directing until his death in a car crash.

Films include: 1912 Seventh Son; Lincoln's Gettysburg Address. '13 The Wreck (+dir). '17 The Co-Respondent (+dir). '18 Too Many Crooks (dir. only). '26 The Sea Wolf (+dir; +exec-prod). '28 Coney Island (dir. only). '30 Little Caesar; The Big Fight; Hurricane (dir. only). '37 The Man Who Made Diamonds (dir. only) (GB).

INCE, Thomas H.

(1882–1924). Director/producer. Born: Thomas Harper Ince; Newport, Rhode Island, USA

The early death of Thomas H. Ince, in mysterious circumstances aboard William Randolph Hearst's yacht, may have prevented his name from becoming one of the most important in cinema history. He wrote, directed and cut his first film in one week. He turned directing and producing into a science, with all components of his films working in complete synchronization for maximum turnout. His studio procedures shaped both the economic and aesthetic outlook of the movie business, and many talented directors and actors began their careers in Ince's tight-scheduled studio. He came from a theatrical family, and it was his failure as a stage actor that led him to turn to the movies for an income. By 1910 he was working for Biograph and from there he moved to Independent Motion Pictures where he was given the chance to direct Mary Pickford movies. The following year he became a director for the New York Picture Company and moved to their Los Angeles studio where he began to insist on tightly structured shooting scripts and production. From that time until his death he was one of the most significant figures in the industry, instigating the building of enormous studios, employing thousands of technicians and actors, and totally changing the face of production. Ince's personal speciality was the Western.

Films as a director include: 1911 Their First Misunderstanding (co-dir); The New Cook. '12 War on the Plains; The Indian Massacre; Custer's Last Raid. '13 The Invaders (co-dir). '14 The Battle of Gettysburg; The Typhoon (feature) (sup; +co-sc. only); The Bargain (sup; +co-sc. only); The Wrath of the Gods, or the Destruction of Sakura Juna (sup. only). '16 Civilization (feature) (sup. only) (re-released in 1930 with musical score and dialogue sequences). '23 Human Wreckage (feature) (sup. only); Anna Christie (feature) (sup. only).

Right: Kon Ichikawa. Below, from left to right: Rex Ingram directing The Arab *(1924); actor Rex Ingram in* Thief of Bagdad; *Jill Ireland; John Ireland in Nicholas Ray's* 55 Days at Peking *(1963)*

INGRAM, Rex

(1895–1969). Actor. Born: Reginald Cliff Ingram; aboard a riverboat, nr. Cairo, Illinois, USA

A muscular black actor with a powerful screen persona, Rex Ingram graduated as a doctor from Northwestern University. For no apparent reason he forsook any idea of practising medicine and went to Hollywood. His film debut was in the silent *Tarzan of the Apes* (1918) as an African native. He was not to be stereotyped thus again, however, and carried on to play many diverse roles, one of the most inspired of these being De Lawd in the film version of *Green Pastures* (1936). Opportunities for black actors, never very great, were even less so in the Thirties and Forties. Consequently

Ingram never really won the recognition he deserved.

Films include: 1918 Tarzan of the Apes. '36 The Green Pastures. '39 The Adventures of Huckleberry Finn. '40 Thief of Bagdad (GB). '42 The Talk of the Town. '43 Cabin in the Sky. '45 A Thousand and One Nights. '60 Elmer Gantry. '64 Your Cheatin' Heart. '67 Hurry Sundown. '68 Journey to Shiloh.

INGRAM, Rex

(1893–1950). Director. Born: Reginald Ingram Montgomery Hitchcock; Dublin, Ireland

The son of an Irish clergyman and classical scholar, the future Rex Ingram emigrated to the USA in 1911 and studied sculpture at Yale. But Vitagraph's *A Tale of Two Cities* opened his eyes to the aesthetic possibilities of the movies, and in 1913 he joined the Edison company as an assistant. He worked on scripts, designed, and acted. He moved to Vitagraph, who used him mainly as an actor, his good looks fitting him for romantic leads. After a brief stay at Fox, where he changed Rex Hitchcock to Rex Ingram and wrote scripts, he became a fully fledged director at Universal in 1916. Four years and twelve films later he went on to Metro, for whom he made his great Twenties classics.

With *The Four Horsemen of the Apocalypse* Ingram rose to the top of his profession, and other triumphs followed in *The Prisoner of Zenda* and *Scaramouche*. But Ingram longed for full creative freedom, and in 1924 he took over the Victorine studios at Nice for Rex Ingram Productions. Here he made his masterpiece, *Mare Nostrum*, and here he worked until sound came. He made one sound film, and retired. He loved Africa, and was fascinated by Islam, but eventually he returned to Hollywood. He wrote novels, but sound had destroyed his concern for film-making. His friend Erich von Stroheim, for whom Ingram tried hard to salvage *Greed*, said that Ingram was the greatest of all directors. That opinion can be defended. Ingram's films are a visual delight, and he is a master of atmosphere. He was superb with actors (Rudolph Valentino, Ramon Novarro and his own wife, the lovely Alice Terry), and won the admiration of great technicians like the cameraman John Seitz and the editor Grant Whytock, who stayed with him for film after film. Rex Ingram died in Hollywood.

Films include: 1916 The Great Problem; Black Orchids (GB: The Fatal Orchids). '17 The Reward of the Faithless; The Flower of Doom. '18 His Robe of Honor. '19 The Day

She Paid. '20 Hearts Are Trumps. '21 The Four Horsemen of the Apocalypse; The Conquering Power. '22 The Prisoner of Zenda; Trifling Women. '23 Where the Pavement Ends; Scaramouche. '24 The Arab. '25 Greed (co-ed. only). '26 Mare Nostrum/Our Sea; The Magician. '27 The Garden of Allah. '29 The Three Passions. '32 Baroud (FR-GB) (FR: Les Hommes Bleus).

IRELAND, Jill

(b. 1936). Actress. Born: Hounslow, Middlesex, England

Trained in ballet, blonde Jill Ireland was on stage at the Chiswick Empire at 12 and then did cabaret work and appeared with the Monte Carlo Ballet. J. Arthur Rank saw her film debut as a dancer in *Oh, Rosalinda!!* and offered her a three-year contract. This led to her best-known role, as the prim young Edwardian woman in *Three Men in a Boat*. She accompanied her first husband David McCallum to America and, when they divorced, married Charles Bronson. She is now seemingly content to play his leading lady in violent crime thrillers such as *Death Wish II*.

Films include: 1955 Oh, Rosalinda!! '56 Three Men in a Boat; The Big Money. '59 Carry on Nurse. '70 Città Violenta (IT-FR) (GB: Violent City). '75 Breakout (USA); Hard Times (USA) (GB: The Streetfighter). '76 Breakheart Pass (USA); From Noon Till Three (USA). '79 Love and Bullets (USA). '82 Death Wish II (USA).

IRELAND, John

(b. 1914). Actor. Born: Vancouver, British Columbia, Canada

Showbusiness for John Ireland began when he took part in a water carnival as a professional swimmer in 1935. Then, from the ridiculous to the sublime, he began touring in a Shakespearian repertory company. His film debut came with *A Walk in the Sun* (1945) and it was at this point that he was seen by Darryl F. Zanuck who signed him and in the Forties and the Fifties cast him in cynical and violent roles. For his supporting role in *All the*

King's Men Ireland was nominated for an Academy Award. In 1953 he co-produced and co-directed *Outlaw Territory* with cameraman Lee Garmes. Ireland's fame was short-lived, however, and his career faltered during the Sixties when he began appearing in fly-by-night Italian productions.

Films include: 1946 My Darling Clementine. '48 Red River; Joan of Arc. '49 I Shot Jesse James; All The King's Men. '51 Little Big Horn (GB: The Fighting Seven). '54 Southwest Passage (GB: Camels West). '57 Gunfight at the OK Corral. '60 Spartacus. '65 I Saw What You Did. '76 Salon Kitty (IT-FR-GER). '78 Tomorrow Never Comes (GB-CAN).

IRENE

(1901–1962). Costume designer. Born: Irene Lentz; Brookings, South Dakota, USA

During the Forties Irene was one of the very top designers in Hollywood. Her elegant, classic styles – tight-fitting tailored suits and romantic, soft-flowing evening gowns – were worn on and off screen by such sophisticated stars as Katharine Hepburn, Joan Crawford and Marlene Dietrich. Having originally wanted to be a musician, Irene entered the film world in 1925 as an extra for MGM. Three years later, after studying at the Wolf School of Design in Los Angeles, she opened her first dress shop and before long it was attracting a fashionable clientele of stars. Soon she began designing 'Irene' originals for movies and was quickly made executive designer at MGM. Unfortunately her executive status meant that she was more involved with supervision and administration than designing. She also had alcohol problems and her private life was a shambles, particularly after an unhappy affair with Gary Cooper.

Films include: 1937 Shall We Dance? '39 Midnight. '42 You Were Never Lovelier. '44 Mrs Parkinson. '45 Weekend at the Waldorf. '48 B. F's Daughter (GB: Polly Fulton); State of the Union (GB: The World and His Wife); The Pirate; Easter Parade. '60 Midnight Lace. '63 A Gathering of Eagles.

IRONS, Jeremy

(b. 1949). Actor. Born: Isle of Wight, England

Tall, slender, reserved, elegant, pale, stylish and very British – that is Jeremy Irons' image, and it has been created as a result of his first two major roles, in the television series *Brideshead Revisited* and the film *The French Lieutenant's Woman*. After a period as a social worker and performing as a busker in London's West End he worked as an assistant stage manager before attending drama school in Bristol. He eventually returned to London and finally obtained the part of Judas in *Godspell*. He then managed to stay in work until he became established with *Brideshead Revisited*.

Films: 1980 Nijinsky. **'81** The French Lieutenant's Woman. **'82** Moonlighting; The Captain's Doll (orig. TV).

IVENS, Joris

(b. 1898). Documentarist. Born: Georg Henri Anton Ivens; Nijmegen, Holland

Ivens was supposed to have taken over his family's photographic business, but during his training in Berlin he came under various political and artistic influences that were destined to alter his outlooks and ambitions. Despite becoming head of the tech-nical department of the Amsterdam branch of the family firm, his involvement with Amsterdam film culture soon led to his moving irrevocably into the world of film-making. During his career he has established himself with some monumental works as a leading documentary maker of international reputation. With his first two films, *The Bridge* and *Rain*, Ivens created a pair of avant-garde classics. His film *Spanish Earth*, narrated by Ernest Hemingway, was a pioneering piece of ciné-journalism which attempted to rouse the world against fascism. He has also made two films about the plight of the Chinese people and he has worked in Cuba and North Vietnam. His political views have sometimes restricted the reception of his films, but this cannot detract from his enormous determination and talent.

Films include: 1928 De Brug (GB: The Bridge). **'29** Regen (GB: Rain). **'33** Misère au Borinage/Borinage (short) (BELG). **'37** Spanish Earth (USA). **'39** The 400 Million (USA). **'40** The Power and the Land (short) (USA). **'46** Indonesia Calling (short) (AUS). **'60** L'Italia Non E un Paese Povero (IT) (USA/GB: Italy Is Not a Poor Country). **'61** Pueblo en Armas (short) (CUBA) (USA/GB: An Armed People). **'70** Rencontre Avec le Président Ho Chi Minh (short) (co-dir) (FR). **'76** Comment Yukong Déplaça les Montagnes (co-dir) (FR) (USA/GB: How Yukong Moved the Mountains) – a film cycle consisting of 12 parts.

IVES, Burl

(b. 1909). Actor/folk singer. Born: Burle Icle Ivanhoe; Hunt City Illinois, USA

Burl Ives travelled the country busking with his banjo, picking up folk songs on his travels, and singing on local radio. He then settled in New York where he studied singing and he was soon performing professionally in a Greenwich Village nightclub. Before long he was appearing on Broadway but his career came to a halt with World War II and army service. After the war he was given his own radio show, and a production of *Sing Out Sweet Land* led to Hollywood offers. His first film roles tended to have him singing out on the range, but it was soon realized that he was a powerful dramatic actor. Between appearances in heavy patriarchal roles in films like *Cat on a Hot Tin Roof*, *East of Eden* and *Desire Under the Elms* he has also found time to undertake many successful concert tours as a folk singer. He won the Best Supporting Actor Oscar for his performance in *The Big Country*.

Films include: 1946 Smoky. **'55** East of Eden. **'58** Desire Under the Elms; The Big Country; Wind Across the Everglades; Cat on a Hot Tin Roof. **'59** Day of the Outlaw; Our Man in Havana (GB). **'64** Ensign Pulver. **'67** Jules Verne's Rocket to the Moon (GB) (USA: Those Fantastic Flying Fools). **'82** White Dog.

IVORY, James

(b. 1928). Director. Born: Berkeley, California, USA

After graduating from the film department at the University of Southern California, James Ivory became fascinated by the art and culture of India. In 1960 he was commissioned by the Asia Society to make a documentary about India. While there he met local producer Ismail Merchant. They began collaborating and, with the important contributions of author/scriptwriter Ruth Prawer Jhabvala, produced films such as the wistful *Shakespeare Wallah*. This was a clever parody of Indian culture juxtaposed with the last vestiges of British colonialism, a theme that was explored in one way or another in several of Ivory's subsequent films.

Films include: 1965 Shakespeare Wallah (IND). **'69** The Guru (USA-IND). **'70** Bombay Talkie (IND). **'72** Savages (USA); Helen, Queen of the Nautch Girls (doc. short) (IND); Mahatma and the Mad Boy (dir) (IND). **'75** The Wild Party (co-prod. co) (USA). **'77** Roseland (USA). **'78** Hullabaloo Over Georgie and Bonnie's Pictures (co-prod. co) (GB-IND). **'79** The Europeans (+ act) (GB). **'81** Quartet (co-prod. co).

IWERKS, Ub

(1901–1971). Animator. Born: Ubbe Ert Iwwerks; Kansas City, Missouri, USA

Iwerks name appeared on the screen credits of the first Mickey Mouse cartoons. He had met Walt Disney while both were working in a commercial art studio in 1919. After a jointly unsuccessful business venture the two went to work for Kansas City Slide Company where they were launched into the heady world of film animation. Iwerks proceeded to gain personal success for his work in animation techniques for which he won Academy Awards in 1959 and 1965. In *Mary Poppins* he blended live action with animation. His attempts at cartoons on his own – *Flip the Frog* and *Willie Whopper* – failed to achieve success, not through lack of artistry but through a lack of story sense and an ignorance of audience demand. After the dissolution of his own company in 1940 Iwerks returned to work for Disney as special-effects adviser.

Films include: 1923–26 Alice in Wonderland (series). **'28** Plane Crazy; Steamboat Willie. **'29** Skeleton Dance. **'31–33** Flip the Frog (series). **'33–34** Willie Whopper (series). **'41** The Reluctant Dragon. **'54** 20,000 Leagues Under the Sea. **'55** Lady and the Tramp. **'61** One Hundred and One Dalmations. **'63** The Birds. **'64** Mary Poppins. **'71** Bedknobs and Broomsticks.

J

JACKSON, Anne

(b. 1926). Actress. Born: Pittsburgh, Pennsylvania, USA

A small, trim redhead of Yugoslav and Irish parentage, Anne Jackson studied at the Neighborhood Playhouse and the Actors' Studio, of which her husband Eli Wallach is also an alumnus. She became primarily a stage actress, appearing in many successful Broadway productions including *Summer and Smoke*. She often acts with her husband and they re-created their stage roles in a one-act play, *The Tiger* by Murray Shisgal, in the film version, *The Tiger Makes Out*. Anne Jackson tends to be at her best when playing worldly-wise women, knowing but not quite cynical, in sophisticated sex comedies.

Films include: 1950 So Young, So Bad. '59 The Journey. '60 Tall Story. '67 The Tiger Makes Out. '68 How to Save a Marriage and Ruin Your Life; The Secret Life of an American Wife. '70 Zigzag (GB: False Witness); Lovers and Other Strangers; Dirty Dingus Magee. '77 Nasty Habits (GB). '79 The Bell Jar. '80 The Shining.

JACKSON, Glenda

(b. 1936). Actress. Born: Birkenhead, Cheshire, England

With her high cheek-bones, wide mouth and intense dark eyes, Glenda Jackson is striking rather than pretty and refuses to conceal that she occasionally looks bedraggled or tired; yet she has won Academy Awards for her roles in a sex drama, *Women in Love*, and a sex comedy, *A Touch of Class*. The daughter of a small builder, she had a strict Presbyterian upbringing that left its mark in her very serious approach to acting and in the strength of personality she brings to her work. When she grew too much to become a ballet dancer, she went to RADA, and then had six years of bit parts alternating with temporary jobs such as working in Boot's Chemists. Then Peter Brook offered her the part of the murderous Charlotte Corday in his Theatre of Cruelty production of Peter Weiss' play *Marat-Sade* in 1964, sponsored by the Royal Shakespeare Company. She had already become a leading actress with the RSC when she repeated this role in the film version and so began her movie career. She then quickly achieved international fame in two films by Ken Russell, *Women in Love* and *The Music Lovers*. These gave her a rather artificial reputation as a sex symbol; but Schlesinger's *Sunday, Bloody Sunday* created for her a less extravagant image as a sensible woman trying to share her bisexual lover with another man, and *A Touch of Class* brought out the lighter side of her formidable talent. Meanwhile she was building up an impressive list of credits on television, both in modern works such as David Mercer's *Let's Murder Vivaldi* and in historical costume drama. On the big screen she tended to revert mostly to neurotic or eccentric and strong-minded women, notably the underrated poet of the London suburbs, Stevie Smith, in *Stevie*, a role she had already played on the stage.

Films include: 1967 The Persecution and Assassination of Jean-Paul Marat as Performed by the Inmates of the Asylum of Charenton Under the Direction of the Marquis de Sade/Marat-Sade. '69 Women in Love. '71 The Music Lovers; Sunday, Bloody Sunday. '72 Mary, Queen of Scots; The Triple Echo. '73 A Touch of Class. '75 The Romantic Englishwoman. '78 The Class of Miss MacMichael; Stevie (USA-GB). '79 Lost and Found.

JACKSON, Gordon

(b. 1923) Actor. Born: Glasgow, Scotland

A fair-haired, blue-eyed Scot, Gordon Jackson played Robert Burns as a boy in a BBC radio play in 1937, and was subsequently recommended to Ealing producer Michael Balcon for the second lead as Tommy Trinder's young Scottish companion in *The Foreman Went to France*. His best Ealing role was as the susceptible son of a tyrannical pharmacist (Mervyn Johns) in Victorian Brighton, led astray and involved in murder by a scheming pub landlady (irresistible Googie Withers) in *Pink String and Sealing Wax*. After decades of solid character work, he finally won international notice as Hudson, the austere and imperturbable butler, in the television series *Upstairs, Downstairs*. He was awarded the OBE in 1979.

Films include: 1942 The Foreman Went to France (USA: Somewhere in France). '43 Millions Like Us. '45 Pink String and Sealing Wax. '46 The Captive Heart. '49 Whisky Galore (USA: Tight Little Island). '60 Tunes of Glory. '62 Mutiny on the Bounty (USA). '65 The Ipcress File. '67 The Night of the Generals (GB-FR). '69 The Prime of Miss Jean Brodie. '77 Golden Rendezvous (USA).

Far left: Anne Jackson in The Secret Life of an American Wife, *in which she poses as a call-girl. Left: Glenda Jackson in* Sunday, Bloody Sunday. *Above: Gordon Jackson in* Run Wild, Run Free *(1969)*

221

JACKSON, Pat

(b. 1916). Director. Born: London, England

Pat Jackson left public school to serve his apprenticeship with the GPO Film Unit, soon rising to assistant editor on Basil Wright's *Song of Ceylon* (1934). In 1938 he began making documentaries, initially as co-director. Jackson established an international reputation with his first feature, a Technicolor dramatized documentary, *Western Approaches*, which told the story of a lifeboat carrying survivors from a torpedoed merchant ship and used as a decoy by a lurking German U-boat. After the war he moved on to features, but a brief foray to Hollywood was unsuccessful. His documentary experience added authenticity to his first hospital film, *White Corridors*, but he was unable to repeat this success with a film about nurses in training, *The Feminine Touch*. His career then led, by way of a proto-Carry On comedy, *What a Carve Up!*, to the Children's Film Foundation (*Seventy Deadly Pills*, *Dead End Creek*) and finally to television.

Films include: 1944 Western Approaches (doc) (USA: The Raider). '50 Shadow on the Wall (USA). '51 White Corridors; Encore *ep* Winter Cruise. '52 Something Money Can't Buy. '56 The Feminine Touch (USA: The Gentle Touch). '58 Virgin Island. '61 What a Carve Up! '62 Don't Talk to Strange Men. '64 Seventy Deadly Pills; Dead End Creek (serial).

JACQUES, Hattie

(1924–1980). Actress. Born: Sandgate, Kent, England

'When you're my size, you're conditioned from childhood to people making jokes against you. You have to learn to make them laugh with, rather than at you.' Hattie Jacques was the most famous fat lady in postwar British cinema and an actress with superb comic timing. She was at her best as the battleaxe matron, or the like, in the Carry On films, enough to make any patient get well quickly. On television she became popular, too, in *Hancock's Half Hour* and as Eric Sykes' soft-hearted sister. Having

discovered her talent to entertain while working in a factory during the war, 'Hat' made her stage debut at the Playhouse Theatre. She did pantomime, revues, toured with the Old Vic company, was Sophie Tuckshop in ITMA on the radio, and had early screen roles in versions of Dickens – *Oliver Twist*, *Nicholas Nickleby*, *The Pickwick Papers*. She was married to actor John Le Mesurier from 1945 to 1965.

Films include: 1946 Green for Danger. '47 Nicholas Nickleby. '48 Oliver Twist. '52 The Pickwick Papers. '58 Carry on Sergeant. '59 Carry on Nurse; Carry on Teacher. '60 School for Scoundrels. '62 The Punch and Judy Man. '67 The Plank (short). '69 Crooks and Coronets (USA: Sophie's Place); Monte Carlo or Bust! '72 Carry on Matron.

JAECKEL, Richard

(b. 1926). Actor. Born: Long Beach, New York, USA

Richard Jaeckel's mother was Millicent Hanley, a former Broadway actress. The family moved to Los Angeles when he was eight and he grew up more interested in athletics than acting. In 1943 he found a job as a messenger boy at 20th Century-Fox where his blond boyish good looks caught the eye of a casting director and he was cast as a rookie marine in *Guadalcanal Diary*. His typecasting in war films was soon interrupted by actual war service. He somewhat reluctantly returned to acting, still sometimes in war films but also in Westerns (where he tended to be the heavy) and other action pictures, occasionally varied by psychological dramas such as *Come Back, Little Sheba*, where he gained good notices and began to become more seriously involved in his career. He was nominated for an Oscar as Best Supporting Actor in *Sometimes a Great Notion* and has matured into a reliable character actor.

Films include: 1943 Guadalcanal Diary. '49 Sands of Iwo Jima. '52 Come Back, Little Sheba. '56 Attack! '57 3:10 to Yuma. '58 The Naked and the Dead. '61 Town Without Pity (USA-GER-SWITZ). '67 The Dirty Dozen (USA-GB). '71 Sometimes a Great Notion (GB: Never Give an Inch). '72

Above, from left to right: Hattie Jacques in Carry on Nurse, *with Joan Hickson; Richard Jaeckel in*

Ulzana's Raid. '73 Pat Garrett and Billy the Kid. '77 Twilight's Last Gleaming (USA-GER).

JAFFE, Sam

(1897–1984). Actor. Born: New York City, USA

The son of a Russian actress and an Irish jeweller, Sam Jaffe gave up teaching mathematics for an acting career in the theatre. By 1930 he was starring in the Broadway production of *Grand Hotel*. His first Hollywood role was as the mad Tsar Peter of Russia, briefly married to Catherine the Great (Marlene Dietrich), in Josef von Sternberg's *The Scarlet Empress*. He was also notable in *Lost Horizon* and the title role in *Gunga Din*. But his best part was as Dr Erwin Riedenschneider, the stiffly correct German crime-planner with a fatal weakness for young girls in *The Asphalt Jungle* – this won him the Best Actor Award at Venice as well as an Oscar nomination for Best Supporting Actor. He also appeared on television (he was in the *Ben Casey* series) and maintained an interest in the stage – he founded the Equity Library Theater for young actors in New York in 1948.

Sometimes a Great Notion; Dean Jagger in Firecreek. *Below: Sam Jaffe in* The Scarlet Empress

Films include: 1934 The Scarlet Empress; We Live Again. '37 Lost Horizon. '39 Gunga Din. '46 13 Rue Madeleine. '47 Gentleman's Agreement. '50 The Asphalt Jungle. '51 The Day the Earth Stood Still. '59 Ben-Hur. '68 La Bataille de San Sebastian (FR-MEX-IT) (GB: Guns for San Sebastian). '80 Battle Beyond the Stars.

JAGGER, Dean

(b. 1903). Actor. Born: Lima, Ohio, USA

From a farming family, Dean Jagger was educated at Wabash College, Indiana, and studied acting with Elias Day at the Conservatory in Chicago. He made his Broadway debut in the mid-Twenties. A stage production in Los Angeles led to a film contract with Fox to play opposite Mary Astor in *The Woman From Hell*, a late silent film that injured his career since he was branded as a 'silent star' and found it difficult to get work. He returned to Broadway and achieved theatrical fame in *Tobacco Road* and *They Shall Not Die*, which won him a Paramount contract until 1936. After another four years on Broadway he returned to Fox (by then 20th Century-Fox) to play the title role of the Mormon leader in *Brigham Young*. This did not make him a star but secured his future

Above: Sidney James in Carry on Girls *(1973), with Joan Sims. Below: the director Miklós Jancsó*

Below: Emil Jannings in The Last Laugh – *a silent film classic directed by F.W. Murnau*

as a character actor. He won an Academy Award as Best Supporting Actor in the air-force picture *Twelve O'Clock High*.

Films include: 1929 The Woman From Hell. '40 Brigham Young. '41 Western Union. '47 Pursued. '49 Twelve O'Clock High. '55 Bad Day at Black Rock. '58 The Proud Rebel. '60 Elmer Gantry. '68 Firecreek; Day of the Evil Gun. '71 Vanishing Point. '80 Alligator.

JAMES, Sidney

(1913–1976). Actor. Born: Johannesburg, South Africa

Sid James, with his crumpled face, his eyes creased in a perpetual grin and his dirty laugh, might have made a memorable Shakespearian clown. He was certainly a good enough actor. Instead he was, for nearly thirty years, an indispensable part of the British film and television comedy scene: in the late Forties and early Fifties generally cast as a small-time hood, spiv or barman (the tough but kind Knucksie in *The Small Back Room*); Tony Hancock's pal in *Hancock's Half Hour*; and, immortally, the resident man-in-charge of the Carry On team. The son of variety

artists, he worked in circuses, South African diamond mines and as a dancer in Vaudeville. During the war he transferred from the anti-tank regiment to the entertainments unit and then came to England where he quickly proved himself as a character and Ealing-comedy actor. It is fitting that alphabetical order should keep him close to Hattie Jacques – like a careless husband on whom it is necessary for a fat wife to keep a constant eye, as in *Carry on Cabby*.

Films include: 1948 No Orchids for Miss Blandish. '49 The Small Back Room (USA: Hour of Glory). '51 The Lavender Hill Mob. '52 I Believe in You. '53 The Titfield Thunderbolt. '54 The Belles of St Trinians. '55 Joe Macbeth. '57 Hell Drivers; The Shiralee. '60 Carry on Constable. '61 What a Come Up!; Carry on Regardless. '63 Carry on Cabby. '65 Carry on Cowboy. '66 Don't Lose Your Head. '68 Carry on up the Khyber. '71 Carry on Henry. '74 Carry on Dick.

JANCSÓ, Miklós

(b. 1921). Director. Born: Vác, Hungary

Whereas other Hungarian directors have had to go to Hollywood or London to achieve an international

reputation, Jancsó has managed it with only occasional excursions to Rome and has made few concessions (apart from his ubiquitous nude girls) to popular taste or comprehension. He graduated from the Academy of Dramatic and Cinematographic Art in 1951 and went into directing newsreels and documentary shorts. His career in features, with one forgettable exception, began in 1962 and *The Round-Up*, an enigmatic story of oppression and betrayal in the days of the Austro-Hungarian Empire, brought him international recognition. His early features were in stark black and white but with *The Confrontation* he moved to sumptuous colour and an increasingly stylized and choreographed method of presentation. He has often depicted episodes in Hungarian (and occasionally European) history, but in a symbolic and allegorical manner close to ritual drama, attacking the repressive aspects of Eastern European Stalinism and expressing a Utopian revolutionary socialist vision. He is renowned for the use of extremely long takes (up to ten minutes), partially improvised within an overall plan; but he also uses more rapid cutting when this is appropriate. *Red Psalm* won him the Best Director prize at Cannes. But the Italian-made *Private Vices, Public Virtues* has been his most widely shown film, no doubt because its orgiastic depiction of erotic freedom made it easy to sell as a sex movie.

Films include: 1951 Kesünkbe Vettuk a Béke Ügyét (doc. short) (co-dir). '59 A Harangok Rómába Mentek (The Bells Have Gone to Rome). '62 Oldás és Kötés (GB: Cantata). '64 Így Jöttem (GB: My Way Home). '65 Szegénylegények (USA/GB: The Round-Up). '67 Csillagosok, Katonák (HUNG-USSR) (USA/GB: The Red and the White). '68 Csend és Kiáltás (USA/GB: Silence and Cry). '69 Fényes Szelek (USA/GB: The Confrontation); Sirokkó/ Sirocco d'Hiver (HUNG-FR) (Winter Wind). '71 Égi Bárány/Agnus Dei; La Pacifista (IT-FR-MONACO) (The Pacifist). '72 La Tecnica e il Rito (IT) (orig. TV) (Technique and Rite); Még Kér a Nép (USA/GB: Red Psalm). '73 Roma Rivuole Cesare (IT-HUNG) (USA: Rome Wants Another Caesar). '75 Szerelmem, Elektra (USA/GB: Elektreia). '76 Vizi Privati, Pubbliche Virtù (IT-YUG) (USA/GB: Private Vices, Public Virtues). '79 Magyar Rapszódia (USA/GB: Hungarian Rhapsody); Allegro Barbaro. '81 A Zsarnok Szive Avagy Boccaccio Magyarorszagon (HUNG-IT) (The Tyrant's Heart, or Boccaccio in Hungary).

JANNI, Joseph

(b. 1916). Producer. Born: Milan, Italy

From the University of Milan, Janni studied film in Rome and worked as an assistant director. He was in England, on his way to an apprenticeship with Disney in the USA, when war broke out and spoiled his plans. But he stayed in England and in 1948 formed his own production company, Victoria Films. *The Glass Mountain*, with its popular theme music, put the newly named Vic Films on the map and revealed Janni's talent for the commercial packaging of movies. He achieved his greatest success in the

Sixties as the producer of John Schlesinger's films, which gave vital chances to Alan Bates (*A Kind of Loving*) and Julie Christie (*Billy Liar*). He moved productively through the Swinging Sixties (*Darling . . .* and Joseph Losey's *Modesty Blaise*) and the socially aware Sixties (Ken Loach's *Poor Cow*), interchanging style for squalor where appropriate. He continued his association with Schlesinger on *Yanks* in the Seventies. Janni has been praised for making films that 'take the women's point of view' – usually in collaboration with Schlesinger and Christie.

Films include: 1949 The Glass Mountain (co-prod). '51 White Corridors (co-prod). '54 Romeo and Juliet (co-prod). '56 A Town Like Alice. '57 Robbery Under Arms. '60 Ombre Bianchi (co-prod) (IT-FR) (USA/GB: Savage Innocents). '62 A Kind of Loving. '63 Billy Liar. '65 Darling. . . '66 Modesty Blaise. '67 Far From the Madding Crowd; Poor Cow. '71 Sunday, Bloody Sunday. '79 Yanks (co-prod).

JANNINGS, Emil

(1884-1950). Actor. Born: Theodor Friedrich Emil Janenz; Rorschach, Switzerland

The most famous of German screen actors, Jannings was a touring player before joining Max Reinhardt in Berlin in 1906. He soon became prominent on stage, and made his first film in 1914. In 1917 Jannings began a notable partnership with Ernst Lubitsch, and by 1927, when he left for Hollywood, he had also worked with Murnau (for whom he gave a moving performance as the old doorman in *The Last Laugh*) and Dupont, whose classic *Varieté* contains another Jannings tour de force. In Hollywood Jannings won the first ever Best Actor Oscar (for *The Last Command* and *The Way of All Flesh*), but sound sent him back to Germany and a final triumph as the professor enslaved by Dietrich in *The Blue Angel*. Jannings was an enthusiastic supporter of the Nazis, and appeared until the end of the war in many of the ponderous vehicles characteristic of the period. He was blacklisted after the war, and though eventually allowed to resume work, died before doing so. Egotistical and hard to work with though he was, Jannings had an enormous talent, his expansive theatrical style and mobility of facial expression being perfectly suited to the slightly overdrawn characters he played in silent days.

Films include: 1914 Im Banne der Leidenschaft. '16 Arme Eva/Frau Eva. '19 Madame Dubarry (GB/USA: Passion); Anna Boleyn (GB/USA: Deception). '21 Danton (USA: All for a Woman). '22 Das Weib des Pharaohs (USA: The Loves of Pharaoh). '24 Das Wachssfigurenkabinett (GB/USA: The Three Waxworks/ Waxworks); Der letze Mann (GB/USA: The Last Laugh). '25 Varieté (GB/USA: Variety); Tartuff/Herr Tärtuff (GB/USA: Tartuffe, the Hypocrite). '26 Faust. '27 The Way of All Flesh (USA). '28 The Last Command (USA); Street of Sin (USA). '30 Der blaue Engel (GB/USA: The Blue Angel). '41 Ohm Krüger. '42 Die Entlassung (GB/USA: Bismarck's Dismissal).

JANSSEN, David

(1930–1980). Actor. Born: David Meyer; Naponee, Nebraska, USA

David Janssen appeared in one or two films as a child actor, and after leaving school played minor roles in small films. Television series made him something of a name, and thereafter he divided his time between the small screen (*The Fugitive, Harry O*) and much better, or at least bigger, parts in films. Sadly, of the thirty-odd movies in which he appeared, usually as a tough loner, not one is in the slightest degree memorable.

Films include: 1960 Hell to Eternity. '61 King of the Roaring 20's (GB: The Big Bankroll). '67 Warning Shot. '68 The Shoes of the Fisherman; The Green Berets. '75 Once Is Not Enough. '81 Inchon.

JARMAN, Derek

(b. 1942). Director. Born: Northwood, London, England

In his films Derek Jarman liberally mixes new and anarchic subjects into the framework of orthodox cultural forms. His three major films have all gained near-cult status – *Sebastiane*, a stark and frank film about homosexuality; *Jubilee*, a visual hash of anarchy, culture and symbolism that made heroes of punk's anti-heroes; and *The Tempest*, a magical, mystical, highly decorative adaptation of Shakespeare's play. Jarman began as a painter, having attended the Slade art school, and it was after his successful first exhibition that he was asked to design the sets and costumes for *Don Giovanni* at the London Coliseum. This resulted in Ken Russell employing him for the same purpose on his film *The Devils*, and it was also around this time that Jarman began making 8mm films. Since then he has continued to make films on a shoestring with each one financing the next – and he has proved himself a master of producing lavish-looking, seductive films even with ludicrously small sums of money.

Films include: 1971 The Devils (des. consultant only). '72 Savage Messiah (des. consultant only). '73 Burning Pyramids. '74 The Art of Mirrors (series made 1970–74). '76 Sebastiane (co-dir; +co-sc). '78 Jubilee (+co-sc). '79 The Tempest (+sc). '80 Broken English: Three Songs by Marianne Faithfull. '81 TG: Psychic Rally in Heaven.

JARRE, Maurice

(b. 1924). Composer. Born: Lyon, France

Maurice Jarre studied music at the Paris Conservatoire, and was taught composition by Arthur Honegger. He worked in the theatre orchestra of the Jean-Louis Barrault Company, and then became musical director at the Théâtre National Populaire in its great days under Jean Vilar. Jarre's first film score came in 1952, for a short film of Georges Franju. He went on to compose for several French features, but from the early Sixties he worked largely abroad, often on big-budget films for renowned directors.

He won Academy Awards for *Lawrence of Arabia* and *Doctor Zhivago*, where he combined restrained scoring with the obligatory epic sweep.

Films include: 1961 Les Amours Célèbres. '62 Lawrence of Arabia; The Longest Day; Cybele ou les Dimanches de Ville d'Avray (FR) (GB/USA: Sundays and Cybele). '65 Dr Zhivago. '66 Paris Brule-t-il? (FR) (GB: Is Paris Burning?). '68 The Fixer. '70 Ryan's Daughter. '75 The Man Who Would Be King. '79 Die Blechtrommel (GER-FR) (GB/USA: The Tin Drum).

JASSET, Victorin

(1862–1913). Producer/director. Born: Funay, France

Jasset was a painter, sculptor and costume designer who entered the theatre, working on ballet and pantomimes. Moving on to the cinema, he produced a monumental *La Vie du Christ* at Gaumont, but his most famous work was done for the Eclair company. Jasset produced and in part directed the *Nick Carter*, *Rifle Bill* and *Zigomar* serials of crime and adventure, which were among the earliest of film serials, considerably antedating the work of Louis Feuillade. He was much influenced by contemporary American film-making, and disliked the stodgy theatricalism of the French *film d'art*. He died in 1913 as the result of an operation, just after making *Protéa*, featuring a lady master-criminal of many disguises.

Films include: 1906 La Vie du Christ (prod). '08 Nick Carter, le Roi des Détectives (serial) (co-dir); Rifle Bill, le Roi de la Prairie (serial). '12 Zigomar, Peau d'Anguille (serial) (co-dir) (GB: Zigomar Eelskin); Zigomar Contre Nick Carter (serial) (co-dir). '13 Protéa.

JAUBERT, Maurice

(1900–1940). Composer. Born: Nice, France

The principal composer of the classic period of the French cinema during the Thirties, Maurice Jaubert worked with nearly all of the main filmmakers of that time. His popular but by no means façile compositions were used to heighten the effects of a scene without drawing attention to the music. He was also a lawyer and only began composing at the age of 28 at the invitation of the director and producer Alberto Cavalcanti. Jaubert was killed in action by enemy aircraft fire at the outbreak of World War II.

Films include: 1929 Le Petit Chaperon Rouge. '32 Quatorze Juillet (USA: July 14th). '33 Zéro de Conduite. '34 L'Atalante; Le Dernier Milliardaire. '36 Mayerling. '37 Un Carnet de Bal (USA: Life Dances On; GB: Christine); Drôle de Drame (USA: Bizarre, Bizarre). '38 Hôtel du Nord; Quai des Brumes (USA: Port of Shadows). '39 Le Jour se Lève (USA: Daybreak); Air Pur.

JEFFRIES, Lionel

(b. 1926). Actor/director. Born: London, England

Educated at Wimborne School in Dorset, Lionel Jeffries was an army officer during the war and then

Above, from left to right: David Janssen in The Green Berets, John Wayne's notoriously hawkish Vietnam film; Lionel Jeffries in Jules Verne's Rocket to the Moon (1967); Isabel Jewell with Ronald Colman in A Tale of Two Cities, the most famous screen version of the Dickens classic. Below: Glynis Johns as a mermaid in Miranda. Far right: British 'lady' Rosamund John in The Upturned Glass. Right: George Jessel

was a marvellously precise, inventive and confident artist. Humphrey Jennings died in Greece, after falling from a cliff while scouting locations for a film.

Films include: **1939** Spare Time. **'40** Spring Offensive; London Can Take It. **'42** Listen to Britain; The Silent Village. **'43** Fires Were Started. **'45** A Diary for Timothy. **'48** Cumberland Story. **'49** Dim Little Island. **'50** Family Portrait.

JESSEL, George

(1898–1981). Actor/producer. Born: New York City, USA

Beginning as a boy singer with Eddie Cantor in vaudeville, Jessel had a varied career outside films, as stage producer, vaudeville comic, writer, composer, popular television host and Master of Ceremonies. In cinema he made occasional acting appearances with no great success, but spent 11 years as a producer with 20th Century-Fox from 1945 onwards. Jessel usually produced musicals, but was also producer of Edmund Goulding's brilliant *film noir*, *Nightmare Alley*. His second wife (of four) was actress Norma Talmadge.

Films include: **1926** Lucky Boy (act). **'29** Love, Live and Laugh (act). **'43** Stage Door Canteen (act). **'44** Four Jills and a Jeep (act). **'45** The Dolly Sisters (prod). **'47** Nightmare Alley (prod). **'49** Dancing in the Dark (prod). **'51** Golden Girl (prod). **'52** Wait 'til the Sun Shines, Nellie (prod). **'69** Can Heironymous Merkin Ever Forget Mercy Humpe and Find True Happiness? (act) (GB).

JEWELL, Isabel

(1909–1972). Actress. Born: Shoshone, Wyoming, USA

Isabel Jewell spent some years in stock companies before her Broadway debut in 1930. Two years later she played a hardboiled telephone operator in the fast-talking comedy *Blessed Event*, and repeated the role in the film version. Through the Thirties and Forties she appeared in many notable films, although usually in small parts. A tiny, fair-haired girl, she resisted being typed, moving easily from dizzy blondes to gangsters' molls or pathetic outcasts, and will always be remembered for her frightened little seamstress going to the guillotine with Ronald Colman in the 1935 *A Tale of Two Cities*.

Films include: **1932** Blessed Event. **'33** Counsellor-at-Law. **'34** Manhattan Melodrama. **'35** A Tale of Two Cities. **'37** Marked Woman; Lost Horizon. **'39** Gone With The Wind. **'40** Northwest Passage. **'41** High Sierra. **'48** The Snake Pit. **'53** Small Town Girl. **'57** Bernardine.

JEWISON, Norman

(b. 1926). Director. Born: Toronto, Ontario, Canada

After attending the University of Toronto, Jewison worked in England as a writer and actor for the BBC. He then went into Canadian television before joining CBS as a director in 1958. Success with musical specials brought him into the movies in 1963. Jewison was better suited to the modest scale of earlier efforts like *Send Me No Flowers* and *The Cincinnati Kid*, though even here there were signs of a tendency to inflate his material. *In the Heat of the Night* was a flashily coarse production that ill deserved its reputation, while the later musicals, if rich in detail, were top-heavy affairs. *F.I.S.T.*, however, was a surprisingly radical American Union film.

Films include: **1963** The Thrill of It All. **'64** Send Me No Flowers. **'65** The Cincinnati Kid. **'66** The Russians Are Coming, the Russians Are Coming. **'67** In the Heat of the Night. **'68** The Thomas Crown Affair. **'71** Fiddler on The Roof. **'73** Jesus Christ Superstar. **'75** Rollerball. **'78** F.I.S.T. **'80** . . . And Justice For All.

JOHN, Rosamund

(b. 1913). Actress. Born: Tottenham, London, England

A very versatile actress, Rosamund John won a scholarship to the Embassy Theatre school after playing a small part in the Ealing production *Secret of the Loch* (1934). Following a period in repertory she was spotted by Robert Donat who enticed her back to the cinema. After a number of important roles in the Forties – as a suffragette in *Fame Is the Spur* and a strong-minded nurse in *The Lamp Still Burns* – she ceased acting. Ultimately, Rosamund John's first love was politics – a career into which she entered via her marriage to the Labour member of Parliament John Silkin in 1950.

Films include: **1942** The First of the Few (USA: Spitfire). **'43** The Gentle Sex; The Lamp Still Burns. **'45** The Way to the Stars (USA: Johnny in the Clouds). **'46** Green for Danger. **'47** The Upturned Glass; Fame Is the Spur; When the Bough Breaks. **'50** No Place for Jennifer. **'57** Operation Murder.

JOHNS, Glynis

(b. 1923). Actress. Born: Pretoria, South Africa

The daughter of Mervyn Johns, Glynis Johns made her film debut in 1938 with *South Riding* – a melodramatic exploration of Yorkshire local politics. From this role as Ralph Richardson's daughter she proceeded to prove her acting adaptability in a number of different roles. Among the most notable of these was as the voluptuous mermaid Miranda in the film of the same name. Her attractive husky voice and piercing blue eyes lent her equally well to both serious and comic roles. She has made most impact in America where, in the early Sixties, she starred in her own television series *Glynis*. Her performance in *A Little Night Music* in the mid-Seventies brought her public acclaim once again. Sadly, illness has hampered her later career.

Films include: **1938** South Riding. **'41** 49th Parallel. **'47** Frieda; An Ideal Husband. **'48** Miranda. **'53** The Sword and the Rose. **'56** Around the World in Eighty Days (USA). **'64** Mary Poppins (USA). **'69** Lock Up Your Daughters! **'73** Vault of Horror.

went to RADA. He was spotted by Hitchcock and cast as the bald-headed drama student in *Stage Fright*. That memorable dome then appeared in over a hundred British and American movies as Jeffries distinguished himself as an excellent character actor. In films like *The Wrong Arm of the Law*, in which he played the bungling Inspector Parker, it shone out in all its unashamed nakedness: a sure sign of the dull, obtuse, supposedly incorruptible copper playing it by the book – and a source of marvellous comedy. In 1970 Jeffries turned director of first-class children's films, commencing with his best work, *The Railway Children*. His self-confessed goal in these movies is wholesome family entertainment with a little bit of child psychology. On television he was the cockney Roman Catholic priest in the comedy series *Father Charlie*.

Films include: **1949** Stage Fright. **'56** The Baby and the Battleship; Lust for Life (USA). **'57** Blue Murder at St Trinian's. **'59** The Nun's Story (USA); Please Turn Over. **'60** Two-Way Stretch; The Trials of Oscar Wilde (USA: The Man With the Green Carnation). **'63** The Wrong Arm of the Law. **'67** Camelot (USA). **'68** Chitty Chitty Bang Bang. **'70** The Railway Children (dir). **'72** Baxter! (dir); The Amazing Mr Blunden (dir). **'75** Royal Flash. **'78** The Water Babies (dir) (GB-POL). **'79** Prisoner of Zenda (USA).

JENNINGS, Humphrey

(1907–1950). Director. Born: Frank Humphrey Jennings; Walberswick, Suffolk, England

Educated at Perse School and Pembroke College, Cambridge, where he gained a First in English, Jennings was a man of many skills. He researched in English literature, wrote poetry, painted with great ability, and was a founder of Mass Observation. He was also an organizer of the important Surrealist Exhibition in London in 1936. He had joined the GPO Film Unit in 1934, and by the end of that year had acted, designed sets, edited and directed. Jennings' genius flowered in his wartime documentaries. These films showed a deep attachment to the best things in English character and English life, and they had the kind of unsentimental romanticism found often in English painting but never, outside Jennings, in English cinema. It is important not to overpraise him: he worked on a small scale, and never ventured outside the documentary framework, but within those limits he

225

JOHNS, Mervyn

(b. 1899). Actor. Born: Pembroke, South Wales

Having begun as a medical student at the London Hospital, Mervyn Johns changed his allegiance to drama and enrolled at RADA. As a start to his long and distinguished career, his first accolade was the award of the RADA gold medal. In 1934 he entered films with *Lady in Danger*. The fact that he became one of Britain's more prominent leading men during the war years could be thought surprising due to his unprepossessing looks. This, however, did not stop him playing some demanding roles, such as the nondescript German spy in *Next of Kin* and the strict disciplinarian in *Pink String and Sealing Wax*. After the death of his first wife he retired to an actor's home but then re-emerged to marry again at the age of 77.

Films include: 1940 Saloon Bar. '42 Next of Kin. '43 San Demetrio, London. '44 Halfway House. '45 Pink String and Sealing Wax; Dead of Night. '46 The Captive Heart. '47 Captain Boycott. '57 The Gypsy and the Gentleman. '61 No Love for Johnny. '62 The Day of the Triffids.

JOHNSON, Ben

(b. 1919). Actor. Born: Pawhuska, Oklahoma, USA

Of mixed Irish-Cherokee descent, Johnson was a cowboy and rodeo steer-roper who won a world championship in 1953. By then, too, his film career was well established. He had doubled for Joel McCrea and John Wayne, and played a bit part in *Fort Apache* which led to his becoming a member of John Ford's stock company. He was excellent in a number of Ford Westerns, and played the lead in *Wagon Master*. His later films included several for Sam Peckinpah, and an outstanding Oscar-winning performance as Sam the Lion, the ageing café, pool-hall and cinema owner in *The Last Picture Show*.

Films include: 1948 Fort Apache; Three Godfathers. '49 Mighty Joe Young; She Wore a Yellow Ribbon. '50 Rio Grande; Wagon Master. '53 Shane. '61 One-Eyed Jacks. '64 Cheyenne Autumn. '65 Major Dundee. '69 The Wild Bunch. '71 The Last Picture Show. '72 Junior Bonner. '79 Terror Train.

JOHNSON, Celia

(1908–1982). Actress. Born: Richmond, Surrey, England

An actress of refined and haunted beauty, Celia Johnson was primarily a stage actress. She became seriously involved in films with Noel Coward and played important roles in all his major films, such as the patriotic *In Which We Serve* and *This Happy Breed*. Her most memorable performance was in *Brief Encounter*, a deeply touching story of a suburban housewife's unconsummated love for a doctor, played by Trevor Howard. Celia Johnson continued to work on the stage and TV until her death. She was a DBE.

Films include: 1942 In Which We Serve. '43 Dear Octopus. '44 This Happy Breed. '45 Brief Encounter. '50 The Astonished Heart. '52 I Believe In You. '53 The Captain's Paradise. '55 A Kid for Two Farthings. '57 The Good Companions. '69 The Prime of Miss Jean Brodie.

JOHNSON, Chic

See OLSEN & JOHNSON

JOHNSON, Nunnally

(1897–1977). Screenwriter/producer/director. Born: Columbus, Georgia, USA

A journalist and writer of short stories, Nunnally Johnson began a screenwriting career with Fox in 1933. Two years later he became an associate producer also. After a period in the Forties with International Pictures, which he helped to form, he returned to Fox, and in the Fifties added direction to his duties. It was as a writer, however, that he was most successful. His was a witty and versatile talent, and most of his scripts were single-handed efforts. Outstanding among them were three for Ford, including that of *The Grapes of Wrath*, and *The Woman in the Window* for Fritz Lang. The very funny gangster satire, *Roxie Hart*, was characteristic of his lighter mood.

Films include: 1917 The Gunfighter. '34 The House of Rothschild. '40 The Grapes of Wrath. '41 Tobacco Road. '42 Roxie Hart (+prod). '44 The Woman in the Window (+prod); The Keys of the Kingdom (co-sc). '57 The True Story of Jesse James. '64 The World of Henry Orient (co-sc). '67 The Dirty Dozen (co-sc).

JOHNSON, Richard

(b. 1927). Actor. Born: Upminster, Essex, England

Debonair and handsome, Richard Johnson has been both a star of the stage and the screen. Before joining the navy at the end of the war he had been part of John Gielgud's repertory company. After successful West End appearances he entered the film world and promptly became the source for much gossip following his romantic exploits. Nevertheless, he proceeded to contribute some fine screen performances. His playboy image in films was relinquished and replaced by a more serious one in the stage performance of *Antony and Cleopatra* (1973), in which he played opposite Janet Suzman.

Films include: 1951 Captain Horatio Hornblower. '59 Never So Few (USA). '63 Cairo (USA). '64 The Pumpkin Eater. '65 Operation Crossbow; The Amorous Adventures of Moll Flanders. '66 Khartoum; Deadlier than the Male. '67 Danger Route. '69 Some Girls Do. '71 Julius Caesar.

JOHNSON, Van

(b. 1916). Actor. Born: Charles Van Johnson; Newport, Rhode Island, USA

Van Johnson began as a Broadway chorus boy, had a brief six month contract in Hollywood and was then signed by MGM. During the Forties he became a successful teen-idol; with his exuberant smile, red hair and freckles, Van Johnson embodied the

Above: Mervyn Johns in The Captive Heart, *a story of life in a POW camp. Below: Ben Johnson in* The Train Robbers *(1973). Bottom: Celia Johnson in* Brief Encounter. *Below right: Richard Johnson in* Hennessy *(1975).*

Bottom: Van Johnson in When In Rome *(1951). Below right: Al Jolson in* Mammy. *Below, far right: Buck Jones in Gordon of Ghost City (1933). Bottom, far right: Carolyn Jones in* Sail a Crooked Ship *(1961)*

archetypal 'boy-next-door' image. As his career continued he was able to escape this typecasting and play more mature and serious roles in a variety of films, such as *The Caine Mutiny* in which he portrayed Lt. Maryk. His screen appearances have now diminished but he can often be seen on the dinner-theatre circuit.

Films include: 1942 The War Against Mrs Hadley. '44 Two Girls and a Sailor; Thirty Seconds Over Tokyo. '45 Thrill of a Romance. '47 High Barbaree. '54 The Siege at Red River; The Last Time I Saw Paris; The Caine Mutiny. '58 The Last Blitzkrieg. '63 Wives and Lovers. '67 Divorce American Style.

JOLSON, Al

(1886–1950). Singer/actor. Born: Asa Yoelson; St Petersburg, Russia

As everyone knows, he was a cantor's son who defied family tradition by going on the stage and becoming a colossal success. The story of Jolson's early life provided the basis for *The Jazz Singer*, the mawkish Warner Brothers film in which he spoke the movies' first words of natural dialogue (and which started his 12-year career as a film star in increasingly sentimental vehicles). Perhaps, in retrospect, Jolson's importance to the cinema was not in that prophetic ad-lib – 'You

ain't heard nothin' yet!' – but in the legend of his own origins, from which he established himself as America's most popular entertainer. Notwithstanding Louise Brooks, Jolson could have been the first star to live out part of his life on film – the prototype for Garbo wanting to be alone, Monroe searching for her 'daddy' throughout her screen career, Flynn playing drunks at the end of his. It is the notion that films and life are one. It only needed Al Jolson to play Al Jolson in *The Jolson Story* in 1946 – but he was refused the part (which went to Larry Parks). In real life, the cantor's son began as a stage extra in New York in 1899, worked in a double act with his brother Harry, blacked up his face and joined a minstrel show which led to him becoming Broadway's chief attraction. The rest is legend. Jolson's third of four wives was actress Ruby Keeler.

Films: 1927 The Jazz Singer. '28 The Singing Fool. '29 Say It With Songs. '30 Mammy; Big Boy. '33 Hallelujah, I'm a Bum (GB: Hallelujah, I'm a Tramp). '34 Wonder Bar. '35 Go Into Your Dance (GB: Casino de Paree). '36 The Singing Kid. '39 Rose of Washington Square; Hollywood Cavalcade (guest); Swanee River. '45 Rhapsody in Blue (as himself). '46 The Jolson Story (voice only). '49 Jolson Sings Again (voice only).

JONES, Buck

(1889–1942). Actor. Born: Charles Frederick Gebhart; Vincennes, Indiana, USA

During the Twenties Western star Buck Jones became one of the greatest heroes of American youth. He believed he had a responsibility to set a good example to those who admired him and he remained true to his clean-cut image. He spent much of his childhood in the saddle on his father's ranch, and his wanderlust finally led him to a Wild West show at the 101 Ranch in Oklahoma. Impelled by his love of heroes, he then enlisted in the US Cavalry and was eventually invalided out. He spent some time drifting between ranches, circuses and various other jobs before ending up in Hollywood where he worked as a double for the cowboy stars undertaking the most hazardous stunts. After a spell breaking in horses for the French government during World War I he returned to Hollywood and signed a contract with William Fox. He soon became immensely wealthy and successful and even bought his own circus. But, inevitably, his popularity waned and he lost his fame, fortune and property. The occasional film was bringing him in some revenue when he died, still a hero, trying to save others in a fire at a fashionable nightclub in Boston.

Films include: 1920 The Last Straw. '24 The Circus Cowboy. '25 Hearts and Spurs. '26 The Fighting Buckaroo. '31 The Avenger. '32 South of the Rio Grande; White Eagle. '34 Rocky Rhodes. '38 Stranger From Arizona. '42 Dawn of the Great Divide.

JONES, Carolyn

(1929–1983). Actress. Born: Amarillo, Texas, USA

From amateur dramatics at high school Carolyn Jones became a disc-jockey at a local radio station to pay for her tuition at the Pasadena Community Playhouse. Shortly before her graduation she was appearing in one of their productions when the writer and producer Aaron Spelling saw her and cast her in his play *The Live Wire*. The consequences of this were that Jones and Spelling married and she was offered a contract with Paramount. This contract was suddenly curtailed after two films, but she continued to work in a great deal and later signed for Warner Brothers, where she was repeatedly cast as a sexy woman of the world. Many had declared her an overnight star, and she never quite sustained her initial popularity mainly because she was misused and miscast. She was nominated for an Academy Award for her acting in *The Bachelor Party*.

Films include: 1952 The Road to Bali. '53 House of Wax; The Big Heat. '54 Desiree. '55 The Seven Year Itch; The Tender Trap. '56 The Invasion of the Body Snatchers. '57 The Bachelor Party. '58 King Creole. '77 The Turning Point.

JONES, Chuck

(b. 1912). Animator/director. Born: Spokane, Washington, USA

With a gang of like-minded innovative animators at Warner Brothers during the Forties, Chuck Jones turned out an unceasing flow of fun cartoons full of puns, parodies and animators' in-jokes. Jones went to California at the age of eight and spent much of his boyhood in Twenties Hollywood working as a child extra in Mack Sennett comedies. He attended art school and then worked as a celluloid washer until he was discovered by the animator Ub Iwerks for whom he then worked. Having moved through the ranks of the early studios, he directed his first cartoon when he was 25, and he was soon working at Warners producing numerous fast-moving, hard-hitting, humorous cartoons. After Warners dissolved their animation department he worked briefly for Disney and MGM before finally forming his own company producing cartoons for television. He is a greatly admired and respected animator, and creator of such famous characters as Daffy Duck, Bugs Bunny and Porky Pig, and his work has been the subject of many retrospectives.

Films include: 1940 Elmer's Candid Camera. '42 The Dover Boys. '44 Hell Bent for Election. '49 Fast and Furryous. '57 What's Opera, Doc? '62 Gay Purr-ee (+co-sc). '64 Unshrinkable Jerry Mouse; To Beep or Not to Beep. '65 Dot and the Line. '70 The Phantom Tollbooth (co-dir; +co-sc).

JONES, James Earl

(b. 1931). Actor. Born: Tate County, Mississippi, USA

James Earl Jones has been called the best Othello in the world – he is certainly an incredibly talented and admired Shakespearian actor, and is particularly renowned for his performances at the New York Shakespeare Festival. It was there, after a spate of appearances in off-Broadway productions, that he first gained recognition, playing Oberon in *A Midsummer Night's Dream*. Despite his undoubted talent his film career has never really given him the recognition he deserves. Possibly his biggest film breakthrough was in *The Great White Hope*; he received an Oscar nomination for his role as the first black heavyweight champion of the world. He was, himself, the son of a boxer-turned-actor, Robert Earl Jones. It was through the encouragement of an English teacher that Jones overcame his stutter and decided to study drama rather than medicine. He has won numerous awards for his stage work and, interestingly, his is the uncredited voice of the evil Darth Vader in *Star Wars* (1977) and its sequels.

Films include: 1967 The Comedians. '70 The Great White Hope; End of the Road. '72 The Man. '74 Claudine. '76 The Bingo Long Travelling All-Stars and Motor Kings; The River Niger; The Scarlet Buccaneer. '77 Exorcist II: The Heretic; A Piece of the Action; The Last Remake of Beau Geste.

JONES, Jennifer

(b. 1919). Actress. Born: Phyllis Isley; Tulsa, Oklahoma, USA

David O. Selznick first auditioned Jennifer Jones three years before he unveiled her to the public as his new protégée in *The Song of Bernadette*. She won the Best Actress Academy Award for this role as the peasant girl who convinces the Catholic Church that her visions of the Virgin Mary are indeed genuine. Jones came from a theatrical family and studied at the American Academy of Dramatic Arts in New York. It was there that she met her first husband Robert Walker and they both left to get married. They spent their honeymoon in Hollywood and managed to land a couple of parts in B movies before returning to New York. Jones worked in radio and live shows before meeting Selznick, and although he was successful in building her into a star her first half dozen major films, particularly *Cluny Brown* and *Duel in the Sun*, were by far the best. Jones and Walker were divorced in 1945 and she and Selznick were subsequently married from 1949 until his death 16 years later. She is now married to the art collector and multimillionaire Norton Simon.

Films include: 1943 The Song of Bernadette. '44 Since You Went Away. '46 Cluny Brown; Duel in the Sun. '48 Portrait of Jennie. '50 Gone to Earth (GB) (USA: The Wild Heart). '52 Ruby Gentry; Carrie. '53 Beat the Devil. '56 The Man in the Gray Flannel Suit. '62 Tender Is the Night. '74 The Towering Inferno.

JONES, L.Q.

(b. 1927). Actor. Born: Justus Ellis McQueen; Beaumont, Texas, USA

With his piercing eyes, angular features and thick blond hair, L.Q. Jones lends his characters a menacing and determined quality, and he has played several small but unforgettable parts in war films and Westerns. However, it is television that has tended to provide him with the more major roles that cinema has failed to offer. He graduated in law, business and journalism and enjoyed varied jobs as a salesman, comedian and rancher before turning to the screen at the suggestion of his friend, actor Fess Parker. He has since found constant work in film and television and has also formed his own production company LQJAF (L.Q. Jones and Friends) turning out successful low-budget films.

Films include: 1955 Target Zero. '56 Love Me Tender. '58 The Naked and the Dead; Torpedo Run; The Young Lions. '59 Warlock. '68 Hang 'Em High. '69 The Wild Bunch. '70 The Ballad of Cable Hogue. '75 A Boy and His Dog (dir; +prod. only).

JONES, Quincy

(b. 1933). Composer/arranger. Born: Chicago, Illinois, USA

Jones is a major figure in contemporary music whose syntheses of jazz and pop – though frowned on by purist critics – have brought him great commercial success. He was educated at the Berklee School of Music in Boston, studied with Nadia Boulanger and Olivier Messiaen in Paris, and played (trumpet) with many great jazz artists, including Billie Holiday, Lionel Hampton and Dizzie Gillespie. He turned to composing and arranging, working with such brilliant vocalists as Frank Sinatra, Ray Charles and Peggy Lee. His flexible musical attitudes also made him much sought-after as a writer of film scores and television themes. He was the first black musician to gain prominence in this field, being nominated for an Oscar for the score of *In Cold Blood*. Frail and delicate (he survived two operations for brain aneurysms in 1974), he continues to work, mainly in the jazz-funk style.

Films include: 1965 The Pawnbroker; Mirage. '67 In the Heat of the Night; In Cold Blood. '68 For Love of Ivy. '69 Bob and Carol and Ted and Alice; The Italian Job (GB); McKenna's Gold. '72 The New Centurions. '78 The Wiz.

JONES, Shirley

(b. 1934). Actress/singer. Born: Smithton, Pennsylvania, USA

A former contestant (as Miss Pittsburgh) in the Miss America Beauty Contest, Shirley Jones established her wholesome appeal in the Rodgers and Hammerstein musicals *Oklahoma!* and *Carousel*. That she could be an excellent actress given the chance was underlined by her performance in a quite different kind of part – as a vengeful prostitute in *Elmer Gantry*, for which she won a Best Supporting

Above: Jennifer Jones. Left: James Earl Jones in The Great White Hope *from the true story of Jack Johnson, a black boxer who has a troublesome affair with a white girl. Below left: L.Q. Jones in* The McMasters *(1970). Below: Shirley Jones as Julie in* Carousel *adapted from the stage musical. Bottom: Louis Jourdan*

Actress Oscar. Her film career hit a lean patch in the mid-Sixties and she worked mainly in television and on stage. An upswing in her popularity followed her playing of Connie Partridge in *The Partridge Family* television series, which also featured David Cassidy, her stepson in real life by her marriage to singer Jack Cassidy in 1956 (they divorced in 1975).

Films include: 1955 Oklahoma! '56 Carousel. '60 Elmer Gantry. '61 Two Rode Together. '62 The Music Man. '63 The Courtship of Eddie's Father. '64 Bedtime Story. '70 The Cheyenne Social Club. '79 Beyond the Poseidon Adventure.

JONES, Tommy Lee

(b. 1947). Actor. Born: San Saba, Texas, USA

Jones has the intelligence and flexibility to be a major star in the Eighties, his burly physique and brooding, beetle-browed features making him equally convincing in sympathetic or villainous roles. The stage supplanted football as Jones' main interest while he was at Harvard. He worked regularly on stage until, with a small part in *Love Story*, he began his film career. His first starring role was as an escaped convict ruthlessly hunted down by police in *Jackson County Jail*. He followed this with a virtuoso performance as Howard Hughes in the 1977 television movie *Howard, the Amazing Mr Hughes*. Successes in *The Eyes of Laura Mars*, as a psychotic-detective, and in *Coal Miner's Daughter*, as the pushy but vulnerable husband of country singer Loretta Lynn, consolidated his career. In both films his commanding physical presence intriguingly complemented the sensitivity of his leading ladies, Faye Dunaway and Sissy Spacek, respectively. He is married to the actress Katherine Lardner.

Films include: 1970 Love Story. '75 Elija's Horoscope (CAN). '76 Jackson County Jail. '77 Back Roads (AUS). '78 The Betsy; The Eyes of Laura Mars. '80 Coal Miner's Daughter.

JORY, Victor

(1902–1982). Actor. Born: Dawson City, Yukon Territory, Canada

He will perhaps be best remembered for his menacing portrayal of Oberon in the Reinhardt-Dieterle *A Midsummer Night's Dream*. But Jory's craggy, saturnine physiognomy and powerful frame (he had been a champion boxer and wrestler) were ideal qualifications for playing heavies in the movies – cruel fathers, evil husbands, tough Western desperados or bloodthirsty Indians. He served a lengthy stage apprenticeship before being signed by 20th Century-Fox, making the first of his 76 film appearances in *Sailors Luck* in 1932. Though

Above: Tommy Lee Jones in The Betsy, *a struggle-for-power melodrama also starring Laurence Olivier. Below: Victor Jory in* The Miracle Worker, *the real-life story of the blind, deaf and dumb girl Helen Keller. Bottom: Erland Josephson in* Face to Face *with Ingmar Bergman directing. Bottom right: Louis Jouvet in* Drôle de Drame

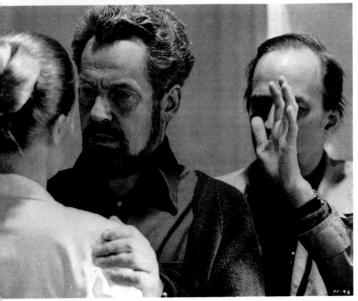

his appearance was sinister, a kindly side to his personality was evident in his pleasant voice – he recorded a number of albums of stories for children. He also possessed strong literary interests, owning a fine library and having a play he had written, *Five Who Were Mad*, performed on Broadway. He appeared in over 200 television shows and was still working in his eightieth year when he died of a heart attack.

Films include: 1933 State Fair. '34 Madame Du Barry. '35 A Midsummer Night's Dream. '38 The Adventures of Tom Sawyer. '39 Gone With The Wind. '49 Canadian Pacific. '62 The Miracle Worker. '64 Cheyenne Autumn. '71 A Time for Dying. '73 Papillon.

JOSEPHSON, Erland

(b. 1923). Actor/director. Born: Stockholm, Sweden

Josephson won widespread recognition as Liv Ullmann's oppressively bland husband in Bergman's 1973 television series *Scenes From a Marriage* (since edited into a film). He has made similar appearances in several of Bergman's more recent films. He specializes in middle-aged professional men, whose relentless stuffiness conceals deep-seated neuroses. Josephson made his acting debut in 1945, beginning his association with Bergman a year later with a small part in *It Rains on Our Love*. He joined the Royal Dramatic Theatre in 1956, and was its creative director between 1966 and 1975 (he succeeded Bergman). He is an established author and an experienced television and film director. Josephson's most recent role was in Makavejev's *Montenegro* – a rare excursion into comedy, though of a peculiarly black type.

Films include: 1946 Det Regnar på Vår Kärlek (USA: It Rains on Our Love; GB: The Man With an Umbrella). '48 Eva. '50 Till Glädje (USA/GB: To Joy). '68 Vargtimmen (USA/GB: Hour of the Wolf). '69 En Passion (USA: The Passion of Anna; GB: A Passion). '72 Viskningar och Rop (USA/GB: Cries and Whispers). '73 Scener ur ett Aktenskap (USA/GB: Scenes From a Marriage). '75

Ansikte mot Ansikte (USA/GB: Face to Face). '78 En och En (USA/GB: One and One) (co-dir. only). '80 Marmeladupproret (+dir) (USA/GB: Marmalade Revolution). '81 Montenegro, or Pigs and Pearls (SWED-GB).

JOURDAN, Louis

(b. 1921). Actor. Born: Louis Genore; Marseilles, France

The son of a hotelier, Jourdan studied acting at the Ecole Dramatique in Paris. He was discovered by the director Marc Allegret who cast this strikingly handsome actor in *Le Corsaire* in 1939. An instant hit, Jourdan starred in nine more films until World War II interrupted his career and he joined the Resistance. After the war, producer David O. Selznick, always on the look out for future stars, invited him to Hollywood to appear in *The Paradine Case*. The American public, especially the female contingent, swooned over Jourdan's dark-eyed suavity and velvety French accent – as did Joan Fontaine in Ophuls' *Letter From an Unknown Woman*, Jourdan's next, and finest, film. Playing a Continental charmer has its limitations, as Jourdan was to discover. Since the Fifties he has found good movie parts hard to come by, settling instead for leads in stage and television.

Films include: 1939 Le Corsaire (FR). '47 The Paradine Case. '48 Letter From an Unknown Woman. '49 Madame Bovary. '54 Three Coins in the Fountain. '56 Julie. '58 Gigi. '60 Can Can. '63 The V.I.P.'s. '76 The Count of Monte Cristo (GB). '77 The Man in the Iron Mask (GB-USA); Silver Bears (GB).

JOUVET, Louis

(1887–1951). Actor/producer. Born: Crozon, Finistère, France

Before World War II, Jouvet became one of France's leading actors and theatre directors. He made little secret of preferring the stage to the screen; nonetheless his lean, wolfish face and clipped, sardonic delivery were well featured in some of the best French movies of the Thirties. He had no formal acting training, but found work with provincial touring companies. From this lowly start Jouvet gradually rose to become a power in the theatre, successively (and successfully) managing the Comédie des Champs Elysees and the Athenée Theatre and becoming a professor at the Paris Conservatoire (which had earlier refused to take him on as a drama student). Jouvet's best postwar role was as a seedy detective in *Quai des Orfèvres*. He died suddenly from a heart attack while rehearsing a play at the Athenée.

Films include: 1933 Knock, ou Le Triomphe de la Médecine (+co-dir) (USA: Dr Knock). '35 La Kermesse Héroïque. '37 Les Bas-Fonds (USA: The Lower Depths); Un Carnet de Bal (USA: Christine); Drôle de Drame (USA: Bizarre, Bizarre). '38 La Marseillaise (USA: Marseillaise); Hôtel du Nord. '39 La Fin du Jour (USA: End of the Day). '40 Volpone. '47 Quai des Orfèvres (USA: Jenny Lamour).

JOY, Leatrice

(1896–1985). Actress. Born: Leatrice Joy Zeidler; New Orleans, Louisiana, USA

Petite, black-haired and doe-eyed, Leatrice Joy was a major silent movie star. She began in films in 1917 and became one of the Twenties most adaptable and personable female leads, being able to appear efficient and sophisticated as well as sweet and yielding. She was something of a trend-setter; she created a vogue for short, bobbed hair and wore men's suits in movies (such as *For Alimony Only*) long before Marlene Dietrich. Clad in a gown by Adrian she looked cool and stunning – it was this elegance that attracted Cecil B. DeMille, who cast her in starring roles in *Manslaughter* and *The Ten Commandments*. At the height of her popularity she married screen heart-throb John Gilbert, though the marriage only lasted two years. With the advent of talkies she seemed to lose interest in movies; her last appearance was in *Love Nest*.

Films include: 1917 A Girl's Folly. '18 One Dollar Bid. '20 The Right of Way; The Invisible Divorce. '22 Minnie; Manslaughter. '23 The Ten Commandments. '26 For Alimony Only. '39 First Love. '49 Air Hostess. '51 Love Nest.

JUNGE, Alfred

(1886–1964). Art director. Born: Görlitz, Germany.

The role of the art director in creating the look of a movie often goes unsung (praise being heaped instead on the director), but Junge's contribution to British film should not be undervalued. He worked as a designer for the State Opera and State Theatre in Berlin and at Ufa studios before the director E. A. Dupont invited him to England to work on *Moulin Rouge* and *Piccadilly*. Junge stayed on, contributing to many fine movies of the Thirties, including *The Man Who Knew Too Much* and *Goodbye, Mr Chips*. In 1942 he entered the most important phase of his career as production designer for Powell and Pressburger, winning an Academy Award for his sets for *Black Narcissus*, in which he brilliantly recreated a Himalayan nunnery in the studio. In 1947 he joined MGM British as head of the art department and he remained there throughout the Fifties.

Films include: 1928 Moulin Rouge. '29 Piccadilly. '34 The Man Who Knew Too Much. '39 Goodbye, Mr Chips. '43 The Life and Death of Colonel Blimp. '46 A Matter of Life and Death. '47 Black Narcissus. '50 The Miniver Story. '52 Ivanhoe. '57 The Barretts of Wimpole Street.

JURADO, Katy

(b. 1927). Actress. Born: Maria Cristina Estella Marcella Jurado Garcia; Guadalajara, Mexico

Tall, black-haired and dark-eyed, Katy Jurado was typecast as a fiery, Mexican señorita in Hollywood Westerns, her most famous moment coming in *High Noon* when she warns her former beau (Gary Cooper) to leave town. From a wealthy ranching background, she was signed up at 16 by Mexican director Emilio Fernandez. She appeared in 27 films and also worked as a magazine columnist. She made her Hollywood debut in *The Bullfighter and the Lady* and endowed all her subsequent roles with passion and brio. She was at her sultry best in *One-Eyed Jacks* and won a Best Supporting Actress Oscar as Spencer Tracy's Indian wife in *Broken Lance*. Her career and private life went into a sad decline during the Sixties: her roles were poor, she was divorced from Ernest Borgnine (they had wed in 1959) and she attempted suicide in 1968. Happily she has since recovered to make further film appearances in Hollywood and her native Mexico.

Films include: 1943 No Maturàs (MEX). '51 The Bullfighter and the Lady. '52 High Noon. '53 Arrowhead. '54 Broken Lance. '56 Trapeze. '58 The Badlanders. '61 One-Eyed Jacks. '62 Barabbas. '68 Stay Away Joe. '73 Pat Garrett and Billy the Kid. '78 The Children of Sanchez (USA-MEX).

JURAN, Nathan

(b. 1907). Director. Born: Austria

Juran moved to the USA with his parents when he was six. He studied architecture and worked as an art director for RKO and 20th Century-Fox. While at Fox he won an Oscar with co-designers Richard Day and Thomas Little for *How Green Was My Valley* in 1941. It was Universal who gave him his first directorial opportunity – *The Black Castle*, starring Boris Karloff. The success of this shocker led to further assignments and Juran came to specialize in action adventures and Westerns, collaborating splendidly with special-effects maestro Ray Harryhausen on *The Seventh Voyage of Sinbad*.

Films include: 1952 The Black Castle. '53 Gunsmoke. '54 Drums Across the River. '57 Twenty Million Miles to Earth; Hellcats of the Navy. '58 The Seventh Voyage of Sinbad. '62 Jack the Giant Killer. '64 East of Sudan; First Men in the Moon. '69 Land Raiders. '73 The Boy Who Cried Werewolf.

JURGENS, Curt

(1912–1982). Actor. Born: Curd Gustaf Anore Gottlieb Jürgens; Munich, Germany

Jurgens is one of the best known German film actors, having appeared in over a hundred movies in his native country and abroad. His classic, blond, Aryan looks and his height (six feet four inches) made him a natural choice as an aristocrat in costume dramas and a Nazi heavy in war films. He started out as a journalist but soon switched to acting, appearing in lead parts at the Burg theatre in Vienna until its closure by the Nazis. He was then pressganged into mainly propaganda movies until imprisoned in a concentration camp during the latter stages of World War II. A well-publicized marriage to actress Eva Bartok in 1955 and a strong performance as a Nazi in *The Devil's General* made him an international star. His more interesting roles include the infatuated schoolmaster in the remake of *The Blue Angel* and Mackie Messer ('Mack the Knife') in the remake of *The Threepenny Opera*.

Films include: 1935 Königswalzer (USA/GB: The Imperial Waltz). '53 Der letzte Walzer (USA/GB: The Last Waltz). '55 Orient-Express (FR-IT); Die Ratten; Des Teufels General (USA/GB: The Devil's General). '57 Bitter Victory (FR-USA). '59 The Blue Angel (USA). '63 Der Dreigroschenoper (GER-FR) (USA/GB: The Threepenny Opera). '65 Lord Jim (GB). '77 The Spy Who Loved Me (GB). '79 Schöner Gigolo – Armer Gigolo (GER) (USA/GB: Just a Gigolo).

JUSTICE, James Robertson

(1905–1975). Actor. Born: James Norval Harald Robertson Justice; Wigtown, Aberdeen, Scotland

A red-bearded, twenty-stone colossus of a man, Justice was best known as the surgeon Sir Lancelot Spratt in the Doctor film series, constantly terrorizing his medical staff with his apoplectic outbursts. His eccentric sense of fun led him to specialize in farce, yet there were touches of pathos in his performances that suggested that he might be capable of more demanding roles. Film acting was just one of his many occupations and interests. He was an expert linguist, a journalist and naturalist, numbered falconry among his other talents (he taught Prince Charles) and held the honorary post of Rector at Edinburgh University.

Films include: 1944 Fiddler's Three; Champagne Charlie. '48 Scott of the Antarctic; Vice Versa. '49 Whisky Galore! (USA: Tight Little Island). '53 The Sword and the Rose. '54 Doctor in the House. '56 Moby Dick; Checkpoint. '57 Doctor at Large. '61 Very Important Person. '63 Doctor in Distress. '65 Doctor in Clover. '68 Chitty Chitty Bang Bang.

Above: Leatrice Joy in Triumph *(1924). Right, from left to right: 'Mexican spitfire' Katy Jurado; Curt Jurgens in* Soft Beds, Hard Battles *(1973), in which he gave excellent support to Peter Sellers; James Robertson Justice in* Some Will, Some Won't *(1970)*

230

KADÁR, Ján

(1918–1979). Director. Born: Budapest, Hungary

Of Slovak origins, Kadár was a student at the Bratislava Film School before the war, and made an early documentary there. Moving to Prague, he was directing features by 1950, and two years later began a long collaboration with Elmar Klos. Kadár was normally in charge of shooting, with Klos acting more as a producer and supervising editing. They made nine features together, and *A Shop on the High Street*, a film of unpretentious realism and acute observation, not only heralded a rebirth of the Czech film but won an Academy Award for the Best Foreign Language Film of 1965. With the fall of Dubcék in 1968, Kadár went to America, worked in television and made three features for the cinema, while Klos remained in Prague and became head of the Prague Film School.

Films include: 1952 Kidnap (co-dir). '55 Hudbaz Marsu (co-dir) (GB: Music From Mars). '58 Tam Na Konečné (co-dir) (GB: The House at the Terminus). '63 Smrt Si Rika Eneelchen. '64 Obzalovany (co-dir). '65 Obchod Na Korze (USA: The Shop on Main Street; GB: A Shop on the High Street). '69 Adrift (USA-CZECH). '70 The Angel Levine (USA). '75 Lies My Father Told Me (CAN). '78 Freedom Road (USA).

KAHN, Gus

(1886–1941). Lyricist. Born: Coblenz, Germany

Gus Kahn was taken to the USA in 1891 and educated in Chicago. He wrote songs for vaudeville, and in the mid-Twenties had risen to songwriter for Broadway shows. When sound came to the cinema, Kahn contributed prolifically. He worked with composers like Sigmund Romberg, George Gershwin and Harry Warren, and his songs were made immortal on film by Fred Astaire and Ginger Rogers (*Flying Down to Rio*), Jeanette MacDonald (*San Francisco, Rose Marie*) and many others. The 1952 film, *I'll See You in My Dreams*, was a biography of Kahn. He was played by Danny Thomas.

Films include: 1927 The Jazz Singer. '33 Flying Down to Rio. '34 Kid Millions; One Night of Love. '35 Thanks a Million. '36 Let's Sing Again; San Francisco. '37 A Day at the Races; Three Smart Girls. '38 Everybody Sing; The Girl of the Golden West. '40 Spring Parade. '41 Ziegfeld Girl.

KAHN, Madeline

(b. 1942). Actress. Born: Boston, Massachusetts, USA

Odd though it may seem, the owner of the most piercing female voice in Hollywood history has a BA degree in Speech Therapy. Madeline Kahn had ambitions as a singer, and worked in musicals and cabaret before Peter Bogdanovich cast her as the straight-laced, dumpy, determined fiancée in *What's Up, Doc?* Since then her kookie humour has enlivened other Bogdanovich films, and has been used to great effect by Mel Brooks, especially in *Blazing Saddles* where Kahn plays a saloon-girl.

Films include: 1972 What's Up, Doc? '73 Paper Moon. '74 Blazing Saddles; Young Frankenstein. '75 Won Ton Ton, the Dog That Saved Hollywood; The Adventure of Sherlock Holmes' Smarter Brother. '77 High Anxiety. '81 History of the World – Part One.

KALATOZOV, Mikhail

(1903–1973). Director. Born: Mikhail Kalatozishvili; Tbilisi, Georgia, Russia

Trained as an economist, Kalatozov entered the Georgian film industry in 1923 and worked as actor, editor and cameraman. Promoted to director in 1928, two years later he made *Salt for Svanetia*, a lyrical documentary about the savage rites of a primitive Caucasian tribe, and one of the masterpieces of Soviet cinema. In disfavour for the 'negativism' of his work, Kalatozov was confined for seven years to administrative duties. By 1939 he was directing again, but during the war he represented the Soviet film industry in Los Angeles, and then was Deputy Minister of film. Free at last in the Fifties to make his own films, he became famous internationally for *The Cranes Are Flying*, a wartime love story which was joint winner of the Best Film Award at the 1958 Cannes Film Festival. An innovative and compassionate film-maker, Kalatozov used interesting and unusual montage and camera angles, combined with sharply effective editing to produce a poetic cinema not overly concerned with politics.

Films include: 1930 Sol Svaneti. '39 Muzhestvo. '41 Valeri Chkalov (USA: Wings of Victory; GB: The Red Flyer). '50 Zagovor Oberechyonnikh (GB: Conspiracy of the Doomed). '54 Verne Druzya (GB: True Friends). '56 Pervyi Eshelon. '58 Letyat Zhuravli (GB/USA: The Cranes Are Flying). '60 Neot Pravlennde Pismo (GB: The Letter That Wasn't Sent). '62 Soy Cuba (USSR-CUBA). '70 La Tenda Rossa (IT-USSR) (GB/USA: The Red Tent).

KALMUS, Herbert T.

(1881–1963). Inventor. Born: Chelsea, Massachusetts, USA

A graduate of the Massachusetts Institute of Technology and a PhD of the University of Zurich, Dr Kalmus experimented with colour film while occupying a number of academic posts. In 1912 he formed the Technicolor Company, and produced a one-reel film in 1917, superimposing red and green images. The process was gradually refined until in 1926 a complete feature, *The Black Pirate*, was produced in two-strip Technicolor. For some time, however, studios preferred to use colour only for selected sequences, until in 1935, in *Becky Sharp*, Kalmus brought in a third strip, sensitive to blue, and three-tone Technicolor arrived. This unique process took in all aspects of filming, from the negative through to the final print, and remained dominant, despite its expense, well into the Fifties.

KANIN, Garson

(b. 1912). Screenwriter/director. Born: Rochester, New York, USA

One day in 1937 the young Kanin pleaded with his boss Samuel Goldwyn for a chance to direct. Goldwyn demurred, saying that the young man had had no experience. 'But, Sir,' said Kanin, 'there was a time when John Ford and Willy Wyler had had no experience.' 'Don't you believe it,' said Goldwyn. Speechless but undeterred, Kanin (who tells the story in *Hollywood*, his nostalgic account of those years) went off to RKO, and by 1941 had made seven films, including some sharp satirical comedies as well as *A Man to Remember*, a moving biography of a small-town doctor. He collaborated with Carol Reed on the award-winning film of the Normandy campaign, *The True Glory*, and then, abandoning direction, he gained a new reputation as playwright and screenwriter. Kanin and his wife, the actress and writer Ruth Gordon, provided superb scripts for director George Cukor and stars Judy Holliday, Spencer Tracy and Katharine Hepburn. Kanin also wrote a book on the latter pair, the closely observed *Tracy and Hepburn*.

Films include: 1938 A Man to Remember (dir). '39 Bachelor Mother (dir; + sc); The Great Man Votes (dir). '40 My Favourite Wife (dir). '45 The True Glory (doc). '48 A Double Life (co-sc). '49 Adam's Rib (co-sc). '50 Born Yesterday (co-sc). '52 The Marrying Kind (co-sc); Pat and Mike (co-sc).

Below: Madeline Kahn in Mel Brooks' horror spoof Young Frankenstein

KAPLAN, Nelly

(b. 1931). Director. Born: Buenos Aires, Argentina

After briefly studying economics, Nelly Kaplan went to Paris at 18 to attend a congress of film archivists. She stayed, becoming a journalist, and then assistant to Abel Gance. She directed some short films, including one on Gance which inspired Kevin Brownlow to make *Abel Gance – The Charm of Dynamite* (1968) as a corrective. Since 1969 Kaplan has directed a number of features. Although she does not consider herself a militant feminist, her films have been concerned with the reversal of sexual roles and the effects of this on oppressors, and she has used humour as a distancing device from the disturbing elements contained.

Films include: **1961** Gustave Moreau, Dessins et Merveilles. **'62** Rodolphe Bresdin. **'63** Abel Gance Hier et Demain (GB: Abel Gance, Yesterday and Tomorrow). **'66** Les Années 25; A la source, la Femme Aimée. **'69** La Fiancée du Pirate (USA: A Very Curious Girl; GB: Dirty Mary). **'71** Papa, les Petits Bateaux. **'76** Néa (FR-GER) (GB: Young Emmanuelle). **'79** Charles et Lucie (USA/GB: Charles and Lucie).

KAPOOR, Prithviraj

(1906–1972). Actor/director. Born: Peshawar, India

Corpulent and jovial, with the air of a friendly puppy, Kapoor was an ugly duckling who grew into a film hero. He was one of the first stars of Hindi films, a producer with his own studio, a director of glittering musicals and fantasies, a member of the Upper House of the Indian Parliament, and the father of three well-known film actors. The eldest, Raj Kapoor (b. 1924: Bombay), plays 'little man' characters, and also directs. Shashi (b. 1938: Calcutta) joined the Geoffrey Kendal Theatre Company, married Jennifer Kendal (the actress Felicity Kendal's sister), and appeared in *Shakespeare Wallah*, James Ivory's film about the troupe. Tall and handsome, Shashi has become a big drawing card in Indian cinema. The third brother, Shammi, has not as yet made quite the same impact.

Films include: **1931** Alam Ara; Shakuntala. **'33** Raj Ram Meera. **'34** Seeta. **'36** Manjil. **'37** Vidyapati. **'39** Dushman. **'41** Sikandar. **'60** Mughal-E-Ajam. **'65** Aasman Mahal. **'71** Kal Aaj Aur Kal.

KARINA, Anna

(b. 1940). Actress. Born: Hanna Karin Blarke Bayer; Copenhagen, Denmark

Karina had appeared in one or two Danish shorts before she left home for Paris at 17. Here she worked in commercials before meeting with Jean-Luc Godard. She played leads in seven of his films, and married him in 1961 (they divorced six years later). The Godard-Karina films map out in many ways the paths they followed throughout their relationship, with Karina able to inject emotion into the

director's intellectual framework. In *Vivre Sa Vie*, *Alphaville* and *Pierrot le Fou*, Karina's radiant self-sufficiency is as complete a portrait of a woman as cinema can offer. When she and Godard parted, his work became arid, and hers ordinary.

Films include: **1959** Pingin oy Skoenne (DEN). **'61** Une Femme Est une Femme (USA/GB: A Woman Is a Woman). **'62** Vivre Sa Vie (USA: My Life to Live; GB: It's My Life). **'64** Bande à Part (USA: Band of Outsiders; GB: The Outsiders). **'65** Pierrot le Fou; Alphaville. **'67** Lo Straniero (IT-FR-ALG) (USA/GB: The Stranger). **'69** The Magus; Justine (USA).

KARLOFF, Boris

(1887–1969). Actor. Born: William Henry Pratt; London, England

The greatest of horror actors was a gentle cricket-lover, the son and brother of distinguished civil servants, and educated at Merchant Taylors' and at Uppingham. As a young man he craved adventure, sailed for Canada in 1909, dug ditches and laid railroad tracks, tried acting with touring companies and found it paid rather better, moved on to the States, and in 1919 got his first movie jobs, as an extra. His first credit came the next year, and through the Twenties he worked steadily, though never in leading parts, and usually as a villain. The turning point came in 1931, when Howard Hawks cast him as the murderous prison barber in *The Criminal Code*, a role he had recently played on stage. This led to better parts such as the role of the Monster in *Frankenstein*. This is one of the most famous creations in cinema, and Karloff, a quiet, slow-moving, watchful actor whose sympathetic nature shone through the trappings of horror, was ideally suited to play it. Unfortunately, it caused him to spend most of his remaining 37 years in the movies in horror-fantasies of one kind or another, but many of the films (*The Mummy*, *The Walking Dead*, *The Old Dark House*, and the trio for Val Lewton) were superb, and he broke away from time to time, playing a gangster (with public-school accent) in *Scarface* and an opera singer (undubbed) in *Charlie Chan at the Opera*. At the very end of his career he played

in Peter Bogdanovich's *Targets*, a film in which a dignified old actor in horror films helps capture a crazy young sniper.

Films include: **1919** His Majesty, the American. **'20** The Last of the Mohicans. **'27** Tarzan and the Golden Lion. **'29** King of the Kongo (serial); The Unholy Night. **'31** The Criminal Code; Five Star Final; The Mad Genius; Frankenstein. **'32** Scarface; The Old Dark House; The Mask of Fu Manchu; The Mummy. **'33** The Ghoul (GB). **'34** The Lost Patrol; The Black Cat (GB: House of Doom). **'35** Bride of Frankenstein; The Raven. **'36** The Invisible Ray; The Walking Dead. **'37** Charlie Chan at the Opera. **'38** Mr Wong, Detective. **'39** Son of Frankenstein. **'47** The Secret Life of Walter Mitty; Unconquered. **'63** The Raven; The Comedy of Terrors. **'68** Targets.

KARLSON, Phil

(1908–1985). Director. Born: Phillip N. Karlstein; Chicago, Illinois, USA

Karlson was an interesting director of crime thrillers during the Fifties. Vivid and full of action, they depicted the kind of environments that might produce corruption and violence. *The Phenix City Story*, in particular, is outstanding in its evocation of urban decay. Based on actual events that led to a murder trial and itself an influence on the real-life verdict, this film is also the most striking example of the director's use of a central figure striving to cut away a web of deceit and deviation. Titles like *Scandal Street*, *Kansas City Confidential* and *Tight Spot* suggest Karlson's tabloid economy and, although he also made Westerns, it is as a thriller director that he awaits major rediscovery. Sadly, his work since the early Sixties has made little impact. After art college he was trained, significantly, in law but preferred writing gags for Buster Keaton and eventually abandoned his course at Loyola University to go on the stage. Then came a long apprenticeship as prop man, assistant director and associate producer at Universal and also Monogram.

Films include: **1945** GI Honeymoon. **'49** The Big Cat. **'51** The Texas Rangers; Lorna Doone. **'52** Scandal Street; Kansas City Confidential. **'55** Five Against the House; Tight Spot; The Phenix City Story. **'59** The

Scarface Mob. **'60** Hell to Eternity; Key Witness. **'62** Kid Galahad.

KAUFMAN, Boris

(1906–1980). Cinematographer. Born: Byelstock, Russia

Kaufman was the brother of the Soviet cinematographer Mikhail Kaufman and the celebrated Kino-Eye documentarist Dziga Vertov (Denis Kaufman). Unlike them he chose to work in the West – initially in France on Jean Vigo's quartet of films and later, after serving with the French Army during World War II, with the National Film Board of Canada, finally settling in the USA. Here he shot films by Elia Kazan (winning the Best Black-and-White Cinematography Oscar for *On the Waterfront* and nominated for *Baby Doll*). Sidney Lumet and others. Kaufman preferred to film in black and white and his best work is in that medium. His connection with Vigo and Vertov – the brothers Kaufman kept closely in touch, describing their work and exchanging ideas – is borne out in the realistic, documentary feel Kaufman's camera brought to glamourless, downbeat, location-shot American dramas. Five years before his death he won the Billy Bitzer Award for 'outstanding contributions to the motion picture industry'.

Films include: 1930 A Propos de Nice (doc). **'31** Taris (doc. short). **'33** Zéro de Conduite (co-photo). **'34** L'Atalante. **'54** On the Waterfront. **'56** Baby Doll. **'57** Twelve Angry Men. **'60** The Fugitive Kind. **'61** Splendor in the Grass. **'62** Long Day's Journey Into Night. **'65** The Pawnbroker; The Group. **'68** Up Tight. **'70** Tell Me That You Love Me Junie Moon.

KAUFMAN, George S.

(1889–1961). Playwright. Born: Pittsburgh, Pennsylvania, USA

A devastatingly witty and prolific dramatist (43 Broadway productions) specializing in wisecracking satirical comedy, Kaufman studiously avoided Hollywood for most of his career. He did, however, draft the Eddie Cantor

film *Roman Scandals*, co-write the Marx Brothers' classic *A Night at the Opera*, and direct *The Senator Was Indiscreet*. Twenty or so of his works have been filmed, most memorably joint efforts with Moss Hart like their breakthrough play *Once in a Lifetime* (a dig at Hollywood), the Pulitzer Prize-winning *You Can't Take It With You*, and the magnificent *The Man Who Came to Dinner*. There were also a couple of stage originals for the Marxes and a further Hollywood connection through his notorious liaison with actress Mary Astor. Kaufman began writing humorous verse in the *New York Mail* and in 1917 was appointed drama editor of the *New York Times*, a post he held for many years.

Films based on Kaufman's plays as writer or co-writer include: 1929 The Cocoanuts. **'30** Animal Crackers. **'31** The Royal Family of Broadway. **'32** Merton of the Movies (GB: Make Me a Star); Once in a Lifetime. **'33** Dinner at Eight; Roman Scandals (co-story only). **'35** A Night at the Opera (co-sc. only). **'37** Stage Door. **'38** You Can't Take It With You. **'40** Dulcy. **'41** The Man Who Came to Dinner. **'42** George Washington Slept Here. **'47** The Senator Was Indiscreet (dir. only) (GB: Mr Ashton Was Indiscreet). **'56** The Solid Gold Cadillac. **'57** Silk Stockings.

KAUFMAN, Mikhail

(b. 1897). Cinematographer/director. Born: Bialystok, Russia

Mikhail Kaufman was, literally, the *Man With a Movie Camera*. It was he who shot for his brother, the director Dziga Vertov, that dazzling exploration of Russian city life; he who supplied the virtuoso camerawork – including some inspired surreal effects – for Vertov to edit into a classic of experimental cinema. Apart from his cinematography for the Kino-Eye group, Mikhail Kaufman directed his own films. *Spring* is a lyrical celebration of that season, featuring some beautiful pellucid photography and

an altogether less frenetic montage style than in Vertov's films. *The Great Victory* is a piece of socialist realism revolving round a ball-bearing factory. Kaufman's younger brother was cinematographer Boris Kaufman, the more well-known of the two because of his work in France and the USA.

Films include: 1923 The Grimaces of Iris; The Three Musketeers. **'24** Kino-Glaz (GB: Kino-Eye). **'25** Moskva (+dir) (Moscow). **'26** Chestaia Tchast Mirva (One Sixth of the Earth). **'29** Cheloviek s Kinoaparatom (GB: Man With a Movie Camera); Vesna (dir. only) (Spring). **'30** Odinnadsati (The Eleventh Hour). **'34** Avio-Mars (dir. only) (Avio March); Velikaia Pobeda (dir. only) (The Great Victor).

KAYE, Danny

(1913–1987). Actor. Born: David Daniel Kaminsky; Brooklyn, New York City, USA

He had the guileless cheek of a soda jerk, the pushy charm (and gobbledegook) of an insurance agent and the balance and dexterity of a waiter, and, in fact, Danny Kaye was all those things before he entered showbusiness in 1938. In the next couple of years he did practically everything it is possible for a young singer-dancer-comedian to do before Moss Hart cast him in his Broadway musical *Lady in the Dark* in 1940. He then married Sylvia Fine who wrote the gags and songs for Kaye that eventually brought him to the attention of Samuel Goldwyn in 1944. From *Up in Arms* to *Hans Christian Andersen* eight years later he was one of the screen's biggest comedy and musical stars – usually a manic, disaster-prone nincompoop upsetting everyone he meets (until he reconciles them to his well-meaningness). His most appropriate film is *The Secret Life of Walter Mitty* – for surely a madcap like Kaye can only occupy a world of daydreams. He was an enormous success on stage at the London Palladium in the early Fifties but his film career tailed off shortly afterwards. In 1955 he won a special Honorary Oscar and in 1982 the Jean Hersholt Humanitarian Award for his unceasing efforts for UNICEF.

Films include: 1944 Up in Arms. **'45** Wonder Man. **'47** The Secret Life of Walter Mitty. **'48** A Song Is Born. **'51** On the Riviera. **'52** Hans Christian Andersen. **'54** Knock on Wood; White Christmas. **'56** The Court Jester. **'58** Merry Andrew. **'63** The Man From the Diner's Club. **'69** The Madwoman of Chaillot (GB).

KAZAN, Elia

(b. 1909). Director. Born: Elia Kazanjoglou; Istanbul, Turkey

Elia Kazan's Greek parents brought him to New York at the age of four, but he remained acutely aware of his European heritage as is evident in two late films based on his own novels, *America, America* and *The Arrangement*. He studied drama at Yale and joined the radical Group Theater, initially as an actor though he was soon directing, notably Clifford Odets' *Waiting for Lefty*. He also directed a short documentary on the South, a region he knew and loved. In the Forties he became a famous Broadway director, putting on plays by Arthur Miller and Tennessee Williams; and he was one of three founders in 1947 of the Actors' Studio, the home of 'Method' acting, with which he was associated until 1962. His feature-film debut was *A Tree Grows in Brooklyn*, which immediately showed his outstanding talent with actors, one of whom, James Dunn, won an Academy Award as Best Supporting Actor. Kazan himself won the Best Director Oscar a couple of years later for *Gentleman's Agreement*, an attack on anti-semitism. He worked three times with the star pupil of the Actors' Studio, Marlon Brando, in *A Streetcar Named Desire*, *Viva Zapata!* and *On the Waterfront*, a union-bashing tale that won Oscars for them both, but is regarded by some as a justification of Kazan's collaboration with HUAC. *East of Eden*, with James Dean, was Kazan's first colour and wide-screen film, showing that his theatrical skills were fully supplemented by cinematic knowhow, though he was still fond of hysterically over-the-top scenes. *Wild River*, his most lyrical film, was set in the Thirties South at the time of the Tennessee Valley Authority (TVA) project, a background familiar to him from his early days. The Sixties produced his most personal films, but he was no longer a reliable box-office director, as he had been in the era of *Baby Doll*. He then concentrated mainly on his career as a novelist, briefly returning in the Seventies to film F. Scott Fitzgerald's classic novel of Hollywood, *The Last Tycoon*. His second wife was actress-director Barbara Loden (1932–1980), who made and starred in *Wanda* (1970).

Films include: 1937 People of the Cumberland (doc. short). **'45** A Tree Grows in Brooklyn. **'46** Boomerang. **'47** Gentleman's Agreement. **'49** Pinky. **'50** Panic in the Streets. **'51** A Streetcar Named Desire. **'52** Viva Zapata. **'54** On the Waterfront. **'55** East of Eden. **'56** Baby Doll. **'57** A Face in the Crowd. **'60** Wild River. **'61** Splendor in the Grass. **'63** America, America (GB: The Anatolian Smile). **'69** The Arrangement. **'76** The Last Tycoon.

Top, from left to right: Prithviraj Kapoor; Raj Kapoor in Jagte Raho *(1957); Shashi Kapoor. Above left: Boris Karloff in* The Body Snatcher *(1945). Above: Anna Karina. Below: Danny Kaye, with the Goldwyn Girls, in his debut as a hypochondriac who joins the army –* Up in Arms. *Below right: Elia Kazan*

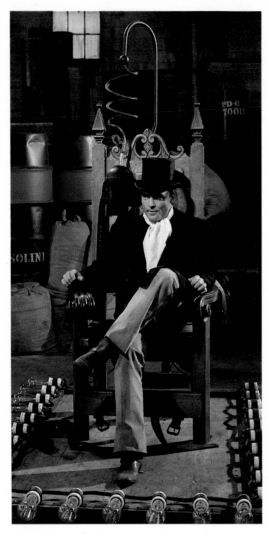

Above: Stacy Keach in The Travelling Executioner *(1970). Above right: Diane Keaton in* Looking for Mr Goodbar. *Top right: Buster Keaton in* The Navigator. *Far right: Ruby Keeler.*

KEACH, Stacy

(b. 1941). Actor. Born: Walter Stacy Keach Jr; Savannah, Georgia, USA

Keach has a distinguished stage training that somehow belies his scarred mouth (the result of four operations to remove a harelip) and bull-like appearance, as if a broad-shouldered boy from Georgia shouldn't be dallying with acting. He is the son of a drama teacher and at first studied economics at the University of California, then attended the Yale school of Drama and the London Academy of Music and Dramatic Art. In 1964 he made his theatre debut as the Player King in *Hamlet* (he has a leaning towards the classics), and four years later appeared as a drunken drifter in his first film, *The Heart Is a Lonely Hunter*. This began a modest but worthy film career as a leading man – often in similar roles. But he is a notable Western villain, too – Doc Holliday in *Doc*, the albino Bad Bob in *The Life and Times of Judge Roy Bean*, Jesse James in *The Long Riders* (in which Keach's brother James played Frank). Keach considers himself a stage actor first and foremost, though in 1972 he branched into direction

with a short, *The Repeater*, followed by an Australian feature, *Road Games*, in 1981.

Films include: 1968 The Heart Is a Lonely Hunter. **'70** End of the Road; Brewster McCloud. **'71** Doc. **'72** The New Centurions (GB: Precinct 45 – Los Angeles Police); The Life and Times of Judge Roy Bean; Fat City. **'74** Luther (GB-CAN-USA). **'78** Up in Smoke. **'80** The Long Riders. **'81** Butterfly; Road Games (+ dir) (AUS).

KEATON, Buster

(1895–1966). Actor/director/ screenwriter. Born: Joseph Francis Keaton; Piqua, Kansas, USA

Keaton is now regarded as the most sophisticated of the great silent comics. Though his films offer a primarily physical world, full of hazards to be overcome acrobatically by Buster, they are laced with inner pain and frustration which, because they are never admitted by Keaton's immobile features, cut far deeper than Chaplin's pathos, Langdon's impotence or Lloyd's naivety. Maybe, though, Keaton was lost in some other dream, beyond mere accomplishment, for at times he seems far, far away. And he wasn't just thinking where to put the camera next: that was something he knew instinctively as a supreme technical director, one whose films are beautiful to look at. He discovered his other major talent as a master of

timing as the youngest of The Three Keatons, his parents' acrobatic comedy act, part of the Mohawk Indian Medicine Company; the batterings he accepted as part of their stage routine must have also taught him never to smile. From 1917 he was in films with Fatty Arbuckle and, after a spell entertaining the troops in France, embarked on the production of his own two-reelers and features under Joseph Schenck. This was his great period, from 1920 to 1928 – the years of *The Paleface*, *The Three Ages*, *Our Hospitality*, *Sherlock Jr*, *The Navigator*, his masterpiece *The General*, and *Steamboat Bill, Jr*. Then came a tragic decline following his move to MGM. For the rest of his career he struggled with alcoholism and found his creative genius lost in bit parts, gagwriting, foreign films and cameo appearances. In the Sixties, though, Keaton's best films were rediscovered and he enjoyed a brief return to the limelight before he died.

Films include: 1917 The Butcher Boy; Fatty at Coney Island (GB: Coney Island). **'20** The Garage; One Week; Neighbors; The Saphead. **'21** The Goat; The Boat; The Paleface. **'22** Cops. **'23** The Three Ages; Our Hospitality; Sherlock Jr (GB: Sherlock Junior); The Navigator. **'25** Seven Chances; Go West. **'26** The General. **'27** College. **'28** Steamboat Bill, Jr; The Cameraman. **'29** Spite Marriage. **'30** Doughboys. **'50** Sunset Boulevard. **'52** Limelight. **'66** A Funny Thing Happened On the Way to the Forum.

KEATON, Diane

(b. 1946). Actress. Born: Diane Hall; Los Angeles, California, USA

Drama studies at Santa Anna college led Keaton to the Neighborhood Playhouse in New York and she attracted attention by not taking her clothes off in *Hair*. Woody Allen chose her as his co-star for the stage version of *Play It Again, Sam* and she entered films in *Lovers and Other Strangers*. No other modern actress is as adept at conveying the barely restrained hysteria that goes with hovering on the near – or far – edge of a love affair. No matter how pretty and likeable she is, in films the Keaton character is a ball of confusion, most notably for Allen – her mentor, friend and former lover. There is a harrowing truthfulness about the way she swaps banalities with him as they test the waters of mutual attraction at the tennis club in *Annie Hall*, or disguises her uncertainty beneath a veneer of arty intellect in *Manhattan*. *Annie Hall* won her an Oscar and deservedly – for she had the difficulty of realizing Allen's conception of Diane Hall herself. Apart from his comedies and maturer works, her credits are now looking very impressive: she was remarkable as a wife subservient to the gangster life in both parts of *The Godfather*; nearly stole *Reds* from Warren Beatty (the arduous making of which put paid to their love affair but brought her another Academy

Above left: Lila Kedrova as the woman trying to get out of Eastern Europe in Alfred Hitchcock's Torn Curtain. *Above: Harvey Keitel in* The Duellists, *directed by Ridley Scott. Below left: Howard Keel in* Annie Get Your Gun. *Below: Brian Keith*

Award nomination); and universally praised as another distraught wife in *Shoot the Moon.*

Films include: 1970 Lovers and Other Strangers. '72 The Godfather; Play It Again, Sam. '73 Sleeper. '74 The Godfather, Part II. '75 Love and Death. '76 I Will . . . I Will . . . for Now; Harry and Walter Go to New York. '77 Annie Hall; Looking for Mr Goodbar. '78 Interiors. '79 Manhattan. '81 Reds. '82 Shoot the Moon.

KEDROVA, Lila

(b. 1918). Actress. Born: Elizabeth Kedrova; Leningrad, USSR

Kedrova gave one of the last great cameos in a Hitchcock film – she was the nervy, flustered and endearing little Polish countess desperate to get out of East Berlin in *Torn Curtain*. It was a role that harked back to her earliest years when her father, a musician who was a favourite of the Tsar, fled with his family to Germany in the aftermath of the Revolution. A prodigy at the piano, apparently encouraged by Shostakovich, at 15 she opted for the Paris stage and became very successful. She was in films from the early Fifties as a red-headed, croaky-voiced character actress specializing in casualties like the drug addict in *Razzia sur la Chnouf*, the alcoholic in *Zorba the Greek* (for which she won the Best Supporting Actress

Oscar) and the dying wife in *Tell Me a Riddle.*

Films include: 1953 Weg ohne Umkehr (GER) (GB: No Way Back). '55 Razzia sur la Chnouf (FR) (GB: Chnouf). '58 La Femme et le Pantin (FR-IT) (GB: A Woman Like Satan). '64 Zorba the Greek (GREECE-USA). '65 A High Wind in Jamaica (GB). '66 Torn Curtain (USA); Penelope (USA). '70 The Kremlin Letter (USA). '73 Soft Beds, Hard Battles (GB) (USA: Undercover Hero). '76 Le Locataire (FR) (GB: The Tenant). '79 Les Egouts du Paradis (FR). '80 Tell Me a Riddle (USA).

KEEL, Howard

(b. 1917). Singer/actor. Born: Harold Clifford Leek; Gillespie, Illinois, USA

Keel took singing lessons while working as a mechanic and, after winning various singing competitions, turned professional. While playing the lead in the West End production of *Oklahoma!* he made his screen debut in a thriller *The Small Voice.* Keel himself had anything but a small voice as he later proved in starring roles in *Annie Get Your Gun, Show Boat, Kiss Me, Kate, Calamity Jane* and *Seven Brides for Seven Brothers.* His many famous songs include the hilariously competitive duet with Betty Hutton, 'Anything You Can Do' (*Annie Get Your Gun*), the dynamic 'Where Is This Life That Late I Lead' (*Kiss Me, Kate*) and

the exuberant 'Bless Your Beautiful Hide' (*Seven Brides for Seven Brothers*). With the decline in popularity of screen musicals in the late Fifties, MGM released him from his contract. He took straight acting roles and worked as a nightclub singer and also on television.

Films include: 1948 The Small Voice (GB) (USA: Hideout). '50 Annie Get Your Gun. '51 Show Boat. '52 Lovely to Look At. '53 Kiss Me, Kate; Calamity Jane. '54 Rose Marie; Seven Brides for Seven Brothers. '55 Kismet. '59 The Big Fisherman. '67 The War Wagon.

KEELER, Ruby

(b. 1909). Actress/dancer. Born: Ethel Hilda Keeler; Halifax, Nova Scotia, Canada

Ruby Keeler was the chorus girl who went out on stage a nobody, came back a star and was then folded in the arms of Dick Powell in a series of Busby Berkeley musical extravaganzas in the Thirties. Her actual life was not so far removed from this Cinderella-style scenario. She had an impoverished childhood in New York and her parents had to scrape together the money to pay for her dancing lessons. As a teenager she became an energetic chorine in night clubs and speakeasies, making her stage debut in *The Rise of Rosie O'Reilly.* A secret marriage to Al Jolson in 1928 made her headline news; a few years later she was cast in the lead in Busby Berkeley's *42nd Street* and stardom was hers. As the vogue for spectacular musicals passed her career lost momentum and the break-up of her marriage to Jolson accelerated its slide. In 1970 she made a nostalgic return to the stage in *No, No Nanette*, staged by Busby Berkeley.

Films include: 1933 42nd Street; Gold Diggers of 1933; Footlight Parade. '34 Dames; Flirtation Walk. '35 Go Into Your Dance (GB: Casino de Paree); Shipmates Forever. '36 Colleen. '38 Mother Carey's Chickens. '41 Sweetheart of the Campus.

KEIGHLEY, William

(1889–1984). Director. Born: William Jackson Keighley Jr; Philadelphia, Pennsylvania, USA

Keighley had 18 years' experience as a stage actor and director in New York by the time he arrived in Hollywood in 1930 to work on the new talking pictures. He served as a dialogue director and assistant director with Howard Betherton before winning his first solo credit with the comedy *Easy to Love.* Gangster films were all the rage in the Thirties and Keighley adapted well to the genre, racking up a series of hits. He became a favourite director of James Cagney (with whom Keighley had worked on Broadway in *Penny Arcade*); he directed the star in several movies, including *G-Men, Each Dawn I Die, The Fighting 69th* and *Torrid Zone.* The actress Genevieve Tobin became Keighley's third wife in 1938 and appeared regularly in his films. His best post-war movie, *The Street With No Name*, harked back to

the rapid-fire realism of his Thirties gangster movies. He retired to Paris in the Fifties, achieving some renown as a still photographer.

Films include: 1934 Easy to Love. '35 G-Men. '36 Bullets or Ballots. '37 The Prince and the Pauper. '38 The Adventures of Robin Hood (co-dir). '39 Each Dawn I Die. '40 The Fighting 69th; Torrid Zone. '41 The Man Who Came to Dinner. '42 George Washington Slept Here. '48 The Street With No Name. '53 The Master of Ballantrae (GB).

KEITEL, Harvey

(b. 1947). Actor. Born: New York City, USA

One of Hollywood's most sought-after character actors since the mid-Seventies specializing in seedy, street-wise roles – a collector for the Mafia in *Mean Streets*, Jodie Foster's pimp in *Taxi Driver* and a sweating, voyeuristic (but shrewdly intelligent) detective in *Bad Timing.* He studied acting with Lee Strasberg and was a member of the Actors' Studio in New York, making his Broadway debut in *Death of a Salesman* in 1965. Three years later he appeared in a student film directed by Martin Scorsese, *Who's That Knocking at My Door?.* Subsequent collaborations with Scorsese – *Mean Streets, Alice Doesn't Live Here Anymore* and *Taxi Driver* established Keitel's movie career. He prepares carefully for each of his roles investing them with powerful – at times almost manic – conviction. In *The Border*, Keitel gave a compelling performance as an unscrupulous border guard.

Films include: 1968 Who's That Knocking at My Door? '73 Mean Streets. '74 Alice Doesn't Live Here Anymore. '76 Taxi Driver; Mother Jugs and Speed; Buffalo Bill and the Indians . . . or Sitting Bull's History Lesson; Welcome to LA. '77 The Duellists (GB). '78 Blue Collar. '80 Saturn 3; Bad Timing. '81 The Border. '82 La Nuit de Varennes (FR-IT).

KEITH, Brian

(b. 1921). Actor. Born: Robert Keith Jr; Bayonne, New Jersey, USA

Following the divorce of his parents, actor/writer Robert Keith and actress Helena Shipman, Keith was brought up by his grandparents. He overcame a prejudice against showbusiness after completing his military service in World War II, taking parts on stage and in radio. Paramount signed up this tall, heavily built actor in 1951, initially casting him in hard-bitten character parts. He specialized in Westerns and action films but as a performer has since proved increasingly versatile. He is also a popular television actor, having appeared in such American series as *Crusader, The Westerner, The Fugitive* and *A Family Affair.*

Films include: 1953 Arrowhead. '57 Run of the Arrow. '65 The Hallelujah Trail. '66 The Russians Are Coming, the Russians Are Coming; Nevada Smith. '69 Gaily, Gaily (GB: Chicago, Chicago). '75 The Wind and the Lion. '76 Nickelodeon (GB-USA). '78 Hooper. '81 The Deadly Companions.

KELLAWAY, Cecil

(1890–1973). Actor. Born: Capetown, South Africa

Round-faced with twinkling blue eyes, Kellaway had had many years of stage experience in South Africa, England and Australia by the time he attracted the attention of RKO by writing and starring in the romantic comedy *It Isn't Done*. He returned to Australia after only 12 months in Hollywood but was persuaded back again by director William Wyler to play Mr Earnshaw in *Wuthering Heights*. Kellaway stayed this time, playing roguish, kindly characters in numerous movies. Highlights of his career were Oscar nominations as Best Supporting Actor for *The Luck of the Irish*, in which he played a leprechaun, and for his portrayal of the patient priest who attempts to overcome Spencer Tracy's prejudice against mixed marriage in *Guess Who's Coming to Dinner?*

Films include: 1937 It Isn't Done (AUS). '39 Wuthering Heights; Intermezzo (GB: Escape to Happiness). '42 I Married a Witch. '44 Frenchman's Creek. '45 Love Letters; Kitty. '46 The Postman Always Rings Twice. '48 Joan of Arc. '50 Harvey. '61 Francis of Assisi. '63 The Cardinal. '64 Hush. . . Hush, Sweet Charlotte. '67 The Adventures of Bullwhip Griffin; Fitzwilly (GB: Fitzwilly Strikes Back); Guess Who's Coming to Dinner? '70 Getting Straight.

KELLER, Marthe

(b. 1945). Actress. Born: Basle, Switzerland

A skiing accident cut short her studies at Basle Opera School of Ballet and Keller turned to straight acting, winning a scholarship to the Stanislavsky School in Munich and eventually appearing in lead roles in the Schiller Theatre in Berlin. She supplied the love interest in *Funeral in Berlin*, then moved to France, being cast by director Phillipe de Broca in *Le Diable par la Queue* and *Les Caprices des Marie* and by Claude Lelouch in *Toute une Vie*. She had romances with both directors and has a son by de Broca. The above movies and good parts on stage and in television established her popularity in France and attracted offers from Hollywood. Tall and blonde, her foreign accent adding beguiling vulnerability to her beauty, she has played Dustin Hoffman's girlfriend in *Marathon Man*, a Garbo-like recluse in *Fedora* and a rich girl dying of cancer in *Bobby Deerfield*. She has been linked romantically with her co-star, Al Pacino, in the latter film.

Films include: 1966 Funeral in Berlin (GB). '69 Le Diable par la Queue (FR-IT) (USA: The Devil by the Tail). '70 Les Caprices de Marie (FR-IT) (USA: Give Her the Moon). '74 Toute une Vie (FR-IT) (USA/GB: And Now My Love). '75 Per le Antiche Scale (IT-FR) (USA/GB: Down the Ancient Staircase).

'76 Marathon Man (USA). '77 Black Sunday (USA); Bobby Deerfield (USA). '78 Fedora (GER-FR).

KELLERMAN, Sally

(b. 1938). Actress. Born: Long Beach, California, USA

Sally Kellerman studied at the Actors' Studio with Jeff Corey and Lee Strasberg, making her film debut in *Reform School Girl*. She went on to play many successful dramatic support roles in films such as *The Boston Strangler*. She is a lanky, sexy, husky-voiced comedienne whose most famous role is perhaps as Major 'Hot Lips' Houlihan in the film *M*A*S*H*, for which she was nominated for an Academy Award.

Films include: 1957 Reform School Girl. '68 The Boston Strangler. '70 M*A*S*H. '72 The Last of the Red Hot Lovers. '73 Lost Horizon; Slither. '76 The Big Bus; Welcome to LA. '79 A Little Romance (FR-IT). '80 Foxes; Loving Couples.

KELLY, Gene

(b. 1912). Actor/dancer/director. Born: Eugene Curran Kelly; Pittsburgh, Pennsylvania, USA

A glimpse of Gene Kelly singing and dancing in the rain tells audiences

Top: Cecil Kellaway as the victim in The Postman Always Rings Twice *(1946), in which an adulterous couple murder the woman's husband but receive their comeuppance. Above: Marthe Keller in* Fedora. *Below: Sally Kellerman in* A Little Romance. *Right: Gene Kelly in* Singin' in the Rain. *Far right: Grace Kelly. Below, far right: Paul Kelly in* Strange Journey *(1946), a tale of treasure-hunters on a desert island*

Opposite page. Left: Jeremy Kemp in The Blue Max. *Centre: Kay Kendall in* The Reluctant Debutante. *Far right: coming to terms with civilian life – Arthur Kennedy as a blind soldier in* Bright Victory

all they need to know about the infectious joy of Hollywood musicals. In contrast to Fred Astaire, Kelly was abrasive, acrobatic and showy as a performer, incorporating ballet and modern dance techniques into his routines. The lead in the 1940 Broadway production of *Pal Joey* led to a contract with MGM, and he made his screen debut with Judy Garland in *For Me and My Gal*. *Cover Girl*, besides teaming Kelly with Rita Hayworth, reunited him with choreographer Stanley Donen with whom he had worked on *Pal Joey*. MGM producer Arthur Freed gradually allowed Kelly and Donen the freedom to make their own kind of musicals, set in real locations with modern characters and stories. Between them they revitalized the portrayal of dance on film, ridding it of 'staginess', and making the routines an integral part of the film's narrative. The highlights of their partnership were *On the Town* and *Singin' in the Rain*, while Kelly himself scored a notable triumph as choreographer and performer in the 20-minute ballet climax of *An American in Paris*. From the late Fifties on, Kelly worked in straight parts and as a director of such films as *Hello, Dolly!* and *The Cheyenne Social Club* (1970). Among his Seventies film appearances he is co-host (with Fred Astaire) of the compilation movies *That's Entertainment!* (1974) and *That's Entertainment, Part 2* (1976).

Films include: **1942** For Me and My Gal. **'44** Cover Girl. **'45** Anchors Aweigh. **'46** Ziegfeld Follies. **'48** The Pirate. **'49** Take Me Out to the Ball Game (GB: Everybody's Cheering); On the Town (co-dir). **'51** An American in Paris. **'52** Singin' in the Rain (co-dir). **'54** Brigadoon. **'60** Inherit the Wind. **'69** Hello, Dolly! (dir. only).

KELLY, Grace

(1928–1982). Actress. Born: Philadelphia, Pennsylvania, USA

Frank Sinatra called her the sensational 'Fair Miss Frigidaire' in *High Society*; Alfred Hitchcock went for her 'sexual elegance', casting her in three movies – *Dial M for Murder*, *Rear Window* and *To Catch a Thief*, clearly fascinated to discover the humour and warmth hidden by her serene facade. She was from a prosperous family with showbiz connections (her uncle was the playwright George Kelly). She trained at the American Academy of Dramatic Art and worked as a model and in television commercials before winning stage parts. MGM signed her up and she made unspectacular appearances in *Fourteen Hours* (1951) and *High Noon*. She did her best work for Hitchcock, but won herself a Best Actress Oscar for her performance as the wife of an alcoholic Bing Crosby in *The Country Girl*. While making *To Catch a Thief* she met Prince Rainier of Monaco; shortly afterwards they were married and she retired from acting.

Films include: **1952** High Noon. **'53** Mogambo. **'54** Dial M for Murder; Rear Window; The Country Girl; Green Fire; The Bridges at Toko-Ri. **'55** To Catch a Thief. **'56** The Swan; High Society.

KELLY, Paul

(1899–1956). Actor. Born: New York City, USA

Paul Kelly began as a child actor – Chick Kelly the Vitagraph Boy – and featured in several of that studio's silent movies. Following stage experience in stock companies and on Broadway, he went to Hollywood, but his career was cut short in 1927 when he was jailed after killing the husband of actress Dorothy Mackaye (whom he later married) in a fight. Producer Darryl Zanuck gave him a fresh start on Broadway in *Broadway Through a Keyhole*. Kelly went on to feature regularly as a tough, granite-jawed supporting actor in A films and leads in B features, reserving his best work for the theatre.

Films include: **1936** Song and Dance Man. **'39** The Roaring Twenties. **'40** Flight Command. **'41** Ziegfeld Girl. **'42** Tough as They Come; Tarzan's New York Adventure. **'47** Fear in the Night; Crossfire. **'53** Gunsmoke. **'54** Johnny Dark.

KEMP, Jeremy

(b. 1935). Actor. Born: Jeremy Walker; Chesterfield, Derbyshire, England

Kemp studied acting at the Central School of Speech and Drama, London, subsequently working in rep and with the Royal Shakespeare Company. Golden-haired, with a brooding countenance – he has been described as 'a sinister-looking bloke with a smile like a razor' – he spent a year as a policeman in the long-running television series *Z Cars*. This established his popularity and several interesting movie roles have since come his way, notably the aristocratic German air ace in *The Blue Max*.

Films include: **1964** Dr Terror's House of Horrors. **'66** The Blue Max. **'68** The Strange Affair. **'70** Darling Lili (USA); The Games (USA). **'72** Pope Joan. **'73** The Blockhouse; The Belstone Fox (USA: Free Spirit). **'76** The Seven-Per-Cent Solution (USA); The Prisoner of Zenda (USA).

KENDALL, Kay

(1926–1959). Actress. Born: Justine McCarthy Kendall; Withernsea, Yorkshire, England

Kay Kendall grew up in show business, her mother an actress and her father a dancer. After joining a chorus line in her early teens, she toured the music halls with her sister Kim. Following a few small roles in minor British films Kay Kendall was given a break and launched as a star in *London Town*, playing opposite Sid Field. The film was a flop, however, and it was not until *Genevieve* that she was recognized as a talented and stylish comedienne. From then on she gave vitality to many productions through her sparkling personality and wonderful sense of comic timing. She married Rex Harrison in 1957. Two years later she died of leukemia.

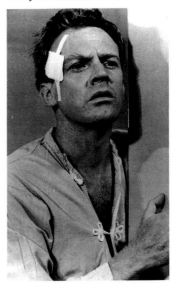

Films include: **1944** Fiddlers Three. **'46** London Town. **'51** Lady Godiva Rides Again. **'53** Street of Shadows (USA: Shadow Man); Genevieve; Meet Mr Lucifer. **'54** Doctor in the House. **'57** Les Girls (USA). **'58** The Reluctant Debutante. **'60** Once More With Feeling (USA).

KENNEDY, Arthur

(b. 1914). Actor. Born: John Arthur Kennedy; Worcester, Massachusetts, USA

Performing in *Richard II* led to Kennedy's becoming a Broadway regular before he was finally spotted by a Warner Brothers scout. His film debut was made in 1940 in *City for Conquest* as James Cagney's brother. He proceeded to play good second leads to big stars like Sinatra and Mitchum. He split his time equally between screen and stage and received a Tony Award for his performance in Arthur Miller's *Death of a Salesman*. He was often, somewhat surprisingly, cast as a vicious villain as, for example, in *The Man From Laramie*.

Films include: **1941** High Sierra. **'46** Boomerang. **'47** Cheyenne. **'51** Bright Victory (GB: Lights Out). **'52** Rancho Notorious; The Lusty Men. **'55** The Man From Laramie. **'57** Peyton Place. **'58** Some Came Running. **'71** My Old Man's Place/Glory Boy.

KENNEDY, Burt

(b. 1923). Director/writer. Born: Muskegon, Michigan, USA

A masterful director of Westerns, over the years Burt Kennedy has gradually altered the tempo and attitudes of his films. His early movies were hard-hitting and tough – films like *The Good Guys and the Bad Guys*, with Robert Mitchum and George Kennedy opposing a new sort of honourless brutality in the West, and *The Rounders*, a film about two poverty-stricken horse-breakers and their relationship with a spirited, unbreakable, wild-eyed roan. He then moved over to paying humorous homage to old Westerns using affectionate re-workings of the genre conventions with spoof Westerns such as *Support Your Local Sheriff* and *Support Your Local Gunfighter*, both starring James Garner. Kennedy came from a theatrical background and joined his family's act 'The Dancing Kennedys' at the age of five. But it was after his World War II service that he began writing, initially for radio and then for television. He also has some very important screenwriting credits to his name with such films as *The Tall T* (1957) and *Comanche Station* (1960), and during the Fifties he had a particularly fruitful partnership with the director Budd Boetticher.

Films include: **1961** The Canadians (GB-CAN). **'64** Mail Order Bride (GB: West of Montana). **'65** The Rounders; The Money Trap. **'67** Welcome to Hard Times (GB: Killer on a Horse); The War Wagon. **'69** Good Guys and Bad Guys; Support Your Local Sheriff. **'71** The Deserter; Support Your Local Gunfighter. **'79** Wolf Lake.

KENNEDY, Edgar

(1890–1948). Actor. Born: Edgar Livingstone Kennedy; Monterey, California, USA

The young Edgar Kennedy wandered around America and finally ended up in Chicago. Using his robust voice he found theatrical work and was finally offered an audition in New York, but he could not afford the fare. He turned to boxing but eventually went back to vaudeville and musical comedy. By 1914 he was working at the Keystone studios and he remained there working with the director Mack Sennett for many years. He was a big, bald man, with a distinctive scowl which made his face his trademark, and he jumbled and wheezed through each scene. He went on to work with various studios and many stars although he never stood in the limelight himself – he was more a scene stealer than a star. He continued to work right up until his death.

Films include: 1932 Little Orphan Annie. '33 Duck Soup; Tillie and Gus. '36 San Francisco. '37 True Confession; A Star Is Born. '40 L'il Abner. '43 Air Raid Wardens. '45 Anchors Aweigh; Captain Tugboat Annie.

KENNEDY, George

(b. 1926). Actor. Born: New York City, USA

George Kennedy first appeared in films playing heavy villainous roles and, despite acquiring a certain degree of sophistication in films like *Charade*, *Cool Hand Luke* and *Death on the Nile*, his basic screen persona has never fundamentally altered. His father was a musician and his mother a dancer, and he was touring in *Bringing Up Father* by the time he was two, and he had his own radio show at the age of seven. He joined the army at 17 and stayed on after the war for a further 16 years working in armed services radio and television. He became an advisor to Phil Silvers on the *Sergeant Bilko* television show and had occasional walk-on parts as an MP. In 1959 he left the army, married and went to Hollywood, where he restarted his acting career in television Western series like *Sugarfoot* and *Cheyenne* and thence progressed to heavies in feature films. He received an Oscar as Best Supporting Actor for his performance in *Cool Hand Luke*.

Films include: 1962 Lonely Are the Brave. '63 Charade. '64 Hush. . . Hush, Sweet Charlotte. '67 The Dirty Dozen (USA-GB); Cool Hand Luke. '68 The Boston Strangler. '73 Lost Horizon. '74 Earthquake. '77 Airport '77. '78 Death on the Nile (GB).

KENT, Jean

(b. 1921). Actress. Born: Joan Mildred Summerfield; Brixton, London, England

With her reddish hair, hazel eyes, vivacious personality and sensual, pouting mouth Jean Kent was one of Britain's most popular sex-symbols during the Forties. She was educated at a convent but toured with her

dancer mother at the age of ten. At 14 she became one of the vaudeville dancers at the Windmill Theatre in London. After a spell in the provinces and a small uncredited film part her career really started when she signed with Gainsborough. Renowned as a hard worker, she did very well playing bad girls in her early small parts and received her first major role as the gypsy in *Caravan* because Margaret Lockwood refused it as too awful. She continued to build successfully on her career by expanding and developing on this same type of character in numerous films. In the Eighties she re-established herself as a leading player in the British television soap-opera *Crossroads*.

Films include: 1944 Fanny by Gaslight; Madonna of the Seven Moons; Champagne Charlie. '45 Waterloo Road. '46 Caravan. '48 Good Time Girl. '49 Trottie True (USA: Gay Lady). '50 The Woman in Question (USA: Five Angles on Murder). '51 The Browning Version. '59 Please Turn Over.

KERN, Jerome

(1885–1945). Composer. Born: New York City, USA

The musicals of Jerome Kern had an enormous impact on the American scene. He was a master of melody and had the ability to adapt difficult books, like *Show Boat*, into musicals. He is generally considered to have been a major influence on the modernization of musical theatre and subsequently on the genre in film, and he also influenced many future composers such as George Gershwin and Richard Rodgers to name only two. His interest in music was encouraged by his mother, who was an aspiring concert pianist. His talent was apparent at an early age and he composed music for high-school shows. Having studied music in New York he went to London in 1903 and found work writing incidental music for shows in the West End. On his return to America he had various jobs as a pianist and vaudeville accompanist, and in 1911 he wrote his first Broadway scores. He was soon established as an important

composer – he produced an astonishing number of popular classics and continued to delight his public until his sudden death from a heart attack in New York.

Films include: 1929 Sally. '34 The Cat and the Fiddle; Music in the Air. '35 Sweet Adeline. '36 Swing Time; Show Boat (co-mus). '37 High, Wide and Handsome. '41 Lady Be Good. '42 You Were Never Lovelier. '44 Cover Girl. '46 Till the Clouds Roll By; Centennial Summer.

KERR, Deborah

(b. 1921). Actress. Born: Deborah Jane Kerr-Trimmer; Helensburgh, Dunbarton, Scotland

The red-haired, genteel daughter of a Scottish architect, Deborah Kerr attended drama school in Bristol where one of her performances won her a ballet scholarship at Sadler's Wells. But she was too old to train seriously for ballet and obtained walk-on parts at the open-air theatre in Regent's Park. Her first bit part in a film, Powell and Pressburger's *Contraband* (1940), was edited out; but she was seen in Gabriel Pascal's *Major Barbara* and

starred in *Love on the Dole*, untypically as a downtrodden working-class girl. Powell and Pressburger gave her a lovely triple role in *The Life and Death of Colonel Blimp*, and she was one of the nuns in *Black Narcissus*. In 1947 she went to Hollywood, where she tended to be even more typecast as a refined lady than in Britain. Despite the famous beach love scene in *From Here to Eternity*, she is best remembered and loved as the prim governess in *The King and I*. *The Sundowners* gave her a rare down-to-earth role as the wife of an itinerant Irishman (Robert Mitchum) in Australia; and shortly before retiring she let herself go as a middle-aged harridan in *The Arrangement*. Her abundant acting talent was evident in both drama and comedy; but her looks and background too often circumscribed her opportunities. She still works occasionally on stage.

Films include: 1941 Major Barbara; Love on the Dole. '43 The Life and Death of Colonel Blimp. '45 Perfect Strangers (USA: Vacation From Marriage). '47 Black Narcissus. '49 Edward, My Son. '53 From Here to Eternity (USA). '56 The King and I (USA); Tea and Sympathy (USA); Heaven Knows, Mr Allison. '58 Separate Tables (USA). '60

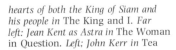

Above, from left to right: Edgar Kennedy in Hot Wires *(1931); George Kennedy; Deborah Kerr as the forthright governess who wins the* hearts of both the King of Siam and his people in The King and I. *Far left: Jean Kent as Astra in* The Woman in Question. *Left; John Kerr in* Tea and Sympathy, *in which a schoolboy is helped by the housemaster's wife. Below left: Evelyn Keyes in* Smuggler's Island *(1951). Below: Guy Kibbee*

The Sundowners (USA). '61 The Innocents. '64 The Night of the Iguana (USA). '69 The Arrangement (USA).

KERR, John

(b. 1931). Actor. Born: New York City, USA

The son of a theatrical family, John Kerr made his acting debut at ten. After studying at Harvard, he appeared on Broadway in *Bernardine* and in *Tea and Sympathy*, where he played opposite Deborah Kerr, later his co-star in the film version. His film debut was as a mentally tormented youth in Vincente Minnelli's *The Cobweb*. Fresh-faced and blue-eyed, he played teenage roles until *South Pacific*, in which he was an officer whose love affair with a half-caste girl (France Nuyen) is overshadowed by race prejudice and death. A few years later he retired from the big screen but he continued to appear occasionally on television, for instance in *The Streets of San Francisco*.

Films include: 1955 The Cobweb. '56 Gaby; Tea and Sympathy. '57 The Vintage. '58 South Pacific. '60 The Crowded Sky. '61 The Pit and the Pendulum; Seven Women From Hell.

KERSHNER, Irvin

(b. 1923). Director. Born: Irvin Kerschner; Philadelphia, Pennsylvania, USA

Following wartime service in the air force, Irvin Kershner studied art at Temple University, Philadelphia, and film at the University of Southern California. After a spell in advertising, he taught photography at USC and made documentary films for the United States Information Service. He worked for three years with the Los Angeles columnist Paul Coates on the television documentary series *Confidential File* before launching into well-made low-budget crime features. Then he began to acquire a cult reputation for offbeat films about eccentrics and losers – *A Fine Madness, Loving* – which ran out of steam with Barbra Streisand in *Up the Sandbox*. After a period of uncertainty, he made the big-time with *The Empire Strikes Back*, the first sequel to *Star Wars* (1977).

Films include: 1958 Stakeout on Dope Street. '59 The Young Captives. '61 The Hoodlum Priest. '63 A Face in the Rain. '64 The Luck of Ginger Coffey (CAN-USA). '66 A Fine Madness. '67 The Flim Flam Man (GB: One Born Every Minute). '70 Loving. '72 Up the Sandbox. '74 S*P*Y*S (GB). '78 The Eyes of Laura Mars. '80 The Empire Strikes Back.

KEYES, Evelyn

(b. 1919). Actress. Born: Port Arthur, Texas, USA

A lively but ladylike blonde, Evelyn Keyes lost her Southern accent only to find herself playing a Southern belle in Cecil B. DeMille's *The Buccaneer* and Scarlett O'Hara's sister in *Gone With the Wind*. She had a lead role in the reincarnation fantasy *Here Comes Mr Jordan*. She showed a flair for comedy as the genie in *A Thousand and One Nights* and for drama as an unfaithful wife in love with a murderous cop (Van Heflin) in Joseph Losey's *The Prowler*. She virtually retired after the mid-Fifties. Her husbands have included the directors Charles Vidor and John Huston and the bandleader Artie Shaw. Her frank autobiography caused a minor sensation in Hollywood, and she has also published a novel, *I Am a Billboard*.

Films include: 1938 The Buccaneer. '39 Gone With the Wind. '41 Here Comes Mr Jordan. '43 Dangerous Blondes. '44 Strange Affair. '45 A Thousand and One Nights. '46 The Jolson Story; Renegades; The Thrill of Brazil; Johnny O'Clock. '48 The Mating of Millie. '51 The Prowler. '53 Rough Shoot (GB) (USA: Shoot First). '55 The Seven Year Itch.

KIBBEE, Guy

(1886–1956). Actor. Born: El Paso, Texas, USA

In his early teens Guy Kibbee worked as a prop boy with a road show, and for nearly thirty years he played showboats, road shows and vaudeville. In 1930 he made his Broadway debut in *The Torch Song* and the following year he began his film career. Round, balding and moon-faced, he mostly played in comedies and Westerns in amiable character roles and sometimes leads, appearing several times with Shirley Temple. His last part was as the judge who goes easy on the baby-rescuing outlaw Robert Hightower (John Wayne) in John Ford's *Three Godfathers*.

Films include: 1931 City Streets; Man of the World; The Crowd Roars. '32 Winner Takes All. '33 42nd Street; Gold Diggers of 1933. '34 Harold Teen (GB: The Dancing Fool). '39 Mr Smith Goes to Washington. '47 Over the Santa Fe Trail (GB: No Escape). '48 Fort Apache; Three Godfathers.

KIDD, Michael

(b. 1919). Dancer/choreographer. Born: Milton Greenwald; New York City, USA

Michael Kidd studied dance and made his stage debut in *The Eternal Road* in 1937. He became a member of the American Ballet at the Metropolitan Opera and worked his way up to soloist, dancing the title role in *Billy the Kid*. He became a choreographer in the Forties, helping to establish a distinctively American style of energetic and acrobatic dancing, which he carried over to the movies in the Fifties in such films as *Guys and Dolls* and *Seven Brides for Seven Brothers*. His film debut as choreographer was based on a Broadway success adapted from the farce *Charley's Aunt*. He first acted (and danced) as one of the three ex-servicemen in *It's Always Fair Weather*. He has directed one film, *Merry Andrew*, with Danny Kaye. He won five Tony Awards in the late Forties and Fifties for his Broadway shows.

Films include: 1952 Where's Charley? '53 The Band Wagon. '54 Knock on Wood; Seven Brides for Seven Brothers. '55 Guys and Dolls; It's Always Fair Weather (actor only). '58 Merry Andrew (+ dir). '68 Star! '69 Hello, Dolly! '75 Smile (actor only). '78 Movie Movie (actor only).

KIDDER, Margot

(b. 1948). Actress. Born: Yellowknife, Northwest Territories, Canada

At 16 Margot Kidder left the last of 12 schools and played a succession of deranged teenagers and juvenile prostitutes on television, besides working as a model. She made her film debut opposite Beau Bridges in *Gaily, Gaily*. She also appeared regularly on television as the girlfriend of the hero (James Garner) in *Nichols*, an offbeat turn-of-the-century Western series. She gave a virtuoso performance in a dual role in Brian De Palma's shocker *Sisters*, and tried her hand as director of a 50-minute film, *Again* (1975), sponsored by the American Film Institute. She has also directed a documentary about the making of Arthur Penn's *The Missouri Breaks* (1976). But she is best known as Lois Lane in the *Superman* films.

Films include: 1969 Gaily, Gaily (GB: Chicago, Chicago). '70 Quackser Fortune Has a Cousin in the Bronx. '72 Sisters (GB: Blood Sisters). '75 The Great Waldo Pepper; The Reincarnation of Peter Proud; 92 in the Shade. '78 Superman, The Movie. '79 The Amityville Horror. '80 Superman II; Willie and Phil. '81 Heartaches (CAN).

KING, Henry

(1888–1982). Director. Born: Christianburg, Virginia, USA

Henry King entered show business as an actor at 21, touring with stock companies. In 1913 he started acting in films, but soon began writing and then directing. His first major success was an army comedy, *23½ Hours Leave*, and his most enduring silent

work was a tale of the rural South, *Tol'able David*. He introduced Ronald Colman to the screen in *The White Sister*, the first of several films he made in Italy. He also discovered Gary Cooper (in *The Winning of Barbara Worth*), Tyrone Power and Jean Peters; and he directed Gregory Peck in two of his best films, *Twelve O'Clock High* and *The Gunfighter*. King was the most important contract-director at Fox (later 20th Century-Fox) during his tenure of over thirty years there. He had a string of hits, including *State Fair, Alexander's Ragtime Band, A Bell for Adano* and *The Song of Bernadette*. He worked in many genres – musicals, Westerns, war films, small-town Americana, literary adaptations – and turned out excellent work in them all. He ended his career with two films relating to F. Scott Fitzgerald, the biographical *Beloved Infidel* and a version of Fitzgerald's last completed novel, *Tender Is the Night* – an appropriate conclusion, since Fitzgerald had finally become the sad poet of the Hollywood King had embodied for half a century.

Films include: 1916 Little Mary Sunshine. '19 23½ Hours Leave. '21 Tol'able David. '23 Fury; The White Sister. '24 Romola. '26 Stella Dallas; The Winning of Barbara Worth. '30 Lightnin'. '33 State Fair. '36 Lloyds of London. '38 In Old Chicago; Alexander's Ragtime Band. '39 Jesse James; Stanley and Livingstone. '43 The Song of Bernadette. '44 Wilson. '45 A Bell for Adano. '49 Prince of Foxes; Twelve O'Clock High. '50 The Gunfighter. '53 The Snows of Kilimanjaro. '57 The Sun Also Rises. '59 Beloved Infidel. '62 Tender Is the Night.

KINNEAR, Roy

(b. 1934). Actor. Born: Wigan, Lancashire, England

Short, round, pudgy-cheeked and funny, Kinnear has made a small place for himself in British films. He became a household name (and face) in the early Sixties as one of the

Above: Henry King directing Rock Hudson. Above right: Margot Kidder. Below left: Roy Kinnear in Taste the Blood of Dracula (1970). *Below right: Leonid Kinskey in* Down

original members of the satirical BBC television show, *That Was the Week That Was*. He broke off his schooling in Edinburgh to go to RADA when he was 17. After national service he appeared on stage, radio and television in Scotland before making his film debut – a few minutes as a bus conductor in *Tiara Tahiti*. More characteristic, though, was his portrayal of Finney, the henchman and general factotum to the villainous Moriarty in *The Adventure of Sherlock Holmes' Smarter Brother*.

Films include: 1962 Tiara Tahiti; The Boys. '63 Sparrows Can't Sing. '65 The Hill; Help! '69 The Bed Sitting Room. '71 Willy Wonka and the Chocolate Factory (USA). '72 Alice's Adventures in Wonderland. '73 The Three Musketeers: The Queen's Diamonds (PAN). '74 Juggernaut. '75 The Adventure of Sherlock Holmes' Smarter Brother.

Argentine Way (1940), a musical directed by Irving Cummings which the critics disliked at the time but managed to elevate Betty Grable and Carmen Miranda to stardom

KINSKEY, Leonid

(b. 1903). Actor. Born: St Petersburg, Russia

Kinskey came to the USA from the USSR in the Thirties having already begun a theatrical career as a mime artiste. His Hollywood debut was in Ernst Lubitsch's delightful masterpiece, *Trouble in Paradise*. Throughout his long career, Kinskey continued to play bartenders, ballet masters and professors, wherever someone with a thick Russian accent was needed.

Films include: 1932 Trouble in Paradise. '33 Duck Soup; Girl Without a Room. '34 We Live Again. '36 The General Died at Dawn. '38 The Great Waltz. '39 The Story of Vernon and Irene Castle. '41 That Night in Rio; Weekend in Havana. '42 Casablanca. '44 That's My Baby! '56 The Man with the Golden Arm.

Above: Klaus Kinski as Woyzeck, the soldier driven to murdering his mistress by a series of cruel misfortunes. Below: Alf Kjellin directing The McMasters. Above right:

Nastassia Kinski displays her grasp of the West Country accent to great effect as the girl destroyed by the men around her in Tess, an adaptation of Thomas Hardy's novel

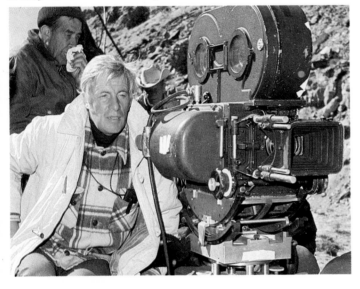

KINSKI, Klaus

(b. 1926). Actor. Born: Nikolas Nakszynski; Zoppot, nr. Danzig (now Poland)

Kinski's Polish parents moved to Berlin when Klaus was a child, and he grew up in extreme poverty. Perhaps in consequence of this, perhaps ironically, he claims to select his film parts on the basis of salary, and has declined offers from Fellini, Visconti and others. As a young man he worked in cabaret, and toured Germany with a poetry recital. He made his first film in 1948, worked steadily from the mid-Fifties, but made no real impact until he teamed up with the director Werner Herzog for *Aguirre, Nosferatu, Woyzeck*, and *Fitzcarraldo*. It proved a perfect matching of actor and director, with Kinski's intense, physical style conveying all the crazed gran-

deur of Herzog's tortured heroes.

Films include: 1948 Morituri (GER). '58 A Time to Love and a Time to Die (USA). '62 The Counterfeit Traitor (USA). '65 Doctor Zhivago (USA). '66 Per Qualche Dollaro in Più (IT-SP-GER) (USA/GB: For a Few Dollars More). '70 La Peau de Torpedo (FR-IT-GER) (USA: Children of Mata Hari; GB: Pill of Death). '73 Aguirre, der Zorn Gottes (GER) (USA/GB: Aguirre, Wrath of God). '75 Lifespan (NETH). '79 Nosferatu: Phantom der Nacht (GER-FR) (USA/GB: Nosferatu, the Vampyre); Woyzeck (GER). '81 Buddy, Buddy (USA). '82 Fitzcarraldo (GER); Android (USA).

KINSKI, Nastassia

(b. 1961). Actress. Born: Nastassja Nakszynski; Berlin, Germany

The breathtakingly beautiful daughter of actor Klaus Kinski was educated in Rome, Munich and Caracas, and

went in her early teens to the USA. There she studied English and took drama courses with Lee Strasberg. She had begun her film career playing a juggler in 1975 in Wim Wenders' *Wrong Movement*, and four years later her perfectly judged performance in the title role of *Tess* made her a star. Her linguistic abilities were further tested in *Exposed*, where she portrayed a farm-girl from the American mid-West, and she starred as the feline heroine of the remake of *Cat People*, winning rave reviews.

Films include: 1975 Falsche Bewegung (GER) (GB: Wrong Movement). '76 To the Devil . . . a Daughter (GB-GER). '78 Cosi Come Sei (IT-SP) (USA: Stay As You Are); Leidenschaftliche Blümchen (GER) (USA: Passion Flower Hotel). '79 Tess (FR-GB). '81 One From the Heart (USA). '82 Exposed (USA-FR); Cat People (USA).

KINUGASA, Teinosuke

(1896–1982). Director. Born: Teinosuke Kokame; Mie Prefecture, Japan

Kinugasa first appeared on stage in 1914, and five years later entered the cinema as an *oyama* or female impersonator. At that time women in Japan were not allowed to act. When they were, in 1922, the *oyamas* went on strike. When the strike failed, Kinugasa became a director, making at least one hundred films and scripting many of them. We can judge him only by the three known in the West. His silent films, *A Page of Madness* and *Crossways*, are extraordinary, featuring an extremely mobile camera, rapid cutting, superimpositions, total reliance on visuals (*A Page of Madness* has no inter-titles), and expressionistic lighting. *Gate of Hell*, a more leisured historical epic shot in superb Eastman Color, won the 1954 Grand Prix at Cannes and the Oscar for Best Foreign Language Film.

Films include: 1926 Kurutta Ippeiji (USA/GB: A Page of Madness). '28 Jujiro (GB: Crossways). '32 Chushingura (The Loyal Forty-Seven Ronin). '33 Futatsu Toro (Two Stone Lanterns). '37 Osaka Natsu No Jin (The Summer Battle of Osaka). '40 Hebihimesaka (Miss Snake Princess). '41 Kawanakajima Kassan (The Battle of Kawanakajima). '47 Joyu (Actress). '52 Daibutsu Kaigen (Saga of the Great Buddha). '53 Jigokumon (USA/GB: Gate of Hell). '61 Okoto to Sasuke (Okoto and Sasuke).

KJELLIN, Alf

(b. 1920). Actor/director. Born: Christian Keleen; Lund, Sweden

Alf Kjellin (pronounced Sha-leen) entered Swedish films as an actor in 1937, and wrote his first screenplay (*Night in the Harbour*) in 1941. Three years later he became internationally known for his moving performance as the young student in Alf Sjöberg's *Frenzy*, which was scripted by a young friend of Kjellin's named Ingmar Bergman. From 1949 he acted in some American films, initially under the pseudonym Christopher Kent, but worked also in Sweden, where he directed his first film, *The Girl in the Rain*, in 1955. Eventually Kjellin settled down in the USA, directed a great deal for television, and a little for the cinema. His *The McMasters* was a touching story of an ex-slave battling with racial hatred.

Films as actor include: 1944 Hets (USA: Torment; GB: Frenzy). '47 Kvinna Utan Ansikte (Woman Without a Face). '49 Madame Bovary (USA). '52 My Six Convicts (USA); The Iron Mistress (USA). '53 The Juggler (USA). '55 Flickan i Regnet (dir. only). '62 Lustgården (dir. only); Siska (dir. only). '63 The Victors (USA). '65 Ship of Fools (USA). '66 Assault on a Queen (USA). '68 Ice Station Zebra (USA). '69 Midas Run (dir. only) (USA) (GB: A Run on Gold). '70 The McMasters (dir. only) (USA) (GB: The McMasters . . . Tougher Than the West Itself!).

KLUGE, Alexander

(b. 1932). Director. Born: Halberstadt, Germany

Kluge had practised as a lawyer and written novels before turning to the cinema in the late Fifties to make a number of short films. In 1962 he was one of a group of young film-makers who signed the Oberhausen Manifesto, calling for state aid for a 'new' German cinema. In 1966 his first feature, *Yesterday's Girl*, was warmly received. Like his later films, it showed an acute political consciousness which was combined in this case with a moving personal story of a girl from the East finding difficulty in accepting the contradictions of a Western society. Always active in film politics, Kluge has relentlessly lobbied to improve matters for German independent film-makers.

Films include: 1966 Abschied von Gestern (GB: Yesterday Girl). '68 Artisten in der Zirkuskuppel: ratlos (GB: Artistes at the Top of the Big Top: Disorientated). '69 Die unbezähmbare Lene Peickert. '71 Der grosse Verhau; Willy Tobler und der Untergang der 6 Flotte. '73 Besitz bürgerin, Jahrgang. '74 Gelegenheitsarbeit einer Sklavin (GB: Occasional Work of a Female Slave). '76 Der starke Ferdinand. '77 Die Menschen, die das Staufer-Jahr Vorbereiten (co-dir). '78 Deutschland im Herbst (co-dir) (GB: Germany in Autumn). '79 Die Patriotin (GB: The Patriot).

KNEF, Hildegard

(b. 1925). Actress. Born: Ulm, Germany

A colourful autobiography describes how in the last days of the war Knef ran away from Berlin in male disguise in order to be with her lover at the front. They were captured by the Russians, but Knef escaped. She was in some of the earliest post-war German films, including the notable *The Murderers Are Amongst Us*, had a brief flirtation with Hollywood in the early Fifties (where her name was changed to Hildegarde Neff), and soon returned to European films. Though often hailed as a second Dietrich, she could never command the classic screen presence of the first, and the quality of most of her films did not help. But she was a brave lady, won a long battle with cancer, and came back to a fine movie at last – Billy Wilder's *Fedora*.

Films include: 1946 Die Mörder sind unter uns (E. GER) (USA: The Murderers Are Amongst Us). '51 Die Sünderin (GB: The Sinner). '52 Diplomatic Courier (USA); Night Without Sleep. '53 Snows of Kilimanjaro (USA); The Man Between (GB). '54 Svengali (GB). '61 Caterina di Russia (IT-FR). '63 Die Dreigroschenoper (GER-FR) (USA/GB: The Threepenny Opera). '78 Fedora (GER-FR).

KNIGHT, Esmond

(b. 1906). Actor. Born: East Sheen, Surrey, England

Educated at Westminster School, Knight first appeared on the professional stage at the Old Vic in 1925, and built a solid reputation doing

everything from Shakespeare to singing and dancing in Cochran musicals. He was also, from 1931, one of the most versatile character actors in British films. He served in the Navy in World War II, and was blinded during action between HMS *Prince of Wales* and the *Bismarck*. Partially regaining his sight, he was able to continue as an actor, and many of his best film roles came in the Forties, notably his village simpleton in *A Canterbury Tale* and his silent holy man in *Black Narcissus*.

Films include: 1931 The Ringer. '36 Pagliacci (USA: A Clown Must Laugh). '39 The Arsenal Stadium Mystery. '40 Contraband. '43 The Silver Fleet. '44 A Canterbury Tale. '47 Holiday Camp; Black Narcissus. '51 The River (IND). '60 Peeping Tom.

KNIGHT, Shirley

(b. 1937). Actress. Born: Goessell, Kansas, USA

The daughter of an Oklahoma farmer turned oil-magnate, Shirley Knight received her acting tuition at the Pasadena Playhouse, and caught the eye of Warner Brothers in a student production of *Look Back in Anger*, in which Dean Stockwell also appeared. Her rise was swift, for in her second year in films she gained an Oscar nomination for her disturbed teenager in *The Dark at the Top of the Stairs*. After a spell on the New York stage, she came to England in 1966 to appear in the film of Leroi Jones' play, *Dutchman*, and later married the English playwright John Hopkins and settled in Britain. Probably her best performance was in Coppola's *The Rain People*. Always adept at playing vulnerable, disturbed, attractive women, she was superb as the fugitive housewife wandering nervily round Pennsylvania with James Caan's retarded hitch-hiker.

Films include: 1959 The Gates of Hell. '60 The Dark at the Top of the Stairs. '62 Sweet Bird of Youth. '65 The Group. '67 Dutch-

man (GB). '68 Petulia. '69 The Rain People. '72 Secrets (GB). '74 Juggernaut (GB). '79 Beyond the Poseidon Adventure. '81 Endless Love.

KNOWLES, Patric

(b. 1911). Actor. Born: Reginald Lawrence Knowles; Horsforth, Yorkshire, England

Learning his trade in provincial repertory, Knowles acted in British films from 1932, and was under contract to the British studios of Warner Brothers. Summoned to Hollywood in 1936, he was fated to be second fiddle to Errol Flynn at Warners, though his looks and physique, trim moustache and English accent would have qualified him for swashbuckling leads elsewhere. But he broke away to work steadily as a reliable support, shading gracefully into character roles, and appearing frequently until the late Fifties. Occasional films since then have included *Chisum*, in which Knowles was effective as an ageing English rancher and mentor of Billy the Kid.

Films include: 1935 Abdul the Damned. '36 Crown v Stevens; The Charge of the Light Brigade (USA). '38 The Adventures of Robin Hood (USA). '39 Torchy Blane in Chinatown (USA). '41 How Green Was My Valley. '43 Frankenstein Meets the Wolf Man (USA). '45 Kitty (USA). '53 Flame of Calcutta (USA). '70 Chisum (USA).

KNOX, Alexander

(b. 1907). Actor. Born: Strathroy, Ontario, Canada

A man with literary ambitions, fulfilled when in later life he became a successful novelist and playwright, Knox attended the University of Western Ontario before working as a journalist. From the *Boston Post* he turned to acting, making his stage debut in that city in 1929. In England in the Thirties, he had fair success on the stage, and made his first film in 1938. Returning to the USA, he built a sterling reputation as a character

Above, far left: Hildegard Knef in Lulu *(1959). Above left: Esmond Knight in* The Winter's Tale *(1966). Above: Shirley Knight on the loose in* The Rain People. *Right: Patric Knowles (left) in Errol Flynn's shadow at Warners, but holding his own in* The Charge of the Light Brigade. *Below: Alexander Knox in* Fräulein Doktor *(1969)*

actor, playing likeable, reliable, literate people, with a notable lead in Henry King's biography of Woodrow Wilson. Once again in Britain from the Fifties, with his wife, the actress Doris Nolan, he has been particularly effective for director Joseph Losey, with remarkable performances in *The Damned* (1962) and *Accident* (1967).

Films include: 1938 The Gaunt Stranger (USA: The Phantom Strikes). '39 Cheer, Boys, Cheer. '44 Wilson. '51 Saturday's Hero (USA) (GB: Idols in the Dust). '54 The Divided Heart. '56 Reach for the Sky. '58 The Vikings. '66 Modesty Blaise. '68 Villa Rides (USA). '70 Puppet on a Chain.

KOBAYASHI, Masaki

(b. 1916). Director. Born: Hokkaido, Japan

Kobayashi studied art at Waseda University and joined Shochiku Studios in 1941. He spent much of his military service as a prisoner during the Sino-Japanese War, subsequently rejoining Shochiku. His wartime experiences formed the basis for the film that made his name as a director, *The Human Condition*, a nine-hour trilogy partly set in a forced labour camp in Manchuria. Although the best of his earlier films, such as *Room With Thick Walls* and *Black River* (which made Tatsuya Nakadai a star), were modern studies of the effects of war, Kobayashi was hailed as a master of Samurai films following the release of *Hara-Kiri*. Its success encouraged him to form his own company, and *Kwaidan*, a collection of supernatural stories, and *Joiuchi*, a study of family loyalty, became his first independent films. Following these examinations of Japanese traditional values, he returned to a contemporary setting for *Kaseki*, the story of a businessman on a European trip who discovers he has only a year to live. Though serious – even gloomy – in theme, Kobayashi's films are beautifully composed; his belief in the essential dignity of Man ensures that despite their intensity of situation they are thought-provoking rather than merely depressing.

Films include: 1955 Kabe Atsuki Heya (Room With Thick Walls). **'57** Kuroi Kawa (Black River). **'59–61** Ningen No Joken, parts 1–3 (part 1, GB: No Greater Love; part 2, GB: Road to Eternity; part 3, GB: A Soldier's Prayer). **'62** Karamiai (The In-

heritance); Seppuku (USA/GB: Hara-Kiri). **'65** Kwaidan. **'67** Joiuchi (USA/GB: Rebellion). **'68** Nippon no Seishun (Hymn to a Tired Man). **'74** Kaseki.

KOCH, Howard

(b. 1902). Screenwriter. Born: New York City, USA

The sophistication and intelligence that were the chief qualities of Koch's writing also contributed to his being hounded relentlessly by the House Un-American Activities Committee in the Fifties for alleged left-wing allegiances. Koch, a graduate from Columbia Law School, initially wrote for the stage and radio, achieving his first major success for his script for Orson Welles' vivid radio adaptation of *War of the Worlds*. Koch then moved to Hollywood, working on movies by many fine directors, including Wyler's *The Letter*, Hawks' *Sergeant York*, Curtiz' *Casablanca* and Ophuls' *Letter From an Unknown Woman*. He won an Oscar for *Casablanca* (with Julius and Phillip Epstein) and was also nominated for *Sergeant York*. Following his blacklisting by the studios in 1951, he wrote under a pseudonym for the rest of the decade. He worked in England during the Sixties, numbering *The Greengage Summer* and *633 Squadron* among his credits.

Films include: 1940 The Sea Hawk (co-sc); The Letter. **'41** Sergeant York (co-sc). **'42** Casablanca (co-sc). **'45** Rhapsody in Blue (co-sc). **'48** Letter From an Unknown Woman. **'50** No Sad Songs for Me. **'51** The Thirteenth Letter. **'61** The Greengage Summer (GB) (USA: Loss of Innocence). **'62** The War Lover (GB). **'64** 633 Squadron (co-sc) (GB). **'67** The Fox (co-sc).

KOCH, Howard W.

(b. 1916). Director/producer. Born: New York City, USA

Koch is better-known as a producer than as a director, having supervised the making of such movie hits as *The Manchurian Candidate*, *The Odd Couple* and *Airplane!* He took the first step towards fulfilling his showbusiness ambitions when he gave up his job as a runner for a Wall Street broker to concentrate on stage management. He moved to Hollywood after a short stay at Universal's New York office, becoming second assistant on John Stahl's *Keys of the Kingdom* (1944). Koch formed Bel Air Productions with Aubrey Schenck in 1953 and turned to directing, varying between grim gangster movies, such as *Big House USA* and *The Last Mile*, and movies that promised more in the title than they delivered on the screen, including *Untamed Youth*, *The Girl in Black Stockings* and *Born Reckless*. From 1961 to 1964 he was vice-president of Frank Sinatra's company, Sinatra Enterprises. He then began the most successful phase of his career as head of production at Paramount, also forming his own production company in 1966.

Films include: 1954 Beachhead (prod). **'55** Big House USA (dir). **'57** Bop Girl (dir); Untamed Youth (dir); The Girl in Black Stockings (dir). **'58** Andy Hardy Comes Home (dir). **'59** The Last Mile (dir); Born Reckless (dir). **'62** The Manchurian Candidate (prod). **'64** Robin and the Seven Hoods (prod). **'65** None But the Brave (prod) (USA-JAP). **'68** The Odd Couple (prod). **'70** On a Clear Day You Can See Forever (prod). **'71** Plaza Suite (prod). **'73** Badge 373 (dir). **'80** Airplane! (prod).

KORDA, Alexander

(1893–1956). Director/producer. Born: Sándor László Kellner; Puszta Turpásztó, Túrkeve, Hungary

Korda was the only British-based producer with the entrepreneurial drive and ambition to rival the great Hollywood movie moguls. He has left a lasting mark (his critics might substitute 'stain') on the British film industry in his attempts to create a cinema that had both a distinct national character and world-wide appeal. Initially a journalist, Korda became active in Hungarian films in 1912, directing over 20 between 1914 and 1919. A right-wing coup induced him to work in Austria and then Germany, where he made (among other movies) *A Modern Dubarry* in 1926 which won him a Hollywood contract with First National. However, it was not until he came to Britain in 1931 and formed London Films that he really came into his own. His sixth production, *The Private Life of Henry VIII*, brought together the talents of his designer brother Vincent, French cameraman Georges Périnal, the writers Lajos Biro and Arthur Wimperis (all of whom worked on many subsequent Korda films) and made stars of the actors Charles Laughton, Robert Donat and Merle Oberon (whom Korda later married – his first wife was actress Maria Corda). The film's world-wide success allowed Korda to set up his own studio at Denham. His studio's films, which include *The Scarlet Pimpernel*, *Things to Come*, *Fire Over England*, *The Four Feathers* and *The Thief of Bagdad*, were characterized by their visual elegance, excellent performances and nostalgic, escapist subject-matter – a mixture of charm and complacency that would be the dominant feature of British filmmaking until the early Sixties. By the end of the Thirties, Korda's extravagant aims had placed him in dire financial straits and he was forced to relinquish control of Denham. He made the patriotic *That Hamilton Woman!* in Hollywood, received a knighthood in 1942, but was unable to maintain any continuity in his career until after World War II, when he re-formed London Films. He took the role of executive producer, using all his considerable charm and influence to encourage investment in his company. He left the directing side to younger men, thereby becoming indirectly responsible for such British classics as Powell and Pressburger's *The Tales of Hoffman*, Reed's *The Third Man*, Lean's *Hobson's Choice* and Olivier's *Richard III*.

Films include: 1926 Eine Dubarry von Heute (dir) (GER) (GB: A Modern Dubarry). **'27** The Private Life of Helen of Troy (dir) (USA). **'33** The Private Life of Henry VIII (dir; +prod). **'34** The Scarlet Pimpernel (prod). **'36** Things to Come (prod); Rembrandt (dir; +prod). **'37** Fire Over England (prod); Elephant Boy (prod). **'39** The Four Feathers (prod). **'40** The Thief of Bagdad (prod). **'41** That Hamilton Woman! (dir; +prod) (USA) (GB: Lady Hamilton). **'48** The Fallen Idol (prod). **'49** The Third Man (prod). **'51** The Tales of Hoffman (prod). **'54** Hobson's Choice (prod). **'56** Richard III (prod).

KORDA, Vincent

(1897–1979). Art director. Born: Vincent Kellner; Puszta Turpásztó, Túrkeve, Hungary

Vincent Korda is best known for his work with his brother Alexander's London Films, and was instrumental in creating a distinctive 'look' for that company's output. He could work wonders with cheap materials, as his castle interiors for *The Private Life of Henry VIII* showed, and had the breadth of vision to create on a grand scale when given the resources, as exemplified by his sets for *Things to Come* and *The Thief of Bagdad* (for which he won an Oscar). Korda studied painting in Budapest, Vienna, Florence and Paris before joining Alexander in 1931 to design the sets for *Marius*, thus initiating a long-standing collaboration, in which Vincent and Alexander's other brother, the director Zoltan Korda, also shared.

Films include: 1933 The Private Life of Henry VIII; The Girl From Maxim's. '35 The Scarlet Pimpernel. '36 Things to Come; Rembrandt. '37 The Man Who Could Work Miracles. '38 The Drum (co-art dir). '40 The Thief of Bagdad (co-art dir). '41 That Hamilton Woman! (USA) (GB: Lady Hamilton). '48 The Fallen Idol (co-art dir). '49 The Third Man (co-art dir). '55 Summer Madness (GB-USA) (USA: Summertime). '62 The Longest Day (co-art dir) (USA). '64 The Yellow Rolls Royce (co-art dir).

KORDA, Zoltán

(1895–1961). Director. Born: Zoltán Kellner; Puszta Turpásztó, Túrkeve, Hungary

Zoltan Korda's film-making career is largely bound up with his older brother Alexander, for whose London Films he directed several entertaining features, often set in Africa or India during the heyday of the British Empire. The best was *The Four Feathers*, which featured superb early Technicolor photography by Georges Périnal and finely orchestrated battle-scenes (Korda had been an officer in the Austro-Hungarian army in World War I), which have since graced several inferior movies. Poor health encouraged Korda to seek the warmer climes of California in the late Thirties, though he continued to direct, making *The Jungle Book* for his brother's company and freelancing for Columbia (*Sahara, Counter-Attack*) and United Artists (*The Macomber Affair*). His best post-war movie was *Cry, the Beloved Country*, based on Alan Paton's novel, which attempted a serious examination of racial problems in South Africa – issues which had been sacrificed on the altar of popular entertainment in his earlier work for London Films.

Films include: 1927 Die Elf Teufel (GER). '33 Cash. '35 Sanders of the River. '37 Elephant Boy (co-dir). '38 The Drum. '39 The Four Feathers. '42 The Jungle Book. '43 Sahara (USA). '45 Counter-Attack (USA). '47 The Macomber Affair (USA). '48 A Woman's Vengeance (+prod) (USA). '52 Cry, the Beloved Country (+ co-prod) (USA: African Fury). '55 Storm Over the Nile (co-dir; + co-prod).

KORNGOLD, Erich Wolfgang

(1897–1957). Composer. Born: Czechoslovakia

Korngold was a child prodigy whose work was performed in Vienna and Leipzig before he was in his teens. In the mid-Thirties, with the Nazi influence pervading Europe, he accepted an invitation by the director Max Reinhardt to arrange Mendelssohn's music for Warner Brothers' production of *A Midsummer Night's Dream*, thus beginning a long and successful association with that studio. He was in a position to choose his projects carefully, frequently selecting historical romances. His stirring, full-blown melodies and swelling crescendos, relying heavily on the string section of the orchestra, ennobled the swashbuckling heroics of Errol Flynn in such films as *Captain Blood, The Adventures of Robin Hood* and *The Sea Hawk* and added poignancy to *The Private Lives of Elizabeth and Essex* and *Kings Row*. He retired from movies in 1947, having won Oscars for his scores for *Anthony Adverse* and *The Adventures of Robin Hood*, composing solely for the concert hall during the last ten years of his life.

Films include: 1935 A Midsummer Night's Dream (mus. arr); Captain Blood; The Story of Louis Pasteur. '36 The Green Pastures; Anthony Adverse. '37 The Prince and the Pauper. '38 The Adventures of Robin Hood. '39 The Private Lives of Elizabeth and Essex. '40 The Sea Hawk. '41 Kings Row. '46 Of Human Bondage.

KORTNER, Fritz

(1892–1970). Actor/director. Born: Vienna, Austria

This full-blooded, intense performer studied at the Academy of Music and Dramatic Arts, Vienna, achieving lasting fame with Max Reinhardt's company in Berlin during the Twenties, particularly for his portrayals of Shylock and Othello. He rapidly became a power in German cinema as a director and actor, perhaps his best-remembered role being that of the respectable Peter Schön, fatally attracted to Louise Brooks' Lulu, in *Pandora's Box*. He left Germany in 1933 to escape the Nazi persecution of the Jews, moved to England, and appeared in four British movies, including the musical *Chu Chin Chow* (as a brigand) and *Abdul the Damned* (as an Oriental despot). He then made Hollywood his home, appearing in anti-Nazi movies and minor roles in major films such as *The Razor's Edge*. He returned to Germany after the war to resume a place at the forefront of serious drama. He played a German-Jewish university professor encountering the aftermath of Nazi anti-Semitism in *The Challenge*, and directed some praiseworthy films, such as *Secrets of the City* and *Sarajevo* (1955), as well as staging productions of Shakespeare, Ibsen and Strindberg.

Films include: 1918 Gregor Marold (+dir). '20 Die Brüder Karamasoff. '23 Schatten (GB: Warning Shadows). '25 Orlacs Hände (GB: The Hands of Orlac). '29 Die Büchse der Pandora (GB: Pandora's Box). '34 Chu Chin Chow (GB). '35 Abdul the Damned (GB). '44 The Hitler Gang (USA). '46 The Razor's Edge (USA). '54 Die Stadt ist voller Geheimnisse (dir; + co-sc) (USA/GB: City of Secrets/Secrets of the City).

KOSCINA, Sylva

(b. 1934). Actress. Born: Zagreb, Yugoslavia

Sylva Koscina found the idea of acting more tempting than that of life at university. She had been spotted by Eduardo De Filippo, offered a screen test which failed and went to Rome determined to persevere in the film world. No doubt as a result of her exotic and sexy looks, bit parts grew into starring roles and she made her film debut in *Il Ferroviere*. Koscina characteristically performed in light comedies and costume dramas. In the late Sixties she worked for Hollywood and starred in such films as *The Secret War of Harry Frigg* with Paul Newman, but she was less an actress than an item of decor.

Films include: 1956 Il Ferroviere (IT) (USA: The Railroad Man; GB: Man of Iron). '57 Gwendalina (IT-FR). '63 Judex (IT-FR). '64 Hot Enough for June (GB). '65 Giulietta Degli Spiriti (IT-FR) (GB: Juliet of the Spirits). '66 Deadlier Than the Male (GB). '68 The Secret War of Harry Frigg (USA); A Lovely Way to Go (USA). '69 L'Assoluto Naturale (IT) (USA: He and She; GB: She and He). '70 Hornet's Nest (USA-IT). '71 Homo Eroticus (IT) (USA: Man of the Year).

KOSMA, Joseph

(1905–1969). Composer. Born: Budapest, Hungary

Kosma studied music in Budapest and in 1933 went to Paris where he met Jacques Prévert with whom he composed more than eighty songs. These were set to Prévert's poetry and became extremely popular. Kosma began to work on film scores from 1936. He saw the art of film music not just as an aural subsidiary but as an entity with its own distinct life. His musical style developed and he collaborated with directors like Renoir, Carné and Paul Grimault – most notably on the latter's short film *Le Petit Soldat*. Kosma also composed symphonies and opera and ballet scores.

Films include: 1935 Le Crime de Monsieur Lange (songs only) (USA: The Crime of Monsieur Lange). '36 Jenny; Une Partie de Campagne. '37 La Grande Illusion (USA: Grand Illusion; GB: The Great Illusion); La Marseillaise (mus. arr; +lyr) (USA: Marseillaise). '38 La Bête Humaine (USA: The Human Beast; GB: Judas Was a Woman). '39 La Règle du Jeu (arr. only). '42 Les Visiteurs du Soir (co-comp) (USA: The Devil's Own Envoy). '45 Les Enfants du Paradis (co-comp) (USA: Children of Paradise). '46 Les Portes de la Nuit (USA: Gates of the Night). '47 Le Petit Soldat. '50 Juliette ou la Clé des Songes. '56 Elena et les Hommes (USA: Paris Does Strange Things; GB: The Night Does Strange Things). '62 Le Caporal Epinglé (USA: The Elusive Corporal; GB: The Vanishing Corporal). '63 In the French Style (USA-FR).

KOSTER, Henry

(b. 1905). Director. Born: Hermann Kosterlitz; Berlin, Germany

Koster is remembered as the director of cheerful Deanna Durbin musicals which saved Universal from bankruptcy in the late Thirties and early Forties. He studied art in Berlin, worked as a cartoonist and commercial artist and broke into movies as a scriptwriter at Ufa and Universal's Berlin studio. He directed his first film in Germany in 1932, *Das Abenteuer der Thea Roland*, then decided to leave the country when the Nazis came to power. He arrived in Hollywood in

1936, making his first Deanna Durbin picture a year later. His work was characterized by solid professionalism allied to a sure touch that brought the best out of lightweight material. His successful track record brought him the prestigious assignment of *The Robe*, the first film in CinemaScope, which was nominated for an Oscar. In general his later work lacked the insouciance of his early movies. Among his last films were the Rodgers and Hammerstein musical *Flower Drum Song* (one of their few misses) and the mawkish *The Singing Nun*.

Films include: 1937 Three Smart Girls. **'39** First Love. **'41** It Started With Eve. **'47** The Bishop's Wife. **'49** The Inspector General. **'50** Harvey. **'51** No Highway (GB) (USA: No Highway in the Sky). **'53** The Robe. **'61** Flower Drum Song. **'66** The Singing Nun.

KOTCHEFF, Ted

(b. 1931). Director. Born: William Theodore Kotcheff; Toronto, Ontario, Canada

Born in Canada of Bulgarian immigrants, Kotcheff, in that land of striving immigrants' sons, made good. He graduated in English and became, at 24, Canada's youngest television director. Kotcheff came to England in 1957, directed plays on television and in the West End, and began his association with fellow countryman, writer Mordecai Richler. Together they worked on *Life at the Top*, *Two Gentlemen Sharing*, *The Apprenticeship of Duddy Kravitz* (from Richler's own novel), and *Fun With Dick and Jane*, the first satire on Seventies recession. Kotcheff also directed the impressive television docu-drama, *Edna the Inebriate Woman*.

Films: 1962 Tiara Tahiti (GB). **'65** Life at the Top (GB). **'69** Two Gentlemen Sharing (GB). **'71** Outback (AUS). **'73** Billy Two Hats. **'74** The Apprenticeship of Duddy Kravitz (CAN). **'77** Fun With Dick and Jane. **'78** Who is Killing the Great Chefs of Europe? (USA-GER) (GB: Too Many Chefs). **'79** North Dallas Forty

KOTTO, Yaphet

(b. 1939). Actor. Born: Harlem, New York City, USA

A powerfully built actor whose aunt ran a well-known dance school in New York (Brando and Dean numbered among its students), Kotto – more than many fellow black actors – has been able to break through the racial stereotype. He's played an engineer in *Alien*, a thief in *The Thomas Crown Affair*, the deposed leader Idi Amin in *Raid on Entebbe*, a barkeeper in *Five Card Stud* and a cool Detroit car worker with brains in *Blue Collar*. At the age of 19, with hardly any stage experience, he was called upon to take over the title role in *Othello*, in a semi-professional theatrical production, when the lead fell ill. This led to Broadway, then television and film. Kotto has directed a film – *The Limit* (1972) – in which he also acted.

Films include: 1968 The Thomas Crown Affair; Five Card Stud. **'70** The Liberation of L.B. Jones. **'72** Across 110th Street; Man and Boy. **'73** Live and Let Die (GB). **'75** Friday Foster. **'76** Raid on Entebbe. **'78** Blue Collar. **'79** Alien. **'80** Brubaker.

KOVACS, Laszlo

(b. 1933). Cinematographer. Born: Hungary

Having studied at the Academy of Film and Theatre Arts in Budapest, Laszlo Kovacs fled Hungary along with fellow cameraman Vilmos Zsigmond and a great deal of footage of the crushing of the Hungarian uprising by Soviet forces. He finally made his way to New York where he rejoined Zsigmond, and they both travelled to Los Angeles in search of film work. Their first short, *Lullaby*, soon gained them recognition, and, through his subsequent collaboration with such directors as Roger Corman and Richard Rush, Kovacs received his cinematographical grounding in the low-budget exploitation movies of

the Sixties. His major break came with Dennis Hopper's *Easy Rider*, a film through which he personally learnt much about America. Kovacs soon became a vital contributor to many of the major movies of the Seventies, working with many new directors like Bob Rafelson, Paul Mazursky and Martin Scorsese. Above all Kovacs understands the needs of his directors and collaborates perfectly with them – but he also makes his own individual mark on a film as he has the ability totally to create and govern its look.

Films include: 1963 Lullaby (short) (co-photo). **'67** Hell's Angels on Wheels. **'69** Easy Rider; That Cold Day in the Park (USA-CAN). **'70** Getting Straight; Five Easy Pieces; Alex in Wonderland. **'71** The Marriage of a Young Stockbroker; The Last Movie. **'72** What's Up, Doc?; The King of Marvin Gardens. **'73** Steelyard Blues; Paper Moon. **'75** Shampoo. **'77** New York, New York; Close Encounters of the Third Kind (add. photo. only). **'79** Heart Beat.

KOZINTSEV, Grigori

(1905–1973). Director. Born: Grigori Mikhailovich Kozintsev; Kiev, Russia

It would be patronizing to call Kozintsev the director who brought Shakespeare to the Russians, but his best known films in the West are *Hamlet* and *King Lear*. He studied at the Academy of Fine Arts in Leningrad and then began his long friendship and collaboration with Leonid Trauberg. Together they organized FEKS (Factory of the Eccentric Actor), an experimental theatre whose aim it was to rid the theatre of its old forms and introduce in their place elements of the music-hall, circus and even cinema. In 1924 the FEKS artists produced an experimental film comedy, *Pokhozdeniya Oktyabriny* (*The Adventures of Oktyabrina*). The Kozintsev-Trauberg partnership peaked, in the silent period, with *New Babylon*, a satirical account of the Paris Com-

mune of 1871. They had made thirteen films together when they split in the mid-Forties. But it is the scale of *Hamlet* and the subtle characterizations therein for which Kozintsev will best be remembered. He shared the Lenin Prize with the actor who played the prince, Innokenty Smoktunovsky.

Films include: 1926 Chertovo Koleso (co-dir) (GB: The Devil's Wheel); Shinel (co-dir) (USA: The Overcoat; GB: The Cloak). **'27** Bratishka (co-dir). **'29** Novyi Vavilon (co-dir) (GB: New Babylon). **'35** Yunost Maksima/The Youth of Maxim (co-dir). **'37** Vozvrascheniye Maksim/The Return of Maxim (co-dir). **'39** Vyborgskaya Storona/The Vyborg (co-dir). **'47** Pirogov. **'53** Belinskii. **'57** Kikhot/Quixote. **'64** Gamlet (GB: Hamlet). **'70** Korolir (GB: King Lear).

KRÄLY, Hans

(1885–1950). Screenwriter. Born: Germany

Kräly came to Hollywood from Germany with Ernst Lubitsch in the early Twenties, after already having collaborated with the director from 1918 on such films as *Carmen* and *Madame DuBarry*. The partnership worked well in Hollywood, too, with *Rosita* (starring Mary Pickford as a Spanish street-singer), *Three Women* and *So This is Paris* coming out in quick succession. Kräly also wrote scripts for Lewis Milestone, Henry Koster and William Wyler, but none quite matched the scintillating wit of those done for Lubitsch.

Films include: 1912 Die Kinder des Generals (GER). **'14** Die ewige Nacht (GER). **'18** Carmen (GER) (USA: Gypsy Blood). **'19** Madame DuBarry (co-sc) (GER) (USA: Passion). **'23** Rosita (co-sc). **'24** Three Women (co-sc). **'26** So This Is Paris (co-sc). **'29** The Last of Mrs Cheyney (co-sc). **'31** Private Lives (co-sc). **'43** The Mad Ghoul.

Below, far left: Fritz Kortner in Schatten. Below left: Sylva Koscina in Hornet's Nest. Below: Yaphet Kotto in Report to the Commissioner (1975)

KRAMER, Stanley

(b. 1913). Producer/director. Born: New York City, USA

Kramer has been criticized for being too liberal and anarchic on one hand, and too commercial on the other. But, if at times his assaults on prejudice and bigotry (*Inherit the Wind, The Defiant Ones, Guess Who's Coming to Dinner?*) are heavy handed, overtly conscientious and tastelessly box-office orientated, at least they have the courage of their convictions. Better still is *High Noon*, a peerless Western thriller and a successful allegory of McCarthyism directed for Kramer by Fred Zinnemann, though *Judgement at Nuremberg* and *On the Beach* – embarrassing in their use of stars – are woefully misguided treatises on holocaust. From New York University, Kramer got nowhere fast either writing scripts at 20th Century-Fox (later at Columbia) or in the research department at MGM. But he got some production experience at the latter studio and, after the war, in which he served in the Signal Corps, established his own production company and embarked on his best spell as a producer of cheap, realistic dramas. In the mid-Fifties he emerged as a director of those outraged 'message' films but ten years later was a spent force.

Films include: 1941 So Ends the Night (assoc. prod). **'42** The Moon and Sixpence (assoc. prod). **'49** Home of the Brave (prod). **'50** The Men (prod); Cyrano de Bergerac (prod). **'51** Death of a Salesman (prod). **'52** High Noon (prod); The Member of the Wedding (prod). **'53** The Wild One (prod). **'54** The Caine Mutiny (prod). **'55** Not as a Stranger (dir; +prod). **'57** The Pride and the Passion (dir; +prod). **'58** The Defiant Ones (dir; +prod). **'60** On the Beach (dir; +prod); Inherit the Wind (dir; +prod). **'61** Judgement at Nuremberg (dir; +prod). **'63** It's a Mad, Mad, Mad, Mad World (dir; +prod). **'65** Ship of Fools (dir; +prod). **'67** Guess Who's Coming to Dinner? (dir; +prod). **'73** Oklahoma Crude (dir; +prod). **'79** The Runner Stumbles (dir; +prod).

KRASKER, Robert

(1913–1981). Cinematographer. Born: Perth, Australia

Krasker studied art in Paris and photography in Dresden. He entered the film industry with Sir Alexander Korda's London Films, working as camera operator on such films as *The Four Feathers* and *The Thief of Bagdad*. In the Forties there was no better cinematographer working in Britain, and Krasker's credits for this period are outstanding. He could range from the black-and-white chiaroscuro intimacy of *The Gentle Sex* and *Brief Encounter* to the Shakespearian pageantry of *Henry V*, shot in truly glorious Technicolor. It was Krasker, too, who created the remarkable effects of hallucination and nightmare – chiaroscuro lighting, vertiginous camera angles, looming close-ups – used by Carol Reed on his two postwar masterpieces, *The Third Man* (winning him the Oscar for Best Black-and-White Cinematography) and *Odd Man Out*. Then came *Senso* for Visconti in Italy and Anthony Mann's

colour epics, *El Cid* – memorable for Krasker's long-shot of the dead hero carried away by his horse at the end – and *The Fall of the Roman Empire*.

Films include: 1939 The Four Feathers (cam. op). **'40** The Thief of Bagdad (cam. op). **'43** The Gentle Sex. **'44** Henry V. **'45** Brief Encounter; Caesar and Cleopatra (co-photo). **'47** Odd Man Out. **'49** The Third Man. **'54** Senso (IT) (GB: The Wanton Countess). **'58** The Quiet American (USA). **'60** The Criminal (USA: The Concrete Jungle). **'61** El Cid (USA-IT). **'64** The Fall of the Roman Empire. **'80** Cry Wolf (short).

KRASNER, Milton

(b. 1901). Cinematographer. Born: Philadelphia, Pennsylvania, USA

Working for Fritz Lang, Milton Krasner made stealthy and feline the appearances of Joan Bennett as the slinky seductress in two great Forties thrillers, *The Woman in the Window* and *Scarlet Street* (1945); he also shot shadows and rain in these pictures like they were menacing entities in their own right. Later Krasner was on hand to bathe in colour, artificial light and sunshine the friendlier charms of Marilyn Monroe in *The Seven Year Itch* and *Bus Stop* (1956). Those two 20th Century-Fox films were beautifully shot in CinemaScope and De Luxe, and it was in widescreen, colour cinematography that Krasner excelled and won himself an Oscar (for *Three Coins in the Fountain*). All of which was a far cry from his beginnings as an assistant cameraman and camera operator at the Vitagraph and Biograph studios in New York in 1918, work which led to his becoming a director of photography at MGM, Universal and RKO in the Thirties.

Films include: 1933 I Love That Man. **'35** Murder in the Fleet. **'38** The Storm. **'42** Arabian Nights. **'44** The Woman in the Window. **'52** Monkey Business. **'54** Three Coins in the Fountain. **'55** The Seven Year Itch. **'59** Home From the Hill. **'62** How the West Was Won (co-photo). **'64** Goodbye Charlie. **'67** The Ballad of Josie. **'70** Beneath the Planet of the Apes.

KRAUSS, Werner

(1884–1959). Actor. Born: Gestunghausen, nr. Coburg, Germany

By World War I Werner Krauss was an experienced stage actor, having made his first appearance at the age of 20 at the Municipal Theatre at Guben. He entered films in 1914 with the assistance of Richard Oswald who directed him in several films. Krauss gradually became one of the leading interpreters of Expressionist films in Germany – as in *The Cabinet of Dr Caligari*, in which he was the crazed old proprietor of a somnambulist in a fairground sideshow. He later became involved with the Nazis and played the title role in *Jud Süss*, a film of Nazi racial propaganda. For his contributions to such productions, Werner Krauss was officially appointed Actor of the State and became vice-president of the Reich Theatre Chamber. After the war Krauss obtained Austrian nationality.

Films include: 1919 Das Kabinett des Dr Caligari (GB: The Cabinet of Dr Caligari). **'20** Die Brüder Karamasoff. **'21** Lady Hamilton. **'24** Das Wachsfigurenkabinett (GB: Waxworks). **'25** Die Freudlose Gasse (USA: Streets of Sorrow; GB: The Joyless Street). **'26** Geheimnisse einer Seele (USA: Secrets of the Soul; GB: Secrets of a Soul); Der Student von Prag (GB: The Student of Prague). **'32** Mensch ohne Namen. **'40** Jud Süss. **'50** Pramien auf den Tod. **'55** Sohn ohne Heimat.

KRISTEL, Sylvia

(b. 1952). Actress. Born: Utrecht, Holland

Long-legged, elegant, lithe and sensual, Sylvia Kristel and the series of *Emmanuelle* movies in which she performs have provided the acceptable face of pornography – a voyeur's paradise of soft-focus soft-porn. Kristel was convent-educated, and it was perhaps the repression she suffered, along with her model's face, that caused her to go in search of fame. She worked as a model and subsequently won the Miss TV Europe contest,

Above left: Sylvia Kristel quietly reflects in Emmanuelle. *Above: Hardy Kruger in* La Tenda Rossa. *Above right: Kris Kristofferson. Right: gentlemanly Otto Kruger on the side of justice in* I Am the Law *(1939). Below: Werner Krauss plays an officer in* Yorck *(1931). Below right: Stanley Kubrick passing a critical eye over* A Clockwork Orange

which led to her first screen role and an affair with the scriptwriter Hugo Claus, by whom she had a son. A few films later she was spotted by the director Just Jaeckin who cast her in the *Emmanuelle* films. She became dissatisfied with her sex-symbol image and has tried to escape from being cast as a nymphomaniac. Her first serious attempt to break out of this mould was not successful – hardly surprising, as it was in the film adaptation of D.H. Lawrence's sexually explicit novel *Lady Chatterley's Lover*.

Films include: 1974 Emmanuelle (FR); Un Linceul n'a pas des Poches (FR); Es War Nicht die Nachtigall (GER) (USA/GB: Julia). **'75** Le Jeu Avec le Feu (FR-IT). **'76** La Marge (FR). **'77** Goodbye Emmanuelle (FR). **'79** The Fifth Musketeer (A-GB); Airport '79 – Concorde (USA) (GB: Airport '80 – Con-

corde). '81 Private Lessons (USA); Lady Chatterley's Lover (GB-FR).

KRISTOFFERSON, Kris

(b. 1936). Singer/actor. Born: Brownsville, Texas, USA

The son of an army general, Kris Kristofferson was a Rhodes Scholar at Oxford, an officer in the army and a teacher of English before he became an award-winning singer and composer at the age of 29. He had his first encounter with the film world when the actor-director Dennis Hopper invited him to write the music for his film *The Last Movie* (1971), and he subsequently played a dope dealer in *Cisco Pike*, for which he had also written the music. A tall, often bearded Texan with a warm smile and an old-fashioned blend of sexuality and niceness, Kristofferson is like an urbanized Huckleberry Finn. He became recognized as an actor after appearing in such films as *A Star Is Born* and *Convoy*, and then briefly gave up acting to return to music. He has since come back to the screen in *Heaven's Gate* amidst great dramas about its epic length and phenomenal cost. He has been married to the singer Rita Coolidge.

Films include: 1971 Cisco Pike. '73 Blume in Love; Pat Garrett and Billy the Kid. '74 Bring Me the Head of Alfredo Garcia (USA-MEX); Alice Doesn't Live Here Anymore. '76 A Star Is Born; The Sailor Who Fell From Grace With the Sea (GB); Vigilante Force. '77 Semi-Tough. '78 Convoy. '80 Heaven's Gate. '81 Rollover.

KRUGER, Hardy

(b. 1928). Actor. Born: Eberhard Krüger; Berlin, Germany

A member of the Hitler Youth at 16, Krüger was taken prisoner by the Americans in 1945. On his release he worked with the Hamburg State Theatre, a touring company and also on the radio. His screen performance in *Liane* was the turning point and he became a popular international leading man. He was invited to Britain by Rank to make *The One That Got Away*, in which he played a German who escapes from a British POW camp with unexpected results. Because of the varied roles he has had, Hardy Kruger has managed to avoid being stereotyped as a blond, bland and unemotional Aryan.

Films include: 1956 Liane, das Mädchen aus dem Urwald (USA/GB: Liane – Jungle Goddess). '57 The One That Got Away (GB). '61 Un Taxi pour Tobruk (FR-GER-SP) (USA: A Taxi for Tobruk; GB: A Taxi to Tobruk). '62 Hatari! (USA). '66 The Flight of the Phoenix (USA). '69 The Secret of Santa Vittoria (USA). '70 Krasnaya Palatka/La Tenda Rossa (USSR-IT) (USA/GB: The Red Tent). '75 Barry Lyndon (USA-GB). '77 A Chacun son Enfer (FR-GER); A Bridge too Far (USA).

KRUGER, Otto

(1885–1974). Actor. Born: Toledo, Ohio, USA

Otto Kruger has often been referred to as one of the most gentlemanly actors in film. His polished acting style and suave bearing meant that he was perfect for roles that called for the elegant touch, on the right and wrong side of the law – he played the judge who hastily tries to leave town when trouble looms in *High Noon*. Of Dutch extraction, Kruger originally trained to be a musician but then turned to acting. While starring on Broadway he made some silent films and in 1932 he started in talkies under contract to MGM. A durable character actor, he continued to work until he was forced to retire from films when, as the result of a stroke, he was no longer able to remember his lines.

Films include: 1933 Turn Back the Clock. '34 Treasure Island; Men in White. '36 Dracula's Daughter. '44 Murder, My Sweet (GB: Farewell My Lovely). '46 Duel in the Sun. '52 High Noon. '54 Magnificent Obsession. '59 Cash McCall. '62 The Wonderful World of the Brothers Grimm. '64 Sex and the Single Girl.

KUBRICK, Stanley

(b. 1928). Director. Born: Bronx, New York City, USA

Encouraged by his father to take up photography, Stanley Kubrick quickly became a full-time employee of *Look* magazine. Not content with this, he soon set out to make his first film, *Day of the Flight* (1950), a documentary which he sold to RKO-Pathé for $4,000. His next two films were features – low-budget tense thrillers financed by borrowed money – on which Kubrick insisted on having creative autonomy. His films have been condemned for being tedious, pretentious and flaccid but it cannot be denied that they are stylish pieces of cinema – directed with deeply personal fervour. Kubrick has an extraordinary degree of pessimism and distrust for institutionalized society and his movies are imbued with a sharp cynicism. *2001: A Space Odyssey*, is preoccupied with themes of transcendence and mortality – mankind chillingly overshadowed by technology. To some a slow and deliberate study, to others a psychedelic trip, *2001*, with its serene and beautiful images, is an undeniable landmark in film technique. In *A Clockwork Orange*, Kubrick presents a terrifying view of a society debased by a violence that some thought to be excessive – but Kubrick's disdain is tinged with a sardonic humour that is magnetic – his imagery lingers in the mind. After the beautiful, elaborate and soulless period picture, *Barry Lyndon*, he made *The Shining*, considered by many to be too mysterious and personal a film for the horror genre. His best work may be *Lolita*, drawing on excellent performances in its rendering of Nabokov's novel, or the Armageddon black-comedy *Dr Strangelove*, or it may be yet to come.

Films include: 1953 Fear and Desire. '55 Killer's Kiss. '56 The Killing. '57 Paths of Glory. '60 Spartacus. '62 Lolita. '64 Dr Strangelove, or How I Learned to Stop Worrying and Love the Bomb. '68 2001: A Space Odyssey. '71 A Clockwork Orange. '75 Barry Lyndon. '80 The Shining.

KULESHOV, Lev

(1899–1970). Director/film theorist. Born: Lev Vladimirovitch Kuleshov; Tambov, Russia

Kuleshov was the first aesthetic theorist of the Soviet cinema. He directed his first film at the age of 18 – *Engineer Prite's Project*, a detective melodrama. From 1918–19 he was at various fronts of the Civil War – shooting newsreel footage of the Red Army – and began experimenting with editing techniques. In 1920 he set up a collective workshop of cinema artists and producers, including Pudovkin, Komanov and Alexandra Khokhlova, whom he married. They put their montage theories into practice in *On the Red Front*, employing the narrative cutting techniques of D.W. Griffith. At

the same time Kuleshov was teaching and was a member of the executive board of the State Institute of Cinematography. After the Civil War, with no film stock available, the workshop set up live stage performances played in a cinematic style – 'films without film' such as *The Extraordinary Adventures of Mr West in the Land of the Bolsheviks*. Kuleshov's writings on film theory were his major contributions to cinema. He remained a near unknown until the early Seventies when there were retrospectives of his work.

Films include: 1918 Proekt Inzhenera Praita (Engineer Prite's Project). '20 Na Krasnom Fronte (On the Red Front). '24 Noebychainiye Prikliucenia Mistera Vesta v Stranye Bolshevikov (The Extraordinary Adventures of Mr West in the Land of the Bolsheviks). '25 Luch Smerti (The Death Ray). '26 Po Zakonu (By the Law). '27 Vashna Znakomaya (Your Acquaintance). '29 Vesely Kanareika (The Happy Canary). '33 Velikii Uteshitel (The Great Consoler); Gorizont (Horizon). '40 Sibiriaki (The Siberians). '43 Kliatva Timura (Timur's Death).

KUROSAWA, Akira

(b. 1910). Director. Born: Tokyo, Japan

In 1951 Kurosawa startled and delighted Western audiences with *Rashomon*, a story of rape and murder told from differing points of view. It won the Golden Lion Award at the Venice Film Festival and put Japanese cinema firmly on the world map. Kurosawa had started out at Toho studios as an assistant to the director Yamamoto, making his directorial debut with *Judo Saga* in 1943. He began his long association with the actor Toshiro Mifune five years later with *Drunken Angel*. Mifune has since starred in many of Kurosawa's famous samurai films such as *Seven Samurai, The Hidden Fortress* (his first CinemaScope picture), *Sanjuro* and *Yojimbo*. These are masterful and influential films, touched with humour, which, though set in the sixteenth century, are full of modern relevance. Kurosawa is a true *auteur*, basing most of his films on his own original ideas, although he has also made highly effective adaptations of Western works such as Shakespeare's *Macbeth* (retitled *Throne of Blood*) and Dostoyevsky's *The Idiot* and *The Lower Depths*. He has also experimented continuously with sound and camera techniques throughout his distinguished career. Severe bouts of depression led to a suicide attempt in 1971, but Kurosawa has since rallied to make *Dersu Uzala*, concerning the relationship between a Russian explorer and his guide, and *Kagemusha*, a splendid return to the samurai film of which he is the master.

Films include: 1943 Sugata Sanshiro (USA/GB: Judo Saga). '45 Tora-no-o/Tora no o o Fumu Otokotachi (USA: The Men Who Tread on the Tiger's Tail; GB: They Who Tread on the Tiger's Tail). '48 Yoidore Tenshi (USA/GB: Drunken Angel). '50 Rashomon. '51 Hakuchi (USA/GB: The Idiot). '52 Ikiru (USA/GB: Living). '54 Shichinin no Samurai (USA/GB: Seven Samurai). '57 Kumonosu-Jo (USA/GB: Throne of Blood); Donzoko (USA/GB: The Lower Depths). '61 Yojimbo; Tsubaki Sanjuro (USA/GB: San-

juro). '65 Akahige (USA/GB: Red Beard). '70 Dodesukaden (USA: Dodeskaden). '75 Dersu Uzala (USSR-JAP). '80 Kagemusha.

KWAN, Nancy

(b. 1939). Actress. Born: Nancy Ka Shen Kwan; Hong Kong

In *The World of Suzie Wong*, her first and only famous film, she played a 'nice' Hong Kong prostitute modelling for an artist (William Holden) who falls in love with her. It made her a star, but only briefly, and it is a shame that this charming, petite Oriental actress has not appeared to greater effect in her films since. The daughter of a Chinese architect and his English wife, she was raised in luxury in England. She studied with the Royal Ballet in London and returned to Hong Kong hoping to open a ballet school. But Hollywood took her and coached her, and she won the part of Suzie Wong after touring as the stage-play understudy. Her Eurasian beauty and impish sense of humour could not sustain her stardom, though she took on varied roles. Still acting, she has extended her career into production with the Nancy Kwan Film Company.

Films include: 1960 The World of Suzie Wong (GB). '61 Flower Drum Song. '62 The Main Attraction (GB). '63 Tamahine. '64 Honeymoon Hotel; Fate Is the Hunter. '65 The Wild Affair. '66 Lt Robinson Crusoe USN. '68 The Wrecking Crew. '70 The McMasters (GB: The McMasters . . . Tougher Than the West Itself!).

KYO, Machiko

(b. 1924). Actress. Born: Osaka, Japan

When Japanese cinema first found popular favour in the West in the early Fifties, the grace and beauty of Machiko Kyo must have been a persuasive factor. She was the lovely actress at the centre of Kurosawa's *Rashomon* – a gentle lady who witnesses the death of her husband – and Mizoguchi's *Ugetsu Monogatari*, as the phantom princess who seduces a poor potter. Versatile, she soon afterwards played, very wittily, a modern prostitute in *The Street of Shame* and, more gravely, a costume-drama concubine in *The Empress Yang Kwei Fei*. Initially Kyo was a dancer at the Shochiku Girls' Opera and later at the Tokyo Nippon Gekijo, where she was discovered for films by the Daiei studio. Early roles displayed only her dancing ability, her break came in *Rashomon* and *Clothes of Deception*. In 1955 she appeared (in English) in *The Teahouse of the August Moon*. By 1964 Kyo had appeared in about eighty films and all of Daiei's bar two.

Films include: 1949 Saigo ni Warrau Otoko (Final Laughter). '50 Rashomon. '51 Itsu Wareru Seiso (Clothes of Deception). '53 Ugetsu Monogatari (USA: Tales After the Rain). '54 Jigokumon (GB: Gate of Hell). '55 Yokihi (JAP-HONG KONG) (GB: The Empress Yang Kwei-Fei). '56 The Teahouse of the August Moon (USA); Akasen Chitai (GB: The Street of Shame). '57 Ana (Hole). '58 Yoru Nosugao (Ladder of Success). '59 Ukigusa (Floating Weeds). '60 Bonchi (The Son). '64 Amai Ase (Sweet Shirt).

Above: the director Akira Kurosawa, on set during the filming of Kagemusha. *Right:* The World of Suzie Wong *lured Nancy Kwan away from her intended career in ballet. Below: Machiko Kyo as the princess who sets out to seduce a pauper in* Ugetsu Monogatari

LA CAVA, Gregory

(1892–1952). Director. Born: Towanda, Pennsylvania, USA

La Cava turned to commercial art after failing as a painter. Working as a cartoonist for newspapers and magazines finally led him into film animation. In the early Twenties he graduated to directing two-reelers and then, in 1922 with *His Nibs*, ventured into feature films. Recognition for La Cava as a director with a firm yet innovative touch came with the arrival of sound. He specialized in directing sophisticated comedies with a style that fused cynicism and improvisation, wit and social comment. He was known for his capacity for transforming poor scripts with his instinct for comedy and ability to draw performances from actors that even they did not know they were capable of. An excellent example of this is *Bed of Roses*, where La Cava turns a trite tale into a scathing comedy of manners.

Films include: 1924 Restless Wives; The New School Teacher. '25 Womanhandled. '26 Let's Get Married; So's Your Old Man; Say It Again. '31 Smart Woman. '32 The Half-Naked Truth. '33 Bed of Roses. '34 Affairs of Cellini. '35 She Married Her Boss; Private Worlds. '36 My Man Godfrey. '37 Stage Door. '40 The Primrose Path (+ prod). '41 Unfinished Business. '42 Lady in a Jam.

LADD, Alan

(1913–1964). Actor. Born: Alan Walbridge Ladd; Hot Springs, Arkansas, USA

Emerging from the shadows at the end of *Citizen Kane*, in which he had a bit part as a reporter, Alan Ladd became a cold killer in *This Gun for Hire* and *The Glass Key*, two films which made him a big Paramount star of the Forties and brought him a regular screen girlfriend in Veronica Lake. He was a small, tough, impassive blond, she an icy, amoral blonde, and together they walked those mean streets with an unequalled coolness and class. Some dull action pictures and *The Great Gatsby* spoiled Ladd's record at the end of the Forties, but in 1953 he played his greatest role as *Shane*, the gentle but lethal gunfighter and the most mythical of Western screen heroes. Ladd's last notable part, following a final decline at Warners and Universal, was as the Hollywood cowboy in *The Carpetbaggers*, but he was already on the skids and died soon after from alcohol and medicine poisoning. He had begun in *The Mikado* at school, trained with Universal and combined acting and journalism during the Depression. His agent-wife Sue Carol promoted his career during the late Thirties and won him his first major parts.

Films include: 1939 Rulers of the Sea; The Green Hornet. '40 Citizen Kane. '42 This Gun for Hire; The Glass Key. '43 China. '44 And Now Tomorrow. '46 Two Years Before the Mast; Calcutta; The Blue Dahlia. '47 Wild Harvest. '48 Whispering Smith; Beyond Glory. '49 The Great Gatsby. '53 Shane. '57 The Big Land. '58 The Proud Rebel. '64 The Carpetbaggers.

LAEMMLE, Carl

(1867–1939). Distributor/production executive. Born: Laupheim, Germany

Raised in a large, bourgeois Jewish family, Laemmle emigrated to New York in 1884. Having achieved minor success as manager of a clothing store in Oshkosh, Wisconsin, after marrying the niece of the owner, he decided to invest in nickelodeons in Chicago. Success led to expansion and to the setting up of the Laemmle Film Service in 1907. Laemmle soon became one of the leading distributors in the business and found himself compelled to defy the monopoly of Edison's Motion Picture Patents Company. Through a mixture of aggressive propaganda against the latter and clever publicity for himself, Laemmle won through. He created the Independent Motion Picture Company of America (IMP) and began for the first time to publicize his stars by their names. In 1912 IMP merged with other smaller companies to form the Universal Film Manufacturing Company, which built a large studio complex, Universal City, opened in 1915. In his later years Laemmle handed over the running of Universal to his son Carl Laemmle Jr (1908–1979) but in 1935, as a result of poor profits, Laemmle Sr was forced to sell Universal for just over $5 million.

Films include: 1909 Hiawatha. '13 Traffic in Souls. '19 Blind Husbands. '22 Foolish Wives. '23 The Hunchback of Notre Dame; White Tiger. '25 The Phantom of the Opera; The Goose Woman. '27 The Cat and the Canary; The Man Who Laughs.

LAFONT, Bernadette

(b. 1938). Actress. Born: Nîmes, France

A product of the French *nouvelle vague*, Lafont trained as a dancer and joined a ballet company. When she was 17, François Truffaut cast her in *Les Mistons* (1957) as the sensual cyclist whom a gang of pre-pubescent mischievous boys – 'mistons' of the title – lust after in the last summer of their innocence, the first summer of their sexual awakening. She then went on to work for a number of France's key directors of the time, including Claude Chabrol, Jacques Rivette and Jean Eustache. She has also appeared in feminist director Nelly Kaplan's first feature, *La Fiancée du Pirate*.

Films include: 1958 Le Beau Serge (GB: Handsome Serge). '59 A Double Tour (FR-IT) (USA: Leda; GB: Web of Passion). '60 L'Eau à la Bouche (USA/GB: Game of Love); Les Bonnes Femmes (FR-IT). '67 Le Voleur (FR-IT) (USA: The Thief of Paris; GB: The Thief). '69 La Fiancée du Pirate (USA: A Very Curious Girl; GB: Dirty Mary). '70 Les Stances à Sophie. '72 Une Belle Fille Comme Moi (USA: Such a Gorgeous Kid Like Me; GB: A Gorgeous Bird Like Me). '73 La Maman et la Putain (GB: The Mother and the Whore). '78 Violette Nozière (FR-CAN).

Far left: Alan Ladd as a salesman who becomes entangled in guerrilla warfare in China. Left: no false modesty for Bernadette Lafont in Une Belle Fille Comme Moi, *here with director François Truffaut*

Left: the ice-cool beauty of Veronica Lake. Above: Barbara La Marr in The White Monkey. Right: Hedy Lamarr in Cecil B. DeMille's Samson and Delilah. Below: handsome Fernando Lamas in Sangaree

LAKE, Veronica

(1919–1973). Actress. Born: Constance Frances Marie Ockelman; Brooklyn, New York City, USA

Having enrolled at the Bliss Hayden School of Acting, Veronica Lake did tests for MGM but was rejected. Luckily she was spotted by Arthur Hornblow Jr of Paramount who changed her name and encouraged her famous blonde 'peek-a-boo' hairstyle. Lake's film debut was made in 1938 in *Sorority House* but her meteoric success took off in 1941 when she starred with Alan Ladd in night-life thrillers, often cast as a shady lady. However, with her glamorous and distinctive looks she was able to adapt to a variety of parts. A notable role was as the reincarnated witch haunting Fredric March in the delightful comedy *I Married a Witch*. At the height of her career she was sought after by such wealthy and powerful men as Aristotle Onassis and Howard Hughes; she was married five times. Veronica Lake's decline was sudden and sad. Having disappeared from view in the Fifties she was discovered as a barmaid in a New York hotel. She died of acute hepatitis.

Films include: 1938 Sorority House. '41 This Gun for Hire; I Wanted Wings; Sullivan's Travels. '42 The Glass Key; I Married a Witch; This Gun for Hire. '43 Star Spangled Rhythm. '46 The Blue Dahlia. '47 Ramrod. '48 The Sainted Sisters.

LA MARR, Barbara

(1896–1926). Actress. Born: Reatha Watson; North Yakima, Washington, USA

Never commonly accepted as a 'great' actress, Barbara La Marr nonetheless had a dominating screen charisma. Coupled with her extraordinary beauty this led to star status and strong adulation from the fans. Life had not been easy and it took some time for Hollywood to accept her. She had several brief, unhappy marriages,

became a professional dancer and then turned to writing screenplays. Public recognition came after her performance in *Cinderella of the Hills* and her best film was *The Prisoner of Zenda*. But she is best known as a heady vamp – a very wicked mixture of sex and cruelty – in the mid-Twenties. Her unsettled career and stormy private life – six marriages in all – were brought to an end by a drug overdose (she had long been addicted) at the age of 29.

Films include: 1920 Harriet and the Piper. '21 The Three Musketeers; Cinderella of the Hills. '22 The Prisoner of Zenda; Trifling Women. '23 Poor Men's Wives; Souls for Sale; The Eternal City. '24 The Shooting of Dan McGrew; The White Moth. '25 The White Monkey. '26 The Girl From Montmartre.

LAMARR, Hedy

(b. 1916). Actress. Born: Hedwig Eva Maria Kiesler; Vienna, Austria

Hedy Lamarr was one of the most beautiful of screen actresses. The darkest of brunettes, she had a flawless, magical face, startling grey eyes – deep and mysterious – and an air of mocking sexuality best exemplified in *Samson and Delilah*. Her father was a

director of the bank of Vienna. At the age of 15 she applied for a job at Sascha Studios in Vienna and as a result received a small role playing a secretary in *Die Blumenfrau von Lindenau*. She later moved to Berlin and the Austro-German film world, and trained with the director Max Reinhardt. Then in 1933 she appeared in the film *Extase*, as a water nymphet in a nude scene – a role that seems to have haunted her throughout her career. After this she abandoned films for a time before moving to Hollywood where she had a screen test with Louis B. Mayer. He changed her name to Lamarr (after silent vamp Barbara La Marr) and loaned her to Walter Wanger for *Algiers*. The film was sensationally received and the result was an enormous publicity build-up for Lamarr by MGM. Unfortunately, however, despite sporadic excellent films, her career never really reached the heights it deserved. By the Fifties she was barely working, though a scandalous biography (she later sued her ghost-writers) kept her in the public eye. The third of her six husbands was the actor John Loder.

Films include: 1931 Die Blumenfrau von Lindenau (A–GER). '33 Extase (CZECH). '38 Algiers. '40 I Take This Woman; Boom Town; Comrade X. '41 Ziegfeld Girl. '42

Tortilla Flat; White Cargo. '47 Dishonored Lady. '49 Samson and Delilah. '50 A Lady Without Passport. '57 The Story of Mankind. '58 The Female Animal.

LAMAS, Fernando

(1915–1982). Actor. Born: Fernando Alvaro Lamas; Buenos Aires, Argentina

While at school in Buenos Aires, Lamas divided his time between drama and sport, and later abandoned his law course at college. He appeared on the stage from the age of 19 and after winning the 1937 South American Freestyle Swimming Championship he was offered work on radio as a result of all his publicity. His screen debut came in 1939, and ten years later an MGM contract enticed him to Hollywood where he appeared in some large-budget movies as a Latin lover. However, audiences were beginning to lose interest in his image by the late Fifties, and he turned to Broadway and television. His widow is the aquatic actress Esther Williams.

Films include: 1942 En el Ultimo Piso. '48 Historia de una Mala Mujer. '51 Rich Young and Pretty. '52 The Merry Widow. '53 Sangaree; Dangerous When Wet; Diamond Queen. '54 Rose Marie. '60 The Lost World. '69 100 Rifles.

Above: Burt Lancaster as a veteran Indian fighter in Ulzana's Raid (1972). Right: Elsa Lanchester in The Bride of Frankenstein. Below: Elissa Landi. Left: Dorothy Lamour on the Road to Bali (1953)

LAMORISSE, Albert

(1922–1970). Director. Born: Paris, France

Having attended film school in Paris and become a photographer, Albert Lamorisse then turned his talents in the direction of documentary film-making. His work was innovative and award-winning, from his first short *Djerba*, made in Tunisia, to his Academy Award winning *Le Ballon Rouge*, a surrealist fairy tale of a lonely boy who rescues a magic balloon which then follows him everywhere. He was particularly keen on the use of aerial photography and was making his last film, *Le Vent des Amoureux*, from a helicopter when he was tragically killed in a crash. A mystical aerial tour of Iran, it was later completed and subsequently received an Academy Award nomination in 1978.

Films include: 1947 Djerba (short). **'51** Bim, le Petit Âne. **'53** Crin-Blanc, Cheval Sauvage (USA: White Mane; GB: Wild Stallion). **'56** Le Ballon Rouge (GB: The Red Balloon). **'60** Le Voyage en Ballon (USA/GB: Stowaway in the Sky). **'65** Fifi la Plume. **'67** Versailles (doc). **'69** Paris Jamais Vu (doc) (GB: Paris Rediscovered). **'71** Le Vent des Amoureux.

LAMOUR, Dorothy

(b. 1914). Actress. Born: Mary Leta Dorothy Kaumeyer; New Orleans, Louisiana, USA

Dorothy Lamour's route to success was via beauty contests, work in a department store in Chicago, singing in a hotel band (she was discovered by the band-leader Herb Kay, who later became her first husband) and on radio shows. Then in 1935 she went to Hollywood where she first donned a sarong and dark body makeup opposite Ray Milland in *The Jungle Princess*. From that time onwards she was rarely to be seen in any other costume as she repeated this appearance in numerous similar roles. She even auctioned two of her sarongs for war bonds and recovered about $2 million for them. Her best known performances are opposite Bing Crosby and Bob Hope in the Road films, playing the perfect, clever foil to their zany humour. Although rarely allowed to stray from her South-Sea beauty image, she had no driving ambition to forsake the role that had put her on the path to such success. She retired in 1953, but was nostalgically reunited in the Sixties with Hope and Crosby for a last Road film, *Road to Hong Kong*, where she lost out in the glamour stakes to the younger Joan Collins.

Films include: 1936 The Jungle Princess. **'37** The Hurricane. **'38** Spawn of the North. **'40** Road to Singapore; Chad Hanna. **'41** Road to Zanzibar. **'42** Road to Morocco. **'44** Rainbow Island. **'45** A Medal for Benny. **'51** The Greatest Show on Earth. **'62** Road to Hong Kong (GB). **'63** Donovan's Reef.

LANCASTER, Burt

(b. 1913). Actor. Born: Burton Stephen Lancaster; New York City, USA

In his early films Burt Lancaster often played haunted, troubled characters – his career began in the brooding films of director Robert Siodmak. He then turned to lighter subjects, becoming a smiling, gallant, swashbuckling hero before again reverting to the more thoughtful topics of films like *Come Back, Little Sheba* and *Birdman of Alcatraz*. In his younger days Lancaster was a gymnast and an acrobat, touring with his diminutive friend Nick Cravat (who later appeared in his more energetic movies), as Lang and Cravat, but his career as a circus performer ended with a hand injury. After the war he found work on Broadway as an army sergeant in *A Sound of Hunting*. At this point he was spotted by the movie industry and made his film debut in *The Killers*. Lancaster soon proved himself a shrewd operator and before long he had started his own production company, Hecht-Hill-Lancaster, with his agent Harold Hecht and the producer James Hill. They went on to produce such memorable movies as *Apache*, *Trapeze* and *Sweet Smell of Success*. Lancaster received the Best Actor Academy Award for his role as the preacher in *Elmer Gantry*, and was voted Best Actor by the British Academy of Film and Television Arts for his superb performance in Louis Malle's *Atlantic City*, proving that, though well into his sixties, he was still a compelling actor.

Films include: 1946 The Killers. **'52** The Crimson Pirate (+co-prod. co) (GB); Come Back Little Sheba. **'53** From Here to Eternity. **'54** Apache (+co-prod. co). **'55** The Rose Tattoo. **'56** Trapeze (+co-prod. co). **'57** Gunfight at the OK Corral; Sweet Smell of Success (+co-prod. co). **'60** Elmer Gantry. **'62** Birdman of Alcatraz (+co-prod. co). **'63** Il Gattopardo (IT-FR)(USA/GB: The Leopard). **'68** The Swimmer. **'72** Ulzana's Raid. **'80** Atlantic City (FR-CAN-USA).

LANCHESTER, Elsa

(1902–1986). Actress. Born: Elizabeth Sullivan; Lewisham, London, England

Having studied with Isadora Duncan as a child, Elsa Lanchester entered the theatre at the age of 16. She became an actress and a singer in night clubs and music halls and was popular in the revue show *Riverside Nights* in London with such songs as 'I've Danced With the Man Who Danced With the Girl Who Danced With the Prince of Wales'. She began working on the stage with the actor Charles Laughton in 1927 and they were married two years later. Their first talking film together was *The Private Life of Henry VIII* in which she played Anne of Cleves. She continued her classical stage work, particularly at the Old Vic, while appearing in films. She made her Hollywood debut in *David Copperfield* and followed that successful film with possibly her most famous performance in *The Bride of Frankenstein*, in a dual role as Mary Shelley and the woman made for the monster. In 1938 she moved permanently to Hollywood with Laughton and in 1950 became an American citizen. She worked as a character actress in films and TV until her death in 1986.

Films include: 1927 One of the Best. **'28** The Constant Nymph. **'31** Potiphar's Wife. **'33** The Private Life of Henry VIII. **'35** David Copperfield (USA); The Bride of Frankenstein (USA); Naughty Marietta (USA); The Ghost Goes West. **'36** Rembrandt. **'38** Vessel of Wrath (USA: The Beachcomber). **'41** Ladies in Retirement (USA). **57** Witness for the Prosecution (USA). **'76** Murder by Death (USA).

LANDI, Elissa

(1904–1948). Actress. Born: Countess Elizabeth Marie Christine Kuehnelt; Venice, Italy

From a blue-blooded background – her grandmother was purportedly the Empress of Austria – Elissa Landi began her stage career in repertory at Oxford. Her film debut was made in 1926 in *London* and her performance as the lynx-eyed shop-girl in Anthony Asquith's *Underground* attracted much attention. Her Hollywood career did not prosper after Fox failed to provide her with suitable vehicles. Nevertheless, Elissa Landi was an actress of fine calibre, able to emote convincing 'goodness' in many films without falling into the trap of sentimental over-acting.

Films include: 1926 London (GB). **'28** Underground (GB); Bolibar (GB); Sin (GB-SWED). **'32** Passport to Hell (GB: Burnt Offering); The Sign of the Cross. **'34** Sisters Under the Skin. **'35** Enter Madame. **'36** Mad Holiday. **'43** Corregidor.

251

LANDIS, Carole

(1919–1948). Actress. Born: Francis Lillian Mary Ridste; Fairchild, Wisconsin, USA

At the age of 16 Carole Landis started her professional career as a dancer and singer in Californian night clubs. With her classic Hollywood glamour-girl looks, blonde hair and the 'best legs in town' she soon broke into films. However, she appeared in very few worthwhile ones although some of her leads in B movies are memorable. Her performance as the dancer wife of deposed police chief (Gene Lockhart) in Douglas Sirk's *A Scandal in Paris* showed how good she could be when working with talented directors. She contributed valuable war work entertaining the troops and selling war bonds.

Films include: 1940 One Million BC; Turnabout. '41 Road Show; I Wake Up Screaming/Hot Spot; Moon Over Miami. '44 Four Jills in a Jeep. '45 A Scandal in Paris/Thieves' Holiday. '46 It Shouldn't Happen to a Dog. '47 Out of the Blue. '48 Lucky Mascot.

LANDIS, John

(b. 1951). Director. Born: Chicago, Illinois, USA

At a surprisingly young age John Landis has made a successful and influential hit at the box office. His films are notable for their manic and insane humour which is saved from being self-indulgent by Landis' intelligent understanding of film genres and how they can be manipulated to good effect. Employed as a mail boy at 20th Century-Fox he graduated, through perseverance and enthusiasm, to production assistant on *Kelly's Heroes* (1970). Following a period as stuntman and bit part actor, Landis returned to Hollywood, wrote his monster movie spoof *Schlock!* and, with money raised from relatives, produced and directed his own script. With *National Lampoon's Animal House* to his credit and *An American Werewolf in London* receiving much critical acclaim, Landis' future looks promising.

Films include: 1973 Schlock! '77 Kentucky Fried Movie. '78 National Lampoon's Animal House. '79 1941 (actor only). '80 The Blues Brothers. '81 An American Werewolf in London.

LANE, Lupino

(1892–1959). Actor/director. Born: Harry Lupino; London, England

Lupino Lane came from a showbusiness background with roots in the circus and the theatre. His stage debut was made at the age of four; by 1913 he was making a name for himself in the West End and started to work in films. He made numerous British comedy shorts but gained widespread popularity when he went to Hollywood during the Twenties. He starred in a large number of two-reelers, now regarded as comedy classics. He returned to England in the Thirties and directed many films in

which he starred. He was the uncle of actress Ida Lupino.

Films include: 1918 His Busy Day. '25 The Fighting Dude. '27 Howdy Dude; Drama de Luxe; Monty of the Mounted. '29 The Love Parade. '30 Golden Dawn; The Yellow Mask. '31 Never Trouble Trouble (+dir); No Lady (+dir); The Love Race (dir. only). '32 Innocents of Chicago (dir. only). '33 Letting in the Sunshine (dir. only). '34 Oh What a Duchess! (dir. only). '35 Trust the Navy. '36 Hot News. '39 The Lambeth Walk.

LANE, Priscilla

(b. 1917). Actress. Born: Priscilla Mullican; Indianola, Iowa, USA

One of a family of four acting sisters – including Rosemary and Lola Lane – vibrant, blonde Priscilla Lane attended the Fagin School of Dramatic Arts in New York. At 14 she was given a contract with Fred Waring and The Pennsylvanians dance band. She proceeded to enjoy success as a singer and comedienne for five years. In 1937 she went to Hollywood, signed a contract with Warner Brothers and appeared in *Varsity Show* with the band. The sisters were made popular in a series of sentimental dramas beginning with *Four Daughters*. Priscilla Lane was able to marry comedy to character roles, as in *Arsenic and Old Lace* in which she played Cary Grant's wife. She made 23 films before retiring in 1948.

Films include: 1937 Varsity Show. '38 Four Daughters. '39 Cowboy From Brooklyn (GB: Romance and Rhythm); Daughters Courageous; Yes My Darling Daughter; The Roaring Twenties; Four Wives. '41 Four Mothers; Blues in the Night. '44 Arsenic and Old Lace. '47 Fun on a Weekend. '48 Body Guard.

LANG Jr., Charles B.

(b. 1902). Cinematographer. Born: Bluff, Utah, USA

Educated at the University of Southern California, Lang worked first in the Paramount Film Laboratory. After a period as camera assistant, he photographed his first films in the late Twenties, and was a director of photography for Paramount from 1929 to 1952. He rose to the top in the Thirties as a subtly creative cinematographer and a master of chiaroscuro, with an Academy Award for *A Farewell to Arms*. Lang photographed over one hundred and fifty films and was at home in every style, as adept with the sombre atmospherics of *Peter Ibbetson* as with the Parisian glitter of *Midnight*. Freelancing from 1952 into the Seventies, Lang proved equally skilful with colour, notably on *The Magnificent Seven* and other Westerns.

Films include: 1927 Ritzy. '30 Tom Sawyer. '32 A Farewell To Arms. '35 Lives of a Bengal Lancer; Peter Ibbetson. '39 Midnight. '47 The Ghost and Mrs Muir. '51 Ace in the Hole. '54 Sabrina. '58 Separate Tables. '59 Some Like it Hot. '60 The Magnificent Seven. '61 One Eyed Jacks. '62 How the West Was Won (co-photo). '63 Charade. '67 Wait Until Dark. '68 Stalking Moon. '69 Bob & Carol & Ted & Alice.

LANG, Fritz

(1890–1976). Director. Born: Vienna, Austria

After studying architecture and painting in Vienna, Lang left Austria in 1910, studied further in Munich and Paris, and travelled the world. By 1913 he was back in Paris, but returned to Austria with the outbreak of war, served in the Austrian army, and was wounded several times. While convalescing he began to write, and was hired by director Joe May. By 1918 he had joined Decla studios in Berlin as editor, and was soon promoted to director. In 1921 *Destiny* brought him fame, and a long series of successes followed. In 1933 the Nazis banned his film *M*, and simultaneously offered him control of the industry. Lang at once left for France, and after one film there went on to the USA. This second career lasted until 1956, and, although erratic, it contained works like *Fury*, *You Only Live Once* and *The Big Heat* which ranked at least as high as his German films. In his late sixties Lang returned to Germany to make three final films, and after retirement from direction appeared, virtually playing himself, as the film-director in Godard's *Le Mépris* (1963, *Contempt*). There is no doubt about Fritz Lang's great skill. His German films were notable for their perfectly controlled spectacle, the magnificent architecture of their sets, and the first statements of the themes which were to run through all his work. These were simple, pessimistic and frightening. Lang saw society as a conspiracy in which the individual was unable to avoid a pre-ordained fate. His cities were in the grip of a paranoia which no other film-maker sensed until the Seventies. His characters could meditate revenge, and sometimes briefly achieve it. But try as they might, they could never escape their fate.

Above: Carole Landis in Dance Hall *(1941). Below: Harry Langdon playing* The Strong Man. *Bottom right: Jessica Lange in* The Postman Always Rings Twice, *Bob Rafelson's version of James M. Cain's novel*

Films include: 1917 Die Hochzeit in Exzentric-Club (sc. only) '19 Halbblut; Die Spinnen (Part 1: Der goldene See) (USA/GB: The Spiders). '20 Die Spinnen (Part 2: Das brillianten Schiff) (USA/GB: The Spiders). '21 Der müde Tod (USA/GB: Destiny); Das indische Grabmal (Part 1: Die Sendung des Yoghis; Part 2: Das indische Grabmal) (USA: Mysteries of India). '22 Dr Mabuse der Spieler (Part 1: Dr Mabuse der Spieler; Part 2: Inferno-Menschen der Zeit. '24 Die Nibelungen/Die Nibelungen: Ein deutsches Heldenlied (Part 1: Siegfried; Part 2: Kriemhilds Rache) (USA: Part 1: Siegfried; Part 2: Kriemhild's Revenge). '27 Metropolis. '28 Spione (USA: Spies). '29 Frau im Mond (USA: By Rocket to the Moon; GB: The Girl in the Moon). '31 M. '32 Das Testament des Dr Mabuse (USA: The Last Will of Dr Mabuse; GB: The Testament of Dr Mabuse). '34 Liliom (FR). '36 Fury (USA). '37 You Only Live Once (USA). '40 The Return of Frank James (USA). '41 Western Union (USA); Man Hunt (USA). '43 Hangmen Also Die! (USA). '44 The Woman in the Window (USA). '45 Scarlet Street (USA). '52 Rancho Notorious (USA); Clash by Night (USA). '53 The Big Heat (USA). '55 Moonfleet (USA). '56 While the City Sleeps (USA); Beyond a Reasonable Doubt (USA). '61 Die tausend Augen des Dr Mabuse (GER–FR–IT) (USA/GB: The Thousand Eyes of Dr Mabuse). '63 Le Mépris (FR) (act. only) (USA: Contempt).

Top: Lupino Lane inherits a fortune in The Lambeth Walk. *Top centre: Priscilla Lane in* Brother Rat and a Baby *(1940). Top right: Fritz Lang. Above: Hope Lange in* In Love and War, *with Jeffrey Hunter. Above right: Frank Langella's 1979* Dracula *was no longer the evil-looking character as portrayed by Bela Lugosi and others*

LANGDON, Harry

(1884–1944). Actor. Born: Council Bluffs, Iowa, USA

For two short years Langdon was the fourth of the great silent comedians, ranking not far behind Chaplin, Keaton and Lloyd. He had spent years with medicine shows, circuses and vaudeville before joining Mack Sennett in 1923. In 1926 the Harry Langdon Corporation was formed, and Langdon took along from Sennett writer/directors Harry Edwards and Frank Capra and the gagman Arthur Ripley. This talented team steered Langdon through three superb comedies, *Tramp, Tramp, Tramp, The Strong Man* and *Long Pants*. But Langdon, as naive as his screen character, came to believe that he could manage alone, dismissed his team, and foundered dismally. His next features failed. In 1931 he was declared bankrupt. He went on, in shorts and lesser parts in features, until his death from a cerebral haemorrhage in 1944, but never looked like regaining his old glory. Langdon's style was unique. A tiny man, with sad, white moon-face, and clad in a child's jacket far too small for him, he played an innocent loose in a frightening world. In a way he was a grotesque version of Keaton, but Keaton's was a comedy of learning while Langdon's was of ignorance. His character had to wait for the world to pass him by. Sadly, it did that to the creator too.

Films include: 1924 Picking Peaches (short). **'26** The Strong Man (+prod); Tramp, Tramp, Tramp. **'27** Long Pants; Three's a Crowd (+dir); His First Flame. **'28** The Chaser (+dir); Heart Trouble (+dir). **'30** A Soldier's Plaything/A Soldier's Pay. **'33** Hallelujah, I'm a Bum/New York/The Heart of New York/Happy Go Lucky/The Optimist (GB: Hallelujah, I'm a Tramp). **'44** Block Busters; Hot Rhythm.

LANGE, Hope

(b. 1931). Actress. Born: Redding Ridge, Connecticut, USA

Belonging to a stage family (her mother an actress, her father a musical arranger for Florenz Ziegfeld), Hope Lange first appeared on Broadway, aged 12, in Sidney Kingsley's *The Patriots*. She studied drama and dance (with Martha Graham), worked in stock and on television, and was signed by 20th Century-Fox, making her film debut in *Bus Stop*. A pretty, gentle blonde, she made only a dozen or so films (and received an Oscar nomination for *Peyton Place*), but appeared more frequently on television. She returned to Broadway in 1977 in *Same Time Next Year*. Her first husband was actor Don Murray, her second was director Alan Pakula.

Films include: 1956 Bus Stop. **'57** The True Story of Jesse James; Peyton Place; The Best of Everything. **'58** Young Lions; In Love and War. **'61** Pocketful of Miracles; Wild in the Country. **'62** How the West Was Won. **'68** Jigsaw (GB: Jigsaw Murder). **'74** Death Wish

LANGE, Jessica

(b. 1950). Actress. Born: Wisconsin, USA

Jessica Lange was almost unknown when she was selected to play the feminine lead in the remake of *King Kong* and given a seven-year contract by Dino De Laurentiis. She had in fact worked in repertory and fringe theatre, modelled, and studied mime. But *King Kong* was received with derision, and Lange had to wait four years for another part, in spite of that contract. She then played the Angel of Death in Bob Fosse's *All That Jazz*, – a major movie but a minor role. She was luckier with *The Postman Always Rings Twice*, in which she was sleazily erotic as the murderous wife. Her few film roles have certainly shown her versatility. The frothy blonde she played in *How to Beat the High Cost of Living* hinted at a potential for stylish comedy.

Films include: 1976 King Kong. **'79** All That Jazz. **'80** How to Beat the High Cost of Living. **'81** The Postman Always Rings Twice. **'82** Frances.

LANGELLA, Frank

(b. 1940). Actor. Born: Bayonne, New Jersey, USA

An accomplished stage actor, Langella had reached Broadway in *The Immoralist* in 1963. He later won critical praise for his roles in *Old Glory* (1965) and *The White Devil* (1966). He shot to screen stardom in the film version of *Dracula*, which he had been playing on Broadway with great success. The part was made to measure for Langella's brooding, darkly romantic good looks.

Films include: 1970 Diary of a Mad Housewife; The Twelve Chairs. **'71** La Maison Sous les Arbres (IT-FR) (USA/GB: The Deadly Trap). **'79** Dracula. **'80** Those Lips, Those Eyes. **'81** Sphinx.

LANSBURY, Angela

(b. 1925). Actress. Born: London, England

Angela Lansbury's grandfather was George Lansbury, noted pacifist and leader of the Labour Party. Her father was Mayor of Poplar in London's East End, her mother the actress Moyna MacGill. Evacuated to the USA at the start of the war, Angela attended drama school in New York, made a brief youthful appearance in Montreal cabaret, went to Hollywood with her mother and was signed by MGM. It was the start of a dazzling career as a character actress on film and in the theatre. Her very first film, the Cukor version of *Gaslight*, won her an Oscar nomination for her performance as the sexy maid. Shortly after she was charmingly sincere as the lovestruck elder sister in *National Velvet*. Such versatility was to carry her happily through the next thirty odd years. The highlights, perhaps, were her hard-as-nails newspaper owner in *State of the Union* and, above all, her murderous Mrs Iselin in *The Manchurian Candidate*, as unrelenting a study in total evil as the cinema can offer. She found time, too, to triumph in stage musicals: *Mame* and *Sweeney Todd* in New York, *Gypsy* in London.

Films include: 1944 Gaslight (GB: Murder in Thornton Square); National Velvet. '45 The Picture of Dorian Gray. '46 Till the Clouds Roll By. '47 If Winter Comes. '48 State of the Union. '55 A Lawless Street. '56 The Court Jester. '58 The Long, Hot Summer. '60 The Dark at The Top of The Stairs. '61 Blue Hawaii. '62 The Manchurian Candidate. '63 In the Cool of the Day. '64 The World of Henry Orient. '65 Dear Heart; The Greatest Story Ever Told; The Amorous Adventures of Moll Flanders; Harlow. '70 Black Flowers for the Bride (GB: Something for Everyone). '71 Bedknobs and Broomsticks. '78 Death on the Nile (GB). '79 The Lady Vanishes (GB). '80 The Mirror Crack'd (GB). '81 The Pirates of Penzance.

LANTZ, Walter

(b. 1900). Animator/producer. Born: New Rochelle, New York, USA

At 15 Lantz went to work as a copy-boy for Hearst newspapers in New York. He took drawing classes, and when Hearst decided to animate some of the papers' cartoon characters, Lantz was given a job in the studio. Later he pioneered techniques of mixing animation with live action. In 1926 he joined Mack Sennett as animator and gagman; moving to Universal two years later, he took charge of the cartoon department. Universal then helped him to finance his own studio, releasing through Universal. Woody Woodpecker was the best known of Lantz's many cartoon characters, the voice being supplied by his wife, the actress Grace Stafford.

Films include: 1929 Weary Willies. '32 The Athlete. '34 Jolly Little Elves. '36 Turkey Dinner. '38 The Big Cat and the Little Mousie. '40 Andy Panda Goes Fishing. '41 Woody Woodpecker. '42 Juke Box Jamboree. '47 Musical Moments From Chopin. '57 Operation Cold Feet. '61 Rough and Tumbleweed. '62 Fowled-Up Birthday.

LANZA, Mario

(1921–1959). Actor/singer. Born: Alfred Arnold Cocozza; New York City, USA

Mario Lanza, a tenor who had reputedly one of the finest 'natural' voices of the century, became a professional singer at 20. After war service with the army air force he entered films with MGM in 1948, having impressed Louis B. Mayer by his singing at the Hollywood Bowl. Throughout his career Lanza had problems with his weight (he was a compulsive eater), temperament and discipline, and was eventually sued by MGM for missing work on *The Student Prince*. The film was released with Edmund Purdom acting, and Lanza dubbing the voice. After this, Lanza made one or two minor films, and died from a heart attack, in Rome, at the age of 38.

Films include: 1949 That Midnight Kiss. '50 Toast of New Orleans. '51 The Great Caruso. '52 Because You're Mine. '54 The Student Prince (voice only). '55 Serenade. '57 Seven Hills of Rome (USA-IT). '59 For the First Time.

LA PLANTE, Laura

(b. 1904). Actress. Born: St Louis, Missouri, USA

Laura La Plante began her film career in Christie comedies in 1919, and first made a real impression in First National's *The Old Swimmin' Hole* in 1921. Moving to Universal, this charming, vivacious blonde was one of the studio's leading stars throughout the Twenties, the period of her finest films. She was effective in romantic drama (*Smouldering Fires*), mystery thrillers (*The Cat and the Canary* and *The Last Warning*), and domestic comedy. In this genre her great triumph was *Skinner's Dress Suit*, directed by her first husband William A. Seiter. Leaving Universal, she went to England in the Thirties and made a few films for her second husband, producer Irving Asher. Since the war she has been in semi-retirement back in America.

Films include: 1921 His Four Fathers; The Old Swimmin' Hole. '23 The Thrill Chaser. '24 Sporting Youth; Excitement. '25 Smouldering Fires. '26 Skinner's Dress Suit. '27 The Cat and the Canary. '29 Showboat; The Last Warning. '34 The Girl in Possession (GB). '46 Little Mister Jim. '57 Spring Reunion.

LARDNER Jr, Ring

(b. 1915). Screenwriter. Born: Ringold Wilmer Lardner Jr; Chicago, Illinois, USA

The son of one of America's greatest humorists, Ring Lardner Jr was working for the *New York Mirror* as a story writer when David O. Selznick employed him to write movie scripts. Despite having worked on such films as *A Star Is Born* and *Nothing Sacred* (both 1937) he received scant credit for his work until *Woman of the Year* for which he shared with Michael Kanin a Best Original Screenplay Oscar. In 1950 he was sentenced to a

year in prison for contempt of the House Un-American Activities Committee. Throughout the McCarthy era he was blacklisted as one of the Hollywood Ten and was forced to write under pseudonyms. His name finally returned to the screen in 1965 with *The Cincinnati Kid*, and he also received new acclaim (and a second Academy Award) for *M*A*S*H*.

Films include: 1939 Meet Dr Christian (co-sc). '40 Courageous Dr Christian (co-sc). '42 Woman of the Year (co-sc). '43 Cross of Lorraine (co-sc). '44 Marriage Is a Private Affair (co-sc. uncredited). '46 Cloak and Dagger (co-sc). '47 Forever Amber (co-sc). '49 The Forbidden Street (GB: Britannia Mews). '58 Virgin Island (co-sc. as Phillip Rush) (GB). '65 The Cincinnati Kid (co-sc). '70 M*A*S*H.

LA ROCQUE, Rod

(1898–1969). Actor. Born: Chicago, Illinois, USA

La Rocque's seems to have been a charmed life. From a famous circus family, he sang falsetto as a boy and was a member of the Chicago Newsboys' Quartet; at 9 he was on stage in *Salomy Jane*. But the voice deepended and he quickly grew to well over six foot and 180 pounds, and was often cast as a heavy. The New York stage led to a film career on the East Coast from 1914 before he eventually signed for Paramount in Hollywood. Here he became a dashing matinée idol, working for such directors as his friend Cecil B. DeMille (*The Ten Commandments* and others) and Ernst Lubitsch (*Forbidden Paradise*). Perhaps his most important role was as the rough Australian sheep-farmer who is left a

Top left: the expansive Angela Lansbury in Death on the Nile. *Top: the star of* Gigolo *(1926) – Rod La Rocque. Above: Mario Lanza as* The Great Caruso. *Below: Charles Laughton as Captain Bligh who is finally cast adrift by his crew in* Mutiny on the Bounty. *Left: Laura La Plante in* Silk Stockings *(1927)*

fortune and becomes a sophisticated man of the world in *The Coming of Amos*. Sound posed no problems for La Rocque and he continued acting until 1941 when he went into real estate brokerage and made a fortune. He was happily married to screen star Vilma Banky from 1927 until his death. Their only professional appearance together was on stage in *The Cherries Are Ripe*.

Films include: 1923 The Ten Commandments. '24 Forbidden Paradise. '25 The Coming of Amos; Braveheart. '26 Gigolo. '27 The Fighting Eagle; Resurrection. '30 Let Us Be Gay. '39 The Hunchback of Notre Dame. '41 Meet John Doe.

LASKY, Jesse L.

(1880–1958). Producer. Born: San Francisco, California, USA

Having appeared in vaudeville as a cornet duo with his sister, Jesse Lasky also dabbled in gold prospecting and nightclub ownership before deciding to make films his career. In 1913 he and a friend, Cecil B. DeMille, joined up with Samuel Goldfish (then Lasky's brother-in-law, later to become Samuel Goldwyn) to form the Jesse L. Lasky Feature Play Company. Their first film was *The Squaw Man*, which was also the first feature film made in Hollywood. In 1916 the company merged with Adolph Zukor's Famous Players Company which later became Paramount. Zukor was the president and Lasky vice-president. The hallmark of Lasky's films was the embodiment of his own sense of optimism and a belief in man's basic nobility. He also loved making adventure movies with a dash of romance. However, even his ingenuity was stretched with the coming of the Depression and he lost a fortune on the Wall Street Crash. Leaving Paramount, he made *The Power and the Glory* for Fox and, after another unsettled period during which time he became severely embroiled in tax difficulties, Lasky joined Warners where he successfully stamped his mark on *Sergeant York*, *The Adventures of Mark Twain* and *Rhapsody in Blue*. He died in 1958 without

completing a project for Paramount that was designed to settle his debts with the tax authorities. In 1980 the Academy of Motion Picture Arts and Sciences organized a major tribute to mark the hundredth anniversary of his birth.

Films include: 1913 The Squaw Man. '23 The Covered Wagon; The Ten Commandments. '27 Wings; Chang; The Rough Riders (GB: The Trumpet Call). '33 The Power and the Glory. '41 Sergeant York. '45 Rhapsody in Blue. '51 The Great Caruso.

LASSALLY, Walter

(b. 1926). Cinematographer. Born: Berlin, Germany

Walter Lassally's family fled to England during World War II, where his father set himself up as a 'one man film unit' producing documentaries and shorts. Walter was naturally interested in the business and worked as a clapper-boy at the Riverside Studios until it closed. During the Fifties he allied himself with Britain's Free Cinema film-makers and worked as a cinematographer for directors such as Lindsay Anderson, Gavin Lambert, Tony Richardson and Karel Reisz. His discreet, trick-free style suited the ideology of the new breed of directors who wanted to make worthwhile films rather than empty confections. *A Taste of Honey* was the first all-location British film, and the free-wheeling, hand-held camera in *Tom Jones* was Lassally's innovation. He has also worked closely with Michael Cacoyannis, winning himself an Academy Award for *Zorba the Greek*, and he continues to experiment – for James Ivory's *Savages* Lassally utilized black and white, sepia toning and colour to great effect.

Films include: 1956 To Koritsi Me Ta Mavra (GREECE) (GB: A Girl in Black). '60 Beat Girl (GB). '61 A Taste of Honey (GB). '62 Electra (GREECE); The Loneliness of the Long Distance Runner (GB). '63 Tom Jones (GB). '64 Zorba the Greek (GREECE-USA). '68 Joanna (GB). '72 Savages (USA). '75 The Wild Party (USA).

LATTUADA, Alberto

(b. 1914). Director. Born: Milan, Italy

The son of renowned composer Felice Lattuada, Alberto qualified as an architect and then became involved in two anti-fascist publications – *Camminare* and *Corrente*. After helping to found the first Italian film library and publishing a book of photographs called *The Square Eye*, he worked as an assistant on Mario Soldati's film *Piccolo Mondo Antico* (1941) before making his own directorial debut with *Giacomo l'Idealista*. His films are visually very stylish, and he has a penchant for literary adaptations. His first major success was *Il Bandito*, a film about a soldier who heroically returns from war but becomes involved in a life of crime. It created a considerable stir in Italy on its release and established Lattuada as a neo-realist director. A consistent theme running through Lattuada's work is that of

rebellion against hypocrisy, but he always avoids preaching by mixing the message with skilful satire and comedy.

Films include: 1942 Giacomo l'Idealista. '46 Il Bandito. '48 Senza Pietà (GB: Without Pity). '49 Il Mulino del Po (GB: The Mill on the River). '50 Luci del Varietà (USA: Variety Lights; GB: Lights of Variety). '52 Anna; Il Cappotto (USA/GB: The Overcoat). '57 Guendalina (IT-FR). '60 I Dolci Inganni (IT-FR) (GB: Les Adolescentes). '65 La Mandragola (IT-FR) (USA/GB: The Mandrake). '73 Sono Stato Io!

LAUGHTON, Charles

(1899–1962). Actor. Born: Scarborough, Yorkshire, England

The son of hoteliers, Laughton was educated at Stonyhurst. He was gassed during World War I but recovered to go to RADA, and quickly developed as a successful stage actor. He entered films with *Piccadilly* in 1929, and in 1931 went to America with the play *Payment Deferred*. He was Nero in *The Sign of the Cross* in Hollywood a year later, but it was back in England that he became a major star, winning an Oscar for his outrageous Henry in *The Private Life of Henry VIII*, the film that put Alexander Korda's London Films on the map. Laughton remained a screen celebrity for the next thirty years and was, perhaps, the greatest of all the cinema's character actors. Certainly he was the only one to challenge the supremacy of sleeker, handsomer leading men. He himself was stout and ugly, a fact that hurt him and contributed to his career-long insecurity, but also to his flamboyant, frequently over-the-top, but sometimes magnificent performances, often as tyrants or ogres: as Captain Bligh in *Mutiny on the Bounty* (his second Oscar nomination), as Mr Barrett in *The Barretts of Wimpole Street*, as Quasimodo in *The Hunchback of Notre Dame*. Laughton was a committed artist who really belonged to the stage, the dramatic confines of movies being too restrictive for his bulging talent – except perhaps as the director of *The Night of the Hunter*, the strangest of fantasy dramas. Late in his career Laughton concentrated on literary readings but enjoyed two last great movie roles, as the counsel in *Witness for the Prosecution* (the third Oscar nomination) and as a Southern senator in *Advise and Consent*. Though homosexual, Laughton was married to actress Elsa Lanchester, who supported him in several films.

Films include: 1928 Daydreams (short). '29 Piccadilly. '32 The Old Dark House (USA); The Sign of the Cross (USA); If I Had a Million (USA). '33 Island of Lost Souls (USA); The Private Life of Henry VIII. '34 The Barretts of Wimpole Street (USA). '35 Les Miserables (USA); Mutiny on the Bounty (USA). '36 Rembrandt. '37 I, Claudius (unfinished). '39 Jamaica Inn; The Hunchback of Notre Dame (USA). '44 The Suspect (USA). '45 Captain Kidd (USA). '47 The Paradine Case (USA). '48 The Big Clock (USA). '54 Hobson's Choice. '55 The Night of the Hunter (dir. only) (USA). '57 Witness for the Prosecution (USA). '62 Advise and Consent (USA).

Above: Laurel and Hardy run into trouble while delivering the deeds to a gold mine in Way Out West. *Top centre: born for stardom; Piper Laurie. Above centre: a sultry and exotic Daliah Lavi in* Lord Jim

LAUNDER & GILLIAT

Launder, Frank (b. 1907). Director/screenwriter/producer. Born: Hitchin, Hertfordshire, England

Gilliat, Sidney (b. 1908). Director/screenwriter/producer. Born: Edgeley, Cheshire, England

Launder worked in rep in Brighton (to avoid the boredom of his daytime job as a civil servant) and in 1928 had his play, *There Was No Signpost*, produced by the theatre company. He joined the scenario department at British International Pictures (BIP), where he first met Gilliat, and later worked at Shepperton, Teddington and Gainsborough studios. Gilliat was personal assistant to Walter Mycroft, scenariochief at BIP, before he progressed to assistant director and screenwriter. He moved on to the Nettlefold studios and as associate producer to Gaumont and Gainsborough, renewing his association with Launder in the late Thirties. Their early scripts together included two fine train thrillers, *The Lady Vanishes* and *Night Train to Munich* (Gilliat had earlier co-written *Rome Express*, and later films would feature trains), and a popular period piece, *The Young Mr Pitt*. Then came the films they also directed and/or produced in partnership (often for their own company, Individual Pictures): *The Rake's Progress, Green for Danger, London Belongs to Me* and their St Trinian's comedies based on the anarchic 'schoolgirls' cartoons by Ronald Searle. If Launder and Gilliat have produced no masterpieces, then at the very least they have excelled at portraying the English as they like to see themselves, usually dotty and eccentric. Thus they put on screen Charters (Basil Radford) and Caldicott (Naunton Wayne), two cricket-mad gents travelling by train; and the rival school heads (Alastair Sim and Margaret Rutherford) in *The Happiest Days of Your Life*. Yet, in contrast, *The Rake's Progress* and *Only Two Can Play* gave genuinely sexy roles to, respectively, Rex Harrison and Jean Kent, and Peter Sellers and Mai Zetterling. And Gilliat's *Waterloo Road* memorably starred John Mills as a squaddie who goes AWOL – escaping across a railway siding – to rescue his girl from the attentions of a wartime spiv (brilliantly played by Stewart Granger), culminating in the most brutally real-istic fistfight seen in British films up to that time.

Films include: 1932 Rome Express (co-sc. Gilliat). **'33** You Made Me Love You (co-sc. Launder); Friday the Thirteenth (co-sc. Gilliat). **'35** Bulldog Jack (co-sc. Gilliat). **'36** Twelve Good Men (co-sc. Launder, Gilliat). **'37** Oh, Mr Porter! (co-sc. Launder). **'38** The Lady Vanishes (co-sc. Launder, Gilliat). **'40** Night Train to Munich (co-sc. Launder, Gilliat). **'41** Kipps (sc. Gilliat). **'42** The Young Mr Pitt (co-sc. Launder, Gilliat); Partners in Crime (short) (co-dir; +co-sc. Launder, Gilliat). **'43** Millions Like Us (co-dir;+co-sc. Launder, Gilliat). **'44** Two Thousand Women (dir;+sc. Launder); Waterloo Road (dir;+sc. Gilliat). **'45** The Rake's Progress (dir. Gilliat; co-sc;+co-prod. Launder, Gilliat). **'46** I See a Dark Stranger (dir. Launder; co-sc;+co-prod. Launder, Gilliat); Green for Danger (dir;+co-sc. Gilliat; co-prod. Launder, Gilliat). **'47** Captain Boycott (dir;+co-sc. Launder; co-prod. Launder, Gilliat). **'48** London Belongs to Me (dir;+co-sc. Gilliat; co-prod. Launder, Gilliat). **'50** The Happiest Days of Your Life (dir;+co-sc. Launder; co-prod. Launder, Gilliat). **'53** The Story of Gilbert and Sullivan (dir;+co-sc. Gilliat; co-prod. Launder, Gilliat). **'54** The Belles of St Trinian's (dir. Launder; co-sc;+co-prod. Launder, Gilliat). **'61** Only Two Can Play (dir. Gilliat; co-prod. Launder, Gilliat). **'72** Endless Night (dir;+sc;+prod. Gilliat; exec. prod. Launder). **'80** The Wildcats of St Trinian's (dir;+sc. Launder; prod. consultant Gilliat).

LAUREL & HARDY

Laurel, Stan (1890–1965). Actor/screenwriter. Born: Arthur Stanley Jefferson; Ulverston, Lancashire, England

Hardy, Oliver (1892–1957). Actor. Born: Oliver Norvell Hardy; Harlem, Georgia, USA

By the age of 6, Laurel was a stage comedian in Glasgow; fourteen years later he understudied Chaplin in one of the Fred Karno sketch troupes that came to America. He stayed, and vaudeville success brought him early film work for Universal and Broncho Billy Anderson. Hardy sang with a minstrel show as a child, went to military college and abandoned a law degree to run a cinema before joining Lubin Motion Pictures as a general assistant. After spells with Vitagraph and comic Larry Semon, he joined Hal Roach's Comedy All Stars who by then included gagman and occasional actor Stan Laurel. They made their first film together, *Lucky Dog*, in 1917, but were not actually teamed until *Putting Pants on Philip* a decade later. In all they made 105 films together, 24 of them features. The collision of two opposites that makes for great screen comedy was perfected by Laurel and Hardy, and those who have followed in their wake – Abbott and Costello,

Above left: John Phillip Law in Diabolik *(1968). Above: Florence Lawrence. Below: Marc Lawrence in* Blind Alley *(1939), a thriller that explores the subconscious mind of a killer. Below left: Peter Lawford*

Martin and Lewis, Lemmon and Matthau, and even Morecambe and Wise – have, indeed, merely followed. Stan and Olly, with their distinctive individual mannerisms, were each uniquely funny characters but the comedy – and tragedy – in their films derives from the endless frustration of the fat, pedantic and graceful Hardy by the thin, incompetent simpleton Laurel – usually resulting in slapstick catastrophe (much of it written by Stan, the creative partner of the act). But, as the disasters themselves never stopped at the physical destruction of all that had been built up – there was always one more brick to drop down on Hardy's head – so the interplay between the boys always went beyond the comic wrecking of the fat man's plans. Though Hardy may beseech Laurel, 'Why don't you do something to help me?', or belt him when things go wrong, a moment later he will say, 'Remember, united we stand, divided we fall'; and they are never funnier than when, with a look and nod, they join up to wreck somebody's car or house (usually James Finlayson's). Theirs is the most touching of screen relationships, one never threatened by ruination, and their incompatability and mutual need has inspired the affection and laughter of audiences for over fifty years.

Films together include: 1917 Lucky Dog. '27 Putting Pants on Philip. '28 Two Tars. '29 Men O' War. '30 Night Owls; Brats. '31 Our Wife; One Good Turn; Beau Hunks (GB: Beau Chumps). '32 The Music Box; Towed in a Hole. '33 Fra Diavolo; Sons of the Desert (GB: Fraternally Yours). '34 Babes in Toyland; The Live Ghost. '35 The Fixer Uppers. '37 Way Out West. '38 Swiss Miss; Block-Heads. '39 The Flying Deuces. '40 A Chump at Oxford. '51 Atoll K (FR-IT) (USA: Robinson Crusoeland/Utopia; GB: Escapade).

LAURIE, Piper

(b. 1932). Actress. Born: Rosetta Jacobs; Detroit, Michigan, USA

Born of a Russian father and Polish mother, Piper Laurie spent her teens in Los Angeles where she became involved in amateur dramatics. Red-haired, hazel-eyed and with an exquisite figure, she was discovered by a Universal talent scout in 1949. As a starlet she was required to do little more than look good and was featured opposite such heart-throbs of the day as Ronald Reagan, Tyrone Power, Rock Hudson and Tony Curtis. She and Curtis were featured four times together and became a very popular comedy-romance team. It was only after she had left Universal and worked on the New York stage that she was able to prove herself as an actress of more than average ability, and on her return to the screen she excelled as the crippled alcoholic girlfriend of a pool-room addict (Paul Newman) in The Hustler. However, she decided to interrupt her career in favour of marriage to the writer Joseph Morgenstern, and after a fifteen-year gap returned to the screen as Margaret White, an obsessively religious neurotic who drives her daughter Carrie to seek a horrifying revenge.

Films include: 1952 No Room for the Groom; Has Anybody Seen My Gal?; Son of Ali Baba. '53 Mississipi Gambler. '54 Johnny Dark. '57 Until They Sail. '61 The Hustler. '76 Carrie. '77 Ruby. '79 Tim.

LAVI, Daliah

(b. 1942). Actress. Born: Daliah Levènbuch; Haifa, Israel

Lavi has all the colour and beauty of a dahlia – a tall, exotic hothouse variety – though her career as a leading lady of international films has now wilted. The daughter of a Russian and his German wife, at 10 she met Kirk Douglas while he was filming The Juggler (1953) in her home town, and she would later star with him in Vincente Minnelli's Two Weeks in Another Town, her first major movie. First came dance-training in Sweden and film appearances in Israel and France. Her fine performance as a possessed girl in the Italian Il Demonio won her a key role in Lord Jim, and she subsequently played a succession of lovely secret-agents in Sixties spy thrillers. She has since enjoyed success as a multi-lingual singer. Her second of three husbands was film producer John Sullivan.

Films include: 1960 Candide, ou l'Optimisme au XXe Siècle (FR) (USA/GB: Candide). '61 Un Soir sur la Plage (FR) (GB: Violent Summer). '62 Two Weeks in Another Town (USA). '63 Il Demonio (IT-FR). '65 Lord Jim (GB). '66 The Silencers (USA). '67 The Spy With a Cold Nose (GB). '68 Nobody Runs Forever (GB) (USA: The High Commissioner). '71 Catlow (GB).

LAW, John Phillip

(b. 1937). Actor. Born: Los Angeles, California, USA

The son of a deputy sheriff and an actress, Law was raised in Hollywood, was a film extra at eight, had a part in John Sturges' The Magnificent Yankee (1950) at 13, and a year later began to train as a mechanical engineer. This was abandoned in favour of a law course at the University of Hawaii, and that in turn for a career as an actor. Elia Kazan coached him and theatre work led to the Italian cinema (where he has made half his films) and a Hollywood breakthrough as a love-sick seaman in The Russians Are Coming, the Russians Are Coming. He has since worked a couple of times for Otto Preminger, and he was the famous German World War I flying ace in Roger Corman's Von Richtofen and Brown. However, it was with a different set of wings, those belonging to the blond, blind angel who gives a lift to Jane Fonda in Barbarella, that Law made his major bid for stardom in the late Sixties.

Films include: 1964 Alta Infedeltà (USA/GB: High Infidelity) (IT-FR). '66 The Russians Are Coming, the Russians Are Coming. '67 Hurry Sundown. '68 Barbarella (FR). '71 Von Richtofen and Brown (GB: The Red Baron); The Love Machine; The Last Movie. '73 The Golden Voyage of Sinbad (GB). '75 The Spiral Staircase (GB). '78 Hooper. '81 Tarzan, the Ape Man.

LAWFORD, Peter

(1923–1984). Actor. Born: London, England

Lawford, the son of Lt General Sir Sidney Lawford, began in showbusiness as a child actor in a British film about trains, Poor Old Bill (1931) and as a cockney kid in MGM's Lord Jeff (1938). He travelled continually with his parents, and was educated by private tutors. Arriving in Hollywood in the early Forties, he worked as an usher in the Westwood Village Theater and landed a contract with MGM, playing roles that asked for little more than charm and good looks, of which he had an abundance. While his acting appearances were unremarkable, his stock in fashionable society increased markedly – he married John F. Kennedy's sister Patricia in 1954 (divorced 1966), and became a member of Sinatra's playboy clique, along with other luminaries like Dean Martin and Sammy Davis Jr. Art (of a sort) imitated life when the buddies appeared together in Ocean's Eleven and Sergeants Three. His many television appearances include leading roles in The Thin Man

series and The Doris Day Show. Probably his most interesting screen role was that of the neurotic studio executive Paul Bern in the biopic Harlow.

Films include: 1942 Random Harvest. '44 The White Cliffs of Dover. '46 Cluny Brown. '60 Ocean's Eleven; Exodus. '62 Advise and Consent; Sergeants Three. '65 Harlow. '68 Skidoo!; Buona Sera, Mrs Campbell. '75 Rosebud.

LAWRENCE, Florence

(1886–1938). Actress. Born: Hamilton, Ontario, Canada

With Florence Lawrence the Hollywood star system was born and famous faces would no longer tolerate tiny salaries. Lawrence earned a mere $25 a picture while at Biograph where she was known simply as 'The Biograph Girl'. But under the guidance of Carl Laemmle at the Independent Motion Picture Company, her name became as well-known as her face; her purse grew fatter, too. The daughter of an actress-manager, Florence began in showbusiness at the age of four as 'Baby Flo, the Child Wonder Whistler'. She broke into movies in 1907 and was D.W. Griffith's first leading lady. She then made fifty movies in eleven months for IMP, but the failure of her marriage to her frequent co-star Harry Salter and a serious accident incurred while making The Pawns of Destiny disrupted her career. Various comebacks failed dismally and the former moviegoers' darling was forced to work as a $75-a-week extra at MGM. The sad state of her career and the failure of two further marriages were contributing factors to her taking her own life (by eating ant poison).

Films include: 1908 The Ingrate. '09 Resurrection; Mrs Jones' Burglar. '10 The Call of the Circus. '11 Nan's Diplomacy; The Hoyden. '12 Angel of the Studio. '14 The Pawns of Destiny. '16 Elusive Isabel.

LAWRENCE, Marc

(b. 1910). Actor. Born: New York City, USA

Watchful and mean-looking, Lawrence is one of Hollywood's most reliable 'baddies'. He has acted in over one hundred movies, progressing from being a henchman in gangster films and Westerns to more substantial roles – Cobb the bookie in The Asphalt Jungle, a Mafia boss in Johnny Cool and a cattle rustler in The Virginian. Lawrence came into films via the stage and radio, making his debut in White Lady in 1933. He made a foray into directing in the late Fifties and early Sixties, his best-remembered film being Nightmare in the Sun (1965). Since then he has returned to playing heavies, looking even more sinister with age.

Films include: 1935 Little Big Shot. '43 The Ox-Bow Incident. '44 The Princess and the Pirate. '46 The Virginian. '48 Key Largo. '50 The Asphalt Jungle. '63 Johnny Cool. '69 Krakatoa: East of Java. '74 The Man With the Golden Gun (GB).

LAWSON, John Howard

(1894–1977). Screenwriter. Born: New York City, USA

Lawson was the main spokesman for the Hollywood Ten – those directors and screenwriters indicted for contempt of Congress for refusing to cooperate with the House Un-American Activities Committee in the late Forties. He was a prime target for the Committee witch-hunters; he was the author of numerous radical plays, including *Success Story* (filmed as *Success at Any Price*) and a campaigner for left-wing causes. He was also one of the founders of the Screen Writers' Guild, formed to protect writers against exploitation by the Hollywood studios, and became its first president in 1933. Lawson's first filmed script was *Dynamite* (1930), DeMille's first talkie. During the late Thirties and the war years he was successful as a writer of anti-fascist films, including *Blockade*, then the only movie to portray the real issues of the Spanish Civil War, and of vividly exciting war films such as *Action in the North Atlantic*. In 1949, his refusal to forswear his left-wing connections in his stand against HUAC led to him being imprisoned for a year and blacklisted by Hollywood. He went into exile in Mexico, returning later to the USA to lecture at universities and write several books on screenwriting.

Films include: 1930 Dynamite (co-sc); Our Blushing Brides (co-sc). '34 Success at Any Price (co-sc). '35 Party Wire (co-sc). '38 Blockade; Algiers. '40 Four Sons. '43 Sahara (co-sc); Action in the North Atlantic. '45 Counter-Attack. '47 Smash-Up/Smash-Up, the Story of a Woman (GB: A Woman Destroyed).

LAWSON, Wilfrid

(1900–1966). Actor. Born: Wilfrid Worsnop; Bradford, Yorkshire, England

Lawson, one of Britain's finest character actors, could conjure a star performance out of a cameo part. He first appeared, aged 16, in *Trilby* at the Pier Pavilion, Brighton and made his West End debut in 1928 in *Sweeney Todd*. He had made a name for himself in George Bernard Shaw's plays, so it was fitting that his appearance as dustman Alfred Doolittle in the film version of the playwright's *Pygmalion* brought him a Hollywood contract. He returned home when war broke out and spent the rest of his life in Britain. His moustachioed, mobile face has been described as a 'squinting, stubbly battlefield' but he could also appear smooth and sophisticated when the part required. Despite being plagued by a drink problem, he managed to give impressive performances right up to the end of his career on stage, film and television.

Films include: 1935 The Turn of the Tide. '38 The Terror; Pygmalion; The Gaunt Stranger (USA: The Phantom Strikes). '40 Pastor Hall. '42 The Great Mr Handel. '44 Fanny by Gaslight (USA: Man of Evil). '57 Hell Drivers. '56 War and Peace (IT–USA). '63 Tom Jones.

LAYDU, Claude

(b. 1927). Actor. Born: Brussels, Belgium

Laydu was both fortunate and unlucky with his first screen role in which he played the unwordly, saint-like priest in Robert Bresson's *Diary of a Country Priest*. His performance was highly praised and awarded, but he never again had as a good a role in another film. He became interested in the theatre at 15 and studied in Paris with the great mime-actor, Jean-Louis Barrault. Laydu played several interesting minor roles after his debut, but stopped acting some years ago.

Films include: 1951 Journal d'un Curé de Campagne (GB: Diary of a Country Priest); Le Voyage en Amérique (GB: Trip to America). '52 Nous Sommes Tous des Assassins (USA: We Are All Murderers; GB: Are We All Murderers?). '55 Attila Flagello Di Dio (IT-FR) (GB: Attila the Hun); Sinfonia d'Amore (FR-IT). '57 La Roue (GB: Wheels of Fate). '60 Le Dialogue des Carmélites (FR-IT) (GB: The Carmelites).

LAYE, Evelyn

(b. 1900). Actress. Born: Evelyn Froud; London, England

From a theatrical background, Evelyn Laye made her West End debut at the Gaiety Theatre in *The Beauty Spot* in 1918. Numerous delightful performances subsequently made her a firm favourite and she attracted offers from Hollywood (where Goldwyn nicknamed her 'the Champagne Blonde') following her appearance on Broadway in Noel Coward's *Bitter Sweet*. She made *One Heavenly Night*, then returned to England, acting on stage and in various film musicals, such as *Princess Charming*, a Ruritanian romance also starring Henry Wilcoxon, and Victor Saville's *Evensong*, in which she played an opera singer who falls in love and gives up the stage. Her later film roles include a fine performance as Jean Simmons' mother in *Say Hello to Yesterday*. She was married to comedian Sonnie Hale from 1926 to 1931. The marriage ended in a stormy divorce which involved another major British musical star, Jessie Matthews. Laye subsequently married the actor Frank Lawton. Though in her eighties, this popular actress continues to work in the theatre and television.

Films include: 1927 The Luck of the Navy. '31 One Heavenly Night (USA). '33 Waltz Time. '34 Princess Charming; Evensong. '35 The Night Is Young. '59 Make Mine a Million. '66 Theatre of Death. '70 Say Hello to Yesterday.

LEACHMAN, Cloris

(b. 1926). Actress. Born: Des Moines, Iowa, USA

For many years, practically the only glimpse moviegoers had had of Cloris Leachman had been as the beautiful murder victim at the beginning of Aldrich's *Kiss Me Deadly*. She studied drama with Elia Kazan at the Actors' Studio in New York and appeared on Broadway in *As You Like It* (which featured Katharine Hepburn as Rosalind). She then concentrated on television, her many parts including the wise-cracking Phyllis in *The Mary Tyler Moore Show* who proved so popular that a whole series was based around her. Cloris Leachman's career has tended to take second place to her family (she married producer/director George H. Englund in 1953 and has five children). She has, however, achieved widespread recognition by winning an Oscar for Best Supporting Actress as the lonely wife who falls for the young hero in *The Last Picture Show*, and followed up this triumph with an Emmy Award for Best Actress in *A Brand New Life*. Both roles amply demonstrated her wide dramatic range as an actress. Her gift for broad comedy has since been underlined in her roles in Mel Brooks' *Young Frankenstein*, *High Anxiety* and *History of the World – Part One*.

Films include: 1955 Kiss Me Deadly. '69 Butch Cassidy and the Sundance Kid. '70 WUSA. '71 The Last Picture Show. '73 Dillinger. '74 Daisy Miller; Young Frankenstein. '75 Crazy Mama. '77 High Anxiety. '81 History of the World – Part One.

LEACOCK, Philip

(b. 1917). Director. Born: London, England

The son of a Canary Islands' planter, Leacock entered the British film industry in 1935 as a camera assistant, becoming a director of documentaries in the Army Kinematograph Service during World War II. He joined the

Above: Wilfrid Lawson in The Wrong Box *(1966). Above right: Claude Laydu as the priest in* Le Journal d'un Curé de Campagne. *Far right: Domicile Conjugal starred Jean-Pierre Léaud. Right: Cloris Leachman as a lonely wife in* The Last Picture Show. *Bottom right: the director David Lean. Below: Evelyn Laye*

Crown Film Unit in 1948 (his credits included *Festival in London*) before making a successful feature film debut with *The Brave Don't Cry*, a docudrama about trapped miners. He became a contract director for Rank, then travelled to Hollywood in 1959. He made a few interesting movies then concentrated on television, directing and/or producing such series as *Route 66*, *Gunsmoke*, *The Defenders* and *Mod Squad*. Leacock's gentle humanitarianism – a legacy from his experience in British documentary in the Thirties and Forties – makes his films appear somewhat old-fashioned today. He is at his best when directing children, as in *The Kidnappers* and *The Spanish Gardener*, or with an anti-war subject such as *The War Lover*.

Films include: 1951 Festival in London (doc). '52 The Brave Don't Cry. '53 Appointment in London; The Kidnappers (USA: The Little Kidnappers). '56 The Spanish Gardener. '59 Take a Giant Step (USA). '60 Let No Man Write My Epitaph (USA); Hand in Hand. '62 The War Lover. '72 Baffled!

LEACOCK, Richard

(b. 1921). Director. Born: Canary Islands

Like his brother Philip, he was raised in the Canaries. He went to Harvard to study physics in 1938 and, in 1943, served as a cameraman in the American army. The most important event in his career as a film-maker may well have been when Robert Flaherty chose him to be his cameraman on *Louisiana Story*. In the mid-Fifties Leacock teamed up with *Life* magazine writer, Robert Drew, to develop

a new screen journalism which eventually became known as Direct Cinema, the American equivalent of *cinéma vérité*. Leacock, Drew and another colleague, D.A. Pennebaker, used light-weight equipment to film events – a presidential nomination (*Primary*), a convention of policemen (*Chiefs*), a Bob Dylan tour (*Dont Look Back*, 1967) – with a potential for ready-made drama. Their detached and ironic view left audiences to draw certain conclusions about the oddities of individual and group behaviour in certain circumstances.

Films include: 1948 Louisiana Story (co-photo). '60 Primary (co-dir). '62 The Chair (co-dir). '63 Crisis (co-dir). '64 A Happy Mother's Day (co-dir). '68 Monterey Pop (co-photo). '70 Chiefs; Sweet Toronto (co-photo); Maidstone (co-photo).

LEAN, David

(b. 1908). Director. Born: Croydon, Surrey, England

The late Fifties and Sixties were perhaps the last time in which the yearning for lavish spectacle on an epic scale could be fulfilled. In many ways, David Lean was the master of the form, the unassuming heir to DeMille's throne though he (and scriptwriter Robert Bolt) took their subjects from contemporary history rather than the Bible, *The Bridge on the River Kwai*, *Lawrence of Arabia*, *Doctor Zhivago*, along with *Ryan's Daughter* – Bolt scripted the last three – were all astonishingly successful. The technical gloss and craftsmanship that radiated from these films failed, however, to conceal a certain emptiness at their core. Raised in a strict Quaker home, Lean entered the film industry as a cutting-room assistant at Gainsborough and within ten years became the highest-paid editor in Britain. In 1942 Noel Coward asked him to co-direct *In Which We Serve*, and this set Lean on course for a string of brilliant successes. *Blithe Spirit* and *Brief Encounter* were followed by two outstanding Dickens' films, *Great Expectations* and *Oliver Twist*. A project to re-make *Mutiny on the Bounty* ran into problems in the late Seventies and, in 1982, Lean announced he was planning to film E.M. Forster's classic novel of English colonialism, *A Passage to India*.

Films include: 1936 As You Like It (ed). '38 Pygmalion (ed). '41 49th Parallel (ed); One of Our Aircraft is Missing (ed). '42 In Which We Serve (co-dir). '44 This Happy Breed. '45 Blithe Spirit; Brief Encounter. '46 Great Expectations. '48 Oliver Twist. '52 The Sound Barrier (USA: Breaking the Sound Barrier/Star Bound). '57 The Bridge on the River Kwai. '62 Lawrence of Arabia. '65 Doctor Zhivago (USA). '70 Ryan's Daughter.

LÉAUD, Jean-Pierre

(b. 1944). Actor. Born: Paris, France

Movie-making is in Léaud's blood – his parents were the screenwriter Pierre Léaud and the actress Jacqueline Pierreux, while the directors François Truffaut and Jean-Luc Godard are among his intimate friends. At 14 he was picked to play Antoine Doinel in Truffaut's study of his own deprived childhood *The 400 Blows*. Léaud was superb as the adolescent to whom every adult is a potential enemy, and Truffaut's fascination with the character of Doinel led him to make several sequels, including *Love at Twenty*, *Stolen Kisses* and *Bed and Board*, in which Léaud substituted an unappealing, predatory earnestness for his earlier sympathetic vitality. In 1962 Léaud began a close working relationship with Godard, working in various capacities behind the camera and appearing in *Masculin-Féminin*, *Made in USA*, *La Chinoise*, *Weekend* and *Le Gai Savoir*. These and Truffaut's films typed Léaud as a furtive embodiment of youthful alienation, both fascinating and slightly repulsive, with his piercing dark eyes staring out from a foxy face framed by lank, black hair. These qualities made him a perfect choice as the egotistical actor who plays on Jacqueline Bisset's better nature in Truffaut's *Day for Night* and as Maria Schneider's irrepressible, movie-mad boyfriend – the complete antithesis to Marlon Brando's ageing romantic – in *Last Tango in Paris*.

Films include: 1959 Les Quatre Cent Coups (USA/GB: The 400 Blows). '59 Le Testament d'Orphée (USA/GB: The Testament of Orpheus). '62 L'Amour à Vingt Ans *ep* Antoine et Colette (FR-IT-JAP-GER-POL) (USA/GB: Love at Twenty). '66 Masculin-Féminin (FR-SWED); Made in USA. '67 Le Départ; La Chinoise, ou Plutôt à la Chinoise; Weekend (FR-IT). '68 Baisers Volés (USA/GB: Stolen Kisses). '69 Le Gai Savoir (FR-GER); Porcile (IT-FR) (GB: Pigsty). '70 Domicile Conjugal (FR-IT) (USA/GB: Bed and Board). '72 Ultimo Tango a Parigi (IT-FR) (GB: Last Tango in Paris). '73 La Nuit Américaine (FR-IT) (USA/GB: Day for Night).

LEDERER, Charles

(1906–1976). Screenwriter. Born: New York City, USA

Lederer's early career was in journalism, but as might be expected of one whose father was a theatrical producer, whose mother was a singer, and whose aunt was actress Marion Davies, he soon turned to Hollywood. A protégé of Charles MacArthur and Ben Hecht, he collaborated on *The Front Page*. He soon established a reputation for sharp-witted and irreverent comedies, especially those made by Howard Hawks, and became a junior member of the Algonquin Round Table, that gathering of prominent New York writers which included Dorothy Parker. He was co-author of the stage musical *Kismet*, which he adapted for the screen in 1955, and which won him a Tony Award.

Films include: 1931 The Front Page. '33 Topaze (co-sc). '40 His Girl Friday; Comrade X (co-sc). '47 Kiss of Death (co-sc). '49 I Was a Male War Bride (co-sc) (GB: You Can't Sleep Here). '51 The Thing. '52 Monkey Business. '53 Gentlemen Prefer Blondes. '55 Kismet (co-sc). '60 Can Can (co-sc); Ocean's Eleven (co-sc). '62 Mutiny on the Bounty.

LEDERER, Francis

(b. 1906). Actor. Born: Frantisek Lederer; Prague, Czechoslovakia

The youngest of three sons of a leather merchant, Lederer won a scholarship to the Prague Academy of Dramatic Art before he was 18. His subsequent stage work established his reputation in Europe, and he went on to make films in France and Germany, working for G.W. Pabst and others. In 1932 he appeared on the New York stage with a musical, *Autumn Crocus*, which won him a Hollywood contract. His early parts were lean and lithe romantic leads, but after World War II he played heavier character roles. He has been involved in a wide range of other activities, including an art gallery and the World Peace Foundation, which he helped to found.

Films include: 1929 Die Büchse der Pandora (GER) (GB: Pandora's Box); Atlantik (GER). '34 Pursuit of Happiness; Romance in Manhattan. '35 The Gay Deception. '36 One Rainy Afternoon. '39 Confessions of a Nazi Spy. '44 The Bridge of San Luis Rey. '46 The Madonna's Secret. '50 A Woman of Distinction.

LEE, Anna

(b. 1914). Actress. Born: Joanna Boniface Winnifrith; Ightham, Kent, England

A sweet-faced blonde, Lee soon became a popular star of British films of the Thirties following her training at drama school. In 1939 she went to the USA with her first husband, director Robert Stevenson. Since then she has worked steadily in a wide variety of supporting and character roles, and is best remembered for her role as Bronwen in John Ford's *How Green Was My Valley*. She has also acted for Fritz Lang and Samuel Fuller. When her film work declined in the Sixties, she became increasingly involved in American television.

Films include: 1932 Ebb Tide. '33 Chelsea Life. '35 Passing of the Third Floor Back. '37 King Solomon's Mines. '41 How Green Was My Valley. '43 Hangmen Also Die! (USA). '48 Fort Apache (USA). '58 The Last Hurrah (USA). '59 The Crimson Kimono. '62 The Man Who Shot Liberty Valance (USA). '65 The Sound of Music; Seven Women.

LEE, Bernard

(1908–1981). Actor. Born: London, England

Now perhaps best remembered as 'M', the boss of super-spy James Bond, Lee began to act at 14 when he followed his father, Edmund Lee, on to the stage. After a period as a fruit salesman, he studied at RADA and toured England with several plays, before working in London rep. Despite a busy stage career, he made over a hundred films, often playing police or military figures, notably in *The Blue Lamp* and *The Third Man*.

Films include: 1934 The Double Event. '36 Rhodes of Africa. '37 The Black Tulip. '47 The Courtneys of Curzon Street. '48 The Fallen Idol. '49 The Third Man. '50 The Blue

Lamp. '51 Calling Bulldog Drummond. '61 Whistle Down the Wind. '62 Dr No. '63 From Russia With Love. '65 Thunderball. '77 The Spy Who Loved Me.

LEE, Bruce

(1940–1973). Actor. Born: Bruce Lee Hsaio Loong; San Francisco, California, USA

Lee left America at an early age when his father took a job acting in Chinese opera in Hong Kong. As a teenager he studied martial arts and achieved great prowess. He returned to America, to study at Seattle University, and was spotted taking part in karate championships by 20th Century-Fox and signed to play in the comic-book television series *The Green Hornet*. Bit-parts in movies followed, but his career took off when he returned to Hong Kong to make a series of martial arts films which exploited his explosive athletic abilities to the full. His last complete film, *Enter the Dragon*, reached the West at a time of increased interest in Oriental culture, and was a huge box-office success. His sudden and mysterious death aged only 32 enhanced his cult reputation.

Films include: 1941 Chin-men nü/Golden Gate Tears/Tears of San Francisco (extra). '69 Marlowe (USA). '71 T'ang-shan ta-hsiung/The Big Boss (also GB title) (USA: Fists of Fury). '72 Ching-wu men/Fist of Fury (also GB title) (USA: The Chinese Connection); Meng lung kuo chiang/Way of the Dragon (also GB title) (+ dir; + sc; + martial arts dir) (USA: Return of the Dragon). '73 Lung-cheng-hu tou/Enter the Dragon (USA–HONG KONG). '78 Szu-wan yu-hsi/Game of Death (GB: Bruce Lee's Game of Death).

LEE, Christopher

(b. 1922). Actor. Born: Christopher Frank Cavandini Lee; London, England

The son of an army officer and an Italian mother, Lee was educated at public schools, attaining fluency in eight languages. Following work in

Above left: shades of Bogart – Francis Lederer in The Madonna's Secret. Above: Bernard Lee confronting difficult moral issues in The Raging Moon (1970), a tale about two physically disabled people who fall in

love. Above: Anna Lee as Bronwen in How Green Was My Valley. Below: Bruce Lee playing with fire in Enter the Dragon. Below left: the cold face of Christopher Lee, another favourite in the Dracula stakes

Intelligence in World War II, he was chosen by Hammer Films to play the Creature in *Curse of Frankenstein*. His tall, sinister, dark good looks led to the lead in *Dracula*, a role he was to repeat many times. The part of the villain in the James Bond movie *The Man With the Golden Gun* in the early Seventies signalled a break with the horror genre, and today he works extensively on American television, typically in blockbusters like Harold Robbins' *The Pirate*.

Films include: 1948 Corridor of Mirrors; Hamlet. '52 The Crimson Pirate (USA). '55 Cockleshell Heroes; Storm Over the Nile. '57 Curse of Frankenstein. '58 A Tale of Two Cities; Dracula (USA: Horror of Dracula). '59 Hound of the Baskervilles. '61 Taste of Fear (USA: Scream of Fear). '74 Man With the Golden Gun. '77 Airport '77 (USA). '78 Circle of Iron (USA) (GB: The Silent Flute).

Top: Janet Leigh as Marion Crane, who becomes the murder victim in one of the most famous sequences Hitchcock ever shot – the horrific shower stabbing in Psycho. Above: Vivien Leigh, attired as Scarlett O'Hara, smiles for the camera while relaxing between takes on the set of Gone With the Wind

LEE, Rowland V.

(1891–1975). Director. Born: Findlay, Ohio, USA

Rowland V. Lee entered showbiz as an actor, first appearing on the stage as a child, with his parents, in stock companies and on Broadway. Educated at Columbia University, he abandoned a budding career on Wall Street and turned to the movies. After a period with director Thomas Ince – interrupted by service in World War I – he turned to making his own films. They were, on the whole, horror or historical adventure dramas, heavily atmospheric and employing predominantly stylized settings.

Films include: 1921 Cupid's Brand. '24 In Love With Love. '26 Alice Adams. '27 Barbed Wire (co-dir). '29 The Mysterious Dr Fu Manchu. '33 Zoo in Budapest. '34 The Count of Monte Cristo. '35 Cardinal Richelieu; The Three Musketeers. '37 Toast of New York. '39 Son of Frankenstein (+prod). '44 The Bridge of San Luis Rey. '45 Captain Kidd. '59 The Big Fisherman (co-sc; +prod. only).

LEENHARDT, Roger

(1903–1985). Director/film critic. Born: Paris, France

A respected and influential critic and film theorist, Leenhardt was born into a rigidly Protestant family, which had a marked effect on his intellectual formation, and encouraged his severe ideals. After studying at the Sorbonne, he worked for several respected journals, becoming a fine critic. From 1933 he made short films, usually documentary studies of arts personalities. In 1947 he won the Grand Prix in Belgium for *Naissance du Cinéma*. He made few features, the best-known being *Les Dernières Vacances*, a sensitive story of adolescent love.

Films include: 1934 L'Orient Qui Vent (co-dir. only); En Crête Sans les Dieux (co-dir. only). '47 Naissance du Cinema. '48 Les Dernières Vacances (feature). '52 Victor Hugo (co-dir). '55 François Mauriac. '59 Daumier. '60 Paul Valéry. '62 Le Rendez-Vous de Minuit (feature) (GB: Rendezvous at Midnight). '63 L'Homme à la Pipe. '65 Corot. '76 Pissarro. '80 Manet ou le Novateur Malgré Lui (unfinished).

LEE THOMPSON, J.

(b. 1914). Director. Born: John Lee Thompson; Bristol, England

J. Lee Thompson wrote his first play while still at school, and had two produced in London before he was 20. Several small parts in films followed a period with the Nottingham Repertory Company, but in 1934 he turned to scenario-writing. After service in World War II with the RAF, he scripted several films before directing his first feature, *Murder Without Crime* (1950). His subsequent films, notably *The Guns of Navarone*, have been fast action adventures.

Films include: 1954 The Weak and the Wicked. '56 Yield to the Night (USA: Blonde Sinner). '57 Woman in a Dressing Gown. '58 Ice Cold in Alex. '59 No Trees in the Street; Tiger Bay. '61 The Guns of Navarone. '72 Conquest of the Planet of the Apes (USA). '73 Battle for the Planet of the Apes (USA). '78 The Greek Tycoon (USA); The Passage.

LEFEBVRE, Robert

(b. 1907). Cinematographer. Born: Paris, France

Lefebvre entered films in 1923 as a camera assistant, working up to become director of photography by 1932. He has worked on many French films, including some with Abel Gance and René Clair, and his reputation as a creator of beautiful visual images was established by *Casque d'Or*.

Films include: 1934 Sapho (co-photo). '36 Un Grand Amour de Beethoven (GB: Beethoven). '38 Katia; Clochemerle. '51 Edouard et Caroline (GB: Edward and Caroline). '52 Casque d'Or (USA: Golden Helmet; GB: Golden Marie). '54 Le Blé en Herbe (GB: Ripening Seed). '55 Les Grandes Manoeuvres (FR-IT) (USA: The Grand Maneuver). '57 Porte des Lilas (FR-IT). '70 Claude et Greta (GB: Any Time Anywhere).

LÉGER, Fernand

(1881–1955). Painter. Born: Argentan, France

The great Cubist painter Fernand Léger was occasionally involved with cinema. He is said to have been fascinated by Chaplin, and in 1921 to have begun an animated cartoon, *Charlot Cubiste*. Three years later, Léger collaborated with the American director Dudley Murphy on an avant-garde short, *Ballet Mécanique*, and the same year he designed striking sets for some scenes of Marcel L'Herbier's *L'Inhumaine*. In 1936 he designed costumes for the British film, *Things to Come*, and in 1946 wrote a sketch for Hans Richter's episode film, *Dreams That Money Can Buy*. Léger died while planning a film which was to have been entitled *Le Ballet des Couleurs*.

Film include: 1921 Charlot Cubiste (unfinished cartoon). '24 L'Inhumaine (set dec); Ballet Mécanique (dir). '36 Things to Come (cost. des) (GB). '46 Dreams That Money Can Buy ep The Girl With the Prefabricated Heart (dir; +sc) (USA).

LEHMAN, Ernest

(b. 1920). Screenwriter. Born: New York City, USA

Educated at the City College of New York, Lehman planned a career in chemical engineering, only to change course and become a writer. He also had a spell as a theatre and film publicity agent, an experience he turned to good account in a story, *Sweet Smell of Success*, which was later filmed from Lehman's own script. Beginning early in the Fifties, he wrote a number of film scripts, almost all adaptations of existing work. A notable exception, however, was *North by Northwest*, a brilliant original specifically written with Hitchcock in mind. Lehman also scripted Hitchcock's last film, *Family Plot*. From the mid-Sixties he has produced occasional films, and he directed and produced *Portnoy's Complaint* from his own adaptation.

Films include: 1948 The Inside Story (co-sc). '54 Executive Suite; Sabrina (co-sc) (GB: Sabrina Fair). '56 Somebody Up There Likes Me; The King and I. '57 Sweet Smell of Success (co-sc). '59 North by Northwest. '60 From the Terrace. '61 West Side Story. '63 The Prize. '65 The Sound of Music. '66 Who's Afraid of Virginia Woolf? (+prod). '69 Hello Dolly! (+prod). '72 Portnoy's Complaint (+dir; +prod). '76 Family Plot. '77 Black Sunday (co-sc).

LEIGH, Janet

(b. 1927). Actress. Born: Jeanette Helen Morrison; Merced, California, USA

Sheer chance brought Janet Leigh, a student of music and psychology at the College of the Pacific, to the attention of MGM in 1946. Norma Shearer saw her portrait at a ski lodge where her parents worked in Northern California, and took it to the studio. It sounds like a publicity story, but Leigh has vouched for it. For some years she played routine ingénue roles, but matured in the Fifties to play a variety of interesting roles. An attractive, intelligent actress, she proved expert in comedy (*My Sister Eileen*), tough Westerns (*The Naked Spur*) and crime dramas (Welles' *Touch of Evil*), but, ironically, will always be identified with the movie in which Hitchcock played havoc with audience expectations (*Psycho*). Leigh's heroine is not only a thief; she is horribly killed one-third of the way through the film. From 1951 to 1962 Janet Leigh was married to Tony Curtis. Their daughter, Jamie Lee Curtis, has made a promising beginning as a screen actress.

Films include: 1947 The Romance of Rosy Ridge. '48 Act of Violence. '49 Little Women; That Forsyte Woman (GB: The Forsyte Saga). '51 Two Tickets to Broadway. '52 Scaramouche. '53 The Naked Spur; Houdini. '54 Prince Valiant; The Black Shield of Falworth. '55 Pete Kelly's Blues; My Sister Eileen. '58 Touch of Evil; The Vikings. '60 Psycho. '62 The Manchurian Candidate. '66 Harper (GB: The Moving Target). '80 The Fog.

LEIGH, Vivien

(1913–1967). Actress. Born: Vivian Mary Hartley; Darjeeling, India

Vivien Leigh arrived in England in 1920 and was educated there. She then studied at RADA and made a first stage appearance in 1934. A five-year contract with Alexander Korda eventually brought her a lead opposite Laurence Olivier (whom she later married) in *Fire Over England*. Visiting him in Hollywood, she was tested for Scarlett O'Hara in *Gone With the Wind*, and although virtually unknown in America was given this most coveted role of the period. Leigh was slim and dainty, with a small oval face and green eyes, and looked perfect as Scarlett. She duly won her Academy Award, a feat she was to repeat for her Blanche Dubois in *A Streetcar Named Desire*, a part she had played on stage. She acted regularly on stage and screen until tuberculosis made her appearances infrequent, and led to her death in 1967.

Films: 1935 Things Are Looking Up; The Village Squire; Gentleman's Agreement; Look Up and Laugh. '37 Fire Over England; Dark Journey; Storm in a Teacup; The First and the Last/21 Days (USA: 21 Days Together). '38 A Yank at Oxford. '39 St Martin's Lane (USA: Sidewalks of London); Gone With the Wind (USA). '40 Waterloo Bridge (USA). '41 That Hamilton Woman! (USA) (GB: Lady Hamilton). '45 Caesar and Cleopatra. '48 Anna Karenina. '51 A Streetcar Named Desire. '55 The Deep Blue Sea. '61 The Roman Spring of Mrs Stone (USA). '65 Ship of Fools (USA).

Right, from left to right: Margaret
Leighton in The Teckman Mystery
(1954); John Le Mesurier in The Alf
Garnett Saga (1972); Jack Lemmon
as the gendarme who falls for a
prostitute (Shirley MacLaine) in Irma
La Douce; Lotte Lenya exhibits the
steely look she reserved for movies
in The Roman Spring of Mrs Stone

LEIGHTON, Margaret

(1922–1976). Actress. Born: Barnt
Green, Worcestershire, England

On the professional stage at 16,
Margaret Leighton always belonged
primarily to the theatre. She was a
leading member of the great Old Vic
company in the late Forties, playing
opposite Olivier and Richardson, and
went on to a distinguished career in
London and in New York, where she
won two Tony awards. A tall, elegant,
dignified blonde, she excelled in playing characters whose calm exterior
could mask a chaos of emotions, and
in two films in particular she was able
to use this ability to the full. The first
was Hitchcock's *Under Capricorn*,
where she played the malevolent
housekeeper Milly, steadily driving
Ingrid Bergman to drink; the other
was Ford's last film, *Seven Women*,
where Leighton's Agatha Andrews,
founder and director of the remote
mission in China, was a disturbing yet
oddly sympathetic portrait of religious
fanaticism.

Films include: 1948 Bonnie Prince Charlie;
The Winslow Boy. '49 Under Capricorn. '50
The Elusive Pimpernel; The Astonished
Heart. '62 Waltz of the Toreadors. '65 Seven
Women. '69 The Madwoman of Chaillot.
'71 The Go-Between. '72 Lady Caroline
Lamb (GB-IT). '75 Great Expectations.

LEISEN, Mitchell

(1898–1972). Director/designer.
Born: Menominee, Michigan, USA

When barely 20, Leisen was already
designing costumes for DeMille's *Male
and Female* (1919), and did the same
for Fairbanks' *Robin Hood* (1922) and
The Thief of Bagdad (1924). On this last
his work was dazzling, and he rose to
art director, staying with DeMille in
that office for eight years and designing, among other films, *King of Kings*
(1927) and *The Sign of the Cross* (1932).
He began to direct for Paramount in
1933. With his gifts as an artist allied
to a bubbling sense of comedy and a
genius for directing actresses, Leisen
was as responsible as anyone (including Lubitsch) for the style and look of
Paramount movies of the Thirties and
Forties. He made great comedies (*Easy
Living, Midnight*), romances that were
both witty and moving (*Remember the
Night, Hold Back the Dawn*), and oddities so odd that they could only be
Leisen. *Murder at the Vanities* (1934)
is a lavish musical *and* a tough, tense
crime film, while *Death Takes a Holiday*
is supernatural fantasy, touching
love story and possessed of the quintessential Paramount look. Leisen's
best movies were from scripts by Preston Sturges and Billy Wilder, and as
they moved into direction in the Forties, so Leisen faded. He went on until

1957, but *Kitty* in 1945 was the last
real Leisen film.

Films include: 1933 Cradle Song. '34 Death
Takes a Holiday. '35 Behold My Wife;
Hands Across the Table. '37 Swing High,
Swing Low; Easy Living. '38 The Big Broad-
cast of 1938. '39 Midnight. '40 Remember
the Night (+ prod); Arise My Love. '41 Hold
Back the Dawn (+ act). '43 No Time for
Love. '44 Lady in the Dark; Frenchman's
Creek. '45 Kitty. '46 To Each His Own. '47
Golden Earrings. '48 Dream Girl. '50 No
Man of Her Own. '57 The Girl Most Likely.

LELOUCH, Claude

(b. 1937). Director/cinematographer.
Born: Paris, France

Claude Lelouch began making
amateur films when he was only 13
and his first short, *La Mal du Siècle*,
won him a prize at the Cannes
Amateur Festival in 1950. In 1956 he
visited America where he made two
shorts but the first piece of his work to
be widely seen was *Quand le Rideau se
Lève*, an illicit documentary made on a
trip to Moscow in 1957 and subsequently shown on American television. His family financed *Le Propre de
l'Homme*, his first feature film, but it
was never released. Then came *Un
Homme et une Femme*, a glossy, romantic drama which won huge acclaim
and was followed up by another success *Vivre Pour Vivre*. By the late
Sixties he had set up his own production company, Les Films 13, employing the composer Francis Lai and
scriptwriter Pierre Uyttenhoeven. As
well as directing, Lelouch often oper-
ates his own camera, explaining: 'I
find it so difficult for a director to hand
over the camera . . . as if Van Gogh
had got a friend to hold his painting
brush for him'. His style is visually
ornate (too lush for some): 'I am
interested in only one thing – people,
then feelings, then life, then love.'

Films include: 1960 Le Propre de l'Homme.
'64 L'Amour avec des Si. '66 Un Homme et
une Femme (+ co-photo) (GB: A Man and a
Woman); Pour un Maillot Jaune (doc.
short) (GB: For a Yellow Jersey). '67 Vivre
pour Vivre (+ photo) (FR-IT) (GB: Live for
Life); Loin du Vietnam (co-dir) (GB: Far
From Vietnam). '70 Le Voyou (+ photo)
(FR-IT) (GB: Simon the Swiss). '71 Smic,
Smac, Smoc (USA: Money, Money, Money).
'74 Mariage. '77 Un Autre Homme, une
Autre Chance (USA: Another Man, Anot-
her Chance; GB: Another Man, Another
Woman). '79 A Nous Deux (FR-CAN). '81
Les Uns et les Autres (+ photo) (USA:
Bolero).

LE MESURIER, John

(1912–1983). Actor. Born: Bedford,
England

The son of a solicitor, Le Mesurier
attended public school in Dorset
before studying drama at the Fay
Compton School of Acting where one
of his classmates was Alec Guinness.
World War II interrupted his career in
repertory but after the war he made
his film debut in *Death in the Hand*. His
mournful appearance, gentle manner
and vague delivery made him an
immensely popular character actor
with British audiences and Le Mesurier soon found himself in the happy
position of being able to pick and
choose his roles (which have often
been as bureaucrats or civil servants).
Preferring comedy – from 1968 he
played Sergeant Wilson in the celebrated television comedy series about
the Home Guard, *Dad's Army* – he
nevertheless excelled in a certain type
of reflective drama, and in 1971 was
named television's Best Actor of the
Year for his portrayal of the dissolution of a human being in *Traitor*. His
first wife was the actress-comedienne
Hattie Jacques.

Films include: 1948 Death in the Hand. '49
Old Mother Riley's New Venture. '56

Private's Progress. '58 I Was Monty's
Double; The Moonraker. '59 I'm All Right
Jack; The Hound of the Baskervilles. '60
School for Scoundrels. '61 Only Two Can
Play. '63 The Pink Panther (USA). '69
Midas Run (USA) (GB: A Run on Gold); The
Magic Christian. '71 Dad's Army. '77 Stand
Up Virgin Soldiers.

LEMMON, Jack

(b. 1925). Actor. Born: John Uhler
Lemmon III; Boston, Massachusetts,
USA

After graduating from Harvard,
Lemmon began acting in New York
where he was soon a regular voice in
radio soap operas. This led him into
television and Broadway until in 1954
he went to Hollywood and scored an
immediate success opposite Judy Holliday in *It Should Happen to You*. Dark-
haired, hazel-eyed, of medium build,
Lemmon seemed to be very much Mr
Average. During his first few years as
a film star he played a great variety of
roles – in musicals (*My Sister Eileen*)
and romantic melodrama (*Fire Down
Below*). But it wasn't until *Some Like it
Hot* and especially *The Apartment* that
he found his true screen persona, that
of the decent man struggling to come
to terms with events going on around
him, and more often than not having
to accept failure. His comedy is of the
manic variety, carried into slapstick at
times and usually expressed by his
vast range of facial expressions. Many
of his roles also include an element of
suffering and moments of incredible
seriousness that, in *Tribute* for example, overflow into crass sentimentality. The same reactions can, however, be harnessed to magnificent
effect in a drama like *Missing*. His
partnership with Walter Matthau was
most fruitful and resulted in some
comedy classics like *The Odd Couple*,
The Fortune Cookie and *The Front Page*.

became interested in an acting career in movies. Beginning with appearances in films made by Selig Polyscope, he was a star name by 1916. He was ambitious to direct, however, and his chance came when he was allowed to make the serial *The Master Key* in 1914. His first wife, Mae Murray, featured in several of his movies until their divorce in 1925. Leonard then married actress Gertrude Olmstead. He had joined the newly-formed MGM in 1924 and remained there for a further 30 years, becoming one of the studio's most reliable craftsmen. His credits include *Susan Lenox: Her Fall and Rise*, starring Greta Garbo and Clark Gable, the multi-Oscar-winning musical *The Great Ziegfeld* and a glossy film version of *Pride and Prejudice*, scripted by Aldous Huxley and starring Laurence Olivier and Greer Garson. He left MGM in 1955 to make *La Donna Più Bella del Mondo* (*Beautiful But Dangerous*) with Gina Lollobrigida in Italy.

Films include: 1922 Fascination. '23 The French Doll. '31 Susan Lenox: Her Fall and Rise. '32 Strange Interlude. '36 The Great Ziegfeld. '37 Maytime. '40 Pride and Prejudice. '45 Weekend at the Waldorf. '53 The Clown. '54 Her Twelve Men.

Lemmon has shown only a fleeting interest in direction, but his understanding of Matthau helped to make *Kotch* (1971) a moving yet humorous look at old age.

Films include: 1954 It Should Happen to You; Phfft! '55 My Sister Eileen; Mister Roberts. '57 Fire Down Below (GB); Operation Mad Ball. '58 Bell, Book and Candle. '59 Some Like it Hot. '60 The Apartment. '62 Days of Wine and Roses. '63 Irma La Douce. '65 The Great Race. '66 The Fortune Cookie (GB: Meet Whiplash Willie). '68 The Odd Couple. '70 The Out-of-Towners. '72 Avanti! '74 The Front Page. '79 The China Syndrome. '80 Tribute (CAN-USA). '81 Buddy, Buddy. '82 Missing.

LENI, Paul

(1885–1929). Director/art director. Born: Stuttgart, Germany

Leni worked as a stage designer for Max Reinhardt and Leopold Jessner and as a poster designer for the cinema before directing his first films in Germany. He also acted as art director on his own films and those of other German directors. In *Backstairs* (co-directed with Jessner) and *Waxworks* Leni used strongly stylized sets, contorted Expressionist acting and exaggerated light and shadow to create a pervasive atmosphere of threat. He went to Hollywood to make four films at the end of the silent period, and successfully transposed his European style. *The Cat and the Canary* is the greatest of haunted house mysteries, all billowing curtains, deserted corridors and cobwebbed clocks, while *The Man Who Laughs* is historical adventure seen as Gothic horror. Leni died of blood poisoning at the age of 44, but his influence survived. Eisenstein's *Ivan the Terrible* owes much of its visual style to *Waxworks*, while the American films set a pattern which Universal in the Thirties and

RKO in the Forties were to follow with profit.

Films include: 1914 Das Panzergewolbe (art dir). '16 Das Tagebuch des Dr Hart. '17 Das Rätsel von Bangalor (co-dir; +co-sc; +art dir); Dornröschen. '19 Die platonische Ehe; Prinz Kuckuck. '20 Patience. '21 Fiesco Die Verschwörung zu Genua. '21 Hintertreppe (co-dir) (Backstairs). '23 Tragödie der Liebe (art dir) (USA/GB: Tragedy of Love). '24 Das Wachsfigurenkabinett (USA: The Three Waxworks; GB: Waxworks). '27 The Cat and the Canary (USA); The Chinese Parrot (USA). '28 The Man Who Laughs (USA); The Last Warning (USA).

LENICA, Jan

(b. 1928). Animator. Born: Poznań, Poland

Lenica studied music and architecture before turning to the graphic arts. He was a magazine illustrator, designed theatre and film posters (winning awards for the latter) and, in 1957, made his first animated film, working at that time in collaboration with Walerian Borowczyk. From 1959 onwards Lenica worked alone, making films in Poland, France, Germany and the USA. His vision is macabre and sardonic, sometimes concerned with a little man lost in a frightening world, sometimes with a dream universe inhabited by flying men, monstrous reptiles and living skeletons. In his film *A*, enormous cut-out letters invade and destroy a peaceful house. Lenica has been compared with the horror writer H.P. Lovecraft and the painter Francis Bacon. His nightmares are certainly as threatening as theirs. Lenica's films have won numerous prizes at international festivals.

Films include: 1957 Strip-Tease (co-dir); Był Sobie Raz (co-dir) (GB: Once Upon a Time). '58 Nagrodzone Uczucie (co-dir) (GB: Requited Feelings/Love Rewarded);

Dom (co-dir) (GB: The House). '59 Monsieur Tête (FR). '61 Nowy Janko Muzykant (Janko the Musician). '62 Labirynt (GB: Labyrinth). '64 Die Nashörner (GER) (GB: Rhinoceros). '65 A (FR). '66 La Femme-Fleur (FR) (GB: Woman Is a Flower). '69 Adam 2. '73 Fantorro, le Dernier Justicier (FR). '74 Landscape (USA). '77 Ubu Roi (GER). '79 Ubu et la Grande Gidouille (FR).

LENYA, Lotte

(1900–1981). Actress/singer. Born: Karoline Blamauer; Vienna, Austria

Lenya made only five films, and 30 years passed between the first one and the second. Her greatness lies as a stage singer, her earthy, passionate voice perfectly attuned to the bitter words of Bertolt Brecht and the sardonic melodies of Lenya's husband Kurt Weill. Her triumph was in *The Threepenny Opera*. On stage she alternated between Lucy and Jenny; in Pabst's film she was Jenny (and rightly, for 'Pirate Jenny' was her greatest song). With the rise of Hitler she and Weill fled to Paris and then New York. Her career was in abeyance until Weill died in 1950. Then she returned, winning a Tony award for *Cabaret*, singing the old songs in a one-woman show, and enjoying herself in occasional movies.

Films: 1931 Die Dreigroschenoper (GER-USA) (GB: The Threepenny Opera). '61 The Roman Spring of Mrs Stone (GB). '63 From Russia With Love (GB). '69 The Appointment (USA). '77 Semi-Tough (USA).

LEONARD, Robert Z.

(1889–1968). Director. Born: Chicago, Illinois, USA

When his family moved to Hollywood in 1907, Leonard, a law student at the University of Colorado, rapidly

LEONE, Sergio

(b. 1921). Director. Born: Rome, Italy

Leone, the son of silent film director Vincenzo Leone, completely revivified the jaded Western in the Sixties, exploiting its traditional characters and situations to create a timeless, savage world peopled by unsmiling, omnipotent heroes and leering, sadistic baddies engaged in ritualistic confrontation. Ennio Morricone's remarkable scores, whistling like the winds in a box canyon, added atmosphere to the proceedings which, though grim in the main, had a certain black humour. Leone entered the Italian film industry at 18, cutting his professional teeth as an assistant on B movies before making his directorial debut with the epic *The Colossus of Rhodes*. He made his first Western, *For a Fistful of Dollars* (a remake of Kurosawa's 1961 samurai film *Yojimbo*) a few years later. It became a box-office blockbuster and made actor Clint Eastwood (till then known only as Rowdy Yates in the television series *Rawhide*) an international star. *For a Few Dollars More*, *The Good the Bad and the Ugly*, and *Once Upon a Time in the West* followed in quick succession, all meeting with huge success. Leone had found a winning formula and astutely stuck to it.

Films include: 1961 Il Colosso di Rodi (IT-SP-FR) (USA/GB: The Colossus of Rhodes). '62 Sodoma e Gomorra (2nd unit dir) (IT-USA) (USA/GB: Sodom and Gomorrah). '64 Per un Pugno di Dollari (IT-GER-SP) (USA/GB: A Fistful of Dollars). '66 Per Qualche Dollaro in Più (IT-GER-SP) (USA/GB: For a Few Dollars More). '67 Il Buono, il Brutto, il Cattivo (USA/GB: The Good, the Bad and the Ugly). '68 C'Era una Volta il West (USA/GB: Once Upon a Time in the West). '72 Giù la Testa (USA: Duck! You Sucker; GB: A Fistful of Dynamite). '83 Once Upon a Time in America (USA).

Above: Joan Leslie in Janie Gets Married *(1945). Right, from left to right: child star Mark Lester in* Eyewitness; *Oscar Levant in* Humoresque; *Jerry Lewis in one of seven roles he played in* The Family Jewels *(1965)*

LERNER, Irving

(1909–1976). Director/producer/editor. Born: New York City, USA

Irving Lerner's first films were made for the anthropology department of Columbia University (where Lerner had formerly been a student). He taught at the Harry Alan Potamkin Film School between 1933 and 1934 and then joined the Rockefeller Foundation's Commission on Human Relations, where he directed and produced progressive documentaries, including *A Place to Live*. During World War II he worked for the Office of War Information, gaining charge of his own film unit. For the rest of his career he alternated between working as an editor on such movies as *God's Little Acre* (1958), *Spartacus* (1960) and *Steppenwolf* (1974) and making taut, low-budget melodramas which tended to be too commercial to become avant-garde classics and too experimental to be box-office hits. They have worn rather better, however, than his one big-budget feature *The Royal Hunt of the Sun*. He died while completing the editing of Martin Scorsese's musical drama *New York, New York* (1977).

Films include: 1941 A Place to Live (doc). **'48** Muscle Beach (doc) (co-dir). **'58** Murder by Contract. **'59** City of Fear. **'60** Studs Lonigan. **'63** Cry of Battle (USA-PHIL). **'69** The Royal Hunt of the Sun (GB).

LeROY, Mervyn

(b. 1900). Director/producer. Born: San Francisco, California, USA

He was six when an earthquake destroyed San Francisco and his father's fortune. Young LeRoy was forced to go to work selling newspapers and after appearing in an amateur play as a singing newsboy he began to enter himself in talent contests, finally ending up in vaudeville. By the early Twenties he was an actor, and decided to go into movies. His first job was as a wardrobe assistant for Famous Players-Lasky and he was soon taking an interest in photography, as well as acting. In the Thirties he joined First National Pictures, a subsidiary of Warner Brothers, and began to direct programme fillers. From there he progressed to features. His hard-edged films usually deal with social problems, although he was quite capable of producing more easy-going entertainment. It was LeRoy who was initially responsible for Warner's supremacy in gangster thrillers and who propelled Edward G. Robinson to stardom in films such as *Little Caesar* and *Five Star Final*. He also made the superb *I Am a Fugitive From a Chain Gang*, starring Paul Muni as the innocent convict who's forced to go on the run. In 1933 LeRoy's vaudeville experience came to his aid and another innovatory series for Warners was launched with the musical *Gold Diggers of 1933*. Finding himself needing larger and larger budgets, he joined MGM in 1938 and became one of their most respected producers. *The Wizard of Oz* was his most successful venture there. During the Fifties he set up his own production company and in the mid-Sixties retired to write his autobiography *Mervyn LeRoy: Take One*. He claimed: 'I never let anything in my private life show in my work . . . at times of stress or tragedy, your work is your staff.'

Films include: 1930 Little Caesar. **'31** Gentleman's Fate; Five Star Final. **'32** I Am a Fugitive From a Chain Gang. **'33** Hard to Handle; Tugboat Annie; Gold Diggers of 1933. **'39** The Wizard of Oz (prod. only). **'41** Johnny Eager. **'42** Random Harvest. **'49** Little Women. **'51** Quo Vadis? **'55** Mister Roberts (co-dir). **'59** The FBI Story. **'62** Gypsy. **'65** Moment to Moment.

LESLIE, Joan

(b. 1925). Actress. Born: Joan Brodel; Detroit, Michigan, USA

A child entertainer, Leslie made her first stage appearance at the age of two. Later she was part of a vaudeville act with her two older sisters and they sang and danced their way all over Canada and the eastern coast of the USA. She was spotted by an MGM scout and chosen to play Robert Taylor's little sister in *Camille*. Soon she was contracted to Warner Brothers where she appeared in such films as *High Sierra* (as the crippled teenager befriended by ex-con Humphrey Bogart) and *Sergeant York*. Throughout her career she found it difficult to play anything other than goody-goody roles. A devout Catholic, she was deeply involved in doing good works and, in 1948, was named 'Girl of the Year' by the Catholic Youth Organization.

Films include: 1936 Camille. **'41** High Sierra; Sergeant York. **'42** The Male Animal; Yankee Doodle Dandy. **'43** The Sky's the Limit. **'44** Hollywood Canteen. **'45** Rhapsody in Blue. **'56** The Revolt of Mamie Stover.

LESTER, Mark

(b. 1958). Actor. Born: Oxford, England

Lester was acting in television commercials at two-and-a-half and in features at six. He became a big star as a sensitive but plucky lead in *Oliver!*, and appeared in several similar movie roles, becoming the world's highest-paid child actor. Perhaps his most interesting role was in *Night Hair Child*. He was cast against type as a demonic child who murders his mother and sleeps with his stepmother (Britt Ekland); this plot made the film something of a *succès de scandale*

at the time. Aged 18, Lester appeared in the dual title role of *The Prince and the Pauper*, a star-studded adaptation of Mark Twain's novel in which at least he was not alone in looking hopelessly awkward.

Films include: 1967 Our Mother's House. **'68** Oliver! **'69** Run Wild, Run Free. **'70** Eyewitness (USA: Sudden Terror). **'71** Melody/SWALK; Black Beauty. **'72** Night Hair Child (USA: What the Peeper Saw); Whoever Slew Auntie Roo? (USA: Who Slew Auntie Roo?). **'73** Scalawag (USA-IT). **'77** The Prince and the Pauper (PAN) (USA: Crossed Swords).

LESTER, Richard

(b. 1932). Director. Born: Philadelphia, Pennsylvania, USA

Lester, the son of a playwright and Hollywood scriptwriter, studied psychology at the University of Pennsylvania, then rapidly worked his way to the position of director with CBS television. He travelled extensively around Europe, settling in England in the mid-Fifties and resuming his career as a director, this time with Independent Television. He made three television shows with the Goons comedy team – Peter Sellers, Spike Milligan and Harry Secombe – making his film debut with an innovative short for which he also wrote the music, *The Running, Jumping and Standing Still Film* (1960). A flair for directing comedy, an interest in pop music and fashion and a flashy film-making technique made him an ideal choice for the Beatles' films *A Hard Day's Night* and *Help!*, the first of which, spurred by the energy of the Beatles' songs, rattled along at a breathless pace, full of wisecracks and neat satire. The second, however, was sprawling and gimmick-ridden, qualities which became increasingly evident in Lester's work, in particular *How I Won the War* (a cult film solely

because of John Lennon's appearance in it) and *The Bed Sitting Room*. The failure of these films led to Lester working as a director of television commercials in France and Italy for several years. He then returned to features, his enthusiasm renewed, to make several excellent popular entertainment movies, including *The Three Musketeers, Juggernaut* and *Robin and Marian*. His handling of *Superman II*, however, showed signs of a relapse into tedious parody.

Films include: 1962 It's Trad, Dad. '64 A Hard Day's Night. '65 The Knack. '66 Help! '67 How I Won the War. '68 Petulia (USA). '69 The Bed Sitting Room. '73 The Three Musketeers: the Queen's Diamonds (PAN). '74 Juggernaut (USA). '75 The Four Musketeers: the Revenge of Milady (PAN-SP). '76 Robin and Marian (USA). '80 Superman II (USA). '83 Superman III.

LEVANT, Oscar

(1906–1972). Pianist/composer/actor. Born: Pittsburgh, Pennsylvania, USA

Levant regarded himself primarily as a concert pianist, with acting in movies coming low down on his scale of priorities. He studied music with Stojovski and Schoenberg, played piano in various dance bands and became a close friend of the composer George Gershwin and a leading interpreter of his works. He went to Hollywood in the late Twenties composing music for several, largely forgotten films. His ready wit endeared him to radio audiences and he began to appear regularly in movies in the Forties. His first major role, as the comic foil for Bing Crosby and Mary Martin in *Rhythm on the River*, was specially written for him. In *Rhapsody in Blue*, the story of Gershwin, he played himself and performed some of Gershwin's music. Though his performance was praised by critics, Levant insisted that he was 'horribly

miscast'. He was clearly happiest playing himself, and did so to great effect in *An American in Paris* as a bohemian composer who patches up a lovers' tiff between Gene Kelly and Leslie Caron. Levant made a point of parading his many insecurities and neuroses in public, particularly on television chat shows, so perhaps the best memory of this talented man is of him joyfully living out all his fantasies as the simultaneous player, conductor and highly appreciative audience of a Gershwin concerto in one of the great set-pieces from that film. He was the author of three semi-autobiographical books, the titles of which alone bear witness to his special brand of humour – *A Smattering of Ignorance, The Importance of Being Oscar* and *The Memoirs of an Amnesiac*.

Films include: 1940 Rhythm on the River. '41 Kiss the Boys Goodbye. '45 Rhapsody in Blue. '46 Humoresque. '49 The Barclays of Broadway. '51 An American in Paris. '52 O. Henry's Full House (GB: Full House); The 'I Don't Care' Girl. '53 The Band Wagon.

LEVIN, Henry

(1909–1980). Director. Born: Trenton, New Jersey, USA

Levin's parents ran a theatrical boarding house, so it is not surprising that he was a frequent performer in vaudeville and amateur shows throughout his youth. He studied economics at the University of Pennsylvania and worked as a bond-trader on Wall Street until, in the mid-Thirties, he turned to directing and acting with small theatre companies. A job with Columbia as a dialogue coach in 1941 led him into film direction and he rapidly acquired a reputation for slick consistency, making 52 features and working with most of the major studios. His films range from tough thrillers such as *The Corpse Came COD* (starring George Brent and

Joan Blondell), musicals like *Jolson Sings Again*, and Westerns such as *The Lonely Man* (starring Jack Palance), to the epic fantasy of *Journey to the Center of the Earth*. He died from a heart-attack on the last day of shooting *Scouts' Honour* for NBC television.

Films include: 1947 The Corpse Came COD. '48 The Mating of Millie. '49 Jolson Sings Again. '52 Belles on Their Toes. '57 April Love; The Lonely Man. '59 Journey to the Center of the Earth. '64 Honeymoon Hotel. '65 Genghis Khan (USA-GER-YUG).

LEVINE, Joseph, E.

(b. 1905). Producer. Born: Boston, Massachussetts, USA

Joseph E. Levine is the last of the Hollywood movie moguls. He worked his way up from obscurity (he was raised in a poor quarter of Boston) to hold a powerful position in a film industry mainly dominated by big-business conglomerates. He ventured into motion pictures in 1938, buying into an art-house cinema in New Haven, Connecticut. He then formed Embassy Films which initially specialized in the distribution of Italian neo-realist films such as *Roma, Città Aperta* (1945, *Rome, Open City*) and *Ladri di Biciclette* (1948, *Bicycle Thieves*). However, it was as the promoter of Italian epics like *Le Fatiche di Ercole* (1958, *Hercules*) and *Ercole e la Regina di Lidia* (1959, *Hercules Unchained*) that he made his name. He used the vast profits he made from these movies to back less commercial films such as – in 1961 – De Sica's *La Ciociara (Two Women)*, Germi's *Divorzio all'Italiana (Divorce – Italian Style)* and Fellini's *Otto e Mezzo* (1963, $8\frac{1}{2}$) and moved into production. He scored his first major screen success with *The Graduate* and continued to alternate between expensive, star-studded films and those with minority appeal. Embassy Films merged with the Avco Corporation in the late Sixties, and Levine became president. He left Avco-Embassy in 1974 to form Joseph E. Levine Presents. Though he has achieved great success as a producer, he has perhaps made a greater contribution to film-making as an innovative and daring distributor, helping to bring a wide range of foreign films before the American public.

Films include: 1964 The Carpetbaggers. '66 Nevada Smith. '67 The Graduate; The Producers. '68 The Lion in Winter (GB). '70 Soldier Blue. '71 Carnal Knowledge. '73 The Day of the Dolphin. '74 Il Portiere di Notte (IT) (USA/GB: The Night Porter). '77 A Bridge Too Far. '78 Magic (co-prod).

LEWIN, Albert

(1898–1968). Director/producer/screenwriter. Born: New York City, USA

Brought up in Newark, New Jersey, Lewin graduated from Harvard and started work as a teacher at the University of Missouri. His first film scenario was accepted in 1924, and work with MGM followed. Personal assistant to Irving Thalberg, Lewin moved to Paramount in 1937 when

Thalberg died, and then struck out on his own. His first film as director, *The Moon and Sixpence* displayed the literary style and interesting approach to narration and dialogue which were to characterize his best work. A heart attack forced him to retire from directing prematurely. But he continued writing for the screen in the Sixties, concluding with *The Wicked Dreams of Paula Schultz* (1968).

Films include: 1942 The Moon and Sixpence. '45 The Picture of Dorian Gray. '47 The Private Affairs of Bel Ami. '51 Pandora and the Flying Dutchman (GB). '53 Saadia. '57 The Living Idol (USA-MEX).

LEWIS, Jerry

(b. 1926). Actor/director. Born: Joseph Levitch; Newark, New Jersey, USA

Lewis in his looniest moments appeared to prove irrefutably that man had indeed descended from apes, and crazy apes at that. He was also a very funny comic whose child-like zaniness might now seem over the top, but to Fifties audiences there were few funnymen who could match him. Lewis teamed up with singer Dean Martin in 1946 and over the next decade they made 16 films together. But Martin tired of playing the straight man (and Lewis probably tired of his partner's cruel asides) and they split up. On his own, Lewis appeared in a number of comedies directed by Frank Tashlin before undertaking writing, producing and directing his own films which included *The Bellboy* (1960), *The Nutty Professor* (1963) and *The Patsy* (1964).

Films include: 1949 My Friend Irma. '50 At War With the Army. '52 Jumping Jacks; The Stooge. '53 Money From Home. '55 You're Never Too Young; Artists and Models. '56 Hollywood or Bust. '58 The Geisha Boy; Rock-a-Bye Baby. '60 Cinderfella. '70 One More Time (dir) (USA-GB). '82 King of Comedy.

LEWIS, Joseph H.

(b. 1900). Director. Born: New York City, USA

A director whose output consisted almost entirely of B movies, Lewis made some interesting films. He began his Hollywood career at MGM, progressed to the editing rooms, and finally got a job as a second-unit director in 1937. His first features followed shortly thereafter and were produced at a rate of two a year. Low on budget, poorly scripted and high on action, the best of them boast striking lighting effects and a tense, paranoic atmosphere. *Gun Crazy*, a Forties Bonnie-and-Clyde story, has been dubbed 'a tone poem of camera movements'. Lewis later directed episodes for television Westerns like *Gunsmoke* and *The Rifleman*.

Films include: 1942 Secrets of a Co-Ed (GB: Silent Witness); The Mad Doctor of Market Street. '45 My Name Is Julia Ross. '46 So Dark the Night. '49 The Undercover Man; Gun Crazy/Deadly Is the Female. '53 Cry of the Hunted. '55 The Big Combo. '57 The Halliday Brand. '58 Terror in a Texas Town.

LEWTON, Val

(1904–1951). Producer. Born: Vladimir Ivan Leventon; Yalta, Russia

Lewton's name is synonymous with a particular type of horror film – a moody, atmospheric shift away from conventional shock and suspense tactics, which owed more to a probing of the psychology of fear than the visual exploitation of blood and guts. After Columbia University he turned to writing and, eventually, films. Instructed by RKO to make low-budget horror movies he produced a string of compelling and spooky films, beginning with *Cat People* – remade forty years later by Paul Schrader – all of which suggested deeper terrors than they portrayed, and most of which were hugely successful. Unwilling to break a winning formula, RKO attempted to limit Lewton's horizons, which resulted in his departure from the studio with a sense of frustration and disappointment which may well have contributed to the heart attack which killed him at 46.

Films include: 1942 Cat People. '43 I Walked With a Zombie; The Seventh Victim. '44 The Curse of the Cat People; Youth Runs Wild; Mademoiselle Fifi. '45 The Body Snatcher; Isle of the Dead. '46 Bedlam. '51 Apache Drums.

L'HERBIER, Marcel

(1890–1979). Director. Born: Paris, France

A very underrated director, L'Herbier is of great importance in the history of the French cinema, though scarcely known abroad. A retrospective season at the National Film Theatre in London in 1979 helped restore his reputation. The son of a magistrate, and himself trained in the law, L'Herbier became first a theatre reviewer, then film critic, moving into production during World War I. A respected theorist, and champion of film-makers' rights, his features were among the first to stress the importance of form and visual flair, combining technical exactitude with the designs of Cavalcanti and Léger. With the coming of sound his work became uneven and sporadic, and in 1954 he abandoned film in favour of television.

Films include: 1919 Rose France. '24 L'Inhumaine. '25 Feu Mathias Pascal (GB: The Late Mathias Pascal). '28 L'Argent. '30 Le Mystère de la Chambre Jaune. '31 Le Parfum de la Dame en Noir. '37 Forfaiture. '40 La Comédie du Bonheur (IT-FR). '41 Histoire de Rire. '42 La Nuit Fantastique (GB: Fantastic Night); L'Honorable Catherine.

LHOMME, Pierre

(b. 1930). Cinematographer. Born: Boulogne, France

One of the early exponents of *cinéma vérité*, Lhomme's first film, *Le Joli Mai*, consisted largely of unrehearsed interviews with Parisians photographed with a hand-held 16mm camera. Gradually, however, Lhomme moved into the mainstream of French cinema

with films like *L'Armée des Ombres*, a moody, atmospheric, study of the French Resistance, using blue-grey colour to good sombre effect which established his reputation as a visual stylist of note. He has since worked with many leading directors, including Robert Bresson.

Films include: 1963 Le Joli Mai (GB: The Lovely Month of May). '66 Le Roi de Coeur (FR-IT) (USA/GB: King of Hearts). '68 La Chamade (FR-IT) (USA/GB: Heartbeat). '69 L'Armée des Ombres (FR-IT) (USA/GB: The Army in the Shadows). '71 Quatre Nuits d'un Rêveur (FR-IT) (USA/GB: Four Nights of a Dreamer). '73 La Maman et la Putain (USA/GB: The Mother and the Whore). '74 Sweet Movie (FR-CAN-GER). '75 La Solitude du Chanteur de Fond; Le Sauvage (FR-IT); La Chair de l'Orchidée (FR-IT-GER). '77 L'Ombre des Châteaux; Dites-Lui que Je T'Aime (GB: This Sweet Sickness). '78 Judith Therpauve. '81 Quartet (GB-FR).

LILLIE, Beatrice

(b. 1894). Actress. Born: Constance Sylvia Munston; Toronto, Canada

She was a scintillating, zany comedienne whose life story reads like the plot of one of her light-hearted revues. The daughter of a government official and a concert singer, Lillie made her debut at 15 singing with her mother. A trip to England in 1914 resulted in a leading part in the stage production *The Daring of Diane*, and she soon established herself as a top showgirl. In 1920 she met and married Sir Robert Peel. Although she started making films shortly thereafter, clowning superbly in the silent *Exit Smiling*, she has always said that the movies came second to her first love, the live stage. As a result her film appearances have been high in quality but lacking in quantity.

Films include: 1926 Exit Smiling. '29 The Show of Shows. '30 Are You There? '38 Dr Rhythm. '44 On Approval (GB). '50 Scrapbook for 1933 (GB). '56 Around the World in 80 Days. '67 Thoroughly Modern Millie.

LINCOLN, Elmo

(1889–1952). Actor. Born: Otto Elmo Linkenhelt; Rochester, Indiana, USA

Big and beefy, possessor of 'the largest chest in Hollywood' (53 inches when expanded), Lincoln intended at the time he left home aged 15 to become an engineer. Instead he ended up playing fairly insignificant strongman parts in early silents, until D. W. Griffith picked him for *The Birth of a Nation*. A variety of work followed, all of it exploiting Lincoln's physique, but most important was the title role in the first *Tarzan of the Apes*. This was a huge success and several sequels followed, but Lincoln felt uneasy acting and acquired a reputation for being temperamental. He worked only sporadically in films thereafter, but in 1950 toured with a circus as 'The Original Tarzan'. He was working as an extra for Columbia at the time of his death from a heart attack.

Films include: 1915 The Birth of a Nation. '16 Intolerance. '18 Tarzan of the Apes;

Romance of Tarzan. '19 Elmo the Mighty (serial); The Fire Flingers. '20 Under Crimson Skies/The Beach Comber. '21 The Adventures of Tarzan (serial). '27 The King of the Jungle (serial). '39 Colorado Sunset.

LINDBLOM, Gunnel

(b. 1931). Actress. Born: Göteborg, Sweden

One of Ingmar Bergman's stock company of actresses, Lindblom was working at the City Theatre in Göteborg when the director discovered her. She worked with Bergman both on the stage and in film and her reputation chiefly rests on the five typically intense, brooding films she made with him. So darkly striking was she as the nymphomaniac in *The Silence* that 20th Century-Fox lured her to America, but only one film, *Rapture*, emerged before she returned to Sweden. As well as much stage work, still with Bergman, she has appeared in Mai Zetterling's *The Girls*, and her own directoral debut, *Summer Paradise*, a likeable study of women's role in society and the family, reveals the influence of her mentors.

Films include: 1952 Kärlek. '57 Det Sjunde Inseglet (USA/GB: The Seventh Seal); Smultronstället (USA/GB: Wild Strawberries). '60 Jungfrukällan (USA/GB: Virgin Spring). '63 Nattvardsgästerna (USA/GB: Winter Light); Tystnaden (USA/GB: The Silence). '64 Älskande Par (USA/GB: Loving Couples). '65 Rapture (USA-FR). '68 Flickorna (USA/GB: The Girls). '69 Fadern (GB: The Father). '77 Paradistorg (dir; +co-sc. only) (USA/GB: Summer Paradise). '81 Sally och Friheten (dir; +co-sc. only).

LINDER, Max

(1883–1925). Actor/director. Born: Gabriel-Maximilien Leuvielle; Cavenne, Bordeaux, France

Perhaps the first truly international star of the silent era, Max Linder and his comedy creation – Max, the debonair, woman-chasing playboy – were hugely popular on both sides of the Atlantic. Linder had started working on shorts for Pathé in 1905, and five years later he was their top star, making films at a rate of one a week. Active service in World War I, however, left him physically depleted and subject to depression. An early trip to America to work for Essanay was marred by language difficulties, and poor health forced his return to France. Although his films there were as popular as ever, his depression deepened, heightened by a disastrous return to the States in the early Twenties. In 1925 he died tragically in a suicide pact with his young wife Hélène; his daughter Maud has done much to keep his memory alive with her compilation film *En Compagnie de Max Linder* (1963).

Films include: 1905 Le Première Sortie d'un Collégien (act. only). '06 Les Débuts d'un Patineur (act. only) (GB: Max's Ice Scream). '09 Max Aéronaute. '10 Le Cauchemar de Max (dir; +sc; +act); Max Cherche une Fiancée (dir; +sc; +act) (GB: Max in Search of a Sweetheart). '11 Max Se Marie (dir; +sc; +act); Max dans Sa Famille (doc)

(dir; +sc; +act). '17 Max Comes Across (dir; +sc; +act) (USA); Max Wants a Divorce (dir; +sc; +act) (USA). '22 The Three Must-Get-Theres (dir; +sc; +act) (USA). '23 Au Secours! (co-sc; +act) (GB: The Haunted House). '24 Der Zirkuskönig (co-dir; +co-sc; +act) (A) (GB: Circusmania).

LINDFORS, Viveca

(b. 1920). Actress. Born: Uppsala, Sweden

Lindfors' childhood stood her in good stead for her subsequent international career. The daughter of an army officer, she travelled extensively, and became proficient in English, German and French. After three years at Stockholm's Royal Dramatic School, she entered films. Working in Italy she achieved a reputation as the highest paid Swedish star ever. In 1946 she went to Hollywood, but the parts she was offered seldom made the most of her talent and strong personality. She moved to New York and the stage, and won three awards for the title role in *Anastasia*. Although she has made several movies since, she has preferred stage and television, touring with her one-woman show, *I Am a Woman*.

Films include: 1940 Snurriga Familjen. '41 Tänk, Om Jag Gifter Mig Med Prästen. '44 Appassionata. '48 To the Victor (USA). '49 Night Unto Night (USA); The Adventures of Don Juan (USA). '50 Backfire (USA); No Sad Songs for Me (USA). '55 Moonfleet. '58 I Accuse (GB). '62 The Damned (GB) (USA: These Are the Damned). '73 The Way We Were (USA). '76 Welcome to LA (USA). '78 A Wedding (USA). '82 Creepshow (USA).

LISI, Virna

(b. 1937). Actress. Born: Virna Lisa Pieralisi; Ancona, Italy

Virna Lisi is best known to English and American audiences for playing bubbly, sexy types such as the over-

Above, from left to right: Beatrice Lillie in her finest film, Exit Smiling; Elmo Lincoln, the first ever Tarzan in Tarzan of the Apes; Max Linder as Max, the man-about-town (just mad about girls) who featured in many films; Virna Lisi in How to Murder Your Wife

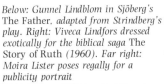

Below: Gunnel Lindblom in Sjöberg's The Father, adapted from Strindberg's play. Right: Viveca Lindfors dressed exotically for the biblical saga The Story of Ruth (1960). Far right: Moira Lister poses regally for a publicity portrait

whelmingly affectionate blonde appearing opposite Jack Lemmon in *How to Murder Your Wife*. She is indeed a very beautiful blue-eyed blonde, but her abilities as an actress have probably been blurred by her dazzling good looks. She has in fact played a wide range of roles in Europe – where she progressed from small supporting parts to become a glamorous star of the Sixties. Her career began when she was studying at business school at the age of 16 and she was offered a film by a producer friend of her parents. From 1953 onwards she appeared in many Italian films in roles decorative rather than dramatic, but nevertheless proved herself a competent actress. She spent two years working in Hollywood but found the typecasting stifling and returned to France, Italy and England where she was able to find a much greater variety of film work.

Films include: 1954 E Napoli Canta; La Corda d'Acciaio. '61 Romolo e Remo (USA/GB: Duel of the Titans). '64 La Tulipe Noire (FR-IT-SP) (USA/GB: The Black Tulip). '65 Casanova '70 (IT-FR); How to Murder Your Wife (USA). '66 Assault on a Queen (USA); Not With My Wife, You Don't! (USA). '67 La Vingt-Cinquième Heure (FR-IT-YUG) (USA/GB: The Twenty-Fifth Hour). '71 The Statue (USA). '72 Barbe-Bleue (FR-IT-GER) (USA/GB: Bluebeard).

LISTER, Moira

(b. 1923). Actress. Born: Cape Town, South Africa

Having made her stage debut while visiting England as a child, Moira Lister returned when she was 20 to pursue her stage career. From that time onwards she worked continually in the public eye – touring with John Gielgud, writing for the *Daily Mail*, appearing in South Africa and Australia in her own one-woman show, working on television and making numerous films. Her rather sophisticated though petulant good looks often resulted in her being given unsympathetic 'other woman' roles. Despite this she has always remained popular and is still much in demand as a radio and television personality.

Films include: 1943 The Shipbuilders. '46 Wanted for Murder. '48 Uneasy Terms; Once a Jolly Swagman (USA: Maniacs on Wheels). '51 Pool of London. '53 The Cruel Sea; Trouble in Store. '55 The Deep Blue Sea. '64 The Yellow Rolls Royce. '67 Stranger in the House. '73 Not Now Darling.

267

LITVAK, Anatole

(1902–1974). Director/writer/producer. Born: Kiev, Russia

Anatole Litvak made a wide variety of films from love dramas to war movies, and all had considerable conviction and power. *The Snake Pit*, for example, was a film so telling that it prompted changes in the laws regarding the treatment of mental illness. Litvak began working in the theatre as a stage hand at the age of 13, and became involved in all aspects of stage craft including acting. In 1925 he went to Berlin, where he worked as an assistant to G. W. Pabst on *Die freudlose Gasse* (1925, *The Joyless Street*), and made countless shorts for Ufa. A brief spell in Paris in the mid–Thirties resulted in his famous version of *Mayerling* with Charles Boyer. By 1940 he had become an American citizen, having moved there four years earlier, and was working very successfully for Warner Brothers. During World War II he enlisted and rose to the rank of colonel, as well as working with the director Frank Capra on the *Why We Fight* series of films. After the war his career remained stable but by 1949 he had returned to Europe, where he remained, living primarily in Paris, although his masterpiece *Decision Before Dawn*, about the Nazis during World War II, was made in Germany.

Films include: 1930 Dolly macht Karrierre (GER). '32 Coeur de Lilas (FR) (+co-sc). '33 Sleeping Car (GB). '35 L'Equipage (FR) (+co-sc). '36 Mayerling (FR). '37 The Woman I Love (GB: The Woman Between); Tovarich. '38 The Amazing Dr Clitterhouse; The Sisters. '39 Confessions of a Nazi Spy. '40 All This, and Heaven Too. '48 The Snake Pit (+co-prod). '51 Decision Before Dawn. '55 The Deep Blue Sea (+co-prod) (GB). '56 Anastasia (GB). '61 Goodbye Again (+prod) (USA-FR). '67 The Night of the Generals (GB-FR).

LIVESEY, Roger

(1906–1976). Actor. Born: Barry, Glamorgan, Wales

The sound, worthy, understated but unmistakable Britishness of Roger Livesey helped him to achieve great popularity during the war years and beyond. Educated at Westminster School and then the Italia Conti Drama School, he had made his stage debut at the age of 11, and during the Twenties and Thirties established himself as a reliable, talented though not especially brilliant star of stage and screen. During the Forties he excelled himself in a series of Powell and Pressburger movies, particularly in *A Matter of Life and Death*, in which he played the motorcycling brainsurgeon. His real *tour de force* was in *The Life and Death of Colonel Blimp*, ageing from dashing young subaltern to bald elderly officer. One of his later roles was a superb cameo as the father of *The Entertainer* (Laurence Olivier), playing a music-hall performer still able to bring the audience to its feet. Towards the end of his career he concentrated on stage and television work, particularly the *Justice* television series with Margaret Lockwood.

Films include: 1934 Lorna Doone. '35 Midshipman Easy. '36 Rembrandt. '38 The Drum. '41 49th Parallel (USA: The Invaders). '43 The Life and Death of Colonel Blimp (USA: Colonel Blimp). '45 I Know Where I'm Going. '46 A Matter of Life and Death (USA: Stairway to Heaven). '60 The Entertainer. '65 The Amorous Adventures of Moll Flanders.

LIZZANI, Carlo

(b. 1917). Director/writer. Born: Rome, Italy

Carlo Lizzani is one of the few Italian directors whose work has become known internationally. He is recognized for his realist, documentary style and his commitment to Marxism, though this has often distracted critics from the merits of his films. Lizzani fought with the resistance during World War II, and he belonged to the group of young writers who wrote for the two leading Italian journals *Bianco e Nero* and *Cinema*. He was also an early neo-realist. He entered films in 1946 as a scriptwriter and director, working with other neo-realists such as Aldo Vergano, Giuseppe De Santis and Roberto Rossellini. He had completed numerous documentaries and shorts by the time he directed his first feature *Achtung! Banditi!* in 1952. Since then, in addition to his politically motivated films, he has made full-length documentaries, and some strictly commercial movies with Dino De Laurentiis and MGM, as well as 'spaghetti' Westerns under the pseudonym Lee W. Beaver.

Films include: 1952 Achtung! Banditi! '53 Amore in Città ep L'Amore Che Si Paga. '54 Cronache di Poveri Amanti. '61 Il Gobbo (IT-FR) (USA/GB: The Hunchback of Rome). '63 Il Processo di Verona. '65 La Guerra Segreta (co-dir) (IT-FR-GER) (USA: The Dirty Game). '66 Svegliati e Uccidi (FR-IT). '67 Un Fiume di Dollari (USA/GB: The Hills). '68 Banditi a Milano. '71 Roma Bene. '78 Kleinhoff Hotel.

LLOYD, Frank

(1886–1960). Director. Born: Glasgow, Scotland

A truly professional film-maker, Frank Lloyd was unpretentious about his craft. Yet many of his films were

among the most famous Hollywood films of the Thirties and have proved to be of lasting merit. Lloyd had been involved in the theatre in Britain so when he left for Canada in 1909 to find work it is not surprising that he joined a travelling theatre company. By 1913 he had arrived in Hollywood, where he began working as an actor at Universal. In the years leading up to the Thirties he learnt his trade, writing and directing for various studios. During World War II he commanded a unit of cameramen overseas. In 1946 he retired, but he returned to film-making six years later after the death of his first wife, actress Alma Heller. He received two Best Director Academy Awards, for *The Divine Lady* and *Cavalcade*, and his film *Mutiny on the Bounty* was voted Best Picture in 1935.

Films include: 1915 The Bay of Seven Islands; The Toll of Youth; Billie's Baby. '16 The Call of the Cumberlands; Sins of Her Parents. '19 Les Miserables. '22 Oliver Twist. '24 The Sea Hawk. '29 The Divine Lady; Drag. '31 East Lynne. '32 A Passport to Hell (GB: Burnt Offering). '33 Cavalcade. '35 Mutiny on the Bounty. '36 Under

Above left: Roger Livesey in I Know Where I'm Going, *a love story with a Scottish setting. Above: Harold Lloyd in trouble as usual in* Hot Water *(1924). Below: Sondra Locke, Clint Eastwood's favourite actress, in* The Gauntlet

Two Flags. '37 Wells Fargo. '41 The Lady From Cheyenne. '54 Shanghai Story. '55 The Last Command.

LLOYD, Harold

(1893–1971). Actor. Born: Burchard, Nebraska, USA

After appearing in Nebraska with various visiting stock companies, Lloyd decided to enter the theatre and enrolled at the School of Dramatic Art in San Diego. He began to play extras in films for Edison and then joined up with Hal Roach to create the comic character Willie Work. A short sortie into the Keystone empire was uneventful, and on returning to Roach Lloyd created Lonesome Luke, largely based on Charlie Chaplin's Tramp. Towards the end of 1917 Lloyd decided to create a more individual trademark and the 'glasses' character was born. Bespectacled, with a three-piece-suit and straw hat, his unassuming figure attained a scholarly look that belied the bizarre and dangerous situations he always found

Above: Gene Lockhart in Down Among the Sheltering Palms *(1953), a South Pacific-style love story. Right: Margaret Lockwood in her most famous role as* The Wicked Lady. *Below: John Loder in* Ourselves Alone *(1936)*

himself in – such as hanging several hundred feet above Los Angeles in *Safety Last*. The humour is based on the naivety and optimism of the all-American boy and, unlike the response to Chaplin's films, the laughter emanates more from the unlikely situations than from emotional involvement. Lloyd's comedies were extremely popular in their day and made him a very rich man – and one of the best loved comics of all time.

Films include: 1922 Grandma's Boy; Doctor Jack. '23 Safety Last. '24 Girl Shy. '25 The Freshman (GB: College Days). '26 For Heaven's Sake. '27 The Kid Brother. '28 Speedy. '32 Movie Crazy. '34 The Cat's Paw. '36 The Milky Way. '46 The Sin of Harold Diddlebock (reissued as Mad Wednesday, 1950).

LOACH, Ken

(b. 1936). Director. Born: Nuneaton, Warwickshire, England

A law student at Oxford, Ken Loach was also president of the Experimental Theatre Club. On leaving university he worked as an actor before becoming a director in rep. He then moved on to directing in fringe theatre before joining the BBC in 1961 as a trainee director. He had been working on the police drama series *Z Cars* when he teamed up with producer Tony Garnett, with whom he enjoyed a very fruitful collaboration on a series of television plays, which led to his chance to direct features. In contrast to his committed political dramas for television, many of his films are about the young, such as *Kes*, *Black Jack* and *Looks and Smiles*, although they have been no less biting and thought-provoking because of this. During the eight-year gap between the films *Family Life* and *Black Jack* Loach's television output remained substantial. Most notable was *Days of Hope*.

Films include: 1967 Poor Cow. '69 Kes. '71 Family Life (USA: Wednesday's Child). '79 Black Jack. '81 Looks and Smiles.

LOCKE, Sondra

(b. 1947). Actress. Born: Shelbyville, Tennessee, USA

Community theatre work led to her first screen role as a young girl who befriends a deaf mute (Alan Arkin) in *The Heart Is a Lonely Hunter*, and she earned herself an Oscar nomination into the bargain. A few years in minor movies and television followed before she was noticed again – in the rat-infested horror film *Willard* – and then, beginning with *The Outlaw Josey Wales*, she became Clint Eastwood's frail, blonde leading lady and, in real life, his girlfriend. *The Gauntlet*, in which she starred as a hooker whom Eastwood's has-been cop has to escort from jail to court, subsequently gave Locke her best chance to steal some of Clint's thunder.

Films include:1968 The Heart Is a Lonely Hunter. '71 Willard. '73 A Reflection of Fear. '74 The Second Coming of Suzanne. '76 The Outlaw Josey Wales. '77 The Gauntlet. '78 Every Which Way But Loose. '80 Bronco Billy; Any Which Way You Can.

LOCKHART, Gene

(1891–1957). Actor. Born: London, Ontario, Canada

Lockhart began his career as a singer and songwriter but soon became one of Hollywood's most eminent character actors. Equally at ease in villainous or crooked parts and in kindly or benevolent ones, he has been compared to Cecil Kellaway and Charles Coburn. His wife Kathleen and daughter June have both also appeared in many films.

Films include: 1922 Smilin' Through. '34 By Your Leave. '36 Mind Your Business. '38 Algiers. '39 Blackmail. '41 All That Money Can Buy/The Devil and Daniel Webster; Meet John Doe. '43 Hangmen Also Die! '45 The House on 92nd Street. '47 Miracle on 34th Street (GB: The Big Heart). '49 The

Inspector General. '56 Carousel; The Man in the Gray Flannel Suit.

LOCKWOOD, Margaret

(b. 1916). Actress. Born: Margaret Day; Karachi, India

Lockwood was the best villainess British cinema ever had. In *The Wicked Lady*, she was gloriously tarty as the highborn girl who becomes a highwaywoman, and her succumbing to James Mason in that film was a shocking thing for Forties audiences. She was paired with Mason in *The Man in Grey*, too, their dark, cruel looks and immoral behaviour making them the most popular stars in Britain. But Lockwood's lovely but witchlike features, her cleavage and beauty spot limited her dramatic chances, and when she broke from type to give a fine acting performance as a straight-talking barmaid in *Cast a Dark Shadow* it damaged her career, and she left films for the stage and television. She returned for the part of Cinderella's stepmother in *The Slipper and the Rose* in 1975. Lockwood had attended the Italia Conti Drama School and RADA. Her stage debut was as a fairy in *A Midsummer Night's Dream* in 1928 and her first film *Lorna Doone* six years later. At first she played girl-next-door roles until her cheeky, headstrong heroine in Hitchcock's *The Lady Vanishes* made her a star.

Films include: 1934 Lorna Doone. '37 Doctor Syn. '38 Bank Holiday; The Lady Vanishes. '39 The Stars Look Down. '43 The Man in Grey. '44 Give Us the Moon. '45 The Wicked Lady. '46 Bedelia. '47 Jassy. '55 Cast a Dark Shadow. '75 The Slipper and the Rose – The Story of Cinderella.

LODER, John

(b. 1898). Actor. Born: John Muir Lowe; London, England

Square-jawed, with brown hair, grey eyes and of large build, John Loder had good parts in a number of prestigious films such as Alfred Hitchcock's *Sabotage*, in which he plays a plain-clothes detective trying to win the confidence of a spy (Oscar Homolka) and the love of his wife (Sylvia Sidney), and John Ford's *How Green Was My Valley*. The son of an army man, he was educated at Eton and Sandhurst before serving in the 15th Hussars during World War I. He was taken prisoner by the Germans and remained there after the war in order to run a pickle factory. It was there that he first became interested in acting and appeared in several German films before returning to England and lead roles in 1927. In 1939 he went to Hollywood where he met his third wife Hedy Lamarr, but Loder was never really star material and he retired to run a lucrative ranch with his fifth wife, Argentinian heiress Alba Larden.

Films include: 1933 The Private Life of Henry VIII. '34 Java Head; Lorna Doone. '36 Sabotage. '37 Dr Syn; King Solomon's Mines. '38 Owd Bob (USA: To the Victor). '41 How Green Was My Valley (USA). '42 Now, Voyager (USA). '58 Gideon's Day (USA: Gideon of Scotland Yard).

LOGAN, Joshua

(b. 1908). Director/playwright. Born: Joshua Lockwood Logan III; Texarkana, Texas, USA

Logan is primarily a man of the theatre whose interest in the cinema peaked in the Fifties, the decade when movies were most influenced by concurrent developments in stage drama. The films he made included *Picnic*, an excellent melodrama starring William Holden and Kim Novak; *Bus Stop*, on which Marilyn Monroe found her most sympathetic director; and *South Pacific*, from his own Pulitzer Prize-winning stage original and one of the most popular musicals of all time. In the Sixties he reconstructed Marcel Pagnol's *Marius* trilogy as *Fanny* and kept up his record for big, lavish musicals with *Camelot*, an unexpected box-office flop, and *Paint Your Wagon*, notable for the singing of Lee Marvin and Clint Eastwood. He'd gone from Culver Military Academy to Princeton University and there won a scholarship to the Moscow Art Theatre to study under the great drama coach Stanislavsky. He was in films as early as 1936, coaching Marlene Dietrich and others on *The Garden of Allah*, but then the theatre claimed him and he has scored many notable successes as actor, playwright and producer on Broadway.

Films include: **1936** The Garden of Allah (dial. dir). '**37** History Is Made at Night (dial. dir); I Met My Love Again (co-dir). '**53** Main Street to Broadway (guest). '**55** Picnic (dir); Mister Roberts (co-sc; co-play basis). '**56** Bus Stop (dir). '**57** Sayonara (dir). '**58** South Pacific (dir). '**60** Tall Story (dir). '**61** Fanny (dir; +prod; +co-play basis). '**64** Ensign Pulver (dir; +prod; +co-sc; +co-play basis). '**67** Camelot (dir). '**69** Paint Your Wagon (dir).

LOLLOBRIGIDA, Gina

(b. 1927). Actress. Born: Subiaco, Italy

The tumbling dark hair, the full and inviting lips, the flared eyes and nose and the luscious body – a man might do a lot for a Lollobrigida. He would ignore the fact that those lips were parted in mockery and that her temper would flare too. Her nickname – 'La Lollo' – spoke of the especially sweet seduction that might be offered by a sultry Italian peasant girl (*Pane, Amore e Fantasia*), a gypsyish circus acrobat (*Trapeze*) or a scantily clad Arabian queen (*Solomon and Sheba*). She played modern-day temptresses and call-girls, too, but that was about the extent of her prescribed range – even though there was a talented actress struggling to get beyond it. The daughter of a furniture-maker, she enrolled at the Rome School of Fine Arts but soon became a model for photographic magazines. The director Mario Costa discovered her and she made her first film in 1946. By the early Fifties she was a star in Europe (her voice being dubbed at first), appearing notably in Christian-Jaque's *Fanfan la Tulipe*, Alessandro Blasetti's *Altri Tempi*, René Clair's *Les Belles de Nuit* and Mario Soldati's *La Provinciale*. Then came the very popular

Pane, Amore e Fantasia, the Hollywood glamour machine and worldwide stardom. In the Sixties she worked in America, Britain, Spain, France and at home but became increasingly typecast as a seductress in weak comedies and thrillers. She now concentrates on her successful career as a photographer and maker of short documentaries and videos.

Films include: **1946** Elisir d'Amore. '**47** Follie per l'Opera. '**52** Fanfan la Tulipe (IT-FR) (GB: The Fearless Little Soldier); Altri Tempi (GB: Infidelity); Les Belles de Nuit (FR-IT) (USA: Beauties of the Night; GB: Night Beauties). '**53** La Provinciale (GB: The Wayward Wife); Beat the Devil (GB-IT). '**54** Le Grand Jeu (IT-FR) (GB: The Card of Fate); Pane, Amore e Fantasia (GB: Bread, Love and Dreams); Pane, Amore e Gelosia (GB: Bread, Love and Jealousy). '**55** La Donna Più Bella del Mondo (GB: Beautiful But Dangerous). '**56** Trapeze (USA). '**58** Anna di Brooklyn (+co-prod) (IT-USA) (USA/GB: Anna of Brooklyn). '**59** Solomon and Sheba (USA). '**61** Go Naked in the World (USA). '**64** Strange Bedfellows (USA). '**68** Buona Sera, Mrs Campbell (USA). '**69** Un Bellissimo Novembre (IT-FR) (USA: That Splendid November). '**75** Portrait of Fidel Castro (doc. short) (dir. only).

LOM, Herbert

(b. 1917). Actor. Born: Herbert Charles Angelo Kuchačevič ze Schluderpacheru; Prague, Czechoslovakia

After attending university in Prague, Lom left Czechoslovakia for England in 1939, where he won scholarships to the Old Vic and Sadler's Wells schools and began broadcasting for the European Service of the BBC. His screen debut was as Hitler in *Mein Kampf My Crimes*, and he subsequently became cast as a European, British-based 'heavy', a type that his appearance – dark hair and eyes and a certain Charles Boyerish manner – encouraged. He was perfect as Napoleon in *The Young Mr Pitt* and *War and Peace*, but then decided to break out of his sinister mould. His playing of a doctor in *And Then There Were None* (1975) led to a similar role in the television series *The Human Jungle* and there was also the Pink Panther

series in which he enjoyed enormous success as the neurotic Inspector Dreyfuss plagued by Peter Sellers' Clouseau. He continues to work on both the large and small screens and is the author of a book about the playwright Christopher Marlowe entitled *Enter the Spy*.

Films include: **1940** Mein Kampf My Crimes. '**42** The Young Mr Pitt. '**45** The Seventh Veil. '**47** Dual Alibi. '**50** The Golden Salamander; Night and the City; State Secret (USA: The Great Manhunt). '**55** The Ladykillers. '**56** War and Peace (IT-USA). '**58** Chase a Crooked Shadow; The Roots of Heaven (USA). '**59** Northwest Passage. '**62** The Phantom of the Opera. '**64** A Shot in the Dark. '**68** Villa Rides (USA). '**78** The Revenge of the Pink Panther.

LOMBARD, Carole

(1908–1942). Actress. Born: Jane Alice Peters; Fort Wayne, Indiana, USA

At 13 she was noticed playing baseball in the street by director Allan Dwan, who gave her the part of a tomboy in *A Perfect Crime*. From high school she went to Fox, survived an automobile accident, and joined the Mack Sennett outfit where she made custard-pie and bathing-belle comedies. The turning point was Howard Hawks' *Twentieth Century* – if Dwan was the first to see that Lombard was one of the boys, then it was Hawks who first allowed her air of sexy superiority to flourish, who first released her acid tongue and her energy for fast oneupmanship in screwball comedy. Lombard became the undisputed queen of that genre – through *My Man Godfrey*, *Hands Across the Table*, *Nothing Sacred*, Hitchcock's *Mr and Mrs Smith* and Lubitsch's *To Be or Not to Be* – yet she was equally at home in straight dramas like *Made for Each Other*. She was a tough, witty, wisecracking blonde, but, though she might kick John Barrymore in the stomach (*Twentieth Century*) and swop punches with Fredric March (*Nothing Sacred*), she was no broad like, say, Jean Harlow: Lombard was beautiful, sophisticated and graceful. Those qualities may have won her her first husband, suave William Powell (even

if he later took up with Harlow); the earthiness and practical joker in her may have won her her second, Clark Gable, to whom she was very happily married from 1939. When, at 34, this delightful actress died in a plane crash, following a successful tour selling war bonds, she was mourned by millions, and the cinema lost one of its great stars. Jill Clayburgh played her, lamely, in *Gable and Lombard* (1976).

Above: Gina Lollobrigida in Go Naked in the World. Right: a publicity shot of Julie London in her heyday as a singer. Below, from left to right: Herbert Lom in Good Time Girl (1948); John Longden in Atlantic; Carole Lombard in Made For Each Other; Sophia Loren in Lady L (1965), which was written and directed by Peter Ustinov

Films include: 1921 A Perfect Crime. '25 Gold and the Girl. '28 The Swim Princess (short). '30 The Arizona Kid. '32 No Man of Her Own. '34 Twentieth Century; Now and Forever; Lady by Choice. '35 Hands Across the Table. '36 Love Before Breakfast; My Man Godfrey. '37 Swing High, Swing Low; Nothing Sacred; True Confession. '39 Made for Each Other. '40 They Knew What They Wanted. '41 Mr and Mrs Smith. '42 To Be or Not to Be.

ŁOMNICKI, Jan

(b. 1929). Director. Born: Poland

After graduating from the film school in Łódź, Łomnicki began his film career as a director with the documentary film studio in Warsaw. The majority of his work has been as documentarist, and he has won many awards for his penetrating studies. *Narodziny Statku* is a poignant essay on the meaning of creative activity as the camera follows the building of a ship from its Dantesque beginnings in the steel foundry to the brilliant day-

light and celebration of launch day. In 1963 he made his debut in feature films with *Wiano*.

Films include: 1956 Mistrz Nikifor. '61 Narodziny Statku. '62 Suita Polska; Kolorow Swiat. '67 Kontrybucja. '69 To Ast. '71 Pawel Wróbel. '74 Nagrody i Odznaczenia. '77 Akcja Pod Arsenlem; Ocalić Miasto (POL-USSR).

LONDON, Julie

(b. 1926). Actress/singer. Born: Julie Peck; Santa Rosa, California, USA

Julie London's first husband, actor-director Jack Webb, once said: 'People forget she was a helluva actress before she ever sung a note'. Certainly London's achievements as a breathy, bluesy vocalist in the Fifties, with a string of fine albums and a smash-hit single to her name. 'Cry Me a River' (which she sang in typically sensual style as Tom Ewell's dream girl in *The Girl Can't Help It*), have overshadowed her acting career. She was discovered working in a Los Angeles store by Alan Ladd's talent-scout wife, Sue Carol, and London subsequently made attractive appearances in several slight melodramas. Dissastisfied with her movie career she began working as a singer in the 881 club in Hollywood, and temporarily gave up film acting. She returned to features in the late Fifties, her roles including the mistress of a radio commentator in *The Great Man* and a dance-hall girl in *Saddle the Wind*. She starred with her second husband, Bobby Troup, in the television series *Emergency*.

Films include: 1945 On Stage Everybody, '47 The Red House. '48 Tap Roots. '49 Task Force. '50 The Return of the Frontiersman. '56 The Great Man; The Girl Can't Help It (as herself). '57 Drango. '58 Saddle the Wind; Man of the West. '59 The Wonderful Country; Night of the Quarter Moon.

LONGDEN, John

(1900–1971). Actor. Born: West Indies

Longden, the son of a Wesleyan minister, worked as a mining engineer in Yorkshire in his teens but gradually found an actor's life more to his liking. Successes in repertory in Liverpool and Birmingham led to roles in silent films. He also starred in two pioneering British talkies, being grave and dogged as Anny Ondra's policeman boyfriend in Hitchcock's *Blackmail* and suitably stiff-upper-lipped as an officer on the Titanic in E. A. Dupont's *Atlantic*. His career faded towards the end of the Thirties, but, despite a drink problem, he continued to appear regularly in small character roles until his retirement in the mid-Sixties. He made a single foray into direction with *Come Into My Parlour* (1932), a thriller co-written with his wife, actress Jean Jay.

Films include: 1929 Blackmail. '30 Atlantic. '31 The Skin Game. '37 Young and Innocent. '38 The Gaunt Stranger (USA: The Phantom Strikes). '41 The Common Touch; The Tower of Terror. '48 Bonnie Prince Charlie. '51 Pool of London. '63 Lancelot and Guinevere (USA: Sword of Lancelot).

LOOS, Anita

(1893–1981). Screenwriter. Born: Sisson, California, USA

Anita Loos' father ran a theatrical newspaper and encouraged Anita in an acting career. However she was determined to be a writer. Her talent was first noticed by the director D. W. Griffith and she accompanied him as a staff-writer from Biograph, first to Mutual then to Triangle studios. Between 1915 and 1917 she scored major successes as the writer of Douglas Fairbanks' movies (the first being *His Picture in the Papers*), witty pieces, satirizing contemporary fads and fashions and directed by her husband-to-be, John Emerson. Anita then left Hollywood for New York, becoming a stylish member of the literary world, a successful playwright and the author of a provocative novel, *Gentlemen Prefer Blondes*, in 1925. The book was filmed in 1928 and 1953, with Ruth Taylor and Alice White, Jane Russell and Marilyn Monroe respectively playing its cheerful, gold-digging heroines. She returned to Hollywood in the late Twenties and joined the writing staff at MGM under Irving Thalberg's supervision, making Jean Harlow a star with her superb script for *Red-Headed Woman*. She worked mainly as a co-author, sharing the screenplay credits on many fine movies, including *San Francisco* (1936) and *The Women* (1939). Following Thalberg's death, she found Hollywood less to her liking and took up residence in New York in the Forties. She continued to write books and plays, scripting, among other things, the musical *Gigi* from the novel by Colette.

Films include: 1916 His Picture in the Papers. '17 The American; Wild and Woolly. '23 Dulcy. '28 Gentlemen Prefer

Blondes. '32 Red-Headed Woman. '33 Hold Your Man. '34 Biography of a Bachelor Girl. '40 Susan and God (GB: The Gay Mrs Trexel). '41 Blossoms in the Dust. '42 I Married an Angel. '53 Gentlemen Prefer Blondes (play basis only).

LOREN, Sophia

(b. 1934). Actress. Born: Sofia Scicolone; Rome, Italy

Loren's rise to international stardom is a publicity man's dream. She was brought up in Puzzuoli, near Naples, the illegitimate child of a would-be actress who encouraged her teenage daughter to enter beauty contests and find work as a model. Sophia became the protegée of producer Carlo Ponti; he helped her obtain bit parts in numerous movies and a lead role in *Aida* (1953), in which her voice was dubbed by prima donna Renata Tebaldi. Her big break came the following year in De Sica's *Gold of Naples*. De Sica's patient direction nurtured her budding dramatic gifts, and her performance brought her wider recognition. Ponti, who married her in 1957, had her learn English and won her a main part in Kramer's *The Pride and the Passion*, with Cary Grant and Frank Sinatra. She went on to grace some routine action films, a neat comedy, *Houseboat*, opposite Grant, and a picaresque Western, *Heller in Pink Tights*, directed by George Cukor. In general her films had up to that point done little to explore her acting talent, touting her as the latest Latin sex-bomb instead. De Sica's *Two Women* changed that, and she won a Best Actress Oscar for her role as a young mother in war-torn Italy. She followed this with a demure, appealing performance in *El Cid* and starred in two more De Sica movies, *Yesterday, Today and Tomorrow* and *Marriage Italian Style*. The early Sixties was the high point of her career; most of her films since then have been disappointing, leaning unfairly on her charm, warmth and resplendent poise. Perhaps the most interesting role was as her own mother in the television adaptation of her biography, *Sophia: Living and Loving*. In 1982 she served a month in prison for income tax irregularities, emerging from detention looking as if she had spent a month in a health farm, and full of indulgent, queenly good humour for the Italian authorities who had had the temerity to convict her.

Films include: 1954 L'Oro di Napoli *ep* Pizze a Credito (USA: Gold of Naples; GB: Every Day's a Holiday/Gold of Naples). '57 The Pride and the Passion (USA). '58 Houseboat (USA). '60 Heller in Pink Tights (USA); The Millionairess (GB). '61 La Ciociara (USA/GB: Two Women); El Cid (USA-IT). '62 Boccaccio '70 *ep* La Riffa (IT-FR). '64 Ieri, Oggi e Domani (USA/GB: Yesterday, Today and Tomorrow); Matrimonio all'Italiana (IT-FR) (USA/GB: Marriage Italian Style). '67 A Countess From Hong Kong (GB); C'Era una Volta (IT-FR) (USA: More Than a Miracle/Once Upon a Time/Happily Ever After; GB: Cinderella – Italian Style). '70 La Moglie del Prete (IT-FR) (USA/GB: The Priest's Wife). '72 Man of La Mancha (USA). '77 Una Giornata Particolare (IT-CAN) (USA/GB: A Special Day).

LORENTZ, Pare

(b. 1905). Director. Born: Clarksburg, Virginia, USA

A former journalist and film critic, Lorentz became one of the American cinema's foremost documentary film-makers with two hugely influential films financed by Roosevelt's 'New Deal' administration in the mid-Thirties – *The Plow that Broke the Plains* and *The River*. The first detailed the plight of farmers in America's Mid-West, which drought had turned into a dust bowl; the second film (which won the documentary prize at the Venice Film Festival) showed how deforestation and overcropping had despoiled the Mississippi valley, climaxing with terrifying shots of the river bursting its eroded banks. Both documentaries approached these economic and ecological problems in a formal, lyrical way, carefully blending music (composed by Virgil Thompson) and narration (by Thomas Chalmers) with visual images to great emotional effect. As head of the US Film Service in 1938, Lorentz provided opportunities for documentarists like Robert Flaherty and Joris Ivens to make films. Lorentz's last film was *The Fight for Life*, showing the problems of childbirth in slum areas. The funds to the US Film Service were abruptly cut off in 1940, and Lorentz moved to RKO as director of production, also making some short films for the armed forces. After World War II he was made Chief of Motion Pictures, Music and Theatre in occupied Germany, helping to plan a documentary on the trials of Nazi war criminals, *Nuremberg/Nürnberg* (1948). He resigned from this post in 1947 and has since only played a minor part in the American film industry.

Films include: 1936 The Plow That Broke the Plains. **'38** The River. **'39** The City (treatment only). **'40** Power and the Land (prod); The Fight for Life.

LORRE, Peter

(1904–1964). Actor. Born: László Löwenstein; Rosenberg, Hungary

Peter Lorre ran away from home at the age of 15 and after working in travelling shows and on the stage in Vienna and Zurich entered films in 1928. Fritz Lang was impressed by what he saw of Lorre in occasional roles as an extra and cast him in his first sound film, *M*, in which Lorre played a psychopathic child murderer. His success lead to his being typecast as a quiet, sinister villain. In 1933 he was forced to flee from Nazi Germany, and he worked briefly in France before arriving in Britain to add a chill to Hitchcock's *The Man Who Knew Too Much*. In Hollywood from 1935, he played the oriental detective Mr Moto in a popular series before appearing in his best-remembered role as the cringing, effeminate Joel Cairo opposite Sydney Greenstreet and Humphrey Bogart in *The Maltese Falcon*. He and Greenstreet appeared together in seven more films, an oddly apt combination with the gross figure of Greenstreet as cool and cruel as the squat Lorre –

with his bulging eyes, nervous twitches and high, wheedling, nasal voice – was sweaty, agitated and vulnerable. Returning to Europe in 1949, Lorre began to produce and direct and continued to travel the world for acting parts until his death from heart failure in 1964. He is said to have enjoyed his all-too-infrequent comedy parts and the few he tackled – for example, in *Arsenic and Old Lace*, *Silk Stockings*, *The Raven* – showed how good he was.

Films include: 1931 M (GER). **'34** The Man Who Knew Too Much (GB). **'35** Mad Love; Crime and Punishment. **'36** The Secret Agent (GB). **'37** Think Fast, Mr Moto. **'38** Mr Moto's Gamble. **'40** Stranger on the Third Floor. **'41** The Maltese Falcon. **'42** Casablanca. **'44** The Mask of Dimitrios; Arsenic and Old Lace. **'45** Confidential Agent. **'51** Die Verlorene (dir) (GER) (USA/GB: The Lost One). **'53** Beat the Devil. **'57** Silk Stockings. **'63** The Raven; The Comedy of Terrors. **'64** The Patsy.

LOSEY, Joseph

(1909–1984). Director. Born: La Crosse, Wisconsin. USA

Losey, a former medical student, came into movies via theatre direction, winning an Oscar for his short film *A Gun in His Hand* (1945). Following his prestigious theatre production of Brecht's *Galileo* starring Charles Laughton, he was signed to RKO by Dore Schary. Losey's first feature was *The Boy With Green Hair*, an allegory about racism. A clear current of social concern ran through his next films, the best of which were the thrillers *The Prowler* and *M* (a remake of Fritz Lang's 1931 movie about the hunt for a child murderer). Losey's progress in Hollywood was abruptly cut short when he was branded a communist by the House Un-American Activities Committee and blacklisted by the studios. He found work in Britain but, apart from his thriller *The Criminal*, his work went largely unnoticed until he teamed up with the playwright Harold Pinter in the Sixties. Together they made *The Servant*, *Accident* and *The Go-Between*, sophisticated and pessimistic studies of the conflict between social role-playing and the fulfilment of personal desires. In these and subsequent works, Losey has shown himself a master at bringing out the best in many extremely talented collaborators, including the cinematographer Gerry Fisher, the designer Carmen Dillon, the composers John Dankworth and Michel Legrand and the actors Dirk Bogarde, Stanley Baker and James and Edward Fox. Since 1974 Losey chose to work mainly in France. His later films tended to founder on the rocks of his own painstaking preoccupation with nuance and detail, lacking the drive of his earlier features. However, a new Losey film was still a major event in international cinema.

Films include: 1948 The Boy With Green Hair. **'51** The Prowler; M. **'56** The Intimate Stranger (under pseudonym; + act) (GB) (USA: Finger of Guilt). **'60** The Criminal (GB) (USA: The Concrete Jungle). **'62** The Damned (GB) (USA: These Are the Damned). **'63** The Servant (GB).

'66 Modesty Blaise (GB). '67 Accident (GB). '71 The Go-Between (GB). '73 A Doll's House (GB-FR). '76 Mr Klein (FR-IT). '80 Don Giovanni (IT-FR-GER). '82 La Truite (FR).

LOUISE, Anita

(1915–1970). Actress. Born: Anita Louise Fremault; New York City, USA

Blonde, blue-eyed and ethereal, Anita Louise has complained that her looks prevented her being considered for serious roles. She made her film debut aged nine under the name of Louise Fremault in *The Six Commandments* (1924). In the Thirties she became a star of costume dramas such as *Madame Du Barry*, *A Midsummer Night's Dream* (as Titania), *The Story of Louis Pasteur*, *Anthony Adverse* and *Marie Antoinette* without making any really lasting impression, aside from being extremely decorative. In 1940 she married Buddy Adler, who was head of production at 20th Century-Fox from 1956 until his death in 1960. Louise made her last movie, *Retreat Hell!*, in 1952 and since then appeared in the television series *My Friend Flicka*, *Mannix* and *Mod Squad*, as well as hosting the chat show *Sunday at the Town Home*. She also became well-known as a champion of various philanthropic causes.

Films include: 1934 Madame Du Barry. **'35** A Midsummer Night's Dream; The Story of Louis Pasteur. **'36** Anthony Adverse. **'37** First Lady; Tovarich. **'38** Marie Antoinette; The Sisters. **'45** The Fighting Guardsman. **'46** The Bandit of Sherwood Forest; The Devil's Mask. **'52** Retreat Hell!

LOURIÉ, Eugene

(b. 1905). Art director/director. Born: Russia

Lourié arrived in Paris in 1921, where he studied painting and design. He met Jean Renoir, who employed him as set designer on four films, including *La Grande Illusion* and *La Règle du Jeu*. When Renoir left France for Hollywood, Lourié followed him to work on *The Southerner* and also designed Charles Chaplin's *Limelight* and Max

Above left: Peter Lorre in The Maltese Falcon. *Above: Joseph Losey directing* The Go-Between. *Right: Bessie Love in* The Dawn of Understanding *(1918). Far right: Arthur Lowe in* Fragment of Fear *(1970). Bottom, far right: Frank Lovejoy in* Retreat Hell! *Bottom right: Montagu Love (centre) with Louis Hayward and Clayton Moore in* The Son of Monte Cristo *(1940). Below: Anita Louise in* Green Light *(1937)*

Ophuls' *The Exile*. Most of his sets are very simple and based on pure lines, for Lourié does not believe in confusing an audience with unnecessary detail. Although his best work was for Renoir, some of his work on low-budget films in the Sixties was very effective, particularly his dramatic use of stark interiors in *Shock Corridor* and *The Naked Kiss*. He has also been involved in special-effects work and has combined this with direction on films such as *The Beast From 20,000 Fathoms* and *The Colossus of New York*.

Films include: 1937 La Grande Illusion (FR) (USA: Grand Illusion; GB: The Great Illusion). **'38** La Bête Humaine (FR) (USA: The Human Beast; GB: Judas Was a Woman). **'39** La Règle du Jeu (FR) (USA: The Rules of the Game). **'45** The Southerner (USA). **'47** The Song of Scheherazade (USA); The Long

Night (USA); The Exile (USA). '51 The River (IND). '52 Limelight (USA). '53 The Beast from 20,000 Fathoms (+ dir) (USA). '58 The Colossus of New York (+ dir) (USA). '63 Shock Corridor (USA). '64 The Naked Kiss (USA). '77 An Enemy of the People (USA).

LOVE, Bessie

(1898–1986). Actress. Born: Juanita Horton; Midland, Texas, USA

With a daughter resembling Mary Pickford and a desperate need for money, Bessie Love's mother sent her to D.W. Griffith's studios in 1915 hoping she would become an actress. She was certainly beautiful – with a heart-shaped face, large eyes, light brown hair and a petite figure – and it was soon apparent that she had acting ability as well. Griffith gave her a role in *Intolerance* and in the next few years Love became popular with audiences, playing female lead op-

posite such stars as Douglas Fairbanks and William S. Hart, generally as an *ingénue*. During the early Twenties she acted on stage, and this stood her in good stead when talkies arrived. Her first screen words were spoken in MGM's musical *Broadway Melody*. In 1935 she decided to settle in England where she lived until her death, entering an eighth decade of movie-making with additional appearances in the theatre and on television. She was superb in a cameo role as the busybody answering service lady in *Sunday, Bloody Sunday* and appeared with James Cagney in *Ragtime* and Warren Beatty in *Reds*.

Films include: 1916 Intolerance. '21 The Sea Lion. '23 Human Wreckage. '25 The Lost World; The King on Main Street. '26 Young April. '27 Dress Parade. '29 The Broadway Melody; Hollywood Revue of 1929. '31 Morals for Women (GB: Farewell Party). '51 No Highway (GB) (USA: No Highway in the Sky). '54 The Barefoot

Contessa (USA-IT). '68 Isadora (GB) (USA: The Loves of Isadora). '71 Sunday, Bloody Sunday (GB). '81 Ragtime; Reds.

LOVE, Montagu

(1877–1943). Actor. Born: Portsmouth, England

Love was educated at Portsmouth Grammar School and Cambridge University and was a newspaper illustrator before he began his acting career. His work on the New York stage led to roles in movies from 1913 onwards. Tall and burly, he became famous in villainous roles, taking the leads in *Rasputin the Black Monk* and *Rough Neck*. He made a successful transition to talkies, inviting much admiration for his melodious, British-accented voice. Love was thus given a much wider variety of roles and gave particularly memorable performances as Henry VIII in *The Prince and the Pauper* and Colonel Weed in *Gunga Din* (based on Kipling's narrative poem). Love's second wife was stage star Marjorie Hollis, whom he married in 1929.

Films include: 1917 Rasputin the Black Monk. '19 Rough Neck. '29 Bulldog Drummond; The Divine Lady. '30 Kismet. '37 The Life of Emile Zola; Parnell; The Prince and the Pauper. '38 The Adventures of Robin Hood. '39 Gunga Din.

LOVEJOY, Frank

(1914–1962). Actor. Born: Bronx, New York City, USA

After the Wall Street Crash of 1929 Lovejoy lost his job as a 'runner' and he turned to acting instead. His Broadway debut was made in *Judgement Day* (1934) and as a result of this he found work on the radio, and soon became one of the most successful and well-paid actors of that medium. In the early Forties he met Stanley Kramer and was drawn to Hollywood.

He first gained public recognition in Kramer's *Home of the Brave*, in which he plays a staid and decent man oblivious, in his acceptance of a black colleague, of the violent racialism felt by others. From this point he was to play similar reliable and earnest types in many of his films.

Films include: 1948 Black Bart (GB: Black Bart, Highwayman). '49 Home of the Brave. '50 In a Lonely Place; The Sound of Fury. '51 I Was a Communist for the FBI; Retreat Hell! '53 The Hitch-Hiker; House of Wax. '54 The Americans. '55 The Crooked Web. '56 Julie. '57 Three Brave Men.

LOWE, Arthur

(1915–1982). Actor. Born: Hayfield, Derbyshire, England

Short, bald, rotund Arthur Lowe did not enter films until after World War II. While serving in the Middle East he became involved in entertaining the troops. On emergence into civilian life he made use of his father's contacts with theatre companies to pursue his career as a character actor. He made his stage debut in 1945 in repertory in Manchester and had a screen role as the reporter at the end of *Kind Hearts and Coronets*. Arthur Lowe's success began on television as Mr Swindley in *Coronation Street*. His film roles did not really amount to much, though Lindsay Anderson made excellent use of him and Lowe's multi-sided performance in *O Lucky Man!* won much acclaim. He added light relief to *The Lady Vanishes*. He is best remembered as Captain Mainwaring, the pompous, irate and very funny mainstay of TV's *Dad's Army*.

Films include: 1949 Kind Hearts and Coronets. '63 This Sporting Life. '68 If. . . . '71 Dad's Army. '72 The Ruling Class. '73 O Lucky Man!; No Sex Please – We're British; Theatre of Blood. '75 Royal Flash. '79 The Lady Vanishes.

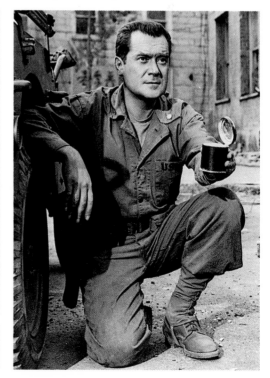

LOWE, Edmund

(1892–1971). Actor. Born: San Jose, California, USA

Edmund Lowe studied for the priesthood before switching to law and ending up teaching English and elocution. Through that job he became involved with actors and entered showbusiness. In 1911 he made his stage debut with Oliver Morosco's stock company and by 1917 was playing on Broadway in *The Brat*. Six feet tall, with blue-grey eyes, brown hair, impressive build and suave manner, Lowe was soon picked up by the movies and in his early roles played romantic heroes – usually with a waxed moustache. His performance opposite Pola Negri in *East of Suez* (1925) established him as a minor screen idol and the following year he gave an interesting performance as a tough, fast-talking sergeant in the war drama *What Price Glory?* (in which he supposedly coined the phrase 'sez you'). Despite never becoming a first-string star, he worked continuously as second lead until his retirement in the early Sixties.

Films include: 1922 Peacock Alley. '23 The Silent Command. '26 What Price Glory? '28 In Old Arizona. '30 Scotland Yard. '33 Dinner at Eight. '42 Call Out the Marines. '43 Murder in Times Square. '45 Dillinger. '56 Around the World in 80 Days. '57 The Wings of Eagles. '58 The Last Hurrah. '60 Heller in Pink Tights.

LOY, Myrna

(b. 1905). Actress. Born: Myrna Williams; Helena, Montana, USA

Loy's professional career began when she joined the chorus line at Grauman's Chinese Theatre at the age of 18. Soon she was getting bit parts in films – mainly as mysterious and exotic *femmes fatales* owing to her slightly oriental appearance and green, almond-shaped eyes. She managed to escape these roles in 1934 with *The Thin Man*, playing the perfect wife, Nora Charles, charming, witty, sexy and sophisticated, opposite William Powell as detective Nick. The film was a great success and led to several sequels. Her popularity now high, Myrna Loy was voted 'Queen of the Movies' (Gable was 'King'). During World War II she worked for the Red Cross returning after the war to co-star in William Wyler's *The Best Years of Our Lives*. She later matured as a character actress – notably as Paul Newman's alcoholic mother in *From the Terrace*. Television work and lively activity in public affairs kept Myrna Loy busy in her later years.

Films include: 1925 Pretty Ladies. '26 Ben-Hur. '27 When a Man Loves; The Jazz Singer. '29 The Black Watch (GB: King of the Khyber Rifles); Show of Shows. '30 Cameo Kirby. '31 Transatlantic; Arrowsmith. '32 The Woman in Room 13; The Mask of Fu Manchu. '34 Manhattan Melodrama; The Thin Man; Stamboul Quest. '36 Wife vs Secretary; The Great Ziegfeld. '37 Parnell. '38 Test Pilot. '39 The Rains Came. '46 The Best Years of Our Lives. '49 The Red Pony. '56 The Ambassador's Wife. '60 From the Terrace. '74 Airport 75. '79 The End.

LUBITSCH, Ernst

(1892–1947). Director/actor. Born: Berlin, Germany

For twenty years the name of Lubitsch was synonymous with all that was witty, naughty and stylish in screen comedy. The son of a tailor, Lubitsch started out in showbusiness as an actor (working with Max Reinhardt's Deutsches Theater) and comedian. He appeared in and scripted or co-scripted a number of movies before devoting his energies to direction, achieving international regard with *Madame Dubarry* (1919) and *Anna Boleyn* (1920), starring Pola Negri and Emil Jannings respectively. He came to Hollywood in 1922 to make *Rosita* (1923) with Mary Pickford. A five-year contract with Warner Brothers followed, for whom he made a series of sophisticated, risqué comedies, including *The Marriage Circle, Forbidden Paradise* and *Lady Windermere's Fan*, which established his unique style, 'the Lubitsch touch'. He moved to Paramount in 1929, winning an Oscar nomination for *The Love Parade*, a light operetta set in the fictitious principality of Sylvania, following this success with such masterpieces as *Trouble in Paradise* and *Design for Living*. He took over as head of production at Paramount, but returned to direction with *Angel* in 1937. Lubitsch left Paramount, making perhaps his most famous film for MGM, *Ninotchka* – a hilarious blend of gentle political satire and romantic comedy starring Greta Garbo and Melvyn Douglas. He developed a serious heart condition in the Forties, although he managed to direct two particularly excellent features, *To Be or Not to Be*, which brilliantly mocked the Nazis, and *Cluny Brown*, a delightful piece of romantic fluff set in pre-war England. In 1947 he won a special Academy Award for a '25-year contribution to motion pictures'. Lubitsch's comic achievements are without equal in the cinema and a host of directors, including Billy Wilder, Preston Sturges and William Wyler have confessed their admiration and indebtedness to his very special genius.

Films include: 1924 The Marriage Circle; Forbidden Paradise. '25 Lady Windermere's Fan. '29 The Love Parade. '32 Trouble in Paradise. '33 Design for Living. '37 Angel. '38 Bluebeard's Eighth Wife. '39 Ninotchka. '42 To Be or Not to Be. '43 Heaven Can Wait. '46 Cluny Brown.

LUCAS, George

(b. 1944). Director/producer. Born: Modesto, California, USA

American Graffiti was not just a massive commercial success (made on a very low budget) but a very personal work for Lucas. The nostalgia for necking, drive-ins and cruising in the America of the Sixties evoked by the film, echoed Lucas' nostalgia for his own adolescence – running his custom-built Fiat around his home town. Ambitions to become a champion racer were terminated by a near-fatal accident and Lucas decided to attend the University of Southern Cal-

ifornia film school where he gained several prizes – notably for the science fiction short *THX-1138*, which won an award at the National Student Film Festival. He then got a scholarship to observe the making of Francis Ford Coppola's *Finian's Rainbow* (1967) and as a result became the protégé of Coppola, who took him on as assistant for *The Rain People*. Lucas' first feature was an extended version of *THX-1138* which, with its distinctive imagery, has now attained cult status. The creator of the epic *Star Wars* – with its ingenious special effects and racy adventure story – has this to say about the film business: 'I hate directing. It's like fighting a 15-round heavyweight bout with a new opponent every day'. He has, however, produced two sequels – *The Empire Strikes Back* and *The Revenge of the Jedi*. And he has worked with enormous success with Steven Spielberg. Lucas' films have been criticized for being brilliant but sterile, lacking atmosphere, revelling in their own technical audacity and, essentially, having no more depth than a comic-strip. On the other hand, audiences love his movies and they have made Lucas a very wealthy man.

Films include: 1969 The Rain People (ass. dir. only). '70 THX-1138; Gimme Shelter (photo. only). '73 American Graffiti. '77 Star Wars. '80 The Empire Strikes Back (exec. prod; +co-sc). '81 Raiders of the Lost Ark (exec. prod; +co-sc). '83 The Revenge of the Jedi (exec. prod; +co-sc).

LUGOSI, Bela

(1888–1956). Actor. Born: Béla Blaskó; Lugos, Hungary

After studying at the Academy of Theatrical Arts in Budapest, Lugosi made his stage debut as Romeo and for many years worked as a romantic lead in Hungarian theatre. In 1921 he settled in America where he appeared in plays and routine films, before creating Dracula on stage and screen and settling down to a career of evil characters who seemed to take him over. He became a personification of the myth of the Count and came to believe his words: 'I am Dracula'. Universal starred him in a stream of villainous roles – vampires, mutants, mad doctors – yet as he continued

Above left: Edmund Lowe in the title role of Chandu the Magician *(1932). Above: Ernst Lubitsch, 'the Sultan of Satire', at work on* The Marriage Circle. *Below: an MGM publicity portrait of Myrna Loy*

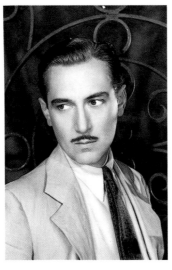

Mysterious Mr Wong; Mark of the Vampire; The Raven. '39 Son of Frankenstein; Ninotchka. '41 The Wolf Man. '42 The Ghost of Frankenstein; The Corpse Vanishes (GB: The Case of the Missing Bride). '45 The Body Snatcher; Zombies on Broadway (GB: Loonies on Broadway). '56 Bride of the Monster; The Black Sheep.

LUKAS, Paul

(1895–1971). Actor. Born: Pál Lukács; Budapest, Hungary

A versatile actor – but one who usually played continental seducers and suave villians – Paul Lukas received his training at the Hungarian Academy of Acting. He made his stage debut in 1916 and was soon appearing in classic roles in Budapest, Vienna and Berlin, often working as guest star for Max Reinhardt. In 1927 he was brought to the USA by Adolph Zukor and made his first American film, *Loves of an Actress*, with Pola Negri. The coming of sound did not defeat him; although he retained his accent he learned English thoroughly. As a result of this Lukas was often cast in mediocre films as villainous Nazis. It was in a very different role, however, that he gained personal and public success. His Broadway performance as a German underground worker fleeing from the Nazis in *Watch on the Rhine* led to a film version for which he won an Oscar as well as the New York Film Critics Award.

Films include: 1930 Anybody's Woman. '32 Thunder Below. '33 Little Women. '35 The Three Musketeers. '38 The Lady Vanishes (GB). '43 Watch on the Rhine. '48 Berlin Express. '50 Kim. '54 20,000 Leagues Under the Sea. '65 Lord Jim (GB).

LUMET, Sidney

(b. 1924). Director. Born: Philadelphia, Pennsylvania, USA

Sidney Lumet began as an actor, first on Yiddish radio with his parents in New York and then in the film *One Third of a Nation* (1938). After service in World War II he returned to acting in television parts. He then opted for directing (350 dramas on television), making his first film, *Twelve Angry Men*, under the auspices of producer

and star Henry Fonda. A tightly structured courtroom drama, it won Lumet wide critical acclaim and an Academy Award nomination. Lumet's subsequent films are exceptional in their use of black-and-white and colour photography and naturalistic 'urban' themes. He excels in the deployment of actors – Peter Finch in *Network*, Al Pacino in *Serpico* and *Dog Day Afternoon* – as characters caught up in moral conflicts or facing up to evil and madness.

Films include: 1957 Twelve Angry Men. '60 The Fugitive Kind. '61 Vu du Pont (FR) (USA/GB: A View From the Bridge). '62 Long Day's Journey Into Night. '64 Fail Safe. '65 The Pawnbroker; The Hill. '67 The Deadly Affair (GB). '71 The Anderson Tapes. '73 Serpico. '74 Murder on the Orient Express. '75 Dog Day Afternoon. '76 Network. '77 Equus (GB). '78 The Wiz. '80 Just Tell Me What You Want. '81 Prince of the City. '82 Deathtrap; The Verdict.

LUMIÈRE, Louis

(1864–1948). Pioneer filmmaker/inventor. Born: Besançon, France

'Oh, I never go to the cinema . . . if I had known what it would come to, I would never have invented it'. So said Louis Lumière in 1930. Thirty-five years previously he and his brother Auguste (1862–1954) presented the world's first projected moving-picture show to a paying public. The sons of a photographer and manufacturer of photographic equipment, the Lumière brothers became fascinated by Edison's Kinetoscope, a peep-show device using celluloid rolls of film that were pulled over an electric light under a magnifying glass. It was Louis who became obsessed with the idea of combining the Kinetoscope with a projector, to show moving images to a larger audience than one. He came up with the Cinématographe, a camera-projector using a claw mechanism to engage the sprocket holes and pull them across the magnifier. The Lumières' first film was *La Sortie des Usines*, a documentary about workers leaving a factory. When it was shown in the Salon Indien at the Grand Café, Boulevard des Capucines, it so amazed the audience that they demanded a repeat showing. More films followed, including *L'Arroseur Arrosé*, the world's first comedy film featuring a gag with a watering hose, and *L'Arrivée d'un Train en Gare de la Ciotat*, which had a train steaming towards the audience, frightening many of them into fleeing their seats. The Lumières sent their show – films, equipment and operatives – all over the world, making them a fortune, but by the 1900s others had taken their developments further and major producers like Pathé and Gaumont were striding ahead. Louis Lumière chose to be content with his conception and retired to the quieter waters of manufacturing photographic and film supplies.

Films include: 1895 La Sortie des Usines; L'Arroseur Arrosé; Charcuterie Mécanique; Demolition d'un Mur; La Mer par Gros Temps; Partie d'Écarté; Promenade des Congressites sur le Bord de la Saône; Le Repas de Bébé. '96 L'Arrivée d'un Train en

Gare de la Ciotat; Les Bains de Diane à Milan. '98 La Vie et la Passion de Jésus-Christ.

LUNDGREN, P. A.

(b. 1911). Art director. Born: Vöstra Harg, Sweden

Lundgren's work is widely believed to surpass that of the best American examples of set design. Following a short period of army service and prior to entering the film industry, he worked as a commercial artist in advertising. Many of his excellent designs have been for Ingmar Bergman – in *The Seventh Seal*, for example, he created a medieval atmosphere with exquisite detail. Lundgren's triumph is that he is able to bring a vividly accurate sense of period to all the films he has designed.

Films include: 1955 Sommarnattens Leende (USA/GB: Smiles of a Summer Night). '57 Det Sjunde Inseglet (USA/GB: The Seventh Seal). '60 Jungfrukällan (USA/GB: The Virgin Spring). '61 Lustgården (USA: Pleasure Garden); Sasom i en Spegel (USA/GB: Through a Glass Darkly). '63 Tystnaden (USA/GB: The Silence). '64 För att inte Tala om Alla Dessa Kvinnor (USA: All These Women; GB: Now About These Women). '69 En Passion (USA: The Passion of Anna; GB: A Passion). '71 Beröringen (USA-SWED) (USA/GB: The Touch); Utvandrarna (USA/GB: The Emigrants). '72 Nybyggarna (USA/GB: The New Land).

LUPINO, Ida

(b. 1918). Actress/director. Born: London, England

Ida Lupino came from a theatrical family (her father was Stanley Lupino) and enrolled at RADA, winning extra parts in films. When her mother, actress Connie Emerald, auditioned for a role in *Her First Affaire* (1933) Ida was given the role instead – that of a Lolita-like adulterous flapper. Her screen career launched, she was offered a contract by Paramount. Her films during the Thirties and Forties usually cast her as dubious, hard women, often from the wrong side of the tracks: in *High Sierra* she was outstanding as Humphrey Bogart's loyal moll; in *The Light That Failed* she is the vicious cockney model who destroys artist Ronald Colman's masterpiece. In the Fifties she turned to directing. Her material is usually unconventional, often dealing with controversial problems. *Outrage*, for example, is about the emotional aftermath of rape. Her own production company failed in the Fifties but she proceeded to direct numerous American television dramas and appeared in more films.

Films include: 1933 Money for Speed (GB). '36 The Gay Desperado. '39 The Adventures of Sherlock Holmes (GB: Sherlock Holmes); The Light That Failed. '40 They Drive by Night. '41 High Sierra. '48 Road House. '50 Never Fear/The Young Lovers (dir; + co-sc. only); Outrage (dir; + co-sc. only). '51 Hard, Fast and Beautiful (dir. only). '53 The Hitch-Hiker (dir; + co-sc. only); The Bigamist (+ dir). '55 The Big Knife. '66 The Trouble With Angels (dir. only). '72 Junior Bonner.

Above: Ida Lupino in Pillow to Post *(1945), one of her few comedy films. Above right: Paul Lukas in* Thunder Below, *a triangular love story. Below: Bela Lugosi bares his fangs in Tod Browning's* Dracula

his career so the quality of the films declined. By the mid-Forties he had become an alcoholic and following a prescription for morphine became a drug addict. His publicity stunts were infamous – he gave many interviews lying in a coffin – and on his death he was buried in Dracula's cloak.

Films include: 1931 Dracula. '32 Murders in the Rue Morgue; White Zombie. '33 Island of Lost Souls; Night of Terror. '35

Above: a publicity photo of Carole Lynley, a popular choice for blonde waifs in the Fifties and Sixties. Below: Ben Lyon as a World War I pilot in Howard Hughes' Hell's Angels

Above: a studio portrait of Diana Lynn. Below: Sue Lyon's publicity promoted her as a sexual delinquent, an image she had gained by her performance in Lolita

LYE, Len

(1901–1980). Animator. Born: Christchurch, New Zealand

Before working his passage to England in 1926, Lye had been living in the Pacific islands where he was greatly influenced by Polynesian art. He then lived on a barge in London and began working on his first film *Tusalava* (1929) with backing from the London Film Society. In the Thirties he was employed by the GPO to make animation documentaries and publicity films. Soon he was experimenting with painting directly onto film, making an abstract animation short *Colour Box*, which was released by the GPO. His following films used the cameraless technique – notably the complex *Trade Tattoo*. He turned to live-action propaganda films in the Forties. He settled in the USA in 1944. From the Fifties Lye concentrated mostly on sculpture and painting.

Films include: 1935 Colour Box. **'36** Birth of a Robot; Rainbow Dance. **'37** Trade Tattoo.

'39 Colour Flight. **'41** Lambeth Walk; Musical Poster; When the Pie Was Opened. **'43** Kill or Be Killed; Planned Crops. **'79** Particles in Space (USA).

LYNCH, David

(b. 1946). Director. Born: Missoula, Montana, USA

David Lynch studied painting at the Pennsylvania School of Fine Arts. He began making short experimental films in 1966 and one of them, *Alphabet*, won him a grant from the American Film Institute. This led to the half-hour film *The Grandmother*, shot on 16mm. He attended the Centre for Advanced Film Studies and embarked on *Eraserhead*, which was five years in the making. A beautifully filmed black-and-white nightmare about an apparent dullard who fathers a mutant, it received limited showings at first but rapidly achieved horror cult status – and it is certainly one of the most unusual and disturb-

ing films ever made. Lynch's next film, *The Elephant Man*, also in black and white, was based on the life of John Merrick (John Hurt) – the worst recorded case of human deformity – and another study of freakishness, though evinced with sympathy and superb atmosphere. It marked Lynch's breakthrough as a major director into mainstream cinema. His next project was a film of Frank Herbert's classic sci-fi saga, *Dune*, shot in colour

Films: 1970 The Grandmother (short). **'77** Eraserhead. **'80** The Elephant Man. **'84** Dune.

LYNLEY, Carol

(b. 1942). Actress. Born: New York City, USA

Blonde, blue-eyed, pretty, wholesome-looking Carol Lynley was a successful child model who progressed to juvenile television roles. At the age of 15 she made her Broadway stage debut and her film debut was in Walt Disney's *The Light in the Forest*. After playing a succession of *ingénue* roles and troubled Fifties teenagers, she was able to adapt to more mature parts in the Sixties and Seventies, also working on stage. She gave a poignant performance as the mother in *Bunny Lake Is Missing* and was one of the passengers facing a watery grave in *The Poseidon Adventure*.

Films include: 1958 The Light in the Forest. **'59** Blue Denim (GB: Blue Jeans); Hound Dog Man. **'61** Return to Peyton Place. **'63** The Cardinal; Under the Yum Yum Tree. **'65** Bunny Lake Is Missing (GB); Harlow. **'67** The Shuttered Room (GB). **'72** The Poseidon Adventure. **'75** The Four Deuces. **'78** The Cat and the Canary (GB). **'79** The Shape of Things to Come (CAN).

LYNN, Diana

(1924–1972). Actress. Born: Dolores Loehr; Los Angeles; California, USA

Success came at the age of 11 for Diana Lynn. She was a prodigy at the piano and played with the Los Angeles Junior Symphony Orchestra. She entered films by chance when she was spotted by Paramount whilst accompanying other musicians on a movie, and was given a speaking part and afterwards a contract. She was soon recognized as a talented comedienne and played in many Forties comedies. With her pert looks and engaging, zany sense of humour she was perfect for 'sister-to-the-star' parts as in *The Major and the Minor*, in which she supported Ginger Rogers. She found it hard, however, to make the transition from child to adult actress and retired from the screen after making *An Annapolis Story* (1955) – continuing to work on television until she died of a stroke.

Films include: 1939 They Shall Have Music (GB: Melody of Youth). **'41** There's Magic in Music. **'42** The Major and the Minor. **'43** Star Spangled Rhythm; The Miracle of Morgan's Creek. **'44** Our Hearts Were Young and Gay. **'46** The Bride Wore Boots. **'49** My Friend Irma. **'50** My Friend Irma Goes West. **'51** Bedtime for Bonzo. **'54** Track of the Cat.

LYON, Ben

(1901–1979). Actor. Born: Atlanta, Georgia, USA

Lyon's family moved to New York when he was very small and on leaving high school he immediately took up acting, appearing in minor stage roles from the age of 17. In 1920 he was offered a film part in Vitagraph's *Heart of Maryland* and soon afterwards Samuel Goldwyn signed him to play the juvenile lead in *Potash and Perlmutter*. During the Twenties he became a very popular star in Hollywood, where he appeared in a variety of romantic, athletic roles that fully exploited his dark good looks. In 1930 he married Bebe Daniels and starred in Howard Hughes' *Hell's Angels*, piloting his own plane in some of the more spectacular airborne sequences. In 1939 the Lyons moved to Britain where they became very popular radio stars through their show *Hi, Gang!* During the war he served as a combat pilot with the RAF, reaching the rank of lieutenant-colonel. On his demob, 20th Century-Fox offered him a contract as their British talent scout and in later years he returned to Hollywood as executive in charge of casting and new talent – in which capacity he claims to have 'spotted' Marilyn Monroe during a screen test. Dividing his time between Britain and Hollywood, he recaptured his radio audience during the Fifties when he and his wife broadcast their show *Life With the Lyons*. In 1977 he was awarded the OBE for his services to Britain during World War II.

Films include: 1923 Potash and Perlmutter; Flaming Youth. **'24** Painted People. **'25** The Pace That Thrills. **'27** For the Love of Mike. **'29** The Flying Marine; The Air Legion. **'30** Hell's Angels. **'33** I Cover the Waterfront. **'41** Hi, Gang! (GB). **'54** Life With the Lyons (GB) (USA: Family Affair).

LYON, Sue

(b. 1946). Actress. Born: Davenport, Iowa, USA

A child model at the age of 12 and a blonde nymphet in various television films, she was discovered by Stanley Kubrick while appearing on *The Loretta Young Show* and won her audition for the lead role in his much publicized *Lolita*. The part placed her firmly in the limelight and typecast her as an openly sexy blonde ripe for exploitation. Unfortunately her turbulent private life then pushed her career into second place. In 1973 she married a man serving a forty-year jail sentence for murder and worked for a time as a cocktail waitress. The following year she filed for divorce. After working her way through husbands and managers as if they were going out of style, she tried to re-establish herself in the film world during the late Seventies, but sadly offers were few and far between.

Films include: 1962 Lolita (GB). **'64** The Night of the Iguana. **'65** Seven Women. **'67** The Flim Flam Man (GB: One Born Every Minute); Tony Rome. **'71** Evel Knievel. **'73** Tarots (SP-IT). **'77** Towing. **'78** Crash!; End of the World.

MacARTHUR, Charles

(1895–1956). Screenwriter.
Born: Scranton, Pennsylvania, USA

MacArthur and Ben Hecht were reporters in Chicago from around 1915 to 1920. They formed a partnership to write *The Front Page*, *Twentieth Century* and other Broadway hits, and in the Thirties they wrote and directed four films at the Paramount studio on Long Island. These included a notable melodrama, *Crime Without Passion*, and a savagely witty fantasy, *The Scoundrel*. MacArthur on his own wrote *The Sin of Madelon Claudet* (1931), a film which brought the Best Actress Oscar to his wife, the famous stage actress Helen Hayes. MacArthur and Hecht had no share, however, in the scripts of any of the three film versions of *The Front Page*.

Films include: 1930 Paid (co-sc). **'31** The Front Page (co-play basis). **'32** Rasputin and the Empress (sc). **'34** Crime Without Passion (co-dir;+co-sc); Twentieth Century (co-sc). **'35** The Scoundrel (co-dir; +co-prod; +co-sc); Once in a Blue Moon (co-dir; +co-prod; +co-sc); Barbary Coast (co-sc). **'36** Soak the Rich (co-dir; +co-prod; +co-sc). **'39** Wuthering Heights (co-sc). **'40** His Girl Friday (co-play basis). **'40** I Take This Woman (story basis). **'47** The Senator Was Indiscreet (sc) (GB: Mr Ashton Was Indiscreet).

McCALLUM, David

(b. 1933). Actor. Born: Glasgow, Scotland

The son of a musician, McCallum attended the Royal Academy of Music and RADA, was property-master at Glyndebourne, and an actor at the Oxford Playhouse. Here he was spotted by director Clive Donner and given a part in his film, *The Secret Place*. After appearing with fair success in a number of mainly routine British films, he went to the USA in the Sixties and starred in the television series *The Man From UNCLE*. His work in film has been sporadic and largely devoid of interest, but someone did once describe him as 'a sex-symbol for the teeny-boppers'.

Films include: 1957 The Secret Place. **'58** Violent Playground; A Night to Remember. **'62** Billy Budd. **'63** The Great Escape (USA-GER). **'65** The Greatest Story Ever Told (USA); The Spy With My Face (USA). **'66**

Around the World Under the Sea (USA). **'68** Sol Madrid (USA) (GB: The Heroin Gang). **'69** Mosquito Squadron. **'76** The Diamond Hunters (S. AFRICA) (USA: The Kingfisher Caper). **'79** Dogs (USA).

McCAMBRIDGE, Mercedes

(b. 1918). Actress. Born: Carlotta Mercedes McCambridge; Joliet, Illinois, USA

Mercedes McCambridge began her career as a radio actress, where her low, vibrant tones were a marked asset. She worked on the Broadway stage in the Forties, and made a first film appearance in 1949, playing a political hatchet-woman in *All the King's Men*. The part won her a Best Supporting Actress Oscar, and set the pattern for the best of her subsequent roles. McCambridge radiated energy, and often venom as well. As Joan Crawford's vengeful enemy in *Johnny Guitar*, driven almost insane by jealousy, she outdid the star for sheer intensity, while in *Touch of Evil*, playing a cameo for her old radio colleague Orson Welles, she transformed herself, unbelievably, into a teenage hoodlum (she was almost 40). In the Sixties she was much affected by a serious accident to her son, but surmounted her difficulties, and made a successful return to Broadway in *Who's Afraid of Virginia Woolf?*

Films include: 1949 All the King's Men. **'51** Lightning Strikes Twice; The Scarf; Inside Straight. **'54** Johnny Guitar. **'56** Giant. **'57** A Farewell to Arms. **'58** Touch of Evil. **'59** Suddenly, Last Summer (GB). **'61** Angel Baby. **'73** The Exorcist (uncredited voice). **'77** Thieves.

McCAREY, Leo

(1898–1969). Director/screenwriter/producer. Born: Los Angeles, California, USA

McCarey studied law at USC, but like many an LA youngster in those heady days, couldn't resist the movies. he assisted Tod Browning at Universal, then spent six years with Hal Roach. McCarey worked for Roach as gag-man, director and writer, and by 1926 was comedy supervisor with overall control of the studio's films. He was instrumental in bringing Laurel and Hardy together, and personally directed some of their best shorts. Going into features in 1929, he became one of the outstanding comedy directors of the Thirties. His successes included

Eddie Cantor's *The Kid From Spain*, the Marx Brothers' classic *Duck Soup*, and the delightful *Ruggles of Red Gap*. This last showed a serious side to McCarey, more fully revealed in *Make Way for Tomorrow*, a delicate study of old age which was a critical triumph and a commercial disaster. McCarey's later work was popular but anonymous, although *Going My Way* won Oscars for Best Film and Best Director. His earlier Best Director award for the superb crazy comedy *The Awful Truth* was infinitely better deserved.

Films include: 1929 The Sophomore. **'31** Indiscreet. **'32** The Kid From Spain. **'33** Duck Soup. **'34** Six of a Kind; Belle of the Nineties/It Ain't No Sin. **'35** Ruggles of Red Gap. **'37** Make Way for Tomorrow; The Awful Truth. **'39** Love Affair. **'42** Once Upon a Honeymoon. **'44** Going My Way. **'45** The Bells of St Mary's. **'52** My Son John. **'57** An Affair to Remember. **'58** Rally 'Round the Flag, Boys!

Below left: David McCallum – 'a sex-symbol for the teeny-boppers'? Below: Mercedes McCambridge – the world's greatest living radio actress according to Orson Welles, in George Stevens' Giant, one of her few film appearances

McCARTHY, Kevin

(b. 1914). Actor. Born: Seattle,
Washington, USA

McCarthy studied journalism at the
University of Minnesota (his sister is
the distinguished writer Mary
McCarthy), but college plays lured
him to stock companies and Broadway. His first great success was as the
disillusioned son Biff in Arthur
Miller's *Death of a Salesman*, and he
made his film debut in the same part,
winning an Oscar nomination for
Best Supporting Actor. McCarthy has
continued to act on stage, television
and screen. His best known film part
remains that of the beleaguered hero of
the first *Invasion of the Body Snatchers*
(he appeared, briefly, in the 1978
remake, too), but he was excellent as a
polished con-man in *A Big Hand for the
Little Lady*, and as an unscrupulous
presidential campaign manager in *The
Best Man* (1964).

Films include: 1951 Death of a Salesman.
'54 Drive a Crooked Road. '55 An Anna-
polis Story (GB: The Blue and the Gold);
Stranger on Horseback. '56 Nightmare;
Invasion of the Body Snatchers. '61 The
Misfits. '63 Gathering of Eagles; The Prize.
'66 A Big Hand for the Little Lady (GB: Big
Deal at Dodge City). '72 Kansas City
Bomber. '78 Piranha; Invasion of the Body
Snatchers. '81 The Howling.

McCAY, Winsor

(1869–1934). Animator. Born:
Spring Lake, Michigan, USA

McCay drew a comic strip for the *New
York Herald* in 1905, and pioneered
the animated cartoon as early as
1907. He made his films for his own
touring vaudeville act, and most of
them were seen in this way rather
than in movie theatres. They lasted a
bare two or three minutes, but in
1917–18 he made *The Sinking of the
Lusitania*, an elaborate nine-minute
effort on which he worked for almost
two years. In the early Twenties he
abandoned animation to become an
editorial cartoonist for the Hearst
press. After McCay's death, many of
his films were found in his garage,
restored, and eventually exhibited.
The *Lusitania* film, though insecure in
technique and disfigured by blatant
propaganda, proved to be imaginatively conceived, with some striking
visual effects.

Films include: 1911 Little Nemo. '12 How a
Mosquito Operates/The Story of a Mos-
quito. '14 Gertie the Dinosaur. '16 Winsor
McCay and his Jersey Skeeters. c.'18–20
Gertie on Tour; The Centaurs; Flip's Circus.
'21 Dreams of the Rarebit Fiend/
Adventures of a Rarebit Eater (series: The
Pet, Bug Vaudeville, The Flying House).

McCLURE, Doug

(b. 1935). Actor. Born: Glendale,
California, USA

A blond, blue-eyed athlete, McClure
paid his way through college in Los
Angeles by modelling and television
commercials, and from the late Fifties
played leads in a number of action
movies. He was better known, however, for his television portrayal of the

easy-going cowboy, Trampas, in the
series *The Virginian* and *The Men From
Shiloh*. In the Seventies McClure paid
regular visits to England to star in
British producer John Dark's successful series of adventure fantasies – ideal
movies for family audiences made at a
time when there was little of that kind
around.

Films include: 1957 The Enemy Below. '59
Gidget. '60 The Unforgiven. '65 Shenan-
doah. '66 Beau Geste. '67 The King's Pirate.
'75 The Land That Time Forgot (GB). '76 At
the Earth's Core (GB). '77 The People That
Time Forgot (GB). '78 Warlords of Atlantis
(GB). '80 Humanoids From the Deep (GB:
Monster).

McCOY, Tim

(1891–1978). Actor. Born: Timothy
McCoy; Saginaw, Michigan, USA

McCoy's father was Irish, and chief of
police at Saginaw. The boy had two
ambitions, both fulfilled – to be an
army officer and a cowboy. He roun-
ded up wild horses, worked as a
cowboy, mixed with Indians, learned
their sign language, and became an
honorary member of the Arapaho
tribe. An artillery major in World War
I, when it ended he became (at 28)
Adjutant General of Wyoming, responsible for Indian affairs. In 1922
Paramount enlisted McCoy to help on
The Covered Wagon. He provided train-
loads of extras and much technical
advice, and organized and appeared
in a stage prologue at Grauman's
Egyptian Theatre. He stayed with the
cinema, and in the Twenties starred in
a number of ambitious Westerns at
MGM, playing an upright cowboy
hero much in the William S. Hart
style. Later on, he made Western
series for Columbia and Monogram,
founded a Wild West show, continuing with his act when well into his
seventies, and was commissioned as
colonel in World War II. And he is said
to have been the fastest draw of all the
Western players, taking just six
frames of film, or a quarter of a
second.

Films include: 1923 The Covered Wagon
(technical advisor). '25 The Thundering
Herd. '26 War Paint. '27 Winners of the
Wilderness. '28 The Law of the Range. '30
The Indians Are Coming (serial). '32 Fight-
ing Fool; Texas Cyclone. '33 Man of Action;
End of the Trail. '40 The Westerner. '42
West of the Law. '56 Around the World in
80 Days. '65 Requiem for a Gunfighter.

McCREA, Joel

(b. 1905). Actor. Born: Pasadena,
California, USA

Educted at Pomona State College, Joel
McCrea made a few stage appearances and played some small parts in
silent films. More prominent from
1929, he had his first real success in
Cukor's *Girls About Town* in 1931, and
for the next 30 years was one of
Hollywood's most popular and dependable leading men. Tall, rugged,
good-looking and exuding integrity,
he was made for outdoor action pictures, but could adapt his slow-
moving, thoughtful style to urban
melodrama (*Dead End*), to crazy
comedy (*The Palm Beach Story*), or to

Top, far left: Kevin McCarthy in Death of a Salesman. Centre, far left: Western star Tim McCoy in Alias John Law (1942). Below, far left: Hattie McDaniel, Hollywood's best-known black actress in the Thirties, in Show Boat. Left: Doug McClure in The King's Pirate. Below left: Jeanette MacDonald in Naughty Marietta

Above: Joel McCrea in Dead End. Below: Malcolm McDowell and Christine Noonan take to the rooftops in Lindsay Anderson's If. . . ., the late-Sixties classic about life and revolution at an English public school. Bottom: Roddy McDowall in Charlie Chan and the Curse of the Dragon Queen (1981)

political thrillers (Foreign Correspondent). There are two great roles which contain the essence of the man. In Preston Sturges' Sullivan's Travels McCrea played a director of movie comedy who goes out to explore the real world and discovers a hell – he most beautifully conveyed a good man's helpless anguish. From the mid-Forties he made Westerns, and in Sam Peckinpah's elegiac Ride the High Country he was an ageing lawman on his last mission, wanting only, he says, to 'enter his house justified'. After that, McCrea retired. It was a good line to sum up a good lifetime in movies. Married since 1933 to actress Frances Dee, with a son who has made a movie or two, McCrea still runs his ranch, is very rich (from real estate as well as all those movies),

and has, once or twice, been tempted out of his well-earned retirement.

Films include: 1932 The Most Dangerous Game/The Hounds of Zaroff; Bird of Paradise. '35 Private Worlds. '37 Dead End. '39 Union Pacific. '40 Foreign Correspondent. '41 The Palm Beach Story; Sullivan's Travels; Reaching for the Sun. '42 The Great Man's Lady. '44 Buffalo Bill. '48 Four Faces West (GB: They Passed This Way). '62 Ride the High Country (GB: Guns in the Afternoon). '76 Mustang Country.

McDANIEL, Hattie

(1895–1952). Actress. Born: Wichita, Kansas, USA

Large, fat, amiable and always amused, Hattie McDaniel was the first American black woman to sing on the radio. She was a superb blues singer, toured with George Morrison's negro orchestra, and in Show Boat, and from 1932 played countless supporting roles, almost always as a maid, in Hollywood movies. As Mammy in Gone With the Wind she won the Academy Award for Best Supporting Actress, and on both radio and television she starred in the Beulah series. It was a restricted career, but she accepted its limitations cheerfully, and once said, unanswerably, 'I would rather play a maid than be one.'

Films include: 1933 I'm No Angel. '35 The Little Colonel. '36 Show Boat. '37 Saratoga. '39 Gone With the Wind. '40 Maryland. '42 They Died With Their Boots On. '44 Since You Went Away. '46 Song of the South. '48 Family Honeymoon; Mickey; Mr Blandings Builds His Dream House.

MacDONALD, Jeanette

(1901–1965). Actress. Born: Philadelphia, Pennsylvania, USA

Jeanette MacDonald was a Broadway chorine in 1920, rose to second lead in The Magic Ring in Greenwich Village, and then to large parts in Broadway musicals of the Twenties like Irene and Tangerine. Paramount tested her, and forgot her. Later on, Ernst Lubitsch looked at the test, and cast her opposite Maurice Chevalier in The Love Parade. In those early musicals with Lubitsch, and above all in Mamoulian's enchanting Love Me Tonight, MacDonald sang sweetly, but also showed herself an accomplished and witty comedienne, with a stylish swagger and a naughty look in her eye. When she moved to MGM, alas, she suffered in endless popular but sentimental musicals with the monolithic Nelson Eddy, and the look became sadder and sadder.

Films include: 1929 The Love Parade. '30 Monte Carlo; The Lottery Bride. '32 One Hour With You; Love Me Tonight. '34 The Cat and the Fiddle. '35 Naughty Marietta. '36 Rose Marie; San Francisco. '37 The Firefly. '49 The Sun Comes Up.

McDOWALL, Roddy

(b. 1928). Actor. Born: Roderick Andrew McDowall; Herne Hill, London, England

McDowall was a child actor in British films from the age of nine, and when the London Blitz came in 1940 was evacuated, with his mother, to the USA. He continued his career in Hollywood, playing rather sad, sensitive children, and had major roles in John Ford's How Green Was My Valley and in Lassie Come Home. Growing up, he studied acting in New York, and achieved great success on the Broadway stage before returning to films in 1960 as a highly versatile supporting player who could also be called upon for off-beat leads. He was touching in Planet of the Apes as a scholarly chimpanzee, but even better as the crazed high-school genius of Lord Love a Duck (1966). In his mid-thirties then, he looked a very convincing eighteen.

Films include: 1939 Just William (GB); Poison Pen (GB). '41 How Green Was My Valley. '43 Lassie Come Home. '44 The White Cliffs of Dover. '63 Cleopatra. '65 Inside Daisy Clover. '67 Planet of the Apes (GB). '71 Escape From the Planet of the Apes. '72 The Poseidon Adventure. '78 The Cat From Outer Space.

McDOWELL, Malcolm

(b. 1943). Actor. Born: Leeds, Yorkshire, England

McDowell shot to fame as Mick Travis, the rebel hero of Lindsay Anderson's allegory of revolution, set in an English public school, If . . . . The film defined McDowell's screen persona – attractively boyish, anti-establishment, arrogant and amoral, pursuing wild bouts of violence and sex with pop-eyed relish. As such, the role of Alex, the gangleader, in Kubrick's horrific epic fantasy A Clockwork Orange fitted him like a glove, while he showed a gentler side opposite Nanette Newman in The Raging Moon, the story of a love-affair between two disabled people. McDowell's own life had a distinct bearing on his early films. The son of a publican, he was educated (like Travis) at a public school. He then worked as a coffee salesman, later incorporating his experiences into Anderson's picaresque saga of success and failure O Lucky Man! Bored with selling door-to-door, he turned to acting, appearing in repertory in the Isle of Wight and joining the Royal Shakespeare Company in 1965 as a spear-carrier. He worked in television for a while until cast by Anderson in If . . . McDowell subsequently formed the SAM production company with Anderson and David Sherwin. His films since the mid-Seventies have been disappointing on the whole, perhaps the best being Anderson's bitter and controversial satire of British society, Britannia Hospital; the worst being the embarrassing soft-core pseudo-epic Caligula, in which McDowell played the loony Roman emperor. He married Margot Dullea in 1975; after their divorce he married actress Mary Steenburgen, who co-starred with him in Time After Time, in 1980. They have one daughter.

Films include: 1968 If . . . . . '70 Figures in a Landscape. '71 A Clockwork Orange; The Raging Moon (USA: Long Ago, Tomorrow). '73 O Lucky Man! '75 Royal Flash. '76 Aces High (GB-FR). '79 Caligula (IT-USA); Time After Time. '82 Britannia Hospital; Cat People.

McENERY, Peter

(b. 1940). Actor. Born: Walsall, Staffordshire, England

McEnery had no drama school training, and after a short spell in repertory worked in the Royal Shakespeare Company from 1961. He had already played a small role in the film *Tunes of Glory* in 1960. In 1966 he was cast by Roger Vadim as Jane Fonda's stepson in *La Curée*. Other offers for continental films resulted, and for some time McEnery was better known there than in England. Back home, and trying to get rid of such unhelpful labels as 'the new Gérard Philipe' and 'England's export Romeo', he played the blond thug in the movie version of *Entertaining Mr Sloane*, but the film was poor and did him little good. His later work has been largely on stage and in television.

Films include: 1960 Tunes of Glory. '61 Victim. '64 The Moon-Spinners. '66 La Curée (FR-IT) (USA/GB: The Game Is Over); The Fighting Prince of Donegal. '67 J'Ai Tué Raspoutine (FR-IT) (GB: I Killed Rasputin). '68 Meglio Vedova (FR-IT) (USA/GB: Better a Widow); Negatives. '70 The Adventures of Gerard; Entertaining Mr Sloane.

McGOOHAN, Patrick

(b. 1928). Actor. Born: Astoria, Long Island, New York, USA

Six months after his birth, McGoohan returned with his parents to Ireland. When he was eight, the family moved to Sheffield, and eventually he joined the local rep as tea-boy. In four years he rose to playing leads, moved to Bristol Old Vic and played Henry V for them in London. He was impressive in early film roles such as that of the crooked lorry driver in *Hell Drivers*, but his career did not really flourish until he went into television, where he starred in the series *Danger Man* and *The Prisoner*. The latter was not an immediate success, but has since acquired a cult reputation. In 1968 McGoohan went to the USA, acted in films, notably in Siegel's *Escape From Alcatraz*, and directed a film musical, *Catch My Soul* (1974).

Films include: 1955 I Am a Camera. '56 Zarak. '57 Hell Drivers; The Gypsy and the Gentleman. '62 Life for Ruth (USA: Walk in the Shadow). '63 Dr Syn Alias the Scarecrow. '68 Ice Station Zebra (USA). '72 Mary, Queen of Scots. '76 Silver Streak (USA). '79 Escape From Alcatraz (USA).

MacGRAW, Ali

(b. 1938). Actress. Born: Alice MacGraw; Pound Ridge, New York, USA

After graduating from Wellesley College, where she studied art history, Ali MacGraw was an editorial assistant on *Harper's Bazaar*, assistant to a fashion photographer, and a highly successful cover-girl. Entering films in 1968, she played the lead one year later in *Goodbye, Columbus* (as a flirtatious college girl), and went on to appear as the doomed heroine of the tear-stained box-office triumph, *Love Story*. In Sam Peckinpah's *The Getaway* she had a strong role as a thief and murderess, but after that her

career faltered, and occasional later films have been fairly unrewarding. Her second husband was Paramount chief Robert Evans, her third the actor Steve McQueen.

Films include: 1968 A Lovely Way to Die (GB: A Lovely Way to Go). '69 Goodbye, Columbus. '70 Love Story. '72 The Getaway. '78 Convoy. '79 Players. '80 Just Tell Me What You Want.

McGRAW, Charles

(1914–1980). Actor. Born: New York City, USA

Raised in Akron, Ohio, McGraw returned to New York at 17, joined the navy, went back to Akron University, and left to become an actor. After an interlude in the boxing ring, he found success in Odets' *Golden Boy* on Broadway in the late Thirties, and moved on to Hollywood in 1942. From then until his macabre death in 1980 (he bled to death after walking through the glass door of a shower) he played tough, gravel-voiced heavies in scores of films, contriving to be in a fair number of very good ones. He was one of the hit-men in Robert Siodmak's version of *The Killers*, the brutal trainer of gladiators in *Spartacus* (ending up in a vat of hot soup), and a bloodthirsty police chief in *The Defiant Ones*.

Left: Charles McGraw in The Narrow Margin, *a thriller about a key prosecution witness' perilous journey by train. Above left: Peter McEnery as the amoral, thuggish protagonist of* Entertaining Mr Sloane

Above left: Patrick McGoohan in Silver Streak. *Above: Ali McGraw in* Love Story. *Below: Dorothy McGuire gave a great performance as the Irish girl Katie Nolan in Elia Kazan's* A Tree Grows in Brooklyn

Films include: 1943 The Moon Is Down; The Mad Ghoul. '46 The Killers. '47 T-Men. '49 Reign of Terror. '52 The Narrow Margin. '57 Slaughter on 10th Avenue. '58 The Defiant Ones. '60 Spartacus. '77 Twilight's Last Gleaming (USA-GER).

McGUIRE, Dorothy

(b. 1918). Actress. Born: Omaha, Nebraska, USA

The daughter of a rich Nebraska lawyer, Dorothy McGuire had acted when a child at the Omaha Community Playhouse, but made no serious attempt at a professional career until school and college were over. She understudied Martha Scott in *Our Town* on Broadway, took over when Scott left for the film version, and in 1941 had a great success in the title role of *Claudia*. McGuire in her turn

went to Hollywood for the film of the play, and began a thirty-year career as a screen actress. She played gentle, loving, but often strong-minded ladies, and as time went on moved smoothly into character roles while preserving all her charm. Her most memorable parts, perhaps, were as the vulnerable dumb girl hunted by a psychopath in Robert Siodmak's *The Spiral Staircase*, and as the Quaker wife striving to keep husband and son out of the Civil War in William Wyler's *Friendly Persuasion*.

Films include: 1943 Claudia. '45 A Tree Grows in Brooklyn; The Spiral Staircase. '46 Till the End of Time. '47 Gentleman's Agreement. '54 Three Coins in the Fountain. '56 Friendly Persuasion. '60 The Dark at the Top of the Stairs. '65 The Greatest Story Ever Told. '71 Flight of the Doves.

Above: John McIntire in the Western television series The Virginian. *Right: Virginia McKenna in* Carve Her Name With Pride. *Below: Frank McHugh, the centre of attention, in* Three Men on a Horse (1936)

McHUGH, Frank

(1898–1981). Actor. Born: Francis Curray McHugh; Homestead, Pennsylvania, USA

On the stage from childhood (his parents ran a stock company), McHugh reached Broadway in *The Fall Guy*, and appeared in his first feature film in 1930. A Warner Brothers contract player, he appeared in over ninety films between 1930 and 1942, and had reached around one hundred and fifty by the end. McHugh played the hero's loyal friend, sometimes with a touch of sadness, but more often as comedy relief, punctuating his performances with a characteristic nervous laugh. He leaves many happy memories, outstanding among them his Quince in the Max Reinhardt *A Midsummer*

Night's Dream, a beautifully judged cameo in a film filled with fine comedy acting.

Films include: 1930 Going Wild; Dawn Patrol. '31 The Front Page. '33 The Mystery of the Wax Museum; Footlight Parade. '35 A Midsummer Night's Dream. '39 The Roaring Twenties. '44 Going My Way. '45 State Fair. '49 Mighty Joe Young. '53 A Lion Is in the Streets. '64 A Tiger Walks. '67 Easy Come, Easy Go.

McINTIRE, John

(b. 1907). Actor. Born: Spokane, Washington, USA

One of Hollywood's outstanding character actors of the Forties and Fifties, McIntire made his first mark as a radio actor, which gave full scope to that slow, rough-edged drawl which

became so familiar in his film career. His wife, actress Jeanette Nolan, starred with him in many radio shows. In the movies McIntire played sheriffs, editors, politicians, with a leavening of humour and a strong undercurrent of integrity. His most famous part was as the local sheriff in *Psycho*, but he was equally good as the olderly lawyer trying to clean up corruption in *The Phenix City Story*, and in a number of Westerns for Anthony Mann. He was also a notable television star.

Films include: 1950 The Asphalt Jungle; Winchester '73. '53 Mississippi Gambler; A Lion Is in the Streets. '54 Apache. '55 The Kentuckian; The Phenix City Story. '60 Who Was That Lady?; Elmer Gantry; Psycho. '74 Herbie Rides Again. '75 Rooster Cogburn.

MACKENDRICK, Alexander

(b. 1912). Director. Born: Boston, Massachusetts, USA

Born in the United States to Scottish parents who were visiting there, Mackendrick went to Glasgow Art School, spent some time in advertising, and became a scriptwriter at Pinewood in 1937. He directed some shorts there, and made a number of wartime documentaries. After the war he returned to writing, now at Ealing, and in 1949 directed his first feature, *Whisky Galore!* This and subsequent Ealing films were both entertaining and visually original, with a mordant humour holding the whimsy in check. After a great success with the black comedy *The Ladykillers*, Mackendrick went to America to make his masterpiece, *Sweet Smell of Success*, a scathing enquiry into corruption in the world of columnists and publicity agents. After that, with the world apparently open to him, he made only three films in twelve years before settling down as dean of the film section of the California Institute of the Arts in 1969. He held the post until 1979, and stayed on as a teacher. It seems a dreadful waste of one of the very few British directors with some claim to be reckoned an *auteur*, but Mackendrick was never willing to compromise much with commercialism, and on one occasion walked out of a £2 million project (*The Guns of Navarone*, 1961) after two weeks' shooting.

Films include: 1949 Whisky Galore! (USA: Tight Little Island). '51 The Man in the White Suit. '52 Mandy (USA: Crash of Silence). '54 The Maggie (USA: High and Dry). '55 The Ladykillers. '57 Sweet Smell of Success (USA). '63 Sammy Going South (USA: A Boy Ten Feet Tall). '65 A High Wind in Jamaica. '67 Don't Make Waves (USA).

McKENNA, Virginia

(b. 1931). Actress. Born: London, England

Virginia McKenna was a pupil at the Central School of Dramatic Art in London, made a West End debut in 1949 in *A Penny for a Song*, and appeared with John Gielgud in *The Winter's Tale*, playing Perdita. She made numerous British films during the Fifties, typically playing the sweet English rose rising to the demands of wartime heroism, but her more interesting parts included Henrietta in *The Barretts of Wimpole Street*, where she was reunited with Gielgud. After some years of semi-retirement she was tempted back to play Joy Adamson in *Born Free*, along with her second husband Bill Travers and a large number of lions. The animal connection has remained through her later films. McKenna's first husband was the actor Denholm Elliott.

Films include: 1952 Father's Doing Fine. '53 The Cruel Sea. '57 The Barretts of Wimpole Street; The Smallest Show on Earth. '58 Carve Her Name With Pride; Passionate Summer. '66 Born Free. '69 Ring of Bright Water. '70 Waterloo (IT-USSR). '74 Swallows and Amazons. '78 Holocaust 2000 (IT-GB) (USA: The Chosen).

MacKENZIE, John

(b. 1932). Director. Born: Edinburgh, Scotland

After studying history at Edinburgh University, and a spell with the city's Gateway theatre, MacKenzie moved to London and the BBC, where the success of his television directorial debut, *Voices in the Park*, opened the door to the film industry. He remains preoccupied with contemporary Scottish themes, both his television plays *Just Another Saturday* and *Just a Boys' Game* providing insights into the seamier aspects of Scots macho, a subject further explored in the controversial study of Gorbals gangster Jimmy Boyle in Southern Television's

A Sense of Freedom. His early movie work attracted little attention, but he scored more recently with another look at gangsters, this time from London's East End, in the funny, exciting and occasionally bloody *The Long Good Friday.*

Films include: 1971 One Brief Summer; Unman, Wittering and Zigo. '72 Made. '80 The Long Good Friday.

McKERN, Leo

(b. 1920). Actor. Born: Reginald McKern; Sydney, Australia

Leo McKern has the sort of looks that get him noticed; big, burly and with a glass eye, he has been described as 'a wayward Toby jug', and the possessor of a 'craggy, beetle-browed face', 'like a round, home-made loaf of bread'. At any rate, they have served him in good stead, for his career has been varied and busy. He began and abandoned engineering for commercial art, served in New Guinea during World War II, and then came to England where he carved out an

impressive reputation on the stage. His film and television work has established him as a character actor of considerable range, from the informer in *Ryan's Daughter* to Chang, the comic villain of the Beatles' *Help!* He recently achieved considerable success as the eccentric barrister *Rumpole of the Bailey* in the popular television series, written by John Mortimer.

Films include: 1957 Time Without Pity. '59 The Mouse That Roared; Yesterday's Enemy. '62 The Inspector (USA: Lisa). '64 A Jolly Bad Fellow; King and Country. '65 Help!; The Amorous Adventures of Moll Flanders. '66 A Man For All Seasons. '70 Ryan's Daughter. '75 The Adventure of Sherlock Holmes' Smarter Brother. '81 The French Lieutenant's Woman.

McLAGLEN, Andrew V.

(b. 1920). Director. Born: London, England

The son of actor Victor McLaglen, he inherited not only his father's burly frame – he is six feet seven inches tall – but his interest in the movies. Brought to America at the age of five, he was raised among Hollywood people and, after a period as a clerk with Republic, graduated to working with his father's friend and director, John Ford, as assistant director on *The Quiet Man* (1952). His own features have revealed the Ford influence – a strong leaning towards hearty action pictures and epic Westerns like *Shenandoah*. He has directed over two hundred and fifty episodes for television series like *Gunsmoke* and *Rawhide*. With *The Wild Geese*, a curiously anachronistic and romantic study of African mercenaries which is nonetheless exciting and entertaining, he proved that, though the Western may have gone out of fashion, its brawling, macho trademarks are still as popular as ever.

Films include: 1957 Gun the Man Down; The Abductors. '63 McLintock! '65 Shenandoah. '68 The Devil's Brigade; Bandolero!;

Above: Leo McKern as the shady publican Tom Ryan in Ryan's Daughter. *Below: Barton MacLane (right) in Fritz Lang's powerful study*

of a convict on the run, You Only Live Once *(1937). Above: Victor McLaglen in John Ford's pro-IRA feature* The Informer

Above: Shirley MacLaine in The Yellow Rolls Royce, *a film in which the only talent she was allowed to display was one for looking casual but chic. Right: Stephen McNally in* Woman in Hiding *(1949). Far right: Fred MacMurray in the black comedy* Murder, He Says

Hell Fighters. '69 The Undefeated. '70 Chisum. '78 The Wild Geese (GB).

McLAGLEN, Victor

(1886–1959). Actor. Born: Tunbridge Wells, Kent, England

McLaglen was made for the role of Quincannon, the two-fisted, hard-drinking sergeant with a bluff humour and a sentimental heart of gold, whom he played in the John Ford Cavalry trilogy. There's a touch of Quincannon in all McLaglen's roles, and a good bit in his real life too. The son of a bishop, he went to South Africa when he was young, and he opted for a life of adventure, joining the British Army under age, wrestling and boxing his way round the world and collecting a face with the rugged, broken-nosed, lived-in look which finally got him work in films. Though without pretensions to serious acting, he became a very big silent star – his best film being *What Price Glory?* (1926) – and won an Oscar in 1935 for his part of Gypo in Ford's *The Informer*. His other famous role was as the tyrannical Irishman brawling with John Wayne, in *The Quiet Man*, while Shirley Temple made him cry in *Wee Willie Winkie*. McLaglen's brothers Arthur, Clifford, Cyril, Leopold and Kenneth all acted in films. His son Andrew is a director.

Films include: 1922 The Glorious Adventure (GB). '24 Winds of Chance. '25 The Unholy Three. '29 The Black Watch (GB: King of the Khyber Rifles). '34 The Lost Patrol. '35 The Informer. '37 Wee Willie Winkie. '39 Gunga Din. '48 Fort Apache. '49 She Wore a Yellow Ribbon. '50 Rio Grande. '52 The Quiet Man.

MacLAINE, Shirley

(b. 1934). Actress. Born: Shirley MacLean Beaty; Richmond, Virginia, USA

Shirley MacLaine tackles her career with a tireless energy; as well as her acting work, she has been a political campaigner, an author and a documentary film-maker. The sister of actor Warren Beatty, she first appeared on stage as a child in the chorus line of the Broadway production of *The Pajama Game*. Discovered by Hal Wallis, she took time out to learn about production techniques while appearing in a variety of comedy, dramatic and musical film roles. Her red-headed good looks, impish humour, natural timing and air of vulnerability made her popular as a kook or a kindly floozie in films like *Irma La Douce* (1963) and *Sweet Charity*. Her best role, though, was as Fran Kubelik, the mixed-up elevator girl in Billy Wilder's *The Apartment*. She has been nominated for three Oscars and has achieved considerable success with her one-woman shows, singing and dancing proving her favourite area of showbiz.

Films include: 1956 The Trouble With Harry; Around the World in 80 Days. '58 Some Came Running. '60 Can Can; The Apartment. '61 The Children's Hour (GB: The Loudest Whisper). '64 The Yellow Rolls Royce (GB). '69 Sweet Charity. '72 The Possession of Joel Delaney. '73 The Other Half of the Sky; A China Memoir (doc) (co-dir; +prod; +sc. only). '77 The Turning Point. '79 Being There.

MacLANE, Barton

(1902–1969). Actor/writer. Born: Columbia, South Carolina, USA

MacLane was one of those actors who worked steadily and competently in films for most of his career – he made over one hundred and fifty without ever quite achieving top status. After Wesleyan University, he went on to New York and studied at the American Academy of Dramatic Art. His athletic build and sports experience made him a natural choice for the role of a football player in *The Quarterback*, and he went on to play a galaxy of heavies – gangsters, convicts and general badmen, including the threatening Lieutenant Dundy in *The Maltese Falcon*. He played the inspector in the Torchy Blane film series in 1936–39, and later did some television work. He died of pneumonia.

Films include: 1926 The Quarterback. '35 G-Men; Man of Iron. '36 Bengal Tiger; Smart Blonde. '39 I Was a Convict. '41 Hit the Road; The Maltese Falcon. '44 The Cry of the Werewolf. '53 The Glenn Miller Story. '61 Pocketful of Miracles. '68 Arizona Bushwhackers.

McLAREN, Norman

(b. 1914). Animator. Born: Stirling, Scotland

One of the greatest exponents of abstract animation. McLaren first became aware of the possibilities film offered while studying at Glasgow's School of Art in the early Thirties. An amateur film, *Seven Till Five* (1933), brought him to the attention of documentary-maker John Grierson, who later offered him a job, first with the GPO Film Unit and subsequently with the National Film Board of Canada. Inventive and original, McLaren has often dispensed with the camera altogether, painting geometric patterns directly on to the film so that they squirm and prance in time to the music in works like *Dots* and *Loops*. *Pas de Deux* superimposed multiple images of ballet dancers onto the same frame, whilst *Neighbours* (1952) used human actors photographed a frame at a time to give them unusual movement. Through example and encouragement, McLaren has done much to widen the public awareness of animation.

Films include: 1937 Book Bargain (anim. only). '38 Love on the Wing. '40 Dots (USA); Loops (USA); Boogie Doodle (USA). '49 Begone Dull Care (co-dir) (CAN). '50 Around Is Around (CAN-GB). '52 Two Bagatelles (CAN). '65 Pas de Deux (CAN).

McLEOD, Norman Z.

(1898–1964). Director. Born: Norman Zenos McLeod; Grayling, Michigan, USA

The son of a clergyman, McLeod studied at the University of Washington before enlisting in the Royal Canadian Air Force in World War I. He went to Hollywood in 1919, and entered the film industry writing gags and scripts. After a spell with Fox, which saw him direct his first feature, *Taking a Chance* (1929), he moved in 1930 to Paramount, and soon established a reputation as a leading comedy director. He worked with an impressive list of stars: the Marx Brothers in *Monkey Business*, W.C. Fields in *It's A Gift*, Bing Crosby and Bob Hope in *Road To Rio*, and Danny Kaye in *The Secret Life of Walter Mitty*. The success of his work was not only due to the cast, however, for McLeod handled his films with such skill and restraint that the results were unpretentious and always entertaining.

Films include: 1931 Monkey Business. '32 Horse Feathers; If I Had a Million *ep* The Forger. '34 It's a Gift. '36 Pennies From Heaven. '42 Panama Hattie. '47 The Secret Life of Walter Mitty; Road to Rio. '48 The Paleface. '54 Casanova's Big Night.

MacMURRAY, Fred

(b. 1908). Actor. Born: Kankakee, Illinois, USA

Tall, dark and heavy featured, with the easy-going air of a door-to-door insurance salesman, Fred MacMurray might have been made for the sophisticated screwball comedies which became his forte. But that bland and friendly mask could quickly slip when there was a scent of a dame or money in the air. MacMurray's insurance man Walter Neff in Billy Wilder's *Double Indemnity* is the perfect study of a weak, bluff but basically ordinary guy corrupted by sex and money, both offered by Phyllis Dietrichson (Barbara Stanwyck) whose husband they subsequently dispose of. Later for Wilder, MacMurray was excellent as the selfish, oily boss messing up the life of his mistress (Shirley MacLaine) in *The Apartment*. It was MacMurray's love of music – he played saxophone in the American Legion Band – which drew him to Hollywood, where he worked as an extra to pay the rent. Discovered when playing with a band on screen, he was cast in *The Gilded Lily* with Claudette Colbert, which not only made him a star but established a romantic comedy duo which was to last for a further six films. Although he continued to specialize in light-hearted roles, including tolerant fathers in television's *My Three Sons* and Disney films, his dramatic roles were the most effective.

Films include: 1935 The Gilded Lily. '36 The Texas Rangers. '37 True Confession. '40 Too Many Husbands. '43 No Time for Love. '44 Double Indemnity. '45 Murder, He Says. '47 The Egg and I. '48 Family Honeymoon. '53 Fair Wind to Java. '54 The Caine Mutiny. '60 The Apartment.

McNALLY, Stephen

(b. 1913). Actor. Born: Horace McNally; New York City, USA

In *Winchester '73* (1950) McNally played the renegade Dutch Henry Brown, who steals the magic rifle from James Stewart, only to lose it again to a poker-playing Indian; it was, perhaps, typical of the supporting roles he played in a score of thrillers, Westerns and general adventure movies. He had first acted at high school, and, although he trained in law at Fordham University, he soon abandoned it for Broadway, where the lead in *Johnny Belinda* won him a contract from MGM under his real name. He later moved to Warner Brothers to star in the film version of his stage hit, but inspired casting gave him the role of the loathsome villain rather than the hero, and made him a reputation which kept him busy throughout the Fifties and Sixties.

Films include: 1948 Johnny Belinda. '49 City Across the River. '52 Duel at Silver Creek. '53 The Stand at Apache River. '54 A Bullet Is Waiting. '55 Violent Saturday. '57 Hell's Crossroads. '58 Johnny Rocco. '65 Requiem for a Gunfighter. '68 Panic in the City. '69 Once You Kiss a Stranger.

MACPHERSON, Jeanie

(1884–1946). Screenwriter.
Born: Boston, Massachusetts, USA

A contemporary of Mary Pickford and Florence Lawrence, Jeanie Macpherson began her career on the stage and entered films in 1908. She started as an actress with Biograph, but began collaborating on scenarios with D.W. Griffith, and later moved to Universal where she had her own unit, writing, directing and acting in two-reelers. She was hired by Cecil B. DeMille to work on the scenario of *The Captive*, and a fruitful relationship developed, which not only kept them in a working partnership for the remainder of her life, resulting in such classics as the first *The Ten Commandments* and *The King of Kings*, but also linked them romantically.

Films include: 1908 Mr Jones at the Ball (actress only). '11 Enoch Arden (actress only). '14 The Ghost Breaker (actress only). '15 Carmen (actress only); The Captive. '17 A Romance of the Redwoods. '19 Male and Female. '23 Adam's Rib; The Ten Commandments. '27 The King of Kings.

McQUEEN, Steve

(1930–1980). Actor. Born: Terence Steven McQueen; Indianapolis, Indiana, USA

On screen, Steve McQueen was a winner, but for all his cool, smooth, tough exterior, there was a restlessness, a sense of being at odds with the world which was wholly in character with the mad car chase in *Bullitt* and the vain attempt to vault the border wire on a motorbike in *The Great Escape*. He had come a long way from his unpromising beginnings, the juvenile delinquent product of a broken home. Disciplined by a spell in the marines, he drifted to Greenwich Village and there gained his first experience of acting, winning himself a place at the Actors' Studio. Small parts on the stage and television followed, but films like *The Magnificent Seven* soon pushed him to stardom and made him a particularly laconic sex symbol. Off-screen he was reputed to be a rebel, obsessed with racing cars and increasingly dissatisfied with the scripts he was offered. A world-weary quality crept into some of his films – for example *Junior Bonner* – while others, such as *An Enemy of the People*, stretched his acting skills at the expense of his popular appeal. Characteristically, he fought hard against the mesothelioma diagnosed in 1979, but it cut short his life a year later at the age of 50.

Films include: 1956 Somebody Up There Likes Me. '60 The Magnificent Seven. '62 Hell Is for Heroes. '63 The Great Escape. '65 The Cincinnati Kid. '66 Nevada Smith. '68 The Thomas Crown Affair; Bullitt. '71 Le Mans. '72 Junior Bonner. '73 Papillon. '74 The Towering Inferno. '77 An Enemy of the People. '79 Tom Horn. '80 The Hunter.

MacRAE, Gordon

(1921–1986). Actor. Born: East Orange, New Jersey, USA

MacRae was a child actor on radio, becoming a singer when his voice developed. After a first film in which he did not sing, he made a musical debut on screen in *Look for the Silver Lining*, with June Haver, and was then paired in several movies with Doris Day. A handsome, amiable fellow, he scored heavily as Curly in the film version of *Oklahoma!* and then replaced Sinatra in the leading role of *Carousel*. He made a final appearance, playing songwriter Buddy DeSylva, in the biopic *The Best Things in Life Are Free*, before concentrating on his singing career.

Films include: 1949 Look for the Silver Lining. '50 The Daughter of Rosie O'Grady; Tea for Two; Return of the Frontiersman. '51 On Moonlight Bay. '53 The Desert Song; By the Light of the Silvery Moon; Three Sailors and a Girl. '55 Oklahoma! '56 Carousel; The Best Things in Life Are Free. '80 The Pilot (CAN).

MACREADY, George

(1909–1973). Actor. Born: Providence, Rhode Island, USA

'At heart', claimed George Macready, 'I'm really a harmless and calm person'. It was difficult to believe of this six-foot-one, blond, blue-eyed, scar-faced actor who specialized in playing villains. Related to the famous tragedian William Charles Macready, George studied Greek and maths at university and worked in a bank and on a newspaper before trying his hand at acting. He made a good impression in Shakespeare and the popular classics on Broadway, and in 1942 he went to Hollywood, playing bad guys as varied as Rita Hayworth's slimy husband in *Gilda* and the incompetent instigator of the court martial in *Paths of Glory* for the rest of his career.

Films include: 1942 Commandos Strike at Dawn. '45 My Name Is Julia Ross. '46 Gilda; The Man Who Dared. '47 The Swordsman. '48 The Big Clock. '49 Knock on Any Door. '50 Rogues of Sherwood Forest. '57 Paths of Glory. '71 The Return of Count Yorga.

MAGNANI, Anna

(1908–1973). Actress. Born: Alexandria, Egypt

Magnani's life and personality made her admirably suited for the role she was most commonly called upon to play, the archetypal Mediterranean woman – earthy, unglamorous yet brash, passionate and sensual. Born in poverty and raised by her grandparents, she was educated in a convent, and paid for her subsequent acting lessons by singing in a nightclub. She moved into films following her marriage to director Goffredo Alessandrini, but made her biggest impact in Rossellini's *Rome, Open City*. She worked with many top Italian directors, among them Vittorio De Sica and Luchino Visconti, and picked up several awards, including an Oscar for *The Rose Tattoo*, the first of the few films that she made in Hollywood. Her later work was mostly for television, but the huge crowds that attended her funeral in Rome proved that she remained popular to the end.

Films include: 1934 La Cieca di Sorrento (GB: The Blind Woman of Sorrento). '41 La Fuggitiva. '45 Roma, Città Aperta (USA:

Rome, Open City). '48 L'Amore *eps* La Voce Umana, Il Miracolo (USA: The Ways of Love; GB: The Miracle). '51 Bellissima. '52 La Carrozza d'Oro (IT-FR) (USA/GB: The Golden Coach). '55 The Rose Tattoo (USA). '60 The Fugitive Kind (USA); Risate di Gioia (IT) (GB: The Passionate Thief). '69 The Secret of Santa Vittoria (USA). '72 Fellini's Roma (IT-FR).

MAGNUSSON, Charles

(1878–1948). Producer. Born: Göteborg, Sweden

Magnusson's talents as a producer made him a major figure in the development of the Swedish film industry. Magnusson started in the movie business as a newsreel cameraman, filming the *Arrival of King Haakon* in 1905 and travelling to the USA to make a special report on Theodore Roosevelt in 1907. Magnusson was head of production at Svensk Biografteatren between 1908 and 1919 and of Svensk Filmindustri between 1919 and 1928. In addition to writing and directing his own films, Magnusson was skilled at recognizing talent when he saw it, signing up in 1912 the directors Victor Sjöström and Mauritz Stiller. He also acquired the screen rights to the work of Selma Lagerlöf, whose novels subsequently formed the basis of such early Swedish classics as Stiller's *Herr Arnes Pengar* and *Gösta Berlings Saga* and Sjöström's *Körkalen*.

Films include: 1909 Värmlanningarna. '12 Tva Svenska Emigrents Aventyr i Amerika. '13 Lojen och Tarar; Ingeborg Holm (GB: Give Us This Day). '17 Thomas Graals Bästa Film (GB: Wanted, a Film Actress). '19 Herr Arnes Pengar (GB: Sir Arne's Treasure). '20

Karin Ingmarsdotter (GB: God's Way). '21 Körkarlen (GB: Thy Soul Shall Bear Witness/The Phantom Carriage/The Stroke of Midnight). '24 Gösta Berlings Saga (GB: The Atonement of Gösta Berling).

MAIN, Marjorie

(1890–1973). Actress. Born: Mary Tomlinson; Acton, Indiana, USA

Marjorie Main, a minister's daughter, started acting in stock companies and vaudeville. She appeared on Broadway in 1916 and on screen (in *A Home Divided*) in 1932. Lean, angular and strong-jawed, with a rasping vocal delivery, she was utterly compelling in her refusal to harbour her evil son, Baby-Face Martin (Humphrey Bogart) in William Wyler's *Dead End*, a fine partner for Wallace Beery in several MGM movies and delightfully hard-boiled as the hillbilly Ma Kettle in *The Egg and I*. This film initiated a series of nine Ma and Pa Kettle films (in which she starred with Percy Kilbride) between 1949 and 1956. She retired from movies in 1957, having stolen scenes in virtually every film she appeared in.

Films include: 1937 Dead End; Stella Dallas. '39 The Women. '41 The Trial of Mary Dugan; Barnacle Bill. '46 Bad Bascomb. '47 The Egg and I. '49 Big Jack; Ma and Pa Kettle. '50 Mrs O'Malley and Mr Malone. '56 Friendly Persuasion.

MAKAVEJEV, Dušan

(b. 1932). Director. Born: Belgrade, Yugoslavia

Makavejev is one of the few contemporary Yugoslavian directors to have achieved international status,

Left: Steve McQueen in The Cincinnati Kid. *Above: George Macready in* Lady Without a Passport *(1950). Right: Anna Magnani in a typically animated pose in* Made in Italy *(1966)*

Above: Karl Malden as General Omar Bradley in Patton. *Right: Marjorie Main in* Ma and Pa Kettle at the Fair *(1952). Below: Gordon MacRae as the tearaway given a chance to help his family from beyond the grave in* Carousel

his films being popular in the West for their anti-authoritarian attitudes and their jokey equating of sexual freedom with personal liberation. Makavejev studied psychology at Belgrade University, and then enrolled in the Academy of Film, Theatre, Radio and Television. He had entered a short film, *Anthony's Broken Mirror*, in the 1957 Cannes Amateur Film Festival and made several documentaries before he directed his first feature, *Man Is Not a Bird*. His subsequent films won several prizes, establishing his reputation abroad while severely jeopardizing his position in his native country. Following the release of *WR – Mysteries of the Organism*, which poked anarchic fun at Russian communism, Makavejev was forced to look elsewhere for employment. He lectured in film in the USA and Canada, then teamed up with Swedish producer Bo Jonsson to make *Montenegro*, a sort of weird and wonderful soap opera about a bored wife who gets involved with the eccentric owners of a sex club, full of surreal humour and joyful eroticism.

Films include: 1966 Čovek Nije Tijca (GB: Man Is Not a Bird). '67 Ljubavni Slucaj/Tragedija Sluzbenice PTT (GB: The Switchboard Operator). '68 Nevinost Bez Zaštite (USA/GB: Innocence Unprotected). '71 WR – Mysterije Organizma (YUG-GER) (USA/GB: WR – Mysteries of the Organism). '74 Sweet Movie (FR-CAN-GER). '81 Montenegro, or Pigs and Pearls (SWED-GB).

MAKK, Károly

(b. 1925). Director. Born: Budapest, Hungary

Makk was an assistant on *2 × 2* (1944), starring the fascist actor Szillassy, retaining this position when Zoltán Várkonyi reshot large sections of it after the Hungarian Liberation. Makk then studied at the Budapest Academy of Dramatic and Film Art (where he later held the post of professor), was an assistant on Géza Radványi's *Valahol Europaban* (1947, *Somewhere in Europe*) and made numerous newsreels and short films. He directed his first feature, *Liliomfi*, in 1954, which was a comedy that made light-hearted fun of the conventions of operetta. This and subsequent movies such as *Tale of 12 Points*, which dealt with a group of people who won a large sum of money, and *House Under the Rocks*, about a peasant trying to save his marriage, gained him an international reputation as an acute observer of the individual's place in society. His work deteriorated during the Sixties but he achieved widespread critical praise for *Love*, made in 1971. He has also directed several plays for television both abroad and in his native Hungary.

Films include: 1955 Liliomfi; 9-Es Kórterem. '57 Mese a 12 Talátról (Tale of 12 Points). '58 Hàz a Sziklàk Alatt (House Under the Rocks). '64 Elveszett Paradicsom (Lost Paradise). '69 Isten És Ember Elótt (Before God and Man). '71 Szerelem (USA/GB: Love). '74 Macskajáték (USA: Cats' Play). '78 Egy Erkólcsós Ejszaka (A Very Moral Night). '82 Die Jäger (GER); Olelkezo Tekintetek (A Certain Kind of Look).

MALDEN, Karl

(b. 1914). Actor. Born: Mladen Sekulovich; Gary, Indiana, USA

With his bulbous, battered nose and small, bright blue eyes, Malden has one of those ugly-attractive faces that seems to invite examination by the camera, expressions of truculence, sympathy, greed, cowardice or twinkling amusement passing over his well-worn countenance in rapid succession. He has proved a versatile film actor, playing everything from priests to gangleaders and cuckolds to generals in a host of movies since the Forties. Born of Yugoslavian parents, Malden studied acting at the Chicago Art Institute. He moved to New York and established a considerable reputation on Broadway in such plays as *Golden Boy*, *Key Largo*, *All My Sons* and *A Streetcar Named Desire*. He began in movies in 1940 with a minor part in *They Knew What They Wanted*, landing a major supporting role in *Boomerang!*, a thriller directed by Elia Kazan (with whom Malden had frequently worked in the theatre). His movie career really took off after he won a Best Supporting Actor Oscar in Kazan's *A Streetcar Named Desire* as Mitch, Blanche DuBois' shy suitor. His only major excursion into direction was with *Time Limit* (1957), a tense drama about an army court martial. His television roles include the likeable detective Mike Stone in *The Streets of San Francisco*.

Films include: 1946 Boomerang! '47 Kiss of Death. '51 A Streetcar Named Desire. '52 Ruby Gentry. '54 On the Waterfront. '56 Baby Doll. '61 One Eyed Jacks. '62 Birdman of Alcatraz; Gypsy. '65 The Cincinnati Kid. '66 Nevada Smith. '67 Billion Dollar Brain. '70 Patton (GB: Patton, Lust for Glory). '71 Wild Rovers. '79 Beyond the Poseidon Adventure; Meteor.

MALICK, Terrence

(b. 1945). Director/screenwriter. Born: Illinois, USA

Malick's two major films have the common theme of young people caught up in violent events they seem incapable of comprehending. In *Badlands*, Martin Sheen and Sissy Spacek drive across the USA leaving a trail of carnage in their wake; in *Days of Heaven* Richard Gere and Brooke Adams escape poverty in the big city to be embroiled in a nightmare world of treachery and violence. Malick was the son of an oil company executive, grew up in Texas and Oklahoma, and was educated at Harvard and Oxford University. He did odd jobs in the Texas oilfields and on farms and taught philosophy before studying at the American Film Institute in Los Angeles. While there he worked in the movie industry re-writing scripts, including that for *Pocket Money*. He made his first feature, *Badlands* (which he also produced and wrote) for a mere $335,000, many of the actors involved agreeing to let payment of their salaries be deferred until the film's release.

Films include: 1972 Lanton Mills (short); Pocket Money (sc. only). '73 Badlands. '74 The Gravy Train (co-sc. only). '78 Days of Heaven.

MALLE, Louis

(b. 1932). Director. Born: Thumeries, France

Louis Malle developed an interest in film-making during days of enforced idleness (through illness) spent at the movies. However, his parents persuaded him to study political science at the University of Paris, a wish he tried to carry out but never followed through as he left the university to study at the Institut des Hautes Etudes Cinématographiques. He became an assistant to the oceanographer Jacques Cousteau, then worked with Robert Bresson, to whom he attributes much of his style, particularly where a discreet handling of authenticity is concerned; his powers of observation were learnt from watching Jacques Tati movies. Malle's debut as a feature-film director came with the well-received thriller *Ascenseur pour l'Echafaud*. From then on his films made an impact in some way or other, many being memorable for the controversy they caused: *Les Amants* was considered too sexually explicit; *Lacombe Lucien* questioned the guilt of French people involved in collaborating with the enemy in World War II; *Le Feu Follet* deals with a man who can't accept adulthood and so commits suicide; *Pretty Baby* (a film banned in many countries) explores child prostitution; and *Atlantic City USA* is a disillusioned look at a decaying city full of ageing adolescents. In 1968 Malle became 'tired of actors, studios, fiction and Paris', sold his house, divorced his wife and went to make a series of – again controversial – documentaries in India, after which he was accused of giving India a poor name. He continues to make films in Europe and America, and is now married to the actress Candice Bergen.

Films include: 1956 Un Condamné à Mort s'Est Echappé (ass. dir. only) (GB: A Man Escaped). '58 Ascenseur pour l'Echafaud (USA: Frantic; GB: Lift to the Scaffold); Les Amants (USA/GB: The Lovers). '60 Zazie dans le Métro (USA/GB: Zazie). '63 Le Feu Follet (FR-IT) (USA: The Fire Within; GB: A Time to Live and a Time to Die). '65 Viva Maria! (FR-IT). '67 Le Voleur (FR-IT) (USA: The Thief of Paris; GB: The Thief). '69 L'Inde Fantôme (doc series) (GB: Phantom India). '74 Lacombe Lucien. '75 Black Moon (FR-GER). '78 Pretty Baby (USA). '80 Atlantic City USA (CAN-FR-USA) (GB: Atlantic City). '81 My Dinner With André (USA).

MALLESON, Miles

(1888–1969). Actor/screenwriter. Born: Croydon, Surrey, England

From the early Thirties until his death, Malleson was one of the best-loved character actors in British films. With wobbling jowls and sad demeanour, he could be a perfect comic foil; he could also relish a touch of the macabre, portraying with an innocent delight characters like his hangman in *Kind Hearts and Coronets* or his hearse-driver in *Dead of Night* (1945). But all this was only a small part of the man. He was a skilled scenarist, and a playwright, stage director and stage actor of note. Malleson was always a champion of progressive causes. During World War I

he worked for the Conscientious Objectors' movement, and his best-known play, *Six Men of Dorset*, was an account of the Tolpuddle Martyrs.

Films include: 1934 Nell Gwyn (+ sc). '40 The Thief of Bagdad (+ co-sc). '41 Major Barbara. '42 Thunder Rock. '49 Kind Hearts and Coronets. '52 The Importance of Being Earnest. '56 Three Men in a Boat. '59 The Hound of the Baskervilles. '60 Peeping Tom.

MALONE, Dorothy

(b. 1925). Actress. Born: Dorothy Eloise Maloney; Chicago, Illinois, USA

Despite winning a Best Supporting Actress Oscar in 1956 for her performance in Douglas Sirk's *Written on the Wind*, Dorothy Malone has had few major opportunities to display her considerable dramatic talent on film, being best known as Constance Mackenzie in the long-running Sixties television series *Peyton Place*. She grew up in Dallas and worked as a model while still at high school. When appearing in a production of *Star Bound* in 1943 at Southern Methodist University, she was spotted by a talent scout and signed by RKO, who first cast her in *The Falcon and the Co-Eds* (1943). She left RKO for Warner Brothers in 1945, shortened her name to Malone and the following year gave a splendid performance as the bespectacled assistant in a bookstore in *The Big Sleep*. She played nice girls for ten years, attracting little attention; then in 1955 she changed her agent, her hair colour (from brunette to blonde) and her image for *Battle Cry*, and was then cast in the part of the nymphomaniac Marylee in *Written on the Wind*. Her life was seriously threatened by illness in the mid-Sixties, and since then her movie appearances have been few and far between. Her first husband (1959–1963) was the actor Jacques Bergerac, formerly married to Ginger Rogers.

Films include: 1944 One Mysterious Night (GB: Behind Closed Doors). '46 The Big Sleep. '49 South of St Louis; Colorado Territory. '54 Private Hell 36; Young at Heart. '55 Battle Cry. '56 Written on the Wind. '57 The Tarnished Angels. '64 Fate Is the Hunter.

MAMOULIAN, Rouben

(b. 1898). Director. Born: Tiflis, Georgia, Russia

That Mamoulian made a mere 16 films in the 29 years of his cinema career will always be a cause for sadness. But what films they were. Before becoming involved in cinema he studied at the Moscow Art Theatre, but he soon abandoned that realistic mode, and in the Twenties built a reputation as a producer of opera and stage musicals. His stage career continued alongside his film work, and *Porgy and Bess, Oklahoma!* and *Carousel* were among his theatrical triumphs. Mamoulian came to the cinema in the first days of sound. *Applause* was a tremendous start, freeing camera and soundtrack from the

constraints that his contemporaries meekly accepted. There followed the finest version of *Dr Jekyll and Mr Hyde*, revelling in the subjective camera; the effervescent *Love Me Tonight*, a musical in which every movement of actors and camera is a dance of joy; and *Queen Christina*, where Mamoulian made Garbo move to the ticking of a metronome in the scene of memorizing the room and ended with a close-up in which she expresses nothing while the image leads the spectator to imagine what he will. The accepted wisdom that after introducing three-colour Technicolor in *Becky Sharp* Mamoulian did nothing is rubbish: *Summer Holiday* and *Silk Stockings* are the most moving, as well as the most elegant, of musicals.

Films: 1929 Applause. '31 City Streets; Dr Jekyll and Mr Hyde. '32 Love Me Tonight. '33 Song of Songs; Queen Christina. '34 We Live Again. '35 Becky Sharp. '36 The Gay Desperado. '37 High, Wide and Handsome. '39 Golden Boy. '40 The Mark of Zorro. '41 Blood and Sand. '42 Rings on Her Fingers. '47 Summer Holiday. '57 Silk Stockings.

MANCINI, Henry

(b. 1924). Composer/arranger. Born: Cleveland, Ohio, USA

Mancini is best known as the composer of the irresistibly sly tenor sax theme for Blake Edwards' Pink Panther films and cartoons, and as the co-writer of the Oscar-winning songs 'Moon River', reflectively strummed on guitar by Audrey Hepburn in

Breakfast at Tiffany's, and 'Days of Wine and Roses', which featured in the film of the same name. He studied at Juilliard and with such musicians as Mario Castelnuovo and Alfred Sunda, and his haunting melodies and his smooth arrangements for brass (the French horn in particular) show the influence of Glenn Miller, with whose orchestra he worked during the Forties as a pianist and arranger. His early credits included the orchestration for *The Glenn Miller Story* (1953) and *The Benny Goodman Story* (1955); he became particularly sought-after as film composer during the Fifties and Sixties following his jazz score for the *Peter Gunn* television series. His wife is Ginny O'Connor, a former singer with the Glenn Miller – Tex Beneke Orchestra, whom he married in 1947.

Films include: 1958 Touch of Evil. '61 Breakfast at Tiffany's; The Second Time Around. '62 Days of Wine and Roses; Hatari! '63 The Pink Panther; Charade. '64 A Shot in the Dark (GB). '65 The Great Race. '66 Two for the Road. '67 Wait Until Dark. '68 The Party. '75 The Return of the Pink Panther (GB).

MANDER, Miles

(1888–1946). Actor. Born: Lionel Mander; Wolverhampton, Staffordshire, England

Educated at Harrow and McGill University in Montreal, Mander became a sheep-farmer in New Zealand in 1908, but then returned to Britain as

Far left: Miles Malleson sporting typically English headgear. Left: a studio publicity portrait of Miles Mander. Below left: Dorothy Malone in Douglas Sirk's The Tarnished Angels, *a melodrama that attempted to capitalize on the success of* Written on the Wind. *Below: Nino Manfredi, the epitome of suavity. Right: Silvana Mangano as the mother of the beautiful boy who obsesses the composer protagonist (played by Dirk Bogarde) in Luchino Visconti's* Death in Venice

novelist, playwright and occasional scriptwriter and director. He scored a hit with *The First Born*, a light commentary on married life which he acted in, directed, and adapted from his own novel and play, but his directorial career never really took off, and it is as an actor that he will be remembered. A confident, natural performer, he played smooth characters with a touch of weakness about them (Grayle in *Murder, My Sweet*), gentlemanly cads (*The Pleasure Garden*), and a variety of crooks, and did them all with style.

Films include: 1925 The Pleasure Garden. '27 The Fake. '28 The Physician; The First Born (+dir; +prod; +co-sc). '29 The Crooked Billet. '33 The Private Life of Henry VIII. '39 Wuthering Heights (USA); The Man in the Iron Mask (USA). '41 That Hamilton Woman! (USA) (GB: Lady Hamilton). '44 Murder, My Sweet (USA) (GB: Farewell, My Lovely).

MANFREDI, Nino

(b. 1921). Actor. Born: Castro dei Volsci, Italy

Graduating with a degree in law, Manfredi turned actor on stage and radio, and before playing his first film role in 1949 was engaged to dub the voices of other actors. For Italian audiences the French matinée idol Gérard Philipe spoke with the voice of Nino Manfredi. But fame in his own right was not long in coming. Although very few of the numerous

films he made have been widely shown outside Italy, he became one of the leading Italian stars of comedy. He played middle-class, middle-aged father figures, worried emigrants, sympathetic underdogs and the like, and varied his comedy with an occasional dramatic role. He also wrote and directed *Per Grazia Ricevuta*, a Cannes prize-winner.

Films include: 1958 Camping. '60 Audace Colpo dei Soliti Ignoti; Le Pillole di Ercole; L'Impiegato. '61 Crimen (IT-FR) (USA: And Suddenly It's Murder; GB: Killing at Monte Carlo). '62 A Cavallo della Tigre (GB: Jailbreak). '63 L'Amore Difficile *ep* L'Avventura di un Soldato (+dir; +co-sc) (GB: Sex Can be Difficult *ep* The Soldier's Adventure). '66 Operazione San Gennaro (IT-FR-GER) (USA/GB: Treasure of San Gennaro). '67 Il Padre di Famiglia (IT-FR) (USA: The Head of the Family). '71 Per Grazia Ricevuta (+dir; +co-sc).

MANGANO, Silvana

(b. 1930). Actress. Born: Rome, Italy

Mangano, born of an English mother, trained as a dancer under Zhia Ruskaya, then worked as a model. She won the 'Miss Rome' beauty contest in 1946 and was cast in small movie parts until, with a sensational performance in a leading role in Giuseppe De Santis' *Bitter Rice*, she became a world-wide star. As a worker in the Po valley rice fields, whose main interests are boogie-woogie, men and money, she was described as 'pneumatic and primitive' by critics. She became a

kind of neo-realist sex goddess, wowing art-house audiences with her voluptuous sensuality. She married the film's producer, Dino De Laurentiis, in 1949 and continued to give powerful movie performances. She preferred to work in Italian cinema, never venturing to Hollywood, unlike her more famous contemporaries, Sophia Loren and Gina Lollobrigida.

Films include: 1948 Riso Amaro (GB: Bitter Rice). '49 Il Lupo della Sila (GB: The Wolf of Sila). '52 Anna. '57 La Diga sul Pacifico (USA: This Angry Age; GB: The Sea Wall). '58 La Tempesta (GB: The Tempest). '60 Jovanka e l'Altri (IT-USA) (USA/GB: Five Branded Women). '62 Barabba (IT) (USA/GB: Barabbas). '67 Le Streghe (IT-FR) (USA: The Witches); Edipo Re (GB: Oedipus Rex). '68 Teorema (GB: Theorem). '69 Scipione Detto Anche l'Africano. '70 Medea (IT-FR-GER). '71 Morte a Venezia (USA/GB: Death in Venice). '75 Gruppo di Famiglia in un Interno (IT-FR) (GB: Conversation Piece).

MANKIEWICZ, Herman J.

(1897–1953). Screenwriter. Born: New York City, USA

Mankiewicz was educated at Columbia University and in Berlin, where he was also correspondent for the Chicago *Tribune*. He returned to become drama editor of the *New York Times* and the *New Yorker*, before moving to Hollywood in 1926. He worked as a writer – and in the early Thirties as producer – on many of the finest movies of the period, and his

incisive, iconclastic wit flavoured movies as various as *Laughter* (1930) (his own favourite work), *Duck Soup* (1933), and *Citizen Kane*. As a highly civilized and sophisticated writer, Mankiewicz was often at odds with his employers (when Warners put him on a Rin-Tin-Tin movie to punish him, he turned in a script that had the dog carry a baby *into* a burning house), and was all too often driven to drink. But his meeting with Welles sparked off his masterpiece. Of course *Citizen Kane* is Welles' film, but it was Mankiewicz, the old journalist, who knew the publisher William Randolph Hearst/Charles Foster Kane, not Welles, and Kane himself is largely Mankiewicz's creation. He dictated that script from his bed (he had broken his leg), with John Houseman keeping him to it, and it is filled with his own experiences. Even Rosebud was no Freudian symbol: it was a bicycle stolen from the infant Mankiewicz at his home in Wilkes-Barre, Pennsylvania. With the exception of *Citizen Kane*, however, Mankiewicz's list of credits does not testify to his creative genius which, in the Forties and early Fifties, was largely misused by Hollywood.

Films include: 1930 The Vagabond King. '31 The Royal Family of Broadway (co-sc). '32 Million Dollar Legs (co-sc). '33 Dinner at Eight (co-sc). '35 After Office Hours. '39 It's a Wonderful World (co-sc). '40 Citizen Kane (co-sc). '44 Christmas Holiday. '45 The Spanish Main (co-sc). '49 A Woman's Secret. '52 The Pride of St Louis.

MANKIEWICZ, Joseph L.

(b. 1909). Director/producer/screenwriter. Born: Wilkes-Barre, Pennsylvania, USA

Joseph Mankiewicz's early career closely followed that of his elder brother Herman. He too was Berlin correspondent of the Chicago *Tribune*, wrote titles for silents, graduated to scripts and became a producer. But for all their shared love of words, the brothers were radically different, with Herman the brilliant, distrusted intellectual, Joseph the trusted studio pro. His credits as producer include *Fury* (1936), *Three Comrades* (1938), and *The Philadelphia Story* (1940), and his work as director (from 1946), albeit literary and theatrical, is witty and humane, modest in its avoidance of visual rhetoric and resting firmly on the things Mankiewicz did best – directing actors, and giving them marvellous lines. *A Letter to Three Wives* and *All About Eve* won Oscars for Best Screenplay and Best Director and *All About Eve* won the Best Picture Award as well. These are fine films, but even better is *People Will Talk*, a film which Mankiewicz builds round the disturbing, silent presence of the veteran Scottish actor Finlay Currie, to whom, when at last he speaks, Mankiewicz gives words that chill the blood.

Films include: 1948 Escape (GB); A Letter to Three Wives. '50 All About Eve. '51 People Will Talk. '53 Julius Caesar. '54 The Barefoot Contessa. '55 Guys and Dolls. '59 Suddenly, Last Summer. '63 Cleopatra. '67 The Honey Pot. '70 There Was a Crooked Man . . . '73 Sleuth (GB).

science fiction, as well as technical works on pottery and porcelain. *The Hireling*, directed by Alan Bridges from a script by Mankowitz, won the Grand Prix at Cannes in 1973.

Films include: **1954** Make Me an Offer! (co-sc). **'55** A Kid For Two Farthings. **'59** Expresso Bongo. **'60** The Millionairess (co-sc). **'61** The Long and the Short and the Tall (co-sc); The Day the Earth Caught Fire (co-sc). **'62** Waltz of the Toreadors. **'70** Bloomfield (co-sc). **'73** The Hireling.

MANN, Abby

(b. 1927). Screenwriter. Born: Abraham Goodman; Philadelphia, Pennsylvania, USA

Educated at Temple and New York universities, Mann travelled widely in Europe before returning to the USA in 1955, where he began a notable career as a television playwright. Two of his film scripts, *Judgement at Nuremburg* and *A Child is Waiting*, have derived from his own television plays. Much of Mann's work consists of documentary-type dramas on political subjects, but he wrote the pilot film which created the vastly popular Kojak character, while in the cinema he provided the screenplay for *The Detective*, one of the best thrillers of the Sixties.

Films include: **1961** Judgement at Nuremburg. **'62** I Sequestrati di Altona (IT-FR) (USA/GB: The Condemned of Altona). **'63** A Child Is Waiting. **'65** Ship of Fools. **'68** The Detective. **'75** Report to the Commissioner (GB: Operation Undercover).

MANN, Anthony

(1906–1967). Director. Born: Emil Bundsmann; San Diego, California, USA

Anthony Mann worked in the New York theatre from the age of 18, progressed to directing, formed his own stock company, and directed on Broadway. After a brief spell as talent scout for David O. Selznick in New York, he went to Hollywood in 1940, and within two years was directing low-budget pictures for RKO and Republic. This period included excellent thrillers like *Desperate* (1947) and *T-Men*, and in 1950 Mann made his first large-scale film, the Western *Winchester '73*. Other outstanding Westerns followed, five of them starring James Stewart. They were distinguished by spectacular outdoor photography, always enhancing rather than merely decorating the theme of the film, by a meticulous sense of detail, and by a rough immediacy which never tries to blur the violence and the pain. Away from the Western, Mann made *The Tall Target* (1951), a taut thriller set on a train carrying Lincoln and his would-be assassins, and *The Glenn Miller Story*, again with Stewart, a nostalgic tribute to the big-band era. He died while making *A Dandy in Aspic* (1968), the film being completed by its star Laurence Harvey.

Films include: **1942** Dr Broadway. **'46** The Bamboo Blonde. **'47** Railroaded; T-Men. **'49** Border Incident. **'50** Side Street. **'52** Bend of the River (GB: Where the River Bends). **'53** The Naked Spur; The Glenn Miller Story. **'54** The Far Country. **'55** The Man From Laramie. **'58** Man of the West. **'60** Cimarron. **'61** El Cid (USA–IT). **'64** The Fall of the Roman Empire. **'65** The Heroes of Telemark (GB).

MANN, Daniel

(b. 1912). Director. Born: Daniel Chugermann; New York City, USA

Daniel Mann had a long and distinguished stage career before entering films. He worked with the Neighborhood Playhouse in New York and with the Actors' Studio, taught drama, and directed on Broadway. Moving to Hollywood in the early Fifties, Mann filmed two plays he had directed on stage, *Come Back, Little Sheba* and *The Rose Tattoo*. His style was theatrical, but he proved a remarkable director of actresses. The stars of both these films, Shirley Booth and Anna Magnani, won Oscars, as did Elizabeth Taylor a few years later in Mann's *Butterfield 8*. But he was lost without such strong material, and his subsequent films have been routine.

Films include: **1952** Come Back, Little Sheba. **'54** About Mrs Leslie. **'55** The Rose Tattoo; I'll Cry Tomorrow. **'56** The Teahouse of the August Moon. **'59** The Last Angry Man. **'60** Butterfield 8. **'62** Five Finger Exercise. **'65** Judith; Our Man Flint. **'68** For Love of Ivy. **'71** Willard. **'72** The Revengers.

MANN, Delbert

(b. 1920). Director. Born: Lawrence, Kansas, USA

After some stage experience, Delbert Mann entered television as an assistant director in 1949, was rapidly promoted, and between 1950 and 1955 directed over one hundred plays. Like other television directors of that time, such as Martin Ritt and Sidney Lumet, Mann moved to the big screen, and his first film, *Marty*, from one of his small-screen plays, won Oscars for Best Picture, Best Director and Best Actor (Ernest Borgnine). *The Bachelor Party*, also adapted from his television version, was another modest and affectionate picture, and *The Dark at the Top of the Stairs* was a shrewd study of domestic conflict. Since then Mann has lost his way, with literary adaptations designed for television, and a disastrous remake of *All Quiet on the Western Front* (1980).

Films include: **1955** Marty. **'57** The Bachelor Party. **'58** Desire Under the Elms. **'60** The Dark at the Top of the Stairs. **'61** The Outsider; Lover Come Back. **'60** That Touch of Mink. **'69** David Copperfield (GB). **'70** The Out-of-Towners.

MANSFIELD, Jayne

(1933–1967). Actress. Born: Vera Jayne Palmer; Bryn Mawr, Pennsylvania, USA

After working in a stock company in Dallas, Jayne Mansfield went to Hollywood in 1954 with film ambitions,

Above: Jayne Mansfield suffers for her art in a studio publicity shot. Below: Fredric March with Myrna Loy in The Best Years of Our Lives

MANKOWITZ, Wolf

(b. 1924). Screenwriter. Born: Cyril Wolf Mankowitz; London, England.

Born in the East End of London to Russian Jewish immigrants, Mankowitz won scholarships which took him to Downing College, Cambridge. In 1949 he and his brother opened an antique shop and Wolf built a reputation as a versatile writer, producing short stories, novels, plays, and eventually screenplays. *Make Me an Offer!*, based on his experience as an antique dealer, was in turn novel, stage play and film. Mankowitz's best work is rich in East End character and idiom, but he has also written imaginative and appeared on television before her film debut in 1955. A publicist's delight, she was almost always cast as a blonde and bosomy Monroe look-alike. She was a critical success on Broadway in *Will Success Spoil Rock Hunter?* and also appeared in the screen version. She may have had acting ability, but her films gave her little chance to show it. Only *The Girl Can't Help It*, *Will Success Spoil Rock Hunter?* and Paul Wendkos' *The Burglar* had much merit in a dismal collection. She was killed in a car crash on her way to a television engagement in New Orleans.

Films include: 1955 Pete Kelly's Blues; Illegal. '56 The Girl Can't Help It. '57 The Burglar; The Wayward Bus; Will Success Spoil Rock Hunter? (GB: Oh, for a Man). '58 The Sheriff of Fractured Jaw (GB). '63 Promises! Promises! '67 A Guide for the Married Man; Single Room Furnished.

MARAIS, Jean

(b. 1913). Actor. Born: Jean Marais-Villain; Cherbourg, France.

The good-looking son of a vet, Jean Marais did his acting apprenticeship on the French stage where he was given walk-on parts until he met and befriended Jean Cocteau. For much of Marais' career Cocteau wrote and directed for him. After his appearance in *Les Parents Terrible* a critic said of him 'he is beautiful', but his acting didn't stand up to much criticism on that occasion. His blond Aryan looks made him a natural for the romantic lead in *L'Eternel Retour* (1943, *Love Eternal*), after which he became an idol. He went from strength to strength during the Forties and Fifties, playing the prince and the beast in *La Belle et la Bête*, Don José in *Carmen* and the title role in Cocteau's popular and successful tale of the nether world, *Orphée*. His popularity continued during the Sixties and Seventies, and he worked with other directors, learning new styles and improving his technique. He remains a sought-after property.

Films include: 1942 Carmen. '46 La Belle et la Bête. '47 Les Chouans. '48 Les Parents Terribles (USA: Intimate Relations); L'Aigle à Deux Têtes (USA: The Eagle With Two Heads; GB: The Eagle Has Two Heads). '50 Le Château de Verre; Orphée (USA: Orpheus). '59 Le Testament d'Orphée (USA/GB: Testament of Orpheus). '61 Napoleon II, l'Aiglon. '65 Le Gentleman de Cocody (FR-IT) (GB: Ivory Coast Adventure). '66 Le Saint Prend l'Affût (FR-IT). '70 Peau d'Ane (GB: The Magic Donkey).

MARCH, Fredric

(1897–1975). Actor. Born: Ernest Frederick McIntyre Bickel; Racine, Wisconsin. USA

At the age of 13 Fredric March was producing his own plays, but on leaving high school he worked in a bank before World War I disrupted his life. It was while recovering from an appendicitis operation some years later that March suddenly decided to follow his instinct and go on stage. His debut

Below: a dashing Jean Marais in Sept Hommes, un Garce *(1967)*

was in David Belasco's *Deburau*, after which he took minor parts in many films during the Twenties. He worked his way up to starring in the talkies, and for several years played romantic leads in dramas and comedies after his portrayal of John Barrymore in the stage play *The Royal Family* won him a Paramount contract. In 1935 he played the Russian count who sweeps Garbo off her feet in *Anna Karenina* and went on to give a marvellous performance as the fading screen idol in *A Star is Born*. From 1937 he chose his roles carefully, and was one of the few American male stars to carry off costume drama with panache. In the latter years of his career he became a character actor of some standing.

Films include: 1931 Dr Jekyll and Mr Hyde; The Royal Family of Broadway. '34 The Barretts of Wimpole Street. '35 Anna Karenina; Les Misérables. '37 A Star is Born. '42 I Married a Witch. '46 The Best Years of Our Lives. '51 Death of a Salesman. '56 The Man in the Gray Flannel Suit. '60 Inherit the Wind. '73 The Iceman Cometh.

MAREY, Étienne-Jules

(1830–1904). Physician/physiologist. Born: Beaune, France.

Étienne Marey had long experimented with graphic methods of recording animal and bird movement, and was beginning to apply photography to his work when he met Eadweard Muybridge towards the end of the 1870s. Muybridge had invented a mechan-

ism whereby a battery of cameras were triggered off as a moving object passed before them. By 1882 Marey had taken this a step further by inventing the *fusil photographique* (photographic gun) which took twelve individual photographs in one second. The recording method – derived from an invention by astronomer Jules Janssen – was ingeniously simple; initially Marey used circular plates which revolved each time the shutter opened to reveal a small area of sensitized surface. Eventually Marey was using a continuous strip of paper film, and when the celluloid film was introduced by Eastman, Marey developed his Chronophotographic camera to capture movement in a rapidly taken succession of images.

MARGOLIN, Janet

(b. 1943). Actress. Born: New York City, USA

Having studied drama at the High School of Performing Arts, Margolin worked as an assistant at the Shakespeare Festival Theatre before making her stage debut as a mentally disturbed girl in *Daughter of Silence*. Her success was immediate and the director Frank Perry cast her in his film *David and Lisa*, in which she gave a stunning performance as the mute girl who begins to talk in couplets and falls in love with a disturbed boy. She was Mary of Bethany in *The Greatest Story Ever Told* and the perfect foil to

Right: the vulnerable beauty of Janet Margolin

Woody Allen as the laundress in *Take the Money and Run*. In 1961 she won the Blum Award for Most Promising Actress, but she worked very irregularly in movies throughout the Seventies. Her dark beauty has been largely wasted in routine vehicles and television series such as *The Defenders* and *Police Story*.

Films include: 1962 David and Lisa. '65 Bus Riley's Back in Town; The Greatest Story Ever Told. '66 The Eavesdropper (USA-ARGENTINA); Nevada Smith. '67 Enter Laughing. '68 Buona Sera, Mrs Campbell. '69 Take the Money and Run. '73 Your Three Minutes Are Up. '77 Annie Hall. '79 Last Embrace.

MÁRIÁSSY, Félix

(1919–1975). Director. Born: Mikosal, Hungary

Fascinated by life in post-war Hungary, Félix Máriássy created a new level of realism in socialist cinema. *Kis Katalin Házassága*, a film reflecting the political climate of the time, and the later *Rokonok* illustrate his eye for the human character and his subtlety when dealing with social relations. Born into an aristocratic family he originally intended to be a designer, but decided to become a film-maker when he was 20. Having served an obligatory apprenticeship as editor and assistant director he made his solo debut in 1949 with *Szabóné*, about problems in a factory and the workers' attempts to overcome them. His films marked a departure from the new Hungarian directors who had placed documentary at the heart of film-making, although he turned to documentaries when illness prevented him from producing regular features. His wife Judith Máriássy wrote most of his films.

Films include: 1949 Szabóné (Anna Szabó). '50 Kis Katalin Házassága (Catherine's Marriage). '54 Rokonok (Relatives). '55 Budapesti Tavasz (Springtime in Budapest). '58 Csemp Eszek (The Smugglers). '59 Álmatlan Évek (Sleepless Years). '62 Pirosbetűs Hétköznapok (HUN-CZ) (Every Day Sunday). '64 Karambol (Goliath). '66 Fugefalevel (Fig Leaf). '68 Kötölék (Bondage). '70 Imposztorok (Impostors).

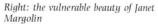

289

MARION, Frances

(1887–1973). Screenwriter. Born: Frances Marion Owens; San Francisco, California, USA

During the silent era Frances Marion wrote films for stars like Lillian Gish, Greta Garbo and Rudolph Valentino, and she intuitively provided the right material for them – honest, emotional stories with the human touch and dynamic plots. She was a shrewd judge of screen talent and gave many performers the right material to begin their glossy careers. She began her own career as a writer on the *San Francisco Examiner* and was one of the first female war correspondents covering World War I battles. A talented painter, model and actress, she decided to go behind the camera and write screenplays after playing a vamp opposite Mary Pickford. She also collaborated with the director (and her second husband) George Hill on a number of films such as *The Big House* and *The Secret Six*. Her string of successes ensured her promotion and she became script supervisor and 'script doctor' at MGM. But she also lost control of her own writing – by 1940 she had stopped writing scripts altogether – and although she tried some directing and producing these independent ventures were not well received. She won two Best Screenplay Academy Awards, for *The Big House* and *The Champ*.

Films include: 1917 Rebecca of Sunnybrook Farm. '20 Humoresque. '26 Stella Dallas. '30 Anna Christie; Min and Bill (co-sc); The Big House. '31 The Secret Six; The Champ. '33 The Prizefighter and the Lady (co-sc) (GB: Everywoman's Man). '36 Riffraff (co-sc); Camille (co-sc).

MARKER, Chris

(b. 1921). Director. Born: Christian François Bouche-Villeneuve; Paris, France

Chris Marker began his career as a novelist. He then produced a photographic study of Korea and from there moved into films, working as assistant to Alain Resnais. His first solo films *Dimanche à Pékin*, *Lettre de Sibérie* and *Cuba Si!* were rather like filmed letters. Perhaps even more remarkable was *La Jetée*, a post-nuclear war film about time and memory made up of hundreds of still photographs. Marker's innovative approach to documentary is more clearly delineated in *Le Joli Mai*, a composite picture of Paris life in May 1962 which illustrates his humanitarian optimism, and which was also one of the films that launched *cinéma vérité*. He then formed SLON (Société pour le Lancement des Oeuvres Nouvelles) – a collection of political film-makers whose main achievement was *Loin du Vietnam*, a collective statement on the Vietnam War, co-ordinated by Marker.

Films include: 1956 Dimanche à Pékin. '58 Lettre de Sibérie. '62 Cuba Si! (CUBA-FR); La Jetée (GB: The Pier). '63 Le Joli Mai (GB: The Lovely Month of May). '67 Loin du Vietnam (prod; + ed. only) (GB: Far From Vietnam). '69 La Bataille des Dix Millions (USA/GB: Cuba: Battle of the 10,000,000). '71 Les Mots Ont un Sens. '77 Le Fond de l'Air Est Rouge.

MARQUAND, Christian

(b. 1927). Actor/director. Born: Marseille, France

Tall, dark, slim, virile and volatile, Christian Marquand is everyone's idea of the French resistance hero. He began as a stage actor at 17 and worked regularly as a leading man in Paris and London. In 1946 he was picked up by Jean Cocteau for a bit part in *La Belle et la Bête*. He soon became a male sex-symbol and played opposite his female counterparts in many French, Italian and Hollywood-made movies, while still continuing with his stage career. He attempted to hide his image by working on the other side of the camera, and after his astonishing success directing the sex-spoof *Candy* he announced that he was giving up acting. Unfortunately few directorial assignments came along and he returned to acting. His later roles in such films as *The Other Side of Midnight*, although non-starring, have been respectable.

Films include: 1947 Quai des Orfèvres (USA: Jenny Lamour). '51 Les Mains Sales (GB: Dirty Hands). '53 Lucrezia Borgia (FR-IT) (GB: Lucretia Borgia). '56 Et Dieu Créa la Femme (USA/GB: And Woman . . . Was Created/And God Created Woman). '58 Une Vie (FR-IT) (USA: End of Desire; GB: One Life). '62 The Longest Day (USA). '63 Les Grands Chemins (dir; + co-sc. only) (FR-IT) (GB: Of Flesh and Blood). '66 The Flight of the Phoenix (USA). '68 Candy (dir. only) (USA-FR-IT). '77 The Other Side of Midnight (USA).

MARSH, Mae

(1895–1968). Actress. Born: Mary Warne Marsh; Madrid, New Mexico

After a disturbed childhood – her father died when Mae was four and shortly after the family moved to San Francisco it was destroyed in the 1906 earthquake – Mae Marsh was encouraged to become an actress by her elder sister who was making musical comedy here career. In 1912 the sisters visited the Biograph studios whereupon D.W. Griffith, attracted by Mae's 'frail appealing look', offered her a contract. By the end of the year she was playing lead roles and in 1913 was groomed as Mary Pickford's successor. *The Birth of a Nation*, in which she plays a nervous girl who eventually leaps to her death while escaping a rapist, established her as a star, a status consolidated by her role in *Intolerance*: as the wife of an innocent man sentenced to death and only reprieved at the last moment she gave a warm, emotional performance scattered with child-like gestures and hops and skips denoting happiness. Her move to Goldwyn proved to be less happy; the films she was given were disappointing and on her marriage in 1918 she retired to devote herself to family life and the security of her husband's wealth. However, after losing most of it in the Wall Street Crash she returned to the screen in the Thirties and continued to take small roles in a variety of movies – many of them for director John Ford – until 1967.

Films include: 1912 Man's Genesis; The Sands of Dee. '13 Judith of Bethulia. '15 The Birth of a Nation. '16 Intolerance. '23 Paddy the Next Best Thing (GB); The White Rose. '34 Little Man, What Now? '40 The Grapes of Wrath. '45 A Tree Grows in Brooklyn. '52 Night Without Sleep; The Quiet Man. '53 The Sun Shines Bright. '56 The Searchers. '61 Two Rode Together.

MARSHALL, E. G.

(b. 1910). Actor. Born: Everett G. Marshall; Owatonna, Minnesota, USA

In an attempt to enter the world of show business E. G. Marshall formed a band, playing the guitar and singing. It performed on the radio and in clubs with moderate success but as interest waned Marshall formed a repertory troupe called The Oxford Players and took them on tour. In 1937 he went to New York and after appearing in several little-known plays he found himself on Broadway in *The Iceman Cometh*. He made his film debut in *The House on 92nd Street* (1945), but his rather nondescript face meant he was given fairly unchallenging roles – he was the governor of a Western state in *Broken Lance* and was a member of the jury in *Twelve Angry Men* – and he concentrates his talents on stage and small screen. He won two Emmy Awards for his starring role in the television series *The Defenders* and has hosted documentaries made by National Geographic.

Films include: 1948 Call Northside 777. '54 The Caine Mutiny; Broken Lance. '55 The Silver Chalice. '56 The Mountain. '57 Twelve Angry Men; Bachelor Party. '58 The Buccaneer. '70 Tora! Tora! Tora! (USA-JAP). '78 Interiors.

MARSHALL, George

(1891–1975). Director. Born: Chicago, Illinois, USA

After being expelled from the University of Chicago in 1912 and trying

his luck as a mechanic and newspaper reporter, Marshall involved himself in the emergence of the film industry first as an extra at Universal, then as a screenwriter and by 1917 he had graduated to direction. He served in World War I, after which he went back to Hollywood where he made many of the Tom Mix Westerns before specializing in comedy. His method of working was to do away with character acting, as he did not hold with the idea of directors and actors spending too much time on films – a hangover from the days when he churned out three-reeler shorts – and he based his humour on sight-and-sound gags as performed by Laurel and Hardy, W. C. Fields, Bob Hope and Lucille Ball. From 1925 to 1930 he was supervising director of all comedies put out by Fox, and then continued to direct throughout his life, in the latter years working in television on series such as *Policewoman*, *Here's Lucy* and *The Odd Couple*.

Films include: 1939 Destry Rides Again; You Can't Cheat an Honest Man. **'40** The Ghost Breakers. **'45** Incendiary Blonde. **'46** The Blue Dahlia. **'47** The Perils of Pauline. **'49** My Friend Irma. **'50** Fancy Pants. **'53** Houdini. **'58** The Sheepman. **'62** How the West Was Won (co-dir). **'69** Hook, Line and Sinker.

MARSHALL, Herbert

(1890–1966). Actor. Born: London, England

Raised in a theatrical family, Marshall joined the Brighton repertory company and made his stage debut with *The Adventures of Lady Ursula* and was soon appearing frequently on the London stage. During World War I he lost his right leg but this did not deter him in the least from his acting career. He became a popular stage performer in both London and New York. Soon after his screen debut in England in 1927 he appeared in his first important film *The Letter*, playing opposite Jeanne Eagels. Although he continued to act on the stage, often with his wife Edna Best, he was ultimately drawn to Hollywood where he settled down to play mature, romantic leads.

Films include: 1929 The Letter. **'30** Murder (GB). **'31** Michael and Mary (GB). The Calendar (GB). **'32** Trouble in Paradise; Blonde Venus. **'33** I Was a Spy (GB). **'40** The Letter; Foreign Correspondent. **'41** The Little Foxes. **'46** Duel in the Sun.

MARSHALL, Tully

(1864–1943). Actor. Born: Nevada City, California, USA

Marshall's career began on stage in 1887 with his New York debut made in *Twelfth Night*, opposite Madame Modjeska. His wife, Marion Fairfax, wrote for him during this period. His stage performances ended when he was spotted by D. W. Griffith who cast him as the High Priest in *Intolerance* (1916), the film which initiated his long and respected career as a screen actor. He proved his versatility and talent in such films as *Oliver Twist* (as Fagin) and *The Hunchback of Notre Dame* (as King Louis XI).

Films include: 1916 Oliver Twist. **'23** The Hunchback of Notre Dame; Richard the Lion-Hearted. **'24** The Stranger. **'25** The Merry Widow. **'27** The Cat and the Canary. **'29** Alias Jimmy Valentine; The Mysterious Dr Fu Manchu. **'30** Redemption. **'35** Black Fury. **'39** Blue Montana Skies.

MARTIN, Dean

(b. 1917). Actor. Born: Dino Crocetti; Steubenville, Ohio, USA

After his high school education, Dean Martin moved to Long Beach, California, with his family and was soon established as a nightclub singer. Then came the renowned teaming up with comedian Jerry Lewis. In the Fifties the two became the highest paid comedy stars in the USA. In 1956 the team dissolved. With his debonair looks and laconic, relaxed manner, Martin easily adapted to romantic leads in his solo films, and appeared in a series of spoof spy movies. He also became a major recording star with the song 'Memories Are Made of This'.

Films include: 1949 My Friend Irma. **'52** Jumping Jacks; The Stooge. **'53** The Caddy. **'55** You're Never Too Young; Artists and Models. **'56** Hollywood or Bust. **'58** Some Came Running. **'59** Rio Bravo. **'60** Bells Are Ringing. **'62** Sergeants Three. **'63** Toys in the Attic; Four for Texas. **'64** Kiss Me, Stupid. **'66** The Silencers. **'67** Rough Night in Jericho. **'68** Bandolero!; Five Card Stud. **'70** Airport. **'75** Mr Ricco.

MARTIN, Mary

(b. 1914). Actress. Born: Weatherford, Texas, USA

Although she had a notable talent for singing and dancing as a child, Mary Martin did not pursue this career

Opposite page. Far left: Christian Marquand in the epic film of the D-Day landings The Longest Day. *Above centre: Mae Marsh in D. W. Griffith's* The Birth of a Nation. *Below centre: E.G. Marshall in* Tora! Tora! Tora! *Right: Herbert Marshall with Garbo in* The Painted Veil *(1934). This Page. Far left: a studio publicity shot of Tully*

straight away. She married early (and gave birth to Larry Hagman, the adored and despised J. R. in television's long-running *Dallas* series) and then, after a quick divorce, opened a dancing school. Her Broadway career began as a result of nightclub appearances and in 1939 she was given a Paramount contract and proceeded to make nine films in three years. She characteristically appeared in light musicals, winning audiences with her verve and vitality rather than by spectacular singing.

Films include: 1939 The Great Victor Herbert. **'40** Rhythm on the River. **'41** Love Thy Neighbour; Kiss the Boys Goodbye; The Birth of the Blues; New York Town. **'43** Star Spangled Rhythm; Happy Go Lucky; True to Life. **'46** Night and Day.

MARTIN, Strother

(1919–1980). Actor. Born: Kokomo, Indiana, USA

While working towards his degree in theatre at the University of Michigan,

Marshall. Above left: Dean Martin propping up the bar in Kiss Me, Stupid. *Above: Mary Martin in* Night and Day, *an anodyne musical biography of Cole Porter. Below: Strother Martin in* Slap Shot, *a no-punches-pulled story about an unsuccessful ice-hockey team, also starring Paul Newman*

Martin became a champion diver. After service in World War II he went to Hollywood as a swimming instructor. He began to appear on television and in small theatre groups through the Fifties and made his screen debut with a small part in *The Asphalt Jungle* (1950). In the Sixties his film career gathered momentum as he appeared in Westerns in character roles, describing himself at the time as a 'specialist in playing prairie scum'. He often appeared with Paul Newman, who was a good friend off-screen, in such films as *Cool Hand Luke* in which he was a vicious prison warden. Lee Marvin once said of him that 'the kind of characters that Strother plays are the ones you can always tell are headed for a cheap funeral'.

Films include: 1959 The Horse Soldiers. **'61** The Deadly Companions. **'62** The Man Who Shot Liberty Valance. **'67** Cool Hand Luke. **'69** Butch Cassidy and the Sundance Kid; The Wild Bunch; True Grit. **'70** The Ballad of Cable Hogue. **'73** Sssssss (GB: Ssssnake). **'75** Rooster Cogburn. **'77** Slap Shot.

MARTINELLI, Elsa

(b. 1935). Actress. Born: Rome, Italy

Born into a poor family of nine children, Elsa Martinelli began earning her keep at the age of 12. Moving from bar work to modelling she entered films with the help of Kirk Douglas who owned a fashion company: her screen debut was opposite him in *The Indian Fighter*. With her exotic, sensual looks, she was signed by Carlo Ponti and returned to Italy where her image rivalled that of Gina Lollabrigida. She has varied her roles to avoid stereotyping, from a magazine photographer in *Hatari!* to a wife discovered in an Ancient Roman brothel in *The Oldest Profession*.

Films include: 1955 The Indian Fighter (USA). '56 Four Girls in Town (USA); La Risaia (USA/GB: Rice Girls). '57 Manuela (GB) (USA: Stowaway Girl). '59 I Battellieri del Volga (GB: The Boatmen). '60 . . . Et Mourir de Plaisir (FR–IT) (GB: Blood and Roses). '62 Hatari! (USA). '63 The VIPs (GB). '67 Maroc 7 (GB); Le Plus Vieux Métier du Monde *ep* Nuits Romaines (FR–IT–GER) (GB: The Oldest Profession *ep* Roman Nights). '76 Il Garofano Rosso.

MARVIN, Lee

(b. 1924). Actor. Born: New York City, USA

Lee Marvin, with his now familiar silver-haired appearance and gravelly voice, took a long time to reach stardom, spending several years on active service in the US Marine Corps before turning to acting. Some thirty films and two hundred and fifty television shows after his screen debut, *You're in the Navy Now*, he landed the lead in *Cat Ballou* and won an Oscar for his dual role as an ancient, moth-eaten ex-gunfighter with a taste for alcohol and his murderous brother. Apart from the idiosyncratic musical *Paint Your Wagon*, his later films have been mostly violent thrillers in which he plays the cynical, tough – and often psychopathic – killer.

Films include: 1951 You're in the Navy Now. '52 Duel at Silver Creek. '53 The Big Heat; The Wild One. '54 The Caine Mutiny. '56 Attack! '62 The Man Who Shot Liberty Valance. '64 The Killers. '65 Cat Ballou. '66 The Professionals. '67 The Dirty Dozen; Point Blank. '68 Hell in the Pacific. '69 Paint Your Wagon. '70 Monte Walsh. '72 Prime Cut. '74 The Klansman. '76 Shout at the Devil. '80 The Big Red One. '81 Death Hunt.

MARX BROTHERS, The

Chico Marx (1887–1961). Actor. Born: Leonard Marx; New York City, USA

Harpo Marx (1888–1964). Actor. Born: Adolph Marx; New York City, USA

Groucho Marx (1890–1977). Actor. Born: Julius Henry Marx; New York City, USA

Zeppo Marx (1901–1979). Actor. Born: Herbert Marx; New York City, USA

The sons of Minnie Schoenberg from Germany and Sam Marx from Alsace were raised in poverty in Manhattan. Groucho was the first to go on stage – as a boy soprano, and then with the Gus Edwards school act. In 1908 Minnie put him, Harpo and another brother, Gummo (born Milton, 1897–1977), into a vaudeville musical act, The Three Nightingales, that would later grow into a comedy team, The Six Mascots, around 1912. This had some success with its *Fun in Hi Skule* skit and especially when the Marxes' uncle, vaudevillian Al Shean, helped refine their stage characters – Harpo donned a red wig and lost his voice, Chico became the Italian straight man, and Groucho stooped and went garrulous. By the early Twenties they were able to tour Britain, and in 1924 they finally made it big on Broadway with *I'll Say She Is* and later with *The Cocoanuts*, which, with the talkies, became their first film. Twelve more would follow, of which four for Paramount (*Animal Crackers, Monkey Business, Horse Feathers* and *Duck Soup*) and two for MGM (*A Night at the Opera* and *A Day at the Races*) are regarded as classics. It is impossible to distil the Marx Brothers' surreal comedy. Theirs was a manic, furiously funny and unmanageable assault on American institutions. Anything that came in their path they would wreck: Groucho with his stream of barbed insults, most of them heaped on long-suffering Margaret Dumont, most of them founded on his lack of sex and money; Chico through remorseless ignorance and double-dealing; and the dumb, inhuman Harpo (he eats plates and drinks ink and loves animals) with his unhinged, uncontrollable, anti-social comic terrorism. It is remarkable that any director could direct them, but Norman Z. McLeod, Leo McCarey and

Above, far left: a publicity shot of Elsa Martinelli. Above left: Lee Marvin in John Boorman's revenge thriller Point Blank. *Above: the four Marx Brothers, (left to right) Zeppo, Groucho, Chico and Harpo in their*

first feature, The Cocoanuts. *Below: James Mason as a schoolmaster in* Child's Play *(1972). Below left: the waifish Giulietta Masina as Gelsomina in Fellini's* La Strada, *the film that made her an international star*

Sam Wood all tried and the Marxes' films are packed with irresistible moments. It all boils down to the divine logic of Fiorello (Chico) reminding Otis B. Driftwood (Groucho) in *A Night at the Opera* that in a Marx Brothers contract 'There ain't no Sanity Clause!'; or Harpo putting to sleep with a spray can of ether the entire cast of *Animal Crackers* – including himself and the blonde he has chased throughout the film.

Films together: 1926 Humorisk (unreleased). '29 The Cocoanuts. '30 Animal Crackers. '31 Monkey Business. '32 Horse Feathers. '33 Duck Soup. *Groucho, Chico and Harpo only:* '35 A Night at the Opera. '37 A Day at the Races. '38 Room Service. '39 At the Circus. '40 Go West. '41 The Big Store. '46 A Night in Casablanca. '49 Love Happy. '57 The Story of Mankind (separate appearances).

MASINA, Giulietta

(b. 1920). Actress. Born: Giulia Anna Masina; Giorgio di Piano, near Bologna, Italy

After making her screen debut in Roberto Rossellini's *Paisà*, Giulietta Masina was the star of several of the Fifties and Sixties films of her husband, Federico Fellini, whom she met

while appearing in a 1942 radio play that he had written. An actress of great depth and passion, her ability to endow the ordinary with touches of the bizarre has enhanced Fellini's movement from his early neo-realist works to his later surreal masterpieces. Her total identification with her husband's career has kept her something of an enigma in the film world. One of the few non-Fellini films she played in was *The Madwoman of Chaillot* in which she reportedly took a small part in order to get Katharine Hepburn's autograph.

Films include: 1946 Paisà (USA/GB: Paisan). '50 Persiane Chiuse (USA/GB: Behind Closed Shutters). '51 Europa '51 (USA: The Greatest Love). '54 La Strada. '55 Donne Proibite (GB: Forbidden Women); Il Bidone (GB: The Swindlers). '57 Le Notti di Cabiria (USA: Nights of Cabiria; GB: Cabiria). '58 Fortunella. '65 Giulietta degli Spiriti (GB: Juliet of the Spirits). '67 Non Stuzzicate la Zanzara. '69 The Madwoman of Chaillot (GB).

MASON, James

(1909–1984). Actor. Born: Huddersfield, Yorkshire, England

The son of a wealthy wool merchant, James Mason had a privileged

292

English upbringing, being educated at Marlborough and Cambridge. After a disastrous start in films when he was removed from Alexander Korda's *The Private Life of Don Juan* (1934) he made his debut in a 'quota quickie' the following year. He reached stardom in the Forties with a series of melodramas for Gainsborough studios, in the first of which, *The Man in Grey*, he portrayed a sadistic aristocrat who delights in humiliating his aristocratic wife. In the Fifties he went to Hollywood, making his mark in films like Hitchcock's *North by Northwest* or alongside Judy Garland in *A Star Is Born*. Apart from his memorable performance in *Lolita*, his later films were generally unworthy of his talents although his presence enhanced movies like the Agatha Christie thriller *Evil Under the Sun*. James Mason's long career was a search for quality roles in quality films, few of which were available to him in Britain in the Forties when his cruel handsomeness made him the country's biggest star. His open criticism of the British industry and his departure for America made him a rebel – but there he was able to mature as the excellent performer he undoubtedly was.

Films include: 1935 Late Extra. '37 The Mill on the Floss. '39 Hatter's Castle. '42 Thunder Rock. '43 The Bells Go Down; The Man in Grey. '44 Fanny by Gaslight. '45 The Seventh Veil; The Wicked Lady. '47 Odd Man Out. '49 The Reckless Moment (USA). '52 The Prisoner of Zenda (USA). '53 The Man Between; Julius Caesar (USA). '54 A Star Is Born (USA). '59 North by Northwest (USA). '60 The Trials of Oscar Wilde (USA: The Man With the Green Carnation). '62 Lolita. '64 The Pumpkin Eater. '66 Georgy Girl. '70 Spring and Port Wine. '73 The Mackintosh Man. '75 Mandingo (USA); Autobiography of a Princess. '77 Cross of Iron (GB-GER). '78 The Boys From Brazil (USA). '81 Evil Under the Sun. '82 The Verdict.

MASON, Marsha

(b. 1942). Actress. Born: St Louis, Missouri, USA

Until the early Seventies Marsha Mason had been almost entirely a stage actress. She had amassed a solid body of stage experience and made two films when she met the screenwriter Neil Simon, the man who was to become her second husband and also have a major influence on her career. Her first starring role saw her opposite James Caan in *Cinderella Liberty*, a performance that gained her a Best Actress Academy Award nomination. She soon received another for her superb portrayal of a single parent who reluctantly agrees to share an apartment with a struggling actor (Richard Dreyfuss) in Simon's story *The Goodbye Girl*. Mason's sense of timing is perfectly suited to Simon's snappy one-liners, and she has since appeared in two more of his films – *The Cheap Detective*, in which she had a cameo role as a glamorous widow, and *Chapter Two*, as the honeymooning wife helping her new husband (Caan) to get over his first marriage. She has also appeared on American television in *Love of Life* and *Dr Kildare*.

Films include: 1966 Hot Rod Hullabaloo. '68 Beyond the Law. '73 Blume in Love; Cinderella Liberty. '77 The Goodbye Girl;

Audrey Rose. '78 The Cheap Detective. '79 Chapter Two; Promises in the Dark. '81 Only When I Laugh (GB: It Hurts Only When I Laugh).

MASSEY, Daniel

(b. 1933). Actor. Born: London, England

Born into a stage family (his father is Raymond Massey; his sister, Anna Massey), Daniel Massey went to Eton and Cambridge before turning to the stage, making his London debut in *The Happiest Millionaire*. Among his most well-known film roles have been Robert Dudley, Elizabeth I's favourite, in *Mary, Queen of Scots* and the young Noel Coward in *Star!* His forte, that of playing effete upper-class gentlemen, however, has been found on television, most notably in *War and Peace* – as Prince Andrei – and as the self-effacing homosexual in *Roads to Freedom*. He was married for a time to the actress Adrienne Corri.

Films include: 1958 Girls at Sea. '60 The Entertainer. '61 The Queen's Guards. '65 The Amorous Adventures of Moll Flanders. '67 The Jokers. '68 Star (USA). '70 Fragment of Fear. '72 Mary, Queen of Scots. '76 The Incredible Sarah. '80 Bad Timing. '81 Victory (USA) (GB: Escape to Victory).

MASSEY, Raymond

(1896–1983). Actor. Born: Toronto, Ontario, Canada

Immortalized as Dr Gillespie in television's long-running hospital soap opera, *Dr Kildare*, Raymond Massey has acted in films since 1931. After serving abroad in World War I, he trained as an actor, making his professional debut in London in an Eugene O'Neill play, *In the Zone*. By 1926 he was a co-owner and manager of the Everyman Theatre where he produced and directed plays as well as acting in them. His screen reputation was built on both sides of the Atlantic with a wide variety of parts from the title role in *Abe Lincoln in Illinois* to James Dean's tyrannical father in *East of Eden*. He was married three times with two of his children – Anna and Daniel – also chosing acting as their career.

Films include: 1931 The Speckled Band. '35 The Scarlet Pimpernel. '37 Fire Over England; The Prisoner of Zenda; The Drum (USA: Drums). '40 Abe Lincoln in Illinois (USA) (GB: Spirit of the People); Santa Fe Trail (USA). '44 Arsenic and Old Lace (USA). '46 A Matter of Life and Death (USA: Stairway to Heaven). '47 Possessed (USA). '55 Seven Angry Men (USA); East of Eden (USA). '62 How the West Was Won (USA). '69 Mackenna's Gold (USA).

MASTROIANNI, Marcello

(b. 1924). Actor. Born: Fontana Liri, Italy

Sophisticated and sexy, yet vulnerable with a haunted look, Marcello Mastroianni has come to represent the epitome of the suave Italian. Whether eating himself to death in *La Grande Bouffe* or playing Federico Fellini's alter ego in *Otto e Mezzo* (among others), his air of relaxed naturalness

Above: Marsha Mason in Chapter Two. *Below: Raymond Massey gave one of his best performances in the dual role of John and Oswald Cabal in H. G. Wells' vision of the future,* Things to Come *(1936). Above right:*

Daniel Massey in The Incredible Sarah, *a biopic about the great French actress Sarah Bernhardt, starring Glenda Jackson. Below: Marcello Mastroianni in* La Moglie Bionda *(1968, Kiss the Other Sheik)*

has enhanced a wide variety of films. He started in films in 1947 with a small part in *I Miserabili* but it was his stage association with director Luchino Visconti that brought him to the attention of the film world. From romantic leads opposite Sophia Loren to the comedy of *Divorce – Italian Style*, working with many leading directors including Alessandro Blasetti, Michelangelo Antonioni, Mauro Bolognini and, of course, Federico Fellini, he has become one of the biggest names of Italian cinema.

Films include: 1948 I Miserabili. '50 Domenica d'Agosto (GB: A Sunday in August). '54 Cronache di Poveri Amanti. '55 La Bella Mugnaia (USA: The Miller's Beautiful Wife; GB: The Miller's Wife). '57 Le Notti Bianche (USA/GB: White Nights). '58 I Soliti Ignoti (USA: Big Deal on Madonna Street; GB: Persons Unknown). '59 La Dolce Vita. '60 Il Bell'Antonio. '61 La Notte (GB: The Night); Divorzio all'Italiana (USA/GB: Divorce – Italian Style). '63 Otto e Mezzo (USA/GB:8½). '64 Ieri, Oggi e Domani (USA/GB: Yesterday, Today and Tomorrow); Matrimonio all'Italiana (USA/GB: Marriage Italian Style). '68 Amanti (USA/GB: A Place for Lovers). '70 Leo the Last (GB). '72 La Grande Bouffe (USA/GB: Blow-Out). '74 Allonsanfan. '77 Una Giornata Particolare (USA/GB: A Special Day). '78 Ciao Maschio/Bye Bye Monkey. '80 La Città delle Donne (USA/GB: City of Women). '82 La Nuit de Varennes (FR-IT).

MATÉ, Rudolph

(1898–1964). Cinematographer/director. Born: Rudolf Mathéh; Kraków, Poland

Rudolph Maté's career in films started in Hungary when Alexander Korda gave him a chance as an assistant cameraman. He worked with Erich Pommer in Berlin and filmed several of Carl Dreyer's most atmospheric works, including the innovative *Vampyr* and *The Passion of Joan of Arc* which delights in close-ups and low-angle shots. In 1934 he went to Hollywood where he filmed some of the classics of the period including King Vidor's melodramatic *Stella Dallas* and the thriller *Gilda* and the lighthearted *Cover Girl*, both starring Rita Hayworth. His films as director were generally disappointing and in the late Fifties he left Hollywood for Europe where he mainly worked for the rest of his life.

Films as cinematographer include: 1928 La Passion de Jeanne d'Arc (FR) (USA/GB: The Passion of Joan of Arc). '32 Vampyr: Der Traum des Allan Gray (GER-FR) (GB: Vampyr: The Strange Affair of David Gray). '35 Dante's Inferno. '36 Dodsworth. '37 Stella Dallas. '41 That Hamilton Woman! (GB: Lady Hamilton). '44 Cover Girl (co-photo). '46 Gilda. Films as director include: '50 No Sad Songs for Me; Union Station; Branded. '53 Second Chance.

MATHIESON, Muir

(1911–1975). Musical director/conductor. Born: Stirling, Scotland

Mathieson has worked as an arranger and conductor on over six hundred movies, including many British cinema classics of the Thirties and Forties. A graduate of the Royal College of Music, he entered the film industry in 1931 as an assistant musical director for Alexander Korda's London Films. His credits there include *Rembrandt*, *Fire Over England* and *Elephant Boy*, but perhaps his most notable achievement was his collaboration with Arthur Bliss on the score of *Things to Come*, one of the first occasions when the composer worked with the film-makers from the scripting to the final editing. The resultant score did much to encourage leading composers such as William Walton, Walter Leigh and William Alwyn into the cinema; Mathieson also persuaded Ralph Vaughan Williams to compose the music for *49th Parallel*. After World War II, he became musical director of the J. Arthur Rank Organization. He also directed several musical documentaries, the best-known being *Instruments of the Orchestra* (1946), and worked extensively as a conductor. In 1957, he was made an Officer of the Order of the British Empire for his contribution to films.

Films include: 1935 The Ghost Goes West; The Scarlet Pimpernel; Sanders of the River. '36 Rembrandt; Things to Come. '37 Fire Over England; Elephant Boy. '38 South Riding. '40 Gaslight (USA: Angel Street). '41 49th Parallel (USA: The Invaders). '44 Henry V; This Happy Breed. '45 Brief Encounter. '54 Doctor in the House. '58 Vertigo (USA). '62 The L-Shaped Room. '64 Becket.

MATTHAU, Walter

(b. 1920). Actor. Born: New York City, USA

A tall, stooping figure, his features as crumpled and creased as his clothes, Matthau has shambled through a series of superb Hollywood comedies with the air of one engaged in a win-or-bust struggle with the morning after the night before. He is, by his own account, the son of a Russian Orthodox priest who endowed Walter with an improbable Slavic mouthful of a surname (Matuschanskayasky) before disappearing out of his life. Matthau served in the air force during World War II, then enrolled at the New School for Social Research Dramatic Workshop. He first appeared on Broadway in the late Forties, scoring his first major success there in 1955 in *Will Success Spoil Rock Hunter?* His early movie roles were generally as seamy, sinister characters, but an award-winning performance on Broadway as Oscar in *The Odd Couple* in 1965, a part especially written for him by Neil Simon, won him major roles in screen comedy. The following year he began his hilariously successful partnership with Jack Lemmon in Billy Wilder's *The Fortune Cookie*. Matthau won a Best Supporting Actor Oscar as a crooked lawyer who magnifies a slight physical injury sustained by his client (Lemmon) to defraud an insurance company. The pair have since starred in the movie version of *The Odd Couple* (directed by Gene Saks), *The Front Page* and *Buddy, Buddy* (both directed by Wilder), Lemmon's nervous energy striking sparks from Matthau's flinty irascibility. Matthau is at his best when rising to the challenge of another strong personality, such as Anne Jackson in *The Secret Life of an American Wife* or George Burns in *The Sunshine Boys*, while he was irresistible as the booze-ridden baseball coach of a team of tough kids in *The Bad News Bears*. He has underlined his great versatility with excellent straight performances in the thrillers *Charley Varrick* and *The Taking of Pelham One Two Three*.

Films include: 1955 The Kentuckian. '56 Bigger Than Life. '58 Kid Creole. '59 Gangster Story (+dir.). '62 Lonely Are the Brave. '63 Charade. '64 Fail Safe; Goodbye Charlie. '66 The Fortune Cookie (GB: Meet Whiplash Willie). '68 The Odd Couple; The Secret Life of an American Wife. '69 Cactus Flower; Hello, Dolly! '71 Plaza Suite; Kotch. '73 Charley Varrick. '74 The Taking of Pelham One Two Three; The Front Page. '75 The Sunshine Boys. '76 The Bad News Bears. '78 California Suite. '81 Buddy, Buddy. '82 The First Monday in October.

MATTHEWS, Jessie

(1907–1981). Actress/dancer/singer. Born: London, England

Jessie Matthews was born in Soho of a large, poor family. Her mother and elder sister fostered her ambitions to become a dancer and Jessie first appeared on stage in 1919 in *Bluebell in Fairyland* at the Metropolitan Theatre. She joined André Charlot's revue company in 1923, understudying Gertrude Lawrence. Two years later she scored a personal triumph when she took over from Lawrence on stage in Toronto. She quickly became a major star of British musicals. She played uncredited bit parts in a couple of Twenties' movies before landing her first main role in the 1931 musical *Out of the Blue*. Her performances in Victor Saville's films, *The Good Companions*, *Evergreen*, *First a Girl* and *It's Love Again* established her as a front rank star. Mischievous and appealing, with large, expressive eyes and beautiful legs, she was a bewitching performer investing her musical comedy roles with a surprisingly modern sexual frankness. She married comedy star Sonnie Hale amidst a blaze of controversy in 1931 (she had been named in his divorce from actress Evelyn Laye). Jessie returned to the stage in the Forties, appearing in *The Lady Comes Across* on Broadway in 1941. She made a single film in Hollywood, *Forever and a Day*, but a nervous breakdown precipitated her return to England. She became a favourite with the armed forces as an entertainer, divorced Hale in 1944 and, after the war, pursued an erratic, troubled stage career. In 1963 she took over the role of Mrs Dale in the highly popular BBC radio serial *Mrs Dale's Diary*, further endearing herself to the British public. One of her most popular songs, 'Over My Shoulder', provided the title of her autobiography, published in 1974.

Films include: 1923 The Beloved Vagabond. '31 Out of the Blue. '33 The Good Companions; Friday the Thirteenth *ep* Millie the Non-Stop Variety Girl. '34 Waltzes From Vienna; Evergreen. '35 First a Girl. '36 It's Love Again. '37 Head Over Heels; Gangway. '38 Sailing Along. '39 Climbing High. '43 Forever and a Day (USA). '44 Victory Wedding (short) (dir. only); Candles at Nine. '47 Life Is Nothing Without Music (short) (dir. only). '58 Tom Thumb.

MATTSSON, Arne

(b. 1919). Director. Born: Uppsala, Sweden

Arne Mattsson became director Per Lindberg's assistant in 1941 and the following year – while doing his national service – directed his first short. By 1944 he was writing scripts and directing for Lux before moving on to work for Svensk Filmindustri and Nordisk Tonfilm. He was little-known outside Sweden until he made *One Summer of Happiness*, a portrait of adolescent passion that aroused much adverse reaction because of its permissiveness when it first hit the American 'art' circuit. The offending scene involved a nude romp by a Swedish lake. Later in his career Mattsson concentrated on stylish thrillers in the Hitchcock vein, such as *The Doll*, the story of a nightwatchman who is destroyed by a female dummy – the object of his passion – that comes to life.

Films include: 1949 Kvinna i Vitt (Woman in White). '52 Hon Dansade en Sommar (USA/GB: One Summer of Happiness). '54 Kärlekens Bröd (GB: The Bread of Love); Salka Valka. '56 Hemsöborna (People of Hemsö). '59 Damen i Svart (Lady in Black); Körkarlen (The Phantom Carriage). '62 Vaxdockan (USA/GB: The Doll). '69 Bamse (USA: Teddy Bear). '70 Ann och Eve (USA/GB: Ann and Eve).

MATURE, Victor

(b. 1916). Actor. Born: Louisville, Kentucky, USA

Victor Mature was promoted by Hollywood as 'The Beautiful Hunk of Male',

Left: Walter Matthau as a bankrobber who is hounded by the Mafia in Charley Varrick. *Above: Jessie Matthews in a 1932 comedy* The Midshipmaid

'Mr Beefcake' and 'The He-Man of the Year'. He himself is modestly self-effacing about his time in movies, saying: 'I spent most of my career battling pharoahs and playing opposite sharks and alligators'. Mature gained much of his early acting experience at the Pasadena Playhouse; indeed he had appeared in over sixty plays before being cast in his first movie, *The Housekeeper's Daughter*, in 1939. He attracted plenty of attention in his next role – as a chivalric caveman saving Carole Landis from dinosaurs in *One Million BC*. After World War II, Mature's career gradually gathered momentum; he played the consumptive Doc Holliday (one of his best performances) in Ford's *My Darling Clementine*, had leading parts in two fine thrillers, *Kiss of Death* and *Cry of the City* and then appeared in his most famous role, as Samson in De-Mille's *Samson and Delilah*. From then on, though Mature gave adept performances in several movies, in particular the Western *The Last Frontier* and the romantic drama *China Doll*, he never really escaped the tag of sweaty epic hero. He officially retired in 1962, but has made occasional film appearances since then, in particular an amusing, self-parodic cameo in De Sica's *After the Fox*.

Films include: 1940 One Million BC (GB: Man and His Mate). '41 No, No, Nanette; The Shanghai Gesture. '42 My Gal Sal. '46 My Darling Clementine. '47 Kiss of Death. '48 Cry of the City. '49 Easy Living; Samson and Delilah. '50 Stella. '52 Androcles and the Lion. '53 The Robe. '55 The Last Frontier. '57 The Long Haul. '58 China Doll. '61 I Tartari/The Tartars (IT). '66 Caccia alla Volpe (IT) (USA/GB: After the Fox). '72 Every Little Crook and Nanny.

MAY, Elaine

(b. 1932). Actress/director/writer. Born: Elaine Berlin; Philadelphia, Pennsylvania, USA

Jack Berlin, a well-known Jewish actor, was producer and director of a travelling theatre company and his daughter began acting for him at the age of six. When May was ten her father died and the family moved to Los Angeles. At 16 she briefly married and drifted into acting, studying under Maria Ouspenskaya (formerly of the Moscow Art Theatre). At the University of Chicago she met Mike Nichols and together they formed an exciting stage partnership, lasting from 1955 to 1961, that specialized in quick-witted, improvized comedy sketches. The pinnacle of their success came with *An Evening With Mike Nichols and Elaine May*, on Broadway in 1960. The following year they went their separate ways, with Nichols becoming a director and May turning to screenwriting and stage direction and, eventually, film direction. Her film-acting debut came in *Enter Laughing* and she went on to star opposite Jack Lemmon in *Luv*. She played a clumsy, somewhat dowdy, moneyed botanist seduced into marrying gold-digger Walter Matthau in *A New Leaf* – a film she also directed. And she cast her own daughter, Jeannie Berlin, as the homely girl ditched on her

honeymoon in favour of a rich blonde in *The Heartbreak Kid*. Most of May's stories are satires on sex, marriage, love, suicide and loneliness, all things obviously close to her heart after her own unhappy teenage marriage.

Films include: 1967 Luv (act); Enter Laughing (act). '68 California Suite (act). '71 Such Good Friends (sc. under pseudonym Esther Dale); A New Leaf (dir; +sc; +act). '72 The Heartbreak Kid (dir). '76 Mikey and Nicky (dir; +sc). '78 Heaven Can Wait (co-sc).

MAY, Joe

(1880–1954). Director. Born: Joseph Otto Mandel; Vienna, Austria

Although never considered to be one of the major figures in German cinema, Joe May played an enormous role in building up the German film industry after World War I, and all his films achieved popular success. He began his showbusiness career in 1909, directing operettas in Hamburg. By 1911 he was working for the Continental Film Company and by 1914 had set up his own film company. He introduced the first serial films to Germany with his detective stories about Stuart Webbs (Ernst Reicher), the most successful of the series being *Die geheimnisvolle Villa*. A few years later he made a comedy police series featuring Joe Debbs (Max Landa), and began his association with Fritz Lang who collaborated on several of the Debbs films. Perhaps his most prolific period came during his time as a director at Ufa from 1926 to 1933; *Asphalt* was a film about 'street life' and was much influenced by the avant-garde documentary work of Walter Ruttmann, particularly *Berlin, die Sinfonie einer Grosstadt* (1927, *The Symphony of a Great City*). May fled to France with the rise of Nazism and in 1934 emigrated to America where his first film – *Music in the Air* – was from fellow immigrant Billy Wilder's script. From then on he churned out routine American products and produced a spate of mystery films, the most notable being *The Invisible Man Returns*. He retired in 1944.

Films include: 1912 In der Tiefe des Schachtes. '14 Die geheimnisvolle Villa. '15 Das Gesetz der Mine. '17 Die Hochzeit in Exzentric-Club. '19 Veritas Vincit; Die Herrin der Welt. '21 Das indische Grabmal (USA: Mysteries of India; GB: The Hindu Tombstone). '23 Tragödie der Liebe. '28 Heimkehr. '29 Asphalt. '31 Paris – Méditerraneé (FR). '34 Music in the Air (USA). '37 Confessions (USA). '39 House of Fear (USA). '40 The Invisible Man Returns (USA).

MAYAKOVSKY, Vladimir

(1894–1930).
Poet/playwright/screenwriter. Born: Bagdadi, Georgia, Russia

Mayakovsky, the self-proclaimed 'soldier-poet of the Revolution', was a leading Bolshevik artist and a prominent member of the Futurist movement. A former student of the Moscow College of Painting, Sculpture and Architecture, Mayakovsky was keen to investigate the possibilities of a new, social-realist cinema but few of his scripts were ever filmed. His two best-known plays, *The Bedbug* and *The Bath House*, were adapted from rejected film scripts. Deeply depressed with the path the Russian Revolution had taken, Mayakovsky committed suicide in 1930. He was posthumously pronounced a genius by Stalin, who ordered that the town where Mayakovsky had been born should henceforth bear the artist's name.

Films include: 1914 Drama v Kabare Futuristov No 13 (actor only) (Drama in the Futurists' Cabaret No. 13). '18 Nye Dlya Deneg Rodivshisya (co-sc; +act) (Creation Can't Be Bought); Barishnya i Khuligan (+act) (The Young Lady and the Hooligan); Zakovannaya Filmoi (+act) (Shackled by Film). '26 Tri (Three).

MAYER, Carl

(1894–1944). Screenwriter. Born: Graz, Austria

Orphaned at 16, Mayer did a variety of jobs in his youth in order to support his younger brothers. Up until 1919 he had no contact with the film world, yet by 1929 he had written some of the best-known and most loved German films. It was his meeting with the poet Hans Janowitz that set him on that particular path and together they created *The Cabinet of Dr Caligari*, an

Expressionist film about a psychiatrist who apparently forces a somnambulist to murder. With its incredible sets and mannered acting, *The Cabinet of Dr Caligari* exercised enormous influence over succeeding German and American horror films. During the writing of the script Mayer had befriended a director, F.W. Murnau, and later worked with him on several films, including *Sunrise*, about a young farmer who tries to murder his wife at the instigation of his mistress but who sees the error of his ways at the eleventh hour. Resisting offers from Hollywood, Mayer wrote *Sunrise* in Europe and saw his efforts rewarded when the film was given two of the first-ever Academy Awards. Leaving Germany in 1932, he worked in Paris and then arrived in London where he worked on *Pygmalion* and *World of Plenty* as well as becoming consultant on films produced for the Ministry of Information.

Films include: 1919 Das Kabinett des Dr Caligari (co-sc) (GB: The Cabinet of Dr Caligari). '21 Hintertreppe (Backstairs). '24 Sylvester (GB: New Year's Eve). '25 Der letzte Mann (USA/GB: The Last Laugh); Tartüff (USA: Tartuffe, the Hypocrite; GB: Tartuffe). '27 Berlin, die Sinfonie einer Grosstadt (co-sc) (GB: The Symphony of a Great City); Sunrise (USA). '28 The Four Devils (USA). '31 Ariane. '32 Der träumende Mund (co-sc) (Dreaming Lips). '37 Dreaming Lips (remake) (co-sc) (GB). '38 Pygmalion (co-sc. uncredited) (GB). '43 World of Plenty (co-sc. uncredited) (GB).

MAYER, Louis B.

(1885–1957). Executive producer. Born: Eliezer Mayer; Minsk, Russia

Mayer was vice-president in charge of production at MGM between 1924 and 1951 (when Dore Schary replaced him), overseeing the process whereby stars such as Greta Garbo, Clark Gable, Spencer Tracy and Judy Garland were created and such films as *Mutiny on the Bounty, A Night at the Opera* (both 1935), *The Wizard of Oz* and *Gone With the Wind* (both 1939) were made. Mayer's father emigrated from Russia to America, setting up as a junk dealer in St John, New Brunswick, Canada. Mayer joined the by now prosperous family business and, in 1907 decided to buy and renovate a rundown motion picture theatre in Haverhill, Massachusetts. His policy of showing top-class films paid off and he was soon running the largest theatre chain in New England. He moved into film distribution and formed his own production company in 1917, his first film being *Virtuous Wives* (1918), starring Anita Stewart. In 1924 Louis B. Mayer Pictures merged with Metro and Goldwyn to form MGM at the instigation of distributor Marcus Loew. Mayer became vice-president, running the conglomèrate like a family business and setting himself up as a widely resented father-figure. Leaving the creative side of the business very much in the hands of his production chief Irving Thalberg (succeeded by Hunt Stromberg and Dore Schary) Mayer ensured that MGM became famous for glossy, star-studded family entertainment. He became one of the most powerful men in Hollywood, capable of making or breaking careers on a whim. Following Thalberg's death in 1936 and the general decline in audience figures during the Forties, Mayer's conservative attitudes to film-making were exposed as increasingly old-fashioned and his previously impregnable position was gradually eroded. A series of disagreements with MGM president Nicholas Schenck resulted in Mayer's being released from his contract and his gradually failing health decreed that he took little further active part in the film industry.

MAYNARD, Ken

(1895–1973). Actor. Born: Vevay, Indiana

A champion at rodeos and a trick rider with circuses and Wild West shows, Maynard entered the movies in 1922 and soon became a popular Western hero, performing his own stunts in a series of quickly-made films which concentrated on pace and lashings of high adventure. He and his palomino, Tarzan, made the transition to sound safely, and Maynard became the first singing cowboy. But by the end of the Thirties his vogue was passing and after abortive attempts at a comeback he retired in 1944. Thirty years later he died forgotten, a poverty-stricken alcoholic, suffering from severe malnutrition.

Films include: 1924 Janice Meredith (GB: The Beautiful Rebel); $50,000 Reward. '26 The Grey Vulture. '27 The Red Raiders. '29 Señor Americano. '30 Lucky Larkin; The Fighting Legion. '34 In Old Santa Fe. '36 Mystery Mountain (serial). '43 Death Valley Rangers; White Horse Stampede; Blazing Frontier.

MAYO, Archie L.

(1891–1968). Director. Born: Archibald L. Mayo; New York City, USA

In Hollywood by 1915, Mayo began as a gagman, directed comedy shorts, and made his first feature in 1926. Up until 1937 he was a contract director at Warners. He spent a few years at Fox before retiring in 1946. No one has ever considered Mayo an *auteur*, but there are some pearls hidden away in his prolific output. *The Doorway to Hell* (1930) is a tense gangster movie, with Lew Ayres and a novice Cagney; *Black Legion* a tough and frightening film about a reborn Ku Klux Klan; and *It's Love I'm After* (1937) a very witty and well-paced comedy which takes Leslie Howard and Bette Davis a long way from their usual pastures.

Films include: 1933 Ever in My Heart; The Life of Jimmy Dolan (GB: The Kid's Last Fight). '36 The Petrified Forest. '37 Black Legion. '38 The Adventures of Marco Polo. '41 Charley's Aunt (GB: Charley's American Aunt). '42 Moontide. '44 Sweet and Low Down. '46 A Night in Casablanca; Angel on My Shoulder.

MAYO, Virginia

(b. 1920). Actress. Born: Virginia Jones; St Louis, Missouri, USA

At 17 Mayo was a ballet dancer with the St Louis Opera Company. Her next occupation, in sharp contrast, was as straight woman to a performing horse in a four-year vaudeville stint. The 'horse' was two men known as the Mayo Brothers – hence Virginia's change of name. The act led on to nightclubs where she worked until landing a Goldwyn contract. She reached Hollywood in 1943 and played opposite Danny Kaye and Bob Hope, and her immaculate blonde beauty made her a favourite pin-up of World War II. She appeared usually, and rather colourlessly, in musicals and costume adventure, but was infinitely better in sluttish roles such as she played in *The Best Years of Our Lives* and *White Heat*.

Films include: 1944 The Princess and the Pirate. '45 Wonder Man. '46 The Best Years of Our Lives. '47 The Secret Life of Walter Mitty. '48 A Song Is Born. '49 Colorado Territory; White Heat. '51 Along the Great Divide; Captain Horatio Hornblower (GB: Captain Horatio Hornblower RN). '55 The Silver Chalice.

MAYSLES, Albert and David

Maysles, Albert (b. 1926). Documentary director. Born: Boston, Massachusetts, USA

Maysles, David (b. 1932). Documentary director. Born: Boston, Massachusetts, USA

Both brothers gained degrees in psychology at Boston University, and Albert taught the subject there for three years. In 1956 they moved into film, eventually joining Robert Drew's documentary team, for which Albert photographed *Primary* (1960). The brothers went on to make their own films, initially attempting to avoid what they considered the journalistic approach of the Drew team. The mundane style of such films as *Salesman* may well have fulfilled this aim, but their other work has favoured the glamorous or the bizarre. *Gimme Shelter*, a film on the Rolling Stones, even included an on-camera murder.

Films include: 1957 The Youth of Poland. '62 Showman. '64 What's Happening! The Beatles in the USA. '66 Meet Marlon Brando; A Visit With Truman Capote. '69 Salesman (co-dirs). '70 Gimme Shelter (co-dirs). '75 Grey Gardens (co-dirs). '78 Running Fence.

MAZURKI, Mike

(b. 1909). Actor. Born: Mikhail Mazurwski; Tarnopol, Austria

Of Ukrainian peasant origin, Mazurki was in the USA from childhood, and was a basketball player and footballer before becoming a heavyweight wrestler. Spotted in Los Angeles by

Above: Louis B. Mayer, the domineering studio boss of MGM. From left to right: Ken Maynard and Doris Hill in Sons of the Saddle (1930); Virginia Mayo in The Best Years of Our Lives; Mike Mazurki as the huge ex-convict Moose Malloy in Murder, My Sweet; Donald Meek in Frank Capra's satire on money-love, You Can't Take It With You; Ralph Meeker as private eye Mike Hammer in Robert Aldrich's apocalyptic thriller Kiss Me Deadly

296

Sternberg, he was offered only a small part in *The Shanghai Gesture* (1941), but the turning point came when he played the vast, slow-witted Moose Malloy, pathetically seeking his lost love in *Murder, My Sweet*. Thereafter his huge frame, battered face and grating voice were featured in hundreds of films. He only ever played the lead once, when he portrayed the simple-minded Yukon trapper in *Challenge to Be Free*.

Films include: 1944 Murder, My Sweet (GB: Farewell, My Lovely). '47 Nightmare Alley; Sinbad the Sailor. '51 Ten Tall Men. '55 Kismet. '59 Some Like It Hot. '63 Donovan's Reef. '65 Requiem for a Gunfighter. '75 Challenge to Be Free. '80 Sam Marlowe, Private Eye.

MAZURSKY, Paul

(b. 1930). Director/screenwriter/actor. Born: New York City, USA

Mazursky studied literature at Brooklyn College, moved to Greenwich Village, acted in off-Broadway plays and on television and entered films, as an actor, in Kubrick's *Fear and Desire*. He then formed a partnership with Larry Tucker to write television material, and together they also wrote the script of the Hy Averback film, *I Love You, Alice B. Toklas!* Their next script, *Bob & Carol & Ted & Alice*, was directed by Mazursky, and this and his third film, *Blume in Love*, were highly praised as penetratingly comic studies of pain-filled middle-class neurosis. This view is not universal, however. It is possible to see Mazursky's work as sophisticated soap opera.

Films include: 1953 Fear and Desire (actor only). '55 The Blackboard Jungle (actor only). '66 Deathwatch (actor only). '68 I Love You, Alice B. Toklas! (co-sc; +co-lyr only). '69 Bob & Carol & Ted & Alice (+co-sc). '70 Alex in Wonderland (+co-sc;

+act). '73 Blume in Love (+sc; +act). '74 Harry and Tonto (+co-sc). '76 Next Stop, Greenwich Village (+sc); A Star Is Born (actor only). '78 An Unmarried Woman (+sc; +act). '79 A Man, a Woman and a Bank (CAN) (actor only). '80 Willie & Phil (+sc; +narr). '81 History of the World – Part One (actor only).

MEEK, Donald

(1880–1946). Actor. Born: Glasgow, Scotland

Small, bald, prim and nervous Donald Meek was as well loved as any character actor of the golden years. He was respectability incarnate, but his youth had been colourful indeed. He was on the stage at eight, an acrobat on a piano-wire; he toured Australia as the child-lead of *Little Lord Fauntleroy*; went back to acrobatics in the USA and sustained severe injuries which confined him henceforth to acting. At 18, tropical fever made him bald. Thus the fates conspired against Meek, and for the movies, in which he acted steadily for the last 13 years of his life. He was always memorable, whether losing his samples of whisky to Thomas Mitchell in *Stagecoach*; thinking himself to sleep in *Mrs. Wiggs of the Cabbage Patch* (1934); after the reward for unmasking Edward G. Robinson in *The Whole Town's Talking*; or, in a rare moment of Meek bravery, as the gutsy little Scottish prospector standing up to the bad guys in *Barbary Coast*. Modern audiences simply don't know how actors like Meek could give joy week in, week out.

Films include: 1929 The Hole in the Wall. '34 The Merry Widow. '35 The Whole Town's Talking (GB: Passport to Fame); The Informer; Barbary Coast; China Seas; Top Hat; Captain Blood. '38 The Adventures of Tom Sawyer; You Can't Take It With You; Little Miss Broadway. '39 Stagecoach; Young Mr Lincoln; Nick Carter – Master Dectective. '45 State Fair. '47 Magic Town.

MEEKER, Ralph

(b. 1920). Actor. Born: Ralph Rathgeber; Minneapolis, Minnesota, USA

Educated at Northwestern University, Meeker acted in college productions there with Charlton Heston, Jean Hagen and Patricia Neal. Moving on to New York, he spent much time in stock companies before reaching Broadway, where, still relatively unknown, he succeeded Brando in the lead in *A Streetcar Named Desire*. This brought him film offers, and a 30-year career as a supporting player and occasional lead. Too often limited to snarling toughs with a yellow streak, Meeker was capable of more complex and thoughtful performances when the chance came. In the mid-Fifties he did have three outstanding parts in quick succession: the arrogant private eye Mike Hammer in *Kiss Me Deadly*; one of the condemned, his swagger visibly crumbling, in *Paths of Glory*; and the Indian-hating Yankee officer in *Run of the Arrow*. Meeker has seldom been as lucky since.

Films include: 1951 Teresa. '52 Glory Alley; Shadow in the Sky. '53 The Naked Spur. '55 Kiss Me Deadly; Big House USA. '57 Run of the Arrow; Paths of Glory. '67 The Dirty Dozen; The St Valentine's Day Massacre. '68 The Detective. '70 I Walk the Line. '71 The Anderson Tapes. '79 Winter Kills. '80 Without Warning.

MEERSON, Lazare

(1900–1938). Art director. Born: Russia

Meerson left Russia after the Revolution, went to Germany, and then on to Paris. A painter and a student of architecture, he entered the cinema at the Pathé studios in Montreuil, and made his first set designs for Jacques Feyder's *Gribiche* (1925). Combining architectural skill with a talent for

authenticity, Meerson paid immense attention to detail, supervised everything personally, and strove always to serve the spirit of the film. The vast city sets which he constructed for films like Clair's *Sous les Toits de Paris* (1930, *Under the Roofs of Paris*) and Feyder's *La Kermesse Héroïque* (1935, *Carnival in Flanders*) brought a new dimension to the French film. Meerson's later work for Korda in England was as stylish if less spectacular.

Films include: 1926 Carmen (FR). '28 Les Deux Timides (FR). '31 Le Million (FR) (USA: The Million); A Nous La Liberté (FR). '33 Le Grand Jeu (FR). '36 As You Like It (GB). '37 Knight Without Armour (GB); Fire Over England (GB); Break the News (GB). '38 The Divorce of Lady X (GB).

MEHBOOB

(1907–1964). Director. Born: Ramjankhan Mehboobkhan; Kashipura, Baroda, India

The son of a policeman, Mehboob ran away to Bombay at 18 and worked as an actor at the Imperial Film Company. Turning to writing, in 1932 he persuaded the studio to let him direct his own script, *Al Hilal*. He became a prolific and successful director, and in 1942 was able to start his own production company. In 1952 Mehboob gained international recognition for *Aan*, the first Indian Technicolor film, and a massive success. Mehboob's earlier films were boldly radical, showing him as a fervent champion of the underdog, and attacking the hoarding mentality of the rich and their attitude to the peasantry. His later films emphasized glamorous production values.

Films include: 1935 Al Hilal. '39 Aurat. '41 Roti. '42 Bahen. '43 Taqdeer (GB: Fate). '48 Amar. '49 Andaz. '52 Aan (GB: Savage Princess). '57 Bharat Mata (GB: Mother India). '60 Son of India.

MEIGHAN, Thomas

(1879–1936). Actor. Born: Pittsburgh, Pennsylvania, USA

A stage actor of note in the early years of this century, Meighan signed a contract with the Lasky company in 1915 and remained a popular leading man until the end of the silent days. Tall and handsome, with an easy, confident manner, he rose to stardom in *The Miracle Man* (as did Lon Chaney and Betty Compson), and appeared in a number of films for DeMille, notably as the butler in *Male and Female* (a version of the Admirable Crichton story) and as the straying husband in *Why Change Your Wife?* Meighan's last great success was as a New York cop in the Howard Hughes/Lewis Milestone film, *The Racket*. He played a few parts in sound films before his death, in 1936, from the after-effects of pneumonia.

Films include: 1914 Dandy Donovan, the Gentle Cracksman. '15 Kindling. '16 The Trail of the Lonesome Pine. '19 The Miracle Man; Male and Female. '20 Why Change Your Wife? '22 Manslaughter. '28 The Racket; The Mating Call. '29 The Argyle Case. '34 Peck's Bad Boy.

MEKAS, Jonas

(b. 1922). Director. Born: Semeniskiai, Lithuania

Taken to a forced labour camp near Hamburg in 1944, Mekas escaped, and until 1949 lived in displaced persons' camps in Germany. In those years he studied film, and on reaching America in 1950 became involved in the avant-garde movement. In 1955 he founded and edited the magazine *Film Culture*, and from 1959 wrote criticism in *The Village Voice*. Since then he has made his own films, and also organized several groups of radical film-makers. Mekas' film, *The Brig*, a record of the Living Theater's stage production, was voted the best documentary of the year at the 1964 Venice Festival, although in fact it was a fictional re-creation of a day in a US Marines punishment block.

Films include: 1961 Guns of the Trees. '63 Film Magazine of the Arts. '64 The Brig; Award Presentation to Andy Warhol. '66 Notes on the Circus. '69 Diaries, Notes and Sketches. '72 Reminiscences From a Journey to Lithuania.

MÉLIÈS, Georges

(1861–1938). Director/producer. Born: Paris, France

The young Méliès was fascinated by stage magic and made a name for himself with his magic shows, which soon incorporated magic lantern presentations. In December 1895, Méliès saw the Lumière film show, bought a projector and began to exhibit. He built a camera and made films himself, at first on the simple actuality lines of the Lumières. Discovering the possibilities of trick work, he set out to make his little films into demonstrations of magic, using double and multiple exposure, stop motion, slow motion and other devices. His films – he made hundreds – are charming, funny, and highly ingenious, but Méliès, in almost twenty years of film-making, did not develop his methods far beyond the mechanical reproduction of theatrical illusion. He was repeating his stage effects – only better. By 1913 his failure to move on was costing him his audience. The studio he had built at Montreuil was sold, and he fell into obscurity, eventually running a toyshop at the Gare Montparnasse. In the Thirties his films were rediscovered and he received the Legion of Honour.

Films include: 1896 Escamotage d'une Dame Chez Robert-Houdin (USA/GB: The Vanishing Lady). '97 Exécution d'un Espion. '98 La Lune à un Mètre (USA/GB: The Astronomer's Dream). '99 L' Affaire Dreyfus (USA/GB: The Dreyfus Case). 1900 Jeanne d'Arc (USA/GB: Joan of Arc). '01 Barbe-Bleue (USA/GB: Bluebeard). '02 Le Voyage dans la Lune (USA/GB: A Trip to the Moon); Le Sacre d'Edouard VII/Le Couronnement du Roi Edouard VII (USA/GB: The Coronation of Edward VII). '12 A la Conquête du Pôle (USA/GB: The Conquest of the Pole).

MELVILLE, Jean-Pierre

(1917–1973). Director. Born: Jean-Pierre Grumbach; Paris, France

Grumbach served with the Free French in World War II. Afterwards, unable to enter the industry by orthodox means, he set up his own production company and began to make films on very low budgets. He was an ardent admirer of the Hollywood films of the Thirties, and his pseudonym, Melville, was a homage to the American author of *Moby Dick*. Melville's

early films, with their economy of means, location shooting, and freshness of approach, were models for the *nouvelle vague* directors and Melville acted, a benevolent father-figure, in films by Jean-Luc Godard and Claude Chabrol. Enjoying larger resources in the Sixties, Melville made a number of superb gangster films. They combined the bleak fatality of American *film noir* with mystical undertones reminiscent of the cinema of Jean Cocteau, with whom Melville had worked long before on *Les Enfants Terribles*. It is tragic that they were either ignored by British distributors or (like *Le Samourai*) torn to pieces by them.

Films include: 1948 Le Silence de la Mer. '50 Les Enfants Terribles. '53 Quand Tu Liras Cette Lettre (FR-IT). '56 Bob le Flambeur. '59 Deux Hommes dans Manhattan. '61 Léon Morin, Prêtre (GB: Léon Morin, Priest). '63 Le Doulos (FR-IT); L'Aîné des Ferchaux (FR-IT). '66 Deuxième Souffle (USA: Second Wind; GB: Second Breath). '67 Le Samouraï (FR-IT) (GB: The Samurai). '69 L'Armée des Ombres (FR-IT) (GB: The Army in the Shadows). '70 Le Cercle Rouge (FR-IT) (GB: The Red Circle). '72 Un Flic (FR-IT) (GB: Dirty Money).

MENJOU, Adolphe

(1890–1963). Actor. Born: Pittsburgh, Pennsylvania, USA

Educated at Cornell, Menjou was in repertory at Cleveland by 1912, and made a few films before World War I service. Resuming in 1921, he rose rapidly as a smartly turned-out, debonair, world-weary and slightly wicked leading man. Lubitsch drew out the best from him in *The Marriage Circle* and *Forbidden Paradise*, and he was memorable too as the sympathetic seducer of *A Woman of Paris*. Sound suited him just as well, and he went on for another 30 years, diversifying his parts as he grew older. Outstanding in his portrait gallery were the cynical editor of *The Front Page* (played, later on, first by Cary Grant and then by Walter Matthau, but not better than by Menjou), the worried producer of *A Star Is Born* and the corrupt general of *Paths of Glory*. He was a superb professional to whom a bad performance was unthinkable.

Films include: 1921 The Sheik. '23 A Woman of Paris. '24 Forbidden Paradise; The Marriage Circle. '29 Fashions in Love. '30 Morocco. '31 The Front Page. '32 A Farewell to Arms. '35 Gold Diggers of 1935. '36 The Milky Way. '37 A Star Is Born. '57 Paths of Glory.

MENZEL, Jiří

(b. 1938). Director/actor. Born: Prague, Czechoslovakia

Menzel was brought up in Nazi-occupied Czechoslovakia. At the age of 19 he was accepted by the Prague Film Faculty, studied with the foremost new Czech directors, and became an assistant to the director Věra Chytilová in 1961. He was drafted into the army two years later, where he made newsreels. His career as a film director gathered momentum from 1965 onwards with his collaborations with the writers Josef

Škvorecký and Bohumil Hrabal. His first full-length feature, and probably his best known film in the West, was *Closely Observed Trains* (co-scripted with Hrabal) which won an Academy Award for Best Foreign Film in 1968. That year Menzel completed the whimsically satirical *Capricious Summer* and *Zločin v šantánu* (made with Škvorecký) shortly before the Russian invasion. His next film, *Skřivánci na nitích* fell foul of an increasingly repressive political climate and was never released. Menzel worked in the theatre for several years before returning to movies in 1976 with *Secluded Near Woods*.

Films include: 1965 Perličky na dně ep Smrt pana Baltazara (GB: Pearls of the Deep ep Mr Baltazar's Death); Zločin v dívčí škole ep Zločin v dívčí škole (Crime at the Girls' School). '66 Ostře sledované vlaky (+act) (USA: Closely Watched Trains; GB: Closely Observed Trains). '68 Rozmarné léto (+act) (USA/GB: Capricious Summer); Zločin v šantánu (+act) (The Crime in the Night Club). '69 Skřivánci na nitích (Larks on a Thread). '76 Na samotě u lesa (GB: Secluded Near Woods). '77 Hra o jablko (actor only) (GB: The Apple Game). '79 Báječní muži s klikou (+act) (GB: Those Wonderful Movie Cranks). '80 Postřižiny (USA: Short Cut).

MENZIES, William Cameron

(1896–1957). Art director/director. Born: New Haven, Connecticut, USA

Menzies is probably the most influential designer in the Anglo-American cinema and was largely responsible for defining the role of the art director as having overall responsibility for the 'look' of a film. His designs, renowned for their exoticism and flamboyance, include the fairy-tale settings of *The Thief of Bagdad* (both the 1924 and 1940 versions), the futurism of *Things to Come* and the lavish spectacle of *Gone With the Wind*, in which his greatest achievement was the burning of Atlanta, a sequence he also directed. Menzies was educated in Scotland and at Yale University, and entered the American film industry after military service in World War I as an assistant to art director Anton Grot on *The Naulahka* (1918). His first credit as an art director was on *Serenade* three years later. With the coming of sound, Menzies often worked as a co-director or director as well as designer of his films. Though his direction of actors left something to be desired, there was no doubt about his consummate skill at orchestrating action on a grand scale.

Films include: 1924 The Thief of Bagdad. '26 The Son of the Sheik. '27 The Dove. '28 Sadie Thompson. '36 Things to Come (dir; +art dir) (GB). '39 Gone With the Wind. '40 Foreign Correspondent (co-art dir); The Thief of Bagdad (co-dir; +co-art dir) (GB). '44 Address Unknown (dir; +prod; +art dir). '56 Around the World in 80 Days.

MERCANTON, Louis

(1879–1932). Director. Born: Switzerland

Mercanton was educated in England and obtained his first professional stage experience in South Africa in 1904. He returned to England to manage Sir Herbert Beerbohm Tree's His Majesty's Theatre and in 1911 became the artistic director of the Anglo-French society, L'Eclipse. He made his film debut as a co-director, with Henri Desfontaines, of *La Reine Elisabeth*, which starred the celebrated stage actress Sarah Bernhardt. Mercanton went on to make three more films with her – *Adrienne Lecouvreur*, *Jeanne Doré* and *Mères Françaises*. Often collaborating with director René Hervil, Mercanton had a successful film career in Britain and France. He was a firm believer in the virtues of shooting in real locations rather than in the studio. His son Jean (1919–1947) acted in many of his films, while his stepson Jacques (b. 1909) became well known in France as a cinematographer.

Films include: 1912 La Reine Elisabeth (co-dir) (USA/GB: Queen Elizabeth). '13 Adrienne Lecouvreur (co-dir). '16 Jeanne Doré; Le Lotus d'Or. '17 Mères Françaises (co-dir). '18 Bouclette (co-dir); Le Torrent (co-dir). '19 L'Appel du Sang. '20 Miarka la Fille à l'Ours. '24 Les Deux Gosses. '28 Vénus. '30 Le Mystère de la Villa Rose (co-dir). '31 Marions-Nous.

MERCER, Johnny

(1909–1976). Lyricist. Born: Savannah, Georgia, USA

Johnny Mercer fully deserves to be listed alongside Cole Porter, Irving Berlin, Lorenz Hart and Oscar Hammerstein II as one of the all-time great lyricists, his work including such standards as 'That Old Black Magic', 'Laura' and 'Something's Gotta Give'. As a young man Mercer travelled to New York with a local theatre group from his home town. He rose to prominence as the vocalist and master of ceremonies with the Paul Whiteman Orchestra and then scored a smash hit in 1933 with 'Lazybones', with music by Hoagy Carmichael. Mercer collaborated during his career with many other fine composers, including Jerome Kern, Harry Warren, Harold Arlen and Henry Mancini, his work for all of them characterized by a love of word play and alliteration. He started working in movie musicals in 1933 and subsequently won Academy Awards for Best Song for 'On the Atchison, Topeka and the Santa Fe' (music by Harry Warren) from *The Harvey Girls*, 'In the Cool, Cool, Cool of the Evening' (music by Hoagy Carmichael) from *Here Comes the Groom* (1951), 'Moon River' from *Breakfast at Tiffany's* and 'Days of Wine and Roses' from the film of the same name (the last two with music by Henry Mancini). Mercer's numerous stage show credits include a 1974 collaboration with composer André Previn, *The Good Companions*, based on the novel by J.B. Priestley.

Films include: 1933 The College Coach (GB: Football Coach). '36 Rhythm on the Range. '41 Birth of the Blues. '42 You Were Never Lovelier. '43 Star Spangled Rhythm; The Sky's the Limit. '46 The Harvey Girls. '54 Daddy Long Legs (+ mus); Seven Brides for Seven Brothers. '61 Breakfast at Tiffany's. '62 Days of Wine and Roses. '70 Darling Lili.

MERCHANT, Ismail

(b. 1936). Producer. Born: Bombay, India

Merchant was educated at Bombay University and studied business administration in New York. He established his reputation by producing a short film, *The Creation of Woman* (1961), and teamed up with the American director James Ivory to film Ruth Prawer Jhabvala's novel about Indian life, *The Householder*, which she herself scripted. The same team produced five more features on Indian themes over the next 15 years, but Merchant diversified by trying his hand at direction and by making five features set in the USA, all directed by Ivory and three of them scripted by Jhabvala. The trio then tackled a European topic – an adaptation of Jean Rhys' novel *Quartet*. Merchant's achievement as an independent producer in raising finance for relatively uncommercial projects over so many years is much to be respected.

Films include: 1963 Gharbar/The Householder (IND). '65 Shakespeare-Wallah (IND). '69 The Guru (USA-IND). '70 Bombay Talkie (IND). '72 Savages (USA); Mahatma and the Mad Boy (short) (+dir)(IND); Helen, Queen of the Nautch Girls (doc. short) (IND). '75 The Wild Party (USA). '77 Roseland (USA). '78 Hullabaloo Over Georgie and Bonnie's Pictures (made for TV but shown in cinemas) (GB-IND). '79 The Europeans (GB). '80 Jane Austen in Manhattan (made for TV but shown in cinemas) (GB-USA). '81 Quartet (co-prod) (GB–FR). '82 Heat and Dust (GB); The Courtesans of Bombay (doc) (+dir) (GB).

MERCOURI, Melina

(b. 1923). Actress. Born: Anna Amalia Mercouri; Athens, Greece

The daughter of a Greek politician who served as a government minister, Melina Mercouri became a stage actress and made her film debut in 1955. Her role as the happy whore of the Piraeus waterfront in *Never on Sunday*, directed by her second husband, Jules Dassin, brought her international fame, an Oscar nomination and the Best Actress prize (shared with Jeanne Moreau) at Cannes. Her strong personality, earthy sexuality and husky voice established her as a distinctive star; but her involvement in politics made her screen appearances increasingly intermittent and earned her seven years' exile from her native country while the right-wing junta ruled. She returned to Greece in 1974 and in 1977 was elected to parliament for Piraeus. She was appointed Minister of Culture and Sciences, a fitting culmination to her career in films, theatre and politics. She is married to the director Jules Dassin.

Films include: 1955 Stella. '57 Celui Qui Doit Mourir (FR-IT) (GB: He Who Must Die); The Gypsy and the Gentleman (GB). '59 La Loi (FR-IT) (USA/GB: Where the Hot Wind Blows). '60 Pote Tin Kyriaki (USA/GB: Never on Sunday). '62 Phaedra (USA-GREECE). '63 The Victors (GB). '64 Topkapi (USA-FR). '65 Les Pianos Mécaniques (FR-SP) (USA: The Uninhibited). '69 Gaily, Gaily (USA) (GB: Chicago, Chicago). '77 Nasty Habits (GB). '78 A Dream of Passion (SWITZ-GREECE).

Above: Melina Mercouri in La Promesse de l'Aube *(1970,* Promise at Dawn*). Below: Burgess Meredith in* The Story of GI Joe

MEREDITH, Burgess

(b. 1908). Actor. Born: Cleveland, Ohio, USA

Burgess Meredith started his career as a reporter on the *Cleveland Plain Dealer* and, after a variety of other jobs, joined Eva LeGallienne's Student Repertory Group in 1929. In the Thirties he became a leading Broadway actor and starred in Maxwell Anderson's *Winterset*. He made his screen debut in the film version, and went on to play troubled nice guys in his early films, such as George in *Of Mice and Men* and the overworked psychoanalyst in *Mine Own Executioner*. He survived accusations of communist sympathies and the television role of 'The Penguin' in *Batman* to become increasingly busy in his later years, notably as the boxer's manager, Mickey, in *Rocky* and its sequels. The actress Paulette Goddard was his third wife (1944–49).

Films include: 1936 Winterset. '39 Of Mice and Men. '45 The Story of GI Joe. '46 The Diary of a Chambermaid. '47 Mine Own Executioner (GB). '62 Advise and Consent. '66 Batman (made for TV but shown in cinemas). '75 Day of the Locust. '76 Rocky. '78 Magic. '79 Rocky II – Redemption. '81 True Confessions. '82 Rocky III.

Above: a studio publicity portrait of Una Merkel. Below: the supercharged musical star Ethel Merman in an early role in We're Not Dressing

Right: Gary Merrill in his best-known film role as Bette Davis' director boyfriend Bill Sampson in Joseph Mankiewicz's All About Eve

MERKEL, Una

(1903–1986). Actress. Born: Covington, Kentucky, USA

A natural blonde with twinkling blue eyes, Una Merkel had acting ambitions from childhood. During the Twenties she worked mostly on the stage, with only occasional film parts, until D.W. Griffith cast her as Lincoln's lost sweetheart Ann Rutledge in *Abraham Lincoln*. After that she was regularly in films as a glamorous comedienne and character actress throughout the Thirties, playing golden-hearted gold-diggers in musicals, a dowdy mother in *Riffraff*, with Jean Harlow, and a cowboy's respectable wife who tangles with Marlene Dietrich in *Destry Rides Again*. She returned to Broadway in 1944 in *Three's a Family*, and thereafter was able to choose character parts in films, television and the theatre. Having played the weak-minded Mrs Winemiller in Tennessee Williams' *Summer and Smoke* on stage, she re-created the role in the film version and was nominated for an Oscar.

Films include: 1930 Abraham Lincoln. '31 Daddy Long Legs. '32 Red-Headed Woman. '33 Bombshell/Blonde Bombshell; 42nd Street. '36 Riffraff; Born to Dance. '37 Saratoga. '39 Destry Rides Again; Some Like It Hot. '52 With a Song in My Heart. '55 The Kentuckian. '61 Summer and Smoke.

MERMAN, Ethel

(1909–1984). Actress/singer. Born: Ethel Agnes Zimmerman; New York City, USA

Having sung in vaudeville and nightclubs, Ethel Merman was offered a six-month contract by Warner Brothers in 1929, but appeared in only one film before returning to the stage. In 1930 she made her Broadway debut in *Girl Crazy* with Ginger Rogers, and her rendition of 'I Got Rhythm' stopped the show. She went on to triumph in over a dozen Broadway musicals, including *Annie Get Your Gun*, *Call Me Madam*, *Gypsy* and *Hello, Dolly!* She belted out songs with great power and was more effective on stage than on film, though she continued to make musical films and was able to re-create her role as Sally Adams, the 'hostess with the mostest' who becomes a United States ambassador, in the film version of *Call Me Madam*.

Films include: 1930 Follow the Leader. '34 We're Not Dressing. '35 The Big Broadcast of 1936. '36 Anything Goes. '38 Alexander's Ragtime Band. '43 Stage Door Canteen. '53 Call Me Madam. '54 There's No Business Like Show Business. '63 It's a Mad, Mad, Mad, Mad World. '65 The Art of Love.

MERRILL, Gary

(b. 1915). Actor. Born: Hartford, Connecticut, USA

After war service, and one film appearance in 1944, Gary Merrill starred in the Broadway production of *Born Yesterday*. He went to Hollywood for a leading role in *Slattery's Hurricane*, and 20th Century-Fox gave him a contract. He played the commanding officer of a group of bomber pilots in *Twelve O'Clock High* and the stage director loved by Margo (Bette Davis) in *All About Eve*. Subsequently Bette Davis became his second wife (1950–60). His rather stern appearance, with tense features and heavy eyebrows, tended to limit his range to serious character parts, with occasional leads. In the Sixties he developed an interest in politics, but his attempt to be nominated as a Republican candidate for Maine's state legislature was unsuccessful.

Films include: 1944 Winged Victory. '49 Slattery's Hurricane; Twelve O'Clock High. '50 All About Eve. '51 Decision Before Dawn. '54 The Human Jungle. '59 The Wonderful Country; The Savage Eye. '66 Cast a Giant Shadow. '68 The Power. '77 Thieves.

METTY, Russell

(1906–1978). Cinematographer. Born: Los Angeles, California, USA

Metty's career began in the Thirties but his most notable period was at Universal in the Fifties when he worked on the colour films of director Douglas Sirk, for which he pioneered several new techniques. His ability to

organize complicated crane shots was demonstrated in the lengthy and elaborate tracking sequence, following Charlton Heston and Janet Leigh as well as a car that is about to explode, at the opening of Orson Welles' *Touch of Evil*. He won the 1960 Oscar for colour cinematography on Stanley Kubrick's *Spartacus*.

Films include: 1936 Sylvia Scarlett. '38 Bringing Up Baby. '46 The Stranger. '54 Taza, Son of Cochise; Magnificent Obsession; Sign of the Pagan. '55 All That Heaven Allows. '56 Written on the Wind. '58 A Time to Love and a Time to Die; Touch of Evil. '59 Imitation of Life. '60 Spartacus. '61 The Misfits. '68 Madigan.

METZNER, Ernö

(b. 1892). Art director. Born: Hungary

Of Jewish origin, Metzner studied at the Budapest Academy of Fine Arts. He worked as a set designer in Germany in the Twenties and early Thirties, notably with the director G.W. Pabst, for whom he made an impressive reconstruction of a coal-mine in *Kameradschaft*. He also directed a few films, including an interesting short, *Überfall* (1929, *Accident*), in the avant-garde abstract style of Hans Richter and Oskar Fischinger. Forced to leave Germany in 1933, he worked in France and England before going to the United States, where he became a Hollywood set designer.

Films include: 1920 Sumurun (USA: One Arabian Night). '26 Geheimnisse einer Seele (USA: Secrets of the Soul; GB: Secrets of a Soul). '29 Das Tagebuch einer Verlorenen (GB: Diary of a Lost Girl/Diary of a Lost One); Die weisse Hölle von Piz Palü (USA: White Hell of Piz Palu; GB: The White Hell of Pitz Palu). '30 Westfront 1918 (USA: Comrades of 1918; GB: West Front, 1918). '31 Kameradschaft (GER-FR) (USA: Comradeship). '33 Du Haut en Bas (FR). '34 Chu Chin Chow (GB). '36 The Robber Symphony (GB-GER). '44 It Happened Tomorrow (USA).

MEYER, Russ

(b. 1923). Director. Born: Oakland, California, USA

Meyer's career has just the hint of seediness that could be expected of a man dubbed 'King of the Nudies'. An amateur film-maker in his youth, he was trained as a combat cameraman in World War II, and later progressed from underwear magazines to photographing *Playboy* centrefolds. His reputation is based on films like *Vixen!*, which cleared $6 million profit and made him 'acceptable' in Hollywood as a creator of glossy, tantalizing porn which seldom delivers quite as much as it promises. Filmed with carefully staged glimpses of nudity within a minimal and irrelevant plot and laced with self-deprecating humour and occasional tongue-in-cheek intellectualism, Meyer's films enjoy a considerable cult status as well as having commercial appeal.

Films include: 1960 The Immoral Mr Teas. '61 Eve and the Handyman. '64 Fanny Hill: Memoirs of a Woman of Pleasure (GER). '66 Mondo Topless. '68 Finders Keepers, Lovers Weepers; Vixen! '70 Beyond the Valley of the Dolls. '75 Supervixens. '76 Up! '79 Beneath the Valley of the Ultravixens.

MIFUNE, Toshiro

(b. 1920). Actor. Born: Tsingtao, China

Japan's best known actor, Mifune is to samurai what John Wayne was to cowboys. In fact, there is considerably more to this short, stocky character actor than the autocratic exterior might reveal. Born in China, he and his parents were repatriated when he was young. After a spell in the army he entered a talent competition at the Toho company in 1945, and his success led to some small movie parts. Akira Kurosawa cast him in his period films *Rashomon* and *Seven Samurai*, both of which had tremendous impact in the West. *Rashomon* won an Oscar, and Mifune became Hollywood's favourite Japanese, called upon whenever a samurai or proud World War II soldier was needed. At home, however, he has appeared in a variety of films, including comedies, which reveal not only his extraordinary presence, but a far greater range than his overseas work has allowed him to express.

Films include: 1950 Rashomon. '54 Shichinin no Samurai (USA/GB: Seven Samurai). '57 Kumonosu-Jo (USA/GB: Throne of Blood); Donzoko (USA/GB: The Lower Depths). '58 Kakushi Toride no San Akunin (GB: The Hidden Fortress). '61 Yojimbo; Tsubaki Sanjuro (GB: Sanjuro). '63 Tengoku to Jigoku (GB: High and Low); Go Juman Nin no Isan (+ dir) (Legacy of the 500,000). '65 Akahige (USA/GB: Red Beard). '66 Grand Prix (USA). '68 Hell in the Pacific (USA). '75 Paper Tiger (GB-GER). '81 Inchon (USA).

MILES, Bernard

(b. 1907). Actor. Born: Uxbridge, Middlesex, England

Miles' origins were humble; his father was a farm labourer and his mother a cook. They were, however, ambitious for their children, and young Bernard was sent to Pembroke College, Oxford. After a period as a teacher he joined the New Theatre, London, and worked in most of the jobs on and off the stage before joining Herbert Farjeon's revue company in 1937, which established his theatrical reputation. His comparatively few film appearances have been distinguished by marvellous character acting: a larger-than-life portrayal of the typically Dickensian 'poor but honest' Joe Gargery in *Great Expectations*, or as Mr Harris, the *petit bourgeois* father whose values are threatened by the prospect of his son's mixed marriage in *Sapphire*. In 1959 Miles opened the Mermaid Theatre in London, and his efforts to keep it going won him a knighthood in 1969, and a life peerage ten years later.

Films include: 1942 In Which We Serve. '44 Tawny Pipit (+ co-dir; + prod; + sc). '46 Great Expectations. '47 Nicholas Nickleby; Fame Is the Spur. '50 Chance of a Lifetime (+ co-dir; + co-prod; + co-sc). '56 Tiger in the Smoke; Moby Dick. '59 Sapphire. '69 Run Wild Run Free.

MILES, Sarah

(b. 1941). Actress. Born: Ingatestone, Essex, England

There is a frailty about Sarah Miles which gives an edge to the sensuality of her mouth and the jittery wilfulness in her eyes. For most of her film career she has excelled in depicting the unstable and irresponsible depths of sexuality; her first role after RADA was as teacher Laurence Olivier's schoolgirl would-be seductress in *Term of Trial*. In Joseph Losey's *The Servant* she was compelling as the amoral, slatternly maid, down from the North and after her employer; and as *Ryan's Daughter* she played merry hell with the lives of her father and admirers alike. Few of her other films have made the most of her, however, and she has often been miscast – as the heroine of the Western *The Man Who Loved Cat Dancing* – or downright wasted, battling against the odds in Michael Winner's leaden remake of *The Big Sleep*.

Films include: 1962 Term of Trial. '63 The Servant. '65 Those Magnificent Men in Their Flying Machines (or How I Flew From London to Paris in 11 Hours 25 Minutes). '66 I Was Happy Here; Blow-Up. '70 Ryan's Daughter. '72 Lady Caroline Lamb (GB-IT). '73 The Hireling; The Man Who Loved Cat Dancing (USA). '78 The Big Sleep.

MILES, Sylvia

(b. 1932). Actress. Born: New York City, USA

There is a story that Sylvia Miles once threw a plate of food over a critic who called her 'New York's party girl'. Certainly there's no denying that she was once the big favourite of the New York theatre crowd; she made her stage debut in 1955, and went on to notch up 36 projects with the Actors' Studio and others. On film, her blowsy, blonde, buxom good looks have brought her a series of riveting cameo roles, notably as the hooker in *Midnight Cowboy*, and a stunning seven-minute appearance in *Farewell, My Lovely*, both of which won her Oscar nominations.

Films include: 1960 Murder, Inc. '61 Parrish. '64 Psychomania. '65 Terror in the City. '69 Midnight Cowboy. '71 The Last Movie; Who Killed Mary What's Ername? '72 Heat. '75 Farewell, My Lovely (GB-USA). '76 The Great Scout and Cathouse Thursday/Wildcat. '79 Shalimar (USA-IND). '81 Evil Under the Sun (GB).

Above: Sarah Miles in Ryan's Daughter. *Below: Sylvia Miles (right) in the horror film* The Sentinel *(1977). Bottom left: Toshiro Mifune in Kurosawa's* Sanjuro. *Bottom right: Bernard Miles in* Never Let Me Go *(1953)*

MILES, Vera

(b. 1930). Actress. Born: Vera Ralston; Boise City, Oklahoma, USA

Vera Miles has nothing if not range. She arrived in Hollywood with her stunt-man husband having won a series of local beauty contests. A spell playing very minor roles for Warner Brothers brought her to Hitchcock's attention, and eventually he gave her the part of Henry Fonda's wife who descends slowly into madness under the pressure in *The Wrong Man*. Conversely, in Ford's *The Searchers* she played a healthy outspoken frontierswoman, while in *Autumn Leaves* she was the wife who torments her husband by flirting with his father. Despite such versatility, her career never quite took off, partly because her second marriage – to 'Tarzan' Gordon Scott – left her pregnant just when Hitchcock could have launched her to fame in *Vertigo* (1958). But she did play the sister in *Psycho*. She has worked extensively on television, and, although not always content with her roles, has earned a reputation as an actress guaranteed to appeal to audiences and sponsors alike.

Films include: 1955 Tarzan's Hidden Jungle; Wichita. '56 The Searchers; Autumn Leaves. '57 The Wrong Man. '60 Psycho. '61 Back Street. '62 The Man Who Shot Liberty Valance. '67 Gentle Giant. '71 The Wild Country.

MILESTONE, Lewis

(1895–1980). Director. Born: Lewis Milstein; near Odessa, Russia

All Quiet on the Western Front, one of the most intelligent war movies ever made, won Milestone not only an Oscar but a reputation as a major director. And yet it was by no means the only achievement of his career. He came to Hollywood at an early age and worked as a film cutter, an experience which was to influence his style as a director considerably. Intent on pursuing his career his own way, he clashed with Howard Hughes and Warner Brothers and was said to be 'difficult', but he took to talkies as few others did. *All Quiet on the Western Front* boasted a number of innovations in its use of sound and its bold visual sweep as well as in its message,

but few from Milestone's extremely varied output of films hit similar heights. His later war films, including *Pork Chop Hill*, were less sure, and his last project, *Mutiny on the Bounty*, foundered on its unusual casting, notably Marlon Brando as Fletcher Christian.

Films include: 1926 The Caveman. '30 All Quiet on the Western Front. '31 The Front Page. '33 Hallelujah, I'm a Bum (GB: Hallelujah, I'm a Tramp). '39 Of Mice and Men. '45 A Walk in the Sun. '46 The Strange Love of Martha Ivers. '48 Arch of Triumph. '50 Halls of Montezuma. '53 They Who Dare. '59 Pork Chop Hill. '60 Ocean's Eleven. '62 Mutiny on the Bounty.

MILIUS, John

(b. 1944). Director/screenwriter. Born: St Louis, Missouri, USA

Big and burly, Milius has more than a little in common with Attila the Hun. He delights in championing unfash-

ionable views, and describes his beliefs as those of a 'Zen fascist'. The son of a shoe manufacturer, he attempted to join the army in a sincere quest for death or glory, but, rejected because of chronic asthma, he turned instead to expressing the virtues of such views through film. *Dirty Harry*, the ruthless, relentless dispenser of rough justice (whom Milius helped to create for Don Siegel's 1971 film), is typical of his characters. So are *Dillinger* and *Conan the Barbarian*, who reject the nicer social conventions in favour of a stern and violent puritanism. Yet, for all Milius' swaggering machismo, there is a thoughtful side to his work, most obvious in *The Wind and the Lion*, which reveals a deeper understanding of the dilemmas and complications behind the conventional concept of heroism. Unlike Attila, Milius does not always take himself too seriously.

Films include: 1969 The Devil's 8 (co-sc. only). '72 Jeremiah Johnson (co-sc. only); The Life and Times of Judge Roy Bean (co-

Left: Ann Miller cuts loose in On the Town. *Above, far left: Vera Miles as Rose, who suffers a mental breakdown when her husband (Henry Fonda) is arrested in Hitchcock's* The Wrong Man. *Above centre: Ray Milland in* Ministry of Fear. *Above: Hayley Mills in* Twisted Nerve. *Below: John Mills in* Oh! What a Lovely War *(1969). Below right: Juliet Mills in Billy Wilder's* Avanti! *Bottom right: Sandra Milo in Fellini's* $8\frac{1}{2}$

sc. only). '73 Dillinger (+sc). '75 The Wind and the Lion (+sc). '78 Big Wednesday (+co-sc). '79 Apocalypse Now (co-sc. only). '81 Conan the Barbarian (+co-sc).

MILLAND, Ray

(1905–1986). Actor/director. Born: Reginald Truscott-Jones; Neath, Glamorgan, Wales

For ten years Milland worked in Hollywood, a charming, romantic supporting actor in light comedy-dramas, steadily being groomed for better things. Fame came, but from an unexpected direction with *The Lost Weekend*, Billy Wilder's nightmarish and adventurous journey into the taboo world of the alcoholic. It won Milland an Oscar, and opened doors which had previously been closed to him though, curiously enough, few of his subsequent films, excepting Hitchcock's *Dial M for Murder*, had much beyond his presence to recommend them. After several interesting

302

low-budget films as director, he moved increasingly towards character parts, lending weight to otherwise turgid projects like *Love Story*. His autobiography, *Wide-Eyed in Babylon*, charts his progress from Guardsman to star with delightful self-deprecating humour.

Films as actor include: 1929 The Flying Scotsman (GB). '32 Payment Deferred. '36 The Jungle Princess. '37 Easy Living; Bulldog Drummond Escapes. '39 French Without Tears (GB). '42 Reap the Wild Wind; The Major and the Minor. '44 Ministry of Fear. '45 The Lost Weekend. '54 Dial M for Murder. '55 The Girl in the Red Velvet Swing; A Man Alone (+dir). '58 The Safecracker (+dir) (GB). '62 Panic in Year Zero (+dir). '63 The Man With the X-Ray Eyes. '70 Love Story. '80 Survival Run.

MILLER, Ann

(b. 1924). Actress/dancer. Born: Lucille Ann Collier; Chireno, Texas, USA

It has been said of Ann Miller that all she could do was dance, and with characteristic modesty she herself lays no great claim to acting. But her dancing was so exuberant and even erotic that that was more than enough. An ambitious mother set her

to dancing aged three as a cure for rickets. After initial apathy in Hollywood, she aroused the interest of Lucille Ball, who was instrumental in getting her some small roles in minor musicals. A contract with MGM followed, and, although she never quite achieved star status, her good looks, long legs and dazzling dancing made her a firm favourite. She was rewarded by being partnered with Fred Astaire in *Easter Parade*. Her film career declined in the Fifties, but she continued to make popular appearances on stage and television into the Seventies.

Films include: 1937 New Faces of 1937. '38 Radio City Revels; You Can't Take it With You. '40 Hit Parade of 1941. '48 Easter Parade; The Kissing Bandit. '49 On the Town. '52 Lovely to Look At. '53 Small Town Girl; Kiss Me Kate. '54 Deep in My Heart. '56 The Opposite Sex.

MILLER, Arthur C.

(1895–1970). Cinematographer. Born: Roslyn, Long Island, New York, USA

Among Miller's several claims to fame is that he gave Shirley Temple her halo – by back-lighting her curly blonde hair. Such effects were very much his trademark, since a similar technique gave the monsoon its spooky fascination in *The Rains Came*, and added a good deal to the spiritual quality to *The Song of Bernadette*. Miller started out experimenting with his Brownie camera, snapping passing beer drays and selling the results to the owners. He established a small company in New York which he later moved to Hollywood, where he soon established a reputation through his craftsmanship and sheer dedication. John Ford was the director he most liked working for, and he won an Oscar for Ford's *How Green Was My Valley*, as well as for *The Song of Bernadette* and *Anna and the King of Siam*.

Films include: 1914 The Perils of Pauline (serial). '23 Bella Donna; The Cheat. '39 The Rains Came. '40 The Mark of Zorro. '41 How Green Was My Valley; Tobacco Road. '43 The Song of Bernadette. '46 Anna and the King of Siam. '48 A Letter to Three Wives. '50 The Gunfighter. '51 The Prowler.

MILLER, David

(b. 1909). Director. Born: Paterson, New Jersey, USA

Miller worked his way up through the ranks. After high school he entered the National Screen Service as a messenger boy, and rose steadily until he was given the chance to direct some of the famous Pete Smith popular educational shorts. Two of his documentaries, *Penny Wisdom* (1937) and *Seeds of Destiny* (1946), won Academy Awards. In his features career he has been either versatile or inconsistent, according to one's point of view; competent rather than creative, he has tackled mostly commercial subjects, from war films like *Flying Tigers* to quality thrillers like *Sudden Fear* and *Midnight Lace*.

Films include: 1941 Billy the Kid. '42 Flying Tigers. '50 Our Very Own. '52 Sudden Fear. '54 Beautiful Stranger (GB) (USA: Twist of Fate). '57 The Story of Esther Costello (GB). '60 Midnight Lace. '62 Lonely Are the Brave. '63 Captain Newman MD. '76 Bittersweet Love.

MILLS, Hayley

(b. 1946). Actress. Born: London, England

Hayley Mills' career highlights the pleasures and pitfalls of being a child star. The daughter of actor John Mills, she went into movies while still only 12. She achieved considerable success as the snub-nosed cherub, a successor to Shirley Temple, on the run with a gunman in *Tiger Bay*, but in the string of Disney films that followed it her sweet English innocence began to wear sickly thin. A coy sex comedy, *The Family Way*, attempted to mature her image, and led to a much-publicized marriage to director Roy Boulting, many years her senior. With blonde hair and angelic good looks, she has been dogged by her past reputation; but her role as the English mother trying to come to terms with the rigours of the African bush in the 1981 television series *The Flame Trees of Thika* has brought her a deserved reassessment.

Films include: 1959 Tiger Bay. '60 Pollyanna (USA). '61 Whistle Down the Wind. '62 In Search of the Castaways (USA: The Castaways). '64 The Moon-Spinners. '65 Sky West and Crooked (USA: Gypsy Girl). '66 The Family Way. '67 Pretty Polly (USA: A Matter of Innocence). '68 Twisted Nerve. '69 Take a Girl Like You. '75 Deadly Strangers.

MILLS, John

(b. 1908). Actor. Born: Felixstowe, Suffolk, England

As the head of Britain's other acting family, more down-market than the Redgraves, Sir John Mills has become something of a national institution. Much of this derives from the fact that he has probably appeared in uniform more than any other actor. Encouraged by his mother, ex-box-office manageress of the Haymarket Theatre, Mills began acting in his spare time, and later packed in his job to travel to London. Here he joined a touring company, and was spotted by Noel Coward. A subsequent role in Coward's stage play *Cavalcade* established his career and led to film offers. In the Forties and Fifties he became England's favourite Englishman, appearing in scores of stiff-upper-lip but sympathetic and human military roles, notably in *In Which We Serve* and *Waterloo Road*. His reputation was seldom higher than following David Lean's esteemed *Great Expectations*, though he won an Oscar as late as 1970 as the village idiot in *Ryan's Daughter*, and was knighted six years later. Although his roles are now more varied, he is often content to add cameo appearances to undistinguished films like *The Big Sleep* (1978). In 1982 he was the old schoolmaster in a stage version of *Goodbye, Mr Chips*.

Films include: 1936 Tudor Rose (USA: Nine Days a Queen). '40 The Green Cockatoo. '42 In Which We Serve. '45 Waterloo Road. '46 Great Expectations. '48 Scott of the Antarctic. '49 The History of Mr Polly (+prod); The Rocking Horse Winner (+prod). '57 Town on Trial. '59 Tiger Bay. '65 Sky West and Crooked (dir; +prod. only)(USA: Gypsy Girl). '66 The Family Way. '79 Zulu Dawn (USA-NETH). '82 Gandhi (GB-IND).

MILLS, Juliet

(b. 1941). Actress. Born: London, England

Like her sister Hayley, Juliet Mills first appeared in films as a child with her father, playing, amongst others, Little Polly in *The History of Mr Polly*. Lacking the cloying sweetness which made her sister a movie star, however, Juliet turned to the stage, which has remained her most successful medium. She first appeared as the lead in *Alice Through The Looking Glass* at the Chelsea Palace, and graduated to work with Sir Michael Redgrave in London and on Broadway. She remains a busy stage actress. Her occasional film appearances have often been in forgettable British comedies, such as *No, My Darling Daughter*, though a brief nude shot added a hint of naughtiness to the cool, crisp English Rose to spice up Billy Wilder's *Avanti!* Her successful performance in this film has not been followed up, except in a few television films. Her third husband is actor Maxwell Caulfield.

Films include: 1942 In Which We Serve. '47 So Well Remembered. '49 The History of Mr Polly. '61 No, My Darling Daughter. '63 Nurse On Wheels. '64 Carry On Jack. '66 The Rare Breed (USA). '69 Oh! What a Lovely War. '70 The Challengers (USA). '72 Avanti! (USA-IT).

MILO, Sandra

(b. 1935). Actress. Born: Alessandra Marini; Milan, Italy

Milo's film career began while she was still at university, when she was offered a part, in *Lo Scapolo*, starring Alberto Sordi and directed by Antonio Pietrangeli. Her exuberant personality attracted numerous offers of film roles and she worked regularly in France as well as her native Italy, for such directors as Renoir, Cayatte and Fellini. Among her best-remembered roles are Carla, the plump, amiable and vulgar mistress of the film director Anselmi in *8½*, a lonely spinster who advertises for a living companion in *La Visita* and the triple role of Susy, Iris and Fanny in *Juliet of the Spirits*.

Films include: 1956 Lo Scapolo (IT-SP); Elena et les Hommes (FR) (USA: Paris Does Strange Things; GB: The Night Does Strange Things). '57 Les Aventures d'Arsène Lupin (FR-IT). '58 Le Miroir à Deux Faces (FR-IT) (GB: The Mirror Has Two Faces). '59 Il Generale della Rovere (IT-FR); La Jument Verte (FR-IT) (USA: The Green Mare; GB: The Green Mare's Nest). '60 Adua e le Compagne (USA: Love à la Carte; GB: Hungry for Love). '61 Fantasmi a Roma (GB: Phantom Lovers). '63 Otto e Mezzo (IT-FR) (USA/GB: 8½). '64 La Visita. '65 Giulietta degli Spiriti (IT-FR) (GB: Juliet of the Spirits). '68 The Bang Bang Kid (SP-USA-IT).

MIMIEUX, Yvette

(b. 1939). Actress. Born: Los Angeles, California, USA

A frail, intelligent-looking blonde, Mimieux has given creditable, if not especially striking, performances in many films. The child of a French father and a Mexican mother, she was spotted in a play by director Vincente Minnelli. He cast her in a small role in *Home From the Hill* (1959). Although her part was later cut, MGM had been impressed by her looks and gave her the part of Weena in *The Time Machine*, based on the novel by H.G. Wells. The characters she played in her next films were mostly insipid creatures, although she was outstanding as the beautiful, straw-haired and retarded teenager who captures a boy's heart in *The Light in the Piazza*. Since the Seventies she has been offered more interesting roles, notably that of Dinah Hunter who becomes caught up in a nightmarish train of events in *Jackson County Jail*.

Films include: 1960 The Time Machine. '62 The Light in the Piazza (GB); Diamond Head; The Wonderful World of the Brothers Grimm; The Four Horsemen of the Apocalypse. '63 Toys in the Attic. '65 Joy in the Morning. '67 The Caper of the Golden Bulls (GB: Carnival of Thieves). '68 Three in the Attic; The Mercenaries (GB) (USA: Dark of the Sun). '70 The Picasso Summer. '76 Jackson County Jail. '81 Mystique.

MINEO, Sal

(1939–1976). Actor. Born: Salvatore Mineo; New York City, USA

With his baby face and dark, soulful eyes, Sal Mineo carried a touch of tragedy with him. It came true for him in *Rebel Without a Cause* when, as Plato, the friend of the hero (James Dean), he is pointlessly gunned down by the police; it came true for him, too, in real life when his career failed to fulfil its potential, and he was stabbed to death outside his Hollywood home, still only in his thirties. There is a cruel irony in this, for at his peak Mineo so excelled in playing tormented teenagers that he was nicknamed 'The Switch-Blade Kid'. Of Sicilian descent, he had appeared on stage as a child, and after some small movie parts made the link with James Dean that was to prove explosive to a whole generation, though he was equally good in the very different role of an Israeli guerrilla in *Exodus*. He won Oscar nominations for both films, but good parts became scarcer when he matured. He passed over a chance to make *The Last Picture Show* (1971) to give the opportunity to Peter Bogdanovich. At the time of his death he was involved in the theatre in Los Angeles. Very much a child – an insecure, twitchy, *angst*-ridden child – of the Fifties, Mineo was lost outside that era of Holden Caulfields.

Films include: 1955 Rebel Without a Cause; Six Bridges to Cross. '56 Giant; Somebody Up There Likes Me; Crime in the Streets. '57 The Young Don't Cry. '59 The Gene Krupa Story. '60 Exodus. '62 The Longest Day. '64 Cheyenne Autumn. '69 Krakatoa: East of Java. '71 Escape From the Planet of the Apes.

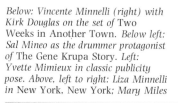

Below: Vincente Minnelli (right) with Kirk Douglas on the set of Two Weeks in Another Town. *Below left: Sal Mineo as the drummer protagonist of* The Gene Krupa Story. *Left: Yvette Mimieux in classic publicity pose. Above, left to right: Liza Minnelli in* New York, New York; *Mary Miles*

Minter in Drums of Fate: *Miou-Miou in* Al Piacere di Rivederla *(1976); a studio portrait of Isa Miranda. Right: Helen Mirren in Michael Powell's Barrier Reef idyll* Age of Consent. *Below right: Carmen Miranda. 'The Brazilian Bombshell', in* Greenwich Village *(1944)*

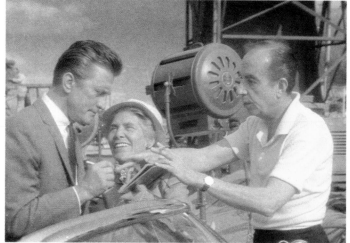

MINNELLI, Liza

(b. 1946). Actress. Born: Los Angeles, California, USA

The daughter of Judy Garland and director Vincente Minnelli who separated when she was only five years old, Liza Minnelli was assured, if she had any talent, of a start in show business. But she was dreadfully burdened in two ways: she had to face the inevitable comparisons with her mother, and she had to grow up in the shadow of that mother's disintegrating life. So far she has survived, though three marriages and some well-publicized affairs hint at another sad and saddening life. In the movies before she was three, in the final shots of her mother's *In the Good Old Summertime* (1949), she was educated in the USA, in Switzerland and briefly at the Sorbonne. At 19 she was the youngest performer to win Broadway's Tony Award. She went on to a successful career as a nightclub singer, but was unlucky in that the withering away of the screen musical severely limited her chances. She was excellent in her adult debut, *Charlie Bubbles*, and had the part of a

lifetime, exactly tailored to her, in *Cabaret*, for which she won the Best Actress Oscar. Her energy is electrifying, her voice like her mother's, perhaps with greater range; that there is no trace of her mother's sincerity and charm is perhaps the fault of the films.

Films include: 1968 Charlie Bubbles (GB). '69 The Sterile Cuckoo (GB: Pookie). '70 Tell Me That You Love Me, Junie Moon. '72 Journey Back to Oz (voice only); Cabaret. '74 That's Entertainment! (as on-screen co-narr). '75 Lucky Lady. '76 A Matter of Time (USA-IT); Silent Movie (uncredited). '77 New York, New York. '81 Arthur.

MINNELLI, Vincente

(1910–1986). Director. Born: Chicago, Illinois, USA

Minnelli had a colourful childhood, touring before he was eight with the Minnelli Brothers Dramatic Tent Show. Growing up, he designed sets and costumes for cinema prologues, and became art director for New York's Radio City Music Hall. In the late Thirties he staged Broadway mu-

sicals, and in 1940 Arthur Freed invited him to join MGM. After a two-year training in film techniques, he directed his first musicals, and was an outstanding contributor to the studio's marvellous record in those years. Two of his early films are classics: the tender, nostalgic *Meet Me in St Louis*, and the gaudily exuberant *The Pirate*. Minnelli followed with the balletic fantasy, *An American in Paris* (Best Picture Oscar), and *Gigi* (Best Picture and Best Director Oscars). These musicals were triumphs of design, and alive with movement; song and dance were firmly integrated with story. Minnelli did not confine himself to musicals. There were also charming comedies like *Father of the Bride*, and dramas that revelled in the odder quirks of human nature (*The Cobweb* and *Lust for Life*).

Films include: 1943 Cabin in the Sky. '44 Meet Me in St Louis. '45 The Clock (GB: Under the Clock); Yolanda and the Thief. '48 The Pirate. '50 Father of the Bride. '51 An American in Paris. '52 The Bad and the Beautiful. '53 The Band Wagon. '54 Brigadoon. '55 The Cobweb. '56 Lust for Life. '58

Gigi; Some Came Running. '59 Home From the Hill. '60 Bells Are Ringing. '62 The Four Horsemen of the Apocalypse; Two Weeks in Another Town. '63 The Courtship of Eddie's Father. '65 The Sandpiper. '70 On a Clear Day You Can See Forever. '76 A Matter of Time (USA-IT).

MINTER, Mary Miles

(1902–1984). Actress. Born: Juliet Shelby; Shreveport, Louisiana, USA

From 1915 to 1922 Minter played winsome, childlike heroines, and was Mary Pickford's chief rival at Famous Players-Lasky. Edward Sloman, who directed her in *The Ghost of Rosy Taylor*, a brilliant film which is virtually the only Minter movie to be seen now, described her as 'the best-looking youngster I ever saw, and the lousiest actress' (quoted in Kevin Brownlow's book *The Parade's Gone By . . .*). In 1922 Minter's career came to a sudden end when the unsolved murder of the director William Desmond Taylor rocked a Hollywood already shaken by the Arbuckle affair. Minter was shown to have been closely involved with Taylor, 25 years her senior. She did not work again.

Films include: 1912 (as Juliet Shelby) The Nurse. '15 The Fairy and the Waif. '16 Youth's Endearing Charm. '17 Melissa of the Hills; Environment. '18 The Ghost of Rosy Taylor. '19 Anne of Green Gables. '20 Nurse Marjorie. '22 Tillie; The Heart Specialist; The Cowboy and the Lady. '23 Drums of Fate.

MIOU-MIOU

(b. 1950). Actress. Born: Sylvette Héry; Paris, France

She began her career in café-theatres, working with actors like Gérard Depardieu and Patrick Dewaere who also had film careers ahead of them. An attractive, natural and fresh-faced girl, with freckles and urchin-cut blonde hair, Miou-Miou became a name in the Seventies with the vast commercial success of *Les Valseuses*. She made a few notable movies, including *Jonas: Qui Aura 25 Ans en l'An 2000* and the charming *F comme Fairbanks*, but many more designed largely to titillate.

Films include: 1972 Elle Court, Elle Court la Banlieue (GB: Love in the Suburbs). '73 Themroc; Les Aventures de Rabbi Jacob (FR-IT) (GB: The Adventures of Rabbi Jacob). '74 Les Valseuses (GB: Making It). 75 Lily, Aime-Moi. '76 F comme Fairbanks; Jonas: Qui Aura 25 Ans en l'An 2000 (FR-SWITZ) (USA/GB: Jonah Who Will Be 25 in the Year 2000). '78 Les Routes du Sud (FR-SP) (GB: Roads to the South). '79 La Dérobade (GB: The Life, the Confessions of a Street-Walker). '80 La Femme-Flic.

MIRANDA, Carmen

(1909–1955). Actress. Born: Maria do Carmo Miranda da Cunha; near Lisbon, Portugal

Miranda moved with her parents to Rio de Janeiro, where she sang in cafés and became a popular radio star. She also appeared in a few Brazilian films. In 1939 she made a hit on Broadway in the musical, *Streets of Paris*, and was signed to a film contract by 20th Century-Fox. In the Forties she enlivened many an otherwise routine musical with her energetic singing and dancing, her extravagant costumes and enormous, fruit-laden head-dresses. She was tiny – just over five feet – but platform soles and heels brought her up to almost six feet and she easily dominated when she was on screen. When she died from a heart attack, her body was taken to Rio to lie in state.

Films include: 1936 Alô, Alô, Carnaval (BRAZ). '38 Banana da Terra (BRAZ). '40 Down Argentine Way. '41 That Night in Rio; Weekend in Havana. '42 Springtime in the Rockies. '43 The Gang's All Here (GB: The Girls He Left Behind). '44 Something for the Boys. '47 Copacabana. '48 A Date With Judy. '50 Nancy Goes to Rio. '53 Scared Stiff.

MIRANDA, Isa

(1909–1982). Actress. Born: Ines Isabella Sampietro; Milan, Italy

Isa Miranda was a lady of many talents. She was a poet, a novelist and a painter, and an extremely beautiful woman who herself was painted by many artists. Born of poor parents in Milan, she worked as a seamstress, then as a secretary and a model. She had played a few small parts in Italian films when Max Ophuls gave her the lead in *La Signora di Tutti*; it brought her a stardom which endured for forty years. She made films in the USA (notably the remake of *Hotel Imperial*,

following Pola Negri), in Britain, in France (a Cannes Best Actress award for *Au-Delà des Grilles*), and in Germany as well as in her native Italy, and starred on the London stage in Tennessee Williams' *Orpheus Descending*.

Films include: 1934 Tenebre; La Signora di Tutti. '35 Passaporto Rosso. '37 Il Fu Mattia Pascal; Scipione l'Africano. '39 Hotel Imperial (USA). '49 Au-Delà des Grilles (FR-IT) (GB: Beyond the Walls). '50 La Ronde (FR). '52 Les Sept Pêchés Capitaux (FR-IT) (USA/GB: Seven Deadly Sins). '55 Summer Madness (GB-USA) (USA: Summertime). '64 The Yellow Rolls Royce (GB). '68 The Shoes of the Fisherman. '74 Il Portiere di Notte (USA/GB: The Night Porter).

MIRISCH, Walter

(b. 1921). Producer. Born: New York City, USA

After World War II Mirisch, still in his early twenties, was producing low-budget movies for Monogram. By 1951 he was executive producer at Allied Artists, and in 1957, with his brother Marvin and half-brother Harold, he founded the Mirisch Corporation, Walter being vice-president in charge of production. The company had neither story department nor studio and rented space when necessary. It financed many good films by directors such as Billy Wilder, John Ford and John Sturges, and won three Best Picture Oscars (for *The Apartment*, 1960, *West Side Story*, 1961, and *In the Heat of the Night*). In 1963 United Artists bought the company, but the brothers retained administrative control.

Films include: 1955 An Annapolis Story (GB: The Blue and the Gold). '58 Man of the West. '60 The Magnificent Seven (exec. prod.). '62 Two for the Seesaw. '66 Hawaii. '67 In the Heat of the Night. '70 They Call Me Mister Tibbs! (exec. prod.). '73 Scorpio. '78 Gray Lady Down; Same Time, Next Year. '79 Dracula.

MIRREN, Helen

(b. 1945). Actress. Born: Chiswick, London, England

Beginning her stage career with the National Youth Theatre, Helen Mirren was a member of the Royal Shakespeare Company from 1967 to 1972, making her film debut at that time in Peter Hall's version of *A Midsummer Night's Dream*. Since then Mirren has divided her time between stage, cinema and television. Many of her stage performances have been highly praised. The cinema has seemed more interested in her sensuous looks and voluptuous figure than in her skills as an actress, though she has had a few interesting parts, such as the intelligent and cultured gangster's moll in *The Long Good Friday*.

Films include: 1968 A Midsummer Night's Dream; Age of Consent (AUS). '72 Miss Julie; Savage Messiah. '73 O Lucky Man! '76 Hamlet. '79 Caligula (IT-USA); S.O.S. Titanic. '80 Hussy; The Long Good Friday; The Fiendish Plot of Fu Manchu (USA). '81 Excalibur (USA).

MITCHELL, Cameron

(b. 1918). Actor. Born: Cameron
Mizell; Dallastown, Pennsylvania,
USA

Cameron Mitchell's lucky break came
in 1939 when he was offered the part
of Christopher Sly in Alfred Lunt's
Broadway production of *The Taming of
the Shrew*. His film career began with
MGM in 1945 (he caught the eye in
John Ford's *They Were Expendable*),
and was considerably advanced by his
stage success as Happy in *Death of a
Salesman*, a role he repeated in the film
version. Mitchell never reached major
stardom, but turned in countless competent performances, usually as aggressive, rough-diamond characters.
His roles became more elevated when
he moved into Italian spectacle – he
played Cesare Borgia and even Julius
Caesar – but he came home, perhaps
thankfully, to *The High Chaparral* and
television fame.

Films include: 1945 They Were Expendable.
'51 Death of a Salesman. '53 How to Marry
a Millionaire. '55 Love Me or Leave Me. '56
Carousel. '57 No Down Payment; Monkey
on My Back. '63 Il Duca Nero (IT). '65
Minnesota Clay (IT-SP-FR). '67 Hombre.
'72 Buck and the Preacher. '80 Without
Warning (GB: The Warning). '82 My
Favorite Year.

MITCHELL, Thomas

(1892–1962). Actor. Born: Elizabeth,
New Jersey, USA

One of the greatest American character actors, Mitchell went to Hollywood to write. Originally a reporter,
then a playwright who moved into
acting, he first appeared on Broadway
in one of his own plays. He was co-
author of *Little Accident*, which
brought him financial independence,
and was filmed three times. Hollywood summoned him to work on
the screenplay of *All of Me* and act as
dialogue director. While there, he was
offered a part in *Craig's Wife*. He was
superb, followed up with *Theodora
Goes Wild* and *Lost Horizon*, and
stayed. Curly-haired, bright-eyed,
wryly mischievous, he had astonishing range, and the knack of almost
always choosing good movies. No
actor had any better year than Mitchell in 1939; he won the Best Supporting Actor Oscar for his drunken
doctor in *Stagecoach*, he was the tragic
Kid in *Only Angels Have Wings*, and he
gave richly satisfying performances in
Mr Smith Goes to Washington and *Gone
With the Wind*. Next year he was
Driscoll in Ford's *The Long Voyage
Home*, a towering performance in a
film marked by outstanding acting.
And so he went on, winding down
when it came to the Fifties, perhaps
lacking the old bravura, but never
losing his magnetic hold.

Films include: 1936 Craig's Wife; Theodora
Goes Wild. '37 Lost Horizon; The Hur-
ricane. '39 Stagecoach; Only Angels Have
Wings; Mr Smith Goes to Washington;
Gone With the Wind. '40 Our Town; The
Long Voyage Home. '43 The Outlaw. '44
The Sullivans; The Keys of the Kingdom.
'46 It's a Wonderful Life. '48 Silver River.
'52 High Noon. '61 Pocketful of Miracles.

MITCHELL, Yvonne

(1925–1979). Actress. Born: Yvonne
Joseph; London, England

A distinguished stage actress and a
successful playwright and novelist –
her play *The Same Sky* won the Festival of Britain prize as the best new
play of 1950 – Yvonne Mitchell made
her film debut in Thorold Dickinson's
The Queen of Spades in 1949, and
showed herself as effective in intense,
emotional parts as she had been in the
theatre. Her outstanding film performance came in 1957 with *Woman
in a Dressing Gown*. As the untidy,
maddening, over-loving wife she gave
a virtuoso display which won her an
acting award at the Berlin Festival. It
was a star performance that was
entirely unglamorous, and perhaps
set a pattern from which other actresses of the Sixties profited.

Films include: 1953 Turn the Key Softly. '54
The Divided Heart. '56 Yield to the Night
(USA: Blonde Sinner). '57 Woman in a
Dressing Gown. '59 Tiger Bay; Sapphire.
'60 Conspiracy of Hearts. '65 Genghis Khan
(USA-GER-YUG). '70 The Corpse (USA:
Crucible of Horror). '72 Demons of the
Mind.

MITCHUM, Robert

(b. 1917). Actor. Born: Bridgeport,
Connecticut, USA

Mitchum had a hard youth during the
Depression – as hobo, coal-miner,
prizefighter – before settling down in
the early Forties with the Long Beach
Theater Guild and learning to act. In
1943 he played bits in around twenty
movies, and gradually climbed the
ladder until in 1945 *The Story of GI Joe*
revealed him as a potential star. Mitchum had timed things well. His
casual, laconic, anti-hero style,
saying little but expressing much, was
perfect for *film noir*, and he played in
some outstanding specimens of the
genre – *Crossfire*, *Out of the Past*,
Pursued. Mitchum has lasted wonderfully well. He has made lots of routine
movies, but every few years there has
been a triumph: the sad rodeo veteran
in Nicholas Ray's *The Lusty Men*, the
demented preacher in *The Night of the
Hunter*, the ageing Westerner of *El
Dorado*.

Films include: 1945 The Story of GI Joe. '46
The Locket. '47 Pursued; Crossfire; Out of

*Below: Robert Mitchum, watching out
for a U-boat, in* The Enemy Below
(1957). Above: Cameron Mitchell in
Buck and the Preacher. *Above right:
Thomas Mitchell as Doc Boone, a
drunk with a heart of gold, in John*

Ford's Stagecoach. *Above right:
Yvonne Mitchell in* Woman in a
Dressing Gown. *Above, far right:
Western hero Tom Mix. Right: Gaston
Modot as Fil de Soie, the blind man,
in* Les Enfants du Paradis

the Past (GB: Build My Gallows High). '52
Macao; The Lusty Men. '54 River of No
Return; Track of the Cat. '55 The Night of
the Hunter. '59 Home From the Hill. '60
The Sundowners. '62 The Longest Day. '67
El Dorado. '68 Lo Sbarco di Anzio (IT) (USA:
Anzio; GB: The Battle for Anzio). '70 Ryan's
Daughter (GB). '73 The Friends of Eddie
Coyle. '75 Farewell, My Lovely.

MITRA, Subatra

(b. 1931). Cinematographer. Born:
India

Interested from schooldays in films
and photography, Mitra was greatly
influenced by watching cameraman
Claude Renoir shooting Jean Renoir's
The River (1951). It was here that he
met Satyajit Ray, who in 1955 engaged Mitra to photograph *Pather
Panchali*. Mitra became Ray's regular
cameraman, working with him on the
rest of the Apu trilogy and other films,
and also photographed the first films
of James Ivory. An innovative lighting
cameraman using sophisticated techniques not often associated with
Indian films, Mitra has proved himself
a master black-and-white cinematographer, and his work has certainly
been crucial to the realization of Ray's
vision.

Films include: 1955 Pather Panchali (USA:
Song of the Little Road). '56 Aparajito
(USA/GB: The Unvanquished). '58 Paras
Pathar (GB: The Philosopher's Stone). '59
Apur Sansar (USA/GB: The World of Apu).
'60 Devi (USA/GB: The Goddess). '62 Kan-
chenjunga. '63 Mahanagar (GB: The Big
City). '65 Shakespeare-Wallah. '68 The
Arch (HONGKONG). '69 The Guru (USA-
IND). '70 Bombay Talkie.

MITRY, Jean

(b. 1907). Theoretician/historian/
director. Born: Jean-René-Pierre
Goetgheluck Le Rouge Tillard des
Acres des Préfontaines; Soissons,
France

Famous as a writer on the theory and
history of the cinema, whose major
work, *Esthétique et Psychologie du
Cinéma*, is among the classics of film
scholarship, Mitry was himself an
active film-maker. He directed and
edited some highly regarded shorts, including the award-winning *Pacific
231* and *Images pour Debussy*, films
which display an acute sensitivity to
the interaction of music and image.
Mitry founded the first film society in
France (1925), and was instrumental
in organizing the Cinémathèque
Française. A professor of cinema at
the French film school, IDHEC, since
1944, he also taught film at the
University of Montreal.

Films include: 1929 Paris Cinéma (co-dir).
'49 Pacific 231 (+ed). '50 Le Paquebot
Liberté (co-dir). '51 Aux Pays des Grands
Causses. '52 Rêverie de Claude Debussy;
Images pour Debussy (+ sc). '53 Le Rideau
Cramoisi (ed) (GB: The Crimson Curtain).
'56 Symphonie Mécanique; Le Miracle des
Ailes. '57 Chopin (co-dir) (GB); La Machine
et l'Homme. '59 Énigme aux Folies-Bergère.

MIX, Tom

(1880–1940). Actor. Born: Thomas
Edwin Mix; Mix Run, Pennsylvania,
USA

There are two life stories of Tom Mix.
The one sedulously propagated
during his stardom had him behaving
heroically in half-a-dozen wars, roun-
ding up outlaws as a US Marshal, and
chatting happily in four Indian languages, as befitted one whose Indian
great-grandfather had translated the
Bible into Osage. The truth, established by a young relative, Paul Mix, is
more prosaic. His war service was
largely imaginary, and ended in de-
sertion; he was, briefly, a deputy
sheriff; and he really was a cowboy
with The Miller Brothers 101 Ranch, a
Wild West show which sued him for
horse-stealing. And this legendary
Westerner was born, not in El Paso, as
he said, but in rural Pennsylvania.
But the poseur was still a great showman. He drifted into the movies with
the Selig company in 1909, starred in
countless short films, and after joining
Fox in 1917 remained at the top until
the end of the silents. His films of the
Twenties were exciting and lavishly
produced, and Mix, a superb rider, did
his own stunts. But he painted a
colourful picture of the West which
was far from realistic, not even, except
in his early days, authentic in dress.
Compare Mix's huge white hat, hand-
carved boots and decorative jackets
with the dress of the real cowboys in
truer Westerns, and in the
background of his own. Mix gradually
faded out in the Thirties, and was
killed in a car-crash, through his own
reckless driving, in 1940.

Films include: 1920 The Daredevil
(+dir; + sc); Rough Riding Romance; The
Untamed. '22 Just Tony; Sky High. '23 The
Lone Star Ranger. '24 The Heartbuster. '25
The Rainbow Trail. '26 The Great Train
Robbery. '32 Destry Rides Again; My Pal,
the King. '35 The Miracle Rider (serial).

MIZOGUCHI, Kenji

(1898–1956). Director. Born: Tokyo,
Japan

The film that introduced Kenji Mizoguchi to the West was *Ugetsu Monogatari*, a story of a potter desperately
trying to continue his craft in a war-
torn medieval village, who meets a
phantom princess and is lured away
to a land of sensual delights. His
earlier films were very different, and
many concerned social issues, especially the oppression of women.
Mizoguchi himself was brought up in
conditions of great poverty (his personal life was always traumatic) and
left school at the age of 13. He spent
his early adult life living near the
Mukojima Studios of the Nikkatsu
Motion Picture Company where he
met Osamu Wakayama, a progressive
director who gave him a job as an
assistant director; and in 1922 he was
given his first opportunity to direct.
Early in his career he was greatly
influenced by Western film-makers,
but he then moved on to create, with
The Life of Oharu, the beginning of a
genre he was to make his own –
personal dramas set in an historical
epoch reconstructed with great detail.
Mizoguchi became one of the most
prominent members of the Japanese
film world – the many positions he
held included head of the All-Japan
Film-Makers League, member of the
Social Studies Committee of the Ministry of Education and, almost up until
the time of his death, president of the
Japan Motion Picture Directors' Association. He is generally regarded as
Japan's greatest ever director. He
certainly one of world cinema's great
pictorialists: a creator of remarkably
beautiful images combining exquisite
decor and camerawork.

Films include: 1922 Ai ni Yomigaeru Hi
(The Resurrection of Love). 36 Naniwa Ereji
(USA/GB: Naniwa Elegy/Osaka Elegy);
Gion no Shimai (USA/GB: Sisters of the
Gion). '39 Zangiku Monogatari (USA/GB:
The Story of the Last Chrysanthemums).
'41 Genroku Chushingura Part I (USA: The
Loyal 47 Ronin; GB: The Loyal 47 of the
Genroku Era). '42 Genroku Chushingura
Part II (USA: The Loyal 47 Ronin; GB: The
Loyal 47 of the Genroku Era). '46 Utamaro o
Meguro Gonin no Onna (USA: Utamaro
and His Five Women; GB: Five Women
Around Utamaro). '49 Waga Koi wa
Moenu (USA: My Love Burns; GB: My Love
Has Been Burning). '52 Saikaku Ichidai
Onna (USA/GB: The Life of Oharu). '53
Ugetsu Monogatari (USA: Ugetsu; GB: Tales
of the Pale and Silvery Moon After the
Rain). '54 Sansho Dayu (USA/GB: Sansho
the Bailiff/The Bailiff); Chikamatsu Mono-
gatari (USA/GB: A Story From
Chikamatsu/The Crucified Lovers). '55
Yokihi (USA: The Princess Yang Kwei-Fei;
GB: The Empress Yang Kwei-Fei); Shin-
Heike Monogatari (GB: New Tales of the
Taira Clan). '56 Akasen Chitai (USA/GB:
The Street of Shame).

MODOT, Gaston

(1887–1970). Actor. Born: Paris,
France

Gaston Modot was a contemporary of
Picasso and Modigliani and was himself, at one time, a painter in Montmartre. He made an impressive start
in silent films in 1910 in the popular
Onésime comedy series and became
one of the leading actors of the French
cinema, working with many of its
major directors during a career that
lasted into the Sixties. A large athletic
man with dark hair and eyes, he
proved himself a versatile actor equally at home in villainous, humorous
or dramatic roles. He played the amorous egoist in Luis Buñuel's *L'Age d'Or*,
and the surly, brutal gamekeeper in
La Règle du Jeu. He also directed occasionally and collaborated on several
scripts.

Films include: 1930 L'Age d'Or; Sous les
Toits de Paris (USA: Under the Roofs of
Paris). '35 La Bandéra (USA: Escape From
Yesterday). '36 Pépé-le-Moko; La Vie Est à
Nous (USA: People of France). '37 La
Grande Illusion (USA: Grand Illusion; GB:
The Great Illusion). '39 La Règle du Jeu
(USA: The Rules of the Game). '45 Les
Enfants du Paradis (USA: Children of Para-
dise). '52 Casque d'Or (USA: Golden Helmet;
GB: Golden Marie). '56 Elena et les Hommes
(USA: Paris Does Strange Things; GB: The
Night Does Strange Things). '58 Les
Amants (GB: The Lovers). '59 Le Testament
du Dr Cordelier (GB: Experiment in Evil).

MOHR, Hal

(1894–1974). Cinematographer.
Born: San Francisco, California,
USA

Hal Mohr helped to make the movies
move. Born the year before the
Lumiére brothers made their first
public presentation of moving film, he
devoted his life to the infant cinema.
Dropping out of high school he built
his own camera out of a projector and
immediately began a career in film
which was to last for over sixty years.
By 1921 he was a director of photography and was soon regarded as one
of Hollywood's most innovative cameramen. His best work was in the silent
cinema of the late Twenties when he
worked with European directors like
Michael Curtiz and Paul Leni. Influenced by the great German directors Mohr produced the most dynamic
examples of Hollywood Expressionism. In the Thirties, after shooting the
first talkie – *The Jazz Singer* – Mohr was
already experimenting with deep-
focus photography on films like *Bullets
or Ballots* and *The Green Pastures* (both
1936), predating *Citizen Kane* (1940)
and the work of Gregg Toland by
several years. In later years he also
worked in television on shows like *Life
With Father* and *I Married Joan*. A
highly respected craftsman, Mohr was
a president of the American Society of
Cinematographers.

Films include: 1926 The Third Degree. '27
The Jazz Singer. '28 The Wedding March.
'29 The Last Performance (GB: Erik the
Great Illusionist). '33 State Fair. '35 Captain Blood; A Midsummer Night's Dream.
'36 The Green Pastures. '39 Destry Rides
Again. '43 The Phantom of the Opera
(co-photo). '52 The Fourposter; Rancho
Notorious. '60 The Last Voyage.

MOLANDER, Gustav

(1888–1973). Director. Born: Helsinki, Finland

A versatile, resourceful director, Gustav Molander became the mainstay of the early Swedish film industry and later started many famous performers, such as Ingrid Bergman, Bibi Andersson and Mai Zetterling, on their careers. His father was the director of the National Theatre in Helsinki and Molander joined the company as an actor in 1909. Four years later he went to Stockholm where he played leading roles with the Royal Dramatic Theatre before becoming a teacher at their drama school for two years. He soon began writing scripts for Mauritz Stiller, and he made his own directorial debut in 1920. Along with Stiller and Sjöström he created the golden age of Swedish silent cinema and when they went to Hollywood Molander stayed on to form a link between the past and the renaissance of Swedish cinema in the Fifties. Ingmar Bergman collaborated with Molander on the scripts of three of his films – *A Woman Without a Face*, *Eva* and *Divorced*. His first wife Karin was an actress; his younger brother Olaf was a director and actor.

Films include: 1922 Thomas Graals Myndling (Thomas Graal's Ward). '27 Hans Engelska Fru (His English Wife). '31 En Natt (GB: One Night). '35 Swedenhielms. '36 Intermezzo. '42 Jacobs Stege (Jacob's Ladder). '47 Kvinna Utan Ansikte (A Woman Without a Face). '48 Eva. '51 Frånskild (Divorced). '54 Herr Arnes Penningar (Sir Arne's Treasure).

MOLINARO, Edouard

(b. 1928). Director. Born: Bordeaux, France

Although of the generation of French *nouvelle vague* directors, Edouard Molinaro is now thought of as a director of stylish, commercially successful comedies, notably *La Cage aux Folles*, about an ageing homosexual couple. Molinaro attended university at the request of his parents but spent much of his time making short films. He won several amateur film awards and in 1949 he began working on features as an assistant director – nine years later he directed his first film *Le Dos au Mur*. At first he directed thrillers but he soon moved on to period comedy (*Mon Oncle Benjamin*) and black comedy (*L'Emmerdeur*), finding his niche with mirth rather than mystery.

Films include: 1958 Les Dos au Mur (GB: Evidence in Concrete). '59 Des Femmes Disparaissent (GB: Girls Disappear). '62 Les Ennemis; Arsène Lupin Contre Arsène Lupin (FR-IT). '64 Une Ravissante Idiote (FR-IT) (GB: A Ravishing Idiot). '67 Oscar. '69 Hibernatus (FR-IT); Mon Oncle Benjamin (FR-IT) (GB: The Amorous Adventures of Uncle Benjamin). '73 L'Emmerdeur (FR-IT) (USA: Pain in the A**). '77 L'Homme Pressé. '78 La Cage aux Folles (FR-IT) (USA: Birds of a Feather). '80 La Cage aux Folles II (FR-IT).

MONROE, Marilyn

(1926–1962). Actress. Born: Norma Jean Baker; Los Angeles, USA

During her lifetime few people could resist Marilyn Monroe, or can do now.

Above: Marilyn Monroe in Let's Make Love. *Below: Ricardo Montalban partners Cyd Charisse in* Fiesta *(1947). Below centre: Yves Montand. Below right: Douglass* Montgomery *in* Woman to Woman. *Bottom: Maria Montez. Bottom right: George Montgomery in* China Girl *(1942). Bottom, far right: Robert Montgomery in* The Lady in the Lake

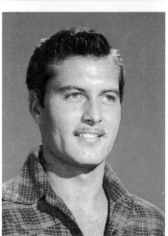

Her allure – she was sloppy, unfettered but magnetic – made a collective cuckold of American men during the Fifties. It still reaches beyond the grave to enchant and claim successive generations of men – and women. More has been written about Monroe than any other star, and probably more than any other woman who has ever lived. Certainly she is the most legendary woman of the twentieth century, and that status derives from her remarkable beauty, her talent, her sexuality, her private life, her mercurial, troubled personality, and the mystery enshrouding her death. It has very little to do with her films, which, with the exceptions of *Gentlemen Prefer Blondes*, *Bus Stop*, *The Seven Year Itch*, *Some Like It Hot* and *The Misfits*, are an extraordinarily bad bunch. It was Monroe's own complaint that her movies turned her into a sex symbol and nothing more, but she was never sufficiently in control of her life or her career to escape an image that she in any case seemed to foster. Of her muddled 36 years there have been too many accounts: it is time she was left in peace and remembered not for the wrecked, fatherless childhood, the marriages, affairs and breakdowns and the final fatal overdose, but for the few moments of greatness she left behind. These include most of her scatterbrained, wildly sexy-but-innocent scenes in *The Seven Year Itch* and *Some Like It Hot* for Billy Wilder; and her songs – 'Diamonds Are a Girl's Best Friend', 'That Old Black Magic' and the electrifyingly erotic 'My Heart Belongs to Daddy', which is the only bearable moment in *Let's Make Love*. Remembered, too, should be the endless shots of Marilyn's brow furrowed in confusion. They denote the perplexity of a voluptuous munitions-factory worker who, via bit-part contracts at 20th Century-Fox and Columbia, was suddenly raised to screen goddess and in the process had her life stolen from her.

Films include: 1947 Dangerous Years. '48 Ladies of the Chorus. '49 Love Happy. '50 The Asphalt Jungle; All About Eve. '51 Let's Make It Legal. '52 Clash by Night; Don't Bother to Knock; Monkey Business. '53 Niagara; Gentlemen Prefer Blondes; How to Marry a Millionaire. '54 River of No Return; There's No Business Like Show Business. '55 The Seven Year Itch. '56 Bus Stop. '57 The Prince and the Showgirl (GB). '59 Some Like It Hot. '60 Let's Make Love. '61 The Misfits. '62 Something's Got to Give (unfinished).

MONTALBAN, Ricardo

(b. 1920). Actor. Born: Mexico City, Mexico

After being educated in America and graduating from school plays to Broadway, Montalban returned to Mexico in 1941, where he made several films before signing the contract that MGM had offered him while he was appearing with Tallulah Bankhead in *Her Cardboard Lover* on Broadway. Tall, dark and possessed of a dashing manner, Montalban soon became popular as a smooth, romantic lead, an image he later tried to vary by taking non-romantic roles in adventures and thrillers. Television offered him more scope to explore his acting talents, and he became the star of the popular television series *Fantasy Island*. He received ecstatic notices for his performance in the television production of George Bernard Shaw's *Don Juan in Hell* and continues to appear on the stage. He is married to Georgiana Young, sister of the actress Loretta Young.

Films include: 1948 On an Island With You. '49 Border Incident. '51 Across the Wide Missouri. '53 Latin Lovers. '54 The Saracen Blade. '64 Cheyenne Autumn. '66 Madame X; The Singing Nun. '69 Sweet Charity. '71 Escape From the Planet of the Apes. '72 Conquest of the Planet of the Apes.

MONTAND, Yves

(b. 1921). Actor. Born: Ivo Livi; Monsummano, Italy

Montand's father was an Italian socialist forced to flee the country with the rise to power of Mussolini. From the age of two Montand was brought up in France and the family lived in poverty around the Marseille dockland. From the age of eleven he worked as a labourer and then became a barman until he began to make his living as a singer in Marseille nightclubs. In 1944 he went to work in the Parisian music-halls and there met Edith Piaf who became his mentor, lover and co-star in the film *Étoile Sans Lumière* (1946). He remained primarily a singer until 1953 when he featured in his first major film *Le Salaire de la Peur*. Already a crooner with a large following, his unusual yet attractive appearance – elegantly loose-limbed with hooded eyes and a wide humorous mouth – led to his becoming a nonchalant lover and heart-throb in generally sub-standard Hollywood films. Returning to France for meatier roles, he continued to work on stage (both as singer and actor) and screen. He is married to the actress Simone Signoret, a relationship that has survived many well-publicized diversions, including an affair with Marilyn Monroe and some controversy over his staunchly socialist politics.

Films include: 1953 Le Salaire de la Peur (FR-IT) (GB: The Wages of Fear). '57 Les Sorcières de Salem (GB: The Witches of Salem). '60 Let's Make Love (USA). '61 Aimez-Vous Brahms? (FR-USA) (USA: Goodbye Again); My Geisha (USA-JAP). '66 Grand Prix (USA). '69 Z (FR-ALGERIA). '70

On a Clear Day You Can See Forever (USA). '72 Tout Va Bien (FR-IT). '73 État de Siège (FR-IT-GER) (GB: State of Siege). '75 Le Sauvage (FR-IT).

MONTEZ, Maria

(1920–1951). Actress. Born: Maria Africa Vidal de Santo Silas; Barahona, Dominican Republic

Known in America as 'The Caribbean Cyclone', Maria Montez was a fantasy movie-queen. With luxurious hair, fiery Latin features, satin complexion and a vibrant voice that throbbed with promise, she was the archetypal seductress. The daughter of a Spanish don who held consular posts throughout the world, she was educated in the Canary Islands before travelling extensively, and eventually ended up in New York as a model. Universal decided that she was ideal for decoration in their movies of the Forties, and she played in a succession of costume extravaganzas (usually as seductive maidens) until her temper and bargaining powers landed her the role of Scheherazade in *Arabian Nights*. On seeing herself in the film she said: 'When I look at myself I am so beautiful, I scream with joy'. From there she went on to other glossy lead roles until after World War II when her sort of frothy escapism became excessive to audiences. She went to live in semi-retirement in France and a comeback bid some years later was thwarted by a spreading waistline. She died of a heart attack.

Films include: 1941 The Invisible Woman. '42 Bombay Clipper. '43 Arabian Nights; White Savage. '44 Ali Baba and the Forty Thieves; Cobra Woman. '45 Sudan. '46 Tangier. '48 Siren of Atlantis. '49 Portrait d'un Assassin (FR). '51 La Vendetta del Corsaro (IT) (GB: Duel Before the Mast).

MONTGOMERY, Douglass

(1909–1966). Actor. Born: Brantford, Ontario, Canada

Of wholesome appearance, six feet tall, brown-haired and hazel-eyed, Douglass Montgomery had a steady, if uneventful, career in films during the Thirties and Forties. While still at school in Los Angeles he began acting at the Pasadena Playhouse where he befriended a young unknown named Clark Gable. Montgomery went on to become a juvenile lead on the New York stage and joined the coveted New York Theater Guild. His film career began with *Paid* in 1930 – until 1933 he used the name Kent Douglass – and after journeying to Hollywood he was offered the lead opposite Katharine Hepburn in *Little Women*. He went back to Canada to join the army at the outbreak of World War II, and later featured in the British film *The Way to the Stars*.

Films include: 1932 A House Divided. '33 Little Women. '34 Eight Girls on a Boat; Little Man, What Now?. '35 The Mystery of Edwin Drood. '39 The Cat and the Canary. '45 The Way to the Stars (USA: Johnny in the Clouds). '46 Woman to Woman (GB). '47 Sinfonia Fatale (IT) (GB: When in Rome). '53 Forbidden (GB).

MONTGOMERY, George

(b. 1916). Actor. Born: George Montgomery Letz; Brady, Montana, USA

One of 15 children from an immigrant Russian family, Montgomery was educated in Montana and became boxing champion at the state university. On graduating he went to study the sport in Hollywood under ex-World Heavyweight Champion Jim Jeffries. His rugged, masculine good looks and physique soon attracted the attention of the studios and during the mid-Thirties he became a stuntman for many action movies. In 1939 he was offered a contract by 20th Century-Fox and played rather characterless but handsome and genial leading men opposite some of their most glamorous leading ladies. Most of his publicity during this time concerned his various romances with Ginger Rogers, Hedy Lamarr and singer Dinah Shore (to whom he was married from 1943 to 1960). After World War II service he was in increasingly weak vehicles and was very wooden as private eye Philip Marlowe in *The Brasher Doubloon*. He continued to appear in films until the early Seventies. He also began writing, producing and directing low-budget adventure films.

Films include: 1941 The Cowboy and the Blonde. '42 Ten Gentlemen From West Point; Roxie Hart. '43 Coney Island. '47 The Brasher Doubloon (GB: The High Window). '48 Belle Starr's Daughter. '51 Sword of Monte Cristo; The Texas Rangers. '65 Satan's Harvest; Battle of the Bulge.

MONTGOMERY, Robert

(1904–1981). Actor/director. Born: Henry Montgomery Jr; New York City, USA

Robert Montgomery enjoyed a privileged childhood until his father died penniless. After working as a railway mechanic and on an oil tanker, he moved to Greenwich Village with the idea of becoming a writer. A friend persuaded him to try acting and he spent several years in repertory before becoming the lead in *Dawn* on Broadway. In 1929 he signed for MGM. He served as an ambulance driver during World War II and was on the first destroyer into Cherbourg on D-Day. He was seen in action by John Ford, who later cast him in *They Were Expendable*. When Ford broke a leg during shooting, Montgomery took over and then carried on to direct *The Lady in the Lake* (1946), in which he also starred as detective Philip Marlowe. This film is an oddity because it was photographed entirely from a subjective point of view through the eyes of Marlowe. He appeared in fewer films after that, preferring to concentrate on politics and television work: his series *Robert Montgomery Presents* was highly regarded.

Films include: 1929 Untamed. '30 The Big House. '31 Inspiration; Private Lives. '36 Petticoat Fever. '37 The Last of Mrs Cheyney; Night Must Fall. '41 Rage in Heaven. '45 They Were Expendable. '47 Ride the Pink Horse (+dir). '48 June Bride. '50 Eye Witness (GB: Your Witness).

MOODY, Ron

(b. 1924). Actor. Born: Ronald Moodnick; Hornsey, London, England

The characters played by versatile Ron Moody tend towards the fantastic. His appearance is difficult to describe for he is a master of disguises and is often unrecognizable underneath a welter of makeup. He came to showbusiness relatively late in his life, for he spent four years in the RAF before studying sociology at the London School of Economics. While there he, Bernard Levin and some of their friends put on annual revues. This led to the stage; Moody worked constantly until he became a household name after his appearance as Fagin in Lionel Bart's *Oliver* – a role he was to re-create on the screen with equal success. Small character parts in a dozen or so films followed, and he has appeared in one or two television plays. Since then Moody has been pursuing his lifelong ambition to write successful musicals – he wrote the story, lyrics and music for *Grimaldi* which sadly flopped, as did *Saturnalia*, an anti-permissive musical that closed at great loss only a few weeks after its opening. His one-man shows are always well-received, but as yet he has not been offered the serious dramatic roles he would like.

Films include: 1959 Follow a Star. '63 The Mouse on the Moon. '64 Murder Most Foul. '68 Oliver! '69 David Copperfield. '70 The Twelve Chairs (USA). '71 Flight of the Doves (USA); Bedknobs and Broomsticks (USA). '74 Dogpound Shuffle (CAN) (GB: Spot). '75 Legend of the Werewolf. '79 The Spaceman and King Arthur (USA: Unidentified Flying Oddball).

MOORE, Colleen

(b. 1900). Actress. Born: Kathleen Morrison; Port Huron, Michigan, USA

When the director D.W. Griffith was unable to get *Intolerance* past the censors, Colleen Moore's uncle, an influential businessman, pulled a few strings to change their minds. In return Griffith took his niece on at the studio. Five feet three inches tall, with one eye blue and the other brown, black hair and a pert and lively personality, Moore became one of the highest paid silent stars and received more fan mail and adulation than most of her contemporaries. Her clothes and style – the bob-haired jazz-baby – were copied throughout the world and her press coverage was enormous. At one stage she was condemned by a women's club for 'flighty actions on the screen'. She usually featured in sentimental, melodramatic love stories concerning innocent country girls sucked into the evil ways of the big city, and the titles were thought very risqué at the time – *Naughty But Nice*, *Her Wild Oat* (1927), *Why Be Good?* (1929). An intelligent woman (Eisenstein said she was the only person in Hollywood he could talk to), she made few films after the coming of sound and concentrated on business and writing. Her books include her autobiography *Silent Star* and a book for business-

women, *How Women Can Make Money in the Stock Market*.

Films include: 1918 Little Orphan Annie. '24 The Perfect Flapper. '25 Sally; The Desert Flower. '26 Irene; Ella Cinders. '27 Naughty But Nice; Orchids and Ermine. '33 The Power and the Glory. '34 The Scarlet Letter.

MOORE, Dudley

(b. 1935). Actor/comedian/composer. Born: Dagenham, Essex, England

The son of an electrician, Dudley Moore went to the Guildhall School of Music and Drama, and won himself an organ scholarship to Magdalen College, Oxford. In 1960 he appeared in the revue *Beyond the Fringe* at the Edinburgh Festival and then starred in a very successful television series, *Not Only But Also*, with Peter Cook. In 1973 the duo took their revue *Good Evening* to Australia and America. Moore stayed in Los Angeles and while attending a group therapy session met Blake Edwards. The director starred him opposite Bo Derek and Julie Andrews in '10', a glossy, romantic comedy, and he was immediately taken to the maternal – and not so maternal – bosom of American womanhood. He had previously appeared in British comedy films (often with Peter Cook) but '10' made him an international star. *Arthur* confirmed his popularity; he was Oscar-nominated for his portrayal of a drunken, spoilt playboy reluctant to marry an heiress in order to secure his inheritance. A cuddly, pint-sized pin-up, five foot three with warm brown eyes and tousled hair, Moore has been described by humorist Jonathan Miller as a 'grubby cherub'. He has been married to actresses Suzy Kendall and Tuesday Weld and there followed a well-publicized romance with Susan Anton. The partnership with Cook continued to flourish on record and in television talk-shows.

Films include: 1966 The Wrong Box. '67 30 Is a Dangerous Age, Cynthia; Bedazzled. '69 The Bed Sitting Room. '78 Foul Play (USA); The Hound of the Baskervilles. '79 '10' (USA). '80 Wholly Moses! (USA). '81 Arthur (USA).

MOORE, Grace

(1901–1947). Singer/actress. Born: Mary Willie Grace Moore; Jellico, Tennessee, USA

Grace Moore's father tried to discourage his daughter's singing aspirations and so, on leaving college, she ran away to New York. Her parents eventually found her singing in Greenwich Village cafés. Refusing to go home, she went to study music in Paris. Irving Berlin put her on stage in his *Music-Box Revue* on her return, and after developing her lyrical, tender voice, she won herself a contract with the Metropolitan Opera Company. As her popularity with opera fans increased, so the film world took an interest. MGM already had Jeanette MacDonald on their books and the golden-haired, violet-eyed, slender and exuberant Moore was the perfect stable-mate. After making a couple of films for MGM she was fired when she put on weight, and went back to the concert circuit until Columbia signed her. *One Night of Love* secured her a place in the hearts of film audiences and she, more than anyone else, was the performer who popularized the operatic movie. Three years before her tragic death in a plane crash while on her way to a concert in Copenhagen, Moore wrote her autobiography, *You're Only Human Once*, a story that read like a film script and was in fact made into the movie *So This Is Love* (1953).

Films include: 1931 New Moon. '34 One Night of Love. '35 Love Me Forever (GB: On Wings of Song). '36 The King Steps Out. '37 When You're in Love (GB: For You Alone); I'll Take Romance. '39 Louise (FR).

MOORE, Kieron

(b. 1925). Actor. Born: Kieron O'Hanrahan; Skibbereen, Co. Cork, Ireland

Having produced two Gaelic plays while at college in Dublin, Kieron Moore was offered a role with the Abbey Theatre and abandoned his medical studies to join the company. He turned down film contract offers from Hollywood to accept a part in the Alexander Korda production *A Man*

Above, left to right: Ron Moody in David Copperfield; Colleen Moore in Orchids and Ermine; Dudley Moore as a songwriter looking for the romance of a lifetime in '10'; Grace

About the House – an offbeat thriller in which he played a charming but slightly sinister lover. Securing his reputation in both British and American films, he won a starring role in the Sixties television series Ryan International. Since 1973, he has worked for the Catholic Fund for Overseas Development and directed two documentaries about its work.

Films include: 1947 A Man About the House; Mine Own Executioner. '48 Anna Karenina. '51 David and Bathsheba (USA). '55 The Blue Peter (USA: Navy Heroes). '60 The League of Gentlemen. '62 The Day of the Triffids. '66 Arabesque (USA-GB). '75 The Progress of Peoples (doc) (dir. only). '78 The Parched Land (doc) (dir. only).

MOORE, Mary Tyler

(b. 1937). Actress. Born: New York City, USA

Mary Tyler Moore, the attractive female star of the highly successful

week tour of *Gigi* and opened the play in New York before succumbing to pneumonia.

Films include: 1940 Citizen Kane. '42 The Magnificent Ambersons. '44 Since You Went Away; Dragon Seed; Mrs Parkington. '47 The Lost Moment. '48 Johnny Belinda; The Woman in White. '62 How the West Was Won. '64 Hush . . . Hush, Sweet Charlotte.

MORE, Kenneth

(1914–1982). Actor. Born: Gerrards Cross, Buckinghamshire, England

After an abortive attempt at fur-trapping in Canada, Kenneth More returned to his native England to get a job as a stage-hand at London's Wind-mill Theatre. Following a spell in repertory and a term of service in the Royal Navy, he found a niche in early television productions. The Fifties saw him making a name in British comedy films like *Genevieve* and *Doctor in the House* and as the war hero Douglas Bader in *Reach for the Sky*. His career took a downward turn in the Sixties until he was chosen for the part of Jolyon in the 26-part television series *The Forsyte Saga*. He continued in sporadic film and television roles until the end of his life. More, jovial and very, very English, was without doubt one of the most popular of all post-war British stars.

Films include: 1948 Scott of the Antarctic. '50 Chance of a Lifetime. '53 Genevieve. '54 Doctor in the House. '55 The Deep Blue Sea. '56 Reach for the Sky. '57 The Admirable Crichton. '58 A Night to Remember; The Sheriff of Fractured Jaw. '59 North West Frontier (USA: Flame Over India). '60 Sink the Bismark! '63 The Comedy Man.

MOREAU, Jeanne

(b. 1928). Actress. Born: Paris, France

Jeanne Moreau, the fascinating star of the *nouvelle vague*, followed her English mother onto the stage where she was discovered by film director Louis Malle in *Cat on a Hot Tin Roof*. He cast her in *Ascenseur pour l'Echafaud* which confirmed her own reputation as well as making Moreau a star. She is a fine actress whose desirability stems from her self-aware sexuality rather than her sometimes dowdy looks. She was used to good effect by directors like Roger Vadim, Jacques Demy and Michelangelo Antonioni, reaching her peak as the apex of the love triangle in François Truffaut's *Jules et Jim*. Her brief attempt at direct-ing in the Seventies, encouraged by Orson Welles, was not a success. She was at one time married to director William Friedkin.

Films include: 1958 Ascenseur pour l'Echafaud (USA: Frantic; GB: Lift to the Scaffold); Les Amants (GB: The Lovers). '59 Les Liaisons Dangereuses 1960. '61 La Notte (FR-IT) (GB: The Night). '62 Jules et Jim (GB: Jules and Jim). '63 Le Feu Follet (USA: The Fire Within; GB: A Time to Live and a Time to Die). '64 The Train (FR-IT-USA). '65 Viva Maria! '66 Campanadas a Medianoche (SP-SWITZ) (GB: Chimes at Midnight). '67 Great Catherine (GB). '76 The Last Tycoon (USA). '82 Querelle (GER-FR); La Truite (FR).

Moore in The King Steps Out; *Kieron Moore; Mary Tyler Moore feels the effects of a 'happiness bug' spread by a pet toucan in* What's So Bad About Feeling Good? *Below, left to right:*

Roger Moore, licensed to kill in his most famous role as James Bond; the stony stare of Agnes Moorehead in La Sage-Femme, le Curé et le Bon Dieu, *(1962,* Jessica); *Kenneth More as the*

indomitable Douglas Bader in Reach for the Sky; *Jeanne Moreau in Joseph Losey's* Eva/Eve *(1962), in which she plays a classy prostitute with her customary sophistication*

television series *The Dick Van Dyke Show*, entered showbiz through ap-pearing in television commercials. Married at 17 to a public-relations executive, she played in the chorus of various shows after the birth of her first child. *The Dick Van Dyke Show* established her as a leading television comedienne and she got her own show, playing a lively, pert bachelor girl. She seemed to be typecast into similar roles in films like *Thoroughly Modern Millie* until Robert Redford cast her as the coldly neurotic mother of *Ordinary People*, proving her acting abilities are not confined to comedy. A shrewd businesswoman, she co-founded (with her second husband, Grant Tinker) MTM Enterprises which produces several popular television series.

Films include: 1967 Thoroughly Modern Millie. '68 What's So Bad About Feeling Good?; Don't Just Stand There. '69 Change of Habit. '80 Ordinary People. '82 Six Weeks.

MOORE, Roger

(b. 1928). Actor. Born: Stockwell, London, England

After working as a tea-boy in a car-toon studio and being an extra in *Caesar and Cleopatra* (1945), Roger Moore went to RADA. He played small parts in several London Arts Theatre productions before being called up during World War II to serve in an entertainment division where he met his second wife, Dorothy Squires. He went to America with her, but returned, several undistinguished films later, to settle in England. On television Moore played *Ivanhoe* and then landed the part of the suave charming crime-fighter, *The Saint*, and was rescued from oblivion. With a growing international image, he was an obvious choice to replace Sean Connery as Secret Agent 007. Alter-nating between James Bond extrava-ganzas and thrillers like *The Wild Geese*, he has become one of England's most bankable modern stars.

Films include: 1955 Diane (USA); The King's Thief (USA). '61 The Sins of Rachel Cade (USA). '69 Crossplot (+prod). '73 Live and Let Die. '74 The Man With the Golden Gun. '77 The Spy Who Loved Me. '78 The Wild Geese. '79 Moonraker (GB-FR); Escape to Athena. '81 For Your Eyes Only (GB-FR). '83 Octopussy.

MOOREHEAD, Agnes

(1906–1974). Actress. Born: Boston, Massachusetts, USA

Agnes Moorehead went to the Amer-ican Academy of Dramatic Arts before joining Orson Welles' Mercury Theatre. Her screen debut was as Kane's mother in *Citizen Kane* and she appeared in several other Welles movies. Her theatre and television work flourished alongside her film career, with nagging wives and bitchy friends becoming her specialities. She was Endora, the cantankerous mother-in-law of television's *Bewit-ched*, and in 1973 completed a 25-

Left: Rita Moreno in The Night of the Following Day *(1968). Above: Frank Morgan in Rouben Mamoulian's musical* Summer Holiday *(1947)*

MORENO, Antonio

(1886–1967). Actor. Born: Madrid, Spain

With his black hair and smouldering eyes, Antonio Moreno was an obvious candidate for a silent romancer. After his successful debut with Rex-Universal, he worked mainly at Vitagraph until 1921, and at various studios, and starred opposite many of the silent queens of the screen – Mary Pickford, the Gish sisters, Gloria Swanson, Clara Bow, Great Garbo amongst others – rivalling Valentino as cinema's Latin lover. He was equally at home in comedy and tragedy, melodrama or romance, earning the nickname 'King of Cliff-hangers' because of his extensive work in serials. At the height of his career he married Daisy Danziger, the daughter of an oil millionaire, but nevertheless continued playing character parts in films like *Creature From the Black Lagoon*.

Films include: 1912 Voice of the Million. '23 The Trail of the Lonesome Pine. '26 Beverly of Graustark; The Temptress; Mare Nostrum. '28 Madame Pompadour. '36 The Bohemian Girl. '38 Rose of the Rio Grande; Valley of the Giants. '47 Captain From Castile. '53 Thunder Bay. '54 Creature From the Black Lagoon. '56 The Searchers.

MORENO, Rita

(b. 1931). Actress. Born: Rosa Dolores Alverio; Humacao, Puerto Rico

Born in Puerto Rico, Rita Moreno moved to New York when a small child and began earning a living, dancing in night clubs at the age of 15. Some years later she was cast in *So Young, So Bad* and signed by MGM who, however, dropped their option after only a year. There followed a period of moving between television, B movies and the occasional good film which led to the part of Rita in *West Side Story* in which her spirited performance won her an Academy Award. Small, with black hair and brown, flashing eyes, she has often been typecast as an Amerindian with hooped earrings and feathers, but got

her own back on Hollywood's caricatures in Dick Lester's satirical *The Ritz*.

Films include: 1950 So Young, So Bad; Pagan Love Song; The Toast of New Orleans. '52 Singin' in the Rain. '53 Latin Lovers. '55 Untamed. '56 The King and I. '61 West Side Story. '68 The Night of the Following Day. '71 Carnal Knowledge. '76 The Ritz.

MORGAN, Frank

(1890–1949). Actor. Born: Francis Philip Wupperman; New York, USA

One of the Wupperman family, famous for making Angostura Bitters, Frank Morgan followed his brother Ralph into vaudeville. Although he appeared in silent films, he only really made his name with the coming of sound when he became an MGM contract player, taking a range of character parts. His endearing absent-minded wizard in *The Wizard of Oz* became something of a stereotype as he continually found himself cast as blustering buffoons. He died at the age of 59, just as he was to begin filming *Annie Get Your Gun* (1950).

Films include: 1933 Reunion in Vienna; Bombshell/Blonde Bombshell. '34 Affairs of Cellini. '36 The Great Ziegfeld. '37 The Last of Mrs Cheyney; Saratoga. '39 The Wizard of Oz. '40 The Shop Around the Corner; Boom Town. '42 Tortilla Flat. '46 The Courage of Lassie. '49 Any Number Can Play; The Great Sinner. '50 Key to the City.

MORGAN, Harry

(b. 1915). Actor. Born: Henry Bratsburg; Detroit, Michigan, USA

From a stock company at Mount Kisco, New York, which included Henry Fonda and Frances Farmer, Harry Morgan (known in his early days as Henry Morgan) moved on to the Group Theatre and Broadway success in *Golden Boy* and *The Gentle People*. In the cinema since 1942, Morgan has played a wide range of character roles, frequently as the hero's sardonic sidekick, but taking in the occasional unscrupulous politician or banker, tough sheriff or kindly doctor. Wellman's *The Ox-Bow*

Incident and Borzage's *Moonrise* saw him at his best. Amid a great deal of television work, his Colonel Sherman Potter in *M*A*S*H* stands out, a very sane old army surgeon coping as best he may with a variety of engaging lunatics.

Films include: 1943 The Ox-Bow Incident (GB: Strange Incident). '46 Dragonwyck. '48 The Big Clock; Moonrise. '49 Madame Bovary. '52 High Noon. '53 The Glen Miller Story. '62 How the West Was Won. '69 Support Your Local Sheriff. '76 The Shootist. '79 The Apple Dumpling Gang Rides Again.

MORGAN, Helen

(1900–1941). Actress/singer. Born: Helen Riggins; Toronto, Ontario, Canada

After appearing in the chorus of a Chicago cabaret, Helen Morgan moved to New York in 1918 to win fame as a torch-singer in the speakeasies of the Prohibition era. She starred on Broadway as the tragic Julie of *Show Boat*, and also in *Sweet Adeline*. Her few films, early in the sound period, included two versions of *Show Boat* (she was particularly moving in James Whale's superb 1936 version), but perhaps her finest screen performance was in her debut film,

Top, far left: Antonio Moreno cracks the whip in a bloody duel from The Temptress, *in which he co-starred with Greta Garbo. Above: Harry Morgan in the spoof Western* Support Your Local Sheriff. *Below: Helen Morgan as the doomed songstress Julie in the Kern and Hammerstein musical* Show Boat

playing the sad burlesque queen Kitty Darling in Rouben Mamoulian's *Applause*. She was troubled for a long time by drinking problems, and died from cirrhosis in 1941. Ann Blyth played her in *The Helen Morgan Story* (1957).

Films include: 1929 Applause; Glorifying the American Girl; Show Boat. '30 Roadhouse Nights. '34 You Belong to Me; Marie Galante. '35 Sweet Music; Go Into Your Dance (GB: Casino de Paree); Frankie and Johnnie. '36 Show Boat.

MORGAN, Michèle

(b. 1920). Actress. Born: Simone Roussel; Neuilly-sur-Seine, France

While working as a film extra to pay for her drama classes, Michèle Morgan was noticed by director Marc Allegret and given a large part in *Gribouille*, opposite the great Raimu. Classically beautiful, remote and enigmatic, Morgan had something in her of the young Garbo. She was a star at 17, partnering Charles Boyer in *Orage* and Jean Gabin in *Quai des Brumes*, but when the war came she went to Hollywood and, away from the directors and the ambiance she had been used to, she was little more than a competent romantic lead. Back in France, she had a triumph as the blind heroine of *La Symphonie Pastorale*, winning the Best Actress award at Cannes, and was gently moving in her one British film, Carol Reed's *The Fallen Idol*. She has continued working in France, through a long series of indifferent films, with only Claude Chabrol's *Landru* being of much consequence, but those first performances have left an indelible image.

Films include: 1937 Gribouille; Orage. '38 Quai des Brumes (USA: Port of Shadows). '40 Untel Père et Fils (USA: The Heart of a Nation). '44 Passage to Marseille (USA). '46 The Chase (USA); La Symphonie Pastorale. '48 The Fallen Idol (GB). '53 Les Orgueilleux (FR-MEX) (USA/GB: The Proud Ones). '63 Landru (FR-IT) (GB: Bluebeard). '66 Lost Command (USA). '75 Le Chat et la Souris (USA: Cat and Mouse; GB: Seven Suspects for Murder).

MORI, Masayuki

(b. 1911). Actor. Born: Tokyo, Japan

The son of a novelist, Takeo Arishima, and educated at Kyoto University, Mori was a stage actor who made his first films for the Toho company in 1942. A strong and sensitive actor, he has given three outstanding performances in films known in the West. He played the title role of the saintly prince in Kurosawa's version of Dostoyevsky's *The Idiot*; he was the husband in the same director's *Rashomon*, the film which first alerted European audiences to Japanese cinema; and most memorably of all, he was Genjuro, the poor potter who marries a ghost princess in Mizoguchi's *Ugetsu Monogatari*.

Films include: 1945 Toro no O o fumu Otokotachi (USA: The Men Who Tread on the Tiger's Tail; GB: They Who Tread on the Tiger's Tail). '47 Anjo-ke no Butokai (A Ball at the Anjo House). '50 Rashomon. '51 Hakuchi (GB: The Idiot); Nusumarete Koi (Stolen Love). '53 Ugetsu Monogatari (USA: Ugetsu; GB: Tales of the Pale and Silvery Moon After the Rain). '55 Yokihi (JAP-HK) (USA: The Princess Yang Kwei-Fei; GB: The Empress Yang-Kwei-Fei). '58 Yoru no Tsuzumi (Adulterous Wife). '61 Onna no Kunsho (Design for Dying). '63 Taiheiyo Hitoribotchi (USA: My Enemy, the Sea; GB: Alone on the Pacific). '77 Ani Imoto (GB: My Brother and Sister).

MORIARTY, Michael

(b. 1941). Actor. Born: Detroit, Michigan, USA

Michael Moriarty made his first professional appearance at the New York Shakespeare Festival before spending a year at drama school in London polishing his craft. On his return to the USA, however, he was obliged to earn his living selling tyres for six months before being taken on by Tyrone Guthrie for his Repertory Company in Minneapolis. He worked there for four years before his 'break' came with a low-budget 'shocker' called *My Old Man's Place* in 1971. His role as the Vietnam veteran in *Who'll Stop The Rain?* was far worthier of his talent, and he achieved world-wide renown for his portrayal of the cold-blooded Nazi, Erik Dorf, in the television series *Holocaust*.

Films include: 1971 My Old Man's Place/Glory Boy. '72 Hickey and Boggs. '73 Bang the Drum Slowly; The Last Detail. '74 Shoot It: Black – Shoot It: Blue. '75 Report to the Commissioner (GB: Operation Undercover). '78 Who'll Stop The Rain? (GB: Dog Soldiers). '82 The Winged Serpent.

MORLEY, Robert

(b. 1908). Actor. Born: Semley, Wiltshire, England

Educated at Wellington College and trained for the stage at RADA, Morley made a first London appearance in 1929. He and Peter Bull established their own repertory company at Perranporth in Cornwall, and then, back in London, Morley played the title role in *Oscar Wilde*. It was a turning point. He repeated the role on Broadway, was invited to Hollywood, and gained an Oscar nomination for his first part, that of Louis XVI in *Marie Antoinette* (1938). Numerous character parts in America and Britain followed. Rotund, triple-chinned, charming and at times choleric, Morley could be a predictable actor, but when the part gave him scope, he could add convincing and often humorous detail to his characterization.

Films include: 1941 Major Barbara. '42 The Young Mr Pitt. '49 The Small Back Room (USA: Hour of Glory). '51 The African Queen (USA-GB). '53 The Story of Gilbert and Sullivan. '56 Around the World in 80 Days. '60 The Trials of Oscar Wilde (USA: The Man With the Green Carnation). '64 Topkapi (USA-FR). '65 The Loved One (USA). '71 When Eight Bells Toll. '78 Who Is Killing the Great Chefs of Europe? (USA-GER) (GB: Too Many Chefs).

MORRICONE, Ennio

(b. 1928). Composer. Born: Rome, Italy

Already regarded as an important composer in the rarefied world of 'serious music', Ennio Morricone has, by his talent, elevated many 'spaghetti' Westerns from dreary routine movies into unforgettable experiences. He has worked on all Sergio Leone's films, and took 'The Good, the Bad and the Ugly' to the top of the charts. The originality and outstanding musicianship of his work combining so perfectly with the images on the screen have won him universal acclaim in both the world of music and the world of film.

Films include: 1964 Prima della Rivoluzione (GB: Before the Revolution); Per un Pugno di Dollari (IT-GER-SP) (USA/GB: A Fistful of Dollars). '65 Pugni in Tasca (GB: Fists in the Pocket). '66 Per Qualche Dollaro in Più (USA/GB: For a Few Dollars More). '67 Il Buono, il Brutto, il Cattivo (IT-GER-SP) (USA/GB: The Good, the Bad and the Ugly). '68 C'Era una Volta il West (USA/GB: Once Upon a Time in the West); La Bataille de San Sebastian (FR-MEX-IT) (GB: The Guns of St Sebastian). '69 Le Clan des Siciliens (FR-IT) (GB: The Sicilian Clan). '71 Il Decamerone (IT-FR-GER) (GB: The Decameron). '74 Mussolini Ultimo Atto (IT). '78 Days of Heaven (USA).

MORRISSEY, Paul

(b. 1939). Director. Born: New York City, USA

While still a student at Fordham University, Morrissey made silent narrative movies laced with brutal black humour. In 1965 he met Andy Warhol, and for a while they worked together, pooling their equipment. Gradually Morrissey took over as director, giving the films a more conventional structure, whereas Warhol wanted the films to look as if no-one had made them (an aim he certainly achieved). Morrissey himself claims that he wants to make movies 'that appeal to a lot of people'.

Films include: 1964 Sleep (co-dir). '66 The Chelsea Girls (prod. ass). '68 Flesh; Lonesome Cowboys (exec. prod). '70 Trash; Women in Revolt. '72 Heat. '73 Carne per Frankenstein (IT-FR) (USA: The Frankenstein Experiment; GB: Flesh for Frankenstein); Dracula Vuole Vivere: Cerca Sangue di Vergine (IT-FR) (USA: Andy Warhol's Dracula; GB: Blood for Dracula). '78 The Hound of the Baskervilles (GB).

Below, left to right: Michèle Morgan in The Vintage *(1957); Masayuki Mori in* Ugetsu Monogatari; *Michael Moriarty in* Who'll Stop the Rain?; *Robert Morley as George III in* Beau Brummel *(1954)*

MORROW, Vic

(1932–1982). Actor. Born: New York City, USA

A horrifying accident while on location when he was filming *Twilight Zone* (he was decapitated by a helicopter) brought an end to a very worthy actor and director. He made an outstanding debut as a juvenile delinquent in *The Blackboard Jungle*, and worked steadily in films and television from then on. His performance as the ruthless baseball coach in *The Bad News Bears* made an unforgettable impact despite the formidable rivalry of Walter Matthau and Tatum O'Neal. Contrasted with his tough detective parts and gangster roles, his baseball coach (underneath the surface nastiness) was touching and vulnerable. Morrow also directed a film – *Deathwatch* (1966).

Films include: 1955 The Blackboard Jungle. '56 Tribute to a Bad Man. '57 Men in War. '60 Cimarron. '61 Portrait of a Mobster. '74 Dirty Mary, Crazy Larry. '75 Un Maledetto Pasticcio (IT-FR-GER) (GB: The Babysitter). '76 The Bad News Bears; The Treasure of Matecumbe. '79 The Evictors.

MORSE, Helen

(b. 1948). Actress. Born: Wembley, London, England

The daughter of a doctor who emigrated to Australia when she was three years old, Helen Morse studied acting in Sydney and graduated at the top of her class. That comes as a surprise to no-one who has seen her work, particularly as the tender but tough mother in the Australian film *Caddie*.

Films include: 1974 Stone; Petersen. '75 Picnic at Hanging Rock. '76 Caddie. '79 Agatha (GB).

MOSTEL, Zero

(1915–1977). Actor. Born: Samuel Joel Mostel; New York City, USA

The son of a rabbi, and a Fine Arts graduate of New York University, Mostel had ambitions to become a painter. But in 1942 he started work as a nightclub comic, moved to radio, the theatre, and Hollywood. He played heavies at first (notably in *The Enforcer*), but suddenly he was blacklisted in the McCarthy witch-hunt, and did little until, in 1958, he returned to Broadway and very quickly won three Tony Awards. These included one for his performance as the slave, Pseudolus, in *A Funny Thing Happened on the Way to the Forum*, a role he repeated on his return to the screen. A large, heavy man, Mostel nevertheless moved with agile grace, and used his mobile face and loud, aggressive voice to produce superb boisterous comedy. He teamed marvellously with nervous Gene Wilder in *The Producers*; and in *The Front*, his last film, he touched on the dark times of his own life, playing an entertainer driven to suicide by blacklisting.

Films include: 1943 Dubarry Was a Lady. '50 Panic in the Streets. '51 The Enforcer (GB: Murder, Inc.). '66 A Funny Thing Happened on the Way to the Forum. '67 The Producers. '70 The Angel Levine. '72 The Hot Rock (GB: How to Steal a Diamond in Four Uneasy Lessons). '73 Marco. '74 Rhinoceros. '76 The Front.

MOWBRAY, Alan

(1896–1969). Actor. Born: London, England

Mowbray began his acting career in England after World War I, but worked in the USA from 1923, and became an American citizen ten years later. In Hollywood from 1931, he was a founder member of the Screen Actors' Guild, and appeared in over two hundred films, playing pretty well anyone who could be given a lofty, imperious and essentially English manner. He could be a perfect butler an immensely dignified lawyer, or a barnstorming actor, a role which he played twice for John Ford, in *My Darling Clementine* and *Wagonmaster*. In Rouben Mamoulian's *Becky Sharp* was another perfect Mowbray role, and if pressed he could forget he was English and manage a Metternich or (on two occasions) a very convincing George Washington.

Films include: 1931 God's Gift to Women (GB: Too Many Women); Alexander Hamilton. '34 The House of Rothschild. '35 Becky Sharp. '36 My Man Godfrey. '37 Topper. '38 Merrily We Live. '41 That Hamilton Woman! (GB: Lady Hamilton). '43 His Butler's Sister. '45 Where Do We Go From Here? '46 My Darling Clementine. '50 Wagonmaster. '52 Androcles and the Lion. '56 The King and I.

MÜLLER, Renate

(1906–1937). Actress. Born: Munich, Germany

The daughter of a Munich film critic, Renate Müller trained for the stage under Max Reinhardt, and appeared in her first film in 1929. She was charming and talented, the perfect heroine of light romantic comedy, who came to the fore in the early days of sound when versions in various languages were often made if a film was thought to have international appeal. She became, therefore, almost as popular in Britain as in Germany. But the Nazis saw her as a symbol of ideal womanhood, and forced her to make propaganda pictures. She fought against this, resulting in her death – supposedly suicide – from a fall from a hotel window.

Films include: 1929 Peter, der Matrose. '30 Liebling der Götter (USA: Darling of the Gods). '31 Die Privatsekretärin (GB version: Sunshine Susie; USA: The Office Girl); Liebeslied (GER-IT). '32 Mädchen zum Heiraten. '33 Walzerkrieg (USA: Waltz Time in Vienna; GB: The Court Waltzes). '36 Allotria (USA: The Private Life of Louis XIV). '37 Togger.

MULLIGAN, Robert

(b. 1925). Director. Born: New York City, USA

Mulligan was a student of theology when the war took him off to be a radio operator in the Marines. After-wards he worked in journalism for a while before entering television at the bottom – a messenger boy for CBS. By the mid-Fifties he was a top television director, and one of several such who moved into the cinema at that time. For a long time Mulligan seemed to be on the edge of making a really notable film. *Fear Strikes Out* was a sympathetic study of a baseball player driven to nervous collapse by his domineering father, and *To Kill a Mockingbird* a timely onslaught on racial prejudice in Alabama. But gradually smoothness and good taste took over, and when Mulligan's producer, Alan J. Pakula, began to direct for himself, it seemed clear that much of the credit for the early successes belonged to him.

Films include: 1957 Fear Strikes Out. '60 The Rat Race; The Great Impostor. '61 Come September. '62 The Spiral Road; To Kill a Mocking Bird. '63 Love With the Proper Stranger. '65 Baby the Rain Must Fall; Inside Daisy Clover. '67 Up the Down Staircase. '71 Summer of '42. '72 The Other. '78 Blood Brothers; Same Time, Next Year.

MUNI, Paul

(1895–1967). Actor. Born: Muni Weisenfreund; Lemberg, Austria-Hungary (later Lwow, Poland, now Lvov, USSR)

Muni was the son of travelling players who emigrated to the USA in 1902. The boy was on the stage at 12, and with the Yiddish Art Theater in New York by 1918. A Broadway success in *We Americans* led to two films; another stage hit, *Counsellor-at-Law*, preceded his first real movie triumph in *Scarface* and a Warners contract. In the Thirties Muni was reckoned a great screen actor; his Zola, Pasteur and Juarez brought critical garlands and (for Pasteur) an Oscar. But looking back now at the profusion of delight that was the Hollywood Thirties, it seems absurd that these reverent, bearded biopics can have been thought great movies; and equally odd that this conscientious impersonator was thought far superior to such hacks as Grant and Tracy. But Muni could do well enough if ever he left his makeup box at home. For example, in *Hi, Nellie!*, a joyful newspaper comedy, Muni plays a reporter demoted to run the agony column. He's a joy, and so is the film.

Films include: 1929 The Valiant. '31 Scarface/Scarface, the Shame of a Nation. '32 I Am a Fugitive From a Chain Gang (GB: I Am a Fugitive From the Chain Gang). '34 Hi, Nellie! '35 Black Fury. '36 The Story of Louis Pasteur. '37 The Good Earth; The Life of Emile Zola. '39 Juarez. '40 Hudson's Bay. '43 Stage Door Canteen. '45 Counter-Attack (GB: One Against Seven). '59 The Last Angry Man.

MUNK, Andrzej

(1921–1961). Director. Born: Kraków, Poland

A graduate of the Polish Film School, Munk worked for some years in documentary before making *The Man on the Track*, the first of his four features, in 1956. One of the outstanding directors of the Polish 'New Wave', Munk at once attracted international attention, and stood out among his contemporaries by virtue of his unromantic view of war and the Resistance, his wry humour, and his sardonic attitude to the pin-prickings of bureaucracy. His best-known film, *Eroica*, was a highly personal view of the Resistance and the prisoner-of-war camps; *Bad Luck* was a kind of Polish Schweik, with its picture of a little man struggling to cope with war and officialdom; *Passenger*, a tragic story of Auschwitz incomplete when Munk was killed in a motor accident, was edited by others for release.

Films include: Documentaries – 1949 Sztuka Młodych (Art of the Young). '50 Zaczęko się w Hiszpanii (It Began in Spain). '51 Nauka Bliżej Życia (Science Closer to Life). '53 Kolejarskie Słdwd (A Railwayman's Word). '55 Blekitny Krzyz (The Men of the Blue Cross); Niedzielny Poranek (GB: One Sunday Morning). '59 Spacerek Starmoiejski (A Walk in the Old City). Features – '56 Człowiek na Torze (GB: The Man on the Track). '57 Eroica. '60 Zezowate Szczęście (GB: Bad Luck). '63 Pasażerka (GB: Passenger).

MURNAU, F.W.

(1888–1931). Director. Born: Friedrich Wilhelm Plumpe; Bielefeld, Germany

Murnau studied philosophy at Heidelberg, and theatre with Max Reinhardt. He was a pilot in World War I, and interned in Switzerland. One year after the war, he was directing his first films. He made 17 in Germany, and a final four in America. Of these, only 12 survive. They form a body of work as startling, and as compelling, as any in cinema. Murnau is hard to pin down. His work has no unifying theme; what runs through it all is an attitude to the image on the screen and to what it can express. There is a sense of life in the whole of every frame. Sometimes this life is expressed through intricate camera movement, as in much of *The Last Laugh* or the opening scenes of *Sunrise*, but it can equally be conjured out of stillness. There is a famous shot in *Schloss Vogelöd* of two figures standing at opposite sides of a huge, unfurnished hall. Nothing happens, although much has taken place before that shot, but the scene pulsates. No other director has had quite that feeling for space, open or confined. It can range from the cramped streets of

Nosferatu, the Vampire to the vast panoramas of *Faust*, yet the films are no mere geometrical exercise, for with that visual sense Murnau has a compassion for suffering, a warm humour, and a feeling for delight. His American masterpiece, *Sunrise*, is now widely acknowledged as one of the great films of all time.

Films include: 1919 Der Knabe in blau/Der Todessmaragd. '20 Der Gang in die Nacht (USA: Love's Mockery). '21 Schloss Vogelöd. '22 Nosferatu, eine Symphonie des Grauens (USA: Nosferatu, the Vampire); Der brennende Acker; Phantom. '24 Die Finanzen des Grossherzogs. '25 Der letzte Mann (USA/GB: The Last Laugh); Tartüff (USA: Tartuffe, the Hypocrite; GB: Tartuffe). *All remaining films USA*: '27 Sunrise – A Song of Two Humans. '28 Four Devils. '30 City Girl/Our Daily Bread; Tabu.

MURPHY, Audie

(1924–1971). Actor. Born: Kingston, Texas, USA

A sharecropper from the backwoods, he killed more Germans and won more decorations in World War II than any other American soldier. Taken up by Hollywood, he became a star playing the scared youth in *The*

Red Badge of Courage. Then came a series of Westerns featuring him as the fresh-faced innocent that he was, and an excellent 'mean' part in *The Unforgiven*. But he lost money in numerous 'business deals', went bankrupt, was charged with attempted murder and died in a private plane crash with four other people. Murphy played himself in the story of his wartime adventures, *To Hell and Back* (1955). He was briefly married to actress Wanda Hendrix.

Films include: 1948 Beyond Glory. '50 The Kid From Texas (GB: Texas Kid – Outlaw). '51 The Red Badge of Courage; The Cimarron Kid. '52 Duel at Silver Creek. '54 Drums Across the River. '58 The Quiet American; Ride a Crooked Trail. '59 Cast a Long Shadow. '60 The Unforgiven. '65 Arizona Raiders. '67 40 Guns to Apache Pass. '69 A Time for Dying (unreleased in USA).

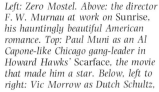

Left: Zero Mostel. Above: the director F. W. Murnau at work on Sunrise, *his hauntingly beautiful American romance. Top: Paul Muni as an Al Capone-like Chicago gang-leader in Howard Hawks'* Scarface, *the movie that made him a star. Below, left to right: Vic Morrow as Dutch Schultz,* infamous Twenties racketeer, in Portrait of a Mobster; *Helen Morse as the put-upon but resilient heroine of* Caddie; *Alan Mowbray in* Merrily We Live; *Renate Müller in* Liselotte von der Pfalz *(1935); Audie Murphy poses in US Cavalry uniform for a studio publicity photograph while on location*

315

MURPHY, George

(b. 1902). Actor/dancer. Born: New Haven, Connecticut, USA

By the age of 25, with no theatrical background, George Murphy was an established Broadway dancer and light actor. When Hollywood beckoned, he answered the call and smiled and danced his way through innumerable musical comedies through the Thirties. The high spot of his career was when he partnered Fred Astaire in *Broadway Melody of 1940*. He gradually drifted away from musicals into rather nondescript straight roles and, as his interest in politics developed, so his involvement in films declined. He retired from the screen in 1952 to concentrate on politics and was elected to the US Senate in 1964.

Films include: 1934 Jealousy; Kid Millions. **'37** Broadway Melody of 1938. **'40** Broadway Melody of 1940. **'41** A Girl, a Guy and a Gob (GB: The Navy Steps Out). **'42** The Powers Girl (GB: Hello! Beautiful); For Me and My Gal (GB: For Me and My Girl). **'44** Show Business. **'48** The Big City. **'50** It's a Big Country. **'52** Talk About a Stranger.

Above: George Murphy in Little Miss Broadway *(1938). Below, left to right: Barbara Murray, whose witty sophistication brightened up* Up Pompeii *(1971); Don Murray in* The Hoodlum Priest *; Mae Murray in* Circe the Enchantress *(1924); Musidora in* Judex

MURRAY, Barbara

(b. 1929). Actress. Born: London, England

A child of theatrical parents, Barbara Murray was a child dancer before appearing as an actress in rep. The Rank Organization took her up in 1947 and she appeared in many films for them. She is a lovely actress, professional to her fingertips, but her career suffered from the handicap of her firmly held religious beliefs which rendered her virtually unemployable for any role requiring an uninterrupted schedule. As a result, her parts have been small and lamentably unworthy of her undoubted talent. She has fared better as a television actress.

Films include: 1948 Anna Karenina; Saraband For Dead Lovers. **'49** Passport to Pimlico; Don't Ever Leave Me. **'50** Tony Draws a Horse. **'53** Meet Mr Lucifer. **'54** The Peckman Mystery; Doctor at Large; Campbell's Kingdom. **'63** Doctor in Distress.

MURRAY, Don

(b. 1929). Actor/director. Born: Donald Patrick Murray; Hollywood, California, USA

Murray is the child of Hollywood parents (his mother was a dancer, his father a dance director), so it was to be expected that this tall, good-looking boy should train for the stage and appear on it. What – possibly – was not to be taken for granted was that he would grow up into a man of strong moral principles. He is a member of the Brethren Community, a religious group devoted to work amongst the poor of all nations, and was a conscientious objector to the Korean War. His career in the movies has been ordered to an enormous extent by his refusal of many parts to which he had a moral objection, but his directorial career, where he had full control of the subject, gave him an opportunity to turn out sound work with a strong social message. He was once married to actress Hope Lange.

Films as actor include: 1956 Bus Stop. **'57** The Bachelor Party; A Hatful of Rain. **'58** From Hell to Texas (GB: Manhunt). **'61** The Hoodlum Priest. **'62** Advise and Consent; Escape From East Berlin (USA-GER) (GB: Tunnel 28). **'64** One Man's Way. **'66** Kid Rodelo (USA-SP). **'70** The Cross and the Switchblade (dir; +co-sc. only). **'71** Happy Birthday Wanda June. **'77** Damien (+dir; +sc). **'81** Endless Love.

MURRAY, Mae

(1889–1965). Actress. Born: Marie Adrienne Koenig; Portsmouth, Virginia, USA

A Broadway dancer and star of the Ziegfeld Follies, Mae Murray made her first film in 1916 and remained a leading star until the end of the silent period. A shimmering blonde, known as 'the girl with the bee-stung lips', Murray was a flamboyant character and, while her youth and vitality lasted, superb in the colourful romances of the time. In her one important film, *The Merry Widow*, she fought bitterly with the director, Erich von Stroheim. Murray wanted froth and fantasy, with her dancing showcased. Stroheim had seen the film rather differently, and MGM's cutters tended to support Murray's interpretation. Her third husband was director Robert Z. Leonard; her fourth, Prince David Mdivani, tried to control her career. Mdivani and she made impossible demands; Murray insisted on living like a princess, and the studios ignored her. She lived on for 34 more years after her last picture, in a fantasy of stardom, a real-life version of Norma Desmond (Gloria Swanson) in *Sunset Boulevard* (1950).

Films include: 1919 A Big Little Person; The Delicious Little Devil. **'20** On With the Dance. **'22** Peacock Alley. **'25** The Masked Bride; The Merry Widow. **'26** Valencia. **'27** Altars of Desire. **'31** Bachelor Apartment.

MUSIDORA

(1889–1957). Actress. Born: Jeanne Roques; Paris, France

As Diana Monti in Louis Feuillade's *Judex*, and as Irma Vep (note the anagram) in his *Les Vampires*, Musidora was a blend of fantasy, sensuality, and exuberant wickedness. She had huge, dark eyes; she wore, when at work, black leotard, hood and tights; she wrought untold havoc in banal Parisian suburbs and in the minds of respectable men. Her glory lasted as long as that of the director whose finest creation she was. After him, she appeared in a few forgotten films, directed one or two more, retired to become a journalist and writer on cinema, and in her last years worked at the Cinémathèque Française.

Films include: 1912 Les Misères de l'Aiguille. **'13** La Tango-Manie. **'15** Les Vampires (serial). **'16** Judex (serial). **'17** Mam'zelle Chiffon. **'18** Vicenta (+dir;+sc). **'19** La Flamme Cachée (+co-dir). **'20** Pour Don Carlos (+co-dir). **'22** Soleil et Ombre (+co-dir). **'24** La Sierra de los Soros (SP) (dir. only). **'26** Le Berceau de Dieu. **'51** La Magique Image (doc) (dir. only).

MUYBRIDGE, Eadweard James

(1830–1904). Photographer/inventor/pioneer. Born: Edward James Muggeridge; Kingston-on-Thames, Surrey, England

Eadweard Muybridge was a Victorian eccentric in the grand manner. Legend has it that he shot a man in a quarrel over a dog; the fact is that he shot his wife's lover. Legend has it that he invented a camera capable of taking rapid photographs in order to win a bet that a galloping horse has all four feet off the ground at once; the fact is that it took him four years of experiment and hard thinking before he came up with the astonishing but simple device of having a row of cameras ranged side by side down a track; the shutters were worked by the horse itself stepping on a cord. Muybridge immediately saw the value of his invention and over the next few years took thousands of photographs of animals and humans in motion. In the early 1880s he projected his series of photographs on a machine he called a Zoopraxiscope, and thus became the inventor of moving photographs. That is the legend: the fact is that this proved to be technically impossible, and Muybridge was obliged to draw each photograph onto a glass disc before they could be projected. Nonetheless in 1888 he met Thomas Edison, who realized the commercial value of his cameras if they could be developed to synchronize with his recently invented phonograph.

NAGEL, Conrad

(1897–1970). Actor. Born: Keokik, Iowa, USA

Tall, fair-haired and with piercing blue eyes, Nagel was nicknamed 'The Prince Consort' in the Twenties following a successful series of romantic leading roles opposite such stars as Gloria Swanson, Bebe Daniels and Pola Negri. Notable among his many well-judged performances were as the writer who falls for Swanson in *The Impossible Mrs Bellew*, as the husband who is nearly poisoned by his wife (Negri) in *Bella Donna* and as the over-principled Angel Clare in *Tess of the d'Urbervilles*. Fine actor though he was (and his career also included many distinguished Broadway appearances), Nagel perhaps worked more profitably behind the scenes in the film industry. He helped found the Academy of Motion Pictures Arts and Sciences with Louis B. Mayer and attempted to organize an actors' union as a branch of the Academy. From the late Thirties on, Nagel played mainly character parts in the movies, and became the host of radio and television shows. He was awarded a special Oscar in 1947 for his work on the Motion Picture Relief Fund.

Films include: 1919 Little Women. '20 The Fighting Chance. '21 Fool's Paradise. '22 The Impossible Mrs Bellew. '23 Bella Donna. '24 Tess of the d'Urbervilles. '25 Sun Up. '26 The Waning Sex. '27 The Girl From Chicago. '32 Kongo. '37 Love Takes Flight (dir. only). '55 All That Heaven Allows. '59 The Man Who Understood Women.

NAISH, J. Carrol

(1900–1973). Actor. Born: Joseph Patrick Carrol Naish; New York City, USA

Naish left school at 14 to work as a song-plugger, then joined Gus Edwards' children's troupe. After World War I service first in the navy and then in the army signal corps in France, he stayed on in Europe, learning several languages and taking various jobs, including a spell with a stage company run by musical comedy star Gaby Deslys. He established himself in Hollywood in the Thirties as an excellent character actor, his gift for mimicry making him capable of playing any nationality – Latins, Russians, Arabs or Orientals. To give an idea of his versatility, he was Loretta Young's Chinese father in *Hatchet Man*, an Italian prisoner of war in *Sahara*, a Mexican peasant in *A Medal for Benny*, and Chief Sitting Bull in *Annie Get Your Gun*. Described as 'Hollywood's one-man UN' by *Time* magazine, Naish has also made many radio and television appearances, taking the lead in *The New Adventures of Charlie Chan* in the late Fifties.

Films include: 1932 Hatchet Man (GB: The Honorable Mr Wong). '39 Beau Geste. '41 Blood and Sand; The Corsican Brothers. '43 Sahara; Batman (serial). '44 House of Frankenstein. '45 A Medal for Benny; The Southerner. '47 The Fugitive. '50 The Black Hand; Annie Get Your Gun. '51 Bannerline. '55 Desert Sand.

NAISMITH, Laurence

(b. 1908). Actor. Born: Lawrence Johnson; Thames Ditton, Surrey, England

Naismith is best known in movies for supporting roles as well-spoken Englishmen, often from respectable medical or seafaring backgrounds. He played a steamboat captain in *Mogambo*, Dr Hawkins in *Boy on a Dolphin*, the heroic Captain Smith who goes down with his ship *The Titanic* in *A Night to Remember* and the First Sea Lord in *Sink the Bismarck!* Naismith was a merchant seaman before he turned to acting. He made his stage debut in 1927 and later formed his own repertory company. During World War II he served in the Royal Artillery; he then returned to the theatre, breaking into movies in 1947.

Films include: 1950 The Happiest Days of Your Life. '53 Mogambo (USA); Cosh Boy (USA: The Slasher); The Beggar's Opera. '54 Carrington VC. '55 The Dam Busters. '57 The Barretts of Wimpole Street; Boy on a Dolphin (USA). '58 The Two-Headed Spy; A Night to Remember. '60 Village of the Damned; Sink the Bismarck! '65 Sky West and Crooked (USA: Gypsy Girl).

NALDI, Nita

(1909–1961). Actress. Born: Anita Donna Dooley; New York City, USA

Nita Naldi was convent-educated, worked as a model and became a dancer with the Ziegfeld Follies. Tall and dark-haired, she was cast by John Barrymore as a Spanish dancer in *Dr Jekyll and Mr Hyde* and rapidly rose to become a sultry, exotic leading lady in the Twenties. She was at her best opposite Rudolph Valentino, spurning him as the veiled, tempestuous, high-born Dona Sol in *Blood and Sand* and ensnaring him in an adulterous imbroglio in *Cobra*. The coming of sound rendered her romantic, vampish persona somewhat obsolete and she retired from movies, though she later made occasional appearances on Broadway and on television.

Films include: 1921 Dr Jekyll and Mr Hyde. '22 Blood and Sand. '23 The Ten Commandments; Lawful Larceny. '24 Sainted Devil; The Breaking Point; What Price Beauty? '25 The Lady Who Lied; The Marriage Whirl; Cobra. '26 The Miracle of Life; The Unfair Sex.

Below, left to right: Conrad Nagel in Kid Gloves (1929); J. Carrol Naish goes Gallic as the detective hero of Enter Arsène Lupin (1944); Laurence Naismith in Lionel Jeffries' fine ghost story for children The Amazing Mr Blunden (1972); Nita Naldi played opposite Valentino in Blood and Sand

NARIZZANO, Silvio

(b. 1926). Director. Born: Montreal, Quebec, Canada

Of Italian-American parentage, Narizzano graduated from Bishop's University in Quebec and joined a theatre group in Ottawa. After experience as an actor and stage manager, he was accepted as a trainee director by the Canadian Broadcasting Corporation. He worked in television, winning awards for his production of *Death of a Salesman* in the USA and for a series of Feydeau farces made for Granada Television in England. The latter success led to his first full directorial assignment, a horror film called *Fanatic*, starring Tallulah Bankhead. His next movie was *Georgy Girl*, an adult comedy that showed the cruel side of London life in the Swinging Sixties, with particularly fine performances from Lynn Redgrave as the shy, awkward Georgy and Charlotte Rampling as her bitchy, selfish flatmate. *Georgy Girl* established Narizzano as a maker of trendy, youth-orientated pictures, but subsequent features such as *Blue*, a dull Western starring heart-throb Terence Stamp and *Loot*, a flashy, patchy adaptation of Joe Orton's black farce, failed to live up to expectations.

Films include: **1960** Under Ten Flags (co-dir) (USA). '65 Fanatic (GB) (USA: Die! Die! My Darling). '66 Georgy Girl (GB). '68 Blue (USA). '71 Loot (GB). '73 Redneck (IT-GB). '75 The Sky Is Falling (USA). '77 Why Shoot the Teacher? (CAN). '78 The Class of Miss MacMichael (GB).

NARUSE, Mikio

(1905–1969). Director/screenwriter. Born: Tokyo, Japan

Naruse's films have been little seen in the West, possibly because distributors have considered them too 'Japanese' in their naturalistic treatment of everyday life and therefore uncommercial. His family was too poor to send him to university and he started work, aged 15, as a prop man at the newly-formed Shochiku film company. He gradually worked his way up to the position of director, making his first feature, *Chambara Fufu* (*Mr and Mrs Swordplay*) in 1930. An unhappy five-year marriage to screen actress Sachiko Chuba behind him, Naruse began his most creative period in the Fifties with a series of films, including *Inazuma*, *Bangiku* (1954) and *Ukigumo*, based on the feminist writings of Tumiko Hayashi (1904–1951), depicting downtrodden women. For Naruse, the claustrophobic roles women were made to play in Japanese society became a particular expression of his generally pessimistic view of the human condition.

Films include: **1934** Kagirinaki Hodo (Street Without End). '35 Tsuma yo Bara no Yo ni (Wife! Be Like a Rose!/Kimiko). '39 Hataraku Ikka (The Whole Family Works). '41 Hideko no Shasho-san (Hideko the Bus Conductor). '51 Meshi (Repast). '52 Okasan (Mother); Inazuma (Lightning). '53 Tsuma (Wife). '54 Yama no Oto (Sound of the Mountain). '55 Ukigumo (Floating Clouds). '56 Nagareru (Flowing). '62 Horoki (A Wanderer's Notebook/Lonely Lane).

NATWICK, Mildred

(b. 1908). Actress. Born: Baltimore, Maryland, USA

Natwick was an excellent character actress who specialized in playing eccentric old ladies even at the beginning of her career. She initially had problems finding stage parts, but got a good break in 1932 when she was invited to join the University Players (which included Henry Fonda, James Stewart, Margaret Sullavan and Joshua Logan). She made her Broadway debut the same year in *Carrie Nation*, and went on to score a number of successes in the theatre, notably as Madame Arcate in Noel Coward's *Blithe Spirit*. Though she entered films in 1940, she remained primarily a stage actress. Her best-known screen appearances were in John Ford's *She Wore a Yellow Ribbon*, as a cavalry officer's wife whom John Wayne attempts to escort to safety, and in the Neil Simon comedy *Barefoot in the Park*, in which she played Jane Fonda's bewildered mother.

Films include: **1940** The Long Voyage Home. '45 Yolanda and the Thief. '47 The Late George Apley; A Woman's Vengeance. '48 The Kissing Bandit; Three Godfathers. '49 She Wore a Yellow Ribbon. '52 The Quiet Man. '56 The Trouble With Harry. '67 Barefoot in the Park. '74 Daisy Miller. '75 At Long Last Love.

NAZIMOVA, Alla

(1879–1945). Actress. Born: Alla Nasimoff; Yalta, Crimea, Russia

Nazimova came from a wealthy Jewish background but was educated at a Catholic school in Switzerland. She gave up a potential career as a violinist for one in acting, becoming a star pupil at the Moscow Academy and then joining Stanislavsky's Moscow Art Theatre. She appeared with her first husband Paul Orleneff in *The Chosen People* (a play banned in Russia) in London, Berlin and New York. The excellent reception she received on Broadway persuaded her to remain in the USA, though her husband returned to Russia. A year later, in 1906, she scored a great success in the title role of Ibsen's *Hedda Gabler*, exciting critical praise for the new naturalism of her acting. Slim and graceful, with large, long-lashed blue eyes, she first appeared in movies in a 1916 film version of her stage hit *War Brides*. The film director Charles Bryant became her second husband. She was at her best in intense, emotional roles, such as Nora in her own film production of Ibsen's *A Doll's House*. Following her divorce from Bryant, she returned to Broadway in 1925. Her enigmatic personality fascinated the public and, in the manner of other European geniuses of the arts, she became known simply by her surname. She reappeared in a handful of Hollywood movies in the Forties, her best role being the ageing Polish countess in *In Our Time*.

Films include: **1916** War Brides. '19 Out of the Fog; The Red Lantern. '21 Camille. '22 A Doll's House. '22 Salome (+prod). '24

Madonna of the Streets. '25 My Son. '40 Escape. '44 The Bridge of San Luis Rey; In Our Time; Since You Went Away.

NAZZARI, Amedeo

(1907–1979). Actor. Born: Salvatore Amedeo Buffa; Cagliari, Sardinia, Italy

Nazzari had a long and distinguished movie career, spanning four decades and including over one hundred films. He was a gentle giant of a man, six feet three inches tall and heavily built, who shunned publicity and lived quietly with his mother and sister prior to his marriage, late in life, to actress Irena Genna. At 20, Nazzari abandoned his engineering studies for acting and toured with various stage companies. He appeared in his first movie, *Ginevra degli Almieri*, in 1935, winning his first starring role the following year in *Cavalleria*. He initially specialized in romantic leads, then played in costume dramas, neo-realist films and gangster pictures. In 1947 he won an Italian Silver Ribbon for Best Actor in *Il Bandito*.

Films include: **1936** Cavalleria. '46 Il Bandito. '47 La Figlia del Capitano (GB: The Captain's Daughter); Un Giorno nella Vita. '49 Il Lupo della Sila (GB: The Wolf of the Sila). '57 Le Notti di Cabiria (IT-FR) (USA: Nights of Cabiria; GB: Cabiria). '59 La Maja Desnuda (IT-USA) (USA/GB: The Naked Maja). '69 Le Clan des Siciliens (FR) (GB: The Sicilian Clan). '72 Joe Valachi – i Segreti di Cosa Nostra (IT-FR) (USA/GB: The Valachi Papers). '76 A Matter of Time (USA-IT).

NEAGLE, Anna

(1904–1986). Actress. Born: Florence Marjorie Robertson; London, England

Neagle, the daughter of a sea captain, began a career as a dancer in her early teens. She played in the chorus of the Broadway tour of *Wake Up and Dream* and had a featured role in *Stand Up and Sing*, both starring Jack Buchanan, who, with producer-director Herbert Wilcox decided to cast her in her first starring role in a movie, *Goodnight Vienna*. Groomed by Wilcox, who produced and directed most of her films and married her in 1943, Neagle became a major British star of stage and screen. Her films alternated between musicals, comedies and historical dramas and she achieved special fame as *Nell Gwyn*, as Queen Victoria in *Victoria the Great* and *Sixty Glorious Years*, as *Nurse Edith Cavell*, as the French Resistance heroine *Odette* and as Florence Nightingale in *The Lady With the Lamp*. She was made a Dame of the British Empire in 1969. She returned to the stage in *My Fair Lady* in 1980.

Films include: **1932** Goodnight Vienna. '33 Bitter Sweet. '34 Nell Gwyn. '37 Victoria the Great. '38 Sixty Glorious Years (USA: Queen of Destiny). '39 Nurse Edith Cavell (USA). '40 Irene (USA). '41 No, No, Nanette (USA). '43 Forever and a Day (USA). '48 Spring in Park Lane. '49 Maytime in Mayfair. '50 Odette. '51 The Lady With the Lamp. '54 Lilacs in the Spring (USA: Let's Make Up). '57 These Dangerous Years (prod. only).

Above: Nazimova as the beautiful, tragic heroine Camille. *Below: Amedeo Nazzari as a Mafia boss in* The Sicilian Clan

Left: Mildred Natwick in her first film, The Long Voyage Home. Above: an unamused but regal Anna Neagle in Victoria the Great

Paul Newman has a word in Patricia Neal's ear in Hud. Below: Tom Neal in Detour (1945). Below right: Pola Negri in Shadows of Paris (1924)

NEAL, Patricia

(b. 1926). Actress. Born: Packard, Kentucky, USA

Neal, a graduate from Northwestern University near Chicago, studied at the Actors' Studio in New York and captured five awards on her Broadway debut, in Lillian Hellman's *Another Part of the Forest*. A contract with Warner Brothers followed in 1948, and she established herself as a fine screen actress with her performance in her second feature, *The Fountainhead*. For three years she had a well-publicized romance with that film's co-star, Gary Cooper. She then met and married the author Roald Dahl in 1953. Successes on stage in New York and London and fewer but better parts in movies further enhanced her reputation, and she was finally accorded the accolade of a Best Actress Oscar for *Hud*, as the sensual, laconic housekeeper who is sexually attacked by the anarchic, drunken Hud (Paul Newman). At the height of her career there occurred a tragic sequence of events; her young daughter died from measles and her baby son was gravely injured in a road accident. Neal herself suffered from a severe stroke that left her paralysed. The heroic recovery she made inspired the television film *The Patricia Neal Story* (1981), starring Glenda Jackson and Dirk Bogarde. She even managed to resume her career, playing supporting parts in feature and television films.

Films include: 1949 John Loves Mary; The Fountainhead; The Hasty Heart (GB). '51 The Day the Earth Stood Still; Weekend With Father. '52 Washington Story (GB: Target for Scandal). '57 A Face in the Crowd. '61 Breakfast at Tiffany's. '63 Hud. '64 Psyche 59 (GB). '65 In Harm's Way. '68 The Subject Was Roses. '72 Baxter! (GB).

NEAL, Tom

(1914–1972). Actor. Born: Evanston, Illinois, USA

Ruggedly handsome and sporting a Clark Gable moustache during the second half of his career, Neal achieved some success as a tough lead in B

features. His career was, however, overshadowed by his turbulent, violent private life. He hit the headlines in 1951 when he put Franchot Tone in hospital following a brawl over actress Barbara Payton. Neal's film career then went into a decline and he took up landscape gardening. This peaceful occupation did not prevent him from getting into trouble, this time of a far more serious kind: in 1965 his third wife was found shot dead and Neal was convicted of manslaughter. He served a six-year jail sentence and died from natural causes a few months after his release.

Films include: 1938 Out West With the Hardys. '39 Within the Law. '42 Flying Tigers; China Girl. '43 Behind the Rising Sun. '45 Crime Inc.; First Yank Into Tokyo (GB: Mask of Fury). '49 Bruce Gentry (serial). '51 Danger Zone. '53 The Great Jesse James Raid (serial).

NEAME, Ronald

(b. 1911). Director/producer/cinematographer. Born: London, England

The son of the silent movie actress Ivy Close and the photographer Elwin Neame, Ronald Neame entered the film industry in 1928 as a clapper-boy at Elstree Studios. By 1934 he was a successful director of photography, working on *Pygmalion* (1938) and *In Which We Serve* (1942), and he then became a producer for Cineguild, the independent company set up by Noel Coward, David Lean and Anthony Havelock-Allan. Neame's credits included such British classics as *Brief Encounter* (1945), *Great Expectations* (1946) and *Oliver Twist* (1948). He made his debut as a director in 1947 with *Take My Life* and notable among his early films were *The Card* and *The Horse's Mouth*, witty and unpretentious showcases for Alec Guinness' acting talents. His career reached a peak in the Sixties with the Scottish army drama *Tunes of Glory*, *I Could Go on Singing* (Judy Garland's last picture) and the film version of Muriel Spark's novel *The Prime of Miss Jean Brodie*, starring Maggie Smith. Neame has since been given various amorphous big-budget movies, the most entertaining of which have been *The Poseidon Adventure* and *The Odessa File*.

Films include: 1952 The Card (USA: The Promoter). '59 The Horse's Mouth. '60 Tunes of Glory. '63 I Could Go on Singing. '69 The Prime of Miss Jean Brodie. '70 Scrooge. '72 The Poseidon Adventure (USA). '74 The Odessa File (GB-GER). '79 Meteor (USA). '82 The First Monday in October (USA).

NEEDHAM, Hal

(b. 1930). Director/stunt man. Born: Tennessee, USA

After leaving school at 14, Needham worked as a logger before becoming a paratrooper. To earn extra money he did part-time stunt work at travelling fairs and earned himself such a good reputation that he was called to Hollywood in the mid-Fifties where he

stood in for John Wayne, Kirk Douglas and, eventually, Burt Reynolds. Needham and Reynolds struck up an immediate rapport and worked together on the television series *Riverboat*. It was at Reynold's insistence that Needham began directing with *Smokey and the Bandit*. The film uses all Needham's expertise as it features car chases, fist fights, falls, horse stunts and crashes, elements used in all his films as director. During his action-packed career Needham has broken his backbone twice, plus fifty or so other bones. In the Seventies he formed Stunts Unlimited, an el..e corps of stunt men who develop an test safety equipment for use in films.

Films as stunt man include: 1957 The Spirit of St Louis. '69 The Undefeated. '73 White Lightning. '75 French Connection II. '76 Nickelodeon (GB-USA); Gator. '77 Smokey and the Bandit (dir. only). '78 Hooper (dir. only). '80 Smokey and the Bandit II (dir. only) (GB: Smokey and the Bandit Ride Again). '81 The Cannonball Run (dir. only).

NEGRI, Pola

(b. 1899). Actress. Born: Barbara Apollonia Chalupiec; Janowa, Poland

Negri became the protégée of Countess Planten and studied ballet at the Imperial Royal Ballet School in Warsaw. When ill-health forced her to give up dancing she took up drama and during World War I made a number of films for Polish director Alexander Hertz. On the invitation of Max Reinhardt she went to Berlin where she met the director Ernst Lubitsch and was signed by Ufa. Together Negri and Lubitsch formed a formidable and successful team. The raven-haired beauty with tragic grey-blue eyes excelled in her characterizations and depth of expression under Lubitsch's guidance. In 1922 she was lured to Hollywood, where all her better qualities as an actress were stripped away, leaving behind a cold, mysterious and self-congratulatory exterior. Most of the roles offered watered down her alluring sexuality, and her much-publicized rivalry with Gloria Swanson, as well as her alleged affair with Rudolph Valentino, only served to alienate her from American audiences. During this period her one film of any note was Lubitsch's *Forbidden Paradise*. However, with the coming of sound she gave up the American struggle and went back to Ufa. Rumours of an affair with Hitler and difficulties with Goebbels forced her to leave Germany and she retired to Hollywood, only being tempted to work again on two films, *Hi Diddle Diddle* (1943) and *The Moon-Spinners* (1964), both of which parodied her own career and self-importance.

Films include: 1918 Carmen (GER) (USA: Gypsy Blood); Die Augen der Mumie Ma (GER) (USA: The Eyes of the Mummy Ma). '19 Madame Dubarry (GER) (USA: Passion). '20 Sumurun (GER) (USA: One Arabian Night). '23 Bella Donna (USA). '24 Forbidden Paradise (USA). '25 A Woman of the World (USA). '27 Barbed Wire (USA); Hotel Imperial (USA). '32 A Woman Commands (USA). '37 Tango Notturno (GER).

NEGULESCO, Jean

(b. 1900). Director. Born: Craiova, Romania

Negulesco served in a French frontline hospital during World War I, and then began a career as an artist, studying under Brancusi; he sold all 150 pictures at his first exhibition. In 1932 he joined Paramount as their theatrical adviser on the rape scene in *The Story of Temple Drake* (1933), for which he designed the scene so that it could be shot without incurring the censor's wrath. Later he spent two months on *The Maltese Falcon* (1941) before John Huston was hired as director. After directing *Singapore Woman* (1941) he made *The Mask of Dimitrios*, in which he created a lively, fast-moving thriller of pre-World War II European intrigue. A sombre mood was successfully captured in the powerful drama *Johnny Belinda*, in which a deaf-mute girl (Jane Wyman) is raped and gives birth to a son. Once he moved to Fox in the Fifties, Negulesco's films became rather lightweight. Nevertheless, they were largely well-received: *How to Marry a Millionaire* was a box-office hit and *Three Coins in the Fountain* was nominated for an Oscar.

Films include: 1944 The Mask of Dimitrios. **'45** Three Strangers. **'46** Humoresque. **'48** Johnny Belinda; Road House. **'50** Three Came Home; The Mudlark. **'52** Phone Call From a Stranger; O. Henry's Full House *ep* 'The Last Leaf'. **'53** How to Marry a Millionaire. **'54** Three Coins in the Fountain.

NEILAN, Marshall

(1891–1958). Director/actor. Born: San Bernardino, California, USA

In 1905 Neilan joined the Barney Bernard stock company and toured America with them. After that he became D.W. Griffith's chauffeur, and it was the great director – always on the lookout for talent – who persuaded him to carry on acting. Kalem studios offered him a contract and he was soon playing leads opposite Ruth Roland. Not content simply to appear in front of the camera, Neilan took to scenario-writing and became a director. He and Mary Pickford worked together on pictures such as *Rebecca of Sunnybrook Farm* and *Daddy Long Legs*, and by 1918 he had become an independent producer. In his mid-Twenties he was renowned for discovering talent and producing a string of money-making movies. Unfortunately, his elevated lifestyle took up more and more of his time, and he entertained lavishly when he should have been on set. Gradually he frittered away his fortune and became notorious for his affairs with leading ladies such as Gloria Swanson and Dorothy Gish. His career and reputation declined sharply and he made his last and ill-received film *Swing It Professor* in 1937.

Films include: 1917 Rebecca of Sunnybrook Farm. **'18** Stella Maris. **'19** Daddy Long Legs. **'20** Dinty. **'21** Bits of Life; The Lotus Eater. **'24** Dorothy Vernon of Haddon Hall.

Below: Franco Nero in Il Mercenario *(1969, A Professional Gun). Right: Anthony Newley in his ego-tripping*

'25 Sporting Venus. **'26** Skyrocket. **'27** Venus of Venice. **'29** The Awful Truth.

NELSON, Ralph

(b. 1916). Director. Born: New York City, USA

Before World War II Nelson acted in the New York theatre, and was stage manager for Alfred Lunt and Lynn Fontanne. After the war he went into television and by the mid-Fifties was a leading director. He graduated to feature films with *Requiem for a Heavyweight* (he had won an Emmy for his television production of the play), and has directed and produced for the cinema through the Sixties and Seventies. Sidney Poitier (for *Lilies of the Field*) and Cliff Robertson (for *Charly*) have won Oscars in Nelson's films but, by and large, this director has met with little critical approval. In the past, a routine commercial director could turn out tasteful and watchable films. Now, it seems, he must choose between oozing sentimentality and gratuitous violence, and Nelson has inflicted plenty of both.

Films include: 1962 Requiem for a Heavyweight (GB: Blood Money); Lilies of the Field. **'63** Soldier in the Rain. **'64** Fate Is the Hunter. **'65** Once a Thief. **'66** Duel at Diablo. **'67** Father Goose; Battle Horns (GB: Counterpoint). **'68** Charly. **'70** . . . Tick . . . Tick . . . Tick; Soldier Blue (+ act). **'71** Flight of the Doves. **'72** The Wrath of God. **'75** The Wilby Conspiracy. **'76** Embryo. **'77** A Hero Ain't Nothing But a Sandwich.

NĚMEC, Jan

(b. 1936). Director. Born: Prague, Czechoslovakia

Jan Němec graduated from the Prague Film School in 1960, and his early short films won a high reputation at Oberhausen and other European festivals. he managed three remarkable features before the Russians invaded Czechoslovakia in 1968 and put a virtual end to his career and that of his wife, the singer Marta Kubišová. Němec's work was most successful in giving visual form to tormented states of mind. *Diamonds of the Night* brought an acute perception to the plight of two young men

escaping from a Nazi transport train, while *The Party and the Guests* was a disturbing study of a banal festivity going nightmarishly wrong. Němec was allowed to leave his country in 1973 and continued to work abroad.

Films include: 1960 Sousto (GB: A Piece of Bread). **'63** Pamět našeho dne (GB: Memory of Our Day). **'64** Démanty noci (GB: Diamonds of the Night). **'65** Perličky na dně *one ep only* (GB: Pearls of the Deep). **'66** O slavnosti a hostech (GB: The Party and the Guests). **'67** Mučedníci lásky (GB: Martyrs of Love); Mother and Son (HOLL). **'68** Oratorio for Prague (FR). **'69** Czechoslovakia 1918–1968 (doc). **'75** Das Rückendekolleté (SWITZ-GER).

NERO, Franco

(b. 1941). Actor. Born: Francesco Sparanero; Parma, Italy

A good-looking, sexy, capable actor, he is best known for his Hollywood role in *Camelot* (he played Sir Lancelot). Never out of work, and seldom out of the gossip columns (he is the acknowledged father of Vanessa Redgrave's child), his films are mainly made for domestic consumption and seldom seen outside Italy.

Films include: 1966 La Bibbia (IT) (USA/GB: The Bible – In the Beginning). **'67** Django (IT-SP); Camelot (USA). **'68** Un Tranquillo Posto in Campagna (IT-FR) (USA/GB: A Quiet Place in the Country); Vendetta (IT-GER). **'69** Bitka na Neretvi (YUG-GER-IT) (USA/GB: The Battle of the River Nerena). **'70** Tristana (SP-IT-FR); The Virgin and the Gypsy (GB). **'71** Drop Out (IT). **'72** Pope Joan (GB). **'82** Querelle (GER-FR).

NEWLEY, Anthony

(b. 1931). Actor/composer. Born: Hackney, London, England

Newley began acting in films while still at the Italia Conti School, and scored a big success as the Artful Dodger in *Oliver Twist*. Later on he left films to compose musicals. He co-wrote, co-composed (with Leslie Bricusse) and directed the very successful *Stop the World – I Want to Get Off*, in which he also starred; then the less fortunate *The Roar of the Greasepaint,*

fantasy Can Hieronymus Merkin Ever Forget Mercy Humppe and Find True Happiness?

the Smell of the Crowd. Newley has directed two films; *Hieronymus Merkin* may have been a disaster, but his direction of *Summertree* won some critical approval.

Films include: 1948 The Guinea Pig; Oliver Twist. **'55** Cockleshell Heroes. **'57** The Good Companions. **'63** The Small Sad World of Sammy Lee. **'67** Doctor Dolittle. **'68** Sweet November. **'69** Can Hieronymus Merkin Ever Forget Mercy Humppe and Find True Happiness? (+dir; +prod; +co-sc; +co-songs). **'71** Summertree (dir. only). **'75** Mister Quilp (USA) (GB: The Old Curiosity Shop (+mus; +lyr). **'78** Sammy Stops the World (USA).

NEWMAN, Alfred

(1901–1970). Composer/music director. Born: New Haven, Connecticut, USA

In Newman's youth he was a cinema pianist, a vaudeville accompanist, and (at 17) conductor of an orchestra. Moving into the New York theatre, by 1927 he was working on important musicals, and was musical director by 1930. In that year Samuel Goldwyn engaged him to score Eddie Cantor's *Whoopee*, and from Goldwyn Newman went to 20th Century-Fox, whose music department he headed from 1939 to 1960. He composed some of the best film scores ever written, and worked on over 250 movies in all. He was at home in every genre, and adept at using traditional musical techniques to elucidate twentieth century ideas. He provided scores for many great directors (Ford above all, but also Hawks, Lang, Wyler, Hitchcock and King), and he won nine Oscars, most of them, ironically, for some of the least distinguished (other than musically) films with which he was concerned. The artful and ironic singer/composer Randy Newman is his son.

Films include: 1938 Alexander's Ragtime Band (mus). **'40** Tin Pan Alley (mus. dir). **'43** The Song of Bernadette (mus). **'47** Mother Wore Tights (mus. dir). **'50** All About Eve (mus). **'52** With a Song in My Heart (mus. dir). **'53** Call Me Madam (mus. dir). **'55** Love Is a Many Splendored Thing (mus). **'56** The King and I (mus. dir). **'58** South Pacific (mus. dir). **'62** How the West Was Won (mus). **'67** Camelot (co-mus. dir)

NEWMAN, Joseph M.

(b. 1909). Director. Born: Logan, Utah, USA

At 15 Newman was an office boy at MGM. He worked his way up, successively becoming an assistant director to Lubitsch, Cukor and Walsh. He then went to England in 1937 to help organize MGM-British and do some second-unit direction. Newman returned home to direct shorts and generally help out (the lovely Donkey Serenade sequence in *The Firefly* (1937) is Newman, not the credited director, Robert Z. Leonard). He made his first feature in 1942 and continued to turn out accomplished, small-scale action films for the next twenty years, putting his experience as a documentary filmmaker during World War II to good account with the convincing realism of their settings. Sadly, his kind of modestly reliable director is now forgotten.

Films include: 1942 Northwest Rangers. **'45** Diary of a Sergeant (doc). **'49** Abandoned. **'50** 711 Ocean Drive. **'52** Red Skies of Montana; Pony Soldier (GB: MacDonald of the Canadian Mounties); The Outcasts of Poker Flat. **'54** The Human Jungle. **'55** This Island Earth. **'56** Flight to Hong Kong. **'59** The Big Circus; Tarzan the Ape Man. **'61** A Thunder of Drums; The George Raft Story (GB: Spin of a Coin).

NEWMAN, Nanette

(b. 1939). Actress. Born: Northampton, England

Nanette Newman came from a theatrical background and first met the producer/director Bryan Forbes when she was 16. They married in 1958, and her career became intertwined with his. She was effective in some early cameo roles, especially as Edith Evans' slatternly neighbour in *The Whisperers* and as the neurotic Julia in *The Wrong Box*, but of her leading parts only that in the tragic romance, *The Raging Moon*, gave her much opportunity. She played the part intended for Elizabeth Taylor in *International Velvet*, but that disaster did no-one concerned much good.

Films include: 1960 The League of Gentlemen. **'62** The L-Shaped Room. **'64** Of Human Bondage. **'66** The Wrong Box. **'67** The Whisperers. **'69** Captain Nemo and the Underwater City. **'71** The Raging Moon (USA: Long Ago, Tomorrow). **'73** Man at the Top. **'75** The Stepford Wives (USA). **'78** International Velvet.

NEWMAN, Paul

(b. 1925). Actor/director. Born: Cleveland, Ohio, USA

Repertory in Wisconsin and Illinois, the Yale School of Drama, television in New York, and a stage part in *Picnic* which attracted the attention of Warners: those were the beginnings of Paul Newman's successful career. His first film hit was as the boxer Rocky Graziano in *Somebody Up There Likes Me*, and he never looked back. Good looks, easy (occasionally too easy) charm, and a fair share of acting ability made him one of the most popular, and bankable, stars of the Sixties and Seventies, and he was in as many good films as he could reasonably expect. Newman was best, perhaps, in roles where there was a touch of insecurity or self-doubt, like Billy the Kid in Penn's *The Left-Handed Gun*, or the pool-player in *The Hustler*, or where this spilled over into near mania, as in *Cool Hand Luke*. While working on the New York stage, he met the actress Joanne Woodward, and they married in 1958. Newman has directed his wife in two notable films, *Rachel, Rachel*, a moving study of a lonely woman, and the little-seen but highly intelligent *The Effect of Gamma Rays on Man-in-the-Moon Marigolds*. He has also been active politically, working for the civil rights movement in America, and serving as a delegate to the 1978 United Nations conference on disarmament.

Films include: 1955 The Silver Chalice. **'56** Somebody Up There Likes Me. **'58** The Left-Handed Gun; Cat on a Hot Tin Roof. **'60** Exodus. **'61** The Hustler. **'63** Hud. **'66** Harper (GB: The Moving Target); Torn Curtain. **'67** Hombre; Cool Hand Luke. **'68** Rachel, Rachel (dir; +prod. only). **'69** Winning (+co-exec. prod); Butch Cassidy and the Sundance Kid (+co-exec. prod). **'70** WUSA (+co-prod). **'71** Sometimes a Great Notion (+dir; +co-exec. prod) (GB: Never Give an Inch). **'72** The Effect of Gamma Rays on Man-in-the-Moon Marigolds (dir; +prod. only); The Life and Times of Judge Roy Bean (+co-exec. prod). **'73** The Sting. **'74** The Towering Inferno. **'76** Buffalo Bill and the Indians . . . or Sitting Bull's History Lesson. **'77** Slap Shot. **'80** Fort Apache, the Bronx. **'81** Absence of Malice. **'82** The Verdict (USA).

NEWTON, Robert

(1905–1956). Actor. Born: Shaftesbury, Dorset, England

Newton was on the stage at 15, in the West End before he was 20 and, soon after that, off to Canada to work on a ranch. Still not settled, he went back to the theatre, appeared in New York in *Private Lives*, came home to run the Shilling Theatre in Fulham, and made his first film in 1933. Over the next twenty years he gave some notable performances in character parts. He was always tempted to overact (most notably as Long John Silver in *Treasure Island*) and his fruity tones and rolling eyes made him an easy target for caricature, but in his earlier years he was more amenable to control, and capable of considerable subtlety. In *Jamaica Inn* and *Poison Pen* he was modest and effective; *Odd Man Out* and *Hatter's Castle* allowed him to go a little over the top without damaging the film; and in *Temptation Harbour*, one of his few leads, he was very good indeed as the honest signalman corrupted by Simone Simon and a large haul of stolen money.

Films include: 1937 Fire Over England; The Squeaker (USA: Murder on Diamond Row). **'39** Jamaica Inn; Poison Pen. **'41** Hatter's Castle. **'44** This Happy Breed; Henry V. **'47** Odd Man Out; Temptation Harbour. **'48** Oliver Twist. **'49** Obsession (USA: The Hidden Room). **'50** Treasure Island. **'52** Blackbeard the Pirate (USA). **'56** Around the World in 80 Days (USA).

NIBLO, Fred

(1874–1948). Director/actor. Born: Frederico Nobile; York, Nebraska, USA

Niblo was the son of Italian immigrants, and entered films in 1917 after long experience as a stage actor and director. He made a number of films for Ince, starring his wife, Enid Bennett, and by the early Twenties was in charge of prestige productions like *The Mark of Zorro* (Fairbanks) and *Blood and Sand* (Valentino). A capable if somewhat plodding director, he took over *Ben-Hur* when it was running into severe production and financial troubles in Italy, and guided the enormous project to spectacular success (the great chariot race, however, was largely the creation of second-unit director B. Reeves Eason). Niblo went on to direct Garbo in *The Temptress* and *The Mysterious Lady*, but his career did not long survive sound, and apart from the odd stint as an actor he retired after an attempt to revive his fortunes in England had failed.

Films include: 1918 A Desert Wooing. **'20** Sex; The Mark of Zorro. **'21** The Three Musketeers. **'22** Blood and Sand. **'24** Thy Name Is Woman; The Red Lily. **'25** Ben-Hur. **'26** The Temptress. **'27** Camille. **'28** The Mysterious Lady. **'30** Way Out West. **'32** Blame the Woman.

Above left: Nanette Newman in The Raging Moon, *a love story set in a home for the disabled. Far left: Paul Newman in* Sometimes a Great Notion, *which he also directed. Left: Robert Newton in* Oliver Twist

321

NICHOLS, Barbara

(1929–1976). Actress. Born: Barbara Nickerauer; New York City, USA

A steady bit player for the twenty odd years of her working life, Nichols had a Brooklyn accent that did for her what a cockney accent did for Michael Caine. She was nearly always the dumb blonde with easy ways and a heart of gold, and the rich Brooklynese gave dimension to roles which would otherwise have been somewhat colourless and characterless. Perhaps the best Nichols part was that of the ambitious cigarette-girl in *Sweet Smell of Success*; she was memorable also in Lang's *Beyond a Reasonable Doubt*.

Films include: 1956 Miracle in the Rain; Beyond a Reasonable Doubt; The King and Four Queens. '57 Sweet Smell of Success; The Pajama Game; Pal Joey. '58 Ten North Frederick; The Naked and the Dead. '59 The Scarface Mob. '60 Who Was That Lady? '61 The George Raft Story (GB: Spin of a Coin).

Above: Jack Nicholson in The Border. *Right: Asta Nielsen. Below, far right: Philippe Noiret in* A Time For Loving, *(1971). Below right: Noël-Noël in* Le Septième Ciel *(1958). Below: the tranquil, urbane David Niven in* Paper Tiger, *in which he attempts to rescue a kidnapped boy*

NICHOLS, Dudley

(1895–1960). Screenwriter/director. Born: Wapakoneta, Ohio, USA

Dudley Nichols, a journalist and fiction-writer, settled in Hollywood in 1929 and rapidly became a leading scenarist. He wrote 13 scripts for John Ford, ranging in style from the dark atmospherics of *The Informer* to the sunny comedy of *Steamboat Round the Bend*, and including the classic Western *Stagecoach*. Nichols also wrote a brilliant Hawks comedy (*Bringing Up Baby*), a Fritz Lang *film noir* (*Scarlet Street*) and two of Jean Renoir's American films. In the Forties he directed three features, among them the film version of Eugene O'Neill's *Mourning Becomes Electra*.

Films include: 1934 The Lost Patrol (co-sc); Judge Priest (co-sc). '35 The Informer; The Crusades (co-sc); Steamboat Round the Bend (co-sc). '36 The Plough and the Stars. '38 Carefree (co-sc); Bringing Up Baby (co-sc). '39 Stagecoach. '40 The Long Voyage Home. '41 Swamp Water. '43 This Land Is Mine (+co-prod). '45 Scarlet Street. '47 Mourning Becomes Electra (+dir; +co-prod). '52 The Big Sky. '57 The Tin Star. '59 The Hangman.

Above: a studio publicity shot of Barbara Nichols taken by Bud Frauer. Left: Anna Q. Nilsson. Below: Leonard Nimoy as Mr Spock, the eminently logical, half-human, half-Vulcan science officer of the starship Enterprise in Star Trek – The Motion Picture

NICHOLS, Mike

(b. 1931). Director. Born: Michael Igor Peschkowsky; Berlin, Germany

Mike Nichols was formerly a cabaret comic with Elaine May before going on to produce many successful Broadway plays and turning his attention westward to Hollywood in the mid-Sixties. His first film was the powerful and unforgettable *Who's Afraid Of Virginia Woolf?* and he won the Best Director Oscar with his second, *The Graduate*. His anti-war sentiments were vividly expressed in the harsh unsentimentality of the black comedy *Catch-22*. Some of Nichols' later films seemed unworthy of their director's remarkable reputation, however.

Films: 1966 Who's Afraid of Virginia Woolf? '67 The Graduate. '70 Catch-22. '71 Carnal Knowledge. '73 The Day of the Dolphin. '75 The Fortune.

NICHOLSON, Jack

(b. 1937). Actor/director. Born: Neptune, New Jersey, USA

After years of frustration working in Roger Corman 'quickies', Nicholson finally got his break when he was called on to replace Rip Torn as the alcoholic Southern lawyer in *Easy Rider*. Once his talent was allowed to flower, he moved from success to success, winning an Oscar for his brilliant portrayal of the rebellious inmate in *One Flew Over the Cuckoo's Nest*. Nicholson has proved an amazingly versatile actor, capable of complex and widely ranging roles. As the loner revisiting his family in *Five Easy Pieces*, as the private-eye of *Chinatown*, as the tough petty officer of *The Last Detail*, and as so many others, he has created a gallery of anti-heroes who are vividly alive, acutely idiosyncratic, maddeningly unforgettable. Nicholson wrote a few scripts back in his Corman days, and in 1971 directed his first film, *Drive, He Said*, a bleak study of a group of eccentric misfits which won much critical praise. Later he made *Goin' South*, also playing the lead role of a hobo reformed by a girl (Mary Steenburgen). Nicholson's fame as one of Hollywood's greats is secure.

Films include: 1958 The Cry Baby Killer. '60 The Little Shop of Horrors. '63 The Terror (+ add. dir. uncredited). '66 The Shooting (+ co-prod.); Ride in the Whirlwind (+ co-prod; + sc). '67 The Trip (sc. only). '69 Easy Rider (+ add. ed. uncredited). '70 On a Clear Day You Can See Forever; Five Easy Pieces. '71 Drive, He Said (dir; + co-prod; + co-sc. only); Carnal Knowledge. '72 The King of Marvin Gardens. '73 The Last Detail. '74 Chinatown. '75 Tommy (GB); Professione: Reporter (SP-IT-FR) (USA/GB: The Passenger); One Flew Over the Cuckoo's Nest. '76 The Missouri Breaks; The Last Tycoon. '78 Goin' South (+ dir). '80 The Shining (GB). '81 The Postman Always Rings Twice; Reds. '82 The Border.

NIELSEN, Asta

(1883–1972). Actress. Born: Copenhagen, Denmark

The greatest star of European silent cinema, Asta Nielsen was on stage for some ten years before making her first film in 1910. Her first husband, Urban Gad, directed her many times; in 1911 they moved from Denmark to Germany, and the remainder of Nielsen's career was in German films. She was pale-faced, striking rather than beautiful, and had huge, expressive dark eyes. Her acting style was quiet, naturalistic and refined, her characterization a model of detail. Pabst's *The Joyless Street* is frequently shown because of the young Garbo, but it also contains a towering performance from Nielsen as a woman driven by poverty to prostitution and murder. She was the first Lulu (in 1923), she played Ibsen's Hedda Gabler and Strindberg's Miss Julie, and even Hamlet, in a version based on the curious book by Edward Vining which sought to show that the prince was in reality a woman. Nielsen made even that bizarre project moving and credible. She made only one sound film, though she continued for a while to act on stage. She returned to Denmark when the Nazis came to power in Germany.

Films include: 1910 Afgrunden (DEN) (The Abyss). '11 Heisses Blut (Hot Blood). '12 Der Totentanz (USA: The Dance of Death). '13 Engelein (Little Angel). '16 Das Liebes-ABC (Alphabet of Love). '19 Rausch (Intoxication). '20 Hamlet (+ co-prod). '21 Fräulein Julie (Miss Julie). '23 Erdgeist (Earth Spirit). '24 Hedda Gabler. '25 Die freudlose Gasse (USA: Streets of Sorrow; reissued as: The Street of Sorrow; GB: The Joyless Street). '27 Dirnentragödie (USA: Women Without Men). '32 Unmögliche Liebe (Unlikely Love Affair).

NILSSON, Anna Q.

(1888–1974). Actress. Born: Anna Querentia Nilsson; Ystad, Sweden

A lovely ash blonde, Anna Nilsson left Sweden to become a model in New York, and by 1911 was in the movies with the Kalem company. She was a star until the late Twenties, when a serious riding accident and the advent of sound combined to damage her career. She did return, however, in cameo roles, and is there in *Sunset Boulevard*, that great tribute to silent films, playing bridge with Stroheim, Keaton and H. B. Warner. Of the films

of her stardom, she is superb in Raoul Walsh's early masterpiece, *The Regeneration*; other notable Nilsson roles were in Tourneur's *Isle of Lost Ships* and Herbert Brenon's *Sorrell and Son*.

Films include: 1915 The Regeneration. '19 Her Kingdom of Dreams; Soldiers of Fortune. '23 Isle of Lost Ships. '26 The Greater Glory. '27 Sorrell and Son. '38 Prison Farm. '42 Girl's Town. '46 The Farmer's Daughter. '47 Magic Town. '50 Sunset Boulevard.

NIMOY, Leonard

(b. 1931). Actor. Boston, Massachusetts, USA

Leonard Nimoy = Mr Spock in the *Star Trek* series, is the usual equation but this serious-minded actor cannot be dismissed quite so lightly. An advocate of the Stanislavsky method of acting, he ran his own school in Hollywood teaching the Russian master's precepts. A fine photographer, Nimoy has also written poetry and plays and an autobiography with the title of *I Am Not Spock*. In the remake of *Invasion of the Body Snatchers* he played the psychiatrist friend of the hero who has himself been 'taken over' by the pod invaders. Thousands of Spock fans were grief-stricken when their hero seemed lost forever at the end of *Star Trek II – the Wrath of Khan*. A sequel was quickly announced.

Films include: 1951 Queen for a Day; Rhubarb. '53 Old Overland Trail. '63 The Balcony. '64 Seven Days in May. '66 Deathwatch. '71 Catlow (GB). '78 Invasion of the Body Snatchers. '79 Star Trek – the Motion Picture. '82 Star Trek II – the Wrath of Khan.

NIVEN, David

(1910–1983). Actor. Born: Kirriemuir, Angus, Scotland

Elegant, urbane and well-spoken, David Niven was classed as a 'British gentleman type' when he began working as a film extra in the Thirties, and he has since made the category his own. He graduated from Sandhurst military academy and served in Malta with the Highland Brigade before abruptly resigning his commission to seek work in Canada and the USA. After a succession of odd jobs, he found himself in Hollywood. He received his first major roles in *Dodsworth* and *The Prisoner of Zenda*, his open, pleasant manner making up for his lack of acting experience. When World War II began Niven was the first Hollywood star to enlist; he joined the Commandos, achieving the rank of Colonel. Afterwards Niven maintained his position as a highly popular movie star. He was particulary adept in light comedy parts, though he won his Oscar in a different kind of role – as the disillusioned, lonely army officer in *Separate Tables*. He wrote two best-selling volumes of reminiscences, *The Moon's a Balloon* and *Bring on the Empty Horses*, as well as novels.

Films include: 1935 Without Regret; Barbary Coast; Splendor. '36 Dodsworth; The Charge of the Light Brigade. '37 The Prisoner of Zenda. '38 Bluebeard's Eighth Wife; Four Men and a Prayer; The Dawn Patrol.

'39 Wuthering Heights; Raffles. '44 The Way Ahead (GB). '46 A Matter of Life and Death (GB) (USA: Stairway to Heaven). '48 Bonnie Prince Charlie (GB). '50 The Elusive Pimpernel (GB) (USA: The Fighting Pimpernel). '53 The Moon Is Blue. '54 Carrington VC (GB) (USA: Court Martial). '56 Around the World in 80 Days. '58 Bonjour Tristesse; Separate Tables. '59 Ask Any Girl. '61 The Guns of Navarone (USA-GB). '67 Casino Royale (GB). '75 Paper Tiger (GB-GER). '80 Rough Cut.

NOËL-NOËL

(b. 1897). Actor/screenwriter. Born: Lucien Noël; Paris, France

A painter and cartoonist, and, after World War I, a singer and songwriter, Noël-Noël entered films at the beginning of the sound period. He won popular success playing on the screen the character of Ademaï, a comic soldier created by an old cabaret colleague, Paul Colline, and in the Forties was the sympathetic star of modest, gentle films like *La Cage aux Rossignols* and *Le Père Tranquille*. Noël-Noël wrote many of his own scripts, and directed one film, *Les Casse-Pieds* (1950), a series of sketches on the subject of bores.

Films include: 1930 Le Prison en Folle. '31 Papa Sans le Savoir; Mistigri. '33 Mannequins; Vive la Compagnie. '34 Mam'zelle Spani. '35 Ademaï au Moyen-Age. '46 La Cage aux Rossignols (GB: A Cage of Nightingales); Le Père Tranquille. '55 Un Fil à la Patte; Les Carnets du Major Thompson (USA: The French They Are a Funny Race; GB: The Diary of Major Thompson).

NOIRET, Philippe

(b. 1931). Actor. Born: Lille, France

A large, heavy man who could play anything from vulnerable hero to comic villain, Noiret had been a stage actor of some note, especially with the Théâtre National Populaire in Paris, before making his first film appearance in Agnès Varda's *La Pointe Courte*. The film that really established him was Louis Malle's *Zazie dans le Métro*, where he played the unhappy uncle whose life is disrupted by the diabolical child. He was perfectly cast as the husband in Franju's *Thérèse Desqueyroux*, and then, in the late Sixties, went off to Hollywood for Cukor's *Justine* and Hitchcock's *Topaz*, two very average films. He came back to work steadily in France through the Seventies, striking up a highly successful partnership with the director Bertrand Tavernier. In the first of their four films together, *L'Horloger de Saint-Paul*, Noiret was outstanding as a quiet widower trying to come to terms with the fact that his son has killed a man.

Films include: 1942 Le Capitaine Fracasse. '55 La Pointe Courte. '60 Zazie dans le Métro (GB: Zazie). '61 Les Amours Célèbres (FR-IT); Tout l'Or du Monde (FR-IT) (GB: All the Gold in the World). '62 Thérèse Desqueyroux (USA/GB: Therese). '64 Les Copains. '69 Topaz (USA); Justine (USA). '73 L'Horloger de Saint-Paul (GB: Watchmaker of Saint-Paul); La Grande Bouffe (FR-IT) (GB: Blow-Out). '81 Coup de Torchon (GB: Clean Slate).

NOLAN, Jeanette

(b. 1911). Actress. Los Angeles, California, USA

From her beginnings as the only woman member of the *March of Time* radio series, she moved on to Orson Welles' Mercury Theatre and repeated her role of Lady Macbeth in Welles' film of the play remarkably effectively. From then on her movie career was assured, and of the many meaty roles she played, the vicious widow of the policeman in *The Big Heat* and the distraught mother who thinks she has found her son, recovered from the Indians, in *Two Rode Together*, are quite unforgettable. She is married to actor John McIntire.

Films include: 1948 Macbeth. '50 No Sad Songs for Me. '51 The Secret of Convict Lake. '53 The Big Heart. '57 April Love. '61 Two Rode Together. '62 The Man Who Shot Liberty Valance. '63 Twilight of Honor (GB: The Charge Is Murder). '66 Chamber of Horrors. '78 Avalanche.

NOLAN, Lloyd

(1902–1985). Actor. Born: San Francisco, California, USA

Lloyd Nolan's forty-odd years as one of Hollywood's most reliable actors began in 1935. Before that, he had studied law at Stanford University, acted at the Pasadena Playhouse, and plugged away until, in 1933, he had a big stage hit as Biff Grimes in *One Sunday Afternoon* (a part played in the movies by Gary Cooper and James Cagney). This brought Nolan a Paramount contract. He played leads – reporters or detectives as a rule – in action films, and was particularly good as the private eye of the excellent Michael Shayne series of the early Forties. He was still around in the Seventies, hard as ever in *Airport* and *The Private Files of J. Edgar Hoover*.

Films include: 1935 G-Men. '37 Wells Fargo. '40 Johnny Apollo; Michael Shayne, Private Detective. '45 A Tree Grows in Brooklyn. '46 The Lady in the Lake. '57 Peyton Place. '68 Ice Station Zebra. '70 Airport. '74 Earthquake. '78 The Private Files of J. Edgar Hoover.

NOLTE, Nick

(b. 1941). Actor. Born: Omaha, Nebraska, USA

Nolte initially wanted to be a professional footballer like his father but, after leaving Pasadena College in 1962, he decided to become an actor. After ten years with various stock companies, he landed a prominent role in the television series *Rich Man, Poor Man*. He then broke into movies, his first two being tasteless and disappointing. Nolte henceforth became more selective and has given several excellent performances – as a has-been football player in *North Dallas Forty*, a tough marine involved in dope-dealing by his weedy friend (Michael Moriarty) in *Who'll Stop the Rain?* and as the hero of the 'beat' generation, Neal Cassady, in *Heart Beat*.

Films include: 1975 Return to Macon County (GB: Highway Girl). '77 The Deep

(USA-GB). '78 Who'll Stop the Rain? (GB: Dog Soldiers). '79 North Dallas Forty; Heart Beat. '81 Cannery Row. '82 48 Hrs.

NORMAN, Leslie

(b. 1911). Producer/director. Born: London, England

Leslie Norman entered the film industry at 14, starting out in the laboratories and cutting rooms at Warner Brothers' Teddington Studios in London. He worked his way up to supervising editor and also co-directed *Too Dangerous to Live* (1939). After army service (much of it in Burma) during World War II, Norman joined Ealing Studios as an editor and cut, among other films, *The Overlanders* (1946), *Nicholas Nickleby* and *Frieda* (both 1947). He then successfully collaborated with director Harry Watt, acting as his producer on a series of films with Australian or African settings – *Eureka Stockade*, *Where No Vultures Fly* and *West of Zanzibar*. He started directing films at Ealing in 1955 with *The Night My Number Came Up*, climaxing this last phase of his distinguished career with the war epics *Dunkirk* (Ealing's most expensive film) and *The Long and the Short and the Tall*. His son is the television film-critic and author Barry Norman.

Films include: 1949 Eureka Stockade (prod). '51 Where No Vultures Fly (prod). '52 Mandy (prod) (USA: Crash of Silence). '53 The Cruel Sea (prod). '54 West of Zanzibar (prod). '56 The Unknown (dir). '57 The Shiralee (dir). '58 Dunkirk (dir). '60 Summer of the Seventeenth Doll (dir) (AUS) (USA: Summer of Passion). '61 The Long and the Short and the Tall (dir); Spare the Rod (dir). '62 Mix Me a Person (dir).

NORMAND, Mabel

(1892–1930). Actress. Born: Staten Island, New York City, USA

Normand came into movies via modelling, making her first film, *Over the Garden Wall*, in 1910. She then worked with Mack Sennett at the Biograph Studios, accompanying the director when he left to form his own company, Keystone, in 1912. For the next ten years she reigned supreme as the queen of silent comedy. Full of moody, restless energy off the screen, vibrant and bewitching on it, she appeared in over one hundred two-reelers, sometimes also directing, with first Charlie Chaplin and then Fatty Arbuckle as frequent partners. In 1914 she co-starred with Marie Dressler and Chaplin in Sennett's *Tillie's Punctured Romance*, the first ever feature-length comedy and a smash hit. She parted company with Sennett in 1918 (ending rumours of their eventual marriage after a long affair) to join Goldwyn. Her career began a gradual decline, largely due to the debilitating effects a wild social life and an addiction to drugs had upon her. She was shattered by two scandals in the early Twenties: in 1922 her close friend the director William Desmond Taylor was murdered and soon afterwards her chauffeur was

convicted of shooting oil millionaire Courtland S. Dines. Her marriage to actor Lew Cody was little more than a party joke. Normand's health deteriorated and she finally succumbed to tuberculosis.

Films include: 1910 Over the Garden Wall. '11 The Squaw's Love. '14 Mabel's Strange Predicament; Mabel at the Wheel (+dir); The Fatal Mallet; Mabel's Busy Day (+co-dir); His Trysting Place; Tillie's Punctured Romance. '15 Mabel and Fatty's Simple Life (+co-dir); Mabel's Wilful Way (+dir). '18 Mickey. '19 Sis Hopkins; When Doctors Disagree. '20 The Slim Princess; What Happened to Rosa? '21 Molly O. '23 The Extra Girl. '27 Should Men Walk Home.

NORTH, Alex

(b. 1910). Composer. Born: Chester, Pennsylvania, USA

North has been nominated for Oscars several times for his perceptive and at times innovatory compositions – his music for *A Streetcar Named Desire* was the first 100 per cent jazz score. Of Russian-Jewish parentage, North studied at the Curtis Institute of Philadelphia, the Juilliard in New York and the Moscow Convervatoire, becoming the first American to join the Union of Soviet Composers. On his return to the USA, he continued his musical education and worked on scores for various documentary films. During army service in World War II he was put in charge of therapeutic self-entertainment programmes in mental hospitals. Subsequent experience in the theatre, with Arthur Miller and Elia Kazan in particular, led to work in Hollywood, beginning in the early Fifties. In addition to composing symphonic works for the concert hall, North has written extensively for television, his credits including *Playhouse 90* and *Rich Man, Poor Man*.

Films include: 1951 A Streetcar Named Desire; Death of a Salesman. '52 Viva Zapata! '60 Spartacus. '61 The Misfits. '63 Cleopatra. '64 Cheyenne Autumn. '66 Who's Afraid of Virginia Woolf? '68 The Shoes of the Fisherman. '81 Dragonslayer.

NORTH, Sheree

(b. 1933). Actress. Born: Dawn Bethel; Los Angeles, California, USA

Sheree North was known for much of the Fifties as 'the girl 20th Century-Fox calls for whenever Marilyn Monroe refuses to make a film', though she has since assumed a strong film identity of her own. She packed a lot of living into her early teens, marrying at 15, having a child then getting a divorce, and working as a model and nightclub dancer. Her highly-charged routine in the Broadway musical *Hazel Flagg* won her a part in the film version *Living It Up* in 1954. She was signed up by 20th Century-Fox and touted as a sex symbol. She made bubbly, personable appearances in several movies, but her career was overshadowed by the likes of Monroe and Jayne Mansfield and she left Hollywood to concentrate on stage and television appearances. She returned to movies in the late

Above: Jeanette Nolan as Lady Macbeth in Orson Welles' fine adaptation of Shakespeare's play. Below: Mabel Normand – a barrel of laughs in Peck's Bad Girl (1919)

Sixties, giving strong character performances as once-glamorous, hard-boiled or crooked ladies in such films as *Madigan*, *Charley Varrick* and *The Shootist*, also playing Monroe's mother in the biopic *Marilyn, the Untold Story*.

Films include: 1954 Living It Up. '55 How to Be Very Popular; The Lieutenant Wore Skirts. '56 The Best Things in Life Are Free. '57 The Way to the Gold. '68 Madigan. '69 The Gypsy Moths. '71 The Organization. '73 Charley Varrick. '76 The Shootist. '81 Marilyn, the Untold Story.

Above: Lloyd Nolan in Dressed to Kill *(1941). Below: Sheree North in* Breakout *(1975). Bottom: Ramon Novarro as the hero of Fred Niblo's silent version of* Ben-Hur

Above: Nick Nolte in Who'll Stop the Rain? *Below: the beatific smile of Kim Novak in a Columbia publicity shot. Bottom: Ivor Novello, British matinee idol of the Twenties*

NOVAK, Kim

(b. 1933). Actress. Born: Marilyn Pauline Novak; Chicago, Illinois, USA

Blonde, green-eyed Kim Novak – big box-office in the Fifties – needed to convey very little in her movies other than the occasional hint of slumbrous sexuality to wow the male sections of an audience. At the same time, the attentiveness she showed on screen towards her fellow actors endows her performances with an unpretentious-

ness and integrity that invites sympathetic attention. In 1953 she toured the USA as 'Miss Deepfreeze', publicizing refrigerators, and a year later won her first part in a movie, a walk-on in *The French Line*. She was signed up by Columbia who turned her into a star to replace Rita Hayworth and rival Marilyn Monroe. Undoubtedly her finest performance was in Hitchcock's *Vertigo*, in the dual role of Madeleine and Judy – a tormenting mystery for the detective hero, played by James Stewart. She had far less interesting roles in her later films and as her

career went into a gentle decline she worked increasingly on television. She was briefly married to actor Richard Johnson, her co-star in *The Amorous Adventures of Moll Flanders*.

Films include: 1955 Picnic. '57 Jeanne Eagels; Pal Joey. '58 Vertigo; Bell, Book and Candle. '60 Strangers When We Meet. '64 Kiss Me, Stupid. '65 The Amorous Adventures of Moll Flanders (GB). '68 The Legend of Lylah Clare. '73 Tales That Witness Madness (GB). '79 Schöner Gigolo – Armer Gigolo (USA/GB: Just a Gigolo). '80 The Mirror Crack'd (GB).

NOVARRO, Ramon

(1899–1968). Actor. Born: Ramon Samaniegos: Durango, Mexico

When Samaniegos Sr settled in Los Angeles in 1914, young Ramon worked as a singing waiter and in vaudeville, and was in the movies, as an extra, by 1917. His break came five years later, when the director Rex Ingram, needing a replacement for Valentino, who had just left the Metro company, cast him as Rupert of Hentzau in his version of *The Prisoner of Zenda*. It was Ingram, too, who had the actor change his name to Novarro. Handsome, athletic and versatile, Novarro was a star until the mid-Thirties; his greatest successes came in Ingram's French Revolution romance, *Scaramouche*, in the legendary *Ben-Hur*, and in Lubitsch's gently nostalgic *The Student Prince*. When his fame faded, Novarro still made occasional appearances in small parts, his final one being in *Heller in Pink Tights*, as late as 1960. For the most part he lived alone in the Hollywood Hills, painting and dealing in real estate. In 1968 he was brutally murdered in his home by petty thieves.

Films include: 1922 The Prisoner of Zenda. '23 Scaramouche. '24 The Arab. '25 Ben-Hur. '27 The Student Prince. '28 Forbidden Hours. '29 The Pagan. '30 Call of the Flesh. '32 Mata Hari. '34 The Cat and the Fiddle; Laughing Boy. '35 The Night Is Young. '37 The Sheik Steps Out. '60 Heller in Pink Tights.

NOVELLO, Ivor

(1893–1951). Actor. Born: Ivor Novello Davies; Cardiff, Wales

The son of choral singer Clara Novello Davies, he himself trained as a singer and also wrote songs, achieving immense success with 'Keep the Home Fires Burning' during World War I. After the war he went on the stage playing, most famously, the romantic Parisian 'apache' character, *The Rat*, in his own play; audiences loved this effete but charming rogue and in 1925 Novello brought him to the screen, with two sequels. In films from 1920, he had rapidly become a pale, soulful matinee idol, often in costume dramas, and through the decade he was Britain's only rival to Hollywood heart-throbs. His own appearances in American films (including D. W. Griffith's *The White Rose*) were unsuccessful, however, and his best picture was Hitchcock's *The Lodger*, in which he played the mysterious young man suspected of murdering young girls. Novello's film career tailed off in the

Thirties. He continued to act in, write and produce musicals until his death, his popularity with legions of female fans undiminished.

Films include: 1920 L'Appel du Sang (FR). '21 Carnival. '22 The Man Without Desire (+prod). '23 The White Rose (USA); Bonnie Prince Charlie. '25 The Rat (+co-sc; +co-play basis). '26 The Triumph of the Rat (+co-sc); The Lodger (USA: The Case of Jonathan Drew). '27 Downhill (+co-sc) (USA: When Boys Leave Home); The Vortex. '28 The Constant Nymph. '29 The Return of the Rat (+co-sc). '31 Once a Lady (USA). '34 Autumn Crocus.

NOYCE, Philip

(b. 1950). Director. Born: Griffith, New South Wales, Australia

Noyce began making films at school and university. In 1970 he became part-time manager of the Sydney Film-maker's Co-operative and in 1973 was selected by Sydney Film School for a year-long training scheme that resulted in a sixty-minute movie, *Backroads*, shown successfully at the Berlin and Cannes film festivals. *Newsfront*, his first feature, was widely acclaimed for its portrayal of a group of Australian newsreel cameramen during the Fifties. Shot like a documentary and intercut with actual newsreel footage, it was an incisive examination of changing Australian society and one of the best – if least exportable – of the 'New Wave' films. Noyce's next important picture was *Heatwave*, an odd mix of a Sixties-style story of civic corruption shot in the style of a Forties *film noir*.

Films include: 1968 Better to Reign in Hell (short). '71 Good Afternoon (doc). '73 Caravan park (short). '74 Castor and Pollux (doc). '76 God Knows Why But It Works (doc). '77 Backroads. '78 Newsfront. '81 Heatwave. '82 The Umbrella Man.

NYKVIST, Sven

(b. 1922). Cinematographer. Born: Moheda, Sweden

Nykvist took over from Gunnar Fischer as Ingmar Bergman's regular cinematographer on *The Virgin Spring* in 1960, although he had worked for Bergman much earlier on *Gycklarnas Afton* (1953, *Sawdust and Tinsel*). He had entered the industry in 1941, rising four years later to lighting cameraman. Nykvist acknowledges a great debt to Bergman and, before him, to Alf Sjöberg, but has himself proved a brilliant and original artist, especially skilful at landscape and at contriving the dream and hallucination sequences of which Bergman has made much use. A cameraman much in demand now, Nykvist has worked abroad too, with other distinguished directors, including Louis Malle and Roman Polanski.

Films include: 1954 Salka Valka. '60 Jungfrukällan (USA/GB: The Virgin Spring). '62 Natt Vardsgästerna (USA/GB: Winter Light). '66 Persona. '70 Erste Liebe (SWED-GER). '71 One Day in the Life of Ivan Denisovitch (GB-NOR). '72 Siddhartha (USA). '75 Ansikte mot Ansikte (USA/GB: Face to Face). '76 Le Locataire (FR) (USA/GB: The Tenant). '78 Pretty Baby (USA). '79 Starting Over (USA).

OAKIE, Jack

(1893–1978). Actor. Born: Lewis Delaney Offield; Sedalia, Missouri, USA

Oakie was brought up in Muskogee, Oklahoma, from where he took his stage name. He began his theatrical career as a chorus boy in George Cohan's *Little Nelly Kelly* and progressed to song-and-dance man, forming a popular vaudeville duo with Lulu McConnell. In 1927 he went to Hollywood and was an instant success. Oakie's twinkling blue eyes and rotund figure made him ideal for comedy: he was Migg Tweeny, an American serviceman who becomes embroiled in the mad principality of Klopskopia ruled over by W. C. Fields in *Million Dollar Legs*, and was cast as Tweedledum in the all-star version of *Alice in Wonderland*. Oakie always tended to play amiable but dumb characters, although he was rather more flamboyant as Napoloni Bacteria (a caricature of Mussolini) in Chaplin's *The Great Dictator*.

Films include: 1929 Close Harmony. '30 Hit the Deck; The Sap From Syracuse (GB: The Sap Abroad); Let's Go Native. '32 Million Dollar Legs. '33 Alice in Wonderland. '35 The Call of the Wild. '40 The Great Dictator. '56 Around the World in 80 Days. '59 The Wonderful Country.

OATES, Warren

(1928–1982). Actor. Born: Depoy, Kentucky, USA

Oates struggled hard to reach the top. He came from a poor hillbilly community, joined the marines, studied at Louisville University, did some amateur acting, and after spells as a dishwasher and cloakroom attendant managed to obtain some bit parts in television. By the end of the Fifties he had broken into the movies as a gangster or Western heavy ('My face looks like two miles of country road', he once said), and his work for directors like Sam Peckinpah (in *The Wild Bunch*) and Monte Hellman (in whose *Two-Lane Blacktop* he was outstanding) led to his being offered many excellent character parts and offbeat leads in movies and television series prior to his sudden, premature death. His last role was as the corrupt chief of the American border guards in *The Border*; this was Oates at his most macho.

Films include: 1958 Up Periscope. '60 The Rise and Fall of Legs Diamond. '62 Ride the High Country (GB: Guns in the Afternoon). '64 Mail Order Bride (GB: West of Montana). '65 Major Dundee. '67 In the Heat of the Night. '69 The Wild Bunch. '71 Two-Lane Black Top. '73 Dillinger. '74 Cockfighter/Born to Kill; Bring Me the Head of Alfredo Garcia (USA-MEX). '79 1941. '82 The Border.

OBERON, Merle

(1911–1979). Actress. Born: Estelle Merle O'Brien: Tasmania, Australia

It is sad to think that this beautiful and capable actress will always be remembered best not for the films she made but for the film which – because of her – was never made. In 1937 she was involved in a serious car accident while filming Josef von Sternberg's *I, Claudius*, and her long weeks of illness (she was seriously concussed and brain damage was feared) stopped production of what would have been (judging from the excerpts still remaining) one of the most remarkable films ever made. She was a bland and passionless Cathy in *Wuthering Heights*, a sad and soulful Lady Blakeney in *The Scarlet Pimpernel* and a vivacious can-can dancer in the 1944 *The Lodger*. Merle Oberon's second husband was the gifted cameraman Lucien Ballard; her first was the producer Alexander Korda, who provided her with the role that made her an international star, that of Anne Boleyn in *The Private Life of Henry VIII*.

Films include: 1933 The Private Life of Henry VIII. '35 The Scarlet Pimpernel. '36 These Three. '39 Wuthering Heights (USA). '40 'Til We Meet Again (USA). '44 Dark Waters (USA); The Lodger (USA). '45 A Song to Remember (USA). '46 Temptation (USA). '73 Interval (+ prod; + co-ed).

O'BRIEN, Edmond

(1915–1985). Actor. Born: New York City, USA

After a brief stay at Fordham University, O'Brien went to the Neighborhood Playhouse School on a scholarship and on graduation played in summer stock and on Broadway. He worked in radio and on stage with Orson Welles' Mercury Theatre group before going to Hollywood on an RKO contract, making his film debut in *The*

Hunchback of Notre Dame. Solidly built, heavily jowled, and essentially sympathetic, he played cops, politicians, writers, all of them with a lively intelligence. He won a Best Supporting Actor Oscar for his fast-talking, sweaty press agent in *The Barefoot Contessa*, and remained active well into the Seventies. But his best time was in the days of *film noir*: *The Killers* (first version), *White Heat* and *D.O.A.* all contain O'Brien performances to cherish.

Films include: 1939 The Hunchback of Notre Dame. '46 The Killers. '49 White Heat; D.O.A. '53 The Bigamist. '54 The Barefoot Contessa (USA-IT). '55 Pete Kelly's Blues. '56 The Girl Can't Help It. '62 Birdman of Alcatraz; The Longest Day. '64 Seven Days in May; Rio Conchos.

O'BRIEN, George

(1900–1985). Actor. Born: San Francisco, California, USA

The son of San Francisco's Chief of Police, and heavyweight champion of the Pacific Fleet in World War I, George O'Brien didn't quite have the background to play the lead in one of the greatest romantic movies of all time. But in *Sunrise* he did just that, and he didn't let Murnau down. His performance as the simple country husband seduced by the city woman was a remarkable study of lost innocence. O'Brien was a stunt double, played a few parts in small films, and was picked out by John Ford to star in the director's first major film, *The Iron Horse*, in 1924. O'Brien played in four more Ford films over the next two years, one of them being *The Blue Eagle*, where his co-star was Janet Gaynor, who would be with him again in *Sunrise*. With sound, O'Brien became typecast as a Western hero, and his movies were normally minor affairs, but John Ford never forgot his old stars, and O'Brien stayed on in the cavalry for *Fort Apache*, *She Wore a Yellow Ribbon*, and even *Cheyenne Autumn* in 1964.

Films include: 1922 White Hands. '25 Thank You; The Fighting Heart (GB: Once to Every Man). '26 The Blue Eagle. '27 Sunrise. '29 True Heaven. '31 The Seas Beneath. '47 My Wild Irish Rose. '48 Fort Apache. '49 She Wore a Yellow Ribbon. '64 Cheyenne Autumn.

O'BRIEN, Margaret

(b. 1937). Actress. Born: Angela O'Brien; Los Angeles, California, USA

Universally acknowledged to be one of the finest child actresses ever, Margaret O'Brien was on the screen from the age of four. She became an international star at the age of seven with her charming and unforgettable performance as Tootie in *Meet Me in St Louis*, for which she received an Academy Award. Her freckled face, disarming smile and solemn husky voice, allied with an acting ability so natural it could only have been so, made her an obvious choice for well-loved characters like Beth in *Little Women* and the bewildered, frightened orphan in *The Secret Garden*. Like many other child stars she failed to make the transition to adult roles, although her appearance as the inept daughter in *Heller in Pink Tights* showed she was still a talented comedienne.

Films include: 1941 Babes on Broadway. '42 Journey for Margaret. '43 Jane Eyre. '44 The Canterville Ghost; Madame Curie; Meet Me in St Louis. '49 Little Women; The Secret Garden. '51 Her First Romance (GB: GIrls Never Tell). '60 Heller in Pink Tights.

O'BRIEN, Pat

(1899–1983). Actor. Born: William Joseph Patrick O'Brien; Milwaukee, Wisconsin, USA

O'Brien and Spencer Tracy were friends from childhood. Together they went to military school, joined the navy and went to drama school in New York. O'Brien made slow progress during the Twenties, but when he played the fast-talking reporter Hildy Johnson in Lewis Milestone's film version of *The Front Page*, he established himself as a star. He appeared regularly over the next twenty years, but the Thirties were his great period, when this rugged Irishman stood for order and decency in many Warner Brothers' gangster films. He formed a notable partnership with James Cagney in movies such as *Ceiling Zero*.

Left: Jack Oakie as a Fascist leader in Charles Chaplin's The Great Dictator. *Above: Warren Oates in Sam Peckinpah's gruesome thriller* Bring Me the Head of Alfredo Garcia. *Above right: Edmond O'Brien in* The Third Voice (1960). *Below: Merle Oberon in* Temptation

Films include: 1931 The Front Page. '32 The Final Edition (GB: Determination. '37 The Great O'Malley; San Quentin. '38 Angels With Dirty Faces. '42 Flight Lieutenant. '43 The Iron Major. '48 Fighting Father Dunne. '52 Okinawa. '54 Ring of Fear. '59 Some Like It Hot. '81 Ragtime.

O'CONNELL, Arthur

(1908–1981). Actor. Born: New York City, USA

A character actor in over seventy Hollywood films, his career started in vaudeville and the legitimate theatre on Broadway. Although he originally wanted to be a priest, one can only be glad the call of the greasepaint prevailed. He was a sensitive, fine actor whose most memorable performance was as Rosalind Russell's reluctant suitor in *Picnic*. His sad-eyed countenance graced such films as *Citizen Kane*, in which, along with Alan Ladd, he made an uncredited appearance, and *Anatomy of a Murder*, in which he played a country lawyer. In Joshua Logan's *Bus Stop* he was excellent as the guardian of the rough rodeo rider (Don Murray) whose passion for a lowly chanteuse (Marilyn Monroe) he tries to curb.

Films include: 1940 Citizen Kane. '48 The Naked City. '56 Bus Stop; The Man in the Gray Flannel Suit; Picnic. '59 Anatomy of a Murder. '61 Pocketful of Miracles; Misty. '65 The Great Race. '66 Fantastic Voyage. '72 The Poseidon Adventure.

O'CONNOR, Donald

(b. 1925) Actor/dancer/composer. Born: David O'Connor; Chicago, Illinois, USA

It is difficult to imagine that this singing, dancing, chirpy, cheeky little man who starred in the *Francis the Talking Mule* series, and also played leading roles in such major musicals as *Singin' in the Rain*, is, in fact, a serious composer of classical music. Born into a circus family, he was on the road as an infant and made his film debut at the age of 11. From then on (apart from two years in the armed forces) he was constantly on the screen until he conducted the Los Angeles Philharmonic Orchestra in his first symphony. Thereafter his screen appearances were sporadic as he concentrated more and more on his music.

Films include: 1938 Tom Sawyer – Detective. '44 The Merry Monahans. '49 Yes Sir, That's My Baby; Francis. '52 Singin' in the Rain. '53 Call Me Madam; Walking My Baby Back Home. '54 There's No Business Like Show Business. '57 The Buster Keaton Story. '74 That's Entertainment!. '81 Ragtime.

Far left: George O'Brien in Noah's Ark (1928). *Left: child star Margaret O'Brien on the set of MGM's* Lost Angel (1943). *Above: Pat O'Brien as a kindly priest in* Angels With Dirty Faces. *Below: Donald O'Connor in* Francis – *a film about a talkative mule. Below left: a studio publicity portrait of Arthur O'Connell*

O'CONNOR, Una

(1880–1959). Actress. Born: Agnes McGlade; Belfast, Northern Ireland

Thin-faced, lugubrious and prone to shrieking, Una O'Connor had been with the Abbey Theatre in Dublin as early as 1911, and then enjoyed success in London and New York before in the Thirties becoming one of Hollywood's army of character players. The chirpy Cockney maid in *Cavalcade* established her, but she was usually a poor afflicted soul, puzzled by *The Invisible Man*, finding something very nasty down a well in *The Bride of Frankenstein* and, of course, a natural for the sad Mrs Gummidge in *David Copperfield*.

Films include: 1929 Dark Red Roses. '33 Cavalcade; The Invisible Man. '34 The Barretts of Wimpole Street. '35 The Informer; David Copperfield; Rose Marie; The Bride of Frankenstein. '38 The Adventures of Robin Hood. '43 This Land Is Mine. '45 The Bells of St Mary's. '46 Of Human Bondage.

ODETS, Clifford

(1906–1963). Playwright/ screenwriter/director. Born: Philadelphia, Pennsylvania, USA

Odets was a gifted dramatist, best known for his work with the New York Group Theater in the Thirties. Several of his plays have been filmed (notably *Golden Boy* and *The Country Girl*), but Odets was more directly involved with the cinema as a screenwriter. His scripts had all the virtues of his plays: vivid characters, strong stories, colourful dialogue and social concern. *Sweet Smell of Success* has deservedly become a classic, but the almost forgotten *Deadline at Dawn*, a crime thriller filled with haunting poetry, is even better. Odets also directed two films, of which *None But the Lonely Heart*, in particular, suggested that he could have excelled in this line too, had he so chosen.

Films include: 1936 The General Died at Dawn. '39 Golden Boy. '44 None But the Lonely Heart (dir; + sc). '46 Deadline at Dawn (sc. only); Humoresque (co-sc. only). '52 Clash by Night (play basis only). '54 The Country Girl (play basis only). '55 The Big Knife (play basis only). '75 Sweet Smell of Success (co-sc. only). '59 The Story on Page One (dir; + sc). '61 Wild in the Country (sc. only).

O'DONNELL, Cathy

(1925–1970). Actress. Born: Ann Steeley; Siluria, Alabama, USA

A petite, fragile beauty, who was outstanding as the compassionate fiancée of the armless veteran in *The Best Years of Our Lives*, she went on to make many worthy appearances, but never managed to reach the heights of her debut film. She came very close, however, as the tragic teenager in Nicholas Ray's early masterpiece, *They Live by Night*, and had goodish parts, too, in *Detective Story* and *The Man From Laramie*.

Films include: 1946 The Best Years of Our Lives. '48 They Live by Night. '50 Side Street; The Miniver Story. '51 Detective Story; Never Trust a Gambler. '52 The Woman's Angle (GB). '55 Mad at the World; The Man From Laramie. '57 The Story of Mankind. '59 Ben-Hur.

OGIER, Bulle

(b. 1939). Actress. Born: Boulogne-sur-Seine, France

Ogier worked in experimental theatre in Paris before her film debut in Jacques Rivette's *L'Amour Fou* (1968). A diminutive honey-blonde, she seemed for a time in danger of being typecast in romantic but neurotic and rather sad roles, but has managed to depart from the pattern playing a character whom one critic described as a 'leather-booted, whip-toting gauleiter' in Barbet Schroeder's essay in sado-masochism, *Maîtresse*. By contrast, Ogier has adapted well to the leisurely improvisations of Rivette, and has also done good things for Buñuel and Alain Tanner.

Films include: 1969 Quarante-Huit Heures d'Amour (GB: Forty-Eight Hours of Love); Et Crac (short). '70 Piège. '71 M Comme Mathieu; La Salamandre (SWITZ) (USA/GB: The Salamander). '73 Le Charme Discret de la Bourgeoisie (FR-SP-IT) (GB: The Discreet Charm of the Bourgeoisie); George Qui? '75 Un Divorce Heureux (FR-DEN). '76 Maîtresse.

O'HARA, Maureen

(b. 1920). Actress. Born: Maureen FitzSimmons; Milltown, Ireland

Said to be John Ford's favourite actress, this beautiful, red-haired Irish actress was ideal for Technicolor, where her lovely colouring was an asset to her undeniable acting ability. By the age of 14 she was already receiving awards in festivals and drama contests. Her roles were usually of the fiery, tempestuous type, which she played to perfection, but her underlying tenderness shone forth particularly in *How Green Was My Valley*, which established her as a Hollywood star of the first order. Lithe, obviously full of health and vigour, she did many of her own stunts in her pictures, and last appeared with John Wayne, whom she partnered to perfection in many films, in *Big Jake*. Her best role was probably as the Irish colleen Wayne finds it necessary to court, marry, fight with and tenderly love in *The Quiet Man*.

Films include: 1939 Jamaica Inn (GB); The Hunchback of Notre Dame. '41 How Green Was My Valley. '43 This Land Is Mine. '47 The Foxes of Harrow. '50 Rio Grande. '52 The Quiet Man. '57 Wings of Eagles. '59 Our Man in Havana (GB). '71 Big Jake.

O'HERLIHY, Dan

(b. 1919). Actor. Born: Wexford, Ireland

A truly outstanding actor who gave a virtuoso performance in Luis Buñuel's *The Adventures of Robinson Crusoe* in which, until the arrival on the screen of Man Friday, he gave an almost wordless and definitive impression of agonizing loneliness. He was just as

memorable as the anguished General Black who is ordered to drop a hydrogen bomb on New York in *Fail Safe*. A qualified architect, he began acting at the Gate and Abbey theatres in Dublin. After making two films in London, he was taken to Hollywood by Orson Welles to play Macduff to Welles' *Macbeth*. When worthy film parts proved unforthcoming, his beautiful, rich voice assured him a healthy income from radio plays.

Films include: 1946 Hungry Hill. '47 Odd Man Out. '48 Macbeth. '51 The Desert Fox (GB: Rommel – Desert Fox). '54 The Adventures of Robinson Crusoe. '58 Home Before Dark. '59 Imitation of Life. '62 The Cabinet of Dr Caligari. '64 Fail Safe. '70 Waterloo (IT-USSR). '74 The Tamarind Seed (GB). '77 MacArthur (GB: MacArthur the Rebel General).

O'KEEFE, Dennis

(1908–1968). Actor. Born: Edward Flanagan; Fort Madison, Iowa, USA

Flanagan's parents were in vaudeville as 'Flanagan and Edwards, the Rollicking Twosome', and from an early age he appeared on stage with them. In the early Thirties the movies beckoned, and he played numerous bit parts, billed, when credited at all, as Bud Flanagan. In 1937 MGM, impressed by his infectious grin and easy confidence, gave him a contract and changed his name. As O'Keefe, he played leads in light comedies and thrillers until the Fifties. He was always a competent and conscientious pro, though seldom severely tested. His films were almost all ephemeral, but two which should last are *The Leopard Man*, which he made for Val Lewton, and *T-Men*, a taut thriller which O'Keefe was partly responsible for scripting.

Films include: 1938 The Bad Man of Brimstone. '41 Topper Returns. '43 Hangmen Also Die!; The Leopard Man. '44 The Story of Dr Wassell. '45 Brewster's Millions. '47 Dishonored Lady; T-Men (+ co-sc). '48 Raw Deal. '54 Angela (+ dir) (IT-USA). '55 Chicago Syndicate. '61 All Hands on Deck.

OLAND, Warner

(1880–1938). Actor. Born: Johan Werner Ohlund; Umea, Sweden

A Swede who made his living playing Orientals, Oland was educated in Boston, and as a young man acted in stage plays by Ibsen and Strindberg. By 1912 he was in the movies, and found himself playing a villainous Japanese baron in the bellicose serial *Patria* (1917). Oland didn't always portray Chinese or Japanese (he notably escaped to be Jolson's cantor father in *The Jazz Singer*), but he did more than his share, lusting after Colleen Moore in *Twinkletoes* (1926), menacing the world as *The Mysterious Dr Fu Manchu*, and fitting perfectly into Sternberg's stylized East in *Shanghai Express*. In his last years he joined the side of the angels, playing Charlie Chan, the philosophical Chinese detective, in some seventeen beautifully tailored B movies. The fourth of seven Chans, he alone will forever be associated with that acute, gentle, epigrammatic man. Oland died from bronchial pneumonia.

Films include: 1912 The Life of John Bunyan; Pilgrim's Progress. '18 The Yellow Ticket. '25 Don Q, Son of Zorro. '27 The Jazz Singer. '29 The Mysterious Dr Fu Manchu. '31 Black Camel; Dishonored; Charlie Chan Carries On. '32 Shanghai Express. '34 The Painted Veil. '37 Charlie Chan at Monte Carlo.

OLBRYCHSKI, Daniel

(b. 1945). Actor. Born: Łowicz, Poland

Daniel Olbrychski first came to public notice reciting poetry in a Polish television competition. He went on to study dramatic art in Warsaw. His second film role, in Andrzej Wajda's *Ashes*, brought him to fame, confirmed when he took over the role of the popular actor Zbigniew Cybulski (who had been killed in an accident) in *Everything for Sale*. He has successfully played a wide range of roles in Wajda's films, but he has also worked with other good directors, notably Krzysztof Zanussi and the Hungarian Miklós Jancsó. Olbrychski is an accomplished amateur sportsman and does his own stunts. Besides films, he acts and sings on television and in the theatre, and has played Hamlet at the National Theatre in Warsaw.

Films include: 1964 Ranny w Lesie (Wounded in the Forest). '65 Popioły (USA/GB: Ashes). '68 Wszstko na Sprzedaz (USA/GB: Everything for Sale). '69 Pan Wolodyjowski (GB: Colonel Wolodyjowski). '70 Krajobraz po Bitwie (GB: Landscape After Battle). '71 Życie Rodzinne (GB: Family Life); Égi Bárány/Agnus Dei (HUNG); La Pacifista (IT-FR-GER) (The Pacifist). '73 Wesele (USA/GB: The Wedding). '74 Ziemia Obiecana (Promised Land). '79 Panxiy z Wilka (POL-FR) (The Young Girls of Wilko). '80 Rycerz (The Knight). '82 La Truite (FR).

OLCOTT, Sidney

(1873–1949). Director. Born: Toronto, Canada

Pioneer director Sidney Olcott, the son of Irish immigrants, was involved in movie-making as early as 1904, acting and generally assisting at Biograph. He began to direct in 1907 with the new Kalem company, and promptly made his mark in film history. Without bothering about copyright, he directed a private version of *Ben-Hur* (the chariot-race plus one reel of interiors), and precipitated a lawsuit that dragged on for four years. Olcott was one of the first to shoot on location, both in Florida (Kalem had a studio at Jacksonville) and in Ireland, where in 1910 and 1911 he led the first American company to film outside the USA. Olcott then went to Egypt and Palestine to make *From the Manger to the Cross*, a feature length film on the life of Christ shot in North Africa and Palestine. This film made vast sums for Kalem, but Olcott was in dispute with the company and his name was removed from the picture. Olcott continued to direct until 1927, working for Famous Players, and making movies with Pickford, Valentino, Swanson and Norma Talmadge. Like other pioneers, such as Thomas H. Ince and Edwin S. Porter, Olcott's contribution was vital.

Films include: 1907 The Sleigh Bells (+ act). '07 Ben-Hur (co-dir). '09 A Florida Feud. '11 The Colleen Bawn (+ act); Rory O'More. '12 Ireland the Oppressed (+ act); From the Manger to the Cross (+ act). '15 Madame Butterfly. '16 Poor Little Peppina; The Innocent Lie. '20 Scratch My Back. '24 The Green Goddess; Monsieur Beaucaire. '27 The Claw.

Left, from top to bottom: Una O'Connor in Cavalcade; *Cathy O'Donnell in* The Best Years of Our Lives; *Bulle Ogier in* La Vallée *(1972)*

Top: Dan O'Herlihy in Sergei Bondarchuk's star-studded epic Waterloo. *Above: Dennis O'Keefe with Constance Moore in* I'm Nobody's Sweetheart Now *(1940)*

Above: Maureen O'Hara in William Dieterle's The Hunchback of Notre Dame. *Above right: Warner Oland. Right: Daniel Olbrychski in* Brzezina *(1970, The Birch Wood)*

329

OLIVEIRA, Manoel de

(b. 1908). Director. Born: Oporto,
Portugal

Manoel de Oliveira's first documentary depicted the everyday lives of working people on the river Douro with great social insight. After a few more documentaries – made with difficulty because he refused to support the prevailing right-wing dictatorship – he made his first feature, *Aniki-Bóbó*, set in Oporto and using children's games to mirror adult moral concerns. He had to wait over twenty years to follow this with a re-enactment of a Holy Week Passion Play, and another decade before he could make his comedy *Past and Present*, a sharp satire on the greedy rich. He became more prolific in the Seventies, finally receiving official support. His more recent *Francisca* was a love-triangle story involving the famous nineteenth-century novelist Camilo Castelo Branco (from whose work Oliveira's previous *Ill-Fated Love* had been adapted), his friend and the woman they both love. The Eighties finally brought Oliveira overdue international recognition.

Films include: 1931 Douro, Faina Fluvial (doc. short) (GB: Hard Work on the River Douro). **'42** Aniki-Bóbó. **'56** O Pinto e a Cidade (doc. short) (GB: The Painter and the Town). **'59** O Pão (doc. short) (Bread). **'63** O Acto da Primavera (The Passion of Jesus). **'64** A Caça (short) (The Hunt). **'72** O Passado e o Presente (Past and Present). **'75** Benilde ou a Virgem Mãe (Benilde: Virgin and Mother). **'79** Amor de Perdição (Ill-Fated Love). **'81** Francisca.

OLIVER, Edna May

(1883–1947). Actress. Born: Edna May Nutter; Malden, Massachusetts, USA

After years on Broadway, Edna May Oliver moved over to films in 1924, a transition for which film fans can be profoundly grateful. She never gave an indifferent performance, and was often brilliant, in particular as the resolute frontierswoman defying the Indians from her stately bed in *Drums Along the Mohawk*, and in a series of definitive characterizations, including Aunt March in *Little Women*, Betsy Trotwood in *David Copperfield*, the Nurse in *Romeo and Juliet* (all those three for George Cukor), and Miss Pross in *A Tale of Two Cities*. Nor was she outshone by the starry cast of *Pride and Prejudice*, in which she was the proud Lady Catherine de Bourgh. Besides playing famous literary characters, she created the role of schoolteacher Hildegarde Withers, heroine of a pleasant series of Thirties detective movies. She was a tall, lean, spinsterish lady with a haughty air, a Hollywood dowager who knew very well that her face was her fortune.

Films include: 1931 Cimarron; Fanny Foley Herself (GB: Top of the Bill). **'32** The Penguin Pool Murder (GB: The Penguin Pool Mystery). **'33** Little Women. **'34** Murder on the Blackboard. **'35** David Copperfield; A Tale of Two Cities; Murder on a Honeymoon. **'36** Romeo and Juliet. **'39** Drums Along the Mohawk. **'40** Pride and Prejudice. **'41** Lydia.

Above: Edna May Oliver in No More Ladies *(1935). Right: Laurence Olivier in his Oscar-winning role of* Hamlet, *which he also produced and directed. Below: Ole Olsen and Chic Johnson in* The Ghost Catchers, *one of the duo's zaniest films*

Below: Anny Ondra in Blackmail. *Right: Ryan O'Neal and his daughter Tatum in* Paper Moon

OLIVIER, Laurence

(b. 1907). Actor/director. Born: Dorking, Surrey, England

Although this great actor's career has alternated between stage and screen since the Thirties, the theatre has retained his true allegiance. He first attracted attention in films as the romantic lead in *Fire Over England* and *Q Planes*, and he then made his mark in Hollywood as Heathcliff in *Wuthering Heights* and Max de Winter in *Rebecca*. Olivier's first film as a director was the widely acclaimed *Henry V*; this was followed by *Hamlet* (which won four Oscars, including one for Olivier as Best Actor), and *Richard III*, arguably the best of his Shakespeare films, in which he gave a definitive performance as the hunchbacked king. His subsequent films have been patchy, though he himself was excellent as Archie Rice in *The Entertainer*, as a teacher accused of molesting a girl pupil in *Term of Trial* and as a sadistic Nazi dentist in *Marathon Man*. For health reasons,

from the Seventies on he has increasingly concentrated on film and television rather than the stage; he was particularly compelling as Lord Brideshead in TV's *Brideshead Revisited* and Clifford Mortimer in *Voyage Round My Father*. His wife is the actress Joan Plowright; he was previously married to actresses Jill Esmond and Vivien Leigh. He was knighted in 1947 and, in 1970 became the first actor to be made a life peer.

Films include: 1930 Too Many Crooks. **'37** Fire Over England; 21 Days (USA: 21 Days Together). **'39** Q Planes (USA: Clouds Over Europe); Wuthering Heights (USA). **'40** Rebecca (USA); Pride and Prejudice (USA). **'41** That Hamilton Woman! (GB: Lady Hamilton); 49th Parallel (USA: The Invaders). **'44** Henry V (+dir; +prod; +co-sc). **'48** Hamlet (+dir; +prod). **'52** Carrie (USA). **'53** The Beggar's Opera. **'56** Richard III (+dir; +prod). **'57** The Prince and the Showgirl (+dir; +co-prod). **'60** The Entertainer. **'62** Term of Trial. **'65** Bunny Lake Is Missing; Othello. **'66** Khartoum. **'69** Oh! What a Lovely War. **'70** Three Sisters (+ dir). **'73** Sleuth. **'76** Marathon Man (USA). **'77** A Bridge Too Far. **'78** The Boys

From Brazil (USA). **'79** Dracula (USA). **'80** The Jazz Singer (USA). **'81** Clash of the Titans.

OLMI, Ermanno

(b. 1931). Director. Born: Bergamo, Italy

Olmi worked as a clerk in the Edison-Volta electric plant – very like one of his own under-privileged heroes – and stayed in the industry to direct and produce sponsored documentary films. In 1959 he made his first feature, *Time Stood Still*, a semi-documentary probing the relationship of two men guarding a dam in the Alps. His next two films, *Il Posto* and *I Fidanzati*, won him an international reputation, confirmed by his later work, of which *The Tree of Wooden Clogs* won the Palme d'Or at Cannes. Olmi's films have something in common with Italian neo-realism – he admits a debt to Rossellini – but their quietness, their unforced concern for people and their feeling for place and environment are very much his own.

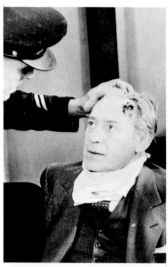

Above: Patrick O'Neal in Castle Keep.
Right: Henry O'Neill in The Getaway
(1941)

Films include: 1959 Il Tempo si è Fermato (GB: Time Stood Still). '61 Il Posto (USA: The Sound of Trumpets; GB: The Job). '63 I Fidanzati (USA: The Fiances; GB: The Engagement). '65 E Venne un Uomo (USA: And There Came a Man; GB: A Man Named John). '69 Un Certo Giorno (GB: One Fine Day). '70 I Recuperanti (orig. TV) (The Scavengers). '71 Durante l'Estate (orig. TV) (During the Summer). '74 La Circostanza (orig. TV) (USA-GB: The Circumstance). '78 L'Albero degli Zoccoli (USA/GB: The Tree of Wooden Clogs).

OLSEN & JOHNSON

Olsen, Ole (1892–1963). Actor. Born: John Sigvard Olsen; Peru, Indiana, USA

Johnson, Chic (1891–1962). Actor. Born: Harold Ogden Johnson; Chicago, Illinois, USA

On leaving Northwestern University, Ole Olsen went into vaudeville and met his lifelong comedy partner. Chic (short for Chicago) Johnson, a pianist, in the office of a music publisher.

They soon developed an ad-lib style that led on to a successful vaudeville career and a number of film appearances. Their big stage hit was *Hellzapoppin'*, a travelling revue which opened in 1938 and became a huge Broadway hit. The film version, hilariously anarchic and surreal (it's a film about the making of a film about a stage show), is affectionately remembered while Olsen and Johnson's eight other features are forgotten.

Feature films: 1930 Oh! Sailor, Behave. '31 Fifty Million Frenchmen; Gold Dust Gertie (GB: Why Change Your Husband?). '36 Country Gentlemen. '37 All Over Town. '42 Hellzapoppin'. '43 Crazy House. '44 Ghost Catchers. '45 See My Lawyer.

ONDRA, Anny

(b. 1903). Actress. Born: Anny Sophie Ondráková; Tarnow, Poland

The golden-haired, brown-eyed daughter of a Czech colonel in the Austro-Hungarian army, Anny Ondra married the actor-director Karel Lamač and became a star of Czech, Austrian and German films. She went to England in 1928, acted in a couple of Graham Cutts' films and played the heroine, pregnant by one man but married to another, in Hitchcock's last silent film, *The Manxman*. The first in a long line of erotic Hitchcockian blondes, she also appeared in his first sound film, *Blackmail*, as a girl who kills a man to save her virtue; her heavy accent necessitated a primitive form of dubbing and her brief spell in English-language films ended. But she continued her career, mainly in Germany, through the Thirties and occasionally thereafter, acting in a wide range of films from heavy drama to comic parody. Divorcing Lamač, she married ex-world heavyweight boxing champion Max Schmeling.

Films include: 1919 Dáma s malou nožkou. '22 Zigeunerliebe (A). '23 Únos bankéře Fuxe. '25 Ich liebe dich (GER). '28 God's Clay (GB); Glorious Youth (orig. title: Eileen of the Trees) (GB). '29 The Manxman (GB); Blackmail (GB). '31 Mamsell Nitouche (also French-language version) (GER-FR). '34 Klein Dorrit (GER). '35 Grossreinemachen (GER) (USA: General Housekeeping). '37 Der Unwiderstehliche (GER) (USA: The Irresistible Man). '51 Schön muss man sein (GER).

O'NEAL, Patrick

(b. 1927). Actor. Born: Ocala, Florida, USA

O'Neal reached the movies via the Neighborhood Playhouse, the Actors' Studio, and a stage part opposite Joan Blondell in *Come Back, Little Sheba*. He has played a number of villains on screen, a rather cruel cast of face helping him, but has occasionally broken away from this stereotype; he gave a notable performance as the art historian Captain Beckman in Sydney Pollack's hallucinatory *Castle Keep*. O'Neal was thoroughly chilling as the sinister Dale Cobra in *The Stepford Wives*, and if his lead in *The Kremlin Letter* was a shade undistinguished, this may well have been due to the poorish script.

Films include: 1965 In Harm's Way; King Rat. '66 Chamber of Horrors; Alvarez Kelly; A Fine Madness. '67 Matchless (IT). '68 Assignment to Kill; Where Were You When the Lights Went Out?; Castle Keep. '70 The Kremlin Letter; El Condor. '73 The Way We Were. '75 The Stepford Wives.

O'NEAL, Ryan

(b. 1941). Actor. Born: Patrick Ryan O'Neal; Los Angeles, California, USA

The son of Hollywood parents, Ryan O'Neal naturally drifted into showbusiness, starting as a stuntman (he is a good swimmer and boxer) and working his way through television series such as the everlasting *Peyton Place* before landing the role of Oliver Barrett IV in the box-office smash *Love Story*. He was much more fun (and certainly had much more fun) in *What's Up, Doc?* as the absent-minded professor; co-starred with his daughter Tatum in the very funny *Paper Moon*; and gave a taut, chilling performance as a gangsters' professional driver in *The Driver*. He is said to have done much of his own stunt work in this film, but this may be mere studio publicity. His acting has sharpened as his career has developed, and his later films have a honed-down keenness lacking in his earlier movies.

Films include: 1969 The Big Bounce. '70 The Games; Love Story. '72 What's Up, Doc? '73 Paper Moon. '75 Barry Lyndon (USA-GB). '76 Nickelodeon. '78 The Driver; Oliver's Story (GB-USA). '79 The Main Event. '81 Green Ice (GB). '82 Partners.

O'NEAL, Tatum

(b. 1963). Actress. Born: Los Angeles, California, USA

The daughter of actor Ryan O'Neal and his first wife, actress Joanna Moore, Tatum O'Neal went to live with her father when her parents divorced. She appeared with him in Peter Bogdanovich's *Paper Moon* as Addie Pray, a self-reliant orphan who teams up with a con-man, and won the Best Supporting Actress Oscar at the age of ten. She was paid a record fee for a child actor to play the girl baseball pitcher in *The Bad News Bears*, and she also appeared in Bogdanovich's comedy of early Hollywood, *Nickelodeon*. She started to grow up as the Olympic equestrian gold medallist in *International Velvet*, and was a teenager in a hurry to lose her virginity at summer camp in *Little Darlings*. In *Circle of Two* she played a girl involved in a relationship with an ageing artist (Richard Burton). Having survived child stardom, she now faces the problem of carving out an adult career.

Films: 1973 Paper Moon. '76 The Bad News Bears; Nickelodeon (GB-USA). '78 International Velvet (GB). '80 Little Darlings; Circle of Two.

O'NEILL, Henry

(1891–1961). Actor. Born: Henry Joseph O'Neill; Orange, New Jersey, USA

After World War I, Henry O'Neill entered the theatre and toured with a number of road shows before joining the Celtic Players and appearing with them in *The Playboy of the Western World* and *The Singer*. His first major Broadway role was as Paddy in Eugene O'Neill's *The Hairy Ape*. During the Depression he was offered a small role in the Hollywood movie *The Kennel Murder Case* and, from then on, he made films his career, only returning to the stage on a couple of occasions. Most of his films were for Warner Brothers and MGM, for whom he played character parts such as clerics, judges and lawyers. His most notable performances were as Father Xavier in *Anthony Adverse* and Colonel Piquart in *the Life of Emile Zola*.

Films include: 1933 The Kennel Murder Case. '34 Madame Dubarry. '36 Anthony Adverse; The Golden Arrow; The Life of Louis Pasteur. '37 The Life of Emile Zola. '41 Billy the Kid. '43 Girl Crazy. '45 Anchors Aweigh. '46 Three Wise Fools. '57 The Wings of Eagles.

O'NEILL, Jennifer

(b. 1949). Actress. Born: Rio de Janeiro, Brazil

On leaving school at 15, tall, leggy, chestnut-haired O'Neill became a model and within a few years was one of New York's best-known faces. Photographers queued to work with her and she appeared in all the national magazines, as well as on television advertising beauty products. After featuring on the cover of *Vogue* she was offered a film contract but refused it on the grounds that she was not interested in doing nude scenes or travelling. Nevertheless, she studied acting and finally accepted two minor roles before screen testing for Howard Hawks' *Rio Lobo*. Opposite John Wayne, O'Neill played a waif of the Texas plains. She went on to appear as Dorothy, who gently initiates a randy adolescent in *Summer of '42*, the film that established her as a star.

Films include: 1969 For Love of Ivy. '70 Rio Lobo. '71 Such Good Friends; Summer of '42. '72 Glass Houses; The Carey Treatment. '75 The Reincarnation of Peter Proud. '76 L'Innocente (FR-IT) (GB: The Innocent). '78 Cloud Dancer. '81 Scanners.

OPHULS, Marcel

(b. 1927). Director. Born: Marcel Oppenheimer; Frankfurt, Germany

The son of director Max Ophuls, Marcel spent his formative years in Hollywood. In 1950 he went to study philosophy at the Sorbonne, but abandoned that in favour of becoming assistant to Anatole Litvak and Julien Duvivier. He also worked for his father on the latter's last film, *Lola Montès* (1955). After three years with an American television company, Ophüls returned to France, where he met Jeanne Moreau, who agreed to finance his comedy *Peau de Banane*, starring herself and Jean-Paul Belmondo. Unfortunately, his next action-feature was a flop. He then spent three years working on *Le Chagrin et la Pitié*, a superb documentary

that attacked French collaboration during World War II and was subsequently banned in France for a number of years. *The Memory of Justice*, a film investigating Nazi atrocities, the French in Algeria and the Americans in Vietnam, was poorly received, and Ophuls has temporarily abandoned film-making in favour of the lecture circuit.

Films include: 1960 Matisse ou le Talent du Bonheur (short) (FR). '62 L'Amour à Vingt Ans *ep* Munich (GER-POL-FR-IT-JAP) (GB: Love at Twenty *ep* Munich). '63 Peau de Banane (FR-IT). '65 Feu à Volonté (FR-SP). '70 Le Chagrin et La Pitié (doc) (SWITZ-GER) (GB: The Sorrow and the Pity). '72 A Sense of Loss (doc) (USA-SWITZ). '75 The Memory of Justice (doc) (USA-GB-GER).

OPHULS, Max

(1902–1957). Director. Born: Max Oppenheimer; Saarbrücken, Germany

Max Ophuls ran away from home to become an actor and by the age of 23 was working as a director at the Vienna Burg-Theatre. By 1930 he was involved in films, becoming Anatole Litvak's dialogue director. With Hitler's rise to power, Ophuls and his family became nomads and he began directing his own films in France, Italy and America. By 1938 he had gained French citizenship and a few years later went to Hollywood where he won an international reputation with films such as *Letter From an Unknown Woman*, *Caught* and *The Reckless Moment*. Returning to France in 1950, he continued his successful career with *La Ronde*, *Madame de . . .* and *Lola Montès*. Ophuls has been described as being excessively romantic, but this never detracts from the unique dramatic style of his films. *Madame de . . .*, *The Reckless Moment*, *Letter From an Unknown Woman* and *Lola Montès* all show women being repressed and ultimately destroyed by the rigid morality of a hypocritical society. Although the subject was not unique

to Ophuls, his manner of dealing with it, using constantly moving cameras to capture the lushness of his decor, turned his films into ornate, seductive masterpieces.

Films include: 1932 Die verkaufte Braut. '36 Komedie om Geld (NETH). '40 De Mayerling à Sarajevo (FR) (GB: Sarajevo). '47 The Exile (USA). '48 Letter From an Unknown Woman (USA); Caught (USA). '49 The Reckless Moment (USA). '50 La Ronde (FR). '53 Madame de . . . (FR-IT). '55 Lola Montès (FR-GER) (GB: The Fall of Lola Montez).

ORRY-KELLY

(1897–1964). Costume designer. Born: Walter Orry Kelly; Kiama, New South Wales, Australia

For over thirty years Orry-Kelly was a leading Hollywood costume designer, his creations having a great influence on American women's styles. For example, the jumper he designed for Ingrid Bergman in *Casablanca* became one of the stardard looks of the Forties. He was an accomplished artist and experienced stage designer when he left Australia for the USA, joining Warner Brothers in 1923. From the Thirties on he became particularly associated with Bette Davis' and Kay Francis' films, his simplicity of line making him completely at ease with period and modern styles. His costumes for the Bette Davis movie *Jezebel* attracted particular publicity, especially the 'red' ballroom gown that Jezebel wears to shock her fiancé and the other guests. (Because the film was made in black and white, the dress looked black on film and had to be remade in another colour.) Orry-Kelly left Warners in 1943 and subsequently worked at 20th Century-Fox, Universal and MGM. He won three Oscars for best costume design – for the MGM musicals *An American in Paris* (shared with Walter Plunkett and Irene Sharaff) and *Les Girls* and Billy Wilder's *Some Like It Hot*.

Films include: 1935 Dangerous. '38 Jezebel. '39 Dark Victory. '41 The Little Foxes. '42

Above, left to right: Jennifer O'Neill in Such Good Friends; the director Max Ophuls; Maureen O'Sullivan as Jane, the most charming companion any apeman could wish for, in Tarzan Finds a Son (1939). Below: Peter O'Toole as Henry II with Richard Burton as the 'troublesome priest' in Becket. Right: Milo O'Shea in The Adding Machine. Below right: a studio publicity shot of Our Gang, the best-loved kids in Hollywood

Casablanca. '44 Mr Skeffington. '45 The Corn Is Green. '46 A Stolen Life. '51 An American in Paris (co-cost. des). '57 Les Girls. '59 Some Like It Hot. '62 Gypsy.

OSBORNE, John

(b. 1929). Playwright/screenwriter. Born: London, England

Although he began his career as an actor, John Osborne is known throughout the world as a playwright. His first play, *Look Back In Anger*, initiated the wave of 'Social Realism' plays which were to sweep the stage in the Sixties. He has worked on most of the script adaptations of his plays and wrote the original screenplay for the Oscar-winning *Tom Jones*.

Films include: 1959 Look Back In Anger (add. dial. only). '60 The Entertainer (co-sc). '63 Tom Jones. '68 Inadmissible Evidence. '70 Erste Liebe (actor only) (SWITZ-GER). '71 Get Carter (actor only). '74 Luther (play basis only) (GB-CAN-USA). '75 The Entertainer (play basis only) (USA). '78 Tomorrow Never Comes (actor only) (GB-CAN).

O'SHEA, Milo

(b. 1925). Actor. Born: Dublin, Ireland

Though spending most of his acting career in the theatre, Milo O'Shea has adapted easily and readily to the cinema. His best-known film role is, undoubtedly, that of Leopold Bloom in *Ulysses*, but he gave a fine performance as Friar Lawrence in *Romeo and Juliet*. He invests his character roles with flair and charm and has been much in demand as a television actor, having appeared in numerous plays and in his own comedy series, *Me Mammy*.

Films include: 1951 Talk of a Million (USA: You Can't Beat the Irish). '67 Ulysses. '68 Romeo and Juliet; Barbarella (FT-IT). '69 The Adding Machine. '70 The Angel Levine (USA); Loot. '72 The Hebrew Lesson (EIRE). '74 Percy's Progress. '79 Arabian Adventure. '82 The Verdict (USA).

OSHIMA, Nagisa

(b. 1932). Director. Born: Tsushima, Japan

The most celebrated – and the most notorious – of Japanese 'New Wave' directors, Oshima studied law at Kyoto University before joining the Shochiku studio in 1954 as an assistant. He made his first feature in 1959, and his first impact on Western audiences with *Boy* ten years later. Working independently since 1965, he has developed a style both experimental and formalist, with heavy political commitment. For Oshima, sex and politics are intertwined, and sexual frustration is paralleled by public violence. *Ai No Corrida* and *Ai No Borei*, both widely shown in the West, deal with people to whom love-making is a dominating passion; only by surrendering to it can they endure the oppression of society.

Films include: 1959 Ai To Kibo No Machi (USA/GB: A Town of Love and Hope). '60

Nihon no Yoru to Kiri (USA/GB: Night and Fog in Japan). '61 Shiiku (USA/GB: The Catch). '66 Hakachu no Torima (USA/GB: Violence at Noon); Ninja Bugeicho (USA/GB: Band of Ninja). '68 Koshikei (USA/GB: Death by Hanging). '69 Shinjuku Dorobo Nikki (USA: Diary of a Shinjuku Burglar; GB: Diary of a Shinjuku Thief); Shonen (USA/GB: Boy). '70 Gishiki (USA/GB: The Ceremony). '76 L'Empire des Sens/Ai No Corrida (FR-JAP) (USA/GB: In the Realm of the Senses/Empire of the Senses). '78 L'Empire de la Passion/Ai No Borei (FR-JAP) (GB: Empire of Passion). '83 Merry Christmas Mr Lawrence (USA).

O'SULLIVAN, Maureen

(b. 1911). Actress. Born: Boyle, Roscommon, Ireland

Maureen O'Sullivan left Ireland for Hollywood in 1930, when director Frank Borzage offered her a part in *Song o' My Heart*. She worked for Fox for a while, and then spent nine years at MGM. A petite, very pretty brunette, and a competent actress with the gift of sincerity, she played supporting roles in some of the company's major films, notably as Henrietta in *The Barretts of Wimpole Street* and Dora in *David Copperfield*, and was Jane to Johnny Weissmuller's Tarzan half a dozen times from 1932 to 1942. Then she retired to bring up her family. She was married to director John Farrow; they had seven children, among whom are actresses Mia and Tisa Farrow. Miss O'Sullivan did emerge from retirement occasionally, however, to work on the Broadway stage and in a few films. She was charming as ever in Boetticher's *The Tall T*; the years seemed to have passed her by.

Films include: 1930 Song o' My Heart. '32 Payment Deferred; Tarzan the Ape Man. '34 The Barretts of Wimpole Street; Tarzan and His Mate. '35 David Copperfield; Anna Karenina. '37 A Day at the Races. '38 A Yank at Oxford. '40 Pride and Prejudice. '53 All I Desire. '57 The Tall T. '65 Never Too Late.

O'TOOLE, Peter

(b. 1932). Actor. Born: Peter Seamus O'Toole; Connemara, Galway, Ireland

Tall and fair-haired with child-like blue eyes, O'Toole studied at RADA, becoming at 23 the Bristol Old Vic's youngest ever leading man before the title role in David Lean's *Lawrence of Arabia* made him an international star. In performance, O'Toole's mock-heroic gestures, like the Emperor's New Clothes, seem to reveal rather than conceal a naked insecurity. His remarkable, almost feminine, handsomeness of feature makes the disclosure of inadequacy doubly disturbing, and not surprisingly critics have periodically castigated him for being self-indulgent as an actor. Though such criticisms (fuelled by stories of his heavy drinking) have some validity, he can be an arresting performer on stage and on film, a fact reflected by his having been nominated for a Best Actor Oscar six times – for his roles in *Lawrence of Arabia*, *Becket*, *The Lion in Winter*, *Goodbye Mr Chips*, *The Ruling Class* and *The Stunt Man*.

Films include: 1960 Kidnapped. '62 Lawrence of Arabia. '64 Becket. '65 Lord Jim; What's New, Pussycat? (USA-FR). '66 How to Steal a Million (USA). '67 The Night of the Generals (GB-FR). '68 The Lion in Winter. '69 Goodbye Mr Chips. '71 Murphy's War; Under Milk Wood. '72 The Ruling Class. '80 The Stunt Man (USA). '82 My Favorite Year (USA).

OUR GANG

Comedy group in series of same name (1922–1944).

The Our Gang series was originated by comedy producer Hal Roach, who decided in 1922 to present a group of children behaving as children actually do, instead of performing precociously in Hollywood style. The series grew out of the Sunshine Sammy comedies, starring young Ernie Morrison as a somewhat stereotyped black boy. He was joined by Allen Clayton 'Farina' Hoskins, who played his tomboy sister (it is claimed that not even Roach knew that the 'girl' was a boy dressed up by an enterprising mother), Mickey Daniels, Jackie Condon, Joe Cobb and the romantic interest, Mary Kornman. Our Gang made 96 silent two-reel shorts and survived the transition to sound, with regular changes of personnel, including the brief addition of future star Jackie Cooper in 1929, and the takeover of the leadership by Spanky McFarland in 1932. Their *Bored of Education* won a Short Subject Oscar in 1936. In 1938 Roach sold the series to MGM, after which it became sugary and moralistic instead of funny, and it gradually declined. The Roach shorts have been re-run on American television under the title *The Little Rascals*, since MGM retained the rights to the *Our Gang* title.

Films include: 1928 Growing Pains. '31 Dogs Is Dogs. '35 Maria's Little Pirates. '36 Pay as You Exit; General Spanky (feature). '37 Framing Youth; Night n' Gales; Mail and Female; Our Gang Follies of 1938. '38 Three Men in a Tub.

OUSPENSKAYA, Maria

(1876–1949). Actress. Born: Tulia, nr. Moscow, Russia

After drama studies and touring in a stock company, Maria Ouspenskaya joined the Moscow Art Theatre in 1911, eventually becoming an instructor. Stanislavsky took his players on tour in the USA in 1923 and Ouspenskaya decided to stay on. At first best-known as a theatre actress and teacher, she re-created her stage role in the film version of *Dodsworth*, receiving an Academy Award nomination for Best Supporting Actress, and beginning a Hollywood career that more than once involved her playing roles as ballet teachers and countesses, and lasted until her death from an accident brought about by smoking in bed. Her formidable Russian presence enlivened many a film.

Films include: 1936 Dodsworth. '37 Conquest (GB: Marie Walewska). '39 Love Affair; The Rains Came; Judge Hardy and Son. '40 Dr Ehrlich's Magic Bullet; Waterloo Bridge; The Mortal Storm; The Man I Married; Dance, Girl, Dance. '41 Kings Row. '48 A Kiss in the Dark.

OWEN, Seena

(1896–1966). Actress. Born: Signe Auen; Spokane, Washington, USA

Of Danish origin, blonde and blue-eyed, Seena Owen played the Princess Beloved in the Babylonian sequences of D. W. Griffith's *Intolerance*. The cinematographer Billy Bitzer called her 'a truly beautiful girl who needed no help from the camera'. While making the film, Griffith is said to have helped bring about her marriage to fellow actor George Walsh (which

ended in divorce in 1924). Her last important role was in Erich von Stroheim's *Queen Kelly*, with Gloria Swanson. Although Seena Owen retired from acting with the coming of sound, she followed the example of her sister, screenwriter Lillie Hayward, and turned her hand to scripts and original stories for the movies during the Thirties and Forties.

Films include: 1914 Out of the Air. '15 Penitentes. '16 Intolerance. '17 Madame Bo-Peep. '20 The Price of Redemption. '22 Sisters. '26 The Flame of the Yukon; Shipwrecked. '28 The Blue Danube; Queen Kelly. '41 Aloma of the South Seas (co-sc. only). '47 Carnegie Hall (co-sc. only).

OZEP, Fedor

(1895–1948). Director. Born: Moscow, Russia

Fedor Ozep (whose name is also transliterated as Fyodor Otsep) adapted Pushkin's *The Queen of Spades* for the director Yakov Protozanov while still a college student. He was made artistic supervisor of the Russ film cooperative in 1918, continuing to write scripts, including the science-fiction film *Aelita*. Ozep turned director and collaborated with Boris Barnet on the three-part adventure serial *Miss Mend*. He then went to Germany to direct the co-production *The Living Corpse*, based on Tolstoy's play, and stayed to make his best-known film, *The Brothers Karamazov*, from Dostoyevsky's novel. Forced to move on to France, where he directed several films, he was interned for a while at the start of World War II and then made his way to Canada and the USA, where he directed his last films, including a Russo-American love story and a tense thriller.

Films include: 1916 Pikovaia Dama (co-sc. only) (GB: The Queen of Spades). '19 Polik-

ushka (co-sc. only). '24 Aelita (co-sc. only). '26 Miss Mend (co-dir; +co-sc.). '28 Kukla s Millionami (co-sc. only) (The Doll With Millions); Zemlya v Plenu (Earth in Chains/The Yellow Passport). '29 Zhivoi Trup/Der lebende Leichnam (USSR-GER) (GB: The Living Corpse). '31 Der Mörder Dimitri Karamazov (GER) (GB: The Brothers Karamazov). '44 Three Russian Girls (co-dir) (USA) (GB: She Who Dares). '47 Whispering City (CAN).

OZU, Yasujiro

(1903–1963). Director. Born: Tokyo, Japan

Drunken and unruly at school, Ozu failed all his exams and became a village schoolteacher. Rescued from this fate by a relative, he started as an assistant cameraman at the Shochiku company's Kamata studios in Tokyo in 1924. He became an assistant director in 1926 and directed his first film in 1927. Many of his early films were student comedies, gangster thrillers and melodramas. Some of his early Thirties films had sound but no dialogue; he did not make his first talkie until 1936. He had by then begun to explore his main concern – Japanese family life and the relationships between the generations. His style was restrained and simple, with an almost static camera, generally at a low-angle point of view. His career was interrupted by World War II, when he worked on propaganda documentaries in Singapore and spent six months as a prisoner of war. From 1949 he resumed his working relationship with Kogo Noda, who had written many of his earlier scenarios, and together they co-scripted Ozu's remaining 13 films, which included most of those well known in the West. Ozu began filming in colour in 1958, using it with great expressive beauty in his last half-dozen films. He remained unmarried, indulged by an affectionate mother, and had little direct personal experience of the complex Japanese family life that he depicted with unmatched sympathy and skill.

Films include: 1927 Zange no Yaiba (The Sword of Penitence). '29 Wakaki Hi (Days of Youth). '31 Tokyo no Gassho (Tokyo Chorus). '32 Umarete wa Mita Keredo (USA/GB: I Was Born, But . . .). '33 Dekigokoro (USA: Passing Fancy). '35 Tokyo no Yado (An Inn in Tokyo). '36 Hitori Musuko (USA: The Only Son). '41 Toda-ke no Kyodai (USA: The Brothers and Sisters of the Toda Family). '48 Kaze no Naka no Mendori (A Hen in the Wind). '49 Banshun (USA: Late Spring). '52 Ochazuke no Aji (USA: The Flavor of Green Tea Over Rice). '53 Tokyo Monogatari (USA/GB: Tokyo Story). '56 Soshun (USA/GB: Early Spring). '58 Higanbana (+co-sc) (USA: Equinox Flower). '59 Ohayo (USA: Ohayo; GB: Good Morning); Ukigusa (USA: Floating Weeds). '61 Kohayagawa-ke no Aki (USA: Early Autumn/The End of Summer). '62 Samma no Aji (USA/GB: An Autumn Afternoon).

Above left: the tiny, bird-like figure of Maria Ouspenskaya in a typical character role in the Forties. Left: Seena Owen with Matthew Betz in The Flame of the Yukon

P

PABST, G. W.

(1885–1967). Director. Born: Georg Wilhelm Pabst; Raudnitz, Bohemia (now Czechoslovakia)

Pabst studied as an engineer but preferred the theatre and by 1905 was acting in Switzerland. In 1910 he went to America and his experiences as a member of a performing German-language troupe controlled by labour unions fired his artistic interest in social problems. After internment in France during World War I, he returned to the stage and in 1921 began acting for and assisting film director Carl Froelich. In 1923, with a medieval tale called *The Treasure*, he began a 33-year career as a director himself, achieving his major successes in the years 1926 to 1931. Unlike his great contemporaries Fritz Lang and F. W. Murnau, Pabst was largely unswayed by the Expressionist movement in German arts, but opted instead for a powerful realism – the better to explore the social themes that preoccupied him in such films as *The Joyless Street* (poverty and exploitation), *The Love of Jeanne Ney* (communism and bourgeois decadence), *Westfront 1918* and *Kameradschaft* (war and nationalism). But Pabst possessed a romantic spirit, too. *Pandora's Box*, which immortalized Louise Brooks as Lulu, is one of the most splendidly erotic films ever made, and *The Threepenny Opera* is a delightful and atmospheric version of the Soho underworld fantasy. The latter, like *Westfront 1918*, was banned by the Nazis, but, although Pabst had brief sojourns in France and the USA, he remained in Germany for the duration of the war, producing little of note. His last, postwar films revealed only his apparent directionlessness. If Pabst is not, in the final analysis, a great film-maker, he was at the very least the maker of some of the cinema's most memorable films: *The Joyless Street*, *Pandora's Box*, *Westfront 1918* and *Kameradschaft*.

Films include: 1923 Der Schatz (USA: The Treasure). '25 Die freudlose Gasse (USA: Streets of Sorrow; GB: The Joyless Street). '26 Geheimnisse einer Seele (USA: Secrets of the Soul; GB: Secrets of a Soul). '27 Die Liebe der Jeanne Ney (USA: Loves of Jeanne Ney; GB: The Love of Jeanne Ney). '28 Begierde/Abwege (GB: Crisis). '29 Die Büchse der Pandora (USA/GB: Pandora's Box); Das Tage-buch einer Verlorenen (GB: Diary of a Lost Girl/Diary of a Lost One). '30 Westfront 1918 (USA: Comrades of 1918; GB: West Front, 1918). '31 Die Dreigroschenoper (GER-USA) (GB: The Threepenny Opera); Kameradschaft (GER-FR) (USA: Comradeship). '33 Don Quichotte (FR) (+English version: Don Quixote). '34 A Modern Hero (USA). '55 Der letzte Akt (A) (USA: The Last Ten Days; GB: Ten Days to Die).

PACINO, Al

(b. 1940). Actor. Born: Alberto Pacino; New York City, USA

Pacino – dark, serious and good-looking – has been an intense and moody anti-hero in the American cinema since the early Seventies when he gave remarkable performances as Michael Corleone in both parts of *The Godfather*. Despite the presence of Brando and De Niro, Pacino was the lifeblood of that saga, the most human male character in it. This superb actor's dedication to his craft is not in doubt but it has been less well-publicized than that of De Niro (Pacino's major contemporary), and he has avoided the trappings of stardom. However, his performances in *The Godfather* films and Sidney Lumet's *Serpico*, as a solitary hippie cop, and *Dog Day Afternoon*, as a bankrobber, suggest there may be no more relevant actor working in the urban battlegrounds of modern American films. Of Sicilian descent, Pacino spent his childhood at the movies and acted out the fantasies he saw on the screen for his grandmother and for his classmates. He joined a children's theatre, acted in experimental workshops, dropped out of the High School of Performing Arts, and drifted from job to job before, in 1966, he was accepted by the Actors' Studio. His screen debut was in *Me, Natalie*. Pacino carefully chooses his parts and when not making films works in the theatre. He received Oscar nominations in consecutive years for *The Godfather*, *Serpico*, *The Godfather, Part II* and *Dog Day Afternoon*, and also for *...And Justice for All*. In 1982 he moved into domestic comedy with *Author! Author!*

Films: 1969 Me, Natalie. '71 The Panic in Needle Park. '72 The Godfather. '73 Scarecrow; Serpico. '74 The Godfather, Part II. '75 Dog Day Afternoon. '77 Bobby Deerfield. '80 . . . And Justice for All; Cruising. '82 Author! Author!

PAGE, Geneviève

(b. 1931). Actress. Born: Geneviève Bonjean; Paris, France

A beautiful blonde with a colourful, outspoken personality, Geneviève Page, the god-daughter of the couturier Christian Dior, studied acting at the Paris Conservatoire. A member of the French National Theatre and the Jean-Louis Barrault company in Paris, she has become a leading French stage actress, specializing in classical and tragic roles. Since 1950 she has made some interesting excursions into films, with a particularly memorable performance as the madam in *Belle de Jour*.

Films include: 1950 Ce Siècle à Cinquante Ans. '55 Cherchez la Femme. '56 The Silken Affair (GB). '60 Song Without End (USA). '61 El Cid (USA-IT). '65 Trois Chambres à Manhattan (USA: Three Rooms in Manhattan). '67 Belle de Jour (FR-IT). '68 Decline and Fall . . . of a Birdwatcher (GB); Mayerling (GB-FR). '70 The Private Life of Sherlock Holmes (GB).

Below left: Al Pacino in Serpico.
Below: Geneviève Page in The Private Life of Sherlock Holmes

PAGE, Geraldine

(b. 1924). Actress. Born: Kirkville, Missouri, USA

Geraldine Page is one of the USA's finest actresses, having been nominated three times as Best Supporting Actress (for *Hondo*, *You're a Big Boy Now* and *Pete 'n' Tillie*) and three times as Best Actress (for *Summer and Smoke*, *Sweet Bird of Youth* and *Interiors*) despite the fact that movies have taken second place to the theatre in her distinguished career. The daughter of an osteopath, she won a scholarship to the Chicago Academy of Fine Arts, then enrolled in the Goodman Theatre Dramatic School. Her performance as a strong-minded widow opposite John Wayne in *Hondo* made her name (she was touted as a 'second Grace Kelly, with a sexy sizzle under a cool exterior'). However, she refused to become sucked into the Hollywood star system, preferring to pick and choose her roles. In films she has tended to portray unhappy or frustrated women on the verge of mental breakdown, although she revealed a lighter side in the Disney musical comedy *The Happiest Millionaire*. In addition to many stage awards, she won Emmys for her performances in the television plays *A Christmas Memory* and *The Thanksgiving Visitor*. The actor Rip Torn became her second husband in 1963. She was previously married to violinist Alexander Schneider.

Films include: 1953 Taxi; Hondo. '61 Summer and Smoke. '62 Sweet Bird of Youth. '66 You're a Big Boy Now. '67 The Happiest Millionaire. '69 Trilogy. '71 The Beguiled. '72 Pete 'n' Tillie. '78 Interiors. '81 Harry's War.

PAGET, Debra

(b. 1933). Actress. Born: Debralee Griffin; Denver, Colorado, USA

With red-gold hair, large eyes and a stunning figure, Debra Paget had the looks to make it big in Hollywood. However, though she was signed up by 20th Century-Fox in her teens and made a fair debut opposite Richard Conte in *Cry of the City*, her career has been erratic. Her best early roles were as exotic young girls – a Red Indian squaw in *Broken Arrow* and *The Last Hunt* and a South Sea Island chief's daughter married to a white man (Louis Jourdan) in *Bird of Paradise* – and her subsequent roles were never strong enough for her to escape this tag. She gave perhaps her finest performance for Fritz Lang in his adventure films set in India, *Der Tiger von Eschnapur* and *Das indische Grabmal*, her leading role as Seetha culminating in an erotic dance with a snake. Briefly the wife (for 22 days) of director Budd Boetticher, she has since married an oil magnate and retired from the screen.

Films include: 1948 Cry of the City. '50 Broken Arrow. '51 Anne of the Indies. '52 Les Miserables. '54 Princess of the Nile. '56 The Last Hunt. '57 The River's Edge. '59 Der Tiger von Eschnapur and Das indische Grabmal (GER-FR-IT) (USA, single feature: Journey to the Lost City/Tigress of Bengal; GB, single feature: Tiger of Bengal). '63 The Terror; The Haunted Palace.

PAGNOL, Marcel

(1895–1974). Playwright/ screenwriter/director. Born: Aubagne, Marseille, France

Pagnol began writing plays as a teenager and, following the success of his *Les Marchands de Gloire* in Paris, decided to give up his teaching career to concentrate on writing. A string of further successes gave him the financial resources to set up his own studio, labs and production and distribution company. The movies that resulted were essentially cinematic records of theatrical performances, but were distinguished by Pagnol's affectionate view of the joys and sorrows of French provincial life in the South of France, his gift for witty dialogue and character observation and by the excellent performances of actors such as Raimu, Fernandel and Pierre Fresnay (who consequently became international stars). His Marius Trilogy – *Marius* (co-directed with Alexander Korda), *Fanny* (directed by Marc Allégret) and *César* (directed by Pagnol himself) – was hugely successful all over the world. Pagnol went on to write and direct such films as *Merlusse* and *La Femme du Boulanger* that have since become classics of the French cinema. Pagnol also wrote novels and an autobiography, suitably entitled for one whose artistic output was so large, *The Days Were Too Short*. He was successively married to the actresses Orane Demazis (Fanny in the Marius Trilogy), Josette Day and Jacqueline Bouvier, the last of whom frequently appeared in his films under the name of Jacqueline Pagnol.

Films include: 1931 Marius (co-dir; +sc). '32 Fanny (sc). '33 Un Direct au Coeur; Jofroi (dir; +sc). '34 Angèle (dir; +sc). '35 Merlusse (dir; +sc). '36 César (dir; +sc); Topaze (dir; +sc). '38 La Femme du Boulanger (dir; +sc) (GB: The Baker's Wife); Schpoutz (dir; +sc). '52 Manon des Sources (dir; +sc) (GB: Manon of the Springs).

PAIGE, Janis

(b. 1922). Actress. Born: Donna Mae Tjaden; Tacoma, Washington, USA

Following the divorce of her parents, Janis Paige moved to Hollywood with her mother, entertaining the troops as a waitress/singer at the Hollywood Canteen. She was soon contracted to Warner Brothers, making her first movie appearance in *Bathing Beauty* in 1944, but grew dissatisfied with supporting roles (she was usually cast as the second lead's girlfriend) and decided to concentrate on the stage. She built up a reputation as an energetic musical star, scoring a huge success in *The Pajama Game* on Broadway in 1954. She returned to Hollywood with a good role as 'America's Swimming Sweetheart', Peggy Dainton, in *Silk Stockings*. In addition to film and stage work, she has appeared extensively on television, having had her own series in the Fifties, *It's Always Jan*. Her third husband was composer/lyricist Ray Gilbert who won an Oscar for Zip-a-Dee-Doo-Dah from Walt Disney's feature *Song of the South* (1947).

Films include: 1944 Bathing Beauty; Hollywood Canteen. '46 Of Human Bondage. '47 Cheyenne. '49 The House Across the Street. '51 Mr Universe. '57 Silk Stockings. '60 Please Don't Eat the Daisies. '61 Bachelor in Paradise. '67 Welcome to Hard Times (GB: Killer on a Horse).

PAINLEVÉ, Jean

(b. 1902). Documentarist. Born: Paris, France

The only son of the mathematician and politician Paul Painlevé (1863–1933), Painlevé studied medicine and then became interested in the possibilities of filming scientific subjects. He made his first film, *Evolution de l'Oeuf*, in 1925 and five years later co-founded L'Institut du Cinéma Scientifique. His underwater films proved especially popular and, like all his work, were characterized by photographic expertise and an imaginative, witty presentation of factual information. Painlevé's films and his efforts to advise and finance likeminded film-makers have done much to reveal the educational possibilities of cinema.

Films include: 1925 Evolution d'un Oeuf. '26 La Pieuvre. '27 Le Bernard-l'Ermite. '28 Oursins. '29 Crabes. '30–'39 La Chirurgie Correctrice et Réparatrice. '33 L'Hippocampe Géologique (GB: The Sea Horse). '36 Evolution de la Chaîne des Alpes. '38 Barbe Bleu (co-dir). '45 Le Vampire. '46 Jeux d'Enfants.

PAKULA, Alan J.

(b. 1928). Producer/director. Born: New York City, USA

Pakula has said of his film *Starting Over*: 'A man and a woman committing themselves to a life together is one of the most heroic acts in the world.' This statement is indicative of the maturity of outlook and thoughtful concern with the individual in (an often inimical) society displayed in Pakula's best work. The son of a printing and advertising executive, Pakula studied liberal arts with a major in drama at Yale University. He then worked as an assistant to the head of Warner Brothers Cartoons and in 1950 became an assistant producer at MGM. He moved to Paramount, producing a series of films directed by Robert Mulligan, including *Fear Strikes Out*, *To Kill a Mockingbird*, *Inside Daisy Clover* and *The Stalking Moon*. Pakula moved into directing with *The Sterile Cuckoo*, a well-observed story of young love on a college campus starring Liza Minnelli. His next film, *Klute*, a steely thriller with compelling performances by Donald Sutherland as a detective and Jane Fonda as a call girl, established his reputation with critics and public alike. *Klute*'s prevailing atmosphere of paranoia and corruption was explored more directly in Pakula's 'political' films, *The Parallax View* and *All the President's Men*. In his subsequent films, the Western *Comes a Horseman* and a light-hearted study of divorce and reconciliation, *Starting Over*, Pakula has maintained his record as one of Hollywood's most intelligent film-makers.

Films include: 1957 Fear Strikes out (prod). '62 To Kill a Mockingbird (prod). '65 Inside Daisy Clover (prod). '68 The Stalking Moon (prod). '69 The Sterile Cuckoo (dir). '71 Klute (dir; +prod). '73 Love and Pain and the Whole Damn Thing (dir; +prod). '74 The Parallax View (dir; +prod). '76 All the President's Men (dir). '78 Comes a Horseman (dir). '79 Starting Over (dir).

PAL, George

(1908–1980). Producer/director. Born: Georg Pál; Cegled, Hungary

Pal graduated with a degree in architecture from the Budapest Academy of Arts and then moved to Eindhoven, Holland to work for a leading advertising agency. He made his first films there – cigarette advertisements in which he experimented with photography and cartoons. He sub-

Above left: Geraldine Page as the neurotic headmistress of a girls' school in The Beguiled, *a torrid drama with an American Civil War setting. Left: Debra Paget in a typical role as Princess of the Nile. Above: the exuberant Janis Paige, looking for a*

husband in Follow the Boys *(1963). Below left: Lilli Palmer in the eighteenth-century romp* The Amorous Adventures of Moll Flanders. *Above: Jack Palance. Right: Eugene Pallette in Frank Capra's* Mr Smith Goes to Washington

sequently introduced a third dimension to his work by using a patented method of animating puppets. The results proved so successful that he decided to go to Hollywood in 1939. He won a contract with Paramount and between 1941 and 1947 produced the famous *Puppetoons* series of short films. He then worked as the producer, head of special effects and later director of science-fiction and fantasy movies, winning Oscars for special effects on *Destination Moon, When Worlds Collide, War of the Worlds, Tom Thumb* and *The Time Machine.*

Films include: 1941 Gaye Knighties (short) (prod). **'42** Jasper and the Choo-Choo (short) (prod). **'43** Good Night, Rusty (short) (prod). **'44** And to Think I Saw It on Mulberry Street (short) (prod). **'47** Tubby the Tuba (short) (prod). **'50** Destination Moon (prod; + sp. eff). **'51** When Worlds Collide (prod; + sp. eff). **'53** War of the Worlds (prod; + special eff). **'54** The Naked Jungle (prod). **'58** Tom Thumb (prod; + sp. eff). **'60** The Time Machine (dir; + prod; + sp. eff). **'62** The Wonderful World of the Brothers Grimm (co-dir; + sp. eff). **'68** The Power (prod). **'75** Doc Savage, Man of Bronze (prod; + co-sc).

PALANCE, Jack

(b. 1918). Actor. Born: Vladimir Palanuik; Lattimer, Pennsylvania, USA

Vladimir Palanuik (the real name of Jack Palance comes in several variations) was the son of a Ukrainian coal miner, an outstanding athlete, and a pilot in World War II. After being badly burned in a crash, he underwent plastic surgery whose results are still visible in his taut, angular features. After the war he went on the New York stage, understudied Anthony Quinn in Elia Kazan's production of *A Streetcar Named Desire,* and impressed Kazan enough to be invited to Hollywood to act in that director's *Panic in the Streets.* In 1953 Palance made his real impact as the gunfighter, Wilson, in *Shane.* His menacing looks and quiet voice made him an impressive actor, too ambiguous and disturbing to be confined forever to heavies, and his later successes were proof of real versatility: the blackmailed film star in *The Big Knife,* the outlaw in *I Died a Thousand Times* and the neurotic producer in Godard's *Contempt.*

Films include: 1950 Panic in the Steets. **'52** Sudden Fear. **'53** Shane; Arrowhead; Second Chance. **'55** The Big Knife; I Died a Thousand Times. **'59** Ten Seconds to Hell (USA-GB). **'60** Austerlitz (FR-IT-YUG) (GB: The Battle of Austerlitz). **'63** Le Mépris (FR-IT) (USA/GB: Contempt). **'65** Once a Thief (FR-USA). **'66** The Professionals. **'72** Chato's Land (GB). **'79** Cocaine Cowboys.

PALLETTE, Eugene

(1889–1954). Actor. Born: Winfield, Kansas, USA

On leaving Culver Military Academy, Eugene Pallette served a gruelling apprenticeship in touring companies before becoming a Hollywood extra and eventually a lead actor. But his love of food and refusal to diet led to an unheroically portly figure and he was demoted to supporting roles, in which he continued to work regularly until the mid-Forties. His deep, foghorn voice became a character asset in the Thirties, when he played rotund, witty types or sometimes elderly men to whom life had brought tragedy or disappointment. He is reputed to have led a semi-reclusive life on a ranch in Oregon for several years, prepared to stave off any anticipated attacks, until he tired of the loneliness in 1948 and made one last return to the screen. In *The Adventures of Robin Hood* Pallette provided the screen's best Friar Tuck.

Films include: 1915 The Birth of a Nation. **'16** Intolerance. **'20** Parlor, Bedroom and Bath. **'21** The Three Musketeers. **'34** Caravan; The Dragon Murder Case; One Exciting Adventure. **'35** Steamboat Round the Bend; All the King's Horses; The Ghost Goes West. **'36** My Man Godfrey. **'37** Clarence; 100 Men and a Girl. **'38** The Adventures of Robin Hood. **'39** Mr Smith Goes to Washington. **'41** The Lady Eve; Swamp Water (GB: The Man Who Came Back). **'43** Heaven Can Wait. **'48** Silver River.

PALMER, Lilli

(1914–1986). Actress. Born: Lillie Marie Peiser; Posen, Germany (now Poland)

Lilli Palmer began her acting career in Germany, but left for France in 1933 and two years later made her film debut in Britain. She stayed for ten years, and then accompanied her husband, Rex Harrison, to Hollywood, where for the first time she had good parts in films of value, notably in Fritz Lang's *Cloak and Dagger* and Robert Rossen's *Body and Soul.* After that interlude she spent the next thirty years working in many countries, but never again received parts worthy of her talents. She was slight, slim and exquisitely refined in youth, and she remained gracious and lovely until her death in 1986.

Films include: 1936 The Secret Agent (GB). **'37** Command Performance (GB). **'45** The Rake's Progress (GB) (USA: Notorious Gentleman). **'46** Cloak and Dagger (USA). **'47** Body and Soul. **'58** Mädchen in Uniform (GER). **'65** Operation Crossbow (GB-IT); The Amorous Adventures of Moll Flanders (GB). **'68** Oedipus the King (GB). **'75** Lotte en Weimar (GER). **'78** The Boys From Brazil (USA).

PALUZZI, Luciana

(b. 1937). Actress. Born: Luciana Paoluzzi; Rome, Italy

Paluzzi's film debut was in a small part as a country girl in *Three Coins in the Fountain*. She came to England for *No Time to Die*, was briefly under contract to Rank, and then made an American film or two before returning to Europe to play a very nasty lady in *Thunderball*. Since then she has appeared in many British, American and Italian films, mainly totally forgettable ones, and she briefly starred in the television series *Fivefingers*. But early in her career she was in Fritz Lang's *Der Tiger von Eschnapur* (1959, *Tiger of Bengal*), and now that that film has been rescued from the butchery first practised on it by British distributors, Paluzzi can at least look back on one good performance in a film certain to survive. She was formerly married to actor Brett Halsey.

Films include: 1954 Three Coins in the Fountain; J'Avais Sept Filles (FR-IT) (GB: I Had Seven Daughters). **'57** La Donne Che Venne dal Mare (IT-FR). **'58** No Time to Die (GB); Sea Fury (GB). **'65** Questa Volta Parliamo di Uomini (USA: Let's Talk About Men); Thunderball. **'67** The Venetian Affair; Chuka. **'69** Captain Nemo and the Underwater City (GB); Noventi-Nueve Mujeres (SP-GER-GB-IT) (GB: 99 Women). **'78** The Greek Tycoon.

PANAMA, Norman

(b. 1914). Screenwriter/producer/director. Born: Chicago, Illinois, USA

Norman Panama and Melvin Frank were fellow students at the University of Chicago, and soon afterwards teamed up to write radio comedy for Milton Berle and Bob Hope. In 1941 Panama and Frank sold the story, *My Favourite Blonde* (1942), to Paramount, and a prolific screenwriting partnership began. In the Fifties they produced and directed from their own scripts until, early in the Sixties, they went their separate ways. Panama as a solo director seldom reached the level of the team's best work (though Frank went on to the success of *A Touch of Class*, 1973), and most of his films were limp marital comedies. But the comedies he and Frank wrote for Bob Hope are among the comedian's best films. *White Christmas* is a classic musical, and *Li'l Abner* (1959), which they directed and produced from their own Broadway musical, based on the Al Capp comic strip, has marvellous numbers directed with enormous verve.

Films include: 1944 The Road to Utopia (co-sc). **'46** Monsieur Beaucaire (co-sc). **'48** Mr Blandings Builds His Dream House (co-prod; +co-sc). **'50** The Reformer and the Redhead (co-dir; +co-prod; +co-sc). **'51** Strictly Dishonourable (co-dir; +co-prod; +co-sc); Callaway Went Thataway (co-dir; +co-prod; +co-sc) (GB: The Star Said No). **'54** Knock On Wood (dir); White Christmas (co-sc). **'56** That Certain Feeling (co-dir; +co-prod; +co-sc). **'60** The Facts of Life (dir). **'62** The Road to Hong Kong (GB) (prod; +co-sc). **'66** Not With My Wife, You Don't (dir). **'69** How to Commit Marriage (dir); The Maltese Bippy (dir). **'76** I Will, I Will . . . For Now.

PANGBORN, Franklin

(1893–1958). Actor. Born: Newark, New Jersey, USA

Pangborn had only one act, but he played it joyously in many Hollywood movies. He was cast as a shop-assistant, a hotel clerk, or minor functionary, appearing neat, prissy, beautifully spoken, and disdainful of almost everyone. His character would then come under pressure, and dissolve into misery. Producers appreciated such actors in those days, and Pangborn found his way into the best movies of his day – *Mr Deeds Goes to Town*, *My Man Godfrey*, *A Star Is Born*, *Stage Door*. Preston Sturges loved Pangborn, and used him whenever he could; so did W. C. Fields, a master of anarchy to whom Pangborn's orderliness was an irresistible target. The sufferings of Pangborn's bank examiner at the hands of Fields in *Bank Dick* have to be seen to be believed.

Films include: 1936 My Man Godfrey; Mr Deeds Goes to Town. **'37** A Star Is Born; Stage Door. **'38** Three Blind Mice. **'40** The Bank Dick (GB: The Bank Detective). **'41** Never Give a Sucker an Even Break (GB: What a Man); Sandy Steps Out. **'42** George Washington Slept Here. **'45** The Horn Blows at Midnight; You Came Along. **'47** Calendar Girl. **'50** Tea for Two. **'57** Oh, Men! Oh, Women!

PAPAS, Irene

(b. 1926). Actress. Born: Irene Lelekou; Corinth, Greece

A striking beauty in the classical vein, Papas was one of Greece's leading actresses by the age of 22. She has since become an international star, working in Europe and in the USA. She is a magnificent actress, usually in tragic or heavily dramatic roles. Her finest performances have been as the widow in *Zorba the Greek*, as the wife of the assassinated politician in *Z*, and as Electra, Helen and Iphigenia in the Greek tragedies she made with Michael Cacoyannis. She went into political exile in the late Sixties, and worked passionately to arouse opinion against the military régime in Greece.

Films include: 1953 Le Infedeli (IT) (USA/GB: The Unfaithfuls). **'55** Atilla, Flagello di Dio (IT-FR) (USA/GB: Attila the Hun). **'56** Tribute to a Bad Man (USA). **'61** The Guns of Navarone (GB). **'62** Electra. **'64** The Moon-Spinners (GB); Zorba the Greek (GREECE-USA). **'67** A Ciascuno il Suo (IT) (USA: To Each His Own). **'69** Z (FR-ALG). **'71** The Trojan Women (USA). **'77** Iphigenia. **'79** Bloodline (USA-GER); Christo si è Fermato a Eboli (IT-FR) (USA: Eboli; GB: Christ Stopped at Eboli). **'81** Lion of the Desert (GB-LIBYA).

PARADZHANOV, Sergei

(b. 1924). Director. Born: Tbilisi, Georgia, USSR

The poetic cinema of Paradzhanov does not fit easily into the canons of socialist realism. Graduating from the Moscow Film Institute in 1951, he made a number of films in Kiev before earning a reputation in 1964 with

Above: Luciana Paluzzi in The Greek Tycoon. *Below: a publicity portrait of Irene Papas. Bottom: Cecil Parker wearing a characteristically bemused expression in* The Pure Hell of St Trinians *(1960)*

Above: Franklin Pangborn in Reveille With Beverley *(1943). Right: Eleanor Parker in* Of Human Bondage, *a film version of W. Somerset Maugham's novel. Below right: Barbara Parkins in* Asylum *(1972)*

Shadows of Our Forgotten Ancestors, a film filled with wild imagery and influenced by Dovzhenko, Ukrainian folklore and religious mysticism. Its successor, *The Colour of Pomegranates*, used a similar style to tell the story of the eighteenth century Armenian poet Sayadin. After this, all Paradzhanov's projects were rejected or halted by the Soviet authorities, and he himself was sentenced, in 1974, to six years in a labour camp for homosexuality and incitement to suicide. Released in 1978, Paradzhanov was again imprisoned in 1982, and there seems little chance that this highly imaginative artist will ever be permitted to work freely again.

Films include: 1955 Andreish (co-dir). **'58** Pervyi Paren (The First Lad). **'61** Ukrainskaya Rapsodiya (Ukrainian Rhapsody). **'65** Teni Zabytykh Predkov (GB: Shadows of Our Forgotten Ancestors). **'69** Sayat Novar (GB: The Colour of Pomegranates). **'71** Kiev's Frescoes (unfinished).

PARKER, Alan

(b. 1944). Director. Born: Islington, London, England

Beginning as a copywriter and maker of television commercials, Parker directed notable television films like *No Hard Feelings* (about the Blitz) and the award-winning *The Evacuees*, and went on to a first cinema feature, *Bugsy Malone*, a gangster musical played by children. Four features since then, two of them made in the USA, have been huge commercial successes, but their critical reception has been far from kind. *Midnight Express* won BAFTA and Golden Globe awards, but was attacked as hysterical, violent and xenophobic, while Parker's directorial style has been described as overblown and dependent on tired cliché. Certainly he is a director aiming at gut-reactions, and at times obtaining them, as with the fascist rally in *Pink Floyd – The Wall*, in dangerous ways.

Films: 1976 Bugsy Malone. '78 Midnight Express. '80 Fame (USA). '81 Shoot the Moon (USA). '82 Pink Floyd – The Wall.

PARKER, Cecil

(1897–1971). Actor. Born: Cecil Schwabe; Hastings, Sussex, England

Although he was educated in Belgium and born with the surname Schwabe, it is difficult to imagine anyone more English than Cecil Parker. He entered films from the legitimate stage, when talkies began in England, with the 1929 version of *The Woman in White*, but really made his mark with his unforgettable portrayal of the caddish, adulterous husband in Hitchcock's *The Lady Vanishes*. His roles, and later his leads, almost always made use of his talent for light comedy and were always a joy to watch. He made only a few films in Hollywood, preferring to confine his stage work and films to England. He was never less than the perfect English gentleman, and even when he played a villain it was always a polite villain.

Films include: 1929 The Woman in White. '38 The Lady Vanishes. '47 Captain Boycott. '48 The First Gentleman (USA: Affairs of a Rogue). '49 The Chiltern Hundreds (USA: The Amazing Mr Beecham). '51 The Man in the White Suit. '52 His Excellency; I Believe in You. '55 The Ladykillers. '62 The Amorous Prawn. '65 A Study in Terror (USA: Fog). '69 Oh! What a Lovely War.

PARKER, Dorothy

(1893–1967). Screenwriter. Born: Dorothy Rothschild; West End, New Jersey, USA

A writer of wit and style, Parker became famous as the drama critic of *The New Yorker* and the darling of the smart set, whose review could make or break a play. Her wit was often malicious, but always wonderfully funny, and her short stories were so perfectly written, with never an unnecessary word, that they have become minor classics. It is not generally known that she was also a serious journalist, and reported with feeling and compassion on the Spanish Civil War. She became increasingly supportive of left-wing causes and was cited by HUAC in the Fifties. Her work as a scriptwriter in Hollywood reached its zenith when she collaborated with her husband, Alan Campbell, and Robert Carson on the memorable 1937 version of *A Star Is Born*, based on a story by director William A. Wellman.

Films include: 1934 Here Is My Heart (uncredited co-sc). '35 One Hour Late (co-sc). '36 Suzy (co-sc); Lady Be Careful (co-sc). '37 A Star Is Born (co-sc). '38 Trade Winds (co-sc). '42 Saboteur (co-sc). '47 Smash-Up/Smash-Up, the Story of a Woman (co-sc) (GB: A Woman Destroyed). '49 The Fan (co-sc) (GB: Lady Windermere's Fan).

PARKER, Eleanor

(b. 1922). Actress. Born: Cedarville, Ohio, USA

Beautiful, red-haired Eleanor Parker, the daughter of a school teacher was spotted by a talent scout at the Pasadena Playhouse and signed up by Warner Brothers. Although her part in her debut film, *They Died With Their Boots On* (1941), ended up on the cutting-room floor, she managed to work her way through bit parts to second leads in B movies in the Forties. This steady training and experience resulted in ten glorious years from *Caged* in 1950 to *Home From The Hill* in 1959, during which she gave excellent performances in every film she was in. From then onwards, however, her roles and her career have unaccountably declined, and since the Sixties she has appeared mainly in supporting roles.

Films include: 1943 Mission to Moscow. '46 Of Human Bondage. '48 The Woman in White. '50 Caged. '51 Detective Story. '52 Scaramouche. '55 Interrupted Melody. '56 The Man With the Golden Arm. '57 Lizzie. '59 Home From the Hill. '65 The Sound of Music. '67 Warning Shot. '79 Sunburn (GB-USA).

PARKINS, Barbara

(b. 1942). Actress. Born: Vancouver, British Columbia, Canada

A leading ballerina with the Vancouver ballet, Barbara Parkins went to Hollywood originally to study jazz dance and techniques. She toured with Donald O'Connor's troupe of dancers, but then abruptly decided to abandon her dancing for an acting career. A cool, beautiful brunette, she made her name in television's *Peyton Place*. As for films, ten years of Hollywood seem to have been quite enough for her and she has since worked solely in Europe and mostly in England. She has not been too lucky with her films. She had a substantial role in John Huston's *The Kremlin Letter*, playing a girl agent, but since then little worthwhile has come her way.

Films include: 1961 20,000 Eyes. '67 The Valley of the Dolls. '70 The Kremlin Letter. '71 Les Maison Sous les Arbres (FR-IT) (USA/GB: The Deadly Trap); The Mephisto Waltz. '74 Christina (CAN). '76 Shout at the Devil (GB). '77 The Disappearance (GB-CAN). '79 Bear Island (GB-CAN).

PARKS, Gordon

(b. 1912). Director. Born: Fort Scott, Kansas, USA

The youngest of 15 children born into a poverty-stricken family, Gordon Parks tried a variety of hard-work-for-low-pay jobs before a 1937 newsreel of a Japanese bombing raid changed his life and he decided to become a photographer. He bought his first camera in a Seattle pawnshop and shortly afterward won the first Julius Rosenwald photography fellowship. He travelled widely, initially for the Office of War Information, then for the Farm Security Administration, documenting the plight of America's poverty-stricken. In 1949 he joined *Life* magazine and became one of the world's most highly respected photojournalists. During the course of all this activity, Parks wrote an autobiographical book, *The Learning Tree*, which was to become his *entrée* into the film world; *The Learning Tree* became the first major production to be directed by a black. *Shaft* followed, and it was this film that made him much sought after. It is a slick private-eye thriller transposing a traditionally white domain to an all-black domain. Sequels followed but Parks still regards film-making as being of less importance to him than his photography, writing and composing. His son, Gordon Parks Jr (1935–79), served in the army, became a still photographer and directed four films, including *Superfly* (1972), before he died in a plane crash.

Films include: 1969 The Learning Tree/Learn Baby Learn. '71 Shaft. '72 Shaft's Big Score! '74 The Super Cops. '76 Leadbelly.

PARKS, Larry

(1914-1975). Actor. Born: Olathe, Kansas, USA

After being active in the Illinois University drama society, Larry Parks began his acting career in summer stock. His early attempts to establish himself on Broadway were not as successful as he would have liked, and on the death of his father he gave up the theatre to work as an inspector on the New York Central Railroad. However, he had got to know John Garfield and Elia Kazan, and when he was offered a part in *Golden Boy* on Broadway he leapt at the chance to resume his acting career. A contract with Columbia followed, and in 1946 he shot to fame portraying Al Jolson in *The Jolson Story* and its popular sequel. Unfortunately his triumph was short-lived, for in 1951 he was called before the House Un-American Activities Committee where he admitted to being a member of the Communist Party during World War II. His career was ruined and he was reduced to theatrical tours in small towns. He later made several films in Europe, then retired from showbusiness to run a real-estate firm.

Films include: 1941 Mystery Ship. '45 Counter-Attack. '46 The Renegades; The Jolson Story. '47 Down to Earth; The Swordsman. '48 The Gallant Blade. '49 Jolson Sings Again. '50 Emergency Wedding (GB: Jealousy). '52 Love Is Better Than Ever (GB: The Light Fantastic). '62 Freud (GB: Freud – The Secret Passion). '68 Tiger By the Tail/Cross-up (GB).

PARRISH, Robert

(b. 1916). Director. Born: Columbus, Georgia, USA

Raised in Hollywood, Robert Parrish became an actor while still a teenager and made his screen debut as the pea-shooting newsboy in Charlie Chaplin's *City Lights* (1931). In 1933 he joined RKO as an assistant editor, and quickly rose to being a film editor. He worked mainly for John Ford in the late Thirties, his touch being apparent in films such as *The Grapes of Wrath*, *Stagecoach* and *The Long Voyage Home* (all 1939) and, after naval service during World War II, resumed his career, working on films such as *Body and Soul* (for which he won himself an Oscar) and *All the King's Men* – a film that flopped at its preview and which was about to be dropped before producer Robert Rossen hired Parrish to edit it; it won the 1949 Academy Award for Best Picture. In the early Fifties he began directing his own movies – *Cry Danger*, *The Purple Plain* (starring Gregory Peck), the 'domestic' Western *Lucy Gallant* and the war-movie *Up From the Beach* (1965) being among his best. By 1955 Parrish had formed his own production company, Trimark Productions, but continued to freelance for the Hollywood majors. He now lives in London and has written an excellent autobiography, *Growing Up in Hollywood*.

Films include: 1936 Mary of Scotland (ed. only). '39 Young Mr Lincoln (ed. only). '47 Body and Soul (co-ed. only). '48 A Double Life (ed. only); Caught (ed. only). '49 All the

King's Men (ed. only). '51 Cry Danger; The Mob. '52 San Francisco Story; Assignment – Paris. '54 The Purple Plain (GB). '55 Lucy Gallant. '58 Saddle the Wind. '59 The Wonderful Country. '63 In the French Style (USA-FR). '68 Duffy (GB). '71 A Town Called Bastard (GB-SP). '74 The Marseille Contract (GB-FR).

PARSONS, Estelle

(b. 1927). Actress. Born: Marblehead, Massachusetts, USA

The highly talented Estelle Parsons moved from politics to serious, topical television programmes, to the stage and thence to Hollywood. Her stage career was triumphant and her film performances equally brilliant. She won an Oscar as Best Supporting Actress for her role as the hysterical wife forced into lawbreaking against her will in *Bonnie and Clyde*, and was nominated for one in *Rachel, Rachel*, in which she gave an outstanding performance as the lesbian religious fanatic. Lamentably, this remarkable actress has had far too few good roles.

Films include: 1963 Ladybug, Ladybug. '67 Bonnie and Clyde. '68 Rachel, Rachel. '69 Don't Drink the Water. '70 The Watermelon Man; I Walk the Line; I Never Sang for My Father. '73 Two People. '74 For Pete's Sake. '75 Foreplay.

PARSONS, Louella

(1884–1972). Columnist. Born: Louella Rose Oettinger; Freeport, Illinois, USA

Far more influential than any producer, director or magnate, Louella Parsons could make or break a star in her daily syndicated column in the Hearst newspapers. She was largely responsible for the banishment of Ingrid Bergman by publishing the news of her affair with the Italian director Roberto Rossellini. As a result, Bergman did not appear in an American film for seven years. Parsons' career as a columnist with Americans began after she wrote a glowing article about Hearst's mistress Marion Davies, who later became a firm friend of hers. Parsons had no pretensions to being a wordsmith, but her column was pithy and her scoops genuine. As she wrote for many Americans to whom English was a second language, her accessible style was an enormous asset. Louella appeared as herself in a couple of films.

Films include: 1937 Hollywood Hotel. '46 Without Reservations. '51 Starlift.

PASCAL, Gabriel

(1894–1954). Producer. Born: Arad, Hungary

Pascal produced and sometimes directed and acted in silent films in Italy, Germany and France. Moving to England in the mid-Thirties, he gained the friendship and confidence of George Bernard Shaw, and was entrusted with the filming of Shaw's plays. Pascal produced four of them. *Pygmalion* and *Major Barbara*, the

second of which he also directed, were marvellously spirited and hugely successful, but *Caesar and Cleopatra* considerably exceeded its budget, and emerged as static and dull. This fiasco put an end to Pascal's career in England, but shortly before his death he managed to produce a version of *Androcles and the Lion* in the USA.

Above: Larry Parks bursts into song in the title role of The Jolson Story. *Below: Estelle Parsons in John Frankenheimer's* I Walk the Line

Films include: 1921 Popoli Morituri (IT). '32 Frederica/Frederike (GER); Unheimliche Geschichten (GER) (The Living Dead). '36 Reasonable Doubt. '38 Pygmalion. '41 Major Barbara (+dir). '45 Caesar and Cleopatra (+dir). '52 Androcles and the Lion (USA).

PASOLINI, Pier Paolo

(1922–1975). Director. Born: Bologna, Italy

Pasolini's father was a Fascist army officer who made his family attend the Catholic church for social rather than religious reasons. Pasolini's mother was from the peasant region of Friuli and had a spiritual and poetic sense of religion much admired by her non-believing young son. Rebelling against his father's views, Pasolini became a Marxist, but more for emotional and cultural reasons than from any strong political leanings. The result of this troubled background was a welter of poems and films that caused outrage, confusion and may perhaps have ultimately led to his murder in 1975. He attended Bologna University and joined the Communist Party before arriving penniless in Rome and living in the slum quarter. Characters from his experiences there litter his novels, *Ragazzi di Vita* (Young Delinquents) and *Una Vita Violenta* (A Violent Life), published during the Fifties. He began to work as a scriptwriter for Franco Rossi and Federico Fellini and, in 1961, made his directorial debut with *Accatone*, a portrait – using the urban dialect – of a Roman pimp. His third feature, *Il Vangelo Secondo Matteo*, was a highly-praised critique of modern morality that heralded a change from merely anti-bourgeois proletarian themes towards a Marxist analysis of Biblical and mythical subjects. After a trilogy of films in which sexuality and mysti-

cism were intertwined, Pasolini moved back to the reality of the 'depraved' twentieth century with a vengeance. Cruelty and pessimism are over-apparent in *Salò o le Centoventi Giornate di Sodoma*; during its making some of the prints were stolen and it was while Pasolini was patching it up that a youth battered him to death for reasons that remain unknown. *Salò*, blending de Sade and fascism, thereby became the nightmare valediction for this extraordinary film-maker.

Films include: 1957 Le Notti di Cabiria (co-sc. only, uncredited) (IT-FR) (GB: Nights of Cabiria). '61 Accattone. '62 Mamma Roma. '64 Il Vangelo Secondo Matteo (IT-FR) (USA/GB: The Gospel According to St Matthew). '66 Uccellacci e Uccellini (USA: Hawks and Sparrows). '67 Edipo Re (USA/GB: Oedipus Rex). '68 Teorema (USA/GB: Theorem). '70 Porcile (IT-FR) (USA/GB: Pigsty). '71 Il Decameron (IT-FR-GER) (USA/GB: The Decameron). '72 I Racconti di Canterbury (IT-FR) (USA/GB: The Canterbury Tales). '74 Il Fiore delle Mille e Una Notte (IT-FR) (USA/GB: Arabian Nights). '75 Salò o le Centoventi Giornate di Sodoma (IT-FR) (USA/GB: Salo or the 120 Days of Sodom).

Right: Nigel Patrick, just one of a host of stars shown doing battle with the German Luftwaffe in Guy Hamilton's World War II epic The Battle of Britain. *Below: Marisa Pavan at the peak of her success in Hollywood in David Miller's medieval drama* Diane, *which also starred Lana Turner*

PASSER, Ivan

(b. 1933). Director. Born: Prague, Czechoslovakia

Ivan Passer's grandmother was a scenarist for silent films, and he developed his interest in the cinema by studying at FAMU, the Prague film school, where he met Miloš Forman, on several of whose early films he collaborated as a scriptwriter. His own first feature as director, *Intimate Lighting*, was a sharply humorous view of two friends, approaching middle age, who meet and discuss their lives. When Passer left Czechoslovakia because of the Russian invasion, he (like Forman) went to New York and started an American career. His first two films in the USA were successful critically but not commercially, and a further two films from other people's scripts made little impact. He then found a powerful story, *Cutter and Bone*, concerning the after-effects of the Vietnam War on the lives of a crippled war veteran, his wife and his best friend. This became Passer's most successful American film to date, *Cutter's Way*. His next project, *The Eagle of Broadway*, was about the Western gunslinger Bat Masterson.

Films include: 1963 Konkurs (co-sc. only) (USA: The Competition/Talent Competition). '65 Lásky jedné plavovlásky (co-sc. only) (USA: Loves of a Blonde; GB: A Blonde in Love); Fádní odpoleone (short) (A Boring Afternoon). '66 Intimní osvětlení (USA/GB: Intimate Lighting). '67 Hoří má panenko (co-sc. only) (CZ-IT) (USA: Song of the Firemen; GB: The Firemen's Ball). '71 Born to Win (USA). '74 Law and Disorder (USA). '76 Crime and Passion (USA). '77 Silver Bears (GB). '81 Cutter's Way (USA).

PASTERNAK, Joe

(b. 1901). Producer. Born: Joseph Herman Pasternak; Szilagy-Somlyo, Hungary

Pasternak emigrated to America when he was 19 and took a job washing dishes on the Paramount lot. The press made a lot out of 'Smiling Joe' the waiter, and as a result he was offered the chance to make a screen test. It was disastrous from an acting point of view, but one of Paramount's directors took pity on him and made him fourth assistant. He was sent off to Europe to scout for talent. Within two years he had become first assistant and after the release of *Help Yourself* (1932), a comedy which he wrote and directed, he was offered a job as assistant editor at Universal. He then began on a career as a producer that was soon to make him 'the king of Hollywood musicals'. *Three Smart Girls* brought Deanna Durbin fame and the nine-film partnership that followed earned them both a fortune. He salvaged Marlene Dietrich's flagging career with *Destry Rides Again* and after joining MGM in 1941 helped transfer Esther Williams' extraordinary swimming talent to the screen. Pasternak's life-story is told in the ghost-written autobiography *Easy the Hard Way*.

Films include: 1937 Three Smart Girls; One Hundred Men and a Girl. '39 Destry Rides Again. '40 Seven Sinners; Spring Parade. '45 Anchors Aweigh. '48 A Date With Judy. '51 The Great Caruso. '53 Latin Lovers. '56 The Birds and the Bees. '62 Billy Rose's Jumbo. '64 Looking for Love. '68 The Sweet Ride.

PASTRONE, Giovanni

(1883–1959). Director/producer. Born: Montechiaro d'Asti, Italy

Pastrone entered the cinema in 1905 as an administrator, and within a few years was producing and directing historical spectacles on an unparalleled scale. *The Fall of Troy* used a cast of 800 for its single reel, and also introduced the heroic strong man, Maciste, who was to be around in Italian epics until the Sixties. But Pastrone's most prestigious film was

Cabiria, an epic of the Punic Wars. *Cabiria* had magnificent sets, was researched with great accuracy, and was highly innovatory in its extensive use of a moving camera. The film changed many people's conception of cinema, and is said to have been a vital influence on Griffith. Pastrone was a skilful promoter of his product. His company, Itala Film, conquered the national market, and Pastrone was enabled to set up a lucrative theatre chain. He himself retired in 1923, but his influence as director, exhibitor and technical innovator was felt in Italian cinema for long after that.

Films include: 1909 Giordano Bruno; Manon Lescaut. '10 La Caduta di Troia; Agnese Visconti. '12 Padre. '14 Cabiria. '15 Maciste; Il Fuoco. '19 Hedda Gabler. '23 Povere Bimbe.

PATHÉ, Charles

(1863–1957). Industrialist/producer. Born: Chevry-Cossigny, France

The most powerful of the early moguls, Pathé got his start in 1893 when he borrowed 1,000 francs to buy a phonograph and set up as a fairground exhibitor. He next obtained an Edison Kinetoscope, and engaged an engineer, Charles Joly, to copy this, and also the new Lumière projector. Soon he was making simple films, and in 1897, with his three brothers, founded the Pathé Frères company. At first the company sold equipment. In 1901 it went into production; the Vincennes studio was built the next year, and production on a large scale began. By 1908 the firm was the world's largest producer of films and was also manufacturing raw film and equipment. It had branches in London and New York, and Pathé himself spent three years in America concentrating on that area of his business. When he returned to France in 1917, however, he was forced to recognize that American films had outstripped him, and that the market for his products, at home and overseas, had shrunk drastically. Charles Pathé retired in 1929; his company finally collapsed in 1934.

PATRICK, Nigel

(1913–1981). Actor. Born: Nigel Dennis Wemyss; London, England

The son of acting parents, Nigel Patrick was on the stage at 18 after a private education. He spent some time in provincial repertory companies before becoming established on the West End stage, where he featured mainly in sophisticated light-comedy. Tall, debonair and well-spoken, Patrick was very much in the Michael Wilding mould and, after his film debut in *Mrs Pym of Scotland Yard*, made himself quite a reputation in *Spring in Park Lane*, *The Browning Version*, *The Sound Barrier* and *The Pickwick Papers*. By 1952 he was one of Britain's top ten actors. He directed two films with little success – *How to Marry a Rich Uncle* and *Johnny Nobody* – and during the Sixties returned to

the stage. He also appeared as an airline security officer in the television series *Zero One*.

Films include: 1939 Mrs Pym of Scotland Yard. '48 Spring in Park Lane. '51 The Browning Version. '52 The Sound Barrier; The Pickwick Papers. '57 How to Marry a Rich Uncle (+dir). '59 Sapphire. '60 The League of Gentlemen; The Trials of Oscar Wilde (USA: The Man With the Green Carnation). '61 Johnny Nobody (+dir). '69 Battle of Britain. '73 The Mackintosh Man.

PAUL, Robert W.

(1869–1943). Inventor/director. Born: Highbury, London, England

In 1894 Robert Paul was a successful scientific instrument maker in London. He was approached to make copies of the Edison Kinematograph, which had not been patented in Britain, and went on to turn out 60 more with improved design. When Edison refused to provide film for these pirate machines, Paul designed a camera, in partnership with Birt Acres, and set about making his own. They also developed a projector and, in 1896, were showing their little films at the Alhambra music-hall in London only two weeks after the Lumière show at the Empire. That same year Paul filmed the Derby. In 1897 he built an open-air studio at Muswell Hill in North London, and an indoor one two years later. Until 1910 he continued to make topical films, comedies and trick films, but then abandoned cinema, which he never regarded as more than a sideline, and returned to his scientific work.

Films include: 1895 Rough Sea at Dover; Arrest of a Pickpocket. '96 The Derby; The Soldier's Courtship; The Terrible Railway Accident; The Twins' Tea Party. '98 The Deserter. 1903 A Chess Dispute. '06 The '?' Motorist. '10 The Butterfly.

PAVAN, Marisa

(b. 1932). Actress. Born: Marisa Pierangeli; Cagliari, Sardinia, Italy

After her father's death in 1950, Pavan and her family went to Hollywood. There they joined her famous twin sister, the actress Pier Angeli. She was screen-tested by producer Sol Siegel and made her debut in *What Price Glory?* as Nicole, a French girl. Her dark, gentle beauty made her perfect casting as an Indian in *Drum Beat* and as an Israelite in *Solomon and Sheba*, but her most famous role was in *The Rose Tattoo*, in which she played Anna Magnani's Italian daughter. For this performance she received a Best Supporting Actress Oscar nomination. She has a secondary career as a singer, and has worked extensively in television.

Films include: 1952 What Price Glory? '54 Down Three Dark Streets; Drum Beat. '55 Diane; The Rose Tattoo. '56 The Man in the Gray Flannel Suit. '57 The Midnight Story (GB: Appointment With a Shadow). '59 John Paul Jones; Solomon and Sheba. '73 L'Événement le Plus Important Depuis que l'Homme a Marché Sur la Lune (FR-IT) (GB: The Slightly Pregnant Man).

PAVLOW, Muriel

(b. 1921). Actress. Born: Lee, Kent, England

Muriel Pavlow's perennially youthful looks and petite build were both an asset and a handicap to her career. On the one hand they enabled her to play a child or adolescent convincingly, but with an adult's maturity and perception. On the other, they condemned her to be typecast as the sweet little thing in every film she was in, and may well have precluded the chance to prove her talent in more exacting roles. Primarily a stage actress (she won great acclaim for her playing of a nine-year-old in *Dear Octopus*), she translated effortlessly to the screen.

Films include: 1937 A Romance in Flanders (USA: Lost on the Western Front). '46 Night Boat to Dublin; The Shop at Sly Corner. '48 Quiet Wedding. '54 Doctor in the House; Conflict of Wings. '56 Reach for the Sky. '57 Doctor at Large. '59 Whirlpool. '61 Murder She Said.

Left: Muriel Pavlow and Derek Farr in The Shop at Sly Corner. *Above: John Payne in* The Eagle and the Hawk. *Below: Katina Paxinou with Gary Cooper in* For Whom the Bell Tolls

PAXINOU, Katina

(1900–1973). Actress. Born: Katina Constantopoulos; Piraeus, Greece

Katina Paxinou studied drama at the Geneva Conservatoire and then set out on a career as an opera singer, her debut being in the 1920 production of *Beatrice*. In 1929 she joined the Marika Cotopouli Company and turned to classical drama. She then joined the Greek National Theatre and was appearing in London when World War II broke out. Unable to return home, she went to America and after several plays on Broadway was offered a contract by Paramount. Her first role was as Pilar in *For Whom the Bell Tolls*: a large, angular woman of enormous gestures, a mane of black hair and a strong bony face, she was ideally cast as the proud, tough, motherly woman 'belonging' to the guerilla leader. She appeared in several more Hollywood movies and in 1946 made *Uncle Silas* in Britain. In 1956 she returned to Athens and, with her husband Alexis Minotis, set up and ran the Royal Theatre of Athens, a venue dedicated to the revival of ancient Greek tragedy.

Films include: 1943 For Whom the Bell Tolls; Hostages. '45 Confidential Agent. '47 Mourning Becomes Electra; Uncle Silas (GB) (USA: The Inheritance). '49 Prince of Foxes. '54 Mr Arkadin/Confidential Report (SP-FR). '59 The Miracle. '60 Rocco e i Suoi Fratelli (IT-FR) (USA/GB: Rocco and His Brothers). '68 Tante Zita (FR) (GB: Zita). '70 Un Été Sauvage (FR-IT).

PAYNE, John

(b. 1912). Actor. Born: Roanoke, Virginia, USA

John Payne studied drama at Columbia, performed on the radio, in university theatre and in stock, and in 1935 reached Hollywood with a Goldwyn contract. He did not really establish himself until the early Forties, when he went to 20th Century-Fox and starred in musicals, usually

opposite Alice Faye or Betty Grable. Later on, he moved into action pictures, and in 1957 temporarily left the cinema to appear in his own television series, *The Restless Gun*. He returned for a few films in the Sixties. Payne's was a career that never really led to anything worthwhile, and ironically enough, his very first film, *Dodsworth*, may well be the only one that endures. His first two marriages were to actresses Anne Shirley and Gloria de Haven.

Films include: 1936 Dodsworth. '40 Star Dust; Tin Pan Alley. '41 Weekend in Havana. '42 Springtime in the Rockies. '43 Hello Frisco Hello. '45 The Dolly Sisters. '51 Crosswinds. '56 Hold Back the Night. '70 The Savage Wild.

PEARSON, George

(1875–1973). Producer/director. Born: Kennington, London, England

Schoolmasters as a class have always been hostile to the cinema. Pearson not only approved of it; he gave up teaching to make movies, and made them for some thirty years. Beginning in 1912 with educational films for Pathé's London branch, he soon moved on to fiction films, working for Pathé, Gaumont, and eventually for his own company. Pearson's *A Study in Scarlet* was one of the first Sherlock Holmes films, and he followed up with the hugely popular 'Ultus' thriller serials, made in the manner of Louis Feuillade (the schoolmaster in him came out here: 'Ultus' is a Latin variant on Feuillade's 'Judex'). In the Twenties Pearson directed Betty Balfour in the 'Squibs' comedies, and made his own favourite film, the patriotic *Reveille*. He worked on after the sound revolution, but mainly on 'quota quickies', and when the war came he became Director-in-Chief at the Colonial Film Unit.

Films include: 1913 The Fool; Sentence of Death. '14 The Live Wire; A Study in Scarlet. '15 Ultus, the Man From the Dead

(USA: Ultus 1 – The Townsend Mystery; Ultus 2 – The Ambassador's Diamond). '18 The Better 'Ole or the Romance of Old Bill (USA: Carry On). '22 Squibs Wins the Calcutta Sweep. '24 Reveille. '26 The Little People. '35 Gentleman's Agreement. '37 The Fatal Hour.

PECK, Gregory

(b. 1916). Actor. Born: Eldred Gregory Peck; La Jolla, California, USA

A graduate of the Neighborhood Playhouse in New York, Peck was on Broadway in 1942, in Emlyn Williams' *The Morning Star*, and in Hollywood two years later, playing a Russian partisan in Jacques Tourneur's *Days of Glory*. *The Keys of the Kingdom* brought him a stardom that has endured for almost 40 years. Tall and handsome, rugged but gentle, Peck usually played heroic figures of total integrity, figures which reflected the actor's own liberal opinions. The Southern lawyer stand-

ing up to racialism in *To Kill a Mockingbird*, which brought him his Best Actor Oscar after four previous nominations, was the finest example of this side of Peck's work, but almost inevitably the rare parts in which he played characters less than totally perfect were more interesting. Frailty and doubt beset him in two Hitchcock films, *Spellbound* and *The Paradine Case*, while Henry King brought superlative performances from him as the Colonel in *Twelve O'Clock High*, a man visibly breaking under strain, and as *The Gunfighter* wearily awaiting the necessary end. Recently, perhaps just to show that he could do it, he essayed a total villain, playing the infamous Dr Mengele in *The Boys from Brazil*, a gripping piece of acting that redeemed a moderate film. From 1967 to 1970 Gregory Peck was President of the Academy of Motion Picture Arts and Sciences.

Films include: 1944 Days of Glory; The Keys of the Kingdom. '45 Spellbound. '46 Duel in

Above: Gregory Peck, strong on integrity in a studio publicity shot. Above right: François Périer in Jean Cocteau's Orphée. *Below: George Peppard in* The Victors

the Sun. '47 Gentleman's Agreement; The Paradine Case. '49 Twelve O'Clock High. '50 The Gunfighter. '53 The Snows of Kilimanjaro; Roman Holiday. '56 The Man in the Gray Flannel Suit; Moby Dick. '58 The Big Country (+ co-prod.) '59 Pork Chop Hill (+prod); Beloved Infidel. '61 The Guns of Navarone (GB). '62 To Kill a Mockingbird; How the West Was Won. '66 Arabesque. '68 The Stalking Moon. '69 Marooned. '70 I Walk the Line. '74 The Dove (prod. only). '76 The Omen. '78 The Boys From Brazil. '80 The Sea Wolves.

PECKINPAH, Sam

(1926–1985). Director/screenwriter. Born: Fresno, California, USA

The descendant of a pioneer family, Peckinpah majored in drama at USC, and worked in the theatre and television before entering the cinema as dialogue director for Don Siegel on *Riot in Cell Block 11* (1954). After building a reputation as a writer and director of television Westerns, he directed his first feature film in 1961.

Peckinpah's was a stormy and controversial career. A strong-willed man, he ran into frequent trouble with producers. He was fired from *The Cincinnati Kid*, and his *Major Dundee* was cut to ribbons. His early movies, especially the reflective Western, *Ride the High Country*, won much critical approval, but *The Wild Bunch*, a harsh and would-be realistic picture of the old West, was marred by what seemed the director's taste for gratuitous violence, and the savagery of *Straw Dogs* was found to be totally unacceptable. Of the later work, *Pat Garrett and Billy the Kid* had something of the earlier sobriety, but other films have re-emphasized the decline of what had appeared a promising talent. David Thomson has cited Peckinpah as an example of what can happen when censorship is removed from a genre involving violence; art chafes against its confines, but cannot do without them.

Films include: 1961 The Deadly Companions. '62 Ride the High Country (GB: Guns in the Afternoon). '65 Major Dundee; The Glory Guys (sc. only). '68 Villa Rides (co-sc. only). '69 The Wild Bunch. '70 The Ballad of Cable Hogue. '71 Straw Dogs (GB). '72 Junior Bonner; The Getaway. '73 Pat Garrett and Billy the Kid. '74 Bring Me the Head of Alfredo Garcia (USA-MEX). '75 The Killer Elite. '77 Cross of Iron (GB-GER). '78 Convoy.

PENN, Arthur

(b. 1922). Director. Born: Philadelphia, Pennsylvania, USA

It is a sad commentary on modern Hollywood that Arthur Penn was able to make only ten films in the first 25 years of his career. He trained as an actor, studying with the Actors' Studio in Los Angeles and with Michael Chekhov, but entered television as a floor manager, and by 1953 was writing and directing plays. In 1958 Penn directed his first film and his first Broadway play. The film, *The Left-Handed Gun*, a striking psychological Western, was a financial failure, and Penn waited four years before being able to transfer his Broadway success, *The Miracle Worker*, to the cinema. From 1965 to 1970 he worked steadily – almost one film a year – for the only

time. He made two films in the mid-Seventies, and in 1982, when it had seemed that his career was over, came *Four Friends*. Penn's films form a consistent body of work. His heroes are outsiders, whether outlaws like Billy the Kid or Bonnie and Clyde, leaving white society for the Indians like the Little Big Man, cut off from normality by deafness (Helen Keller) or conspiracy (Mickey One). In different ways they fight back, and Penn uses their struggle as an allegory of the individual in society today. These are not easy films, and they teach no easy lessons. Penn is a marvellous director of actors, and his films have an attractive surface, but beneath it the uncomfortableness persists.

Films: 1958 The Left-Handed Gun. '62 The Miracle Worker. '65 Mickey One. '66 The Chase. '67 Bonnie and Clyde. '69 Alice's Restaurant. '70 Little Big Man. '73 Visions of Eight *ep* The Highest. '75 Night Moves. '76 The Missouri Breaks. '82 Four Friends (GB: Georgia's Friends).

PENNEBAKER, D.A.

(b. 1926). Director. Born: Donn Alan Pennebaker; Evanston, Illinois, USA

Pennebaker studied engineering at Yale, set up his own electronics firm, moved into advertising, and eventually into writing and directing experimental films. In 1959 he joined Richard Leacock and others in an equipment-sharing film co-operative, Filmakers. In 1963 Pennebaker was able to set up his own company. His best known films, *Monterey Pop* and *Dont Look Back*, were shot on 16mm, blown up to 35mm, and widely distributed outside the normal commercial channels. Pennebaker has always used the *cinéma vérité* approach, with the camera simply a recording instrument, but this method still involves selection and editing, and as Pennebaker has said, almost every one of his films is a personal journal.

Films include: 1959 Opening in Moscow. '60 Primary (co-dir); Balloon (co-dir). '61 David. '62 Jane (co-dir). '63 Mr Pearson (CAN). '67 Dont Look Back. '68 Monterey Pop; Two American Audiences; Beyond the Law (co-photo. only). '69 One P.M. '70 Sweet Toronto; Maidstone (co-photo. only).

PEPPARD, George

(b. 1928) Actor. Born: Detroit, Michigan, USA

A product of the Actors' Studio, this tall, lean, good-looking star is a good actor and a worthy leading man. Obviously frustrated by the lack of meaty roles, in 1978 he mortgaged his home, raised every penny he could and produced, directed and starred in a film entitled *Five Days From Home*. Unfortunately, this was not the success he had hoped for, and he was obliged to return to somewhat pedestrian films. His best known roles are in *The Blue Max*, as a fighter pilot, and *Breakfast at Tiffany's*.

Films include: 1957 The Strange One (GB: End as a Man). '59 Pork Chop Hill. '61 Breakfast at Tiffany's. '62 How the West

Was Won. '63 The Victors (GB). '64 The Carpetbaggers. '65 Operation Crossbow (GB-IT) (USA: The Great Spy Mission). '66 The Blue Max (GB); Tobruk. '68 P.J. (GB: New Face in Hell). '78 Five Days From Home (+dir; +prod). '79 De l'Enfer à la Victoire (IT-FR) (USA: From Hell to Victory). '81 Race for the Yankee Zephyr (NZ-AUS).

PEREIRA, Hal

(1910–1983). Art director. Born: Chicago, Illinois, USA

Having served his apprenticeship in the theatre, Hal Pereira moved to Paramount in 1942 and had the good fortune to work under the supervision of the great Hans Dreier, the man responsible for the rich, glowing, no-expense-spared interiors which became known as the Paramount Look. On Dreier's retirement, Pereira became the supervisory art director. An art director not only requires knowledge of period, but also has to have an inborn sense of a film's mood and of how to enrich and enhance it. Pereira had this ability. He also had extraordinary versatility and could design sets for films varying from the vast outdoor feeling of *Shane*, to the depressed claustrophobic atmosphere of *Double Indemnity* and the happy Bohemianism of *The Odd Couple*.

Films as co-art dir. include: 1944 Double Indemnity; Ministry of Fear. '46 Blue Skies. '50 The Goldbergs (GB: Molly). '51 When Worlds Collide; The Greatest Show on Earth. '52 Carrie. '53 Shane. '54 The Naked Jungle. '56 The Ten Commandments. '58 Vertigo. '63 Hud. '68 The Odd Couple.

PÉRIER, François

(b. 1919). Actor. Born: François-Gabriel-Marie Pillu; Paris, France

Périer was in films and on the stage before he was 20, and has had a career of unbroken success in both his chosen spheres. In his early films he played light romantic and comedy roles. He reached the top partly through his own talent – his easy naturalism was well suited to the screen – but largely because he had the luck, or the acumen, to be in so many films by fine directors. Carné, Duvivier, Autant-Lara, Clair – all of them found parts for Périer. Growing older, he moved happily into solid character roles, still with the knack of finding good movies. He was memorable in *Gervaise*, as a disabled workman corrupted by idleness; in *Orphée*, as Heurtebise, the Angel of Death; in Chabrol's *Juste Avant la Nuit* (1971), as a man whose best friend confesses to the murder of his (Périer's) wife; and perhaps best of all, as the Inspector of Police patiently finding his way through the maze of Melville's *Le Samouraï* (1967).

Films include: 1938 Hôtel du Nord; La Fin du Jour. '39 Le Duel. '41 Les Jours Heureux. '42 Lettres d'Amour. '47 Le Silence Est d'Or (USA: Man About Town). '50 Orphée (USA: Orpheus). '53 Villa Borghese (IT-FR). '56 Gervaise. '57 Le Notti di Cabiria (USA/GB: Nights of Cabiria); Je Reviendrai à Kandara. '74 Stavisky . . . (FR-IT). '78 Le Raison d'État (FR-IT).

PERIES, Lester James

(b. 1921). Director. Born: Ceylon (now Sri Lanka)

From 1939 Peries was a journalist in London, and while there made two amateur shorts. He returned to Ceylon in 1949 as assistant to the British documentarist Ralph Keene, made his first professional documentary in 1954, and his first feature three years later. Peries' films use simple themes, and are concerned more with the personal problems of the characters than with social issues. They were the first films to give Sinhalese cinema any international prominence; Peries' first feature, *Rekava*, brought him a reputation abroad, and his later work has maintained it. The films have dealt with village life and family jealousies, personal rivalries, ambitions, the sadness of being ugly or growing old – gentle material quietly and touchingly used.

Films include: 1957 Rekava (GB: The Line of Destiny). '68 Golu Hadawatha (Silence of the Heart). '69 Akkara Patta (Five Acres of Land). '75 The God King (GB: Sri Lanka). '76 Dese Nise (The Eyes); Madol Duwia (Enchanted Island); Ahasin Pola Watha (White Flowers for the Dead). '79 Veera Puran Appu (Rebellion). '81 Baddegama (Village in the Jungle). '82 Kaliyugaya (Changing Village, Part 2).

PÉRINAL, Georges

(1895–1965). Cinematographer. Born: Paris, France

Périnal's was an outstanding career spanning half a century. He was a camera assistant as early as 1913, worked on short films in the Twenties for Jean Grémillon, and at the end of the decade began his celebrated collaboration with René Clair. The luminous beauty of the night scenes in *Sous les Toits de Paris* (1930) is a testament to Périnal's skill, and Clair's films never looked half as good without him. In the mid-Thirties Périnal went to England to work for Alexander Korda, and spent many of his remaining years there. He won an Oscar for his colour photography on *The Thief of Bagdad* (1940), and did distinguished work for Carol Reed (*The Fallen Idol*, 1948) and Powell and Pressburger (*The Life and Death of Colonel Blimp*).

Films include: 1928 Maldone; La Tour; Les Nouveaux Messieurs (co-photo.) (USA: The New Gentlemen). '29 Gardiens de Phare. '30 Le Sang d'un Poète (co-photo). '31 A Nous la Liberté. '32 Quatorze Juillet (USA: July 14th). '33 The Private Life of Henry VIII (GB). '36 Rembrandt (co-photo) (GB). '43 The Life and Death of Colonel Blimp (GB) (USA: Colonel Blimp). '47 Nicholas Nickleby (GB). '57 A King in New York (GB). '58 Bonjour Tristesse (USA). '60 Oscar Wilde (GB).

PERKINS, Anthony

(b. 1932). Actor. Born: New York City, USA

The son of the well-known actor Osgood Perkins, Anthony began working in summer stock while still a schoolboy. His tall, lean, lanky frame and nervous, sensitive face – with its lopsided, appealing grin – made him a natural for gawky, misunderstood adolescents, and he had an early movie success in this line as the baseball player Jim Piersall, suffering at the hands of his domineering father in *Fear Strikes Out*. The culmination, of course, was his brilliant Norman Bates in *Psycho*, but it would be a pity if this, unforgettable though it is, caused other Perkins roles to be overlooked. The anguished revolutionary of *WUSA* (1970), the sculptor trapped in the labyrinthine ways of Chabrol's *Ten Days' Wonder*, the beleaguered Josef K. of Welles' *The Trial*: these were varying facets of a fine actor still maturing, still widening his range.

Films include: 1956 Friendly Persuasion. '57 The Lonely Man; Fear Strikes Out. '58 The Matchmaker. '60 Psycho. '61 Goodbye Again (USA-FR). '62 The Trial (FR-IT-GER). '70 Catch-22. '72 The Life and Times of Judge Roy Bean; Le Décade Prodigieuse (FR-IT) (USA/GB: Ten Days' Wonder). '74 Murder on the Orient Express (GB). '78 Remember My Name. '80 North Sea Hijack (GB) (USA: Ffolkes). '83 Psycho II.

PERRINE, Valerie

(b. 1944). Actress. Born: Galveston, Texas, USA

Very much a child of her times, Valerie Perrine ran away from her comfortable, middle-class home, dropped out of college, went to Europe to 'find herself', experimented with drugs, was a 'hippie', lived on welfare, was a stripper in Las Vegas, appeared in *Playboy*, and finally settled down to become a very good actress. Although she was nominated for an Academy Award as Lennie Bruce's stripper-junkie wife in *Lenny* she gave a far more heart-felt and moving performance as W.C. Fields' mistress in *W.C. Fields and Me*. She was Lex Luthor's girl in *Superman, The Movie*, and then gave a brilliant performance as Jack Nicholson's sexy, dumb, spendthrift, affectionate wife in *The Border*.

Films include: 1972 Slaughterhouse – 5. '73 The Last American Hero. '74 Lenny. '76 W.C. Fields and Me. '77 Mr Billion. '78 Superman, The Movie. '79 The Electric Horseman; Agency (CAN). '80 Can't Stop the Music; Superman II. '81 The Border.

PERRY, Frank

(b. 1930). Director. Born: New York City, USA

After considerable experience in stock companies, Perry studied direction under Lee Strasberg, and later joined the Theatre Guild, where he met his first wife, Eleanor Perry, who was to collaborate on the scripts of all his films until they separated in 1970. In 1960 they wrote a screenplay, *Somersault*, sold it to Hollywood, and with the money produced their first film, *David and Lisa*. This study of two disturbed teenagers was extremely well received, and gained Perry an Oscar nomination. It remains his best film, but *The Swimmer*, with Burt Lancaster swimming home through lush suburbia, is an imaginative and deeply pessimistic allegory, while *Doc*

interestingly translates the legend of Wyatt Earp and Doc Holliday into contemporary perspectives. But with the years Perry's work has coarsened. His 1981 film *Mommie Dearest*, a bizarre and tasteless account of Joan Crawford and her daughter, was far removed from the delicacy of *David and Lisa*.

Films include: 1962 David and Lisa. '68 The Swimmer. '69 Last Summer; Trilogy (+ prod); Ladybug, Ladybug. '70 Diary of a Mad Housewife. '71 Doc. '72 Play It as It Lays. '75 Rancho Deluxe. '81 Mommie Dearest.

PETERS, Bernadette

(b. 1948). Actress. Born: Bernadette Lazzara; New York City, USA

Bernadette Peters was a television personality from the age of five years, moved on to children's parts in the legitimate theatre and thence to Hollywood. A petite, blue-eyed blonde, she tended to be cast against her looks as hookers and other tough females, until she got the part of Eileen, the shy schoolteacher who, also, is forced to become a tart in the remarkable film *Pennies From Heaven*. In *Annie* she was back to villainesses again, playing Lillie St Regis with lightness and humour.

Films include: 1973 Ace Eli and Rodger of the Skies. '74 The Longest Yard (GB: The Mean Machine). '76 W.C. Fields and Me; Silent Movie. '79 The Jerk. '81 Heart Beeps. '82 Pennies From Heaven; Annie.

Above: Anthony Perkins as the murderous victim of an oedipal complex in Psycho. *Below: Jean Peters in* A Man Called Peter. *Right: Bernadette Peters in Mel Brooks'* Silent Movie. *Far right: Valerie Perrine, supervamping in* Superman, The Movie. *Below right: Gérard Philipe in* Juliette ou la Clé des Songes *(1951). Below, far right: Leslie Phillips in* In the Doghouse *(1961)*

PETERS, Jean

(b. 1926). Actress. Born: Elizabeth Jean Peters; Canton, Ohio, USA

Hollywood lost one of its most attractive leading ladies when in 1957 Jean Peters married the eccentric multimillionaire Howard Hughes and retired from the screen. When a student at Ohio State University, she had won a campus popularity contest which carried with it a trip to Hollywood and a screen test; 20th Century-Fox promptly signed her, and she made her debut opposite Tyrone Power in *Captain From Castile*. She was usually cast as a spirited lady in that kind of costume piece, her lusty pirate wench in *Anne of the Indies* being a choice example, but she had a wide range, as her two best movies showed. In Samuel Fuller's *Pickup on South Street* she was superb as a gum-chewing broad who is, fairly innocently, involved in espionage, while in Robert Aldrich's *Apache* she gave a moving portrait of gentle devotion as the

Indian girl in love with Burt Lancaster. In 1971 Jean Peters divorced Hughes, who had become a recluse; later she married film executive Stanley Hough and resumed her acting career in television.

Films include: 1947 Captain From Castile. '49 It Happens Every Spring. '51 Anne of the Indies. '52 Viva Zapata!; O. Henry's Full House (GB: Full House). '53 Niagara; Pickup on South Street. '54 Three Coins in the Fountain; Apache. '55 A Man Called Peter.

PETRI, Elio

(1929–1982). Director. Born: Rome, Italy

In his early days Petri was the film critic of the Italian communist paper, *L'Unita*. He had always been in left-wing politics, and social satire and protest had become increasingly marked in his films. For a while he wrote scripts for other directors. Giuseppe De Santis' neo-realist classic, *Roma Ore 11* (1953, It Happened in Rome), not only had a script in part by Petri, but was based on a book of reportage by him. Petri directed some documentaries, then directed and co-wrote an impressive first feature, *L'Assassino*, with Mastroianni as a man guiltless of a murder but pain-

fully aware of his lack of social responsbility. *La Decima Vittima* was a modish but enjoyable futuristic thriller, while *Investigation of a Citizen Above Suspicion*, an unnerving story of a police chief who commits murder and challenges his colleagues to convict him, won Petri the Oscar for Best Foreign Film.

Films include: 1954 Nasce un Campione (short). '57 I Sette Contadini (short). '61 L'Assassino (IT-FR) (USA: Lady-Killer of Rome). '62 I Giorni Contati (GB: The Days Are Numbered). '64 Il Maestro di Vigevano. '65 La Decima Vittima (IT-FR) (USA/GB: The 10th Victim). '67 A Ciascuno il Suo (+ co-sc) (USA: To Each His Own). '70 Indagine su un Cittadino al di Sopra di Ogni Sospetto (USA/GB: Investigation of a Citizen Above Suspicion). '73 La Proprietà Non È Più un Furto. '76 Todo Modo. '79 Stanza Delle Buone Notizie.

PHALKE, D.G.

(1870–1944). Director. Born: Dhundiraj Govind Phalke; Trimbakeshwar, India

D.G. Phalke was the father of the Indian film industry. He saw his first film, *The Life of Christ*, in his forties and was so impressed that he determined to make the life of Lord Krishna. However, the first film he made (and the first film ever to be made in India) was, perhaps wisely, *Raja Harischandra* in 1913; to be followed by *The Legend of Mohini* before *The Birth of Lord Krishna* appeared in 1918. He brought his films to England where they were received with acclaim by the trade and the press. His films excelled in trick photography, animation, colour, and spectacular backgrounds, and the subjects were mythological to appeal to the mass audience. He has often been likened to Méliès for his trick effects. His daughter appeared in some of his films, causing a social furore. He made his last film in 1937, and died in poverty, almost forgotten.

Films include: 1913 Raja Harischandra (King Harischandra); Mohini Bhasmasur (The Legend of Mohini). '14 Satyavan Savitri. '17 Lanka Dahan (The Burning of Lanka). '18 Shri Krishna Janma (The Birth of Lord Krishna). '19 Kalya Mardan (The Childhood of Krishna). '23 Sati Mahananda. '26 Bhakta Prahlarda (Saint Prahlarda). '32 Setu Bandhan (The Bridging of Lanka). '37 Gangavataran.

PHILIPE, Gérard

(1922–1959). Actor. Born: Cannes, France

Gérard Philipe began his stage career in Paris in 1942, after studying at the Conservatoire d'Art Dramatique. Soon he was offered film roles and came to fame as a sensitive schoolboy in an aborted love affair with an older woman in Claude Autant-Lara's *Le Diable au Corps*. For the next 12 years he was constantly working for many of the top French film-makers – René Clair, Max Ophuls, Marcel Carné, for instance – and established himself internationally as a dashing romantic hero in *Fanfan la Tulipe*. He continued his stage career, producing plays for

the Théâtre National Populaire, and ventured as far as England for one film, but never went to Hollywood, though he was regarded as Charles Boyer's natural successor. He made a film in Mexico with Luis Buñuel but became ill during the production and died soon afterwards of a heart attack at the age of 36.

Films include: 1944 Les Petites du Quai aux Fleurs. '46 L'Idiot. '47 Le Diable au Corps (GB: Devil in the Flesh). '49 La Beauté du Diable (USA: Beauty and the Devil; GB: Beauty and the Beast). '50 La Ronde. '52 Fanfan la Tulipe; Les Belles de Nuit (FR-IT) (USA: Beauties of the Night; GB: Night Beauties). '54 Knave of Hearts (GB) (USA: Lovers, Happy Lovers); Le Rouge et le Noir (FR-IT) (GB: Scarlet and Black). '58 Montparnasse 19 (FR-IT) (GB: The Lovers of Montparnasse). '59 Les Liaisons Dangereuses 1960 (GB: Les Liaisons Dangereuses). '60 La Fièvre Monte à El Pao (FR-MEX) (GB: Republic of Sin).

PHILLIPS, Leslie

(b. 1924). Actor. Born: London, England

A product of the Italia Conti School, Leslie Phillips started working at the age of 12 and hasn't stopped since. An able light-comedian, he first became known in Britain through the radio show *The Navy Lark*. He has appeared as the likeable, silly charmer in countless shows in the theatre, the movies, and on television. In a desperate struggle to break away from this image he co-produced *Maroc 7*, in which he played a dramatic role, but the film was not a success.

Films include: 1938 A Lassie From Lancashire. '52 The Sound Barrier. '57 Les Girls (USA). '58 I Was Monty's Double. '59 Carry On Nurse; Carry On Teacher; Please Turn Over; The Navy Lark. '61 Very Important Person. '67 Maroc 7 (+ co-prod). '73 Not Now Darling. '76 Spanish Fly (GB-SP). '77 Not Now Comrade.

PIALAT, Maurice

(b. 1925). Director. Born: Cunlhat, Puy de Dôme, France

Maurice Pialat had made a living as a painter and occasional actor, but turned to films in 1952. He made a number of short films, one of which, *L'Amour Existe*, won an award at Venice, and worked in television before making his first feature, *L'Enfance Nue*, in 1967. Acted by nonprofessionals, the film was a moving evocation of childhood, centred on the fortunes of an unwanted boy farmed out to other families, and was awarded the Prix Jean Vigo. In his four features since then, Pialat has used the same intimate, gentle style to deal with the problems of terminal illness (*La Gueule Ouverte*), rebellious youth (*Passe Ton Bac d'Abord*), and precarious relationships (*Loulou* and *Nous ne Vieillirons pas Ensemble*).

Films include: 1961 L'Amour Existe (short). '63 Voyages en Turquie et en Arabie Séoudite (doc). '68 L'Enfance Nue. '72 Nous ne Vieillirons pas Ensemble (FR-IT) (USA: We Won't Grow Old Together). '74 La Gueule Ouverte. '76 Passe Ton Bac d'Abord. '80 Loulou.

PICCOLI, Michel

(b. 1925). Actor. Born: Jacques Daniel Michel Piccoli; Paris, France

An important and illustrious international actor of both stage and screen, Michel Piccoli has worked for almost every important director there is. In return he has given even to the smallest part a distinction which has added immeasurably to the film. The list of those who have directed him sparkles like a diamond necklace: Renoir, Buñuel, Melville, Resnais, Clouzot, Hitchcock, Godard, and so on. His balding, elegant appearance, coupled with his intelligent, sardonic playing, has made him a truly memorable actor. He is in the enviable position of heading his own production company, Films 66, and of being able to pick and choose amongst the parts offered to him, preferring to act in films of boldness and originality.

Films include: 1945 Sortilèges (GB: The Sorcerer). '49 Le Point du Jour. '55 French Cancan (FR-IT) (USA: Only the French Can). '56 La Mort en ce Jardin (FR-MEX) (USA: Gina; GB: Evil Eden). '63 Le Doulos; Le Mépris (FR-IT) (USA/GB: Contempt). '64 Le Journal d'une Femme de Chambre (FR-IT) (USA/GB: The Diary of a Chambermaid). '66 La Guerre Est Finie (FR-SWED) (GB: The War Is Over). '67 Les Demoiselles de Rochefort (USA/GB: The Young Girls of Rochefort); Belle de Jour (FR-IT). '69 Dillinger è Morto (IT) (GB: Dillinger Is Dead); La Voie Lactée (FR-IT) (USA/GB: The Milky Way); Topaz (USA). '70 Les Choses de la Vie (USA/GB: The Things of Life). '71 La Décade Prodigieuse (USA/GB: Ten Days' Wonder). '72 Le Charme Discret de la Bourgeoisie (FR-SP-IT) (USA/GB: The Discreet Charm of the Bourgeoisie). '73 Themroc; Les Noces Rouges (USA: Wedding in Blood; GB: Red Wedding); La Grande Bouffe (FR-IT) (USA/GB: Blow-Out). '76 F comme Fairbanks. '80 Salto nel Vuoto (IT-FR) (Leap Into the Void); Atlantic City USA (CAN-FR-USA) (GB: Atlantic City). '82 Une Chambre en Ville (GB: A Room in Town).

PICHEL, Irving

(1891–1954). Director/actor. Born: Pittsburgh, Pennsylvania, USA

A graduate of Harvard, and for a time a stage actor, Pichel was signed by MGM as a writer in 1927. This was short-lived, but in the early Thirties he began a fruitful career as actor and director. As an actor he was impressive: tall, handsome and dignified, with a richly expressive voice (every inch a Harvard man), he played characters as diverse as the hectoring attorney in Sternberg's *An American Tragedy*, Fagin in Herbert Brenon's *Oliver Twist*, and even, in *British Agent*, Josef Stalin himself. He directed from 1932 until his death. Much of his work was routine, but there were high spots. His first effort, *The Most Dangerous Game* (made with Ernest Schoedsack), is a darkly exciting horror film; and *Destination Moon* a splendid piece of sci-fi. Pichel also produced Jean Renoir's first American film, *Swamp Water*. After that experience, Pichel wrote that Renoir was the best director he had ever known; reluctantly, he shot a new ending to the film when their employer, Darryl Zanuck, rejected Renoir's conclusion.

Films include: 1930 The Right to Love (act). '31 An American Tragedy (act). '32 Madame Butterfly (act); The Most Dangerous Game/The Hounds of Zaroff (co-dir). '33 Oliver Twist (act); I'm No Angel (act). '34 British Agent (act). '35 She (dir). '37 Beware of Ladies (act). '40 Earthbound (dir). '41 Swamp Water (prod) (GB: The Man Who Came Back). '42 The Pied Piper (dir). '46 The Bride Wore Boots (dir). '48 Miracle of the Bells (dir); Mr Peabody and the Mermaid (dir). '50 Destination Moon (dir). '53 Martin Luther (dir). '54 Day of Triumph (co-dir).

PICK, Lupu

(1886–1931). Director/actor. Born: Jassy, Romania

Lupu Pick (also known as Lupu-Pick) worked on stage in Hamburg and Berlin and entered the cinema in 1915 as an actor. In 1917 he founded his own company, Rex, and two years later began to direct. During the Twenties he became the leading exponent of the *kammerspiel* film; this genre, which marked a break from the Expressionist fantasies that previously dominated German screens, consisted of sparse, intimate, psychological dramas about ordinary people trapped by destiny. Most typical of Pick's work were *Shattered*, about the disruption of a stationmaster's humdrum existence when a visiting inspector seduces his daughter (a film without intertitles), and *Sylvester*, the story of a grocer whose wife and mother each try to possess him. Both films were scripted by Carl Mayer, but this fruitful partnership ended when he and Pick quarrelled over *Der letzte Mann* (1925, The Last Laugh), eventually directed by F.W. Murnau. After acting in Fritz Lang's *Spione*, Pick went to England to make *Eine Nacht in London* and to France for *Napoleon auf St Helena* from a script by Abel Gance. But he was now past his best. He died from gastric poisoning.

Films include: 1917 Die Pagode (act); Es Werde Licht! (act). '18 Die Weltspiegel (dir); Die Liebe des Van Royk (dir). '19 Nacht des Grauens (act); Kitsch (dir). '21 Scherben (dir) (USA/GB: Shattered). '23 Sylvester (dir) (GB: New Year's Eve). '25 Das Haus der Lüge: '26 Die letzte Droschke von Berlin (act). '28 Spione (act) (USA: Spies); Eine Nacht in London (dir). '29 Napoleon auf St Helena (dir). '31 Gassenhauer (dir).

PICKENS, Slim

(1919–1983). Actor. Born: Louis Bert Lindley; Kingsburgh, California, USA

Slim Pickens spent over fifteen years on the rodeo circuit before being spotted by a talent scout and offered a job in *Rocky Mountain*, starring Errol Flynn. After years in low-budget Westerns, he got his big chance as the sheriff in Marlon Brando's grim *One-Eyed Jacks*, and consolidated it with his performance as the bomb-riding Major King-Kong in *Dr Strangelove*. After that he had many big films to his credit, and with his distinctive twangy drawl seemed to be equally at home in comic and dramatic parts.

Films include: 1950 Rocky Mountain. '54 The Outcast. '61 One-Eyed Jacks. '64 Dr

Strangelove, Or How I Learned to Stop Worrying and Love the Bomb (GB). '66 Stagecoach. '67 Will Penny. '70 The Ballad of Cable Hogue. '72 The Cowboys. '73 Pat Garrett and Billy the Kid. '74 Blazing Saddles. '79 Beyond the Poseidon Adventure. '80 Honeysuckle Rose.

PICKFORD, Mary

(1893–1979). Actress/producer. Born: Gladys Mary Smith; Toronto, Canada

In April 1909, Gladys Smith, a child actress whose name had been changed by the Broadway producer David Belasco to Mary Pickford, was engaged by D.W. Griffith to work for him at Biograph. She made 80-odd one-reel films for Griffith, worked briefly for other companies, came back to Griffith for the best-known of her early films, such as The New York Hat, and then, in 1913, settled to a career in features at Famous Players. She was already an actress of great skill, charm and versatility, by no means always playing children (as the myth has it), but ingénues, Indian maidens, tomboys, anything asked of her. She was soon the most popular of all stars, and perhaps the best-known woman in the world. And she fought hard for what she knew she deserved, winning in 1916 a contract guaranteeing her $10,000 per week. She worked at this period for Tourneur, DeMille and other fine directors, but to a degree she was, and remained, her own producer. From 1920 on she made her films for United Artists, of which she and her second husband, Douglas Fairbanks, were founder members. Then came her great Twenties films, many of them happily surviving, so that audiences now can still see the heroines of Little Annie Rooney, Sparrows, My Best Girl, and many others. She made four sound films, winning an Oscar for her Southern flirt in the tragic Coquette, and showing in her last film, Secrets, all the grace, sensitivity and charm that had held her following for almost a quarter of a century. Her last husband was actor Charles 'Buddy' Rogers.

Above, far left: the garrulous Slim Pickens in Gordon Douglas' remake of the John Ford classic Stagecoach. *Far left: Michel Piccoli. Left: Mary Pickford in* Rebecca of Sunnybrook Farm. *Above: Walter Pidgeon in* How Green Was My Valley. *Below: Harry Piel, whose devil-may-care style helped maintain his popularity with German audiences*

Films include: 1909 Her First Biscuits. '10 An Arcadian Maid; Wilful Peggy. '12 The New York Hat. '14 Hearts Adrift (+ sc); Tess of the Storm Country. '15 Cinderella. '17 The Poor Little Rich Girl; Rebecca of Sunnybrook Farm. '18 Stella Maris. '19 Daddy Long Legs. '20 Pollyanna; Suds. '23 Rosita. '24 Dorothy Vernon of Haddon Hall. '25 Little Annie Rooney. '26 Sparrows. '27 My Best Girl. '29 Coquette; The Taming of the Shrew. '33 Secrets. '48 Sleep, My Love (co-prod. only).

PIDGEON, Walter

(1897–1984). Actor. Born: East St John, New Brunswick, Canada

After a short stage career, Pidgeon entered the cinema in 1926, and when sound came his pleasant baritone voice was in some demand for early musicals. During the Thirties his progress was hampered by illness, but he had a few good roles with MGM towards the end of the decade, and played the lead in their Nick Carter detective series. Stalwart, reliable, given to smoking his pipe and looking on with eyes gently twinkling, Pidgeon made an obvious partner for ladylike Greer Garson in well-bred movies like Madame Curie and Mrs Miniver, and spent too much time in such undemanding roles. But he was actor enough to make the films bearable, and waited patiently for better chances. One such came along in Fritz Lang's Man Hunt, where Pidgeon was a big-game hunter trying for even bigger game at Berchtesgaten; another was as the pastor in John Ford's How Green Was My Valley, his sobriety balancing Maureen O'Hara's fire.

Films include: 1926 Mannequin. '28 Melody of Love/Madelon. '37 Saratoga. '39 Nick Carter, Master Detective. '41 Man Hunt; How Green Was My Valley; Blossoms in the Dust. '42 Mrs Miniver. '44 Madame Curie. '62 Advise and Consent. '68 Funny Girl. '78 Sextette.

PIEL, Harry

(1892–1963). Director/actor. Born: Düsseldorf, Germany

Harry Piel was an immensely busy and prolific director and actor who specialized in adventure films and comedies. A German equivalent to Douglas Fairbanks, he was well-rounded rather than slimly lithe but was able to do his own stunts, and had a light and humorous touch. He began directing in 1912 and took up occasional acting as well in 1915. From 1920 he both acted in and directed virtually all of his films, frequently partnered by his wife, Dary Holm. His output fell off a little after the coming of sound but he still averaged two films a year until 1938.

Films include: 1912 Dämonen der Tiefe (dir. only). '15 Die grosse Wette. '16 Unter heisser Sonne (Under a Hot Sun). '18 Das amerikanische Duell. '21 Der Reiter ohne Kopf (3-part serial). '29 Sein Bester Freund/Ein Abenteuer mit fünfzehn Hinden (USA: His Best Friend). '30 Er oder ich. '32 Der Geheimagent/Ein Mann fällt vom Himmel (GB: Secret Agent). '37 Sein bester Freund (USA: His Best Friend). '51 Der Tiger Akbar.

PINELLI, Tullio

(b. 1908). Screenwriter. Born: Turin, Italy

A student of law and political science, Tullio Pinelli changed course and began to write for the theatre, radio, and in 1941 for the cinema. He did outstanding work in the Forties for Alberto Lattuada (Senza Pietà) and Pietro Germi (Il Cammino della Speranza), but best of all was Pinelli's work for Federico Fellini. He wrote, wholly or in part, all Fellini's films up to Juliet of the Spirits, and if one finds the realistic, smaller-scale films like I Vitelloni, La Strada and Il Bidone far more attractive then the flamboyant machines of Fellini's later period, some of the credit for this may well be given to Pinelli.

Films as co-sc. include: 1945 L'Adultera. '46 Il Bandito. '47 La Figlia del Capitano (GB: The Captain's Daughter); Senza Pietà (GB: Without Pity). '49 In Nome della Legge (GB: In the Name of the Law). '50 Il Cammino della Speranza (GB: Road to Hope). '53 I Vitelloni (IT-FR) (GB: The Spivs). '54 La Strada. '55 Il Bidone (IT-FR) (GB: The Swindlers); La Dolce Vita. '65 Giulietta degli Spiriti (IT-FR) (GB: Juliet of the Spirits). '75 Amici Miei (IT) (USA: My Friends). '79 Viaggio con Anita (IT-FR) (USA: Travels With Anita).

PINTER, Harold

(b. 1930) Playwright/ screenwriter. Born: Hackney, London, England

The son of a Portuguese-born Jewish tailor, Harold Pinter was educated at Hackney Downs Grammar School and trained as an actor at RADA and the Central School. He then acted on the radio and with a touring company in Ireland. He had begun writing as a child, mainly poetry and stories, and wrote a short play, The Room, for Bristol University in 1957. His first full-length play, The Birthday Party, was staged in 1958. In 1959 he won critical acclaim with The Caretaker; he also write the script for the 1963 film version. In the same year his screenplay for The Servant, from Robin Maugham's novel, was the beginning of a fruitful collaboration with director Joseph Losey. Pinter has written original plays for television and radio; but all of his screenplays are adaptations, including several from his own stage plays. His terse, allusive style is well suited to film, though his versions of other people's novels, for example John Fowles' The French Lieutenant's Woman, have generally been more successful than the films based on his own plays. His first wife, actress Vivien Merchant (1929–82), frequently appeared in his stage and television plays and had leading roles in Accident and The Homecoming. His second wife is the writer Lady Antonia Fraser.

Films: 1963 The Caretaker (from own play) (USA: The Guest); The Servant (+ act). '64 The Pumpkin Eater. '66 The Quiller Memorandum (GB-USA). '67 Accident (+ act). '68 The Birthday Party (from own play). '71 The Go-Between. '73 The Homecoming (from own play) (GB-USA). '74 Butley (dir. only) (GB-USA-CAN). '76 The Last Tycoon (USA). '81 The French Lieutenant's Woman. '83 Betrayal (from own play).

PINTOFF, Ernest

(b. 1931). Director/animator. Born: Watertown, Connecticut, USA

Ernest Pintoff graduated from the University of Syracuse with a degree in Fine Art. A trumpet player, he turned professional jazz musician for a few years before joining a group of animators, who in 1945 set themselves up as United Productions of America (UPA), and working as a cartoonist on such projects as *The Wounded Bird* and *Blues Pattern*. In 1957 he joined Terrytoons and created the Flebus character, a simple figure who wants everyone to love him. From 1960 Pintoff acted as an independent animator and director and gained universal recognition with *The Violinist* and *The Interview*, in which an unforthcoming jazz musician is interviewed by a less-than-knowledgeable television chat-show presenter. *The Critic* was the pinnacle of his animated success. He won an Oscar for this film in which a series of abstract shapes appear on the screen and an elderly man is overheard conversing about a possible interpretation of the spectacle; he decides the blobs look like 'two cockroaches mating' and finally concludes that the film is 'symbolic of junk'. In the mid-Sixties Pintoff decided to broaden his scope and now concentrates on live action films like *Harvey Middleman – Fireman* and *Jaguar Lives* and television projects such as *Kojak* and *Hawaii Five O*.

Films include: 1956 Blues Pattern (short); The Wounded Bird (short). **'58** Flebus (short). **'59** The Violinist (short). **'60** The Interview (short). **'61** The Shoes (short). **'62** The Old Man and the Flower (short). **'63** The Critic (short). **'65** Harvey Middleman – Fireman. **'79** Jaguar Lives. **'81** St Helens.

PISIER, Marie-France

(b. 1944). Actress. Born: Dalat, Indochina (Vietnam)

It is a doubtful compliment to be known as 'the thinking man's Bardot', and one which Marie-France Pisier should rightly resent. Holding, as she does, degrees in law and political science, she is keenly involved in the Women's Liberation Movement and took part in the 1968 student demonstrations in Paris. But, although she lacks the blatant sexuality of Brigitte Bardot, she has, nonetheless, an ineffable air of femininity about her which enables her to play the mysterious temptress to perfection. She won a César (the French equivalent of an Oscar) for her role in *Cousin Cousine*, which led her to Hollywood and a lead in *The Other Side of Midnight*, but she seems more at home in French movies. She was delightful in a couple of small roles for François Truffaut, poised and beautiful as the mysterious governess in Jacques Rivette's *Céline et Julie Vont en Bateau* and deliciously enigmatic in de Gregorio's *Sérail*. She could make little out of the bland material of *Chanel Solitaire*, but showed everyone else up (and looked half her age) in the glossy American television mini-series *Scruples*, again playing a rising fashion designer.

Films include: 1962 L'Amour à Vingt Ans ep Paris (FR-IT-JAP-GER-POL). **'64** Le Mort d'un Tueur (FR-IT); Les Yeux Cernés (IT-FR). **'67** Trans-Europ Express. **'68** Baisers Volés (GB: Stolen Kisses). **'74** Céline et Julie Vont en Bateau (USA/GB: Celine and Julie Go Boating). **'75** Cousin Cousine. **'76** Sérail. **'77** The Other Side of Midnight (USA). **'79** Les Soeurs Brontë; French Postcards (GER-FR-USA). **'82** Chanel Solitaire (FR-GB); Les As des As (FR-GER).

PITT, Ingrid

(b. 1943). Actress. Born: Natasha Petrovana; Poland

The daughter of Russian parents, Ingrid Pitt began her acting career as a member of the Berliner Ensemble at the Bertolt Brecht Theatre. Reputedly she made a daring escape from East Berlin and went to New York, later living on an Indian reservation for a while. Then came stunt work in Spanish-made Westerns and a breakthrough in *Where Eagles Dare* as Heidi the German girl who slaps Richard Burton's face. This had brought her to England where she stayed on to become Hammer Films' resident fierce, blonde and buxom horror queen, sexily preying on young girls in *Countess Dracula* and *The Vampire Lovers*. Since the early Seventies she has matured into a tough and attractive character actress – playing a terrorist in the SAS movie *Who Dares Wins*, but given better acting parts in such prestigious television drama as *Artemis '81* and *Smiley's People*. Twice married, Ingrid Pitt is also building a reputation for herself as an authoress.

Films include: 1966 El Sonido Prehistorico (SP). **'68** Where Eagles Dare. **'70** The Vampire Lovers; Countess Dracula. **'71** The House That Dripped Blood. **'72** Nobody Ordered Love. **'74** The Wicker Man. **'82** Who Dares Wins.

PITTS, ZaSu

(1898–1963). Actress. Born: Parsons, Kansas, USA

In the sound period the talents of ZaSu Pitts were employed almost entirely for comedy. With her pale face, wide, staring eyes and fluttery hands, she was the perfect casting for eccentric spinsters (*Mrs Wiggs of the Cabbage Patch*), cousins up from the country

(*Life With Father*), and the like, and the audiences who laughed at her in those films, and in the two-reel slapstick comedies with Thelma Todd, had forgotten, or never known, that Pitts had been, for a brief but wonderful time, one of the screen's great tragic actresses. She began in 1917, a gawky adolescent supporting Mary Pickford. She caught the fancy of King Vidor, who made *Better Times* around her portrait of a lovelorn girl at boarding-school, and then came five years of nondescript movies until Stroheim saw in her the Trina for his *Greed*. She played a young bride brutalized by her husband, turning to the only comfort she has, the money she so zealously hoards. As a picture of nerve-racked obsession, it was, and remains, unsurpassed on film. Stroheim kept her on to play, with equal brilliance, the crippled heiress of *The Wedding March*, and she had a notable tragic role, too, in Ludwig Berger's *Sins of the Fathers* (1928). Sound came, her voice was comic and she was dropped from *All Quiet on the Western Front* (1930). Once more Stroheim, his own career almost beyond repair, called on her for *Walking Down Broadway*, but other hands mangled the film (released as *Hello Sister*), and for ZaSu Pitts it was eccentric comedy or oblivion. She had no real choice.

Films include: 1917 The Little Princess; Rebecca of Sunnybrook Farm. **'19** Better Times. **'24** The Fast Set. **'25** Greed. **'26** Mannequin. **'28** The Wedding March. **'32** Westward Passage. **'33** Hello Sister. **'34** Mrs Wiggs of the Cabbage Patch. **'35** Ruggles of Red Gap. **'47** Life With Father. **'63** It's a Mad, Mad, Mad, Mad World.

PLANER, Franz

(1894–1963). Cinematographer. Born: Karlsbad (now Karlovy Vary), Czechoslovakia

Franz Planer began his career as a portrait photographer before entering German films in 1919. He arrived in Hollywood in 1937, changed his name to Frank and became one of Max Ophuls' favourite cameramen, imbuing *Letter From an Unknown Woman* with a magical quality through his fluid camera movement. He went on to work for John Huston (*The Unforgiven*), Edward Dmytryk (*The Caine Mutiny*) and Stanley Kramer (*The Pride and the Passion*), and in 1962 was nominated for an Oscar for his work on his last film, William Wyler's *The Children's Hour*.

Films include: 1920 Der Ochsenkrieg (GER). **'32** Liebelei (GER). **'34** Maskerade (A). **'38** Holiday (GB: Free to Live). **'47** The Exile. **'48** Letter From an Unknown Woman; One Touch of Venus. **'49** Criss Cross. **'50** Cyrano de Bergerac. **'51** Death of a Salesman. **'53** The 5,000 Fingers of Doctor T. **'54** The Caine Mutiny; 20,000

Above, left to right: an enigmatic Marie-France Pisier in French Postcards; *Ingrid Pitt in* Where Eagles Dare; *ZaSu Pitts in* The Perfect Marriage *(1946); Sidney Poitier in* In the Heat of the Night. *Far left: Donald Pleasence in* Dracula. *Left: Suzanne Pleshette in* Rome Adventure. *Below: Christopher Plummer as the Inca ruler Atahualpa in* The Royal Hunt of the Sun, *from Peter Shaffer's play*

Leagues Under the Sea. '57 The Pride and the Passion. '58 The Big Country. '59 The Nun's Story. '60 The Unforgiven. '61 Breakfast at Tiffany's; The Children's Hour (GB: The Loudest Whisper).

PLEASENCE, Donald

(b. 1919). Actor. Born: Worksop, Nottinghamshire, England

Balding and rather small, with protruding blue eyes and a rasping hiss in his voice, Donald Pleasence gives an eccentric or sinister turn to his characterizations even when he is not, as usual, playing the villain. But he can finally switch to pathos, whether as the tramp in *The Caretaker*, defeated in his scheming, or as the unhappy husband of a faithless second wife (Françoise Dorléac), mourning his first wife, in *Cul-de-Sac*. As the relentlessly pursuing psychiatrist in *Halloween*, he appears only marginally less psychopathic than his murderous young patient, whom he would rather kill than cure. Pleasence started his acting career in the theatre after arranging variety shows at a POW camp in Germany during World War II. He made his London debut in 1946 in Peter Brook's production of *The Brothers Karamazov* and appeared on Broadway in the early Fifties with Laurence Olivier's touring company. By the mid-Fifties he was becoming well-known in television drama and began taking supporting roles in British films. From the mid-Sixties he was also seen in American films and became widely known for the role of James Bond's adversary, Blofeld, in *You Only Live Twice*. The actress Angela Pleasence is his daughter.

Films include: 1954 The Beachcomber. '59 Look Back in Anger. '60 Sons and Lovers. '63 Dr Crippen; The Great Escape (USA); The Caretaker (USA: The Guest). '65 The Greatest Story Ever Told (USA). '66 Cul-de-Sac; Fantastic Voyage (USA). '67 You Only Live Twice; Will Penny (USA). '70 Soldier Blue (USA). '74 The Black Windmill; The Apprenticeship of Duddy Kravitz (CAN). '76 The Last Tycoon (USA); The Eagle Has Landed. '78 Halloween (USA). '79 Dracula

(USA). '81 Escape From New York (USA). '82 The Thing (USA).

PLESHETTE, Suzanne

(b. 1937). Actress. Born: New York City, USA

Born into a theatrical family, Suzanne Pleshette was educated at Manhattan's High School for the Performing Arts and at Syracuse University. Her Broadway debut was in *Compulsion* and her first film was *The Geisha Boy*, with Jerry Lewis. Producer-director Delmer Daves gave her a co-starring role in *Rome Adventure*, opposite Troy Donahue, to whom she was also married for a few months. She played the schoolteacher who sacrifices her life in *The Birds* and later appeared in several Disney films. Her film career failed to mature and almost faded out in the Seventies, though she continued to work in television. Neither medium has made full use of her beauty and talent.

Films include: 1958 The Geisha Boy. '62 Rome Adventure (GB: Lovers Must Learn). '63 The Birds. '64 Youngblood Hawke. '65 The Ugly Dachshund. '66 Nevada Smith. '67 The Adventures of Bullwhip Griffin. '68 Blackbeard's Ghost. '71 Support Your Local Gunfighter. '76 The Shaggy DA. '79 Hot Stuff.

PLUMMER, Christopher

(b. 1927). Actor. Born: Toronto, Ontario, Canada

Educated in Montreal, Christopher Plummer made his stage debut in Ottawa, and gained wide experience of Shakespeare and the classics. He reached Broadway in 1954, and starred in Shakespearian roles at Stratford, Ontario. His early film parts were in *Stage Struck* and Nicholas Ray's *Wind Across the Everglades*. After a gap of six years, he gained recognition in *The Fall of the Roman Empire* and, especially, as Von Trapp in *The Sound of Music*. He was also notable as the ruthless film producer in *Inside Daisy Clover*. His later film career, despite his impressive presence, has lacked any particular direction, apart from an inclination to period pieces and uniformed or aristocratic roles. But he showed a capacity for comedy in *The Return of the Pink Panther*. Plummer has been married to actress Tammy Grimes, ex-newspaper-woman Patricia Lewis and actress Elaine Taylor.

Films include: 1958 Stage Struck; Wind Across the Everglades. '64 The Fall of the Roman Empire. '65 The Sound of Music; Inside Daisy Clover. '67 The Night of the Generals (GB-FR). '69 Lock Up Your Daughters! (GB). '75 The Return of the Pink Panther (GB); The Man Who Would Be King (GB). '78 International Velvet (GB). '79 Starcrash.

PLUNKETT, Walter

(1902–1982). Costume designer. Born: Oakland, California, USA

Having given up law studies at Berkeley, Walter Plunkett became an actor and dancer in vaudeville and

then a self-taught designer for the New York stage and the Metropolitan Opera. He came to Hollywood in 1925, working as a dancer in Erich von Stroheim's *The Merry Widow*, in which he partnered another future costume designer for the movies, Irene. In 1926 Plunkett was made head of wardrobe at FBO, which later became RKO, where he was a costume designer. He worked on several Katharine Hepburn films, freelanced for a while and joined Selznick International in 1937, where his most notable contribution was to *Gone With the Wind*. After that he concentrated chiefly on historical films, mainly at MGM from 1946 to 1965. He was meticulous in detail, basing his work on extensive research and the use of authentic fabrics, but he also designed costumes to express mood and personality, carefully adapting them to the individual actor or, especially, actress.

Films include: 1926 Ain't Love Funny. '33 Little Women. '36 Mary of Scotland. '39 Stagecoach; Gone With the Wind. '46 Duel in the Sun. '49 That Forsyte Woman (GB: The Forsyte Saga). '51 An American in Paris. '52 Singin' in the Rain. '53 Young Bess; The Actress. '57 Raintree County. '58 Some Came Running. '61 Pocketful of Miracles. '62 How the West Was Won. '65 Seven Women.

POITIER, Sidney

(b. 1924). Actor/director. Born: Miami, Florida, USA

Tall, clean-cut, intelligent, Sidney Poitier almost single-handedly transformed the image of the black on the American screen from the Fifties onward, latterly as director as well as actor. He grew up in the Bahamas, the son of a tomato farmer whose business collapsed, so that Poitier had to leave school at 13 to help support the family. After army service as a physiotherapist, he joined the American Negro Theater. Some critical success on Broadway led to film parts, as a medical intern in *No Way Out* and a progressive clergyman in *Cry, the Beloved Country*. He progressed from supporting to lead roles, winning an Oscar nomination for *The Defiant Ones* and the Best Actor award for *Lilies of the Field*. The increasing blandness of his image was disrupted by his tough detective, Virgil Tibbs, in *In the Heat of the Night*; and he gained increased control of his career when he began to direct himself in the Seventies, at first in a Western and a tear-jerking romance, but finding his form in comedies aimed at black audiences. Poitier is a noble presence in the cinema and he may yet produce a masterpiece.

Films as actor include: 1950 No Way Out. '52 Cry, the Beloved Country (GB) (USA: African Fury). '55 The Blackboard Jungle. '56 Edge of the City (GB: A Man Is Ten Feet Tall). '57 Something of Value. '58 The Defiant Ones. '59 Porgy and Bess. '61 A Raisin in the Sun. '63 Lilies of the Field. '67 In the Heat of the Night; To Sir, With Love (GB); Guess Who's Coming to Dinner? '68 For Love of Ivy (+co-sc). '72 Buck and the Preacher (+dir). '73 A Warm December (+dir) (GB-USA). '74 Uptown Saturday Night (+dir). '77 A Piece of the Action (+dir). '80 Stir Crazy (dir. only).

POLANSKI, Roman

(b. 1933). Director/screenwriter/
actor. Born: Paris, France

Despite more tragedy in his life than
most men could bear, Roman Polanski was in 1979 able to complete a
film – *Tess* – of such simple beauty that
his erratic genius seemed an even
more eccentric quality. The ennobling
stoicism of Thomas Hardy's heroine
Tess of the d'Urbervilles (played with
great delicacy by Nastassia Kinski) in
that movie matched Polanski's own;
significantly, it was dedicated to
Sharon Tate, his actress-wife who was
slaughtered by the Charles Manson
gang in 1969 and who had originally
recommended the novel to her husband. Not that *Tess* is indicative of
Polanski's films, most of which are
bizarre and ironic studies in fear or the
supernatural: *Repulsion, Cul-de-Sac,
Rosemary's Baby, Macbeth.* Though
Chinatown stands out from the rest as
an accessible and gripping *film noir*
thriller, it, too, is motivated by disturbing forces, by corruption and
incest. Polanski's world may often be
absurd, comic and gentle, but bloody
knives seem to provide the only answers to the human nightmare, even,
ultimately, in *Tess*. Polanski's mother
died at Auschwitz, but he escaped to
become a child actor in the Kraków
Theatre in his parents' native Poland.
By 1953 he was in films, appearing in
Andrzej Wajda's *A Generation* among
others. He then entered the Lodz Film
School and graduated with an award-
winning short, *Two Men and a Wardrobe*, having already assisted the director Andrzej Munk. Polanski's feature debut, *Knife in the Water*, established him as a major Polish director. He worked in France and went to
London for *Repulsion*, which starred
Catherine Deneuve as a withdrawn
young girl terrorized into murder.
Rosemary's Baby, with Mia Farrow as
a girl impregnated by the devil,
marked his Hollywood debut. Sharon
Tate was herself pregnant when she
and her party of friends were butchered. Polanski's career survived
that, though he has been unable to
work in Hollywood since 1977 when
he left America to avoid certain imprisonment for a charge of statutory
rape. *Tess* was made in France. In
1981 Polanski returned to Warsaw to
direct and act in the play *Amadeus*. His
next film was the lavish *Pirates*, regarded by Polanski as one of his most
important projects.

Films include: 1953 Trzy Opowieści (act)
(POL). '55 Pokolenie (act) (POL) (USA/GB:
A Generation). '58 Morderstwo (short)
(POL); Dwaj Ludzie z Szafa (short) (POL)
(USA/GB: Two Men and a Wardrobe). '60
Zezowate Szczęście (ass. dir) (POL). '61 Le
Gros et le Maigre (short) (FR) (USA/GB: The
Fat and the Lean). '62 Nóż w Wodzie (POL)
(USA/GB: Knife in the Water). '65 Repul-
sion (GB). '66 Cul-de-Sac (GB). '67 Dance of
the Vampires (GB) (USA: The Fearless Vam-
pire Killers, or Pardon Me, But Your Teeth
Are in My Neck). '68 Rosemary's Baby
(USA). '71 Macbeth (GB). '72 Che? (IT-FR-
GER) (USA: Diary of Forbidden Dreams; GB:
What?). '74 Chinatown (USA). '76 Le Lo-
cataire (FR) (USA/GB: The Tenant). '79
Tess (FR-GB). '83 Pirates (ISRAEL).

POLGLASE, Van Nest

(1898–1968). Art director. Born:
New York City, USA

Polglase studied architecture, interior
decoration and design at Beaux Arts
and afterwards joined a firm of architects. From 1919 he was assistant art
director with Famous Players-Lasky
in New York and in 1927 went to
work for the studio (by then Paramount) in Hollywood. In 1929 he
moved to MGM and in 1932 was hired
by David O. Selznick to supervise art
direction at RKO. At one time Polglase
had as many as 110 set decorators
working under him, and, although it
is not certain how much creative
control he exerted over them, there is
little doubt that (with Carroll Clark)
he was responsible for the great,
glossy, white art-deco ballrooms and
nightclubs that provided a fantasy
world for Fred Astaire and Ginger
Rogers to dance in. He had built a
magnificent medieval set for *The
Hunchback of Notre Dame* and helped
design, too, the looming, alienating
vastnesses of *Citizen Kane*. A drink
problem cost Polglase his job at RKO
and in 1943 he moved to Columbia,
where he realized the tawdry, night-
time glitter of *Gilda*. Polglase continued to work until 1957, latterly as a
freelance. He died of burns when his
clothes accidentally caught fire. He
was nominated for six Oscars.

Films as art dir, or co-art dir: 1925 A Kiss in
the Dark. '28 The Magnificent Flirt. '33
Flying Down to Rio. '34 The Gay Divorcee
(GB: The Gay Divorce). '35 Roberta; Top
Hat. '36 Follow the Fleet; Mary of Scotland.
'37 Shall We Dance? '38 Carefree. '39 Love
Affair; The Hunchback of Notre Dame. '40
My Favourite Wife; Citizen Kane. '41 Sus-
picion. '46 Gilda. '57 The River's Edge.

POLITO, Sol

(1892–1960). Cinematographer.
Born: Palermo, Sicily

Polito was educated in New York. He
entered films as a still photographer
and then became a camera assistant.
He began to shoot films for Mutual in
1918 and worked for most of the
major studios during the silent era,
eventually settling at Warner Brothers in 1933. There, he and another emigré cinematographer, Tony
Gaudio, were largely responsible for
establishing the dramatically lit and
textured Warners house-style of the
Thirties. Polito worked most rewardingly with Mervyn LeRoy, Michael
Curtiz and Irving Rapper. He retired in
1949, having received Oscar nominations for his black-and-white
photography on *Sergeant York* and
colour photography on *The Private
Lives of Elizabeth and Essex* (with W.
Howard Greene) and *Captains of the
Clouds*. His son Eugene is also a
cinematographer.

Films include: 1917 Queen X. '29 Seven
Footprints to Satan. '32 I Am a Fugitive
From a Chain Gang (GB: I Am a Fugitive
From the Chain Gang). '33 42nd Street. '36
The Petrified Forest; The Charge of the
Light Brigade (co-photo). '38 The Adven-
tures of Robin Hood (co-photo). '39 The
Private Lives of Elizabeth and Essex (co-

*Above: Roman Polanski directs Jack
Nicholson in a scene from* Chinatown.
Below: Michael J. Pollard in Bonnie

*and Clyde. Right: the Chaplinesque
silent-movie comedian Snub Pollard
and his famous moustache*

photo). '40 The Sea Hawk. '41 Sergeant
York. '42 Now, Voyager; Captains of the
Clouds. '44 Arsenic and Old Lace. '46 A
Stolen Life (co-photo). '49 Anna Lucasta.

POLLACK, Sydney

(b. 1934). Director. Born: Lafayette,
Indiana, USA

Pollack is a competent director in the
commercial cinema, especially good
at drawing sensitive, understated performances from such actors as Robert
Redford and Jane Fonda, and most of
his films are visually striking. They
are increasingly socially concerned,
too – *Absence of Malice* powerfully
indicts bad journalism and political
manoeuvering – but it must be said
that few of them have any bite. They
are conscientious but cautious pictures, seemingly afraid of offending.

However, *This Property Is Condemned*
is a fine adaptation of a Tennessee
Williams play; *They Shoot Horses,
Don't They?* skilfully recreates a Depression dance marathon; and *Jeremiah Johnson* is a beautifully told
story of a lone trapper, snowbound
and periodically challenged by mar-
auding Indians. Against those, *The
Way We Were* is an irksome piece of
sentiment and *The Yakuza* a dreadful
waste of Robert Mitchum. Pollack
studied at the Neighborhood
Playhouse and appeared on Broadway and television. He also taught
drama. He won a cluster of
Emmy nominations for his work as a
television director before making his
first film, *The Slender Thread*, in 1965.

Films include: 1965 The Slender Thread.
'66 This Property Is Condemned. '68 The
Scalphunters. '69 Castle Keep; They Shoot

Horses, Don't They? '72 Jeremiah Johnson. '73 The Way We Were. '75 The Yakuza; Three Days of the Condor. '77 Bobby Deerfield. '79 The Electric Horseman. '81 Absence of Malice.

POLLARD, Michael J.

(b. 1939). Actor. Born: Michael J. Pollack; Passaic, New Jersey, USA

Diminutive, wispy-haired, impish Pollard studied at the Actors' Studio and made his Broadway debut in *Comes the Day* with George C. Scott. He then appeared on stage with Warren Beatty in *A Loss of Roses* and then came his big break; he was cast as C. W. Moss, the inarticulate but good-natured garage hand turned gangster robbing banks with Beatty and Faye Dunaway in *Bonnie and Clyde*. He received an Oscar nomination for Best Supporting Actor and on the strength of that was offered

further good roles. He was the prisoner of war leading a group of escapees across the Austrian mountains in *Hannibal Brooks*, and starred as the country-boy ace mechanic exploited by Big Halsy (Robert Redford) in *Little Fauss and Big Halsy*. He also played Billy the Kid as a half-witted psychopath in *Dirty Little Billy*. His television credits include *Gunsmoke*, *The Virginian* and *I Spy*.

Films include: 1962 Hemingway's Adventures of a Young Man. '63 Summer Magic. '66 The Wild Angels; The Russians Are Coming, the Russians Are Coming. '67 Enter Laughing; Bonnie and Clyde. '68 Jigsaw (GB: Jigsaw Murder). '69 Hannibal Brooks (GB). '70 Little Fauss and Big Halsy. '72 Dirty Little Billy. '80 Melvin and Howard.

POLLARD, Snub

(1886–1962). Actor. Born: Harold Frazer; Melbourne, Australia

Snub Pollard was a popular slapstick comedian in silent days. His trademarks were an immense, drooping moustache, derby hat and string tie, striped shirt and white gloves; his manner was frenetic and his eyes forever rolling. He joined Hal Roach in 1915 and worked in Harold Lloyd movies. In 1919 he had his own series of one-reelers. In the Twenties the studio tried to build him up by promoting him to two-reel comedies, but Pollard was never quite funny enough, or original enough, for star status. An attempt to run a company of his own failed, and in the sound period he made only the occasional appearance in small parts in features.

Films include: 1919 Start Something (short). '22 The Dumb-Bell (short); The Bow Wows (short); Years to Come. '23 The Courtship of Miles Sandwich (short). '32 Make Me a Star. '34 Cockeyed Cavaliers. '38 Starlight Over Texas. '57 Man of a Thousand Faces. '61 Pocketful of Miracles.

POLONSKY, Abraham

(b. 1910). Director/screenwriter. Born: New York City, USA

Andrew Sarris names Polonsky, Chaplin and Losey as the three major casualties of Fifties blacklisting. But Chaplin's work was almost finished, and Losey built a new career in Europe, while Polonsky, who had directed one film, and that often reckoned a masterpiece, had to wait until 1970 before he directed again. He came from a Russian immigrant family, taught at City College in New York, wrote fiction and radio scripts – some of them for Orson Welles' Mercury Theatre – and after war service went to Hollywood as a scriptwriter. He wrote the acclaimed boxing melodrama, *Body and Soul*, starring John Garfield; and was then asked to write and direct Garfield's next film, *Force of Evil*. Then HUAC destroyed him, though not financially, for he wrote for television and doctored other men's film scripts, but as a creative artist. When he came back in 1970 with *Tell Them Willie Boy Is Here*, about an Indian boy as abused by society as Polonsky himself had been,

the film was careful, intelligent, even moving, but the vital spark had gone.

Films include: 1947 Body and Soul (sc. only); Golden Earrings (co-sc. only). '49 Force of Evil. '51 I Can Get It for You Wholesale (sc. only). '68 Madigan (co-sc. only). '69 Tell Them Willie Boy Is Here. '71 Romance of a Horse Thief (USA-YUG).

POMMER, Erich

(1889–1966). Producer. Born: Hildesheim, Germany

As a young man Pommer joined the French Gaumont company and by the age of 20 was head of their central European office. In 1913 he moved to the French Eclair company, but on the outbreak of World War I returned home to fight for his country. After being invalided out of the army, he resumed his career by founding the Deutsche Eclair (Decla) company and in 1919 produced the first of his masterpieces, *The Cabinet of Dr Caligari*. Decla then merged with Bioscop and eventually became part of Ufa when Pommer joined the latter's board of directors. He was still regarded primarily as a businessman, but his natural flair for creating excitement and adventure, and tailoring the stories to fit his stars, soon made him a much respected impresario and he gained a massive reputation for being able to extract the best and most extraordinary performances from all members of his cast and crew. Directors who worked for him included Lubitsch and Lang. The marvellous atmosphere created in *The Blue Angel* was a Pommer triumph, for he had to harness the erratic temperaments of both the 'new' star Marlene Dietrich and director Josef von Sternberg. With the rise of the Nazis, Pommer began a period of self-imposed exile which took him to Paris, London – where he worked with Alexander Korda on *Fire Over England* and formed Mayflower Pictures with Charles Laughton – and Hollywood. After World War II Pommer returned to Germany to try and rebuild the film industry there, producing several unremarkable films before retiring to Hollywood in 1956.

Films include: 1919 Das Kabinett des Dr Caligari (GB: The Cabinet of Dr Caligari). '25 Varieté (GB: Vaudeville). '26 Faust. '27 Metropolis. '30 Der blaue Engel (USA/GB: The Blue Angel). '37 Fire Over England (GB); Troopship (GB) (USA: Farewell Again). '39 Jamaica Inn (GB); Hotel Imperial (USA). '40 Dance Girl Dance (USA).

PONTECORVO, Gillo

(b. 1919). Director. Born: Gilberto Pontecorvo; Pisa, Italy

The younger brother of Professor Bruno Pontecorvo, the Harwell scientist who defected in 1950, Gillo Pontecorvo is himself a Marxist, and his concern with imperialism and colonialism has been very clear in his major films. He worked as an assistant director, directed documentary shorts, and made his first feature in 1957. His second film, *Kapò*, the story of a young Jewess in Auschwitz,

gained some international recognition, but with the third, *The Battle of Algiers*, Pontecorvo won the Golden Lion at Venice and enormous acclaim. This film of the Algerian struggle for independence was terse, exciting, and essentially fair-minded; it used real locations and many non-professional actors, and looked, and perhaps was, totally authentic. Pontecorvo went on to make *Queimada!*, which starred Marlon Brando in a story of slavery in the West Indies, but it lacked the urgency of the earlier work. Pontecorvo's later films have scarcely been seen in Britain or America.

Films include: 1956 Die Windrose *ep* Giovanna (E. GER). '58 La Grande Strada Azzurra (IT-FR-YUG). '60 Kapò (IT-FR). '66 La Battaglia di Algeri (IT-ALGERIA) (GB: Battle of Algiers). '69 Queimada! (IT-FR) (USA: Burn!). '79 Ogro (IT-SP-FR).

PONTI, Carlo

(b. 1910). Producer. Born: Magenta, Milan, Italy

Carlo Ponti graduated in law from the University of Milan and practised as an attorney for three years, during which time he handled the affairs of many influential people. One of them was a high-ranking member of a film distribution company who left his business in Ponti's care when he was forced to leave Italy. Armed with this authority, Ponti then spent the early Forties overseeing the production of films by many of Italy's greatest directors. After World War II Ponti joined Lux Films (1945–49) and was instrumental in the rejuvenation of the Italian film industry with such films as Luigi Zampa's *Vivere in Pace* (1946, *To Live in Peace*), which brought him praise from critics the world over, and *Senza Pietà*. During this period Ponti discovered a young actress named Sophia Loren, and by 1960 had established her as a star, *Two Women* winning her an Oscar. They were married in Mexico in 1957, a coupling deemed to be bigamy in Italy (although he had divorced his first wife Giuliana Fiastri a few years previously). They were forced to annul the marriage; Ponti became a French citizen in 1965 and was granted a French divorce from Fiastri, thus enabling him to re-marry Loren. In 1950 Ponti joined Dino De Laurentiis in a successful four-year partnership that saw the production of some of Italy's most exciting films, including Federico Fellini's *La Strada*. Ponti then went on to expand his activities to Europe and Hollywood. In 1979 he was sentenced to two years imprisonment (which as a French citizen he was not required to serve) for illegally exporting capital from Italy.

Films include: 1941 Piccolo Mondo Antico. '47 Senza Pietà. '51 Europa '51 (USA: The Greatest Love). '54 La Strada. '56 War and Peace (IT-USA). '61 La Ciociara (FR-IT) (GB: Two Women). '64 Ieri, Oggi e Domani (IT-FR) (USA/GB: Yesterday, Today and Tomorrow); Matrimonio all'Italiana (IT-FR) (USA/GB: Marriage, Italian Style). '65 Lady L (USA-FR-IT); Dr Zhivago (USA). '66 Blow-up (GB). '75 Professione: Reporter (IT-FR-SP) (USA/GB: The Passenger).

POPESCU-GOPO, Ion

(b. 1923). Animator/director. Born:
Bucharest, Romania

Popescu-Gopo completed his first
animated cartoon in 1938, and after
war service attended the School of
Sculpture in Bucharest. In 1950 a
national animation studio was set up
and, with his father, Popescu-Gopo
made *The Naughty Duckling*, the first
Romanian cartoon with colour and
sound. He became known abroad
when his *A Short History* won the
Golden Palm at Cannes in 1957. Over
the years he has won more than fifty
international awards. His best cartoons have been whimsical accounts
of historical or cultural events, full of
gentle poetry and ingenious gags.
From the early Fifties he also made
live-action- (usually science-fiction)
films. In 1969 he was appointed Head
of the Cinema and Television section
of the World Health organization.

Films include: 1955 Surubul Lui Marinică.
'56 Scurtă Istorie (GB: A Short History);
Fetita Mincinoasă. '58 Sapte Arte. '59 O
Poveste Ca In Basme. '60 Homo Sapiens.
'64 Allo, Allo. . . . '67 De 3 Ori Bucuresti *ep*
Orasul Meu. '68 Sancta Simplicitas. '75
Uno, Doi, Trei. . . .

PORTEN, Henny

(1888–1960). Actress. Born:
Magdeburg, Germany

Henny Porten was the first popular
star of the German cinema. The
daughter of opera singer Franz
Porten, she began her career in
around 1906, but her great period
came soon after World War I, when
she worked for directors like Lubitsch,
Jessner and Dupont. Porten's acting
was restrained and natural, and she
had great range. She was excellent in
comedy: in Lubitsch's *Kohlhiesel's
Daughters* she played both daughters,
the pretty Gretl and the plain Liesl, in
a virtuoso display of sheer technique.
In more serious vein, her moving
Anna Boleyn survives (Lubitsch
again), as does her unhappy maidser-
vant in Jessner's *Hintertreppe*. In the
Nazi period she appeared rarely, for
her second husband was a Jew, but
she came back afterwards, and even
in the Fifties was playing the occasional lead.

Films include: 1917 Die Ehe der Luise
Rohrbach. '19 Rose Bernd (+ prod). '20
Anna Boleyn (USA: Deception); Kohlhies-
els Töchter (Kohlhiesel's Daughters). '21
Hintertreppe (+ prod) (Backstairs). '23
INRI. '23 Der Kaufmann von Venedig (GB:
The Jew of Mestri). '28 Zuflucht (+prod)
(GB: Refuge). '31 Luise, Königin von Preu-
ssen. '44 Familie Buchholz. '54 Carola
Lamberti – Eine vom Circus (E. GER) (GB:
Woman of the Circus). '55 Das Fräulein von
Skuderi (E. GER-SWED).

PORTEN, Cole

(1893–1964). Composer/lyricist.
Born: Peru, Indiana, USA

Porter inherited a fortune from his
grandfather, a coal and timber millionaire. After studying at Yale University and Harvard Law School, he
decided to devote himself to music.

Heartbroken at the failure of his first
Broadway venture, *See America First*
in 1916, he joined the French Foreign
Legion, transferring to the French
army during World War I. After the
war he spent much of his time in
Paris, studied at the Schola Cantorum
and gained a world-wide reputation
as a *bon viveur*. In 1928 the musical
Paris became the first of his many
Broadway hits, which included *Silk
Stockings*, *Can-Can* and *Kiss Me, Kate*
(all of which were later adapted for the
screen). Despite a serious riding accident in 1937 that confined him to a
wheelchair for the rest of his life,
Porter consolidated his position as one
of the greatest American songwriters
with a steady output of songs that
combined haunting melodies with
witty, racy and romantic lyrics. In
1946 Warner Brothers released a film
biopic of Porter's life, *Night and Day*,
with Cary Grant in the leading role.

Films include: 1929 The Battle of Paris. '34
The Gay Divorcee (GB: The Gay Divorce).
'36 Born to Dance. '37 Rosalie. '40 Broad-
way Melody of 1940. '41 You'll Never Get
Rich. '43 Something to Shout About. '48
The Pirate. '53 Kiss Me, Kate. '56 High
Society. '57 Les Girls. '60 Can-Can.

PORTER, Edwin S.

(1869–1941). Pioneer/director. Born:
Edwin Stanton Porter; Connellsville,
Pennsylvania, USA

After numerous jobs and three years'
naval service, Edwin S. Porter became

interested in film equipment through
a job with the firm that marketed the
Edison Vitascope. He began experimenting with projection and in partnership with William J. Beadnell invented
the Beadnell 'Improved Projector'. In
1900 fire gutted their factory and
Porter became a freelance photographer, worked his way into the Edison
company and finally emerged as film-
production chief. His first pictures for
the company were rough vaudeville
shows or landscapes, but influenced
by the pioneering Georges Méliès,
Porter began to experiment with non-
stop motion photography and innovative cutting. Edison accused him of
'cutting his people in half', believing –
as he did – that the camera ought to
show a person in entirety. Porter
remained unperturbed and his *The
Great Train Robbery*, a 12-minute
short that marked the birth of the
Western and packed out the Nickelodeons, was extraordinary in its use
of camera (the closing shot is of a
bandit in close-up, firing his revolver
at the audience), trick photography
and editing – all techniques that
became standard when D. W. Griffith
started to develop Porter's ideas.
Other companies flocked to outdo *The
Great Train Robbery*, but Edison refused to relax his outmoded ideas and
in 1909 Porter formed Rex Films. On
its unfortunate demise he joined the
company that was to become Famous
Players. With less chance to shine in
feature-length adaptations of literary
works and the like, Porter retired but
continued to experiment with colour

technology, synchronized sound and
3-D projects until his death.

Films include: 1902 The Life of an Amer-
ican Fireman. '03 The Great Train Robbery;
Uncle Tom's Cabin. '04 The Night Before
Christmas. '05 Stolen by Gypsies. '06 The
Life of a Cow-Boy. '07 Rescued From an
Eagle's Nest. '08 The Face on the Barroom
Floor. '10 Peg Woffington. '11 The Strike at
the Mines. '13 Tess of the Storm Country.
'14 Eternal City.

PORTER, Eric

(b. 1928). Actor. Born: London,
England

Eric Porter's ambition to be an actor
never faltered from the time he acted
in school plays at Wimbledon College.
He went from school to Stratford-on-
Avon, where he 'carried a spear', from
there to repertory in the Bristol and
London Old Vic Companies. He entered films in the Sixties and has since
played tough character roles and
leads in a good number of films. There
is no doubt, however, that in the
public mind he is best known as
Soames in the television production of
The Forsyte Saga, although he is also a
notable Shakespearian actor.

Films include: 1964 The Fall of the Roman
Empire (USA); The Pumpkin Eater. '68 The
Lost Continent. '71 Hands of the Ripper;
Nicholas and Alexandra (USA). '72 Antony
and Cleopatra (GB-SP-SWITZ). '73 The Day
of the Jackal (GB-FR); The Belstone Fox;
Hitler: The Last Ten Days (GB-IT). '78 The
Thirty-Nine Steps.

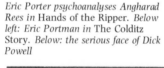

Films include: **1935** Maria Marten; Abdul the Damned. **'41** 49th Parallel; One of Our Aircraft Is Missing. **'43** Millions Like Us. **'44** A Canterbury Tale. **'45** Great Day. **'46** Daybreak. **'47** Dear Murderer. **'48** Corridor of Mirrors. **'55** The Colditz Story. **'62** Freud (USA) (GB: Freud – The Secret Passion). **'67** The Whisperers.

POST, Ted

(b. 1918). Director. Born: Brooklyn, New York City, USA

Ted Post is essentially a stage and television director, having made only a dozen or so cinema films since his debut in 1956. He trained as a theatre director by directing plays for the labour unions. By 1950 he had built a high reputation; that was the time of live television drama, and Post moved into television as a director. Live television went, but Post stayed – for 600 odd productions, including countless episodes of *Peyton Place*, *Rawhide*, *The Virginian*, and such. His best known films for the big screen, *Hang 'Em High* and *Magnum Force*, have been described as showing Post's 'belief in the destructive nature of social conformity'; others have seen in them a glorification of mindless violence.

Films include: **1956** The Peacemaker. **'59** The Legend of Tom Dooley. **'68** Hang 'Em High. **'70** Beneath the Planet of the Apes. **'73** Magnum Force; The Haddad Experiment. **'75** Whiffs (GB: C.A.S.H.). **'78** Good Guys Wear Black; Go Tell the Spartans.

POTTER, H. C.

(1904–1977). Director. Born: Henry Codman Potter; New York City, USA

A graduate of the Yale School of Drama, Potter founded the Hampton Players, one of the first summer-stock theatres on the Eastern circuit, and directed there for eight years before making his first film in 1936. It seems that Potter is now remembered mainly for his comedies, and certainly the zany *Hellzapoppin'* was beautifully handled by him, but his dramatic pictures were infinitely more rewarding. *Beloved Enemy* (Potter's debut) was a moving film about the Irish patriot Michael Collins; *The Shopworn Angel* (1938) was a perfect vehicle for Margaret Sullavan; and *The Time of Your Life* (1948) did full justice to William Saroyan's best play, and contained one of James Cagney's most sensitive performances.

Films include: **1936** Beloved Enemy. **'37** Wings Over Honolulu. **'38** Romance in the Dark. **'39** The Story of Vernon and Irene Castle; Blackmail. **'42** Hellzapoppin'. **'43** Victory Through Air Power (co-dir). **'48** Mr Blandings Builds His Dream House. **'50** The Miniver Story (GB). **'57** Top Secret Affair (GB: Their Secret Affair).

POWELL, Dick

(1904–1963). Actor/director/producer. Born: Richard E. Powell; Mountain View, Arkansas, USA

Few actors have changed their image in mid-career as totally and as suc-

cessfully as Powell. He joined Warners in the early Thirties in time for the heyday of that studio's musicals. He was a cherubic, clean-cut, singing juvenile in *42nd Street* and all the rest, but there was a naughty twinkle in his eye and a relish in his voice as he went 'Pettin' in the Park' – and elsewhere – with chaste Ruby Keeler and all those Busby Berkeley chorines. He moved off to Paramount for light comedy without song in Preston Struges' *Christmas in July*, and then suddenly emerged as Raymond Chandler's tough private eye Philip Marlowe in *Murder, My Sweet*. He was a revelation, solid, human, and his own man. He stayed in *film noir* for *Cornered* and a few more, showed a talent for broad comedy in *You Never Can Tell*, and then had a stab at direction. He made competent action movies, with the submarine drama *The Enemy Below* rather better than the rest, produced a deal of television drama, and was the comfortable host of a chat-show in his last years. He was married to Joan Blondell, and then to June Allyson, who survived him.

Films include: **1933** 42nd Street; Gold Diggers of 1933. **'34** Flirtation Walk. **'40** Christmas in July. **'43** Star Spangled Rhythm. **'44** It Happened Tomorrow; Murder, My Sweet (GB: Farewell My Lovely); Johnny O'Clock. **'45** Cornered. **'51** You Never Can Tell. **'52** The Bad and the Beautiful. **'53** Split Second (dir; + prod). **'56** The Conqueror (dir; + prod). **'57** The Enemy Below (dir; + prod).

POWELL, Eleanor

(1912–1982). Dancer/actress. Born: Springfield, Massachusetts, USA

Almost able to dance before she could walk, Powell first attracted attention doing acrobatics on the beach at Atlantic City. She was offered a revue job at the Ritz Grill and at the age of 16 landed herself a place in Gus Edwards' revue in New York. It was but a short step to musicals on Broadway, closely followed by an MGM contract in 1935. A brilliant, exuberant tap dancer, she has been described as a 'disciplined hurricane' by one critic and, after her tremendous debut in *Broadway Melody of 1936*, another critic said she lent 'a sort of poetry to a slightly eccentric art'. Perhaps her most treasured accolade came from Fred Astaire, who considered her a better dancer than himself after their appearances together in *Born to Dance* and *Broadway Melody of 1940* – in both of which she matched him tap for tap. She is said to have covered four miles during her dancing in *George White's Scandals* and her stamina stood her in undoubted stead when she appeared in a forty-minute non-stop routine at the London Palladium in 1949. After her marriage to Glenn Ford in 1943 Powell more or less retired from the screen – a timely departure, for by then the tap-dancing musical was going out of style.

Films include: **1934** George White's Scandals. **'35** The Broadway Melody of 1936. **'36** Born to Dance. **'37** Rosalie. **'40** Broadway Melody of 1940. **'41** Lady Be Good. **'42** Ship Ahoy. **'43** Thousands Cheer. **'50** Duchess of Idaho.

Far left: Henny Porten, the first German movie queen in Monika Vogelsang *(1919). Left: Eleanor Powell tapping her way to stardom in* The Broadway Melody of 1936. *Above:*

Eric Porter psychoanalyses Angharad Rees in Hands of the Ripper. *Below left: Eric Portman in* The Colditz Story. *Below: the serious face of Dick Powell*

PORTMAN, Eric

(1903–1969). Actor. Born: Halifax, Yorkshire, England

In Michael Powell's World War II idyll *A Canterbury Tale*, the mysterious village JP Thomas Culpepper – who strikes in the darkness of the blackout to pour glue on girls' hair – is crowned with a halo of sunlight just as the train carriage he is sitting in enters a tunnel. Culpepper, the self-elected protector of pastoral England (whose night-time depradations prevent the girls going out with soldiers) and seemingly a miracle-worker, was brilliantly played in this film by Eric Portman. His frigid, supercilious exterior hides a great romantic heart but

his actions hint at kinkiness, and only an actor as good as Portman could convey so much in a single characterization – or was worthy of such on-screen deification. His other fine portrayal for Powell was as the cold-blooded Nazi U-boat commander in *49th Parallel*; Portman, though, was equally at ease as a bluff, working-class shop steward in Launder and Gilliat's *Millions Like Us*. He was the son of a wool-merchant, and he began his working career as a menswear salesman. In 1924 he joined Robert Courtneidge's touring Shakespeare company and made his London stage debut. He began his intermittent 34-year film career in *Marie Marten* in 1935.

POWELL, Jane

(b. 1929). Actress. Born: Suzanne
Burce; Portland, Oregon, USA

A child singer who had had her own
radio programme since she was 11,
Jane Powell was signed at 16 to a
long-term contract with MGM. For
ten years or so she played happily
carolling adolescents in musical romances. She was petite and pretty, and
had a pleasant personality, but apart
from *Seven Brides for Seven Brothers*
the films were unmemorable. MGM
obviously wanted to create a second
Deanna Durbin, but Durbin had
better writers and better directors.
Powell's career faded in the late Fifties, and she moved into television
and the theatre, with a highlight in
1973 when she appeared on Broadway in *Irene*.

Films include: 1944 Song of the Open Road.
'46 Holiday in Mexico. **'48** A Date With
Judy. **'51** Royal Wedding (GB: Wedding
Bells). **'53** Three Sailors and a Girl; Small
Town Girl. **'54** Seven Brides for Seven
Brothers. **'55** Hit the Deck. **'56** The Birds and
the Bees. **'57** The Girl Most Likely. **'58** The
Female Animal; Enchanted Island.

POWELL, Michael

(b. 1905). Director/producer/
screenwriter. Born: Canterbury,
Kent, England

When a retrospective of his films was
put on at the National Film Theatre in
London, Michael Powell insisted that
the season should begin with a film –
any film – by Rex Ingram. Seldom has
any great director owed so clear a debt
to another; even more seldom has a
heritage been turned to such personal
and imaginative use. Powell went, at
19, to work for Ingram at Nice. He
watched the making of *Mare Nostrum*
(1926), and he acted in *The Magician*
and *The Garden of Allah*. Then he came
home, was briefly a cameraman and
screenwriter, directed quickies
through the Thirties (with a maturing
style visible in such good little films as
The Phantom Light), and by the end of
the decade was entrusted with larger
projects like *The Spy in Black*. In 1938
the partnership with Emeric Pressburger began. Powell and Pressburger
formed the Archers company, and
from 1942 to 1956 all their films were
written, directed and produced in
tandem. From 1943, Powell and Pressburger made five successive masterpieces, from *Colonel Blimp* to *Black
Narcissus*, with, in between, *A Canterbury Tale, I Know Where I'm Going* and
A Matter of Life and Death. They were
eccentric and wayward, visually
superb (in part due to the great art
director Alfred Junge) and structured
round great set-pieces. But they were
something else too. These films were
essentially English, not just in their
feeling for the landscape – though *A
Canterbury Tale* shows that as no other
English movie has – but in their
understatement, their control of intense passion, their casual decency.
Powell had one fine film left after the
partnership dissolved, the dark and
terrible *Peeping Tom* – a film critically
reviled in its day, but now winning
acceptance as crucial to understand-

ing Powell's complex art. Its director
is active still: at 75 he went to America
as senior adviser to Francis Ford
Coppola's Zoetrope studios.

Films include: 1926 The Magician (act)
(USA). **'27** The Garden of Allah (act) (USA).
'31 Two Crowded Hours (dir); Rynox (dir;
+ co-sc). **'34** Something Always Happens
(dir). **'35** The Phantom Light (dir). **'36** The
Man Behind the Mask (dir). **'37** The Edge of
the World (dir; + sc). **'39** The Spy in Black
(dir) (USA: U-Boat 29). **'40** The Thief of
Bagdad (co-dir). **'41** 49th Parallel (dir; +
prod; + co-sc) (USA: The Invaders). *As co-
dir, co-prod, co-sc:* One of Our Aircraft Is
Missing (+ act). **'43** The Life and Death of
Colonel Blimp (USA: Colonel Blimp). **'44** A
Canterbury Tale. **'45** I Know Where I'm
Going. **'46** A Matter of Life and Death (USA:
Stairway to Heaven). **'47** Black Narcissus.
'48 The Red Shoes. **'49** The Small Back
Room (USA: Hour of Glory). **'50** The Elusive
Pimpernel (co-dir; + co-sc) (USA: The
Fighting Pimpernel). **'51** The Tales of Hoff-
mann. **'56** The Battle of the River Plate
(USA: Pursuit of the Graf Spee). **'60** Peeping
Tom (dir; + prod; + act). **'68** Age of
Consent (dir; + co-prod) (AUS). **'72** The
Boy Who Turned Yellow (dir).

POWELL, Robert

(b. 1944). Actor. Born: Salford,
Lancashire, England

Robert Powell works mainly for television and the stage, and his international reputation was earned playing Jesus in the Franco Zeffirelli television epic *Jesus of Nazareth*. However,
he has also played many diversified
parts in films, including the lead in the
second re-make of *The Thirty-Nine
Steps* and the title role in Ken Russell's
frenzied *Mahler*. His gaunt, sculpted
face and piercing blue eyes give him a
distinctive appearance, and the
seriousness of his demeanour adds
distinction to his roles.

Films include: 1967 Robbery. **'69** The
Italian Job. **'72** Running Scared; The
Asphyx; Secrets; Asylum. **'74** Mahler. **'75**
Tommy. **'77** The Four Feathers. **'78** The
Thirty-Nine Steps. **'80** The Survivor.

POWELL, William

(1892–1984). Actor. Born:
Pittsburgh, Pennsylvania, USA

One of the finest players in the history
of the American screen, William
Powell was on the New York stage by
1912, and in films ten years later,
making his debut as a minor villain in
the John Barrymore *Sherlock Holmes*.
Through the Twenties Powell was in
interesting films by good directors, but
never really stood out until Sternberg
cast him as the arrogant film director
in *The Last Command* (1928). From
then on Powell's career flourished,
and sound, revealing his rich voice
with its ironic modulations and impeccable timing, completed his
triumph. Elegant, perfectly turned
out, eyebrow raised in quizzical
wonder at the oddness of the world, he
played comedy, melodrama, thriller
with equal insouciance. He was two of
the screen's finest private detectives –
first the haughty Philo Vance, then, in
that great partnership with Myrna
Loy, the genial bibulous Nick Charles.

354

He was intensely moving in *One Way Passage* as a murderer returning on ship to certain execution; irresistibly funny as tramp turned butler in *My Man Godfrey*; and serenely dominating the spectacle of *The Great Ziegfeld*. His last great role was as Clarence Day in *Life With Father*. But it is difficult to recall a bad film in which he appeared. He was the first husband of Carole Lombard.

Above, far left: Jane Powell in the MGM musical Nancy Goes to Rio *(1950). Above left: Robert Powell in* Asylum. *Left: the directors Michael Powell and Emeric Pressburger on the set of* One of Our Aircraft Is Missing. *Below left: Paula Prentiss in* What's New Pussycat?. *Above: William Powell in* For the Defense *(1930). Below: Tyrone Power as the swashbuckling* Captain From Castile. *Below right: Albert Préjean in René Clair's first talkie* Sous les Toits de Paris

POWER, Tyrone

(1913–1958). Actor. Born: Cincinnati, Ohio, USA

Tyrone Power Sr (1869–1931) was a matinée idol of Broadway and silent movies who died on the set of *The Miracle Man* (1932). His son, Tyrone Power, made his own film debut in 1932. This Tyrone was affable, extremely handsome, and a more-than-competent actor. From around 1937 he was the top male star at 20th Century-Fox, frequently submerged in opulent costume dramas. But he could be a compelling actor with half a chance, and directors like Henry King (*Alexander's Ragtime Band*) and Mamoulian (*Blood and Sand*) drew fine performances from him. When in 1946 he returned to the screen after war service, he was sometimes cast in parts that took him far away from his romantic past. *Nightmare Alley*, in which he played an alcoholic who is degraded to a fairground freak, was perhaps his finest achievement. His popularity was fading by the Fifties, but ironically enough his films were getting better, and he did good things for Ford and Wilder before, like his father, he too died on the set, from a heart attack while working for King Vidor on *Solomon and Sheba* (1959).

Films include: 1932 Tom Brown of Culver. '36 Girls' Dormitory. '38 Alexander's Ragtime Band. '41 Blood and Sand. '47 Captain From Castile; Nightmare Alley. '50 The Black Rose. '51 The House in the Square (GB) (USA: I'll Never Forget You). '53 Mississippi Gambler. '55 The Long Gray Line. '56 The Eddie Duchin Story. '57 Seven Waves Away (GB) (USA: Abandon Ship); Witness for the Prosecution.

Films include: 1922 Sherlock Holmes (GB: Moriarty). '29 Interference; The Canary Murder Case. '30 Street of Chance. '31 Man of the World. '32 One Way Passage. '34 The Thin Man. '36 The Great Ziegfeld; My Man Godfrey; Libelled Lady. '47 Life With Father. '55 Mister Roberts.

PRÉJEAN, Albert

(1893–1979). Actor. Born: La Varenne-St Hilaire, Paris, France

A good-looking, likeable Gallic type, Préjean was a former acrobat, nightclub singer and World War I air ace when he entered movies as a stunt man in a version of *The Three Musketeers*. His first acting part was in René Clair's directorial debut *Paris Qui Dort*, the first of five delightful comedy-dramas they made together. Of these, Préjean's best roles were in *The Italian Straw Hat*, in which he is the luckless bridegroom Fadinard, forced to replace a hat chewed up by his horse on his way to his wedding, and in the formative French sound film *Sous les Toits de Paris*, in which he is the street singer who loses his girl when he is wrongfully arrested. Other roles that the popular Préjean essayed were Inspector Maigret (three times) and Mack the Knife in *L'Opéra de Quat' Sous*, the French-language version of Pabst's *The Threepenny Opera*.

Films include: 1921 Les Trois Mousquetaires (GB: The Three Musketeers). '23 Paris Qui Dort (GB: The Crazy Ray). '24 Le Voyage Imaginaire. '27 Un Chapeau de Paille d'Italie (GB: The Italian Straw Hat). '28 Les Nouveaux Messieurs (USA: The New Gentlemen). '30 Sous les Toits de Paris (USA: Under the Roofs of Paris). '31 L'Opéra de Quat' Sous (French-language version of Die Dreigroschenoper, GER-USA) (GB: The Threepenny Opera). '36 Jenny. '43 Au Bonheur des Dames. '44 Cécile Est Morte. '47 Les Frères Bouquinquant. '51 Je N'Ai Que Toi au Monde (FR-BELG). '62 De la Poudre et des Balles.

PREMINGER, Otto

(1906–1986). Director/producer/actor. Born: Vienna, Austria

For several years Preminger combined the study of law with acting and directing, most notably for Max Reinhardt at the Theatre der Josefstadt in Vienna. He had directed a single film, *Die grosse Liebe*, when 20th Century-Fox offered him a contract in 1935. He accepted, eager to escape the rise of Nazism in Europe. Preminger's autocratic temperament led to clashes with Darryl F. Zanuck, Fox's head of production, and it was several years before the huge success of *Laura* (which he produced and directed) established his Hollywood career. Over the next fifteen years Preminger made several movies that challenged contemporary views of morality – in particular *The Moon Is Blue*, *Bonjour Tristesse* (which starred his discovery Jean Seberg) and *Anatomy of a Murder*. During the Sixties he became known as the producer and director of big-budget features based on best-selling novels, in which lavish spectacle tended to obscure the acute psychological observation of his earlier work. He later returned to smaller-scale productions with *The Human Factor*, based on the novel by Graham Greene. Preminger's professional reputation as a martinet, noted for reducing actresses (and actors) to tears, led to him being known in Hollywood as 'Otto the Terrible'. As if to deliberately foster this image, he made various convincing appearances as a Nazi in war films, in particular as the POW commandant in Billy Wilder's *Stalag 17* (1953).

Films include: 1932 Die grosse Liebe (A). '44 Laura. '45 Fallen Angel. '47 Forever Amber. '49 The Fan (GB: Lady Windermere's Fan). '52 The Moon Is Blue. '54 Carmen Jones. '56 The Man With the Golden Arm. '57 Saint Joan (GB). '58 Bonjour Tristesse. '59 Porgy and Bess; Anatomy of a Murder. '60 Exodus. '62 Advise and Consent. '63 The Cardinal. '65 In Harm's Way; Bunny Lake Is Missing (GB). '75 Rosebud (+ prod). '79 The Human Factor (GB-USA).

PRENTISS, Paula

(b. 1939). Actress. Born: San Antonio, Texas, USA

Paula Prentiss has been called 'a one-girl Goon Show with sex appeal'. Ever since her early films opposite the likes of Jim Hutton and Rock Hudson she has specialized in zany comedy roles, such as the highly provocative Nurse Duckett in *Catch-22* and the stripper with a taste for abstract poetry in *What's New, Pussycat?*. She originally studied science but soon switched to Northwestern University to study drama. It was there that she met her future husband, actor Richard Benjamin, and her film career began soon afterwards when she was spotted by a Hollywood talent scout. Her popularity further increased with the successful American television series *He and She*, in which she and Benjamin co-starred. She has since managed to mature, without losing her comic gifts, as shown in Billy Wilder's *Buddy, Buddy*, in which she plays the estranged wife of Jack Lemmon's suicidal television censor.

Films include: 1961 Bachelor in Paradise. '64 Man's Favorite Sport?; The World of Henry Orient; Looking for Love. '65 What's New, Pussycat? (USA-FR). '70 Catch-22. '71 Born to Win. '72 Last of the Red Hot Lovers. '74 The Parallax View. '75 The Stepford Wives. '81 Buddy, Buddy.

PRESLEY, Elvis

(1935–1977). Singer/actor. Born: Elvis Aaron Presley; Tupelo, Mississippi, USA

Just a poor country boy, the survivor of twins, Elvis Presley grew up in poverty in a small Mississippi town and, from 1945, in Memphis, Tennessee, the city in which he was later to build a $100,000 mansion, named Graceland, on Elvis Presley Boulevard. In 1953, working as a truck driver, he made an amateur recording as a present for his mother. In 1955 he was signed by RCA Victor and in 1956 'Heartbreak Hotel' brought him to fame. As a hip-waggling young rock'n'roll rebel, dark and sneering, he shocked the older generation and was idolized by the younger. He made four films, including the challenging, aggressive *Jailhouse Rock* before being drafted into the army. Somewhat tamed, he returned to sing ballads in mostly innocuous movies where he was usually torn between an insipid country blonde and a sophisticated brunette from the city. Only as a half-breed Indian living as part of a white family in *Flaming Star* did he consistently suggest the dark, dangerous quality that had been much of his original appeal. He continued making two or three films a year until the end of the Sixties, when increasing overweight became an embarrassment. Then, surprisingly and successfully, he returned to the live concert appearances he had long abandoned – the film records of these tours are considerably more engaging than most of his later features. Worn out by dietary and medical over-indulgences, he died of a heart attack at 42. He married Priscilla Beaulieu in 1967, and they divorced in 1973.

Films include: 1956 Love Me Tender. '57 Loving You; Jailhouse Rock. '58 King Creole. '60 GI Blues; Flaming Star. '61 Wild in the Country. '62 Follow That Dream; Kid Galahad; Girls! Girls! Girls! '64 Kissin' Cousins; Viva Las Vegas (GB: Love in Las Vegas). '65 Girl Happy. '69 The Trouble With Girls; Change of Habit. '70 Elvis – That's the Way It Is (doc). '72 Elvis on Tour (doc).

PRESSBURGER, Emeric

(b. 1902). Director/producer/ screenwriter. Born: Miskolc, Hungary

Pressburger had been a journalist and a writer of film-scripts in Austria and Germany before leaving for France with the Nazis rise to power. A short time later he came to England, and continued as a filmwriter until the partnership with Michael Powell was formed in 1938. Pressburger did some solo work, little of it memorable, but unless the films which he wrote in Europe should one day surface, his reputation must rest upon his contribution to the films of the partnership. As writer and producer it may well have been immense.

Films include: 1930 Abschied/So sind die Menschen (co-sc) (GER) (USA/GB: Farewell). '31 Ronny (co-sc) (GER). '33 Une Femme au Volant (sc) (FR). '35 La Vie Parisienne (co-sc) (FR). '38 The Challenge (co-sc). '39 The Spy in Black (sc) (USA: U-Boat 29). '40 Contraband (sc) (USA: Black-out). '41 49th Parallel (co-sc) (USA: The Invaders). As co-dir, co-prod, co-sc: One of Our Aircraft Is Missing. '43 The Life and Death of Colonel Blimp (USA: Colonel Blimp). '44 A Canterbury Tale. '45 I Know Where I'm Going. '46 A Matter of Life and Death (USA: Stairway to Heaven). '47 Black Narcissus. '48 The Red Shoes. '49 The Small Back Room (USA: Hour of Glory). '50 The Elusive Pimpernel (co-dir; + co-sc) (USA: The Fighting Pimpernel). '51 The Tales of Hoffmann. '53 Twice Upon a Time (dir; + prod; + sc). '56 The Battle of the River Plate (USA: Pursuit of the Graf Spee). '57 Miracle in Soho (prod; + sc. only). '72 The Boy Who Turned Yellow (sc. only).

PRESTON, Robert

(b. 1918). Actor. Born: Robert Preston Meservey; Newton Highlands, Massachusetts, USA

Tall, rugged Robert Preston has had a consistently steady career since his relatively easy entry into show business at the age of 20. He joined the Pasadena Playhouse on leaving high school, and was given a Paramount contract two years later. He was immediately assigned to lead roles in B movies and second lead in higher-quality material such as *Union Pacific*, in which he plays a gambler whose wife (Barbara Stanwyck) loves another man and eventually murders her husband, and *Beau Geste*, in which he plays the youngest brother. After serving in World War II he returned to Paramount and worked a few times with Alan Ladd – the latter had become the bigger star since working with Preston for the first time on *This Gun For Hire* in 1942. Gradually Preston became disenchanted with the roles supplied for him by Paramount, and after a few films for RKO he decided to return to the boards, winning himself a Tony Award for his role in *The Music Man* on Broadway. He has since had considerable success on television and in the Eighties has returned to the screen in Blake Edwards' *S.O.B.* (1981) and *Victor/ Victoria* (1982).

Films include: 1938 King of Alcatraz. '39 Union Pacific; Beau Geste. '40 North West Mounted Police. '42 Reap the Wild Wind; This Gun for Hire. '47 The Macomber Affair. '49 Tulsa. '55 The Last Frontier. '60 The Dark at the Top of the Stairs. '62 The Music Man. '63 All the Way Home. '72 Junior Bonner. '73 Mame.

PRÉVERT, Jacques

(1900–1977). Poet/screenwriter. Born: Neuilly-sur-Seine, France

Jacques Prévert's association with the Surrealist movement in the Twenties greatly influenced his writing, though he was excluded from membership of the actual group by its leader, André Breton. In 1932 he joined the left-wing theatre Groupe Octobre and also began writing full-length film scripts with *L'Affaire Est dans le Sac*, directed by his brother Pierre (born 1906), whose later comedy films, *Adieu Léonard* and *Voyage-Surprise*, he also co-wrote with him. Jacques' only

Above: Elvis Presley swops a guitar for macho military chic in a publicity shot. Below: Vincent Price, mellifluous Master of the Macabre in Roger Corman's The Masque of the Red Death. *Above right: Robert Preston as Professor Harold Hill,* The Music Man. *Right: Marie Prevost as a Mack Sennett Bathing Beauty. Far right: Dennis Price in his best movie role, as the ruthless social climber of Robert Hamer's black comedy* Kind Hearts and Coronets, *the most celebrated of all the Ealing films*

script for Jean Renoir was *Le Crime de Monsieur Lange*, syndicalist propaganda within a charming tale of love and murder. But he began to collaborate regularly with Marcel Carné from *Jenny* onwards, culminating in *Le Jour Se Lève* and *Les Enfants du Paradis*. The partnership nearly ended with the failure of their *Les Portes de la Nuit*, based on a ballet by Prévert, which included the song 'Les Feuilles Mortes' (Autumn Leaves), with his words and Joseph Kosma's music. By then, Prévert's poetry had reached best-seller status with the publication of *Paroles* (1945) and *Histoires* (1946), again containing many lyrics set to music by Kosma. Prévert continued to write occasional scripts after the Forties, but his poetry became his main interest; and he was thoroughly out of step with the *nouvelle vague* when it came at the end of the Fifties.

Films include: 1928 Souvenirs de Paris ou Paris Express (short). '33 L'Affaire Est dans le Sac (GB: It's in the Bag). '35 Le Crime de Monsieur Lange (USA: The Crime of Monsieur Lange). '36 Jenny (co-sc). '37 Drôle de Drame (USA: Bizarre, Bizarre). '38 Quai des Brumes (USA: Port of Shadows). '39 Le Jour Se Lève (co-sc) (USA: Daybreak). '43 Adieu Léonard (co-sc). '45 Les Enfants du Paradis

(USA: Children of Paradise). '46 Les Portes de la Nuit (USA: Gates of the Night). '47 Voyage-Surprise (co-sc). '49 Les Amants de Vérone. '50 Souvenirs Perdus (co-sc); La Marie du Port (co-sc). '61 Les Amours Célèbres *ep* Agnès Bernauer (FR-IT).

PREVIN, Andre

(b. 1929). Composer/arranger/ conductor. Born: Berlin, Germany

A child prodigy at the piano, Previn escaped to California with his family in 1939 and put out a successful album of piano jazz at 16. In the same year he joined MGM as an orchestrator and arranger while continuing his musical studies. He soon also became a prolific composer, at first of film scores but then also of art-music, which became his main interest when he was appointed principal conductor of the London Symphony Orchestra in 1968. Though he wrote dozens of original film scores, his Oscars were all for adaptations – *Gigi*, *Porgy and Bess*, *Irma La Douce* and *My Fair Lady*. He has been married to jazz singer Betty Bennett, songstress Dory Previn and actress Mia Farrow.

Films as composer include: 1955 Bad Day at Black Rock. '60 Elmer Gantry; Pepe (USA-MEX). '62 The Four Horsemen of the Apocalypse; Long Day's Journey Into Night. '63 Two for the Seesaw. *Films as arranger include:* **1953** Kiss Me Kate. '58 Gigi. '59 Porgy and Bess. '60 Bells Are Ringing. '63 Irma La Douce. '64 My Fair Lady. '75 Rollerball.

PREVOST, Marie

(1898–1937). Actress. Born: Mary Bickford Dunn; Sarnia, Ontario, Canada

The movies have treated many people cruelly, but none more so than Marie Prevost. She was dark, curly-haired, pert and pretty, and briefly one of Mack Sennett's Bathing Beauties. She went on in the early Twenties to Universal for a series of romantic comedies, playing flirtatious flappers and good-hearted vamps. Warners signed her in 1922, and she reached her height in three films for Ernst Lubitsch. In *The Marriage Circle* she dominated the film as the happily amoral wife of staid Adolphe Menjou, while her ruthless little gold-digger in *Three Women* was equally brilliant. The slow decline began with the talkies. Sound itself presented no problems, but she suffered increasingly from weight problems, and by the mid-Thirties had virtually dropped out of films. Dieting did not help, and eventually she stopped eating almost completely. She lived alone, divorced from her husband and former co-star Kenneth Harlan, and penniless, and in January 1937 was found dead: the worst case of malnutrition the doctors had ever seen.

Film include: 1917 Her Nature Dance. '22 Kissed; The Beautiful and Damned. '23 The Wanters. '24 The Marriage Circle; Three Women. '25 Kiss Me Again. '26 Up in Mabel's Room. '28 The Godless Girl. '30 Paid (GB: Within the Law); Ladies of Leisure. '35 Hands Across the Table. '36 13 Hours by Air.

PRICE, Dennis

(1915–1973). Actor. Born: Dennistoun Rose-Price; Twyford, Berkshire, England

The son of a general, and destined for the Church, Price changed his plans, and after Oxford went to the Embassy School of Acting and thence into repertory. Invalided out of the army in 1942, he went back to the theatre, was spotted by director Michael Powell and given the part of the young soldier in *A Canterbury Tale*. It was a happy beginning in a superb film, and they were few and far between in Price's career. But he played sardonic, polished characters in scores of British films, with a justly admired performance as the murderous poor relation in *Kind Hearts and Coronets*, and memorable cameos in *Victim* and *The Wrong Arm of the Law*. His film career ended sadly in cheap horror pictures, but by that time he had enjoyed great success in television, playing P. G. Wodehouse's butler Jeeves in a celebrated BBC series.

Film include: 1944 A Canterbury Tale. '46 Caravan; Hungry Hill. '47 Holiday Camp. '48 Good Time Girl. '49 The Bad Lord Byron; Kind Hearts and Coronets. '59 I'm All Right Jack. '61 Victim. '63 The Wrong Arm of the Law. '65 A High Wind in Jamaica. '70 Venus in Furs. '73 Theatre of Blood.

PRICE, Vincent

(b. 1911). Actor. Born: St Louis Missouri, USA

The air of cultivation that Vincent Price exudes on screen is not acting. He gained his degrees in art history and English at Yale, and in Fine Arts at London, and all his life has been a connoisseur and collector of art. He began acting on the English stage, joined Orson Welles' Mercury Theatre, and went into the movies in 1938. He played historical characters as diverse as Raleigh, Clarence, Richelieu, Charles II and the Mormon Joseph Smith; he had a nice line in charming but effete young men (particularly memorable in *Laura*), and played the occasional horror role, revelling in the old Lionel Atwill part of the demented sculptor in *House of Wax*. In the Sixties came the famous series of Roger Corman adaptations from Edgar Allan Poe. They gave Price a wide variety of characters, and they were striking enough, but they finished him as a serious actor. He never escaped from the genre, and only *Witchfinder-General* and the Dr Phibes movies stretched him at all.

Films include: 1938 Service de Luxe. '44 Laura. '46 Dragonwyck. '51 His Kind of Woman. '53 House of Wax. '54 The Mad Magician. '58 The Fly; House on Haunted Hill. '59 The Tingler. '60 Fall of the House of Usher/House of Usher. '61 The Pit and the Pendulum. '62 Confessions of an Opium Eater (GB: Evils of Chinatown). '63 The Raven. '64 The Masque of the Red Death (GB-USA). '68 Witchfinder-General (GB) (USA: The Conqueror Worm). '75 Journey Into Fear (GB-CAN). '83 Monster Club; Ruddigore.

PROTOZANOV, Yakov

(1881–1945). Director. Born: Moscow, Russia

The first Russian director to develop an individual style, Protozanov began as an actor, but was directing by 1911. His early films were sentimental romantic dramas, but in 1916 he made a decorative and finely acted version of Pushkin's *The Queen of Spades*, and the next year, after the Revolution in February had shaken the tight Tsarist censorship, came his *Father Sergius*, a harrowing study, based on Tolstoy, of corruption in the church. Protozanov fled the Civil War to work in France, but returned in 1924 to direct his best-known film, the science-fiction *Aelita*, famous for its Constructivist sets, but also filled with robust comedy. He worked on until his death in 1945, with at least two more remarkable films to his credit: the Civil War romance, *The Forty-First*, and a light Oriental fantasy, *Adventures in Bokhara*, which was his last film, and delighted English audiences in those wartime years when Soviet films were widely shown.

Films include: 1911 Pesnya Katorzhanina (The Prisoner's Song). '16 Pikovaia Dama (GB: The Queen of Spades). '18 Otets Sergii (Father Sergius). '20 Justice d'Abord (FR). '23 L'Ombre du Péché (FR). '24 Aelita. '27 Sorok Pervyi (GB: The Forty-First). '28 Byelyi Orel (The White Eagle). '34 Marionetki (Marionettes). '43 Nasreddin v Bukhare (GB: Adventures in Bokhara).

PROVINE, Dorothy

(b. 1937). Actress. Born: Deadwood, South Dakota, USA

After studying drama at Washington University, Dorothy Provine rapidly landed a Warner Brothers contract. Blonde, slim and perky, and able to sing and dance, she seemed destined for musicals, but by 1958, when she arrived, musicals were withering away, and at first the studios forced a tough-girl image upon her. She played the title role in *The Bonnie Parker Story*, a low-budget precursor of *Bonnie and Clyde*, and was still a bad girl in *Riot in Juvenile Prison*. But then she had some television successes, and more glamorous movie roles followed. Few of her films were very good, unfortunately, but she did play the feminine lead in the amusing *Who's Minding the Mint?* and stood up well to the competition of a very strong comedy cast.

Films include: 1958 The Bonnie Parker Story. '59 Riot in Juvenile Prison; The 30 Foot Bride of Candy Rock. '63 Wall of Noise; It's a Mad, Mad, Mad, Mad World. '64 Good Neighbor Sam. '65 The Great Race; That Darn Cat! '66 Se Tutte le Donne del Mondo (USA-IT) (USA: Kiss the Girls and Make Them Die). '67 Who's Minding the Mint? '68 Never a Dull Moment.

PRYOR, Richard

(b. 1940). Actor/comedian. Born: Peoria, Illinois, USA

Richard Pryor started out as a singer and pianist in nightclubs, adding comedy material drawn from his youthful experiences to create lively sketches of black life. Becoming well-known as a stand-up comic on the nightclub circuit led to television appearances on the Ed Sullivan and Johnny Carson shows and parts in television drama. After a few bit parts in films he made an impact as Piano Man in *Lady Sings the Blues*, the biopic of jazz singer Billie Holiday (played by Diana Ross), and he then moved on to leading roles, comic and dramatic. He was badly burned at his home in 1980 in an accident, but was able to resume both films and live appearances. Two filmed records of his nightclub acts have added to his popularity, and he has also turned out several LPs which further reveal his richly irreverent sense of humour.

Films include: 1967 The Busy Body. '72 Lady Sings the Blues. '73 Wattstax; Some Call It Loving. '74 Uptown Saturday Night; Blazing Saddles (co-sc. only). '76 Silver Streak. '78 Blue Collar. '79 Richard Pryor Live in Concert; The Muppet Movie. '80 Stir Crazy. '82 Some Kind of Hero; Richard Pryor Live on the Sunset Strip. '83 Superman III – The Legend Grows.

PUDOVKIN, Vsevolod

(1893–1953). Director/actor. Born: Penza, Russia

Pudovkin studied at the State Film School under Vladimir Gardin, and then was a member of Lev Kuleshov's experimental workshop. At this time he worked as a writer, assistant director, and actor, and gave some striking performances, notably as the villain of Kuleshov's *The Death Ray*. Pudovkin's reputation as a great director rests on the three major films he made between 1926 and 1928: *Mother*, drawn from Maxim Gorky's work on the revolutionary education of a mother; *The End of St Petersburg*, which, together with Eisenstein's *Oktyabr* (1927, *October*), celebrated the tenth anniversary of the October Revolution; and *Storm Over Asia*, about an attempt by the English during the Civil War to put a captured partisan on the throne of Mongolia. In these films Pudovkin exploited the theories which he discussed at length in his seminal books, *Film Technique* and *Film Acting*. His basic principle was that the timing of shots and the significance of their order was the source of their power. As regards acting, Pudovkin emphasized the place of stillness, concentration, and empathy with the spectator. Great screen actors had always realized this; Pudovkin spelt it out. Later on, although he largely avoided the trouble with the authorities that destroyed

Eisenstein, his work lacked the creative drive of his silent films. *Deserter* and *Suvorov* are worthy films, but the fires are out.

Films include: 1921 Serp i Molot (act; + ass. dir. only). '25 Luch Smerti (act; + ass. dir; + art dir. only) (The Death Ray). '26 Mat' (GB: Mother); Mekhanika Golovnovo Mozga (GB: Mechanism of the Brain). '27 Konyets Sankt Peterburga (GB: The End of St Petersburg). '28 Potomok Chingis-Khana (USA/GB: Storm Over Asia). '29 Zhivoi Trup (USSR-GER) (actor only) (GB: The Living Corpse). '32 Prostoi Sluchai (GB: A Simple Case). '33 Dezertir (GB: Deserter). '39 Minin i Pozharsky (Minin and Pozharsky). '41 Suvorov (co-dir). '43 Vo Imya Rodini (co-dir) (GB: In the Name of Our Fatherland). '46 Admiral Nakhimov (+ act). '48 Tri Vstrechi (co-dir) (Three Encounters). '50 Zhukovsky.

Above: Dorothy Provine. Below: Richard Pryor in Bustin' Loose *(1981). Below right: Edna Purviance in* The Adventurer *(1917), one of many silent films in which she partnered Charlie Chaplin. Above right: Denver Pyle in* Guardian of the Wilderness

PURVIANCE, Edna

(1894–1958). Actress. Born: Paradise Valley, Nevada, USA

A fine pianist with hopes of making music her career. Purviance was working as a secretary to make ends meet when Charles Chaplin discovered her. Struck by her beauty – blonde hair, blue-grey eyes, full figure and immaculate turn-out – he signed her up at their first meeting: 'I doubted whether she could act or had any humour . . . she would at least be decorative to my comedies'. She made her debut as a young wife enjoying a flirtation with a drunk (Chaplin) in an hotel in *A Night Out*. This was the beginning of an eight-year partnership that was beautifully balanced and included a brief affair in 1916. She understood Chaplin's pathos and theatricality, fitting into the often forlorn mood of his films with the quiet endurance and graceful innocence demanded of her: she was sensitive and moving as the downtrodden gypsy girl in *The Vagabond*; enchanting as the French nurse in *Shoulder Arms* and as the unmarried mother who abandons her child in *The Kid*; and tried to match up to the sophistication of her own star-vehicle *A Woman of Paris*, a formative Hollywood comedy of manners and morals. Unfortunately her notices for *A Woman of Paris* were not good and her working relationship with Chaplin more or less ended. But she remained on the Chaplin payroll and may have appeared as an extra in *Monsieur Verdoux* (1947) and *Limelight* (1952).

Films include: 1915 A Night Out; The Champion; Work; The Bank. '16 Carmen/Charlie Chaplin's Burlesque on Carmen; The Vagabond; The Rink. '17 Easy Street; The Immigrant. '18 A Dog's Life; Shoulder Arms. '21 The Kid. '23 A Woman of Paris. '26 A Woman of the Sea (unreleased).

PUTTNAM, David

(b. 1941). Producer. Born: Southgate, London, England

David Puttnam has been the most successful British independent producer of the late Seventies and early Eighties, winning the Best Picture Oscar with *Chariots of Fire*, his sporting tribute to British Olympic prowess. The son of a Fleet Street press photographer, he started out as an advertising whizzkid, moved on to open a photographic agency and formed a partnership with Sandy Lieberson in 1969 to produce such films as *That'll Be the Day* and *Mahler*. He went solo with *The Duellists* and moved to Hollywood in the late Seventies as a tax exile, but returned to lend his abilities to the long-awaited revival in British films. He has helped to launch such previously unknown directorial talents as Ridley Scott and Alan Parker. Before the success of *Chariots of Fire*, *Midnight Express* won an Academy Award for Best Screenplay (Adaptation).

Films as producer or executive producer include: 1971 Melody/S.W.A.L.K. '73 That'll Be the Day; Swastika (doc). '74 Stardust; Mahler. '75 Lisztomania; Brother, Can You Spare a Dime? (doc). '76 Bugsy Malone. '77 The Duellists. '78 Midnight Express. '79 Agatha. '80 Foxes (USA). '81 Chariots of Fire. '83 Local Hero.

PYLE, Denver

(b. 1920). Actor. Born: Bethune, Colorado, USA

Named after the capital city of his native state, Denver Pyle studied at Colorado State University before working in the Texas and Oklahoma oilfields. In 1941 he enlisted in the navy. Wounded in action off Guadalcanal, he was medically discharged in 1942 and subsequently studied acting. He made his film debut in 1946. Soon he was playing chief villain in Roy Rogers and Gene Autry Westerns, and moved on to working for Arthur Penn in *The Left-Handed Gun* and John Ford in *The Horse Soldiers* and *The Man Who Shot Liberty Valance* (1962). He is best remembered as Hamer, the relentless Texas Ranger who pursues the young outlaws, in Penn's *Bonnie and Clyde*.

Films include: 1948 The Man From Colorado; Devil Ship. '49 Hellfire; Streets of San Francisco. '52 Oklahoma Annie. '55 To Hell and Back; Ten Wanted Men. '58 The Left-Handed Gun. '59 The Horse Soldiers. '65 Shenandoah. '67 Bonnie and Clyde. '68 Bandolero!; Five Card Stud. '77 Guardian of the Wilderness.

QUAID, Randy

(b. 1953). Actor. Born: Houston, Texas, USA

Tall, with untidy curly hair and pale bulging eyes, Randy Quaid was in his second year at college when Peter Bogdanovich cast him in a small role in *The Last Picture Show*. Two more Bogdanovich pictures followed, and then a major role as the young sailor-prisoner in *The Last Detail*. He was the naive epileptic exploited by Duddy Kravitz (Richard Dreyfuss) in *The Apprenticeship of Duddy Kravitz*; and he has continued to play mostly simple or somewhat retarded characters with increasing skill. His younger brother Dennis (born 1954) followed him to Hollywood and made his debut in *September 30, 1955* (1977), which examined the impact of James Dean's death on seven adolescents. He was a high-school quarterback in *Breaking Away* (1979). Both brothers appeared, as the Miller brothers, in *The Long Riders*.

Films include: 1971 The Last Picture Show. '72 What's Up Doc? '73 Paper Moon; The Last Detail. '74 The Apprenticeship of Duddy Kravitz (CAN). '75 Breakout. '76 The Missouri Breaks; Bound for Glory. '78 Midnight Express (GB). '80 Foxes; The Long Riders.

QUALEN, John

(b. 1899). Actor. Born: John Oleson; Vancouver, British Columbia, Canada

Qualen was the sharp-nosed little Swedish immigrant usually seen pattering round his wife's kitchen as she attends to meals for the heroes in John Ford Westerns like *The Searchers* and *The Man Who Shot Liberty Valance*. A regular member of Ford's stock company, he was also memorable as Muley in *The Grapes of Wrath* and the sailor Axel in *The Long Voyage Home*. Qualen's parents were Norwegian but he was brought up in Illinois. He first gained recognition for his performances as the Swedish janitor in the Broadway and screen versions of *Street Scene*. Then Ford's *Arrowsmith* launched their long association.

Films include: 1931 Street Scene; Arrowsmith. '38 Five of a Kind. '40 The Grapes of Wrath; His Girl Friday; The Long Voyage Home. '41 All That Money Can Buy/The Devil and Daniel Webster. '42 Casablanca. '47 The Fugitive. '54 The High and the Mighty. '56 The Searchers. '62 The Man Who Shot Liberty Valance. '64 Cheyenne Autumn. '65 The Sons of Katie Elder. '66 A Big Hand for the Little Lady (GB: Big Deal at Dodge City). '68 Firecreek. '73 Frasier the Sensuous Lion.

Above: Randy Quaid as the hulking, slow-witted, mild-mannered prisoner escorted by Jack Nicholson and Otis Young in Hal Ashby's The Last Detail. *Right: the ferret-faced John Qualen in John Ford's* The Grapes of Wrath

QUAYLE, Anthony

(b. 1913). Actor. Born: Ainsdale, Lancashire, England

From Rugby School and RADA, Quayle surprisingly became the straight man in a music-hall comedy team. It was a brief aberration. By 1932 he was with the Old Vic, and by 1936 his reputation was such that he was playing with Ruth Gordon in *The Country Wife* on Broadway. After the war his career as stage actor and producer flourished. From 1948 to 1956 he was director of the Shakespeare Memorial Theatre, and since then has alternated between films and the stage – he had previously played only a few relatively small parts on screen. Quayle's natural style has always worked perfectly on film. He has normally played tough, efficient, reliable characters. The time-serving Wolsey of *Anne of the Thousand Days* was a change of pace that won him an Oscar nomination, and his sympathetic attorney in *The Wrong Man* could well have done.

Films include: 1948 Saraband for Dead Lovers. '55 Oh, Rosalinda!! '56 Battle of the River Plate (USA: Pursuit of the Graf Spee). '57 The Wrong Man; Woman in a Dressing Gown. '58 Ice Cold in Alex. '61 The Guns of Navarone. '65 A Study in Terror (USA: Fog). '69 McKenna's Gold (USA); Anne of the Thousand Days. '76 The Eagle Has Landed.

QUIMBY, Fred

(1886–1965). Cartoon producer. Born: Minneapolis, Minnesota, USA

Quimby's name appears on the best of the Tom and Jerry cartoons made at MGM by William Hanna and Joseph Barbera. It has been claimed that he was an old studio executive with no sense of humour: maybe then he was like the authoritarian bulldog who only emerges from his kennel to lay down the law to the dynamic duo – and to keep the fun flowing at a frantic pace. Certainly, he was as effective, for many of those cartoons are master-pieces and seven of them won Oscars. Quimby first came to the attention of film exhibitors as a showman and designer of theatres. In 1920 he became general manager for Pathé Distribution and in 1924 went to Fox as head of shorts production. Two years later he began his thirty-year tenure as production boss of shorts at MGM, and in 1937 he personally supervised the building of their big cartoon studio, eventually gathering round himself some six hundred employees. As well as Hanna and Barbera, the talent he fostered included Rudolf Ising and Tex Avery, respective creators of Barney the Bear and Droopy the Dog. Quimby retired in 1955 and two years later the MGM cartoon department closed.

Films include: 1939 The Bear That Couldn't Sleep. '40 The Milky Way; Puss Gets the Boot. '43 Yankee Doodle Mouse; Dumb Hounded; Red Hot Riding Hood. '44 Mouse Trouble. '45 Quiet Please! '46 The Cat Concerto. '49 The Little Orphan. '52 Two Mouseketeers. '53 Johann Mouse.

QUINE, Richard

(b. 1920). Director. Born: Detroit, Michigan, USA

Moving to Los Angeles at six, Richard Quine became a child actor in theatre and films and continued acting in supporting roles into adulthood, quitting in 1950. He co-directed a B picture at Columbia in 1948, and became a dialogue director. He graduated to directing in 1951 and made some second features and crime thrillers before specializing mainly in comedies and musicals. Blake Edwards wrote the scripts for eight of his films between 1952 and 1962, five of them in collaboration with Quine, and the duo also wrote the stories for Edwards' first two films as director. After 1960 Quine left Columbia to freelance, with some success when he stuck to comedy; but his penchant for heavy drama, already apparent in *Strangers When We Meet*, did not advance his career and his credits became increasingly intermittent in the Seventies. He is likely to be remembered mainly for his Fifties comedies (*Operation Mad Ball*) and musicals (*My Sister Eileen*).

Films include: 1951 Purple Heart Diary (GB: No Time for Tears). '53 Cruisin' Down the River. '54 Drive a Crooked Road; Pushover; So This Is Paris. '55 My Sister Eileen. '56 The Solid Gold Cadillac. '57 Operation Mad Ball. '58 Bell, Book and Candle. '59 It Happened to Jane. '60 Strangers When We Meet; The World of Suzie Wong (GB). '63 Paris When It Sizzles. '64 Sex and the Single Girl. '65 How to Murder Your Wife. '70 The Moonshine War. '79 The Prisoner of Zenda.

Above: Anthony Quayle as a stalwart Roman soldier in Anthony Mann's gripping epic The Fall of the Roman Empire *(1966). Below: Anthony Quinn – whose portrayals of salty peasants get more and more grizzled and philosophical as the years go by – in* The Passage *(1978), directed by J. Lee Thompson*

QUINN, Anthony

(b. 1915). Actor. Born: Chihuahua, Mexico

Quinn's mother was Mexican, his father an Irish fruit-picker who became property-man at the Selig company's Zoo in early Hollywood. Quinn was in the movies by 1936, but although he married Katherine, Cecil B. De Mille's adopted daughter, he was confined for a long time to small parts. Some of them were memorable, in particular his Crazy Horse in *They Died With Their Boots On* and his Mexican lynch victim in *The Ox-Bow Incident*, and his eventual promotion to leads was no surprise. A Broadway success in *A Streetcar Named Desire* helped him on his way, he won two Supporting Actor Oscars, for *Viva Zapata!* and *Lust for Life*, and he gave what remains his finest performance when he went to Italy to star for Fellini as the circus strong man, Zampano, in *La Strada*. Back in America, Quinn became a very big name in the Sixties, but his brutal, earthy, swaggering roles in films like *Zorba the Greek* did him little good as an actor, and he became sadly typed as sort of combination life-force and all-in wrestler. At times, though, as in the engaging and terribly underrated *Flap*, where he played a drunken but heroic Indian, he revealed that there was still an actor there.

Films include: 1938 Bulldog Drummond in Africa. '41 They Died With Their Boots On. '43 The Ox-Bow Incident (GB: Strange Incident). '51 The Brave Bulls. '52 Viva Zapata! '54 La Strada (IT). '56 Notre Dame de Paris (GB: The Hunchback of Notre Dame); Lust for Life. '62 Requiem for a Heavyweight (GB: Blood Money); Lawrence of Arabia (GB); Barabbas (IT). '64 Zorba the Greek (GREECE-IT). '65 A High Wind in Jamaica. '68 The Shoes of the Fisherman. '69 The Magus (GB). '70 Flap (GB: The Last Warrior). '78 The Greek Tycoon. '81 High Risk.

R

RADEMAKERS, Fons

(b. 1920). Director. Born: Roosendael, Holland

The most respected of Dutch directors, Rademakers was a stage actor and producer until in 1955 he went into films, working as assistant to Jean Renoir, Vittorio De Sica and others. From 1956 he directed his own films. Rademakers is a confessed admirer of Ingmar Bergman, and hence adept at dealing with fantasy and psychological conflict. He is effective with modest projects like *My Friend* (the real-life story of a Belgian judge who tries to kill his wife), but his most important film is probably *Max Havelaar*, a three-hour study of pervasive corruption in Java, in which Rademakers probes beyond colonialism to explore prejudice and dishonesty at all levels.

Films include: 1959 Dorp aan de Rivier (GB: Doctor in the Village). '60 Makkers, Staakt un Wild Geraas (GB: That Joyous Eve). '61 Het Mes (GB: The Knife). '63 Als Twee Druppels Water (GB: The Spitting Image).

'66 De Dans van de Reiger (GER-HOLL) (GB: The Dance of the Heron). '71 Mira. '73 Niet voor de Poesen (HOLL-BELG) (GB: Because of the Cats). '76 Max Havelaar (HOLL-INDONESIA). '79 Mijn Vriend of het Vergorgen Leven van Jules Depraeter (BELG-HOLL) (GB: My Friend/The Judge's Friend).

RADFORD, Basil

(1897–1952). Actor. Born: Chester, Cheshire, England

Radford was the archetypal eccentric Englishman. He teamed up with Naunton Wayne and as the comedy duo Charters and Caldicott – cricket-obsessed gentlemen who let the horrors of everyday living pass them by – scored such a hit in Alfred Hitchcock's *The Lady Vanishes* that they began their own radio show. The duo's career remained interlinked, but Radford also proved himself well able to handle solo 'serious' roles by playing the owner of a small engineering firm with a pig-headed work force in *Chance of a Lifetime*.

Films include: 1936 Broken Blossoms. '37 Young and Innocent. '38 The Lady Vanishes. '40 Night Train to Munich. '43 Millions Like Us. '45 The Way to the Stars (USA: Johnny in the Clouds); Dead of Night *ep* Golfing. '46 The Captive Heart. '49 Passport to Pimlico; Whisky Galore! (USA: Tight Little Island). '50 Chance of a Lifetime. '51 The Galloping Major.

RAFELSON, Bob

(b. 1935). Director. Born: New York City, USA

Leaving home at 14, Rafelson worked as a rodeo-rider, ocean-liner hand and jazz musician before enrolling at Dartmouth College to read philosophy. In 1953 he began writing plays and, while doing his military service in Japan, took up disc-jockeying and working on films produced by the Shochiku company. On his return to America he became an associate producer at Universal and then moved on through Revue Productions and Desilu to Screen Gems. In 1966 he devised *The Monkees* television show

with Bert Schneider, a comedy series centred around a zany pop group that then took off in the music business as a result of the show's popularity. Rafelson directed three of the episodes and went on to produce The Monkees' feature film *Head*, which he co-wrote with Jack Nicholson, star of Rafelson's next two features *Five Easy Pieces* and *The King of Marvin Gardens*. These are outstanding films of American family life, sad, affectionate and both realistic and melodramatic. Nicholson also starred in Rafelson's steamy remake of *The Postman Always Rings Twice*, a more commercial project than he had hitherto attempted.

Films include: 1968 Head. '70 Five Easy Pieces. '72 The King of Marvin Gardens. '76 Stay Hungry. '81 The Postman Always Rings Twice.

RAFFERTY, Chips

(1909–1971). Actor. Born: John Goffage; Broken Hill, New South Wales, Australia

Rafferty was a sheep-shearer, big-game hunter and gold-prospector before he entered films as an extra in *Come Up Smiling* (1939). He became popular playing heroic soldiers in *Forty Thousand Horsemen* (1940) and *Rats of Tobruk* (1944). He then persuaded director Harry Watt to cast him as the rugged cattle-drover in *The Overlanders* (1946), a role that perfectly suited his craggy 'Gary Cooper' looks, slow drawl and strong, silent manner. Rafferty became a familiar face to British audiences when Ealing gave him a contract and took him to England to appear opposite Googie Withers in *The Loves of Joanna Godden*. During the Forties he continued making movies in Europe and Australia and in the Sixties went to America for *Mutiny on the Bounty* and *The Sundowners*. In the mid-Fifties Rafferty formed his own production company but met with little success.

Films include: 1947 Bush Christmas (GB); The Loves of Joanna Godden (GB). '49 Eureka Stockade (GB) (USA: Massacre Hill). '53 The Desert Rats (USA). '56 Walk Into Paradise (+ prod; + co-sc) (AUS-FR) (USA: Walk Into Hell); Smiley (AUS-GB). '60 The Sundowners (USA). '62 Mutiny on the Bounty (USA). '66 They're a Weird Mob. '70 Skullduggery (USA). '71 Wake in Fright (AUS-USA) (USA/GB: Outback).

Above: Basil Radford in the comedy thriller Night Train to Munich, *directed by Carol Reed. Right: the rangy figure of Chips Rafferty in Harry Watt's* The Overlanders

RAFT, George

(1895–1980). Actor. Born: George Ranft; New York City, USA

One of a large family brought up in the Hell's Kitchen area of New York, Raft worked his way up from a hoofer in local dance-halls to Broadway. In 1929 he made his film debut in *Queen of the Nightclubs*. The sleek, good-looking Raft then appeared as Spencer Tracy's henchman in *Quick Millions* and a succession of similar gangster roles followed – including his famous portrayals of a coin-tossing hood in *Scarface* and an ex-fighter trying to find class to go with his wealth in *Night After Night*. In mid-career his private and social life began to make the news; while dancing in his New York club days he had supposedly fallen in with the Mafia; his nightclub in Havana was closed by the Castro regime; and in 1966 he was refused entry to England by the Home Office because of his gangland connections. His career had declined by the Forties, and by the early Fifties he had virtually retired. He died not, as might have been expected, the victim of a hitman's bullet, but from leukaemia.

Films include: 1929 Queen of the Nightclubs. '31 Quick Millions. '32 Scarface; Night After Night. '34 Bolero. '35 Rumba. '37 Souls at Sea. '39 Each Dawn I Die. '40 They Drive By Night (GB: Road to 'Frisco). '48 Race Street. '54 Rogue Cop. '59 Some Like It Hot. '67 Casino Royale (GB). '72 Hammersmith Is Out.

RAIMU

(1883–1946). Actor. Born: Jules Muraire; Toulon, France

The young Raimu was an extra in music-hall at the Toulon Casino. He went on to become a popular artist in variety, café-concerts and revue. But there was always a straight actor lurking in this heavily-built, sad-faced man, and he went, briefly, to the Comédie Française, before settling in the Thirties to be one of the great character actors of French cinema. His style was the essence of Provence – as was his accent – and it was as the cafe owner César in Marcel Pagnol's Marius Trilogy that he made his screen reputation. Raimu uniquely combined pathos with a reassuring strength. Orson Welles once said that he was the greatest actor he had seen.

Films include: 1912 L'Homme Nu. '31 Marius. '32 Fanny. '36 César. '37 Un Carnet de Bal (USA: Life Dances On; GB: Christine). '38 La Femme du Boulanger (GB: The Baker's Wife). '40 Untel Père et Fils (USA: The Heart of a Nation). '42 Les Inconnus dans la Maison (GB: Strangers in the House). '43 Le Colonel Chabert. '46 L'Homme au Chapeau Rond.

RAINER, Luise

(b. 1912). Actress. Born: Vienna, Austria

The brief career of Luise Rainer is one of the classic Hollywood mysteries. She was a stage actress with Max Reinhardt in Vienna, and had made one or two films when MGM carried her off to star (replacing Myrna Loy) in *Escapade*. She was a petite brunette with wide, soulful eyes, too ready perhaps to fill with tears, and, with her accent, not easy to cast. But her next two films each brought her the Best Actress Oscar, first for her Anna Held, the sad first wife of *The Great Ziegfeld*, and then for her almost silent Chinese peasant girl in *The Good Earth*. In the next two years she made five more films for MGM. Some of them did badly at the box-office, and the studio dropped her (or she walked out: accounts vary). Whatever really happened, Rainer made only one more film, and apart from very rare stage and television appearances has lived quietly in London for many years with her American publisher husband Robert Knittel.

Films: 1930 Ja, der Himmel über Wien (A). '32 Sehnsucht 202 (GER-A). '33 Heut' kommt's drauf an (GER). '35 Escapade. '36 The Great Ziegfeld. '37 The Good Earth; The Emperor's Candlesticks; Big City. '38 The Toy Wife (GB: Frou-Frou); The Great Waltz; Dramatic School. '43 Hostages.

RAINS, Claude

(1889–1967). Actor. Born: London, England

Claude Rains had a high reputation as a stage actor when, in his mid-forties, he made the oddest of all film debuts. James Whale cast him as *The Invisible Man*. So this fine actor, renowned for his mobile and expressive features, played his first major film part in bandages or invisible. The voice – rich, vibrant and sardonic – did all the work. For the next thirty-odd years Rains played leads and character parts, and for the first half of that period he was scarcely in a bad film. He played many sympathetic parts (the father in *Four Daughters*, the psychiatrist in *Now, Voyager*) and many villains, but the unique thing about Rains was that even his villains became sympathetic. *Notorious* is the classic example, but the same thing happened with his murderous crime expert in *The Unsuspected*, his Spanish don in *Anthony Adverse*, and a score of others. 'I'm only a poor corrupt official,' says Rains' police chief in *Casablanca*, but the smile and the twinkle with which he says it make one forget the corruption in admiration of the man.

Films include: 1933 The Invisible Man. '35 The Clairvoyant (GB). '36 Anthony Adverse. '38 Four Daughters. '39 Mr Smith Goes to Washington. '42 Now, Voyager; Casablanca. '43 The Phantom of the Opera. '44 Mr Skeffington. '45 Caesar and Cleopatra (GB). '46 Notorious. '47 The Unsuspected. '59 This Earth Is Mine. '62 Lawrence of Arabia (GB).

RAIZMAN, Yuli

(b. 1903). Director. Born: Moscow, Russia

A graduate of Moscow University, where he studied literature and art, Raizman began his film career as a literary consultant, actor and assistant director. He made his own first film in 1927, and a year later directed the remarkable *Katorga*. This film, set in a Siberian prison camp before the Revolution, employs a unique blend of Eisensteinian montage, Expressionist lighting, and caricatured, satirical acting. Criticized originally for its alleged pessimism, it now seems extraordinarily forceful and invigorating. Raizman made nearly twenty films over the next 40 years, but few are known in the West. One exception is *The Last Night*, which paints a vivid picture of a provincial town awaiting the Revolution.

Films include: 1928 Katorga (Penal Servitude). '30 Zemlya Zhazhdyot (The Earth Thirsts). '37 Poslednaya Noch (GB: The Last Night). '40 Podniataia Zelina (Virgin Soil Upturned). '42 Mashenka. '49 Rainis. '55 Urok Sisni (GB: The Lesson of Life). '58 Kommunist (GB: The Communist). '61 A Yesli Eto Liubovi (What If It's Love). '68 Tvoi Sovremennik (Your Contemporary). '82 Chastnaya Zhizn (Private Life).

RALSTON, Esther

(b. 1902). Actress. Born: Bar Harbor, Maine, USA

As a child Esther Ralston was on the vaudeville stage with her parents, and made her first film at the age of 12, playing an angel in *The Deep Purple* (1914). Her film career proper began a few years later, with several Westerns and a small part in Chaplin's *The Kid* (1921). She was one of the loveliest girls ever to appear in the movies, a classic blue-eyed blonde, publicized as the 'American Venus', and reached stardom with her role as Mrs Darling in Herbert Brenon's enchanting *Peter Pan*. She was in other important silents for Brenon and James Cruze, and had the leading part in Sternberg's *The Case of Lena Smith*. She played a peasant girl who becomes a servant in her lover's house: it was almost certainly her finest role, but sadly, no prints survive. Esther Ralston went on in sound films until 1941.

Films include: 1916 Phantom Fortunes. '24 Peter Pan. '25 Lucky Devil. '27 Children of Divorce. '29 The Case of Lena Smith; Betrayal; The Wheel of Life. '31 The Prodigal. '32 Rome Express (GB). '34 Sadie McKee. '40 Tin Pan Alley.

RAMPLING, Charlotte

(b. 1946). Actress. Born: Sturmer, Cambridgeshire, England

Charlotte Rampling was educated in France, and after working as a model obtained a small part in *The Knack* (1965). Then the Boulting brothers gave her the lead in *Rotten to the Core*, and her career was launched. She is a fluent linguist, and takes advantage of this to appear in French and Italian as well as English-speaking films, notably *The Night Porter*. A sensual-looking, brown-haired beauty, she was ideally cast as the silky, treacherous Velma in the serviceable remake of *Farewell, My Lovely*. Another good part was that of the neurotic actress Dorrie in *Stardust Memories*, made by her friend Woody Allen.

Films include: 1965 Rotten to the Core. '66 Georgy Girl. '69 La Caduta degli Dei (IT-GER) (USA/GB: The Damned). '71 Addio

Fratello Crudele (IT) (USA/GB: 'Tis Pity She's a Whore). '72 Asylum. '74 Zardoz; Il Portiere di Notte (IT) (USA/GB: The Night Porter); Caravan to Vaccarès (GB-FR). '75 Farewell, My Lovely (GB-USA). '80 Stardust Memories (USA). '82 The Verdict (USA).

RANDALL, Tony

(b. 1920. Actor. Born: Leonard Rosenberg; Tulsa, Oklahoma, USA

An urbane comedian with impeccable timing and a highly expressive face, Randall is particularly good in roles with a touch of zany fantasy, and was a perfect balance to down-to-earth Rock Hudson and Doris Day in several comedies, giving superb characterizations as a bored dilettante in *Pillow Talk*, a manic advertising man in *Lover Come Back*, and as the supposedly dying Hudson's solicitous friend in *Send Me No Flowers*. He won an Emmy Award for the TV series *The Odd Couple*, and had previously appeared in the play on stage.

Films include: 1957 Will Success Spoil Rock Hunter? (GB: Oh, for a Man!); Oh, Men! Oh, Women! '59 The Mating Game; Pillow Talk. '60 The Adventures of Huckleberry Finn; Let's Make Love. '61 Lover Come Back. '64 The Seven Faces of Dr Lao; Send Me No Flowers. '66 The Alphabet Murders (GB); Our Man in Marrakesh (GB) (USA: Bang, Bang, You're Dead). '72 Everything You Always Wanted to Know About Sex, But Were Afraid to Ask. '79 Scavenger Hunt.

Left: an atmospheric studio portrait of George Raft. Above: Raimu in Marcel Pagnol's César. Above right: Luise Rainer in The Emperor's Candlesticks. Above, far right: Esther Ralston in The Spotlight (1927). Right: Tony Randall in the Doris Day vehicle Pillow Talk. Below right:

Charlotte Rampling in Visconti's powerful study of greed and corruption set during the rise of Nazism, The Damned. Bottom: Renato Rascel in Seven Hills of Rome (1957). Below left: Claude Rains in The Unsuspected – as a criminologist, Victor Grandison, who commits the perfect murder

RANK, J. Arthur

(1888–1972). Film magnate. Born: Joseph Arthur Rank; Hull, Yorkshire, England

A Methodist, a Victorian, and heir to a flour-milling fortune, Rank entered films in 1933 as founder of a small company making religious pictures, and the following year went into commercial features with his British National company. In conflict with the distributors, he became his own distributor and exhibitor, and during the war years expanded enormously. He acquired control of the Gaumont and Odeon circuits, the Denham, Gainsborough and Gaumont studios, took over Elstree and built Pinewood. Thus for some twenty-five years he virtually monopolized the British industry. By the time he gave up the chairmanship of Rank in 1962 (he had been created a baron in 1957), the interests of the organization included bowling alleys, television rentals, petrol stations, ballrooms and bingo halls, to which last sad function many of their once flourishing cinemas had sunk. Unlike his counterparts in Hollywood, Rank made no impact at all on the films that were made under his aegis.

RAPPER, Irving

(b. 1898). Director. Born: London, England

Rapper was taken as a child to live in New York, and while at New York University was already directing and acting in stage productions. He went to Hollywood in the mid-Thirties as a dialogue director, settling at Warner Brothers, where he worked with Michael Curtiz, William Dieterle and Anatole Litvak. He became a full director in 1941, and through the Forties made stylish and literate (if a trifle stagy) pictures. Always skilled at directing actors, Rapper drew several splendid performances from Bette Davis, and out of the lush sentiment and larger-than-life characters of *Now, Voyager* he fashioned a minor masterpiece. He left Warners at the end of the decade, and his later work was much less interesting.

Films include: 1941 Shining Victory; One Foot in Heaven. '42 Now, Voyager. '44 The Adventures of Mark Twain. '45 The Corn Is Green; Rhapsody in Blue. '46 Deception. '47 The Voice of the Turtle. '49 Anna Lucasta. '50 The Glass Menagerie. '56 The Brave One. '78 Born Again.

RASCEL, Renato

(b. 1912). Actor. Born: Renato Ranucci; Turin, Italy

Rascel's parents were opera singers, and at eight the boy was singing with the Sistine Chapel choir. In films by the mid-Thirties, he proved able to move with unerring instinct from comedy to tragedy. His work as a comedian has been enhanced by his small stature; his subtle observations of the humiliations handed out to small men makes his humour particularly endearing especially in films like *The Secret of Santa Vittoria* and *The Overcoat*.

Films include: 1942 Pazzo d'Amore. '51 Io Sono il Capataz. '52 Napoleone; Il Cappotto (USA/GB: The Overcoat). '54 La Passegiata (+dir). '56 The Monto Carlo Story (USA-IT-FR). '57 Arrivederci Roma. '59 Policarpo, Ufficiale di Scrittura. '61 Gli Attendenti. '69 The Secret of Santa Vittoria (USA).

Below: Basil Rathbone as Guy of Gisborne in The Adventures of Robin Hood. Right: Gregory Ratoff in Abdulla the Great (1954). Centre right: Aldo Ray in The Day They Robbed the Bank of England. Far right: the director Nicholas Ray

RATHBONE, Basil

(1892–1967). Actor. Born: Johannesburg, South Africa

The American screen's most distinguished villain was British to the core. Hollywood claimed him in 1924. Lean-faced, intellectual, icily commanding, he waited until sound came to give up the theatre and devote himself to films. When he did, the incisive, dismissive voice combined with his other assets to make a remarkable actor. People remember him as a superb swashbuckling villain (though never a heavy – in his duels with Flynn and Power he was nimble and light-footed as a cat), and as the movies' best Sherlock Holmes, but he was much more. He was a strangely moving Karenin, opposite Garbo; magnificent as the war-weary commanding officer in the second *Dawn Patrol* (1938); a very deadly Tybalt in the Cukor *Romeo and Juliet* (1936). He had few leads, but those few were impressive: conniving killers in *Kind Lady* (1935) and *Love From a Stranger* (1937), and a very human and credible Richard III in *Tower of London* (1939). He played Holmes 14 times, ending in 1946. *The Last Hurrah* (1958), for John Ford, was the only worthwhile film out of the last ones he made.

Films include: 1923 The School for Scandal (GB). '25 The Masked Bride. '35 David Copperfield; Anna Karenina; The Last Days of Pompeii; A Tale of Two Cities; Captain Blood. '38 The Adventures of Marco Polo; The Adventures of Robin Hood. '39 The Hound of the Baskervilles; The Adventures of Sherlock Holmes. '44 The Scarlet Claw. '54 Casanova's Big Night.

RATOFF, Gregory

(1897–1960). Actor/director. Born: St Petersburg, Russia

In the Russian army in World War I, Ratoff emigrated to America after the Revolution and worked in the New York Yiddish Theatre and on Broadway, as actor and as director. His earliest film work was as an actor, specializing in explosive Europeans, and even after he turned in 1936 to direction he still put in the odd stint before the cameras, most memorably perhaps in *All About Eve*. As a director he was happiest when he had actors as expansive as himself, and he got enjoyable performances out of Peter Lorre, Erich von Stroheim and (in *Black Magic*) Orson Welles. In quieter vein, Ratoff directed Ingrid Bergman in her first American film, *Intermezzo*.

Films as actor include: 1932 What Price Hollywood? '34 George White's Scandals; Let's Fall in Love. '50 All About Eve. '57 The Sun Also Rises. '60 Once More, With Feeling; Exodus. Films as director include: '39 Intermezzo (GB: Escape to Happiness). '41 The Corsican Brothers. '43 Something to Shout About; The Heat's On (GB: Tropicana); Song of Russia. '45 Where Do We Go From Here? '49 Black Magic. '60 Oscar Wilde (GB).

RATTIGAN, Terence

(1911–1977). Playwright/ screenwriter. Born: London, England

Educated at Harrow and Oxford University, Terence Rattigan decided not to follow his father into the diplomatic service but to become a playwright instead. *First Episode*, written in collaboration with a fellow-student, was performed in London and New York. His first big success was the comedy *French Without Tears*, which he helped to adapt for the screen. He served during World War II at the Foreign Office, continuing to write for the cinema. After the war he essayed serious drama with *The Winslow Boy*, about a cadet accused of stealing, and *The Browning Version*, a gloomy view of public school life. Both were made into successful films. He remained primarily a man of the theatre but was

swept aside by the mid-Fifties revolution in English drama, which made his plays about middle-class malaise seem outdated and irrelevant. But he continued to write screenplays for plush productions into the Seventies. He was knighted in 1971.

Films include: 1939 French Without Tears (co-sc. from own play). '45 The Way to the Stars (co-sc) (USA: Johnny in the Clouds). '48 The Winslow Boy (co-sc. from own play). '51 The Browning Version (from own play). '52 The Sound Barrier (USA: Breaking the Sound Barrier/Star Bound). '55 The Deep Blue Sea (from own play). '57 The Prince and the Showgirl (from own play). '58 Separate Tables (co-sc. from own play) (USA). '63 The VIPs (USA: International Hotel). '64 The Yellow Rolls Royce. '69 Goodbye Mr Chips.

RAY, Aldo

(b. 1926). Actor. Born: Aldo Da Re; Pen Argyl, Pennsylvania, USA

The son of Italian immigrants, Aldo Ray served in the US Navy during World War II as a frogman in the Pacific. He played a small part for director David Miller in *Saturday's Hero* while campaigning for election as constable of Crockett, California, which he won. Despite his tough-guy appearance he was so popular and easy-going that he made no arrests and resigned after eight months. He returned to Hollywood and was quickly given the lead opposite Judy Holliday in George Cukor's *The Marrying Kind*. He was also a dim boxer for Cukor in *Pat and Mike*, and went on to play tough sergeants in several war films. After the Fifties he dropped mostly to minor roles, often in minor films. By the late Seventies he was down to working in a pornographic Western, *Sweet Savage – Bad Girl of the West* (1979), because, as he frankly admitted, he needed the cash. An instinctive rather than an intellectual actor, he has basically played characters not unlike himself.

Films include: 1951 Saturday's Hero (GB: Idols in the Dust). '52 The Marrying Kind; Pat and Mike. '55 Battle Cry. '57 Men in War. '58 The Naked and the Dead. '59 The Siege of Pinchgut (GB). '60 The Day They

Robbed the Bank of England (GB). '67 Riot on Sunset Strip. '68 The Green Berets. '75 Psychic Killer. '81 The Glove.

RAY, Nicholas

(1911–1979). Director. Born: Raymond Nicholas Kienzle; Galesville, Wisconsin, USA

While still at school, Ray wrote a radio series that won him a scholarship to the University of Chicago. He studied architecture with Frank Lloyd Wright before working in theatre and radio in New York. After experience as assistant director to Elia Kazan on *A Tree Grows in Brooklyn* (1945), he directed *They Live by Night*, a touching tale of a young gangster and his true love, doomed in a world that has no place for them. Made in 1947, it was not generally released until 1949, when it was more praised in France and England than in the USA. He went on to make other stories of misfits and youngsters in trouble, notably *Rebel Without a Cause*, his first big success. This was followed by a variety of assignments, culminating in two epics, shot in Spain, that marked the end of his Hollywood career. By this time he was becoming a cult director and his silence seemed to reinforce his integrity. He lived in Europe for some six years, working on one unfinished film. He returned to live in New York and did some teaching at Harpur College, where he made *We Can't Go Home Again* with his students. His friendship with the German director Wim Wenders led to an acting appearance in *The American Friend* and a final collaboration, when he was dying of cancer, in *Lightning Over Water*. He married actress Gloria Grahame in 1948 and dancer Betty Utey in 1952.

Films include: 1948 They Live by Night. '49 Knock on Any Door. '50 In a Lonely Place. '51 On Dangerous Ground. '52 The Lusty Men. '54 Johnny Guitar. '55 Rebel Without a Cause. '56 Bigger Than Life. '57 The True Story of Jesse James (GB: The James Brothers); Bitter Victory. '58 Party Girl. '61 King of Kings. '63 55 Days at Peking. '73 We Can't Go Home Again. '77 Der amerikanische Freund (actor only) (GER-FR) (USA/GB: The American Friend). '80

Lightning Over Water/Nick's Movie (co-dir; +appearance as himself).

RAY, Satyajit

(b. 1921). Director. Born: Calcutta, India

After taking a degree at Calcutta University, Ray went on to study at Shantiniketan, founded by the Nobel-prizewinning poet Rabindranath Tagore. While working as a commercial artist he helped to set up the Calcutta Film Society in 1948 and he was encouraged in his ambition to film the Bengali novel *Pather Panchali* by Jean Renoir, who came to India to make *The River* (1951). He started shooting part-time in 1952, exhausting his own resources and eventually being helped out by the West Bengali government. The film won a prize at the 1956 Cannes Film Festival, putting Indian cinema on the world map and enabling Ray to complete *Aparajito* and *Apur Sansar*, the remaining films of what was to remain his most admired work, the Apu Trilogy. Having brought Apu from childhood in a village to adulthood in the city, Ray moved on to deal with the problems of modern life, including those of women, in such films as *Mahanagar* and *Company Limited*, but he also explored the past (*Charulata*, *Distant Thunder*) and kept in touch with village life, sometimes seen from a city perspective (*Days and Nights in the Forest*). Always interested in children's literature, he made several films for children, including *The Adventures of Goopy and Bagha* and *The Golden Fortress*. Having previously worked in the Bengali language, which limited his market in India, Ray made *The Chess Players* in Hindi-Urdu and English, contrasting the impatient dynamism of the British soldiers who take over the kingdom of Oudh with the appealing indolence of the Indians who allow them to do so. Ray was awarded an honorary doctorate by Oxford University in 1978 and a special Golden Lion at the 1982 Venice Film Festival.

Films include: 1955 Pather Panchali (USA: Song of the Little Road). **'56** Aparajito (USA/GB: The Unvanquished). **'58** Jalsaghar (USA/GB: The Music Room). **'59** Apur Sansar (USA/GB: The World of Apu). **'60** Devi (USA/GB: The Goddess). **'62** Kanchenjunga. **'63** Mahanagar (USA/GB: The Big City). **'64** Charulata (USA: The Lonely Wife). **'66** Nayak (USA/GB: The Hero). **'68** Goopy Gyne Bagha Byne (USA/GB: The Adventures of Goopy and Bagha). **'69** Aranyer Din-Ratri (USA/GB: Days and Nights in the Forest). **'71** Seemabadha (USA/GB: Company Limited). **'73** Ashani Sanket (USA/GB: Distant Thunder). **'75** Sonar Kella (USA/GB: The Golden Fortress). **'77** Shatranj ke Khilari (USA/GB: The Chess Players). **'80** Hirok Rajar Deshe (GB: The Kingdom of Diamonds). **'81** Pikoo (short) (FR); Sadyati (GB: Deliverance).

RAYE, Martha

(b. 1916). Actress. Born: Margaret Theresa Yvonne Reed; Butte, Montana, USA

A comedienne and singer known for her huge mouth and loud booming voice, Martha Raye was in vaudeville at three in her parents' act. She was a nightclub singer in Hollywood when she was discovered by Paramount, making her film debut opposite Bing Crosby in 1936. Other musical roles followed and her comic ability was given an opportunity in *Hellzapoppin'*. Her finest role was with Chaplin in *Monsieur Verdoux* as the only one of his bigamous wives whom he is unable to murder. After this she concentrated on television and live appearances. She spent much of her time entertaining the troops during World War II and in Korea and Vietnam, receiving for this the Jean Hersholt Humanitarian Award in the Oscar ceremonies of 1969. She had survived a suicide attempt in 1956, and in 1967 she starred on Broadway in *Hello, Dolly!* In the Seventies she played the housekeeper in the television series *McMillan and Wife*. She divorced her sixth husband in 1962.

Films include: 1936 Rhythm on the Range; The Big Broadcast of 1937. **'37** Artists and Models. **'40** The Boys From Syracuse. **'42** Hellzapoppin'. **'44** Four Jills in a Jeep; Pin-Up Girl. **'47** Monsieur Verdoux. **'62** Jumbo. **'79** Airport '79 – Concorde (GB: Airport '80 – The Concorde).

REAGAN, Ronald

(b. 1911). Actor/politician. Born: Tampico, Illinois, USA

Elected Governor of California in 1966 and 1970, and President of the United States in 1980, Ronald Reagan has made both political and movieland history in a way that dwarfs his second-rate career as a film actor. Of lower-middle-class Scottish and Irish origins, he graduated from Eureka College in 1932 and became a sports announcer on radio. Given a seven-year contract at Warners in 1937, he played the lead as a radio announcer in *Love Is on the Air* after a few minor parts. His first major A-film role was opposite Bette Davis in *Dark Victory*, and his most famous part was as the victim of punitive leg amputation in *Kings Row* ('Where's the rest of me?'). After war service he was reduced to supporting roles and concentrated on union activities with the Screen Actors Guild, of which he became president in 1947. Married to actress Jane Wyman from 1940 to 1948, he met young actress Nancy Davis through SAG and married her in 1952. She was a staunch anticommunist, and partly under her influence, he moved from liberal to conservative in views and from Democrat to Republican in party. Meanwhile, back on the screen, he was in a couple of good Allan Dwan Westerns in the mid-Fifties, and played a convincing villain for Don Siegel in *The Killers*, conniving with his devious mistress (Angie Dickinson) to bemuse a naive racing driver (John Cassavetes) and involve him in crime. In 1959 Reagan was re-elected president of SAG and in 1960 he headed a successful strike for better pay and conditions for actors. This was, ironically, his first step on the path to the White House.

Films include: 1937 Love Is on the Air (GB; Radio Murder Mystery). **'38** Brother Rat. **'39** Dark Victory. **'40** Knute Rockne – All American; Santa Fe Trail. **'41** Kings Row. **'43** This Is the Navy. **'49** The Hasty Heart (GB). **'51** Bedtime for Bonzo. **'54** Cattle Queen of Montana. **'55** Tennessee's Partner. **'57** Hellcats of the Navy. **'64** The Killers.

REDFORD, Robert

(b. 1937). Actor. Born: Santa Monica, California, USA

Robert Redford left the University of Colorado in 1957 and spent a year travelling and painting in Europe. From 1958 he studied theatrical design at the Pratt Institute in New York and acting at the American Academy of Dramatic Arts. He began to get acting parts on television and on Broadway, where he eventually starred in Neil Simon's *Barefoot in the Park*. After several increasingly important film roles, it was his re-creation of the lead in *Barefoot in the Park* on-screen that brought him stardom, massively confirmed by the success of *Butch Cassidy and the Sundance Kid*, where he effectively partnered Paul Newman. He set up his own production company to make such films as *Downhill Racer* and *The Candidate*, and was reunited with Newman in *The Sting*, which brought him an Oscar nomination. An isolated figure who has had little to do with conventional Hollywood life, Redford was determined to control his career and use it to express his liberal views, for instance in the Watergate film *All the President's Men*. Turning director, he won an Oscar at his first attempt with *Ordinary People*.

Films include: 1962 War Hunt. **'65** Inside Daisy Clover. **'66** The Chase. **'67** Barefoot in the Park. **'69** Butch Cassidy and the Sundance Kid; Tell Them Willie Boy Is Here; Downhill Racer. **'72** Jeremiah Johnson; The Candidate (+co-exec. prod.). **'73** The Way We Were; The Sting. **'74** The Great Gatsby. **'75** The Great Waldo Pepper; Three Days of the Condor. **'76** All the President's Men (+co-exec. prod.). **'79** The Electric Horseman. **'80** Brubaker; Ordinary People (dir. only).

REDGRAVE, Lynn

(b. 1943). Actress. Born: London,
England

After studying at the Central School of
Speech and Drama, Lynn Redgrave
appeared in the Royal Court Theatre
as Helena in *A Midsummer Night's
Dream*. She made her film debut in
Tom Jones and the same year (1963)
she joined the National Theatre company. Her first and best starring role
was as the gawky but good-hearted
heroine of *Georgy Girl*, which brought
her an Academy Award Best Actress
nomination against her sister Vanessa (Liz Taylor won). She went to live
in the United States in 1966 and
married actor-director John Clark in
1967. She continued to appear in both
British and American films, including
a miscalculated impersonation of the
Dutch madam Xaviera Hollander in
The Happy Hooker; but her movie
career waned in the Seventies. She
scored a big hit on Broadway in *Black
Comedy* and starred in an American
television sitcom series, *House Calls*.

Films include: 1963 Tom Jones. '64 The Girl
With Green Eyes. '66 Georgy Girl; The
Deadly Affair. '67 Smashing Time. '69 The
Virgin Soldiers. '72 Everything You Always
Wanted to Know About Sex, But Were
Afraid to Ask (USA). '73 The National
Health. '75 The Happy Hooker (USA). '76
The Big Bus (USA). '80 Les Séducteurs *ep*
Sketch Anglais (FR-IT) (USA: Sunday
Lovers).

REDGRAVE, Michael

(1908–1985). Actor. Born: Bristol,
Somerset, England

From a theatrical family, Michael
Redgrave was educated at Clifton College, Bristol, and Magdalene College,
Cambridge. After teaching at Cran-
leigh, he made his stage debut in 1934
at the Liverpool Playhouse and joined
the Old Vic company in 1936. In the
same year he played a small part for
Hitchcock in *The Secret Agent*, which
led to the starring role as a madcap
musicologist and amateur spy in *The
Lady Vanishes*. He continued to be
primarily a theatre actor but had
some notable film roles, such as the
mad ventriloquist taken over by his
dummy in *Dead of Night*. A brief
sojourn in Hollywood in the late Forties produced an Academy Award
nomination as Best Actor for *Mourning Becomes Electra*. In the early Fifties
he was the unhappy schoolmaster in
The Browning Version and a lively Jack
Worthing in *The Importance of Being
Earnest*. From the late Fifties he played
mainly supporting roles; and soon
after his impressive cameo as the
small-boy messenger grown to old age
in *The Go-Between* he gave up the
cinema, perhaps partly because he
became afflicted with Parkinson's Disease. He married actress Rachel Kem-
pson (born 1910) in 1935; their son
Corin (born 1939) and daughters
Vanessa and Lynn followed them into
acting careers. He was knighted in
1959.

Films include: 1936 The Secret Agent. '38
The Lady Vanishes. '41 Kipps (USA: The
Remarkable Mr Kipps). '45 The Way to the
Stars (USA: Johnny in the Clouds); Dead of

Night *ep* The Ventriloquist. '47 Fame Is the
Spur; Mourning Becomes Electra (USA). '48
Secret Beyond the Door (USA). '51 The
Browning Version. '52 The Importance of
Being Earnest. '54 Mr Arkadin/Confidential
Report (SP-FR). '55 The Dam Busters. '57
Time Without Pity. '58 The Quiet American
(USA). '62 The Loneliness of the Long
Distance Runner. '65 The Heroes of Tele-
mark. '69 Oh! What a Lovely War. '71 The
Go-Between; Nicholas and Alexandra
(USA).

Above: the Redgrave family – Lynn in
The National Health *(top left);*
Vanessa in Isadora *(top) and Michael*
(as a ventriloquist) in Dead of Night.
Below: Donna Reed in See Here,
Private Hargrove

REDGRAVE, Vanessa

(b. 1937). Actress. Born:
Blackheath, London, England

Too tall for ballet, Vanessa Redgrave
turned to acting and became a star of
the Royal Shakespeare Company at
Stratford-on-Avon, playing a notable
Rosalind in *As You Like It*. Her first
important screen role was as the
dazzling ex-wife of a gentle madman
(David Warner) in *Morgan, a Suitable
Case for Treatment*, winning her an
Oscar nomination; and her enigmatic
role in *Blow-Up* added to her movie
reputation. She was married to director Tony Richardson (1962–67), with
whom she made a couple of dud films;
but she had a child by one of her co-
stars, Franco Nero, in her first American venture, *Camelot*. Her big attempt
at Art was as the American dancer
Isadora Duncan; but *Isadora* was a

flop, though it brought her a second
Best Actress Oscar nomination. The
topic had been pre-empted by Ken
Russell in a small-scale but brilliant
television treatment, with Vivian Pick-
les. But Russell did little for Redgrave
when he directed her as a sensual nun
in *The Devils*. Her political involvement with the Workers' Revolutionary Party seemed to coincide
with a decline in her film career, but
she made a partial recovery in bringing to life the worthy histrionics of
Julia, in which she was ably partnered
by Jane Fonda and won herself an
Academy Award as Best Supporting
Actress. She followed this with a 1981
Emmy for her television role as a
Jewish member of a concentration-
camp women's orchestra in *Playing
for Time*, which was scripted by Arthur
Miller.

Films include: 1958 Behind the Mask. '66
Morgan, a Suitable Case for Treatment; A
Man for All Seasons; Blow-Up. '67 Camelot
(USA). '68 Charge of the Light Brigade;
Isadora (USA: The Loves of Isadora). '69
Oh! What a Lovely War. '71 The Devils. '72
Mary, Queen of Scots. '74 Murder on the
Orient Express. '77 Julia (USA). '79 Agatha;
Yanks; Bear Island (GB-CAN).

REED, Carol

(1906–1976). Director. Born: Putney
London, England

Carol Reed started his career as an
actor in 1923 and became personal
aide to the popular thriller-writer
Edgar Wallace, overseeing the stage
and film versions of his stories. Then
he undertook theatrical and film assignments for Basil Dean, who had set
up Associated Talking Pictures (later
Ealing Studios), and directed his first
film in 1935. He began to win a
reputation with the coal-mining story
The Stars Look Down and the war film
The Way Ahead; and he collaborated
with Garson Kanin on the Oscar-
winning documentary *The True Glory*.
The peak of his career came in the late
Forties with the IRA tragedy *Odd Man
Out* and two Graham Greene tales, *The
Fallen Idol* and *The Third Man*, followed
by the unusual (for him) sexual tensions of *Outcast of the Islands*. He was
knighted in 1952 and promptly went
into creative decline, briefly recovering with his third Greene subject, *Our
Man in Havana*. He finally won Oscars
for himself and the picture with the
Dickensian musical *Oliver!* The heady
days when Reed was considered equal
to David Lean and superior to Michael
Powell seem unlikely to return; but
his contribution to the British cinema
in his heyday was substantial.

Films include: 1935 Midshipman Easy
(USA: Men of the Sea). '38 Bank Holiday.
'39 The Stars Look Down. '40 Night Train
to Munich (USA: Night Train). '41 Kipps
(USA: The Remarkable Mr Kipps). '44 The
Way Ahead. '45 The True Glory (doc) (co-
dir). '47 Odd Man Out. '48 The Fallen Idol.
'49 The Third Man. '51 Outcast of the
Islands. '53 The Man Between. '55 A Kid for
Two Farthings. '56 Trapeze (USA). '58 The
Key. '59 Our Man in Havana (USA). '63 The
Running Man. '65 The Agony and the
Ecstasy (USA). '68 Oliver! '70 Flap (USA)
(GB: The Last Warrior). '71 Follow Me
(USA: The Public Eye).

REED, Donna

(1921–1986). Actress. Born: Donna Mullenger; Denison, Iowa, USA

A pretty and vivacious leading lady of the Forties and Fifties, Donna Reed won her Best Supporting Actress Oscar for her part as a prostitute – played with sympathetic restraint – in *From Here to Eternity*. She was usually cast as the wholesome sweetheart who wins her man, as in her 1941 debut, *The Getaway*, in which she played a criminal's sister loved by a detective. Excellent roles were provided for her in *They Were Expendable*, set in the Pacific in World War II, and *It's a Wonderful Life*, where she was radiant as James Stewart's wife. Born on a farm, Reed had trained to be a secretary but took a screen test at MGM with another unknown, Van Heflin. After some forty films she became the hostess of *The Donna Reed Show* on television, which ran from 1958 to 1966. She then pursued her interests in photography, travel and world peace, acting only occasionally.

Films include: 1941 The Getaway; The Bugle Sounds. '44 See Here, Private Hargrove. '45 They Were Expendable. '46 It's a Wonderful Life; Faithful in My Fashion. '51 Saturday's Hero (GB: Idols in the Dust). '52 Scandal Sheet (GB: The Dark Page). '53 From Here to Eternity. '54 The Last Time I Saw Paris. '56 Beyond Mombasa (GB). '60 Pepe (USA-MEX).

REED, Oliver

(b. 1938). Actor. Born: Wimbledon, London, England

The nephew of director Carol Reed, he left school at 17 and hustled as a strip-club bouncer and fairground boxer before joining the Royal Army Medical Corps. Work as a film extra brought him a part in the BBC television serial *The Golden Spur* and he soon emerged as a lead in Hammer horror movies. Michael Winner took him under his wing for several films set during the Swinging Sixties. Ken Russell then relied upon him to bring a sweaty reality into his own cinematic fantasy world: Reed was excellent as a hulking Gerald Crich in *Women in Love* (notoriously wrestling in the nude with Alan Bates), as the sensual priest Grandier in *The Devils*, and as the Teddy Boy holiday-camp 'greencoat' who becomes the step-father of *Tommy*. Since then it has been a long bout of hell-raising and leads in big-budget but inconsequential films. The battered, bull-like Reed is an original, especially good at playing upper-class yobs and costume heroes or villains, often with comic charm.

Films include: 1958 The Square Peg. '60 'Beat' Girl; The Curse of the Werewolf; The Two Faces of Dr Jekyll. '62 The Damned (USA: These Are the Damned). '64 The System. '66 The Trap. '67 The Jokers; I'll Never Forget What's-'is-Name. '68 Oliver! '69 Women in Love. '71 The Devils. '73 The Three Musketeers: the Queen's Diamonds (PAN). '75 Tommy; Royal Flash; The Four Musketeers: the Revenge of Milady (PAN-SP). '78 The Class of Miss MacMichael. '81 Lion of the Desert (GB-LIBYA-USA). '82 Venom.

Top: Oliver Reed in Hannibal Brooks *(1969). Top right: Christopher Reeve in* Superman, The Movie. *Above: Steve Reeves flexes his muscles in* Hercules Unchained. *Below: Serge Reggiani in* Manon

REEVE, Christopher

(b. 1952). Actor. Born: New York City, USA

Is he man or Superman? It will always be impossible now to dissociate this actor from the role of the famous comic-strip hero. But Reeve is an intelligent, talented performer, one who easily held his own with Marlon Brando, Glenn Ford and Gene Hackman in *Superman, The Movie*. He started acting in local rep at the age of nine, completed a degree at Cornell University and took an advanced acting programme at the Juilliard School. He worked with the National Theatre in London and the Comédie Française in Paris, then in an American television soap opera (as a womanizing villain) and on Broadway with Katharine Hepburn in *A Matter of Gravity*. *Gray Lady Down* marked his screen debut but he was still unknown when he was offered the part of the crime-fighting 'man of steel' and his innocuous alter ego, Clark Kent, in a film that quickly demanded two sequels. In *Deathtrap* he played a homosexual playwright who conspires with another (Michael Caine) to kill the latter's wife.

Films: 1978 Gray Lady Down; Superman, The Movie. '80 Somewhere in Time; Superman II. '82 Deathtrap. '83 Superman III – The Legend Grows.

REEVES, Steve

(b. 1926). Actor/bodybuilder. Born: Glasgow, Montana, USA

Reeves had little acting ability but a top-heavy tenement of muscle for a body that made him very popular in Italian epics in the late Fifties and early Sixties. Formerly Mr America, Mr World, Mr Universe and Le Plus Bel Athlète du Monde, he made a name for himself in showbiz by flexing his muscles in cabaret. In 1954 he landed a part in the film *Athena* and attracted the attention of Italian entrepreneur Pietro Francisci who was looking for a star to play *Hercules*. The resultant film and its follow-up *Hercules Unchained* – both packed with feats of strength and voluptuous heroines to drape themselves over Reeves' torso – were promoted in America by Joseph E. Levine and enjoyed colossal success. Reeves continued to play mythological musclemen until the mix-Sixties when epics of that kind went out of vogue and his stardom waned. He retired to California to raise horses on his ranch.

Films include: 1954 Athena (USA). '58 Le Fatiche di Ercole (IT) (USA/GB: Hercules); Ercole e la Regina di Lidia (IT-FR) (USA/GB: Hercules Unchained). '59 Gli Ultimi Giorni di Pompeii (IT-SP-MON) (USA/GB: The Last Days of Pompeii); Il Terrore dei Barbari (IT) (USA/GB: Goliath and the Barbarians). '61 Il Ladro di Bagdad (IT-FR) (USA/GB: The Thief of Bagdad). '62 Romolo e Remo (IT) (USA/GB: Duel of the Titans). '63 Il Figlio di Spartaco (USA: The Slave; GB: The Son of Spartacus). '68 Vivo per la Tua Morte (IT) (USA: A Long Ride From Hell).

REGGIANI, Serge

(b. 1922). Actor. Born: Reggio Emilia, Italy

The dark, slightly built Reggiani made his name in some of the best post-war French films. He was the despicable collaborator in Marcel Carné's *Les Portes de la Nuit*, the suicidal brother in Henri-Georges Clouzot's *Manon*, the soldier involved with a prostitute and a housemaid in Max Ophuls' *La Ronde*, and, perhaps best of all, the young man driven to murder twice in Jacques Becker's *Casque d'Or*. These were romantic films underscored with tragedy, and Reggiani's uncertain demeanour and handsome looks suited them perfectly. A naturalized Frenchman, he had a couple of film parts as a teenager then trained as a hairdresser before acting lessons brought him to the Conservatoire. Stage work followed, then Louis Daquin gave him a supporting part in *Le Voyageur de la Toussaint* in 1943. He remained a top actor from the Fifties until the Seventies and enjoyed considerable success as a singer.

Films include: 1943 Le Voyageur de la Toussaint. '44 Le Carrefour des Enfants Perdus. '46 Les Portes de la Nuit (USA: Gates of the Night). '49 Manon. '50 La Ronde. '51 Secret People (GB). '52 Casque d'Or (USA: Golden Helmet; GB: Golden Marie). '73 Il Gattopardo (IT) (USA/GB: The Leopard). '69 L'Armée des Ombres (IT-FR) (GB: The Army in the Shadows). '77 Une Fille Courue de Fil Blanc; Violette et François.

REID, Beryl

(b. 1920). Actress. Born: Hereford, England

Entertaining Mr Sloane begins with a slow vertical tilt up the garishly-dressed, buxom body of a girl leaning raffishly against a gravestone as she slurps at an iced-lolly. Her face, though, when it is revealed, belongs to the not-so-girlish Beryl Reid, and it is typical of this excellent character actress that she has wickedly deluded us into believing that the plump, raucous and vulgar old predator she plays is something entirely different. Her other memorable film roles were as June Buckridge, the bitchy lesbian actress who loses her girlfriend (Susannah York) in *The Killing of Sister George*, a truly brilliant performance; and as the saucy, raddled Mrs Slipshod in *Joseph Andrews*. It is to be regretted that few other good screen parts have come her way but she has compensated with distinguished theatre and television work. A dancer and soubrette on stage at 17, she quickly graduated to comedy, making a name for herself in BBC Radio's *Educating Archie*. Her first film was *The Belles of St Trinian's* (1954).

Films include: 1956 The Extra Day. '60 Two-Way Stretch. '68 Inspector Clouseau; The Killing of Sister George (USA); Star! (USA). '70 Entertaining Mr Sloane. '72 Dr Phibes Rises Again. '77 Joseph Andrews. '78 Carry On Emmanuelle.

REID, Wallace

(1891–1923). Actor. Born: William Wallace Reid; St Louis, Missouri, USA

In 1910 Wallace Reid entered the movies and, by 1914, had appeared in scores of short films, many of which he also directed. He played Jeff, the fighting blacksmith, in *The Birth of a Nation*, an effective cameo which helped to make him a very big star. With Famous Players from 1915, Reid was a romantic idol, tall, fair-haired and full of boyish charm. He was in some excellent films (notably DeMille's *The Golden Chance* and *Joan the Woman*), and also in the 'Wallace Reid Racing Features', swiftly made motor-racing adventures which owed almost everything to the star. Tragically, Reid became a drug-addict after morphine treatment following a serious train accident. His last films were made with intense difficulty. He entered a sanatorium in 1922, and died the following year, aged only 31.

Films include: 1910 The Phoenix. '15 The Birth of a Nation; Enoch Arden (GB: As Fate Ordained). '16 The Golden Chance; The House With the Golden Windows; Joan the Woman. '17 The Devil Stone. '19 The Valley of the Giants; The Roaring Road. '20 Double Speed. '22 Nice People.

REINIGER, Lotte

(1899–1981). Animator. Born: Berlin, Germany

The pioneer and leading exponent of silhouette films, Lotte Reiniger created an enchanting world of moving cut-out fairytale figures that has its own unique place in cinema history. She began her career making silhouettes from black paper of the personalities of the Reinhardt theatre company, and made her first film, *The Ornament of a Loving Heart* (1919), in the tradition of Eastern shadow theatre. In 1923 she began the first full-length animated feature, finishing *The Adventures of Prince Achmet* three years later. In the sound era she began a series of short films based on operas, the best-known being *Papageno* and *Carmen*. She continued to create such exquisitely choreographed confections almost up until her death, working in Britain (with the GPO Film Unit) and Canada after the mid-Thirties, completing a successful series of shadow plays for the BBC and moving into 'silhouette colour' with *Jack and the Beanstalk* in 1955. After the death of her husband and collaborator, Carl Koch (1892–1963), she did not work for ten years but eventually returned to lecture and hold workshops on shadow animation throughout Europe and America. Her film-making technique remained almost unchanged from the Twenties. She used 'trick tables', with glass tops illuminated from below, on which the cut-out paper figures were arranged and fixed against backgrounds built up with layers of semi-transparent paper to give an illusion of depth; these were shot frame-by-frame from above.

Films include: 1919 Das Ornament des verliebter Herzens (GB: The Ornament of a Loving Heart). '21 Der fliegende Koffer (GB: The Flying Coffer). '22 Aschenputtel (GB: Cinderella). '26 Der Abenteuer des Prinzen Achmed (GB: The Adventures of Prince Achmet). '33 Carmen. '35 Galathea; Papageno; Der kleine Schornsteinfeger (GB: The Little Chimney Sweep). '53 Snow White and Rose Red (GB). '55 Jack and the Beanstalk (GB). '75 Aucassin and Nicolette (CAN). '78 The Rose and the Ring (CAN).

REISNER, Charles F.

(1887–1962). Director/screenwriter/songwriter/producer/actor. Born: Charles Francis Reisner; Minneapolis, Minnesota, USA

Charles Reisner had a great natural flair for comedy, and his tremendous ability for devising elaborate gags and visual jokes was utilized by nearly all of the major comic stars of his time. He entered films during World War I as an actor in Universal's one-reelers and then became a gag-man for Mack Sennett. He soon began working with Charles Chaplin and assisted and wrote gags on *A Dog's Life* (1918). He continued to collaborate with Chaplin on all but one of his films until the completion of *The Gold Rush* (1925). Reisner then went to Warner Brothers where he directed Sydney Chaplin in a series of feature comedies, and it was during the years that followed that he directed many of the great

Above left: Beryl Reid in the eighteenth-century romp Joseph Andrews, *adapted from Henry Fielding's novel. Above: Duncan Renaldo in his most famous role as the Cisco Kid in* The Daring Caballero. *Right: a publicity portrait of Lee Remick. Below right: the solemn, unruffled Michael Rennie. Below: Wallace Reid in Cecil B. DeMille's* The Affairs of Anatol *(1921)*

comedians. By 1950 he had moved to television, writing the *Nightwatchman* series.

Films as director include: 1926 The Better 'Ole. **'28** Steamboat Bill, Jr. **'29** Hollywood Revue of 1929. **'31** Reducing. **'32** Flying High. **'37** Murder Goes to College. **'41** The Big Store. **'44** Meet the People; Lost in a Harem. **'50** Travelling Saleswoman.

REISZ, Karel

(b. 1926). Director. Born: Ostrava, Czechoslovakia

Educated in Reading, England, Reisz fought with the Czech squadron of the RAF during World War II. He then went to Cambridge and became a film journalist, writing for *Sight and Sound* and co-editing *Sequence*. He also wrote a book, *The Technique of Film Editing*, and became Programme Selection Officer for the British Film Institute. With Gavin Lambert, Lindsay Anderson and others, Reisz founded the Free Cinema movement which revitalized the British documentary in the Fifties with its free-flowing studies of working-class people; Reisz's most notable contribution was *We Are the Lambeth Boys*, focusing on kids in a Kennington youth club. This socially-concerned series of films directly presaged the British 'New Wave' and Reisz's first feature, *Saturday Night and Sunday Morning*, a strong adaptation of Alan Sillitoe's novel about a disgruntled, boozing, womanizing young factory-worker (the role that made a star of Albert Finney). Grim

and downbeat, it stands alongside the early films of Tony Richardson, John Schlesinger and Lindsay Anderson as a vociferous document of Northern, working-class angst. Reisz moved less easily into the Swinging Sixties, though *Morgan, a Suitable Case for Treatment* and *Isadora* successfully maintained his preoccupation with the social misfit. Like most of his contemporaries he has since worked in Hollywood, but he returned to Britain for his most celebrated film *The French Lieutenant's Woman*, a good-looking and clever adaptation of John Fowles' double-ended Victorian novel about a mysterious fallen women (Meryl Streep) – Reisz again evoking sympathy for the outcast.

Films: 1955 Momma Don't Allow (doc) (co-dir). **'57** Every Day Except Christmas (doc) (co-prod. only). **'59** We Are the Lambeth Boys (doc); March to Aldermaston (doc) (assoc. prod. only). **'60** Saturday Night and Sunday Morning. **'63** This Sporting Life (prod. only). **'64** Night Must Fall. **'66** Morgan, a Suitable Case for Treatment. **'68** Isadora (USA: The Loves of Isadora). **'74** The Gambler (USA). **'78** Who'll Stop the Rain? (USA) (GB: Dog Soldiers). **'81** The French Lieutenant's Woman.

RELPH, Michael

(b. 1915). Producer/director/screenwriter/art director. Born: Broadstone, Dorset, England

The son of actor George Relph, he entered films in 1932 as an assistant art director for Michael Balcon at Gaumont-British. Having established himself as an art director at Warners and a prominent theatrical designer, he rejoined Balcon at Ealing as an art director and, from 1945, as associate producer. His set design for *Saraband for Dead Lovers* won him an Oscar nomination. He formed a long-standing partnership with director Basil Dearden, often co-writing as well as directing and producing in the Fifties. Later he specialized in producing, forming Allied Film Makers in the early Sixties. In 1971, the year of Dearden's death, he became chairman of the Film Producers Association of Great Britain, a post he held until 1976 (he was also chairman of the British Film Institute's Production Board). Going back into film-making as executive in charge of production for Boyd's Co., he was responsible for

setting up *Scum, The Tempest* (both 1979) and *Sweet William* (1980).

Films include: 1944 Champagne Charlie (art dir). **'46** The Captive Heart (assoc. prod). **'47** Nicholas Nickleby (art dir); Frieda (assoc. prod). **'48** Saraband for Dead Lovers (assoc. prod; + art dir). **'49** Kind Hearts and Coronets (assoc. prod). **'50** Cage of Gold (assoc. prod). **'55** The Ship That Died of Shame (prod; + co-sc). **'57** Davy (dir). **'58** Rockets Galore (dir) (USA: Mad Little Island). **'59** Sapphire (prod). **'61** Victim (prod).

REMICK, Lee

(b. 1935). Actress. Born: Boston, Massachusetts, USA

For such a calm, refined beauty, Lee Remick has played a disarming range of teases and sexpots. She began as a Southern temptress – tossing her hair down in court in *Anatomy of a Murder* – and though she is generally a genteel lady now, the men are still left tormented – for example, Robin Ellis as her American admirer in *The Europeans*. Perhaps her most shocking role was as the young alcoholic wife in *Days of Wine and Roses*, a portrayal of disintegration that deservedly won her an Oscar nomination. The daughter of a New York actress, she was educated privately. Modelling and dance training led her to acting in summer stock and swiftly to Broadway and television work. Her first film part was as a nubile majorette in *A Face in the Crowd*. Most of her performances still dwell on that sublime combination of exhibitionism and control, not that she isn't occasionally warm, motherly and distraught – as in *The Omen*. She starred prestigiously as Winston Churchill's mother in the television costume-drama series *Jennie*.

Films include: 1957 A Face in the Crowd. **'58** The Long Hot Summer. **'59** Anatomy of a Murder. **'62** Days of Wine and Roses. **'63** The Wheeler Dealers (GB: Separate Beds). **'65** Baby, the Rain Must Fall; Hallelujah Trail. **'68** No Way to Treat a Lady. **'70** Loot (GB). **'71** A Severed Head (GB). **'76** The Omen. **'77** Telefon. **'78** The Medusa Touch (GB-FR). **'79** The Europeans (GB). **'80** Tribute (CAN-USA).

RENALDO, Duncan

(1904–1980). Actor. Born: Renault Renaldo Duncan; Valladolid, Spain or Camden, New Jersey, USA

Renaldo was deserted by his Scottish father and Romanian mother when a baby. He arrived in the USA in the early Twenties, hoping to become a portrait painter. Unable to realize this aim, he became involved with the film industry, working as an actor and writer, first in New York and then Hollywood. In 1932 Renaldo was imprisoned, allegedly for illegally entering the USA. Pardoned by President Franklin Delano Roosevelt, he returned to Hollywood, where after a brief spell as a Latin lover type, he came to specialize in Westerns. He appeared in some 160 movies, but achieved most fame as the Cisco Kid, a role he played in such films as *The Daring Caballero* and in a long-running television series in the Fifties. Renaldo's co-star

in the latter was Leo Carrillo, who played the Kid's faithful sidekick, Pancho.

Films include: 1929 The Bridge of San Luis Rey; Pals of the Prairie. **'31** Trader Horn. **'39** Zaza. **'41** Outlaws of the Desert. **'43** For Whom the Bell Tolls; Border Patrol. **'44** The San Antonio Kid. **'49** The Daring Caballero. **'59** Zorro Rides Again.

RENNIE, Michael

(1909–1971). Actor. Born: Bradford, Yorkshire, England

Tall, hollow-cheeked and serious-looking, Rennie worked as a car salesman and factory manager before an encounter with a Gaumont-British casting director led to his becoming Robert Young's stand-in in Alfred Hitchcock's *The Secret Agent* (1936). In order to gain acting experience, Rennie worked in repertory in York and Windsor for a couple of years. He then returned to films, achieving featured billing in *Ships With Wings* and star status in the Margaret Lockwood vehicle *I'll Be Your Sweetheart*. He went to Hollywood in 1951, where for eight years he enjoyed a flourishing career as a supporting actor. He returned to England in 1959 a minor star, and took the lead role of Harry Lime in the successful television series *The Third Man*.

Films include: 1941 Ships With Wings. **'45** I'll Be Your Sweetheart; The Wicked Lady; Caesar and Cleopatra. **'47** White Cradle Inn (USA: High Fury). **'51** The Day the Earth Stood Still (USA). **'53** The Robe (USA). **'55** Soldier of Fortune (USA); The Rains of Ranchipur (USA). **'57** Island in the Sun (USA). **'67** Hotel (USA). **'68** The Power (USA). **'69** Krakatoa: East of Java (retitled Volcano for TV showings) (USA).

RENOIR, Claude

(b. 1914). Cinematographer. Born: Paris, France

The son of the actor Pierre Renoir, Claude Renoir learned his craft from the cinematographers Jean Bachelet, Marcel Lucien and Joseph Louis Mundwiller, and made an excellent debut with *Toni* (directed by his uncle, Jean Renoir). Between 1939 and 1942, Renoir served with the Cinematic Service of the navy. With the end of World War II, his career really took off and he found himself constantly in demand. This remarkably gifted photographer has done much evocative and memorable work, perhaps the finest example of his skill being his superb colour photography of Jean Renoir's film *The River*, set in India.

Films include: 1934 Toni. **'36** Une Partie de Campagne (not released until 1949). **'37** La Grande Illusion (ass. cam) (USA: Grand Illusion; GB: The Great Illusion). **'38** La Bête Humaine (ass. cam) (USA: The Human Beast; GB: Judas Was a Woman); Prison sans Barreaux (GB: Prison Without Bars). **'46** Jéricho (GB: Behind These Walls). **'48** La Grande Volière; L'Impasse des Deux Anges. **'51** The River (IND). **'56** Elena et Les Hommes (USA: Paris Does Strange Things; GB: The Night Does Strange Things). **'68** Barbarella (FR-IT). **'75** French Connection II (USA). **'77** The Spy Who Loved Me (GB). **'78** Attention! Les Enfants Regardent.

RENOIR, Jean

(1894–1979). Director. Born: Paris, France

The son of the Impressionist painter Auguste Renoir (lovingly described in his book *Renoir, My Father*), Jean Renoir served as a cavalry officer and a pilot during World War I, then married his father's last model, Catherine Hessling and was drawn into film-making. More than any other director, Renoir created a world where people are as natural as landscape; he watched them through his deep focus, gave them space to breathe and live, kept the framework loose so that his marvellous actors, Simon, Gabin, Jouvet and the rest, could improvise a little as they inhabited their characters fully. And when he came to his masterpiece, *La Règle du Jeu*, and made it in total awareness that it was his masterpiece, he acted too, as magisterially as any of them, a portrait of the artist as blunderer in spite of himself. When it first appeared, *La Règle* was hissed from the screen, and *Boudu* and *Toni*, too, took years to find an audience. The films of his American exile, *Swamp Water* and *Diary of a Chambermaid*, so long belittled, now seem in their eccentric naturalness to be essential Renoir. To Truffaut and to Godard he was French cinema; to everyone who cares for film he has always some new insight, some fresh delight. But one correction, for the record. Renoir's 'Everyone has his reasons' has been quoted more often than any line of film, to prove Renoir's all-embracing understanding. But what Octave says in *La Règle* is in fact, 'The most terrifying thing in the world is that everyone has his reasons', and that is a little different – less comforting, less easy and less evasive. There were no simple answers for Jean Renoir.

Films include: 1924 La Fille de l'Eau. '26 Nana. '28 La Petite Marchande d'Allumettes (co-dir). '31 La Chienne. '32 Boudu Sauvé des Eaux (USA: Boudu Saved From Drowning). '34 Toni. '35 Le Crime de Monsieur Lange (USA: The Crime of Monsieur Lange). '36 La Vie Est à Nous (doc) (USA: People of France); Une Partie de Campagne (+act) (not released until 1949). '37 Les Bas-Fonds (USA: The Lower

Depths); La Grande Illusion (USA: Grand Illusion; GB: The Great Illusion). '38 La Bête Humaine (+act) (USA: The Human Beast; GB: Judas Was a Woman). '39 La Règle du Jeu (+act) (USA: The Rules of the Game). '41 Swamp Water (USA) (GB: The Man Who Came Back). '45 The Southerner (USA). '46 Diary of a Chambermaid (USA); The Woman on the Beach (USA). '51 The River (IND). '52 Le Carosse d'Or/La Carozza d'Oro (IT-FR) (GB: The Golden Coach). '55 French Cancan (USA: Only the French Can). '59 Le Déjeuner sur l'Herbe (USA: Picnic on the Grass). '69 Le Petit Théâtre de Jean Renoir (FR-IT-GER).

RENOIR, Pierre

(1885–1952). Actor. Born: Paris, France

The son of Impressionist painter Auguste Renoir and the elder brother of film director Jean Renoir, Pierre Renoir established himself as a major character actor in the theatre and on the screen. He studied at the Paris Conservatoire and appeared at the Odéon and Porte Saint Martin theatres before joining the army when World War I broke out. After being severely wounded he returned to the stage in 1916. He formed a long and successful partnership with the actor Louis Jouvet, and from 1946 worked with Jean-Louis Barrault at the Théâtre

Marigny. He gave many fine film performances, playing Charles Bovary in *Madame Bovary*, Inspector Maigret in *La Nuit du Carrefour*, Louis XVI in *La Marseillaise* (all directed by his brother Jean) and, most famous of all, the sinister Jericho in Marcel Carné's *Les Enfants du Paradis*.

Films include: 1911 La Dieue. '32 La Nuit du Carrefour. '34 Madame Bovary. '37 La Marseillaise. '38 Le Patriote (USA: The Mad Emperor). '39 Pièges (GB: Snares). '41 Histoire de Rire (USA Foolish Husbands). '45 Les Enfants du Paradis (USA: Children of Paradise); Peléton d'Exécution (USA: Resistance). '46 Mission Spéciale. '49 Scandale aux Champs-Elysées. '51 Knock (USA/GB: Dr Knock).

Far left: the director Jean Renoir. Left: Pierre Renoir as Louis XVI in La Marseillaise. *Below, left to right: Anne Revere in* National Velvet; *Clive Revill in* A Severed Head, *based on*

RESNAIS, Alain

(b. 1922). Director. Born: Vannes, France

A sickly child, Alain Resnais developed a passion for serious literature and music, but also for comics and sub-literary thrillers, all interests which survived into adulthood. He made amateur films on 8mm and 16mm, studied acting and went to IDHEC, the French film school, to train as an editor but left after one year. He worked as a professional editor until the late Fifties and was an amateur maker of art films until his first 35mm film as director, *Van Gogh*, launched him as a documentarist in

the novel by Iris Murdoch; Fernando Rey in one of his less distinguished films, Guns of the Magnificent Seven *(1969), the third in the famous series of Western adventures*

1948. He made some of the best documentary shorts of the Fifties, including the concentration-camp study *Night and Fog*, before turning to features with *Hiroshima, Mon Amour*, scripted by the novelist (and later filmmaker) Marguerite Duras. This set the pattern, already established on several of his documentaries, of his collaboration with distinguished writers, including Alain Robbe-Grillet, Jean Cayrol, Jorge Semprun and David Mercer. But Resnais still developed his own distinctive style – based on complex editing and an elaborate relationship of image, text and music – and his preoccupations with time, memory, the failures and flaws in human relationships and a paradoxical optimism and warmth are based on his left-wing political commitment. His lack of commercial appeal in the Sixties severely limited his career in the Seventies but he made a comeback with *My American Uncle*, which achieved popular success without any compromise of his thematic or ideological principles.

Films include: 1948 Van Gogh (doc. short) (+ed). '50 Guernica (doc. short) (co-dir; +ed). '55 Nuit et Brouillard (doc. short) (USA/GB: Night and Fog). '57 Toute la Mémoire du Monde (doc. short) (+ ed). '59 Hiroshima, Mon Amour (FR-JAP). '61 L'Année Dernière à Marienbad (FR-IT) (USA/GB: Last Year in Marienbad). '63 Muriel, ou le Temps d'un Retour (FR-IT) (USA/GB: Muriel). '66 La Guerre Est Finie (FR-SWED) (USA/GB: The War Is Over). '67 Loin du Vietnam (co-dir) (USA/GB: Far From Vietnam). '68 Je T'Aime, Je T'Aime (+co-sc). '74 Stavisky . . . (FR-IT). '77 Providence (FR-SWITZ). '80 Mon Oncle d'Amérique (GB: My American Uncle).

Left: Burt Reynolds as a footballing convict in Robert Aldrich's tough comedy The Longest Yard. *Above: the ever-exuberant Debbie Reynolds in the musical* The Unsinkable Molly Brown, *directed by Charles Walters from Richard Morris' musical play*

REVERE, Anne

(b. 1907). Actress. Born: New York City, USA

Anne Revere studied at the American Laboratory Theatre, making her Broadway debut in 1931. Apart from her appearance in the 1934 movie *Double Door*, she remained a stage actress until the Forties, when she became successful as a supporting actress (specializing in maternal roles) in Hollywood. She won an Oscar in 1945 playing Elizabeth Taylor's mother in *National Velvet*. Blacklisted by the House Un-American Activities Committee in 1951, she returned to the theatre, winning a Tony Award for her performance in *Toys in the Attic*. She began acting in television in 1962, appearing in such series as *The Edge of Night*, *A Time for Us* and, in the Seventies, *The Six Million Dollar Man*, but she had to wait until 1976 for her next major film role.

Films include: 1940 One Crowded Night. '43 The Song of Bernadette. '44 The Keys of the Kingdom; Standing Room Only; National Velvet. '45 Fallen Angel. '46 Dragonwyck. '47 Gentleman's Agreement; Body and Soul. '51 A Place in the Sun. '76 Birch Interval.

REVILL, Clive

(b. 1930). Actor. Born: Wellington, New Zealand

This versatile, energetic character actor is something of a master of disguise, having played a flamboyant Russian in *The Private Life of Sherlock Holmes*, an Italian hotel manager in *Avanti!* and an inscrutable Chinaman in *One of Our Dinosaurs Is Missing*. At the age of 20, he gave up a career in accountancy to come to England and study acting at the Old Vic Theatre School. Having appeared in repertory and with the Royal Shakespeare Company, he established himself with the role of the narrator in the Peter Brook production of *Irma La Douce*, which had a successful run on Broadway. He made his film debut in *The Headless Ghost* (1959), but did not work regularly in movies until the mid-Sixties.

Films include: 1965 Bunny Lake Is Missing. '66 Modesty Blaise; Kaleidoscope; A Fine Madness (USA). '68 The Shoes of the Fisherman. '70 The Private Life of Sherlock Holmes. '72 Avanti! (USA-IT). '73 The Legend of Hell House. '74 The Black Windmill. '75 One of Our Dinosaurs Is Missing.

REY, Fernando

(b. 1915). Actor. Born: La Coruña, Spain

A carefully trimmed beard and moustache endows Rey with the patrician air of a Spanish grandee, and he has become famous in movies – especially those directed by Luis Buñuel – as a polished, practised sophisticate whose surface urbanity conceals an uncontrollable libido. He was particularly excellent as the would-be seducer of a novitiate nun in *Viridiana*, as the debauched guardian of a crippled girl in *Tristana* (both by Buñuel) and, in rather a different kind of role, as an erudite, reclusive writer in *Elisa, Vida Mia*, for which he won the Award as Best Actor at the 1977 Cannes Film Festival. The son of a high-ranking army officer, Rey drifted into film acting as an extra in the mid-Thirties and subsequently worked on Spanish-dubbed versions of American and British films, dubbing the voices of such stars as Tyrone Power, Humphrey Bogart and Laurence Olivier, long after he had become a successful actor in his own right. Probably his most famous role was that of the elegant master criminal in William Friedkin's nail-biting police thriller *The French Connection*.

Films include: 1954 Mare Nostrum (IT-SP); Comicos. '59 Sonatas (SP-MEX). '61 Viridiana (SP-MEX). '63 The Ceremony (SP-USA). '65 Campanadas a Medianoche (SP-SWITZ) (USA: Falstaff; GB: Chimes at Midnight). '70 Tristana (SP-IT-FR). '71 The French Connection (USA). '72 Le Charme Discret de la Bourgeoisie (FR-SP-IT) (GB: The Discreet Charm of the Bourgeoisie). '75 French Connection II (USA). '76 Le Désert des Tartares (FR-IT-IRAN-GER) (USA: The Desert of the Tartars). '77 Cet Obscur Objet du Désir (FR-SP) (USA/GB: That Obscure Object of Desire).

REYNAUD, Émile

(1844–1918). Animation pioneer. Born: Montreuil, France

Émile Reynaud was the most important figure in the pre-history of film animation. In 1877 he patented the Praxinoscope, a moving peepshow toy using mirrors instead of a shutter for increased brilliance. In 1882 he combined this with a projector to produce a variety of animated cartoons, initially on paper but from 1888 on celluloid. In 1889 he displayed his Théâtre Optique at the Universal Exhibition in Paris but it took another three years to prepare a programme for public exhibition in 1892 at the Musée Grevin, the Pantomimes Lumineuses. With occasional changes of programme, the show ran for eight years and was seen by half a million spectators. But it was overtaken by the Lumières' Cinématographe, though Reynaud used photographic means to produce *Guillaume Tell* and *Le Premier Cigare*. After 1900 Reynaud gradually sank into poverty and, a forgotten and disappointed man, died in a sanatorium at Ivry.

Films include: 1889 Un Bon bock. '90 Clown et Ses Chiens. '91 Pauvre Pierrot. '94 Rève au Coin du Feu. '96 Guillaume Tell. '97 Le Premier Cigare.

REYNOLDS, Burt

(b. 1936). Actor/director. Born: Waycross, Georgia, USA

Brought up in Florida, where his ex-cowboy father was a police chief, Burt Reynolds won a football scholarship to Florida State University but his sporting career was ended by a car accident and he turned to acting, joining the Hyde Park Playhouse in New York. Given a television contract by Universal, he appeared in the series *Riverboat*, *Hawk* and *Gunsmoke*, often as an Indian (he is part-Indian by origin). He made his film debut in 1961 but his movie career made little headway until the late Sixties. He became well-known in the early Seventies through his amusingly irreverent appearances on television chat shows and his role in *Deliverance*, which both established and undermined his characteristic macho image. Associated with violent action movies (in which he often does his own stunts), he has a strong liking for humour and also an evident desire to develop more sensitive and even romantic aspects of his screen image, as when he played a tough cop in love with a high-class call-girl (Catherine Deneuve) in *Hustle* and a hopeful divorcé in *Starting Over*. He has attempted singing and dancing a couple of times, and has directed three films, the conventional *Gator*, the unusual black comedy of would-be suicide *The End*, and the vice-squad thriller *Sharky's Machine*. He was married to television actress Judy Carne (1963–66) and has filled the gossip columns with other romances, including a long-term relationship with the Fifties pop singer Dinah Shore.

Films as actor include: 1961 Angel Baby. '69 Sam Whiskey. '72 Fuzz; Deliverance; Everything You Always Wanted to Know About Sex, But Were Afraid to Ask. '73 Shamus; The Man Who Loved Cat Dancing; White Lightning. '74 The Longest Yard (GB: The Mean Machine). '75 W.W. and the Dixie Dancekings; At Long Last Love; Lucky Lady; Hustle. '76 Silent Movie; Gator (+ dir); Nickelodeon (GB-USA). '77 Smokey and the Bandit; Semi-Tough. '78 The End (+ dir); Hooper. '79 Starting Over. '80 Rough Cut; Smokey and the Bandit II (GB: Smokey and the Bandit Ride Again). '81 The Cannonball Run; Paternity; Sharky's Machine (+ dir). '82 The Best Little Whorehouse in Texas.

REYNOLDS, Debbie

(b. 1932). Actress. Born: Mary Francis Reynolds; El Paso, Texas, USA

At school Debbie Reynolds showed more ability as a majorette than as an actress but, by the time she had reached her mid-teens and become 'Miss Burbank', she had been offered a contract with Warner Brothers. By 1950 she had made the move to MGM where she was successfully cast in many lightweight films and musicals – most notably *Singin' in the Rain* with Donald O'Connor and Gene Kelly. Her image in these early films and in the publicity hand-outs was one of blindingly bland normality. She tried to escape from all that with some attempts at slapstick comedy, but she was not encouraged by the film companies and her films became increasingly anaemic. Having survived her own, fairly disastrous, televison show she threw caution to the wind and destroyed her girl-next-door typecasting by playing the ageing but still sexy Thirties vamp in the chiller *What's the Matter With Helen?*. Her first husband was the actor Eddie Fisher and their daughter is the actress Carrie Fisher.

Films include: 1950 Three Little Words. '52 Singin' in the Rain. '53 I Love Melvin; The Affairs of Dobie Gillis. '54 Susan Slept Here. '55 The Tender Trap. '57 Tammy and the Bachelor (GB: Tammy). '62 How the West Was Won. '64 The Unsinkable Molly Brown. '66 The Singing Nun. '67 Divorce American Style. '71 What's the Matter With Helen?.

RICHARDSON, Ralph

(1902–1983). Actor. Born: Cheltenham, Gloucestershire, England

Ralph Richardson's film appearances have always been interesting but his relatively few starring roles are particularly memorable. In *The Fallen Idol*, for example, he gave a superbly subtle performance as the embassy butler constructing an exciting fantasy world for the ambassador's lonely son while his own life crumbles around him. Richardson's first job was as office boy in an insurance company but an inheritance of £500 enabled him to enrol at Brighton School where his interest soon turned from art to acting. By 1920 he had joined the St Nicholas Players and gained considerable repertory experience. Six years later he made his West End debut in *Yellow Sands*. In 1930 he joined the Old Vic Company and soon became a well-established stage actor in addition to embarking on his screen career. His rich oboe-toned voice proved capable of a wide range of emotional expression, and he played such diverse characters as the jealous brother of a sea captain in *Java Head*; the straight-laced schoolteacher fiancé of a chorus girl in *Friday the Thirteenth* and the peppery old general who finds his whisky turned to water in *The Man Who Could Work Miracles*. The peak of his film career was in the Thirties and Forties but throughout the following decades his enormous reputation as a stage actor remained unchanged. He continued to play major roles on the stage and occasionally on television until his death in 1983. He was knighted in 1947.

Films include: 1933 The Ghoul; Friday the Thirteenth. '34 Java Head. '36 Things to Come. '37 The Man Who Could Work Miracles. '38 South Riding; The Citadel. '39 The Four Feathers; The Lion Has Wings. '46 School for Secrets. '48 Anna Karenina; The Fallen Idol. '49 The Heiress (USA). '52 The Sound Barrier (USA: Breaking the Sound Barrier/Star Bound). '62 Long Day's Journey Into Night (USA). '69 Oh! What a Lovely War; The Bed Sitting Room. '73 O Lucky Man! '81 Time Bandits; Dragonslayer.

RICHARDSON, Tony

(b. 1928). Director. Born: Cecil Antonio Richardson; Shipley, Yorkshire, England

As president of the Oxford University Dramatic Society Tony Richardson was responsible for such productions as *The Duchess of Malfi*. On joining the BBC as a producer he remained involved in stage productions and in 1956 became associate director of the English Stage Company and produced their first play, *Look back in Anger* – thus founding a long and successful collaboration with John Osborne that continued into films. His film debut *Momma Don't Allow* (1955) was a modest jazz documentary, co-directed with Karel Reisz. In 1958 he founded his own production company, Woodfall Films, which went on to produce most of the 'kitchen sink' dramas of the Sixties as well as the enormously successful *Tom Jones*. After a patchy subsequent career he has emerged as

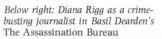

Below: Ralph Richardson as a would-be murderer in the period black comedy The Wrong Box *(1966)*

Below right: Diana Rigg as a crime-busting journalist in Basil Dearden's The Assassination Bureau

Right: Walter Rilla as a Nazi propagandist in The Lisbon Story, *an ironic role for a refugee from Hitler's Germany*

a more American-influenced director with *The Border*, starring Jack Nicholson as a border guard trying to be a decent citizen in a hot-bed of violence and corruption. Richardson was married to the actress Vanessa Redgrave from 1962 to 1967.

Films include: 1959 Look Back in Anger. '60 The Entertainer. '61 A Taste of Honey. '62 The Loneliness of the Long-Distance Runner. '63 Tom Jones. '65 The Loved One (USA). '67 The Sailor From Gibraltar. '68 Charge of the Light Brigade. '70 Ned Kelly. '77 Joseph Andrews. '81 The Border (USA).

RICHTER, Hans

(1888–1976). Director. Born: Berlin, Germany

Invalided out of the Kaiser's army in 1916, Hans Richter joined up with the Dadaists in Zurich and eventually in Berlin. An outspoken opponent of Nazism, he was forced to flee Germany and travelled around Europe before emigrating to America. There he made *Dreams That Money Can Buy*, a Surrealist fantasy starring his fellow emigrés Marcel Duchamp and Fernand Léger. He became a professor at the City College in New York and was director of its Institute of Film Techniques. Richter is perhaps best known for his black and white shorts made in the Twenties – films to be experienced

rather than understood. Much of his work was innovative – he was one of the earliest exponents of experimental cinema – and he may have been the first film-maker to use negative film as an image in its own right. His film *Ghosts Before Breakfast*, made in Germany, continued his explorations of the external real world and the cinematic dream world and became a mini-classic of experimental film. The later 8×8 is a fairy tale for adults, mixing equal parts of Lewis Carroll and Freud, with a cast that reads like a Who's Who of Surrealists. He was also considered a leading authority on Dadaism as well as being a painter and collagist.

Films include: 1926 Film Studie. '28 Vormittagsspuk (GB: Ghosts Before Breakfast); Inflation. '29 Rennsymphonie; Alles dreht sich, alles bewegt sich!; Zweigroschenzauber. '46 Dreams That Money Can Buy (USA). '56 8 × 8 (USA); Dadascope Part I (USA). '63 Alexander Calder: From the Circus to the Moon (USA). '67 Dadascope Part II (USA).

RIEFENSTAHL, Leni

(b. 1902). Director/actress. Born: Berlin, Germany

The most memorable aspect of the propaganda documentaries made by Leni Riefenstahl is her use of intercut-

ting and montage effects – for through the use of these methods she gives her films great rhythm, atmosphere and awesome power. She came from an artistic family and was a student at the Academy of Art in Berlin. She entered films as an actress when she was 23 but soon realized the possibilities of working behind the camera. Riefenstahl directed, produced and starred in her first film, *The Blue Light*, in 1932, and it was this film that brought her to Hitler's notice. He commissioned her to make a documentary on the Nazi Party Rally at Nuremburg. The resulting two films, particularly the second, *Triumph of the Will*, were extraordinary pieces of documentary film-making and prime examples of the use of propaganda. There is, perhaps no more terrifying espousal of an evil cause than *Triumph of the Will*. She went on to use the same techniques in *Olympia*, another superbly constructed film, but the authorities were not so impressed as the film showed a black man, Jesse Owens, beating the unbeatable Aryans. Very little of importance followed. Having spent some time in prison camps after the war, she has since proved herself a highly talented and highly respected photographer.

Films include: 1926 Der heilige Berg (actress only) (GB: The Holy Mountain). '32 Das blaue Licht (+ prod; + act) (GB: The Blue

Light). '34 Triumph des Willens (doc) (USA/GB: Triumph of the Will). '36 Olympia (Pt 1: Fest der Volker; Pt 2: Fest der Schönheit) (doc) (+ sc) (USA: The Olympic Games; GB: Berlin Olympiad). '53 Tiefland (+ sc; + act) (unfinished).

RIGG, Diana

(b. 1938). Actress. Born: Doncaster, Yorkshire, England

Clad in leather and striking a karate-chop pose, Diana Rigg *was* Emma Peel, a tongue-in-cheek Avenger alongside her trusty Steed. For many television viewers who know her from *The Avengers* it would be hard to envisage her as the excellent Shakespearian actress she undoubtedly is. Rigg spent her early childhood in India before returning to England to complete her education. At 17 she attended RADA, where she was in the same class as Glenda Jackson and Susannah York. She made her professional debut in 1957 in Brecht's *Caucasian Chalk Circle* and soon afterwards joined the Royal Shakespeare Company. She turned to television in the mid-Sixties, having success in England with *The Avengers* but failing in America with her show *Diana*. In the meantime she had started to appear in movies – she was the ill-fated Mrs Bond in *On Her Majesty's Secret Service* opposite George Lazenby.

With a few exceptions her films have not been particularly notable and she remains far better known for her television and stage work.

Films include: 1968 A Midsummer Night's Dream. '69 The Assassination Bureau; On Her Majesty's Secret Service. '70 Julius Caesar; Hospital (USA). '73 Theatre of Blood. '77 A Little Night Music (USA-A-GER). '81 Evil Under the Sun; The Great Muppet Caper.

RILLA, Walter

(1895–1980). Actor. Born: Neukirchen, Saarbrücken, Germany

A graduate of Königsberg University, Rilla worked as a journalist and drama critic before turning to acting. He made his stage debut in 1921 and rapidly became a front rank star of German and French films. Alexander Korda persuaded him to play the brother to Merle Oberon's Lady Blakeney in *The Scarlet Pimpernel*. Shortly afterwards Rilla settled in England. His first major part in British films was as a handsome, womanizing banker in *Black Eyes*. Among his other notable character performances were as the leader of a gang of smugglers in *The Golden Salamander* and as a villainous director of German propaganda films in *The Lisbon Story*. His son is the writer, television producer and film director Wolf Rilla (b. 1920), whose

movies include *Bachelor of Hearts* (1958) and *Village of the Damned* (1960).

Films include: 1922 Hanneles Himmelfahrt (GER). '26 Der Geiger von Florenz (GER). '35 The Scarlet Pimpernel. '37 Victoria the Great. '39 Black Eyes. '46 The Lisbon Story. '50 State Secret (USA: The Great Manhunt); The Golden Salamander. '51 Behold the Man (dir; + prod). '63 Cairo (USA). '65 The Face of Fu Manchu. '67 I Giorni dell'Ira (IT) (USA/GB: Day of Anger).

RISI, Dino

(b. 1917). Director. Born: Milan, Italy

Dino Risi came from a medical family and he himself trained as a doctor specializing in psychiatry. He became interested in cinema in Milan and studied film in Switzerland while interned there during World War II. He had already made friends with directors Mario Camerini and Alberto Lattuada who gave him work as an assistant director. On his return to Italy after the was he began to direct documentaries, making his first, the award-winning *Bersaglieri della Signora*, in 1945. From 1951 onwards he gave up psychiatry to concentrate entirely on feature films. It was his third feature, *Il Segno di Venere*, a comedy starring Sophia Loren, that really launched his career. Since then he has become one of Italy's major directors with films that gently and humorously observe life.

Films include: 1946 Barboni (doc). '52 Vacanze col Gangster. '55 Il Segno di Venere (GB: Sign of Venus); Pane, Amore e . . . . . (GB: Scandal in Sorrento). '57 La Nonna Sabella (IT-FR) (GB: Oh! Sabella!). '61 Un Amore a Roma (IT-FR-GER). '62 Il Sorpasso (USA: The Easy Life). '75 Profumo di Donna (USA: Scent of a Woman; GB: That Female Scent). '76 Telefoni Bianchi. '77 Anima Persa (IT-FR).

RISKIN, Robert

(1897–1955). Writer. Born: New York City, USA

Robert Riskin began writing plays in 1912 while still at college. By the time he went to Hollywood under contract to Columbia in 1931 he was already a successful playwright. He met Frank Capra and they co-scripted *The Miracle Woman*, an adaptation from Riskin's play *Bless Your Sister*, thus beginning a fruitful collaboration that included all of Capra's famous social comedies in the Thirties. After 1941 Riskin concentrated mainly on production, founding Equitable Pictures with his brother Everett, although he wrote his last script in 1961 – again for Capra. He was married to the actress Fay Wray. Riskin won a deserved Oscar for his script for *It Happened One Night* and he might have won more. He was the greatest contributor to Capra's populist world other than the director himself, and he wrote with a genuine feeling for the American people.

Films include: 1931 The Miracle Woman; Platinum Blonde. '32 American Madness. '33 Lady for a Day. '34 It Happened One Night; Broadway Bill. '36 Mr Deeds Goes to Town. '37 Lost Horizon. '38 You Can't Take

it With You. '41 Meet John Doe. '51 Here Comes the Groom. '61 Pocketful of Miracles.

RITCHIE, Michael

(b. 1938). Director. Born: Waukesha, Wisconsin, USA

Educated at Harvard, Michael Ritchie began his career as an assistant producer in television in the early Sixties and moved on to directing segments of such popular series as *The Man From UNCLE* and *Dr Kildare*. He also worked on documentaries, which may help to explain the style of his feature debut, *Downhill Racer*, the ski-racing film for which he was hired by Robert Redford. He worked with Redford again on *The Candidate*, a strong political critique, and developed his semi-documentary manner in his amused look at local beauty contests, *Smile*. He returned to sport and finally achieved commercial success with the Little League baseball story *The Bad News Bears* and the football comedy *Semi-Tough*.

Films include: 1969 Downhill Racer. '72 Prime Cut; The Candidate. '75 Smile. '76 The Bad News Bears. '77 Semi-Tough. '78 The Bad News Bears Go to Japan (prod. only). '79 An Almost Perfect Affair. '80 The Island.

RITT, Martin

(b. 1920). Director. Born: New York City, USA

A Communist until the Soviet-German Pact of 1939, Martin Ritt started out as an actor, his political views leading him to join the radical Group Theatre, where he met the playwright Clifford Odets, Lee Strasberg, Elia Kazan and Nicholas Ray. He made his New York Debut in Odets' *Golden Boy* in 1937 and, apart from war service, continued acting in the theatre for a decade. Then he turned to television, initially as an actor but soon as a director, gaining a considerable reputation. In 1951 he was blacklisted for his former Communist Party membership and went back to the theatre, as well as teaching at the Actors' Studio, where he encouraged such students as Paul Newman, Joanne Woodward and Rod Steiger. He entered the cinema with *Edge of the City*, a tough tale of the New York waterfront and interracial friendship, based on the television play *A Man Is Ten Feet Tall*. He has consistently taken a radical attitude to racialism (*The Great White Hope*) and unionism (*Norma Rae*) and he confronted the old scandal of blacklisting in *The Front*. His style is forceful rather than subtle but he regularly gets good performances from his leading actors – Patricia Neal, Melvyn Douglas and Sally Field won Oscars under his direction, and he was nominated for Best Director with *Hud*.

Films include: 1956 Edge of the City (GB: A Man Is Ten Feet Tall). '58 The Long Hot Summer. '59 The Sound and the Fury. '63 Hud. '65 The Spy Who Came in From the Cold (GB). '67 Hombre. '68 The Brotherhood. '70 The Molly Maguires; The Great White Hope. '72 Sounder. '76 The Front. '79 Norma Rae.

RITTER, Thelma

(1905–1969). Actress. Born: Brooklyn, New York City, USA

Thelma Ritter's harsh voice, plain face and small stature could not conceal a heart as big as all outdoors; and a cynical urban wit added to her appeal. As a kid in Brooklyn she was already an entertainer and actress, playing in stock companies even before studying at the American Academy of Dramatic Arts. She worked in theatre and radio until a former neighbour, director George Seaton, gave her a small role in *Miracle on 34th Street*. Darryl F. Zanuck was delighted with her and bigger parts followed. She was frequently the heroine's wordly-wise friend who had lived and suffered but came up smiling. She was nominated six times for the Best Supporting Actress Academy Award but never won.

Films include: **1947** Miracle on 34th Street (GB: The Big Heart). **'48** A Letter to Three Wives. **'49** Father Was a Fullback. **'50** All About Eve. **'51** The Mating Season; The Model and the Marriage Broker. **'52** With a Song in My Heart. **'53** Pickup on South Street. **'59** Pillow Talk. **'61** The Misfits. **'62** Birdman of Alcatraz. **'65** Boeing-Boeing. **'68** What's So Bad About Feeling Good?

THE RITZ BROTHERS

Al Ritz (1901–1965). Actor. Born: Al Joachim; Newark, New Jersey, USA

Jim Ritz (1903–1985). Actor. Born: Jim Joachim; Newark, New Jersey, USA

Harry Ritz (1906–1986). Actor. Born: Harry Joachim; Newark, New Jersey, USA .

The Ritz Brothers' slapstick antics and zany musical numbers enlivened several routine musicals during the Thirties and Forties, with Allan Dwan's musical version of *The Three Musketeers* (in which they played Aramis, Porthos and Athos, with Don Ameche as D'Artagnan and Binnie Barnes as a radiant Lady De Winter) showing them to particular advantage. The sons of Austrian immigrants, the Ritz Brothers came into being when Harry and Jim joined up with the eldest brother Al who had already made a name as a solo performer in vaudeville. They became successful on Broadway in the early Thirties and at the same time began appearing in movies. The brothers continued to perform in cabaret until Al's death in 1965. Harry and Jim made cameo appearances in *Won Ton Ton, the Dog That Saved Hollywood* (1975); Harry also featured in *Silent Movie* (1976).

Films include: **1936** Sing Baby Sing; One in a Million. **'37** You Can't Have Everything. **'38** The Goldwyn Follies. **'39** The Three Musketeers; The Gorilla; Pack Up Your Troubles. **'42** Behind the Eight Ball (GB: Off the Beaten Track). **'43** Never a Dull Moment.

RIVA, Emmanuelle

(b. 1927). Actress. Born: Chénimenil, France

Alain Resnais' *Hiroshima, Mon Amour* gave the part of an actress tormented by memories of her love for a German soldier to screen débutante Emmanuelle Riva, and in it she gave one of the great haunting performances of modern cinema. Formerly a dressmaker, she came to Paris to audition for the stage and studied drama at L'École Dramatique. A successful stage career preceded her entry into films. After she was widely acclaimed in *Hiroshima, Mon Amour*, similar passionate, tragic parts came her way, notably in *Léon Morin, Prêtre* and *Thérèse Desqueyroux*. A grey-eyed, brown-haired beauty, she is considered one of the most sensitive but dazzling actresses in French films, though works rarely now.

Films include: **1959** Hiroshima. Mon Amour (FR-JAP); Le Huitième Jour. **'60** Kapò (IT-FR). **'61** Léon Morin, Prêtre (FR-IT) (GB: Leon Morin, Priest). **'62** Thérèse Desqueyroux (USA/GB: Thérèse); Climats (GB: Climates of Love). **'64** Le Gros Coup (FR-IT). **'65** Thomas l'Imposteur (GB: Thomas the Impostor). **'76** Le Diable au Coeur (USA: The Devil in the Heart). **'82** Gli Occhi, La Bocca (IT-FR).

RIVETTE, Jacques

(b. 1928). Director. Born: Rouen, France

Rivette is an unorthodox, uncommercial director who came ashore with the *nouvelle vague*. With one exception, *La Religieuse*, an adaptation from Diderot, he has refused to be absorbed into the mainstream, and his movies are encumbered with neither straightforward narratives nor any clear message, other than that film itself is a language for communication. Rivette has no regard for the conventions of the cinema industry – accordingly *L'Amour Fou* was four hours long (nine hours shorter, however, than the original *Out One*) and mixed both 16mm and 35mm film. *Céline and Julie Go Boating*, meanwhile, is an endless, free-flowing comedy about two girls and the stream of events that befall them, with imagination and the nature of cinema as much the subjects of the film – and Rivette's entire milieu – as anything else. He was a critic on *Cahiers du Cinéma* and *Arts*, and assisted Renoir, Becker, Rohmer and Truffaut before making his first short in the early Fifties and his first feature – *Paris Nous Appartient* – in 1959.

Films include: **1949** Aux Autre Coins (short) (not distributed). **'50** Le Quadrille (short) (not distributed). **'56** Le Coup du Berger (short). **'60** Paris Nous Appartient (GB: Paris Belongs to Us). **'65** Suzanne Simonin, la Religieuse de Diderot (USA: La Religieuse/The Nun). **'68** L'Amour Fou. **'74** Out One: Spectre; Céline et Julie Vont en Bateau (USA/GB: Celine and Julie Go Boating). **'76** Noroît (USA: Northwest Wind); Duelle (USA: Women Duelling).

ROACH, Hal

(b. 1892). Producer. Born: Harold Eugene Roach; Elmira, New York, USA

Hal Roach entered films in 1912 as a $5-a-day cowboy and set up as a producer-director in 1915 after receiving a small legacy. Harold Lloyd was his first star, to be followed by Our Gang (in a series featuring children),

Will Rogers, Charlie Chase and, particularly, Laurel and Hardy. Roach directed only occasionally after 1920 but produced features as well as shorts in the Twenties and Thirties, winning Academy Awards with Laurel and Hardy's *The Music Box* and Our Gang's *Bored of Education*. By the mid-Thirties he was beginning to concentrate on features instead of two-reel and three-reel shorts, working in collaboration with his son Hal Roach Jr (1921–1972), with whom he co-directed *One Million BC*. He claimed that his forte was visual comedy, with the emphasis on imitating childish actions. This and his attention to developing character personalities had carried him successfully through the transition from silents to sound films. After war service producing films for the Signal Corps and the US Army Air Force, he tried to switch to television production, but with mixed results. The company finally failed, and the studios were demolished in the mid-Sixties. Appropriately, Hal Roach's last success was the compilation film *The Crazy World of Laurel and Hardy*. Roach shares with Mack Sennett the credit for most of the best slapstick comedy that Hollywood produced so abundantly in its golden age.

Films as producer or executive producer include: **1921** Never Weaken (short). **'26** There Ain't No Santa Claus (short). **'27** Putting Pants on Philip (short). **'32** Helpmates (short); The Music Box (short). **'36** Bored of Education (short). **'37** Topper; Way Out West. **'38** There Goes My Heart; Swiss Miss; Merrily We Live. **'39** Of Mice and Men; Topper Takes a Trip. **'40** A Chump at Oxford; One Million BC (+co-dir). **'41** Topper Returns. **'42** The Devil With Hitler. **'48** Who Killed Doc Robin? **'66** The Crazy World of Laurel and Hardy (compilation) (co-prod).

ROBARDS Sr, Jason

(1892–1963). Actor. Born: Hillside, Michigan, USA

After attending the American Academy of Dramatic Arts, Jason Robards appeared on Broadway before entering films, usually as a hero in low-budget features. With the coming of sound he switched to character roles – he played William Herndon, Lincoln's law partner, in D. W. Griffith's *Abraham Lincoln* and a greedy builder in *Mr Blandings Builds His Dream House*. He continued to appear on stage, his last role on Broadway being in *The Disenchanted* in 1958, with his son Jason Robards Jr.

Films include: **1921** The Gilded Lily. **'25** Stella Maris. **'27** Hills of Kentucky. **'30** Abraham Lincoln. **'32** Docks of San Francisco. **'34** All of Me. **'39** I Stole a Million. **'44** Madamoiselle Fifi. **'46** Bedlam. **'47** Riffraff. **'48** Mr Blandings Builds His Dream House. **'61** Wild in the Country.

ROBARDS Jr, Jason

(b. 1922). Actor. born: Chicago, Illinois, USA

Serving in the navy, Jason Robards Jr survived the attack on Pearl Harbor in 1941. He studied at the American Academy of Dramatic Arts, joined a stock company in 1951 and five years later gained critical recognition in Eugene O'Neill's *The Iceman Cometh*. His screen career did not really get going until the Sixties but he quickly

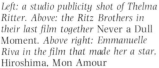

Left: a studio publicity shot of Thelma Ritter. Above: the Ritz Brothers in their last film together Never a Dull Moment. *Above right: Emmanuelle Riva in the film that made her a star,* Hiroshima, Mon Amour

Right: Rachel Roberts in Murder on the Orient Express. *Below: Jason Robards Jr in* The Ballad of Cable Hogue. *Below left: Jason Robards Sr in* Lightnin' *(1930), a Will Rogers vehicle directed by Henry King*

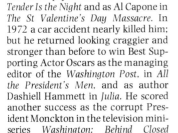

rose to starring roles – for example, as the failed psychiatrist Dick Diver in *Tender Is the Night* and as Al Capone in *The St Valentine's Day Massacre*. In 1972 a car accident nearly killed him; but he returned looking craggier and stronger than before to win Best Supporting Actor Oscars as the managing editor of the *Washington Post*, in *All the President's Men*, and as author Dashiell Hammett in *Julia*. He scored another success as the corrupt President Monckton in the television miniseries *Washington: Behind Closed Doors*. He has also continued to star on Broadway. Lauren Bacall was the third of his four wives.

Films include: 1959 The Journey. **'61** By Love Possessed. **'62** Tender Is the Night;

Long Day's Journey Into Night. **'65** A Thousand Clowns. **'66** A Big Hand for the Little Lady (GB: Big Deal at Dodge City). **'67** The St Valentine's Day Massacre. **'68** Isadora (GB) (USA: The Loves of Isadora). **'73** Pat Garrett and Billy the Kid. **'76** All the President's Men. **'77** Julia. **'80** Melvin and Howard.

ROBBE-GRILLET, Alain

(b. 1922). Novelist/ screenwriter/ director. Born: Brest, France

Educated at the National Agronomic Institute in Paris, Alain Robbe-Grillet worked at the National Institute of Statistics (1945–48) and as an agricultural engineer for the Institute of

Tropical Fruits (1949–51), a post that entailed much overseas travel. He published his first novel, *Les Gommes (The Erasers)* in 1953 and soon became a leading light of the *nouveau roman* (New Novel) school, a group of novelists who emphasized the description of events and the external world at the expense of the psychological analysis traditionally associated with the French novel. He became literary advisor to Les Editions de Minuit, which published several of these writers. He was also drawn to the cinema, which already had many of the qualities he tried to attain in his novels. He wrote the original script for *Last Year in Marienbad*, directed by Alain Resnais, a baffling story of a woman torn between two men and between past and present. He turned director with *L'Immortelle*, an ambiguous tale of a professor who has a love affair with a mysterious woman in Istanbul before they both die in suspicious circumstances. *Trans-Europ Express* concerns film-makers who, to while away a journey, invent a suspense story about a criminal obsessed with sadistic

sexuality and find it coming to life around them. Robbe-Grillet has continued to make enigmatic and erotic films as well as publishing occasional novels.

Films include: 1961 L'Année Dernière à Marienbad (sc. only) (USA/GB: Last Year in Marienbad). **'63** L'Immortelle (FR-IT-TURK). **'67** Trans-Europ Express (+act). **'68** L'Homme Qui Ment (FR-CZECH) (USA: The Man Who Lies). **'70** L'Eden et Après (FR-CZECH) (USA: Eden and After). **'73** Glissements Progressifs du Plaisir. **'75** Le Jeu Avec le Feu (FR-IT).

ROBERTS, Rachel

(1927–1980). Actress. Born: Llanelly, Carmarthen, Wales

The daughter of a Welsh Baptist minister, Rachel Roberts won prizes at RADA for her comedy talent and during her early stage career was a lively revue artist. She began playing small film parts in 1952 and she was in the Old Vic company in 1954–56. Not a beauty, but a powerful and expressive actress, she came into her own with the new realism of the Sixties, notably as Albert Finney's married mistress in *Saturday Night and Sunday Morning* and Rugby League football-player Richard Harris' widowed landlady in *This Sporting Life*, a role that won her an Academy Award nomination. She continued to appear on stage – for instance, as the lively Liverpool tart *Maggie May* in Lionel Bart's musical – and became well-known on American television. In the Seventies she undertook varied assignments but only a few good roles came her way. She took her own life in 1980. She was married to the actors Alan Dobie (1955–61) and Rex Harrison (1962–71).

Films include: 1954 The Weak and the Wicked. **'60** Saturday Night and Sunday Morning. **'63** This Sporting Life. **'69** The Reckoning. **'73** The Belstone Fox; O Lucky Man! **'74** Murder on the Orient Express. **'75** Picnic at Hanging Rock (AUS). **'78** Foul Play (USA). **'79** Yanks.

375

ROBERTSON, Cliff

(b. 1925). Actor. Born: La Jolla, California, USA

Originally a journalist and then a stage actor, Cliff Robertson made his film debut in *Picnic* and played the young John F. Kennedy in the wartime adventure *PT-109*. He won an Academy Award as *Charly*, a mentally subnormal man who briefly becomes a genius after surgery and has an affair with his lovely psychologist (Claire Bloom). Robertson then directed the rodeo picture *J. W. Coop*. In the mid-Seventies his career went adrift when he accused David Begelman, production chief of Columbia, of embezzling $10,000 in his name. Begelman admitted the truth of this and similar charges, losing his Columbia job but continuing to flourish, while Robertson was unable to find work in Hollywood for over three years. Then, when he had started in *Brainstorm*, production was closed down following the death of his co-star Natalie Wood. He has done some excellent work in television, winning an Emmy for *The Game* and being nominated for *The Two Worlds of Charly Gordon*. He also played the much-fraught head of the CIA in *Washington: Behind Closed Doors*. He married actress Dina Merrill in 1966.

Films include: 1955 Picnic. '56 Autumn Leaves. '58 The Naked and the Dead. '60 Underworld USA. '63 PT-109; Sunday in New York. '68 Charly. '71 J. W. Coop (+dir; +prod; +co-sc). '72 The Great Northfield Minnesota Raid. '74 Man on a Swing. '75 Three Days of the Condor. '76 Obsession; Shoot (CAN). '80 The Pilot (+dir; +co-sc) (CAN).

ROBESON, Paul

(1898-1976). Singer/actor. Born: Princeton, New Jersey, USA

The son of a slave who had become a Protestant minister, Paul Robeson won a scholarship to Rutgers College and excelled himself in athletics and football. While at Columbia University Law School he began acting, and in 1921 he made his professional

debut in *Simon the Cyrenian*. He achieved great success in his friend Eugene O'Neill's *All God's Chillun Got Wings* and *The Emperor Jones* and also had a silent screen debut in *Body and Soul*. Possessed of an especially deep and resonant bass baritone, he gave concert tours in America and Europe and his renditions of 'Ole Man River' made him a legend. He spent much of the Thirties in Britain and brought his towering presence to such films as *Sanders of the River* and *King Solomon's Mines*, while in Hollywood he made *Show Boat* and, finally, *Tales of Manhattan*. In the Forties Robeson appeared in his acting triumph *Othello*, on Broadway and on tour, but he was now under serious attack from the American authorities for his vociferous opposition to racism and fascism and his left-wing views, which had won him many friends in the USSR. In 1950 his passport was confiscated and not until 1958 could he collect the Stalin Peace Prize that he had been awarded in 1952. He died lonely and neglected after a long period of ill-health. Robeson was the first to admit that his screen work was poor but the dignity and presence he lent to the films he appeared in consolidated his colossal stature both as performer and fighter for racial equality.

Films: 1925 Body and Soul. '30 Borderline (GB). '33 The Emperor Jones. '35 Sanders of the River (GB). '36 Show Boat; Song of Freedom (GB). '37 My Song Goes Forth (doc) (GB); Big Fella (GB); Jericho (GB); King Solomon's Mines (GB). '39 The Proud Valley (GB). '42 Native Land (doc); Tales of Manhattan. '54 Lied de Strôme (compilation) (E. GER).

ROBEY, George

(1869-1954). Actor. Born: George Edward Wade; London, England

The son of an engineer whose financial difficulties forced his removal from Cambridge University, George Robey seemed set to follow his father's career until his comic and vocal talents led to his professional stage debut in London in 1891. Appearing in the guise of a sort of saucy country parson with an ill-fitting bowler hat and big,

black eyebrows, he rapidly established himself as the most popular and celebrated comedian of the variety stage – 'the prime minister of mirth'. By 1900 he was in films. There were to be only a few memorable roles in his fifty-year flirtation with the cinema, but he was very impressive as the bumbling, cowardly Ali Baba in *Chu Chin Chow*; as the lecherous, gullible sugar-daddy in Carol Reed's *A Girl Must Live*; and as Falstaff in Laurence Olivier's *Henry V*, a role he had successfully played in the straight theatre in 1935.

Films include: 1900 The Rats. '13 Good Queen Bess. '16 The Anti-Frivolity League; £66 13s 9¾d for Every Man, Woman and Child. '23 Don Quixote. '33 Don Quixote. '34 Chu Chin Chow. '39 A Girl Must Live. '42 Salute John Citizen. '43 Variety Jubilee. '44 Henry V. '52 The Pickwick Papers.

ROBINSON, Edward G.

(1893–1973). Actor. Born: Emmanuel Goldenberg; Bucharest, Romania

He had a leering Mongolian face, a squat, unheroic frame and a rasping voice, but for all that Edward G. Robinson was one of the mightiest actors of the American cinema. As aggressive in his delivery as Cagney and often as dry as Tracy, like them he had that indefinable magnetic presence that made him a great star as well as performer. And to the gangster Rico in *Little Caesar*, the insurance investigator in *Double Indemnity*, the victims of *femme fatale* Joan Bennett in *The Woman in the Window* and *Scarlet Street* and the ace poker player in *The Cincinnati Kid*, he brought both sympathy and humanity – though most of the roles were studies in villainy or vanity. He came to America with his family at the age of ten and studied at City College of New York, and the American Academy of Dramatic Arts. He planned his career carefully, going into stock in 1913 and building up his reputation on Broadway from 1915. *Little Caesar* made him a film star and brought him many more roles as gangsters, tough newspapermen or

Above, far left: Cliff Robertson as Lieutenant John F. Kennedy in PT-109. Above left: Paul Robeson in the African adventure film Jericho. *Above: George Robey in* A Girl Must Live. *Below: a studio portrait of May Robson*

cops in his long stay at Warner Brothers, which also saw him take on biopics and comedies. During the war Robinson broadcast to European underground movements from England in nine different languages, but despite his patriotism to the Allied cause his liberal views and supposed links with the Communist Party led to his appearance in front of the House Un-American Activities Committee. He was cleared but his film career had suffered. He returned to the stage, achieving major successes in *Darkness at Noon* and *Middle of the Night*, adding to earlier triumphs in Ibsen and Shaw. The Sixties saw him back in vogue as a powerful character actor in movies.

Films include: 1923 The Bright Shawl. '30 Little Caesar. '31 Five Star Final. '35 The Whole Town's Talking (GB: Passport to

Left: Flora Robson in Holiday Camp, *in which she starred with Dennis Price and Jack Warner*

Fame); Barbary Coast. '36 Bullets or Ballots; Kid Galahad. '38 The Amazing Dr Clitterhouse. '39 Confessions of a Nazi Spy. '40 Dr Ehrlich's Magic Bullet (GB: The Story of Dr Ehrlich's Magic Bullet). '44 Double Indemnity; The Woman in the Window. '45 Scarlet Street. '48 All My Sons; Key Largo. '56 The Ten Commandments. '62 Two Weeks in Another Town. '64 Cheyenne Autumn. '65 The Cincinnati Kid. '69 Mackenna's Gold. '72 Soylent Green.

ROBISON, Arthur

(1886–1935). Director. Born: Chicago, Illinois, USA

Of German-Jewish parents, Robison, though born in the USA, was brought up in Germany. He studied medicine at Munich University and worked as a doctor before turning to acting and in 1914 entering films as a writer and director. While most of his work is now forgotten, he remains famous as the director of Warning Shadows, a nightmarish journey into a cuckolded husband's private hell. Co-scripted by Robison and Rudolf Schneider, superbly filmed by cinematographer Fritz Arno Wagner and containing excellent performances by Fritz Kortner as the husband and Ruth Wegher as his tantalizing, faithless wife, the film is one of the finest examples of German Expressionist cinema.

Films include: 1923 Zwischen Abend und Morgen; Schatten (GB: Warning Shadows). '26 Manon Lescaut. '27 Der letzte Walzer (GB: The Last Waltz). '29 The Informer (GB). '33 Des jungen Dessauers/Grösse Liebe. '34 Fürst Woronzeff. '35 Mach' Mich Glücklich; Der Student von Prague (GB: The Student of Prague).

ROBSON, Flora

(1902–1984). Actress. Born: South Shields, Co. Durham, England

Plain but expressive features, a beautiful speaking voice and a regal air made Flora Robson ideal for queenly roles in films. Thus, she was a delightful Elizabeth I (flattered by the attentions of Errol Flynn and his monkey) in The Sea Hawk and also in Fire Over England; and played the Empress Elizabeth in Catherine the Great, the Empress of China in 55 Days at Peking and – always a good sport – the Queen of Hearts in Alice's Adventures in Wonderland. But she was equally effective as old Nellie Dean in Wuthering Heights, as Esther in Holiday Camp and as Sister Philippa in Black Narcissus. Few of these roles could have tested her. She was one of the finest, and most deeply respected, character players of the British theatre, and her greatest stage triumph was in an altogether different part, as the tragic Edinburgh prostitute in The Anatomist. After RADA, she made her stage debut as Queen Margaret in Will Shakespeare. She then worked in rep, often in Shakespeare, and had four years as a welfare worker before returning to four decades of success on stage and screen, appearing in her first film, Dance Pretty Lady, in 1931. She became a Dame of the British Empire in 1960.

Films include: 1931 Dance Pretty Lady. '34 Catherine the Great. '37 Fire Over England; I, Claudius (unfinished). '39 Wuthering Heights (USA). '40 The Sea Hawk (USA). '43 Saratoga Trunk (USA). '47 Black Narcissus; Holiday Camp. '54 Romeo and Juliet (GB-IT). '63 55 Days at Peking (USA). '64 Guns at Batasi. '65 Seven Women (USA). '72 Alice's Adventures in Wonderland. '79 A Man Called Intrepid (GB-CAN-USA).

ROBSON, Mark

(1913–1978). Director. Born: Montreal, Quebec, Canada

The army, naval academy and Political Science studies left less impression on Mark Robson than part-time work in the property department at Fox. From 1935 he worked as a cutter at RKO and was employed, uncredited, on Orson Welles' Citizen Kane (1940) and The Magnificent Ambersons (1942). Robson then joined Val Lewton's unit and edited Cat People (1942) before directing his own first feature, The Seventh Victim, an especially dark and disturbing entry in the Lewton horror cycle. Other films directed by Robson at this stage in his career explored the corruption and callousness in American society, notably in Champion and Home of the Brave. Then came the unashamed sentiment of The Inn of the Sixth Happiness with Ingrid Bergman as missionary Gladys Aylward, two tacky but well-handled soap operas in Peyton Place and Valley of the Dolls, a study of Gandhi's assassination in Nine Hours to Rama, and finally the disaster movie Earthquake – which literally made the cinema seats shudder.

Films include: 1943 The Seventh Victim. '45 Isle of the Dead. '49 Champion; Home of the Brave. '54 The Bridges at Toko-Ri. '57 The Little Hut; Peyton Place. '58 The Inn of the Sixth Happiness (GB). '63 Nine Hours to Rama (GB); The Prize. '65 Von Ryan's Express. '66 Lost Command. '67 Valley of the Dolls. '74 Earthquake.

ROBSON, May

(1858–1942). Actress. Born: Mary Jeanette Robison; Melbourne, Australia

May Robson became a popular character actress of stage and screen, specializing in sympathetic elderly ladies. She scored her greatest success as the star of Frank Capra's Lady for a Day, being nominated for a Best Actress Oscar for her portrayal of 'Apple Annie', who is given the chance by gangsters to pose as a rich woman to impress her visiting daughter. She also made fine contributions to such movies as Dinner at Eight (as the cook, Mrs Wendel), Anna Karenina (as Countess Vronsky), A Star Is Born (as Janet Gaynor's encouraging grandmother) and Bringing Up Baby (as the kindly, bemused dowager Mrs Random). Educated in England, Belgium and France, she married at 16, moved to the USA and was then widowed at the age of 20 with a young son. Her work as a dressmaker and jewellery designer led to contact with the theatre and thence to acting. The misprinting of her real name in a programme led to her adopting the stage name May Robson; her first major success came as the lead in the long-running play The Rejuvenation of Mary, a role she also repeated on film.

Films include: 1915 How Molly Made Good (as herself). '27 The Rejuvenation of Aunt Mary. '31 Mother's Millions. '32 If I Had a Million. '33 Dinner at Eight; Lady for a Day. '34 Lady by Choice. '35 Anna Karenina. '37 A Star Is Born. '38 The Adventures of Tom Sawyer; Bringing Up Baby. '41 Joan of Paris.

ROC, Patricia

(b. 1918). Actress. Born: Felicia Reise; Hampstead, London, England

A slender, brown-haired, innocent-looking Gainsborough lady with an engaging smile, Patricia Roc is best remembered as the good girl wronged by her cousin (Margaret Lockwood) in The Wicked Lady, and as the pretty factory worker in Millions Like Us. After RADA she acted on stage in Nuts in May and attracted the attention of Alexander Korda who offered her a bit part in The Rebel Son. She quickly became a popular leading lady of the Forties though her roles tended to be wholesome and unexciting, and she must have welcomed the chance to go to Hollywood, the first British star to do so under J. Arthur Rank's scheme for lease-lend between British and American studios. In 1949 she married French cameraman André Thomas and subsequently worked in Paris and Rome, but with little success.

Films include: 1939 The Rebel Son. '42 Let the People Sing. '43 Millions Like Us. '45 The Wicked Lady; Johnny Frenchman. '46 Canyon Passage. '47 The Brothers; Jassy; Holiday Camp. '49 The Perfect Woman; The Man on the Eiffel Tower (FR-USA). '57 The Hypnotist (USA: Scotland Yard Dragnet). '60 Bluebeard's Ten Honeymoons.

ROCHA, Glauber

(1938–1981). Director. Born: Victoria da Conquista, Bahia, Brazil

Rocha studied law and worked as a film critic and journalist. In 1962 he completed his first feature film as director, *Barravento*, followed by superb films like *Black God, White Devil* and *Antonio das Mortes* which made him a prominent contributor to the re-vitalized Brazilian cinema – *Cinema Nôvo*. These films reflected Rocha's interest in his country, its roots, tradi-tions, conflicts, violence, mysticism and primitivism, but their powerful, lyrical imagery, backed with rich musical soundtracks and contained within essentially allegorical frame-works, were also strident calls to revolution in the face of oppression and exploitation. He spent the Seven-ties in Europe, writing, teaching and trying to raise money for his movies. His last film, *Age of the Earth*, made after his return to Brazil, is a powerful demand for reconciliation between Catholicism and Marxism through the agency of the Third World.

Films include: 1958 O Patio (short). **'62** Barravento. **'64** Deus e o Diabo na Terra do Sol (GB: Black God, White Devil). **'65** Amaz-onas (short). **'66** Maranhâo (short). **'67** Terra em Transe (GB: Earth in Revolt). **'69** Antonio das Mortes. **'70** Der Leone Have Sept Cabeças (IT-FR) (GB: The Lion Has Seven Heads); Cabeças Cortadas (BRAZ-SP). **'75** Claro (IT). **'80** Aibade da Terra/Age of the Earth.

RODGERS, Richard

(1902–1979). Composer. Born: Long Island, New York, USA

Richard Rodgers was the most ver-satile, popular American composer, freely adapting his prolific gift for melody to almost any style, from the jazzy to the balladic, the folksy to the Oriental. From a musical family, he began composing when still a child. He met the first of his great lyricist collaborators, Lorenz Hart, at Col-umbia University; the pair rapidly became a successful songwriting team. Between 1921 and 1923 Rod-gers studied at the Institute of Musical Art in New York, then from 1925 on, in partnership with Hart, wrote a series of hit songs, the first being 'Manhattan'. The pair made their mark in Hollywood during the Thirties with such films as the Maurice Chev-alier vehicle *Love Me Tonight*. Their greatest musical, *Pal Joey*, was per-formed on Broadway in the Forties and filmed in a cleaned-up version in the Fifties. The team broke up in 1942, when the irascible Hart refused to work on *Oklahoma!* Rodgers then joined up with Oscar Hammerstein II and the two produced a series of smash hit stage and screen musicals. Follow-ing Hammerstein's death in 1960, Rodgers wrote his own lyrics, his last stage musical being *I Remember Mama*.

Films include: 1930 Spring Is Here. **'32** The Phantom President; Love Me Tonight. **'33** Hallelujah, I'm a Bum. **'35** Mississippi. **'40** The Boys From Syracuse. **'45** State Fair. **'48** Words and Music. **'55** Oklahoma! **'56** Carousel; The King and I. **'57** Pal Joey. **'58** South Pacific. **'62** Jumbo; State Fair. **'65** The Sound of Music. **'66** The Swinger.

ROEG, Nicolas

(b. 1928). Director. Born: London, England

An enigmatic, puzzling talent whose films are distinguished by their com-plex structures and visual beauty, Roeg had few peers in the British cinema of the Seventies, though he was often neglected when the critical laurels were dealt out. Maybe this was due to the inaccessibility of his films, and Roeg's reluctance to pander to mere entertainment. Each film he makes is a genuinely harrowing ex-perience – the superb colour photo-graphy, the rapid cross-cutting and the distortion of time zones combining beautifully in remarkable studies of people in places where they shouldn't be: a gangster hiding out with a rock star in *Performance*; white children lost in the Australian outback in *Walkabout*; a middle-class couple in the nightmare Venice of *Don't Look Now*; an alien in America in *The Man Who Fell to Earth*; and a psychology professor ravishing the comatose body of his girlfriend in *Bad Timing*. Roeg began as a still photographer, joined MGM as a clapper-boy, and worked as an editor and scriptwriter before emerging as a cameraman on such prestigious English films as *Law-rence of Arabia* (1962), *Nothing But the Best* and *The Masque of the Red Death* (both 1964), *Fahrenheit 451* (1966) and *Far From the Madding Crowd* (1967).

Films include: 1970 Performance (co-dir). **'71** Walkabout (AUS). **'73** Don't Look Now (GB-IT). **'76** The Man Who Fell To Earth. **'80** Bad Timing. **'83** Eureka.

ROGERS, Ginger

(b. 1911). Actress. Born: Virginia Katherine McMath; Independence, Missouri, USA

Ginger Rogers' bubbly good looks and innocent sense of fun injected a new and very modern vitality into movie musicals. No ethereal Ruritanian princess warbling light operetta, Ginger was clearly flesh and blood; she danced with gusto and grace and sang the latest Berlin and Gershwin tunes as they were meant to be sung, in broad American. She and Fred Astaire were an irresistibly hip combi-nation that audiences everywhere could (and still can) identify with. His witty, romantic pursuit of her in all their movies had the effect of trans-forming her from a nice, jolly girl into everyman's dream of romance; her innate charm made it easy to see her through Fred's dewy eyes. Urged on by her ambitious mother, Lela Rogers (who later became a Hollywood scriptwriter), Ginger won amateur Charleston contests, formed a vaudeville act called Ginger and the Red-Heads and was then signed up by Paramount producer Walter Wanger in 1929 while appearing in the Broad-way musical *Top Speed*. She made her movie debut in 1930 in *Young Man of Manhattan* and three years later com-menced her ten-film partnership with Astaire in RKO's *Flying Down to Rio*. After a decade of musical comedy, she was clearly keen to prove herself as a performer in a wide variety of films.

Below: Ginger Rogers in Shall We Dance? *(1937). Right: Roy Rogers and his faithful 'four-legged friend',* Trigger, *in a studio publicity shot. Far right: Will Rogers in* Doctor Bull *(1933), directed by John Ford*

Her Academy Award winning role in *Kitty Foyle* did just that. Of her films after the main split from Astaire, only *Tom, Dick and Harry, Roxie Hart, The Major and the Minor* and *Monkey Business* were particularly outstand-ing. She made her last screen appear-ance as Jean Harlow's mother in *Harlow* in the mid-Sixties but con-tinued a successful Broadway career in such shows as *Mame* and *Hello, Dolly!* She has married five times, her second husband being the actor Lew Ayres, her fourth the actor Jacques Bergerac and her fifth (briefly) the actor, producer and director William Marshall.

Films include: 1930 Young Man of Manhat-tan. **'33** Gold Diggers of 1933; Flying Down to Rio. **'35** Roberta; Top Hat. **'36** Swing Time. **'39** The Story of Vernon and Irene Castle. **'40** Kitty Foyle. **'41** Tom, Dick and Harry. **'42** Roxie Hart; The Major and the Minor. **'49** The Barkleys of Broadway. **'52** Monkey Business. **'65** Harlow.

ROGERS, Roy

(b. 1912). Actor. Born: Leonard Slye; Cincinnati, Ohio, USA

During the Depression Rogers worked in a shoe factory and as a fruit-

picker, but his singing and guitar-playing took him into radio. When Republic were involved in a quarrel with their cowboy star Gene Autry, they signed Rogers (then billed as Dick Weston) as a possible replacement, and by 1938 he was starring and singing in B-Westerns. Rogers' vogue lasted until the early Fifties. His amiable good looks and simple sin-cerity went down well, and the team built around him was equally popu-lar. His wife, Dale Evans, was often his heroine; toothless Gabby Hayes his sidekick; and a beautiful golden pa-lomino named Trigger his horse.

Films include: 1935 Tumbling Tum-bleweeds. **'38** Under Western Stars. **'39** The Arizona Kid. **'40** Robin Hood of the Pecos. **'42** Sons of the Pioneers; Red River Valley. **'43** King of the Cowboys. **'44** Yellow Rose of Texas. **'46** My Pal Trigger. **'50** Heart of the Rockies. **'52** Son of Paleface. **'75** Mackin-tosh and TJ.

ROGERS, Will

(1871–1935). Actor. Born: William Pen Adair Rogers; Colagh, Oklahoma, USA

A one-man antidote to all the sham, pomposity and pretentiousness of the

Below: Gilbert Roland in Lewis Milestone's comedy My Life With Caroline (1942)

world, Will Rogers developed his own drawling, freewheeling style of verbiage – and his famed, homespun philosophy – to accompany his lasso-slinging act on stage. In such movies as *Judge Priest* and *Steamboat Round the Bend* (inevitable he should work for the populist John Ford), *Down to Earth, Business and Pleasure, Ambassador Bill* and *They Had to See Paris*, Rogers personified the gentle, small-town, independent do-gooder, and his frank good sense and shrewd, un-classic features made him a particular favourite with film audiences of the Depression: they felt comfortable in his presence. He was educated at Kemper Military Academy, then travelled to Argentina to seek his fortune. He ended up on a cattle boat shipping mules from Buenos Aires to South Africa for the Boer War. He stayed on in South Africa, performing rope tricks in a Wild West show, but soon returned home and joined the Ziegfeld Follies as a cowboy act. He made his first film, *Laughing Bill Hyde*, in 1918. When Will Rogers died in a plane crash 17 years later, all of America mourned him.

Films include: 1919 Jubilo. **'22** The Ropin' Fool. **'23** Two Wagons – Both Covered. **'27** Strolling Thru Europe With Will Rogers. **'29** They Had to See Paris. **'31** A Connecticut Yankee (GB: The Yankee at King Arthur's Court). **'32** Ambassador Bill; Down to Earth; Business and Pleasure. **'33** State Fair. **'34** Judge Priest; David Harum. **'35** Steamboat Round the Bend.

ROGOSIN, Lionel

(b. 1924). Director. Born: New York City, USA

Inspired by the films of De Sica and Flaherty, Rogosin turned his back on his Yale education and successful business career in 1954 to develop and express his social conscience through the drama-documentary film. The first result, *On the Bowery*, was a sympathetic study of the victims of New York's skid row, whilst *Come Back Africa*, which includes extraordinary footage filmed secretly in one

of South Africa's black townships, remains a powerful and damning indictment of apartheid and the pass system. Rogosin's technique is to use real scenes and people in planned dramas; 'They must be allowed to express themselves in their own manner, but in accordance with the abstractions and themes which . . . the director must be able to see in them'. In his turn, Rogosin has influenced the naturalistic approach of directors like John Cassavetes.

Films include: 1955 On the Bowery. **'59** Come Back Africa. **'65** Good Times, Wonderful Times. **'66** Oysters Are in Season (short); How Do You Like Them Bananas? (short). **'70** Black Roots. **'72** Black Fantasy. **'73** Woodcutters of the Deep South. **'74** Arab Israeli Dialogue (short).

ROHMER, Eric

(b. 1920). Director. Born: Maurice Scherer; Nancy, France

Eric Rohmer wrote film criticism for *La Gazette du Cinéma* and then for its successor, *Cahiers du Cinéma*, which he edited from 1957 to 1963. He started making shorts in the early Fifties, left his first feature incomplete and finished his second, *Le Signe du Lion*, in 1959. In 1957 he collaborated with Claude Chabrol on a famous book about Hitchcock as a Catholic moralist. He began his series *Six Contes Moraux* (Six Moral Tales) with a 16mm short, *La Boulangère de Monçeau* (1962) and a 16mm short feature, *La Carrière de Suzanne* (1963). He broke off to make documentaries for French television, and then completed the series with four 35mm films, three in colour. It was the black-and-white *Ma Nuit Chez Maud*, a philosophical disquisition with tantalizing sexual overtones (or maybe the other way round) that made his international reputation, confirmed by *Claire's Knee*. In the six tales, usually a man in love with one woman is tempted by another yet finally returns to the first – but the theme is played with complex variations. After a couple of historical excursions, *Die*

Marquise von O, a remarkable version of Heinrich von Kleist's novella about the social consequences of an unexplained pregnancy, and *Perceval le Gallois*, Rohmer began a new series, possibly a less rigorous one, with the charming *La Femme de l'Aviateur*.

Films include: 1959 Le Signe du Lion (GB: The Sign of Leo). **'67** La Collectionneuse (GB: The Collector). **'69** Ma Nuit Chez Maud (USA: My Night at Maud's; GB: My Night With Maud). **'70** Le Genou de Claire (USA/GB: Claire's Knee). **'72** L'Amour l'Après-Midi (USA: Chloe in the Afternoon; GB: Love in the Afternoon). **'76** Die Marquise von O (GER-FR)(USA/GB: The Marquise of O). **'78** Perceval le Gallois (USA: Perceval). **'81** La Femme de l'Aviateur (GB: The Aviator's Wife). **'82** Le Beau Mariage (GB: A Good Marriage).

RÖHRIG, Walter

(b. 1893; deceased). Art director. Born: Germany

Röhrig was a stage designer in Zürich and a member of the Der Sturm group of artists. Employed as a painter at the Ufa studios in Berlin, he became involved in *The Cabinet of Dr Caligari* project with Hermann Warm and Robert Herlth, the latter of whom was to be Röhrig's regular collaborator. The distorted, painted sets of *The Cabinet of Dr Caligari* dominated the film, but in their work for Lang and Murnau, Herlth and Röhrig designed sets which, although always striking in their own right, were at the service of the director and actors. So they designed drab, realistic interiors for *The Last Laugh*; graceful period decoration for *Tartuffe*; a great deal of model work and some expressionist architecture for *Faust*. It is hard to separate Röhrig's contributions from his partner's, but it is known that in Lang's *Destiny* Röhrig was responsible for the design of the framing story, the city square, and the vistas of moonlit hills. Later Röhrig worked with Herlth on *The Congress Dances* and *Morgenrot*, two finely designed films, but then, in the Nazi period, was confined to commercial routine.

Films as art dir, or co-art dir. include: 1919 Das Kabinett des Dr Caligari (GB: The Cabinet of Dr Caligari). **'21** Der müde Tod (USA/GB: Destiny). **'25** Der letzte Mann (GB: The Last Laugh); Zur Chronik von Grieshuus (GB: The Chronicles of the Grey House); Tartüff (GB: Tartuffe). **'26** Faust. **'28** Four Devils (USA). **'31** Der Kongress Tanzt (USA: The Congress Dances). **'33** Morgenrot. **'35** Amphitryon. **'41** Heimkehr (A-GER). **'42** Rembrandt.

ROLAND, Gilbert

(b. 1905). Actor. Born: Luis Antonio Damasco Alonso; Ciudad Juarez, Mexico

With his slick, dark, Latin looks and lithe, athletic build, it is hardly surprising that Roland made his name as a romantic lead. Of Spanish/Mexican origin, Roland moved to California when he was young, and broke into acting as an extra. He made his reputation as Armand opposite Norma Talmadge in *Camille*, and survived the transition to sound with the timely help of diction lessons. His ability to speak fluent Spanish helped him secure roles in films like the beautifully photographed melodrama *Men of the North*; when 20th Century-Fox stopped the production of Spanish films in 1935 Roland was dropped as a male lead but survived playing various characters called Lopez in *Juarez* and *The Sea Hawk*. Between 1946 and 1947 he appeared six times as The Cisco Kid, and in the Sixties he made several 'spaghetti' Westerns in Italy. Renowned as a tennis player and a lover of Clara Bow, Roland's relaxed personality has made him a survivor and a particular favourite with his colleagues.

Films include: 1925 The Plastic Age. **'27** Camille. **'30** Men of the North (English-language and Spanish-language versions). **'37** Last Train From Madrid. **'39** Juarez. **'40** The Sea Hawk; Rangers of Fortune. **'49** We Were Strangers. **'52** The Bad and the Beautiful. **'64** Cheyenne Autumn. **'71** The Christian Licorice Store. **'79** Cabo Blanco (USA-SP).

379

ROLAND, Ruth

(1892–1937). Actress. Born: San Francisco, USA

Ruth Roland's childhood reads like a synopsis of every Hollywood film about vaudeville. Her father was an ex-newspaper man who ran the Columbia Theatre, San Francisco, and left Ruth's mother, a talented singer, soon after the baby was born. Taught to yodel and gurgle Tyrolean lullabies by her Swiss grandmother, Ruth made her stage debut at the age of two, and was the first professional child actress to play Hawaii! She entered films in 1911, and appeared in 200 silents in the next three years. *The Red Circle* of 1915, in which she starred as an heiress damned by a family curse, established her reputation, and she became a queen of the serials, notable for her prolific output and huge popularity. In 1923, however, she retired from serials, and gradually faded from the movie business, content to live off the huge profits from the astute investments she had begun as early as 1914. She died tragically from cancer aged only 44.

Above: a studio publicity shot of Ruth Roland. Below: Ruth Roman as a society girl in Alfred Hitchcock's Strangers on a Train

Films include: 1911 A Chance Shot. '13 While Father Telephoned. '15–'16 The Red Circle (serial). '17 The Neglected Wife (serial). '18 Hands Up! (serial). '19 The Adventures of Ruth (serial). '20 Ruth of the Rockies (serial). '23 Ruth of the Range (serial). '26 The Masked Woman. '30 Reno. '36 From Nine to Nine (CAN).

ROMAN, Ruth

(b. 1923). Actress. Born: Norma Roman; Lynn, Massachusetts, USA

Ruth Roman came to New York in 1940 and spent three hard years going the rounds of producers' offices before getting a bit part as a Wave in *Stage Door Canteen* (1943). She bought a one-way ticket to Los Angeles, was screen-tested by Warner Brothers, but was not given a contract. She hung on in Hollywood, taking the odd bit part and only making regular appearances as the Queen of the Jungle in a Universal serial. Finally in 1949 the producer Dore Schary cast her in the RKO thriller *The Window*. A further role that year, in the gritty Stanley Kramer production *Champion*, established her name. In the course of her successful, busy career she has moved from glamorous leads to middle-aged character parts. Her best remembered film roles were as Farley Granger's upper-middle-class fiancée in *Strangers on a Train* and as a sexy gangster's moll doing her angst-ridden husband's dirty work in *Joe Macbeth*. She began working in television in the mid-Sixties and appeared regularly in various movies and such series as *Dr Kildare* and *Ironside*.

Films include: 1945 Jungle Queen (serial). '49 The Window; Champion. '50 Three Secrets. '51 Lightning Strikes Twice; Strangers on a Train. '55 Joe Macbeth (GB). '74 A Knife for the Ladies. '77 Day of the Animals.

ROMANCE, Viviane

(b. 1909). Actress. Born: Pauline Ronacher Ortmanns; Roubaix, France

This sensual French leading actress was formerly a model and chorus girl at the Moulin Rouge. She got into movies via a bit part in Jean Renoir's *La Chienne* in 1931; five years later she was starring opposite Jean Gabin in Julien Duvivier's *La Belle Équipe*, as an alluring but faithless wife. When her popularity began to fade, after a decade or so at the top, she attempted to produce her own films aided by her husband, producer Clément Duhour, without much success. She broke a ten-year absence from film-making to take the part of Mme Gabrielle in Claude Chabrol's *Nada* in 1973.

Films include: 1936 La Belle Équipe (USA: They Were Five). '37 Mademoiselle Docteur (USA/GB: Street of Shadows); Le Puritain; La Maison du Maltais (USA/GB: The House of the Maltese). '40 Angelica. '41 Une Femme dans la Nuit. '42 Carmen. '48 Le Carrefour des Passions (USA/GB: Crossroads of Passion). '49 Maya (+prod). '50 Passion (+prod). '63 Mélodie en Sous-Sol (FR-IT) (GB: The Big Snatch).

ROMERO, Cesar

(b. 1907). Actor. Born: New York City, USA

To a whole generation of wide-eyed youngsters, Romero will remain forever the inane, giggling arch-enemy of the Caped Crusader, *Batman*, a truly terrible fate indeed for a man who was once the archetypal Latin lover. He gave up serving in a New Jersey department store in favour of showbiz, and worked as a dancer in musical comedies in nightclubs and on Broadway before entering films in 1932. After a spell with Universal and MGM, he earned a long-term contract with 20th Century-Fox, though he later went freelance and moved into television. Like most actors of Spanish origin, he was doomed to play the Cisco Kid, in several films including *The Gay Caballero* (1940). He still occasionally appears in movies, whenever

Left: Viviane Romance in L'Affaire du Collier de la Reine *(1946). Above: Cesar Romero in the motor-racing drama* The Racers *(1956)*

a suave and charming foreign playboy is needed.

Films include: 1934 The Thin Man. '35 Clive of India. '37 Wee Willie Winkie. '42 Orchestra Wives; Springtime in the Rockies. '49 The Beautiful Blonde From Bashful Bend. '54 Vera Cruz. '56 Around the World in 80 Days. '60 Ocean's Eleven. '63 Donovan's Reef. '66 Batman. '68 Hot Millions (GB); Skidoo!

ROMERO, George A.

(b. 1939). Director. Born: New York City, USA

As they say in all the corniest horror movies, George Romero must have been a strange child. After all, at the age of 14 he was arrested for throwing a burning dummy off a roof whilst filming his first amateur movie, *The Man From the Meteor*. The unhealthy influence of science-fiction continued to pervade his otherwise normal education, at Suffield College, Connecticut, and the Carnegie-Mellon Institute in Pittsburgh, and resulted in a Future Scientists of America Award for another 8mm effort *Earthbottom*. With *Night of the Living Dead* his unusual preoccupations came to the fore, and branded him a master of horror with a fascination for depicting the bloody demise of flesh-eating zombies. *Hungry Wives*, about the stultifying effects of American suburbia, and *Knightriders*, in which modern knights joust on motorbikes, had some interesting ideas, but generally Romero is happiest wasting the undead; has anyone *really* seen him out in the daylight?

Films include: 1968 Night of the Living Dead. '71 There's Always Vanilla/The Affair. '73 The Crazies; Hungry Wives (GB: Season of the Witch). '77 Martin. '79 Dawn of the Dead (GB: Zombies). '81 Knightriders. '82 Creepshow.

ROMM, Mikhail

(1901–1971). Director. Born: Irkutsk, Russia

Romm began in the Russian film industry as a scriptwriter and assistant director before joining Mosfilm and making a brilliant first feature, *Boule de Suif*, based on the Maupassant novella. He followed this success with two historical films about Lenin which brought Romm worldwide acclaim – *Lenin in October* and *Lenin in 1918*. For many years Romm divided his time between film-making (he won five Stalin prizes in the course of his career) and teaching film directing at the Moscow Cinematography Institute. After being neglected for many years in the West he re-established his international reputation with *Nine Days of One Year*.

Films include: 1934 Pyshka (GB: Boule de Suif). '37 Lenin v Oktyabre (Lenin in October). '39 Lenin v 1918 Godu (Lenin in 1918). '41 Mechta (Dream). '45 Chelovek no 217 (GB: Girl no 217). '48 Russkii Vopros (The Russian Question). '56 Ubistvo na Ulitsye Dante (Murder on Dante Street). '61 Devyat dnei Odnogo Goda (GB: Nine Days of One Year). '65 Obyknovennyi Fashism (doc) (Ordinary Fascism).

RONET, Maurice

(1927–1983). Actor. Born: Nice, France

Ronet gave many elegant film performances (most notably for the director Claude Chabrol), as the misfit hero Paul in *The Champagne Murders*, as the lover murdered by a jealous husband in *La Femme Infidèle* and as the suicide in *Le Feu Follet*. From a theatrical background, Ronet studied acting at the Paris Conservatoire, obtained extensive experience with Jean-Louis Barrault's company and received his first major film role in *Rendez-Vous de Juillet*. In addition to pursuing an international career as a movie actor, he made occasional forays into directing, beginning in 1965 with *Le Voleur du Tibidabo*. The director Jean-Luc Godard commemorated Ronet's affair with his then wife, Anna Karina, in *Une Femme Mariée* (1964, *A Married Woman*).

Films include: 1949 Rendez-Vous de Juillet. '53 Lucrèce Borgia (FR-IT) (GB: Lucretia Borgia). '60 Plein Soleil (FR-IT) (GB: Blazing Sun; reissued as Purple Noon). '63 Le Feu Follet (FR-IT) (USA: The Fire Within; GB: A Time to Live and a Time to Die). '64 La Ronde (FR-IT). '66 La Ligne de Démarcation. '67 Le Scandale/The Champagne Murders; La Route de Corinthe (FR-IT). '68 La Femme Infidèle (FR-IT). '69 La Piscine (USA: The Swimming Pool; GB: The Sinners). '79 Bloodline (USA-GER). '82 La Balance.

ROONEY, Mickey

(b. 1920). Actor. Born: Joe Yule Jr; New York City, USA

Born into a vaudeville family, he appeared on stage before he was a year old. His mother subsequently took him to Hollywood where he got his first film part playing a midget in *Not to Be Trusted*. He then became Mickey McGuire and appeared in over sixty shorts and second features, usually as a slum kid or orphan. McGuire became Rooney, and he gave a miraculous performance as a whooping Puck in *A Midsummer Night's Dream* and emerged – via the rehabilitation of his teenage thug in *Boys Town* – as the brash, freckle-faced Andy Hardy in the MGM series that made him a world-famous star. Starring in dozens of musicals and comedies in the next decade – notably with lifelong friend Judy Garland in *Strike Up the Band* and *Babes on Broadway* – Rooney grew up: only barely, but enough to become a millionaire, to marry and divorce Ava Gardner (the first of eight wives whose alimonies made him a bankrupt) and to go to war. His exuberance outlasted the public taste for it, however, and MGM gave him short shrift when he tried to maintain his stardom in the late Forties. Amid dozens of empty projects in the remainder of his film career, only *Baby Face Nelson*, in which he played to perfection the pig-faced psychopath, showed that Rooney was still a fine actor. He has made more films, ending up as the small, plump, bearded old dreamer who befriends boy and horse in *The Black Stallion* – the lad from *National Velvet* still looking for winners. He has toured with his band, been nominated for three Emmys for his television work (to add to his three Oscar nominations and Special Oscar Award) and had a smash hit on Broadway in *Sugar Babes*, but he still seems to be searching for a channel for his ever-abundant energies.

Films include: 1927 Not to Be Trusted; Orchids and Ermine. '35 A Midsummer Night's Dream. '37 A Family Affair. '38 Boys Town; Love Finds Andy Hardy. '39 Babes in Arms. '40 Strike Up the Band. '41 Life Begins for Andy Hardy; Babes on Broadway. '43 The Human Comedy. '44 National Velvet. '47 Summer Holiday. '54 Drive a Crooked Road. '56 The Bold and the Brave. '57 Operation Mad Ball; Baby Face Nelson. '61 Breakfast at Tiffany's '63 It's a Mad, Mad, Mad World. '72 Pulp. '79 The Black Stallion.

ROSAY, Françoise

(1891–1974). Actress. Born: Françoise de Nalèche; Paris, France

Six feet tall with a resonant voice, Françoise Rosay was a mainstay of the French cinema in the Thirties. She studied acting at the Comédie Française and made her first screen appearance as early as 1913 in *Falstaff*. She married the Belgian-born director Jacques Feyder in 1917. She went with him to Hollywood in 1928 and worked in a couple of films there. But it was the films she made with him on their return to France, particularly *La Kermesse Héroïque*, that established her as a star. She was separated from him for part of World War II and spent some time in England, symbolizing the Free French spirit in her support for General de Gaulle. She adorned several British films in the Forties. After Feyder's death in 1948, she returned to the USA for several film appearances and she continued to work in European films until her own death. She also remained a notable theatre actress, and during the war she co-authored a book about the art and craft of films, *Le Cinéma Notre Métier* (1944), with her husband.

Films include: 1913 Falstaff. '31 Le Rosier de Madame Husson. '33 Le Grand Jeu (GB: The Great Game). '35 La Kermesse Héroïque (USA/GB: Carnival in Flanders). '36 Jenny. '37 Un Carnet de Bal (USA: Life Dances On; GB: Christine); Drôle de Drame (USA: Bizarre, Bizarre). '42 Une Femme Disparaît (SWITZ) (USA: Portrait of a Woman; GB: A Woman Disappeared). '44 The Halfway House (GB). '45 Johnny Frenchman (GB). '48 Saraband for Dead Lovers (GB). '59 The Sound and the Fury (USA). '62 The Longest Day (USA). '73 Der Fussgänger (GER) (USA: The Pedestrian).

ROSE, William

(1918–1987). Screenwriter. Born: Jefferson City, Missouri, USA

William Rose came to England during World War II, serving in the Canadian Black Watch regiment, and married in 1943. After the war he settled in Britain, becoming a scriptwriter at Ealing and elsewhere. His American view of Britain as cosy, old-world and traditional chimed in well with the nostalgia of the time, not thoroughly disrupted until the advent of the Angry Young Men era and the rise of CND. But he brought a certain welcome asperity to this approach, notably in his scripts for director Alexander Mackendrick, *The Maggie* and *The Ladykillers*. Having celebrated the joys of old cars (*Genevieve*) and old cinemas (*The Smallest Show on Earth*) in his non-Ealing ventures, he started working in the USA and developed a more varied repertoire, from zany comedy to the race-problem comedy of manners *Guess Who's Coming to Dinner*, which brought him an Academy Award. He was based in Jersey, Channel Islands.

Films include: '48 Once a Jolly Swagman (GB) (USA: Maniacs on Wheels). '53 Genevieve (GB). '54 The Maggie (GB) (USA: High and Dry). '55 Touch and Go (GB) (USA: The Light Touch); The Ladykillers (GB). '57 The Smallest Show on Earth (GB) (USA: Big Time Operators). '63 It's a Mad, Mad, Mad World. '66 The Russians Are Coming, the Russians Are Coming. '67 Guess Who's Coming to Dinner. '69 The Secret of Santa Vittoria.

ROSENBERG, Stuart

(b. 1928). Director. Born: New York City, USA

After studying Irish literature at New York University, Stuart Rosenberg went into television and made his name directing segments of the distinguished law-enforcement series *The Defenders* and *The Untouchables* in the early Sixties. His cinema career got off to a tentative start when he left *Murder, Inc.* in sympathy with the Screen Actors Guild strike that interrupted production and it was finished by the producer Burt Balaban. Rosenberg's television association with liberal causes was sustained by his first major film, *Cool Hand Luke*, an exciting prison-break melodrama with all-out star performances from Paul Newman and George Kennedy (who won an Academy Award). But Rosenberg's subsequent films were a curiously mixed bag, including some thrillers before he drifted into the fashionable horror genre to little effect. The departure of director Bob Rafelson from Robert Redford's *Brubaker* brought Rosenberg full circle to the theme of prison reform. It has been argued that his television work reveals a more consistent authorial personality than his cinema films.

Films include: 1960 Murder, Inc. (co-dir). '67 Cool Hand Luke. '69 The April Fools. '70 Move; WUSA. '72 Pocket Money. '73 The Laughing Policeman (GB: An Investigation of Murder). '75 The Drowning Pool. '76 Voyage of the Damned (GB). '79 The Amityville Horror. '80 Brubaker.

Below: Katharine Ross in The Longest Hundred Miles. *Right: Leonard Rossiter in* Rising Damp

Below: the Italian director who consistently redefined cinema's social role – Roberto Rossellini

ROSHER, Charles

(1885–1974). Cinematographer. Born: London, England

Charles Rosher was perhaps one of the most technically innovative cameramen of the early days of the cinema, and throughout his career he continued to achieve astounding results. As a lighting expert and experienced still photographer Rosher knew how to make the best of a star, and he was one of the first Hollywood cameramen to combine artificial light with daylight on locations. He had originally intended to enter the diplomatic service but decided to study photography instead and attended the Regent Street Polytechnic in London. In 1908 he travelled to America where he eventually took up filming news events. Three years later he moved to Los Angeles to help set up one of the first Hollywood film studios, for the Centaur Film Company, and he soon began shooting two-reelers at their Nestor studios. He subsequently became Mary Pickford's favourite cameraman at United Artists – her films proving a great tribute to Rosher's work as their photography is regarded as among the finest of the silent period. He also shared the first cinematography Oscar for his work as co-photographer on Murnau's *Sunrise*. Later in his career Rosher moved on to colour photography and was responsible for many excellent MGM musicals.

Films include: 1912 Early Days in the West. '19 Daddy Long Legs (co-photo).'21 Little Lord Fauntleroy. '22 Tess of the Storm Country. '23 Rosita. '25 Little Annie Rooney (co-photo). '27 Sunrise (co-photo). '30 Atlantic (GB-GER). '44 Kismet. '45 Yolanda and the Thief. '46 The Yearling (co-photo). '50 Annie Get Your Gun. '51 Showboat. '53 Kiss Me Kate. '55 Jupiter's Darling (co-photo).

ROSI, Francesco

(b. 1922). Director. Born: Naples, Italy

Rosi has weathered the years better than his more illustrious contemporaries. While Fellini and Antonioni have wandered off into odder and

odder byways, Rosi has gone on making his middle-of-the-road, 'old-fashioned' movies with unimpaired skill. He was a law student, a radio writer and director, then in the film industry as assistant to Visconti. He made his first feature in 1958, and won international attention four years later with *Salvatore Giuliano*, a film about the notorious Sicilian bandit which revealed the passionate social concern that was to inform all Rosi's mature work. In the Sixties his career wavered a little, but *The Mattei Affair* was a startling return to form with its documentary-like investigation of the strange history of a great petroleum tycoon; *Illustrious Corpses* boldly attacked right-wing terrorism and its place in the Italian state; while his masterpiece, *Christ Stopped at Eboli*, added a new and deeply felt humanity to the political dimensions of the earlier work.

Films include: 1958 La Sfida (IT-SP). '59 I Magliari. '61 Salvatore Giuliano. '63 Mani Sulla Città (USA/GB: Hands Over the City). '65 Il Momento della Verità (IT-SP) (USA/GB: The Moment of Truth). '67 C'Era una Volta (IT-FR) (USA: More Than a Miracle; GB: Cinderella – Italian Style). '70 Uomini Contro (IT-YUG). '72 Il Caso Mattei (GB: The Mattei Affair). '73 Lucky Luciano (IT-FR). '76 Cadaveri Eccellenti (IT-FR) (USA/GB: Illustrious Corpses). '79 Cristo si è Fermato a Eboli (IT-FR) (USA: Eboli; GB: Christ Stopped at Eboli). '81 Tre Fratelli (IT) (GB: Three Brothers).

ROSS, Herbert

(b. 1927). Director. Born: New York City, USA

Having worked as a chorus boy, model, choreographer, television producer and stage director, at the age of 42 Herbert Ross was given his first opportunity to direct films and eight years later he became an overnight movie celebrity with the one-two punch of *The Turning Point* and *The Goodbye Girl*. His stage experience began when he worked as a teenage Shakespearian actor, but he abandoned acting for ballet and then moved to choreography having suffered a broken ankle. He eventually choreographed and produced *The*

Martha Raye Show and *The Milton Berle Show* for television. He then divided his time between stage and screen choreography, working with the likes of Barbra Streisand, Natalie Wood and Cliff Richard. Since his delayed debut as a director he has continued to work on successful lightweight entertainment films.

Films include: 1969 Goodbye Mr Chips. '70 The Owl and the Pussycat. '72 Play It Again Sam. '75 The Sunshine Boys; Funny Lady. '77 The Turning Point; The Goodbye Girl. '78 California Suite. '80 Nijinsky. '82 Pennies From Heaven.

ROSS, Katharine

(b. 1943). Actress. Born: Los Angeles, California, USA

Katharine Ross shot into the public eye as the girl who leaves her own wedding to disappear on a bus with *The Graduate* (Dustin Hoffman). She also received an Academy Award nomination for the role and won the Golden Globe Award as most promising female newcomer of the year. Her acting career began at 17 when she joined the Actors' Workshop in San Francisco. Besides her stage work she was cast in a small part in an episode of the *Sam Benedict* television series. After a few minor film roles her first break came with *Games* in which she played a society beauty on the brink of madness. Simone Signoret then brought her to the attention of director Mike Nichols and *The Graduate* followed. Despite the acclaim she received for this performance her career has not lived up to expectations.

Films include: 1967 Games; The Graduate; The Longest Hundred Miles. '68 Hell Fighters. '69 Butch Cassidy and the Sundance Kid; Tell Them Willie Boy Is Here. '70 Fools. '72 They Only Kill Their Masters; Get to Know Your Rabbit. '75 The Stepford Wives. '78 The Betsy; The Swarm.

ROSSELLINI, Roberto

(1906–1977). Director. Born: Rome, Italy

In his time Rossellini was accused of being a fascist, a communist, a payer

of lip-service to the Church, a blasphemer, and an immoral adulterer. He began his career in Mussolini's Italy, making films with the blessing of the regime in the early Forties. At the end of World War II he astonished audiences with the landmark neo-realist films, *Rome, Open City* and, a year later, *Paisà*. In the Fifties he began his cycle of films – *Stromboli* and *Viaggio in Italia* being the best known – with Ingrid Bergman who, fascinated by Rossellini, left America to live and work with him. During this period he suffered the vituperation of critics who despised these seemingly arid films and ridiculed his search for a style that would reveal his characters' inner states of mind. Finally he turned to television where he began exploring historical subjects and continued to experiment with new narrative forms, as in *La Prise de Pouvoir par Louis XIV* (1966, *The Rise of Louis XIV*), which brought the political machinations and physical reality of the past vividly to life. But it is the films made at the end of the war for which he will be best remembered, films that attempted to portray the reality of contemporary events to a nation which had been convincingly seduced by the illusions of order, affluence and power paraded before it for twenty years by Mussolini's rhetoric. The war shattered those fantasies, but the Italians did not want to be reminded of their folly – they didn't like Rossellini's films. The Americans, however, took *Rome, Open City* to heart, and saw in *Paisà* the real filmed alongside the fictional, where partisans 'acted' alongside professional actors. These and, indeed, most of his other films influenced film-makers everywhere. In nearly all of post-war European cinema there is evidence to be found of one of the world's major directors.

Films include: 1941 La Nave Bianca (co-dir). '42 Un Pilota Ritorna. '43 L'Uomo della Croce. '45 Roma, Città Aperta (USA: Rome, Open City; GB: Open City). '46 Paisà (USA/GB: Paisan). '47 Germania, Anno Zero (IT-GER) (USA/GB: Germany, Year Zero). '48 L'Amore: episode one/Una Voce Umana; episode two/Il Miracolo (GB: The Miracle). '50 Francesco Giullare di Dio (USA/GB: Flowers of St Francis);

Stromboli/Stromboli, Terra di Dio (USA: God's Land). '51 Europa '51 (USA: The Greatest Love). '54 Viaggio in Italia (IT-FR) USA: Strangers; GB: The Lonely Woman/Journey to Italy). '59 India; Il Generale Della Rovere (IT-FR). '72 Blaise Pascal (orig. TV). '74 Anno Uno (orig. TV) (GB: Italy, Year One).

ROSSEN, Robert

(1908–1966). Director/screenwriter. Born: Robert Rosen; New York City, USA

Brought up in Manhattan's Lower East Side, Robert Rossen became interested in the theatre and directed Richard Maibaum's The Tree in 1930. Warner Brothers gave him a scriptwriting contract and he worked on several effective crime melodramas in the late Thirties. These reflected the social concerns that led him into the Communist Party, which he left in 1947. He turned director in 1946 with the thriller Johnny O'Clock, followed by the powerful boxing story Body and Soul. His study of Southern politics, All the King's Men, based on Robert Penn Warren's novel about Louisiana governor Huey Long, won the Best Picture Oscar; Rossen himself was nominated as both director and writer. Then, in 1951, he was blacklisted by HUAC; in 1953 he named names and was eventually able to work again, though he never returned to Hollywood. He made mostly dud films throughout the rest of the Fifties, but returned to form with The Hustler, a sombre study of a pool-player's abortive love affair, starring Paul Newman and Piper Laurie. The film helped to revive a dying indoor sport, and once again Rossen was nominated for Academy Awards as director and writer. His last film, Lilith, was well received in France, where it confirmed his growing reputation as an auteur.

Films include: 1937 Marked Woman (co-sc). '39 The Roaring Twenties (co-sc). '41 The Sea Wolf (sc). '45 A Walk in the Sun (sc). '46 Johnny O'Clock (dir; + sc). '47 Body and Soul (dir). '49 All the King's Men (dir; + prod; + sc). '51 The Brave Bulls (dir; + prod). '56 Alexander the Great (dir; + prod; + sc). '57 Island in the Sun (dir). '59 They Came to Cordura (dir; + co-sc). '61 The Hustler (dir; + prod; + co-sc). '64 Lilith (dir; + prod; + co-sc).

ROSSI, Franco

(b. 1919). Director. Born: Florence, Italy

Graduating with a degree in literature Franco Rossi began his cinematic career as an assistant director, mainly to Renato Castellani. He moved on to become a dubbing director before trading the cinema for radio, where he produced effective and imaginative plays. He then returned to the cinema as a director in 1952. Although his first two films were rather lacking in exciting subject matter his third, Il Seduttore, a comedy about a man having trouble in reconciling fantasy and fact, was well received. Possibly his best film is Amici per la Pelle, a gentle and moving story of two boys, beautifully filmed and both intuitive and informative about the world of children. His later film, Smog, created

a great stir with censors and was attacked in America as being anti-American and in Italy for not showing anti-American traits. Despite this the film won the Critics Award at the Venice Film Festival.

Films include: 1951 I Falsari. 54 Il Seduttore. '55 Amici per la Pelle (GB: Friends for Life). '57 Amore a Prima Vista (IT-SP). '62 Smog. '64 Tre Notti d'Amore ep La Moglie Bambina (FR-IT). '66 Non Faccia la Guerra, Faccia l'Amore (IT-SP). '67 Una Rosa per Tutti (GB: Everyman's Woman). '69 Le Avventure di Ulisse (+ co-sc); Giovinezza Giovinezza (+ co-sc) (USA: Youth March). '76 Pure as a Lily/Come una Rosa al Naso (GB-IT). '77 L'Altra Metà del Cielo.

ROSSITER, Leonard

(1927–1985). Actor. Born: Liverpool, England

Leonard Rossiter looked like a salesman – smooth, fast-talking and a bit ragged around the edges, particularly when it came to his portrayal of the rapacious Rigsby in the British television series Rising Damp and as the hero of The Fall and Rise of Reginald Perrin. The son of a bookie and barber, Rossiter went into the army and on being demobbed wanted to attend university but could not afford it and took a job in insurance. Inspired by his participation in amateur productions he gave up the security of his work and took up acting. Some years in rep led to a London debut in 1956 and by the early Sixties he was appearing on television in such series as Z Cars, in which he played a chief inspector. He made his first film appearance in John Schlesinger's A Kind of Loving, which led to a better and funnier part as Billy's harassed undertaker boss in Billy Liar. Since then his film and television career flourished and he became a household name, but despite this his first love was theatre and he would turn down film roles in order to perform live. His popularity was further enhanced by his propensity for spilling large glasses of vermouth over the long-suffering Joan Collins in Cinzano commercials.

Films include: 1962 A Kind of Loving. '63 Billy Liar; This Sporting Life. '65 King Rat (USA). '65 Hotel Paradiso. '67 The Devil's Own. '68 Oliver!; 2001: A Space Odyssey. '74 Butley (USA-GB-CAN). '76 The Pink Panther Strikes Again. '80 Rising Damp. '82 Britannia Hospital.

ROSSON, Hal

(b. 1895). Cinematographer. Born: Harold Rosson; New York City, USA

The brother of directors Arthur and Richard Rosson, he began in films as a bit-part player for Vitagraph in 1908. He also did stunt work, and in 1915 was apprenticed as a cameraman. Rosson shot many films – mostly for MGM – in both the silent and sound era. Though he was one of the first big-studio cameramen to exploit the possibilities of colour – sharing a Special Oscar for The Garden of Allah (Dietrich's first colour film) and contributing greatly to the artistic merits of The Wizard of Oz and On the Town – he did his best work in black and white. Red Dust (starring Jean Harlow,

Rosson's wife from 1933 to 1935) owes greatly to the moody jungle darkness he gave it; The Red Badge of Courage is a stark, grey and frightening war film; and The Asphalt Jungle is reinforced by Rosson's shooting of harsh, realistic cityscapes.

Films include: 1915 David Harum. '20 Heliotrope. '32 Red Dust. '36 The Garden of Allah. '37 Captains Courageous. '39 The Wizard of Oz. '40 Boom Town. '44 Thirty Seconds Over Tokyo. '46 Duel in the Sun. '49 On the Town. '50 The Asphalt Jungle. '51 The Red Badge of Courage. '67 El Dorado.

ROTA, Nino

(1911–1979). Composer. Born: Milan, Italy

Rota studied music at the Santa Cecilia Academy in Rome, and composition and conducting at the Curtis Institute in Philadelphia. He came to the cinema through Ildebrando Pizzetti, who had taught him in Rome. Pizzetti had written film scores, and through an introduction Rota was commissioned to score Castellani's Zaza (1943). Pizzetti also brought Rota to the notice of Fellini, and a long partnership ensued. For 25 years Rota wrote Fellini's scores, his music perfectly echoing the anxieties of the films. He composed also, in a more operatic style, for Visconti, and although he never went to the USA, he worked on many British and American films made in Europe, sharing an Oscar for The Godfather, Part II.

Films include: 1949 In Nome della Legge (GB: In the Name of the Law); The Glass Mountain (GB); Obsession (GB) (USA: The Hidden Room). '54 La Strada. '56 War and Peace (IT-USA). '57 Le Notti di Cabiria (IT-FR) (USA: Nights of Cabiria; GB: Cabiria). '59 La Dolce Vita. '60 Rocco e i Suoi Fratelli (IT-FR) (USA/GB: Rocco and His Brothers). '63 Otto e Mezzo (USA/GB: 8½); Il Gattopardo (IT-FR) (USA/GB: The Leopard). '65 Giulietta degli Spiriti (IT-FR) (GB: Juliet of the Spirits). '68 Romeo and Juliet (GB-IT). '70 Waterloo (IT-USSR). '72 The Godfather (USA). '74 The Godfather, Part II (co-mus) (USA).

ROTHA, Paul

(1907–1984). Director/author. Born: London, England

A painter, designer and art critic, Rotha began his film career with John Grierson at the Empire Marketing Board. He then became deeply involved in the documentary movement, directing films from the mid-Thirties for many institutions. Rotha's films invariably expressed deep social concern. Gradually he became a producer rather than a director. From 1953–55 he was head of BBC documentaries; he was also a founder of the Federation of Documentary Film Units, and chairman of the British Film Academy. He found time to direct one or two fictional features, and wrote copiously on film. His Documentary Film remains a standard text. His history of the cinema, The Film Till Now, has also been highly influential, but Rotha's idealism and hatred of commercialism blinded him to the merits of American cinema in

particular, and many of the book's judgements now read very oddly indeed.

Films include: 1933 Contact (doc). '35 Shipyard (doc). '36 Cover to Cover (doc) (prod. only). '37 Today We Live (doc) (prod. only). '43 World of Plenty (doc). '45 Land of Promise (doc). '47 A City Speaks (doc). '51 No Resting Place. '53 World Without End (co-dir). '59 Cradle of Genius (doc). '61 Das Leben von Adolf Hitler (doc) (GER) (GB: The Life of Adolf Hitler). '63 De Overval (HOLL) (GB: The Silent Raid).

ROTUNNO, Giuseppe

(b. 1923). Cinematographer. Born: Rome, Italy

In 1940 Rotunno went to work in the Cinecittà studios as a still photographer, but his anti-Fascist views lost him his job and he became a newsreel cameraman. With the German occupation, Rotunno tried to escape to Greece, was captured and interned. After the war he rapidly made his way up, becoming a director of photography by 1955. Rotunno has produced fine work in black-and-white, such as White Nights and Rocco and His Brothers, (both for the director Luchino Visconti), and in colour, including Visconti's The Leopard and the Fellini Satyricon; the uncanny, atmospheric lighting of the last-named film perhaps remains his finest achievement. On occasional trips to America he has worked on films like Carnal Knowledge and All That Jazz.

Films include: 1955 Pane Amore e . . . (USA/GB: Scandal in Sorrento). '60 On the Beach (USA); Rocco e i Suoi Fratelli (IT-FR) (USA/GB: Rocco and His Brothers). '66 La Bibbia (USA: The Bible – in the Beginning). '67 Le Streghe (IT-FR) (USA: The Witches). '68 Candy (USA-IT-FR). '69 The Secret of Santa Vittoria (USA); Fellini Satyricon (IT-FR). '71 Carnal Knowledge (USA). '72 Fellini's Roma (IT-FR). '79 All That Jazz (USA).

ROUCH, Jean

(b. 1917). Director. Born: Paris, France

Armed with degrees in literature and civil engineering, Rouch went to West Africa, and used his camera as a recording tool to describe tribal life and customs more accurately than any words. Slowly, film took over, and by the mid-Fifties Rouch was making full-length documentaries on Africa, one of which, Moi, Un Noir, won the prestigious Prix Delluc for the best French film of its year. With films like Chronique d'un Été, made in collaboration with Edgar Morin, Rouch used his cinéma vérité methods to describe life in France, and not only transformed the look and scope of documentary, but strongly influenced the whole generation of nouvelle vague film-makers in their search for a more direct reality.

Films include: 1956 Les Fils de l'Eau (doc). '58 Moi, un Noir (doc) (GB: I, a Negro). '60 La Pyramide Humaine. '61 Chronique d'un Eté (co-dir) (GB: Chronicle of a Summer). '65 La Chasse au Lion a l'Arc (doc) (GB: The Lion Hunters). '66 La Goumbe des Jeunes Noceurs (doc). '67 Le Jaguar. '70 Petit à Petit. '75 Cocorico! Monsieur Poulet (co-dir) (FR-NIGERIA).

ROUNDTREE, Richard

(b. 1942). Actor. Born: New Rochelle, New York, USA

Blaxploitation's James Bond, Roundtree was a college drop-out (he was at Southern Illinois on a football scholarship) who went through many jobs, from town hall janitor to advertising model, before joining New York's Negro Ensemble Company in 1967. In the movies from 1970, he became famous as the black super-sleuth Shaft in three films and a television series, smartly dressed, cool, ruthless and very hip indeed. Roundtree has come a long, long way from Stepin Fetchit, but one could argue that both views of blacks are equally demeaning.

Films include: 1970 What Do You Say to a Naked Lady? '71 Shaft. '72 Embassy (GB); Shaft's Big Score! '73 Charley One-Eye (GB); Shaft in Africa. '74 Earthquake. '79 Escape to Athena (GB); Game for Vultures. '81 Inchon. '82 One Down Two to Go.

ROWLANDS, Gena

(b. 1934). Actress. Born: Cambria, Wisconsin, USA

Gena Rowlands went from the University of Wisconsin to the American Academy of Dramatic Arts, where she met and married a fellow-student, the future director John Cassavetes. Rowlands scored a Broadway success in *The Middle of the Night*, opposite Edward G. Robinson, and in 1958 went on to Hollywood. Her film appearances have been irregular but striking. She has played in a number of her husband's films, and in *A Woman Under the Influence* gained critical praise and several awards. Here she played a blue-collar worker's wife on the verge of nervous breakdown, and her part in *Opening Night*, for which she won the Best Actress Award at Berlin, was similarly nervy. She then broke splendidly from type in *Gloria*, as a brassy but brave lady holding her own against some very nasty hoodlums.

Films include: 1958 The High Cost of Loving. '62 The Spiral Road; Lonely Are the Brave. '63 A Child Is Waiting. '67 Tony Rome. '68 Faces. '71 Minnie and Moskowitz. '74 A Woman Under the Influence. '77 Opening Night. '78 The Brink's Job. '80 Gloria.

ROY, Bimal

(1909–1966). Director. Born: Dacca, Bengal, India

Born into a rich Dacca family, Roy entered films in 1932 as an assistant cameraman. He rose rapidly to director of photography and, in 1943, to director, working first in Calcutta and then Bombay. Of his early films, *Udayer Pathey* has been described as the 'first experimental low-budget film of the Indian cinema'; in spite of its unknown cast, it was massively popular. Roy gained international recognition in 1953 with *Two Acres of Land*, which was concerned with inequality in an anachronistic society.

Films include: 1944 Udayer Pathey. '49 Mantra Mugdha. '53 Do Bigha Zamin

Left: Charles Ruggles (left) in Breaking the Ice *(1938). Above left: Richard Roundtree in* Shaft. *Above: Gena Rowlands in* Gloria

(GB: Two Acres of Land). '55 Biraj Bahu; Amanat (co-dir). '56 Devdas. '57 Gotama the Buddha (co-dir). '59 Madhumati. '62 Kabuliwala. '64 Bandini.

RÓZSA, Miklós

(b.1907). Composer. Born: Budapest, Hungary

One of the few film-music composers to have created successful concert music (chamber and symphonic works), Rózsa, who had been an outstanding pupil at the Leipzig Conservatory, first became involved with cinema when the director Jacques Feyder, impressed by his ballet *Hungaria*, asked him to compose the music for *Knight Without Armour*. This was made in England, and Rózsa stayed on to work for the film's producer, his fellow-Hungarian Alexander Korda. In 1940 Rózsa followed Korda to Hollywood, where he was still working in the Eighties. In the Forties he wrote scores for some of the most celebrated *films noirs* – Double Indemnity, *The Killers* (1946), Criss Cross – trying always with his music to complete the film's psychological effect rather than merely illustrate. Later he worked mainly on more spectacular movies, adopting a richer, full-blooded style, but his more recent scores, like those for Resnais' *Providence* and Wilder's

Fedora (1978), have seen a return to a more intimate scale. Rózsa won three Oscars – for *Spellbound*, *A Double Life* (1948) and *Ben-Hur*.

Films include: 1937 Knight Without Armour (GB). '40 The Thief of Bagdad (GB). '41 That Hamilton Woman! (GB: Lady Hamilton). '44 Double Indemnity. '45 Spellbound; The Lost Weekend. '48 The Naked City (co-mus). '49 Criss Cross. '56 Lust for Life. '59 Ben-Hur. '73 The Golden Voyage of Sinbad (GB). '77 Providence (FR-SWITZ).

RUBENS, Alma

(1897–1931). Actress. Born: Alma Smith; San Francisco, California, USA

One of the classic beauties of silent films, Alma Rubens grew up in San Francisco where she was convent-educated, but before she was twenty was in Hollywood, playing a slave-girl in *Intolerance* (1916). She appeared in several early Douglas Fairbanks films, and by the early Twenties was a star in her own right. Her life ended tragically. She became a morphine addict, first snared, it is said, by the same actor who had introduced Wallace Reid, Barbara La Marr and others to drugs, and after spells in hospitals, an arrest for possession of morphine, and other unhappy events, she died at the age of 33. Her career had ended two

years earlier; her last film, one of the few to survive, was Henry King's *She Goes to War* (1929).

Films include: **1916** The Half Breed. **'17** The Firefly of Tough Luck. **'18** Madame Sphinx. **'21** The Moonshine Menace. **'22** Restless Souls; The Valley of Silent Men. **'23** Enemies of Women. **'24** Under the Red Robe; The Price She Paid. **'25** East Lynne. **'29** Show Boat.

RUGGLES, Charles

(1886–1970). Actor. Born: Los Angeles, California, USA

Until the coming of sound Charles Ruggles was primarily a stage actor, although he had appeared in a few films before he began working regularly in the cinema in 1929. He went on to become one of the mainstays of Paramount's great comedies of the Thirties. In *Trouble in Paradise* and other Lubitsch films he played worldly sophisticates with enormous

charm. No one could cough more eloquently, or raise an eyebrow more quizzically than Ruggles, and he brought his almost apologetic sense of fun to some of the finest comedies of the period. He was delicious as the spendthrift nephew in *Love Me Tonight*; set aside his usual polish to play the rough Westerner in *Ruggles of Red Gap*; and made a wonderful series of husband-and-wife movies, in which he was mercilessly henpecked by Mary Boland. In his later years he went back for a time to the theatre, winning a Tony for *The Pleasure of His Company*.

Films include: **1915** Peer Gynt. **'23** The Heart Raider. **'29** Gentlemen of the Press. **'32** If I Had a Million; Trouble in Paradise; Love Me Tonight. **'33** Mama Loves Papa. **'35** Ruggles of Red Gap. **'37** Exclusive. **'38** Bringing up Baby. **'47** It Happened on Fifth Avenue. **'60** All in a Night's Work. **'61** The Pleasure of His Company. **'65** The Ugly Dachshund. **'66** Follow Me, Boys.

RUGGLES, Wesley

(1889–1972). Director. Born: Los Angeles, California, USA

In 1914 Wesley Ruggles came from stock and musical comedy to Keystone as an actor. Within three years he was directing, and worked steadily, as a competent Hollywood professional, until 1944. Ruggles was saddled with some ludicrous movies (such as *The Leopard Woman*, 1920, described by William K. Everson as 'a mélange of vampery, espionage, regeneration and jungle adventure which really has to be seen to be disbelieved'), but was a shrewd hand with comedy, making the best Mae West film, *I'm No Angel*, and the gorgeous Carole Lombard comedy, *True Confession*. He also made the spectacular Western, *Cimarron*, which won an Oscar for Best Picture in 1931. In 1944 Ruggles was signed by Rank to make a lavish British musical, *London Town*, starring Sid Field. The film was a disaster, and Ruggles retired.

Films include: **1917** For France. **'29** Street Girl; Condemned. **'31** Cimarron. **'33** I'm No Angel. **'34** Bolero. **'36** Valiant Is the Word for Carrie. **'37** True Confession. **'38** Sing, You Sinners. **'40** Too Many Husbands; Arizona. **'46** London Town (GB) (USA: My Heart Goes Crazy).

RÜHMANN, Heinz

(b. 1902). Actor/director. Born: Essen, Germany

Rühmann had a distinguished stage career in Germany, where from 1926 to 1932 he worked with Max Reinhardt in Berlin, and went on to leads in plays as diverse as *Harvey*, *Death of a Salesman* and *Waiting for Godot*. Innocent, charming and sprightly, Rühmann was adept at comedy, and made his first hit in films in a popular musical of 1930, *Die Drei von der Tankstelle*, with Lilian Harvey. But he could handle grimmer roles with as much skill, and was excellent in an early Robert Siodmak thriller, *Der Mann, der seinen Mörder sucht*, as a distressed little chap who hires someone to kill him, and spends the movie trying to escape. He made over a hundred films in Germany, and very few elsewhere.

Films as actor include: **1930** Die Drei von der Tankstelle. **'31** Der Mann, der seinen Mörder sucht (USA: Inquest). **'38** Kleider machen Leute (GB: Clothes Make the Man). **'44** Der Engel mit dem Saitenspiel (dir. only). **'53** Briefträger Müller (+ co-dir). **'60** Der brave Soldat Schwejk (USA: The Good Soldier Schweik). **'63** Das Haus in Montevideo. **'65** Ship of Fools (USA). **'70** Die Feuerzangenbowle. **'71** Der Kapitan.

RULE, Janice

(b. 1931). Actress. Born: Mary Janice Rule; Cincinnati, Ohio, USA

Janice Rule studied dance in Chicago, danced in nightclubs and on Broadway, and also acted on the New York stage. Since 1951 she has made occasional film appearances, and from around the mid-Sixties has frequently

made an impression in parts where she can show a sense of irony and wry amusement. She was outstanding in *The Swimmer*, coming near to stealing the film as Burt Lancaster's embittered ex-mistress, and also in *Gumshoe*, a *film noir* parody where she was as enigmatically wicked as any of those shady ladies of the Forties. She is married to actor Ben Gazzara.

Films include: **1951** Goodbye My Fancy. **'52** Holiday for Sinners. **'56** Gun for a Coward. **'58** Bell, Book and Candle. **'66** The Chase; Alvarez Kelly. **'68** The Swimmer. **'71** Gumshoe (GB). **'73** Kid Blue. **'77** Three Women.

RUMAN, Sig

(1884–1967). Actor. Born: Siegfried Albon Rumann; Hamburg, Germany

One of Hollywood's immortal character players, Ruman had acted on stage in Germany before going to America in 1923. He joined a German-language company in New York, reached Broadway, and played a first film part (a bit as a bailiff) in *The Royal Box* in 1929. Five years later he moved to Hollywood for good, and went on providing marvellous cameos to the end of his life. Usually cast as a blustering, opinionated Teuton (and much tormented by the Marx Brothers in this role), Ruman was better still in his occasional sympathetic parts. He was superb in *Ninotchka* as a Russian commissar overwhelmed by Paris; wildly funny in Lubitsch's black comedy *To Be or Not To Be*; and intensely moving as the harassed but great-hearted proprietor of the airline in *Only Angels Have Wings*.

Films include: **1934** The World Moves On. **'35** Under Pressure; A Night at the Opera. **'37** Seventh Heaven; A Day at the Races; Nothing Sacred. **'39** Ninotchka; Only Angels Have Wings. **'42** To Be or Not To Be. **'43** The Song of Bernadette. **'53** Stalag 17. **'54** White Christmas.

RUSH, Barbara

(b. 1927). Actress. Born: Denver, Colorado, USA

While at the University of California at Santa Barbara, Rush won the University Players' Best Actress of the Year award. A scholarship to the Pasadena Playhouse Theatre Arts College followed, and a year later her career began when this hazel-eyed, attractive brunette was spotted by Paramount. She appeared regularly through the Fifties and Sixties, often playing leads. Two of her performances stand out from the rest: in Nicholas Ray's *Bigger Than Life* Rush was moving as the distraught wife watching James Mason going mad, while in a fine Sixties Western, *Hombre*, she suffered bravely as Fredric March's alienated wife held as a hostage by bandits.

Films include: **1950** The Goldbergs (GB: Molly). **'51** The First Legion; Quebec; When Worlds Collide. **'53** It Came From Outer Space. **'54** Magnificent Obsession. **'55** Captain Lightfoot. **'56** Bigger Than Life. **'60** Strangers When We Meet. **'67** Hombre. **'80** Can't Stop the Music.

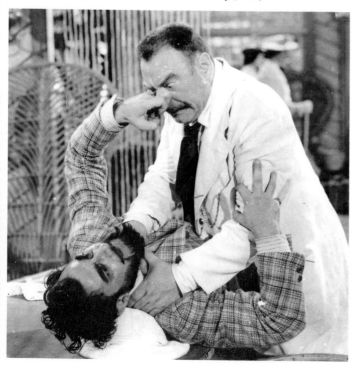

Below left: German actor-director Heinz Rühmann. Left: Alma Rubens in Enemies of Women. *Above: Janice Rule in* Alvarez Kelly, *a Western set during the Civil War*

Above: Barbara Rush as the wife of a teacher who becomes addicted to cortisone in Bigger Than Life. *Below Sig Ruman adjusts Fritz Feld's necktie in* Victory *(1940)*

RUSSELL, Gail

(1924–1961). Actress. Born: Chicago, Illinois, USA

A sad victim of Hollywood pressures, Gail Russell's career flourished with Paramount for a brief period in the late Forties. She was extremely beautiful, dark-haired, blue-eyed, quiet and gentle in manner, and gave effective performances in films like the supernatural thriller, *The Uninvited*, Borzage's *Moonrise*, and Losey's *The Lawless*. But a painful shyness and fear of the cameras made her drink in order to continue. She became an alcoholic, her Paramount contract lapsed, and her marriage to actor Guy Madison broke up. Her roles became fewer and poor, and in 1961, after a last part in *The Silent Call*, supporting a small boy and a dog, she was found dead in her apartment after a final drinking bout. The studios had known of her illness for many years, but had been content to hush it up.

Films include: 1944 Lady in the Dark; Our Hearts Were Young and Gay; The Uninvited. '45 Salty O'Rourke. '48 Moonrise; The Night Has a Thousand Eyes. '49 Wake of the Red Witch; Captain China; El Paso. '50 The Lawless (GB: The Dividing Line). '51 Air Cadet (GB: Jet Men of the Air). '56 Seven Men From Now. '61 The Silent Call.

RUSSELL, Jane

(b. 1921). Actress. born: Ernestine Jane Geraldine Russell; Bemidji, Minnesota, USA

The daughter of an actress, Jane Russell studied drama at Max Reinhardt's Theatrical Workshop and with the veteran actress Maria Ouspenskaya. These serious beginnings were forgotten in the outburst of publicity which greeted her film debut in Howard Hughes' *The Outlaw*. She was billed as 'mean – moody – magnificent', and the world was invited to gaze in wonder at her abundant curves. It took her some time to prove that she was a very good comedienne, viewing her own erotic pretensions with ironic amusement, but with *The Paleface*, opposite Bob Hope, and still more with her delicious Dorothy in *Gentlemen Prefer Blondes*, she managed it in the end. Russell was excellent, too, in exotic melodrama, playing slightly shady but good-at-heart ladies with style and vigour. Her perfect partner was Robert Mitchum. He shared Russell's ability not to take the world – or the movie – too seriously, and they were splendid together in *His Kind of Woman* and *Macao*.

Films include: 1943 The Outlaw. '48 The Paleface; Mountain Belle (released 1952). '51 His Kind of Woman. '52 Macao. '53 Gentlemen Prefer Blondes. '54 The French Line. '56 Hot Blood; The Revolt of Mamie Stover. '57 The Fuzzy Pink Nightgown. '70 Darker Than Amber.

RUSSELL, Ken

(b. 1927). Director. Born: Southampton, Hampshire, England

The *enfant terrible* of the the British cinema, Russell, after serving in the RAF, became a dancer and, briefly, an actor before studying photography at South-West Essex Technical College in Walthamstow, where he met and collaborated with his first wife, costume designer Shirley Russell. He made several amateur films in the late Fifties and freelanced for BBC television before replacing John Schlesinger as a director for the arts programme *Monitor*. Here he began a series of biographical studies of composers and other artists, culminating in the portrait of Delius in old age, *Song of Summer* (1968), that many consider his best work. His movie career started inauspiciously with a weak seaside comedy, continued with an anonymous blockbuster and became recognizably his own with a coarse adaptation of D. H. Lawrence's novel *Women in Love*. He resumed his interest in composers and other artists, following a scandalous television film on Richard Strauss, with an overheated study of Tchaikovsky, *The Music Lovers*, soon surpassed by the whirling images of *Mahler* and *Lisztomania*. He also essayed musical adaptations with the charming, if heavy-handed, *The Boy Friend* and the outrageous, decidedly overwrought *Tommy*. Unusual among British directors in pinning his faith to images (and to music), Russell has carried inventiveness to previously unexplored realms of bad taste and inconsequence. Yet the brilliant talent that created the best of his television fictionalized documentaries has never entirely been extinguished. He returned to television in 1978 with a two-part film on Wordsworth and Coleridge before his first American venture, the psychedelic *Altered States*.

Films include: 1958 Amelia and the Angel (short). '64 French Dressing. '67 Billion Dollar Brain. '69 Women in Love. '71 The Music Lovers; The Devils; The Boy Friend. '72 Savage Messiah. '74 Mahler. '75 Tommy; Lisztomania. '77 Valentino. '80 Altered States (USA).

RUSSELL, Kurt

(b. 1951). Actor. Born: Springfield, Massachusetts, USA

With his blond mop of hair, youthful face and blue eyes, Kurt Russell still seems not far removed from the child actor who kicked Elvis Presley on the shin in *It Happened at the World's Fair* in 1963. That was Russell's film debut, though he had been in television for some time. Sixteen years later, Russell played Presley (with the songs dubbed) in John Carpenter's television movie *Elvis*, and stayed on with Carpenter for *Escape From New York*, in which he was effective as an embittered veteran, oozing malice as he stalked a ruined Manhattan in search of the President.

Films include: 1963 It Happened at the World's Fair. '66 Follow Me, Boys. '68 The Horse in the Gray Flannel Suit. '69 The Computer Wore Tennis Shoes. '73 Charley and the Angel. '74 Superdad. '78 The One and Only. '79 Elvis (GB: Elvis – The Movie) (orig. TV). '80 Used Cars. '81 Escape From New York; The Fox and the Hound (voice only). '82 The Thing.

Top: Gail Russell in El Paso. *Top right: Kurt Russell as the macho hero of John Carpenter's* Escape From New York. *Above: Jane Russell's finest hour – posing for* The Outlaw. *Below: Ann Rutherford in an MGM publicity photograph from around 1937–38 when she was an emergent star*

RUSSELL, Rosalind

(1908–1976). Actress. Born: Waterbury, Connecticut, USA

A graduate of the American Academy of Dramatic Arts, Rosalind Russell was on Broadway by 1930 and at MGM on contract four years later. Used at first in dramatic roles, she seemed refined and a trifle pallid, but when her first real chance came, as the house-proud perfectionist driving her husband to despair in *Craig's Wife*, she seized on it superbly. *Night Must Fall* and *The Citadel* added to her range; and then came the inspired switch to comedy with *His Girl Friday*. Along with Jean Arthur, Russell was the perfect incarnation of the Hawksian woman – independent, devastatingly witty, a professional to her fingertips. When they stopped making that kind of movie, Russell went back to heavier drama, and for a while to the stage, but there were a few films left to revive old memories, and in *Auntie Mame*, *Gypsy* and *Rosie* she was still as spirited and as attractive as ever.

Films include: 1934 Evelyn Prentice. **'37** Live, Love and Learn; Night Must Fall. **'38** Man-Proof; The Citadel. **'39** The Women. **'40** His Girl Friday. **'42** My Sister Eileen. **'46** Sister Kenny. **'47** Mourning Becomes Electra. **'58** Auntie Mame. **'62** Gypsy. **'67** Rosie. **'71** Mrs Pollifax – Spy.

RUTHERFORD, Ann

(b. 1922). Actress. Born: Vancouver, British Columbia, Canada

Ann Rutherford, a pretty, perky performer with brown hair and eyes, was always destined to act in the shadows of bigger stars, like Vivien Leigh in *Gone With the Wind*. She was on stage as a child and from 11 in Hollywood where she worked for radio and had a film debut, as Joan Arlen, in *Student Tour* in 1934. Some low-budget Westerns followed and she then took on the role of Polly Benedict, Mickey Rooney's girlfriend, in the Andy Hardy series that kept her in the public eye well into the Forties. She was naughty Lydia in *Pride and Prejudice* and had good supporting parts in *The Secret Life of Walter Mitty* and *The Adventures of Don Juan* before retiring from the screen in 1950. She returned after an absence of 22 years to play the wisecracking telephone operator in *They Only Kill Their Masters*.

Films include: 1935 Waterfront Lady. **'36** The Singing Vagabond. **'37** You're Only Young Once. **'38** Love Finds Andy Hardy; Out West With the Hardys. **'39** Judge Hardy and Son; Gone With the Wind. **'40** Pride and Prejudice. **'47** The Secret Life of Walter Mitty. **'49** The Adventures of Don Juan (GB: The New Adventures of Don Juan). **'50** Operation Haylift. **'72** They Only Kill Their Masters. **'75** Won Ton Ton, the Dog That Saved Hollywood.

RUTHERFORD, Margaret

(1892–1972). Actress. Born: Balham, London, England

Margaret Rutherford was a teacher of elocution and piano who arrived in the theatre in her thirties as an Old Vic student. It was not until 1933 that she reached the West End, but after that her careers on the stage and in films flourished side by side. With her jutting chin and body seemingly on the point of toppling over, Rutherford looked a delightful eccentric, and her characters matched her looks. On stage she was a superb Arcati (the bicycling medium in *Blithe Spirit*). For the movies she repeated some of her stage successes, was the epitome of a bossy headmistress in *The Happiest Days of Your Life*, and made for Agatha Christie's Miss Marple. This much loved actress received an OBE in 1961, and was made Dame of the British Empire in 1967. Her husband, the actor Stringer Davis, played small parts in almost all her films.

Films include: 1943 The Demi-Paradise. **'45** Blithe Spirit. **'48** Miranda. **'49** Passport to Pimlico. **'50** The Happiest Days of Your Life. **'53** Trouble in Store. **'59** I'm All Right Jack. **'63** The VIPs. **'61** Murder She Said. **'64** Murder Most Foul. **'67** A Countess From Hong Kong.

RUTTENBERG, Joseph

(1889–1983). Cinematographer. Born: St Petersburg, Russia

Ruttenberg was in the USA at the age of four, worked for a Hearst newspaper in Boston, and by 1907 was a staff photographer on the *Boston American*. His first moving picture photography was for a local newsreel which he originated, and in 1915 he entered the film industry proper as a cameraman for Fox, where he stayed until 1926. In the Thirties he joined MGM, and rose rapidly to the top, with outstanding work on some of the studio's finest films (*Fury*, *Three Comrades*, *The Philadelphia Story*). Ruttenberg worked on until 1968. He had been in the industry for 53 years, had won four Oscars, and, what mattered perhaps more, the American Society of Cinematographers' much-valued Milestone Award.

Films include: 1917 Thou Shalt Not Steal. **'31** The Struggle. **'36** Fury. **'37** A Day at the Races. **'38** Three Comrades. **'39** The Women (co-photo). **'40** Waterloo Bridge; The Philadelphia Story. **'41** Dr Jekyll and Mr Hyde. **'54** Brigadoon. **'58** Gigi. **'60** Butterfield 8 (co-photo). **'68** Speedway.

RUTTMANN, Walter

(1887–1941). Director. Born: Frankfurt, Germany

Ruttmann was a brilliant experimental film-maker who sold his talents to the Nazi movement. A painter in his youth, he began to work in abstract film in the early Twenties. He contributed the 'Dream of the Falcons' sequence to Fritz Lang's *Die Nibelungen*, provided special effects for Lotte Reiniger and Paul Wegener, and in 1927 made his famous documentary about Berlin, *The Symphony of a Great City*, the forerunner of a long line of city-symphony films. This film has been much criticized for elevating form and rhythm above content, and for lacking human feeling, but it remains a supremely thrilling experience. In the Nazi period Ruttmann made documentaries glorifying the state; he also collaborated on the editing of Leni Riefenstahl's *Olympia* (1936, *Berlin Olympiad*). In 1941 he was mortally wounded while working on a documentary on the Eastern Front.

Films include: 1924 Die Nibelungen, Part I: Siegfried (animation sequence 'Dream of the Falcons' only). **'21–'25** Opus I–IV. **'27** Berlin, die Symphonie einer Grossstadt (GB: The Symphony of a Great City). **'29** Melodie der Welt. **'31** In der Nacht. **'33** Acciaio (IT). **'35** Stuttgart. **'36** Düsseldorf. **'37** Mannesmann. **'38** Weltstrasse See. **'41** Krebs.

RYAN, Robert

(1909–1973). Actor. Born: Chicago, Illinois, USA

Ryan made his first significant mark in *Crossfire*, playing a psychotic anti-semitic soldier who murders a Jew. Other notable roles in a whole string of good films rapidly followed. He played another obsessed veteran in *Act of Violence*, a paranoid millionaire in *Caught*, and was then superb in a sympathetic role as the boxer on the way out in *The Set-Up*. Versatile enough to be equally adept with heavies and heroes, and always suggesting a passionate conviction behind his rugged good looks, Ryan went on turning in impeccable performances on screen and stage right up to the year of his death. Ironically, this man who had so often in his films played bigoted and intolerant characters was in private life a quiet though committed liberal, who fought for the abolition of the House UnAmerican Activities Committee.

Films include: 1940 Golden Gloves (GB: Ex-Champ). **'46** The Woman on the Beach. **'47** Crossfire. **'48** Act of Violence; Caught. **'49** The Set-Up. **'52** Clash by Night. **'55** Bad Day at Black Rock. **'62** Billy Budd (GB). **'67** The Dirty Dozen. **'69** The Wild Bunch. **'73** The Outfit.

RYDELL, Mark

(b. 1934). Director/actor. Born: New York City, USA

Rydell was a jazz pianist in New York, a student at the Neighborhood Playhouse and the Actors' Studio, and an actor on stage and television (he crops up memorably as a sweet-voiced singer in a marvellous episode of *Sergeant Bilko*). He went to Hollywood as a television director, and in 1968 made his first cinema feature, a well-received version of D. H. Lawrence's *The Fox*. Obviously adept with literary material, Rydell went on to make *The Reivers* from a William Faulkner novel. One or two unremarkable films followed, but his careful family study, *On Golden Pond*, was a superb return to form. Admittedly he really only had to stand aside and let Hepburn and the Fondas get on with it, but he stood aside with admirable modesty and discretion.

Films include: 1956 Crime in the Streets (actor only). **'67** The Fox. **'69** The Reivers. **'72** The Cowboys. **'73** Cinderella Liberty; The Long Goodbye (actor only). **'76** Harry and Walter Go to New York. **'79** The Rose. **'81** On Golden Pond.

Above: Rosalind Russell as the beautiful actress with The Velvet Touch (1948) for murder – a fine role in a fine theatrical melodrama

Above: Margaret Rutherford as Miss Marple in Murder at the Gallop *(1963). Below: Robert Ryan in the violent Western* Lawman *(1971)*

S

SABU

(1924–1963). Actor. Born: Sabu Dastagir; Karapur, Mysore, India

When Alexander Korda decided to film Kipling's story *Elephant Boy* in India, a search uncovered an orphaned and illiterate boy working in the Maharaja's stables who could handle elephants with skill. Under good direction the child showed a lively, intelligent and natural acting ability; and he was well cast in further Korda productions in Eastern roles particularly suiting a cheeky, energetic yet charming personality. He was best in *The Thief of Bagdad* (1940), and as Mowgli in another Kipling creation, *The Jungle Book*. Now a star, Sabu remained in Hollywood, only returning to make two Powell and Pressburger productions: *Black Narcissus* and *The End of the River*. His film career from then onward was increasingly less sucessful as he lost his boyish looks, and film tastes edged away from fantasy adventures. He died of a heart attack at 39.

Films include: 1937 Elephant Boy. '38 The Drum. '40 The Thief of Bagdad. '42 The Jungle Book (USA). '44 Cobra Woman (USA). '47 The End of the River; Black Narcissus. '49 Song of India (USA). '51 Savage Drums (USA). '52 Buon Giorno Elefante (IT) (USA/GB: Hello Elephant!). '63 Rampage (USA). '64 A Tiger Walks (USA).

SADOUL, Georges

(1904–1967). Historian/critic/theorist. Born: Nancy, France

Georges Sadoul has been cited as the first author to apply economics, politics and technique to the study of film. His books – among them *History of World Cinema* (1949), *Dictionary of Films* and *Dictionary of Film-makers* (both 1965) – were based on his own vast collection of material, have been translated into 22 languages and are considered standard works of reference. Originally a student of law, he was involved with the Surrealist movement and in the Thirties became a Marxist. He was a film critic for the communist daily paper *L'Humanité* and the left-wing weekly *Les Lettres Françaises*. His political persuasions greatly influenced his writings, of which his work on the early history of

the cinema and on French film is considered particularly invaluable.

SAINT, Eva Marie

(b. 1924). Actress. Born: Newark, New Jersey, USA

Eva Marie Saint has made relatively few screen appearances in a long career. She studied at the Actors' Studio in New York, and for the following five years she was well-known in soap operas where she was dubbed 'The Helen Hayes of Television'. After winning critical acclaim for her belated Broadway debut in 1953, she was cast by Elia Kazan opposite Marlon Brando in *On the Waterfront*. She won an Academy Award for this screen debut as the innocent Edie Doyle determined to uncover her brother's murder by a dockland gang. Choosing well for her next few films, she scored with a serious, intense performance in Zinnemann's *A Hatful of Rain* as the long-suffering, expectant wife of a drug addict; and she is perhaps most familiar as the cool, blonde double-agent, Eve Kendall, in Hitchcock's *North By Northwest*. However her film appearances have been sporadic and since 1972 she has worked almost entirely on television.

Films include: 1954 On the Waterfront. '56 That Certain Feeling. '57 A Hatful of Rain; Raintree County. '59 North by Northwest. '60 Exodus. '65 The Sandpiper. '66 The Russians Are Coming, the Russians Are Coming; Grand Prix. '68 The Stalking Moon. '70 Loving. '72 Cancel My Reservation.

ST CLAIR, Malcolm

(1897–1952). Director. Born: Los Angeles, California, USA

Malcolm St Clair entered the film industry as an extra in the Mack Sennett company in 1915. A former sports cartoonist, he became a gag-writer and eventually a director with Sennett and then as an independent when he made, among others, two early Buster Keaton movies. The success of his first feature-length comedy, *George Washington Jr*, assured him of a Paramount contract. Riding high on a crest of a wave of Chaplin and Lubitsch creations, St Clair produced

some of the most popular social comedies of the mid-Twenties, delicately executed by Adolphe Menjou and Florence Vidor in the smash hits of 1925 and 1926: *Are Parents People?* and *The Grand Duchess and the Waiter*. However he failed to adapt to the sound film. Between 1935 and 1948 he worked mainly on B feature productions, apart from a few inferior late Laurel and Hardy films, and revived his early Sennett days by directing the Keystone chase sequence in *Hollywood Cavalcade* (1939).

Films include: 1919 Rip and Stitch Tailors (short) (co-dir). '21 The Goat (short) (co-dir). '22 The Blacksmith (short) (co-dir). '24 George Washington Jr. '25 Are Parents People? '26 The Grand Duchess and the Waiter; The Show-Off. '28 Gentlemen Prefer Blondes. '29 The Canary Murder Case. '43 The Dancing Masters. '48 Fighting Back.

ST JOHN, Al

(1893–1963). Actor. Born: Alfred St John; Santa Ana, California, USA

Pale, pop-eyed, gangling Al St John was for some years one of the funniest of Mack Sennett's Keystone Kops. And he also supported his uncle Roscoe Arbuckle, an obvious mean and skinny foil to the fat man's antics. In

the early Twenties he wrote and directed his own shorts. When sound came St John returned to vaudeville, where he had started his showbiz career at the age of eight. He was soon back in Hollywood, however, briefly worked with Arbuckle again, and was eventually teamed with William Boyd as Luke in *Hopalong Cassidy Returns*. For many years afterwards he played his increasingly grizzled Fuzzy Q. Jones character, supporting the top B-Western stars.

Films include: 1913 Algy on the Force. '14 Mabel's New Job; Tillie's Punctured Romance. '16 Fatty and Mabel Adrift. '20 Speed (+dir). '22 The City Chap (+dir). '23 The Salesman (+dir). '31 No Greater Love; The Painted Desert. '36 Hopalong Cassidy Returns. '37 The Outcasts of Poker Flat. '38 Moonlight on the Range. '46 The Lone Rider Fights Back. '51 Thundering Trail (GB: Thunder on the Trail).

ST JOHN, Jill

(b. 1940). Actress. Born: Jill Oppenheim; Los Angeles, California, USA

One of Hollywood's greatest clichés is that beneath the gorgeous bosom of every glamour star a serious actress is dying of frustration. Just now and then, it really does seem to be true.

388

Certainly Jill St John was almost *too* successful in her early career. The daughter of wealthy restaurateurs, she appeared on stage at the age of five, was a regular on the radio series *One Man's Family*, made her television debut in *A Christmas Carol*, and was signed up by Universal as a budding starlet aged 16. The same year she married one millionaire, Neil Dublin, and three years later another, Lance Reventlow. Her film parts have mostly exploited her stunning red hair and curvaceous figure, leading to the ultimate in male fantasy, a role as a Bond girl in *Diamonds Are Forever*. Yet St John studied at UCLA at an early age, and her old flame Henry Kissinger dubbed her 'one of the brightest women I have ever met'. Only recently has she been able to escape the confines of her sexist stereotype, turn-

Above: Jill St John as the sexy Tiffany Case in Diamonds Are Forever.
Right: Al St John in The Salesman.
Below, from left to right: Sabu in The Jungle Book; *Eva Marie Saint in* A Hatful of Rain; *S.Z. Sakall in* Thank Your Lucky Stars; *Renato Salvatori as the confused boxer in* Rocco and His Brothers; *Dominique Sanda in* The Conformist

ing in an impressive performance as the insane warden of a woman's prison in *The Concrete Jungle*.

Films include: 1958 Summer Love. '59 Holiday for Lovers. '60 The Lost World. '61 The Roman Spring of Mrs Stone (GB). '62 Tender Is the Night. '63 Come Blow Your Horn; Who's Minding the Store?; Who's Been Sleeping in My Bed? '64 Honeymoon Hotel. '66 The Liquidator (GB). '67 Tony Rome. '71 Diamonds Are Forever (GB). '82 The Concrete Jungle.

SAKALL, S. Z. ('Cuddles')

(1884–1955). Actor. Born: Eugene Gero; Budapest, Hungary

The enduring image of Sakall is of a fat, flustered, middle-aged German – he played Rick's assistant in *Casablanca* – slapping his wobbly cheeks in disbelief and muttering in a heavy accent 'Nah! Nah! Nah!'. It was a role he perfected so well and played so often that even studio heads, not usually famed for their affectionate natures, knew him as 'Cuddles', but it disguises the fact that he had an earlier, thriving career in Europe before Hitler took a personal dislike to his brand of musical comedy and forced him to start again elsewhere. Born in poverty, Sakall started writing music-hall sketches when he was 16,

and graduated to gag-writing for a well-known Budapest comic. After World War I he went to Vienna, playing a variety of roles on the Austrian and German stage, acting with Max Reinhardt and appearing in the first German talkie, *Zwei Herzen im ¾ Takt*. In 1954 he wrote an autobiography, *The Story of Cuddles*.

Films include: 1916 Suszterherceg (HUNG). '30 Zwei Herzen im ¾ Takt (GER). '37 The Lilac Domino (GB). '40 It's a Date. '41 Ball of Fire. '42 Yankee Doodle Dandy; Casablanca. '43 Thank Your Lucky Stars. '46 The Time, the Place and the Girl. '49 In the Good Old Summertime. '54 The Student Prince.

SALTZMAN, Harry

(b. 1916). Producer. Born: Sherbrooke, Quebec, Canada

Harry Saltzman seems to have an eye for a current trend – initially producing the kitchen-sink British films of the late Fifties and then catching the spirit of the modern era with the technology-ridden James Bond films alongside more brutal, realistic spy movies such as *Funeral in Berlin* and *Billion Dollar Brain*. Though born in Canada, he worked mostly in America where he produced *The Robert Montgomery Show* for television. He then began working in England where he joined forces with Tony Richardson and John Osborne to found Woodfall Films, and the British 'New Wave' followed. Next came his partnership with Albert 'Cubby' Broccoli and the beginning of the Bond phenomenon. Saltzman branched off into the more down-to-earth espionage films like *The Ipcress File* and in 1975, after an unhappy partnership, he sold the rights of the Bond films to Broccoli. Saltzman has since become primarily involved with stage production.

Films include: 1959 Look Back in Anger. '60 Saturday Night and Sunday Morning; The Entertainer. '62 Doctor No. '63 From Russia With Love. '64 Goldfinger. '65 The Ipcress File; Thunderball. '66 Funeral in Berlin. '67 Billion Dollar Brain; You Only Live Twice. '69 The Battle of Britain. '71 Diamonds Are Forever. '73 Live and Let Die. '74 The Man With the Golden Gun. '80 Nijinsky (exec. prod) (USA).

SALVATORI, Renato

(b. 1933). Actor. Born: Forte dei Marmi, Italy

Salvatori's career underwent a remarkable change of direction. While he was working at the resort of Viareggio, his dark, muscular good looks won him an accidental film debut as a romantic juvenile, and led to a series of similar roles. After work with Visconti, Rossellini and De Sica, however, he emerged as a powerful character actor, specializing in simple peasants or brutish villains, rendering each with an effective mix of subtlety and force. He was at his most characteristic in *Rocco and His Brothers*, playing a boxer seduced by easy money and petty crime, who ends up murdering his girl. He has also acted in over a hundred French films.

Films include: 1952 Le Ragazze di Piazza di Spagna (USA: Three Girls From Rome; GB: Girls of the Spanish Steps). '57 Poveri ma Belli (IT-FR) (GB: Girl in a Bikini). '58 I Soliti Ignoti (USA: Big Deal on Madonna Street; GB: Persons Unknown). '59 Nella Città l'Inferno (IT-FR) (GB: Caged). '60 Era Notte a Roma (IT-FR) (USA: It Was Night in Rome); Rocco e i Suoi Fratelli (IT-FR) (USA/GB: Rocco and His Brothers). '62 Smog; Les Grands Chemins (FR-IT) (GB: Of Flesh and Blood). '64 Tre Notti d'Amore (IT-FR). '69 Z (FR-ALGERIA). '70 Queimada! (IT-FR). '73 Etat de Siège (FR-IT-GER) (GB: State of Siege). '79 La Luna (USA: Luna).

SANDA, Dominique

(b. 1948). Actress. Born: Dominique Varaigne; Paris, France

Rebelling against her strict Catholic upbringing when her parents refused to let her attend art school, Dominique Sanda became a sought-after model for women's magazines. Robert Bresson cast her as the tragic heroine, driven to suicide, in his Dostoyevsky adaptation, *Une Femme Douce*, on the strength of hearing her voice on the telephone. She followed this with a Turgenev adaptation for Maximilian Schell. She played the proud, doomed Jewish girl in *The Garden of the Finzi-Continis* and the lesbian wife of an anti-Fascist Italian exile in Bernardo Bertolucci's *The Conformist*. She was also excellent – controlled and cool but deeply emotional – in a later Bertolucci film, *1900*. In 1976 she shared the best actress award at Cannes for her role in *The Inheritance*. She first attempted an English-language role in *The Mackintosh Man* (in which she shockingly shoots the chief spy, played by James Mason). Following a teenage marriage and divorce, she had a child by actor-director Christian Marquand.

Films include: 1969 Une Femme Douce (USA/GB: A Gentle Creature). '70 Erste Liebe (GER-SWITZ) (USA/GB: First Love); Il Conformista (IT-FR-GER) (USA/GB: The Conformist); Il Giardino dei Finzi-Contini (IT) (USA/GB: The Garden of the Finzi-Continis). '73 L'Impossible Objet (USA: Story of a Love Story; GB: Impossible Object); The Mackintosh Man (GB). '74 Steppenwolf (USA). '76 Novecento/1900 (IT-FR-GER); Eredità Ferramonti (IT) (USA: The Inheritance). '78 Utopia. '79 Cabo Blanco (USA-SP). '82 Une Chambre en Ville (GB: A Room in Town).

SANDERS, George

(1906–1972). Actor. Born: St Petersburg, Russia

George Sanders called his 1960 auto-biography *Memoirs of a Professional Cad* and a dozen years later took his own life from 'boredom'. The gossip columns fed on his four marriages, particularly the second, to Zsa Zsa Gabor (1949–1957), and the fourth, to her sister Magda Gabor (1970). He was born in Russia of English parents but left at the time of the Revolution in 1917. Educated at Bedales and Manchester Technical School, he went into the tobacco business, travelling in Argentina and Brazil. Returning to England he took up acting and soon he made his way to Hollywood in 1936. For a while he played the Saint and the Falcon (a role he handed over to his brother, Tom Conway) as well as more rewarding roles, often as suave Nazis. He scored a hit as the Gauguinesque painter who abandons his family in *The Moon and Sixpence* and won a Best Supporting Actor Oscar for his role as an acerbic drama critic who adopts a moronic girlfriend (Marilyn Monroe) in *All About Eve*. He also worked two or more times each with such directors as Alfred Hitchcock, Fritz Lang and Douglas Sirk, and once with Roberto Rossellini in *Viaggio in Italia*, an experience he found disconcerting in comparison with Hollywood's efficiency. His most memorable role in the latter part of his career was as the voice of the tiger Shere Khan in *The Jungle Book*.

Films include: 1936 Find the Lady (GB). '39 The Saint in London. '40 Rebecca; Foreign Correspondent. '41 Man Hunt. '42 The Moon and Sixpence. '45 A Scandal in Paris. '47 Forever Amber. '49 The Fan (GB: Lady Windermere's Fan). '50 All About Eve. '52 Ivanhoe (GB). '53 Call Me Madam. '54 Viaggio in Italia (IT-FR) (USA: Strangers; GB: The Lonely Woman/Journey to Italy). '55 Moonfleet. '56 While the City Sleeps. '57 The Seventh Sin. '65 The Amorous Adventures of Moll Flanders (GB). '66 The Quiller Memorandum (GB-USA). '67 The Jungle Book (voice only). '69 The Best House in London (GB). '70 The Kremlin Letter.

SANDRELLI, Stefania

(b. 1946). Actress. Born: Viareggio, Italy

She was discovered through her appearances on the beach and in the Miss Ninfetta competition (in which she came second). Her first film, *Gioventù di Notte*, brought the body of a woman and the mind of a child to the public, while *Divorce –Italian Style* made her a star. She quickly matured into a sexy and sophisticated lead in French and Italian art-house movies. In Germi's *Sedotta e Abbandonata* she played a young girl in need of love who becomes the victim of antiquated prejudices, and the role not only enriched her visible charms – dark eyes, beautiful complexion and swan-like neck – but revealed her true acting ability and underlying light-heartedness. She has since done her most notable work for Bertolucci in *1900* and *The Conformist*, in which her impassive lesbian dance with Domi-

nique Sanda provided one of the most erotic sequences in Seventies cinema.

Films include: 1961 Gioventù di Notte; Divorzio all'Italiana (GB: Divorce – Italian Style); Il Federale (USA: The Fascist). '64 Sedotta e Abbandonata (IT-FR) (USA/GB: Seduced and Abandoned). '66 Io la Conosceve Bene (IT-GER-FR); Tendre Voyou (FR-IT) (USA: Tender Scoundrel). '67 L'Immorale (IT-FR). '70 Il Conformista (IT-FR-GER) (USA/GB: The Conformist). '72 Alfredo, Alfredo (IT-FR). '74 Delitto d'Amore. '75 L'Ingorgo (IT-FR-GER-SP). '76 Novecento/1900 (IT-FR-GER).

SANDRICH, Mark

(1900–1945). Director. Born: Mark Rex Sandrich; New York City, USA

The director of no less than five classic Fred Astaire/Ginger Rogers movies, Sandrich started out as prop man before working his way up through a series of successful comedies for RKO to *The Gay Divorcee*. He brought the most efficient, methodical approach to musicals, be it in his perfected use of playback, synchronizing action to pre-recorded soundtrack, his insistence that dance numbers be an integrated part of the plot, or the use of shadows and camera-angles. Sandrich was working on an adaptation of Irving Berlin's *Blue Skies* when a heart attack cut short his career at the age of 44.

Films include: 1928 Runaway Girls. '33 Melody Cruise (+ co-sc). '34 Hips, Hips, Hooray; The Gay Divorcee (GB: The Gay Divorce). '35 Top Hat. '36 Follow the Fleet. '37 Shall We Dance? '38 Carefree. '42 Holiday Inn. '44 Here Come the Waves; I Love a Soldier.

SARAFIAN, Richard C.

(b. 1927). Director. Born: New York City, USA

The son of Armenians, Sarafian was a bartender, boarding-house manager and researcher for *Life* magazine before he became an assistant with a documentary film company. He then wrote several scripts and in the Sixties directed for television series such as *Bronco*, *77 Sunset Strip*, *Bonanza* and *Ben Casey*. *Andy*, the story of a retarded boy, was his first important feature. Sarafian's films are charac-

Above left: a publicity portrait of George Sanders, always the suavest of villains. Above: Stefania Sandrelli in Il Diavolo nel Cervello *(1972, Devil in the Brain). Below: John Saxon in the John Sturges Western* Joe Kidd *(1972), about a ruthless bounty hunter*

terized by their outdoor locations – the highways of *Vanishing Point*, the mud-flats of *Man in the Wilderness*, the mountains of *The Man Who Loved Cat Dancing* – and rebel heroes; they also use visual metaphors to stress the irregular inner workings of society. Though Sarafian has not broken into the big league, he remains an interesting director of offbeat movies, several of which have achieved cult status.

Films include: 1965 Andy. '69 Run Wild, Run Free (GB). '70 Fragment of Fear (GB). '71 Vanishing Point (GB); Man in the Wilderness (USA-SP). '73 The Man Who Loved Cat Dancing; Lolly Madonna XXX (GB: The Lolly Madonna War). '76 The Next Man. '79 Sunburn (USA-GB).

SARANDON, Susan

(b. 1946). Actress. Born: Susan Tomaling; New York City, USA

In *Joe* Susan Sarandon played a wayward teenager who is eventually gunned down by her father. It was a

Below: ill-fated Gia Scala. Above: Susan Sarandon in The Other Side of Midnight. *Above right: Michael Sarrazin in* A Man Called Gannon. *Above, far right: Telly Savalas as Herbie Hassler in the British comedy* Crooks and Coronets *(1969)*

very different role from the sort which most actresses are required to undertake to launch their careers, but it is in accordance with the approach of a lady who considers herself a character actress rather than a starlet, who attended the University of Washington, but no acting lessons, and who has always chosen her roles to suit her own considerable self-exploration and development, rather than for her career alone. Although she has appeared in a couple of television soap operas – 'a good training ground' – and achieved a cult following for her part in *The Rocky Horror Picture Show*, her reputation rests on more substantial portrayals in films like *Atlantic City USA*, for which she won an Oscar nomination.

Films include: 1970 Joe. '74 The Front Page. '75 The Great Waldo Pepper; The Rocky Horror Picture Show. '77 The Other Side of Midnight. '78 King of the Gypsies; Pretty Baby. '79 Something Short of Paradise. '80 Atlantic City USA (FR-CAN-USA) (GB: Atlantic City); Loving Couples.

SARRAZIN, Michael

(b. 1940). Actor. Born: Jacques Michel André Sarrazin; Quebec City, Quebec, Canada

Because of his youthful, soulful good looks, Michael Sarrazin has often been stuck playing juvenile leads, albeit in films as varied as the nightmarish study of Depression dancing marathons *They Shoot Horses, Don't They?* to the faintly ludicrous psychic thriller *In Search of Gregory* and the pretentious adventure *Caravans*. Sarrazin entered films after passing through eight schools and finally dropping out. He worked for the CBC and at a Toronto theatre whilst still in his teens, and the parts he played in four National Film Board of Canada historical documentaries brought him to the attention of a Universal talent scout. His subsequent film work has been prolific and varied, though many of the films have been plagued with distribution and cutting problems. He has perhaps never quite made the impact he could have, and is better known in Canada and America than in Britain.

Films include: 1967 Gun Fight in Abilene; The Flim Flam Man (GB: One Born Every Minute). '69 A Man Called Gannon; Eye of the Cat; They Shoot Horses, Don't They? '70 In Search of Gregory (IT-GB). '71 The Pursuit of Happiness. '74 For Pete's Sake. '76 The Gumball Rally. '78 Caravans (IRAN-USA).

SAURA, Carlos

(b. 1932). Director. Born: Huesca, Aragón, Spain

Carlos Saura studied engineering (1950–53) while developing an interest in photography that led him to Madrid's film school (1953–57), where he stayed on for six more years as a lecturer until sacked for his political views. Growing up under Fascism in Franco's Spain, and as a child living through the Civil War, he was one of the first directors to tackle analytically political and social subjects as they pertained to Spain. Predictably he ran into censorship problems. *The Hunt*, an acute analysis of the bourgeoisie at the time, won the Silver Bear at Berlin in 1966. *Cousin Angelica*, the first Spanish film to deal with those who lost the Civil War, won the Jury Prize at Cannes in 1974; and *Raise Ravens*, seen from the viewpoint of a nine-year-old child, shared the Special Jury Prize at Cannes in 1976. *Blood Wedding*, a brilliantly staged ballet film, was a tribute to the poet and playwright Federico García Lorca, murdered in the Civil War; and *Tender Hours* returned to the theme of growing up in Spain in the Franco era.

Films include: 1958 Cuenca (short). '60 Los Golfos (GB: The Hooligans). '66 La Caza (GB: The Hunt). '67 Peppermint Frappé. '69 La Madriguera (USA: The Honeycomb). '73 Ana y los Lobos. '74 La Prima Angélica (USA: Cousin Angelica). '76 Cría Cuervos (USA: Cria!; GB: Raise Ravens). '77 Elisa, Vida Mia. '78 Los Ojos Vendados! '79 Mama Cumple 100 Años (SP-FR). '81 Deprisa, Deprisa (FR-SP); Bodas de Sangre (GB: Blood Wedding); Dulces Horas (GB: Tender Hours). '82 Antonieta (FR-MEX-SP).

SAUTET, Claude

(b. 1924). Director. Born: Montrouge, Paris, France

While training as a sculptor, Claude Sautet became a music critic and ran an educational centre for delinquent children. He studied film at IDHEC (1946–48), worked as an assistant director and made his first short in 1951. He became a scriptwriter and adapted novels for the screen; Georges Franju's *Les Yeux Sans Visage* (1959, *Eyes Without a Face*) was one of many scripts he worked on. He turned director in 1956, at first making gangster movies in *film noir* style but soon developing sociological and psychological interests in the problems of everyday life – work, love, age. His best-known film, *Les Choses de la Vie*, starring Michel Piccoli and Romy Schneider, attempted a stream-of-consciousness approach.

Films include: 1951 Nous N'Irons Plus au Bois (short). '56 Bonjour Sourire. '60 Classe Tous Risques (FR-IT) (GB: The Big Risk). '65 L'Arme à Gauche (FR-SP-IT) (GB: Guns for the Dictator). '70 Les Choses de la Vie (GB: The Things of Life). '71 Max et les Ferrailleurs. '72 César et Rosalie (FR-IT-GER) (USA/GB: César and Rosalie). '74 Vincent, François, Paul . . . et les Autres (USA: Vincent, François, Paul . . . and the Others). '76 Mado (FR-GER-IT). '78 Une Histoire Simple. '80 Un Mauvais Fils.

SAVALAS, Telly

(b. 1924). Actor. Born: Aristotele Savalas; Garden City, Long Island, New York, USA

'Who loves ya, baby?', the catchphrase of Savalas' shaven-headed, lolly-pop-licking television cop *Kojak*, effectively celebrates the turning point in the career of an actor hitherto fated to be hated. Savalas entered the movies late; born to Greek parents, he studied at Columbia University, worked for the US State Department, and headed the news section of one of the big American television networks before arriving at the movies by the back door. Asked to find an actor one day, he turned up for the audition himself. Over six feet tall and rugged, with a cruel set of features, he was picked to play Burt Lancaster's cell mate in *Birdman of Alcatraz*, and seemed doomed to play villains from Blofeld in *On Her Majesty's Secret Service* to the tough, brutal GI in *The Dirty Dozen*. With *Kojak*, however, he arose smooth and sexy from the ashes of past misdemeanours, and his reputation is now sufficiently sophisticated to make him a mainstay of glossy drinks commercials.

Films include: 1962 Birdman of Alcatraz; Cape Fear. '65 The Greatest Story Ever Told; Battle of the Bulge. '67 The Dirty Dozen (USA-GB). '69 On Her Majesty's Secret Service. '70 Kelly's Heroes (USA-YUG). '75 Inside Out (GB-GER); The Diamond Mercenaries (SWITZ) (USA: Killer Force).

SAVILLE, Victor

(1897–1979). Director/producer. Born: Birmingham, Warwickshire, England

During the Thirties Victor Saville was a mainstay of the British film industry. He was both prolific and well-respected as producer and director – particularly of musicals – especially when working with Jessie Matthews, from whom he encouraged excellent performances in *The Good Companions*, *Evergreen* and *First a Girl*. The son of an art dealer, Saville's first dealings with the film industry came when a friend of the family gave him a job in his firm, running a small Coventry cinema in the evenings and working in a film distribution office by day. He soon became involved in production and in 1920 formed Victory Motion Pictures with Michael Balcon. Then, while producing for Gaumont, he made his directorial debut with *The Arcadians*. His own production company, Burlington Films, followed, but it was on his return to Gaumont as a director in 1930 that he enjoyed his greatest successes. Six years later he again formed his own production company, Victor Saville Productions, and the films that followed included possibly his best one, *South Riding*. In 1938 he took over from Balcon as head of production at MGM British, and with the outbreak of World War II he moved to Hollywood where he again worked primarily as a producer. He returned to England in the late Fifties but retired after making only a couple of films.

Films include: 1923 Woman to Woman (co-prod. only). '27 The Arcadians (+ prod). '29 Kitty. '31 Sunshine Susie (+ co-sc) (USA: The Office Girl). '33 The Good Companions. '34 Evergreen. '35 First a Girl. '36 It's Love Again. '38 South Riding (+ prod); The Citadel (prod. only). '39 Goodbye, Mr Chips (prod. only). '53 I, the Jury (prod. only) (USA). '54 The Long Wait (USA). '55 Kiss Me Deadly (exec. prod. only) (USA). '61 The Greengage Summer (prod. only) (USA: Loss of Innocence).

SAXON, John

(b. 1935). Actor. Born: Carmen Orrico; New York City, USA

Of Italian descent, the son of a building contractor, John Saxon paid his way through drama classes with Stella Adler by working as a model. A photograph in *True Story* magazine brought him a Universal contract and he played leading roles as mixed-up youngsters until he became the oldest teenager in movies. He played a psychotic soldier in Robert Redford's debut film, *War Hunt*, but after that he sank to taking mostly supporting roles, sometimes in European productions, though he starred in a television series, *The Doctors*. He again acted with Redford in *The Electric Horseman*, but this time round Redford was the star and Saxon (though playing his boss) the support.

Films include: 1955 Running Wild. '58 The Reluctant Debutante; Summer Love. '60 Portrait in Black; The Unforgiven. '62 War Hunt. '63 The Cardinal. '66 The Appaloosa (GB: South West to Sonora). '69 Death of a Gunfighter. '78 The Bees. '79 The Electric Horseman.

SCALA, Gia

(1934–1972). Actress. Born: Giovanna Sgoglio; Liverpool, England

Born of an Italian father and Irish mother, Gia Scala was brought up in Italy. She went to New York in her teens and studied acting with Stella Adler, becoming an American citizen in 1956. Given a Universal contract, she had a small part in *All That Heaven Allows* and a major one as an actress being tested for the lead in a biblical epic in *Four Girls in Town*. For Columbia she played the widow of a murdered union leader in *The Garment Jungle*. The most memorable role in the later part of her brief career was as the traitor, allegedly dumb after Gestapo torture, who is summarily executed by her compatriot (Irene Papas) in *The Guns of Navarone*. After this, her career went downhill, not helped by her alcoholism. She died of an overdose of drink and drugs.

Films include: 1955 All That Heaven Allows. '56 Four Girls in Town. '57 The Big Boodle (GB: Night in Havana); The Garment Jungle; Tip on a Dead Jockey (GB: Time for Action); Don't Go Near the Water. '58 The Tunnel of Love; The Two-Headed Spy (GB). '59 The Angry Hills (GB). '60 I Aim at the Stars (GER-USA). '61 The Guns of Navarone (GB). '66 Operation Delilah (USA-SP).

SCHAFFNER, Franklin J.

(b. 1920). Director. Born: Tokyo, Japan

Epics are, perhaps, to directors what animals and children are to actors; they sort the men from the boys. Schaffner's reputation rests squarely on his output of big-budget films, and displays a remarkable ability to prevent the spectacle from smothering all before it. The son of missionary parents, Schaffner tried to break into acting on his return to the States after a spell in the navy, with little success. Instead he transferred to directing, acquiring a great deal of experience in the CBS television department. Once in Hollywood he quickly established himself as a reliable, untemperamental, flexible craftsman who could be trusted to make the most of a very large amount of money. What if *Nicholas and Alexandra* is a little bland – there's plenty of gritty medieval realism in *The War Lord*, inventive and thoughtful science-fiction in *Planet of the Apes*, and sophisticated thrills in *The Boys From Brazil* to make up for it. *Patton*, for which Schaffner won an Oscar, remains that rare commodity – an excellent, intelligent, grand-scale war movie.

Films include: 1963 The Stripper (GB: Woman of Summer). '64 The Best Man. '65 The War Lord. '67 The Double Man (GB); Planet of the Apes. '70 Patton (GB: Patton; Lust for Glory). '71 Nicholas and Alexandra. '73 Papillon. '76 Islands in the Stream. '78 The Boys From Brazil. '81 Sphinx.

SCHARY, Dore

(1905–1980). Producer/screenwriter. Born: Isidore Schary; Newark, New Jersey, USA

Schary was unusually soft-spoken and self-effacing for a Hollywood tycoon and he seemed to have been somewhat ill at ease in the exercizing of executive power. The child of immigrant parents who had built up a successful catering business, he left school at 14, worked in various jobs, then decided at 19 to go to high school, cramming 4 years study into 10 months. He then worked as a reporter and as an actor/writer/director in Cincinnati which led to a writing contract with Columbia. Following his first Broadway success, *Too Many Heroes* in 1937, he joined MGM as a scriptwriter, working on such films as *Boys Town* (1938) and *Edison the Man* (1940). He made his directorial debut with a series of popular, low-budget movies, though their liberal political content fuelled disagreements between him and MGM. He left in 1943 to pursue a successful career as a producer for Vanguard Films, spent 1947 at RKO (in which he produced *Crossfire*, an exposé of anti-semitism in the armed forces) and then returned to bolster MGM's declining fortunes as chief of production, a post he retained, despite repeated clashes with studio boss Louis B. Mayer, until 1956. Of the films made under his aegis at MGM, *Bad Day at Black Rock* was probably closest to his own personal political views. During the McCarthy era he was one of the few major

Hollywood producers to maintain a semblance of integrity. Not least among his achievements was his fostering of the directors Nicholas Ray, and Joseph Losey, both of whom made their first feature under him at RKO.

Films include: 1944 I'll Be Seeing You. '45 The Spiral Staircase. '46 The Farmer's Daughter. '47 Crossfire. '50 The Asphalt Jungle. '51 An American in Paris; The Red Badge of Courage. '52 Singin' in the Rain; Ivanhoe (GB). '53 Julius Caesar; Mogambo. '54 Seven Brides for Seven Brothers. '55 Bad Day at Black Rock.

SCHATZBERG, Jerry

(b. 1927). Director. Born: New York City, USA

Leaving the University of Miami after one year, Jerry Schatzberg took many odd jobs, eventually becoming a successful fashion photographer for *Vogue* and other magazines, and opening his own studio. After directing several television commercials, he put together a film project about a fashion model who has a nervous breakdown, which he ultimately directed as *Puzzle of a Downfall Child*, starring Faye Dunaway. His next two films helped to make a star of Al Pacino; *Scarecrow*, in which Pacino played one of a pair of drifters (with Gene Hackman), shared the Golden Palm at Cannes in 1973. Schatzberg nonetheless found it difficult to establish more than a minor cult reputation, mainly in France, until he tackled more robust material with his political fable *The Seduction of Joe Tynan*, starring Alan Alda, and his study of a country-and-western singer, played by Willie Nelson, in *Honeysuckle Rose*.

Films: 1970 Puzzle of a Downfall Child. '71 The Panic in Needle Park. '73 Scarecrow. '76 Dandy, the All American Girl (GB: Sweet Revenge). '79 The Seduction of Joe Tynan. '80 Honeysuckle Rose. '83 Misunderstood.

SCHEIDER, Roy

(b. 1935). Actor. Born: Orange, New Jersey, USA

Scheider's rise to fame has been less than meteoric. He began acting while a student and after a stretch in the air force joined the Lincoln Center Repertory Company, and finally broke into television. In the movies he seemed destined to play a variety of excellent supporting roles, often exploiting his lean, finely-muscled build – as Jane Fonda's pimp in *Klute*, or Dustin Hoffman's brother in *Marathon Man*. He first gained some deserved attention, as well as an Oscar nomination, as Gene Hackman's partner in *The French Connection*, and his most popular role so far has undoubtedly been as the honest, ordinary small-town cop trying to cope with the menacing shark in *Jaws*. The extent of his range and talent was demonstrated by his leading role in Bob Fosse's musical drama, *All That Jazz*.

Films include: 1964 The Curse of the Living Corpse. '68 Star. '70 Loving. '71 Klute; The

French Connection. '73 The Seven-Ups. '75 French Connection II; Jaws; Sheila Levine Is Dead and Living in New York. '76 Marathon Man. '77 Sorcerer (GB: Wages of Fear). '79 Last Embrace; All That Jazz.

SCHELL, Maria

(b. 1926). Actress. Born: Margarete Schell; Vienna, Austria

Schell made her film debut, under the name Gritli Schell, with her mother in Siegfried Steiner's *Steinbruch*. It was not until 1954 that she created any impression, and that may have been because she made four consecutive films, including René Clément's *Gervaise* (in which she had the title role) and Visconti's *Le Notti Bianche*, in four different countries. These films quickly cast her in the mould of the vulnerable and emotional heroine, which she went on to play in a series of mediocre and rather superficial dramas, though she did win a Best Actress Award at Cannes for *Die letzte Brücke*. In the Sixties she retired from films to devote time to her family but returned in 1968 with *99 Women*. Since then she has worked intermittently in film (she had a small part in *Superman, The Movie*) and television.

Films include: 1942 Steinbruch (SWITZ). '49 Der Engel mit der Posaune (A). '52 Dr Holl (GER) (USA: Angelika; GB: Affairs of Dr Holl). '53 Die letzte Brücke (A-YUG) (GB: The Last Bridge). '56 Rose Bernd (GER). '57 Le Notti Bianche (IT-FR) (GB: The White Nights). '58 The Brothers Karamazov (USA). '59 The Hanging Tree (USA). '68 99 Mujeres (SP-IT-GER-GB) (USA/GB: 99 Women). '74 The Odessa File (GB-GER). '78 Superman, The Movie (USA). '79 Schöner Gigolo – armer Gigolo (GER) (USA/GB: Just a Gigolo).

SCHELL, Maximilian

(b. 1930). Actor/director. Born: Vienna, Austria

Schell, a tall, thin, handsome and intense leading man, won the 1961 Best Actor Oscar playing a German defence attorney in *Judgement at Nuremberg*, whereupon he found himself lost in largely mediocre movies until the end of the decade when he began to direct – his first movie being *First Love*. More worthy films – including *The Pedestrian, End of the Game* and *Tales From the Vienna Woods* – as director have followed and his acting career has also been rejuvenated with two Oscar nominations for his performances in *Man in the Glass Booth* and *Julia*. The son of a playwright-poet and a prominent Viennese actress, he was one of four children (including his older sister Maria) who all chose acting as a career. He began his education at Zurich University and went on stage in the early Fifties. Schell made his debut in *The Young Lions* in Hollywood.

Films include: 1958 The Young Lions (actor) (USA). '61 Judgement at Nuremberg (actor) (USA). '62 I Sequestroni di Altona (actor) (IT-FR) (USA/GB: The Condemned of Altona; Five Finger Exercise (actor) (USA). '64 Topkapi (actor) (USA-FR). '67 The Battle Horns (actor) (USA) (GB: Counterpoint). '68 Das Schloss (prod; + act) (USA/GB: The Castle). '70 Erste Liebe (dir)

Above: Roy Scheider, the versatile star of All That Jazz. *Below: Maria Schell, the put-upon heroine of many international films. Above right: her brother Maximilian Schell in* The Battle Horns. *Above, far right: Joseph Schildkraut as a sly King Herod in* Cleopatra

(GER-SWITZ) (USA: First Love). '73 Der Fussgänger (dir) (USA/GB: The Pedestrian). '74 The Odessa File (actor) (GB-GER). '75 Der Richter und sein Henker (dir; +prod; +co-sc) (GER-IT) (USA: End of the Game); Man in the Glass Booth (actor) (USA). '77 Cross of Iron (GB-GER); Julia (actor) (USA). '79 Geschichten aus dem Wienerwald (+dir; +prod; +act) (GER-A) (USA/GB: Tales From the Vienna Woods).

SCHENCK, Joseph M.

(1878–1961). Producer. Born: Rybinsk, Russia

The Schenck family emigrated to the USA in 1893. Joseph and his younger brother Nicholas gradually built up a

thriving drugstore business. They then expanded by successfully exploiting the lucrative possibilities of amusement parks. One of these, Paradise Park, was bought by entrepreneur Marcus Loew, who, in 1912, invited the Schencks to become partners in his chain of theatre and film theatres, Consolidated Enterprises. Joseph Schenck left in 1917 and quickly rose to fame as the producer of Fatty Arbuckle and Buster Keaton films. Schenck's wife, Norma Talmadge (they had wed in 1917), starred in several of his films, which also featured her sisters Constance and Natalie (Keaton's wife). Schenck became the highly successful chairman of the board of United Artists in 1924 and president in 1927. He then left to establish 20th Century Productions with himself as president. When in 1935 his company merged with the Fox Film Corporation, he became chairman of the new company, 20th Century-Fox. He was forced to resign in 1941 after being convicted of income tax irregularities, but was reappointed executive head of production in 1943 (he resigned the following year). His last major venture was the formation of the Magna Corporation with producer Mike Todd to promote the Todd-AO wide-screen system. Schenck was awarded a special Oscar for services to the film industry in 1952.

Films include: 1917 Butcher Boy. '18 Salome. '22 Polly of the Follies. '23 Three Ages. '24 Sherlock Jr; The Navigator; Her Night of Romance. '25 Seven Chances. '26 The General. '28 Steamboat Bill Jr; The Battle of the Sexes. '29 New York Nights. '30 Dubarry, Woman of Passion; The Bat Whispers. '33 Secrets.

SCHENCK, Nicholas M.

(1881–1969). Executive producer. Born: Rybinsk, Russia

Nicholas M. Schenck and his elder brother Joseph joined Marcus Loew's Consolidated Enterprises in 1912 in executive positions. Nicholas re-

mained with the company when Joseph left to become an independent producer and, with the death of Loew in 1927, became president of Loew's Inc (which had become the parent company of MGM in the early Twenties). Schenck took little active part in the more creative side of film-making, leaving that side of the business to Louis B. Mayer and his head of production, Irving Thalberg. In the mid-Fifties, following a row among Loew's stockholders fomented by Mayer (who had lost his job at MGM in 1951), Schenck was forced to relinquish the presidency and to accept nominal position of chairman. His place was taken by Arthur Loew (Marcus' son) and then by Joseph R. Vogel. Schenck retired from motion pictures in 1958.

SCHILDKRAUT, Joseph

(1895–1964). Actor. Born: Vienna, Austria

The son of the internationally known actor Rudolf Schildkraut, Joseph Schildkraut, a former student of the Imperial Academy of Music, studied with the character actor Albert Basserman and at the American Academy of Dramatic Arts in New York. He made successful appearances for Max Reinhardt's company in Berlin between 1913 and 1917; he then went back to the USA. He made his American film debut in 1921 but, though he appeared in over sixty films, had few chances to impress. His best roles were as Captain Dreyfus in *The Life of Emile Zola* (for which he won an Oscar as Best Supporting Actor) and as Otto Frank, the heroine's father, in *The Diary of Anne Frank*. His undoubted talents as an actor were better appreciated on Broadway and later on television. He published an autobiography, *My Father and I*, in 1959.

Films include: 1915 Schlemiel (GER). '21 Orphans of the Storm. '25 Road to Yesterday. '27 The King of Kings. '28 The Blue Danube (GB: Honour Above All). '29 Show Boat. '32 The Blue Danube (GB). '34 Viva Villa; Cleopatra. '37 The Life of Emile Zola.

'38 Suez. '39 The Three Musketeers; Pack Up Your Troubles (GB). '40 The Shop Around the Corner. '59 The Diary of Anne Frank. '65 The Greatest Story Ever Told.

SCHLESINGER, John

(b. 1926). Director. Born: London, England

Schlesinger entered the film industry via the directing of short pieces for the BBC television series *Tonight* and *Monitor*. A prize at the Venice Film Festival for his documentary film *Terminus* established his reputation, which was further enhanced by his first feature *A Kind of Loving*, a bittersweet love story with a distinctive Northern working-class tang, which made a star of Alan Bates. The same flavour was present in his next movie, the inventive, outspoken comedy *Billy Liar*, which gave Julie Christie her first leading role. Schlesinger then emphasized her freewheeling, spirit-of-the-Sixties image in the widely praised *Darling* . . . . The director was soon riding the crest of a wave of public and critical popularity, although Thomas Hardy fans disliked his glamorous version of *Far From the Madding Crowd*. The Oscar-winning *Midnight Cowboy* occasionally lapsed into mawkishness, but there was no denying its powerful success in capturing the feel of New York low-life; and, while *Sunday, Bloody Sunday* was not flawless, it was one of the very few films to attempt a truthful, unsensational portrayal of a homosexual relationship. The wave finally broke with *Day of the Locust*: despite being his most challenging film and containing several fine performances, it was mangled by the critics and a disaster at the box-office. Schlesinger later recovered his commercial standing with *Marathon Man*, only to lose it again with *Yanks* and the disastrous British-backed flop *Honky Tonk Freeway*. It is a maxim in Hollywood that a director is only as good as his last picture; however, it would be somewhat unfair to apply it too strictly in any assessment of Schlesinger as a film-maker.

Films include: 1961 Terminus (doc). '62 A Kind of Loving. '63 Billy Liar. '65 Darling . . . '67 Far From the Madding Crowd. '69 Midnight Cowboy (USA). '71 Sunday, Bloody Sunday. '73 Visions of Eight *ep* The Longest (USA). '75 Day of the Locust (USA). '76 Marathon Man (USA). '79 Yanks (USA). '81 Honky Tonk Freeway.

SCHLÖNDORFF, Volker

(b. 1939). Director. Born: Wiesbaden, Germany

Schlöndorff was active before the New German Cinema emerged in the Seventies, but he has contributed as much to that movement as Fassbinder, Herzog or Wenders, and one of his films, *The Tin Drum*, is an undoubted masterpiece. After high school in Paris, he attended the French film school IDHEC and assisted Alain Resnais on *L'Année Dernière à Marienbad* (1961, *Last Year in Marienbad*), Louis Malle on *Zazie dans le Métro* (1960, *Zazie*) and Jean-Pierre Melville on several films. He worked in television reportage and returned to Germany for his feature debut *Young Törless*, which shared the International Critics Award at Cannes in 1966. Schlöndorff proceeded to alternate between commercial subjects, like the adultery drama *Die Moral der Ruth Halbfass*, and more serious, probing films, such as *Michael Kohlhaas*, about a 16th-century horse-trader's revolt against injustice, and *The Sudden Fortune of the Poor People of Kombach*, about poverty-stricken farmers. His reputation grew with *The Lost Honour of Katharina Blum*, the story of a woman who is forced into political consciousness when she becomes the victim of a smear campaign after befriending a terrorist. *The Tin Drum*, a remarkable version of Günter Grass' novel, is about a boy who decides to stop growing at the age of three and through whose eyes the audience witnesses the cataclysmic events of Central Europe in the Thirties and Forties. A beautifully made film – both surreal and naturalistic, rich in comedy and tragedy – it was an international hit and identified Schlöndorff as a major talent and won the 1979 Best Foreign Film Oscar. It was followed by *Circle of Deceit*, in which a German journalist suffers a crisis of conscience as he covers the bloody destruction of Beirut. Shot on real locations and using real incidents, this film doubles as a terrifying piece of reportage. Schlöndorff is married to the film director and actress Margarethe von Trotta.

Films include: 1966 Der junge Törless (GER-FR) (GB: Young Törless). '67 Mord und Totschlag (USA/GB: A Degree of Murder). '69 Michael Kohlhaas – der Rebell (GER) (GB: Michael Kohlhaas). '71 Der plötzliche Reichtum der armen Leute von Kombach (GB: The Sudden Fortune of the Poor People of Kombach). '72 Stroh Fever (USA: A Free Woman); Die Moral der Ruth Halbfass. '75 Die verlorene Ehre der Katharina Blum (GB: The Lost Honour of Katharina Blum). '76 Der Fangschuss (GER-FR). '78 Deutschland im Herbst (co-dir) (GB: Germany in Autumn). '79 Die Blechtrommel (GER-FR) (USA/GB: The Tin Drum). '81 Die Fälschung (GER-FR) (USA/GB: Circle of Deceit).

SCHNEER, Charles H.

(b. 1920). Producer. Born: Norfolk, Virginia, USA

Credit is due to Schneer for his belief in the appeal of myth and magic in the cinema. Long before 'sword and sorcery' films became the vogue in the Eighties, he and his collaborator, the model-animator and special-effects genius Ray Harryhausen, had brought to life the heroes, gods and beasts of ancient legend in a series of spectacular and popular fantasy films. The most famous of them was *Jason and the Argonauts*, with its angry stone giant, its Neptune, its scorpions, harpies and sword-wielding skeletons. On graduating from Columbia University, Schneer served as an assistant at Columbia Pictures in New York from 1939 to 1942. After the war he embarked as a producer with Universal, later returning to Columbia, and in 1956 became president of Morningside Productions where he began working with Harryhausen. In 1960 Schneer formed his British production company, American Films. His non-Harryhausen pictures include the story of rocket expert Werner von Braun, *I Aim at the Stars*, and the Tommy Steele musical *Half a Sixpence*.

Films include: 1957 Hell Cats of the Navy; Twenty Million Miles to Earth. '58 The Seventh Voyage of Sinbad. '59 Battle of the Coral Sea. '60 I Aim at the Stars (GER-USA); The Three Worlds of Gulliver (GB). '63 Jason and the Argonauts. '67 Half a Sixpence (GB-USA). '73 The Golden Voyage of Sinbad (GB). '77 Sinbad and the Eye of the Tiger. '81 Clash of the Titans (GB).

SCHNEIDER, Maria

(b. 1935). Actress. Born: Paris, France

There's an aura of fragile, amoral, self-destructive exoticism surrounding Maria Schneider, born of a subtle mix of her own background and the reputation which has dogged her since she had the dangerous honour of starring in *Last Tango in Paris*, Bertolucci's claustrophobic tale of a middle-aged American's degraded affair with a young Parisian. Schneider grew up with her Romanian gypsy mother, unaware of the identity of her father, actor Daniel Gélin, until she was 16. She appeared in several films, including one for Vadim, to little avail, until *Last Tango* catapulted her into the public eye. The resulting media attention focused on her apparently wild private life as much as her career. In 1975 she turned in a good performance opposite Jack Nicholson in Antonioni's fatalistic and wistful study of a man seeking a new life, *The Passenger*, but nothing else has tapped her potential.

Films include: 1972 Ultima Tango a Parigi (FR-IT) (GB: Last Tango in Paris); La Vieille Fille (FR-IT). '75 Professione: Reporter/The Passenger (IT-FR-SP); The Baby Sitter – Un Maledetto Pasticcio (IT-FR-GER) (GB: Wanted: Babysitter). '77 Lo Sono Mia (IT-GER). '78 Voyage au Jardin des Morts; Violanta (SWITZ). '79 La Dérobade (GB: The Life/The Confessions of a Streetwalker). '80 Mama Dracula (IT-BELG).

SCHNEIDER, Romy

(1938–1982). Actress. Born: Rosemarie Albach-Retty; Vienna, Austria

Born to one of Austria's leading theatrical families – her father was an actor at the Vienna Volk-Theatre, and her mother a famous star of stage and screen – Romy Schneider seemed destined for great things, but after an initial energetic burst, her career faltered. As a teenager, she had achieved stardom in *Sissi*, a romantic series about the Austro-Hungarian Royal Family. A friendship with Alain Delon introduced her to the French cinema, but, surprisingly, she decided to retire just as international success threatened in the late Fifties. She was, however, lured back to play well-received roles in *Boccaccio '70* and *The Trial*, which re-established her career. She won César Awards for *Une Histoire Simple* and *L'Important C'Est d'Aimer*, but many of her French films were not seen abroad, and some of her American work was mediocre. Much more might have been expected of her had she not died tragically of a heart-attack.

Films include: 1962 Boccaccio '70 (IT-FR); Le Procès (FR-IT-GER) (GB: The Trial). '63 The Cardinal (USA). '65 What's New, Pussycat? (USA-FR). '70 Les Choses de la Vie (FR-IT) (GB: Things of Life). '72 César et Rosalie (USA/GB: César and Rosalie); The Assassination of Trotsky (GB-FR-IT). '73 Ludwig (IT-FR-GER). '74 L'Important C'Est d'Aimer (FR-IT-GER) (USA/GB: The Main Thing Is to Love). '78 Une Histoire Simple.

SCHOEDSACK, Ernest B.

(b. 1893). Director. Born: Ernest Beaumont Schoedsack; Council Bluffs, Iowa, USA

Schoedsack worked as a cameraman at Keystone before going to the front as a cameraman for the US Signal Corps during World War I. He travelled on documentary assignments as a journalist after the war, and in 1926 met his old forces colleague Merian C. Cooper. The two were hired by Paramount to make a film about Abyssinian emperor Haile Selassie, which was followed by two more ethnic documentaries, *Grass*, shot in Persia, and *Chang*, shot in Siam. Schoedsack and Cooper then shot location scenes for *The Four Feathers*, and Schoedsack filmed *Rango* in Sumatra and co-directed *The Most Dangerous Game* for RKO in Hollywood. Producer and director then collaborated on *King Kong*, co-scripted by Schoedsack's wife Ruth Rose. *Kong* does not bear the stamp of a director and Schoedsack's main contribution may have been to harness together the various elements that made it the best of all adventure-fantasy films and to keep his cameras at a usually respectful distance. Many of the thrills, though, are due to him. It was the highlight of his career, but *Dr Cyclops* is a classic horror film and *Mighty Joe Young*, with the *King Kong* production team re-united, another atmospheric gorilla-in-the-city yarn. Before retiring Schoedsack and Rose worked on *This Is Cinerama*, the first modern wide-screen film, featuring its hair-raising rollercoaster ride.

Films: 1926 Grass (doc) (co-dir). '27 Chang (doc) (co-dir). '29 The Four Feathers (co-dir). '31 Rango. '32 The Most Dangerous Game (co-dir) (GB: The Hounds of Zaroff). '33 King Kong (co-dir); Blind Adventure; Son of Kong. '34 Long Lost Father. '35 The Last Days of Pompeii. '37 Trouble in Morocco; Outlaws of the Orient. '40 Dr Cyclops. '49 Mighty Joe Young. '52 This Is Cinerama (co-dir, uncredited).

SCHORM, Evald

(b. 1931). Director. Born: Prague, Czechoslovakia

Originally an opera-singer, Evald Schorm studied at FAMU, the Prague Film School, from 1957 to 1962, graduating in the same year as Věra Chytilová and Jiří Menzel. He made a number of highly respected documentaries (1962–66), probing deeply into the realities of Czechoslovakian life, particularly that of the working class, and was considered the philosopher of the Czech 'New Wave'. His first feature film, the anti-Stalinist *Everyday*

Courage, ran into official opposition at home, despite winning a prize, and it was awarded the Critics' Prize at the Pesaro Film Festival. *The Return of the Prodigal Son* attempted to analyse why the revolution had been betrayed by bureaucratic compromise, and *Five Girls Like a Millstone Round One's Neck* studied the actual state of contemporary class relations through a tale of five teenage girls. Schorm played the role of the one nonconformist guest in Jan Němec's *The Party and the Guests*. His last film, *The Seventh Day, the Eighth Night*, a study of fear in modern society, was banned. Rather than go into exile after the Russians invaded in 1968, Schorm gave up making films and turned to opera production.

Films include: 1964 Každý den odvahu/Odvahu pro vsední den (Everyday Courage). '65 Perličky na dně *ep* Dům radosti (GB: Pearls of the Deep *ep* The House of Happiness). '66 Návrat ztraceného syna (The Return of the Prodigal Son); O slavnosti a hostech (actor only) (GB: The Party and the Guests). '67 Pět holek na krku (Five Girls Like a Millstone Round One's Neck). '68 Pražské noci *ep* O chlebových střevíčcích (Prague Nights *ep* Supper of Bread). '69 Farářův konec (End of a Priest); Den sedmý, osmá noc (The Seventh Day, the Eighth Night).

SCHRADER, Paul

(b. 1946). Screenwriter/director. Born: Grand Rapids, Michigan, USA

The product of an ultra-strict Dutch Calvinist upbringing, Paul Schrader attended a Calvinist college, intending to become a minister. He did not see his first film until he was 17. He moved to New York, broke with his past and took an MA in cinema studies at the University of California at Los Angeles (UCLA). He then became a research fellow at the American Film Institute, edited the film magazine *Cinema* (1970–72) and published *Transcendental Style in Film: Ozu, Bresson, Dreyer* in 1972, an austere study of three art-film directors. But he also began to write scripts for Hollywood, alone or in collaboration, and sold the first in 1974. He wrote tough, violent films, of which *Taxi Driver* (directed by Martin

Far left: Maria Schneider as Jeanne, a study in lust, in Last Tango in Paris. *Left: Romy Schneider as the sensual empress in* Lugwig. *Below: Hanna Schygulla as the vicious lesbian in* The Bitter Tears of Petra von Kant

Scorsese) became the best-known. He turned director with *Blue Collar*, a scathing portrayal of corruption in a Detroit car factory. *Hardcore* plunged a Grand Rapids businessman (George C. Scott) into the Californian pornographic underworld in search of his missing teenage daughter. *American Gigolo* tried to apply Bressonian starkness to the study of a sexual professional (Richard Gere). With *Cat People*, not his own project, he attempted to update the 1942 minor classic. Schrader's violent, sexy, puritan films are the anomalous products of the clash between his own contradictory temperament and the commercial demands of Hollywood genres.

Films as screenwriter include: 1975 The Yakuza (co-sc). '76 Taxi Driver; Obsession. '79 Old Boyfriends (co-sc). '80 Raging Bull (co-sc). *Films as director:* '78 Blue Collar (+co-sc). '79 Hardcore (+sc) (GB: The Hardcore Life). '80 American Gigolo (+sc). '82 Cat People.

SCHROEDER, Barbet

(b. 1941). Producer/director/actor. Born: Teheran, Iran

Having graduated from the Sorbonne with a degree in philosophy Barbet Schroeder worked as a jazz tour organizer in Europe, a photo-journalist for six months in India and as a film critic for *Cahiers du Cinéma*. In 1963 he was Jean-Luc Godard's assistant on *Les Carabiniers* and then, through his connections at *Cahiers du Cinéma*, he was asked by the director Eric Rohmer to act in *La Boulangère de Monceau* – and he ended up also producing the film. Then in 1964 he formed his own production company, Les Films du Losange. He went on to produce the rest of Rohmer's films in his *contes moraux* series as well as films by Claude Chabrol, Godard and Jacques Rivette. He began directing in 1969 with the film *More*, and he has also made documentaries on New Guinea and General Amin.

Films as producer include: 1964 La Boulangère de Monceau (short); La Carrière de Suzanne (short). '65 Paris vu Par. . . . '67

La Collectioneuse (USA/GB: The Collector). '69 Ma Nuit Chez Maud (USA: My Night at Maud's; GB: My Night With Maud); More (dir. only). '70 Le Genou de Claire (GB: Claire's Knee). '71 Sing-Sing (doc) (dir. only); La Vallée (GB: The Valley – Obscured By Clouds) (dir); L'Amour, l'Après-Midi (USA: Chloe in the Afternoon; GB: Love in the Afternoon). '74 Out One: Spectre (co-prod); Céline et Julie Vont au Bateau (USA/GB: Céline and Julie Go Boating); General Idi Amin Dada (doc) (dir. only) (GB: General Amin). '76 Maîtresse (dir) (USA/GB: Mistress).

SCHÜFFTAN, Eugen

(1893–1977). Cinematographer. Born: Breslau, Germany (now Wrocław, Poland)

Having been a painter, architect and caricaturist, Eugen Schüfftan began working on animated films. In 1923 he invented the Schüfftan (or Shuftan) Process whereby reflected images of models or painted or photographed backgrounds could be combined in the camera with a live-action foreground. The process was used in Fritz Lang's *Metropolis* (1927), Hitchcock's *Blackmail* (1929) and, indeed, in hundreds of other films as it became an essential element in a cinematographer's bag of tricks. Becoming a lighting cameraman, Schüfftan developed a distinctive style in monochrome, with a strong, grey, subtly varying texture. He left Germany in 1933 to work in France with such directors as Max Ophuls and Marcel Carné. In 1940 he moved on to the United States, and thereafter he alternated between working in the USA and Europe, mainly France. He won an Academy Award for the black-and-white cinematography of Robert Rossen's *The Hustler*, capturing brilliantly the sordid atmosphere of poolrooms, the excitement of the game and the tense atmosphere of an unhappy love affair. He was known in the USA as Eugene Shuftan.

Films include: 1929 Menschen am Sonntag (GB: People on Sunday). '32 Die Herrin von Atlantis/L'Atlantide (co-photo). '35 La Tendre Ennemie (co-photo) (FR). '36 The Robber Symphony (GB-GER). '37 Drôle de Drame (co-photo) (FR) (USA: Bizarre, Bizarre). '38 Quai des Brumes (co-photo) (FR) (USA: Port of Shadows). '39 Sans Lendemain (FR). '44 It Happened Tomorrow (tech. dir. only) (USA). '59 La Tête Contre les Murs (FR) (GB: The Keepers); Les Yeux Sans Visage (FR-IT) (USA: The Horror Chamber of Dr Faustus; GB: Eyes Without a Face). '61 The Hustler (USA). '64 Lilith (USA). '65 Trois Chambres à Manhattan (FR) (USA: Three Rooms in Manhattan).

SCHULBERG. B. P.

(1892–1957). Producer/writer. Born: Benjamin Percival Schulberg; Bridgeport, Connecticut, USA

By the end of the Twenties, B. P. Schulberg was an immensely powerful man – his name appeared on the main title of every Paramount film produced in Hollywood. He began his career as a reporter in New York, then became assistant editor on a film paper and started writing scripts. By the time he went to Paramount in 1925 he had worked as a screenwriter

and publicity agent and formed the production company that made the film *Shadows* (1921). He also contracted Clara Bow and made her famous as the 'It' girl through his clever publicity methods. Within three years he was made head of Paramount's West Coast studios and vice-president in charge of production. He was a man in the Thalberg mould, a creative producer who was much loved, but he fell foul of cutthroat studio politics of the Thirties and was ousted from power. In 1932 he became an independent producer, and he retired in 1945. His son is the writer Budd Schulberg.

Films include: 1921 Stranger Than Fiction. '22 The Infidel. '23 The Lonely Road; The Virginian. '24 The Breath of Scandal; Black Oxen. '26 Mantrap; Dancing Mothers. '29 Abie's Irish Rose. '35 Crime and Punishment. '37 The Great Gambini.

SCHULBERG, Budd

(b. 1914). Novelist/screenwriter. Born: New York City, USA

Brought up in Hollywood, the son of producer B. P. Schulberg, one-time production chief of Paramount, Budd Schulberg was educated at Dartmouth College in faraway New England. He returned as a scriptwriter in the late Thirties but a disastrous collaboration with F. Scott Fitzgerald on *Winter Carnival*, set in his *alma mater*, did not help his career, though it provided material years later for his novel *The Disenchanted* (1950). An earlier novel, *What Makes Sammy Run?*, published in 1941, shocked Hollywood with its behind-the-scenes portrait of a power-hungry Jewish producer, arguably drawn with anti-semitic overtones. Schulberg served with the navy and the OSS during the war. Afterwards he turned against the communist associations of his youth and testified before HUAC, naming names of former left-wing colleagues. By then he lived on a Pennsylvania farm, writing novels and stories, two of which were later filmed. He collaborated with director Elia Kazan, who had also talked to HUAC, to make *On the Waterfront*, widely seen as a justification for informing as well as an attack on corrupt unions. They both won Oscars for their contributions and Schulberg returned to screenwriting for a few years, working with Kazan on *A Face in the Crowd* and Nicholas Ray on *Wind Across the Everglades*. In 1982 he published *Moving Pictures: Memories of a Hollywood Prince.*

Films include: 1937 A Star Is Born (add. dial. only). '38 Little Orphan Annie. '39 Winter Carnival. '41 Weekend for Three (story basis only). '43 City Without Men. '54 On the Waterfront. '56 The Harder They Fall (novel basis only). '57 A Face in the Crowd (from own story). '58 Wind Across the Everglades.

SCHÜNZEL, Reinhold

(1888–1954). Actor/director. Born: Hamburg, Germany

Not a few of the movie people who fled the Hitler regime in the Thirties ended up in Hollywood, as often as not

playing stereotyped Nazis. Schünzel had a long and respected career in Germany, which included acting roles in *The Threepenny Opera* and Lubitsch's *Madame DuBarry*. As a director, he was much influenced by Lubitsch, most obviously in *Amphitryon*, a saucy mythological frolic which had Jupiter descending on a contemporary war-widow. In 1938 he emigrated to America, and, though he directed a few films there, including *The Ice Follies of 1939*, he made a greater impact in several minor but compelling acting roles, usually playing Nazis in anti-Nazi dramas like *The Hitler Gang.*

Films include: 1919 Madame Dubarry (USA: Passion); Maria Magdalena (+dir); Liebe im Ring (dir. only). '21 Lady Hamilton; Luise Millerin. '25 Der Hahn im Korb. '31 Die Dreigroschenoper (GER-USA) (USA: The Threepenny Opera). '32 Unheimliche Geschichten; Das Schöne Abenteuer (dir. only). '33 Viktor und Viktoria (dir. only); Saison in Kairo (dir. only). '35 Amphitryon (dir. only). '37 Land der Liebe (dir. only). '38 Rich Man, Poor Girl (dir. only) (USA). '39 The Ice Follies of 1939 (dir. only) (USA); Balalaika (dir. only) (USA). '41 New Wine (dir. only) (USA) (GB: The Great Awakening). '43 Hangmen Also Die! (USA); Hostages (USA). '44 The Hitler Gang (USA); The Man in Half Moon Street (USA). '46 Dragonwyck (USA); Notorious (USA). '48 Berlin Express (USA).

SCHYGULLA, Hanna

(b. 1943). Actress. Born: Katowice, Poland

Born in Poland but brought up in Munich, Germany, Hanna Schygulla has gradually come to the fore with a series of telling performances in films directed by Rainer Werner Fassbinder (with whom she went to drama school), most notably in the lead of *The Marriage of Maria Braun*. This film brilliantly utilized her strong, many-sided personality, giving her the chance to be by turns sensual, romantic, distressed, pragmatic and tough-minded; its story of a woman's material and emotional survival in post-war Germany can be seen as a metaphor for her country's remarkable post-war recovery. More important, however, *The Marriage of Maria Braun* is one of the very few truly empathic studies of essentially female emotional attitudes and experiences by a male director. Her subsequent roles, in particular in *Lili Marleen*, have tended to promote her as a latter-day Dietrich, focusing on her undeniable attractiveness in fishnet stockings to the exclusion of all else, and it remains to be seen whether she can escape this stereotype.

Films include: 1968 Der Bräutigam, die Komödiantin und der Zuhälter (GB: The Bridegroom, the Comedian and the Pimp). '69 Liebe ist kälter als der Tod (GB: Love Is Colder Than Death). '71 Rio das Mortes; Warnung vor einer heiligen Nutte; Mathias Kneissl. '72 Die bitteren Tränen der Petra von Kant (GB: The Bitter Tears of Petra von Kant). '74 Fontane Effi Briest (GB: Effi Briest). '79 Die Ehe der Maria Braun (GB: The Marriage of Maria Braun); Die dritte Generation (GB: The Third Generation). '80 Berlin – Alexanderplatz (GER-IT). '81 Lili Marleen; Die Fälschung (GER-FR) (GB: Circle of Deceit). '82 La Nuit de Varennes (FR-IT); Antonieta (FR-MEX-SP).

SCOFIELD, Paul

(b. 1922). Actor. Born: Hurstpierpoint, Sussex, England

Paul Scofield is all you might expect of The Great British Actor – tall, dignified, possessed of a noble bearing, with craggy features and a perfectly modulated voice. Above all, he is more at home on the stage than in front of the cameras. Educated at Varndean School for Boys, Scofield had his first role as a walk-on at Brighton's Theatre Royal in 1936. Since then he has gone on to greater things, the Stratford-on-Avon Shakespeare Company and National Theatre among others. He is notoriously choosy about his film work – 'It's not that I don't like films, it's that I like the theatre better' – and his movies have by and large been disappointing. *A Man for All Seasons*, though it won him an Academy Award, is an uninspired screen version very much tied to its theatrical origins. So was *King Lear*. More satisfactory, perhaps, is *The Train*, in which Scofield plays an art-loving Nazi trying to prevent Resistance man Burt Lancaster from liberating a carriage-load of stolen treasures. A little easier on television, Scofield has appeared in several adaptations, of Noel Coward and Graham Greene stories. He was awarded the CBE in 1956.

Films include: 1955 That Lady. '58 Carve Her Name With Pride. '64 The Train (USA-FR-IT). '68 A Man for All Seasons; Tell Me Lies. '70 King Lear; Bartleby. '72 Scorpio (USA). '73 A Delicate Balance.

SCOLA, Ettore

(b. 1931). Director/screenwriter. Born: Trevico, Italy

In the late Forties, Scola worked as a journalist and illustrator for various humorous and satirical magazines. Around this time he also began working on film scripts, and had obtained extensive scriptwriting experience by the time he made his debut as a director in 1964 with *Si Permette Parliamo di Donne*. Scola's scripts for other directors as well as his own films tend to focus sympathetically on those mistreated, humiliated or neglected by society. Especially notable among his films are *Brutti Sporchi e Cattivi*, a gutsy comedy set in a shanty town on the outskirts of Rome, which won an award for Best Direction at the 1976 Cannes Film Festival, and *A Special Day*, which won a Special Jury prize at Cannes the following year.

Films include: 1954 Due Notti con Cleopatra (sc) (USA/GB: Two Nights With Cleopatra). '55 Lo Scapolo (sc). '63 La Visita (sc). '64 Si Permettete Parliamo di Donne. '65 La Congiuntura; Made in Italy (sc). '69 Il Commissario Pepe. '72 La Più Bella Serata della Mia Vita. '76 Brutti Sporchi e Cattivi. '77 Una Giornata Particolare (IT-CAN) (GB: A Special Day). '82 La Nuit de Varennes (FR-IT).

SCORSESE, Martin

(b. 1942). Director. Born: Flushing, Long Island, New York, USA

An asthmatic, sickly child, Scorsese spent much of his youth watching movies in New York's Little Italy. Later the lure of making movies led him to give up an early ambition to be a priest and to study film at New York University. He graduated in 1966 but stayed on as a teacher in the film department until 1970. During this period he directed his first feature, *Who's That Knocking at My Door?* His first major directorial opportunity, however, came courtesy of producer Roger Corman, who hired him to direct *Boxcar Bertha*. The film was sufficiently successful for Scorsese to obtain backing for a much more personal film, born of his own Italian-American background, *Mean Streets*, a disquieting and electric movie about a young collector for the Mafia who represses his conflicting feelings concerning his Mafia elders, his religion, his girl and his buddies. This film and *Taxi Driver* (which made stars of Harvey Keitel and Robert De Niro), both brilliant and brutal views of modern city life, established Scorsese as one of America's leading directors. The feeling and empathy for music and musicians that was the best feature of Scorsese's next film, *New York, New York*, found full expression in his documentary of The Band's last concert, *The Last Waltz*; he then returned to the emotional front-line of *Mean Streets* and *Taxi Driver* with *Raging Bull*, a compelling biography of the boxer Jake LaMotta.

Films include: 1964 What's a Nice Girl Like You Doing in a Place Like This? (short). '68 Who's That Knocking at My Door? '70 Woodstock (doc) (ass. dir;+sup. ed). '72 Boxcar Bertha (+act). '73 Mean Streets (+act). '74 Italianamerican (doc) (+appearance as himself); Alice Doesn't Live Here Anymore. '76 Taxi Driver (+act). '77 New York, New York. '78 The Last Waltz (doc) (+appearance as himself). '80 Raging Bull (+act). '82 King of Comedy.

SCOTT, George C.

(b. 1927). Actor. Born: George Campbell Scott; Wise, Virginia, USA

Scott is apparently a prickly and explosive man and difficult to work with, but he has shown none of the lust for glory of *Patton*, refusing to accept the Best Actor Oscar for his gargantuan performance as the controversial general. He has refused an Emmy Award, too, and generally shown such contempt for showbusiness that it is sometimes difficult to think of him as a star. There is no disputing, however, that he is one of the most powerful actors of his generation, General Patton being just one in a gallery of supreme character portrayals that include the sardonic prosecuting attorney in *Anatomy of a Murder*, the contemptuous promoter in *The Hustler*, the long-suffering, philandering General 'Buck' Turgidson in *Dr Strangelove*, Rochester in *Jane Eyre* and the devout father in *Hardcore*. He is a master of comedy (*The Yellow Rolls Royce* and *Movie, Movie*), dwarfs spectacle films with his aggressive attack (*Patton* and *The Hindenburg*), and, despite the broken nose, rasping voice and air of a man about to burst into an uncontrollable rage, is frequently warm-hearted and sympathetic. After four years in the marines, he attended the University of Missouri School of Journalism but switched to English and Drama and began to act. Then came a slow apprenticeship in stock before he made it to Broadway and had a film debut in *The Hanging Tree*. He has also directed two movies – *Rage* and *The Savage Is Loose* – but neither was successful. Scott has married and divorced actress Colleen Dewhurst twice and is currently married to Trish Van Devere who has appeared with him in several films.

Films include: 1959 The Hanging Tree; Anatomy of a Murder. '64 The Yellow Rolls Royce (GB); Dr Strangelove, or How I Learned to Stop Worrying and Love the Bomb (GB). '70 Patton. '71 Jane Eyre (GB); The Last Run. '72 Rage (+dir). '74 The Savage Is Loose (+prod; +dir). '75 The Hindenburg. '77 Islands in the Stream. '79 Hardcore. '80 The Changeling (CAN).

SCOTT, Lizabeth

(b. 1922). Actress. Born: Emma Matzo; Scranton, Pennsylvania, USA

'What a fall guy I am – thinking just because you're good to look at, you'd be good all the way through' quoth Burt Lancaster in *I Walk Alone*, summing up Lizabeth Scott at her best: turning her fragile, candid looks to suitably treacherous end as a double-dealing blonde torch singer. Scott's career was fairly short, and, though she played a wide range of characters, she is best remembered for her incarnations of a tough good-time girl, such as the worthless, hard-drinking corrupter of honest men in *Bad for Each Other*. Despite touring for nine months with *Hellzapoppin'* shortly after leaving the Alvienne School of Drama in Manhattan, Scott had a long time to wait for her break into movies and several false starts, notably a spell spent working as Tallulah Bankhead's stand-in. Eventually modelling work with *Harper's Bazaar* brought her to the notice of Hal Wallis, but ('My personal life . . . is the most important thing') she went into semi-retirement in 1957.

Films include: **1945** You Came Along. **'47** Desert Fury; Dead Reckoning; I Walk Alone. **'48** Pitfall. **'49** Easy Living; Paid in Full. **'50** Dark City; The Company She Keeps. **'51** Two of a Kind. **'53** Bad for Each Other. **'72** Pulp.

SCOTT, Randolph

(b. 1903). Actor. Born: George Randolph Scott; Orange County, Virginia, USA

It is unlikely that the code of decency operated by the Randolph Scott hero ever existed in the real West – perhaps that's why he was always a loner. The character he created in the Ranown Cycle – seven excellent, low-budget Westerns directed by Budd Boetticher, five of them produced by Harry Joe Brown with Scott as associate producer – was a grim, resolute solitary hardened by experience, but still honest, chivalrous and handsome (though weatherbeaten). And his course through those highly moral, very successful films – from *Seven Men From Now* to *Comanche Station* – helped make him a very rich man (his personal wealth in 1970 was estimated at over $35 million). There were other highlights in his long, distinguished career: the Mamoulian musical *High, Wide and Handsome*, earlier Westerns like *Jesse James* and *Abilene Town*, a series of six more directed by André De Toth that preceded the Ranown Cycle, and his last valedictory outing, *Ride the High Country*, in which he and Joel McCrea were weary old Westerners riding to a final showdown. As a young man Scott studied engineering at the University of North California but opted for an acting career and the Pasadena Playhouse. He entered films in Allan Dwan's *The Far Call* and acted mostly

in romances and musicals at Paramount in the Thirties before the Western genre finally claimed him and elevated him to one of its noblest representatives.

Films include: **1929** The Far Call. **'33** The Cocktail Hour. **'34** Lone Cowboy. **'35** Roberta. **'36** The Last of the Mohicans. **'37** High, Wide and Handsome. **'39** Susannah of the Mounties; Jesse James. **'40** My Favourite Wife. **'41** Belle Starr; Western Union. **'46** Abilene Town. **'56** Seven Men From Now. **'57** The Tall T; Decision at Sundown. **'58** Buchanan Rides Alone. **'59** Ride Lonesome; Westbound. **'60** Comanche Station. **'62** Ride the High Country (GB: Guns in the Afternoon).

SCOTT, Ridley

(b. 1939). Director. Born: South Shields, Co. Durham, England

A former student at the Royal College of Art and the RCA Film School, Scott joined BBC Television as a set designer in the mid-Sixties. He quickly graduated to directing, working on episodes of such series as *Z Cars* and *The Informer*. He left the BBC in 1967 and spent the next ten years as a freelance director making hundreds of commercials. It took him five years to set up his first film, *The Duellists*, distinguished by superb colour photography, the film was a highly accomplished debut, deservedly winning a Special Jury Prize at Cannes. An evident love of special effects, combined with a craftsmanlike determination to tell a good story with well-drawn characters, have been the main features of Scott's subsequent movies, notably *Alien*.

Films include: **1977** The Duellists. **'79** Alien. **'82** Blade Runner.

SCOTT, Zachary

(1914–1965). Actor. Born: Austin, Texas, USA

Scott obtained his first professional acting experience in repertory in England in his late teens. On his return to the USA he worked extensively in stock and on Broadway, then, in 1943, was signed up by Warner Brothers, who were on the look-out for good-looking leading men to replace the many stars that had joined the armed forces. A superficial coldness of demeanour as an actor made him ideal casting as a handsome but ruthless character – a gentleman of the gutter or lecherous heel. His best role of this kind came as Monte Beragon in *Mildred Pierce*, though he indicated his versatility with a sympathetic performance in Jean Renoir's *The Southerner*. His film career began to decline in the Fifties and his films, with the exception of Luis Buñuel's *The Young One*, gave him little opportunity to shine.

Films include: **1943** The Mask of Dimitrios. **'45** Mildred Pierce; The Southerner. **'46** Her Kind of Man. **'47** Cass Timberlane. **'49** Flamingo Road. **'50** Born to Be Bad. **'51** Let's Make It Legal. **'53** Appointment in Honduras. **'60** The Young One/La Joven (USA-MEX) (GB: Island of Shame).

SEATON, George

(1911–1979). Director/scriptwriter/ producer. Born: South Bend, Indiana, USA

After spells of writing for radio and acting, George Seaton became the voice of the Lone Ranger in a radio series. MGM noticed him and brought him to Hollywood where he worked on many scripts including the Marx Brothers' *A Day at the Races*. In 1945 he turned to directing and seven years later he began his fruitful partnership with the producer William Perlberg, a collaboration that was particularly productive over the next ten years. Then in 1970 Seaton wrote and directed *Airport* for Universal, a film that was to produce the studio's biggest

gross until *Jaws* in 1975. Seaton was also a tireless worker for the Hollywood film community – he served three terms as President of the Academy of Motion Picture Arts and Sciences and was President of the Screenwriters' Guild in addition to winning the Jean Hersholt Humanitarian Award.

Films include: **1937** A Day at the Races (co-sc. only). **'40** Doctor Takes a Wife (sc. only). **'43** The Song of Bernadette (sc. only). **'45** Diamond Horseshoe (dir; +sc). **'51** Rhubarb (co-prod. only). **'54** The Bridges at Toko-Ri (co-prod. only). **'56** The Proud and the Profane (dir; +sc). **'57** The Tin Star (co-prod. only). **'64** 36 Hours (+co-prod; +co-sc). **'70** Airport (dir; +sc).

SEBERG, Jean

(1938–1979). Actress. Born: Marshalltown, Iowa, USA

In 1979 Jean Seberg was found dead in her car, where she had lain for a week before anyone had missed her. This lonely death is in complete contrast to her initial introduction to the public when, at 17, her beautiful features and submissive manner were thrust into the limelight by Otto Preminger, who chose her to star in his much publicized film *Saint Joan*. He then starred her in *Bonjour Tristesse*, as a bored French teenager seducing an older man. Despite their notoriety neither of these films was particularly successful. Seberg then left America for France and played Patricia in *Breathless*, her best role. She became involved in political issues but tended to be used by opportunists, and at the same time her life became increasingly turbulent and tragic. In 1970 she suffered a miscarriage – an emotional shock from which she would never recover.

Films include: **1957** Saint Joan (GB). **'58** Bonjour Tristesse. **'59** The Mouse That Roared (GB). **'60** A Bout de Souffle (FR) (USA/GB: Breathless). **'61** La Récréation (FR) (GB: Playtime). **'64** Lilith. **'66** A Fine Madness. **'69** Pendulum; Paint Your Wagon. **'70** Airport. **'75** Le Chat et la Souris (FR) (USA: Cat and Mouse; GB: Seven Suspects for Murder).

SEGAL, George

(b. 1934). Actor. Born: Great Neck, Long Island, New York, USA

From Columbia University, Segal played jazz, acted and did odd jobs before being conscripted into the army. In 1957 he made his New York stage debut and, following nightclub work, appeared with the original cast of the hit revue *The Premise*. A film part in *The Young Doctors* began his Hollywood career. He has since enjoyed regular starring parts, often in marital comedies to which he brings an air of geniality or frustration. His best roles include his wily prison camp internee in *King Rat*, the young biology professor in *Who's Afraid of Virginia Woolf?* (for which he was nominated for an Oscar), and the brash executive abroad who falls in love with an Englishwoman (Glenda Jackson) in *A Touch of Class*. Pleasant-looking with sandy brown hair, Segal has emerged as a likeable, popular player of neurotic middle-class guys, but he has not sought relentlessly for challenging parts.

Films include: 1961 The Young Doctors. '62 The Longest Day. '64 Invitation to a Gunfighter. '65 Ship of Fools; King Rat. '66 Who's Afraid of Virginia Woolf?; The Quiller Memorandum (USA-GB). '67 The St Valentine's Day Massacre. '68 No Way to Treat a Lady. '70 Loving; The Owl and the Pussycat; Where's Poppa? '73 Blume in Love; A Touch of Class (GB). '74 California Split. '75 The Black Bird. '77 Fun With Dick and Jane. '79 Lost and Found. '80 The Last Married Couple in America. '81 Carbon Copy.

SEITZ, George B.

(1888–1944). Director. Born: George Brackett Seitz; Boston, Massachusetts, USA

Seitz came from a well-to-do Quaker family, and via magazine illustration, stock, and a little playwriting, reached Pathé as a scriptwriter in 1913. He wrote and acted in Pearl White serials, and directed her in *The Fatal Ring* and others. Until the mid-Twenties Seitz was Hollywood's top serial director. He also made countless action features, and reached his peak in the Thirties, working for MGM on what were nominally B movies, but they had such superb pace and polish that they competed with the studio's major projects. Seitz worked at high speed, turning out half-a-dozen pictures a year and revelling in the pressures. He made most of the Andy Hardy films, and kept them amazingly watchable, but his thrillers were the real Seitz. Almost fifty years on, movies like *Kind Lady* (nice Aline MacMahon menaced by murderous Basil Rathbone) still live vividly in the memory.

Films include: 1917 The Fatal Ring (+act). '19 Bound and Gagged (serial) (+act). '20 Velvet Fingers (serial) (+act); Rogues and Romance (+act). '26 Desert Gold. '30 Murder on the Roof. '32 Docks of San Francisco; The Widow in Scarlet. '35 Times Square Lady; Kind Lady. '37 Under Cover of Night. '38 Judge Hardy's Children; Love Finds Andy Hardy. '42 A Yank on the Burma Road (GB: China Caravan).

SEITZ, John F.

(1893–1979). Cinematographer. Born: Chicago, Illinois, USA

The younger brother of George B., John Seitz entered films in 1909 as a laboratory technician, and was a director of photography by the time he was 20. In 1920 Seitz joined Rex Ingram at Metro, and a famous partnership began. Seitz photographed all Ingram's films from *Shore Acres* to *The Magician* in 1926. Seitz was noted for the intensity of his low-key lighting, and for his inventiveness. It was Seitz who perfected the matte shot (on Ingram's *Trifling Women*) and patented it later, and who was one of the very few photographers ever to receive credit in studio advertising. He marked time in the Thirties, but afterwards had a whole new, and dazzling, career at Paramount, where he worked on the best films of Preston Sturges and on Billy Wilder's masterpieces. The threatening shadows of *Double Indemnity* are due to Seitz; so are the sparkle of *The Miracle of Morgan's Creek* and the lowering atmospherics of *Sunset Boulevard*.

Films include: 1918 Beauty and the Rogue. '20 Shore Acres. '21 The Four Horsemen of the Apocalypse. '22 The Prisoner of Zenda; Trifling Women. '23 Scaramouche. '26 The Magician. '36 Poor Little Rich Girl. '39 The Adventures of Huckleberry Finn. '41 Sullivan's Travels. '43 The Miracle of Morgan's Creek. '44 Double Indemnity. '45 The Lost Weekend. '50 Sunset Boulevard. '60 Guns of the Timberland.

SELIG, William N.

(1864–1948). Pioneer producer. Born: Chicago, Illinois, USA

William Selig (he was not a Colonel, though always addressed as such) ran a minstrel show before the Edison Kinetoscope caught his fancy one day in 1895. Selig developed a camera, and the Selig Polyscope projector, and in 1896 was making movies in a loft in Chicago. Selig prospered. Surviving a lawsuit for infringement of patents, he joined the Motion Picture Patents combine as a licensed operator. He sent a company under director Francis Boggs on a tour of America, filming as they went, and on a vacant lot in Los Angeles this company made *The Power of the Sultan* (1907), the first story film ever made in California. Two years later Selig set up studio in Los Angeles. He scored a tremendous hit with *Hunting Big Game in Africa* (1909) purporting to show President Roosevelt shooting a lion in Africa. In fact Roosevelt had gone back on a promise to Selig that a cameraman could accompany him, and Selig faked the whole thing in his Chicago studio. Selig was among the first to produce features in America (*The Spoilers* was a huge success in 1914), and the company went on until in 1918 it was squeezed out by bigger operators. Selig was famous for animal pictures, and his Zoo was almost as well known as his studios. He made quite a few human stars, too, notably Kathlyn Williams and Tom Mix.

Films include: 1905 Trapped by Bloodhounds or Lynching. '07 The Count of Monte Cristo at Cripplecreek. '08 Dr Jekyll and Mr Hyde. '09 Hunting Big Game in Africa. '10 Ranch Life in the Great Southwest; Davy Crockett; The Wizard of Oz. '11 Lost in the Jungle. '13 The Adventures of Kathlyn (serial). '16 The Garden of Allah. '21 The Hunger of the Blood.

SELLARS, Elizabeth

(b. 1923). Actress. Born: Glasgow, Scotland

Abandoning early ambitions to become a barrister (she had enrolled at Lincoln's Inn), Sellars went to RADA, repertory, and the Bristol Old Vic. In the West End her great success was as the housemaster's wife in *Tea and Sympathy*. She appeared in a number of British films between 1948 and her marriage in 1960, and occasionally thereafter, but was highly critical of the kind of parts she was usually offered. 'We're expected to sink back into the background and look nice,' she said. But one or two films did give her more of a chance than that. In *The Shiralee* she was a faithless and vicious wife, and in *The Hireling* an alcoholic mother. She continues to act in television.

Films include: 1952 The Gentle Gunman. '54 The Barefoot Contessa (USA-IT); Desiree (USA). '56 The Last Man to Hang? '57 The Shiralee; The Man in the Sky. '60 The Day They Robbed the Bank of England. '63 55 Days at Peking (USA). '67 The Mummy's Shroud. '73 The Hireling.

SELLERS, Peter

(1925–1980). Actor. Born: Southsea, Hampshire, England

Peter Sellers had an extraordinary talent for mimicry and a patchy, uneven film career. Despite the success of the Pink Panther films (and other international vehicles) which came in a rush at the end of his career, they all pale beside the original 1963 film and the cheap but bright British comedies that made him a legendary comedian in the late Fifties. The best of these is *I'm All Right Jack*, in which he played the pompous, pathetic shop-steward Fred Kite – one of the great British character studies. There

have been three other strokes of genius, covering seven characters: the East End crook Pearly Gates and his French-hairdresser alter ego in *The Wrong Arm of the Law*; the whining Quilty and the suburban intellectual in Kubrick's *Lolita*; and the President, the British officer and the crippled, maniacal ex-Nazi in *Dr Strangelove*, again for Kubrick. But his randy Welsh librarian made to look ridiculous by the sexiness of Mai Zetterling in *Only Two Can Play* must not be forgotten either. Sellers was born into a theatrical family and began his career as a comic and impressionist with ENSA. His array of funny voices led him to radio and the famous comedy series, *The Goon Show*. He made his film debut in *Penny Points to Paradise* in 1951, was one of the gang in *The Ladykillers*, and from then on worked tirelessly, usually in films which enabled him to adopt different characterizations. A perfectionist and a moody and difficult man, he was married four times (actresses Britt Ekland and Lynne Frederick were his second and fourth wives). Sellers was nominated for Oscars for *Dr Strangelove* and his last film *Being There*. He died of a heart attack.

Films include: 1951 Penny Points to Paradise. '55 The Ladykillers. '57 The Smallest Show on Earth. '59 I'm All Right Jack. '60 Two Way Stretch; The Millionairess. '61 Mr Topaze (+dir) (USA: I Like Money); Only Two Can Play. '62 Lolita (USA-GB). '63 The Wrong Arm of the Law; The Pink Panther (USA). '64 Dr Strangelove, or How I Learned to Stop Worrying and Love the Bomb; The World of Henry Orient (USA); A Shot in the Dark (USA-GB). '65 What's New, Pussycat? (USA-FR). '66 The Wrong Box; Caccia alla volpe (IT-GB-USA) (USA/GB: After the Fox). '67 Casino Royale. '68 I Love You, Alice B. Toklas (USA). '70 Hoffman; There's a Girl in My Soup. '75 The Return of the Pink Panther. '79 The Prisoner of Zenda (USA); Being There (USA). '82 Trail of the Pink Panther.

SELZNICK, David O.

(1902–1965). Producer. Born: Pittsburgh, Pennsylvania, USA

He was born plain David, adopting the O for euphony, or vanity, in his mogul days. The son of pioneer producer Lewis J. Selznick, David worked for his

Above, far left: George Segal as one half of The Last Married Couple in America. *Above left: Elizabeth Sellars as the faithless wife in* Hunted *(1952). Above: Peter Sellers as Inspector Clouseau in* A Shot in the Dark. *Below: the tragic silent comic Larry Semon*

father in sales and promotion until Lewis' empire collapsed in 1923. Three years later he took a job in the story department of MGM, and rose to associate producer. Often at logger-heads with Louis Mayer, Selznick moved to Paramount, and in 1931 to RKO. Here his abilities had scope. He found new talents like Cukor and Hepburn, and produced films of the quality of *What Price Hollywood?* and *King Kong.* In 1933 Mayer (by now his father-in-law) called him back. For three years he had his own unit at MGM, making *David Copperfield, Anna Karenina* and *A Tale of Two Cities.* In 1936 Selznick set up his own company. He turned out masterpieces like *A Star Is Born* and *Nothing Sacred,* and became engrossed in the long drama of producing *Gone With the Wind.* Selznick's company continued with fair success through the Forties, until in 1948, $12 million in debt, he was forced to close down, and did little thereafter. Selznick was the first genuinely important independent

producer of the sound period. His stamp was on every one of his films, and he pursued his passion for film-making into every detail of his studio's operation. His unending stream of memos (they were published, and give a superb insight into the man) is easy to deride, but reveals a shrewdness, a breadth of technical knowledge, and a knowledge of human nature that no other producer could match. There were weaknesses. He had little literary judgement: rightly seeing *Gone With the Wind* and *Rebecca* as potential moneymakers, he also thought them good books. He had scant patience with men who had their own ideas: there was an uneasy relationship with Hitchcock, a split with King Vidor, and the firing of Huston and Cukor. But perhaps the sheer drive and total love for the medium out-weigh all this. Here was a man who exemplified the glories, as well as the secret flaws, of Hollywood. Selznick's first wife was Irene, the daughter of Louis B. Mayer; his second was Jennifer Jones, the actress to whose career he devoted so much of his care in his later days.

Films include: 1924 Roulette. **'32** What Price Hollywood?; A Bill of Divorcement. **'33** Topaze; Dinner at Eight; King Kong (exec. prod.). **'34** Manhattan Melodrama. **'35** David Copperfield; Anna Karenina; A Tale of Two Cities. **'37** A Star Is Born; Nothing Sacred. **'39** Intermezzo: a Love Story (GB: Escape to Happiness); Gone With the Wind (+uncredited sc; +uncredited dir). **'40** Rebecca. **'44** Since You Went Away. **'45** Spellbound. **'46** Duel in the Sun (+uncredited dir). **'57** A Farewell to Arms (co-prod. only).

SELZNICK, Myron

(1898–1944). Agent/producer. Born: Pittsburgh, Pennsylvania, USA

Myron Selznick, the elder brother of producer David O. Selznick, was groomed by his father Lewis to take over the production side of the Lewis J. Selznick Enterprises. With the collapse of the Selznick Organization, Myron found it impossible to obtain similar work with another studio and instead formed an agency of star talent. His pugnacity and skill at playing studio off against studio en-

sured the best deals for his clients – which at one time included Mary Astor, Katharine Hepburn, Carole Lombard, Myrna Loy, Ginger Rogers, Fred Astaire, George Raft, Gary Cooper, Henry Fonda, Charles Laughton and Fredric March. At his peak in the Thirties he was powerful enough to force studios to accept 'packages' of stars, supporting actors, directors and screenwriters. Unfortunately he fell victim to alcoholism, which ruined his career and ultimately caused his death at the age of 45.

SEMON, Larry

(1889–1928). Actor/director/screenwriter. Born: Lawrence Semon; West Point, Missouri, USA

His father was Zera the Great, vaudeville magician and acrobat, and Larry Semon, though he worked for a time as a newspaper cartoonist, was drawn into showbiz as a writer-director of comedy shorts for Vitagraph. By the end of 1917 he was acting as well – a white-faced clown who exaggerated his ugliness and was perpetually in a whirl of pratfalls, exploding props and chases. He made some classic shorts, such as *The Sawmill,* but he fell out with Vitagraph over budgets and had to go independent. Believing that a succession of gags was more important than developing a comic character, he was unable to make the transition to features successfully, despite his keenness on pet projects such as *The Wizard of Oz,* in which he played the Straw Man to Oliver Hardy's Tin Man. His reputation declined with such features as *The Perfect Clown* (which he did not direct himself) and *Spuds.* He tried serious acting in Josef von Sternberg's *Underworld,* but his career was virtually finished. Early in 1928 he went bankrupt and a few months later, following a nervous breakdown, he died of pneumonia. He had married two of his leading ladies, Lucille Carlisle and then Dorothy Dwan.

Films (shorts unless otherwise specified) include: 1916 The Man From Egypt (dir; +co-sc. only). **'17** Rough Toughs and Roof Tops. **'18** Babes and Boobs; Bathing Beauties and Big Boobs. **'19** Between the Acts. **'20** The Sportsman. **'22** The Sawmill. **'23** The Barnyard. **'24** Trouble Brewing (co-dir; +co-sc; +act); The Girl in the Limousine (feature) (dir; +actor only). **'25** The Wizard of Oz (feature) (co-dir; +co-sc; +act); The Perfect Clown (feature) (actor only). **'26** Stop, Look and Listen (feature) (dir; +co-sc; +act). **'27** Spuds; Underworld (actor only). **'28** A Simple Sap.

SEN, Mrinal

(b. 1923). Director. Born: East Bengal, India

Sen came from a middle-class family, moved to Calcutta at 17, and read physics. He became involved in left-wing politics, went on to journalism, and in the late Fifties to film-making. A prolific director, Sen has always tried to get away from the image, popular in the West, of a mystical, contemplative India. Instead, as a Marxist, he has concerned himself with poverty and the exploitation of

the poor, with the remnants of colonialism, with the threat of famine, and the clash between tradition and modernity. Sen's earlier work owed much to the French *nouvelle vague.* Later on he adopted an agit-prop style with echoes of Brecht, but his recent films have revealed a subtler handling of narrative linked with the ever-present political commitment.

Films include: 1956 Raat Bhore. **'59** Neel Akashar Neechey. **'60** Baishey Sravana. **'64** Pratinidhi. **'67** Matira Manisha. **'71** Ek Adhuri Kahani; Interview. **'72** Calcutta '71. **'74** Padatic. **'80** Ekdin Pratidin (GB: And Quiet Rolls the Dawn). **'83** Kharij.

SENNETT, Mack

(1880–1960). Director/producer/actor. Born: Michael Sinnott; Richmond, Quebec, Canada

When Mack Sennett was 17, his family moved to Connecticut, and Mack worked as a labourer before going to New York in 1902 to try his luck on the stage. Through burlesque, vaudeville and the chorus he reached the Biograph studios in 1908 and was engaged as an actor. From D.W. Griffith and cameraman Billy Bitzer Sennett learned rapidly, and two years later was directing comedy. He left in 1912 and, with two book-makers, Kessel and Bauman, formed the Keystone Company in Los Angeles. This was Sennett's peak period. Keystone's fast, zany action comedy became immensely popular. Sennett produced, often directed, and always edited. He was a master of timing, and his final cut ensured that the break-neck pace never flagged. He made the reputations of comedians like Roscoe (Fatty) Arbuckle, Mack Swain and Edgar Kennedy, and the actress Mabel Normand. Chaplin began at Keystone, too. The Keystone Kops were formed, and Sennett's anarchism took a further step towards the comedy of the absurd. He joined Ince and Griffith under the Triangle banner, and extended his range. The Bathing Beauties appeared, and Gloria Swanson made romantic comedies with Bobby Vernon. Independent from 1917, Sennett went gaily on until sound, but little new, save perhaps his discovery of Harry Langdon, came along in the Twenties. In the Thirties he was struggling. The old days of licensed lunacy in the streets of Los Angeles would not come back. He made several shorts with W.C. Fields for Paramount, and one with Keaton (the only time they worked together) for Educational, and retired, broke.

Films include: 1909 The Curtain Pole (actor). **'10** The Masher (actor). **'11** Comrades (dir; +actor); The Lonedale Operator (sc). **'13** Mabel's Dramatic Career (co-dir; +act). **'14** Kid Auto Races at Venice (prod); Between Showers (prod); Mabel at the Wheel (prod; +act); The Face on the Bar-Room Floor; Tillie's Punctured Romance (feature) (prod; +dir) **'17** Teddy at the Throttle (prod). **'18** Mickey (feature) (prod). **'21** Molly O (feature) (prod; +co-sc). **'22** Suzanna (feature) (prod; +sc). **'25** Boobs in the Woods (prod; +sc). **'32** Ye Olde Saw Mill (feature) (dir; +prod; +co-sc.). **'39** Hollywood Cavalcade (actor). **'49** Down Memory Lane (appearance as himself).

Above: Jean Servais, a world-weary face of the French cinema. Above right: Athene Seyler as Miss Witherfield in The Pickwick Papers. *Above, far right: the dark beauty of Jane Seymour. Below: Delphine Seyrig in* Last Year in Marienbad

SERVAIS, Jean

(1910–1976). Actor. Born: Antwerp, Belgium

Servais reached stardom in his forties in Jules Dassin's *Du Rififi Chez les Hommes* (1955, *Rififi*), playing Tony the embittered ex-con who leads the raid on a large Paris jeweller's. With his long, sad face and deep, rich voice, Servais made the man a memorable figure, and went on to further successes with Dassin and Buñuel. He also made one or two American films. He had studied acting at the Brussels Conservatoire, and worked busily on stage and screen from the early Thirties. On stage he had acted with Jean-Louis Barrault's company; on screen he had been Marius in Raymond Bernard's *Les Misérables*, and had worked for Yves Allégret, Jacques Becker and Max Ophuls before the breakthrough with *Rififi*.

Films include: 1933 Les Misérables. '34 Angèle. '39 Quartier Sans Soleil. '50 Le Château de Verre. '52 Le Plaisir. '53 Rue de l'Estrapade (GB: Françoise Steps Out). '57 Celui qui Doit Mourir (FR-IT) (GB: He Who Must Die). '58 Les Jeux Dangereux (GB: Dangerous Games). '59 Du Rififi Chez les Femmes (FR-IT) (GB: Rififi and the Women). '65 Thomas l'Imposteur (GB: Thomas the Imposter). '66 Lost Command (USA).

SEYLER, Athene

(b. 1889). Actress. Born: London, England

She won the RADA Gold Medal in 1908 and appeared on stage in *The Truants*, her brilliant performances commencing a career that would last over half a century. She appeared on screen for the first time in *The Adventures of Mr Pickwick* in 1921 and acted in many more literary adaptations over the years, dozens of comedies and anything at all that required a small, plump, lovable, quirky maiden aunt or the like. In 1950 she was made President of the Council of RADA and in 1959 was awarded the CBE.

Films include: 1921 The Adventures of Mr Pickwick. '31 The Perfect Lady. '35 Drake of England. '37 The Mill on the Floss; The Sky's the Limit. '47 Nicholas Nickleby. '52 The Pickwick Papers. '53 The Beggars' Opera. '57 How to Murder a Rich Uncle. '58 The Inn of the Sixth Happiness. '60 Make Mine Mink. '63 Nurse on Wheels.

SEYMOUR, Jane

(b. 1950). Actress. Born: Joyce Frankenburg; London, England

An unsmiling, glossy brunette specializing in beautiful bitches and cold villainesses, Jane Seymour made her screen debut as a music-hall girl in *Oh! What a Lovely War*. This followed performances with the Festival Ballet Company and in pantomime, and led to work in prominent British television series (including *The Strauss Family* and *The Onedin Line*) and lead glamour parts in big-budget movies, such as the voodoo-practising Solitaire in *Live and Let Die* and the exotic Princess Farah in *Sinbad and the Eye of the Tiger*. Since moving to Hollywood in the Seventies she precariously maintained her big-screen stardom and was absorbed into American television drama series such as *East of Eden*, in which she was the cruel and selfish Cathy. She has had three much-publicized marriages.

Films include: 1969 Oh! What a Lovely War. '70 The Only Way (PAN-DEN-USA). '72 Young Winston. '73 Live and Let Die; The Best Pair of Legs in the Business. '77 The Four Feathers; Sinbad and the Eye of the Tiger (USA). '78 Battlestar Galactica (USA). '80 Somewhere in Time (USA); Oh Heavenly Dog (USA).

SEYRIG, Delphine

(b. 1932). Actress. Born: Beirut, Lebanon

Born in Lebanon of parents who were from Alsace, Delphine Seyrig spent a wandering youth in Greece, Paris and, during the war years, New York, where her archaeologist father was a cultural attaché. Returning to France, she appeared on the Paris stage from 1952 to 1955. In 1956 she went back to New York to study at the Actors' Studio, made a minor film debut in the Underground movie *Pull My Daisy*, but mainly acted on stage, notably in Arthur Miller's adaptation of Ibsen's *An Enemy of the People*. Alain Resnais saw her in this and cast her as the lead in *Last Year in Marienbad*, making her a star of the art-movie circuit. Her subsequent roles for Joseph Losey, François Truffaut and Luis Buñuel, often as a tantalizing blonde (though her hair is naturally auburn), confirmed this position and made her widely known internationally for her image of cool, sophisticated sexuality and her elegantly musical voice. She has shown a political interest in feminism and worked with such directors as Marguerite Duras and Chantal Akerman, but most of her later films remain unfortunately little seen abroad.

Films include: 1959 Pull My Daisy (short) (USA). '61 L'Année Dernière à Marienbad (FR-IT) (USA/GB: Last Year in Marienbad). '63 Muriel, ou le Temps d'un Retour (FR-IT) (USA/GB: Muriel). '67 La Musica; Accident (GB). '68 Baisers Volés (USA/GB: Stolen Kisses). '69 La Voie Lactée (FR-IT) (GB: The Milky Way). '70 Peau d'Ane (GB: The Magic Donkey). '71 Le Rouge aux Lèvres (BELG-FR-GER) (USA/GB: Daughters of Darkness). '72 Le Charme Discret de la Bourgeoisie (FR-IT-SP) (USA/GB: The Discreet Charm of the Bourgeoisie). '73 A Doll's House (GB-FR); The Day of the Jackal (GB-FR). '74 The Black Windmill (GB). '75 Aloise; India Song; Jeanne Dielman, 23 Quai du Commerce, 1080 Bruxelles (BELG-FR). '76 Son Nom de Venise dans Calcutta Désert. '77 Repérages (SWITZ-FR) (USA: Faces of Love). '80 Le Chemin Perdu (SWITZ-FR-BELG).

SHAMROY, Leon

(1901–1974). Cinematographer. Born: New York City, USA

After studying engineering at Columbia, Shamroy entered films in 1920 as a lab technician at Fox. A director of photography from 1927, he worked with Robert Flaherty on a documentary about the Acoma Indians, and with Paul Fejos on the brilliant experimental feature, *The Last Moment*. In the Thirties Shamroy worked for Schulberg, Selznick and others (Lang's *You Only Live Once* is a notable example of his black-and-white photography), and in 1938 became 20th Century-Fox's leading cinematographer. Shamroy used light and colour with great skill, often changing the natural light, and employing coloured filters and gelatines to accentuate mood and emotional overtones. He photographed the first CinemaScope feature, *The Robe*, and won four Academy Awards.

Films include: 1933 Three-Cornered Moon. '37 You Only Live Once. '38 The Young in Heart. '39 The Adventures of Sherlock Holmes. '42 Roxie Hart; The Black Swan; Ten Gentlemen From West Point. '43 Stormy Weather. '44 Wilson. '45 Leave Her to Heaven; A Tree Grows in Brooklyn. '47 Forever Amber; Twelve O'Clock High. '53 The Robe. '56 The King and I. '58 South Pacific (co-photo). '63 Cleopatra. '67 Planet of the Apes.

SHARAFF, Irene

(b. 1910). Costume designer. Born: Boston, Massachusetts, USA

Irene Sharaff studied at the New York School of Fine and Applied Arts, the Art Students' League and Grande Chaumière in Paris. She designed her first theatre costumes for *Alice in Wonderland* in 1933 and went on to a long career in designing for plays, musicals, ballets and television. Her stage experience made the transition to film easy when the Arthur Freed unit at MGM brought her from Broadway to work on musicals. Later, she worked on both stage and screen versions of *The King and I, West Side Story, Flower Drum Song* and *Funny Girl*. Frequently nominated for Oscars, she won five times, for *An American in Paris, The King and I, West Side Story, Cleopatra* and *Who's Afraid of Virginia Woolf?* She had a superb sense of colour, first demonstrated in *Meet Me in St Louis*, and could encompass a wide range of styles, as her costumes for the ballet sequence, based on Impressionist and Post-Impressionist paintings, in *An American in Paris* showed.

Films include: 1943 I Dood It (co-cost. des); Girl Crazy (co-cost. des). '44 Meet Me in St Louis (co-cost. des). '51 An American in Paris (co-cost. des). '53 Call Me Madam. '54 Brigadoon; A Star Is Born (co-cost. des). '55 Guys and Dolls. '56 The King and I. '59 Porgy and Bess. '60 Can Can. '61 West Side Story; Flower Drum Song. '63 Cleopatra (co-cost des). '66 Who's Afraid of Virginia Woolf? '67 The Taming of the Shrew (co-cost. des) (IT-USA). '68 Funny Girl. '69 Hello, Dolly!

SHARIF, Omar

(b. 1932). Actor. Born: Michael Chalhoub; Alexandria, Egypt

At his peak Sharif brought sophistication, sensitivity and smouldering sex appeal to several major films and for a while was the living proof that it wasn't necessary for a male star to be overtly macho to make female hearts flutter in the Sixties. His curly black hair and moustache and his liquid eyes announced the exotic allure of a refined, latterday Latin lover, but – via

prestigious roles as the fierce Arab friend of *Lawrence of Arabia* and as *Doctor Zhivago* – he became sadly typecast as an all-purpose foreign prince. Greyer and heavier in his fifties, he has not lost his charm but his career has become negligible. Of Lebanese and Syrian descent, Sharif studied mathematics and physics at Victoria College in Cairo and worked in the family lumber business for five years. An old friend offered him a part in the Egyptian film *Serae Fil Wadi* (*The Blazing Sun*) in 1954 and a year later he married its star Faten Hamama (divorced 1966), subsequently appearing with her several times as he emerged as Egypt's top star. He then appeared in Jacques Baratier's *Goha* (1958) before *Lawrence of Arabia* won him an Oscar nomination and a lucrative Columbia contract. Then came stardom – and mediocrity. Away from film sets, Sharif has courted such actresses as Barbra Streisand, Catherine Deneuve and Dyan Cannon, and he is a bridge player of international standing.

Films include: 1962 Lawrence of Arabia (GB). '64 The Yellow Rolls Royce (GB). '65 Doctor Zhivago (USA); Genghis Khan (USA-GER-YUG). '67 Night of the Generals (GB-FR). '68 Mayerling; Funny Girl (USA). '69 McKenna's Gold (USA); Che! (USA). '71 The Horsemen (USA). '81 Inchon (USA).

SHATNER, William

(b. 1931). Actor. Born: Montreal, Quebec, Canada

Shatner supported himself at McGill University by working for the CBC. He then joined the National Repertory Theatre of Ottawa and acted in television before his first film part as Alexei in *The Brothers Karamazov*. He had a couple of good movie roles in *Judgement at Nuremberg* and *The Intruder*, but he achieved fame as the stern, solid Captain Kirk in television's *Star Trek* and its successful movie spin-offs. Attempts to break away from the Kirk image in movies like *The Devil's Rain* have not altered the course of Shatner's career, and it seems he knows on which side his bread is buttered.

Films include: 1958 The Brothers Karamazov. '61 Judgement at Nuremberg. '62 The Intruder (GB: The Stranger). '64 The Outrage. '72 Dead of Night. '75 The Devil's Rain. '77 Kingdom of the Spiders. '79 Riel (CAN). '79 Star Trek – The Motion Picture. '82 Star Trek II: The Wrath of Khan.

SHAUGHNESSY, Mickey

(1920–1985). Actor. Born: Joseph Charles Shaughnessy; New York City, USA

A boxer who preferred the stage, Shaughnessy had a nightclub act as a singing comedian before his film career began in 1952, when he played Judy Holliday's brother in *The Marrying Kind*. The combination of toughness with comic touches made him a popular supporting actor through the Fifties and early Sixties. His better roles included a punch-drunk fighter in *Designing Woman*, the town badman in *The Sheepman*, and, more seriously, Sergeant Leva in *From Here to Eternity*.

Films include: 1952 The Marrying Kind. '53 From Here to Eternity. '57 Designing Woman; Don't Go Near the Water; Jailhouse Rock. '58 The Sheepman. '60 North to Alaska. '62 How the West Was Won. '64 A House Is Not a Home.

SHAW, Robert

(1927–1978). Actor. Born: Westhoughton, Lancashire, England

From RADA Robert Shaw went on to a seven-year stint in small roles at Stratford and the Old Vic, and made his first film, *The Dam Busters*, in 1955. He reached stardom in 1963 as an impassive professional assassin in *From Russia With Love*, and the same year gave a most moving performance as the gentle, retarded brother in *The Caretaker*. In his last years he had leads in major American films like *The Sting* (impressive as a gang-boss, victim of a massive con) and *The Taking of Pelham 123* (a ruthless killer again). But behind all the heavy parts there was a family man (he had ten children by his three wives) and an

Above, from left to right: Omar Sharif as the prince who has a suicide pact with his mistress in Mayerling; *William Shatner in* Star Trek – the Motion Picture; *Robert Shaw in* Force Ten From Navarone *(1978). Below: Mickey Shaughnessy in* The Sheepman

intellectual. He wrote novels, of which *The Hiding Place* and *The Man in the Glass Booth* were highly praised, and adapted the latter for the stage. It played successfully in London and in New York.

Films include: 1955 The Dam Busters. '63 From Russia With Love; The Caretaker (USA: The Guest). '65 Battle of the Bulge (USA). '66 A Man for All Seasons. '69 The Royal Hunt of the Sun. '72 Young Winston. '73 The Hireling; The Sting (USA). '74 The Taking of Pelham 123 (USA). '75 Jaws (USA). '76 Robin and Marian (USA).

SHAW, Run Run

(b. 1906). Producer. Born: Shao Yi-fu; Shanghai, China

Born in Shanghai, where his father owned a cinema, Run Run Shaw and his older brother Run Me Shaw moved to Singapore in 1927 and opened a cinema-renting business. In 1941, when the Japanese took over, they buried their money and dug it up again at the end of the war. In 1957 they moved to Hongkong, started in film production and began to build up a chain of cinemas. By 1972 they controlled the largest privately-owned film circuit in the world, showing Shaw-produced films. Established in 1961, their 46-acre lot on Clearwater Bay has in the Seventies turned out about twenty-five films a year, all in wide-screen and colour since 1977. No unions are permitted in Shaw Movietown, which provides what Asian audiences want – low-budget Kung Fu and karate thrillers – but in later years the company has expanded into international productions. Run Me Shaw died in 1973. Run Run Shaw was, by the time of his knighthood in 1978, one of the wealthiest men in the British Commonwealth.

Films include: 1959 Chiang shan mei jen (GB: The Kingdom and the Beauty). '63 Liang Shan-po yü Chu Ying-t'ai/The Love Eterne. '64 Ta-ti nü-erh/Sons of the Good Earth. '66 Ta tsui hsia/Come Drink With Me. '68 Chin yen-tzu/The Golden Swallow (GB: The Girl With The Thunderbolt Kick). '72 Tien-hsia ti-yi ch'üan/Invincible Boxer (USA: Five Fingers of Death; GB: King Boxer). '74 Shao-lin wu tzu (GB: Five Shaolin Masters). '75 Ch'ing-kuo ch'ing-ch'eng (USA/GB: Empress Dowager); Hung ch'uan hsiao tzu/Disciples of Shaolin. '76 Ying-t'ai ch'i hsüeh (USA/GB: The Last Tempest).

SHEARER, Moira

(b. 1926). Actress/dancer. Born: Moira King; Dunfermline, Scotland

Red-haired and possessed of a wistful beauty, Moira Shearer danced with the Sadler's Wells Ballet from 1942, and in a few years was dancing major roles. She became famous in films with her first part, that of the ballerina who dances herself to death in Powell and Pressburger's The Red Shoes. Shearer made three more films before her virtual retirement in the mid-Fifties to devote herself to her family. She is married to broadcaster and novelist Ludovic Kennedy, and has four children. In 1960 she made a notable film appearance, again for Michael Powell, as a film extra who is murdered in Peeping Tom, and had a London stage hit in 1974 in Man and Wife.

Films: 1948 The Red Shoes. '51 The Tales of Hoffman. '53 The Story of Three Loves (USA). '55 The Man Who Loved Redheads. '60 Peeping Tom; Un Deux Trois Quatre (FR) (GB: Black Tights).

SHEARER, Norma

(1900–1983). Actress. Born: Edith Norma Shearer; Montreal, Canada

Norma Shearer and her sister were taken to New York by their mother

Below, left to right: Moira Shearer in The Red Shoes; Norma Shearer in The Barretts of Wimpole Street;

when she was fifteen. A hoped-for stage career did not materialize, but Norma played small roles in New York films (she is visible in Griffith's Way Down East), allegedly caught the eye of Irving Thalberg, and by 1923 was in Hollywood on a contract with Louis B. Mayer Productions, soon to merge with Metro and Goldwyn. In 1927 she married Thalberg, a clear advantage, but she had already done well in films like He Who Gets Slapped, with Lon Chaney. Her finest silent role was in Lubitsch's The Student Prince, where she struck just the right note of tender fragility, but she was versatile enough, and excellent as an ambitious chorine in Monta Bell's Upstage (1926). The Thirties brought her leads in the studio's prestige pictures. Her ill-advised Juliet is better forgotten, but she was good in several films for Sidney Franklin, as Amanda in Private Lives, as the unhappy heroine of Smilin' Through, and as Elizabeth Barrett (not perhaps suggesting a poetess, but moving as a lady in love). She won one Best Actress Oscar, for The Divorcee, one of the few movies in which she strayed from virtue. After Thalberg died she had one more success, in The Women, and a failure or two, and in 1942 retired. Never a great actress, Shearer had elegance, poise and charm and, when MGM let her loose, spirit and wit in abundance.

Films include: 1920 The Flapper; Way Down East; The Stealers. '24 He Who Gets Slapped. '25 A Slave of Fashion. '27 The Student Prince. '29 The Trial of Mary Dugan; The Last of Mrs Cheyney; Their Own Desire. '30 The Divorcee. '31 A Free Soul; Private Lives. '32 Strange Interlude; Smilin' Through. '34 The Barretts of Wimpole Street. '36 Romeo and Juliet. '38 Marie Antoinette. '39 The Women.

SHEEN, Martin

(b. 1940). Actor. Born: Ramon Estevez; Dayton, Ohio, USA

Martin Sheen's central performance as the American High Command's hired assassin in Apocalypse Now was overlooked by the critics at the time of the film's release. Robert Duvall and Marlon Brando's studies of Vietnam madness in that film won all the accolades, but Sheen's war-lagged, incredulous soldier – who provides the film noir-style voice-over narration – is probably the most authentic portrait yet of the effect of the war on an ordinary American. Sheen has great control: earlier he had played the James Dean lookalike who casually embarks on a murder spree in Badlands, not so much with sang froid as with complete and utter blankness. He was, as a result, typed to some extent in dark, intense, humourless roles, but he has remained in demand. At 17, Sheen won a local televison show contest which eventually led to work in off-Broadway group theatre, a breakthrough on Broadway in The Subject Was Roses, much television and a film debut in The Incident.

Martin Sheen in the television movie Sweet Hostage (1975); Ann Sheridan in Nora Prentiss (1947)

Films include: 1967 The Incident. '68 The Subject Was Roses. '70 Catch-22. '72 Rage. '73 Badlands. '77 The Cassandra Crossing (GB-IT-GER). '79 Apocalypse Now; Eagle's Wing (GB). '80 The Final Countdown. '81 Loophole (GB). '82 Gandhi (GB-IND).

SHELDON, Sidney

(b. 1917). Screenwriter. Born: Chicago, Illinois, USA

A graduate of Northwestern University, Sheldon was a radio announcer and songwriter before going to Hollywood. He was a story analyst for David Selznick, and after spells at Universal and Fox rose to scriptwriter in the early Forties. After war service he became a writer-producer at MGM, and this period saw his best films. He scripted Annie Get Your Gun, and had a hand in Easter Parade, but they were highlights in a generally undistinguished career. He directed two routine films, Dream Wife and The Buster Keaton Story, and much later, after his movie days were over, turned novelist with some success. The Other Side of Midnight and Bloodline were both bestsellers and were filmed in 1977 and 1979 respectively.

Below: Cybill Shepherd in Daisy Miller. Below right: Dinah Sheridan with John Gregson in the classic comedy Genevieve. Below, far right: Lowell Sherman in George Cukor's What Price Hollywood? (1932)

Films include: 1942 Fly by Night (GB: Secret of G32); She's in the Army. **'47** The Bachelor and the Bobbysoxer (GB: Bachelor Knight). **'48** Easter Parade (co-sc). **'50** Annie Get Your Gun. **'51** Rich Young and Pretty (co-sc). **'53** Dream Wife (+dir; +prod). **'55** Anything Goes. **'56** Pardners; The Birds and the Bees (co-sc). **'57** The Buster Keaton Story (+dir; +prod).

SHEPHERD, Cybill

(b. 1950). Actress. Born: Memphis, Tennessee, USA

A beauty contest winner and fashion model, Cybill Shepherd was selected by Peter Bogdanovich to play the leading role of the high-school flirt in *The Last Picture Show*. This was perfect casting, and she was very good indeed, but an association with Bogdanovich and two more leads in his films followed, and her inexperience was painfully manifest. Critical reaction was harsh, and Shepherd moved off to continue her career in Europe. Since then she has worked back in America in summer stock, gathering experience perhaps for a further crack at Hollywood.

Films include: 1971 The Last Picture Show. **'72** The Heartbreak Kid. **'74** Daisy Miller. **'75** At Long Last Love. **'76** Taxi Driver; Special Delivery. **'77** Silver Bears (GB). **'79** The Lady Vanishes (GB).

SHERIDAN, Ann

(1915–1967). Acress. Born: Clara Lou Sheridan; Denton, Texas, USA

Ann Sheridan won a beauty contest which carried with it a Paramount screen test, and the studio signed her. After a number of small parts under her own name, and a few rather better ones as Ann, she switched to Warners and immediately flourished. Her new studio billed her as the 'Oomph' girl, and they did not mislead. She had luxuriant red hair, hazel eyes, full lips, and an irresistible smile and sense of fun. Warners liked to cast her as a sultry dame; Sheridan created the impression that she was the girl next door enjoying every minute of the make-believe. She was lucky in being at Warners at just that time, when the studio was in top form with its crime movies and tough melodramas, and she had actors like Cagney to partner her. She made the very best of her

luck. Perhaps best of all was her torch-singer in *Torrid Zone*, but the girl from the wrong side of the tracks in *Kings Row*, and the wisecracking waitress in *They Drive By Night* weren't far behind. Warners amazingly dropped her in 1948, and she hit back with one of her finest performances, in Hawks' *I Was a Male War Bride*. Her best Fifties part was as a spunky lady living down her past in Douglas Sirk's *Take Me to Town*, and she was charming as ever in *Come Next Spring* (1956), but at the end of the decade she retired, save for television, where she was active until almost her last months. She died of cancer, aged only 51.

Films include: 1934 Search for Beauty; Bolero; Mrs Wiggs of the Cabbage Patch. **'35** Behold My Wife. **'38** Angels With Dirty Faces. **'40** Torrid Zone; They Drive By Night (GB: Road to 'Frisco). **'41** Kings Row. **'44** Shine On Harvest Moon. **'49** I Was a Male War Bride (GB: You Can't Sleep Here). **'52** Steel Town. **'53** Take Me to Town. **'57** Woman and the Hunter (KENYA) (GB: Triangle on Safari).

SHERIDAN, Dinah

(b. 1920). Actress. Born: Dinah Mec; Hampstead, London, England

Despite her image as a typical English rose, Dinah had a German mother and a Russian father. While attending the Italia Conti acting school she made her stage debut at the age of 11 at the Holborn Empire and entered films four years later. Having at last established herself as a leading lady in the record-breaking comedy *Genevieve*, she married her boss, Sir John Davis, and abandoned her career to become a wife and mother. Since her marriage ended in 1965 she has re-established herself as a serious character actress, more often seen on the stage and in television than in films.

Films include: 1936 Irish and Proud of It. **'42** Salute John Citizen. **'45** 29 Acacia Avenue (USA: The Facts of Love). **'48** Calling Paul Temple. **'49** The Huggetts

Abroad; Dark Secret. **'51** Where No Vultures Fly. **'52** The Sound Barrier. **'53** The Story of Gilbert and Sullivan; Genevieve. **'70** The Railway Children.

SHERMAN, Lowell

(1885–1934). Actor/director. Born: San Francisco, California, USA

Sherman came from a theatrical family, and was an important stage actor himself by 1914, when Famous Players signed him to appear with Mary Pickford in *Behind the Scenes*. After that he did little of note in the cinema until 1920, when he was outstanding as a sympathetic villain in Griffith's *Way Down East*. He went on through the Twenties playing smooth, sophisticated types (he was Garbo's lover in *The Divine Woman*, the actress' only lost film), ending in 1932 with a superb performance as an alcoholic director in *What Price Hollywood?* By then Sherman was more interested in direction. *She Done Him Wrong* (Mae West) and *Morning Glory* (Katharine Hepburn) suggested a fine director in the making, and Sherman was entrusted with *Becky Sharp* (1935), the first feature in the new three-strip Technicolor. Unhappily, he died during shooting, and Rouben Mamoulian began again from scratch.

Films as actor include: 1920 Way Down East. **'25** Satan and Sables. **'28** The Divine Woman. **'29** Phipps; Evidence. *Films as director include:* **1931** The Royal Bed (+act) (GB: The Queen's Husband); Bachelor Apartment (+act); High Stakes (+act). **'32** Ladies of the Jury. **'33** She Done Him Wrong; Morning Glory; Broadway Thru a Keyhole. **'35** Night Life of the Gods.

SHERMAN, Vincent

(b. 1906). Director. Born: Vienna, Georgia, USA

Sherman came to Hollywood in 1933 as an actor, and later turned scriptwriter and dialogue director at Warners before becoming a full director there. 'You were lucky to get one film in six you really liked,' he once said, but he always turned out a solid professional job, and when the one-in-six came along he could be very good indeed. *Underground* was an excellent anti-Nazi thriller, and *Old Acquaintance* and *Mr Skeffington* two fine vehicles for Bette Davis. The best of Sherman's later films, *The Garment Jungle*, an exposé of racketeering in the clothing industry, was in fact a salvage effort, for the film had been begun, and then abandoned, by Robert Aldrich. Sherman made no cinema films after 1967, but was much in demand for television movies.

Films as actor: 1933 Counsellor-at-Law. **'34** Speed Wings; One Is Guilty; The Crime of Helen Stanley; Hellbent for Love; Midnight Alibi; Girl in Danger. *Films as director include:* **1940** Saturday's Children; The Man Who Talked Too Much. **'41** Underground. **'43** Old Acquaintance. **'44** Mr Skeffington. **'49** The Adventures of Don Juan. **'50** The Damned Don't Cry. **'57** The Garment Jungle (co-dir). **'61** The Second Time Around. **'67** Cervantes (FR-IT-SP) (USA: The Young Rebel).

SHEYBAL, Vladek

(b. 1933). Actor. Born: Kremieniec, Poland.

Caught carrying Molotov cocktails through the German lines during the Warsaw rising, Sheybal survived a concentration camp and found fame as an actor in Wajda's poignant Polish Resistance saga *Kanał*. In 1958 he defected to the West and, after studying at Oxford, acted in several BBC plays including David Mercer's *The Birth of a Private Man* and Ken Russell's *The Debussy Film*. This led him back to feature films, where with his sharp cruel nose and pale hypnotic eyes he has tended to be cast as sinister, sardonic characters such as the decadent artist Loerke in *Women in Love*, and the Sternberg-like movie director De Thrill in *The Boy Friend*.

Films include: 1957 Kanał (POL) (USA: They Loved Life). '62 The Apple. '63 From Russia With Love. '67 Billion Dollar Brain; Casino Royale. '69 Women in Love. '70 Leo the Last. '71 The Boy Friend. '75 The Wind and the Lion (USA). '80 Shogun (USA-JAP).

SHIELDS, Brooke

(b. 1965) Actress. Born: New York City, USA

Daughter of a Revlon executive and actress Terri Shields, she was chosen to pose in Ivory Snow soap commercials at the age of 11 months and, with the help of her shrewd and ambitious mother, grew up to be America's top child model. She made her film debut in 1977, stabbed to death by a religious maniac in *Alice, Sweet Alice*, and won an international reputation for herself as a 12-year-old prostitute in Louis Malle's controversial *Pretty Baby*. Developing into a lithe and leggy teenager (trenches had to be dug for her to prevent her dwarfing co-star Christopher Atkins in *The Blue Lagoon*), she now combines acting with modelling.

Films include: 1977 Alice, Sweet Alice (GB: Communion). '78 Gypsies; Pretty Baby. '79 Tilt; Wanda Nevada; Just You and Me, Kid. '80 The Blue Lagoon. '81 Endless Love.

SHIMKUS, Joanna

(b. 1943). Actress. Born: Halifax, Nova Scotia, Canada

Brought up in Montreal, Joanna Shimkus went to Paris at 19 as a model and stayed for five years. Jean Aurel cast her in *De l'Amour* and Jean-Luc Godard gave her the part of a girl who thinks she has mixed up her letters to her two lovers and so loses them both in his sketch for *Paris Vu Par . . .* She played the lead role in *Les Aventuriers*, which established her internationally. In Joseph Losey's *Boom!* she played Elizabeth Taylor's secretary, giving the only understated performance in a film of overblown histrionics. Her first American film was *The Lost Man*, in which she was a social worker aiding a militant leader, played by Sidney Poitier, whom she later married. She was marvellously English and Twentyish in *The Virgin and the Gypsy*, based on D. H. Lawrence's story; however her career unaccountably faded out in the early Seventies.

Films include: 1965 De l'Amour (FR-IT) (GB: All About Loving); Paris Vu Par . . . *ep* Montparnasse-Levallois (FR) (GB: Six in Paris). '67 Les Aventuriers (FR-IT) (GB: The Last Adventure). '68 Tante Zita (FR) (GB: Zita); Ho! (FR-IT) (GB: Ho! 'Criminal Face'); Boom! (GB). '69 The Lost Man (USA). '70 The Virgin and the Gypsy (GB). '71 The Marriage of a Young Stockbroker (USA). '72 A Time for Loving (GB) (USA: A Room in Paris).

SHIMURA, Takashi

(1905–1982). Actor. Born: Ikuno, Japan.

Brought up strictly in a family with an authentic Samurai tradition, Shimura became interested in the theatre while at university and in 1930 turned professional. Four years later he began acting in films. In 1943 he moved to the Toho studio and started an association with director Akira Kurosawa which was to last right up to *Kagemusha*. His brilliant performances for Kurosawa – as the woodcut-

ter in *Rashomon*, as the rueful warrior leader in *The Seven Samurai* and as the dying civil servant in *Ikuru* – established him as one of Japan's leading actors.

Films include: 1943 Sugata Sanshiro (Judo Saga). '45 Zoku Sugata Sanshiro (Judo Saga, Part II); Tora no O o Fumu Otok-otachi (USA: The Men Who Tread on the Tiger's Tail; GB: They Who Tread on the Tiger's Tail). '48 Yoidore Tenshi (USA/GB: Drunken Angel). '50 Rashomon. '52 Saikaku Ichidai Onna (USA/GB: The Life of Oharu); Ikiru (USA/GB: Living). '54 Gojira (USA: Godzilla, King of the Monsters; GB: Godzilla); Schichinin no Samurai (USA/GB: Seven Samurai). '57 Kumonosu-jo (USA/GB: Throne of Blood). '58 Kakushi Toride no San-Akunin (USA/GB: The Hidden Fortress). '61 Yojimbo. '65 Akahige (USA/GB: Red Beard). '80 Kagemusha.

SHINDO, Kaneto

(b. 1912). Director. Born: Hiroshima, Japan

The son of a farmer, Shindo entered the film industry in 1934 as an assistant art director, soon graduating to art director and then to scriptwriter. His first film as director came in 1951, but he continued to write, not only for his own films but for directors such as Yoshimura and Masamura. Of Shindo's prolific output three films known in the West confirm his status. *Children of Hiroshima* was an intensely moving account of the sufferings of his native city during and after the nuclear attack; *The Island*, which won First Prize at the Moscow Festival in 1961, was an extraordinary account of the primitive living conditions of a farmer and his family on a lonely island, filmed without one word of dialogue; and *Onibaba* was a chilling ghost story, whose eerie narrative was enhanced by exquisite art direction by Shindo himself.

Films as writer-director include: 1951 Aisai Monogatari (Story of a Beloved Wife). '52 Genbaku no Ko (Children of Hiroshima). '53 Onna no Issho (A Woman's Life). '54 Dobu (Gutter). '60 Onna no Saka (Women

Above, from left to right: Vladek Sheybal in Andrzej Wajda's Kanał; *Brooke Shields shipwrecked and in love in* The Blue Lagoon; *Joanna Shimkus in* The Virgin and the Gypsy, *directed by Christopher Miles. Below: Sylvia Sidney in* Pick Up

of Kyoto). '61 Hadaka no Shima (The Island). '63 Haha (Mother). '65 Onibaba (The Hole). '67 Sei no Kigem (Libido). '68 Tsuymushi Onna to Yowamushi Otoko (Operation Negligé). '69 Kagero (Heat Wave Island).

SHIRLEY, Anne

(b. 1918). Actress. Born: Dawn Evelyeen Paris; New York City, USA

Anne Shirley retired from the screen at 26, when she married producer Adrian Scott, but she had been in films for 23 years. As a child she was credited as Dawn O'Day. At the age of four she was in Herbert Brenon's *Moonshine Valley* (1922), as a moppet reconciling her alcoholic father to her mother, and her family moved to California so that she could work more steadily. In 1930 she was in

Above: Takashi Shimura in Akira Kurosawa's Living. *Above right: the lovely Anne Shirley in John Ford's* Steamboat Round the Bend. *Below: Simone Signoret in* Manèges, *one of the films directed by her first husband, Yves Allégret*

Murnau's *City Girl*, and four years later landed the title role of *Anne of Green Gables* and changed her name to suit the part. She became an attractive and spirited ingénue, with memorable performances as the swamp girl Fleety Belle in John Ford's *Steamboat Round the Bend*, as the daughter, Laurel, in the remake of *Stella Dallas*, and, in her last film, as Claire Trevor's daughter in *Murder, My Sweet*. She married three times. Her first husband was actor John Payne, her second was Scott, her third the screenwriter Charles Lederer.

Films include: 1934 Anne of Green Gables. '35 Steamboat Round the Bend; Chasing Yesterday. '36 Chatterbox; M'Liss; Make Way for a Lady. '37 Stella Dallas. '38 A Man to Remember. '40 Vigil in the Night. '44 Murder, My Sweet (GB: Farewell, My Lovely).

SIDNEY, George

(b. 1911). Director. Born: New York City, USA

Born into a theatrical family, Sidney had a small part in a Tom Mix film in 1923 and played in vaudeville bands before joining MGM in 1932. In the Thirties he was a second-unit director and a director of shorts, and in 1940 and 1941 won Short Subject Oscars. In 1941 he also made his first feature. He stayed with MGM until 1955, and then spent seven years with Columbia. He was MGM's most successful director in the Forties, his hits including the Gene Kelly musical *Anchors Aweigh*, the Judy Garland vehicle *The Harvey Girls* (1946) and a rollicking version of *The Three Musketeers*, starring Kelly and Lana Turner. In the Fifties he ensured continuing success with film versions of long-running Broadway musicals such as Irving Berlin's *Annie Get Your Gun*, Jerome Kern's *Show Boat*, Cole Porter's *Kiss Me, Kate* and Rodgers and Hart's *Pal Joey*.

Films include: 1941 Free and Easy. '42 Pacific Rendezvous. '45 Anchors Aweigh. '47 Cass Timberlane. '48 The Three Musketeers. '50 Annie Get Your Gun. '51 Show Boat. '53 Kiss Me, Kate. '57 Pal Joey. '67 Half a Sixpence (USA-GB).

SIDNEY, Sylvia

(b. 1910). Actress. Born: Sophia Kosow; New York City, USA

Best known for her roles as sweet, tearful slum-girls in Thirties Depression movies like *City Streets* (1931), *Ladies of the Big House, You Only Live Once* and *Dead End*, Sylvia Sidney tired of the sameness of the parts offered her in Hollywood films and increasingly devoted her energies to her first love, the stage. She had received her initial training at the Theatre Guild school and made her Broadway debut at 15 in *Prunella*. As an older character actress she returned to films and was nominated for an Oscar for her role in *Summer Wishes, Winter Dreams*. She has also made impressive television appearances, winning an Emmy for

her performance in a two-part episode of *The Defenders*. In 1982 she made a welcome appearance in Wim Wenders' *Hammett*.

Films include: 1927 Broadway Nights. '31 An American Tragedy. '32 Ladies of the Big House. '33 Pick Up; Jennie Gerhardt. '36 The Trail of the Lonesome Pine; Fury; Sabotage (GB) (USA: A Woman Alone/Hidden Power). '37 You Only Live Once; Dead End. '39 One Third of a Nation. '45 Blood on the Sun. '56 Behind the High Wall. '73 Summer Wishes, Winter Dreams. '77 God Told Me To/Demon; Damien: Omen II; I Never Promised You a Rose Garden. '82 Hammett.

SIEGEL, Don

(b. 1912). Director. Born: Donald Siegel; Chicago, Illinois, USA

Educated at Jesus College, Cambridge and RADA, Don Siegel was a film librarian and assistant editor at Warners before taking over responsibility for inserts and montages. From 1934 until 1942 he made hundreds of these and he also worked as an assistant director and second-unit director from 1939 to 1943. With this superb training behind him, it is hardly surprising that he made two Oscar-winning films in the same year, 1945. But they were shorts; and though he averaged a film a year for the next 35 years, he won no more Oscars. This was not because he had lost his talent, but because he specialized in action genres – mostly thrillers and Westerns – which had little prestige in their native land. However he was admired by French critics, who discovered Siegel as an *auteur* on the basis of his low-budget Fifties pictures such as *Riot in Cell Block 11, Invasion of the Body Snatchers, Baby Face Nelson* and *The Lineup*. Having directed Elvis Presley in *Flaming Star* and Ronald Reagan in *The Killers*, Siegel looked for new worlds to conquer and found television. Apart from television films and pilots, he became a successful series producer. Rich but bored, he began an effective screen partnership with Clint Eastwood that culminated in *Dirty Harry* and helped Eastwood to get started as a director himself. Siegel

has also brought out the best in such top male stars as Walter Matthau (*Charley Varrick*) and John Wayne (*The Shootist*). Women tend to play marginal or ambiguous roles in his films, though sometimes with considerable force – Carolyn Jones in *Baby Face Nelson*, Angie Dickinson in *The Killers*, Susan Clark in *Coogan's Bluff*, Geraldine Page in *The Beguiled*. Siegel has been married to actresses Viveca Lindfors and Doe Avedon.

Films include: 1945 Star in the Night (short); Hitler Lives (doc. short). '46 The Verdict. '49 Night Unto Night; The Big Steal. '54 Riot in Cell Block 11. '56 Invasion of the Body Snatchers. '57 Baby Face Nelson. '58 The Lineup. '60 Flaming Star. '62 Hell Is For Heroes. '64 The Killers; The Hanged Man (orig. TV). '67 Strangers on the Run/Death Dance at Banner (orig. TV). '68 Madigan; Coogan's Bluff. '70 Two Mules for Sister Sara. '71 The Beguiled; Play Misty for Me (actor only); Dirty Harry. '73 Charley Varrick. '74 The Black Windmill (GB). '76 The Shootist. '77 Telefon. '79 Escape From Alcatraz. '80 Rough Cut. '82 Jinxed.

SIGNORET, Simone

(1921–1985). Actress. Born: Simone Kaminker; Wiesbaden, Germany

Simone Signoret's family split up during World War II when her Jewish father escaped to England to join the Free French, and Simone, in Paris, supported her mother and sisters by working as an English tutor and typist. But a childhood friend, Alain Resnais, had instilled in her a passion for film, and she began as an extra, rose swiftly, and by 1946 was playing leads. She first made her mark in *Dédée d'Anvers* (1948) and *Manèges* (1950), two excellent films directed by Yves Allégret, whom she married. She was warm, intense and beautiful, and seemed to live every moment of her parts. The prostitute in *La Ronde* brought international fame, reinforced by her glowing performance in Jacques Becker's *Casque d'Or* and her alarming study of a murderess in Clouzot's *Les Diaboliques*. She divorced Allégret and married the singer and actor Yves Montand. She made films abroad, winning an Oscar for her tragic heroine in *Room at the Top*, where she showed up the film for the shallow thing it was, and there were notable American appearances in *Ship of Fools* and *Games*. With the years she grew heavier, moved slowly, and her face seemed ravaged, but the magnetism was strong as ever, the sympathy undiminished. She devoted much of her time to left-wing political causes, but she must have longed for Ophuls again, or any other of the directors of her youth.

Films include: 1946 Les Démons de l'Aube. '50 La Ronde. '52 Casque d'Or (USA: Golden Helmet; GB: Golden Marie). '53 Thérèse Raquin (FR-IT). '55 Les Diaboliques (GB: The Fiends). '57 Les Sourcières de Salem (FR-E. GER) (USA: The Witches of Salem). '59 Room at the Top (GB). '62 Term of Trial. '65 Ship of Fools (USA). '67 Games (USA). '69 L'Armée des Ombres (FR-IT) (GB: The Army in the Shadows). '70 L'Aveu (FR-IT) (USA: The Confession). '77 La Vie Devant Soi (USA: Madame Rosa). '78 Judith Therpauve; L'Adolescente (FR-GER) (USA: The Adolescent).

SILVA, Henry

(b. 1928). Actor. Born: New York City, USA

With his bright, empty eyes and sharp high cheekbones, Henry Silva has for decades been among the screen's most convincing villains. Born in Spanish Harlem of poor Puerto Rican parents, he did not learn English until he was eight. He did odd jobs to pay for acting lessons at the Actors' Studio. This led to Broadway and then to films, usually in supporting roles, though he was the lead, a ruthless contract killer, in *Johnny Cool*, with Elizabeth Montgomery, and played the title role in *The Return of Mr Moto*. He has also played lead roles in several Italian films and in television, but was most especially frightening as a dope-addicted assassin in *Sharky's Machine*.

Films include: 1952 Viva Zapata! '57 A Hatful of Rain. '60 Ocean's Eleven. '62 The Manchurian Candidate. '63 Johnny Cool. '65 The Return of Mr Moto (GB); The Reward. '66 The Plainsman. '79 Love and Bullets; Buck Rogers in the 25th Century. '81 Sharky's Machine.

SILVERA, Frank

(1914–1970). Actor. Born: Kingston, Jamaica

Silvera's distinctly Hispanic appearance decreed that, though West Indian born, he was frequently cast by Hollywood as a Mexican in Westerns, including *Viva Zapata!* (his first movie), *Guns of the Magnificent Seven* and the television series *The High Chaparral*. He made his professional stage debut in 1934. Despite being a founder of a black theatre company – The Theatre of Being – he played few black roles on screen, *Toys in the Attic* being an honourable exception. He regularly acted in and directed plays in New York and California, and was a Professor of Drama at California State University; his untimely death was the result of accidental electrocution at home.

Films include: 1952 Viva Zapata! '53 Fear and Desire. '55 Killer's Kiss. '59 Crime and Punishment USA. '62 Mutiny on the Bounty. '63 Toys in the Attic. '65 The Greatest Story Ever Told. '67 The St Valentine's Day Massacre; Hombre. '69 Guns of the Magnificent Seven.

SILVERS, Phil

(1912–1985). Actor. Born: New York City, USA

Silvers was a boy singer in vaudeville and a burlesque comedian, made a few musical shorts, and in 1940 debut in features. Through the Forties he played supporting roles, usually in 20th Century-Fox musicals and comedies, and had a Broadway hit in *Top Banana*, but it was *The Phil Silvers Show* on television (originally entitled *You'll Never Get Rich*) which made him a top comedian. Silvers played Sergeant Ernie Bilko, boss of the motor-pool and king of the rackets, in a series that was superbly written and is still, after countless revivals, one of the best comedy shows on the air. Silvers talked non-stop, was wildly inventive, desperately unscrupulous, and totally endearing; the cinema never gave him anything to match.

Films include: 1940 Hit Parade of 1941; You're in the Army Now; Tom, Dick and Harry. '42 My Gal Sal; Footlight Serenade; Four Jills in a Jeep; Roxie Hart. '44 Cover Girl. '63 It's a Mad, Mad, Mad, Mad World. '66 A Funny Thing Happened on the Way to the Forum. '68 Buona Sera, Mrs Campbell.

SIM, Alastair

(1900–1976). Born: Edinburgh, Scotland

Appropriately enough in view of his popular performances as the eccentric headmaster in *The Happiest Days of Your Life* and, switching sex, headmistress Miss Frinton in *The Belles of St Trinian's*, this uniquely comic character actor was at one time a teacher of phonetics and elocution. Though involved in amateur dramatics since his student days, it was not until 1930 that he threw caution to the winds and embarked on a career as a professional actor. After four hard years he achieved success as the Mad Hatter in a stage production of *Alice in Wonderland* and was quickly taken up by the British film industry. By the late Forties he was a firm favourite in films and on the stage and entered into fruitful working relationships with playwright James Bridie and film-makers Launder and Gilliat – for whom he gave his most impressive film performance as the sly, enigmatic Inspector Cockrill in the eerie and chilling comedy thriller, *Green for Danger*.

Films include: 1936 Keep Your Seats Please. '37 The Squeaker (USA: Murder on Diamond Row). '39 Inspector Hornleigh. '45 Waterloo Road. '46 Green for Danger. '47 Hue and Cry; Captain Boycott. '50 The Happiest Days of Your Life. '51 Scrooge. '54 The Belles of St Trinian's. '60 School for Scoundrels. '75 Royal Flash.

SIMMONS, Jean

(b. 1925). Actress. Born: Crouch Hill, London, England

Simmons won her debut part in her teens as Margaret Lockwood's sister in the Gainsborough musical *Give Us the Moon* (1944). As a very promising Rank starlet, she played her first major role as the young, snobbish Estella in David Lean's *Great Expectations* and was nominated for an Oscar for her interpretation of Ophelia in *Hamlet* before marrying Stewart Granger and following him to Hollywood. After several memorable performances – most notably as Sarah Brown in *Guys and Dolls* and as Sister Sharon Falconer in her second husband Richard Brooks' *Elmer Gantry* – she appeared with decreasing frequency in films, though making occasional television appearances and scoring a big success on stage in Stephen Sondheim's musical *A Little Night Music*.

Above: Henry Silva as one of the four rapists pursued by Gregory Peck in Henry King's The Bravados *(1958). Above right: Frank Silvera in* Key

Witness (1960). Below: Phil Silvers in his own television show as the smartest operator in the US Army, Sergeant Bilko

Films include: 1945 The Way to the Stars (USA: Johnny in the Clouds). '46 Great Expectations. '47 Black Narcissus. '47 Uncle Silas (USA: The Inheritance). '48 Hamlet. '49 The Blue Lagoon. '50 So Long at the Fair; Cage of Gold. '53 The Actress (USA); Young Bess (USA). '54 Desiree (USA). '55 Guys and Dolls (USA). '60 Elmer Gantry (USA); Spartacus (USA). '65 Life at the Top. '67 Rough Night in Jericho (USA). '69 The Happy Ending (USA). '75 Mr Sycamore (USA).

SIMON, Michel

(1895–1975). Actor. Born: François Simon; Geneva, Switzerland

Having been a boxer and photographer, Michel Simon made his music-hall debut at Montreuil-sous-Bois as an acrobatic dancer. In 1920 he joined the Pitoëff troupe in Geneva and so came to Paris to start a brilliant stage career. He made some silent films – he was one of the judges in Dreyer's *The Passion of Joan of Arc* – but did not become a screen star until the coming of sound added his deep, hoarse voice to his shambling appearance to complete his screen image. He won great popularity as Clo-Clo in *Jean de la Lune*, worked with Jean Renoir playing a man who kills his faithless mistress in *La Chienne*, performed unforgettably as the irredeemable tramp in *Boudu Saved From Drowning*, and was the eccentric mate of a barge in Jean Vigo's *L'Atalante*. The Thirties were Simon's greatest years but he continued to work until his death, winning the prize for best actor at Berlin as late as 1967 for his role as an anti-semitic farmer who befriends an eight-year-old Jewish boy in occupied France in *Le Vieil Homme et l'Enfant*. He was also oustanding as the understandably jealous old husband of a beautiful and virtuous young wife in *Blanche*.

Films include: 1925 Feu Mathias Pascal (GB: The Late Mathias Pascal). '28 La Passion de Jeanne d'Arc (USA/GB: The Passion of Joan of Arc). '31 Jean de la Lune; La Chienne. '32 Boudu Sauvé des Eaux (USA: Boudu Saved From Drowning). '34 L'Atalante. '37 Drôle de Drame (USA:

Bizarre, Bizarre). '38 La Fin du Jour (USA: End of a Day); Quai des Brumes (USA: Port of Shadows). '47 Panique. '49 La Beauté du Diable (FR-IT) (USA: Beauty and the Devil; GB: Beauty and the Beast). '64 The Train (USA-FR-IT). '67 Le Vieil Homme et l'Enfant (USA: Claude; GB: The Two of Us). '71 Blanche. '75 L'Ibis Rouge.

SIMON, Neil

(b. 1927). Playwright/screenwriter. Born: Bronx, New York City, USA

Neil Simon began writing for radio in partnership with his brother. He moved to television in the Fifties, writing for Sid Caesar's *Your Show of Shows*, Red Buttons, Jackie Gleason and Phil Silvers' Sergeant Bilko. He started to write plays, scoring his first hit on Broadway with *Come Blow Your Horn* in 1961. Although this was filmed a couple of years later, it was not until the mid-Sixties that Simon wrote his first screenplay, *After the Fox*. Since then he has mixed adap-

tations from his Broadway hits with original scripts for the cinema. His clever one-liners, his shrewd treatment of middle-class (especially New York Jewish) angst and the award-winning roles he provides for actors have made him the most popular playwright in American theatre history as well as the dominant personality in successful pictures that are usually brought to the screen by relatively anonymous directors like Herbert Ross and Gene Saks. Following the death of his first wife, Simon married actress Marsha Mason, who served him well in such films as *The Goodbye Girl* and the autobiographical *Chapter Two*, in which she virtually played herself.

Films include: **1966** Caccia alla Volpe (co-sc) (IT-USA-GB) (USA/GB: After the Fox). '67 Barefoot in the Park (from own play). '68 The Odd Couple (from own play). '70 The Out-of-Towners. '71 Plaza Suite (from own play). '72 The Last of the Red Hot Lovers (from own play); The Heartbreak Kid. '74 The Prisoner of Second Avenue (from own play). '75 The Sunshine Boys (from own play). '76 Murder by Death. '77 The Goodbye Girl. '78 The Cheap Detective; California Suite (from own play). '79 Chapter Two. '80 Seems Like Old Times. '81 Only When I Laugh (GB: It Hurts Only When I Laugh).

SIMON, Simone

(b. 1914). Actress. Born: Marseille, France

The daughter of a French mine operator and an Italian mother, Simone Simon was educated in several countries and finally settled in Paris to study sculpture. She soon turned to dress-designing and modelling, which led to film work, initially in operetta and light comedies. She became famous in

Marc Allégret's *Lac aux Dames* and eventually went to Hollywood in the mid-Thirties, but returned to France to play the temptress in *La Bête Humaine* for Jean Renoir, who called her 'a kitten, not a vamp'. Returning to Hollywood, she had some good parts in Val Lewton's productions, especially as the supernatural women of *Cat People* and *Curse of the Cat People*. Dissatisfied with her American film work, she went on the stage in the USA before returning after the war to France, where she acted in a couple of Max Ophuls' films; but her career virtually came to an end in the mid-Fifties.

Films include: **1931** Le Chanteur Inconnu. '34 Lac aux Dames. '37 Seventh Heaven (USA); Love and Hisses (USA). '38 La Bête Humaine (USA: The Human Beast; GB: Judas Was a Woman). '41 All That Money Can Buy/The Devil and Daniel Webster (USA). '42 Cat People (USA). '44 Curse of the Cat People (USA); Mademoiselle Fifi (USA). '47 Temptation Harbour (GB). '50 La Ronde. '52 Le Plaisir. '56 The Extra Day (GB).

SINATRA, Frank

(b. 1915). Singer/actor. Born: Hoboken, New Jersey, USA

In the mid-Forties America and England were Sinatra-crazy. He arrived in New York in 1930 intent on being a singer and within 12 years he had become the idol of the bobby-soxers. Despite having made several splendid Hollywood musicals that allowed Sinatra to shine, he did not really find fame as an actor until his popularity as a singer waned in the Fifties. It was his astonishingly excellent Oscar-winning portrayal of Maggio in the dramatic *From Here to Eternity* that saw a change in his ailing fortunes – and as he turned from musicals to serious acting so the crooning side of his talent also regained favour with a maturing audience. From then on he became Frank Sinatra 'singer *and* actor', and with his powerful performance as a junkie in *The Man With the Golden Arm*, alongside several serious war films, his acting ability was confirmed without doubt. Over the years Sinatra's image has changed from singer to all-round entertainer and personality; his skeletal face and gawky, almost emaciated body have gone and with age have come added weight and hair transplants. His live appearances have become rare spectaculars staged at venues like Caesar's Palace and Madison Square Garden, his marriages to actresses Ava Gardner and Mia Farrow have been widely reported, as have his connections with both members of showbiz cliques and the mob, but above all he remains a charismatic performer as well as a shrewd businessman.

Films include: **1943** Higher and Higher. '45 Anchors Aweigh. '49 On the Town. '51 Meet Danny Wilson. '53 From Here to Eternity. '54 Suddenly. '55 Guys and Dolls. '56 The Man With the Golden Arm; Johnny Concho; High Society. '57 The Joker Is Wild; Pal Joey. '59 A Hole in the Head. '62 The Manchurian Candidate. '65 Von Ryan's Express. '67 Tony Rome. '68 The Detective. '70 Dirty Dingus Magee. '80 The First Deadly Sin.

Above: Alastair Sim in the Ealing comedy Hue and Cry. *Above right: Jean Simmons as an Indian girl in* Black Narcissus. *Right: Michel Simon in* Beauty and the Beast. *Below: Frank Sinatra as a New York cop in* The Detective. *Below left: Simone Simon in* Seventh Heaven

SINDEN, Donald

(b. 1923). Actor. Born: Plymouth, Devon, England

Though he had intended to pursue a career as an architect and surveyor, Sinden, the son of a country chemist, was noticed by impresario Charles F. Smith while appearing in an amateur production at the Brighton Little Theatre and invited to join a company entertaining the troops. Rejected for naval service because of his asthma, he underwent a brief training at drama school and established himself as a promising Shakespearian actor before being chosen by Charles Frend for the role of naval officer Lockhart in *The Cruel Sea*. A suave leading man in British films in the Fifties, he moved on to character parts but came to work increasingly in the theatre – playing Othello and King Lear with the Royal Shakespeare Company – and in television where he was the unperturbable butler to Elaine Stritch's scatty American, Mrs. McNab, in *Two's Company*.

Films include: 1953 The Cruel Sea; Mogambo (USA). '54 Doctor in the House. '55 An Alligator Named Daisy. '56 Tiger in the Smoke. '59 The Captain's Table. '60 The Siege of Sidney Street. '73 The Day of the Jackal (GB-FR). '75 That Lucky Touch.

SIODMAK, Robert

(1900–1973). Director. Born Memphis, Tennessee, USA.

Though a childhood brawl left him with permanently impaired eyesight, Siodmak became a master in the use of light to create chillingly dramatic atmospheres in films like *Phantom Lady*, *The Spiral Staircase* and *The Killers*. Born in America while his parents were there on a business trip, he grew up in Leipzig and Dresden where his father worked as a bank official, and began acting with repertory companies after attending the university at Marburg. Following a brief and unsuccessful diversion into the banking business, he returned to show-business, writing titles for imported American films. In 1929 he made his debut as a director with *Menschen am Sonntag* in collaboration with Edgar G. Ulmer and worked at Ufa until 1934 when Goebbels branded him a 'corrupter of the German family' for his film *Brennendes Geheimnis*. He wisely fled to Paris where he stayed until 1940, making low-budget melodramas with a strong sexual element like *Le Chemin de Rio* (1936), *Traffic in Souls*), *Mollenard* (1938) and *Pièges* (1939, *Shares*). The day before the Germans entered Paris, he left for Hollywood where he rapidly established himself as a proficient and talented director of psychological thrillers. Never really at home in America – his unease is, perhaps, expressed through his films – he left for Europe in 1951 and resumed his career in Germany.

Films include: 1929 Menschen am Sonntag (GER) (co-dir) (USA: People on Sunday). '31 Der Mann, der seinen Mörder sucht (GER) (USA: Looking for His Murderer); Voruntersuchung (GER) (USA: Inquest). '33 Bren-

nendes Geheimnis (GER) (USA: The Burning Secret). '36 La Vie Parisienne (FR) (English-language version: Parisienne Life); Mister Flow (FR) (USA: Compliments of Mr Flow). '41 West Point Widow (USA). '43 Son of Dracula (USA). '44 Cobra Woman (USA); Phantom Lady (USA); Christmas Holiday (USA); The Suspect (USA). '45 The Spiral Staircase (USA). '46 The Killers (USA). '48 Cry of the City (USA). '49 Criss Cross (USA). '52 The Crimson Pirate (GB). '55 Die Ratten (GER). '57 Nachts, wenn der Teufel kam (GER) (USA: The Devil Strikes at Night). '66 Custer of the West (SP).

SIRK, Douglas

(1900–1987). Director. Born: Claus Detlev Sierk; Hamburg, Germany

Brought up by his Danish parents in Skagen, Jutland, he returned to Hamburg as a teenager and after studying law, philosophy and art history established himself as one of Germany's leading theatrical producers. His left-wing sympathies and bold expressive designs aroused the hostility of the Nazis and in 1934 he switched to film as a safer field in which to work. Since he was making highly successful melodramas with no obviously political message, his position became much more secure, but feeling himself a prisoner in his own country, he fled in 1937. Eventually reaching America, he found no film work at first; but in a few years he established himself. His strong visual sense and facility with melodrama led to a highly successful career as a director of 'women's weepies' like *Magnificent Obsession* and *All That Heaven Allows*. Dismissed as florid and novelettish by contemporary critics – though very popular at the box-office – Sirk's films can now be seen as impressive and incisive examinations of emotional relationships in American society. In 1959 he retired, for health reasons, to Switzerland. Though he never directed another film, he resumed his theatrical work in Germany and taught at the Academy of Film and Television in Munich. He has been a seminal influence on young German film-makers, particularly the late Rainer Werner Fassbinder.

Films include: 1935 Das Mädchen vom Moorhof (GER). '39 Boefje (HOLL). '42 Hitler's Madman. '47 Lured (GB: Personal Column). '48 Sleep, My Love; Shockproof. '52 Has Anybody Seen My Gal? '53 All I Desire. '54 Taza, Son of Cochise; Magnificent Obsession; Sign of the Pagan. '55 Captain Lightfoot; All That Heaven Allows. '56 Written on the Wind. '57 The Tarnished Angels. '58 A Time to Love and a Time to Die. '59 Imitation of Life.

SJÖBERG, Alf

(1903–1980). Director. Born: Stockholm, Sweden

Before Bergman, Sjöberg was Sweden's best known modern director, a theatrically-trained rebel who rejected the conventionality of Swedish movies in the Thirties in favour of a more original approach, boldly visual in its attempt to revive the heyday of the silent cinema, yet complex in plot and idea, a mixture of realism

Below: the urbane Donald Sinden (seated) with Dirk Bogarde in Doctor in the House, *directed by Ralph Thomas. Right: Red Skelton in* Merton of the Movies. *Far right: Alison Skipworth in* Madame Racketeer

and Expressionism. Sjöberg's early films were sufficiently unusual to make him an artistic outcast, but *Frenzy*, a study of the tyranny of school life, which Bergman, significantly scripted, won him international acclaim. His bold interpretation of Strindberg's *Miss Julie* earned him the Cannes Grand Prix in 1951, but his subsequent films became over-theatrical, and, disillusioned with film, Sjöberg returned to the stage, where he remained highly regarded until his death, aged 77, in a car crash.

Films include: 1929 Den Starkaste (co-dir) (GB: The Strongest). '39 Med Livet som Insats; Den Blomstertid. '41 Hem Från Babylon. '42 Himlaspelet (GB: Road to Heaven). '44 Hets (USA: Torment; GB: Frenzy). '45 Resan Bort. '46 Iris och Löjtnantshjärta (GB: Iris). '49 Bara en Mor (GB: Only a Mother). '51 Fröken Julie (GB: Miss Julie). '53 Barabbas. '54 Karin Månsdotter. '55 Vildfåglar (GB: Wild Birds). '60 Domaren (GB: The Judge). '66 Ön (GB: The Island). '69 Fadern (GB: The Father).

SJÖMAN, Vilgot

(b. 1924). Director/screenwriter. Born: David Harald Vilgot Sjöman: Stockholm, Sweden

While still a student Vilgot Sjöman appeared in a school production directed by Ingmar Bergman, thus beginning a long association with the director. In the years leading up to his own debut as a director in 1962, Sjöman worked as a novelist, critic and essayist, wrote film scripts and studied film in California before acting as Bergman's assistant on *Nattvardsgästerna* (1962, *Winter Light*). Bergman's influence can be seen in Sjöman's first

film *The Mistress*, an intimate, psychological drama about an emotional love triangle. Sjöman's later movies deal with sexual themes and sexual politics and have often encountered problems with some censors who see the films as pure pornography. Sensational elements, such as the explicit sex sequences in *I Am Curious – Yellow*, tend to cloud over other more serious aspects of the films. In a later film, *Jag Rodnar*, he himself plays a director trying to make a film in the Philippines while coming to terms with the cultural shock of living there.

Films include: 1952 Trots (sc. only). '62 Älskarinnan (+sc) (GB: The Mistress). '64 491; Klänningen (GB: The Dress). '66 Syskonbädd (+sc) (USA/GB: My Sister, My Love). '67 Jag Är Nyfiken – Gul (+sc) (USA/GB: I Am Curious – Yellow). '68 Jag Är Nyfiken – Bla (+sc) (GB: I Am Curious – Blue). '70 Ni Ljuger (+sc). '71 Lyckliga Skitar (+sc) (USA/GB: Blushing Charlie). '77 Tabu. '79 Linus. '81 Jag Rodnar.

SJÖSTRÖM, Victor

(1879–1960). Director. Born: Silbodal, Värmland, Sweden

Sjöström spent much of his early life in the United States, returning in his teens to his native Sweden to become a stage actor. In 1912 he entered films with Svenska Bio, the leading Swedish company, and for 12 years worked for them as script editor, writer, director and actor. Together with his colleague Mauritz Stiller, in whose films he occasionally acted, Sjöström made the Swedish cinema the equal of all of its rivals. Much of his work was shot on location, and he had a feeling for landscape and the interaction of character and nature that perhaps

only Griffith could share. From 1917, with *Terje Vigen*, Sjöström could do no wrong. There was the brooding tragedy of *The Outlaw and his Wife*, the rural tragi-comedy of *The Woman He Chose*, the mysticism of *The Phantom Carriage*, and much more. Then, in 1923, Sjöström went to Hollywood. He made an effective Lon Chaney film, *He Who Gets Slapped*, some films that are lost, and two total masterpieces, *The Scarlet Letter* and *The Wind*. In these films Sjöström (now Seastrom) used landscape with all the intensity of his Swedish days, added an adroit handling of melodrama, and enjoyed an empathy with Lillian Gish that resulted in performances of frightening conviction. In 1930 Sjöström returned to Sweden, made one film there and a final one in England, and devoted himself to acting. In 1957 the long career ended, and gloriously, with his supremely moving portrait of the old doctor in Ingmar Bergman's *Wild Strawberries*.

Films include: **1917** Terje Vigen (+ act) (GB: A Man There Was); Tösen Från Stormyrtorpet (GB: The Woman He Chose). **'18** Berg-Ejvind och Hans Hustru (+ act) (USA: You and I; GB: Love, the Only Law; retitled: The Outlaw and His Wife). **'19** Ingmarssönerna (two parts) (+ act). **'21** Körkarlen (+ act) (USA: The Stroke of Midnight; GB: Thy Soul Shall Bear Witness/The Phantom Carriage). **'24** He Who Gets Slapped (USA). **'25** The Tower of Lies (USA). **'26** The Scarlet Letter (USA). **'28** The Wind (USA); The Divine Woman (USA); The Masks of the Devil (USA). **'57** Smultronstället (actor only) (GB: Wild Strawberries).

SKELTON, Red

(b. 1913). Actor. Born: Richard Bernard Skelton; Vincennes, Indiana, USA

Skelton's father was a clown who died before he was born. By the time he was 14 he was working the Mississippi showboats as a comic, and a year later he joined the circus as a clown. Vaudeville, where he began to develop the character sketches which were to make his name, brought him his first taste of fame, and in 1940 he

signed a 13-year contract with MGM. With *DuBarry Was a Lady*, in which he played a dreamer convinced he was Louis XV, he achieved full-fledged stardom, and featured in many more musicals and comedies. Typically, he turned his red hair and mobile features to good effect in tumbling slapstick, acting out routines like 'Guzzler's Gin', reducing his booze salesman character to cross-eyed drunkenness as he samples the goods he is advertising. In 1953 Skelton moved into television and, by the time he retired in 1971, he was a multi-millionaire.

Films include: **1938** Having Wonderful Time. **'41** Whistling in the Dark. **'42** Panama Hattie. **'43** DuBarry Was a Lady; I Dood It (GB: By Hook or By Crook). **'44** Bathing Beauty. **'46** Ziegfeld Follies. **'47** Merton of the Movies. **'48** The Fuller Brush Man (GB: That Mad Mr Jones); A Southern Yankee. **'49** Neptune's Daughter. **'50** Three Little Words. **'53** The Clown.

SKIPWORTH, Alison

(1875–1952). Actress. Born: Alison Groom; London, England

Stately and imposing, educated privately by tutors from Oxford University, Alison Skipworth was perfectly suited to the roles of assorted queens, duchesses and heiresses. Not that she was born to money; she first went on the stage in 1895 to supplement the meagre income of her husband, artist Frank Markham-Skipworth. She travelled to New York with *The Artist's Model*, and quickly carved out an impressive reputation on Broadway. Aside from the solitary silent appearance in 1921, she did not break into films until 1930, and from then until her retirement in 1942 worked steadily, providing a perfect comedy foil, notably for W.C. Fields, with whom she appeared in *If I Had a Million, Tillie and Gus, Alice in Wonderland* and *Six of a Kind*.

Films include: **1921** Handcuffs or Kisses. **'30** Strictly Unconventional; Outward Bound; Oh, For a Man!; DuBarry, Woman of Passion. **'32** Madame Racketeer (GB: The Sporting Widow); Night After Night; If I Had a

Million. **'33** Tillie and Gus; Alice in Wonderland. **'34** Six of a Kind. **'35** Becky Sharp; The Devil Is a Woman. **'36** Satan Met a Lady. **'38** Wide Open Faces.

SKLADANOWSKY, Max

(1863–1939). Film pioneer. Born: Berlin, Germany

Skladanowsky's fame rests on his achievement in having pipped the Lumière brothers to the post by a few weeks, by showing moving pictures to the public for the first time. It was not a lasting triumph, however, nor a very real one, for his system proved much less successful than his rivals' and he was forced to abandon it shortly afterwards. Apprenticed first to a photographer, and then to a glass-painter, young Max, not surprisingly, sought to combine the two. He toured Germany with his brother Emile and father Carl, putting on magic lantern shows which he sought to make ever more complex. His first attempt at movement involved shooting a series of stills and printing each frame to make a 'flip-book'. A device he displayed at the Berlin Wintergarden in November 1895 was a greater success, but since it involved two interlinked projectors with alternating images, it became obsolete when the Lumières presented their far more sophisticated device within the month.

Films include: **1895–96** The Maid of Orleans; The Pleasant Marriage; The Nocturnal Suitor; Napoleon on St Helena; The Chase of a Fly or the Revenge of Mrs Schultze.

SKOLIMOWSKI, Jerzy

(b. 1938). Director. Born: Warsaw, Poland.

Skolimowski co-scripted *Innocent Sorcerers*, directed by Andrjez Wajda, and on the director's recommendation, he entered Łódź Film School in 1960. Skolimowski then collaborated on another innovative Polish film, Roman Polanski's *Knife in the Water*, and directed an award-winning documentary on boxing. His graduation

film, *Identification Marks: None*, heralded a series of personal films reflecting the younger generation's feeling of alienation in the Sixties. His idiosyncratic style culminated in a collection of visual sketches in *Barrier*, and a provocative anti-Stalinist film, *Hands Up!*, which was censored by the government and hastened his leaving Poland. Skolimowski's witty orchestration of small natural events gradually serves to undermine an apparent surface normality. A London public swimming pool houses an adolescent's tragic infatuation with an older girl in *Deep End*; and a cricket match is played by inmates of a mental asylum in *The Shout*. His recent film, *Moonlighting*, creates a series of tragi-comic events among Poles working in London. It reinforces his theme of alienation while surreptitiously reflecting the political dilemma in Poland. Skolimowski has also appeared as an actor, most notably as a prima-donna press photographer holed up in Beirut in Volker Schlöndorff's *Die Fälschung* (1981, *Circle of Deceit*).

Films include: **1960** Niewinni Czarodzieje (co-sc. only) (GB: Innocent Sorcerers). **'62** Nóż Wodzie (co-sc. only) (GB: Knife in the Water). **'65** Rysopis (GB: Identification Marks: None); Walkower (GB: Walkover). **'66** Bariera (GB: Barrier). **'67** Le Départ (BELG). **'68** Reçe do Góry (GB: Hands Up!). **'70** The Adventures of Gerard (GB-SWITZ); Deep End (USA-GER). **'72** Herzbube (GER-USA) (GB: King, Queen, Knave/Sex, Love and Murder). **'78** The Shout (GB). **'82** Moonlighting (GB).

SKOURAS, Spyros P.

(1893–1971). Executive producer. Born: Skourohorion, Greece

Skouras, one of the most powerful figures in Hollywood in the Forties and Fifties, was a Greek shepherd's son who arrived penniless in the USA in 1910 with two of his brothers, Charles and George. They settled in St Louis and gradually worked their way up from the bottom until, by the mid-Twenties, they had control of all of the city's movie theatres. When their chain of cinemas was bought by Warner Brothers, Skouras became manager of Warners' distribution circuit. In 1931 he joined Paramount and the following year became manager of Fox's Metropolitan Theatres in New York. Following the merger with 20th Century in 1935, Skouras' power in 20th Century-Fox rose steadily until, in 1942, he became president. One of his major coups as head of the studio was his decision to acquire the options on and invest heavily in the CinemaScope wide-screen process, thus temporarily combating the rise of television. The biblical epic *The Robe* (1953) became the first CinemaScope movie and was a resounding commercial success. Skouras remained president of 20th Century-Fox until 1962, when he was ousted following recriminations about the escalating costs of *Cleopatra* (1962). He stayed on as chairman for seven years, being in part responsible for the studio's most profitable movie, *The Sound of Music* (1965). His last years were spent as president of a shipping line.

SLEZAK, Walter

(1902–1983). Actor. Born: Vienna, Austria

The son of a famous opera singer, Walter Slezak was studying medicine in Vienna when he was noticed by the director Michael Kertész (later Curtiz) who gave him the juvenile lead in *Sodom und Gomorrha* (1922). Suddenly Slezak found himself launched on an acting career and he signed with Ufa, appearing in a number of German films before going to America in 1930. One of his roles was as the treacherous young model loved by an artist in Carl Theodor Dreyer's superb *Michael*. Once there he concentrated on plays and musicals for 12 years before making his Hollywood debut in 1942, and he continued to work regularly in films and on Broadway, receiving a Tony Award in 1955 for his performance in *Fanny*. In 1959 he fulfilled a lifelong ambition to emulate his father by singing the role of Zsupan in *The Gypsy Baron* at the Metropolitan Opera – the first of several operatic appearances. In his early American films he tended to be cast as the fool or villain; age allowed him the opportunity to play such parts as the wizened old book dealer Strossel in *The Wonderful World of the Brothers Grimm*.

Films include: **1924** Michael (GER) (USA: Chained; GB: Heart's Desire). **'26** Junges Blut (GER). **'27** Die Lorelei (GER). **'42** Once Upon a Honeymoon. **'44** Lifeboat; The Princess and the Pirate. **'48** The Pirate. **'57** Ten Thousand Bedrooms. **'62** The Wonderful World of the Brothers Grimm. **'67** The Caper of the Golden Bulls (GB: Carnival of Thieves). **'69** The Mysterious House of Doctor C (SP-USA). **'72** Treasure Island (GB-GER-SP).

SLOANE, Everett

(1909–1965). Actor. Born: New York City, USA

For many people the 1929 Wall Street crash meant ruin; for Everett Sloane it meant abandoning the career he had started on leaving the University of Pennsylvania. He joined New York's Cherry Lane Theatre Group, and earned some measure of success with a couple of radio shows, but it was not until he joined Orson Welles' Mercury Theatre in 1937 that his career took off. Three years later he travelled to Hollywood to make a film debut most actors surely dream of, as the hero's colleague Bernstein, one of the narrators of *Citizen Kane*. Not surprisingly, Sloane found himself much in demand as a supporting character actor, and remained busy for the rest of his career playing a variety of roles, from the rich and crippled villain of *The Lady From Shanghai* (again with Welles) to the broad comedy of his last film, *The Disorderly Orderly*. He died from an overdose of sleeping pills, and was presumed to have committed suicide in the belief that he was going blind.

Films include: **1940** Citizen Kane. **'42** Journey Into Fear. **'47** The Lady From Shanghai. **'49** Prince of Foxes. **'50** The Men. **'51** The Enforcer (GB: Murder, Inc). **'56** Lust for Life; Patterns (GB: Patterns of Power). **'50** Home From the Hill. **'64** The Patsy; The Disorderly Orderly.

SLOCOMBE, Douglas

(b. 1913). Cinematographer. Born: London, England

Having been educated in Paris, Douglas Slocombe began working as a freelance journalist and photographer in 1933 and was filming in both Amsterdam and Poland just prior to their respective invasions. The footage he shot there was then used in Herbert Klein's documentary *Lights Out in Europe* (1940). Then during World War II Slocombe was asked by Alberto Cavalcanti to film for Ealing Studios – and he remained there for the next 17 years, becoming a director of photography in 1945. He later began a long association with camera operator Chic Waterson when he teamed up with him on *Cage of Gold* (1950). Despite an earlier preference for more literary topics, the Seventies saw Slocombe becoming more involved with adventure movies and he went on to produce some spectacular work for the tongue-in-cheek yarn *Raiders of the Lost Ark*.

Films include: **1945** Dead of Night (co-photo). **'47** It Always Rains on Sunday. **'49** Kind Hearts and Coronets. **'51** The Man in the White Suit. **'61** The Young Ones (USA: It's Wonderful to Be Young). **'62** The L-Shaped Room. **'63** The Servant. **'68** The Lion in Winter. **'71** The Music Lovers. **'73** Jesus Christ Superstar (USA). **'74** The Great Gatsby (USA). **'77** Julia (USA); Close Encounters of the Third Kind (co-photo) (USA). **'79** The Lady Vanishes. **'81** Raiders of the Lost Ark (USA).

SMITH, Alexis

(b. 1921). Actress. Born: Margaret Alexis Fitzsimmons Smith; Penticton, British Columbia, Canada

A ballet dancer in the Hollywood Bowl production of *Carmen* at 13, she studied at Hollywood High and majored in drama at Los Angeles City College. She was offered a Warners contract at 19 and appeared opposite Errol Flynn in *Dive Bomber* and *Gentleman Jim*. Starring in the B-movie *Steel Against the Sky*, Alexis Smith met actor Craig Stevens, whom she married in 1944. She was a tall, stately and attractive leading lady but never became a big star because, as she admits, 'I typed myself – I played all my roles alike because I didn't know any better.' The best of those roles were in the musical bipics of Cole Porter (*Night and Day*) and George

Gershwin (*Rhapsody in Blue*), and also in *The Constant Nymph*. After *The Young Philadelphians* in 1959, Smith turned to the stage and television, but she returned to movies in the Seventies, playing everyone's favourite aunt Sarah Blue in *Casey's Shadow*, and other tailor-made parts.

Films include: **1941** Steel Against the Sky; Dive Bomber. **'42** Gentleman Jim. **'43** The Constant Nymph. **'44** The Adventures of Mark Twain. **'45** Rhapsody in Blue. **'46** Night and Day; Of Human Bondage. **'47** The Two Mrs Carrolls. **'54** The Sleeping Tiger (GB). **'59** The Young Philadelphians (GB: The City Jungle). **'78** Casey's Shadow. **'82** La Truite (FR).

SMITH, C. Aubrey

(1863–1948). Actor. Born: Charles Aubrey Smith; London, England

Sir Aubrey was an Englishman from his backbone to his stiff upper lip. His old school tie was a Charterhouse one, he'd been to Cambridge, and played cricket for England in Australia and South Africa. Six feet two inches tall, with bushy brows, Roman nose and imposing physique, he had that quiet gentility and confidence which

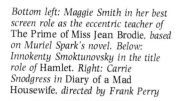

Far left: Walter Slezak (top) in the Vincente Minnelli musical The Pirate; *Everett Sloane (below) in* Patterns. *Centre left: a studio publicity portrait of Alexis Smith taken by Scotty Welbourne. Left: C. Aubrey Smith in* An Ideal Husband. *Below left: Kent Smith in* Nora Prentiss

Bottom left: Maggie Smith in her best screen role as the eccentric teacher of The Prime of Miss Jean Brodie, *based on Muriel Spark's novel. Below: Innokenty Smoktunovsky in the title role of* Hamlet. *Right: Carrie Snodgress in* Diary of a Mad Housewife, *directed by Frank Perry*

marked him out as an officer and a gentleman, firmly but justly suppressing the restless natives on the fringes of the Empire, from *The Lives of a Bengal Lancer* to *The Four Feathers*, whilst dishing out fatherly advice to gung-ho subalterns along the way. He had begun acting on the stage, working with Ellen Terry and Mrs Patrick Campbell, and he entered films in 1915. Though it took fifteen years to establish himself, he had become, by the time of his death, the acknowledged leader of the British colony in Hollywood. He received the OBE in 1938, and was knighted in 1944.

Films include: 1918 Red Pottage (GB). '20 The Face at the Window (GB). '22 The Bohemian Girl (GB). '31 Trader Horn. '33 Queen Christina. '34 Cleopatra; The Scarlet Empress. '35 The Lives of a Bengal Lancer; Clive of India. '36 Little Lord Fauntleroy. '37 The Prisoner of Zenda; Wee Willie Winkie. '38 Four Men and a Prayer. '39 The Four Feathers (GB). '41 Dr Jekyll and Mr Hyde. '48 An Ideal Husband. '49 Little Women.

SMITH, Kent

(1907–1985). Actor. Born: Frank Kent Smith; New York City, USA

Educated at Harvard University, Kent Smith made his first New York stage appearance in 1932 and acted in many plays before moving to the screen. His part in *Cat People* established him and although he never became a star he made his mark in many fine films. He also starred in the long-running television series *Peyton Place* and throughout the Seventies was to be seen regularly as a silver-haired character actor in television movies.

Films include: 1942 Cat People; Hitler's Children. '43 Forever and a Day. '44 Curse of the Cat People. '45 The Spiral Staircase. '49 The Fountainhead. '50 The Damned Don't Cry. '52 The Silent Voice (GB: Paula). '60 Strangers When We Meet. '68 The Money Jungle. '69 Death of a Gunfighter. '72 Pete 'n' Tillie.

SMITH, Maggie

(b. 1934). Actress. Born: Margaret Natalie Smith; Ilford, Essex, England.

Though Maggie Smith's film appearances have been few and occasionally uneven, they have always made an impression. In her first big role, as the devoted but ignored secretary in *The VIPs*, she stole the acting honours out from under Richard Burton and Liz Taylor. Her sharp, dry wit won her an Oscar in *The Prime of Miss Jean Brodie*, as the Scottish teacher who takes 'her gels' under her wing. With delicious irony she played an English actress failing to win an Oscar in *California Suite* – and won one herself for the role. Nevertheless, if not primarily a stage actress, she has at least spent most of her time on it. Educated at Oxford, she studied drama at the Oxford Playhouse School, and toured France and Germany before going into revue. After a season at the Old Vic, 1959–60, she joined the National Theatre at the invitation of Sir Laurence Olivier, playing Desdemona to his *Othello*, a role she repeated in the screen version.

Films: 1958 Nowhere to Go. '62 Go to Blazes. '63 The VIPs (USA: International Hotel). '64 The Pumpkin Eater. '65 Young Cassidy (USA); Othello. '67 The Honey Pot (USA-IT). '68 Hot Millions. '69 The Prime of Miss Jean Brodie; Oh! What a Lovely War. '72 Travels With My Aunt. '73 Love and Pain and the Whole Damn Thing (USA). '76 Murder by Death (USA). '78 Death on the Nile; California Suite (USA). '81 Clash of the Titans. '81 Quartet (FR-GB); Evil Under the Sun. '82 Ménage à Trois.

SMOKTUNOVSKY, Innokenty

(b. 1925). Actor. Born: Krasnoyarsk, Siberia, USSR

The biggest box-office star of the Soviet cinema from the mid- to late Sixties, he began by abandoning his acting course just after the war.

Instead he worked as an extra in crowd scenes in movies and acted in stage comedies. Changing to serious roles, he achieved a great theatrical success as Prince Myshkin in *The Idiot* and was acclaimed for his screen performance in *Soldaty*. Smoktunovsky has since played major film parts in adaptations from Tolstoy, Dostoyevsky and Chekhov, but he is best known for his remarkable portrayal of Hamlet in Kozintsev's film – subsequently being referred to as 'the Russian Hamlet'.

Films include: 1956 Soldaty. '61 Devyat Dnei Odnogo Goda (GB: Nine Days of One Year). '62 Mozart i Salieri (USA: Requiem for Mozart). '64 Gamlet (GB: Hamlet). '66 Beregis Automobilya (USA: An Uncommon Thief; GB: Watch Your Car). '68 Zhivoi Trup. '70 Dyadya Vanya; Tschaikovsky (USSR-USA); Prestuplenie i Nakazanie. '79 Barjerata (BULG).

SNODGRESS, Carrie

(b. 1945). Actress. Born: Park Ridge, nr. Chicago, Illinois, USA

Carrie Snodgress never bothered to change her unglamorous-sounding name, but it didn't prevent her from becoming a promising film actress for a while. After drama studies in Chicago and much television work, she had a film debut opposite James Caan in *Rabbit, Run* and the excellent role of the bored Tina Balser who has an unpleasant affair with an egoist (Frank Langella) in *Diary of a Mad Housewife*. Her performance as a woman trying to cope with domestic drabness and the selfishness of others was particularly moving and won her an Oscar nomination. She failed to capitalize on it, however, and left Hollywood to live with rock singer Neil Young for six years. She returned in 1978 to play Kirk Douglas' girlfriend in *The Fury*.

Films: 1970 Diary of a Mad Housewife; Rabbit, Run. '78 The Fury.

SNOW, Michael

(b. 1929). Director. Born: Canada

A painter, sculptor, photographer and avant-garde film maker whose work remains to say the least enigmatic, Snow specializes in shooting very little for a long time. As a result, predominant shapes and colours form a visual rhythm which varies in tempo and distorts into abstraction as the camera shifts from slow to fast scans, and swoops from high to low. *Wavelength*, a 45-minute single zoom of a New York interior, taken over several days, was heralded as an emblem of a new era in avant-garde cinematography; *Back and Forth* consisted of 52 minutes of a suburban campus classroom, varied only by a change from a horizontal camera motion to a vertical one near the end.

Films include: 1964 New York Eye and Ear Control. '67 Standard Time. '68 Wavelength. '69←→ (Back and Forth); Dripping Water. '71 La Region Centrale. '75 Rameau's Nephew By Diderot (Thanx to Denis Young) By Wilma Schoen. '76 Breakfast.

SOKOLOFF, Vladimir

(1889–1962). Actor. Born: Moscow, Russia

Sokoloff played an Italian in *Cloak and Dagger*, a Frenchman in *The Life of Emile Zola*, a Mexican in *The Magnificent Seven*, and even a Japanese in *To the Ends of the Earth*. In fact he was a Russian, who cut his acting teeth at the Moscow Art Theatre before emigrating in 1923. He went to Germany and made his first film two years later. In Paris he played in Gance's *Napoléon*, later going to America with Max Reinhardt's company, finally arriving in Hollywood in 1937. He achieved his greatest success in *For Whom the Bell Tolls*, playing, for a change, a Spaniard.

Films include: 1927 Napoléon (FR) (GB: Napoleon); Die Liebe der Jeanne Ney (GER) (GB: The Love of Jeanne Ney). '30 Westfront 1918 (GER) (USA: The Western Front 1918). '31 Die Dreigroschenoper (GER-USA) (USA: The Threepenny Opera). '32 L'Atlantide/Die Herrin von Atlantis (GER). '37 Les Bas-Fonds (FR) (USA: The Lower Depths); The Life of Emile Zola (USA); Conquest (USA) (GB: Marie Walewska). '43 For Whom the Bell Tolls (USA). '45 Scarlet Street (USA); A Royal Scandal (USA) (GB: Czarina). '46 Cloak and Dagger (USA). '48 To the Ends of the Earth (USA). '60 The Magnificent Seven (USA).

SOMMER, Elke

(b. 1940). Actress. Born: Elke Schletz; Berlin, Germany

May Britt, Britt Ekland, Anita Ekberg and Elke Sommer – the blonde Nordic sex symbol was very popular in the Fifties and Sixties, but how to tell one from the other? Elke Sommer perhaps had the softest features and the warmest nature of them all and her characters seemed both sexy and innocent at once. Though she had few good chances, she was memorable sitting in a car in a traffic jam with Peter Sellers – both stark naked – in *A Shot in the Dark*; as Paul Newman's guide around Stockholm in *The Prize*; and as the –

unaccountably – spurned wife in *The Oscar*. After university and modelling this minister's daughter brought her linguistic abilities (she is fluent in seven languages) to Italian, German, French and Spanish movies before making her English-speaking debut in *Don't Bother to Knock*. In the Seventies she worked mainly in television and on the stage in an attempt to get away from merely decorative roles in films. She is married to writer Joe Hyams.

Films include: 1961 Don't Bother to Knock (GB). '63 The Victors (GB); The Prize (USA). '64 A Shot in the Dark (GB). '65 The Money Trap (USA); The Art of Love (USA). '66 Boy, Did I Get a Wrong Number! (USA); The Oscar (USA); Deadlier Than the Male (GB). '67 A Venetian Affair (USA). '75 Carry on Behind (GB). '79 The Prisoner of Zenda (USA); The Double McGuffin (USA).

SONDERGAARD, Gale

(1900–1985). Actress. Born: Edith Holm Sondergaard; Litchfield, Minnesota, USA

Following her education at the University of Minnesota, Sondergaard studied drama, intent on a stage career. By the time her second husband, director Herbert Biberman, took her to Hollywood, she had an established Broadway reputation. Her first film appearance, in *Anthony Adverse*, was such a success, however, that she won an Academy Award, and her dark eyes, hair, high cheekbones and perfect diction made her much in demand as a villainess. In 1951 Biberman fell foul of the House Un-American Activities Committee and went to jail as one of the Hollywood Ten. Sondergaard testified in his defence, and as a result did not work for five years. She returned to the stage and television and worked on a documentary about the blacklisting, *Hollywood On Trial* (1976).

Films include: 1936 Anthony Adverse. '37 The Life of Emile Zola. '39 The Cat and the Canary. '40 The Mark of Zorro; The Bluebird; The Letter. '42 My Favourite Blonde. '43 Appointment in Berlin. '44 The Spider Woman. '47 Road to Rio. '69 Slaves. '76 Return of a Man Called Horse.

SORDI, Alberto

(b. 1919). Actor. Born: Rome, Italy

A gifted mimic, Sordi broke into show-business by the unlikely means of winning an MGM Oliver Hardy sound-alike contest when he was 13. A spell in Italian music halls followed, and in 1938 he made his first film, a step on the road which took him to the top of Italy's popularity polls as a comic. With his dark looks, square face and beaked nose, he has acted in a wide range of comedies, and is at his most typical in *I Know That You Know That I Know*, a film he also directed, as a private eye reporting on the behaviour of a jealous VIP. He works extensively on television where he has his own very successful show.

Films include: 1938 La Principessa Tarakanova. '53 I Vitelloni (IT-FR) (GB: The Spivs). '59 La Grand Guerra (IT-FR) (USA/GB: The Great War). '61 Tutti a Casa (IT-FR) (USA: Everybody Go Home). '62 Il Mafioso; Una Vita Difficile. '63 Il Diavolo (USA/GB: To Bed – or Not to Bed). '67 Un Italiano in America. '68 Riusciranno i Nostri Eroi. . . . '78 Le Temoin (IT-FR) (GB: The Witness). '82 Io So Che Tu Sai Che Io So (+dir) (USA/GB: I Know That You Know That I Know).

SOTHERN, Ann

(b. 1909). Actress. Born: Harriette Lake; Valley City, North Dakota, USA

Ann Sothern specialized in playing a particular type of heroine popular in the Thirties, pert, bubbly and blonde. *Maisie*, the Brooklyn showgirl, her purest incarnation, was featured in no less than ten films made in only eight years. For Miss Sothern, who had been taught to dance as one of a trio of sisters by their mother, and who had broken into films via the Christie Comedies, this required a change of appearance, if not of style – she had to dye her natural red hair platinum blonde. Once the dizzy moll parts began to fade, she moved increasingly into character acting, displaying considerable presence, though she continued to sing and dance in Broadway shows like *Lady Be Good*. Despite occasional bouts of ill-health, her career flourished in the Fifties with two television shows, *Private Secretary* and *The Ann Sothern Show*. She was married and divorced from actors Roger Pryor and Robert Sterling.

Films include: 1929 Show of Shows. '30 Doughboys. '38 Trade Winds. '39 Maisie.

Above, from left to right: Vladimir Sokoloff in Cloak and Dagger; *Elke Sommer as a glamorous murder suspect investigated by the bungling Inspector Clouseau (Peter Sellers) in Blake Edwards'* A Shot in the Dark; *Gale Sondergaard in the spooky*

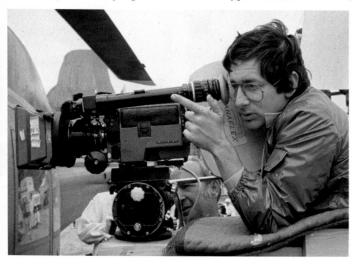

comedy The Time of Their Lives *(1946); Alberto Sordi in* Contestatzione Generale *(1970). Far left: Ann Sothern in* Maisie. *Left: Sissy Spacek in Robert Altman's* Three Women. *Below: the director Steven Spielberg – creator of* Jaws *and* E.T.

'40 Brother Orchid. '41 Lady Be Good. '42 Panama Hattie. '48 A Letter to Three Wives. '53 The Blue Gardenia. '65 Sylvia. '73 The Killing Mind. '75 Crazy Mama.

SPAAK, Charles

(1903–1975). Screenwriter. Born: Brussels, Belgium

The Spaak family must surely rate as among Belgium's most distinguished. Charles' father Paul was a director of Belgium's de la Monnaie Theatre in Brussels; brother Paul-Henri became a premier of Belgium; and Charles' own offspring include daughters Catherine and Agnes, both well-known actresses. Charles was interested in writing from childhood and, following a failed exam, abandoned his education in law and went to Paris instead to work as director Jacques Feyder's secretary. Spaak went on to work for many of the top French film-makers of the Thirties, including Feyder, Renoir, Grémillon and

Cayatte. His work imparted to their projects a unity of style and inspiration, common to films as different as *La Kérmesse Heroïque*, a classic comedy set in a small Flemish village, where the women turn table on their menfolk, and *La Grande Illusion*, an idealistic pacifist World War I film which reflected the views of the European intelligentsia in the troubled late Thirties.

Films include: 1928 Les Nouveaux Messieurs (co-sc) (GB: The New Gentlemen). '35 La Kérmesse Héroïque (co-sc) (USA/GB: Carnival in Flanders). '37 Les Bas-Fonds (co-sc) (USA: The Lower Depths). La Grande Illusion (co-sc) (USA: Grand Illusion; GB: The Great Illusion). '38 La Fin du Jour (co-sc). '41 Premier Bal. '46 L'Homme au Chapeau Rond (co-sc) (USA: The Eternal Husband). '50 Justice Est Faite (co-sc) (GB: Justice Is Done). '52 Nous Sommes Tous des Assassins (co-sc) (USA: We Are All Murderers; GB: Are We All Murderers?). '53 Thérèse Raquin (co-sc). '56 Crime et Chatiment (USA/GB: Crime and Punishment). '74 La Main à Couper (co-sc) (GB: And Hope to Die).

SPACEK, Sissy

(b. 1949). Actress. Born: Mary Elizabeth Spacek; Quitman, Texas, USA

Spacek is small, thin, pale, freckled and uncertain-looking, and one of the most accomplished actresses in the American cinema. Versatility and a willingness to attempt any role seem to be the keys to her success, though she is best known for her teenagers. In her first two films, *Prime Cut* and *Badlands*, she was totally convincing as 15-year-olds – one an unwilling prostitute, the other a delinquent on the run. In *Carrie* she was very disturbing as a high-school girl with telekinetic powers; in *Coal Miner's Daughter* thoroughly believable both as a 13-year-old Loretta Lynn and as the star grown up. She performed Lynn's own country and western songs in that film and claimed the Best Actress Oscar. Since then she has movingly conveyed the growing agony of a woman who suspects her husband is dead in *Missing*, and the problems facing a young wartime widow in *Raggedy Man*, this last directed by her husband Jack Fisk. A first cousin of actor Rip Torn, she stayed with him and his wife Geraldine Page in New York after winning a singer-songwriter contest and while looking for a start in the music industry. She broke into movies via modelling, drama training with Lee Strasberg and television work.

Films: 1970 Trash. '72 Prime Cut. '73 Badlands. '74 Phantom of the Paradise (set dresser only). '76 Carrie; Welcome to LA. '77 Three Women. '78 Verna; USO Girl. '79 Heart Beat. '80 Coal Miner's Daughter. '82 Missing; Raggedy Man.

SPIEGEL, Sam

(1903–1986). Producer. Born: Jaroslau, Poland

No streetwise illiterate furrier or glove manufacturer like some of his Hollywood forbears, but a bona fide graduate in economics, dramatic literature and languages from the University of Vienna, Spiegel came to California to lecture in 1927, got Hollywood under his skin and stayed on to translate scripts for MGM and Universal. He went to Berlin in 1929 as head of Universal's production office there but, with Hitler's ascent to power, was on the move again until he landed in Hollywood, via Vienna and Paris in 1940. From then on Spiegel (also known as S.P. Eagle from the early Forties) worked as an independent producer. With John Huston he formed Horizon Pictures after the war (they made The African Queen together) but the association ended in 1953 when Huston left. S.P. Eagle once again became Spiegel and set about proving that nothing succeeds like success. Few producers were ever as successful as he was. His films got bigger and bigger and won more and more prizes. They were always literate, finely acted and, latterly, bedecked with no-expenses-spared production values and if, in the final analysis, they usually delivered less than they promised, that was still

more than many of his Hollywood contemporaries could do at the time.

Films include: 1942 Tales of Manhattan. '46 The Stranger. '51 The African Queen (USA-GB). '54 On the Waterfront. '57 The Bridge on the River Kwai (GB). '59 Suddenly, Last Summer (GB). '62 Lawrence of Arabia (GB). '66 The Chase. '67 Night of the Generals (GB-FR). '71 Nicholas and Alexandra. '76 The Last Tycoon.

SPIELBERG, Steven

(b. 1947). Director. Born: Cincinnati, Ohio, USA

Spielberg has emerged as the most consistently 'box-office' of the Seventies generation of Hollywood filmmakers. Indeed, the phenomenal commercial appeal of his films has made him not just one of the wealthiest men in America but probably the most financially successful director of all time. Four of the six films he made between 1975 and 1982 were in the top five most popular, most discussed and – in all likelihood – most universally entertaining films of those years. *Jaws, Close Encounters of the Third Kind, Raiders of the Lost Ark* and *E.T. The Extra-terrestrial* were closely followed by a film he helped write and produce, *Poltergeist* (1982); only *1941* failed, perhaps unfairly. It seems remarkable that Spielberg didn't direct *Star Wars*, but then it *was* made by his close colleague George Lucas, producer of what is arguably Spielberg's own best film, *Raiders of the Lost Ark*. That highly acclaimed picture had the following ingredients: witty, thrill-a-minute adventure with a surprise at every turning; a gripping but not too serious plot; a tough, intelligent, handsome, likeable hero (Harrison Ford); a tough, pretty heroine (Karen Allen); an excellent supporting cast; ravishing photography and sets; exotic locations; and, perhaps most important, awesome special effects and a barrage of electric shocks to the audience. It proved that, beyond all others, Spielberg and Lucas were the film packagers *par excellence*. At 13 Spielberg had won a film contest with his 40-minute film, *Escape to Nowhere*. After graduating from California State College he was able to arrange finance for *Amblin'*, a short about a couple of hitchhikers, and during 1970–72 he worked prodigiously directing for television before a couple of road movies, *Duel* (a television film released in cinemas) and *Sugarland Express*, brought him a wider audience. The shark saga *Jaws* reputedly became the biggest grosser in history within 78 days of its release and Spielberg has never looked back. *E.T.*, a heart-rending tale about a friendly alien, broke all records and Spielberg became a millionaire on its merchandizing spin-offs alone. It is likely that Spielberg is now in the position of a Corman or Coppola to further the careers of other young film-makers with a *Raiders* or a *Close Encounters* up their sleeves.

Films include: 1969 Amblin'. '71 Duel. '74 The Sugarland Express. '75 Jaws. '77 Close Encounters of the Third Kind. '78 I Wanna Hold Your Hand. '79 1941. '81 Raiders of the Lost Ark. '82 E.T. The Extra-terrestrial.

Left: Robert Stack in the tough The Scarface Mob (1959). Above: Sylvester Stallone in Rocky, which made him an international star. Above right: Terence Stamp as a lonesome cowboy in Blue. Below: Maureen Stapleton in Melvin Frank's Lost and Found

STACK, Robert

(b. 1919). Actor. Born: Los Angeles, California, USA

An outstanding amateur athlete, Stack achieved fame on his movie debut as the first actor to kiss Deanna Durbin on screen. His budding movie career was interrupted by navy service during World War II and he did not obtain a major film role until 1951 in *The Bullfighter and the Lady*. He was later nominated for an Oscar for his performance as Kyle Hadley in Douglas Sirk's *Written on the Wind*, but became best known as a television actor, playing Eliot Ness in *The Untouchables*. He has continued to work in a wide variety of roles in the USA and abroad.

Films include: 1939 First Love. '**40** The Mortal Storm. '**42** To Be or Not to Be. '**51** The Bullfighter and the Lady. '**54** The High and the Mighty. '**57** Written on the Wind. '**60** The Last Voyage. '**66** Paris, Brule-t-il? (FR) (USA/GB: Is Paris Burning?). '**78** Un Second Souffle (FR) (USA/GB: Second Wind). '**79** 1941.

STAHL, John M.

(1886–1950). Director/producer. Born: New York City, USA

Stahl had worked as an actor and stage director before entering the film industry as a co-producer and director in 1914. He subsequently formed Tiffany-Stahl Productions and then joined Universal, becoming pre-eminent from the Thirties on as a maker of domestic melodramas, then termed 'women's' pictures. Two of his best films, *Imitation of Life* and *Magnificent Obsession*, were later remade in the Fifties by Douglas Sirk. Stahl left Universal for 20th Century-Fox during the Forties and was still under contract to that studio at the time of his death.

Films include: 1920 Greater Than Love. '**21** Suspicious Wives. '**31** Strictly Dishonorable. '**32** Back Street. '**34** Imitation of Life. '**35** Magnificent Obsession. '**44** Keys of the Kingdom. '**45** Leave Her to Heaven. '**47** The Foxes of Harrow. '**48** The Walls of Jericho.

STALLONE, Sylvester

(b. 1946). Actor/screenwriter/ director. Born: New York City, USA

Of Sicilian origin, Sylvester Stallone was born in the tough Hell's Kitchen section of New York City. In 1951 his family moved to the Washington, D.C. area; and when his parents divorced, he went to live with his mother in Philadelphia. A problem child, he was fostered out; but his athletic skills won him a scholarship to an American college in Switzerland. In 1967 he briefly attended a drama course at the University of Miami. By 1970 he was doing odd jobs in New York, including cinema usher, and beginning to get a few bit acting roles; he also began writing scripts and stories. He was encouraged by getting one of the leads (along with Henry Winkler) in a low-budget independent feature, the hilariously funny and well-observed New York comedy *The Lords of Flatbush*, which won some good reviews and a British release. In 1974 Stallone went to Hollywood, getting bit parts in films and television, and wrote a boxing script, *Rocky*, which he sold at a low price on condition that he played the lead and had a share of the profits. The film was a huge, unexpected success and spawned two sequels. Becoming an overnight star, Stallone was also able to appear in other films, trading on his image – in the witty *Paradise Alley*, his directorial debut, he was a New York sharpie who manoeuvres his brother into becoming a star wrestler. He went on to direct the *Rocky* sequels; but having exhausted this vein, he will need new outlets for his undoubted talents.

Films as actor include: 1971 Bananas (uncredited). '**74** The Lords of Flatbush; The Prisoner of Second Avenue. '**75** Capone; Deathrace 2000; Farewell, My Lovely (GB-USA). '**76** Rocky (+sc). '**78** No Place to Hide; F.I.S.T. (+co-sc); Paradise Alley (+dir; +sc). '**79** Rocky II – Redemption (+dir; +sc). '**82** Rocky III (+dir; +sc); First Blood (+co-sc).

Left: Western star Charles Starrett. Below left: Barbara Stanwyck, svelte incarnation of the film noir dangerous lady in Double Indemnity. *Above: Lionel Stander in* Pulp *(1972). Below: Anthony Steel in* Albert RN *(1953), a POW comedy-drama*

STAMP, Terence

(b. 1940). Actor. Born: Stepney, London, England

The son of a Thames tugboat captain, Terence Stamp won a scholarship to the Webber-Douglas drama school. He worked in repertory and then got his first big break when Peter Ustinov cast him in the lead in his movie version of *Billy Budd*; he was an instant hit, being nominated for an Oscar. Offers from Hollywood and elsewhere came thick and fast, but Stamp preferred to pick and choose his roles. He won the Best Actor Award at Cannes for his role in *The Collector*, but probably his best performance was as Sergeant Troy in John Schlesinger's *Far From the Madding Crowd*. Stamp and his long-time girlfriend, the model Jean Shrimpton, were the 'perfect couple' of the Sixties; with the end of that decade Stamp's career declined. After a lengthy absence from the screen he returned to play the super-villain General Zod in *Superman, The Movie* and *Superman II*.

Films include: 1962 Billy Budd; Term of Trial. '65 The Collector (GB-USA). '66 Modesty Blaise. '67 Far From the Madding Crowd; Poor Cow. '68 Blue (USA); Theorem (GB-USA). '78 Superman, The Movie (USA). '80 Superman II (USA).

STANDER, Lionel

(b. 1908). Actor/director/screenwriter/producer. Born: New York City, USA

Stander began in showbusiness as a dialect specialist at the Fred Allen Theater in the late Twenties. Experience as a radio actor and in Fatty Arbuckle and Harold Lloyd comedies led to a regular career in Hollywood from the mid-Thirties on, his gravelly voice encouraging producers to cast him in tough, though frequently comic supporting roles. Blacklisted by the House Un-American Activities Committee in 1950, Stander was unable to secure parts in movies for 13 years and gave up acting to work as a stockbroker. He made his comeback in 1963, when the director Tony Richardson cast him in his stage production of Brecht's *The Resistible Rise of Arturo Ui*; a small role in *The Loved One* followed. He moved to Italy in 1967, becoming a stalwart performer in 'spaghetti' Westerns and subsequently appearing in numerous international features.

Films include: 1926 Men of Steel. '32 The Crowd Roars. '35 The Scoundrel. '36 Mr Deeds Goes to Town. '37 A Star Is Born. '43 Hangmen Also Die! '48 Call Northside 777. '65 The Loved One. '68 C'Era una Volta il West (IT) (USA/GB: One Upon a Time in the West). '77 The Cassandra Crossing (GB-IT-USA); New York, New York.

STANWYCK, Barbara

(b. 1907). Actress. Born: Ruby Stevens; New York City, USA

The sensual half-smile of deceit, provoked by the thought of all that money, and the languid self-satisfaction that comes from having no remorse, plus the hot-cold thrill of murder that makes her eyes dance: Barbara Stanwyck's Phyllis Dietrichson in *Double Indemnity* is one of the most riveting profiles of female callousness in the cinema. It is Stanwyck's greatest role though, as one of Hollywood's best actresses, she brought bite and immediacy to all her parts. Melodrama bitches and more murderesses (*The Strange Love of Martha Ivers* and *The File on Thelma Jordon*), malcontent mothers (*Stella Dallas*) and hard, professional types (*Meet John Doe* and *Executive Suite*) became specialities of Stanwyck – names like Martha, Stella, Thelma and Phyllis fitting like a glove her shrewd, oppressive 35-year-old dames. But to see her as the vivacious stripper Sugarpuss O'Shea leading Gary Cooper astray in *Ball of Fire* and as the cardsharp tripping up Henry Fonda in *The Lady Eve* is to see one of America's wittiest comedy actresses in action. *Remember the Night* and *Clash by Night* were among the films that cast her as still dubious but more sympathetic women. Stanwyck was an orphan who at 13 worked in a New York department store and other un-skilled jobs before she became a chorus girl in the Ziegfeld Follies. She made her stage debut in *The Noose* on Broadway in 1926 and starred in *Burlesque*. In Hollywood she became a star of early Warners and Columbia talkies, working well with Frank Capra and William Wellman. She remained a star well into the Sixties, co-starring in her final film *The Night Walker* with her second ex-husband Robert Taylor, and moving gracefully into television with her own Western series, *The Big Valley*. In 1982 she was awarded an honorary Oscar, long overdue.

Films include: 1927 Broadway Nights. '30 Ladies of Leisure. '31 Night Nurse; The Miracle Woman. '32 Forbidden; The Bitter Tea of General Yen. '35 Annie Oakley. '36 The Plough and the Stars. '37 Stella Dallas. '39 Union Pacific; Golden Boy. '40 Remember the Night. '41 The Lady Eve; Meet John Doe; Ball of Fire. '44 Double Indemnity. '45 My Reputation. '46 The Strange Love of Martha Ivers. '48 Sorry, Wrong Number. '49 The File on Thelma Jordon. '50 No Man of Her Own; The Furies. '52 Clash by Night. '53 Blowing Wild. '54 Executive Suite. '57 Forty Guns. '62 Walk on the Wild Side. '65 The Night Walker.

STAPLETON, Maureen

(b. 1925). Actress. Born: Troy, New York, USA

Stapleton can be homely or matronly as the role demands. In *Plaza Suite* she displayed a fine talent for comedy, but she is usually considered a dramatic actress and gave excellent performances in *Interiors* (as the vulgar new wife) and *Reds* (as Emma Goldman). She was nominated for Oscars for both (as she was for her film debut, *Lonelyhearts*) and won for *Reds*. Stapleton went to New York City direct from school, studied at the Herbert Berghoff acting classes in her spare time, and graduated to the Actors' Studio once her first stage work had given her some experience. Her performance as Serafina Rose in Tennessee Williams' *Rose Tattoo* established her reputation.

Films include: 1958 Lonelyhearts. '60 The Fugitive Kind. '63 Bye Bye Birdie. '69 Trilogy. '70 Airport. '71 Plaza Suite. '78 Interiors. '79 The Runner Stumbles; Lost and Found. '81 Reds.

STARRETT, Charles

(1903–1986). Actor. Born: Athol, Massachusetts, USA

Handsome Charlie Starrett, well over six feet tall in stetson and spurs, was one of the unsung heroes of Hollywood's Wild West. Between 1936 and 1952 he starred in 115 Westerns. His best loved character was the Durango Kid, first played in 1940. Though he was always among the top ten most popular cowboys, he never quite made it to number one. In fact, as the heir to a precision tools firm, his career might have turned out very differently had he not been called upon to play a football extra in *The Quarterback* while at Dartmouth College. He went straight into stage acting and was spotted by a Paramount talent scout. His first film roles were as romantic leads but he quickly became a cowboy star. He retired – only 48 and very wealthy – when television forced the phasing out of small-scale Hollywood Westerns.

Films include: 1926 The Quarterback; Fighting Buckaroo. '32 The Mask of Fu Manchu. '33 Sweetheart of Sigma Chi. '34 Silver Streak. '36 Along Came Love. '38 The Colorado Trail. '40 The Durango Kid. '41 The Pinto Kid. '46 The Desert Horseman (GB: Checkmate). '49 The Blazing Trail (GB: The Forged Will). '52 The Rough, Tough West.

STAUDTE, Wolfgang

(1906–1983). Director/actor/screenwriter. Born: Saarbrücken, Germany

Staudte trained as an actor with Max Reinhardt and made his stage debut in Berlin in 1929. He joined the film industry in 1933 as the writer and producer of short advertising films. Before directing his first feature film, *Akrobat Schö-ö-ön*, he acted in the infamous, anti-semitic, Nazi propaganda film *Jud Süss* (1940). After World War II Staudte became one of the key figures in the reconstruction of the German film industry, directing and scripting several compelling and thoughtful films that were strongly anti-Nazi in theme.

Films as director include: 1943 Akrobat Schö-ö-ön (+ sc). '46 Die Mörder sind unter uns (+ sc) (GB: The Murderers Are Amongst Us). '51 Der Untertan (+ co-sc) (GB: The Underdog). '55 Ciske – Ein kind braucht Liebe (+ sc) (HOLL-GER). '57 Rose Bernd. '58 Kanonen-Serenade (+ co-sc) (GER-IT) (GB: Il Capitano). '60 Kirmes (+ sc). '63 Die Dreigroschenoper (USA/GB: The Threepenny Opera). '78 Zwischengleis.

STEEL, Anthony

(b. 1920). Actor. Born: Chelsea, London, England

Once the British public demanded Boy's Own heroics from Anthony Steel, uncomplicated adventures to go with his formal comic-book good looks. Yet, by the late Seventies, all they required of him was a role in television's *Crossroads*. At least they treated him better in Europe, where his parts were rather more controversial. Appropriately, Steel was the son of an officer in the Indian Army, and served in the Grenadier Guards throughout the war. He drifted into acting by chance, alternating small-screen roles with the stage until *The Wooden Horse* established his name. His popularity began to wane in the mid-Fifties, and he left for Italy and Germany. An earlier spell in Hollywood had not been a great success; married to Swedish stunner Anita Ekberg, he was constantly dismissed as 'Mr Ekberg'.

Films include: 1948 Saraband for Dead Lovers. '50 The Blue Lamp; The Wooden Horse. '53 The Malta Story. '54 West of Zanzibar; The Sea Shall Not Have Them. '55 Storm Over the Nile. '56 Checkpoint. '76 The Story of O. '79 The World Is Full of Married Men.

STEELE, Barbara

(b. 1938). Actress. Born: Birkenhead, Cheshire, England

Tall, dark-haired and green-eyed, Barbara Steele was spotted acting in repertory in Brighton and signed up by the Rank Organization to be groomed for stardom. She made a few films for that studio before 20th Century-Fox bought up her contract. During the actors' strike in Hollywood in 1960 she went to Italy and appeared in the first of many horror movies she has since made in that country. The highlights of her career were her roles in Roger Corman's *The Pit and the Pendulum*, based on the Edgar Allan Poe short story, and Federico Fellini's 8½. She continues to make occasional appearances in movies and was the associate producer of television's *Winds of War*.

Films include: 1958 Bachelor of Hearts. '59 Sapphire. '60 La Maschera del Demonio (IT) (USA/GB: Black Sunday). '61 The Pit and the Pendulum (USA). '63 Otto e Mezzo (IT-FR) (USA/GB: 8½); Lo Spettro (IT) (GB: The Spectre). '65 La Danza Macabre (IT-FR) (GB: Castle of Blood). '74 Caged Heat (USA). '78 Piranha (USA); Pretty Baby (USA); La Clé sur la Porte (FR). '80 The Silent Scream (USA-GB).

STEENBURGEN, Mary

(b. 1954). Actress. Born: Newport, Arkansas, USA

A tall, sweet-faced brunette with a perfect figure and an air of fragility, Steenburgen struck an incongruous note nearly raping her husband (Woody Allen) in *A Midsummer Night's Sex Comedy*, but then she likes slightly offbeat roles. Her credits are excellent: the woman who tries to redeem the 'bum' (Jack Nicholson) in *Goin' South*; the liberated bank clerk who falls for H.G. Wells (Malcolm McDowell – her real-life husband) in *Time After Time*; Melvin's down-to-earth wife Lynda in *Melvin and Howard* (her Oscar role); and the immigrant mother in *Ragtime*. She studied drama at Hendrix College, worked in the famous Doubleday's bookshop in New York, worked as a waitress, and joined a community theatre group. There she was spotted by a television talent scout who brought her to the attention of Jack Nicholson, and he himself cast her in *Goin' South*.

Films: 1978 Goin' South. '79 Time After Time. '80 Melvin and Howard. '81 Ragtime. '82 A Midsummer Night's Sex Comedy.

STEIGER, Rod

(b. 1925). Actor. Born: West Hampton, New Jersey, USA

Steiger won an Oscar for his portrayal of a white Southern cop in *In the Heat of the Night*, a powerful, potentially violent man, basically honest but confused and very nearly corrupted by racism. In many ways it's a typical performance, for Steiger, physically big and heavy-jowled, is at his best exploring the insecurities which lie below the surface of social misfits, be they dangerous men – violent on a grand scale like Napoleon or Al Capone – or the victims of violence pushed to the limit, like the concentration camp survivor in *The Pawnbroker*. At 16, he joined the navy, and when he left it five years later he began acting as a hobby while working as a civil servant. He went on to study acting seriously at the New York Theatre Wing, The Actors' Workshop and finally The Actors' Studio, and emerged a committed exponent of the Method. Steiger's reputation as a screen actor was established with his stunning performance as Brando's brother in *On the Waterfront*. His range is quite extraordinary, even if he occasionally verges on ham. He was bizarre as the psychopath in *No Way to Treat A Lady*, funny as the effeminate embalmer in *The Loved One*, and hugely moving in *W.C. Fields and Me*. The Seventies were not kind to him, bringing the collapse of his third marriage, depression, loneliness and heart trouble which required a serious operation, and a string of mostly second-rate films.

Films include: 1951 Teresa. '54 On the Waterfront. '55 Oklahoma! '56 The Harder They Fall. '57 Run of the Arrow; Across the Bridge. '59 Al Capone. '63 Mani Sulla Città (IT) (GB: Hands Over the City). '65 The Pawnbroker; The Loved One. '67 In the Heat of the Night. '68 No Way to Treat a Lady. '69 The Illustrated Man; Three Into Two Won't Go (GB). '70 Waterloo (IT-USSR). '71 Happy Birthday Wanda June. '72 Giù la Testa (IT) (USA: Duck! You Sucker; GB: A Handful of Dynamite). '73 Lucky Luciano (IT-FR). '76 W.C. Fields and Me. '79 The Amityville Horror. '81 The Chosen.

STEINER, Max

(1888–1971). Composer. Born: Maximilian Raoul Steiner; Vienna, Austria

Max Steiner composed the score for at least half of everybody's favourite movies. He created those haunting melodies which help the memory of *Casablanca* to linger, provided the fragile backdrop to Fay Wray's screams in *King Kong* and, most of all, added the sweeping symphonies to the sweeping, symphonic *Gone With the Wind*. In all, he was nominated for Academy Awards no less than a remarkable 26 times, and he won them for *Now, Voyager*, *Since You Went Away* and *The Informer*. Classically trained, under Mahler and Fuchs at the Viennese Imperial Academy of Music, Steiner came to England in 1904 and was working there when Flo Ziegfeld spotted him ten years later. In Hollywood he became Music Director of RKO, and was borrowed by Selznick and Warners. His output was prodigious – he wrote over 200 scores in all, completed *King Kong* in just two weeks – and he is widely regarded as a pioneer of screen composition.

Films include: 1929 Rio Rita. '33 King Kong. '35 The Informer. '36 Garden of Allah; Little Lord Fauntleroy. '37 A Star Is Born; The Life of Emile Zola. '38 Jezebel. '39 Gone With the Wind. '40 All This, and Heaven Too. '42 They Died With Their Boots On; Casablanca; Now, Voyager. '44 Since You Went Away. '45 Rhapsody in Blue. '46 The Big Sleep. '48 Treasure of the Sierra Madre; Key Largo. '56 The Searchers.

Below left: Ford Sterling in His Pride and Shame *(1916). Left: Robert Stephens in* The Private Life of Sherlock Holmes. *Above, from left to right: Barbara Steele in* The Spectre; *Mary Steenburgen in* Melvin and Howard; *Rod Steiger in* Happy Birthday Wanda June; *Anna Sten in* They Came to Blow Up America *(1943). Below: Connie Stevens in* Never Too Late. *Below left: Jan Sterling in* Ace in the Hole

STEN, Anna

(b. 1910). Actress. Born: Annel (Anjuschka) Stenskaya Sudakevich; Kiev, Ukraine, Russia

Goldwyn brought the slim, beautiful, blonde Sten to America in the Thirties, tried to train her for English-language movies, spent a fortune on publicity and still her career in Hollywood fizzled. Born of a Swedish mother and a Ukrainian father, she was raised in Russia, studied at the Film Academy and joined a repertory company in Moscow. She made a number of films, most notably *Girl With the Hatbox, The Yellow Passport, The House on Trubnaya Square* and *Storm Over Asia*, before going to Germany to work at Ufa studios (where she made *The Brothers Karamazov*, directed by her husband Fedor Ozep). That was when Goldwyn heard of Sten and tried to do for her what had been done for Garbo and Dietrich.

Films include: 1927 Devushka s Korobkoi (Girl With the Hatbox). '28 Dom na Trubnoi (USSR) (GB: The House on Trubnaya Square); Potomok Chingis Khana (USSR) (Storm Over Asia); Zemlya v Plenu (The Yellow Passport/Earth in Chains). '31 Bomben auf Monte Carlo (GER); Sturme der Leidenschaft (GER); Der Mörder Dimitri Karamazov (GER) (GB: The Brothers Karamazov). '34 Nana. '35 The Wedding Night. '40 The Man I Married. '44 Three Russian Girls. '55 Soldier of Fortune.

STEPHENS, Robert

(b. 1931). Actor. Born: Bristol, Somerset, England

Despite the fact that the stage is his first love, since his screen debut in 1960 Robert Stephens has made several very creditable appearances on film, from art teacher Teddy Lloyd in *The Prime of Miss Jean Brodie* to the masterfully weary Sherlock Holmes in *The Private Life of Sherlock Holmes*. After studying at the Northern Theatre School in Bradford, Stephens spent six years in rep. He first became known in London, and later in New York, in John Osborne's play *Epitaph* in 1958. He then spent three years at the Royal Court Theatre in London before being invited to join the National Theatre – of which he was also appointed associate director in 1967. It was also there that he met and co-starred with his future wife (now divorced) Maggie Smith.

Films include: 1961 A Taste of Honey. '63 Cleopatra (USA); The Small World of Sammy Lee. '66 Morgan, a Suitable Case for Treatment. '68 Romeo and Juliet (GB-IT). '69 The Prime of Miss Jean Brodie. '70 The Private Life of Sherlock Holmes. '72 Travels With My Aunt (USA); Asphyx. '77 The Duellists.

STERLING, Ford

(1885–1939). Actor. Born: George Ford Stitch; La Crosse, Wisconsin, USA

A gesticulating, grimacing silent comic with specs and a greasepaint goatee, Ford Sterling was the captain of the Keystone Kops, and one of their original recruits. He had originally joined Mack Sennett at Biograph after running away as a boy to become a circus clown and appearing in vaudeville. In films he first achieved fame playing a farcical bearded Dutchman. He had his own series, the Sterling Comedies, and directed many of his own films. In the sound era Sterling played the White King in *Alice in Wonderland* and a few other roles before the loss of a leg spoiled his career.

Films include: 1911 Abe Gets Even With His Father. '14 Between Showers. '16 The Manicurist (+dir). '17 Stars and Bars (+dir); A Woman in the Case. '22 Oh, Mabel Behave (+co-dir). '26 Everybody's Acting; The Show Off. '28 Gentlemen Prefer Blondes. '33 Alice in Wonderland. '35 Behind the Green Lights; Black Sheep.

STERLING, Jan

(b. 1923). Actress. Born: Jane Sterling Adriance; New York City, USA

Blonde and skinny, Sterling was good at playing mean characters whose temper and behaviour left much to be desired, especially by her boyfriends, lovers and husbands. Nowhere was this better seen than in *Ace in the Hole* where she played the sluttish wife of a man who has been buried alive in a cave-in. She teams up with a heartless opportunist reporter (played by Kirk Douglas) to exploit the crowds who assemble during the unsuccessful rescue attempt. Sterling was born into a socially prominent family and spent much of her early life in Europe and studied at the Fay Compton School of Dramatic Arts in London. She still lives there but returns to Hollywood occasionally.

Films include: 1948 Johnny Belinda. '50 Caged; Mystery Street. '51 Ace in the Hole; The Mating Season. '52 Flesh and Fury. '54 The Human Jungle; The High and the Mighty. '55 Female on the Beach. '58 High School Confidential. '68 The Angry Breed.

STERNBERG, Josef von

(1894–1969). Director. Born: Jonas Sternberg; Vienna, Austria

Sternberg came to the USA as a young boy, returned to Vienna and was back again in his teens, scratching a living in odd film jobs. He went to Hollywood in 1924 and made the waterfront melodrama *The Salvation Hunters* on a minimal budget. His next few projects collapsed or, like his film with Edna Purviance for Chaplin, went unreleased. Joining Paramount, he made the early gangster picture *Underworld* and established his reputation as an arrogant genius. After several prolific years he went to Germany and with *The Blue Angel* began the partnership with Marlene Dietrich that was to continue through six more American films, including *Shanghai Express* and *The Scarlet Empress*. His extraordinarily evocative visual style combined with her masklike beauty to create a new kind of ambiguous eroticism. Leaving her and Paramount in 1935, he seemed to lose direction, with only *The Shanghai Gesture* representing a return to his stylized form. His last film was *The Saga of Anatahan*. He published his revealing but uninformative autobiography, *Fun in a Chinese Laundry*, in 1965. Sternberg must figure among the top half-dozen stylists in the history of the cinema: his films shimmer with light (Dietrich photographed through a mist of veils, shrouds, silks and sequins), artificiality and sexual cruelty. They are confections for voyeurs and connoisseurs of high art in the cinema alike.

Films include: 1921 The Highest Bidder (ass. dir). '25 The Salvation Hunters. '26 A Woman of the Sea/The Sea Gull (unreleased). '27 Underworld. '28 The Last Command; The Drag Net; The Docks of New York. '29 The Case of Lena Smith; Thunderbolt. '30 Der blaue Engel (GER) (English-language version; The Blue Angel, USA-GB, 1931); Morocco. '31 Dishonored; An American Tragedy. '32 Shanghai Express; Blonde Venus. '34 The Scarlet Empress. '35 The Devil Is a Woman; Crime and Punishment. '37 I, Claudius (unfinished) (GB). '41 The Shanghai Gesture. '51 Jet Pilot (released in 1957). '52 Macao. '53 The Saga of Anatahan (JAP) (USA: Ana-Ta-Han).

STEVENS, Connie

(b. 1938). Actress/singer. Born: Concetta Ann Ingolia; New York City, USA

A petite, blue-eyed, doll-faced blonde who could play the ingénue and sing as well, Connie Stevens started in minor soap operas, made her Broadway debut in *The Star Spangled Girl* and worked the Las Vegas nightclub circuit. She began her screen career by playing teen roles in popular romances, the best of them directed by Delmer Daves, and this image stayed with her until she made *The Grissom Gang*, directed by Robert Aldrich. She was a popular recording artist for some years and also appeared regularly on television in such series as *Hawaiian Eye*. Her second husband was actor-singer Eddie Fisher.

Films include: 1957 Young and Dangerous. '58 Party Crashers. '61 Parrish; Susan Slade. '63 Palm Springs Weekend. '65 Two on a Guillotine; Never Too Late. '66 Way, Way Out. '71 The Grissom Gang; The Last Generation. '78 Sergeant Pepper's Lonely Hearts Club Band (USA-GER).

STEVENS, George

(1905–1975). Director. Born: Oakland, California, USA

George Stevens went to Hollywood in 1921. He intended to be an actor but became an assistant cameraman instead. From 1927 to 1930 he worked for Hal Roach, photographing Laurel and Hardy and Our Gang shorts. He then started directing shorts and, in 1933, made his first feature. He soon progressed to vehicles for Katharine Hepburn (*Alice Adams* and, later, *Woman of the Year*) and Astaire and Rogers (*Swing Time*). He had a light hand with comedy and romance and occasionally adventure until his war service with the US Army Signal Corps, which involved filming sometimes grim newsreel footage. His later projects were often heavily ambitious, though *Shane*, a poetic Western seen through the eyes of a child, won great popularity, and *Giant* was enlivened by James Dean's last performance. After Stevens' over-reverent treatment of *The Diary of Anne Frank*, there was nowhere to go but to *The Greatest Story Ever Told*, the story of Jesus. *The Only Game in Town*, with an overweight Elizabeth Taylor vamping Warren Beatty in Las Vegas, was a final epilogue to a career that had once promised to be light, bright and truly American in the best Hollywood tradition. Stevens' over-serious valuation of his own talent was reinforced by Best Director Oscars for *A Place in the Sun* (based on Theodore Dreiser's novel *An American Tragedy*) and *Giant*. His son, George Stevens Jr, was director of the American Film Institute from 1967 to 1979.

Films include: 1935 Alice Adams; Laddie; Annie Oakley. '36 Swing Time. '39 Gunga Din. '42 Woman of the Year; Talk of the Town. '43 The More the Merrier. '51 A Place in the Sun. '53 Shane. '56 Giant. '59 The Diary of Anne Frank. '65 The Greatest Story Ever Told. '70 The Only Game in Town.

STEVENS, Inger

(1934–1970). Actress. Born: Inger Stensland; Stockholm, Sweden

Inger Stevens arrived in the USA with her divorced father in 1947. Three years later, aged 16, she ran away from home, taking various jobs (including that of chorus girl) and also studying at the Actors' Studio. Appearances in commercials led to roles in television drama and on the Broadway stage. She broke into films in 1957 with *Man on Fire*, playing opposite Bing Crosby. The lead in the television series *The Farmer's Daughter* made her a star but her troubled personal life adversely affected her acting career. Two of her best film roles were in *Cry Terror*, as one of a family held hostage by a maniac, and in *Madigan*, in which she played Richard Widmark's lonely wife. Sadly this strikingly beautiful actress committed suicide in 1970.

Films include: 1957 Man on Fire. '58 Cry Terror. '59 The World, the Flesh and the Devil. '64 The New Interns. '67 A Guide for the Married Man. '68 Firecreek; Madigan; 5-Card Stud; Hang 'Em High; House of Cards.

STEVENS, Stella

(b. 1936). Actress. Born: Estelle Eggleston; Hot Coffee, Mississippi, USA

Stella Stevens to some extent fell into the Marilyn Monroe-clone trap, playing voluptuous blonde glamorous girls, from bubbly virgins to tarts who've heard all the come-ons before. She was married at 15, a mother a year later, a single parent a year after that. Her first big success was as Apassionata von Climax in *Li'l Abner*. She appeared nude in Playboy magazine (which did no harm to her career), and went on to star opposite many of the big names of the Sixties including Elvis Presley, Glenn Ford, Jerry Lewis and Bobby Darin. In the Seventies Stevens' performance opposite Jason Robards Jr in *The Ballad of Cable Hogue* (1970) re-established her as an actress of some depth.

Films include: 1959 Say One For Me; Li'l Abner. '61 Man-Trap; Too Late Blues. '62 Girls! Girls! Girls! '68 How to Save a Marriage and Ruin Your Life. '69 The Mad Room. '72 The Poseidon Adventure. '76 Nickelodeon. '78 The Manitou.

STEVENSON, Robert

(1905–1986). Director. Born: Buxton, Derbyshire, England

After studying engineering at Cambridge University, Robert Stevenson entered the film industry writing titles for Paramount–British Newsreel. In 1930 he joined Michael Balcon at Gainsborough as a writer and soon graduated to directing Jack Hulbert comedies. He stayed at Gainsborough until 1938, achieving critical respect with the historical epic *Tudor Rose*, starring Nova Pilbeam and John Mills, and the doggy *Owd Bob*. Then he rejoined Balcon, who had moved to Ealing; but as a pacifist he left for Hollywood at the outbreak of World War II. His biggest early success there

was *Jane Eyre*, with Joan Fontaine and Orson Welles; but a string of commercial failures exiled him to television for five years in the early Fifties. He joined the Walt Disney studio in 1956, making a key contribution to the development of live-action pictures. His best film for Disney was *Mary Poppins*, with Julie Andrews. He was at one time (1934–44) married to actress Anna Lee.

Films include: 1936 Jack of All Trades (USA: The Two of Us); Tudor Rose (USA: Nine Days a Queen). '38 Owd Bob (USA: To the Victor). '39 Young Man's Fancy. '41 Back Street (USA). '43 Jane Eyre (USA). '49 The Woman on Pier 13/I Married a Communist (USA). '59 Darby O'Gill and the Little People (USA). '61 The Absent-Minded Professor (USA). '62 In Search of the Castaways (USA: The Castaways). '64 Mary Poppins (USA). '71 Bedknobs and Broomsticks (USA). '76 The Shaggy D.A.

STEWART, Alexandra

(b. 1939). Actress. Born: Montreal, Quebec, Canada

While studying art in Paris, Alexandra Stewart worked as a photographic model, appearing on the cover of *Elle* magazine and in a Christian Dior commercial. This led to her being offered parts in French films and she rapidly gained an international reputation as an attractive, versatile actress. Among her best roles were a beautiful spy in *Zeppelin* and as Warren Beatty's supportive girlfriend in *Mickey One*.

Films include: 1958 Le Bel Âge (FR) (GB: Love Is When You Make It). '59 Les Motards (FR). '60 Exodus (USA). '61 Les Mauvais Coups (FR) (USA: Naked Autumn). '63 Le Feu Follet (FR-IT) (USA: The Fire Within; GB: A Time to Live and a Time to Die). '65 Mickey One (USA). '67 Maroc 7 (GB). '68 La Mariée Était en Noir (GB: The Bride Wore Black). '71 Zeppelin (GB). '78 In Praise of Older Women (CAN). '79 Agency (CAN). '82 Chanel Solitaire (FR-GB).

STEWART, Anita

(1895–1961). Actress. Born: Anna Stewart; Brooklyn, New York City, USA

Though later a poised Twenties beauty, she began in films as an innocent, pretty maiden. Anita Stewart was working for her local film company in Brooklyn, Vitagraph, by the time she was 16. She formed a romantic on-screen partnership with Earle Williams, notably in *His Phantom Sweetheart*, directed by her brother-in-law, Ralph Ince. She briefly had her own production company, with Louis B. Mayer in charge, and made *Virtuous Wives*, directed by George Loane Tucker. She signed with First National in 1919 and continued to star until the end of the silent era. She retired as, and remained, one of the wealthiest women in Hollywood.

Films include: 1912 The Wood Violet. '13 The Swan Girl. '15 His Phantom Sweetheart; The Juggernaut; The Goddess (serial). '17 The Girl Philippa. '18 Virtuous Wives. '19 A Midnight Romance; Mary Regan. '25 Never the Twain Shall Meet. '28 Sisters of Eve.

STEWART, Donald Ogden

(1894–1980). Screenwriter. Born: Columbus, Ohio, USA

A judge's son, he went to Yale and began to write after failing in stockbroking. His first film assignment was an adaptation of *Brown of Harvard* in 1926; his first play was *Rebound*, produced on Broadway four years later. Stewart had rapidly acquired a reputation as a particularly prolific and sophisticated satirist excelling in witty explorations of American high society. Perhaps most notable was his Oscar-winning screenplay for *The Philadelphia Story*, with Katharine Hepburn as a spoilt society goddess. Stewart's strong social conscience led to his joining the Hollywood Anti-Nazi League and writing a stirring

Far left: Inger Stevens in Don Siegel's Madigan. *Left: Stella Stevens in Sam Peckinpah's* The Ballad of Cable Hogue. *Above: Alexandra Stewart in*

François Truffaut's La Nuit Américaine *(1973, Day for Night). Above: Anita Stewart in* The Great White Way *(1924)*

Above: James Stewart in the Western Firecreek *(1967). Below: Paul Stewart in the bruising boxing picture* Champion, *directed by Mark Robson*

STEWART, James

(b. 1908). Actor. Born: Indiana, Pennsylvania, USA

The tall, lean possessor of that famous, querulous drawl, James Stewart was an important leading man and a modest, much-loved star for over thirty years, but he was really a character actor whose outstanding career went through several different phases. He began as a heavy, but his early successes were as the young, gangling, bashful idealist at the centre of Frank Capra's *Mr Smith Goes to*

Washington and *You Can't Take It With You*, as the pacifist marshal embarrassed by Dietrich's frankness in *Destry Rides Again* and as a suitor competing with Cary Grant for Katharine Hepburn in the screwball comedy *The Philadelphia Story*. He then moved into genial, perplexed and occasionally choleric middle age – as a drunk conversing with a giant rabbit in *Harvey*; and as a man unable to realize the good he has done in the Christmas-time magic of *It's a Wonderful Life*, again for Capra. But in the Fifties, in a superb series of Westerns by Anthony Mann (from *Winchester '73* to *The Man From Laramie*), Stewart played an honest man who was also bitter, anguished, bad-tempered and selfish. It seemed that youthful naivete had given way to deep depression and the transition was astounding. Not only Mann, but Hitchcock, too, spotted the actor's maturer characterization and in *Vertigo* and *Rear Window* the girl-shy Stewart of the Thirties has become a man with morbid sexual obsessions; Otto Preminger even had him as an attorney holding up a pair of panties in court in *Anatomy of a Murder*. These were all great performances – and there was one more, as Ranse Stoddard, apparently *The Man Who Shot Liberty Valance* until the numbing deception is revealed. After that, Stewart succumbed to mediocre films, but he had already done enough. His background was an architecture degree from Princeton University and theatre work with the University Players, who included friends and later screen co-stars Margaret Sullavan and Henry Fonda. Stewart was nominated for Best Actor five times, winning for *The Philadelphia Story*. During World War II he was a bomber pilot and rose to the rank of colonel with a very distinguished record.

Films include: 1935 Murder Man. '36 Wife Versus Secretary. '37 Seventh Heaven. '38 You Can't Take It With You. '39 Mr Smith Goes to Washington; Destry Rides Again. '40 The Shop Around the Corner; The Mortal Storm; The Philadelphia Story. '47 It's a Wonderful Life. '48 Call Northside 777; Rope. '50 Winchester '73; Broken Arrow; Harvey. '52 Bend of the River (GB: Where the River Bends). '53 The Naked Spur; The Glenn Miller Story. '54 Rear Window; The Far Country. '55 The Man From Laramie. '56 The Man Who Knew Too Much. '57 The Spirit of St Louis. '58 Vertigo. '59 Anatomy of a Murder. '62 The Man Who Shot Liberty Valance. '70 The Cheyenne Social Club. '76 The Shootist.

STEWART, Paul

(1908–1986). Actor. Born: New York City, USA

A leading member of Orson Welles' Mercury Theatre company, Stewart co-directed rehearsals for and acted in Welles' notorious radio drama *The War of the Worlds*, had a film debut as Kane's crafty valet in *Citizen Kane*, and worked for the Office of War Information. He was a sinister hood in *Johnny Eager* and played other callous gangsters, doubtful scientists and double-dealing or incompetent army officers, anyone, in fact, who couldn't be trusted. He directed screen tests

and second units, plays on Broadway and for television. His distinguished acting career stretched into the Seventies and he was a notable Flo Ziegfeld in *W.C. Fields and Me*.

Films include: 1940 Citizen Kane. '41 Johnny Eager. '49 The Window; Twelve O'Clock High; Champion. '52 Deadline USA (GB: Deadline); The Bad and the Beautiful. '53 The Juggler. '54 Deep in My Heart. '55 The Cobweb. '58 King Creole. '63 A Child Is Waiting. '65 The Greatest Story Ever Told. '75 The Day of the Locust. '76 W.C. Fields and Me. '78 Revenge of the Pink Panther (GB). '81 S.O.B.

STILLER, Mauritz

(1883–1928). Director. Born: Mowsche Stiller; Helsinki, Finland

The child of Russian-Polish parents, Stiller fled from Finland to Sweden to escape conscription into the Czarist army. He built up a reputation as a theatre actor, and it was as an actor that he was engaged, in 1911, by the Svenska Bio company. Within a year he was writing and directing, and with Victor Sjöström he created the first golden age of Swedish film. Stiller was more versatile and less literary-minded than Sjöström, and it was with a series of brilliant comedies that he first attracted attention. In *Thomas Graal's Best Film* and *Love and Journalism* he drew enchanting humour from the tribulations of his heroes, while the superb *Erotikon* was a sophisticated look at sexual rivalry which deeply influenced the comedies of Lubitsch. But before *Erotikon* Stiller had made his best film *Sir Arne's Treasure*; for this he had gone out, like Sjöström, into the Swedish countryside, and brought back a film filled with a harsh and bitter poetry. In the Twenties Stiller continued in this vein, and his last Swedish film *Gösta Berlings Saga*, a complex epic much influenced by Griffith, not only introduced Garbo but drew the attention of MGM. Stiller and Garbo duly arrived in America. Which of the two L.B. Mayer originally wanted is still debated; what is certain is that Stiller failed in America almost as conclusively as Garbo succeeded. Stiller was an autocrat who demanded a total control which of course he did not get. He completed only two films, one of which, *Hotel Imperial*, showed much of the true Stiller style. His health failed, and he returned to Sweden, directed one stage production, and died.

Films include: 1916 Kärlek och Journalistik (GB: Love and Journalism). '17 Thomas Graals Bästa Film (GB: Thomas Graal's Best Film); Alexander den Store (GB: Alexander the Great). '19 Sången om den Eldröda Blomman (GB: The Flame of Life); Herr Arnes Pengar (USA: Sir Arne's Treasure; GB: Snows of Destiny; retitled Sir Arne's Treasure). '20 Erotikon/Riddaren au Igår (GB: Bonds that Chafe). '21 Gunnar Hedes Saga/En Herrgardssagen (USA: The Blizzard; GB: The Judgement; retitled Gunnar Hede's Saga). '24 Gösta Berlings Saga (USA: The Legend of Gösta Berling; GB: The Atonement of Gösta Berling). '26 The Temptress (USA). '27 Hotel Imperial (USA); The Woman on Trial (USA). '28 The Street of Sin (co-dir) (USA).

anti-fascist script for *Keeper of the Flame*. Inevitably this led to his blacklisting. In 1951 Stewart retired quietly to England, taking on only the occasional writing job.

Films include: 1926 Brown of Harvard. '30 Laughter (co-sc). '31 Tarnished Lady. '34 The Barretts of Wimpole Street. '38 Holiday (co-sc); Marie Antoinette (co-sc). '40 The Philadelphia Story; Kitty Foyle (co-sc). '41 That Uncertain Feeling. '42 Keeper of the Flame. '47 Cass Timberlane.

STOCKWELL, Dean

(b. 1936). Actor. Born: North Hollywood, California, USA

Growing up in Hollywood, Stockwell made his film debut in 1945 at the age of nine. Before that, though, he had already worked on radio and television. With his impish face and brown curly hair (dyed the appropriate colour for Joseph Losey's *The Boy With Green Hair*) and his not inconsiderable acting skills, he became a much sought-after juvenile performer and won an award for his role in *Gentleman's Agreement*. He graduated to leading young adult roles but few parts matched the talent he was able to show in, for example, *The Werewolf of Washington* (1973).

Films include: 1945 Valley of Decision; Anchors Aweigh. **'46** The Green Years. **'47** Gentleman's Agreement. **'48** The Boy With Green Hair. **'49** Down to the Sea in Ships. **'60** Sons and Lovers (GB). **'62** Long Day's Journey Into Night. **'76** Tracks. **'79** She Came to the Valley.

STONE, Andrew L.

(b. 1902). Director/producer/ screenwriter. Born: Oakland, California, USA

Stone joined the San Francisco Film Exchange while a student at the University of California during the Twenties. He moved to Universal and then began to direct short films for Paramount, his first being *Dreary House* in 1928. He rose to special prominence during the Fifties and Sixties as the director/writer and producer of suspense films, often working in collaboration with his wife, Virginia, who acted as musical editor and financial organizer. His career declined in the early Seventies with the commercial failure of two classical composer biopics, one about Greig, *Song of Norway*, and the other about Johann Strauss, *The Great Waltz*.

Films include: 1939 The Great Victor Herbert. **'52** Confidence Gill; The Steel Trap. **'56** Julie. **'58** Cry Terror. **'60** The Last Voyage. **'61** Ring of Fire. **'62** The Password Is Courage (GB). **'70** Song of Norway. **'72** The Great Waltz. **'77** Rollercoaster (co-dir).

STONE, Lewis

(1878–1953). Actor. Born: Louis Stepford Stone; Worcester, Massachusetts, USA

At the age of 20 Lewis Stone went prematurely grey and was already taking on the distinguished look that he was to put to good use in his ensuing film career. Between fighting in the Spanish-American war and World War I he made his screen debut and his earlier interest in writing turned to an interest in acting. After World War I he concentrated on his film work and he soon graduated to the lead roles that led to him signing with MGM, where he remained for the rest of his career. He made the transition to talkies with *The Trial of Mary Dugan* opposite Norma Shearer, and appeared with Garbo in two silents and two talkies. A master of the use of the subtle glance or gesture, he was to

have appeared in *Sabrina* (1954) when he died of a heart attack.

Films include: 1922 The Prisoner of Zenda. **'23** Scaramouche. **'29** The Trial of Mary Dugan; Wild Orchids. **'32** Grand Hotel. **'33** Queen Christina. **'35** David Copperfield. **'41** The Bugle Sounds. **'52** Scaramouche; The Prisoner of Zenda. **'53** All the Brothers Were Valiant.

STOPPA, Paolo

(b. 1906). Actor. Born: Rome, Italy

Before World War II, Stoppa was one of Italy's best-known stage actors. He began appearing in films in the Thirties, achieving great acclaim in *Miracle in Milan*, playing the treacherous villain Rappi in Vittorio De Sica's fable about the poor inhabitants of a shanty town on the outskirts of Milan who are confronted by a greedy landowner. Stoppa went on to appear in some notable films of the Sixties, among them *Rocco and His Brothers* and *Once Upon a Time in the West*.

Films include: 1949 La Beauté du Diable (FR-IT) (GB: Beauty and the Beast). **'51** Miracolo a Milano (USA/GB: Miracle in Milan). **'60** Rocco e i Suoi Fratelli (IT-FR) (USA/GB: Rocco and His Brothers). **'63** Il Gattopardo (IT-FR) (USA/GB: The Leopard). **'64** Becket (GB). **'66** Caccia alla Volpe (USA-IT) (USA/GB: After the Fox). **'68** C'Era una Volta il West (USA/GB: Once Upon a Time in the West). **'79** Suor Omicidi (GB: Killer Nun).

STORARO, Vittorio

(b. 1940). Cinematographer. Born: Rome, Italy

Vittorio Storaro was the most talented cinematographer to emerge in Italy during the Sixties and in the following decade he made his mark on the international scene, winning Oscars for *Apocalypse Now* and *Reds*. He was trained at Rome's Centro Sperimentale and initially worked in short films. His first feature was Franco Rossi's *Giovinezza, Giovinezza*, but it was as Bernardo Bertolucci's regular cameraman that he became known overseas. He says: 'Photography, for me, means writing with light.' He

combines a sensuous quality of realism with an effective degree of stylization that is particularly successful in capturing the past and making it live.

Films include: 1969 Giovinezza, Giovinezza. **'70** La Strategia del Ragno (GB: The Spider's Stratagem); Il Conformista (IT-FR-GER) (USA/GB: The Conformist). **'72** Ultimo Tango a Parigi (IT-FR) (GB: Last Tango in Paris). **'76** Novecento/1900 (IT-FR-GER). **'79** La Luna (USA: Luna); Apocalypse Now (USA); Agatha (GB). **'81** Reds (USA). **'82** One From the Heart (USA).

STORCK, Henri

(b. 1907). Documentarist. Born: Ostend, Belgium

Storck's enthusiasm for film resulted in his abandoning a painting career, but his lyrical film-making style reflects the influence of Ostend artists such as James Ensor, Leon Spillaert and Constant Permeke. Storck's early films were well-received by critics; he also assisted Jean Vigo on *Zéro de Conduite* (1933) and collaborated with Joris Ivens on *Borinage*. In 1938 he founded the Belgian Royal Film Archive and he managed to continue making movies in Belgium during World War II (despite his left-wing sympathies), most notably the patriotic hymn to peasant life *Symphonie Paysanne*. His later work, such as *Le Monde de Paul Delvaux*, about the Belgian surrealist painter, has tended to reflect his early fascination with painting.

Films include: 1932 Histoire du Soldat Inconnu. **'33** Borinage (co-dir). **'36** Regards sur la Belgique Ancienne. **'37** Les Maisons de la Misère. **'46** Le Monde de Paul Delvaux. **'47** Symphonie Paysanne (in five parts). **'49** Au Carrefour de la Vie. **'52** La Fenêtre Ouverte. **'57** Couleurs du Feu. **'66** Jeudi on Chantera comme Dimanche (exec. prod).

STRADLING Sr, Harry

(1902–1970). Cinematographer. Born: England

The nephew of Mary Pickford's cameraman Walter Stradling, Harry Stradling Sr went to America as a young man and filmed many routine movies. He made his reputation in

France with his cinematography for Jacques Feyder's *La Kermesse Héroïque*, in which he boldly and successfully attempted to capture the quality of Flemish paintings on the screen. In England Feyder and Stradling created a low-key, impressionistic Moscow for *Knight Without Armour*, and Stradling's way with lighting also enhanced *South Riding, Pygmalion* and *The Citadel*. Back in the USA he made extraordinary use of double-exposure in *The Corsican Brothers*, in which Douglas Fairbanks Jr had twin roles; won an Oscar for his glowing close-ups of Hurd Hatfield in *The Picture of Dorian Gray*; and tuned into Nicholas Ray's Trucolor vision of *Johnny Guitar*. He gave life to Eliza Doolittle again, this time in colour, and won a second Oscar for *My Fair Lady*. After shooting Barbra Streisand's first four movies, he then put her in the care of his son, Harry Stradling Jr (who had first assisted his father on *Guys and Dolls*) on *The Way We Were* (1973). Harry Jr, nominated for Oscars for that and *1776* (1972), still has a long way to go before he reaches his father's total of 13 nominations.

Films include: 1927 Burnt Fingers (USA). **'34** La Dame aux Camélias (FR). **'35** La Kermesse Héroïque (FR) (USA/GB: Carnival in Flanders). **'37** Knight Without Armour (GB). **'38** South Riding (GB); Pygmalion (GB). **'41** The Corsican Brothers (USA). **'45** The Picture of Dorian Gray (USA). **'54** Johnny Guitar (USA). **'55** Guys and Dolls (USA). **'64** My Fair Lady (USA). **'68** Funny Girl (USA).

Below: Lee Strasberg, actor and influential teacher of the Method. Right: Meryl Streep in The French Lieutenant's Woman. *Far right: Barbra Streisand in* Funny Girl

STRASBERG, Lee

(1901–1982). Actor/teacher. Born: Israel Strasberg; Budzanow, Poland

Trained as an actor in the USA by Richard Boleslavsky and Maria Ouspenskaya, former students of the Moscow Art Theatre's Constantin Stanislavsky, Lee Strasberg made his stage debut in 1925. He helped to found the radical Group Theatre in the Thirties, directing many plays, and in 1948 he became artistic director of the recently-founded Actors' Studio, which taught the Method style of psychological realism to such distinguished students as Marlon Brando, Marilyn Monroe, Paul Newman, Rod Steiger, Kim Stanley, James Dean, Montgomery Clift and Al Pacino, among many others. In 1969 Strasberg set up his own Institute of the Theatre in New York and Los Angeles. In 1974 he began a new career as a character actor in films with the role of gangster Hyman Roth in *The Godfather, Part II*, for which he won an Oscar nomination. The second of his three wives was Paula Strasberg, one-time on-set coach to Marilyn Monroe, and their daughter is the actress Susan Strasberg (born 1938), whose film career got off to a promising start in the mid-Fifties but has since been rather scrappy.

Films: 1974 The Godfather, Part II. '77 The Cassandra Crossing (GB-IT-GER). '79 Boardwalk; Going in Style. '80 . . . And Justice for All. '82 Lookin' to Get Out.

STRAUB, Jean-Marie

(b. 1933). Director. Born: Metz, Lorraine, France

Straub and his wife Danièle Huillet, with whom he works in close collaboration, are exponents of 'minimalist' film-making. Their films are austere in the extreme and are not easy to comprehend by those who see the cinema existing only in the terms laid down by orthodox narrative films. Straub's films are nevertheless highly organized in their use of sound and image, and are as much about the processes of film-making as they are about their ostensible subjects; consequently they can seem tedious to those who seek entertainment, and offensive to audiences who wish to see the conventional aspects of storytelling on screen. In many ways, Straub's films are about the audiences' attitudes and responses towards the paradoxical complexities of structured randomness. Straub grew up in German-occupied Lorraine and studied literature at Strasbourg before moving to Paris where he worked as an assistant to Abel Gance, Jean Renoir, Jacques Rivette and his favourite director Robert Bresson. In 1958 he moved to Germany with Huillet as a protest against the colonial war in Algeria, and they made their first film there.

Films include: 1963 Machorka-Muff (GER-MONACO). '65 Nicht Versöhnt oder Es hilft nur Gewalt, wo Gewalt herrscht (GER) (USA/GB: Not Reconciled). '68 Chronik der Anna Magdalena Bach (IT-GER) (USA/GB: Chronicle of Anna Magdalena Bach); Der Bräutigam, die Komödiantin und der Zuhälter (GER) (USA/GB: The Bridegroom, the Comedienne and the Pimp). '70 Les Yeux Ne Veulent Pas en Tout Temps Se Fermer ou Peut-être Qu'un Jour Rome Se Permettra de Choisir à Son Tour (GER-IT) (USA/GB: Eyes Do Not Want to Close at All Times or Perhaps One Day Rome Will Permit Herself to Choose in Her Turn; or Othon). '72 Geschichtsunterricht (GER-IT-FR) (GB: History Lessons). '75 Moses und Aron (GER-FR-IT). '76 Fortini/Cani (IT-FR-GER-GB-USA). '79 Dalla Nube alla Resistenza (IT-FR-GER-GB) (GB: From the Cloud to the Resistance). '82 Trop Tôt, Trop Tard (FR-EGYPT) (GB: Too Early, Too Late).

STREEP, Meryl

(b. 1950). Actress. Born: Mary Louise Streep; Baking Ridge, New Jersey, USA

One of the brightest new stars to emerge in the late Seventies, blonde strong-featured Meryl Streep has an impeccable academic background – Vassar, Dartmouth, the Yale School of Drama – and first established herself on Broadway. She also played Shakespeare, scoring a notable hit in the title role of *The Taming of the Shrew*. She made her screen debut in *Julia* and was nominated for a Best Supporting Actress Academy Award for her role as the girl who stays home while her menfolk are in Vietnam in *The Deer Hunter*. She also won an Emmy for her part in the 1978 television series *Holocaust*. After a marvellous cameo as Woody Allen's lesbian ex-wife in *Manhattan*, she moved to lead roles as a senator's mistress in *The Seduction of Joe Tynan* and as an estranged wife who loses custody of her child in *Kramer vs Kramer*. After her dual role as a Victorian outcast and a modern movie star in *The French Lieutenant's Woman*, she was in a Robert Benton thriller, *Still of the Night*, and played a Polish woman haunted by memories of Auschwitz in *Sophie's Choice*.

Films: 1977 Julia. '78 The Deer Hunter. '79 Manhattan; The Seduction of Joe Tynan; Kramer vs Kramer. '81 The French Lieutenant's Woman. '82 Still of the Night; Sophie's Choice.

STREISAND, Barbra

(b. 1942). Actress/singer. Born: Barbara Joan Streisand; New York City, USA

Streisand is one of the very few genuine superstars, and her name ensures the success of whatever project she involves herself in, whether film, stage show or record. A former switchboard operator and theatre usherette, Streisand made a name for herself as a nightclub singer before a part in the Broadway musical *I Can Get It for You Wholesale* made her a star; she continued up the showbiz ladder with a recording contract with CBS, a string of hit records (including 'People'), numerous television and stage appearances and the lead part of Fanny Brice in the musical *Funny Girl*. When the show was filmed four years later in 1968, Streisand tied with Katharine Hepburn for the Best Actress Oscar. Her other awards include a special Tony in 1970 as 'Best Actress of the Decade' and a 1976 Oscar for the song 'Evergreen', co-written with Paul Williams, which she sang in *A Star Is Born*. Aside from *Hello, Dolly!*, her films have generally been box-office hits – largely thanks to her personal dynamism. She somehow manages to be both a kooky, awkward ugly duckling and a graceful swan at the same time, winning the maximum sympathy/admiration from her legions of fans, who are in no way alienated by reports of her being temperamental and overbearing. She was formerly married to the actor Elliott Gould, and has since been courted by some of Hollywood's leading men.

Films include: 1968 Funny Girl. '69 Hello, Dolly! '70 On a Clear Day You Can See Forever; The Owl and the Pussycat. '72 What's Up Doc?; Up the Sandbox. '73 The Way We Were. '74 For Pete's Sake. '75 Funny Lady. '76 A Star Is Born (+exec. prod.). '79 The Main Event/Love Is the Main Event. '83 Yentl (+dir; +co-prod); All Night Long.

STRICK, Joseph

(b. 1923). Director. Born: Pittsburgh, Pennsylvania, USA

An independent director with more nerve than talent. Strick has had an uneven career in films ever since he co-directed an hilarious short on preening bodybuilders, *Muscle Beach*. His semi-documentary feature *The Savage Eye* was meant to be perceptive and ironic, but ended up looking vulgar and exploitative. And most of his later features suffered from a similar lack of subtlety or sensitivity in adapting the works of such respected writers as James Joyce and Jean Genet. Strick's reputation was briefly restored in 1970 when he won an Oscar for his uncompromising short documentary *Interviews With My Lai Veterans*, filmed shortly after he was sacked from *Justine* (1969), his only big studio assignment.

Films include: 1948 Muscle Beach (doc. short) (co-dir). '49 Jour de Fête (doc. short) (FR) (GB: The Village Fair). '53 The Big Break (doc). '59 The Savage Eye. '63 The Balcony; An Affair of the Skin. '67 Ulysses (GB); The Legend of the Boy and the Eagle. '69 Ring of Bright Water (GB). '70 Tropic of Cancer; Interviews With My Lai Veterans (doc. short). '73 Janice. '77 Portrait of the Artist as a Young Man.

421

STRODE, Woody

(b. 1914) Actor. Born: Woodrow Strode; Los Angeles, California, USA

A towering six-foot-four-inch former professional footballer and wrestler, Woody Strode made an isolated film appearance in 1941 and started acting regularly in the Fifties. His first important role was as Franklin in Lewis Milestone's Korean War film *Pork Chop Hill* and his next good opportunity was in the title role as the black soldier accused of rape and murder in John Ford's *Sergeant Rutledge*. He made several more films with Ford, notably as John Wayne's sidekick in *The Man Who Shot Liberty Valance*. Later he diversified, appearing and sometimes starring in Italian as well as American films. He is married to Luuikialuana Kaliealoa.

Films include: 1952 Caribbean (GB: Caribbean Gold). '53 City Beneath the Sea. '56 The Ten Commandments. '59 Pork Chop Hill. '60 Sergeant Rutledge; Spartacus. '61 Two Rode Together. '62 The Man Who Shot Liberty Valance. '65 Seven Women. '68 C'Era una Volta il West (IT) (USA/GB: Once Upon a Time in the West). '72 The Gatling Gun. '76 Winterhawk. '79 Key West Crossing.

STROHEIM, Erich von

(1885–1957). Director/actor. Born: Erich Oswald Stroheim; Vienna, Austria

One of the major talents of the silent period, Erich von Stroheim had virtually his entire career as a director compressed into the decade from 1919 through 1929. During these years he was one of the best-known director-personalities in the film world. After a short period in the Austrian army, Stroheim emigrated to the USA in 1906 and arrived in Hollywood in 1914. He soon established himself as a bit player, assistant director and art director within the Griffith organization. During the late 1910s he gained an international reputation as an actor, specializing in villainous German officers, and was popularly known as 'The Man You Love to Hate'. In 1918 he managed to interest producer Carl Laemmle in financing his first feature as a director, actor and writer, *Blind Husbands*. This picture emerged as a witty and sophisticated work and demonstrated Stroheim's assurance as a uniquely gifted filmmaker. He followed this with *The Devil's Passkey*, a film which is lost today, and then embarked on his ambitious production of *Foolish Wives*. The high point of his early directing career, the picture emerged as a triumph of art direction – co-designed by Stroheim himself and the young Richard Day – and featured his most fully realized Continental rogue. Stroheim's eye for details of costume and decor and sensitivity to nuances of behaviour led him to extend and develop the film to such a length that it brought him into conflict with the Universal studio's new young producer, Irving Thalberg. The released version was badly cut and further conflict with Thalberg led to Stroheim's dismissal from his next film, *Merry-Go-Round*. Next hired by the Goldwyn Company, he embarked on his most memorable film, a nine-hour adaptation of the Frank Norris novel *McTeague*, filmed on location in and around San Francisco and Death Valley. Renamed *Greed*, the film combined naturalistic scenes with bizarre subplots and fantasy sequences which were cut from the badly mutilated release version. A reworking of *The Merry Widow* story for MGM turned out to be a big box-office hit, but Stroheim moved rapidly on to Paramount where he starred in and directed *The Wedding March*, set in the decadent Vienna of the declining Hapsburg empire and planned as a two-part picture that was never completed. Similarly *Queen Kelly* in 1928 was only partly filmed when Stroheim was sacked by producer-star Gloria Swanson. With his career as a director virtually finished due to his alleged extravagance – he got one last chance to direct at Fox in 1932 – Stroheim turned to writing and acting. He made a memorable appearance as the prison camp commandant in Renoir's *La Grande Illusion* and was equally effective as the butler in *Sunset Boulevard*.

Films include: 1915 Captain McLean (actor only); The Birth of a Nation (ass. dir; + act). '16 Intolerance (ass. dir; + act). '18 The Hun Within (actor only). '19 Blind Husbands (+ act). '20 The Devil's Passkey. '22 Foolish Wives (+ act). '23 Merry-Go-Round (add. dir. only, uncredited). '25 Greed; The Merry Widow. '28 The Wedding March; Queen Kelly (unfinished). '29 The Great Gabbo (actor only). '32 The Lost Squadron (actor only). '33 Walking Down Broadway/ Hello, Sister (some scenes only). '37 La Grande Illusion (actor only) (FR) (USA: Grand Illusion; GB: The Great Illusion). '50 Sunset Boulevard (actor only).

STROMBERG, Hunt

(1894–1968). Producer. Born: Louisville, Kentucky, USA

Gaining his first experience as a newspaper reporter in St Louis, then as a film publicist in New York, Stromberg naturally gravitated to Hollywood where he served as a producer with occasional screenwriting and directing credits during the mid-Twenties. Hired by MGM in 1925 as one of that group of 'production supervisors' directly responsible to production chief/executive producer Irving Thalberg, he remained with the studio for 17 years. Thalberg's illness late in 1932 led to Stromberg's promotion to full producer status and his career benefitted accordingly. He produced more than his share of hits, with a special preference for musicals, like the Jeanette MacDonald–Nelson Eddy cycle, and comedies. He had his biggest prestige and box-office success in 1936 with *The Great Ziegfeld* which won the Oscar for Best Picture. He also handled two of the studio's first Technicolor productions, *Sweethearts* and King Vidor's tale of Rogers' Rangers, *Northwest Passage*.

Films include: 1921 The Foolish Age. '24 The Siren of Seville (+ dir); The Fire Patron (+ dir). '26 The Torrent. '28 Our Dancing Daughters; White Shadows in the South Seas. '29 The Single Standard. '32 Red Dust.

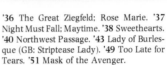

'36 The Great Ziegfeld; Rose Marie. '37 Night Must Fall; Maytime. '38 Sweethearts. '40 Northwest Passage. '43 Lady of Burlesque (GB: Striptease Lady). '49 Too Late for Tears. '51 Mask of the Avenger.

STROUD, Don

(b. 1944). Actor. Born: Honolulu, Hawaii, USA

Despite his lack of any formal training, Stroud has made quite a name for himself as a character actor, specializing in the obsequious, the bigoted and the homicidal. He had worked in a wide variety of jobs before he became Troy Donahue's stunt double for the *Hawaiian Eye* television series. Further television appearances, in *Ironside* and *The Virginian*, led to movies, his first major role being in the Clint Eastwood vehicle *Coogan's Bluff*.

Films include: 1967 The Ballad of Josie. '68 Coogan's Bluff; Madigan; Journey to Shiloh. '70 Bloody Mama; Games; Angel Unchained. '71 Von Richthofen and Brown (GB: The Red Baron). '77 Choirboys. '78 The Buddy Holly Story.

STRUSS, Karl

(1891–1981). Cinematographer. Born: New York City, USA

One of the dedicated cameramen who contributed so much to the quality of Hollywood pictures during the Twenties, Struss had previously made a name for himself as a young freelance still photographer with his own studio in Manhattan. He arrived in California in 1919 and was immediately hired by Cecil B. DeMille who recognized his mastery of cinematography. Struss worked on MGM's *Ben-Hur*, but excelled himself, in collaboration with Charles Rosher, on the Murnau masterpiece *Sunrise* which earned them the first Oscar for Cinematography in 1927. He spent most of the Thirties at Paramount where he was Oscar-nominated for *Dr Jekyll and Mr Hyde* and for DeMille's *The Sign of the Cross* the following year. But unfortunately his talent was largely wasted on routine assignments thereafter.

Films include: 1920 Something to Think About. '25 Ben-Hur (co-photo). '27 Sunrise. '28 Drums of Love. '29 The Taming of the Shrew. '30 Abraham Lincoln. '31 Dr Jekyll and Mr Hyde. '32 The Sign of the Cross. '33 The Island of Lost Souls. '34 Belle of the Nineties. '40 The Great Dictator (co-photo). '41 Aloma of the South Seas. '52 Limelight (co-photo). '54 Cavalleria Rusticana (IT). '59 Counterplot.

STURGES, John

(b. 1911). Director. Born: Oak Park, Illinois, USA

After serving a long apprenticeship in the art department and cutting rooms of RKO during the Thirties, Sturges got his first opportunity to direct on a number of documentaries and training films during the war and collaborated with director William Wyler on the feature-length, wartime documentary *Thunderbolt* (1945). Under contract to Columbia, he directed a series of B pictures during the late Forties and continued in more or less the same vein at MGM, although with slightly larger budgets and better material. In 1954 he was given the opportunity to direct *Bad Day at Black Rock*, a tense and exciting thriller with a modern Western setting and a

Top, far left: Woody Strode in The Deserter *(1971). Top left: Don Stroud in* Coogan's Bluff. *Left: Erich von Stroheim in* The Wedding March, *which he also directed. Above: Margaret Sullavan in* Three Comrades, *directed by Frank Borzage from the novel by Erich Maria Remarque. Below: Barry Sullivan in* The Bad and the Beautiful

strong social theme. The picture was a pet project of MGM production chief Dore Schary and turned out to be a big success for all concerned with Oscar nominations going to Sturges, Spencer Tracy and writer Millard Kaufman. Sturges went on to direct a number of well-known Westerns including *Gunfight at the OK Corral*, *The Magnificent Seven* and *Hour of the Gun* along with action pictures like *The Great Escape*, but the quality of his films declined during the Seventies and he eventually retired. Sturges best movies – especially those starring Steve McQueen – are still exciting to watch.

Films include: 1946 The Man Who Dared. '53 Escape From Fort Bravo. '55 Bad Day at Black Rock. '57 Gunfight at the OK Corral. '58 The Law and Jake Wade; The Old Man and the Sea. '59 Last Train From Gun Hill. '60 The Magnificent Seven. '62 Sergeants Three. '63 The Great Escape (USA-GER). '67 Hour of the Gun. '68 Ice Station Zebra. '72 Joe Kidd. '74 McQ. '76 The Eagle Has Landed (GB).

STURGES, Preston

(1898–1959). Director/screenwriter. Born: Edmond P. Biden; Chicago, Illinois, USA

The meteoric rise and fall of Preston Sturges is one of the most baffling phenomena of the American cinema. He burst on the scene as a writer-director in 1940 with *The Great McGinty* which won him a Best Screenplay Oscar, and for four years he continued to turn out a series of lively and entertaining pictures dealing satirically with American life. But by late 1944 his career was virtually finished, at the same time that two of his last and best movies, *The Miracle of Morgan's Creek* and *Hail the Conquering Hero*, were being nominated for Screenplay Oscars. Born into an eccentric socialite family, he spent much of his youth travelling with his divorced mother and studying at various private schools in Europe and the USA, adopting the name of his mother's second husband and his stepfather, Solomon Sturges. After trying his hand at various jobs he turned to playwriting during the late Twenties and moved on to Hollywood a few years later. He wrote the scripts for about a dozen pictures, including *Diamond Jim* (1935), *Easy Living* (1937) and *Remember the Night* (1940), the last two directed by Mitchell Leisen. Under contract to Paramount from 1937, he persuaded the studio to let him direct in 1940 and immediately made his mark as one of the leading writer-directors in Hollywood. He made superb use of such Hollywood stalwarts as Joel McCrea and Dick Powell, and provided Henry Fonda and Barbara Stanwyck with their best comedy roles ever in *The Lady Eve*, while drawing on the talents of the best character actors to fill out the many eccentric bit parts and cameo roles in the background. Although he had an excellent sense of comic timing and loved the occasional burst of knockabout action, for him the actors and dialogue came first. Following his stay at Paramount, he had a brief and abortive association

with producer Howard Hughes which resulted in only one completed picture, *The Sin of Harold Diddlebock*, starring Harold Lloyd and re-released in 1950 as *Mad Wednesday* in a badly mutilated version. And finally two disappointing pictures for 20th Century-Fox brought his Hollywood career to a close during the late Forties.

Films include: 1940 The Great McGinty (GB: Down Went McGinty). '41 The Lady Eve; Sullivan's Travels; The Palm Beach Story. '43 The Miracle of Morgan's Creek. '44 The Great Moment; Hail the Conquering Hero. '46 The Sin of Harold Diddlebock (reissued as Mad Wednesday, 1950). '48 Unfaithfully Yours. '49 The Beautiful Blonde From Bashful Bend. '55 Les Carnets du Major Thompson (FR) (USA: The French, They Are a Funny Race; GB: The Diary of Major Thompson).

SUCKSDORFF, Arne

(b. 1917). Documentary director. Born: Stockholm, Sweden

Arne Sucksdorff became a master of nature cinematography in Sweden during the Forties. Brought up on a farm, surrounded by wildlife, he saw poetic qualities in the creations of nature and succeeded in transferring his stars – foxes, otters, owls, gulls, rabbits and the seasons themselves – to the screen, their magical qualities unimpaired. In the late Thirties he abandoned his natural-science studies at the University of Stockholm in favour of theatrical direction under the celebrated German actor Rudolf Klein-Rogge. He then took up photography and, after winning a prize in a film magazine, he decided to make his name as a nature film-maker. His first major short was *En Sommarsaga* (1941), a film he financed himself. It was so well received that the Svensk Filmindustri gave him a grant to make a series of documentaries and he produced some of his best work for them: *Vinden Fran Väster* (1942) follows the Lapp people on their migration from the valleys to the plains where they spend the summer; *Sarytid* (1948) shows the annual reindeer round-up. Nature and animals speak for themselves and commentary is unnecessary. In 1951 Sucksdorff went freelance and two years later made his first feature. *The Great Adventure* took him two years to complete and shows how two boys learn by experience that a wild animal will always know instinctively what is best for him, accepting care during the hard winter months but being only too happy to be off once spring returns. Sucksdorff continued to make features during the Fifties, many of them centred around human beings, but he returned to wildlife in 1971 when he directed and shot the animal sequences for *Mr Forbush and the Penguins*.

Films include: 1944 Gryning. '45 Skuggor Över Snön. '47 Dem Drömda Dalen (GB: The Dream Valley); Människor i Stad (GB: Rhythm of a City). '48 En Kluven Värld. '50 Ett Hörn i Norr (GB: The Living Stream). '51 Vinden och Floden (GB: The Wind and the River); Indisk (GB: Indian Village). '53 Det Stora Äventyret (GB: The Great Adventure). '65 Mit Hem är Copacabana.

SULLAVAN, Margaret

(1911–1960). Actress. Born: Margaret Brooke; Norfolk, Virginia, USA

A student at the E.E. Clive Dramatic Academy, Margaret Sullavan joined the famous University Players along with James Stewart, Joshua Logan and Henry Fonda, who became her first husband. By 20 she was on Broadway playing the lead in *A Modern Virgin*. It was while she was appearing in *Dinner at Eight* that she was noticed by film director John Stahl and cast in *Only Yesterday*, a huge success. Sullavan continued in melodramas and weepies through the Thirties, making four excellent films for Frank Borzage – *Little Man, What Now?*, *Three Comrades*, *The Shining Hour* and *The Mortal Storm* – and most often partnering James Stewart. In those films she generally played an ordinary girl who was also an ethereal figure of redemption. In *Little Man, What Now?* she is a penniless newlywed in the Germany of the Twenties, in *Three Comrades* she is dying of tuberculosis, in *The Mortal Storm* she is facing up to Nazism, but Borzage would light up and close in on her pretty, smiling face and her breathy, husky voice would rise in a paean of hope. Nor was this ham acting: the slight and delicate Sullavan was always subtle, alert, unsentimental and moved by the stories of her films. Her own life was less of a dream. Sullavan was unhappy in Hollywood and in 1943 returned to the stage. Her marriages in turn to Fonda, director William Wyler and agent Leland Hayward all broke up and she eventually took a fatal overdose of barbiturates when deafness struck.

Films include: 1933 Only Yesterday. '34 Little Man, What Now? '35 The Good Fairy. '38 Three Comrades; The Shopworn Angel; The Shining Hour. '40 The Shop Around the Corner; The Mortal Storm. '41 Back Street; Appointment for Love. '43 Cry Havoc. '50 No Sad Songs for Me.

SULLIVAN, Barry

(b. 1912). Actor. Born: Patrick Barry; New York City, USA

Barry Sullivan studied law before working as a theatre usher while trying to establish himself as an actor. He reached his target in 1936 when he made his Broadway debut in *I Want a Policeman*. He began his screen career in 1942 with *We Refuse to Die* and scored a moderate success in his next movie, the Western *The Woman of the Town* (1943). Dark-haired, smooth and rarely to be caught smiling, Sullivan carved himself a career as a second-grade star in low-budget crime stories and usually portrayed a man whose charming exterior masks the mind of a ruthless manipulator. Since the Fifties he has appeared in countless television movies and series.

Films include: 1944 Rainbow Island; Lady in the Dark. '46 Suspense. '47 The Gangster. '48 Bad Men of Tombstone. '49 The Great Gatsby. '52 The Bad and the Beautiful. '54 Loophole. '56 The Maverick Queen. '57 Forty Guns. '69 Tell Them Willie Boy Is Here. '72 The Candidate.

SULLIVAN, Francis L.

(1903–1956). Actor. Born: London, England

Francis L. Sullivan made his first stage appearance in *Richard III* at the Old Vic in 1921 and subsequently toured with Charles Doran's Shakespeare Company until 1931 when he entered films. Sharp-eyed, florid in appearance and with a deep, plummy voice, Sullivan weighed in at a massive 19 stone and played parts suited to his massive girth. He was Jaggers in *Great Expectations* and Mr Bumble in *Oliver Twist*. His characters usually incorporated a touch of villainy but he also often appeared as stern lawyers or unyielding judges.

Films include: 1932 The Missing Rembrandt. '33 The Wandering Jew. '38 The Citadel. '41 Pimpernel Smith (USA: Mister V). '45 Caesar and Cleopatra. '46 Great Expectations. '48 Oliver Twist; The Winslow Boy. '50 Night and the City. '55 Hell's Island (USA): The Prodigal (USA).

SURTEES, Robert

(1906–1985). Cinematographer. Born: Covington, Kentucky, USA

Surtees served his apprenticeship as an assistant to Gregg Toland and Joseph Ruttenberg during the late Twenties. He spent the following decade at various Hollywood studios before emerging as a leading lighting cameraman in his own right during the Forties. He spent twenty years at MGM, graduating from small black-and-white pictures like *Thirty Seconds Over Tokyo* (1944) and *Our Vines Have Tender Grapes* (1945) to major colour epics including *Quo Vadis?, Oklahoma!* and the remake of *Ben-Hur*, for which he won his third Oscar. An adaptable and seemingly ageless professional, he continued to be active throughout the Seventies and contributed his expertise to the work of the new generation of directors such as Mike Nichols (*The Graduate*) and Peter Bogdanovich, for whom he must have seemed the ideal choice to photograph the nostalgic *The Last Picture Show* in black-and-white. His son, Bruce Surtees, has emerged as one of the leading American cinematographers during the past decade.

Films include: 1948 A Date With Judy. '49 Intruder in the Dust. '50 King Solomon's Mines. '51 Quo Vadis? (co-photo). '52 The Bad and the Beautiful. '53 Mogambo (co-photo). '55 Oklahoma! '59 Ben-Hur. '62 Mutiny on the Bounty. '67 The Graduate. '71 The Last Picture Show. '73 The Sting. '76 A Star Is Born. '77 The Turning Point. '78 Same Time, Next Year.

SUTHERLAND, Donald

(b. 1935). Actor. Born: St John, New Brunswick, Canada

On graduating from the University of Toronto, Sutherland studied acting at the London Academy of Music and Dramatic Art and gained his first professional experience in repertory in England. After appearing in an Italian horror movie and various British films, he became famous, and something of a cult figure to boot, as the gangling, bespectacled and super-

casual Hawkeye Pierce in Robert Altman's Korean War satire, *M*A*S*H*. A fascinatingly low-key performance as a policeman in Alan J. Pakula's multi-layered thriller *Klute*, opposite Jane Fonda, consolidated his position as a front-rank star, one that he has carefully maintained by mixing the occasional warm and sympathetic role – in *Don't Look Now*, *Invasion of the Body Snatchers* and *Ordinary People* – with more challenging portrayals of psychosis: the repressed Homer Simpson in John Schlesinger's *Day of the Locust*, a Fascist in Bertolucci's *1900* and a morbid sensualist in Fellini's *Casanova*.

Films include: 1964 Il Castello dei Morti Vivi (IT-FR) (GB: Castle of the Living Dead). '67 The Dirty Dozen (GB). '70 M*A*S*H (USA); Kelly's Heroes (USA-YUG). '71 Klute (USA). '73 Steelyard Blues; Don't Look Now (GB). '74 S*P*Y*S (GB-USA). '75 Day of the Locust (USA). '76 Novecento/1900 (IT-FR-GER); The Eagle Has Landed (GB); Il Casanova di Federico Fellini (IT) (USA/GB: Fellini's Casanova). '78 National Lampoon's Animal House (USA); Invasion of the Body Snatchers (USA). '80 Ordinary People (USA). '81 Eye of the Needle (GB).

SUTHERLAND, Edward

(1895–1974). Director. Born: London, England

After vaudeville, Sutherland became, in 1914, a stunt man in Helen Holmes serials, a supporting comic at Mack Sennett's Keystone and then an assistant director to Charlie Chaplin on *A Woman of Paris* (1923) and *The Gold Rush* (1925). Hired by Paramount, in 1926 he directed W.C. Fields on his first important movie, *It's the Old Army Game* The two men were to become close friends and regular working partners. Also starring in the film was Louise Brooks, Sutherland's wife from 1926 to 1928, but he failed to draw out her luminous talent. In the sound era, Sutherland made *Palmy Days* (1931) with Eddie Cantor and a series of vehicles for Fields, of which *Poppy* (1936) was probably the most successful. His career waned after he left Paramount in the mid-Thirties, as he moved on to work with Laurel and Hardy on *The Flying Deuces* (1939) and then with Abbott and Costello on *One Night in the Tropics* (1940). His films seemed increasingly out of tune with the times, reaching a nadir with *Abie's Irish Rose* in 1946. In 1949 he went into television as producer and director of the *Martin Kane* series.

Films include: 1927 Love's Greatest Mistake. '28 Tillie's Punctured Romance. '30 Burning Up. '31 Gang Buster. '33 Murders in the Zoo; Too Much Harmony. '38 Every Day's a Holiday. '43 Dixie. '44 Secret Command. '45 Having Wonderful Crime. '56 Bermuda Affair (GB).

SUZMAN, Janet

(b. 1939). Actress. Born: Johannesburg, South Africa

Although one of today's leading stage actresses, Janet Suzman has only seldom appeared in film roles worthy of her talents. After she had gained a

degree she left her native South Africa partly for political reasons, but also to study acting. She trained at the London Academy of Music and Dramatic Art and gained experience in regional repertory theatres before joining the Royal Shakespeare Company in the early Sixties. She soon won a reputation as a passionate yet intellectual actress in leading classical roles, especially in Shakespeare. Her film debut came in 1971, as the Tsarina in the leaden *Nicholas and Alexandra*. Rather more interesting have been her later performances as Frieda, D.H. Lawrence's wife, in *Priest of Love* and as the adulterous wife of a seventeenth-century English landowner in Peter Greenaway's intriguing costume drama, *The Draughtsman's Contract*. She is married to RSC director Trevor Nunn.

Films include: 1971 Nicholas and Alexandra (USA). '72 A Day in the Death of Joe Egg. '74 The Black Windmill. '76 Voyage of the Damned. '81 Priest of Love. '82 The Draughtsman's Contract.

SWAIN, Mack

(1876–1935). Actor. Born: Salt Lake City, Utah, USA

Six feet two inches tall with a burly physique, Swain, an experienced vaudevillian, became well known as a moustachioed villain, tying the heroine to the railroad tracks or vying with the hero for her attentions in a host of Keystone comedies from 1914 onwards. He became popular enough to star in his own series of two-reelers playing the rumbustious, leering Ambrose. At the beginning of his career he had been associated with Charlie Chaplin's films, and it was Chaplin who rescued Swain's ailing fortunes by giving him his most famous role, that of Jim McKay, Charlie's huge and treacherous prospector partner, in *The Gold Rush*. Swain continued to work regularly in movies up to his death, playing the occasional lead role.

Films include: 1914 Caught in a Cabaret; His Trysting Place; His Musical Career; Mabel's Married Life; Caught in the Rain; Tillie's Punctured Romance; Ambrose's First Falsehood. '23 The Pilgrim. '25 The Gold Rush. '31 Finn and Hattie. '33 The Midnight Patrol.

SWANSON, Gloria

(1899–1983). Actress. Born: Chicago, Illinois, USA

Gloria Swanson was, in the Twenties, the epitome of glamour and frivolousness in the movies and fifty years later she was still celebrating the notion of stardom. She made her film debut at the Essanay Studios in Chicago in 1915 but soon moved to Hollywood, married co-star Wallace Beery and played in Mack Sennett two-reel comedies. Preferring drama to slapstick, she joined Triangle in 1918, and in 1919 moved to Artcraft-Paramount to make the first of six 'daring' sexual comedies for Cecil B. DeMille, including *Male and Female* and *The Affairs of Anatol*. In 1920 she began her six-year reign at Paramount, frequently being directed by Sam Wood and Allan Dwan. Fortified by her third marriage,

Above: Francis L. Sullivan as Mr Bumble in Oliver Twist. *Right: Gloria Swanson in* Madame Sans-Gêne. *Above, centre right: Mack Swain in an early Sennett comedy. Above, far right: Blanche Sweet in* Always Faithful. *Centre right: Nora Swinburne in* Quo Vadis? *Far right: Sylvia Syms in* Expresso Bongo. *Below: Donald Sutherland in* Steelyard Blues. *Bottom: Janet Suzman in* A Day in the Death of Joe Egg

to the Marquis de la Falaise de la Coudraye in 1925 (it lasted until 1931), she decided to set up her own production company, releasing through United Artists, when her Paramount contract expired in 1926. Her first two pictures were moderate hits and she was nominated for an Oscar for her role as a prostitute in *Sadie Thompson*; but her third production, *Queen Kelly*, directed by Erich von Stroheim, was never properly completed, its combination of deviant sexuality and over-budget production proving too much for her resources. A truncated version, briefly seen overseas, was not shown in the USA until the early Fifties. Her first talkie, *The Trespasser*, brought her a second Academy Award nomination and was also a box-office hit. After that, her career went rapidly downhill. She was in serious financial difficulties and an MGM contract produced only one loan-out picture for Fox. Her first attempt at a comeback in 1941 was a failure; but in 1950 she was reunited with Stroheim (as an actor) in Billy Wilder's *Sunset Boulevard*. Her performance as the ageing silent film star Norma Desmond brought her fame with a new generation and her third Oscar nomination. It hardly sparked off a new film career, though she made a couple of minor pictures in the Fifties; but it enabled her to work in the theatre and television, and she had a cameo role in *Airport 1975*.

Films include: 1915 The Fable of Elvira and Farina and the Meal Ticket (short). '16 Hearts and Sparks (short). '17 A Pullman Bride. '18 Society for Sale. '19 Don't Change Your Husband; For Better, For Worse; Male and Female (GB: The Admirable Crichton). '20 Why Change Your Wife?; Something to Think About. '21 The Great Moment; The Affairs of Anatol. '23 Bluebeard's Eighth Wife; Zaza. '24 Manhandled. '25 Madame Sans-Gène. '27 The Love of Sunya. '28 Sadie Thompson; Queen Kelly (unfinished). '29 The Trespasser. '31 Indiscreet. '33 A Perfect Understanding (GB). '34 Music in the Air. '41 Father Takes A Wife. '50 Sunset Boulevard. '74 Airport 1975.

SWEET, Blanche

(1895–1986). Actress. Born: Chicago, Illinois, USA

One of that talented group of young actresses who first made their name in the early films of D.W. Griffith, Blanche Sweet arrived at Biograph in 1909, the same year as Mary Pickford and two years younger – she was only 14 at the time – but already an experienced stage actress. In spite of her youth, she often appeared on the screen as an intelligent and resourceful heroine in such pictures as *The Lonedale Operator* and in Griffith's first important feature, *Judith of Bethulia*, in which she played the title role. The following year she accepted an offer from the Lasky Company and appeared in DeMille's *The Warrens of*

Virginia. Married for a time to the director Marshall Neilan, she and her husband contributed a few of the earliest productions to the newly-formed MGM – *Tess of the d'Urbervilles* and *The Sporting Venus* – but her career was in decline and she retired shortly after the coming of sound.

Films include: 1909 A Man With Three Wives (short). '11 The Lonedale Operator (short); The Last Drop of Water (short). '13 The Massacre (short); Judith of Bethulia. '14 Home, Sweet Home; The Avenging Conscience (GB: Thou Shalt Not Kill). '15 The Warrens of Virginia. '23 Anna Christie. '24 Tess of the d'Urbervilles. '25 The Sporting Venus. '29 Always Faithful. '30 The Woman Racket (GB: Lights and Shadows).

SWINBURNE, Nora

(b. 1902). Actress. Born: Elinore Swinburne Johnson; Bath, Somerset, England

A distant relative of the Victorian poet Algernon Charles Swinburne, Nora Swinburne made her stage debut at ten, trained as a dancer at Rossholm College and then went on to RADA. After modelling in a fashion commercial, she made her feature film debut in 1920. Her peak period was the Forties, when she played a succession of neurotic middle-aged women in Gainsborough melodramas, such as the sickly, miserable mother of Fanny (Phyllis Calvert) in *Fanny by Gaslight*,

the shrewish farmer's wife in *Jassy* and a stately Spanish matron in *Christopher Columbus*. Her role as the gentle mother of a British family in India in Jean Renoir's *The River* may have been a welcome change. She continued in occasional film parts until the end of the Sixties. The actor Esmond Knight was her third husband.

Films include: 1920 Branded. '25 A Girl of London. '30 Alf's Button. '38 The Citadel. '43 The Man in Grey. '44 Fanny by Gaslight (USA: Man of Evil). '47 Jassy. '49 Christopher Columbus. '51 The River (IND); Quo Vadis? (USA). '55 The End of the Affair. '69 Anne of the Thousand Days.

SYMS, Sylvia

(b. 1934). Actress. Born: Woolwich, London, England

Blonde, blue-eyed and petite, Sylvia Syms completed her studies at RADA and was soon launched into a film career in a series of teenage roles, including the title part in Herbert Wilcox's *My Teenage Daughter*, with Anna Neagle playing her mother. She coped valiantly in *Victim* with the difficult part of the wife of a barrister (Dirk Bogarde) who is suddenly confronted with his homosexuality. But during the course of the Sixties and after, her film roles became fewer and father between, although she worked steadily in television and on the stage.

Films include: 1956 My Teenage Daughter (USA: Teenage Bad Girl). '57 Woman in a Dressing Gown. '58 Ice Cold in Alex; Bachelor of Hearts. '59 Expresso Bongo. '60 Conspiracy of Hearts. '61 Victim. '62 The Punch and Judy Man. '72 Asylum.

SZABÓ, István

(b. 1938). Director/screenwriter. Born: Budapest, Hungary

Szabó was one of the first of that new generation of film school graduates in Hungary, Czechoslovakia and Poland who revitalized the Eastern European cinema during the Sixties. After studies at the Budapest Academy of Dramatic and Film Art, he gained his first professional experience as a director of a number of prize-winning shorts. Graduating to features during the mid-Sixties, he had a major success with only his second attempt *Father*, which made effective and ironic use of flashback techniques and shared the Grand Prix at the 1967 Moscow Film Festival. He has remained active throughout the Seventies and won the Silver Bear Award at the 1979 Berlin Festival for his intimate and intense character drama, *Confidence*. Next came *Mephisto*, a universally acclaimed masterpiece about a brilliant German actor who is compromised by the Nazis.

Films include: 1961 Koncert (GB: Concert). '62 Variaciok Egy Temara (Variations on a Theme). '63 Te (GB: You). '65 Almodozasok Kora (GB: The Age of Daydreaming). '67 Apa (GB: Father). '70 Szerelmesfilm (A Film About Love). '74 Túzoltó Utca 25 (USA: 25 Fireman's Street). '77 Budapesti Mesek (Tales of Budapest). '79 Bizalom (GB: Confidence). '81 Mephisto.

TALMADGE, Constance

(1900–1973). Actress. Born: New York City, USA

The natural comedienne of the family and the youngest of the three famous sisters, Constance began her movie career in a series of comedy shorts in 1914. Griffith offered her the role of the Mountain Girl in the Babylonian episode of *Intolerance* and her exuberant and lively performance completely justified his confidence in her. She went on to establish herself as a leading comedy actress of the silent cinema and one of the mainstays of First National during the Twenties, only slightly less famous than her actress sister Norma. She retired at the end of the silent era.

Films include: 1916 Intolerance. '17 The Honeymoon. '19 The Veiled Adventure; A Temperamental Wife. '21 Lessons of Love. '22 East Is West. '25 Her Sister From Paris. '26 Duchess of Buffalo. '27 Venus of Venice; Breakfast at Sunrise.

TALMADGE, Norma

(1897–1957). Actress. Born: Niagara Falls, New York, USA

The most famous and eldest of the Talmadge sisters (the middle sister, Natalie, was best known for her marriage to Buster Keaton), Norma began her career at Vitagraph in 1910, then moved on to Triangle. Her marriage to producer Joseph Schenck in 1916 led to the formation of her own, highly successful production company and her pictures continued to be released through First National during the Twenties. She had her biggest hit with *Secrets*, directed by Frank Borzage. Clarence Brown, who directed her in *Kiki*, regarded her as 'the greatest pantomimist that ever drew breath', though her career was destroyed by the coming of sound: 'Madame DuBarry with a Brooklyn accent wasn't too convincing and she never made another film.'

Films include: 1911 A Tale of Two Cities. '17 Panthea. '21 The Passion Flower; The Sign on the Door. '22 Smilin' Through. '23 Within the Law; Ashes of Vengeance; The Voice From the Minaret. '24 Secrets. '26 Kiki. '27 Camille. '29 New York Nights. '30 DuBarry, Woman of Passion.

TALMADGE, Richard

(b. 1896 or 1898). Actor/stunt man/second-unit director. Born: Ricardo or Sylvester Metzetti or Metezzeti; Munich, Germany or Switzerland

One of those daring young men who provided the spectacular stunts in many early Hollywood pictures, Talmadge defied all the odds to live to a ripe old age and was still directing action and stunt sequences as late as *Circus World* (1964) and *Hawaii*. A European immigrant who arrived in Hollywood during the late 1910s, he adopted the name of Talmadge although unrelated to the famous Talmadge sisters. By the Twenties he was already starring in his own action movies with such titles as *The Speed King*, *Laughing at Danger* (1924) and *The Wall Street Whiz*, all in the tradition of Douglas Fairbanks with whom he worked as an occasional stunt double. With the coming of sound he switched to working as a second-unit director of action sequences and remained active in that capacity for over thirty years.

Films include: 1921 Now or Never. '22 The Cub Reporter. '23 Danger Ahead; The Speed King. '25 The Wall Street Whiz. '26 The Merry Cavalier. '30 The Poor Millionaire. '31 Yankee Don (GB: Dare Devil Dick). '34 Pirate Treasure (serial). '65 Never Too Late; What's New, Pussycat? '66 Hawaii.

TAMBLYN, Russ

(b. 1934). Actor/dancer. Born: Los Angeles, California, USA

A child actor and dancer on the stage (and radio) from an early age, Tamblyn hit his stride during the Fifties and early Sixties when his friendly face and lively personality brightened the look of many Hollywood comedies and musicals, although he was occasionally offered dramatic parts, too. He played Gideon, the youngest and most irrepressible of the Pontipee brothers in *Seven Brides for Seven Brothers*, a role which demonstrated his acrobatic dancing abilities. He was perfectly cast as *Tom Thumb* in 1958, and his abilities as a dancer were stretched to the limit by choreographer and co-director Jerome Robbins in filming *West Side Story* three years later. Inevitably his career declined during later years and he was reduced to appearing in such forgettable flicks as *Dracula vs Frankenstein* and *Win, Place or Steal*.

Films include: 1948 The Boy With Green Hair. '54 Seven Brides for Seven Brothers. '57 Peyton Place. '58 Tom Thumb (GB). '61 West Side Story. '62 How the West Was Won; The Wonderful World of the Brothers Grimm. '65 Son of a Gunfighter (USA-SP). '73 Dracula vs Frankenstein. '74 Win, Place or Steal (GB: Another Day at the Races). '76 Black Heat.

TAMIROFF, Akim

(1899–1972). Actor. Born: Baku, Russia

Educated at Moscow University followed by the Moscow Art Theatre School of Acting, Tamiroff went on tour with the Art Theatre in 1923 and decided to remain in New York. He subsequently joined Nikita Balieff's Chauve-Souris repertory company before the coming of sound lured him to Hollywood. Short and dark, he turned his slightly sinister appearance and heavy accent to good advantage, developing into a leading Hollywood character actor, a position he maintained for almost twenty years. Outstanding performances included the title role in *The General Died at Dawn* and the Spanish Resistance leader Pablo in *For Whom the Bell Tolls*, both of which earned him Oscar nominations. In the Fifties he returned to Europe and appeared in a number of pictures with Orson Welles – *Mr Arkadin* (1954), *Touch of Evil* (1958), as Sancho Panza in the uncompleted *Don Quixote* (1955) and *Le Procès* (1962, *The Trial*).

Films include: 1935 The Lives of a Bengal Lancer; The Story of Louis Pasteur. '36 The General Died at Dawn. '38 The Buccaneer; Dangerous to Know; Spawn of the North; King of Alcatraz. '39 Union Pacific. '40 The Way of All Flesh. '43 For Whom the Bell Tolls. '49 Force of Evil; Easy Living.

TANAKA, Kinuyo

(1909–1977). Actress/director. Born: Shimonoseki, Japan

Japan's first woman director began her career as an apprentice in a musical troupe, joining the Shochiku film company as an actress in 1924. She became a top star in the Thirties and continued to act for many of the greatest Japanese directors, including Ozu, Gosho, Kinoshita and especially Mizoguchi, after she began directing in 1953. She is best known abroad for her Mizoguchi roles as the unhappy heroine in *The Life of Oharu*, the potter's wife in *Ugetsu Monogatari* and the mother sold into prostitution in

Sansho Dayu. The films she directed were mostly not seen overseas but she had a late triumph in winning the Best Actress Award at the 1975 Berlin Film Festival for *Sandakan House no 8*. She was at one time married to director Hiroshi Shimizu and appeared in several of his films.

Films as actress include: 1928 Hazukashi Yume (Intimate Dream). '30 Kinuyo Monogatari (Story of Kinuyo). 33 Izu no Odoriko (GB: The Dancing Girl of Izu). '46 Josei no Shori (The Victory of Women). '47 Joyu Sumako no Koi (Loves of Actress Sumako). '48 Yoru no Onna Tachi (Women of the Night). '52 Okasan (Mother); Saikaku Ichidai Onna (USA/GB: The Life of Oharu). '53 Ugetsu Monogatari (USA: Ugetsu; GB: Tales of the Pale and Mysterious Moon After the Rain). '54 Sansho Dayu (GB: Sansho the Bailiff). '59 Higanbana (USA: Equinox Flower). '65 Akahige (USA/GB: Red Beard). '74 Sandakan Hachiban Shokan-Bokyo (Sandakan House no 8). *Films as director include:* 1953 Koibumi (Love Letters). '55 Tsukiwa Noborinu (The Moon Has Risen);

Chibusa yo Eien Nare (The Eternal Heart). '60 Ruten no Ohi (Wandering Princess). '61 Onna Bakari no Yoru (Women's Night). '62 Oghin-Sama (USA: Love Under the Crucifix).

TANDY, Jessica

(b. 1909). Actress. Born: London, England

A much-acclaimed actress who has appeared with distinction on both the London and New York stages, Jessica Tandy has played relatively few film roles during the course of her career. Slim and sensitive-looking, she is best known to modern film audiences for her role as the disturbed mother of Tippi Hedren in Hitchcock's allegorical thriller, *The Birds*. She was married to Jack Hawkins during the Thirties and to American actor Hume Cronyn from 1942. The couple have frequently appeared together on the stage with great success.

Films include: 1932 The Indiscretions of Eve (GB). '44 The Seventh Cross. '45 The Valley of Decision. '46 The Green Years; Dragonwyck. '47 Forever Amber. '51 The Desert Fox (GB: Rommel – Desert Fox). '63 The Birds. '74 Butley (USA-GB-CAN). '81 Honky Tonk Freeway.

TARADASH, Daniel

(b. 1913). Screenwriter. Born: Louisville, Kentucky, USA

A graduate of Harvard University and the Harvard Law School, Taradash emerged as one of the most prestigious Hollywood scriptwriters for a short period during the early and mid-Fifties. *Rancho Notorious* for Fritz Lang was followed by the Oscar-winning script of *From Here to Eternity* and then *Picnic*. His sole attempt at directing – *Storm Center* (1954) – reflected his interest in subjects with a strong social content. Although he has served as president of both the Writers Guild of America and the Academy of Motion Picture Arts and Sciences, his recent writing credits, on such pictures as *Doctors' Wives* and *The Other Side of Midnight*, have been far from memorable.

Films include: 1949 Golden Boy (co-sc). '49 Knock On Any Door (co-sc). '52 Rancho Notorious; Don't Bother to Knock. '53 From Here to Eternity. '55 Picnic. '58 Bell Book and Candle. '71 Doctors' Wives. '77 The Other Side of Midnight.

TARKOVSKY, Andrei

(1932–1987). Director. Born: Zavroshe, USSR

With only a handful of feature films to his credit since his debut in 1962, Tarkovsky has nevertheless established himself as the leading director of the modern Soviet cinema. Each of his projects has been the result of years of careful preparation and attention to details of script, setting and photography, with Tarkovsky himself actively involved in the scripting and design in particular. A graduate of the Soviet State Film School in Moscow, he directed a pair of interesting shorts before embarking on his first feature, *Ivan's Childhood*, a sensitively handled portrait of a young orphan boy during World War II which shared the top prize at the Venice Film Festival. Then Tarkovsky turned to a highly ambitious treatment of the life of the fifteenth-century ikon painter *Andrei Rublev*, set against the background of one of the most turbulent periods in Russian history. This remarkable and original work was completed during 1965–66 but was suppressed by the Soviet authorities, and Tarkovsky himself appears to have fallen into official disfavour for a time, with a gap of six years before the appearance of his third feature *Solaris*, a thought-provoking science-fiction film based on the novel by Stanislaw Lem. He followed this with *Mirror*, dealing again with childhood and adolescence in his most personal and complex work to date. And finally in *Stalker* he ventured into a Kafkaesque, futuristic world with strong echoes of Beckett, Cocteau's *Orphée* (1950) and Mozart's *The Magic Flute* to create a modern cinematic masterpiece.

Films include: 1959 Segodnya Otpuska Nye Budyet. '61 Katok i Skripka (GB: The Steamroller and the Violin). '62 Ivanovo Detstvo (USA: My Name Is Ivan; GB: Ivan's Childhood). '65 Andrei Rublev. '69 Odin Shans iz Tisyachi (co-sc. only). '72 Solaris. '75 Zerkalo (GB: Mirror). '79 Stalker.

Below, left to right: Constance Talmadge and her pet pooch in a publicity portrait; her more famous sister Norma in The Woman Disputed *(1928); Russ Tamblyn in* Tom Thumb, *directed by George Pal. Above: the swashbuckling Richard Talmadge in* Stepping Lively *(1924). right: Akim Tamiroff in Cecil B. DeMille's Western railroad saga,* Union Pacific. *Right: Kinuyo Tanaka in* Madamu to Nyobo *(1931), directed by Heinosuke Gosho. Below right: Jessica Tandy in* The Desert Fox

TASHLIN, Frank

(1913–1972). Director/animator/screenwriter. Born: Weehawken, New Jersey, USA

Having worked as a cartoonist on a newspaper comic strip and as a gagman, Tashlin developed into one of the leading Hollywood animators, also writing scripts and directing, as part of the top animation team at Warner Brothers during the late Thirties. However, by the late Forties he had switched to writing live-action comedy scripts for Bob Hope and Red Skelton and made a natural transition to writer-director just as Hollywood was moving into wide-screen filming on a big scale. Tashlin succeeded in combining his flair for outrageous, cartoon-like, almost surreal gags and love of social parody with a strong visual sense which was ideally suited to the wide screen and bright pop-art colours. From the mid-Fifties he alternated between Jerry Lewis comedies for Paramount (filmed in VistaVision) and glossy CinemaScope productions at 20th Century-Fox, most notably *The Girl Can't Help It* and *Will Success Spoil Rock Hunter?*, both starring Jayne Mansfield. Unfortunately, his career ran out of steam during the Sixties.

Films include: 1951 The Lemon Drop Kid (co-sc; + add. dir. uncredited). '52 Son of Paleface. '55 The Lieutenant Wore Skirts. '56 Hollywood or Bust; The Girl Can't Help It. '57 Will Success Spoil Rock Hunter? (GB: Oh, For a Man!). '60 Cinderfella. '64 The Disorderly Orderly. '66 The Glass Bottom Boat. '68 The Private Navy of Sergeant O'Farrell.

TATI, Jacques

(1908–1982). Director/actor. Born: Jacques Tatischeff; Le Pecq, France

As a young man Tati's interest in sport was turned to good use when he found he could combine it with his talent for mime. What emerged was a delightful and hilarious series of sporting sketches which proved to be a big hit on the music-hall stage and led to his first short film in 1932, *Oscar, Champion de Tennis*. Tati first became seriously involved in the cinema during the postwar years when he spent some time developing and improving on a feature-length theme which emerged in 1949 as the entertaining comedy *Jour de Fête* – in which he played the central role of the village postman. For his next feature he created his most famous comic character, Monsieur Hulot, with whom he is closely identified. Tall, thin and ungainly, with a peculiarly stiff-limbed gait, he is forever getting himself into awkward predicaments and leaving a trail of disaster in his wake. *Monsieur Hulot's Holiday*, Tati's satirical treatment of summer holidays by the sea, included closely observed portraits of all the characters and was so rich in detail as to demonstrate his claim to be taken seriously as a film-maker and not just a comedian. Similarly, in the Oscar-winning *Mon Oncle* he extended his range to colour which is used effectively in contrasting the Hulot world of old streets and houses with the vulgar modern houses and offices. Filming in 70mm Tati extended his satirical treatment of the modern world in *Playtime* and turned his eye on the modern automobile in *Traffic*, sadly his last completed feature.

Films include: 1932 Oscar, Champion de Tennis (short). '35 Gai Dimanche (short). '47 L'Ecole des Facteurs (short). '49 Jour de Fête (USA: Day of the Fair). '53 Les Vacances de Monsieur Hulot (Monsieur Hulot's Holiday). '58 Mon Oncle (My Uncle) (FR-IT). '68 Playtime. '70 Trafic (Traffic) (FR-IT).

TAUROG, Norman

(1899–1981). Director. Born: Chicago, Illinois, USA

During his career of over forty years as a Hollywood director Taurog proved himself a capable and dependable craftsman with a special preference for comedy, children's pictures and musicals, but with no distinctive style of his own. His films ranged from W.C. Fields comedies at Paramount – *If I Had a Million* (1932), *Mrs Wiggs of the Cabbage Patch* (1934) – to MGM musicals like *Broadway Melody of 1940* and *Words and Music* (1948) and on to Dean Martin and Jerry Lewis comedies during the Fifties, and finally a series of forgettable Elvis Presley vehicles for producer Hal Wallis during the Sixties. Originally on the stage as a successful child actor, Taurog failed to make any impact as a leading man in films. But he soon turned his interest to film-making instead. Gaining some experience as a property man and cutter and then as a director of two-reel comedies, he graduated to features with the coming of sound and won an Oscar in 1931 for *Skippy*, scripted by Joseph L. Mankiewicz and starring the young Jackie Cooper, but he was content to remain a contract director for the remainder of his career.

Films include: 1928 The Farmer's Daughter. '31 Skippy; Huckleberry Finn. '38 Boys Town; The Adventures of Tom Sawyer. '40 Broadway Melody of 1940. '55 You're Never Too Young. '60 GI Blues. '61 Blue Hawaii. '62 Girls! Girls! Girls! '68 Live a Little, Love a Little.

TAVERNIER, Bertrand

(b. 1941). Director. Born: Lyons, France

Bertrand Tavernier was educated at the Lycée Henri IV in Paris, where he shared a desk with another future director, Volker Schlöndorff. In the early Sixties he worked as a press officer for producer Georges de Beauregard, who made many of the *nouvelle vague* films. Tavernier became an influential critic, writing for several magazines but particularly the traditionally left-wing *Positif*. He wrote a book, *Trente Ans du Cinéma Américain*, and contributed to one on the Western. He wrote scripts, directed episodes and finally made a late debut (by modern Franch standards) in 1973 with *L'Horloger de Saint-Paul*, set in his native Lyons, and co-scripted by

Left: Jacques Tati in his brilliant comedy, Monsieur Hulot's Holiday. *Below: Alma Taylor in* Anna the Adventuress. *Below right: Don Taylor in William Wellman's* Battleground

him with the veteran writers Aurenche and Bost, who had been somewhat discredited since the advent of the *nouvelle vague*. It examined the reactions of a middle-aged man when his son kills a brutal factory guard. *Que la Fête Commence . . .* was a story of love and intrigue set in the Paris of 1719. *Le Juge et l'Assassin* was about a magistrate more interested in furthering his political career than in justice when he interrogates a child-murderer. *Une Semaine de Vacances* was a quiet study, again set in Lyons, of a young woman who takes a week off to examine her life. *Coup de Torchon* was a colonial black comedy set in French Africa in the Thirties. Typically Tavernier's films concern a crisis at which values are reassessed, and he explores contradictions with wit and humanity.

Films include: 1973 L'Horloger de Saint-Paul (GB: The Watchmaker of Saint-Paul). '75 Que la Fête Commence . . . (USA: Let Joy Reign Supreme). '76 Le Juge et l'Assassin. '77 Des Enfants Gâtés (USA/GB: Spoiled Children). '79 La Mort en Direct (FR-GER) (USA/GB: Death Watch). '80 Une Semaine de Vacances (GB: A Week's Holiday). '81 Coup de Torchon (GB: Clean Slate).

TAVIANI, Paolo and Vittorio

Taviani, Paulo (b. 1931). Director/screenwriter. Born: San Miniato de Pize, Italy

Taviani, Vittorio (b. 1929). Director/screenwriter. Born: San Miniato de Pize, Italy

Educated at the University of Pisa, the Taviani brothers began making documentaries in 1954 with Valentino Orsini (born 1926) and he also collaborated on their first two features. The brothers work closely together in both writing and directing their films. They have established themselves among the most important Italian film-makers of their generation, noted for their thoughtful and fearless political stance, though until the success of *Padre Padrone*, which won both the Golden Palm and the International Critics Prize at Cannes, they were comparatively little-known abroad. That film was a sympathetic study of a young Sardinian shepherd boy who obtained an education despite the opposition of his traditionalist and heavy-handed father. *Sovversivi* concerned four 'subversives' who attend the funeral of the Communist leader Palmiro Togliatti and become revolutionaries, while *Sotto il Segno dello Scorpione* was a political allegory reflecting the turmoil of Italy in the late Sixties.

Films include: 1962 Un Uomo da Bruciare (co-dir). '64 I Fuorilegge del Matrimonio (co-dir). '67 Sovversivi. '69 Sotto il Segno dello Scorpione. '71 San Michele Aveva un Gallo. '74 Allonsanfàn. '77 Padre Padrone. '79 Il Prato (USA: the Meadow). '81 La Notte di Sàn Lorenzo (GB: The Night of Sàn Lorenzo).

TAYLOR, Alma

(1895–1974). Actress. Born: London, England

Alma Taylor started her acting career at the age of 12, and at 15 was starring for the producer Cecil Hepworth as Tilly the Tomboy, with Chrissie White as her friend Sally. She was a romantic heroine in both versions of *Comin' Thro' the Rye*, and she had a reputation for wearing beautiful clothes. Hepworth was a tireless technical innovator, and in 1920 she was able to play a dual role, appearing on the screen as both characters simultaneously, in *Anna the Adventuress*, a year before Mary Pickford achieved the same feat in *Little Lord Fauntleroy*. Alma Taylor's career gradually declined during the Twenties, but she continued playing character parts into the sound era, making something of a comeback in the Fifties, and also worked in television.

Films include: 1909 The Little Milliner and the Thief (short). '10 Tilly the Tomboy Goes Boating (short); Tilly the Tomboy Buys Linoleum (short). '11 Tilly and the Mormon Missionary (short). '12 Oliver Twist. '14 The Heart of Midlothian. '16 Annie Laurie; Comin' Thro' the Rye. '20 Anna the Adventuress. '23 Comin' Thro' the Rye (remake). '31 Deadlock. '32 Bachelor's Baby. '36 Everybody Dance. '54 Lilacs in the Spring. '56 Lost (USA: Tears for Simon). '57 Blue Murder at St Trinian's.

Right: a wedding for Elizabeth Taylor in Father of the Bride. *Far right: Robert Taylor as Lancelot in* Knights of the Round Table. *Bottom: Rod Taylor in* The Mercenaries

TAYLOR, Don

(b. 1920). Actor/director. Born: Freeport, Pennsylvania, USA

A tall, boyish-looking actor who was frequently cast in roles younger than his true age, Taylor found it difficult to make the transition to directing: 'It wasn't easy at first because I was a happy actor and nobody took me seriously.' Best remembered for his roles as Elizabeth Taylor's bridegroom and husband in *Father of the Bride*, and *Father's Little Dividend* (1951), and in war films like *Battleground* (1949) and *Stalag 17*, he began directing for television during the late Fifties and later graduated to television movies and occasional feature films. Taylor developed a special interest in fantasy subjects during the Seventies when he directed such pictures as *Escape From the Planet of the Apes*, *The Island of Dr Moreau* and *The Final Countdown*.

Films include: 1943 The Human Comedy. '44 Winged Victory. '48 The Naked City. '50 Father of the Bride. '53 Stalag 17. '61 Everything's Ducky (dir. only). '62 The Savage Guns (USA-SP). '64 Ride the Wild Surf (co-dir. only). '67 Jack of Diamonds (co-dir. only). '71 Escape From the Planet of the Apes (dir. only). '73 Tom Sawyer (+ dir). '76 The Great Scout and Cathouse Thursday (dir. only). '77 The Island of Dr Moreau (dir. only). '78 Damien – Omen II (dir. only). '80 The Final Countdown.

TAYLOR, Elizabeth

(b. 1932). Actress. Born: London, England

A strikingly beautiful child, Elizabeth Taylor was signed to a long-term contract by MGM and remained with that studio for almost twenty years. She had the good fortune to appear in a pair of MGM's earliest Technicolor productions – *Lassie Come Home* and *National Velvet* – both big box-office hits which immediately launched her to stardom. Teenage roles followed and she easily made the transition to young adult parts, teamed with Spencer Tracy in *Father of the Bride* and with Montgomery Clift in *A Place in the Sun*. In spite of her great beauty, her talent as an actress was always suspect, and although she made a good stab at Maggie the Cat in *Cat on a Hot Tin Roof*, her Oscar for *Butterfield 8* was more of a sympathy award – she was seriously ill at the time – than a genuine recognition of her talent.

During the Sixties she matured as an actress and was more deservedly awarded her second Oscar for her bitchy wife, opposite her then husband, Richard Burton, in *Who's Afraid of Virginia Woolf?* Rarely out of the headlines due to her various illnesses and highly publicized marriages to such well-known movie figures as Michael Wilding, Mike Todd, Eddie Fisher and Richard Burton (twice), she is clearly a survivor and has taken on the role in the Eighties of the 'grande dame' of the American cinema, venturing onto the stage for the first time in a highly successful production of Lillian Hellman's *The Little Foxes* both in the USA and in London.

Films include: 1947 There's One Born Every Minute. '43 Lassie Come Home. '44 National Velvet. '49 Little Women. '50 Father of the Bride. '51 A Place in the Sun. '57 Raintree County. '58 Cat on a Hot Tin Roof. '59 Suddenly, Last Summer. '60 Butterfield 8. '63 Cleopatra. '66 Who's Afraid of Virginia Woolf? '67 The Taming of the Shrew.

TAYLOR, Robert

(1911–1969). Actor. Born: Spangler Arlington Brough; Filley, Nebraska, USA

A tall, handsome romantic lead, Taylor appeared in dozens of costume and action pictures during his 25 years at MGM. He originally studied music and medicine at Doane College in Nebraska and then at Pomona College, California. A successful screen test led to a number of minor pictures at Fox, Universal and MGM during the mid-Thirties, and he had his first major successes with *Magnificent Obsession* and *Camille*. Taylor developed into a reliable, if dull, leading man during the following years at MGM. If his performance in *Quo Vadis?* as Marcus Vinicius, the commander of a Roman legion who is converted to Christianity, failed to convince, the picture was still a big box-office hit. And he coped rather better with the title role of the British-made *Ivanhoe*.

The decline in his career during later years reflected the decline into mediocrity of MGM, once the leading Hollywood studio. The first of Taylor's two wives was Barbara Stanwyck.

Films include: 1934 Handy Andy. '35 Magnificent Obsession. '36 The Gorgeous Hussy. '36 Camille. '37 Personal Property (GB: The Man in Possession); Broadway Melody of 1938. '38 A Yank at Oxford (GB); Three Comrades. '39 Stand Up and Fight. '40 Flight Command; Waterloo Bridge; Escape. '41 Billy the Kid. '41 Johnny Eager. '43 Bataan; Song of Russia. '46 Undercurrent. '49 Conspirator (GB). '50 Devil's Doorway. '51 Quo Vadis?; Westward the Women. '52 Ivanhoe (GB). '53 Knights of the Round Table (GB). '54 Rogue Cop. '56 The Last Hunt. '58 Party Girl.

TAYLOR, Rod

(b. 1929). Actor. Born: Rodney Taylor; Sydney, Australia

After studying painting at college, Taylor pursued a career as a painter for a short period before he turned to acting instead. Some stage and film experience led to Hollywood where he arrived in the mid-Fifties and immediately secured supporting roles in a number of major studio productions including *The Virgin Queen*, *Giant* (1956) and *Raintree County* (1957). Rugged in appearance, he played the lead in a variety of relatively minor American and British pictures during the Sixties, but had his most memorable role as the resourceful hero of Hitchcock's *The Birds* in 1963. More recently he has divided his time between film and television and has formed his own company, Rodler Inc., for television-film production.

Films include: 1951 The Stewart Expedition. '54 Long John Silver. '55 The Virgin Queen. '60 The Time Machine. '63 The Birds; The VIPs (GB) (USA: International Hotel); Sunday in New York. '65 Young Cassidy. '66 The Glass Bottom Boat; The Liquidator. '67 The Mercenaries. '68 The Hell With Heroes; Nobody Runs Forever (GB) (USA: The High Commissioner). '70 Zabriskie Point. '73 The Train Robbers. '77 The Picture Show Man (AUS).

429

TEAL, Ray

(1902–1976). Actor. Born: Grand Rapids, Michigan, USA

Ray Teal played the saxophone to work his way through the University of California and by 1936 was a stage band conductor. He made his film debut in 1938, and was soon established as a Western character, often a short-fused gunslinger or a corrupt sheriff. After making about 130 films, not all Westerns, he landed the role of the sheriff in the television series *Bonanza* (1959–73) and thereafter appeared only occasionally in cinema films.

Films include: 1938 Western Jamboree. '40 Northwest Passage. '46 The Best Years of Our Lives. '47 Brute Force. '48 Joan of Arc. '50 The Men. '51 Ace in the Hole (USA retitling for TV: The Big Carnival); The Wild North. '58 Saddle the Wind. '60 Inherit the Wind. '61 One-Eyed Jacks. '63 Cattle King (GB: Guns of Wyoming). '70 Chisum.

TEMPLE, Shirley

(b. 1928). Actress. Born: Santa Monica, California, USA

The most popular child star in the history of the cinema, Shirley Temple virtually single-handedly effected the survival of the ailing Fox studio during the mid-Thirties and became a mainstay of the new 20th Century-Fox under Darryl Zanuck. Curly-haired and dimpled, she came across on the screen as not just cute but sensible and talented as well, reflecting her undoubted abilities as a singer, dancer and actress. The peak of her career was concentrated into a four-year period from 1934 through 1938 when she starred in over twenty features, including *Little Miss Marker*, John Ford's *Wee Willie Winkie* and *Rebecca of Sunnybrook Farm*. Regularly appearing at the top of the star popularity polls, she received a special Oscar in 1934. During the Forties she was cast as a teenager in hit movies like *Since You Went Away* and *The Bachelor and the Bobbysoxer*, but she no longer lit up the screen as she had done as a child and she retired from films after 1949. Known by her married name of Shirley Temple Black, she entered politics in the late Sixties and enjoyed a measure of success as an ambassador and chief of protocol.

Films include: 1932 War Babies (short). '33 The Kid's Last Fight (short); Merrily Yours (short). '34 Pardon My Pups (short); Stand Up and Cheer; Little Miss Marker (GB: Girl in Pawn). '35 Little Colonel (GB: The Little Colonel); Curly Top; The Littlest Rebel. '36 Poor Little Rich Girl; Dimples. '37 Wee Willie Winkie. '38 Rebecca of Sunnybrook Farm. '39 The Little Princess. '40 The Blue Bird. '44 Since You Went Away. '47 The Bachelor and the Bobbysoxer (GB: Bachelor Knight). '48 Fort Apache.

TERRY, Alice

(b. 1900). Actress. Born: Alice Frances Taafe; Vincennes, Indiana, USA

By the time she was 15 Alice Terry was working as an extra at Thomas Ince's studios (she plays several parts in his epic *Civilization*). In 1917 she met the director Rex Ingram. Four years later they were married, a union which endured until Rex's death in 1950. Alice played a small part in Ingram's *Shore Acres*, the lead in his next film, *Hearts Are Trumps*, and leads in all his remaining films save two. Alice Terry is the least honoured of the great silent film actresses. She was always cool and restrained (which led critics of her day to undervalue her), and her acting had a clarity and inner truth which are as valid today as ever they were. 'She thinks her role rather than acts it,' Liam O'Leary quotes Ingram as saying, and that was as true of Terry as it was of Garbo or Brooks. Her quiet assurance dominates *The Four Horsemen of the Apocalypse*, while the scene in *Mare Nostrum* in which she walks to her execution is one of the silent cinema's passages of total self-absorption and supreme art. And it is Terry as much as Ingram who makes it so. She retired when Ingram did, and now lives quietly in the San Fernando Valley.

Films include: 1916 Not My Sister; Civilization. '20 Shore Acres; Hearts Are Trumps. '21 The Four Horsemen of the Apocalypse; The Conquering Power. '22 Turn to the Right; The Prisoner of Zenda. '23 Where the Pavement Ends; Scaramouche. '24 The Arab. '26 Mare Nostrum; The Magician. '27 The Garden of Allah. '29 The Three Passions.

TERRY-THOMAS

(b. 1911). Actor. Born: Thomas Terry Hoare-Stevens; London, England

Terry-Thomas gained his earliest acting experience on the radio and on stage. During the late Fifties he was cast in a number of films – including such Boulting Brothers comedies as *Private's Progress, Carleton-Browne of the F.O.* and *I'm All Right Jack* – and developed into one of the mainstays of the British comedy scene. With his faintly unconvincing upper-class accent and stylish appearance to balance the fine moustache and gap-toothed smile, he naturally fitted the role of the sophisticated comic villain although he often doubled as a butler or chauffeur. He was much in demand during the Sixties when he divided his time between American and British productions, but his style of comedy has gone out of fashion during more recent years.

Films include: 1949 Helter Skelter. '56 Private's Progress. '57 Blue Murder at St Trinians. '59 Carleton Browne of the F.O. (USA: Man in a Cocked Hat); I'm All Right Jack; The Hound of the Baskervilles. '60 School for Scoundrels. '65 Those Magnificent Men in Their Flying Machines; How to Murder Your Wife (USA). '71 The Abominable Dr Phibes.

TESHIGAHARA, Hiroshi

(b. 1927). Director. Born: Tokyo, Japan

Teshigahara studied painting at the Tokyo Art Institute, then worked on a number of documentary shorts during the Fifties before setting up his own company to produce his first feature, *Pitfall*. His second feature, the powerful, allegorical and highly erotic *Woman of the Dunes*, was based on the novel by Kobo Abe. It tells of an entomologist who spends a night with a woman living in the sand dunes and then finds that he is trapped with her. A remarkable work which won the Special Jury Prize at Cannes and was nominated for a Best Foreign Film Oscar, it proved a one-shot effort, and Teshigahara was never able to match its success. In 1966 he directed a moderately interesting thriller, *The Face of Another*, and, in the Seventies, *Summer Soldiers*, a feature-length semi-documentary about American deserters from the Vietnam War who are forced to lead an underground existence on the run from the authorities in Japan.

Films include: 1953 Hokusai (short). '59 José Torres Cohort. '62 Otoshi Ana (Pitfall). '64 Suna no Onna (GB: Woman of the Dunes). '66 Tanin no Kao (The Face of Another). '68 Moetsukita Ghizu (USA: The Ruined Map). '71 Summer Soldiers.

TETZLAFF, Ted

(b. 1903). Cinematographer/director. Born: Theodore Tetzlaff; Los Angeles, California, USA

Attracted to films at an early age, Tetzlaff advanced rapidly from photographic lab assistant to camera assistant and then director of photography during the Twenties. As a leading cameraman under contract to Columbia and then Paramount his assignments were mainly routine, although there was *My Man Godfrey* (1936) for Universal and a pair of Mitchell Leisen-Preston Sturges comedies of note – *Easy Living* (1937) and *Remember the Night* (1940). Tetzlaff, however, made his mark at RKO after the war, serving as lighting cameraman on Hitchcock's masterpiece *Notorious*, then made one further notable contribution to Forties *film noir* as the director of an outstanding thriller, *The Window*, in 1949. He directed a number of forgettable features during the Fifties before retiring from filmmaking.

Films include: 1926 Atta Boy (photo. only). '41 The Road to Zanzibar (photo. only). '45 The Enchanted Cottage (photo. only); Notorious (photo. only). '47 Riff Raff. '48 Fighting Father Dunne. '49 Johnny Allegro (Hounded); The Window. '50 The White Tower. '53 Time Bomb (GB) (USA: Terror on a Train). '55 Son of Sinbad. '59 The Young Land.

THALBERG, Irving G.

(1899–1936). Producer. Born: Irving Grant Thalberg; New York City, USA

Although he suffered from ill-health and died at an early age, Thalberg had an influence on Hollywood filmmaking which lasted long after his death. He served as the model for F. Scott Fitzgerald's *The Last Tycoon* and was honoured by the Academy of Motion Picture Art and Sciences who instituted an annual producer award in his name in 1937. Starting out as a secretary to Carl Laemmle, the head of Universal Pictures, he worked his way up to producer status during the early Twenties. In 1923 he joined Louis B.

430

Mayer Pictures and became a key figure in the formation of MGM the following year. With Mayer as studio chief, Thalberg functioned as an active chief of production supervising many of the prestige productions and with a staff of 'production supervisors' answerable to him. This system reflected a new attempt to put studio film-making on a more sound financial basis and meant a shift in power from the leading producer-directors like Rex Ingram and Erich von Stroheim, whose services were inherited by the new studio, to a greater producer control over the individual directors. (Thalberg's own reputation was partly based on his success in controlling the alleged extravagance of Stroheim at Universal and MGM.) In fact, Thalberg's reign at MGM lasted only eight and a half years till the end of 1932 when his illness led to a downgrading of his position. He continued to function as the producer of such prestige films as *The Barretts of Wimpole Street* (1934) and *Romeo and Juliet* (1936) starring his wife, Norma Shearer, and won his third Best Picture Oscar for *Mutiny on the Bounty* (1935) – his previous winners had been *Broadway Melody* (1929) and *Grand Hotel* (1932). But his authority had been reduced and Louis B. Mayer now ran the studio alone.

Far left: little Shirley Temple in Poor Little Rich Girl. *Left: Terry-Thomas in Stanley Kramer's star-studded caper,* It's a Mad, Mad, Mad, Mad World *(1963). Above: Ray Teal in* Decision at Sundown *(1957), directed by Budd*

THEODORAKIS, Mikis

(b. 1925). Composer. Born: Khios, Greece

Mikis Theodorakis is perhaps best known for his work with the Greek director Michael Cacoyannis, particularly for the film *Zorba the Greek*. However his strong, simple melodies, driving bouzoukis, hypnotic rhythms, plus the immediacy and the emotionalism of his music, have made for attractive and distinctive scores for such films as Michael Powell's Resistance drama *Ill Met by Moonlight* and Sidney Lumet's *Serpico*. The son of a minor government official who had been thrown out of work by the Greek dictator Metaxas, Theodorakis began musical studies as a small boy at Patras Conservatory, becoming known as something of a child prodigy. In 1943 he moved to study in Athens but was arrested for belonging to an anti-German partisan movement. During the Greek Civil War he was arrested again as a left-wing democrat, and imprisoned and tortured. On his release in 1954 he went to Paris where he established a reputation as a fine composer. Six years later he returned to Greece and his popular melodies turned him into his country's best-loved composer. In 1964 he entered Parliament and in

Boetticher. Above: Alice Terry in Where the Pavement Ends, *directed by her husband Rex Ingram. Below: Dame Sybil Thorndike in* Alive and Kicking. *Below left: Ernest Thesiger in* A Place of One's Own *(1945)*

the same year he achieved his first great film score success with *Zorba the Greek*. However, with the *coup d'état* in 1967 he was imprisoned for the third time and his music banned. In 1970 he was finally released after international protests.

Films include: 1953 Eva. '57 Ill Met by Moonlight (GB) (USA: Night Ambush). '61 The Shadow of the Cat (GB). '62 Electra; Phaedra (USA-GR). '64 Zorba the Greek (GR-USA). '69 Z (FR-ALG). '71 The Trojan Women (USA). '73 Etat de Siège (FR-IT-GER) (GB: State of Siege). '73 Serpico (USA). '77 Iphigenia.

THESIGER, Ernest

(1879–1961). Actor. Born: London, England

After a public school education at Marlborough College, Ernest Thesiger studied at the Slade School of Art at University College, London, where he developed his talents as a watercolourist and needleworker. (He also became a leading authority on embroidery.) But he soon turned to acting, making his first stage appearances in 1909. Apart from a brief period of service in World War I before being wounded in 1915, he continued to be a leading member of the English acting profession for half a century, being associated in particular with the plays of George Bernard Shaw. His film debut was in 1918, as William Pitt in a life story of *Nelson*. His theatrical manner, his fastidiously modulated voice, his almost cadaverous emaciation and his hawk-like features were generally exploited in a series of eccentric character roles, often in literary or theatrical adaptations. Amongst the most memorable were as the epicene mad scientist Dr Praetorius in *The Bride of Frankenstein* (one of his few American films) and as the evil capitalist Sir John Kierlaw in *The Man in the White Suit*, immensely old and frail but kept alive by drugs and the force of his greed. Thesiger was awarded the CBE in 1950.

Films include: 1918 Nelson. '21 The Adventures of Mr Pickwick. '35 The Bride of Frankenstein (USA). '44 Henry V. '45 Caesar and Cleopatra. '47 The Ghosts of Berkeley Square. '48 The Winslow Boy. '51 Scrooge; The Man in the White Suit. '59 The Battle of the Sexes. '60 Sons and Lovers.

THOMAS, Gerald

(b. 1920). Director. Born: Hull, Yorkshire, England

Best known as the director of the highly successful Carry On series of comedies, Thomas is the younger brother of film director Ralph Thomas and began his career as an assistant editor and editor during the postwar period. He graduated to directing in 1956 and turned out a number of cheap and efficient thrillers like *The Vicious Circle*, starring John Mills. Thomas developed a close working relationship with producer Peter Rogers of Romulus films and they went on to collaborate on the long-running Carry On pictures beginning in 1958 with *Carry On Sergeant* and only ending 20 years and 28 titles later with *Carry On Emmannuelle*.

Films include: 1956 Circus Friends. '57 The Vicious Circle (USA: The Circle). '58 Carry On Sergeant. '60 Watch Your Stern. '61 Raising the Wind. '62 Twice Round the Daffodils. '65 The Big Job. '67 Follow That Camel. '78 Carry On Emmannuelle.

THOMAS, Ralph

(b. 1915). Director. Born: Hull, Yorkshire, England

Gaining his first experience during the Thirties as a clapper boy and assistant editor, Thomas then turned to journalism and saw service during the war before returning to the film industry in 1946. The best of his early pictures was a Hitchcockian thriller *The Clouded Yellow* (1950), starring Trevor Howard, Kenneth More and Jean Simmons as the heroine in distress. In 1954 in collaboration with producer Betty Box he initiated the successful series of Doctor comedies with *Doctor in the House*, featuring Dirk Bogarde as Simon Sparrow and James Robertson Justice as the formidable Sir Lancelot Spratt. Thomas went on to work with Bogarde on other pictures, including a remake of *A Tale of Two Cities*, while returning periodically to the Doctor movies during the early Sixties. More recently he has directed a number of weak spy thrillers and sex spoofs.

Films include: 1949 Helter Skelter. '54 Doctor in the House. '55 Doctor at Sea. '57 Campbell's Kingdom; Doctor at Large. '58 A Tale of Two Cities. '59 The 39 Steps; Upstairs and Downstairs. '60 Doctor in Love. '63 Doctor in Distress. '64 Hot Enough for June. '65 Doctor in Clover. '66 Deadlier Than the Male. '70 Doctor in Trouble.

THORNDIKE, Sybil

(1882–1976). Actress. Born: Gainsborough, Lincolnshire, England

One of the *grandes dames* of the English stage, Sybil Thorndike made only sporadic forays into the film studios. A parson's daughter, she was set for a career as a concert pianist until a broken wrist turned her to acting: she made her debut in 1904. She was leading lady in Lillian Baylis's Old Vic company, but is most memorably connected with the title role of George Bernard Shaw's *Saint Joan*, which she first performed in 1934. Her main characteristics, as an actress and as a person, were energy, warmth and sincerity. These were evident in many of her film roles, although these also reveal her range and versatility – from Nurse Edith Cavell in the controversial *Dawn* to the villainous Mrs Squeers in *Nicholas Nickleby* and Queen Victoria in *Melba*. She was married to the actor and director Sir Lewis Casson for over sixty years. She was created a Dame Commander of the British Empire in 1931 and a Companion of Honour in 1970.

Films include: 1927 Hindle Wakes. '28 Dawn. '36 Tudor Rose (USA: Nine Days a Queen). '41 Major Barbara. '47 Nicholas Nickleby. '49 Britannia Mews (USA: Forbidden Street); Stage Fright. '50 Gone to Earth (USA: The Wild Heart). '51 The Magic Box. '53 Melba. '57 The Prince and the Showgirl. '58 Alive and Kicking. '59 Jet Storm.

THORPE, Richard

(b. 1896). Director. Born: Rollo Smolt Thorpe; Hutchinson, Kansas, USA

Having gained a variety of experience as a young actor on the stage, Thorpe arrived in Hollywood in 1921. He quickly found himself becoming more interested in directing than acting and turned out a large number of pictures, mainly cheap comedies and Westerns, during the following years. Signed up as a director by MGM in 1935, Thorpe remained with this studio for over twenty years, directing a steady average of three pictures per year throughout most of this period. Handling the MGM Tarzan cycle of the late Thirties and early Forties, he was, incredibly, the initial director on the studio's lavish Technicolor production, *The Wizard of Oz* (1939), but was quickly replaced. He made some minor contributions to MGM's Forties musical cycle, but had his biggest commercial hits with *The Great Caruso* and *Ivanhoe*, the first of a series of lavish costume epics. One of his MGM assignments during this period was the early Elvis Presley vehicle, *Jailhouse Rock*. Thorpe's career wound down during the Sixties and he retired in 1967.

Films include: 1923 Three O'Clock in the Morning (actor only). '30 The Utah Kid. '44 Follow the Boys. '51 The Great Caruso. '52 The Prisoner of Zenda; Ivanhoe. '54 The Student Prince. '57 Jailhouse Rock. '61 The Honeymoon Machine. '63 Fun in Acapulco. '65 The Truth About Spring; That Funny Feeling. '67 The Last Challenge (GB: The Pistolero of Red River).

THE THREE STOOGES

Fine, Larry (1911–1975). Comedian. Born: New York City, USA

Howard, Moe (1905–1975). Comedian. Born: New York City, USA

Howard, Shemp (1900–1955). Comedian. Born: Samuel Howard; New York City, USA

The two Howard brothers, Moe and Shemp, began in vaudeville with Ted Healy, as his Stooges, and when joined by tuber-nosed Larry Fine they became The Three Stooges and decided to go it alone. In the early Thirties Shemp was replaced by his brother Curly (Jerome Howard, 1906–52) but Shemp returned when Curly became ill in 1946. On Shemp's death he was replaced by Joe Besser and then Joe De Rita. The team made about two hundred shorts between 1934 and 1958. Their films are full of rather obvious humour – clowning and slapstick of a vaudeville, burlesque nature, but their career managed to ride the ups and downs of the film industry and changes in public taste. They also managed this, surprisingly, without altering many of their gags, jokes or routines.

Feature films include: 1930 Soup to Nuts. '34 Hollywood Party. '59 Have Rocket Will Travel. '60 Three Stooges Scrapbook; Stop! Look! Laugh! (compilation of shorts). '61 Snow White and the Three Stooges. '62 The Three Stooges Meet Hercules; The Three Stooges in Orbit. '63 The Three Stooges Go

Around the World in a Daze; It's a Mad, Mad, Mad, Mad World. '65 The Outlaws Is Coming.

THULIN, Ingrid

(b. 1929). Actress. Born: Solleften, Sweden

Ingrid Thulin is best known as one of the leading actresses in the films of Ingmar Bergman over a period of almost twenty years. She represents the deeper, troubled side of the Bergman female persona in contrast to the more lively, extrovert qualities of Bibi Andersson (with whom she appeared in *Wild Strawberries* and *So Close to Life*) or the more openly sensual qualities of Eva Dahlbeck (*So Close to Life*) or Gunnel Lindblom (*The Silence*). She has also worked occasionally with other European directors, most notably as Yves Montand's mistress in Alain Resnais' *La Guerre Est Finie* and as the powerful scheming, Lady Macbeth-like wife of Dirk Bogarde in Visconti's *The Damned*.

Films include: 1948 Dit Vindarna Bär (Where the Winds Lead). '52 Möte Med Livet (Meeting Life). '54 Två Sköna Juveler (Two Rascals). '57 Smultronstället (USA/GB; Wild Strawberries). '58 Nära Livet (GB: So Close to Life); Ansiktet (USA: The Magician; GB: The Face). '62 The Four Horsemen of the Apocalypse (USA). '63 Tystnaden (USA/GB: The Silence). '66 La Guerre Est Finie (FR-SWED) (GB: The War Is Over). '69 La Caduta degli Dei (IT-GER) (USA/GB: The Damned). '72 Viskingar och Rop (USA/GB: Cries and Whispers). '78 En och En (One and One). '82 Brusten Himmel (dir. only) (GB: Broken Sky).

TIERNEY, Gene

(b. 1920). Actress. Born: New York City, USA

Sultry, beautiful Gene Tierney came from an affluent society background and was educated in private schools in Connecticut and Switzerland. After working briefly as a model and as a Broadway actress, she was signed to a contract by 20th Century-Fox. Her exotic appearance photographed well in colour – her early Technicolor pictures included *Belle Starr* (1941), in the title role, and the Lubitsch fantasy *Heaven Can Wait* (1943); she received an Oscar nomination for her performance as the disturbed wife of Cornel Wilde in *Leave Her to Heaven*. But she is probably best remembered today for her cool and assured performance in the Otto Preminger thriller *Laura* which turned her into a major star.

Films include: 1941 Sundown; Tobacco Road. '42 Rings on Her Fingers. '44 Laura. '45 A Bell for Adano; Leave Her to Heaven. '46 Dragonwyck; The Razor's Edge. '50 Night and the City (GB). '53 Never Let Me Go. '62 Advise and Consent. '63 Toys in the Attic. '64 The Pleasure Seekers.

TIOMKIN, Dimitri

(1899–1979). Composer/music director. Born: St Petersburg, Russia.

One of the most celebrated and renowned of Hollywood composers, Tiomkin was educated at the St

Petersburg Conservatory of Music and St Petersburg University. He first pursued his career in Europe as a concert pianist, conductor and composer before emigrating to the USA in 1925. Although working regularly in Hollywood throughout the Thirties and earning the first of his many Oscar nominations for his scores for two Frank Capra films, *Lost Horizon* and *Mr Smith Goes to Washington*, Tiomkin came into his own during the Fifties when he won Oscars for *High Noon* (both score and song), *The High and the Mighty* and *The Old Man and the Sea*. During these years he was much in demand to provide the lush scores required for lavish epics like *Giant, The Alamo* and *55 Days at Peking*. In 1970 he returned to Russia to serve as executive producer on one of his pet projects, a lavish biopic of *Tchaikovsky* (1971).

Films include: 1937 Lost Horizon. '39 Mr Smith Goes to Washington; Only Angels Have Wings. '41 The Corsican Brothers. '42 The Moon and Sixpence. '44 The Bridge of San Luis Rey. '46 Duel in the Sun. '49 Champion. '52 High Noon. '54 The High and the Mighty; Dial M for Murder. '56 Giant. '58 The Old Man and the Sea. '60 The Alamo. '61 The Guns of Navarone (GB). '63 55 Days at Peking.

TISSE, Edward

(1897–1961). Cinematographer. Born: Eduard Kazimirovich Tisse; Lithuania

Active as a newsreel cameraman during World War I and during the years of revolutionary conflict in Russia which extended into the early Twenties, Tisse also worked on many documentaries and science films as well. But he shot to prominence as the close collaborator of director Sergei Eisenstein over a period of more than twenty years beginning with *Strike* in 1924 and ending with the two-part *Ivan the Terrible* (1944–46). His strong sense of composition – he was trained as a painter and still photographer – and his technical mastery contributed immeasurably to the powerful black-and-white imagery found in all of Eisenstein's works. His occasional work with other Soviet directors, however, never came close to matching his achievements with the great Eisenstein.

Films include: 1918 Signàl (Signal). '21 Golod . . . Golod . . . Golod (Hunger . . . Hunger . . . Hunger). '25 Stachka (GB: Strike); Bronenosets Potemkin (USA/GB: Battleship Potemkin); Yevreiskoye Schastye (Jewish Luck). '27 Oktyabr (USA: Ten Days That Shook the World; GB: October). '28 Staroye i Novoye/Generalnaya Liniya (GB: The Old and the New/The General Line). '35 Aerograd. '38 Aleksandr Nevskii (GB: Alexander Nevsky). '44 Ivan Grozny (GB: Ivan the Terrible). '56 Besmertnyi Garnizon (The Immortal Garrison).

TOBIAS, George

(1901–1980). Actor. Born: New York City, USA

A burly character actor, George Tobias tended to be cast as the hero's down-to-earth loyal, but rather bemused, New Yorker pal, although he

did play his share of bad guys too. He gained his early acting experience on the stage with the Provincetown Players, the Theatre Guild and the Theatre Union, before heading west for Hollywood in the late Thirties. His most successful film-acting period was during the Forties, mostly for Warners, and after 1958 he concentrated on television work, appearing in such shows as *Bewitched* and *Medical Center*.

Films include: 1939 Ninotchka; The Hunchback of Notre Dame. '40 They Drive By Night (GB: The Road to 'Frisco). '42 Yankee Doodle Dandy. '44 The Mask of Dimitrios. '45 Mildred Pierce. '47 Sinbad the Sailor. '51 Ten Tall Men; Rawhide. '53 The Glenn Miller Story. '57 Silk Stockings. '58 Marjorie Morningstar. '70 The Phynx.

TODD, Ann

(b. 1909). Actress/director. Born: Hartford, Cheshire, England

Ann Todd attended the Central School of Speech and Drama in London, where she studied elocution and fencing, with the aim of becoming a teacher. She made her acting debut, at the age of 18, quite by accident when the Arts Theatre Club called her in at very short notice to appear in one of their productions. After making her West End debut in *Baa Baa Black Sheep* she had many supporting theatre and film roles until her big break when she was cast as a sensitive pianist opposite James Mason in *The Seventh Veil*. Her career continued to flourish though in the late Fifties she turned to writing, producing and directing travel documentaries, making only the occasional film appearance. Her third husband was the director David Lean (they are now divorced).

Films include: 1937 The Squeaker (USA: Murder on Diamond Row); Action for Slander. '38 South Riding. '39 Poison Pen. '41 Ships With Wings. '45 The Seventh Veil; Perfect Strangers (USA: Vacation From Marriage). '47 The Paradine Case (USA). '50 Madeleine. '52 The Sound Barrier (USA: Breaking the Sound Barrier/Star Bound). '66 Thunder in Heaven (dir; +prod; +sc. only). '67 Thunder of the Gods (dir; +sc; +prod. only). '74 Thunder of Silence (dir; +prod.; +sc only). '79 The Human Factor (USA-GB).

TODD, Michael

(1907–1958). Producer. Born: Avram Goldenbogen; Minneapolis, Minnesota, USA

A flamboyant showman, Todd had a spectacular series of Broadway hits beginning with *The Hot Mikado* in 1939 and on through the Mae West vehicle *Catherine Was Great* to *The Naked Genius*, starring Joan Blondell who was briefly married to Todd during the Forties. From 1950 on he turned his interest to the cinema. He was one of the founders of the Cinerama company and co-directed the first hit in the new three-screen process, *This Is Cinerama* (1952). During 1954 he helped develop a 65mm process which he christened Todd-AO and which was used for *Oklahoma!* (1955). The following film, *Around the World in 80 Days* (1956), was Todd's pet project. It was personally produced by him and ended up a phenomenal box-office hit and popular success and won the Oscar for Best Picture. He was briefly married to Elizabeth Taylor before his death in a plane crash in 1958.

TODD, Richard

(b. 1919). Actor. Born: Richard Andrew Palethorpe-Todd; Dublin, Ireland

A successful stage actor from 1937 with a break for war service, Todd made a promising entry into films during the late Forties. He won an Oscar nomination for his performance in his third picture, *The Hasty Heart*, as the Scottish soldier with only a short time to live. And he then played the hero on the run in the Hitchcock thriller *Stage Fright*. Much of the rest of his career was routine as he appeared regularly in undistinguished pictures throughout the Fifties and Sixties, with memorable parts – like that of Wing Commander Guy Gibson in *The Dam Busters* – only few and far between.

Films include: 1948 For Them That Trespass. '49 The Hasty Heart; Stage Fright. '50 Portrait of Clare. '51 Lightning Strikes Twice (USA). '52 The Story of Robin Hood and His Merrie Men. '53 Rob Roy, the Highland Rogue. '55 The Dam Busters. '57 Yangtse Incident. '61 The Long and the Short and the Tall. '65 Operation Crossbow (GB-IT). '79 Home Before Midnight.

Below left: an early Seventies portrait of Ingrid Thulin. Left: The Three Stooges (top to bottom) Curly, Moe and Larry. Above: a publicity shot of Gene Tierney. Above right: Ann Todd in The Sound Barrier, directed by her then husband, David Lean. Below: Richard Todd in A Man Called Peter (1955), a film about Peter Marshall who became US Senate Chaplain. Below left: George Tobias in The Judge Steps Out (1947)

Far left: Thelma Todd in You Made Me Love You (1933), directed by Monty Banks. Left: Sidney Toler as the Chinese detective in Charlie Chan in Panama (1940). Above: Italian star Ugo Tognazzi. Below: the vivacious Lily Tomlin in 9 to 5.

TODD, Thelma

(1905–1935). Actress. Born: Lawrence, Massachusetts, USA

A stunningly beautiful blonde comedienne, Thelma Todd brightened up a number of Hollywood shorts and features during her tragically short life. After completing her schooling in Massachusetts, she worked as a schoolteacher and part-time model, then won the Miss Massachusetts beauty contest before she was attracted into pictures. A genuinely talented and uninhibited actress, she benefited from the coming of sound and her popularity grew during the early Thirties when she played opposite the Marx Brothers in *Monkey Business* (1931) and *Horse Feathers* (1932) and had her own comedy series of shorts for producer Hal Roach. She died in 1935 of carbon monoxide poisoning in mysterious circumstances.

Films include: 1929 Seven Footprints to Satan. '30 The King (short); Another Fine Mess (short). '31 The Maltese Falcon; Rough Seas. '32 Alum and Eve (short). '33 The Bargain of the Century (short); Fra Diavolo; Air Hostess; Cheating Blondes. '35 After the Dance. '36 The Bohemian Girl.

TOGNAZZI, Ugo

(b. 1922). Actor. Born: Cremona, Italy

Along with Alberto Sordi, Vittorio Gassmann and Marcello Mastroianni, Ugo Tognazzi has managed to find fame not only in his native Italy but also internationally. He was working as an accountant when he became interested in acting through amateur productions and he soon became involved with theatre revues and variety acts. *One, Two, Three*, his own highly popular television series, followed and as a result he was offered film roles. He quickly became a top box-office star in Italy, appearing in 12 films in 1959 and he has subsequently found fame abroad with such roles as Jane Fonda's rugged lover in *Barbarella*.

Films include: 1953 Amore in Città. '61 Il Federale (USA: The Fascist). '63 La Marcia su Roma (IT-FR); La Terrazza (ARG) (USA: The Terrace). '64 Alta Infedeltà (IT-FR) (USA/GB: High Infidelity). '66 Io la Conosceve Bene (IT-GER-FR). '67 L' Harem; L'Immorale (IT-FR) (USA: The Climax). '68 Barbarella (FR-IT). '71 La Califfa. '73 La Grande Bouffe (FR-IT) (GB: Blow-Out). '78 La Cage aux Folles (FR-IT) (USA: Birds of a Feather). '80 I Viaggiatori della Sera (IT-SP); Sono Fotogenico (IT-FR).

TOLAND, Gregg

(1904–1948). Cinematographer. Born: Charleston, Illinois, USA

Rising rapidly from errand boy to camera assistant and finally to director of photography, Toland was signed to a contract by independent producer Samuel Goldwyn in 1929. Allowed a large measure of freedom by Goldwyn, with whom he remained throughout the rest of his career, he pioneered in the adoption of many new camera techniques such as the use of coated lenses and faster film stocks. But he is best remembered for his introduction of deep-focus compositions in collaboration with directors Orson Welles and William Wyler on *The Little Foxes*, *The Best Years of Our Lives* and especially *Citizen Kane*. Incredibly, although nominated five times, he won only one Oscar, for *Wuthering Heights*, but also co-directed the Oscar-winning documentary *December 7th* with John Ford.

Films include: 1929 The Rescue; Bulldog Drummond. '30 Raffles. '35 Les Misérables. '37 Dead End. '39 Wuthering Heights. '40 The Grapes of Wrath; Citizen Kane. '41 The Little Foxes. '43 December 7th (doc. short) (co-dir). '46 The Best Years of Our Lives. '48 Enchantment.

TOLER, Sidney

(1874–1947). Actor. Born: Warrensburg, Missouri, USA

Sidney Toler was an American character actor who abandoned a successful stage career to enter films early in the sound era. He played supporting roles in scores of Hollywood films before taking over the role of Charlie Chan, the wily oriental detective, in 1938, on the death of Warner Oland, the previous Chan. His first film in this part was *Charlie Chan in Honolulu*. He played Chan in over twenty-five movies until his death, and his large screen presence was greatly responsible for the continuing popularity of the character.

Films include: 1929 Madame X. '31 Strictly Dishonorable. '32 Blonde Venus. '35 Call of the Wild. '39 Charlie Chan in Honolulu; King of Chinatown. '44 Charlie Chan in the Secret Service. '45 The Red Dragon. '46 Dark Alibi.

TOMLIN, Lily

(b. 1939). Actress. Born: Mary Jean Tomlin; Detroit, Michigan, USA

Not everyone involved in *Laugh-In*, the popular television comedy show of the Seventies, continued to be successful but it did spell fame for Lily Tomlin who emerged from the show a popular, zany, very American comedienne. *Laugh-In* was the turning point of a career which had begun when she quit Wayne State University to work locally in cabaret. Further appearances in New York led to her performing comic monologues on *The Garry Moore Show*. Her film roles, though few, have been remarkably varied. She was true to type in *The Late Show*, a thriller spoof, but won considerable critical acclaim in a straight role in *Nashville*. *Moment by Moment*, a mawkish love story starring John Travolta, was altogether less inspiring, but Tomlin was perfect as *The Incredible Shrinking Woman* and made up the strangest of comedy trios with Jane Fonda and Dolly Parton in *9 to 5*.

Films include: 1975 Nashville. '77 The Late Show. '78 Moment by Moment. '80 9 to 5. '81 The Incredible Shrinking Woman.

TOMLINSON, David

(b. 1917). Actor. Born: Henley-on-Thames, Oxfordshire, England

Trained in the theatre, David Tomlinson went into films in 1935. Uppercrust, stiff-upper-lip, but with a natural gift for comedy, he fell easily into a variety of archetypal English RAF or army types or silly-ass roles, in everything from The Huggetts comedy series to war dramas like *The Wooden Horse*. He showed to particular advantage in *Mary Poppins*, in which he played a staid and stern middle-class father finally liberated from the worries of materialism by his children and their singing nanny. He has since excelled playing amiable, eccentric character roles in light-hearted films aimed at the younger generation, notably *Bedknobs and Broomsticks*.

Films include: 1941 Quiet Wedding. '45 The Way to the Stars (USA: Johnny in the

Clouds). '46 School for Secrets. '47 Master of Bankdam. '48 Here Come the Huggetts. '50 The Wooden Horse. '56 Three Men in a Boat. '64 Mary Poppins (USA). '66 The Liquidator. '69 The Love Bug (USA). '71 Bedknobs and Broomsticks (USA). '80 The Fiendish Plot of Dr Fu Manchu (USA).

TONE, Franchot

(1903–1968). Actor. Born: Stanislaus Pascal Franchot Tone; Niagara Falls, New York, USA

Franchot Tone was the son of a wealthy industrialist, sophisticated, charming and handsome. He was first bitten by the acting bug while attending Cornell University, and went on to establish a promising reputation on Broadway. Once under contract to MGM, however, he found himself

Above: David Tomlinson in The Chiltern Hundreds (1949), from the play by William Douglas Home. Below: Franchot Tone in Lost Honeymoon (1947). Right: Regis Toomey in Other Men's Women (1931), directed by William Wellman. Below, far right: the hearty Topol as a Mexican in the Western A Talent for Loving

lumbered with a series of playboy roles, usually as the hero's best friend. This was even true of his two best movies, in *The Lives of a Bengal Lancer* he was Gary Cooper's flippant but true-blue brother officer, and in *Mutiny on the Bounty* he was the wet-behind-the-ears Midshipman Byam, driven by Bligh's cruelty to join Fletcher Christian. At one time Tone was seventh in the list of most popular Hollywood stars, but his stock began to slip in the Forties and Fifties. He was married four times, his wives including the actresses Joan Crawford, Jean Wallace and Barbara Peyton. In the latter part of his career he was widely rumoured to have a drinking problem and received some bad publicity following an ugly bar-room brawl with actor Tom Neal. He returned to New York and produced an adaptation of *Uncle Vanya*, which he later filmed, and finally won some interesting character roles in the early Sixties.

Films include: 1932 The Wiser Sex. '33 Bombshell/Blonde Bombshell. '35 The Lives of a Bengal Lancer; Mutiny on the Bounty. '36 The King Steps Out. '37 The Bride Wore Red. '38 Three Comrades. '43 Five Graves to Cairo. '44 Phantom Lady. '58 Uncle Vanya (+ co-dir). '62 Advise and Consent. '65 Mickey One. '68 Nobody Runs Forever (USA: The High Commissioner).

TONTI, Aldo

(b. 1910). Cinematographer. Born: Rome, Italy

Aldo Tonti was the director of photography on *Ossessione*, Luchino Visconti's study of lust and murder,

loosely based on James M. Cain's novel, *The Postman Always Rings Twice*. Tonti's superb, sombre use of real locations gave the film a documentary authenticity that strongly influenced Italian film-makers and heralded the emergence of the neo-realist movement in post-war Italy, in which Tonti was heavily involved. He had entered the industry in 1934, working his way up from camera assistant to director of photography in five years. His subsequent work, with the exception of his collaborations with Rossellini (including *Europa '51* and *Dov'è la Libertà?*) and Fellini (*Nights of Cabiria*), has not been widely appreciated outside his native country. He has made occasional appearances in front of the camera, mostly in comic roles.

Films include: 1939 Sei Bambine e il Perseo. '42 Ossessione (co-photo). '47 Senza Pietà (GB: Without Pity). '51 Europa '51 (USA: The Greatest Love). '52 Dov'è la Libertà?; La Lupa. '54 Ulisse (co-photo) (GB: Ulysses). '56 War and Peace (IT-USA). '57 Le Notti di Cabiria (IT-FR) (USA: Nights of Cabiria; GB: Cabiria). '59 Ombre Bianche (USA/GB: The Savage Innocents). '62 Barabba/Barabbas. '66 Cast a Giant Shadow (USA). '67 Reflections in a Golden Eye (USA). '72 Joe Valachi; I Segreti di Cosa Nostra (IT-FR) (USA/GB: The Valachi Papers). '76 The Count of Monte Cristo (USA). '79 Ashanti (SWITZ).

TOOMEY, Regis

(b. 1902). Actor. Born: Pittsburgh, Pennsylvania, USA

Toomey entered films a few years after leaving the University of Pittsburgh,

in 1929, and was still working fifty years later. He has made over one hundred and fifty films in all, usually as second rank good guys, sometimes the hero's friend who cops it to prove that the goodies are not all invulnerable, in gangster movies like *G-Men*, war dramas like *Dive Bomber*, and Westerns like *They Died With Their Boots On*. In the Sixties he played Gene Barry's buddy in *Burke's Law* on TV.

Films include: 1929 Alibi. '30 The Light of Western Stars. '35 G-Men. '40 His Girl Friday; Northwest Passage. '41 Dive Bomber. '42 They Died With Their Boots On. '44 Phantom Lady. '45 Spellbound. '46 The Big Sleep. '52 My Six Convicts. '55 Guys and Dolls. '56 Dakota Incident. '64 Man's Favorite Sport. '79 C.H.O.M.P.S.

TOPOL

(b. 1935). Actor. Born: Chaim Topol; Tel Aviv, Palestine

The enduring image of Topol is of a Jewish Anthony Quinn, with the same earthy zest for life, but with perhaps a little more melancholy, growling his way through the song 'If I Were A Rich Man'. In fact, Topol already had a budding acting career before *Fiddler on The Roof* brought him international fame and won him an Oscar nomination. He gained his first acting experience during his military service, with the Israeli Army entertainment unit, and several films followed there. In the late Sixties he worked in Britain, and played opposite David Niven in a drama about the repatriation of Soviet exiles after World War II, *Before Winter Comes*. In London he starred in the stage version of *Fiddler on The Roof*, which opened the door for the subsequent film success. Since then he has made few film appearances; but Joseph Losey cast him in the title role of *Galileo*, his version of Bertolt Brecht's play.

Films include: 1964 Sallah. '66 Cast a Giant Shadow (USA). '68 Every Bastard a King; A Talent For Loving (GB). '69 Before Winter Comes (GB). '71 Hatarnegol: Fiddler on the Roof (USA). '72 Follow Me (GB) (USA: The Public Eye). '74 Galileo (GB- CAN). '79 The House on Garibaldi Street (USA).

TORN, Rip

(b. 1931). Actor. Born: Elmore Rual Torn; Temple, Texas, USA

Torn never intended to be an actor at all, though he has developed into an excellent one. He studied animal husbandry at the University of Texas, and went to Hollywood in search of instant stardom and the money to buy a ranch. Instead he ended up with all the other aspiring stars, washing dishes. He did finally manage to get some television parts, and followed these up with a trip to New York to study at the Actors' Studio. His film career picked up not long afterwards. Throughout the Sixties and Seventies he appeared in a variety of character roles, often playing unstable, explosive and violent types. He took the lead role, a country-and-western singer, in *Payday* (1973). He also played Richard Nixon on television in *Blind Ambition* in 1979. He is the husband of actress Geraldine Page, and Sissy Spacek is a first cousin.

Films include: 1956 Baby Doll. '57 A Face in the Crowd. '59 Pork Chop Hill. '61 King of Kings. '62 Sweet Bird of Youth. '65 The Cincinnati Kid. '72 Slaughter. '76 The Man Who Fell to Earth (GB). '78 The Private Files of J. Edgar Hoover; Coma. '79 The Seduction of Joe Tynan.

TORRE NILSSON, Leopoldo

(1924–1978). Director. Born: Buenos Aires, Argentina

Argentina's best known director, Torre Nilsson began his film career at the age of 15, assisting his father, Leopoldo Torres Rios, also a director. For a while it looked as if young Leopoldo might turn to writing, since he wrote a novel in his twenties, and, although he returned to film in 1950, he retained a love of literature which was to influence many of his subjects. By the end of the decade he had emerged as one of the best filmmakers in South America, his *La Casa del Angel* being favourably noticed at Cannes in 1957. Apart from a few politically expedient historical epics, his work mostly comprised dramas set in modern Argentina, often concerned with the corruption of innocence, and filmed with a distinctive, heavy visual style. Although his 1976 film, *Piedra Libre*, a typically sharp look at South American society, was disapproved of by Argentina's ruling regime, his premature death led to his revaluation there as an artist of the first order.

Films include: 1950 El Crimen de Oribe (co-dir) (Oribe's Crime). '54 Dias de Odio (Days of Hatred). '56 Graciela; La Casa del Ángel (GB: House of the Angel). '58 El Secuestrador (GB: The Kidnapper); La Caída (USA/GB: The Fall). '60 Fin de Fiesta (The Party's Over). '61 La Mano en la Trampa (ARG-SP) (USA/GB: The Hand in the Trap); Piel de Verano (+ prod; + co-sc) (USA/GB: Summer Skin). '63 La Terrazza (USA: The Terrace). '64 El Ojo de la Cerradura/The Eavesdropper (ARG-USA). '68 Martín Fierro (+ co-prod; + co-sc). '72 Los Siete Locos (The Seven Madmen). '74 Boquitas Pintadas (GB: Painted Lips). '76 Piedra Libre (Free for All).

TOTHEROH, Rollie

(1890–1967). Cinematographer. Born: Roland H. Totheroh; San Francisco, California, USA

Rollie Totheroh was director of photography on most of Charlie Chaplin's best-known films. Totheroh started work as a cartoonist on a San Francisco newspaper before he got a job at the Essanay Studios in Chicago as a cameraman. When Chaplin joined Essanay from Keystone in 1915, Totheroh was assigned to his films. The two worked well and stayed together when Chaplin moved on again to First National. Totheroh's credits read like a list of Chaplin's greatest: *The Tramp, Easy Street, The Immigrant, The Pawnshop, The Kid, The Great Dictator* – right up to *Limelight*, which Totheroh was lured out of retirement to help to make in 1952.

Films include: 1915 The Tramp. '16 The Vagabond (co-photo); The Pawnshop (co-photo). '17 Easy Street (co-photo); The Immigrant (co-photo). '21 The Kid. '23 A Woman of Paris (co-photo). '25 The Gold Rush. '31 City Lights (co-photo). '36 Modern Times (co-photo). '40 The Great Dictator (co-photo). '47 Monsieur Verdoux (co-photo); Song of My Heart. '52 Limelight (co-photo).

TOTÒ

(1898–1967). Actor. Born: Antonio de Curtis Gagliardi Ducas Comnuno di Bisanzio; Naples, Italy

From a poor family, Totò went on the stage following military service in World War I. Tall and slim, with the absurd gravity of the natural clown, he soon became a favourite in the music-hall, and played comedy roles in straight productions. His film debut in 1936 introduced him to a wider audience, and over the following 30 years he went on to make scores of movies, including a whole Totò series; by the time of his death from a heart-attack, he was Italy's best-loved comedy star.

Films include: 1937 Fermo con le Mani. '48 Totò al Giro d'Italia. '52 Guardie e Ladri (GB: Cops and Robbers). '54 L'Oro di Napoli (USA: Gold of Naples; GB: Every Day's a Holiday/Gold of Naples); I Tre Ladri (IT-FR); Totò all'Inferno. '55 Destinazione Piovarolo. '58 I Soliti Ignoti (USA: Big Deal on Madonna Street; GB: Persons Unknown). '61 I Due Marescialli. '62 Totò Diabolicus. '63 Toto Contro i Quattro. '67 Le Streghe (IT-FR) (USA: The Witches).

TOTTER, Audrey

(b. 1918). Actress. Born: Joliet, Illinois, USA

In the Forties Audrey Totter often played tough, hard-boiled blondes, as cold as ice on the outside, and often with a heart of flint. She began acting straight from high school, working in Chicago stock companies, and graduated to New York, where she played in so many radio dramas and soap-operas that she became known as 'the girl with a thousand voices'. Her early screen roles were small and varied, but a major supporting role in *The Postman Always Rings Twice* established her and she went on to star

in a series of melodramas with titles like *Tension* or *The Unsuspected*. Her career declined in the Fifties, though from 1972 she played a tough nurse, this time with a heart of gold, in television's *Medical Center*.

Films include: 1944 Main Street After Dark. '46 The Postman Always Rings Twice; Lady in the Lake. '47 The Unsuspected. '49 Any Number Can Play; Tension; The Set Up. '55 Women's Prison; A Bullet for Joey. '64 The Carpetbaggers. '68 Chubasco. '79 The Apple Dumpling Gang Rides Again.

TOURNEUR, Jacques

(1904–1977). Director. Born: Paris, France

Producer Val Lewton said of Tourneur's *Cat People*, 'Our formula is simple . . . three scenes of suggested horror, then one of actual violence'. If Lewton had the ideas, his director Jacques Tourneur had the talent to realize them. Constrained by low budgets to employ few actors and accessible locations, Tourneur used sharp lighting and moody black-and-white photography to suggest something animal lurking just out of view, an intangible extension of the audience's unease. Jacques must have inherited some of his craft from his father, director Maurice Tourneur. The two came to America in 1914, and Jacques began work as a scriptboy, assistant and actor on his father's productions. He first met Lewton when the two were involved in minor jobs on *A Tale of Two Cities* (1935). Their work together proved to be Tourneur's best – not only *Cat People*, but *I Walked with a Zombie* and *The Leopard Man* are regarded as classics of the horror genre. His films declined in the Fifties; he later moved to television, but his projects were undistinguished.

Films include: 1931 Tout ça ne Vaut pas l'Amour/Un Vieux Garçon (FR). '34 Les Filles de la Concierge (FR). '39 They All Come Out; Nick Carter – Master Detective. '42 Cat People. '43 I Walked With a Zombie; The Leopard Man. '47 Out of the Past (GB: Build my Gallows High). '50 The Flame and the Arrow. '52 Way of a Gaucho. '57 Night of the Demon (GB). '63 The Comedy of Terrors. '65 War Gods of the Deep (USA-GB) (GB: City Under the Sea).

TOURNEUR, Maurice

(1876–1961). Director. Born: Paris, France

Tourneur started work as a book illustrator and poster designer, but gave this up in favour of military service in North Africa. On his return he became assistant to sculptor Auguste Rodin. In 1900 he moved to the stage, working as an actor and then a designer. In 1912 a quarrel with director André Antoine caused him to join the Eclair film studios. His talent and reputation were such that in 1914 he was sent to run the company's studio in Fort Lee, New Jersey, USA and he went on to make many prestigious titles, including *Treasure Island* and *The Last of the Mohicans*. In 1926 another quarrel, this time with MGM over the production of *The Mysterious Island*, caused him to return to France. He continued to make films until 1949, when he was crippled in a car accident. From then until his death he worked as a translator, turning American mysteries – ever his favourite tales – into French. His son was the director Jacques Tourneur, who inherited his father's sense of atmosphere and ability to tell a story.

Films include: 1914 The Man of the Hour. **'17** The Poor Little Rich Girl; A Doll's House. **'18** The Blue Bird. **'19** The Last of the Mohicans (co-dir). **'20** Treasure Island '23 The Christian. **'26** Aloma of the South Seas. **'28** L'Equipage (FR). **'29** The Mysterious Island (some scenes only). **'40** Volpone (FR). **'48** L'Impasse des Deux Anges (FR).

TRACY, Spencer

(1900–1967). Actor. Born: Spencer Bonaventure Tracy; Milwaukee, Wisconsin, USA

The words most frequently used when describing Spencer Tracy are 'reliability', 'sincerity', 'integrity'. Of his own acting talent, he once said 'A good performance depends on the role, and what the actor brings of himself to it . . . I bring Spencer Tracy to it'. Therein lies the key to his

Top, far left: Rip Torn in Coma. Top left: Totò in Pier Paolo Pasolini's Uccellacci e Uccellini (1966). *Left: Audrey Totter as an unfaithful wife in* Tension. *Above: Bill Travers as game-warden George Adamson in* Born Free

success; the apparently effortless way he assumed the mantle of each character rang constantly true with his audience, and led to him being labelled the best movie actor in the world. A chance success with the Ripon College drama group encouraged Tracy to take up acting and in 1922 he enrolled in the American Academy of Dramatic Arts in New York. He had obtained several years experience on Broadway before the lead role in the prison drama *The Last Mile* brought him to John Ford's attention; Tracy made his movie debut in *Up the River*, a lightweight crime film. For several years he was cast in sympathetic supporting parts, since producers felt his rugged looks were not sufficiently distinguished for leads. In 1937 he won an Academy Award for *Captains Courageous*, however, and the following year another for *Boys Town*, and his reputation was made. He went on to become one of Hollywood's most popular stars, winning Oscar nominations for a further seven films, including the brooding allegory of the McCarthy witch-hunts, *Bad Day at Black Rock*. Tracy had married the stage actress Louise Treadwell in 1923 and though they were separated for many years his Catholic beliefs prevented him from divorcing her, despite a well publicized romance with Loretta Young in the early Thirties and a close relationship with Katharine Hepburn lasting twenty-five years. He made nine films with her, including the classic comedies *Woman of the Year* (their first movie together), *Adam's Rib* and *Pat and Mike*. In his later films he often played cantankerous but good-hearted father-figures; his last, Stanley Kramer's *Guess Who's Coming To Dinner?* (completed a fortnight before he died), was no exception.

Films include: 1930 Up the River. **'31** Quick Millions. **'32** Sky Devils; The Power and the Glory (GB: Power and Glory); A Man's Castle. **'33** 20,000 Years in Sing Sing. **'36** Fury; San Francisco. **'37** Captains Courageous. **'38** Boys Town. **'40** Northwest Passage. **'41** Dr Jekyll and Mr Hyde. **'42** Woman of the Year; Keeper of the Flame.

Left: Spencer Tracy as a reporter in George Cukor's melodrama Keeper of the Flame, *which also starred Katharine Hepburn. Above: Henry Travers as a detective story addict in Hitchcock's* Shadow of a Doubt

'49 Adam's Rib. **'50** Father of the Bride. **'52** Pat and Mike. **'55** Bad Day at Black Rock. **'58** The Old Man and the Sea. **'61** Judgement at Nuremburg. **'67** Guess Who's Coming to Dinner?

TRAUBERG, Leonid

(b. 1902). Director. Born: Odessa, Russia

Leonid Trauberg became interested in theatre in his youth, and turned to film when he met director Grigori Kozintsev in the early Twenties. They founded FEKS (Factory of the Eccentric Actor) and collaborated on several important Soviet films, notably The Maxim Trilogy, a dramatization of the Russian Revolution seen through the eyes of a Bolshevik. Their film *Prostiye Lyudi* was the first production to be completed after World War II, but it fell foul of official disapproval (and was not shown until 1956). Trauberg and Kozintsev ended their collaboration shortly after. Out of favour with the political authorities for a decade, Trauberg has since made few films. His younger brother, Ilya, is a respected director of documentaries.

Films include: 1924 Pokhozdeniya Oktyabriny (co-dir) (The Adventures of Oktyabrina). **'26** Chertovo Koleso (co-dir) (The Devil's Wheel); Shinel (co-dir) (USA: The Overcoat; GB: The Cloak). **'27** SVD (co-dir). **'29** Novyi Vavilon (co-dir) (GB: New Babylon). **'31** Odna (co-dir) (GB: Alone). **'35** Yunost Maksima (co-dir) (The Youth of Maxim). **'37** Vozvrasheniye Maksim (co-dir) (The Return of Maxim). **'39** Vyborgskaya Storona (co-dir) (The Vyborg). **'43** Aktrosa (GB: The Actress). **'56** Prostiye Lyudi (co-dir) (Plain People). **'58** Sli Soldaty (Soldiers Were Marching). **'60** Mortviye Dushi (Dead Souls). **'61** Volnil Veter (co-dir) (Free Wind).

TRAUNER, Alexander

(b. 1906). Art Director. Born: Sándor Trauner; Budapest, Hungary

Trauner came to Paris to pursue a career as a painter but instead became an assistant to set designer Lazare Meerson, working with him on several films during the Thirties, including *Le Million* (1931) At the start of war and the German occupation, Trauner, being a Jew, was forced into hiding; however he continued to provide designs, notably for Marcel Carné, for whom he created the evocative backgrounds for *Les Enfants du Paradis*. Invited by Billy Wilder to go to America in the Fifties, he has been based there since. His work is characterized by a subtle mix of realism and romance, harnessing naturalism to the themes of the plot. He was responsible for the marvellously 'lived in' locale of *The Apartment*, re-created war-time Rome for *The Night of the Generals*, Victorian England for *The Private Life of Sherlock Holmes*, and exotic Kafiristan in *The Man Who Would Be King*.

Films include: 1933 L'Affaire Est dans le Sac (FR) (ass. art dir) (GB: It's in the Bag). **'37** Drôle de Drame (FR) (USA: Bizarre, Bizarre). **'38** Quai Des Brumes (FR) (USA: Port of Shadows). **'39** Le Jour se Lève (FR) (USA:

Daybreak). **'45** Les Enfants du Paradis (FR) (USA: Children of Paradise). **'52** Othello (MOROCCO). **'55** Land of the Pharoahs (USA). **'59** The Nun's Story (USA). **'60** The Apartment (USA). **'63** Irma La Douce (USA). **'67** The Night of the Generals (GB-FR). **'70** The Private Life of Sherlock Holmes (GB). **'75** The Man Who Would Be King (GB). **'76** Mr Klein (FR-IT).

TRAVERS, Bill

(b. 1922). Actor. Born: Newcastle-upon-Tyne, England

Tall, dark and rugged but with a soft-spoken air which suggests a certain shyness when in human company, Bill Travers has overcome the actor's traditional dislike of working with unpredictable, upstaging animals, and found his niche in wildlife films. His earlier career was varied; he turned to acting after war service, and played in many film and television roles, from classics like *Romeo and Juliet* to Westerns like *Duel at Diablo*. In 1957 he married Virginia McKenna, his second wife, and several years later they appeared in *Born Free*, based on Joy Adamson's popular book about her and her husband's attempts to raise an orphaned lioness, Elsa. Since then Travers has specialized in animal films such as *Ring of Bright Water*, based on Gavin Maxwell's book about a tame otter, *The Belstone Fox* and *An Elephant Called Slowly*.

Films include: 1949 Conspirator. **'50** The Wooden Horse. **'51** The Browning Version. **'54** Romeo and Juliet (GB-IT). **'56** Bhowani Junction. **'57** The Barretts of Wimpole Street; The Smallest Show on Earth. **'66** Duel at Diablo (USA); Born Free. **'68** A Midsummer Night's Dream. **'69** Ring of Bright Water; An Elephant Called Slowly. **'74** The Lion at World's End (doc). **'73** The Belstone Fox (USA: Free Spirit).

TRAVERS, Henry

(1874–1965). Actor. Born: Travers Heagerty; Berwick-on-Tweed, Northumberland, England

Travers' most memorable role was as Clarence the angel, second class, who descends to earth to rescue James Stewart from suicide by showing him how life would be without him in Frank Capra's comedy *It's A Wonderful Life*. It was an appropriate climax to the career of this elderly, thin-mouthed, crumple-faced actor who spent most of his time playing irresistibly benign old gentlemen. Travers began his career on the British stage, then graduated to Broadway, where he established himself as a character actor. He did not enter films until he was in his fifties, but even so worked in a surprisingly high number of quality productions, *High Sierra* and *Random Harvest* among them. He was nominated for an Oscar as Best Supporting Actor in *Mrs Miniver*.

Films include: 1933 Reunion in Vienna; The Invisible Man. **'34** Death Takes a Holiday. **'39** Dark Victory. **'41** High Sierra; Ball of Fire. **'42** Mrs Miniver; Random Harvest. **'43** Shadow of a Doubt. **'46** It's a Wonderful Life; The Yearling. **'49** The Girl From Jones Beach.

TRAVOLTA, John

(b. 1954). Actor. Born: Englewood, New Jersey, USA

For a couple of brief summers in the late Seventies, John Travolta became a teen-idol, a sexy, glamorized James Dean, king of the disco and the high-school hop. It was the culmination of a meteoric career which began when he dropped out of school at 16 and joined a New Jersey stock company. He finally made it to Broadway where he made a notable impression in the stage musical *Grease* and in the television series *Welcome Back, Kotter*. In 1977 he was Tony Manero, strutting his way through the disco and burning with *Saturday Night Fever*. The film version of *Grease* was no less a success, though Travolta's career is in danger of fading away as quickly as the film's catchy but instantly forgettable tunes. Not even his likeable personality and good looks could save *Moment by Moment*, while *Urban Cowboy* was simply *Saturday Night Fever* for Western addicts. Only *Blow Out*, a competent thriller, suggests hope for a mature career.

Films include: 1975 The Devil's Rain. '76 Carrie. '77 Saturday Night Fever. '78 Grease; Moment by Moment. '80 Urban Cowboy. '81 Blow Out.

TREVOR, Claire

(b. 1909). Actress. Born: Claire Wemlinger; New York City, USA

In *Stagecoach* Claire Trevor plays Dallas, the saloon gal run out of town by upright citizens, tough on the outside but coming through as the Duke's lady before the final shoot-out. Trevor had a hard-bitten, heart-of-gold look about her, and excelled in playing such parts. She began acting after attending Columbia University and the American Academy of Dramatic Arts, and graduated from stock companies to Broadway. Her first films were Vitaphone shorts filmed in Brooklyn, but she soon moved to Hollywood, playing a stream of fallen ladies and hoodlums' molls. She was nominated for Oscars for *Dead End* and *The High and the Mighty*, and won one as Best Supporting Actress for *Key Largo*.

Films include: 1933 Life in the Raw. '37 Dead End. '39 Stagecoach. '41 Honky Tonk. '44 Murder, My Sweet (GB: Farewell, My Lovely). '46 Crack-Up. '48 Key Largo. '54 The High and the Mighty. '55 Man Without a Star. '62 Two Weeks in Another Town. '65 How to Murder Your Wife. '67 The Cape Town Affair (USA-S. AFRICA).

TRINDER, Tommy

(b. 1909). Actor. Born: Thomas Edward Trinder; Streatham, London, England

All chin, grin and pork-pie hat, Tommy Trinder exudes cheerful cockney music-hall confidence. One of the last of the old variety troupers, the same generation as Arthur Askey, Trinder first trod the boards in London, at Collins' Music Hall, in 1921, and has scarcely been off them

since. By the late Thirties he was appearing at the London Palladium, and his boisterous humour, quick-fire gags and catch-phrase 'You lucky people!' made him a great success. His film career dates from about the same time, and included several movies for Ealing, notably *The Foreman Went To France*, a morale-booster set in the aftermath of the French collapse of World War II. Since then he has worked on the big screen only occasionally – his last film was the vulgar Australian romp, *Barry McKenzie Holds His Own* – but he has tackled radio and television with characteristic energy and still makes regular appearances in variety shows and pantomimes.

Films include: 1938 Almost a Honeymoon. '40 Sailors Three. '42 The Foreman Went to France. '43 The Bells Go Down. '44 Fiddlers Three; Champagne Charlie. '50 Bitter Springs. '55 You Lucky People. '59 Make Mine a Million. '64 The Beauty Jungle. '70 Under the Table You Must Go. '74 Barry McKenzie Holds His Own (AUS).

TRINTIGNANT, Jean-Louis

(b. 1930). Actor/director. Born: Piolenc, France

His career interrupted by war service in Algeria, Trintignant had the distinction of being discovered twice, playing opposite sensual female stars both times. He gave up studying law to train as an actor. Struggling to overcome a thick provincial accent and natural shyness, he developed an economic acting style which conveyed much by doing little, and gave him an aura of depth and mystery. His first taste of fame came when he starred with Bardot in 1956 in Vadim's *And God Created Woman*. The Algerian war then interrupted his career for three years. He once again achieved recognition, this time opposite Anouk Aimée, in *A Man and a Woman*. Since then he has remained a leading light in the French cinema, winning a Best Actor Award at

Cannes for *Z*. His second wife, Nadine, once editor of films for Godard and others and now a director in her own right, has cast her husband in several of her films. Trintignant himself turned to directing in 1973.

Films include: 1955 Si Tous les Gars du Monde (GB: Race for Life). '56 Et Dieu Créa la Femme (USA/GB: And Woman . . . Was Created/. . . And God Created Woman). '59 Les Liaisons Dangereuses 1960 (GB: Les Liaisons Dangereuses). '66 Paris Brûle-t-il? (USA/GB: Is Paris Burning?); Un Homme et une Femme (GB: A Man and a Woman). '67 Trans-Europ Express. '68 Les Biches (FR-IT) (GB: The Does). '69 Z (FR-ALGERIA); Ma Nuit Chez Maud (GB: My Night With Maud). '70 Il Conformista (IT-FR-GER) (USA/GB: The Conformist). '71 Sans Mobile Apparent (FR-IT) (USA: Without Apparent Motive). '72 L'Attentat (FR-IT-GER) (USA: The French Conspiracy; GB: Plot). '73 Une Journée Bien Remplie (+dir) (FR-IT). '78 L'Argent des Autres. '82 Colpire al Cuore (IT); La Nuit de Varennes (FR-IT).

TRNKA, Jiří

(1912–1969). Animator. Born: Pilsen, Czechoslovakia

Trnka's 1965 film *The Hand* depicted the conflict between a puppet gardener, seeking to protect a flower, and a real human hand, by comparison enormous, which finally dominates and destroys him. Not only was this an eloquent plea for individual freedom – courageous in the context of Sixties Czechoslovakia – it was a startling example of the original way Trnka used the puppet medium. Trnka had become interested in puppets as a child, winning a competition organized by puppeteer Josef Skupa, who persuaded Trnka's parents to send him to Prague's School of Art and Crafts. An early attempt to run a puppet theatre failed, and Trnka worked as a book illustrator throughout World War II. Over the next twenty years he was to establish an international reputation as a filmmaker. His puppets are extraordinary creations, with a distinct visual style perfectly suited to Trnka's use of the camera, and a life and personality all

Far left: John Travolta as the disco-dancing champion of Saturday Night Fever. *Left: Claire Trevor in the blackmail drama* Crossroads *(1942). Below: an 'eyes and teeth' publicity shot of Tommy Trinder*

their own. Much of his work, like *Old Czech Legends* and *The Emperor's Nightingale*, had a strong fairy-tale content. His films won numerous prizes at film festivals; his early death deprived the world of a highly original artist.

Films include: 1946 Zvířátka a Petrovští (The Animals and the Brigands); Dárek (The Gift). '47 Špaliček (The Czech Year). '48 Císařův slavík (The Emperor's Nightingale). '49 Arie prérie (The Song of the Prairie). '53 Staré pověsti české (Old Czech Legends). '55 Dobrý voják Švejk (The Good Soldier Schweik). '59 Sen noci svatojánské (A Midsummer Night's Dream) '62 Kybernetická babička (The Cybernetic Granny) '64 Archanděl Gabriel a paní Husa (The Archangel Gabriel and Mother Goose). '65 Ruka (The Hand).

TROELL, Jan

(b. 1931). Director/cinematographer. Born: Limhamn, Skåne, Sweden

Troell's films, so far few in number, are characterized by a warmth and affection which is unusual in Swedish cinema. A schoolteacher for nine years – an experience he was to draw on for his painful study of a teacher's relationship with his class, *Who Saw Him Die?* – he first began making short films when he met director Bo Widerberg in the early Sixties. His best known films are *Here Is Your Life*, a sensitive study of a young man's coming of age in Sweden during World War I, and *The Emigrants*, a lengthy adaptation as usual photographed by Troell himself, of a well-known Swedish novel about the perils faced by Scandinavians emigrating to the USA in the nineteenth century. In 1974 Troell made *Zandy's Bride* in America, and he seems likely to continue to work abroad.

Films include: 1965 4 × 4 *ep* Uppehåll i Myrlandet (SWED-DEN-NOR-FIN) (Interlude in the Marshland). '67 Här Har du Ditt Liv (GB: Here Is Your Life). '68 Ole Dole Doff (GB: Who Saw Him Die?). '71 Utvandrarna (GB: The Emigrants). '72 Nybyggarna (USA: The New Land). '74 Zandy's Bride (USA). '77

Below: Jean-Louis Trintignant in Bernardo Bertolucci's The Conformist. *Right: the director François Truffaut, face to face with aliens in* Close Encounters of the Third Kind. *Far right: Forrest Tucker in* Barquero

Bang! '79 Hurricane (USA). '82 Ingenjör Andrées Luftfärd (SWED-GER-NOR) (USA: The Flight of the Eagle).

TRUFFAUT, François

(1932–1984). Director. Born: Paris, France

One of France's most sympathetic film-makers, François Truffaut was closely associated with the *nouvelle vague* of the late Fifties. Truffaut's love affair with the movies began as an escape from a miserable, turbulent childhood, which included a spell in a reformatory. A factory worker at 15, he spent all his spare time at the cinema, especially the old movies at the Cinémathèque Française. His intense interest led him, in 1951, to a job as a film critic on *Cahiers du Cinéma*, the influential film magazine, where he gained a reputation for his caustic pen, and formed lasting friendships with André Bazin, Resnais, Godard and Rohmer. After a short spell of National Service, from which he deserted, was caught and dishonourably discharged, he founded his own film company, Les Films du Carrosse, in 1958. He made two short films and then found international critical acclaim with his first feature *Les Quatre Cents Coups*, winning the Grand Prix for direction at the Cannes Festival in 1959. It was a largely autobiographical story of Antoine Doinel, a streetwise 12-year-old, played by Jean-Pierre Léaud, the beginning of a long association with the young actor. Truffaut followed this with *Tirez sur le Pianiste*, starring singer Charles Aznavour in a wistful black-comedy thriller. Truffaut always acknowledged his debt to old masters such as Vigo, Renoir and Hitchcock, and in addition to scripting all his own films, often collaborated with contemporary film-makers, writing and co-producing. He also enjoyed acting and appeared in his own films – *L'Enfant Sauvage*, *La Nuit Américaine* and *La Chambre Verte*. He was also seen as the French scientist, Lacombe, in Spielberg's *Close Encounters of the*

Third Kind (1977). Truffaut's films are always marked by a distinctive gentleness, a graceful humour, and a truly personal cinematic sense.

Films include: 1957 Les Mistons (short) (USA/GB: The Mischief Makers). '59 Les Quatre Cent Coups (USA/GB: The 400 Blows). '60 Tirez sur le Pianiste (USA: Shoot the Piano Player; GB: Shoot the Pianist). '62 Jules et Jim (USA/GB: Jules and Jim). '64 La Peau Douce (USA: The Soft Skin; GB: Silken Skin). '66 Fahrenheit 451 (GB). '68 La Marieé Était en Noir (FR-IT) (USA/GB: The Bride Wore Black); Baisers Volés (USA/GB: Stolen Kisses). '70 L'Enfant Sauvage (USA/GB: The Wild Child); Domicile Conjugal (FR-IT) (USA/GB: Bed and Board). '71 Les Deux Anglaises et le Continent (USA: Two English Girls; GB: Anne and Muriel). '73 La Nuit Américaine (FR-IT) (USA/GB: Day for Night). '75 L'Histoire d'Adèle H. (USA/GB: The Story of Adèle H.). '78 La Chambre Verte (USA/GB: The Green Room). '79 L'Amour en Fuite (GB: Love on the Run). '80 Le Dernier Métro (USA/GB: The Last Metro). '81 La Femme d'à Côté (GB: The Woman Next Door). '82 Un Homme d'à Côté.

TRUMBO, Dalton

(1905–1976). Screenwriter. Born: James Dalton Trumbo; Montrose, Colorado, USA

The plots and stars of films like *Our Vines Have Tender Grapes* and *Thirty Seconds Over Tokyo* may not readily spring to mind now, but in the early Forties they were earning Dalton Trumbo $75,000 a script; today Trumbo is remembered more for his dramatic clash with the House Un-American Activities Committee than for anything he actually wrote. A manual worker until the magazine *Vanity Fair* published his first article, Trumbo made his name with a pacifist novel, *Johnny Got His Gun*. In Hollywood he earned a reputation as being a fast, reliable writer of box-office successes, until, in the wave of anti-communist paranoia which swept post-war America, he was

named for his leftist views. Trumbo was one of the 'Hollywood Ten' who refused to cooperate with HUAC; as a result he went to jail, and was blacklisted by Hollywood. He continued to write scripts under pseudonyms, for a greatly reduced fee, and, much to the industry's embarrassment, won an Oscar for *The Brave One* under the name Robert Rich in 1956. His comeback finally came when he was openly credited for his work on *Exodus* and *Spartacus* in 1960. In 1971 he made his debut as a director, making a film version of *Johnny Got His Gun*. Unfortunately poor health prevented him from continuing in this new career, though he carried on writing for the screen for a couple of years.

Films include: 1936 Road Gang. '40 Kitty Foyle (co-sc). '43 A Guy Named Joe. '44 Thirty Seconds Over Tokyo. '45 Our Vines Have Tender Grapes. '51 The Prowler (co-sc. uncredited). '56 The Brave One (co-sc. under pseudonym Robert Rich). '60 Spartacus; Exodus. '62 Lonely Are the Brave. '65 The Sandpiper (co-sc). '68 The Fixer (USA-HUN). '71 Johnny Got His Gun (dir; + sc). '73 Executive Action; Papillon.

TRUMBULL, Douglas

(b. 1942). Special effects director/director. Born: Los Angeles, California, USA

Douglas Trumbull is a talented young technician who, after illustrating training films of the US armed services, livened up the screen and brought new dimensions to special effects with his work on *2001: A Space Odyssey*. He then directed his own film, *Silent Running*, about an astronaut and three robots (Huey, Dewey and Louey, named after Donald Duck's three nephews) orbit-

ing the sun with a spacecraft full of plants. He is very much into experimenting with lighting effects – notably in his work on *Close Encounters of the Third Kind*.

Films include: 1968 2001: A Space Odyssey. '72 Silent Running (+ dir). '77 Close Encounters of the Third Kind. '79 Star Trek – The Motion Picture. '82 Blade Runner. '83 Brainstorm (dir).

TUCKER, Forrest

(1919–1986). Actor. Born: Plainfield, Indiana, USA

Despite his tall, rugged looks, it never quite seemed possible to take Forrest Tucker seriously in the villainous roles he usually played in the early part of his career. He decided to give acting a try while on holiday in California in 1940; after a false start, interrupted by war service, he settled down to playing the baddy in action pictures and Westerns, such as *Gunfighters* or *Bugles in the Afternoon*. His eyes, however, lacked that ruthlessness which makes a truly villainous villain; instead there was a hint of affability. Sure enough, by the Sixties he was beginning to choose roles with a touch more humour, like the grizzled, over-the-top mountain man in *Barquero*. Also, he sent the whole lot up in the knockabout television cavalry series, *F Troop*. He appeared regularly in films and on television until his death.

Films include: 1940 The Westerner. '42 Keeper of the Flame. '46 The Yearling. '47 Gunfighters. '49 Sands of Iwo Jima. '52 Bugles in the Afternoon. '53 Pony Express. '57 The Quiet Gun. '68 The Night They Raided Minsky's. '70 Barquero; Chisum. '77 Final Chapter – Walking Tall.

TUCKER, George Loane

(1881–1921). Director. Born: George S. Loane; Chicago, Illinois, USA

When George Loane Tucker, director of *The Miracle Man*, died in 1921, the magazine *Photoplay* headed his obituary 'The First of the Immortals'. And the playwright and critic Robert E. Sherwood, writing in 1925, put Tucker on a par with Griffith, Ingram and Flaherty. Such was the man's reputation in his day. But neglect and mischance have led to the loss of almost all his films. He had studied law at the University of Chicago, worked in various jobs on railroads and, around 1904, followed his mother to the stage. He entered films in about 1908, and by 1911 was sharing directing chores with the young Thomas Ince. In 1913 he made one of the first American features, an exposé of the white slave racket called *Traffic in Souls*. This film survives, a brilliantly handled melodrama years ahead of its time. Later that year Tucker came to Britain. His dozen or so English features included versions of *The Prisoner of Zenda*, *The Manxman* and *The Christian*. The films were lavishly produced, finely reviewed, and did much to open up American markets to the British product. Back home by 1916, he worked for Goldwyn, and then, for his own Mayflower company, he made *The Miracle Man*. This story of con-men and fake miracles made Lon Chaney and Betty Compson stars; it enjoyed enormous fame, and one tantalizing fragment is all that remains.

Films include: 1911 Their First Misunderstanding (co-dir). '13 Traffic in Souls. '15 The Prisoner of Zenda (GB); The Christian (GB). '16 The Man Without a Soul (GB) (USA: I Believe); The Manxman (GB). '17 The Cinderella Man; Dodging a Million. '18 Virtuous Wives. '19 The Miracle Man. '21 Ladies Must Live.

TUFTS, Sonny

(1911–1970). Actor. Born: Bowen Charlton Tufts III; Boston, Massachusetts, USA

Sonny Tufts' story is a bizarre and tragic one. It began well enough; the son of a wealthy banker, Tufts wanted to sing as a child, and after Yale was able to pursue his wish and have his voice trained professionally. A solitary film role and several years spent singing in nightclubs followed, until he broke into films in a big way in 1943. Some critics have suggested uncharitably that his success was due to the fact that so many more talented performers were fighting in the armed services, but Tufts had a pleasant singing voice and an attractive, easygoing, hearty personality. By the end of the decade, however, his career began to flag. His private life became increasingly riotous, and he was sued by several showgirls for allegedly biting them in the thigh. It was also widely rumoured that he was an alcoholic. His name became a household joke, and he found work impossible to get. His attempts at a comeback failed, and he died of pneumonia.

Films include: 1939 Ambush. '43 So Proudly We Hail! '45 Bring on the Girls; Miss Susie Slagle's. '46 Swell Guy. '47 Variety Girl; Easy Come, Easy Go. '52 Gift Horse (GB) (USA: Glory at Sea). '55 The Seven Year Itch. '56 Come Next Spring. '65 Town Tamer.

TURNER, Florence

(1885–1946). Actress. Born: New York City, USA

Florence Turner was one of the first silent stars, being widely promoted as 'The Vitagraph Girl'. She had begun acting on the stage as a child, and her career blossomed from the moment she joined Vitagraph as a wardrobe mistress and actress in 1906. She first visited London in 1913, with her director friend Larry Trimble, and spent the next few years commuting between Britain and America. She starred in many of the best early British movies. The advent of sound had ruined her career by the early Thirties. Had it not been for the charity of MGM, who kept her on for the odd bit part and extra work, she would have been forced to retire completely by the end of the decade.

Films include: 1907 How to Cure a Cold. '08 The New Stenographer; Richard III; The Merchant of Venice. '11 A Tale of Two Cities. '14 Through the Valley of Shadows (GB). '15 My Old Dutch (GB). '25 The Road to Ruin. '27 College. '31 Ridin' Fool.

TURNER, Lana

(b. 1920). Actress. Born: Julia Jean Mildred Frances Turner; Wallace, Idaho, USA

Lana Turner's life story epitomizes the dark, dangerous side of Hollywood glamour. Supposedly discovered skipping school one day in a drugstore off Sunset Boulevard, she had a raw, smouldering sex appeal to go with her devastating blonde looks. Initially packaged as 'the Sweater Girl', a ploy which accentuated her obvious charms, she went on to become a top pin-up during World War II and was MGM's most manufactured glamour girl during the Fifties. Now and then – as in *Peyton Place*, for which she won an Oscar nomination – she turned in a fine performance, but she is chiefly remembered for her image rather than for her acting. Her private life was extraordinarily scandalous; in addition to being married seven times, most famously to the bandleader Artie Shaw and the former movie Tarzan Lex Barker, her hoodlum boyfriend, Johnny Stompanato, was knifed to death by her daughter in her kitchen. Despite this, or perhaps because of it, she remained a box-office draw. In 1970 she appeared in a television series appropriately entitled *The Survivors*.

Films include: 1937 They Won't Forget. '38 Love Finds Andy Hardy. '41 Ziegfeld Girl; Dr Jekyll and Mr Hyde. '46 The Postman Always Rings Twice. '47 Cass Timberlane. '52 The Merry Widow; The Bad and the Beautiful. '57 Peyton Place. '59 Imitation of Life. '65 Love Has Many Faces. '66 Madame X. '76 Bittersweet Love.

Left: Sonny Tufts in Swell Guy. *Above: Florence Turner in the silent version of* Far From the Madding Crowd *(1914), directed by Larry Trimble. Below: Lana Turner as the unscrupulous Milady in MGM's lavish* The Three Musketeers *(1948)*

Above: Ben Turpin looks both ways in Hollywood (1923). Above right: Cicely Tyson in Bustin' Loose *(1981). Right: a Paramount publicity portrait of Helen Twelvetrees from the early Thirties. Below: a publicity shot of Rita Tushingham in the Sixties*

to thrillers he turned out two superb efforts in *The Glass Key* and *This Gun for Hire*. The latter film made Alan Ladd a star in the Forties.

Films include: 1922 The Cradle Buster. '25 Miss Bluebeard. '26 The Untamed Lady; Kid Boots. '27 Love 'Em and Leave 'Em. '29 The Greene Murder Case. '30 True to the Navy. '33 Roman Scandals. '35 The Glass Key. '42 This Gun for Hire; Lucky Jordan. '59 Island of Lost Women.

TWELVETREES, Helen

(1907–1958). Actress. Born: Helen Marie Jurgens; New York City, USA

Twelvetrees really was her name, her first husband being one Clark Twelvetrees. She was educated at the Brooklyn Heights Seminary, and then attended the American Academy of Dramatic Arts. She had had some stage experience when Fox offered her a contract in 1929. That year, too, she was chosen as a Wampas Baby Star (one of a good crop which included Jean Arthur and Loretta Young). Until the mid-Thirties Twelvetrees, a small and pretty golden-haired girl, had some success in leads in mainly routine pictures; a long-term contract with the second-rank Pathé studio scarcely helped her. But she appeared in one notable film, playing the heroine of Tay Garnett's grim underworld melodrama, *Her Man*. She also appeared opposite Maurice Chevalier in *A Bedtime Story*. She died, a suicide, in 1958.

Films include: 1929 The Ghost Talks. '30 The Grand Parade; Her Man; The Cat Creeps. '31 Millie; Bad Company. '32 State's Attorney (GB: Cardigan's Last Case). '33 A Bedtime Story. '35 Times Square Lady; She Gets Her Man. '39 Unmarried (GB: Night Club Hostess).

TYSON, Cicely

(b. 1942). Actress. Born: New York City, USA

Slim and elegant, Cicely Tyson was born of West Indian immigrant parents, with a religious mother who thought the cinema was sinful. Nevertheless, she became a reputable stage actress via modelling and the Actors' Studio, making her stage debut in 1959. She was appearing in Genet's *The Blacks* in New York when, in 1963, George C. Scott chose her to play Jane in the American television series *East Side, West Side*, which made her a national star. Her screen break came when Harry Belafonte put her in *Odds Against Tomorrow*. She had several good film roles before making an impressive impact in Martin Ritt's *Sounder*, which brought her an Oscar nomination. In the Seventies she played leading television drama roles in *Roots* and *The Autobiography of Miss Jane Pitman*.

Films include: 1959 Odds Against Tomorrow. '66 A Man Called Adam. '67 The Comedians (USA-BERM-FR). '68 The Heart Is a Lonely Hunter. '72 Sounder. '76 The River Niger; The Blue Bird (USA-USSR). '77 A Hero Ain't Nothin' But a Sandwich. '79 Airport '79 – Concorde (GB: Airport '80 – Concorde).

TURPIN, Ben

(1869–1940). Actor. Born: Bernard Turpin; New Orleans, Louisiana, USA

The cross-eyed comedian Ben Turpin began in vaudeville and burlesque, and entered films with Essanay in Chicago in 1907. He was not successful, but came back in 1914 and appeared in some of Chaplin's earliest films. Turpin became a leading comedian when he joined Mack Sennett in 1917, and remained popular until the end of the silent period. He was small, acrobatic and bellicose, and a great hand at parody, delighting in mocking romantic heroes of the day, and adopting breeches and monocle for his celebrated impersonation of Stroheim. But his cross-eyes made him, and it is alleged that he took out

insurance with Lloyd's against their ever becoming uncrossed. (Sennett himself is the authority for this unlikely tale.)

Films include: 1909 Midnight Disturbance. '15 A Night Out. '16 Carmen. '18 The Battle Royal. '21 A Small Town Idol. '23 The Shriek of Araby. '25 The Marriage Circus. '27 The College Hero. '29 The Show of Shows; The Love Parade. '32 Million Dollar Legs. '40 Saps at Sea.

TUSHINGHAM, Rita

(b. 1942). Actress. Born: Liverpool, England

Rita Tushingham was working at the Liverpool Playhouse with the Liverpool Players Company when she was chosen from a group of over two hundred young hopefuls to play the

lead role in Tony Richardson's film *A Taste of Honey*. For her performance as the pregnant teenager with a seedy mother, black lover and gay friend, Tushingham won a British Film Academy Award, a Cannes Film Festival Award and a New York Critics' Award. After this success she found herself typecast for the next decade as Northern anti-heroines of a somewhat pathetic nature in offbeat films such as *The Knack*, *The Leather Boys* and *Smashing Time*. Rather plain in appearance – mousy with huge eyes, widemouthed and large-toothed – she is a highly sensitive and effective performer but has had little success in recent years. During the Seventies she appeared in a string of forgettable Italian films.

Films include: 1961 A Taste of Honey. '63 The Leather Boys. '64 The Girl With Green Eyes. '65 The Knack; Dr Zhivago (USA). '66 The Trap. '67 Smashing Time. '68 Diamonds for Breakfast.

TUTTLE, Frank

(1892–1963). Director. Born: New York City, USA

Tuttle was educated at Yale, where he was President of the Dramatic Association. On graduation he worked as an editorial assistant on *Vanity Fair* magazine, and in the early Twenties entered Paramount as a writer. Tuttle wrote the script of the classic Gloria Swanson comedy, *Manhandled* (1924), but by that time had begun directing. He had a stylish and inventive way with the polished comedy the studio was so good at and directed Bebe Daniels, Swanson, Louise Brooks and (six times) Clara Bow – a dazzling array of talent and a gift to a craftsman like Tuttle. Brooks has said that Tuttle achieved his effects by making everyone play perfectly straight. Certainly her Tuttle film, *Love 'Em and Leave 'Em*, shows that the method worked. In the Thirties he spent too much time on indifferent musicals (one genre it seemed Paramount just couldn't manage without Lubitsch or Mamoulian) but when he moved over

Left: Liv Ullmann in Ingmar Bergman's Face to Face. Below: Mary Ure in the World War II adventure Where Eagles Dare. Right: Peter Ustinov as Hercule Poirot in Evil Under the Sun

UCHIDA, Tomu

(1898–1972). Director. Born: Okayama, Japan

An actor from 1920, Tomu Uchida joined the Nikkatsu company in 1923 as an assistant director to Kenji Mizoguchi and Minoru Murata, and became a director in 1927. His early films were farcical and satirical comedies but in the Thirties he moved towards realism in the *shomin-geki* genre, concerned with ordinary lower-middle-class life, as in his semi-documentary *Earth*. Out of favour with the right-wing wartime government, he retreated to Manchuria, joined the Chinese enemy and became a communist. Returning to Japan in 1954, he joined the Toei company and specialized in *jidai-geki* or period films and, among other films, made the five-part Miyamoto Musashi series in the early Sixties.

Films include: 1927 Kyoso Mikka-kan; Kutsu (Pain). '36 Jinsei Gekijo (Theatre of Life). '39 Tsuchi (Earth). '57 Dotanba (The Eleventh Hour). '58 Senryo-jishi (The Thief Is Shogun's Kin). '61 Miyamoto Musashi I (Untamed Fury). '62 Miyamoto Musashi II (Duel Without End). '64 Kiga Kaikyo (Hunger Straits). '68 Jinsei Gekijo – Hishakaku to Kiratsune (Kaku and Tsune). '72 Shinken Shobu (Swords of Death).

UCICKY, Gustav

(1901–1961). Director. Born: Vienna, Austria

Ucicky began directing in 1927 with *Café Electric*, starring a young Marlene Dietrich, but his best work belonged to the sound period. Before the Nazis gained power he had made *Hokuspokus*, with Laurence Olivier making a screen debut in the English version, and *Morgenrot*, a restrained and moving submarine drama which was probably his finest film. He then went on to make careful, soothing, covertly propagandistic works for the Nazis. *The Broken Jug*, an almost verbatim version of Kleist's play, was one of Hitler's favourite movies – and

contained some dreadful overacting from Emil Jannings. Ucicky could always call on star names, like Hans Albers, Paula Wessely, Gustav Gründgens, Werner Krauss, but stars and director were hog-tied by the politics of the time.

Films include: 1927 Café Electric (A-GER). '30 Hokuspokus (English-language version: The Temporary Widow); Das Flötenkoncert von Sanssouci. '32 Mensch ohne Namen. '33 Morgenrot (GB: Dawn). '35 Das Mädchen Johanna. '36 Unter heissem Himmel. '37 Der zerbrochene Krug (GB: The Broken Jug). '40 Der Postmeister; Ein Leben lang. '43 Am Ende der Welt; Späte Liebe. '44 Das Herz muss schweigen.

ULLMANN, Liv

(b. 1939). Actress. Born: Tokyo, Japan

The daughter of an aircraft engineer who moved from Tokyo to Toronto at the outbreak of World War II, Liv Ullmann was brought to Norway after the death of her father. She studied acting in London and, after establishing a reputation for herself as a leading lady of the Norwegian stage and appearing in a number of films, she was introduced to Ingmar Bergman who asked her to co-star with Bibi Andersson in *Persona*. Forming a close relationship with the director (they lived together for three years and had a child), she rapidly won international acclaim appearing in several of his films and was brought to Hollywood to star in the remake of *Lost Horizon*. Though acknowledged as an actress of outstanding ability she did not have the parts she deserved in Hollywood films and continued to do her best work with Bergman in Germany. In 1981 she took a year off from acting to tour Europe as goodwill ambassador for the United Nations Children's Fund.

Films include: 1966 Persona (SWED). '68 Vargtimmen (SWED) (USA/GB: Hour of the Wolf); Skammen (SWED) (USA: The Shame; GB: Shame). '69 En Passion (SWED)

(USA: The Passion of Anna; GB: A Passion). '72 Pope Joan (GB); Viskningar och Rop (SWED) (USA/GB: Cries and Whispers). '73 Scener ur ett Äktenskap (SWED) (USA/GB: Scenes From a Marriage) (orig. TV); Lost Horizon (USA). '74 Ansikte mot Ansikte (SWED) (USA/GB: Face to Face) (orig. TV). '77 A Bridge Too Far (USA); Das Schlangenei (GER-USA) (USA/GB: The Serpent's Egg). '78 Herbstsonate (GER) (USA/GB: Autumn Sonata).

ULMER, Edgar G.

(1904–1972). Director. Born: Edgar George Ulmer; Vienna, Austria

No one wore Murnau's mantle more proudly than Ulmer; no one could have worn it in less auspicious surroundings. He studied architecture in Vienna, designed sets for Reinhardt, went with him to the USA with *The Miracle*, and returned to Germany to assist Murnau on his last films there. Accompanying Murnau to Hollywood, he shared in the triumph of *Sunrise*. Back again in Germany, he made his debut as a director, working with Robert Siodmak on *Menschen am Sonntag*. In 1930 he settled for good in America, spent three years as an art director, directed from 1933 on, and made, he calculated, 128 movies, rapidly, cheaply and obscurely. In 1935 he made *The Black Cat* for Universal, a classic of atmospheric horror, with Lugosi and Karloff fighting it out in a castle built over the carnage of a World War I battlefield. The next few years saw him filing in New York, making movies in Yiddish and even Ukrainian. Working from minuscule budgets, he created occasional masterpieces, like *Detour*, made with a stationary car, back-projection, and a couple of tatty interiors. So he went on to the mid-Sixties, in the USA, Mexico, Italy, Spain and Germany. No stars appeared for Ulmer: Zachary Scott and Sydney Greenstreet in *Ruthless* were the nearest he came to that. The camera had to do instead, and Ulmer moved his camera, framed his shots, and let his film flow sweetly on in the way Murnau had done. Ulmer made absurd material sublime.

Films include: 1929 Menschen am Sonntag (co-dir; + co-sc) (GER) (GB: People on Sunday). '34 The Black Cat (GB: The House of Doom). '44 Bluebeard. '45 Detour. '46 The Strange Woman. '48 Ruthless. '51 The Man From Planet X. '55 Murder Is My

Beat/Dynamite Anchorage; The Naked Dawn. '57 The Daughter of Dr Jekyll. '61 L'Atlantide (co-dir) (FR-IT) (GB: The Lost Kingdom). '65 Sette Contro la Morte (+ prod) (IT-GER) (USA: The Cavern).

UNSWORTH, Geoffrey

(1914–1978). Cinematographer. Born: London, England

Britain's most prestigious colour cinematographer began his career as camera assistant at the Gaumont British studios at Shepherds Bush, and joined Technicolor in 1937. After working as camera operator on Powell and Pressburger's *The Life and Death of Colonel Blimp* (1943) and *A Matter of Life and Death* (1946), he made his debut as director of photography in 1946 on the French Revolution melodrama *The Laughing Lady*. After joining the Rank Organization he displayed his flair for lush, atmospheric colour photography on costume pictures like *Jassy* and *Blanche Fury*. Building up a reputation as a masterly international cameraman he contributed to prestigious projects like Stanley Kubrick's *2001: A Space Odyssey*, *Murder on The Orient Express* and *Superman, The Movie*. He died of a heart attack in Brittany while creating the lush lyrical visuals of Roman Polanski's *Tess*.

Films include: 1947 Jassy. '48 Blanche Fury (ext. photo. only). '49 The Blue Lagoon. '56 A Town Like Alice. '58 A Night to Remember. '64 Becket. '68 2001: A Space Odyssey. '72 Cabaret (USA). '74 Murder on the Orient Express. '78 Superman, The Movie. '79 Tess (co-photo) (FR-GB).

URBAN, Charles

(1871–1942). Pioneer producer. Born: Cincinnati, Ohio, USA

Urban came to England from America at the turn of the century. He had developed a projector known as the Bioscope, and like many another inventor found that Edison's patents stood in his way. In England he produced documentaries and newsreels, and worked with the British pioneer G.A. Smith on the early colour process called Kinemacolor. Urban returned to America in the hope that he might popularize his system there. But it proved short-lived and, apart from a series of scientific documentaries which he made in the Twenties, Urban had little further importance on the cinema scene.

Films include: 1904 The Old Chorister. '05 Natural Laws Reversed. '07 Hanky Panky Cards. '08 The Lightning Postcard Artist. '09 The Wizard's Walking Stick. '10 The Plans of the Fortress. '11 The Durbar at Delhi. '12 The Dancer's Dream. '13 The Scarlet Letter (USA). '21 Science of the Soap Bubbles; From Egg to Chick; Ancient Customs of Egypt.

URE, Mary

(1933–1975). Actress. Born: Glasgow, Scotland

The tragically short life of Mary Ure encompassed success in the stage and screen versions of *Look Back in Anger*, a gutsy performance as Clara Dawes

in *Sons and Lovers*, and marriages to playwright John Osborne and actor Robert Shaw. After being chosen to play the Virgin Mary in a Mystery play while at school in York, she decided on a career as a drama teacher and enrolled at the Central School of Speech and Drama in London. Her promising performances there convinced impresario Hugh Beaumont that she had the makings of a fine actress and in 1954 he gave her the opportunity of a London debut in Anouilh's *Time Remembered*. Her success led to a film contract with Alexander Korda and her appearance in *Storm Over the Nile* a year later. But it was her role as the long-suffering wife Alison in *Look Back in Anger*, which she created on stage in 1956, that really established her. Her two marriages rather interfered with her career but she seemed to have made the difficult transition from attractive ingénue to middle-aged character actress when she died from a mixture of alcohol and barbiturates.

Films include: 1955 Storm Over the Nile. '57 Windom's Way. '59 Look Back in Anger. '60 Sons and Lovers. '62 The Mind Benders. '64 The Luck of Ginger Coffey (CAN-USA). '67 Custer of the West (SP). '68 Where Eagles Dare. '73 A Reflection of Fear (USA).

USTINOV, Peter

(b. 1921). Actor. Born: London, England

The talented and versatile Peter Ustinov was educated first at Westminster School and then at stage school, and made his professional debut at the age of 18 at the Players Theatre Club, where he both wrote and appeared in revue sketches. Although his portly presence, exuberant personality and amazing ability to mimic almost any accent firmly established him in comic character roles such as Hercule Poirot and Charlie Chan, acting has been only one facet of his varied career. He wrote his first play at the age of 19, and co-wrote his first film, *The Way Ahead* (1944), during his army service in World War II; he has continued to write prolifically for screen and theatre. His early appearances on film, such as *Vice Versa* and *Quo Vadis?*, in which he played an eccentric and memorable Nero, made his name as a comic performer who nevertheless remained unmistakably himself. He won Oscars for Best Supporting Actor for *Spartacus* and *Topkapi*, and has received many other screen awards. He co-directed *Private Angelo* and the film version of *Romanoff and Juliet*, based on his own play. Ustinov is a witty and entertaining raconteur and a popular choice for television chat shows; he has been married three times.

Films include: 1940 Hallo Fame! '41 One of Our Aircraft Is Missing. '49 Private Angelo (+co-dir; +sc; +co-prod). '50 Odette. '51 The Magic Box; Quo Vadis? (USA). '54 Beau Brummel. '60 Spartacus (USA). '61 Romanoff and Juliet (+dir; +prod; +sc. from own play) (USA). '64 Topkapi (USA-FR). '78 The Thief of Baghdad (GB-FR). '79 Ashanti (SWITZ). '81 Evil Under the Sun; Charlie Chan and the Curse of the Dragon Queen (USA).

Above: Brenda Vaccaro in Midnight Cowboy. *Top: Rudolph Valentino in* The Four Horsemen of the Apocalypse, *his first leading role*

VACCARO, Brenda

(b. 1939). Actress. Born: New York City, USA

After attending the Neighborhood Playhouse dramatic school in Manhattan, Vaccaro struggled through the usual hazards of bit-part acting, supporting herself by working as waitress, bathing-suit model, candy-packer, before getting a break in a television soap-opera, *True Story*. In 1969 she made an impressive film debut in Garson Kanin's *Where It's At*. She was nominated for an Oscar for her role as tough magazine editor Linda Riggs in *Jacqueline Susann's Once Is Not Enough*.

Films include: 1969 Where It's At; Midnight Cowboy. '70 I Love My Wife. '71 Summertree; Going Home. '75 Jacqueline Susann's Once Is Not Enough. '76 Death Weekend (CAN) (USA: The House by the Lake). '77 Airport '77. '78 Capricorn One.

VADIM, Roger

(b. 1928). Director. Born: Roger Vadim Plemiannikov; Paris, France

Vadim's films lie in a strange hinterland between the pornographic and the pretentious. He will be remembered less for them than for the myths and icons he created – most notably that of Brigitte Bardot, his first wife. In 1956 he directed, and she starred, in *Et Dieu Créa la Femme*, regarded at the time as sensationally sexually explicit. It was a massive box-office hit, especially in the USA. Although this success may have helped to pave the way for the *nouvelle vague*, Vadim's own subsequent movies have tended to lack narrative coherence and have substituted an adolescent prurience for intellectual content. They have been redeemed, on the other hand, by a certain technical facility and an eye for sumptuous images. Their most striking features have usually been the bodies of his wives – Annette Stroyberg and Jane Fonda (*Barbarella*) after Bardot – or mistresses like Catherine Deneuve, who bore his son. The latest was Cindy Pickett in *Night Games*, a critical and commercial flop.

Films include: 1956 Et Dieu Créa la Femme (USA/GB: . . . And God Created Woman/And Woman Was Created). '59 Les Liaisons Dangereuses 1960. '62 Les Sept Péchés Capitaux (USA/GB: Seven Capital Sins *ep* L'Orgueil) (+sc); Le Vice et la Vertu (USA/GB: Vice and Virtue). '64 La Ronde (FR-IT) (USA: Circle of Love). '66 La Curée (FR-IT). (USA/GB: The Game Is Over) (+prod). '68 Barbarella (FR-IT). '71 Pretty Maids All in a Row (USA). '79 Night Games (USA).

VALENTINO, Rudolph

(1895–1926). Actor. Born: Rodolfo Guglielmi; Castellaneta, Italy

Valentino came from a comfortably-off Italian family, and was a graduate of the Royal Academy of Agriculture in Genoa at 17. Dissatisfied with his prospects, he left for Paris in 1912, and was in New York the following year. He found a job as a professional dancing partner, went into show business when invited to replace Clifton Webb in a dancing act, and reached Hollywood in 1917. For three years he played small parts, usually Latins and often mildly villainous. Then the influential June Mathis, a leading writer at Metro, insisted that he be given the lead in Rex Ingram's *The Four Horsemen of the Apocalypse*. His six years of astonishing fame followed. He married twice. His first wife was actress Jean Acker. This was a brief union, and Valentino then married the talented designer Natasha Rambova, who attempted with little success to steer her husband towards 'art' films. The public, however, preferred the romantic lover of *The Sheik*. In his short life Valentino was adulated by women, and frequently resented by men (and by fan-magazines too). He died in 1926, from a perforated ulcer; unprecedented scenes marked his funeral. But behind the ballyhoo and the extremes of love and hate there was a very good actor. *The Conquering Power* and *Blood and Sand* show a Valentino visibly maturing, almost at times a character actor; in *Monsieur Beaucaire*, and above all in *The Eagle*, he displays a sense of irony and fun that demolishes the pretensions of the former and makes the latter into sheer delight. The legend and the reality have little in common.

Films include: 1918 A Society Sensation (GB: The Little Duchess) (as M. Rodolpho De Valentina). '19 Eyes of Youth. '21 The Four Horsemen of the Apocalypse; The Conquering Power; The Sheik. '22 Moran of the Lady Letty; Blood and Sand. '24 Monsieur Beaucaire; A Sainted Devil. '25 Cobra; The Eagle. '26 The Son of the Sheik.

goodbye and returned to Italy. After her brilliant performance as the countess torn between passion and patriotism in Visconti's *Senso* she was sought after by French and Italian art-film directors – Franju, Pasolini, and above all Bertolucci, for whom she played the most memorable role of her later career, as the fading beauty who holds the key to the mystery of *The Spider's Stratagem*.

Films include: 1940 Manon Lescaut; Piccolo Mondo Antico. '46 Eugenia Grandet. '47 The Paradine Case (USA). '49 The Third Man (GB). '54 Senso. '59 Les Yeux Sans Visage (FR-IT) (GB: Eyes Without a Face). '61 Une Aussi Longue Absence (FR-IT) (USA/GB: The Long Absence). '67 Edipo Re (GB: Oedipus Rex). '70 La Strategia del Ragno (GB: The Spider's Strategem). '77 Suspiria. '79 La Luna (USA: Luna).

VALLONE, Raf

(b. 1917). Actor. Born: Raffaele Vallone; Tropea, Italy

Vallone's rugged physique and virile good looks made an immediate hit in his first film, De Santis' steamy neorealist *Bitter Rice*. He played league football for Turin while a university student there and, after graduating, went into journalism as a sports reporter and music and film critic. Having quickly established himself as one of Italy's top stars, he built up an international reputation not only for his films but also for stage appearances in Rome, Paris and London – most notably as the protagonist of Arthur Miller's *A View From the Bridge* – a role he re-created for the screen. Since the mid-Sixties Vallone has worked in Hollywood, as well as Europe, and appeared in some rather meretricious blockbusters. He is married to a former co-star, Elena Varzi.

Films include: 1948 Riso Amaro (GB: Bitter Rice). '50 Il Cammino della Speranza (USA/GB: Road to Hope). '53 Thérèse Raquin (FR-IT). '61 El Cid (USA-IT); Vu du Pont (FR) (USA/GB: A View From the Bridge). '62 Phaedra (USA-GREECE). '69 The Italian Job (GB). '77 The Other Side of Midnight (USA). '78 The Greek Tycoon (USA). '81 Lion of the Desert (GB-USA-LIBYA).

VALLEE, Rudy

(1901–1986). Actor. Born: Hubert Vallee; Island Pond, Vermont, USA

Clutching his familiar megaphone, the moon-faced, bespectacled crooner Vallee was the first entertainer to cause mass swooning among his fans. He gave up the idea of being a pharmacist when he learnt to play the saxophone. He had a band while a student at the University of Maine and, after graduating from Yale, he formed The Connecticut Yankees. Jazz era success on radio and in vaudeville led him to Hollywood in 1929 and, despite his proclaimed dislike of the place, he starred in many light romances as well as musical shorts during the Thirties. Later he switched to comic character parts – often the bumbling millionaire who fails to win the girl. Although not classically tall, dark and handsome, he was a self-declared womanizer and was tagged 'The Vagabond Lover' after one of his biggest hit songs and his first film. His third wife was the actress Jane Greer. In 1975 he published a stage play, *Let the Chips Fall*.

Films include: 1929 The Vagabond Lover. '34 George White's Scandals. '38 Gold Diggers in Paris (GB: The Gay Impostors). '41 Too Many Blondes. '43 Happy Go Lucky. '47 The Bachelor and the Bobby Soxer (GB: Bachelor Knight). '48 So This Is New York; Unfaithfully Yours. '67 How to Succeed in Business Without Really Trying. '68 The Night They Raided Minsky's (narr. only). '75 Sunburst.

VALLI, Alida

(b. 1921). Actress. Born: Alida Maria Altenburger; Pola, Italy

As a stunningly beautiful Italian film star, Valli was signed up by David O. Selznick and played the enigmatic murder suspect Maddalena Paradine in Hitchcock's *The Paradine Case*. Selznick also cast her as Harry Lime's sad, loyal mistress in *The Third Man* but by 1951 she had kissed Hollywood

Above: Alida Valli in Carol Reed's The Third Man. Top: Rudy Vallee in Sweet Music (1935). Below: a studio publicity shot of Raf Vallone

Above: Lee Van Cleef in Ehi Amico . . . C'e Sabata, hai chiuso (1969, Sabata). Above right: Charles Vanel in Maddalena (1953). Right: an MGM portrait of luscious Mamie Van Doren. Far right: Dick Van Dyke in Carl Reiner's The Comic (1969), about a silent movie comedian

VAN CLEEF, Lee

(b. 1925). Actor. Born: Somerville, New Jersey, USA

Lee Van Cleef made a striking screen debut as one of the menacing trio of gunslingers in *High Noon*. After war service in the US Navy, he had been spotted in amateur theatricals by Joshua Logan, who cast him in the stage version of *Mr Roberts*. This professional experience enabled him to give a distinctively sinister edge to the many Western and gangland villains he played during the Fifties. His career was given a major fillip by the 'spaghetti' Westerns of the mid-Sixties, which made him a star in Europe. Most memorable are *For a Few Dollars More* and *The Good, the Bad and the Ugly*, in which Sergio Leone's camera lingers on his rangy frame, his cruelly impassive expression and his demonic smile with almost operatic intensity.

Films include: 1952 High Noon. '57 The Lawless Breed; Gunfight at the OK Corral. '58 The Young Lions. '62 How the West Was Won. '66 Per Qualche Dollaro in Più (IT-GER) (USA/GB: For a Few Dollars

More). '67 La Resa dei Conti (IT-SP) (GB: The Big Gundown); Il Buono, il Brutto, il Cattivo (IT) (GB: The Good, the Bad and the Ugly). '77 Killers. '79 The Hard Way (EIRE).

VAN DOREN, Mamie

(b. 1933). Actress. Born: Joan Lucille Olander; Rowena, South Dakota, USA

One of the B-feature platinum blondes spawned by Marilyn Monroe's success in the mid-Fifties, Mamie Van Doren started out as a secretary before modelling and touring the night-club circuit as a singer. She had a brief spell in repertory theatre before going into the movies and appearing in a string of lurid melodramas produced for MGM by Albert Zugsmith. Also featured in several of these was her husband, band leader Ray Anthony. They often exploited contemporary moral panics about dopetaking teenagers (*High School Confidential*), beatniks (*The Beat Generation*) and organized crime (*The Big Operator*). Lacking Monroe's calculating vulnerability or Jayne Mansfield's caricatured excesses, Mamie Van Doren became the siren of sleaze, a Fifties fantasy of delirious female sensuality incarnate.

Films include: 1953 The All American (GB: The Winning Way). '55 Ain't Misbehavin'; Running Wild. '58 Teacher's Pet; High School Confidential. '59 The Beat Generation; Girls Town; The Big Operator. '60 College Confidential. '67 You've Got to Be Smart. '72 The Candidate.

VAN DYKE, Dick

(b. 1925). Actor. Born: West Plains, Missouri, USA

Best known for his long-running, award-winning television show with Mary Tyler Moore, Dick Van Dyke first worked in the entertainment world as a radio announcer with the United States Air Force in World War II. After nightclub experience and a morning variety show on Los Angeles

TV, he eventually graduated to acting on Broadway and stardom in both the stage and screen versions of *Bye, Bye Birdie*. A tall, versatile and amiable comedian, Van Dyke was perhaps a bit lightweight for a Hollywood leading man. English audiences will always treasure the awfulness of his cockney accent in *Mary Poppins*.

Films include: 1963 Bye, Bye Birdie. '64 What a Way to Go!; Mary Poppins. '65 The Art of Love. '66 Lt Robinson Crusoe USN. '67 Divorce American Style; Fitzwilly (GB: Fitzwilly Strikes Back). '68 Never a Dull Moment; Chitty Chitty Bang Bang (GB). '79 The Runner Stumbles.

VAN DYKE, Willard

(1906–1986). Documentary director. Born: Denver, Colorado, USA

After graduating from the University of California, he had a number of jobs – including an apprenticeship with the photographer Edward Weston – before working as a cameraman on Pare Lorentz's documentary *The River*. After a brief involvement with the left-wing production group, Frontier Films, he made his directorial debut in collaboration with Ralph Steiner on *The City*, a documentary on urban planning (said to have been inspired by the poems of Carl Sandburg) for the New York World Fair in 1939. During the war he worked for the Office of War Information's Overseas Motion Picture Bureau. *San Francisco* was the official film on the establishment of the United Nations, and he continued to produce cautious, sponsored documentaries on many social themes. He was director of the Museum of Modern Art's film department 1965–1973.

Films include: 1938 The River (co-photo). '39 The City (co-dir; +co-prod; +photo). '40 Valley Town; The Children Must Learn (+sc). '42 The Bridge. '43 Steeltown. '45 San Francisco. '47 The Photographer. '64 Rice. '68 Shape of Films to Come.

VAN DYKE, W.S.

(1889–1943). Director. Born: Woodbridge Strong Van Dyke II; San Diego, California, USA

'One-Take Woody', as they called him later, had seen a great deal of open-air action – as lumberjack, gold-miner, railroader and mercenary – before entering the movies as assistant to D.W. Griffith on *Intolerance*. Within a year he was directing action pictures himself, and in 1918 made a major film, *Lady of the Dugout*, a gritty, realistic Western with ex-outlaw Al Jennings. Staying with Westerns for most of the Twenties, Van Dyke won a reputation for speed and competence, amply demonstrated in 1926; when he saved MGM a lot of money by making two Tim McCoy Westerns simultaneously. Then came his famous days. He went with Robert Flaherty to film *White Shadows in the South Seas*, and to Africa for the magnificent *Trader Horn*. He directed the first teaming of Loy and Powell in *Manhattan Melodrama*, and took the partnership through four of the Thin Man series, films which give as unsentimental a picture of a happy marriage as any director managed. He shot the superb earthquake spectacle *San Francisco*, and gave the movie a rich humanity. He would do anything that MGM gave him, from *Marie Antoinette* to Andy Hardy; however much Van Dyke may have hated some of his assignments, it never showed on the screen.

Films include: 1916 Intolerance (ass. dir; +act). '18 Lady of the Dugout. '27 Spoilers of the West. '28 White Shadows in the South Seas. '31 Trader Horn. '32 Tarzan the Ape Man. '34 Manhattan Melodrama; The Thin Man. '36 San Francisco; Love on the Run. '38 Marie Antoinette. '40 I Take This Woman; I Love You Again. '42 I Married an Angel; Cairo; Journey for Margaret.

VANEL, Charles

(b. 1892). Actor. Born: Rennes, France

One of France's most popular and durable character actors, Vanel has appeared in over two hundred films since his debut in 1912. Internationally he is best known for his roles in *Les Diaboliques*, as Yves Montand's co-driver in *Wages of Fear* and as Cary Grant's restaurateur friend in Hitchcock's *To Catch a Thief*. Well into his eighties, Vanel was marvellous as the aged peasant visited by his three sons – one a judge, another a teacher and the third a factory worker – in *Three Brothers*. He was voted Best Actor 1953 at the Cannes Film Festival, which also organized a special tribute to him in 1970. He directed two films, *Dans La Nuit* (1929) and *Le Coup de Minuit* (1935).

Films include: 1912 Jim Crow. '25 Âme d' Artiste (GB: The Heart of an Actress). '27 L'Esclave Blanche. '33 Les Miserables. '35 L'Equipage. '42 La Loi du Nord. '44 Le Ciel Est à Vous. '53 Le Salaire de la Peur (USA/GB: Wages of Fear). '54 L'Affaire Mauritzius (FR-IT) (GB: On Trial). '55 To Catch a Thief (USA); Les Diaboliques (GB: The Friends). '81 Tre Fratelli (IT) (GB: Three Brothers).

VAN EYCK, Peter

(1913–1969). Actor. Born: Götz von Eick; Steinwehr, Germany

With his blond, Teutonic good looks, Van Eyck was fated to play mostly sinister Nazi villains. Educated in Berlin, he began his career as a musician, but left for the USA in the early Thirties when Hitler came to power. He worked as an arranger for Irving Berlin among others, moving to Hollywood when his first wife Ruth Ford was given a contract. He did not break into movies himself until 1943, the same year as he became an American citizen, when actors who could impersonate German soldiers convincingly were much in demand. After service in the army, he returned to Hollywood to play a series of menacing character roles before moving back to Europe in 1959. He settled in Switzerland and appeared frequently in films of variable quality.

Films include: 1943 The Moon Is Down; Five Graves to Cairo. '51 The Desert Fox (GB: Rommel – Desert Fox). '53 Le Salaire de la Peur (FR-IT) (GB: Wages of Fear). '54 Mr Arkadin/Confidential Report (SP-FR). '56 Attack! '57 Der gläserne Turm (GER) (GB: The Glass Tower). '61 Die tausend Augen des Dr Mabuse (GER-FR-IT) (GB: The Thousand Eyes of Dr Mabuse). '62 The Longest Day; Ein Toter sucht seinen Mörder (GER-GB) (USA: The Brain; GB: Vengeance). '63 Station Six Sahara (GB-GER). '65 The Spy Who Came in From the Cold (GB). '69 The Bridge at Remagen.

VAN FLEET, Jo

(b. 1919). Actress. Born: Oakland, California, USA

Trained at the New York Neighborhood Playhouse, Jo Van Fleet made her Broadway debut in 1946 and won a number of theatrical awards before making her first film appearance, as James Dean's brothel-keeping mother, in *East of Eden*. For this she was awarded the Oscar for Best Supporting Actress. Her main commitment has remained to the stage – she is a member of the Actors' Studio – and her film roles have been sporadic, but usually impressive.

Films include: 1955 East of Eden; The Rose Tattoo; I'll Cry Tomorrow. '57 Gunfight at the OK Corral. '60 Wild River. '67 Cool Hand Luke. '68 I Love You, Alice B. Toklas! '69 80 Steps to Jonah. '71 The Gang That Couldn't Shoot Straight. '76 Le Locataire (FR) (GB: The Tenant).

VAN PEEBLES, Melvin

(b. 1933). Director. Born: Melvin Peebles; Chicago, Illinois, USA

A tailor's son from Chicago's South Side, Van Peebles spent three years in the US Air Force after graduating from university. He experimented with a number of the arts while living in San Francisco before attending graduate shool in Holland, where he also worked as an actor. In Paris he published five novels, one of which – *La Permission* – he eventually filmed as *The Story of a Three-Day Pass*. This tale of a black GI's weekend with a white French girl was selected as the French entry for the San Francisco

Film Festival in 1968, where it won a cult reputation. Columbia hired him to direct *The Watermelon Man*, after which he set up the outrageous *Sweet Sweetback's Baadasssss Song*, which he produced, directed, scripted, edited and acted in himself. It was a critical flop, but a hit with black audiences in the USA. Van Peebles has also written and directed two Broadway musicals.

Films include: 1967 La Permission (FR) (USA: The Story of a Three Day Pass). '70 The Watermelon Man. '71 Sweet Sweetback's Baadasssss Song (+ prod; + sc; + ed; + mus; + act).

VARDA, Agnès

(b. 1928). Director. Born: Brussels, Belgium

Of Greek-French parentage, Varda was raised in Paris where she studied photography and became the official stills photographer for the Théâtre National Populaire. Having been thus involved with theatre, she then decided to try film-making and – self-confessedly knowing nothing about it – formed a co-operative, bought a cine-camera and made her first film, *La Pointe Courte*, based loosely on William Faulkner's novel *The Wild Palms*. There followed a series of shorts for the French Tourist Office and seven years later (armed with considerably more experience) she made her second feature *Cléo de 5 à 7*, the film that established her as a force to be reckoned with. In this film Varda explores the mind and life of a pop-singer awaiting the life-or-death results of a medical examination. *Le Bonheur* secured Varda's reputation for making interesting, if somewhat off-the-wall films and has an amoral view of happiness in a style that owes much to the influence of her husband Jacques Demy. Criticisms that have been levelled against Varda are that she tends to make everything look like a series of stills photographs and that a lot of unnecessary decoration is incorporated into the plot. However, there is no doubt that her penchant for elegance and her awareness of visual detail show her to have an original talent that can only grow, and *L'Une Chante, l'Autre Pas* proves her instinctive feel for a good story. To date Varda has always written her own screenplays and she is deservedly one of France's most successful women directors.

Films include: 1955 La Pointe Courte. '58 L'Opéra Mouffe (short); Du Côté de la Côte (doc. short) (GB: The Riviera – Today's Eden). '61 Cléo de 5 à 7 (FR-IT) (GB: Cleo From 5 to 7). '65 Le Bonheur (GB: Happiness). '66 Les Créatures (FR-SWED). '67 Loin du Vietnam (GB: Far From Vietnam). '68 Black Panthers (short). '69 Lions Love (USA). '75 Daguerréotypes. '77 L'Une Chante, l'Autre Pas (FR-BELG-CURAÇAO) (GB: One Sings, the Other Doesn't). '81 Mur Murs (FR-USA); Documenteur.

VARNEL, Marcel

(1894–1947). Director. Born: Paris, France

After studying at college, Varnel took up acting, became a stage director and went to America to direct plays and operettas on Broadway. In 1931 he

Above: Peter Van Eyck in Vengeance *(1962). Above right: Jo Van Fleet as one of the intimidating dwellers of an apartment block in Roman Polanski's* The Tenant. *Right: Diane Varsi in* Peyton Place. *Below: Robert Vaughn in the spy thriller* The Venetian Affair

was contracted by Fox to direct *Silent Witness* and other films and two years later began working for British International Pictures in England. Moving on to Gainsborough, he skilfully handled some of Will Hay's comedies and later directed George Formby. He is a director with one great film to his name – *Oh, Mr Porter!*, a British comedy classic with Hay at his best as a bungling stationmaster on a run-down rural halt in Ireland, foiling gunrunners with the help of the fat youth Albert (Graham Moffatt), the ancient Harbottle (Moore Marriott) and the prehistoric steam engine, Gladstone.

Films include: 1932 Silent Witness (co-dir) (USA); Chadhu the Magician (USA). '33 Infernal Machine (USA). '34 Girls Will Be Boys (GB). '35 Dance Band (GB); I Give My Heart (GB). '37 Oh, Mr Porter! (GB). '38 Alf's Button Afloat (GB); Hey! Hey! USA! (GB). '40 Let George Do It (GB). '41 Hi Gang! (GB). '44 He Snoops to Conquer (GB). '46 This Man Is Mine (GB).

Above: Lupe Velez in Mexican Spitfire, the second in a popular series of comedies made by RKO, in which she appeared as a young businessman's mercurial Mexican wife. Right: Lino Ventura. Below: an MGM publicity portrait of sinister Conrad Veidt

VARSI, Diane

(b. 1938). Actress. Born: San Mateo, California, USA

Ash-blonde, all-American-teenager-type Varsi was the product of a broken home and by the age of 20 already had two divorces to her credit. After various jobs she went to study drama in Los Angeles and her performances on stage in *Gigi* led to the role of Lana Turner's mixed-up daughter in *Peyton Place*. She received an Oscar nomination for her performance and had the talent and studio publicity behind her to carve out a successful career. Yet, after three more appearances she announced that she was retiring from Hollywood – at the age of 21 – in order to 'run away from destruction'. A couple of hard years changed her mind but Hollywood was not about to give her a second easy chance and Fox – whose contract she had walked out on – barred her from work. After a brief return to the screen in the late Sixties and early Seventies

she set about reviving her career in the late Seventies with a role in *I Never Promised You a Rose Garden*.

Films include: 1957 Peyton Place. '58 10 North Frederick. '59 Compulsion. '68 Wild in the Streets; Killers Three. '70 Bloody Mama. '71 Johnny Got His Gun. '77 I Never Promised You a Rose Garden.

VAUGHN, Robert

(b. 1932). Actor. Born: New York City, USA

The son of Walter Vaughn and Broadway stage star Marcella Gandel, Vaughn studied journalism in Minnesota before deciding to become an actor. In 1951 he was a finalist in the Philip Morris inter-collegiate radio-acting contest and went on to study drama at the Los Angeles City College. On graduating with a BA he went on to his MA and PhD in political science and then took up a job with the Albuquerque Summer House Theatre as their resident director and leading man. During their production of *End as a Man* he was offered his first film, *Hell's Crossroads*, by Hecht-Lancaster Productions and two years later he was nominated for an Oscar

for his performance as Chester Gwynn, an heir being rooked out of his inheritance, in *The Young Philadelphians*. He was one of *The Magnificent Seven* but his career really took off with the television series *The Man From UNCLE* in which he played super-cool spy Napoleon Solo. Tall, dark, usually well-dressed and with a cool, calculated manner of speech, Vaughn then found himself cast as the sinister assistant DA swopping threats with hero Steve McQueen in *Bullitt* and the 'bad guy' in *Clay Pigeon*. He has since appeared in a handful of spy films for both the small and big screens.

Films include: 1957 Hell's Crossroads; No Time to Be Young. '59 The Young Philadelphians (GB: The City Jungle). '60 The Magnificent Seven. '63 The Caretakers (GB: Borderlines). '67 The Venetian Affair. '68 Bullitt. '71 Clay Pigeon (GB: Trip to Kill). '74 The Towering Inferno. '78 Brass Target. '79 Good Luck Miss Wyckoff.

VEIDT, Conrad

(1893–1943). Actor. Born: Hans Walter Konrad Veidt; Potsdam, Germany

Like so many of the great names in German cinema, Veidt received his early training from Max Reinhardt, at whose theatre he was acting by the time he reached 20. In films by 1917, he became famous two years later when he played the somnambulist Cesare in *The Cabinet of Dr Caligari*. Tall and lean, with finely sculpted features, piercing eyes, and a dancer's grace of movement, Veidt was supremely suited to the Expressionist style, and gave memorable performances as Ivan the Terrible in *Waxworks*, as the haunted pianist in *The Hands of Orlac*, as *The Student of Prague*, and other such possessed characters. He could be restrained and gentle too, and one of his best films, Murnau's *Der Gang in die Nacht*, shows this side of him to perfection. Veidt was in Hollywood for the final silent years, with another macabre triumph in *The Man Who Laughs*, and then returned briefly to Germany before moving to England to escape the Nazis (his wife was Jewish). He played a wide range of parts in British films (best of all, perhaps, the saintly Stranger in *The Passing of the Third Floor Back*), went back to America to finish *The Thief of Bagdad* (1940), and spent his last four years there before his death from a heart attack. In those years the times forced him to play Nazis, but at least he had *Casablanca* to play one of them in.

Films include: 1919 Wahnsinn (+dir); Das Kabinett des Dr Caligari (GB: The Cabinet of Dr Caligari). '20 Satanas; Der Januskorpf. '21 Der Gang in die Nacht; Das indische Grabmal (USA: Mysteries of India; GB: The Hindu Tombstone). '24 Das Wachsfigurenkabinett (USA: Three Wax Works; GB: Waxworks); Nju. '25 Orlacs Hände (A) (GB: The Hands of Orlac). '26 Der Student von Prag (USA: The Man Who Created Life; GB: The Student of Prague). '28 The Man Who Laughs (USA). '31 Der Kongress Tanzt (USA: The Congress Dances; GB: Congress Dances). '32 Rome Express (GB). '35 The Passing of the Third Floor Back (GB). '41 A Woman's Face (USA). '42 Casablanca (USA).

VELEZ, Lupe

(1908–1944). Actress. Born: Maria Guadalupe Velez de Villalobos; San Luis Patosi, Mexico

Now she is probably best remembered for her spectacular Seconal suicide in 1944, four months pregnant, jilted by her lover and hopelessly in debt. But although her torrid private life always overshadowed her acting career, Lupe Velez had managed to invest some of her earlier screen performances with her fiery energy. After a convent education and a brief career as a dancer, the Mexican teenager arrived in Hollywood and was signed by Hal Roach in 1926 to play in comedy shorts. Douglas Fairbanks spotted her and cast her opposite himself in *The Gaucho*. Other memorable roles were in Griffith's *Lady of the Pavements* and DeMille's *The Squaw Man*: later she was consigned to the self-parodying role of 'The Mexican Spitfire' in quickie farces with Leon Errol. Small, curvaceous and tempestuous Lupe Velez's affairs – with John Gilbert, Gary Cooper and Randolph Scott among others – were often the talk of Hollywood. But it was her explosive marriage to Johnny Weissmuller (Tarzan) that fuelled the gossip columns from 1933 until the inevitable divorce in 1938. After that both her love life and her career were on the slide.

Films include: 1927 Sailors Beware (short); The Gaucho. '29 Tiger Rose; Lady of the Pavements. 31 The Squaw Man (GB: The White Man). '34 Strictly Dynamite. '39 The Girl From Mexico; Mexican Spitfire. '41 Six Lessons From Madame La Zonga. '42 Honolulu Lu. '43 Redhead From Manhattan.

VENTURA, Lino

(b. 1919). Actor. Born: Angelo Borrini; Parma, Italy

Lino Ventura's family moved to Paris when he was a small boy and he grew up there. He worked at various jobs before becoming a professional wrestler. Director Jacques Becker, looking for gangster types in 1953, gave him a part in *Touchez Pas au Grisbi*, a big box-office success that started Ventura on a new career. He played gangsters in three of his next four films and frequently thereafter. Besides his Italian origins, his heavy physique and weary, lived-in face made him a convincing yet somehow sympathetic villain, who could also be the hero, as in Jean-Pierre Melville's superb *Le Deuxième Souffle*, a study of internecine warfare among gangsters who also find time to carry off an occasional major robbery. Ventura has sometimes been on the right side of the law – he was the investigating policeman in pursuit of right-wing terrorists in *Illustrious Corpses*.

Films include: 1954 Touchez Pas au Grisbi (GB: Honour Among Thieves). '60 Classe Tous Risques (FR-IT) (GB: The Big Risk). '66 Le Deuxième Souffle (GB: Second Breath). '69 Le Clan des Siciliens (FR-IT) (GB: The Sicilian Clan). '72 Joe Valachi – I Segreti di Cosa Nostra (IT-FR) (USA/GB: The Valachi Papers). '74 La Gifle (FR-IT). '76 Cadaveri Eccellenti (IT-FR) (GB: Illustrious Corpses). '78 The Medusa Touch (GB-FR); Un Papillon sur l'Epaule. '79 L'Homme en Colère (FR-CAN). '80 Sunday Lovers (FR-IT).

447

VERA-ELLEN

(1926–1981). Actress. Born: Vera-Ellen Westmeyr Rohe; Cincinnati, Ohio, USA

Trained as a dancer from early childhood, Vera-Ellen appeared as a Rockette at the Radio City Music Hall, as an entertainer with the Ted Lewis Band and at Billy Rose's Diamond Horseshoe, and in Broadway musicals before being spotted by Sam Goldwyn. He cast her opposite Danny Kaye in *Wonder Man* when she was still 19. The limitations of her singing and acting were made up for by her cute, wide-eyed energy and, above all, by her wonderful dancing with partners like Fred Astaire, Gene Kelly and Donald O'Connor. She was the elusive Miss Turnstiles, the poster queen being sought by the three sailors on leave in New York in *On the Town*. She retired in 1956 at the age of 30, and died of cancer in 1981.

Films include: 1945 Wonder Man. '46 The Kid From Brooklyn; Three Little Girls in Blue. '47 Carnival in Costa Rica. '48 Words and Music. '49 On the Town. '52 The Belle of New York. '53 Call Me Madam. '54 White Christmas. '57 Let's Be Happy (GB).

VERNEUIL, Henri

(b. 1920). Director. Born: Achod Malakian; Rodosto, Turkey

Born of Armenian parentage, Verneuil lived in France from the age of four. After working as a journalist, radio commentator, film critic and magazine editor, he began directing short films in 1946. His first feature followed in 1952 – La Table au Crevés, starring Fernandel. He went on to direct several vehicles for the comedian, as well as a string of thrillers featuring Jean Gabin. Even in the Sixties during the height of the *nouvelle vague*, he continued to turn out traditional blockbusters for the mass market.

Films include: 1947 Escale au Soleil (short). '52 La Table au Crevés (GB: Village Feud). '54 L'Ennemi Public No. 1 (FR-IT) (GB: Public Enemy No. 1). '55 Des Gens Sans Importance. '59 La Vache et le Prisonnier (FR-GER) (GB: The Cow and I). '60 Le Président (FR-IT) (USA: Money, Money, Money; GB: The President). '62 Un Singe en Hiver (USA: A Monkey in Winter; GB: It's Hot in Hell). '63 Mélodie en Sous-Sol (FR-IT) (USA: Any Number Can Win; GB: The Big Snatch). '64 Cent Mille Dollars au Soleil (FR-IT) (USA: Greed in the Sun). '65 Week-End à Zuydcotte (FR-IT) (USA/GB: Weekend at Dunkirk). '69 Le Clan des Siciliens (FR-IT) (GB: The Sicilian Clan). '71 Le Casse (FR-IT) (USA/GB: The Burglars). '73 Le Serpent (FR-IT-GER) (USA TV: Night Flight From Moses; GB: The Serpent). '75 Peur sur la Ville (FR-IT) (GB: Night Caller). '76 Le Corps de Mon Ennemi. '79 I Comme Icare. '82 Mille Milliards de Dollars.

VERNON, John

(b. 1932). Actor. Born: Regina, Saskatchewan, Canada

After studying at RADA in London in the early Fifties, Vernon played in rep at Hornchurch, Essex, for a year before returning to Canada to work in classical theatre, films and television. The lead role in the Canadian television series *Wojeck* won him national recognition, and this led to his first part on Broadway in *The Royal Hunt of the Sun*. Since his Hollywood debut as Mal Reese in *Point Blank* where he is the deserved victim of a spectacular defenestration, he has played many villains or corrupt officials, as in three Don Siegel movies, *Dirty Harry*, *Charley Varrick* and *The Black Windmill*, and the Chicago racketeer in *Brannigan*. He is married to former actress Nancy West.

Films include: 1954 1984 (voice only) (GB). '64 Nobody Waved Goodbye (CAN). '67 Point Blank. '69 Justine; Topaz; Tell Them Willie Boy Is Here. '71 Dirty Harry. '72 Fear Is the Key (GB). '73 Charley Varrick. '74 The Black Windmill (GB). '75 Brannigan (GB). '76 The Outlaw Josey Wales. '78 National Lampoon's Animal House. '81 Crunch/The Kinky Coaches and the Pom-Pom Pussycats.

VERTOV, Dziga

(1896–1954). Director. Born: Denis Arkadievich Kaufman; Bialystok, Russia (now Poland)

The Kaufman family moved to Moscow in 1915. Denis studied medicine, wrote verse and fiction, and adopted his pseudonym of Dziga Vertov (which means 'spinning top'). Soon after the October Revolution he began to work on newsreels and compilation films, and in 1922 started the screen magazine *Kino-Pravda*. Vertov believed that the eye of the camera could record a greater truth than the human eye; he used montage, superimpositions, slow and rapid motion to enhance this truth. His classic *Man With a Movie Camera* is the most joyous of documentaries – a city symphony which delights in the act of filming, and views its characters with sympathy and affection. Vertov welcomed sound, used it inventively, and made a lyrical masterpiece in *Three Songs of Lenin*, which joined archive material to folk songs of the peasants of Uzbekistan in order to celebrate the life and teaching of Lenin. It was virtually the last true work of Vertov. As the plodding didacticism of socialist realism took over in the Thirties, there was no place for his surging enthusiasm and his quirkish individual eye. Vertov's brothers were also famous in cinema. Mikhail was often Denis' cameraman, while Boris emigrated to France, where he was Vigo's photographer, before going on to a notable career in America.

Films include: 1919 Godovshchina Revolyutsii (Anniversary of the Revolution). '21 Istoriya Grazhdanskoi Voini (History of the Civil War). '24 Kino-Glaz (GB: Kino-Eye). '26 Shagai, Soviet (Stride, Soviet). '29 Cheloviek s Kinoaparatom (GB: Man With a Movie Camera). '31 Entuziazm/Simfoniya Donbassa (Enthusiasm/Symphony of the Donbas). '34 Tri Pesni o Lenine (GB: Three Songs of Lenin). '37 Kolybelnaya (Lullaby).

VIDAL, Gore

(b. 1925). Novelist/playwright/screenwriter. Born: West Point, New York, USA

The ageing *enfant terrible* of American letters, Gore Vidal is the grandson of the first senator from Oklahoma; but his own considerable political ambitions have not yet led to elected office. Instead he has expressed his views through his many novels and essays. He had already published a

number of these when he turned to television in 1953 and then to the movies a couple of years later. For MGM he scripted *The Catered Affair*, from Paddy Chayefsky's television play, and *I Accuse!*, about Zola's part in the Dreyfus affair, as well as working uncredited on William Wyler's *Ben-Hur* (1959). He collaborated with Tennessee Williams on *Suddenly, Last Summer*, based on Williams' play, and adapted his own play, *The Best Man*, a political drama directed for the screen by Franklin J. Schaffner. He had no direct part in the unfortunate version of his novel *Myra Breckinridge*, starring Raquel Welch and Mae West, but must take some responsibility for the disastrous *Caligula*, 'based on an original screenplay by Gore Vidal'.

Left: Vera-Ellen as Ivy Smith, 'Miss Turnstiles', and Gene Kelly as a star-struck sailor on shore leave in On the Town. *Below left: the director Luchino Visconti finding little to smile about*

while making The Damned, *his masterful study of decadence in Thirties German high society. Below: John Vernon in* The Black Windmill. *Bottom: the director King Vidor*

VIDOR, Charles

(1900–1959). Director. Born: Budapest, Hungary

After serving as a lieutenant in World War I, Charles Vidor went to the Ufa studios in Germany as an assistant director. He moved to Hollywood in the mid-Twenties, working in various capacities until he was able to finance and direct a short film in 1929. In 1932 he co-directed his first feature, *The Mask of Fu Manchu*, at MGM. After directing at several studios, he joined Columbia in 1939 and there made two of Rita Hayworth's best vehicles, the musical *Cover Girl* and the melodrama *Gilda*, as well as the Chopin biopic *A Song to Remember*. But he fell out with production chief Harry Cohn in 1946 and finally left Columbia in 1948. His most notable films of the Fifties were acerbic views of showbiz life: *Love Me or Leave Me*, the story of singer Ruth Etting (Doris Day) involved with a gangster (James Cagney), for which writer Daniel Fuchs won an Oscar; and *The Joker Is Wild*, in which Frank Sinatra played singer Joe E. Lewis, who is attacked by gangsters, loses his voice and becomes a stand-up comedian. *The Swan* made heavy weather of Grace Kelly's penultimate appearance as a society girl about to marry a prince. And the remake of Hemingway's novel *A Farewell to Arms* was a dull flop, only enlivened by Vittorio De Sica's supporting role as a syphilitic army surgeon. The old-fashioned Liszt biopic *Song Without End* was completed by George Cukor after Vidor's death.

Films include: 1929 The Bridge (short). '40 My Son, My Son. '43 The Desperadoes. '44 Cover Girl. '52 Hans Christian Andersen. '55 Love Me or Leave Me. '56 The Swan. '57 The Joker Is Wild; A Farewell to Arms. '60 Song Without End (co-dir).

VIDOR, King

(1894–1982). Director. Born: Galveston, Texas, USA

As a boy, King Vidor was enthralled by cinema. He took tickets and helped with projection at a local picture house, and at 15 had a camera and photographed a hurricane that had attacked Galveston. The film was shown in that district, and Vidor's future decided. In 1915 he and his wife, the future star Florence Vidor, set out for California. Vidor got work as an extra, wrote scripts with small success, directed a few shorts, and a first feature in 1919. It was the start of a 40-year-long career. He worked at MGM for most of the Twenties. It was the time of his two silent masterpieces *The Big Parade* and *The Crowd*, but the time too of other Vidor films that fall little short: the delicious Marion Davies comedies, *The Patsy* and *Show People*; a quiet, domestic film, *Happiness*, with the great stage star Laurette Taylor; a magnificent *La Bohème* with Gish and Gilbert. With sound, Vidor made the astonishing *Hallelujah*, with its black cast; *Our Daily Bread* with its Russian montage; a deeply-felt Civil War film in *So Red the Rose*. In their different ways, *Northwest Passage* and *An American Romance* (Vidor's epic of the steel industry) carried on the theme of life as struggle which had run through his work from *The Crowd* onwards. Late Vidor could be odd. The passionate melodramatics of *The Fountainhead* or *Ruby Gentry* might be absurd, but they had a kind of grandeur; and there was no faltering in his last great work, a version of *War and Peace* undaunted by the complexity of the novel and seizing its essence with unerring aim. Vidor was married three times: to Florence, to Eleanor Boardman, star of *The Crowd*, and to the writer Elizabeth Hill.

Films include: 1919 The Turn in the Road. '22 Peg o' My Heart. '24 Happiness; Wine of Youth. '25 The Big Parade. '26 La Bohème. '28 The Crowd; The Patsy; Show People. '29 Hallelujah. '31 Street Scene. '34 Our Daily Bread. '35 So Red the Rose. '38 The Citadel (GB). '40 Northwest Passage. '44 An American Romance. '46 Duel in the Sun. '49 The Fountainhead. '52 Ruby Gentry. '56 War and Peace (USA-IT). '59 Solomon and Sheba.

VIGO, Jean

(1905–1934). Director. Born: Paris, France

Vigo was the son of the anarchist known as Miguel Almereyda, who died in prison during World War I under circumstances never satisfactorily explained. Vigo spent wretched years at a boarding school, studied briefly at the Sorbonne, and moved to the South for his health's sake. He was tubercular, and in his short life spent much time in sanatoria. He became briefly an assistant to the great cameraman Léonce-Henry Burel; then he bought his own camera, and made a satirical documentary, *A Propos de Nice*, which contrasted the sunlit luxury of the Riviera rich with the squalor barely hidden from view. The short feature, *Zéro de Conduite*, harked

back to Vigo's unhappy schooldays. Eccentric, surreal, intensely poetical, but toughly realistic in its picture of childhood, the film was derided by its first critics, and banned in France for 12 years for its subversive view of authority. It is now an accepted masterpiece. Vigo had time for one more film, *L'Atalante*. A simple story of two lovers on a barge, a parting and a reconciliation, the film was mangled by its distributors, and not until long after Vigo's death was anything like a full version seen. *L'Atalante* is a great film – an unsentimental allegory that tempers its lyricism with pain. Vigo is not forgotten: the Prix Jean Vigo is one of the most sought-after annual film awards in France.

Films: 1930 A Propos de Nice (doc). '31 Taris, Champion de Natation (doc. short). '33 Zéro de Conduite. '34 L'Atalante.

VISCONTI, Luchino

(1906–1976). Director. Born: Count Don Luchino Visconti, Duke of Modrone; Milan, Italy

Descended from the thirteenth-century rulers of Milan and given the traditional aristocratic education – horse-breeding and classics – Visconti nevertheless developed a strong interest in music and the theatre. In the mid-Thirties he decided on a career in films and apprenticed himself to Jean Renoir. After helping out on *Les Bas Fonds* and *Une Partie de Campagne*, he returned to Italy in 1939 to collaborate with Renoir on an opera film, *La Tosca*, a project disrupted by the outbreak of war. After failing to convince the censors of the desirability of filming *L'Amante di Gramigna*, a story by Sicilian novelist Giovanni Verga, Visconti made his directorial debut with an adaptation of a James M. Cain novel, *The Postman Always Rings Twice*, *Ossessione*, as it was called, emerged in 1942, a forerunner of Italian neo-realism. He then turned to the theatre and established himself as an innovative and adventurous director. (His production of *As You Like It*, for example, had sets designed by Salvador Dali.) Returning to the cinema he directed, at irregular intervals, a sequence of immaculately stylish films, of which *Senso*, combining his interest in opera and in Italian history and his belief in the destructive force of uncontrollable passion, is his masterpiece – though other films vie for that position.

Films include: 1936 Une Partie de Campagne (ass. dir, uncredited) (FR). '37 Les Bas-Fonds (ass. dir, uncredited) (FR) (USA: The Lower Depths). '40 La Tosca (ass. dir). '42 Ossessione. '48 La Terra Trema. '51 Bellissima. '54 Senso (GB: The Wanton Countess). '57 Le Notti Bianche (USA/GB: White Nights). '60 Rocco e i Suoi Fratelli (IT-FR) (USA/GB: Rocco and His Brothers). '63 Il Gattopardo (USA/GB: The Leopard). '65 Vaghe Stelle dell'Orsa (USA: Sandra; GB: Of a Thousand Delights). '67 Lo Straniero (IT-FR-ALG) (USA/GB: The Stranger). '69 La Caduta degli Dei (IT-GER) (USA/GB: The Damned). '71 Morte a Venezia (USA/GB: Death in Venice). '73 Ludwig (IT-FR-GER). '75 Gruppo di Famiglia in un Interno (IT-FR) (GB: Conversation Piece). '76 L'Innocente (IT-FR) (GB: The Innocent).

Films include: 1956 The Catered Affair (GB: Wedding Breakfast). '58 The Left-Handed Gun (TV play basis only); I Accuse! (GB). '59 The Scapegoat (co-sc) (GB); Suddenly, Last Summer (co-sc) (GB). '60 Visit to a Small Planet (TV play and play basis only). '66 Paris Brûle-t-il? (co-sc) (FR) (USA/GB: Is Paris Burning?). '69 The Last of the Mobile Hotshots. '70 Myra Breckinridge (novel basis only). '79 Caligula (IT-USA).

449

VITTI, Monica

(b. 1931). Actress. Born: Maria Luisa Ceciarelli; Rome, Italy

Though she is best known outside Italy as the complex, opaque, equivocal heroines of Antonioni films, Monica Vitti began her career on the stage as a sparkling, versatile comedienne and her first film was the comedy *Ridere, Ridere, Ridere*. After directing her in a number of stage plays Antonioni cast her in the role of Claudia in *L'Avventura*, his first internationally successful film. After three more Antonioni films, she sought a new image as the comic-strip heroine of Joseph Losey's *Modesty Blaise*, and went on to become Italy's leading screen comedienne in films like *La Ragazza con la Pistola*, *Dramma della Gelosia* and *Amore Mio Aiutami*.

Films include: **1954** Ridere, Ridere, Ridere. '**60** L'Avventura (USA: The Adventure). '**61** La Notte (FR-IT) (GB: The Night). '**62** L'Eclisse (IT-FR) (GB: The Eclipse). '**64** Deserto Rosso (IT-FR) (USA/GB: Red Desert). '**66** Modesty Blaise (GB). '**68** La Ragazza con la Pistola (IT-GB) (USA: The Girl With a Pistol). '**69** Amore Mio Aiutami. '**70** Dramma della Gelosia – Tutti i Particolari in Cronaca (USA: The Pizza Triangle; GB: Jealousy Italian Style). '**74** Le Fantôme de la Liberté (FR) (GB: The Phantom of Liberty). '**79** An Almost Perfect Affair (USA).

VLADY, Marina

(b. 1938). Actress. Born: Marina de Poliakoff-Baidaroff; Clichy, France

The daughter of a Russian emigré, Marina's intended career was as a ballet dancer. Her two elder sisters (Hélène Vollier and Odile Versois) went into films, though; and she made her screen debut at 11 as a roller-skating adolescent in *Orage d'Eté*. After marrying director Robert Hossein at 17 she won the Best Actress Award at Cannes for her role as the cynically sensual young bride killing off her elderly husband with over-vigorous love-making in *L'Ape Regina*. She is best known outside France as the working-class Parisian housewife who supplements her income by part-time prostitution in Godard's *Two or Three Things I Know About Her*, but with her exquisitely oblique grey eyes and air of feline menace she has graced large numbers of European films with her presence. Her third husband was the Russian actor and singer, Vladimir Vysotsky, who died in 1980.

Films include: **1949** Orage d'Eté. '**56** Pardonnez Nos Offenses (GB: Forgive Us Our Trespasses). '**63** Una Storia Moderna: L'Ape Regina (IT-FR) (USA: The Conjugal Bed). '**66** Campanadas a Medianoche (SP-SWITZ) (USA/GB: Chimes at Midnight/ Falstaff). '**67** Deux ou Trois Choses que Je Sais d'Elle (FR) (GB: Two or Three Things I Know About Her). '**69** Sirokkó/Sirocco d'Hiver (HUNG-FR). '**73** Le Complot (FR-SP-IT). '**77** Ök Ketten (HUNG) (GB: The Two of Them); Il Triangolo delle Bermude (IT) (USA: The Bermuda Triangle). '**79** The Thief of Baghdad (GB-IT).

VOGLER, Rüdiger

(b. 1942). Actor. Born: Warthausen, Germany

After studying at Heidelberg University, Vogler launched straight into a successful career as a stage actor.

Left: Marina Vlady in La Princesse de Clèves *(1961), directed by Jean Delannoy. Above: Jon Voight, fighting for his life on a weekend trip in hillbilly country in John Boorman's* Deliverance, *scripted from his own*

novel by James Dickey. Right: Gian Maria Volonté as a sadistic bandit leader in For a Few Dollars More. *Below: Rüdiger Vogler in Wim Wenders'* Alice in the Cities. *Below left; Monica Vitti in* L'Avventura

Though he made his reputation primarily as a talented comic, he also acted in the avant-garde plays of Peter Handke, and starred in his television film *Die Chronik der Lafenden Ereignisse*. It was Handke who introduced him to director Wim Wenders who, after giving him small parts in *The Scarlet Letter* and *The Goalkeeper's Fear of the Penalty* (from a novel by Handke), cast him in the leading role for *Alice in the Cities*, *Wrong Movement* and *Kings of the Road*. Here, as a travelling projector mechanic, he manages to combine underplayed humour with profound dissatisfaction at the state of German society.

Films include: **1972** Die Angst des Tormanns beim Elfmeter (GER-A) (GB: The Goalkeeper's Fear of the Penalty). '**73** Der scharlachrote Buchstabe (GER-SP) (GB: The Scarlet Letter). '**74** Alice in den Städten (GB: Alice in the Cities). '**75** Falsche Bewegung (USA: The Wrong Move; GB: Wrong Movement). '**76** Im Lauf der Zeit (USA/GB: Kings of the Road). '**79** Letzte

Liebe. '**81** Bleirne Zeit (USA: Marianne and Juliane; GB: The German Sisters).

VOIGHT, Jon

(b. 1938). Actor. Born: Yonkers, New York, USA

Blond, blue-eyed, 6ft-2½ins tall, Jon Voight shot to fame as the over-optimistic hustler, Joe Buck, in *Midnight Cowboy*. The son of a professional golfer, he was brought up in surburban New York and it was while attending the Catholic University in Washington that he began to think seriously of an acting career. After training at the Neighborhood Playhouse in Manhattan, he spent a period with a repertory company in Vermont and gradually accumulated stage and television experience before breaking into films in 1967. Determined not to be trapped by success, he resisted all attempts to typecast him as the sort of dumb pretty-boy he had played in *Midnight Cowboy*. Though

this has resulted in him working in films all too infrequently, he was impressive as an un-macho liberal playing against Burt Reynolds' super-he-man in *Deliverance* and won an Oscar for his performance as an anti-war Vietnam veteran in *Coming Home*.

Films include: 1967 Hour of the Gun. '69 Out of It; Midnight Cowboy. '70 Catch-22; The Revolutionary (GB). '72 Deliverance. '73 The All-American Boy. '74 Conrack; The Odessa File (GB-GER). '75 Der Richter und sein Henkel (GER-IT) (USA: End of the Game). '78 Coming Home. '79 The Champ. '82 Lookin' to Get Out.

VOLONTÉ, Gian Maria

(b. 1933). Actor. Born: Milan, Italy

After acting for two years with pro-vincial repertory companies, Volonté decided on the benefits of formal train-ing and enrolled at the Academy of Dramatic Arts in Rome for three years. His stage debut after leaving in 1957 was in Racine's *Phèdre*, and it was as a classical actor on stage and occasionally television that he acq-uired his reputation. Tall, dark and handsome, he found little difficulty breaking into films but after establish-ing himself in a series of cardboard epics and spaghetti Westerns he con-served his talents for films with a serious social message. Though he appears in Godard's avant-gardish *Vent d'Est*, he has played his most rewarding roles in provocative poli-tical films, in particular Petri's *Investi-gation of a Citizen Above Suspicion*, the title role in Rosi's *Lucky Luciano* and *Christ Stopped at Eboli*.

Films include: 1960 Under Ten Flags (USA-IT). '61 Ercole alla Conquista di Atlantide (IT-SP) (GB: Hercules Conquers Atlantis); La Ragazza con la Valigia (IT-FR) (USA/GB: Girl With a Suitcase). '64 Per un Pugno di Dollari (USA/GB: A Fistful of Dollars). '66 Per Qualche Dollaro in più (IT-GER-SP) (USA/GB: For a Few Dollars More). '70 Le Vent d'Est (FR-IT-GER); Indagine su un Cittadino al di Sopra di ogni Sospetto

(USA/GB: Investigation of a Citizen Above Suspicion); Le Cercle Rouge (FR-IT) (GB: The Red Circle). '71 Sacco e Vanzetti (IT-FR) (USA: Sacco and Vanzetto). '72 Il Caso Mattei (USA/GB: The Mattei Affair). '73 Lucky Luciano (IT-FR). '79 Cristo si e Fermato a Eboli (GB: Christ Stopped at Eboli).

VON SEYFFERTITZ, Gustav

(1863–1943). Actor. Born: Vienna, Austria

Gustav von Seyffertitz was one of the greatest heavies of silent and early sound films. He was a veteran of the European and American stage, and over fifty when he made his first film in 1917. Until World War I was safely over, he disguised his film appear-ances by adopting the unlikely if ultra-English name of G. Butler Clon-blough, but in the Twenties could sail under his own colours, and emerged, tall, eagle-beaked and full of menace, as a magnificent villain. In *Sherlock Holmes*, with John Barrymore, he was a marvellous Moriarty; he turned Mary Pickford's *Sparrows*, in which he played a devilish baby-farmer, into a frightening experience; and he was regularly, and effectively, in atten-dance in the films of his fellow-Viennese, Josef von Sternberg.

Films include: 1917 Countess Charming. '18 Old Wives for New. '22 Sherlock Holmes (GB: Moriarty). '25 The Eagle; The Goose Woman. '26 Sparrows. '27 The Student Prince. '28 The Docks of New York. '29 The Case of Lena Smith. '30 The Bat Whispers. '32 Shanghai Express. '39 Nurse Edith Cavell.

VON SYDOW, Max

(b. 1929). Actor. Born: Carl Adolf Von Sydow; Lund, Sweden

The son of a professor of folklore at Lund University, this gaunt, powerful actor trained at the Royal Dramatic Theatre School in Stockholm and began his career with provincial rep-ertory companies. At the Malmö Mu-nicipal Theatre he met Ingmar Berg-man, who, after directing him in several stage plays, cast him as the angst-ridden knight Antonius Block in *The Seventh Seal*. In 1965 he made his Hollywood debut as Jesus Christ in *The Greatest Story Ever Told* but re-sisted the lure of Hollywood stardom and continued to live and work in Sweden. It was only after playing a venerable old Jesuit with a weak heart, the title role in *The Exorcist*, that he moved with his family to Los Angeles. His role as the powerless, embittered King Osric who assigns Conan the task of retrieving his way-ward daughter from the Children of Doom in *Conan the Barbarian* is typical of the cameo character parts he now plays.

Films include: 1951 Fröken Julie (USA/GB: Miss Julie). '57 Det Sjunde Inseglet (USA/GB: The Seventh Seal); Smultronstäl-let (USA/GB: Wild Strawberries). '60 Jungfrukallan (USA/GB: The Virgin Spring). '65 The Greatest Story Ever Told (USA). '66 The Quiller Memorandum (GB-USA). '68 Vargtimmen (USA/GB: Hour of the Wolf). '73 The Exorcist (USA). '74 Steppenwolf (USA). '76 Cadaveri Eccelenti (IT-FR) (GB: Illustrious Corpses). '77 Exorc-ist II: The Heretic (USA). '79 Hurricane (USA). '81 Conan the Barbarian (USA).

VUKOTIĆ, Dušan

(b. 1927). Animator/director. Born: Bileća, Yugoslavia

Vukotić studied architecture at the University of Zagreb and started car-tooning in the late Forties as a regular contributor to the satirical magazine *Kerempuh*. In 1951 he was made head of his own animation unit at Du-zafilm, and made his first film *How Kicó Was Born*. Duzafilm went out of business in 1953 and Vukotić and his colleagues reverted to making ad-vertising cartoons at Zagrebfilm, where they eventually established an animation studio. Vukotić made some brilliant satires on film genres, *Cowboy Jimmy* and *Concerto for Sub-Machine Gun* included, and in 1961, with *Sur-ogat*, became the first cartoonist to take the Best Animated Film Academy Award out of America, and the first Yugoslav to win an Oscar. *Surogat* showed a little holidaymaker at the seaside who blows up inflatables and eventually creates a whole warring social environment. The Zagreb school of animation lost its leading light when, in 1963, Vukotić left to work on live features like the children's film *The Seventh Continent*. With Vukotić's example, it had broken away from the cute, Disneyish style that had hitherto dominated world animation, and evolved its own terse, adult, grotesque, surreal and black-humoured modes that would leave the cartoon changed forever.

Films include: 1951 Kako se Ridio Kicó (How Kicó Was Born). '52 Začarini Dvorac u Dudincima (The Haunted Castle at Du-dinić). '56 Nestašni Robot (The Playful Robot). '57 Cowboy Jimmy. '58 Koncert za Mašinsku Pušku (GB: Concerto for Sub-Machine Gun); Strah (The Great Fear). '59 Piccolo. '61 Surogat (GB: Ersatz/The Sub-stitute). '62 Igra (GB: Play). '67 Siedma Pevnina (CZECH-YUG) (The Seventh Con-tinent). '68 Mrlja na Savjesti (GB: A Stain on His Conscience); Opera Cordis. '69 Ars Gratis Artis. '77 Akcija Stadion (Operation Stadium).

W

WAGNER, Fritz Arno

(1889–1958). Photographer. Born: Schmiedefeld am Rennsteig, Germany

After completing his education at the École des Beaux Arts in Paris, Wagner began his career as a newsreel reporter with Pathé Frères. In 1919 he started work in silent feature films as director of photography, and with Lang's *Der müde Tod* and Murnau's *Nosferatu* he became known as a master of the classic German Expressionist period with his understated, atmospheric style. Among his first sound films were G.W. Pabst's *Westfront 1918, Die Dreigroschenoper* and *Kameradschaft*. He remained in Germany throughout World War II and from 1945 to 1948 directed the newsreel *Welt im Bild*.

Films include: 1921 *Der müde Tod* (GB: Destiny). '22 *Nosferatu, eine Symphonie des Grauens* (USA: Nosferatu, the Vampire). '23 *Schatten* (GB: Warning Shadows); *Zwischen Abend und Morgen*. '27 *Der Liebe der Jeanne Ney* (co-photo) (GB: The Loves of Jeanne Ney). '29 *Napoleon auf St Helena*. '30 *Die Jagd nach dem Glück; Westfront 1918* (co-photo) (USA: Comrades of 1918; GB: West Front, 1918). '31 *M* (co-photo); *Die Dreigroschenoper* (GER-USA) (USA: The Threepenny Opera); *Kameradschaft* (GER-FR) (USA: Comradeship). '32 *Das Testament des Dr Mabuse* (co-photo) (GB: The Testament of Dr Mabuse). '37 *Der zerbrochene Krieg* (GB: The Broken Jug). '58 *Ohne Mutter geht es nicht*.

WAGNER, Robert

(b. 1930). Actor. Born: Detroit, Michigan, USA

After military college, he began acting with many small parts in films before his first starring role in *Prince Valiant*. In the Fifties his clean-cut good looks made him a teenage pin-up, and his starring career spanned over twenty years and included roles in *The Pink Panther, The Towering Inferno* and *Airport '79 – Concorde*. In the late Sixties he made a deliberate decision to concentrate on television, and achieved international fame with *It Takes a Thief*, and the series *Hart to Hart*. Married successively to Natalie Wood and Marion Marshall, both marriages ending in divorce, he was remarried to Natalie Wood at the time of her death in 1981.

Films include: 1951 *Let's Make it Legal*. '52 *What Price Glory?* '53 *Prince Valiant*. '54 *Broken Lance*. '56 *The Mountain*. '57 *The True Story of Jesse James*. '63 *The Pink Panther*. '66 *Harper* (GB: The Moving Target). '69 *Winning*. '72 *Madame Sin*. '74 *The Towering Inferno*. '79 *Airport '79 – Concorde* (GB: Airport '80 – Concorde).

WAJDA, Andrzej

(b. 1926). Director/screenwriter. Born: Suwalki, Poland

Wajda's work has continually reflected the fluctuating social and political climate of his country, examining the sensitive areas of the national historical consciousness with a perceptiveness and humanity that make him not only his country's but also one of world cinema's most important figures. Having fought for the Polish Resistance during World War II, he studied painting at the Kraków Academy of Fine Arts and direction at the State Film School at Łódź. During this time he worked as an assistant to the director Aleksander Ford on three short films; his diploma film and his first feature was *A Generation*, a moving and passionate view of the Polish Resistance. His next two films, *Kanał* and *Ashes and Diamonds*, continued to explore Poland's wartime experience and the birth pangs of the new Communist state with increasing assurance and depth. The development of Wajda's gifts as a film-maker coincided with a temporary easing of political restraints in Poland during the late Fifties. Wajda's features were among the first post-war Polish films to be widely seen in the West and deservedly brought him international acclaim. His subsequent work for the cinema and television has been remarkably diverse in theme and content. During the late Seventies he reaffirmed his position as Poland's most authoritative social and political commentator with *Man of Marble*, a brave and moving film about a woman director's attempt to make a documentary about a worker hero discredited by the state for refusing to toe the party line. The film raised fundamental issues of the individual's right to free expression and self-determination and explored the degree to which such rights were tolerated by a superficially 'permissive' political regime. These ques-

tions were investigated in the later *Man of Iron*, a drama/documentary celebrating the birth of the (now outlawed) free trade union Solidarity.

Films include: 1955 *Pokolenie* (USA/GB: A Generation/Light in Darkness). '57 *Kanał* (USA: They Loved Life). '58 *Pooiół i Diament* (USA/GB: Ashes and Diamonds). '59 *Lotna*. '60 *Niewinni Czarodzieje* (USA/GB: Innocent Sorcerers). '61 *Samson*. '65 *Popioły* (USA/GB: Ashes). '67 *Gates to Paradise* (GB-YUG). '68 *Wszystko na Sprzedaz* (USA/GB: Everything for Sale). '70 *Krajobraz po Bitwie* (USA/GB: Landscape After Battle); *Brzezina* (USA/GB: The Birch Wood). '74 *Ziemia Obiecana* (USA/GB: Land of Promise). '76 *Człowiek z Marmur* (+ prod) (USA/GB: Man of Marble). '78 *Bez Znieczulenia* (USA/GB: Rough Treatment). '79 *Panxiy z Wilko* (POL-FR) (USA: The Maids of Wilko; GB: The Young Girls of Wilko). '80 *Dyrygent* (USA/GB: The Conductor). '81 *Człowiek z Żelaza* (USA/GB: Man of Iron).

WALBROOK, Anton

(1900–1967). Actor. Born: Adolf Anton Wilhelm Wohlbruck; Vienna, Austria

From a long line of circus clowns, Walbrook defied family tradition and opted for a career as a straight actor. After training with Max Reinhardt he gradually established himself as a talented and versatile stage actor. Though he made his film debut in 1922 (*Mater Dolorosa*), it was not until

the early Thirties that he began seriously to devote his energies to films. After becoming a popular romantic leading man in films like *Walzerkrieg* he left for Hollywood in 1937 and came to Britain shortly afterwards. As a fervent anti-Nazi he played 'good German' roles in *49th Parallel* and *The Life and Death of Colonel Blimp* with great conviction, and captured the public's imagination with his romantic flyer/pianist playing the Warsaw Concerto over the ruins of Poland in *Dangerous Moonlight*. His most enduring role, though, was as the obsessive impresario who drives ballerina Moira Shearer into a splendid dance of death in *The Red Shoes*.

Films include: 1931 *Salto Mortale* (GER) (GB: The Circus of Sin). '33 *Viktor und Victoria* (GER); *Walzerkrieg* (GER). '37 *Michael Strogoff* (USA) (GB: The Soldier and the Lady); *Victoria the Great* (GB). '40 *Gaslight* (USA: Angel Street). '41 *Dangerous Moonlight* (USA: Suicide Squadron); *49th Parallel* (GB). '43 *The Life and Death of Colonel Blimp* (GB) (USA: Colonel Blimp). '48 *The Red Shoes* (GB). '50 *La Ronde* (FR). '55 *Lola Montès* (FR-GER) (GB: The Fall of Lola Montes).

WALBURN, Raymond

(1887–1969). Actor. Born: Plymouth, Indiana, USA

He was a Hollywood character actor whose speciality was blustering, pompous, lovable rogues, particularly

452

good in films by Frank Capra and Preston Sturges. Raised in Oakland, California, he went into acting in 1912 and never stopped working in stock and theatres all over the USA. He entered films in 1929 in *The Laughing Lady*, and in 1934 went to Hollywood under contract to Columbia. From then on he worked steadily until his retirement in the early Sixties, on the death of his first wife. He then remarried and was tempted back to the stage by Hal Prince to be in the Broadway hit production of *A Funny Thing Happened on the Way to the Forum* in 1962.

Films include: 1929 The Laughing Lady. '34 The Count of Monte Cristo. '36 The Great Ziegfeld; Mr Deeds Goes to Town. '37 High, Wide and Handsome; Thin Ice (GB: Lovely to Look At). '38 Professor Beware. '40 Christmas in July. '44 Hail the Conquering Hero. '47 Mad Wednesday/The Sin of Harold Dibblebock. '50 Riding High. '55 The Spoilers.

WALD, Jerry

(1911–1962). Producer/screenwriter. Born: Jerome Irving Wald; New York City, USA

A dynamic, vigorous character, Jerry Wald studied journalism and then wrote a popular radio column for the New York *Graphic* newspaper. By 1933 he was producing film shorts featuring radio stars for RKO and Warners. He went to Hollywood in 1934 for Warners as a writer, but by 1941 had changed to production. In almost a decade he produced over 65 films for Warners, the cream of those years. In 1950 he formed a production company with Norman Krasna, then in 1952 joined Columbia as vice-president in charge of production. In 1956 he formed Jerry Wald Productions, releasing through 20th Century-Fox. He was presented with the Irving G. Thalberg Award at the 1949 Oscar ceremony.

Films include: 1940 They Drive By Night (sc. only) (GB: Road to Frisco). '42 All Through the Night. '43 Destination Tokyo. '45 Objective, Burma!; Mildred Pierce. '47 Dark Passage. '48 Key Largo; Johnny Belinda. '50 Caged; The Glass Menagerie. '52 Clash by Night. '57 Peyton Place. '60 Sons and Lovers (GB). '61 Wild in the Country.

WALKEN, Christopher

(b. 1943). Actor. Born: Queens, New York City, USA

Walken is a creative New York actor who began his career as a child in television parts and film walk-ons. He made his Broadway debut at 16 in Kazan's production of *J.B.* After graduating from university he returned to the stage as a chorus dancer in various musicals, then managed to switch to drama roles via the original stage production of *A Lion in Winter*. His adult film career debut came in *Me and My Brother*. Since then he has had some fine parts, including Diane Keaton's strung-out brother in *Annie Hall*, Nick in *The Deer Hunter*, for which he won the Academy Award for Best Supporting Actor, and Nathan D. Champion, the sensitive hired-gun in *Heaven's Gate*.

Films include: 1968 Me and My Brother. '71 The Anderson Tapes. '77 Roseland; Sentinel; Annie Hall. '78 The Deer Hunter. '79 Last Embrace. '80 The Dogs of War (GB); Heaven's Gate. '82 Pennies From Heaven.

WALKER, Clint

(b. 1927). Actor. Born: Hartford, Illinois, USA

An amiable giant, Walker was raised in Illinois and at school he excelled in football and wrestling. He enlisted in the merchant marine in 1944, and after the war took his family on the road and worked as an oil man in Texas, a bouncer in Long Beach and a deputy sheriff in Las Vegas before Van Johnson persuaded him to give acting a try. With no previous experience he landed the leading role as Cheyenne Bodie in the long-running television series *Cheyenne*. His first film part was in *The Ten Commandments*. He has since worked regularly in film and television.

Left, from left to right: Robert Wagner in Michael Anderson's All the Fine Young Cannibals *(1960); Anton Walbrook in* Dangerous Moonlight; *Raymond Walburn in* Death Flies East *(1935). Above: Christopher Walken in Herbert Ross'* Pennies From Heaven

Films include: 1956 The Ten Commandments. '58 Fort Dobbs. '64 Send Me No Flowers. '65 None But the Brave (USA-JAP). '66 Night of the Grizzly. '67 The Dirty Dozen (USA-GB). '69 Sam Whiskey. '70 The Phynx. '72 Pancho Villa (SP). '77 The White Buffalo.

WALKER, Helen

(1921–1968). Actress. Born: Worcester, Massachusetts, USA

After working in repertory and on Broadway, Helen Walker was signed to co-star in *Lucky Jordan* opposite Alan Ladd in 1942. Most of her subsequent roles were as female leads in B features or as a supporting actress in main features. One of her most effective performances was as the icy, ruthlessly ambitious psychologist who teams up with Tyrone Power's sham spiritualist in *Nightmare Alley*. Her career was marred by a near-fatal car crash in 1946, and she retired from films in 1955.

Films include: 1942 Lucky Jordan. '45 Brewster's Millions; Murder, He Says; People Are Funny. '46 Cluny Brown; Her Adventurous Night. '47 Nightmare Alley. '48 Call Northside 777. '53 Problem Girls. '55 The Big Combo.

WALKER, Joseph

(1892–1985). Cinematographer. Born: Denver, Colorado, USA

A former electrical engineer who worked for a time in the film labs before graduating to lighting cameraman. Walker shot a variety of pictures at a number of different studios during the Twenties before arriving at Columbia in 1927. He spent the rest of his career at Columbia where he reigned as the leading cameraman throughout the Thirties and most of the Forties. As director Frank Capra's favoured collaborator, he photographed every Capra picture from *Flight* (1929) through 1939 and won an Oscar nomination for his efficient work on *You Can't Take It With You*. A workmanlike craftsman in black-and-white, he proved that he could film equally effectively in colour, winning his third Oscar nomination for *The Jolson Story*.

Films include: 1921 The Girl From God's Country. '34 It Happened One Night. '36 Mr Deeds Goes to Town. '37 Lost Horizon. '38 You Can't Take it With You. '41 Here Comes Mr Jordan. '46 The Jolson Story. '50 Born Yesterday. '52 The Marrying Kind; Affair in Trinidad.

Above: a grizzled Clint Walker in Gold of the Seven Saints *(1961). Below: Helen Walker making up with Dennis*

O'Keefe (left) and William Bendix in Allan Dwan's romantic farce Abroad With Two Yanks *(1944)*

453

WALKER, Robert

(1918–1951). Actor. Born: Salt Lake City, Utah, USA

After early training at the American Academy of Dramatic Arts, he gained a number of bit parts in Hollywood films and was signed to a contract by MGM in 1943. His big break came the following year in the service comedy, *See Here, Private Hargrove*, and in the Selznick production *Since You Went Away*, in which he played opposite his wife, Jennifer Jones. Slight of build and sensitive-looking, he proved the perfect partner for Judy Garland in *The Clock* (1945) as the shy soldier on leave in New York City. His personal life deteriorated after his divorce from Jennifer Jones, but he had one last outstanding role as the sinister, psychopathic killer in Hitchcock's superb thriller *Strangers on a Train* shortly before his sudden, premature death.

Films include: 1943 Bataan. '44 Madame Curie; See Here, Private Hargrove; Since You Went Away; Thirty Seconds Over Tokyo. '45 The Sailor Takes a Wife. '46 Till the Clouds Roll By. '47 The Sea of Grass; The Beginning or the End; Song of Love. '48 One Touch of Venus. '51 Strangers on a Train. '52 My Son John.

WALLACH, Eli

(b. 1915). Actor. Born: New York City, USA

Educated at the University of Texas and City College of New York, Wallach gained a variety of experience on the stage during the early Fifties. Small and dark with beady eyes and an intense nervous style of acting, he made an impressive debut in the Elia Kazan/Tennessee Williams film *Baby Doll* and played a sympathetic supporting role in the star-studded *The Misfits*. Wallach appeared regularly in American and international productions throughout the Sixties and Seventies as a heavy, most memorably as the nasty Mexican bandit leader in *The Magnificent Seven* and as the 'ugly' opposite Clint Eastwood in *The Good, The Bad and the Ugly*.

Films include: 1956 Baby Doll. '60 The Magnificent Seven. '61 The Misfits. '62 How the West Was Won. '66 How to Steal a Million. '67 Il Buono, il Brutto, il Cattivo (IT-GER-SP) (USA/GB: The Good, the Bad and the Ugly). '73 Cinderella Liberty. '76 Aces High (GB-FR). '79 Firepower (GB). '80 The Hunter.

WALLIS, Hal B.

(1898–1986). Producer. Born: Harold Brent Wallis; Chicago, Illinois, USA

Wallis took various jobs as a teenager to help support his family and ended up as a cinema manager. He arrived at Warner Brothers in 1922, and remained with the studio for over twenty years, rising from the publicity department to studio manager and then to producer. Initially his activities were overshadowed by studio chief Darryl Zanuck, but after Zanuck's departure in 1933, Wallis took over his post and played a major role in the success of the studio during the following years. *The Life of Emile*

Zola won Warners its first Best Picture Oscar in 1937 and Wallis was rewarded with the Irving G. Thalberg Award for 1938. He received the award again in 1943 when his production of *Casablanca* was again the top winner shortly before he left Warners. As an independent producer releasing his films through Paramount for twenty-odd years, the few pictures of note – *The Rose Tattoo* (1955) and *Gunfight at the OK Corral* (1957) – were sandwiched between the Martin and Lewis comedies and Elvis Presley vehicles. Later he produced a number of costume epics in Britain.

Films include: 1930 The Dawn Patrol; Little Caesar. '32 I Am a Fugitive From a Chain Gang (GB: I Am a Fugitive From the Chain Gang). '35 A Midsummer Night's Dream. '39 Juarez. '40 Dr Ehrlich's Magic Bullet (GB: The Story of Dr Ehrlich's Magic Bullet). '41 The Maltese Falcon. '42 Casablanca. '50 September Affair. '52 Come Back, Little Sheba. '69 Anne of the Thousand Days (GB). '75 Rooster Cogburn.

WALLS, Tom

(1883–1949). Actor/director. Born: Kingsthorpe, Northamptonshire, England

The son of a butcher, Tom Walls was a jockey and a London policeman before he made his stage debut in 1905. He will always be associated most closely with the series of farces he produced and starred in at the Aldwych Theatre. Many were transferred to the screen, usually with Walls directing. His bluff, roguish characterization was the perfect foil to the monocled inanity of his co-star, Ralph Lynn. During the war years, he turned more to character roles. A keen racegoer, Walls owned the winner of the 1932 Derby.

Films include: 1930 Rookery Nook (+dir) (USA: One Embarrassing Night); On Approval (+dir). '33 A Cuckoo in the Nest (+dir). '35 Stormy Weather (+dir); Foreign Affairs (+dir). '38 Old Iron (+dir); Crackerjack (USA: The Man With a Hundred Faces). '44 The Halfway House; Love Story. '45 Johnny Frenchman. '48 Spring in Park Lane. '49 The Interrupted Journey.

Above, from left to right: Robert Walker as the effeminate, murderous Bruno in Strangers on a Train; *Eli Wallach in* The Magnificent Seven; *Kay Walsh in David Lean's* This Happy Breed; *Ray Walston in* Kiss Me, Stupid; *Jessica Walter, playing a lovelorn psychopath (right), attacks*

her boyfriend's cleaning lady (Clarice Taylor) in Play Misty for Me. *Below, from left to right: Tom Walls (left) with Ralph Lynn in* A Cuckoo in the Nest; *the director Raoul Walsh, who lost an eye while making* In Old Arizona; *a studio publicity shot of Henry B. Walthall*

WALSH, Kay

(b. 1914). Actress. Born: London, England

Starting out as a chorus dancer, Kay Walsh became a vivacious female lead in many British films from the Thirties to the Fifties. Her later career was marred by ill-health, but from the Sixties she has periodically played some effective character roles. Hers were often cockney parts – as Queenie, the bad girl of the family in *This Happy Breed*, as Marlene Dietrich's blackmailing dresser in Hitchcock's *Stage Fright* and as Nancy, the kind-hearted girlfriend of the villainous Bill Sykes in *Oliver Twist*. In this she was directed by David Lean, to whom she was married at the time. Also a writer, she worked on the adaptation of Dickens' *Great Expectations* for Lean's 1948 screen version.

Films include: 1934 How's Chances? '42 In Which We Serve. '44 This Happy Breed. '47 The October Man. '48 Vice Versa; Oliver Twist. '49 Stage Fright. '55 Cast a Dark Shadow. '62 The L-Shaped Room. '72 The Ruling Class.

WALSH, Raoul

(1887–1980). Director/actor. Born: New York City, USA

After travelling widely as a youth and working in a variety of jobs, including a period as a cowhand, Walsh began acting in films in 1910. He was given his first big break by D. W. Griffith who employed him as an assistant director and actor – he played John Wilkes Booth in *The Birth of a Nation* – and then as a director. Walsh is best remembered today for his years at Warners (1939–51) when he directed Bogart, Cagney and Flynn in many of

(1911–1982). Choreographer/director. Born: New York City, USA

Walters first made his name as an actor, dancer and choreographer on Broadway during the Thirties. In 1942 he was signed up by producer Arthur Freed who was just then assembling a new musical unit at MGM. Walters remained at the studio for over twenty years, virtually his entire career in films, working on many of MGM's best known and most popular musicals. He served as dance director on a dozen pictures during 1943–46, then got his first chance to direct with *Good News*, followed by a pair of Fred Astaire musicals – *Easter Parade* with Judy Garland and *The Barkleys of Broadway*, with Fred reteamed with Ginger Rogers for the first time in ten years. Walters was best known for his sensitive handling of female stars – Judy Garland experiencing a problematical end to her career at MGM in *Summer Stock*, Joan Crawford making a musical comeback in *Torch Song* and Grace Kelly in *High Society*. He received his only Oscar nomination for *Lili*, starring Leslie Caron, and was still around to direct two of MGM's last musicals in the Sixties, *Jumbo* and *The Unsinkable Molly Brown*, but by then the studio was in decline and the magic was gone.

Films include: 1947 Good News. '48 Easter Parade. '49 The Barkleys of Broadway. '50 Summer Stock (GB: If You Feel Like Singing). '52 The Belle of New York. '53 Lili; Dangerous When Wet; Torch Song. '55 The Tender Trap. '56 High Society. '60 Please Don't Eat the Daisies. '62 Jumbo. '64 The Unsinkable Molly Brown.

WALTHALL, Henry B.

(1878–1936). Actor. Born: Shelby City, Alabama, USA

After a number of years as a successful stage actor in New York, Walthall joined D. W. Griffith's film troupe at the Biograph Studio in 1909. Dark, handsome and sensitive-looking, he soon developed into one of Griffith's leading actors, playing opposite Mary Pickford and later Blanche Sweet. By the time that Griffith was ready to make the transition from two-reelers to features (during 1913–14), Walthall had become the director's favourite male lead. He starred in *Judith of Bethulia* as Holofernes, played the composer John Howard Payne in *Home Sweet Home* and the romantic hero in *The Avenging Conscience*. But his most famous and memorable role was that of the Little Colonel in *The Birth of a Nation*. Although he worked regularly in films throughout the rest of his life, and was briefly reunited with Griffith, playing a small role in *Abraham Lincoln*, he could never match the success which he had achieved during those early years.

Films include: 1909 A Convict's Sacrifice. '13 Judith of Bethulia (reissued as: Her Condoned Sin). '14 Home Sweet Home; The Avenging Conscience. '15 The Birth of a Nation; The Raven. '26 The Scarlet Letter. '29 The Bridge of San Luis Rey. '30 Abraham Lincoln. '33 42nd Street. '34 Viva Villa! '35 A Tale of Two Cities. '36 China Clipper.

Silver Streak. He made his name as the devil in both the Broadway and Hollywood versions of *Damn Yankees*. His biggest starring role, in Billy Wilder's *Kiss Me, Stupid*, came about when he was brought in as a last-minute replacement for Peter Sellers who had suffered a heart attack. But the picture flopped and Walston returned to supporting roles.

Films include: 1957 Kiss Them for Me. '58 Damn Yankees (GB: What Lola Wants); South Pacific. '60 Portrait in Black; The Apartment; Tall Story. '62 Convicts Four (GB: Reprieve). '64 Kiss Me, Stupid/It Happened in Climax, Nevada. '67 Caprice. '69 Paint Your Wagon. '73 The Sting. '76 Silver Streak. '77 The Happy Hooker Goes to Washington. '82 Fast Times at Ridgemont High (GB: Fast Times).

WALTER, Jessica

(b. 1940). Actress. Born: New York City, USA

After completing her studies at the New York High School of the Performing Arts, Jessica Walter gained her first acting experience in summer stock and then on the Broadway stage. She was cast in a number of pictures during the mid-Sixties, mainly in bitchy and unlikeable roles – as Libby, the pushiest member of *The Group*, and Pat, the bored ex-model, indifferent wife and difficult mistress in *Grand Prix*. Her best role in the cinema to date was provided by Clint Eastwood who recognized her ability to project a tough, knowing quality, initially friendly and pleasant but potentially vindictive, even dangerous when crossed. The picture was *Play Misty for Me*, Eastwood's debut as a director, and he generously allowed her to steal it with what was clearly the best part.

Films include: 1964 Lilith. '65 The Group. '66 Grand Prix. '68 Bye, Bye, Braverman. '71 Play Misty for Me. '76 Number One. '79 Golden Girl.

their most popular pictures of the Forties. He gave Bogart a major boost to stardom by casting him as Roy Earle, the gangster on the run in *High Sierra*, after George Raft had turned down the role, and directed Errol Flynn in a number of films including *Gentleman Jim* and the excellent (though historically ludicrous) war adventure *Objective, Burma!* Walsh had his first major hits during the Twenties with Douglas Fairbanks in *The Thief of Bagdad*, and Victor McLaglen in *What Price Glory?* and its sequel. He remained active as a director throughout the Fifties, handling mainly Westerns and war pictures and had his last major hit with *Battle Cry* in 1955.

Films include: 1914 The Life of General Villa (some scenes only); The Death Dice. '15 The Birth of a Nation (ass. dir; + act). '23 Lost and Found on a South Sea Island (GB: Lost and Found). '24 The Thief of Bagdad. '25 East of Suez. '26 What Price Glory? '28 Sadie Thompson (+ act); In Old Arizona (co-dir). '30 The Big Trail. '37 Artists and Models. '40 Dark Command; They Drive by Night (GB: Road to Frisco). '41 High Sierra. '42 They Died With Their Boots On; Gentleman Jim. '45 Objective, Burma! '47 Pursued. '49 White Heat. '51 Distant Drums. '55 Battle Cry. '56 The Revolt of Mamie Stover. '64 A Distant Trumpet.

WALSTON, Ray

(b. 1918). Actor. Born: New Orleans, Louisiana, USA

A veteran stage actor, Walston arrived in Hollywood during the late Fifties and had a number of good character parts in films and television during the following years. Short, slim and slightly sleazy-looking, he was most effective playing slyly wicked villains or henchmen, as in

WANAMAKER, Sam

(b. 1919). Actor/director. Born: Chicago, Illinois, USA

Educated at Drake University with early stage experience at the Goodman Theatre in Chicago, Wanamaker's early film career was cut short by blacklisting for his left-wing political activities. He left for England in the Forties where he became active in the theatre as actor and director, then added to his stage activities by working as a writer, director and actor on television during the Sixties, with occasional film appearances. Slim, tough and confident-looking, he was effective as the Russian agent in *The Spy Who Came in From the Cold*. More recently he has extended his activities into directing films, most notably *Catlow*, a Spanish-made Western, and the Ray Harryhausen fantasy *Sinbad and the Eye of the Tiger*.

Films include: 1949 Give Us This Day (GB) (USA: Salt to the Devil). '62 Taras Bulba. '63 Man in the Middle (GB). '65 Those Magnificent Men in Their Flying Machines (or How I Flew From London to Paris in 11 Hours 25 Minutes) (GB); The Spy Who Came in From the Cold (GB). '67 The Day the Fish Came Out (GREECE); Warning Shot. '69 The File of the Golden Goose (dir. only). '70 The Executioner (dir. only) (GB). '71 Catlow (dir. only) (GB). '76 Voyage of the Damned (GB). '77 Sinbad and the Eye of the Tiger (dir. only).

WANGER, Walter

(1894–1968). Producer. Born: Walter Feuchtwanger; San Francisco, California, USA

An intelligent, well-educated (he is a graduate of Dartmouth College) and independent-minded producer, Walter Wanger did not fit easily into the studio-run film-making of the Thirties. After a short period at Columbia (*The Bitter Tea of General Yen*) and MGM (*Gabriel Over the White House* and *Queen Christina*), he began to produce independently. During the late Thirties his films were released through Paramount (*The Trail of the Lonesome Pine*) and through United Artists – John Ford's *Stagecoach* and *The Long Voyage Home* and Alfred Hitchcock's *Foreign Correspondent*. After a short period at Universal he formed his own production company. During later years he alternated between effective offbeat black-and-white productions like Fritz Lang's *Scarlet Street* and Max Ophuls' *The Reckless Moment*, both starring Wanger's wife Joan Bennett, and the Don Siegel pictures *Riot in Cell Block 11* and *Invasion of the Body Snatchers*, and disastrously expensive costume epics like *Joan of Arc* and *Cleopatra*. He spent some time in prison in the early Fifties for shooting Bennett's agent, allegedly in a jealous rage.

Films include: 1932 The Bitter Tea of General Yen. '33 Queen Christina; Gabriel Over the White House. '36 The Trail of the Lonesome Pine. '37 You Only Live Once; History Is Made at Night. '38 Algiers; Blockade. '39 Stagecoach. '40 Foreign Correspondent; The Long Voyage Home. '45 Scarlet Street. '47 Smash-Up/Smash-Up, the Story of a Woman (GB: A Woman Destroyed). '48 Joan of Arc. '49 The Reckless Moment. '54 Riot in Cell Block II. '56 Invasion of the Body Snatchers. '63 Cleopatra.

WARD, Simon

(b. 1941). Actor. Born: London, England

The son of a car-dealer, Simon Ward was educated at Alleyn's School, Dulwich, the birthplace of the National Youth Theatre which he joined when he was 13 and acted with for eight years. After an unhappy three years at RADA, he worked with repertory companies in Northampton, Birmingham and Oxford and made occasional West End appearances before getting his big chance in Joe Orton's *Loot* in 1967. Small roles in films followed, though he seemed to get more rewarding parts in television plays – *Carried by Storm*, *Flowering Cherry*, *Smith as Killer* – until he was cast in the title role of *Young Winston*. His subsequent work in films has achieved no very outstanding results, though he was likeable as James Herriot in *All Creatures Great and Small*.

Films include: 1968 If. . . . '69 Frankenstein Must Be Destroyed; I Start Counting. '72 Young Winston. '73 The Three Musketeers: the Queen's Diamonds (PAN); Hitler: the Last Ten Days (GB-IT). '75 All Creatures Great and Small. '76 Aces High (GB-FR). '78 Holocaust 2000 (GB-IT) (USA: The Chosen). '79 Zulu Dawn (USA-HOLL). '81 The Monster Club.

WARDEN, Jack

(b. 1920). Actor. Born: Newark, New Jersey, USA

Red-haired and solidly built, he had some early experience as a professional boxer. Warden's first acting successes were on stage and in films during the Fifties. He typically projects the image of the cynical, streetwise character like the misanthropic salesman juror in *Twelve Angry Men* or Eddie, the experienced 'office bachelor' who takes charge of organizing a night on the town in *The Bachelor Party*. During more recent years he has matured into one of the leading Hollywood character actors, appearing in *All the President's Men* and winning Oscar nominations for his supporting roles in two Warren Beatty pictures, *Shampoo* and *Heaven Can Wait*.

Films include: 1953 From Here to Eternity. '57 The Bachelor Party; Twelve Angry Men. '58 Run Silent, Run Deep. '59 The Sound and the Fury; That Kind of Woman. '75 Shampoo. '76 All the President's Men. '78 Heaven Can Wait. '80 . . . And Justice For All. '82 The Verdict (USA).

WARHOL, Andy

(1927–1987). Painter/director/producer. Born: Andrew Warhola; Cleveland, Ohio, USA

Most widely publicized of all the underground film-makers who rose to prominence during the Sixties, Warhol came to films via art studies (at Carnegie Institute of Technology), early work as a fashion illustrator and as a Pop Art painter. As a director he

is best known for a minimalist technique which involves positioning the camera and letting it run on, with occasional slight camera movements, but allowing the actors to develop and improvise a performance unbroken by subsequent cuts or editing. At its most tedious this method produced such numbing and unwatchable minimalist works as *Sleep* and *Empire*, running six or eight hours. But his later short pictures featured his own troupe of camp and outrageous 'superstars' including Edie Sedgwick, Mario Montez and Viva, some of them quite talented and witty in front of the camera. The best of the shorts, like *Hedy* and *Bike Boy*, were entertaining and perceptive sketches, while his best feature, *Lonesome Cowboys*, was a camp send-up of the Western genre starring Viva as a local ranch-owner and Taylor Mead as her lovably degenerate houseboy. Warhol's later pictures, as a producer, were directed by Paul Morrissey, including *Trash*.

Films include: 1963 Tarzan and Jane Regained . . . Sort Of; Eat; Sleep; Kiss/Andy Warhol Serial. '64 Blow Job; Batman Dracula; Empire (co-dir). '65 Kitchen; Hedy. '66 The Chelsea Girls. '67 ****/Four Stars; Bike Boy. '68 Lonesome Cowboys; Blue Movie/Fuck/Viva and Louis; Flesh (prod). '70 Trash (prod). '72 Women in Revolt/Sex/Andy Warhol's Women (co-dir); Heat (prod).

Top left: Sam Wanamaker in the murder mystery Warning Shot. *Above left: Jack Warden in* All the President's Men. *Above: Simon Ward in the title role of* Young Winston. *Below: David Warner in* Work Is a Four-Letter Word, *in which his co-star was singer Cilla Black*

WARNER, H. B.

(1876–1958). Actor. Born: Henry Byron Warner; London, England

Warner was a tall, slender, dignified English actor who went to America in 1905 with a touring theatre group and reached the pinnacle of his career at 51 playing Jesus Christ in Cecil B. DeMille's *The King of Kings*. He was from a family of actors going back five generations and his thoroughly professional services were much in demand for most of his life. During the Thirties he gained quite a reputation as a character actor and was especially memorable as Lord Melbourne in the British film *Victoria the Great* and as Chang, the suave, philosophical second-in-command of Shangri-La, in Frank Capra's version of *Lost Horizon*.

Films include: 1916 The Market of Vain Desire; The Vagabond Prince. '26 Whispering Smith. '27 The King of Kings. '29 The Trial of Mary Dugan. '36 Mr Deeds Goes to Town. '37 Lost Horizon; Victoria the Great (GB). '38 Bulldog Drummond in Africa. '49 El Paso. '50 Sunset Boulevard. '56 The Ten Commandments.

WARNER, Jack

(1894–1981). Actor. Born: Jack Waters; London, England

Though he was born into a very musical cockney family, performing as a child in his father's E. W. Waters Bijou Orchestra, Jack had an early ambition to be a racing-driver and for many years he worked as a mechanic. In 1927 he joined the Sutton Amateur Dramatic Society and his variety act with Jeff Darnell proved so popular that in 1934 they went professional. After splitting from Darnell, he gained a reputation as a reliable and versatile variety comedian. He made his film debut in 1943 in *The Dummy Talks* but his film career only really began with his role as a cockney corporal in Ealing's POW camp drama, *The Captive Heart*. For a while he resisted typecasting, playing a black-marketeer in *Hue and Cry*, a traitor in *Against the Wind* and an escaped convict in *My Brother's Keeper*. However, his success as the good-tempered bus-driver Joe Huggett in *Holiday Camp* led to a string of Huggett pictures; and his 'typical British bobby', George Dixon, in *The Blue Lamp*, proved so popular that after being killed by a young Dirk Bogarde, the character was resurrected to star in over five hundred episodes of BBC television's *Dixon of Dock Green*.

Films include: 1946 The Captive Heart. '47 Hue and Cry; It Always Rains on Sunday; Holiday Camp. '48 Against the Wind; My Brother's Keeper; Here Come the Huggetts. '50 The Blue Lamp. '51 Scrooge. '54 Forbidden Cargo. '58 Carve Her Name With Pride.

WARNER, Jack L.

(1892–1978). Producer. Born: Jack Leonard Warner; London, Ontario, Canada

The youngest and best known of the four Warner brothers, Jack headed the studio which they founded together in the Twenties for over thirty years. Throughout most of this period it operated as one of the leading film companies in the world, legendary for its early venture into sound with *The Jazz Singer* and its hard-hitting gangster pictures and Thirties musicals, but with many prestige productions to its credit as well, like the Oscar-winning *The Life of Emile Zola* and *This Is the Army*. After assisting their father in various business ventures the brothers operated a nickelodeon for a time (1905–1907), moved into film distribution and then began producing their own pictures with mixed results. The Warner Brothers studio was formed in 1923 with Harry (1882–1958) and Albert (1884–1967) in charge of the financial and business side, while Jack and Sam (1888–1927) supervised the production of films, Jack on the West Coast and Sam in New York where he pursued the studio's first experiments with sound before his early death. A hard-headed businessman, Jack had a number of disputes with his leading stars like Bette Davis and James Cagney, but was generally regarded as a fair-minded boss. He was very active up to the mid-Fifties along with his two brothers, Albert, who then retired, and Harry, who died in 1958. During the Sixties he continued to supervise a few prestige productions, such as *My Fair Lady* and *Camelot*. He received the Irving G. Thalberg Award in 1958.

Films as producer or executive include: 1918 My Four Years in Germany (USA-GER). '27 The Jazz Singer. '30 Little Caesar. '37 The Life of Emile Zola. '42 Casablanca. '43 This Is the Army. '53 House of Wax. '55 Rebel Without a Cause; East of Eden. '56 Moby Dick (GB); Giant. '64 My Fair Lady. '67 Camelot.

WASHBOURNE, Mona

(b. 1903). Actress. Born: Birmingham, England

After opting for a career as an actress rather than a concert pianist, Mona Washbourne found herself playing in variety revues such as the Modern Follies and the Fol-de-Rols and in repertory theatres working in a different play every week. It was not until 1937 that she broke into the West End but her performance in *Mourning Becomes Electra* solidly established her as a gifted character actress. In 1948 she made her film debut when the Terence Rattigan play she had been appearing in, *The Winslow Boy*, was filmed by Anthony Asquith. Since then she has made regular appearances in films, generally playing slightly eccentric mother figures: Billy's wittering, neurotic mother in *Billy Liar*; the overwhelmingly maternal matron in *If. . . .*; and, most memorably, Glenda Jackson's aunt in *Stevie*. Since 1980 she has won a new popularity as Marjorie, the warm, brave widow who runs the grocery store in the television series *The Shillingbury Tales*.

Films include: 1948 The Winslow Boy. '54 Doctor in the House. '57 The Good Companions. '60 The Brides of Dracula. '63 Billy Liar. '68 Mrs Brown You've Got a Lovely Daughter; If . . . . '69 The Bed Sitting Room. '70 Fragment of Fear. '73 O Lucky Man! '75 Mister Quilp/The Old Curiosity Shop. '78 Stevie (USA-GB).

Top: Underground film-maker Andy Warhol. Top right: H. B. Warner in The Gamblers (1929). *Above: Mona Washbourne as the matron and Peter Jeffrey as the head of a public school under fire from anarchistic pupils in* If. . . . *Below: Jack Warner as George Dixon in* The Blue Lamp

WARNER, David

(b. 1941). Actor. Born: Manchester, England

One of the key British actors of the Sixties – he was the Royal Shakespeare Company's youngest-ever Hamlet and represented a whole generation as the mad Marxist hero of *Morgan, a Suitable Case for Treatment* – Warner emerged from a bleak period in the Seventies to become a highly sought-after character actor in Hollywood and British films. With his big, ungainly body and air of gloomy introspection, he has inevitably been cast as disturbed or villainous characters, from his first film role as Blifil, Susannah York's repulsive suitor in *Tom Jones* to his later appearances as evil geniuses in *Time Bandits* and *Tron*. Having devoted most of his energy to film he has had little time to develop a stage career which, after training at RADA and experience in major roles with the RSC, had looked extremely promising.

Films include: 1963 Tom Jones. '66 Morgan, a Suitable Case for Treatment. '68 The Bofors Gun. '69 The Sea Gull. '70 The Ballad of Cable Hogue. '71 Straw Dogs. '74 From Beyond the Grave. '76 The Omen (USA). '77 Providence (FR-SWITZ). '78 The Thirty-Nine Steps. '79 S.O.S. Titanic. '81 Time Bandits. '82 Tron.

WATERS, Ethel

(1896–1977). Actress/singer. Born: Chester, Pennsylvania, USA

Born into poverty and forced to work in menial jobs as a teenager, she first made her name as a cabaret singer at the age of 17 and went on to star in vaudeville, on radio and on the Broadway stage. She was one of the first black performers to receive star billing and appeared in a number of films, including *On With the Show* and *Tales of Manhattan*. But she is best remembered today for three roles in particular: as the intelligent and understanding Aunt Dicey in *Pinky*, which earned her an Oscar nomination; and in the film versions of two of her biggest stage successes, the long-suffering wife Petunia in the all-black musical *Cabin in the Sky* and as Berenice in *The Member of the Wedding*.

Films: 1929 On With the Show. '34 Gift of Gab. '42 Tales of Manhattan; Cairo. '43 Cabin in the Sky; Stage Door Canteen. '49 Pinky. '52 The Member of the Wedding. '56 The Heart Is a Rebel. '59 The Sound and the Fury.

WATERSTON, Sam

(b. 1940). Actor. Born: Cambridge, Massachusetts, USA

Waterston started making movies in the mid-Sixties, in between seasons with the New York Shakespeare Festival, and has remained the sort of actor to whom challenging roles are more important than fame and fortune. His studied dedication has enabled him to emerge very creditably from films like *The Great Gatsby* (in which he played the narrator Nick Carraway) and *Heaven's Gate* (in which he played Canton, the vicious leader of the Stock Growers Association), which have been critical and box-office disasters. Success in films has not prevented him from continuing his stage career – playing as often in small off-Broadway theatres as in big prestige productions. His television roles include an extremely impressive portrayal of J. Robert Oppenheimer in the BBC's seven-part series based on the troubled life of the radical scientist who helped to invent the atom bomb.

Films include: 1966 The Plastic Dome of Norma Jean. '67 Fitzwilly (GB: Fitzwilly Strikes Back). '72 Savages. '74 The Great Gatsby. '75 Rancho DeLuxe. '76 Journey Into Fear. '78 Capricorn One; Interiors. '79 Eagle's Wing (GB). '80 Sweet William (GB); Heaven's Gate.

WATKIN, David

(b. 1925). Cinematographer. Born: England

Working his way up within a documentary unit to lighting cameraman in the mid-Fifties, Watkin graduated to features ten years later. His documentary background appealed to director Richard Lester who was just introducing a new look into British feature films. Lester selected him for two pictures in 1965, appreciating his ability to light quickly and naturally and provide the very contrasty black-and-white tones for *The Knack* while contributing to the freewheeling, spontaneous feel of the Beatles comedy *Help!* During the following years Watkin developed into one of the leading British lighting cameramen, and continued to work regularly with Lester throughout the Seventies. His filming of *The Three Musketeers* and its sequel was outstanding: he helped turn these ordinary decorative period romances into films full of sunshine and poetry. He also photographed some American films, including the large-budget World War II satire *Catch-22*, directed by Mike Nichols.

Films include: 1965 Help!; The Knack. '66 Mademoiselle (GB-FR). '67 Marat-Sade/The Persecution and Assassination of Jean-Paul Marat as Performed by the Inmates of the Asylum of Charenton Under the Direction of the Marquis de Sade. '68 Charge of the Light Brigade. '70 Catch-22 (USA). '71 The Devils; The Boy Friend. '73 The Three Musketeers: The Queen's Diamonds (PAN). '75 The Four Musketeers: The Revenge of Milady (PAN-SP). '76 To the Devil . . . a Daughter (GB-GER).

WATKINS, Peter

(b. 1935). Director. Born: Norbiton, Surrey, England

Educated at Christ College, Cambridge, and RADA, Watkins worked for a time as an assistant producer on commercials, but began directing and financing his own amateur anti-war films during the late Fifties. He attracted world-wide attention with his dramatic and compelling reconstruction of the historical battle of *Culloden* for BBC television. His next production, an uncompromising depiction of the possible horrors of nuclear war, *The War Game*, was never shown by the BBC, but was screened in cinemas and won an Oscar. After the failure of two features in a row, Watkins apparently learned from his mistakes – he went on to make *Punishment Park* in the USA, a chillingly effective futuristic picture about brutality and repression by a possible American police state of the future. He returned to Sweden to write and direct a remarkable three-and-a-half-hour biopic of the life of the Norwegian painter *Edvard Munch*. Justifiably bitter about the way in which he and his films have been treated in his home country, Watkins has continued to pursue his career abroad ever since the late Sixties, mainly in Scandinavia.

Films include: 1964 Culloden (orig TV). '65 The War Game. '67 Privilege. '69 Gladiatorerna (SWED) (USA: Gladiators; GB: The Peace Game). '71 Punishment Park (USA). '76 Edvard Munch (SWED-NOR). '77 Aftenlandet (DEN) (Evening Land).

WATLING, Jack

(b. 1923). Actor. Born: Chingford, Essex, England

Jack Watling went to the Italia Conti stage school in 1937 and was in West End stage plays as well as films in his teens. He joined the Royal Air Force in 1944 and re-established himself in films after the war. Frequently cast as a minor villain or dubious character,

Above, from left to right: Ethel Waters (right) with Julie Harris in The Member of the Wedding; *Sam Waterston in* Dandy, the All-American Girl *(1976); Jack Watling in the Ealing comedy* Meet Mr Lucifer *(1953). Far left: David Wayne gets a peck from Marilyn Monroe in* We're Not Married *(1952). Left: John Wayne and his son Pat on location for* Rio Grande. *Below: Naunton Wayne in* Highly Dangerous *(1950)*

he graduated to lead roles in low-budget comedies and thrillers in the Fifties and early Sixties, as well as supporting roles in major productions. He remained youthful-looking into middle age, but his film career tailed off after the mid-Sixties. His daughters, Dilys and Deborah Watling, are actresses frequently seen on television.

Films include: 1938 Sixty Glorious Years. '43 We Dive at Dawn. '44 The Way Ahead. '48 The Winslow Boy. '51 White Corridors. '56 Reach for the Sky. '57 The Admirable Crichton (USA: Paradise Lagoon). '58 Gideon's Day (USA: Gideon of Scotland yard). '60 Sink the Bismarck! '65 The Nanny. '73 Father Dear Father. '74 11 Harrowhouse.

WATT, Harry

(b. 1906). Director. Born: Edinburgh, Scotland

A drop-out from Edinburgh University, Watt joined the documentary film unit of the Empire Marketing Board under John Grierson in 1931. He developed into one of the leading British documentary directors with such films as *Night Mail* for the GPO Film Unit and *Target for Tonight*, a short feature about the RAF for the Crown Film Unit. He easily made the transition to feature films at Ealing during the Forties, directing *The Overlanders*, based on a true story about an Australian cattle drive during the war. And he travelled to Africa to film *Where No Vultures Fly* (in Technicolor) about a game warden in East Africa. For his last feature he returned to Australia with American star Aldo Ray to make an effective and underrated thriller about a convict on the run, *The Siege of Pinchgut*.

Films include: 1934 Man of Aran (doc) (ass. dir); Radio Interference (doc). '36 Night Mail (doc) (co-dir). '38 North Sea (doc). '39 Jamaica Inn (2nd unit dir); The First Days (doc) (co-dir). '40 Britain Can Take It/London Can Take It (doc) (co-dir); Welfare of the Workers (doc) (prod only). '41 Target for Tonight (doc). '43 Nine Men. '44 Fiddlers Three. '46 The Overlanders (AUS). '49 Eureka Stockade (AUS) (USA: Massacre Hill). '51 Where No Vultures Fly (USA: Ivory Hunter). '58 People Like Us (doc). '59 The Siege of Pinchgut (AUS) (USA: Four Desperate Men).

WAXMAN, Franz

(1906–1967). Composer. Born: Franz Wachsmann; Königshütte, Germany (now Chorzow, Poland)

Franz Waxman seemed destined to become one of Germany's great composers until the rise of Hitler forced a change of direction. A piano player from childhood, he started work as a bank clerk but abandoned this in favour of music academies at Dresden and Berlin, and the lure of café society. He worked on several films of the period – including *Der blaue Engel* (1930, *The Blue Angel*) – but in 1933 was beaten up in the street by Nazi sympathizers because he was a Jew. He left Germany and went first to France and then America, where he slotted easily into the life of a Hollywood composer; he became head of Universal's music department soon after his arrival, went on to become the conductor of MGM's orchestra, and finished up music director at Warners. His credits are long and impressive, ranging from *The Bride of Frankenstein* to *Peyton Place*, a couple of films with Hitchcock, and *Sunset Boulevard* and *A Place in the Sun* for which he won Oscars. Waxman was also the founder and director of the Los Angeles Music Festival.

Films include: 1935 The Bride of Frankenstein. '40 Rebecca. '44 Mr Skeffington. '47 The Paradine Case. '48 Whiplash. '49 Task Force. '50 Sunset Boulevard. '51 A Place in the Sun. '53 Stalag 17. '54 Magnificent Obsession. '57 Sayonara; Peyton Place. '59 The Nun's Story. '62 Taras Bulba.

WAYNE, David

(b. 1914). Actor. Born: Wayne McMeekan; Traverse City, Michigan, USA

David Wayne first appeared on the stage in amateur productions at the age of six, but a spell as a student at Michigan State University, in business, and with a marionette show was to intervene before he returned to it professionally. In 1937 he appeared in New York with Fredric March in *The American Way*, but his career was soon interrupted again, this time by service as a voluntary ambulance driver in World War II. On his return, however, he began to establish an enviable reputation on Broadway with shows like *Finian's Rainbow* and, later, *The Teahouse of The August Moon*. He played a wide variety of character roles in films from the Fifties, ranging from sophisticated, sparkling comedy in *How to Marry a Millionaire* to po-faced science fiction in *The Andromeda Strain*. He also worked on television, in the series *Norby* and *The Good Life*.

Films include: 1949 Adam's Rib. '50 The Reformer and the Redhead; Stella. '51 M. '53 How to Marry a Millionaire. '54 Hell and High Water. '55 The Tender Trap. '59 The Last Angry Man. '61 The Big Gamble. '71 The Andromeda Strain. '74 The Front Page; Huckleberry Finn.

WAYNE, John

(1907–1979). Actor. Born: Marion Michael Morrison; Winterset, Iowa, USA

Since Wayne's death, and as the relevance of his hawkishness recedes, it has become less fashionable to knock his critical standing. There have never been any doubts about his giant stardom – he is the biggest box-office draw in history – or his place in the public's affection, but there is, rightly, a growing realization that he was a great screen actor, too. In the 1982 *Sight and Sound* critics' poll (held every ten years) *The Searchers* had climbed into the position of eleventh best film ever, and the power of that remarkable odyssey movie lies equally in John Ford's direction and Wayne's awesome performance as Ethan Edwards, a man with unbearable feelings. In *The Searchers* – as in Howard Hawks' *Red River* – Wayne achieved so much by showing the dilemmas and doubts that afflict all men, even supposedly self-sufficient men like Ethan and Tom Dunson; the working out of those mental problems, without, finally, killing to solve them, is the key to Wayne's genuine heroism. Forget the stock image of Wayne as a two-fisted cowboy star: underneath there is a fierce moral battle taking place and a yearning in the breast of the masculine man to be tender. Maybe it is less hawkishness than 'Hawks-ishness' that motivates Wayne – a sharing of Hawks' belief in professional friendships, the elevating companionship of women and the sense of belonging, something ultimately denied to Ford's Wayne heroes in both *The Searchers* and *The Man Who Shot Liberty Valance*. That last film, though, is the finest tribute to the actor – more nostalgic than either

True Grit (his Oscar movie) or *The Cowboys* – for in it James Stewart's Eastern lawyer returns to the West to pay homage to Wayne's deceased Tom Doniphon, who becomes a Western legend. It is the same moving message engraved on the gold watch given to Nathan Brittles, the retiring cavalry officer played by Wayne in *She Wore a Yellow Ribbon*, that brings tears to the old man's eyes: 'Lest we forget.' Wayne was a footballer at the University of Southern California who got a props job with Tom Mix at Fox and then worked on the sets and as an extra on a couple of Ford films. Their long friendship would last until Ford's death in 1973 but Wayne didn't become a star until *Stagecoach* in 1939, following a ten-year apprenticeship in over a hundred films, mostly B Westerns, often at Republic. From then he would act in comedies, adventure films, epics, war films, crime thrillers and even an Irish romance (Ford's *The Quiet Man*) – but it was as a troubled, ageing Westerner that he joined the screen immortals and found a permanent place in everyone's heart.

Films include: 1927 Mother Machree (ass. prop man; +extra). '30 The Big Trail. '39 Stagecoach. '40 The Dark Command; The Long Voyage Home. '45 They Were Expendable. '48 Red River; Fort Apache; Three Godfathers. '49 She Wore a Yellow Ribbon; The Sands of Iwo Jima. '50 Rio Grande. '52 The Quiet Man; Big Jim McLain (+co-exec. prod). '53 Hondo. '56 The Searchers. '57 The Wings of Eagles. '59 Rio Bravo; The Horse Soldiers. '60 The Alamo (+dir; +prod). '62 Hatari!; The Man Who Shot Liberty Valance. '63 Donovan's Reef; McLintock! '67 El Dorado. '68 The Green Berets (+co-dir; +exec. prod). '69 True Grit. '70 Rio Lobo. '72 The Cowboys. '76 The Shootist.

WAYNE, Naunton

(1901–1970). Actor. Born: Henry Wayne Davies; Llanwonno, Glamorgan, Wales

At the end of the Thirties, Naunton Wayne and Basil Radford had a monopoly on playing bumbling Englishmen abroad. They first struck a chord in *The Lady Vanishes*, as the two old-school-tie types whose appreciation of the world is limited to cricket, uninterrupted by the worst Hitchcock can throw at them. They went on to work together in a similar vein for Ealing and others for over a decade; they are the fumbling, bureaucratic civil servants in *Passport to Pimlico*. The clean-shaven, solemn-looking Wayne had worked extensively on the stage in light comedy roles before his entrance into film in 1930. Though both he and Radford continued to pursue parallel solo careers, they were at their best together, and, despite the likes of *The Titfield Thunderbolt*, Wayne's performances did not have quite the same magic following Radford's death in 1952.

Films include: 1932 The First Mrs Fraser. '38 The Lady Vanishes. '39 A Girl Must Live. '40 Night Train to Munich (USA: Night Train). '43 Millions Like Us. '49 Passport to Pimlico. '51 Circle of Danger. '53 The Titfield Thunderbolt. '59 Operation Bullshine. '61 Nothing Barred.

WEAVER, Sigourney

(b. 1949). Actress. Born: Susan Weaver; New York City, USA

The daughter of English actress Elizabeth Inglis and American television pioneer Sylvester 'Pat' Weaver, Sigourney Weaver was brought up in a showbiz atmosphere and decided on a career as an actress at an early age. After gaining experience in a political theatre group while studying English at California's Stanford University, she went on to the Yale School of Drama and established herself as a promising and versatile actress in off-Broadway plays like Christopher Duray's *Titanic* and Alberto Innaurato's *Gemini*. She was seized upon by director Ridley Scott to play the part of Ripley, the tough-minded heroine of *Alien*, and made an impressive lead debut. After being hailed as an exciting new star, she held out for another film in which the female role was central to the action and not merely an accessory to the male lead, eventually finding it in Peter Yates' *Eyewitness* where she plays a cool and sophisticated reporter, perilously involved with a lovesick admirer and a gang of Vietnamese diamond smugglers.

Films include: 1977 Annie Hall. '79 Alien (GB). '81 Eyewitness (GB: The Janitor).

WEBB, Clifton

(1893–1966). Actor. Born: Webb Paramallee Hollenbeck; Indianapolis, Indiana, USA

For an actor remembered for playing rather sharp elderly gentlemen, Clifton Webb's early career was remarkably varied. He was picked out of his dancing class at the age of seven to appear in a children's theatre. As soon as he was old enough, he abandoned school and took up painting and singing. By the time he was 19 he was a well-known ballroom dancer, and was appearing regularly on the stage in light comedies and musicals. In the early Twenties he moved to London and played several straight dramatic roles. On Broadway he spent three seasons with *Blithe Spirit*. His first major film part came as a result of his friendship with Otto Preminger, who cast him as Waldo Lydecker, the cultured, elegant but ice-cold villain of *Laura*. This performance won him an Oscar nomination, and led to similar roles, but he toned the image down to a more amiable waspishness to play the aloof babysitter tormenting his charges in the comedy *Sitting Pretty*. He went on to play the same character, Mr Belvedere, in several sequels, abandoning villains for good. When Mr Belvedere had run his course, Webb simply recast him in an older mould as the old gentleman who refuses to conform in *The Remarkable Mr Pennypacker*.

Films include: 1920 Polly With a Past. '25 New Toys. '44 Laura. '46 The Razor's Edge. '48 Sitting Pretty. '52 Dreamboat. '53 Titanic. '54 Three Coins in the Fountain. '55 The Man Who Never Was (GB). '57 Boy on a Dolphin. '59 Holiday for Lovers; The Remarkable Mr Pennypacker. '62 Satan Never Sleeps (GB: The Devil Never Sleeps).

WEBB, Jack

(1920–1982). Actor/director. Born: Santa Monica, California, USA

Despite acting roles in such revered films as *Sunset Boulevard*, Webb is chiefly remembered for *Dragnet*, a crime series which first appeared on the radio in 1949. Webb had entered radio following his World War II service with the US Army Air Force, initially as an announcer and subsequently as an actor. He conceived, directed and acted in *Dragnet*, originating the tough, gritty, yet accessible style which made it so popular. In 1951 the series moved to television, with Webb himself playing the leading role, Detective Joe Friday. Finally, in 1954, it reached the big screen, its popularity unabated. Unfortunately, few of Webb's other projects were to be so well-received. *Pete Kelly's Blues* (1955) was a gangster tale with the same terse style, sugared with an atmospheric jazz score, but the rest of his work remained undistinguished. He returned to the small screen, and for a while was head of Warner Television, during which time he produced several new series, including *Emergency*.

Films as actor include: 1948 He Walked by Night. '50 Sunset Boulevard; Halls of Montezuma; The Men; Dark City. '51 Appointment With Danger. '54 Dragnet (+dir; +prod). '57 The D. I. '59 30 (+dir) (GB: Deadline Midnight). '61 The Last Time I Saw Archie (+dir).

WEBBER, Robert

(b. 1924). Actor. Born: Santa Ana, California, USA

Robert Webber is one of Hollywood's stock of supporting character actors, always there whenever a crooked businessman or seedy con-artist is needed, yet never quite in the full glow of the limelight. He began acting on the stage in the early Forties, turned to films after World War II service with the marines and has worked consistently since, both in America and Europe. He was one of the *Twelve Angry Men*, swayed by Henry Fonda's eloquence in the jury-room, became entangled with *The Dirty Dozen*, and appeared in Sam Peckinpah's bloodbath of Jacobean proportions, *Bring Me the Head Of Alfredo Garcia*.

Films include: 1957 Twelve Angry Men. '65 The Sandpiper; The Third Day. '66 Harper (GB: The Moving Target). '67 The Dirty Dozen (USA-GB); Don't Make Waves. '74 Bring Me the Head of Alfredo Garcia (USA-MEX). '77 The Choirboys. '78 Revenge of the Pink Panther (GB). '79 'IO'. '81 S.O.B.

WEBER, Lois

(1882–1939). Director. Born: Allegheny City, Pennsylvania, USA

From a musical comedy and melodrama, Lois Weber joined Gaumont Talking Pictures Company in about 1907 (sound-on-cylinder movies did not catch on, but they made them as early as that). She wrote, directed, and played the lead in her first film. Soon she was joined, as director and

Above left: Sigourney Weaver as the intrepid heroine of Alien. *Above: Clifton Webb in one of his most villainous roles in Otto Preminger's* Laura. *Below: Robert Webber in Martin Ritt's* The Great White Hope *(1970). Left: Jack Webb fires from the hip in a studio publicity portrait*

lead, by her husband Phillips Smalley, but Weber was always the creative force of the partnership. They went on to Reliance, Rex and Universal, and by about 1913 Weber was one of the leading American directors. An astonishing short thriller, *Suspense*, made by her that year survives. Weber uses triangular split-screen effects, an overhead close-up, and shots through a staircase, and employs reflections in a car's wing-mirror to illustrate a car-chase. For sheer delight in technique, *Suspense* is hard to equal. Weber went on to features. She directed Anna Pavlova in the dancer's only film, *The Dumb Girl of Portici*, an attractive costume spectacle, and made a number of films notable for their social crusading. Weber's *Where*

Are My Children? was an attack on abortion; other films attacked capital punishment and racial prejudice. In 1917 she founded her own company. It was not a success commercially, but a surviving picture from the period, *The Blot*, a searing study of middle-class poverty, shows her skill undiminished. The last film of Weber's 400-odd was made in 1934. Five years later she died in Hollywood.

Films include: 1912 The Troubadour's Triumph. '13 The Female of the Species (+act); Suspense. '15 Hypocrites. '16 The Dumb Girl of Portici (co-dir); Where Are My Children? (co-dir). '17 The Mysterious Mrs M. '19 When a Girl Loves. '21 The Blot. '26 The Marriage Clause. '27 The Angel of Broadway. '34 White Heat.

Above: Paul Wegener being made up for his part in Der Golem und die Tänzerin by costume designer Rochus Gliese (with brush). Below: the call of the jungle – Johnny Weissmuller in Tarzan Finds a Son, the fourth of his twelve outings as Edgar Rice Burroughs' famous hero

WEGENER, Paul

(1874–1948). Actor/director. Born: Bischdorf, Germany

From 1906 Wegener was a member of Max Reinhardt's Deutsches Theater company; a huge, imposing figure, he played many leads in the classical repertory; he also learned from Reinhardt the art of lighting and chiaroscuro, and made full use of this when he came to direct for the cinema. His film debut was as the student in Stellan Rye's *The Student of Prague* in 1913. Soon Wegener was directing, though he preferred to have with him as co-director a film craftsman like Carl Boese, Rochus Gliese or Henrik Galeen, so that it is not easy to determine Wegener's own contribution. But he loved the macabre and the fantastic, and the last of his three Golem films, made in 1920, is a classic of the genre, and Wegener himself, as the man made from clay, is the first and the most touching of the great movie monsters. Through the Twenties Wegener's acting took precedence; he dominates such fine films as Von Gerlach's *Vanina* and Rex Ingram's *The Magician*. With the Nazi period Wegener returned to direction, and continued to act, but his work of this period is never seen, and seems to be of little interest.

Films as actor include: 1913 Der Student von Prag (GB: The Student of Prague). '14 Der Golem (+co-dir). '16 Der Rattenfänger von Hameln (+co-dir); Der Yoghi (+co-dir). '17 Der Golem und die Tänzerin (+co-dir). '20 Der Golem – Wie er in die Welt kam (+co-dir) (GB: The Golem). '20 Sumurun (USA: One Arabian Night). '21 Das Weib des Pharao (USA: The Loves of Pharaoh). '22 Vanina. '26 The Magician (USA). '28 Alraune. '32 Unheimliche Geschichten. '38 Stärker als die Liebe. '42 Der grosse König.

WEILL, Claudia

(b. 1947). Director. Born: New York City, USA

Distantly related to composer Kurt Weill, Claudia Weill began making amateur films at Radcliffe College, and went on to study painting under Oskar Kokoschka. Her early films were mostly experimental or documentary shorts, though she did direct episodes for television's *Sesame Street*. She shared an Academy Award in 1975 for co-directing with Shirley MacLaine a full-length study of China, *The Other Half of the Sky*. Her first feature, *Girlfriends*, a softly feminist and feminine study of the strains modern living imposes on the relationship between two girls, was largely financed privately, though it did receive a network distribution from Warners.

Films include: 1969 Radcliffe Blues (doc) (FR). '71 This Is the Home of Mrs Leviant Graham (doc) (co-dir). '74 Joyce at 34 (doc). '75 The Other Half of the Sky: a China Memoir (doc) (co-dir). '78 Girlfriends. '80 It's My Turn.

WEIR, Peter

(b. 1944). Director. Born: Sydney, Australia

Deservedly the best known director to have emerged from Australia's 'New Wave', Weir began his career in a Sydney television station, making his first film to entertain his colleagues at a Christmas party. *The Cars That Ate Paris*, his first feature, raised a ripple of interest because of its quirky humour and bizarre subject matter: the revenge of apparently driverless cars on a small bush community which has hitherto survived by murdering chance passers-by. His next film, the haunting *Picnic at Hanging Rock*, was among the first movies to alert the outside world to the Australian renaissance, and Weir followed it with another psychic drama *The Last Wave*. Despite the mixed reactions to *Gallipoli*, which many critics approached expecting an apocalyptic and typically visionary exploration of war itself, and who were disappointed with the eloquent and moving requiem for a lost generation they instead received, Weir remains one of the most exciting and interesting directors working in Australia in the Eighties.

Films include: 1971 Homesdale. '74 The Cars That Ate Paris. '75 Picnic at Hanging Rock. '77 The Last Wave. '81 Gallipoli.

WEISS, Jiří

(b. 1913). Director. Born: Prague, Czechoslovakia

Weiss is another of that generation of European film-makers whose careers were drastically changed by the cataclysmic events in Europe in the Thirties and Forties. Originally a law student, he had abandoned that in favour of journalism, and in the early Thirties was directing his own 16mm amateur documentary shorts, one of which won an Award at Venice. With the German invasion, however, Weiss was forced to flee. He went to London, where he worked with the Crown Film Unit, making such films as *The Rape of Czechoslovakia*. Once the war ended, Weiss was able to return to his home country, and, taking advantage of the newly nationalized film industry, began to make features. His work was among the best from the post-war generation, but his reputation was submerged somewhat by the advent of the creative upsurge in Czech cinema in the Sixties.

Films include: 1939 The Rape of Czechoslovakia (GB). '42 Eternal Prague (GB). '43 Before the Raid (GB). '47 Uloupená Hranice (GB: The Stolen Frontier). '53 Muj Přítel Fabián (GB: My Friend the Gypsy/My Friend Fabian). '56 Hra o Zivot (GB: Life Was the Stake/No Middle Road). '58 Vlčí Jáma (GB: Wolf Trap). '59 Taková Láska (GB: Appassionata). '60 Romeo, Julia a Tma (GB: Romeo, Juliet and Darkness; USA: Sweet Light in a Dark Room). '62 Zbabělec (GB: The Coward); Zlaté Kapradí (The Golden Fern). '67 Vražda po Česky (GB: Murder Czech Style).

WEISSMULLER, Johnny

(1904–1984). Actor. Born: Peter John Weissmuller; Windber, Pennsylvania, USA

There can't be many openings in the film industry for yodelling swimmers, but as Hollywood's most famous Tarzan, Weissmuller found his. He entered films on the strength of his reputation in the pool, which had won him five gold medals in the 1924 and 1928 Olympics. His first screen appearances were in sporting shorts, but MGM approached him to play *Tarzan, the Ape Man* in 1932, and his natural agility, magnificent physique and ability to spout 'Me Tarzan – you Jane' lines with a wild-man innocence made him a natural success in the part. He went on to play the role twelve times, opposite a variety of comely mates, and, when the series began to run out of steam, switched to a television 'white hunter' variant, *Jungle Jim*. Weissmuller's private life was punctured by some much-publicized traumas, notably with spitfire actress Lupe Velez, the third of his six wives, and by ill-health which thwarted any comeback his cameo appearance in *The Phynx* (1970) might have heralded.

Films include: 1929 Grantland Rice (doc); Glorifying the American Girl. '32 Tarzan, the Ape Man. '34 Tarzan and His Mate. '36 Tarzan Escapes. '39 Tarzan Finds a Son. '41 Tarzan's Secret Treasure. '42 Tarzan's New York Adventure. '43 Tarzan Triumphs; Tarzan's Desert Mystery. '45 Tarzan and the Amazons. '46 Tarzan and the Leopard Woman; Swamp Fire. '47 Tarzan and the Huntress; Tarzan and the Mermaids. '50 Captive Girl. '52 Jungle Jim in the Forbidden Land. '53 Savage Mutiny. '54 Cannibal Attack. '76 Won Ton Ton, the Dog That Saved Hollywood.

WELCH, Raquel

(b. 1940). Actress. Born: Raquel Tejada; Chicago, Illinois, USA

From the moment Raquel Welch staggered out of the sea, her skimpy prehistoric costume wet and awry from the attentions of a passing pterodactyl in *One Million Years BC*, she was set on the road to stardom. Not that it had come overnight. In 1961 her marriage to high-school sweetheart James Welch had collapsed, and she had left Chicago for San Diego State College and the chance to appear in local repertory theatre. Her first film roles were not encouraging, but a meeting with agent Patrick Curtis was to change that. By the end of the Sixties, a heavy media campaign, centred upon Raquel's striking looks and Amazonian figure, had turned her into one of the world's great sex-symbols, despite surprisingly few on-screen appearances. Her rare good acting roles, as in *The Wild Party*, suggested a talent that had been forgotten beneath the glamorous ballyhoo. In the late Seventies she moved into television movies and began looking for more serious roles in the cinema.

Films include: 1964 Roustabout; A House Is Not a Home. '65 A Swingin' Summer. '66 One Million Years BC (GB). '68 Lady in Cement. '70 Myra Breckinridge. '71 Hannie Caulder. '73 The Three Musketeers: the Queen's Diamonds (PAN). '75 The Four Musketeers: the Revenge of Milady (PAN-SP); The Wild Party. '77 L'Animal (FR). '81 The Swindle.

WELD, Tuesday

(b. 1943). Actress. Born: Susan Ker Weld; New York City, USA

In the mid-Fifties Tuesday Weld was marketed by Hollywood as a teenage sex symbol, egging on the young sons of America to do naughty things at campus hops and drive-in movies. Public titillation was increased by widespread emphasis in the gossip columns on her emotional instability and rebellious image. A child model from the age of three, Weld made her film debut aged 13 in a low-budget musical, *Rock, Rock, Rock* (in which her voice was dubbed by Connie Francis). After many years of poor roles, two performances – as Steve McQueen's girlfriend in *The Cincinnati Kid* and as a beguiling psychopath opposite Anthony Perkins in *Pretty Poison* – brought her belated critical respect as an actress and made her something of a cult figure. Unfortunately, the movies she has turned down for various reasons – *Lolita, Bonnie and Clyde* and *True Grit* among them – are a good deal better than most of those she has appeared in. Her first husband was screenwriter Claude Harz; her second, actor Dudley Moore (they divorced in 1978).

Films include: 1956 Rock, Rock, Rock. '58 Rally 'Round the Flag, Boys! '59 The Five Pennies. '60 Sex Kittens Go to College. '61 Wild in the Country. '65 The Cincinnati Kid. '68 Pretty Poison. '71 A Safe Place. '72 Play It as It Lays. '77 Looking for Mr Goodbar. '80 The Serial.

WELLES, Orson

(1915–1985). Director/actor/screenwriter. Born: George Orson Welles; Kenosha, Wisconsin, USA

As a child, Welles showed precocious talent in many arts, writing, painting, acting. He attended the Todd School at Woodstock, where he directed and acted in Shakespeare and other classics. At 16 he set off for Europe, and began his professional career acting at the Gate Theatre in Dublin. Before he was 20 he was acting on Broadway. In 1937, with John Houseman, he founded the Mercury Theatre, where he produced and acted in some of the most original and vivid stage productions of the time. In 1939 Welles went to Hollywood with an RKO contract giving him total control within the limits of his budget. The result was *Citizen Kane*, a film which in 1962, 1972 and again in 1982 headed the Top Ten lists in a worldwide critical poll. His next film, *The Magnificent Ambersons*, although shortened and drastically re-edited in his absence, has gradually gained acceptance as a masterpiece. From then on, Welles and the studios were at loggerheads, and his opportunities were few. Yet he contrived to make superb dark thrillers like *The Lady From Shanghai* and *Touch of Evil*; on tiny budgets he made Shakespeare films stunning in their visual audacity; and he wandered the world acting in other directors' films to finance his own ventures. His acting often verged on parody, but when it

mattered he could be controlled and startling, as he was in *Jane Eyre, Moby Dick* and *Compulsion*. The waste of Welles' genius was appalling, yet he accomplished so much. Some of film's proudest achievements are his: the sense of passing time in *The Magnificent Ambersons*; the battle of darkness and light in *Macbeth*; the rueful farewell to greatness in *Chimes at Midnight*; and the tingling energy in every foot of *Citizen Kane*.

Films include: 1940 Citizen Kane (dir; + co-sc; + act). '42 The Magnificent Ambersons (dir; + sc; + narr); Journey Into Fear (actor). '43 Jane Eyre (actor). '46 The Stranger (dir; + co-sc. uncredited; + act). '47 The Lady From Shanghai (dir; + sc; + act). '48 Macbeth (dir; + sc; + act). '49 Prince of Foxes (actor); The Third Man (actor); Black Magic (actor). '50 The Black Rose (actor). '52 Othello (dir; + sc; + act) (MOROCCO). '54 Mr Arkadin/Confidential Report (dir; + sc; + act). '56 Moby Dick (actor). '58 The Long, Hot Summer (actor); Touch of Evil (dir; + sc; + act); The Roots of Heaven (actor). '59 Compulsion (actor). '62 Le Procès (dir; + sc; + act) (FR-IT-GER) (USA/GB: The Trial). '63 The VIPs (GB) (USA: International Hotel). '66 Campanadas a Medianoche (dir; + sc; + act) (USA: Falstaff; GB: Chimes at Midnight); A Man for All Seasons (actor). '68 Histoire Immortelle (dir; + sc; + act) (FR) (USA/GB: The Immortal Story). '70 Catch-22 (actor); Waterloo (actor) (IT-USSR). '71 La Décade Prodigieuse (actor) (FR) (USA/GB: Ten Days' Wonder). '73 Vérités et Mensonges/F for Fake (dir; + co-sc; + act) (FR-IRAN-GER). '76 Voyage of the Damned (actor) (GB). '79 The Muppet Movie (actor) (GB). '81 The Man Who Saw Tomorrow (narr).

Far left: shapely Raquel Welch in One Million Years BC. *Centre left: Tuesday Weld in* The Cincinnati Kid. *Left: Orson Welles immortalizes himself at his first attempt as* Citizen Kane. *Below: the immortal curves of Mae West in* I'm No Angel. *Below left: Jack Weston in* A New Leaf. *Below, centre left: Oskar Werner in* Interlude – a Swinging Sixties love story

WELLMAN, William

(1896–1975). Director. Born: William Augustus Wellman; Brookline, Massachusetts, USA

An adventurous and colourful character, Wellman first established his reputation as a young pilot in World War I, then made his name as a film director ten years later with a dramatic World War I flying picture, *Wings*, which won the first Best Picture Oscar. His varied and distinguished career extended over a period of thirty years and included Oscar nominations for two of his biggest hits, *Battleground* and *The High and the Mighty*, although the only other Oscar he ever won was for co-writing the original story for *A Star Is Born*, which he also directed. Wellman worked for all the major Hollywood studios. After a short period as an actor, property man and assistant director, he began directing Buck Jones Westerns at Fox during 1923–4, then moved over to Paramount for *Wings* and *Beggars of Life* (1928), starring Louise Brooks. He distinguished himself at Warners during the early Thirties with *The Public Enemy*, one of the best of the early gangster cycle, and a Depression picture *Wild Boys of the Road* (1933), featuring his future wife Dorothy Coonan. Reaching the peak of his career, Wellman directed two of the earliest Technicolor pictures for Selznick, *A Star Is Born* and *Nothing Sacred*, in 1937. A number of colour productions during the following years were interspersed with such notable black-

and-white films as *The Ox-Bow Incident*, an early example of the serious, psychological Western, and *The Story of GI Joe*, which provided Robert Mitchum with his first starring role.

Films include: 1923 The Man Who Won. '24 The Vagabond Trail. '27 Wings. '31 The Public Enemy (GB: Enemies of the Public). '36 Robin Hood of El Dorado. '37 A Star Is Born; Nothing Sacred. '38 Men With Wings. '39 Beau Geste; The Light That Failed. '42 Roxie Hart. '43 The Ox-Bow Incident (GB: Strange Incident). '45 The Story of GI Joe (USA retitling for TV: War Correspondent). '49 Battleground. '51 Across the Wide Missouri; Westward the Women. '54 The High and the Mighty; Track of the Cat. '58 Lafayette Escadrille (GB: Hell Bent for Glory).

WENDERS, Wim

(b. 1945). Director/screenwriter. Born: Düsseldorf, West Germany

Wenders, in company with such directors as Werner Herzog and Rainer Werner Fassbinder, is one of the key figures in the modern renaissance of German cinema. He studied at the Munich Film School between 1967 and 1970, making several short films and a debut feature, *Summer in the City*, which, with his next film, *The Goalkeeper's Fear of the Penalty*, won him an international audience. These and his subsequent works are absorbing, contrapuntal studies of two very different ideological traditions – the inspirational idealism and romantic sense of brotherhood and belonging which is central to American popular culture, and a specifically Northern European sense of existential anxiety and alienation. In one of Wenders' most respected films, *The American Friend*, Jonathan, the European protagonist, suffers (significantly) from a disease of the blood but experiences genuine liberation through his growing personal commitment to a flamboyant American 'outlaw' involved in swindling and contract killing. Wenders' own 'American Friend', the filmmaker Nicholas Ray (who has had a lasting influence on many other European directors), acted in this film and worked with Wenders on *Lightning Over Water* shortly before his death in 1979. Wenders' fascinating love affair with things American has continued with *Hammett*, in which the writer who virtually invented the private-eye thriller, Dashiell Hammett, becomes caught up in one of his own scenarios. Produced by Francis Ford Coppola (who is said to have directed part of it), the film is a nostalgic celebration of Forties *film noir* studio style and stereotypes, underpinned by Wenders' thematic preoccupations with loneliness, illusion and disillusion.

Films include: 1970 Summer in the City (+act). '72 Die Angst des Tormanns beim Elfmeter (GER-A) (GB: The Goalkeeper's Fear of the Penalty). '73 Der scharlachrote Buchstabe (GER-SP) (GB: The Scarlet Letter). '74 Alice in den Städten (GB: Alice in the Cities). '75 Falsche Bewegung (USA: The Wrong Move; GB: Wrong Movement). '76 Im Lauf der Zeit (+prod) (USA/GB: Kings of the Road). '77 Der amerikanische Freund (GER-FR) (USA/GB: The American

Friend). '80 Lightning Over Water/Nick's Movie (co-dir; +appearance as himself) (GER-SWED). '82 Der Stand der Dinge (GB: The State of Things); Hammett (USA).

WERNER, Oskar

(1922–1984). Actor. Born: Vienna, Austria

An intelligent and sensitive actor, Oskar Werner started his career in the theatre in Vienna where he was a noted stage actor long before his film debut in *Angel With the Trumpet* in 1949. He achieved international recognition when he played Jules in Truffaut's *Jules et Jim*, and his bleak, blond looks earned him the role of the cool East German interrogator in *The Spy Who Came in From the Cold*. In 1965 he was nominated for an Oscar for his performance as the melancholy ship's doctor in *Ship of Fools*.

Films include: 1949 Angel With the Trumpet (GB). '51 Decision Before Dawn (USA); The Wonder Kid (GB). '55 Lola Montès (FR-GER) (GB: The Fall of Lola Montès); Der letzte Akt (USA: The Life of Hitler; GB: Ten Days to Die). '62 Jules et Jim (FR) (GB: Jules and Jim). '65 The Spy Who Came in From the Cold (GB); Ship of Fools (USA). '66 Fahrenheit 451 (GB). '68 Interlude (GB). '76 Voyage of the Damned (GB).

WERTMULLER, Lina

(b. 1928). Director/screenwriter. Born: Arcangela Felice Assunta Wertmuller von Elgg; Rome, Italy

The daughter of a lawyer of aristocratic Swiss stock, Lina Wertmuller began her career as a teacher but her interest in the theatre led her to enrol at the Sharoff Theatre Academy in Rome. After a decade as a stage actress, she entered films as an assistant on Fellini's *Otto e Mezzo* (1963, 8½). She then wrote and directed her own first film, *The Lizards*, concerned with layabouts in southern Italy. This was successful in Italy. In 1964 she set up her own production company, Liberty Films, in association with the actor Giancarlo Giannini, who starred in many of her later films. He won the Best Actor Award at Cannes in 1973 for *Love and Anarchy*; but their first big international success was the concentration-camp comedy-drama *Seven Beauties*. This led to a short-lived contract with Warners, dissolved after one picture. Wertmuller works closely with her husband, set designer and sculptor Enrico Job. Her cult success in the United States has been variously attributed to her socialist and feminist views and to her betrayal of these same views by a cynically superficial approach.

Films include: 1963 I Basilischi (GB: The Lizards). '65 Questa Volta Parliamo di Uomini (GB: Let's Talk About Men). '67 Non Stuzzicate la Zanzara (Don't Sting the Mosquito). '72 Mimi Metallurgico Ferito nell'Onore (USA: The Seduction of Mimi). '73 Film d'Amore e d'Anarchia (USA: Love and Anarchy). '74 Tutto a Posto e Niente in Ordine (USA: All Screwed Up). '76 Pasqualino Settebellezze (USA/GB: Seven Beauties). '78 The End of the World in Our Usual Bed in a Night Full of Rain (IT-USA). '79 Fatto di Sangue fra Due Uomini per

Causa di una Vedova, Si Sospettano Moventi Politici (USA: Revenge; GB: Blood Feud).

WEST, Mae

(1892–1980). Actress. Born: New York City, USA

Eighty years separate Mae West's last film and her stage debut at five years old. Even in childhood the future could be discerned – she was publicized as 'The Baby Vamp'. After years in burlesque, vaudeville and revue, she wrote and produced her play, *Sex*, on Broadway. This was in 1926. The police moved in, and the star was briefly jailed. But she triumphed soon afterwards with *Diamond Lil*, and in 1932 made the first of her legendary Paramount comedies. Only in her first three films did she have full rein; after that the censorship clampdown weakened but could not destroy her. In 1943 she made what seemed for long to be her farewell film, and returned to the stage. In her sixties, she starred in nightclubs. Then, very late in life, she made two more films. The energy and resilience were remarkable; the quality of the movies was not. Looking back today on the films of her prime, it is hard to credit that she was ever considered a corrupting influence. As a sex symbol she was amply voluptuous, but at the same time she was parodying herself and all other sex goddesses. Never has sexual suggestiveness been so humorously artful and yet so essentially innocent. She wrote her own dialogue, and contributed largely to her screenplays, and the zestful timing with which she delivered those epigrams was beyond imitation. Mae West was a force of nature, and the cinema has not had many like her.

Films: 1932 Night After Night. '33 She Done Him Wrong (+play basis); I'm No Angel (+sc). '34 Belle of the Nineties/It Ain't No Sin (+sc). '35 Goin' to Town. '36 Klondike Annie (+sc; +play basis); Go West, Young Man (+sc). '38 Every Day's a Holiday. '40 My Little Chickadee (+co-sc). '43 The Heat's On (GB: Tropicana). '70 Myra Breckinridge. '78 Sextette.

WESTON, Jack

(b. 1925). Actor. Born: Cleveland, Ohio, USA

Interested in acting from an early age, Jack Weston won a theatre scholarship to the Cleveland Playhouse when he was 16, but was soon drafted into the army to serve in World War II. After demobilization he studied at the American Theatre Wing in New York from 1948 to 1950, and eventually gained a part in the television series *Gunsmoke*, which led to roles in the theatre. In 1958 he made his film debut in *Stage Struck*, and he has since played a succession of comic rogues, exploiting his image as a plump, clumsy and conniving character.

Films include: 1958 Stage Struck. '60 Please Don't Eat the Daisies. '61 The Honeymoon Machine. '63 Palm Springs Weekend. '65 Mirage; The Cincinnati Kid. '67 Wait Until Dark. '68 The Thomas Crown Affair. '69 The April Fools; Cactus Flower. '71 A New Leaf. '72 Fuzz. '76 The Ritz.

WEXLER, Haskell

(b. 1926). Cinematographer/producer/director. Born: Chicago, Illinois, USA

Haskell Wexler's father built him a small studio when he was in his teens so that he could make amateur films. After studying at the University of California, he filmed several documentaries in Chicago with director Irvin Kershner, with whom he later worked on *The Hoodlum Priest*. His first feature as cinematographer was *The Savage Eye*, a hysterical semi-documentary view of Los Angeles life. He made a civil-rights documentary, *The Bus*, while consolidating his reputation for black-and-white cinematography by winning an Oscar for *Who's Afraid of Virginia Woolf?* His deep-focus colour photography for *In the Heat of the Night* demonstrated his versatility; and soon afterwards he directed his only feature film, *Medium Cool*, which showed a sensitive concern for the morality of newsreel coverage in depicting (with much on-the-spot footage) the disturbances around the 1968 Democratic Convention in Chicago. He went on to co-direct documentaries with such luminaries as Jane Fonda and Emile De Antonio, while continuing his career in feature films as a lighting cameraman. He won another Oscar for *Bound for Glory*, the story of folksinger Woody Guthrie.

Films as cinematographer include: 1959 The Savage Eye. '61 The Hoodlum Priest; Angel Baby. '63 A Face in the Rain. '64 The Best Man; The Bus (doc) (+dir; +prod; +sc). '66 Who's Afraid of Virginia Woolf? '67 In the Heat of the Night. '68 The Thomas Crown Affair. '69 Medium Cool (+dir; +co-prod; +sc). '70 Gimme Shelter (doc) (co-photo). '74 Introduction to the Enemy (doc) (+co-dir; +co-prod; +co-sc) (GB: Vietnam Journey). '75 One Flew Over the Cuckoo's Nest (co-photo). '76 Underground (doc) (+co-dir; +co-prod; +co-sc); Bound for Glory. '78 Coming Home.

WHALE, James

(1889–1957). Director. Born: Dudley, Worcestershire, England

During the Twenties James Whale worked in the English theatre as an actor, designer and producer. In 1928 he produced R. C. Sherriff's *Journey's End*, and its success took Whale to America, where he directed the film version in Hollywood, and stayed on for twenty more films. Whale's horror films have always been well known, but his other work, so rarely seen, also contains enormous pleasures. The fluid camerawork and flair for a dramatic angle so notable in the *Frankenstein* films and *The Old Dark House* are always present; so is the rich theatricality that makes films like *By Candlelight* and *The Great Garrick* so entrancing. Above all, Whale's films are supremely civilized. *Remember Last Night?* is a deliciously sophisticated comedy-thriller; *One More River* perfectly captures a particular kind of English decency; and Ernest Thesiger, that eccentric character actor whom Whale enjoyed so intensely, is always ready to offer gin or a cigar in the most unlikely circumstances. Whale retired

in 1941 and turned to painting. The last few films given him were mostly uninteresting; he never achieved the status to choose for himself. He made one more film in 1949, a version of a Saroyan play, that showed much of the old visual imagination. He died in 1957, drowned in his own swimming pool.

Films include: 1930 Journey's End (USA-GB). '31 Frankenstein. '32 The Old Dark House. '33 The Kiss Before the Mirror; The Invisible Man; By Candlelight. '34 One More River (GB: Over the River). '35 The Bride of Frankenstein; Remember Last Night? '36 Show Boat. '37 The Road Back; The Great Garrick. '39 The Man in the Iron Mask. '49 Hello Out There.

WHEELER & WOOLSEY

Wheeler, Bert (1895–1968). Actor/comedian. Born: Albert Jerome Wheeler; Paterson, New Jersey, USA

Woolsey, Robert (1889–1938). Actor/comedian. Born: Oakland, California, USA

Wheeler was on the vaudeville stage from childhood and had an act with his wife, Betty, in *The Ziegfeld Follies of 1923*. In 1927 Florenz Ziegfeld partnered him with an ex-jockey, Robert Woolsey, in the Broadway musical *Rio Rita*. For over a decade they were one of the most successful teams of zany comics in showbiz. In 1929 they repeated their stage roles in the film version of *Rio Rita*, including their famous slapping routine. After that they averaged a couple of films a year until Woolsey's death in 1938. Wheeler made a few solo films and continued to work on the stage and, for a while in the Fifties, in television.

Films include: 1929 Rio Rita. '30 Cuckoos; Dixiana; Half Shot at Sunrise; Hook, Line and Sinker. '31 Caught Plastered. '32 Girl Crazy. '34 Hips, Hips, Hooray; Cockeyed Cavaliers. '35 The Nitwits. '37 High Flyers.

WHEELER, Lyle

(b. 1905). Art director. Born: Woburn, Massachusetts, USA

After working as a magazine illustrator and industrial designer, Lyle Wheeler joined MGM as a sketch artist in 1931 and became an assistant art director under Cedric Gibbons. He worked on several Jean Harlow pictures, including *Reckless* (1935). He then worked on all of David O. Selznick's projects in the late Thirties, including the first in colour, *The Garden of Allah*, and the most famous, *Gone With the Wind*, for which Wheeler received the first of his four Oscars and the only solo one (he shared Oscars for *Anna and the King of Siam*, *The Robe* and *The Diary of Anne Frank*). In 1944 he was appointed supervising art director at 20th Century-Fox and in 1947 he became head of the art department. During the period 1944–62 he had a hand in every 20th Century-Fox production; and he oversaw the studio's change from the black-and-white Forties to the colour and CinemaScope of the Fifties. Following a studio reorganiz-

Left: Stuart Whitman as the most intrepid of Those Magnificent Men in Their Flying Machines, *the frantic comedy about an early London to Paris air race. Above: Bert Wheeler (left) and Robert Woolsey and a look that says it all. Below: dependable character actor James Whitmore*

ation he went freelance and worked on several assignments for producer-director Otto Preminger, among others.

Films include: 1936 The Garden of Allah. '37 A Star Is Born. '39 Gone With the Wind. '40 Rebecca. '46 Anna and the King of Siam; My Darling Clementine. '53 The Robe; Call Me Madam; Gentlemen Prefer Blondes. '56 The King and I. '58 South Pacific; The Long, Hot Summer. '59 The Diary of Anne Frank. '62 Advise and Consent. '64 The Best Man. '70 Tell Me That You Love Me, Junie Moon.

WHITE, Carol

(b. 1943). Actress. Born: London, England

Encouraged by her father, a scrap-metal dealer and part-time entertainer, Carol White made her film debut as a young teenager in a children's film and played a schoolgirl in *Carry On Teacher*. In 1962 she married the first of her three husbands, singer Michael King of the King Brothers, and had two sons. She was semi-retired when she was cast in the television film *Up the Junction* (1965), directed by Ken Loach. She had an even greater success with *Cathy Come Home* (1966), the famous tear-jerker about a girl losing her home and consequently her children.

She also starred in Loach's first cinema feature, *Poor Cow*, as a criminal's girlfriend who turns to prostitution when he is jailed. Her career remained buoyant in the late Sixties and early Seventies, and she was in several American productions.

Films include: 1956 Circus Friends. '59 Carry On Teacher. '60 Beat Girl; Never Let Go; Linda. '67 Poor Cow; I'll Never Forget What's-'is-Name. '68 The Fixer (USA-HUNG). '71 Dulcima. '72 Made. '77 The Squeeze. '79 The Spaceman and King Arthur. '82 Nutcracker.

WHITE, Pearl

(1889–1938). Actress. Born: Green Ridge, Missouri, USA

Pearl White was a child actress, a circus rider until a spinal injury ended that career, and a modest performer in stock who had settled for a secretarial job with a film company by 1910. She was barely 21, and seemed a failure. But chance brought her the lead in a modest Western. She was alert, pretty, and confident in her

Above: Carol White in I'll Never Forget What's-'is-Name. *Above right: serial queen Pearl White. Above, far right: Billie Whitelaw in* Night Watch *(1973). Right: Mary Wickes in* June Bride *(1948). Below: Dame May Whitty in* The Lady Vanishes *– as the eponymous Miss Froy*

bearing, and she appeared in countless small films until, with the vogue for adventure serials, *The Perils of Pauline, The Exploits of Elaine* and their successors brought her enormous fame. Through the years of World War I, in fact, Pearl White had no rival, in Europe or America. The serials (the best of them were directed by a skilful Frenchman, Louis Gasnier) were built round mystery and suspense, much in the manner of Feuillade. Sadly, very few episodes survive. In the early Twenties Pearl White starred in a few feature films, but the new departure was unsuccessful, and she returned briefly to serials before retiring in 1924. Her last film was made in France, and she continued to live there until her early death.

Films include: 1910 The Life of Buffalo Bill. 13 Pearl as a Detective. '14 The Perils of Pauline (serial). '15 The Exploits of Elaine (serial); The New Exploits of Elaine (serial). '16 The Iron Claw (serial); Pearl of the Army (serial). '19 The Black Secret (serial). '20 The White Moll. '22 The Broadway Peacock. '23 Plunder (serial). '24 Terreur (FR) (USA: Perils of Paris).

WHITELAW, Billie

(b. 1932). Actress. Born: Coventry, England

Brought up in Bradford, as a child she acted at the Bradford Civic Playhouse and played the boy detective Henry Bones on BBC radio's *Children's Hour*. Though she made her film debut in a low-budget thriller *The Fake* in 1953, it was in television plays like *No Trams to Lime Street, A Resounding Tinkle,* and *Lena, Oh My Lena* (for which she received the Best Television Actress Award of 1960) that Billie Whitelaw established her reputation as a tough, bold, sensual actress. She has since played opposite Albert Finney in *Charlie Bubbles* and *Gumshoe* but, apart from the racist Rhodesian mistress of Leo (Marcello Mastroianni) in John Boorman's *Leo the Last,* she has not had the roles she deserves on the big screen. In 1982 she was the stern, steely secretary in Chris Petit's offbeat thriller *An Unsuitable Job for a Woman.* She continues to prove herself one of Britain's best actresses.

Films include: 1953 The Fake. '57 Miracle in Soho. '58 Carve Her Name With Pride. '61 No Love for Johnnie. '64 Becket. '68 Charlie Bubbles; Twisted Nerve. '70 Start the Revolution Without Me (USA-CZECH). '70 Leo the Last. '71 Gumshoe. '72 Frenzy. '76 The Omen. '78 The Water Babies (GB-POL). '82 An Unsuitable Job for a Woman.

WHITMAN, Stuart

(b. 1926). Actor. Born: San Francisco, California, USA

Having been a top light-heavyweight boxer in the army, Stuart Whitman left the service in 1948 to study law and drama at Los Angeles City College. He had a small part in his debut film, *When Worlds Collide,* but television appearances boosted his career and one of these, as a prizefighter in the play *Dr Christian,* brought him his first lead role in a film, *Johnny Trouble.* He was signed to a seven-year contract by 20th Century-Fox in 1958, and this was the period when he was a minor star, being nominated for a Best Actor Oscar for his part as a reformed child molester in *The Mark,* a British-made production. Since 1965 he has continued his career in Hollywood and Europe, usually as a second lead, and been active in television. He played the Reverend Jim Jones, who led his followers to mass suicide, in *Guyana – Crime of the Century;* and in 1980 he bought the rights to *Gunga Din,* hoping to produce and star in it.

Films include: 1951 When Worlds Collide; The Day the Earth Stood Still. '57 Johnny Trouble. '58 China Doll. '60 The Story of Ruth; Murder, Inc. '61 The Mark (GB). '62 The Longest Day. '64 Shock Treatment. '65 Those Magnificent Men in Their Flying Machines (GB). '77 Death Trap. '79 Key West Crossing. '80 Guyana, el Crimen del Siglo (MEX-SP-PAN) (USA: Guyana: Cult of the Damned; GB: Guyana – Crime of the Century). '81 The Monster Club (GB).

WHITMORE, James

(b. 1921). Actor. Born: White Plains, New York, USA

Whitmore was educated at Yale, saw service with the marines in World War II, and by the end of the Forties had appeared on Broadway and made his first film. His second, *Battleground,* brought him an Oscar nomination for Best Supporting Actor. Whitmore's thirty-odd years in the movies have seen him play very few leads, but he has proved a sterling character player, ruggedly sympathetic, careworn but durable. Memorable roles include his sad crook in *The Asphalt Jungle,* a veteran cop striving to pro-

tect his delinquent son in *Madigan,* and a dignified chimpanzee (President of the Assembly) in *Planet of the Apes.* With that last one behind him, Whitmore went on to play two real presidents, Truman in *Give 'Em Hell Harry!* and Theodore Roosevelt in *Bully.*

Films include: 1949 Battleground. '50 The Asphalt Jungle; The Next Voice You Hear. '53 Kiss Me Kate. '55 Oklahoma! '64 Black Like Me. '67 Planet of the Apes. '68 Madigan. '72 Chato's Land (GB). '75 Give 'Em Hell Harry! '77 Das Schlangenei (GER-USA) (GB: The Serpent's Egg). '78 Bully.

WHITTY, Dame May

(1865–1948). Actress. Born: Liverpool, England

May Whitty was the daughter of a journalist (editor of the *Liverpool Post*) and the wife of stage actor Ben Webster. She had a long and successful stage career in Britain and America, and in 1918 she was created Dame Commander of the British Empire. She made one or two silent films, but her film career proper did not start until she settled in Hollywood for the last twelve years of her life. With the outbreak of war she was often cast as the embodiment of English determination, but she was a versatile and spirited lady who always communicated the zest she brought to her characters. She won an Oscar nomination for her murder victim in *Night Must Fall;* returned to England to be the Lady who vanished for Hitchcock; was richly earthy as Napoleon's mother in *Conquest;* and enjoyed a ripe piece of villainy in *My Name Is Julia Ross.*

Films include: 1915 Enoch Arden. '37 Night Must Fall; Conquest/Marie Walewska. '38 The Lady Vanishes (GB). '41 Suspicion. '42 Mrs Miniver. '43 Flesh and Fantasy. '44 Madame Curie; Gaslight (GB: The Murder in Thornton Square). '45 My Name Is Julia Ross; Devotion. '47 If Winter Comes.

WICKES, Mary

(b. 1916). Actress. Born: Mary Wickenhauser; St Louis, Missouri, USA

An experienced stage player, she came into films in the early Forties, and scored an immediate hit as Monty Woolley's unfortunate nurse in *The Man Who Came to Dinner.* Wickes was tall, angular and determined, and could deliver a wisecrack with the best of them. She was far too often wasted in saccharine confections like *Good Morning, Miss Dove,* and even in her better movies her parts were smaller than one would have wished. Her brisk, no-nonsense approach, however, was always stimulating. Even when they made her a nun in the dire *The Trouble With Angels,* Wickes salvaged a line or two from the wreck.

Films include: 1941 The Man Who Came to Dinner. '42 Now, Voyager. '43 Higher and Higher. '49 Anna Lucasta. '51 On Moonlight Bay. '53 The Actress. '54 White Christmas. '55 Good Morning, Miss Dove. '60 Cimarron. '62 The Music Man. '65 How to Murder Your Wife. '66 The Trouble With Angels. '72 Snowball Express.

WICKI, Bernhard

(b. 1919). Actor/director. Born: St Pölten, Austria

Having attended various acting schools, Bernhard Wicki then went on to appear in over twenty films, but his roles did not satisfy him and his perfectionism pushed him into direction. He became an assistant to Helmut Käutner and made his first film *Warum sind sie gegen uns?*, a documentary, in 1958. As a director his work has been greatly influenced by the neo-realists Vittorio De Sica and Roberto Rossellini. Among Wicki's best-known films are *The Bridge*, which used inexperienced young actors in order to obtain spontaneous performances, and *The Miracle of Malachias*, for which he received the Best Director Award at the Berlin Film Festival.

Films as actor include: 1954 Die letzte Brücke (A-YUG) (GB: The Last Bridge). '55 Kinder. Mütter und ein General. '56 Tierarzt Dr Vlimmen, '57 Züricher Verlobung. '58 La Chatte (GB: The Face of the Cat). '59 Die Brücke (dir. only) (USA/GB: The Bridge). '61 La Notte (FR-IT) (GB: The Night); Das Wunder des Malachias (dir; +co-sc. only) (USA: The Miracle of Malachias). '62 The Longest Day (co-dir. only) (USA). '64 Der Besuch (dir. only) (GER-FR-IT) (USA/GB: The Visit). '65 The Saboteur – Code Name 'Morituri' (dir. only) (USA).

WIDERBERG, Bo

(b. 1930). Director. Born: Malmö, Sweden

Widerberg started his professional life as a novelist and film critic in the Fifties and made a big impact in 1962 with his abrasive assessment of the state of the Swedish film industry, *Visions in Swedish Film*. His directorial debut came the following year (after co-directing the short *Pojken och Draken* for television in 1961) and his first two full-length features, *The Pram* and *Raven's End*, both dealt with young people grappling with a realistic environment, marking a breakaway from the Bergman cult of screen allegories. Apparently committed to realism and social comment, Widerberg followed with two films in contemporary Swedish settings; but he then achieved international acclaim and commercial success with the fairytale-like *Elvira Madigan*, an account of a tragic love affair between a Swedish count and a tightrope walker, filmed in great splashes of Impressionistic colour. He returned to social themes with *Ådalen '31*, a reconstruction of an incident in 1931 when Swedish soldiers opened fire and killed strikers, and *Joe Hill*, a biography of the Swedish singer and songwriter who helped to found the International Workers of the World. In 1976 the thriller *The Man on the Roof* broke Swedish box-office records; *Victoria*, exquisitely filmed, returned to the tragic love-story format.

Films include: 1963 Barnvagnen (GB: The Pram). '64 Kvarteret Korpen (GB: Raven's End). '65 Kärlek 65 (GB: Love 65). '66 Heja Roland! (+ novel basis) (USA: Thirty Times Your Money). '67 Elvira Madigan. '69 Den Vita Sporten (doc) (co-dir) (GB: The White Sport); Ådalen 31. '71 Joe Hill (USA-SWED)

(GB: The Ballad of Joe Hill). '74 Fimpen (USA/GB: Stubby). '76 Mannen pa Taket (USA/GB: The Man on the Roof). '79 Victoria (SWED-GER).

WIDMARK, Richard

(b. 1914). Actor. Born: Sunrise, Minnesota, USA

Blond, wiry Richard Widmark grew up in Chicago and attended Lake Forest College, Illinois, where he subsequently taught speech and drama for two years before becoming a professional actor. Work in radio drama in New York led to his Broadway debut as juvenile lead in a comedy *Kiss and Tell*, and roles in some of Elia Kazan's stage productions followed. He made a big impact in 1947 with his first film *Kiss of Death*, in which he played the sadistic gangster Tommy Udo. This won him an Academy Award nomination, and established him as a Hollywood star. He followed it with a portrait of a crook abroad in the London underworld of Jules Dassin's *Night and the City*, and the doctor fighting bubonic plague in Kazan's *Panic in the Streets*. A succession of degenerate villains and neurotic heroes followed. After leaving Fox when his seven-year contract expired, he widened his range of roles and for the next twenty years he played a succession of starring parts in films such as John Wayne's *The Alamo*, John Ford's *Two Rode Together* and *Cheyenne Autumn* and Stanley Kramer's *Judgement at Nuremberg*, in which he played the prosecutor. He also branched out into production with *Time Limit*, a film about brainwashing in Korea. His portrayal of the brutal cop in *Madigan* led to a spin-off television series. Although working less in recent years, he continues to appear in cameo parts and television films. He is married to the screenwriter Jean Hazelwood.

Films include: 1947 Kiss of Death. '50 Night and the City (GB); Panic in the Streets; Halls of Montezuma. '53 Pickup on South Street. '54 Broken Lance. '55 The Cobweb. '56 The Last Wagon. '57 Time Limit (+prod). '58 The Tunnel of Love. '60 The Alamo. '61 Two Rode Together; Judgement at Nuremberg. '64 Cheyenne Autumn. '66 Alvarez Kelly. '68 Madigan. '74 Murder on the Orient Express (GB). '82 Who Dares Wins (GB).

WIENE, Robert

(1881–1938). Director. Born: Sachsen, Germany

Robert Wiene inherited *The Cabinet of Dr Caligari* from Fritz Lang. The script and the famous Expressionist designs were ready when *Die Spinnen* (1919, *The Spiders*) called Lang away, and Wiene, who had been directing for five years without making much impact, replaced him. But though Wiene was in no sense the film's creator, its impact on him was immense, and its traces can be seen in the best of his later work. *Genuine*, a lurid story of sadism and murder, has something of *Caligari*'s dreamlike spell. *Raskolnikow*, a version of *Crime and Punishment* with a cast of Russian exiles and sets by Andre Andreiev of *Die Dreigroschenoper* (1931, *The Threepenny Opera*) fame, steamrollers

Dostoyevsky's subtleties, but has breathtaking images. And *The Hands of Orlac* is both horror movie and Expressionist dance. Wiene had been a stage actor and director before coming to the cinema to direct Emil Jannings in *Arme Eva*. He was a prolific director, making about forty films, the great majority of little account, before the Nazis came to power and he took refuge in France. He died there in 1938 while working on *Ultimatum*, finished by Robert Siodmak.

Films include: 1914 Arme Eva (co-dir). '19 Das Kabinett des Dr Caligari (GB: The Cabinet of Dr Caligari). '20 Genuine. '23 INRI; Raskolnikow. '24 Orlacs Hände (A) (GB: The Hands of Orlac). '26 Die Königin vom Moulin-Rouge (A); Der Rosenkavalier (A). '30 Der Andere. '31 Panik in Chikago. '34 Eine Nacht in Venedig (GER-HUNG). '38 Ultimatum (co-dir) (FR).

WILCOX, Herbert

(1890–1977). Producer/director. Born: Cork, Ireland

After World War I service in the RFC, Wilcox was a film salesman, distributor and, by 1922, producer. After an initial failure with the offbeat *The Wonderful Story*, he changed tack, imported American stars (including Mae Marsh and Dorothy Gish) and concentrated on pleasant entertainment. Wilcox flourished; he founded British National and built Elstree. Ousted from British National, he formed British and Dominions, which enjoyed extraordinary success. In 1932 Wilcox made his first film with Anna Neagle. They went on to make over thirty together, and became a British institution. They married in 1943, and were inseparable. Neagle made only two films, after 1932, not directed by her husband. The Wilcox–Neagle films were varied in quality. *Nell Gwyn* and *Peg of Old Drury* were lively period romps; the Queen Victoria films were tasteful, worthy and dull; the 'London series' of the Forties agreeable and undemanding. Perhaps Wilcox should have directed less; he was an imaginative producer and a daring entrepreneur, but a moderate director.

Films include: 1922 The Wonderful Story (prod). '23 Paddy the Next Best Thing (prod). '28 Dawn (dir; +prod). '30 Rookery Nook (prod) (USA: One Embarrassing Night). '32 The Little Damozel (dir; +prod). '34 Nell Gwyn (dir; +prod). '35 Peg of Old Drury (dir+prod). '37 Victoria the Great (dir+prod). '40 Irene (dir; +prod) (USA). '45 I Live in Grosvenor Square (dir; +prod). '48 Spring in Park Lane (dir; +prod). '50 Odette (dir; +prod). '55 King's Rhapsody (dir; +prod). '59 The Lady Is a Square (dir; +co-prod).

WILCOXON, Henry

(1905–1984). Actor/producer. Born: Dominica, West Indies

Brought up in the West Indies, Henry Wilcoxon went to England when he was 16 and became a stage actor, first at the Birmingham Repertory Theatre and later on the London stage; his screen debut came in 1931 with *The Perfect Lady*. His tall, rugged good looks caught the attention of Cecil B.

Above: Bernhard Wicki in Die gläserne Zelle (1978). Right: Gene Wilder as a modern-day fairytale magician in Willy Wonka and the Chocolate Factory. Below: Billy Wilder directing his barbed tribute to film-making, Fedora, in 1977

DeMille, who cast him as Marc Antony in the Hollywood production of *Cleopatra*. He remained in the USA and became a naturalized citizen, enlisting in the navy during World War II, after boosting the British in *Mrs Miniver*. His association with DeMille continued after the war, and he was associate producer on *The Greatest Show on Earth* and *The Ten Commandments*, and producer for *The Buccaneer*. His marriage to actress Joan Woodbury ended in divorce.

Films as actor include: 1931 The Perfect Lady (GB). '32 The Flying Squad (GB). '34 Cleopatra. '35 The Crusades. '36 The Last of the Mohicans. '39 Tarzan Finds a Son. '41 That Hamilton Woman (GB: Lady Hamilton). '42 Mrs Miniver. '49 Samson and Delilah; A Connecticut Yankee in King Arthur's Court/Connecticut Yankee (GB: A Yankee in King Arthur's Court). '51 The Greatest Show on Earth (+assoc. prod). '56 The Ten Commandments (+assoc. prod). '58 The Buccaneer (prod. only).

WILDE, Cornel

(b. 1915). Actor. Born: Cornelius Louis Wilde; New York City, USA

Cornel Wilde first intended to become a doctor but became increasingly

interested in acting and started his career in supporting roles on stage in stock theatre and in New York. His good looks, muscular physique and fencing skill won him the role of Tybalt and job of fencing instructor on Olivier's production of *Romeo and Juliet* on Broadway in 1940, and this led to a contract with Warner Brothers. After a series of swashbuckling roles in B movies with both Warners and Fox, he achieved stardom as Chopin in *A Song to Remember*, for which he received an Oscar nomination, and this led to better roles. In 1955 he formed his own production company to make action-packed adventure films, including *The Naked Prey*. After his marriage to actress Patricia Knight ended in divorce, he married actress Jean Wallace, who co-starred with him in many of his own productions.

Films include: 1940 The Lady With Red Hair. '41 High Sierra. '45 A Song to Remember; A Thousand and One Nights. '46 The Bandit of Sherwood Forest. '47 It Had to Be You. '51 The Greatest Show on Earth. '57 Beyond Mombasa; Omar Khayyam (GB). '65 The Naked Prey (+dir) (USA-SA). '69 The Comic. '79 Behind the Iron Mask/The Fifth Musketeer (A-GB).

WILDER, Billy

(b. 1906). Director. Born: Samuel Wilder; Vienna, Austria

A journalist in Vienna and Berlin, Wilder entered films in 1929, when he worked on the script of Edgar G. Ulmer and Robert Siodmak's *Menschen am Sonntag* (1929, *People on Sunday*). He co-wrote a number of German films, until his forced departure in 1933. Wilder was a Jew, and many of his family died in the camps. After directing one film in France, he reached Hollywood, and by the end of the Thirties, in collaboration with Charles Brackett, had written such comedy classics as *Midnight* and *Ninotchka* (both 1939). In 1942 Wilder directed his first American film. The partnership with Brackett lasted until 1950; they scripted together, Brackett produced, Wilder directed. In 1957 the second crucial partnership began, between Wilder and the Romanian-born writer I. A. L. Diamond; it has endured until the present day. Wilder's work has included crime thrillers, romantic comedies, black comedies, films of social crusading, studies of human eccentricity. It has engendered much controversy. Many

of his films were accused of tastelessness when they first appeared; these same films are now attacked for their lurking sentimentality. Both charges have some foundation, but neither has much relevance to Wilder's best work. *Double Indemnity* makes no concessions to comfort; *The Apartment* is a painful admission of selfishness and venality; *Sunset Boulevard* does not diminish Swanson or Stroheim. And Wilder has achieved a marvellous serenity with age. In his middle sixties he could devise the radiant comedy of *Avanti!*, and in *Fedora*, made when he was over 70, he could view the ravages of time without regret. Wilder won Best Director Oscars for *The Lost Weekend* and *The Apartment*, and each was also named Best Film. He also shared Best Screenplay awards for *Sunset Boulevard* and *The Apartment*.

Films include: 1933 Mauvaise Graine (co-dir) (FR). '42 The Major and the Minor. '43 Five Graves to Cairo. '44 Double Indemnity. 45 The Lost Weekend. '50 Sunset Boulevard. '51 Ace in the Hole/The Big Carnival. '53 Stalag 17. '54 Sabrina (GB: Sabrina Fair). '55 The Seven Year Itch. '57 Witness for the Prosecution. '59 Some Like It Hot. '60 The Apartment. '61 One, Two, Three. '63 Irma La Douce. '66 The Fortune Cookie (GB: Meet Whiplash Willie). '70 The Private Life of Sherlock Holmes (GB). '72 Avanti! '74 The Front Page. '78 Fedora (GER). '81 Buddy, Buddy.

WILDER, Gene

(b. 1934). Actor. Born: Gerald Silberman; Milwaukee, Wisconsin, USA

The son of a Russian peasant who had emigrated to the USA at the age of 11

and founded a successful bottle-making plant, Wilder studied acting in his home town of Milwaukee and at the University of Iowa, and in 1956 went to England to complete his training at the Bristol Old Vic. Finding the traditional techniques used there uncongenial, he returned to New York and spent four years at Lee Strasberg's Actors' Studio. He met Mel Brooks through a mutual friend, Anne Bancroft, while appearing in *Mother Courage* in New York, and enthusiastically agreed to play a part in the film he was trying to get off the ground, called *Springtime for Hitler*. Three years later, when Brooks eventually made the film (as *The Producers*), Wilder had already made an impressive screen debut as the frightened young undertaker taken for a ride by *Bonnie and Clyde*. Though it was with Brooks that he established his reputation as a frenetic, uncontrollable comic, his talents have been well used in other films – most notably in Woody Allen's *Everything You Always Wanted To Know About Sex, But Were Afraid to Ask* as a doctor in love with his patient's pet sheep. In 1975 he began directing his own films.

Films include: 1967 Bonnie and Clyde; The Producers. '70 Quackser Fortune Has a Cousin in the Bronx. '71 Willy Wonka and the Chocolate Factory. '72 Everything You Always Wanted to Know About Sex, But Were Afraid to Ask. '74 Blazing Saddles; Young Frankenstein; The Little Prince (GB). '75 The Adventure of Sherlock Holmes' Smarter Brother (+dir; +sc) (GB). '76 Silver Streak. '77 The World's Greatest Lover (+dir; +prod; +sc). '80 Stir Crazy.

WILDING, Michael

(1912–1979). Actor. Born: Westcliff-on-Sea, Essex, England

Michael Wilding was the first to admit his own limitations as an actor: 'I was the worst actor I ever came across with no talent at all except perhaps a penchant for mimicry.' But his good looks and debonair charm won him a devoted following in British films of the Forties, and in 1949 he was voted Britain's most popular male star. After spending his early childhood in Russia, where his father worked as a linguist for British Military Intelligence, he was educated at Christ's Hospital Blue Coat School, and at 17 embarked on a career as an artist. He discovered he had a facility for acting and made his debut in the Austrian film *Pastorale* in 1933. After gaining experience acting with theatre repertory companies he returned to films in the early Forties and shot to stardom partnering Anna Neagle in a series of escapist extravaganzas set among the upper classes. An extremely handsome, charming man, he was married four times, to actresses Kay Young, Elizabeth Taylor and Margaret Leighton, and to American heiress Susan Neil.

Films include: 1933 Pastorale (A). '40 Tilly of Bloomsbury. '41 Kipps. '52 In Which We Serve. '43 Dear Octopus (USA: The Randolph Family). '46 Piccadilly Incident. '47 The Courtneys of Curzon Street; An Ideal Husband. '48 Spring in Park Lane. '49 Under Capricorn; Maytime in Mayfair; Stage Fright. '52 Derby Day. '61 The Naked Edge. '70 Waterloo (IT-USSR).

WILLIAM, Warren

(1895–1948). Actor. Born: Warren Krech; Aitkin, Minnesota, USA

Warren William's father was a newspaper publisher, and his son worked briefly for him as a reporter, but after World War I service he turned to the stage and trained at the American Academy of Dramatic Arts. In the Twenties he was successful on Broadway, and under his real name appeared in a few silent films, playing the lead in Fox's *The Town That Forgot God* in 1922. From 1931 until his death he concentrated on films. A tall, elegant, smoothly spoken and dominating actor, he played lawyers, detectives, gentlemanly kinds of crooks and, although largely confined to B movies, he was working in a day when B movies could be very good. He was a convincing Caesar in DeMille's *Cleopatra*, and a notable hero of crime series, doing his stint as Perry Mason, Philo Vance, and the Lone Wolf. He was superb as Dick Powell's prim brother in *Gold Diggers of 1933*, keeping his dignity as his world crumbled, and showing a talent for comedy too often concealed.

Films include: 1923 Plunder (serial). '32 The Mouthpiece; The Dark Horse; Three on a Match. '33 Gold Diggers of 1933; Lady for a Day. '34 Cleopatra; The Case of the Howling Dog. '36 Satan Met a Lady. '38 Arsène Lupin Returns. '39 The Lone Wolf Spy Hunt (GB: The Lone Wolf's Daughter). '46 Fear. '47 The Private Affairs of Bel Ami.

WILLIAMS, Billy Dee

(b. 1937). Actor. Born: New York City, USA

Born into a musical family in Harlem, Williams made his stage debut at the age of nine in *The Firebrand of Florence* but preferred painting to acting and won a scholarship to the National Academy of Fine Art and Design. His interest in acting was revived when he worked as an extra in television shows to supplement his grant and he began studying drama under Sidney Poitier. After making a film debut in 1959 he worked mainly in the theatre (notably in *A Taste of Honey*) and television (*The FBI, The Interns, Mission Impossible, The Mod Squad, Brian's*

Song) before going on to big-screen success as Diana Ross's leading man in *Lady Sings the Blues*. Since then he has played a barnstorming baseball player in *The Bingo Long Traveling All-Stars and Motor Kings*, and impersonated the 'King of Ragtime' in *Scott Joplin*, but is probably best known for his portrayal of the tough, flamboyant boss of a mining colony, Lando Calrissian, in *The Empire Strikes Back*.

Films include: 1959 The Last Angry Man. '70 The Out-of-Towners. '71 Lost Flight. '72 Lady Sings the Blues; The Final Comedown. '74 The Take. '75 Mahogany. '76 The Bingo Long Traveling All-Stars and Motor Kings. '77 Scott Joplin. '80 The Hostage Tower; The Empire Strikes Back. '81 Nighthawks.

WILLIAMS, Cindy

(b. 1947). Actress. Born: Van Nuys, California, USA

Cindy Williams rose to prominence as Laurie, Ron Howard's cheerleader steady girlfriend, in *American Graffiti*, and has become one of America's top television stars through her role as Shirley in the immensely popular series *Laverne and Shirley*. She spent her childhood in Irving, Texas, and after acting in school plays enrolled in the theatre arts department of Los Angeles City College. She obtained small parts in television and made her film debut in Corman's *Gas-s-s-s*.

Films include: 1970 Gas-s-s-s, or It Became Necessary to Destroy the World in Order to Save It. '71 Drive, He Said. '72 Travels With My Aunt. '73 American Graffiti; The Killing Kind. '74 The Conversation. '75 Mr Ricco. '76 The First Nudie Musical. '79 More American Graffiti (GB: Purple Haze).

WILLIAMS, Elmo

(b.1913). Executive producer/editor/director. Born: Lone Wolf, Oklahoma, USA

Williams' varied career has encompassed work as a film editor, director and producer. Editing British films distributed by Paramount in the Thirties, he returned to America in 1938 and after working at RKO and on government films with Frank Capra during the war, set up his own production unit to make television programmes. Despite winning an Emmy for his Regal Pale Beer commercial, the business fared badly and during the Fifties he again worked as editor – winning an Oscar for his work on *High Noon* (1952) – and made his directorial debut with another Western *The Tall Texan* in 1953. As a producer he was given charge of 20th Century-Fox's British operations in the late Sixties. After producing *Tora! Tora! Tora!* he became worldwide head of production for Fox. In 1973 he went independent, forming Ibex Productions, supported by Iranian funds. When this collapsed after the fall of

the Shah, he founded Gaylord Productions in 1980.

Films as producer include: 1953 The Tall Texan (dir. only). '54 The Cowboy (doc) (+dir). '57 Apache Warrior (dir. only); Hell Ship Mutiny (co-dir. only). '66 The Blue Max (exec. prod) (GB). '70 Tora! Tora! Tora! (USA-JAP). '77 Sidewinder One. '78 Caravans (IRAN-USA).

WILLIAMS, Emlyn

(b. 1905). Actor/playwright/screenwriter/director. Born: Mostyn, Flint, Wales

Though he was from a poor North Wales family, intelligence, application and parental encouragement enabled Emlyn Williams to win scholarships to Holywell County School and Christ Church, Oxford. After taking part in many productions of the Oxford University Dramatic Society he made his stage debut in *And So to Bed* and a year later acted in his own play *Glamour*. By the early Thirties he had become a successful and prolific actor and playwright, and after making an impressive debut as Lord Lebanon in *The Frightened Lady* appeared regularly in British films, often as a smoothly obnoxious charmer and swindler. In 1949, paying homage to his Welsh roots, he wrote, directed and acted in *The Last Days of Dolwyn*. His most successful play, *Night Must Fall*, has been twice filmed with Robert Mont-

Far left: Warren William in Smarty *(1934). Centre left: Billy Dee Williams in* Mahogany. *Left: Cindy Williams in* Travels With My Aunt. *Below, far left: Emlyn Williams in* Major Barbara. *Below left: Kathlyn Williams in* Romance of the Sahara *(1920). Below: MGM's swimming star Esther Williams. Right: Treat Williams in* Prince of the City

Andy Hardy's Double Life. Several small parts followed, each with the obligatory swimming sequence, until her flair for music and comedy finally won her star billing with *Fiesta.* Her subsequent films, notably the aptly-named *Million Dollar Mermaid*, consolidated her popularity and boasted characteristically lavish and colourful underwater ballet sequences. By the early Fifties, however, the public taste for musicals was beginning to fade. Williams attempted, unsuccessfully, to move into straight acting, and virtually retired from films shortly after. With her third husband, actor Fernando Lamas, she has spent her time teaching swimming to handicapped children.

Films include: 1942 Andy Hardy's Double Life. '**44** Bathing Beauty. '**46** Ziegfeld Follies; The Hoodlum Saint; Easy to Wed. '**47** Fiesta. '**48** On an Island With You. '**49** Take Me Out to the Ball Game (GB: Everybody's Cheering); Neptune's Daughter. '**50** Duchess of Idahoe; Pagan Love Song. '**52** Million Dollar Mermaid. '**53** Dangerous When Wet.

WILLIAMS, John

(b. 1932). Composer. Born: Long Island, New York, USA

John Williams was one of the most successful movie soundtrack composers of the Seventies, happiest when creating the stirring, sweeping musical drama to accompany some of the biggest films of the decade: *The Towering Inferno, Star Wars, Close Encounters of The Third Kind, The Empire Strikes Back, Superman, The Movie* and *Superman II.* He was educated at UCLA and the Juilliard School of Music, and shifted away from an early career as a jazz pianist and recording artist in favour of first television and then films in the early Sixties. He has won Academy Awards for *Fiddler on The Roof, Jaws* and *Star Wars*; and the success of *Star Wars* made him one of the few film composers since the Forties to become a household name.

Films include: 1960 I Passed for White. '**66** How to Steal a Million. '**69** Goodbye, Mr Chips (GB). '**71** Jane Eyre (GB); Fiddler on the Roof. '**74** The Towering Inferno; Earthquake. '**75** Jaws. '**77** Close Encounters of the Third Kind; Star Wars. '**78** Superman, The Movie; The Fury. '**80** The Empire Strikes Back; Superman II.

WILLIAMS, Kathlyn

(1888–1960). Actress. Born: Butte, Montana, USA

Kathlyn Williams was the star of America's first serial. After stage experience and a brief spell at Biograph, she joined the Selig Company in Chicago in 1910, billed as 'The Selig Girl' in the days when real names were rarely made public. She appeared in many animal films, a Selig speciality, and in Westerns with Tom Mix. In 1913 came the serial, *The Adventures of Kathlyn*, with more wild animals, and the following year she starred in an elaborate nine-reel version of *The Spoilers.* Kathlyn Williams was a dignified, gentle lady, hard to picture as a serial queen, and she may have been happier when she moved on to Paramount and romantic dramas. Through the Twenties she played important parts in major films, and made occasional cameo appearances until the Forties. *Conrad in Quest of His Youth* gives a rare chance to judge her quality; as a middle-aged woman renouncing a younger lover, she acts with conviction and a most moving restraint.

Films include: 1910 The Fire Chief's Daughter. '**11** The Two Orphans. '**13** The Adventures of Kathlyn (serial); The Love of Penelope. '**14** The Spoilers. '**20** Conrad in Quest of His Youth. '**23** The Spanish Dancer. '**24** Wanderer of the Wasteland. '**28** Our Dancing Daughters. '**29** The Single Standard. '**33** Blood Money. '**47** The Other Love.

WILLIAMS, Richard

(b. 1933). Animator. Born: Toronto, Ontario, Canada

Interested in drawing from the age of two, Williams carefully cultivated his talents and after three years at Ontario College of Art joined the Disney Studio in Burbank. His experience there very much affected his own style of animation, but he found insufficient expression for his creative talents and after leaving came to England in 1955. Finding employment with George Dunning's TV Cartoons, he worked on television commercials by day, and toiled on his own film, *The Little Island*, by night. Taking careful note that it was more successful with the critics than at the box office, he applied a more commercial formula to his next important film *Love Me, Love Me, Love Me*, and earned enough money from it to establish his own studio – Richard Williams Animation. This has been highly successful in producing commercials and title credit sequences, most notably for *What's New, Pussycat?* (1965), *Casino Royale* (1967) and *Charge of the Light Brigade* (1968) – as well as major animation films such as *A Christmas Carol* and *Raggedy Ann and Andy.*

Films include: 1958 The Little Island; The Story of the Motor-Car Engine (+ co-dir). '**62** A Lecture on Man; Love Me, Love Me, Love Me. '**63** Circus Drawings (unfinished). '**65** The Dermis Probe. '**72** A Christmas Carol (USA). '**77** Raggedy Ann and Andy (USA). '**81** The Thief Who Gave Up/The Thief and the Cobbler/Nasruddin (work in progress).

WILLIAMS, Tennessee

(1911–1983). Playwright/screenwriter. Born: Thomas Lanier Williams; Columbus, Missouri, USA

The son of a shoe salesman and a Southern belle, Williams survived a bad bout of diphtheria and at the age of 14 won a prize for an essay on the subject 'Can a Good Wife Be a Good Sport?' After three years at the University of Missouri he was dragooned into the shoe industry by his father but following a nervous breakdown committed himself firmly to writing. His play *Battle of the Angels* was staged by the Theatre Guild in New York and proved a resounding flop, but it did lead to him acquiring a dedicated and assertive agent (Audrey Wood) who managed to get him a six-month scriptwriting contract with MGM. Though none of his work was used it gave him the opportunity to write his semi-autobiographical play *The Glass Menagerie*. Its production on Broadway in 1945 carried Williams to the forefront of American playwrights and was the first of a string of spectacular successes – *A Streetcar Named Desire, The Rose Tattoo, Suddenly, Last Summer, Cat on a Hot Tin Roof, The Night of the Iguana* – many of which Williams himself turned into film scripts.

Films include: 1950 The Glass Menagerie (co-sc. from own play). '**51** A Streetcar Named Desire (from own play). '**55** The Rose Tattoo (from own play). '**56** Baby Doll (play basis only). '**58** Cat on a Hot Tin Roof (play basis only). '**59** Suddenly, Last Summer (co-sc. from own play) (GB). '**60** The Fugitive Kind (co-sc. from own play). '**61** The Roman Spring of Mrs Stone (novel basis only) (GB). '**62** Sweet Bird of Youth (play basis only). '**64** The Night of the Iguana (play basis only). '**68** Boom! (from own play) (GB). '**69** The Last of the Mobile Hotshots (play basis only).

WILLIAMS, Treat

(b. 1948). Actor. Born: Rowayston, Connecticut, USA

Big, thick-set and not particularly handsome, Williams initially seemed more at home as an athlete than as an actor. Bravely discarding his macho image he began playing Shakespeare with the Fulton Repertory Company in Pennsylvania during college vacations and showed sufficient promise to go straight into understudying the lead part, Danny Zuko, in the Broadway production of *Grease.* After making his film debut as a naive detective investigating goings-on in a sleazy, gay bath-house in *The Ritz*, he played the US Army captain who foils the machiavellian attempt to kidnap Churchill in *The Eagle Has Landed* and landed the starring role of Berger, the hippie who dances on the tables and swings from the chandelier in Miloš Forman's *Hair.* After that vital if rather shallow role, he gave a virtuoso performance as Danny Cielo, the conscience-ridden New York cop who attempts to fight police corruption without betraying his friends in *Prince of the City.*

Films include: 1976 The Ritz; Deadly Hero; The Eagle Has Landed. '**79** Hair. '**80** Why Should I Lie? '**81** Prince of the City; The Pursuit of D. B. Cooper.

gomery in 1937 and Albert Finney in 1964 playing the role of the fatally charming psychopath who carries around the head of one of his victims in a hat box.

Films as actor include: 1932 The Frightened Lady. '**33** Friday the 13th. '**39** Jamaica Inn. '**41** Major Barbara. '**49** The Last Days of Dolwyn (+ dir) (USA: Woman of Dolwyn). '**50** Three Husbands (USA). '**51** The Scarf (USA). '**52** Ivanhoe. '**62** The L-Shaped Room. '**69** David Copperfield. '**70** The Walking Stick.

WILLIAMS, Esther

(b. 1923). Actress. Born: Los Angeles, California, USA

'I'm a swimmer, not an actress' might seem an unusual comment from a lady who was one of MGM's most popular stars in the late Forties, but then Esther Williams' talent was unusual. She had taken to water like the proverbial fish as a child, and by the age of 15 had won all the major American swimming championships. She was all set to enter the Olympics but World War II intervened, and she went instead to the University of Southern California. While there she was talked into taking part – along with Johnny Weissmuller – in the Aquacade at the San Francisco Exposition. She was spotted by MGM talent scouts, and made her movie debut opposite Mickey Rooney in

WILLIAMSON, Nicol

(b. 1938). Actor. Born: Hamilton, Lanark, Scotland

Williamson moved to films after notching up a considerable reputation as a stage actor. He began by working with the Dundee Repertory Company, graduated to the Royal Court and the Royal Shakespeare Company, and won a Tony Award for his part in the Broadway production of *Inadmissible Evidence*, which subsequently became his first film role. A powerful presence, he specializes in playing intense, aggressive characters – 'bulls in china shops', as one critic put it. He was the sadistic soldier tormenting his superior in *The Bofors Gun*, and the bullying Afrikaaner security-man in the racial thriller set in South Africa, *The Wilby Conspiracy*. He is also admired in the classics – his *Hamlet* led to an invitation to perform at the White House; and, as proof of his range, he was a sympathetic Sherlock Holmes in *The Seven-Per-Cent Solution*. Since then his film roles have become somewhat eccentric, notably his Merlin in *Excalibur*.

Films include: 1968 Inadmissible Evidence; The Bofors Gun. '69 Laughter in the Dark (GB-FR); Hamlet; The Reckoning. '73 Le Moine (FR-IT-GER) (GB: The Monk). '75 The Wilby Conspiracy (USA). '76 Robin and Marian (USA); The Seven-Per-Cent Solution (USA). '77 The Goodbye Girl (USA). '78 The Cheap Detective (USA). '81 Excalibur (EIRE-USA).

WILLS, Chill

(1903–1978). Actor. Born: Seagoville, Texas, USA

Pick a John Wayne Western that features a grumbling older buddy and the chances are he was played by one of three actors: Walter Brennan, Andy Devine or Chill Wills. Wills grew up in a vaudeville background, travelling the South-west's theatres from childhood. In the early Thirties he formed a singing group, Chill Wills and the Avalon Boys, and their appearance in several Westerns introduced Wills to a career which was to survive long after the group broke up in 1938. Much sought-after as a character support, he continued working until a year before his death. His credits include *Billy the Kid* and *The Alamo* – for which he won an

Oscar nomination as Best Supporting Actor – and his distinctive gravelly voice was used by Francis the Talking Mule.

Films include: 1937 Way Out West. '41 Billy the Kid. '44 Meet Me in St Louis. '45 Leave Her to Heaven. '49 Francis (voice only). '56 Giant. '60 The Alamo. '63 McLintock!; The Cardinal. '70 The Liberation of L. B. Jones. '73 Pat Garrett and Billy the Kid.

WILSON, Michael

(1914–1978). Screenwriter. Born: McAlester, Oklahoma, USA

Michael Wilson began his career as a writer of short stories and taught to supplement his somewhat precarious income. After three years in the marines he went to Hollywood in 1940 where he wrote many a Western for William Boyd before World War II service suspended his artistic activities. On his return he began to work on more prestigious films and in 1951 shared the Oscar for Writing (Screenplay) for his work on *A Place in the Sun*, a tangled web of love, deception and tragedy. Unhappily his triumphant progress abruptly halted that same year with his blacklisting by the industry for failing to affirm or deny his rumoured associations with the Communist Party before the House UnAmerican Activities Committee. He was then barred from employment by the major studios but did manage to work on an independent film – namely Herbert Biberman's *Salt of the Earth* – and some major productions without credit (*Friendly Persuasion, The Bridge on the River Kwai, Lawrence of Arabia*). Only in the Sixties was he able to resume working under his own name.

Films include: 1943 Border Patrol. '51 A Place in the Sun. '52 Five Fingers. '54 Salt of the Earth. '56 Friendly Persuasion (uncredited). '57 The Bridge on the River Kwai (co-sc. uncredited). '62 Lawrence of Arabia (co-sc. uncredited). '65 The Sandpiper. '67 Planet of the Apes. '69 Che! (co-sc).

WINDSOR, Marie

(b. 1922). Actress. Born: Emily Marie Bertelson; Marysvale, Utah, USA

Marie Windsor was once acutely described as 'looking like Loretta Young

with touches of Edmond O'Brien'. She was darkly and silkily beautiful (a one-time Miss Utah, before radio, television and training from Maria Ouspenskaya took her into the movies), but until she mellowed in the Sixties she was a tough and lethal lady, and one of the glories of Fifties thrillers. She made an early mark as the racketeer's sultry wife in *Force of Evil*, and went on to drive many a good man to distraction and worse. Two Windsor girls are unforgettable. In *The Killing* she was Elisha Cook's vicious, greedy wife, and sent the little man to a very messy end, while in *The Narrow Margin* her gangster's moll turned out to be a gallant policewoman. Audiences who thought they knew their Windsor had the shock of their lives.

Films include: 1947 Song of the Thin Man. '49 Force of Evil. '52 The Narrow Margin; The Sniper. '56 The Killing. '57 The Unholy Wife; The Girl in Black Stockings. '63 Critic's Choice. '64 Bedtime Story. '71 Support Your Local Gunfighter. '73 The Outfit. '75 Hearts of the West (GB: Hollywood Cowboy). '76 Freaky Friday.

WINKLER, Henry

(b. 1945). Actor. Born: New York City, USA

Henry Winkler's on-screen performances might be few, but already he's created a reputation that will be hard to shake off; to a generation of Seventies television viewers he will forever be Arthur Fonzerelli, the Fonz himself, super-cool hero of the nostalgic high-school comedy series, *Happy Days*, a role not dissimilar to the one he played in *The Lords of Flatbush* (co-starring Sylvester Stallone). The son of a lumber merchant, Winkler attended Emerson College and Yale Drama School. He worked with stock companies and had several minor stage roles before the Fonz launched him to tremendous popularity. So far he seems uncertain of how to proceed, his film parts being few and largely undistinguished. Only *The One and Only*, in which he played a flamboyant wrestling star, aroused any interest.

Films include: 1974 The Lords of Flatbush; Crazy Joe (USA-FR). '77 Heroes. '78 The One and Only. '82 Night Shift.

WINNER, Michael

(b. 1935). Director. Born: London, England

Michael Winner's films are not to everyone's taste. He has been consistently panned by the critics for his gimmicky style and unashamedly exploitative content. Yet the phenomenal success of *Death Wish*, a thriller in which a victim of tragic crimes pursues a bloody revenge, demonstrates, if nothing else, a keen appreciation of public tastes and moods. Educated in law at Cambridge, Winner became involved in the movie industry at an early age, writing film reviews while in his teens. In the Fifties he went to work for the BBC, making television features, and his big-screen debut followed with *Climb Up the Wall* (1960). He has always had an eye for commercial subjects – or trendy settings, as witness his several Swinging Sixties movies – and excels with tough thrillers or brutal Westerns, like *Lawman* or *Chato's Land*. He works frequently with granite-faced hard-man actor Charles Bronson, and in many ways their styles are complementary – terse, fast-moving, violent, strong on action, short on words.

Films include: 1961 Some Like It Cool. '65 You Must Be Joking. '67 I'll Never Forget What's-'is-Name. '71 The Nightcomers; Lawman (USA). '72 Scorpio (USA); Chato's Land; The Mechanic (USA) (GB: Killer of Killers). '74 Death Wish (USA). '77 The Sentinel (USA). '78 The Big Sleep. '79 Firepower. '82 Death Wish II (USA). '83 The Wicked Lady.

WINNINGER, Charles

(1884–1969). Actor. Born: Athens, Wisconsin, USA

After half a lifetime of hard work, one part, which he played on stage and screen, made Winninger famous. He had been in vaudeville as a child, and made his way up through stock companies to Broadway, the Ziegfeld Follies, and in 1927 to the original production of *Show Boat*, in which he

Dwan's The Inside Story *(1948), set in the Depression; Shelley Winters at her blowsy best in the private-eye thriller* Harper; *Norman Wisdom finding* Trouble in Store, *the film that made him a star; Joseph Wiseman in the Mafia thriller* The Valachi Papers *(1972), directed by Terence Young*

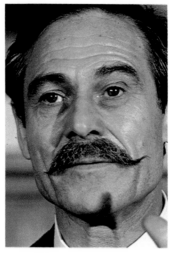

played Cap'n Andy. In the cinema he had been in silent slapstick shorts and a few features, and then, in 1936, repeated his role in the second (and classic) film of *Show Boat*. Twenty years as a character actor followed. Short and tubby, genial and supremely decent, Winninger stood for old-fashioned values in a changing world; and that was what he symbolized when he played his finest part, that of the brave little judge, Billy Priest, in John Ford's *The Sun Shines Bright*.

Films include: 1924 Pied Piper Malone. '26 Summer Bachelors. '31 Bad Sister; Night Nurse. '36 Show Boat. '37 Three Smart Girls; Nothing Sacred. '39 Destry Rides Again. '41 Ziegfeld Girl. '43 Flesh and Fantasy. '45 State Fair. '53 The Sun Shines Bright. '60 Raymie.

WINTERS, Shelley

(b. 1922). Actress. Born: Shirley Schrift; East St Louis, Illinois, USA

Shelley Winters was brought up in Brooklyn, and played in summer stock while still at high school. She worked hard at her profession, studying under Elia Kazan at the Actors' Studio, and with Charles Laughton and Michael Chekhov in Hollywood. On Broadway she was in *Oklahoma!* and *A Streetcar Named Desire*; in the cinema she began in 1943, but had little real chance until in *A Double Life* (1948) she made a vivid impression as the little waitress strangled by Ronald Colman's deranged actor. The best of Winters' early roles always betrayed a touching vulnerability. In *A Place in the Sun* she was unforgettable as another born victim, the factory girl drowned by her lover, while in *The Night of the Hunter* she posed for one of the cinema's most bizarre images, sitting in a sunken car, her throat cut and her hair waving in the current. She went back in the mid-Fifties to the stage. When she returned, it was to play matronly roles. She was plump, warm, often rowdy, and no longer a victim. She won two Best Supporting

Actress Oscars, for *The Diary of Anne Frank* and *A Patch of Blue* (1965), and was joyously unrestrained in *Lolita*, *Harper* and many more. Two of Winters' three marriages were to actors – Vittorio Gassmann and Anthony Franciosa.

Films include: 1948 Red River; Cry of the City. '49 The Great Gatsby. '51 A Place in the Sun. '54 Executive Suite. '55 The Night of the Hunter; I Died a Thousand Times. '59 The Diary of Anne Frank. '62 Lolita. '63 The Balcony. '66 Harper (GB: The Moving Target). '68 The Scalphunters. '70 Bloody Mama. '72 The Poseidon Adventure. '76 Next Stop, Greenwich Village.

WISDOM, Norman

(b. 1920). Actor. Born: London, England

Wisdom left school at 14 and after a few odd jobs joined the army as a band boy. He made his first stage appearance at Collins' Music Hall in Islington in 1946 and two years later acted in a minor screen comedy *A Date With a Dream*. He soon became well known on television and in 1953 starred in his first film vehicle, *Trouble in Store*, playing an incompetent department-store floorwalker. Well-meaning little Norman, with his boyish face, infectious laugh, twisted cap, impossible suit and appalling clumsiness, then became Britain's biggest comedy star, averaging one film a year for Rank until the mid-Sixties. His films, full of slapstick and pathos, generally cast him as the kind-hearted underdog who comes up trumps and wins the initially disdainful girl; the early pictures were directed by John Paddy Carstairs and Wisdom was usually partnered with irascible, supercilious Jerry Desmonde or down-to-earth Northerner Edward Chapman. In 1968 Wisdom gave a fine performance as a burlesque performer in the Hollywood film *The Night They Raided Minsky's*. He has also worked on Broadway (earning a Tony nomination for *Walking Happy*), had his own show in the West End and his own television series. He gave a harrowing straight performance as a man dying in hospital in the television play *Going Gently*.

Films: 1948 A Date With a Dream. '53 Trouble in Store. '54 One Good Turn. '55 As Long as They're Happy (uncredited guest);

Man of the Moment. '56 Up in the World. '57 Just My Luck. '58 The Square Peg. '59 Follow a Star. '60 There Was a Crooked Man; The Bulldog Breed. '61 The Girl on the Boat. '62 On the Beat. '63 A Stitch in Time. '65 The Early Bird. '66 The Sandwich Man; Press for Time. '68 The Night They Raided Minsky's (USA). '69 What's Good for the Goose.

WISE, Robert

(b. 1914). Director. Born: Winchester, Indiana, USA

Forced by family hardship to drop out of college, Wise took a menial job at RKO, where his brother David was an accountant. He soon became a sound-effects cutter, assistant editor and editor, and in that capacity worked with Welles on *Citizen Kane* (1940) and *The Magnificent Ambersons* (1942). Wise has been bitterly, and perhaps unfairly, attacked for mutilating the latter. He was faced with an impossible task when Welles left for a wartime assignment with the film unfinished, and the fact that the film's stature increases with the years shows how well he managed. One scene entirely directed by him, the death of the old Major, is as good as anything in the picture. Val Lewton then promoted Wise to director; Wise completed *Curse of the Cat People*, and made two small, perfect films in *Mademoiselle Fifi* and *The Body Snatcher*. Still at RKO, he had further B-movie successes with *Born to Kill* and *The Set-Up*, but left when Howard Hughes took over the studio. Nothing in his later career matches that early work. His Fifties films were polished, likeable routine, with *Executive Suite* by some way the best. In the Sixties and after his films were large-scale, commercially successful, and deadly dull. *The Sound of Music* and *West Side Story* won Best Director Oscars for Wise, and were also declared Best Picture. The mind boggles, and seeks refuge in memories of the days with Lewton.

Films include: 1944 Curse of the Cat People (co-dir); Mademoiselle Fifi (TV retitling: The Silent Bell). '45 The Body Snatcher. '47 Born to Kill (GB: Lady of Deceit). '49 The Set-Up. '51 The House on Telegraph Hill; The Day the Earth Stood Still. '54 Executive Suite. '58 I Want to Live. '61 West Side Story (co-dir). '65 The Sound of Music. '71 The Andromeda Strain. '79 Star Trek – The Motion Picture.

WISEMAN, Frederick

(b. 1930). Documentary director/producer/editor. Born: Boston, Massachusetts, USA

Trained as a lawyer, Frederick Wiseman lectured in law at Boston University. He became involved in films as producer of Shirley Clarke's feature about delinquent youths in Harlem, *The Cool World* (1963). In 1966 he co-founded the Organization for Social and Technical Innovation (OSTI), which aimed to intervene in problematic social issues. In 1967 he directed his first and most controversial film, *Titicut Follies*, about life in a state hospital for the criminally insane. His subsequent documentaries were frequently concerned with institutions of various sorts (a school, a hospital, the police, the army, a law court), depicted without commentary in *cinéma-vérité* style, but with some implied comment in the editing. In the late Seventies he concentrated on American official activities overseas; and in the early Eighties he made his first fiction film, *Seraphita's Diary*, the story of a model in which nearly all the roles are played by one actress, the model Apollonia Van Ravenstein.

Films include: 1967 Titicut Follies. '68 High School. '69 Law and Order. '70 Hospital. '71 Basic Training. '72 Essene. '73 Juvenile Court. '74 Primate. '75 Welfare. '76 Meat. '77 Canal Zone. '78 Sinai Field Mission. '79 Manoeuvre. '80 Model. '82 Seraphita's Diary (feature).

WISEMAN, Joseph

(b. 1918). Actor. Born: Montreal, Quebec, Canada

Educated in Detroit, Wiseman began appearing with stock companies in 1936 and two years later made his stage debut as a soldier in *A Rebellion in Illinois*. He has acted on stage and screen ever since. Of gaunt and sly appearance, he usually features in sinister, villainous roles such as that of Dr No in the Bond movie of the same name.

Films include: 1951 Detective Story. '52 Les Miserables; Viva Zapata! '57 The Garment Jungle. '62 Dr No (GB). '65 Once a Thief (FR-USA). '68 The Night They Raided Minsky's. '71 Lawman. '74 The Apprenticeship of Duddy Kravitz (CAN). '78 The Betsy.

471

WITHERS, Googie

(b. 1917). Actress. Born: Georgette Lizette Withers; Karachi, India

The daughter of a British army captain and his Dutch wife, Googie Withers was sent to a convent school in London at the age of eight and then attended the Italia Conti dance and drama school. She had her first stage experience at the age of 13 and while appearing in cabaret two years later was spotted by a film producer and given a small part in *The Girl in the Crowd* (1934). There then began a string of stage appearances and, from the mid-Thirties, roles as darkly glamorous or seductively bitchy ladies in thrillers and comedies. At the height of her career she left Britain to live in Australia with her husband, the actor John McCallum, but returned to take the occasional film and television role. In the early Seventies she was notably successful as the governor of a women's prison in the British television series *Within These Walls*.

Films include: 1936 Accused. '38 The Lady Vanishes. '41 Jeannie; One of Our Aircraft Is Missing. '44 On Approval. '45 Pink String and Sealing Wax. '47 It Always Rains on Sunday. '50 Night and the City. '51 White Corridors. '56 Port of Escape.

WITHERS, Jane

(b. 1926). Actress. Born: Atlanta, Georgia, USA

Jane Withers' violent outbursts, sneering cynicism and lashing tongue were a refreshing change from the saccharine cuteness of most Hollywood child stars – she was Shirley Temple's alter ego. In *Bright Eyes* (1934) Withers plays the sadistic brat Joy Smythe who menaces the adorable Temple. Withers was steered into a showbusiness career by a mother determined to make the most of her daughter's talents. She was a capable impersonator and dancer and at the age of three was singing and acting in her own radio show. At the age of five, veteran Jane was moved to Hollywood by her mother, where endless visits to agents and studios paid off when she was selected as an extra for *Handle With Care*. From that time she was a busy actress and one who would still be in films 30 years later. As a child she once made 31 movies in an eight year stretch. She then continued as a star through her teens and twenties until she married in 1947, emerging later from her semi-retirement to appear in *Giant*.

Films include: 1932 Handle With Care. '35 Paddy O'Day; Ginger; This Is the Life. '36 Little Miss Nobody; Pepper. '37 The Holy Terror. '38 Keep Smiling. '40 High School. '56 Giant. '63 Captain Newman MD.

WOLF, Konrad

(1925–1982). Director. Born: Hechingen, Germany

The son of Friedrich Wolf, a doctor and writer of anti-Nazi plays, Konrad Wolf and the rest of his family left Germany for the Soviet Union following persecution by Hitler. Wolf was educated there and later fought in the Soviet army. He went on to study film in Moscow and associated and

worked with such renowned filmmakers as Dovzhenko and Pudovkin. He became assistant to Joris Ivens, the Dutch documentary director, and began to make his own feature films in East Germany in 1954. His best internationally-known work is *Stars*, a tragic story of love between a German NCO and a Greek Jewess, with the Star of David as a symbol for the doomed couple – the film won a gold medal at the Vienna Film Festival.

Films include: 1955 Einmal ist Keinmal; Genesung. '57 Lissy. '58 Die Sonnesucher. '59 Sterne (E. GER-BUL) (GB: Stars). '60 Leute mit Flügeln. '61 Professor Mamlock. '64 Der geteilte Himmel. '67 Der kleine Prinz. '71 Gota (E. GER-USSR). '74 Der nackte Mann auf dem Sportplatz. '77 Mama, ich lebe.

WOLFIT, Donald

(1902–1968). Actor. Born: Newark-on-Trent, Nottinghamshire, England

The son of an accountant and a strict Wesleyan mother, Wolfit first took a job teaching in a preparatory school in Eastbourne, but he had had theatrical experience in World War I concerts, and in 1920 joined Charles Doran's Shakespearian Company. In 1924 he made his London debut in *The Wandering Jew* and after experience with the Sheffield Repertory Company, the Old Vic and the Stratford Memorial Theatre, established his own company in 1937. After doubling for Charles Laughton in *Down River* he made his film debut proper in *Death at Broadcasting House* in 1934. But he remained predominantly a stage actor and most of his major screen appearances were in British films of the Fifties. He excelled as *Svengali*, and played the pompous self-made businessman whose daughter marries working-class adventurer Laurence Harvey in *Room at the Top* and lives unhappily with him in *Life at the Top*.

Films include: 1934 Death at Broadcasting House. '52 The Pickwick Papers. '54 Svengali. '58 I Accuse!; Blood of the Vampire. '59 Room at the Top. '60 The Hands of Orlac. '62 Lawrence of Arabia. '63 Dr Crippen. '64 Becket. '65 Life at the Top. '68 Charge of the Light Brigade.

WONG, Anna May

(1907–1961). Actress. Born: Wong Liu Tsong (Frosted Yellow Willow); Los Angeles, California, USA

Anna May Wong was the archetypal inscrutable Oriental enchantress, playing her roles with an elegance and poise for which she was renowned. A fullblooded Chinese born in America, she worked as an extra before gaining recognition as a slave girl in *The Thief of Bagdad* with Douglas Fairbanks Sr. After making more silent films she went to Europe. It was there that she acted on the stage and also made several films, the most notable being *Piccadilly* with Charles Laughton. She then returned to Hollywood and the talkies, bringing her own brand of sullen oriental allure aboard *Shanghai Express*. She appeared in a few films during World War II and her last appearance was in *Portrait in Black* with Lana Turner and Anthony Quinn.

Films include: 1919 The Red Lantern. '22 The Toll of the Sea. '24 The Thief of Bagdad. '26 The Desert's Toll; A Train to Chinatown. '27 Streets of Shanghai. '29 Piccadilly (GB). '30 The Flame of Love (GB). '31 Daughter of the Dragon. '32 Shanghai Express. '41 Ellery Queen's Penthouse Mystery. '60 Portrait in Black.

WOOD, Natalie

(1938–1981). Actress. Born: Natasha Gurdin; San Francisco, California, USA

One of the few Hollywood child stars who made the transition to teenage roles and adult star. Natalie Wood was one of the most universally popular actresses of her generation. Petite, dark and attractive, she first made her name in a pair of pictures for Warner Brothers during the mid-Fifties. She played James Dean's sensitive teenage girlfriend in Nicholas Ray's *Rebel Without a Cause* and was the kidnapped pioneer girl turned Indian squaw who is hunted by John Wayne and Jeffrey Hunter in *The Searchers*. Still playing a teenager in *West Side Story*, she had a major success as the Puerto Rican heroine, Maria, and had one last big personal hit as the sexy, 'swinging' young wife in Paul Mazursky's parody of the new liberated life style of the Sixties, *Bob & Carol & Ted & Alice*. Her career was showing signs of a revival when she was tragically drowned at sea. At the time she was remarried to her first husband, actor Robert Wagner, following an intervening marriage.

Top left: Googie Withers in the title role of Ealing's The Loves of Joanna Godden (1947). Top: 13-year-old Jane Withers in Chicken Wagon Family *(1939). Above: a Juliet for the Sixties – Natalie Wood as Maria in* West Side Story. *Below: Joanne Woodward as the shy schoolteacher in* Rachel, Rachel, *directed by Paul Newman*

Films include: 1943 Happy Land. '46 Tomorrow Is Forever. '47 Miracle on 34th Street (GB: The Big Heart). '55 Rebel Without a Cause. '56 The Searchers. '58 Marjorie Morningstar. '61 Splendor in the Grass; West Side Story. '62 Gypsy. '63 Love With the Proper Stranger. '65 Inside Daisy Clover; The Great Race. '66 This Property Is Condemned. '69 Bob & Carol & Ted & Alice. '80 The Last Married Couple in America. '83 Brainstorm.

WOOD, Sam

(1883–1949). Director. Born: Samuel Grosvenor Wood; Philadelphia, Pennsylvania, USA

After some early stage and film experience as an actor Wood worked as an assistant director for two years under Cecil B. DeMille in the late 1910s.

Left: Anna May Wong in Shanghai Express. *Below left: Edward Woodward in uniform for* Stand Up Virgin Soldiers. *Bottom left: Monty Woolley in* The Man Who Came to Dinner. *Below: Donald Wolfit in* Becket. *Right: Hank Worden in* Wagonmaster

Remaining at Paramount after promotion to full director status, he was fortunate in getting two of the studio's top stars, Wallace Reid and Gloria Swanson. He directed Reid at his peak in a number of pictures during 1919–20 and Swanson during 1921–23. Signed by MGM in 1927, he remained with that studio for 13 years turning out two or three pictures per year, mainly routine productions, although his career began to pick up during the late Thirties. Two Marx Brothers comedies – *A Night at the Opera* and *A Day at the Races* – were followed by *Goodbye, Mr Chips* which earned an Oscar for Robert Donat and a first nomination for Wood. At RKO in 1940 he extracted another Oscar-winning performance, this time from Ginger Rogers as *Kitty Foyle*, as well as a second nomination for himself before directing Ronald Reagan in *Kings Row* at Warners. Wood returned to Paramount for the most expensive and ambitious film of his career, a two-and-a-half-hour Technicolor adaptation of Hemingway's *For Whom the Bell Tolls*. Although it turned out to be a big hit, the rest of Wood's career was all downhill.

Films include: 1920 Double Speed. **'21** Under the Lash. **'35** A Night at the Opera. **'37** A Day at the Races. **'39** Goodbye, Mr Chips. **'40** Our Town; Kitty Foyle. **'41** Kings Row. **'42** The Pride of the Yankees. **'43** For Whom the Bell Tolls. **'48** Command Decision. **'50** Ambush.

WOODWARD, Edward

(b. 1930). Actor. Born: Croydon, Surrey, England

Woodward started work in the office of a sanitary engineer but gave this up in favour of the Royal Academy of Dramatic Art. A spell with Farnham Repertory was followed by the usual spiral of theatre roles which the

actor has not abandoned, despite his long run as *Callan* on television. His work in that medium has been consistently good – for example, his Sir Samuel Hoare in *Churchill: The Wilderness Years*. In movies he has usually been cast in supporting roles, at his most effective in thrillers, though he was excellent as the ambivalent hero of the Australian film set in the Boer War, *Breaker Morant*.

Films include: 1955 Where There's a Will. **'64** Becket. **'72** Young Winston; Sitting Target. **'73** Hunted. **'74** Callan; The Wicker Man. **'77** Stand Up Virgin Soldiers. **'80** Breaker Morant (AUS). **'82** Who Dares Wins.

WOODWARD, Joanne

(b. 1930). Actress. Born: Thomasville, Georgia, USA

The daughter of a publisher, Joanne Woodward was educated at Louisiana State University, and moved to New York to enrol as a student at the Neighborhood Playhouse. She appeared in television plays before her film debut in 1955. In her second film, *A Kiss Before Dying*, she made a vivid impression as a college girl murdered by her lover, and in 1957 won the Best Actress Oscar for her brilliant portrayal of a split personality in *The Three Faces of Eve*. The following year she married Paul Newman, who directed her in two of her best roles, as the spinster teacher of *Rachel, Rachel*, and the slatternly mother of *The Effect of Gamma Rays on Man-in-the-Moon Marigolds*. A robust, intelligent-looking blonde, with a Southern accent that tends to vary in intensity from film to film, she has always excelled at the playing of losers, usually involved in difficult relationships. Her very rare appearances in comedy have shown a notable talent, but she has always returned to her struggling victims. No-one has ever played such parts better. *Summer Wishes, Winter Dreams* came near to sentimental soap-opera, but Woodward's neurotic wife made it seem a masterpiece at the time. Away from the screen, she and Newman have devoted much time and energy to liberal causes.

Films include: 1955 Count Three and Pray. **'56** A Kiss Before Dying. **'57** The Three Faces of Eve. **'58** The Long, Hot Summer. **'60** The Fugitive Kind. **'63** The Stripper (GB:

Woman of Summer). **'66** A Big Hand for the Little Lady (GB: Big Deal at Dodge City). **'68** Rachel, Rachel. **'70** WUSA. **'71** They Might Be Giants. **'72** The Effect of Gamma Rays on Man-in-the-Moon Marigolds. **'73** Summer Wishes, Winter Dreams. **'75** The Drowning Pool.

WOOLLEY, Monty

(1888–1963). Actor. Born: Edgar Montillion Woolley; New York City, USA

Born in the hotel his father owned at Fifth Avenue and 42nd Street, Monty Woolley was educated at both Yale and Harvard universities. He returned to Yale to teach, taking time out to serve with the US Army in World War I. He left Yale in the mid-Thirties to direct for the Broadway stage, and made his acting debut in 1936 in *On Your Toes*. The following year he was in his first film, *Live, Love and Learn*. His most famous film role, first created on the stage, was as the crusty, unwelcome wheelchair-bound house guest Sheridan Whiteside in *The Man Who Came to Dinner*. He was nominated for Oscars for *The Pied Piper* and *Since You Went Away*; and, as Cole Porter's former professor, he played himself in the biopic *Night and Day*.

Films include: 1937 Live, Love and Learn. **'38** The Girl of the Golden West; Three Comrades. **'39** Never Say Die. **'41** The Man Who Came to Dinner. **'42** The Pied Piper. **'43** Holy Matrimony. **'44** Irish Eyes Are Smiling; Since You Went Away. **'46** Night and Day. **'48** Mrs Tatlock's Millions. **'55** Kismet.

WOOLSEY, Robert

see WHEELER & WOOLSEY

WORDEN, Hank

(b. 1901). Actor. Born: Norton Earl Worden; Rolfe, Iowa, USA

One of the lesser members of John Ford's stock company, Hank Worden earns his place in history on the strength of one great role in one great movie. First seen as a headstrong Southern recruit in *Fort Apache*, Worden went on to be one of the evil Clegg tribe in *Wagonmaster*, could be seen in *The Quiet Man* if you looked very carefully (in the boxing flashback), and then played the sweet simpleton, Mose Harper, in *The Searchers*. All Mose wants is a roof over his head – and a rocking-chair; and after many years he has them, and is fulfilled. The part is crucial to the film, and this small-part player plays it with tender appreciation. He was in other Westerns for Hawks and Fuller, notably as Poordevil in *The Big Sky*, but Mose fitted him like a glove, and could not be repeated. Worden had been a cowhand and a rodeo rider and attended the University of Nevada before he entered films as an extra in DeMille's *The Plainsman* (1936).

Films include: 1948 Fort Apache; Three Godfathers; Red River. **'50** When Willie Comes Marching Home; Wagonmaster. **'52** The Quiet Man; The Big Sky. **'56** The Searchers. **'57** The Buckskin Lady; Forty Guns. **'59** The Horse Soldiers. **'60** Sergeant Rutledge. **'70** Rio Lobo. **'82** Hammett.

WRAY, Fay

(b. 1907). Actress. Born: Alberta, Canada

Fay Wray's career contained a central irony. Although she is remembered, above all, as the heroine of *King Kong*, identified for ever with the girl on the summit of the Empire State Building, that film did her little good. After it, she soon sank to second features, and retired in 1942 after marrying the screenwriter Robert Riskin. But before *Kong* there had been a great deal. Wray was brought up in Los Angeles, in films at 15, and playing leads in prestige pictures by the end of the Twenties. She was the demurely innocent heroine of Stroheim's *The Wedding March*, and the good-bad girl of Sternberg's *Thunderbolt*, and she made some notable horror films before *King Kong* and her entry into legend. Long afterwards, in the Fifties, she came back to play a few character roles.

Films include: **1925** The Coast Patrol. **'28** The Wedding March. **'29** The Four Feathers; Thunderbolt. **'32** Doctor X; The Most Dangerous Game (GB: The Hounds of Zaroff). **'33** The Mystery of the Wax Museum; King Kong; The Bowery. **'34** The Affairs of Cellini. **'35** The Clairvoyant (GB). **'41** Adam Had Four Sons. **'55** The Cobweb. **'58** Summer Love.

WRIGHT, Basil

(b. 1907). Documentary director/ producer. Born: London, England

Educated at Cambridge, Basil Wright joined John Grierson in 1929 at the Empire Marketing Board Film Unit, which in 1933 became the General Post Office (GPO) Film Unit. In 1934 Wright made his most famous solo film, *Song of Ceylon*, for the Ceylon Tea Propaganda Board; and in 1936 he co-directed *Night Mail* with Harry Watt. Like Grierson, he left the GPO in 1937 and formed his own film unit. In 1939 he joined Film Centre, founded by Grierson, to produce films for the Ministry of Information; and in 1945 he became a producer for the Crown Film Unit, wartime successor to the old GPO Film Unit, where he worked on Humphrey Jennings' *A Diary for Timothy*. In the Fifties he directed films again, collaborating with Paul Rotha on *World Without End* and with Michael Ayrton on *Greek Sculpture*. In 1974 he published *The Long View*, a personal history of the cinema.

Films as director include: **1930** Conquest (co-dir). **'32** The Country Comes to Town. **'33** Industrial Britain (co-dir). **'34** Song of Ceylon. **'35** Coalface (co-dir). **'36** Night Mail (co-dir). **'37** Children in School. **'39** The Face of Scotland. **'45** A Diary for Timothy (prod. only). **'46** A Defeated People (prod. only). **'51** Waters of Time (co-dir). **'53** World Without End (co-dir). **'58** The Immortal Land (+co-prod). **'59** Greek Sculpture (co-dir; +co-prod). **'60** A Place for Gold (+prod).

WRIGHT, Teresa

(b. 1918). Actress. Born: Muriel Teresa Wright; New York City, USA

After a brief period in the theatre, Teresa Wright was signed to a con-

tract by producer Sam Goldwyn. She was fortunate in her early film career, which included three films for director William Wyler, and earned an Oscar nomination for *The Little Foxes* and the Best Supporting Actress Oscar for *Mrs Miniver*. She was particularly memorable as Charlie, with the same name and a dangerous attachment to her schizophrenic and murderous Uncle Charlie (Joseph Cotten) in Hitchcock's *Shadow of a Doubt*. Friendly and attractive-looking, she was most often cast as the girl-next-door type, but was effective in a stronger role as the girlfriend and wife of the tortured hero (Robert Mitchum) in Raoul Walsh's psychological Western *Pursued*. In later years she divided her time between the stage, television and the occasional film. She was appealing as one of the sad middle-aged patrons of the New York ballroom in *Roseland*.

Films include: **1941** The Little Foxes. **'42** Pride of the Yankees; Mrs Miniver. **'43** Shadow of a Doubt. **'46** The Best Years of Our Lives. **'47** The Trouble With Women; Pursued. **'58** The Restless Years (GB: The Wonderful Years). **'77** Roseland. **'80** Somewhere in Time.

WYLER, William

(1902–1981). Director. Born: Mulhouse, Alsace, Germany (now France)

During the course of a career which spanned 45 years and over forty feature films, Wyler became known as one of Hollywood's most solid and dependable directors. His attraction to scripts and stories of the highest

Left: 'twas beauty killed the beast – Fay Wray as Ann in King Kong. *Above: Teresa Wright in* Pride of the Yankees. *Below: the American director William Wyler while filming* The Collector. *Bottom: Keenan Wynn as one of 24 leading characters in Robert Altman's* Nashville (1975)

quality led him to film adaptations of many literary works. And he won respect as a sensitive but demanding director of actors. First offered a job by Universal boss Carl Laemmle, young Wyler emigrated to the USA in 1922 and took up a post first in the studio's New York office and then in Hollywood. He quickly developed an interest in film-making and graduated from prop man to cutter and assistant director before launching on his career as a director of two-reel Westerns. Near the end of his stay at Universal Wyler directed John Barrymore in *Counsellor-at-Law* (1933) and Margaret Sullavan, who became his first wife, in *The Good Fairy* (1935). Although the quality of his productions had improved, he aspired to better things and left Universal's low budgets behind him in 1935 as he began a fruitful six-year collaboration with independent producer Sam Goldwyn. He alternated between play adaptations of note, like *The Children's Hour* (retitled *These Three*), *Dead End* and *The Little Foxes*, with film versions of novels including *Dodsworth* and *Wuthering Heights*. Reaching his prime as a director, Wyler was nominated for an Oscar three years running, then won the award for *Mrs Miniver* and again for the Goldwyn production *The Best Years of Our Lives*. Wyler demonstrated his versatility during the following years, alternating between thrillers, comedies and dramatic pictures. At the age of 55 he embarked on his first big-budget costume epic, a three-and-a-half-hour remake of *Ben-Hur* for MGM; the picture went on to become a box-office success and win a record eleven Oscars, including a third for Wyler.

Films include: 1925 Ben-Hur (prod. ass. only). '29 Hell's Heroes. '30 The Storm. '36 These Three; Dodsworth. '37 Dead End. '38 Jezebel. '39 Wuthering Heights. '40 The Westerner; The Letter. '41 The Little Foxes. '42 Mrs Miniver. '44 The Memphis Belle (short). '46 The Best Years of Our Lives. '51 Detective Story. '52 Carrie. '53 Roman Holiday. '55 The Desperate Hours. '56 Friendly Persuasion. '58 The Big Country. '59 Ben-Hur. '65 The Collector (USA-GB). '66 How to Steal a Million. '68 Funny Girl. '70 The Liberation of L. B. Jones.

WYMAN, Jane

(b. 1914). Actress. Born: Sarah Jane Fulks; St Joseph, Missouri, USA

Educated at the University of Missouri, Jane Wyman first made her name as a radio singer and bit actress in films. From 1935 through 1944 she appeared in over forty pictures, most of them long forgotten, with such titles as *The King and the Chorus Girl* (1937), *The Kid From Kokomo* (1939) or *Tugboat Annie Sails Again*, the last co-starring Ronald Reagan, a fellow contract player at Warners whom she married in 1940. There was a noticeable improvement in her parts from 1945 when she graduated to more intelligent and mature roles which obviously suited her. She played the long-suffering girlfriend of an alcoholic (Ray Milland) in *The Lost Weekend* and Gregory Peck's sensible pioneer wife in *The Yearling*, earning an Oscar nomination. And two years later she won the Oscar for her moving performance as the deaf mute in *Johnny Belinda*. She divorced Ronald Reagan in 1948. She had two good roles for director Douglas Sirk in the mid-Fifties – in *Magnificent Obsession* and *All That Heaven Allows* – but virtually retired from films soon after. Her demure appearance and worried air were assets in dramatic roles but may have limited her range of parts and confined her appeal mainly to women.

Top: Jane Wyman in Stage Fright, *her only Hitchcock film. Above: Ed Wynn as Jerry Lewis' godfather in* Cinderfella (1960). *Below: Dana Wynter in her star role as a German girl –* Fraulein *– helping GIs in postwar Berlin. Below right: Diana Wynyard in* Cavalcade

Films include: 1935 King of Burlesque. '36 Gold Diggers of 1937. '37 Mr Dodd Takes the Air. '40 Tugboat Annie Sails Again. '41 You're in the Army Now. '45 The Lost Weekend. '46 The Yearling. '48 Johnny Belinda. '49 Stage Fright (GB). '50 The Glass Menagerie. '54 Magnificent Obsession. '55 All That Heaven Allows. '60 Pollyanna. '69 How to Commit Marriage.

WYNN, Ed

(1886–1966). Actor. Born: Isaiah Edwin Leopold; Philadelphia, USA

An old-fashioned slapstick comedy actor, Ed Wynn was the son of immigrants from Europe. He ran away in his teens to join a travelling actors' company, finally working his way up to the New York stage where he achieved a considerable reputation in the Ziegfeld Follies. Less favourable publicity exposed a row with one-time rival W.C. Fields and his involvement with an actors' strike resulted in blacklisting. Nevertheless he remained hugely popular, first on stage and later on the radio and in films, but in the Thirties a series of disastrous business ventures ruined him. In the Forties he bounced back, this time playing film and television character parts. His re-emergence culminated in an Oscar nomination for his acting in *The Diary of Anne Frank*. He continued to work in both serious and comic roles up to his death. His son is actor Keenan Wynn, who aided and supported his father's return to films as a character actor.

Films include: 1927 Rubber Heels. '33 The Chief. '34 Babes in Toyland. '56 The Great Man. '59 The Diary of Anne Frank. '60 Cinderfella. '64 The Patsy; Mary Poppins. '65 The Greatest Story Ever Told; That Darn Cat! '67 The Gnome-Mobile.

WYNN, Keenan

(1916–1986). Actor. Born: Francis Xavier Aloysius Wynn; New York City, USA

The son of comedian Ed Wynn, Keenan was educated at St John's Military Academy and got his early acting experience on the stage and on radio. He has had an incredibly prolific career in films ever since he was first signed by MGM as a character actor during the early Forties. Most often called upon to play cantankerous drunks or irascible men in uniform, he was especially good as the officious colonel suspicious of 'Limey' Peter Sellers (in an RAF officer's uniform) in Kubrick's *Dr Strangelove*. And he even got a rare opportunity to sing and dance in a comical double act

with James Whitmore as a pair of not-too-tough gangsters in *Kiss Me Kate*. The scriptwriter Tracy Keenan Wynn is his daughter.

Films include: 1942 For Me and My Gal (GB: For Me and My Girl). '43 Lost Angel. '44 See Here, Private Hargrove. '46 Ziegfeld Follies. '50 Annie Get Your Gun. '51 Kind Lady. '52 Holiday for Sinners. '53 All the Brothers Were Valiant; Kiss Me Kate. '56 Man in the Gray Flannel Suit. '59 The Scarface Mob. '64 Dr Strangelove, or How I Learned to Stop Worrying and Love the Bomb (GB). '65 The Great Race. '67 Point Blank. '80 Just Tell Me What You Want.

WYNTER, Dana

(b. 1930). Actress. Born: Dagmar Spencer-Marcus; London, England

An attractive, intelligent – she studied at Rhodes University in Southern Rhodesia before going on the stage – and sophisticated-looking brunette, Dana Wynter had a brief Hollywood career of note during the mid-Fifties. Her most memorable role was that of Becky, Kevin McCarthy's faithful girlfriend in Don Siegel's *Invasion of the Body Snatchers* and the last of the townspeople to succumb to the invaders. During the Sixties her film roles became fewer and farther between although she continued to appear regularly on television. In 1982 she played the role of the Queen in the American television movie *The Royal Romance of Charles and Diana*.

Films include: 1951 White Corridors (GB). '56 Invasion of the Body Snatchers; D-Day, the Sixth of June. '57 Something of Value. '58 Fraulein. '59 Shake Hands With the Devil. '60 Sink the Bismarck (GB). '63 The List of Adrian Messenger. '70 Airport. '75 Le Sauvage (FR-IT).

WYNYARD, Diana

(1906–1964). Actress. Born: Dorothy Isobel Cox; London, England

Wynyard made her stage debut in London in 1925 and then quickly proceeded to New York and Hollywood. From 1932 she was under contract to MGM and made half a dozen films for them – beginning opposite the Barrymores in *Rasputin and the Empress* – and one for Fox, Noel Coward's *Cavalcade*, for which she was nominated for an Oscar. Back in England she was outstanding as the terrorized wife in *Gaslight* and brought her cool, stately beauty to *An Ideal Husband*, *The Prime Minister* and *Tom Brown's Schooldays*. She also appeared in *Kipps* and in 1943 married its director Carol Reed, though they were divorced four years later. She once claimed, 'I don't really want to be a film star' and it was more for her stage work that she became a CBE in 1953.

Films include: 1932 Rasputin and the Empress (USA). '33 Men Must Fight (USA); Cavalcade (USA); Reunion in Vienna (USA). '39 On the Night of the Fire (USA: The Fugitive). '40 Gaslight (USA: Angel Street). '41 The Prime Minister; Freedom Radio (USA: A Voice in the Night); Kipps. '47 An Ideal Husband. '51 Tom Brown's Schooldays. '56 The Feminine Touch (USA: The Gentle Touch). '57 Island in the Sun (USA).

YZ

YAMADA, Isuzu

(b. 1917). Actress. Born: Osaka, Japan

Originally trained as a samisen player, Isuzu Yamada began film acting at 14 because her mother was a friend of the head of Nikkatsu's Kyoto studio. She was an effective heroine in several Mizoguchi films of the mid-Thirties, including *Sisters of the Gion*, usually playing a more-or-less golden-hearted prostitute. The director Teinosuke Kinugasa was one of her six husbands, and she appeared in a couple of his films in the late Forties. She is best known in the West for her later roles in several of Akira Kurosawa's films, especially as the Lady Macbeth character, Asaji, in *Throne of Blood*. She has also had a distinguished career on the stage. The actress Michiko Saga is her daughter.

Films include: 1931 Adauchi Sanshu (The Revenge Champion). '34 Orizuru Osen (Osen of the Paper Cranes). '36 Naniwa Hika/Naniwa Ereji (Osaka Elegy/Naniwa Elegy); Gion no Shimai (GB: Sisters of the Gion). '55 Hiroshima. '57 Kumonosu-Jo (USA/GB: Throne of Blood); Donzoko (USA/GB: The Lower Depths); Shitamachi (Downtown). '58 Shiki no Aiyoku (The Four Seasons of Love). '60 Bonchi (The Son). '61 Yojimbo. '67 Ooku Maruhi Monogatari (The Shogun and His Mistress).

YAMAMURA, So

(b. 1910). Actor/director. Born: Naka, Japan

Strong-featured, beetle-browed Yamamura began as a character actor in the Forties. He played a doctor in Ozu's *Tokyo Story* and appeared for Mizoguchi in *The Loves of Actress Sumako* and *The Empress Yang Kwei-Fei*, and for Kobayashi in *No Greater Love* and *The Inheritance*. In 1970 he was the Admiral Yamamoto in *Tora! Tora! Tora!* but Yamamura had a brief but interesting directing career in the Fifties. His first film, *The Crab-Canning Ship*, showed the revolt of workers on crab-fishing and canning ships in the Twenties – it was obviously influenced by Eisenstein's *Bronenosets Potemkin* (1925, *Battleship Potemkin*) – and implied a leftist criticism of pre-war Japan. *Black Tide* was an interesting fictionalized account of the mysterious death of the president of Japan's National Railways.

Films include: 1946 Inochi Arukaghiri (actor) (For Life). '47 Joyu Sumako no Koi (actor) (USA: The Love of Sumako the Actress; GB: The Loves of Actress Sumako). '53 Tokyo Monogatari (actor) (GB: Tokyo Story/Their First Trip to Tokyo); Kanikosen (dir) (The Crab-Canning Ship). '54 Kuroi Ushio (dir; +act) (Black Tide). '55 Yokihi (actor) (USA: The Princess Yang Kwei-Fei; GB: The Empress Yang Kwei-Fei). '58 The Barbarian and the Geisha (actor) (USA). '59 Kashimanada no Onna (dir) (Maidens of Kashima Sea); Hahakogusa (dir; +act) (Mother and Her Children); Ningen no Joken (actor) (No Greater Love). '60 Furyu Fukagawa Uta (dir) (The Song of Fukagawa). '62 Karamiai (actor) (The Inheritance). '63 Futen Rojin Nikki (actor) (Diary of a Mad Old Man). '70 Tora! Tora! Tora! (actor) (USA-JAP).

YATES, Peter

(b. 1929). Director. Born: Aldershot, Hampshire, England

Of all the British directors of the Sixties who spent some time in the USA, Yates was the only one who stayed on and was able to adapt himself entirely to a wide range of American subjects and stars. After studying at RADA he gained his first experience as an actor, director and stage manager in various British repertory companies. Turning to films during the early Fifties, Yates worked as an assistant editor and third assistant director before working his way up to full director status. Taking advantage of his brief experience in the world of professional racing, Yates staged a car chase through the streets of London in his third feature, *Robbery*, which attracted the interest of Steve McQueen. This led to *Bullitt*, his first American film, which turned out to be a big hit. A variety of features followed, ranging from thrillers like *The Friends of Eddie Coyle*, starring Robert Mitchum, to black comedy like *Mother, Jugs and Speed*. But Yates had his two biggest successes during the late Seventies with the undersea adventure thriller *The Deep* and *Breaking Away*, an entertaining and enjoyable social comedy which received Oscar nominations for Best Picture and Director.

Films include: 1963 Summer Holiday. '64 One Way Pendulum. '67 Robbery. '68 Bullitt (USA). '69 John and Mary (USA). '71 Murphy's War. '72 The Hot Rock (USA) (GB: How to Steal a Diamond in Four Uneasy Lessons). '73 The Friends of Eddie Coyle (USA). '74 For Pete's Sake (USA). '76 Mother, Jugs and Speed (USA). '77 The Deep (USA). '79 Breaking Away (USA). '81 Eyewitness (USA) (GB: The Janitor).

YORK, Michael

(b. 1942). Actor. Born: Fulmer, Buckinghamshire, England

Michael York is from that generation of actors, Michael Caine included, who rose to prominence in the Swinging Sixties, good-looking and with a glamour in direct contrast to the austerity of the British 'New Wave' which had gone before. York's first taste of acting was at Oxford University followed by a spell in rep in Dundee, and he moved unusually quickly into film work. His early roles were varied, from typical Sixties fare like *Smashing Time* to the Anglo-Italian *Romeo and Juliet*. Blond-haired, bright eyed and 'posh', York has usually been cast as the athletic young hero: to good effect as the enthusiastic but innocent d'Artagnan in *The Three Musketeers* and *The Four Musketeers* but less memorably in *Logan's Run*, *The Island of Doctor Moreau* and *The Riddle of the Sands*. His best roles, though, were in *Accident*, as the aristocratic university student, and in *Cabaret*, as Sally Bowles' friend and lover.

Films include: 1967 The Taming of the Shrew (IT-USA); Accident; Smashing Time. '68 The Strange Affair; Romeo and Juliet (GB-IT). '72 Cabaret (USA); Fratello Sole, Sorella Luna (IT-GB) (USA/GB: Brother Sun, Sister Moon). '73 The Three Musketeers: the Queen's Diamonds (PAN). '74 Murder on the Orient Express. '75 The Four Musketeers: the Revenge of Milady (PAN-SP); Conduct Unbecoming; Logan's Run. '77 The Island of Doctor Moreau (USA). '79 The Riddle of the Sands.

YORK, Susannah

(b. 1941). Actress. Born: Susannah Yolande Fletcher; London, England

Trained for the stage at RADA, Susannah York had only a brief career in the theatre before she was attracted to the cinema during the early Sixties. Blonde and blue-eyed with a sweet and innocent-looking face, she soon developed into a leading young star of the Anglo-American cinema, appearing in such films as *Freud*, the Oscar-winning *Tom Jones* and *A Man for All Seasons*, in which she played Sir Thomas More's daughter. She received her only Oscar nomination for her performance as the pathetic Alice who undergoes a sad deterioration during the course of the dance marathon in *They Shoot Horses, Don't They?* During the Seventies she still projected that blend of maturity and innocence which was perfectly suited for the idealized role of Superman's mother in *Superman, The Movie*, though *The Shout* and other films showed her moving into sexier and nastier roles with much conviction.

Films include: 1960 Tunes of Glory; There Was a Crooked Man . . .'61 The Greengage Summer (USA: Loss of Innocence). '62 Freud. '63 Tom Jones. '66 A Man for All Seasons. '68 The Killing of Sister George (USA). '69 Oh! What a Lovely War; They Shoot Horses, Don't They? (USA). '71 Jane Eyre. '72 Images (EIRE). '75 Conduct Unbecoming. '78 The Shout; Superman, The Movie. '83 Yellowbeard.

YORKIN, Bud

(b. 1926). Director. Born: Alan David Yorkin; Washington, Pennsylvania, USA

Yorkin is the director half of a partnership with producer-writer Norman Lear formed in 1959. They contributed some of the most successful comedy programmes on American television during the Sixties and early Seventies. The best-known were *All in the Family* and *Sanford and Son*. Yorkin and Lear also collaborated on a number of feature films, including the Frank Sinatra vehicle, *Come Blow Your Horn*; a historical spoof, *Start the Revolution Without Me*; and a comedy thriller, *The Thief Who Came to Dinner*, starring Ryan O'Neal as a computer analyst turned jewel thief. The best of their pictures, however, was a witty and perceptive social comedy, *Divorce American Style*, with lively performances from Debbie Reynolds, Jason Robards and Jean Simmons. Originally educated at Carnegie Tech and Columbia University, Yorkin joined the staff of NBC in 1949. He produced and directed many television specials during the Fifties, most notably *An Evening With Fred Astaire*, which won a number of Emmy Awards in 1958, the year before he launched his partnership with Lear.

Films include: **1963** Come Blow Your Horn. **'65** Never Too Late. **'67** Divorce American Style. **'68** Inspector Clouseau (GB). **'70** Start the Revolution Without Me (USA-CZECH). **'71** Cold Turkey (exec. prod. only). **'73** The Thief Who Came to Dinner.

YOSHIMURA, Kozaburo

(b. 1911). Director. Born: Hiroshima, Japan

Kozaburo Yoshimura started work in 1929 at the Shochiku studios in Tokyo as assistant director to Yasujiro Shimazu, but he had to wait ten years to be promoted to director. On his return to the film industry after World War II he displayed a new-found maturity in *A Ball at the Anjo House*, scripted by writer-director Kaneto Shindo, with whom he set up an independent production unit. His subsequent career has proved him to be a challenging and versatile director, capable of veering from period spectaculars such as *A Tale of Genji* to contemporary satire in *Ishimatsu of the Forest* and social protest in *Cape Ashizuri*.

Films include: **1934** Nukiashi Sashiashi. **'47** Anjo-Ke no Butokai (A Ball at the Anjo House); Zo o Kutta Renchu (The Fellows Who Ate the Elephant). **'49** Mori no Ishimatsu (Ishimatsu of the Forest). **'51** Genji Monogatari (A Tale of Genji). **'52** Nishijin no Shimai (The Sisters of Nishijin). **'54** Ashizuri Misaki (Cape Ashizuri). **'55** Ginza no Onna (Women of the Ginza). **'57** Yoru no Cho (Night Butterflies). **'60** Onna no Saka (Women of Kyoto). **'68** Atsui Yoru (A Hot Night).

YOUNG, Clara Kimball

(1891–1960). Actress. Born: Chicago, Illinois, USA

Born into a theatrical family, Clara Kimball Young made her stage debut at the age of three. After working in vaudeville she started her film career with the Vitagraph Company in 1909, playing in comedies and costume dramas. Her dark-haired good looks caught the eye of Lewis J. Selznick, who put her under contract with the newly-formed World Film Corporation, and she starred in *Camille* and *Trilby*. Selznick later helped her to form the Clara Kimball Young Film

Corporation which produced her own films. After she divorced her first husband, actor James Young, who had guided her to stardom, she married Harry Garson, and under his management her career plummeted. She returned to vaudeville in the Twenties, but made a screen comeback in the Thirties in a series of character parts. She finally retired in the early Forties.

Films include: **1909** Washington Under the American Flag. **'12** Cardinal Wolsey. **'13** Beau Brummel. **'14** My Official Wife. **'15** Camille; Trilby. **'22** The Worldly Madonna. **'23** Woman of Bronze. **'35** She Married Her Boss; His Night Out. **'42** Mr Celebrity.

YOUNG, Gig

(1913–1978). Actor. Born: Byron Elsworth Barr; St Cloud, Minnesota, USA

Young's career began in confusion and ended in tragedy. He worked his way up through high-school dramatics to the Pasadena Playhouse and a contract with Warner Brothers. His first minor roles went out under his own name until it was realized that another actor was using the name Byron Barr. Young was playing a character called Gig Young in the film *The Gay Sisters* at the time, and adopted the name as his own. He spent much of his time playing supporting roles, often playboys or lovers in comedies and romances, though he won two Oscar nominations, for *Come Fill the Cup* and *Teacher's Pet*, and finally an Oscar for *They Shoot Horses, Don't They?* Late in his career he turned to thrillers and horror films like *The Shuttered Room* and *The Killer Elite*. He was found dead in his bedroom with his last wife, and is thought to have shot her and then committed suicide. He had previously been married (1956–63) to actress Elizabeth Montgomery, his third wife.

Films include: **1942** The Gay Sisters. **'47** Escape Me Never. **'48** The Woman in White. **'51** Only the Valiant; Come Fill the Cup. **'52** Holiday for Sinners. **'54** Young at Heart. **'57** Desk Set (GB: His Other Woman). **'58** Teacher's Pet. **'59** Ask Any Girl. **'62** That Touch of Mink. **'67** The Shuttered Room (GB). **'69** They Shoot Horses, Don't They? **'70** Lovers and Other Strangers. **'74** Bring Me the Head of Alfredo Garcia (USA-MEX). **'75** The Killer Elite. **'78** Game of Death (HK) (GB: Bruce Lee's Game of Death).

YOUNG, Loretta

(b. 1913). Actress. Born: Gretchen Michaela Young; Salt Lake City, Utah, USA

The youngest of three sisters whose mother ran a Hollywood boarding-house, Gretchen was in the movies as a child of four. She retired to go to school, but came back at 14 and was playing leads almost at once. Changing her name to Loretta, she enjoyed a quarter of a century of stardom. She was pretty rather than glamorous, a healthy, open-air, no-nonsense girl, but capable too of a wistful sweetness that her better roles turned to advantage. One such came when she was barely 15, the waif of the circus in *Laugh, Clown, Laugh*; another was in *Platinum Blonde*, as a journalist painfully in love; a third in *A Man's Castle*, as a lost girl sheltered by Spencer Tracy in a shack in a lumber-yard. For those one could forgive the routine movies that filled most of her working life. But she did win the Best Actress Oscar, for *The Farmer's Daughter* in 1947. This was a lively political satire in which Loretta struggled gamely with a Swedish accent. She retired in 1953 and became the hostess of the Loretta Young Show on television. Her sister, Elizabeth Jane (b. 1910), played leading parts, as Sally Blane, in the Thirties, but most of her films were modest affairs.

Films include: **1917** The Primrose Ring. **'27** Naughty But Nice. **'28** Laugh, Clown, Laugh. **'31** Platinum Blonde. **'32** The Hatchet Man (GB: The Honourable Mr Wong). **'33** Zoo in Budapest; A Man's Castle. **'35** The Crusades. **'36** The Unguarded Hour. **'37** Love Is News. **'38** Suez. **'46** The Stranger. **'47** The Farmer's Daughter. **'53** It Happens Every Thursday.

Left: Susannah York as the officer's widow subjected to Conduct Unbecoming *in colonial India. Above: Clara Kimball Young in* Enter Madame *(1922). Below: Loretta Young as the socialite heroine of* The Doctor Takes a Wife *(1940)*

Below, from left to right: Isuzu Yamada in Nagareru *(1956, Flowing); So Yamamura as Admiral Yamamoto in* Tora! Tora! Tora!*; Michael York as a clumsy d'Artagnan in* The Three Musketeers; *a publicity portrait of Gig Young*

YOUNG, Robert

(b. 1907). Actor. Born: Chicago, Illinois, USA

'Bob Young is a director's dream, thoroughly prepared for every scene he works in, with a maximum of enthusiasm and intelligence.' This was written by King Vidor, who directed Young in perhaps his best part, that of *H. M. Pulham, Esq.* It says much for Young that the enthusiasm and intelligence were undimmed in 1941, after ten years playing amiable young men in bland MGM pictures, with only the occasional *Three Comrades* or *The Mortal Storm* to stretch him a little. But the Forties did treat him rather more kindly, with Lang's *Western Union*, two films for Vidor, and the *film noir* masterpiece, *Crossfire*. Even so, this alert, polished and capable actor deserved better things, and it was no surprise that in the mid-Fifties he opted for television, particularly the *Father Knows Best* and *Marcus Welby MD* series.

Films include: 1931 The Sin of Madelon Claudet (GB: The Lullaby). '32 Strange Interlude (GB: Strange Interval). '34 Death on the Diamond. '35 Remember Last Night? '38 Three Comrades; The Shining Hour. '40 Northwest Passage; The Mortal Storm. '41 Western Union; H. M. Pulham, Esq. '43 Claudia. '45 The Enchanted Cottage. '47 Crossfire. '54 Secret of the Incas.

YOUNG, Roland

(1887–1953). Actor. Born: London, England

After London University, RADA and the London stage, Young went to America in 1912 and settled there. He made only two silent films, his debut being as Watson to John Barrymore's Holmes, but with sound he established himself as one of Hollywood's finest supporting players. Young was small, balding, urbane and wistful, with an inimitable closed-lips delivery. He had leads in the Topper films, as a little man hard-pressed by mischievous ghosts, and was a notable Uriah Heep in *David Copperfield*. *Ruggles of Red Gap* gave him a superb part as an English Earl out West, playing 'Pretty Baby' on the drums with Leila Hyams, and *The Philadelphia Story* used him even better. Young was Hepburn's Uncle Willie, observing the proceedings with the quizzical tolerance that was his trademark.

Films include: 1922 Sherlock Holmes (GB: Moriarty). '24 Grit. '31 The Guardsman. '32 One Hour With You. '35 David Copperfield; Ruggles of Red Gap. '36 The Man Who Could Work Miracles (GB). '37 Topper. '38 Topper Takes a Trip. '40 The Philadelphia Story. '41 Two-Faced Woman. '45 And Then There Were None (GB: Ten Little Niggers). '53 That Man From Tangier.

YOUNG, Terence

(b. 1915). Director. Born: Shanghai, China

Educated at Cambridge, Young entered the British film industry as a scriptwriter during the Thirties and Forties. He developed into an efficient director of mainly routine international co-productions during the Fifties which most often featured a wide assortment of American stars like Alan Ladd (*The Green Beret*, 1953), Olivia de Havilland (*That Lady*, 1954) and Jayne Mansfield (*Too Hot to Handle*). His career took off during the Sixties when he directed the first James Bond picture, *Dr No*, and went on to two of the sequels – *From Russia with Love* and *Thunderball*, all starring Sean Connery. Although he attempted other types of pictures, like a remake of the costume romance *Mayerling*, Young was at his best directing action pictures and thrillers like *Wait Until Dark*, starring Audrey Hepburn, and three Charles Bronson vehicles. More recently he was involved with two disastrous projects starring Laurence Olivier – the Moonie-financed $40-million war epic *Inchon*, filmed in 1979 but not released until 1981, and the spy thriller *The Jigsaw Man*, which was abandoned in 1982 before filming was completed.

Films include: 1946 Theirs Is the Glory (co-sc. only) (USA: Men of Arnhem). '48 Corridor of Mirrors; One Night With You. '51 Valley of the Eagles. '55 Storm Over the Nile (co-dir). '60 Un, Deux, Trois, Quatre! (FR) (GB: Black Tights); Too Hot to Handle; Dr No. '63 From Russia With Love. '65 Thunderball; The Amorous Adventures of Moll Flanders. '67 Wait Until Dark (USA). '68 Mayerling (GB-FR). '71 Soleil Rouge (FR-IT-SP) (USA/GB: Red Sun). '72 Joe Valachi: I Segreti di Cosa Nostra (IT-FR) (USA/GB: The Valachi Papers). '81 Inchon.

YOUNG, Victor

(1900–1956). Composer/musical director. Born: Chicago, Illinois, USA

Young was one of Hollywood's finest and most prolific composers and arrangers. He contributed to more than 300 films, an achievement that was recognized at his death by his finally being awarded an Oscar for his music for *Around the World in 80 Days*. From a poor, though musical, background, Young studied the violin at the Imperial Conservatory, Warsaw, and made his first professional appearance with the Warsaw Philharmonic. He was interned in Russia in the last months of World War I but, after various adventures, was back in the USA by 1920. He first became involved with the movie industry when he took the post of assistant director of the Balaban and Katz cinema chain in Los Angeles, writing and arranging music for up to five films a week. Further work as a musical director in radio led to a contract with Paramount in 1936. In addition to his many film scores, he wrote the music for the Broadway show *Seventh Heaven* and co-wrote many songs, including 'Sweet Sue' (his first hit), 'Can't We Talk it Over?' and 'Love Me Tonight'.

Films include: 1936 Anything Goes; Big Broadcast of 1937. '37 Artists and Models. '41 The Palm Beach Story. '42 Reap the Wild Wind. '43 For Whom the Bell Tolls. '48 The Paleface; The Emperor Waltz. '50 Rio Grande. '51 The Greatest Show on Earth. '53 Shane. '54 Three Coins in the Fountain. '55 Stategic Air Command. '56 Around the World in 80 Days.

YUTKEVICH, Sergei

(1904–1985). Director. Born: St Petersburg, Russia

The young Yutkevich was a painter, caught up in the artistic ferment of the early Twenties. He joined Kozintsev and Trauberg at their Factory of the Eccentric Actor (FEKS), and did some stage design, and then worked as assistant and designer on Abram Room's classic *Tretya Meshchanskaya* (1927, *Bed and Sofa*), directing some scenes himself. As solo director Yutkevich made two silent films which revealed a director who took delight in good-looking visuals, and a first sound film, *The Golden Mountains*, notable for the complex counterpointing of sound and image. Unlike many Soviet directors, Yutkevich was a survivor, but even he was briefly in disfavour when accused of 'cosmopolitanism' in the Forties. Cosmopolitan in his film tastes he assuredly was; he loved Feuillade and Pearl White, Olivier's *Hamlet* (1948) and Mickey Rooney's Puck, and Welles' *Othello* (1952), to which his own version,

slow and spectacular, stood in striking contrast. It won a prize at Cannes, though, just as Welles' film had. In the Thirties Yutkevich ran a training programme for young directors; through him, Mark Donskoi stayed in the cinema. And he scored one notable 'first': his *The Great Warrior Skanderbeg* was the first feature film ever made in Albania.

Films include: 1928 Kruzheva (Lace). '29 Chyorni Parus (The Black Sail). '31 Zlatye Gori (GB: The Golden Mountains). '32 Vstrechnyi (co-dir) (GB: Counterplan). '38 Chelovek s Ruzhyom (The Man With a Gun). '43 Noviye Pokhozdeniya Shveika (New Adventures of Schweik). '51 Przhevalskii. '54 Veliki Voin Albanii Skanderbeg (USSR-ALB) (The Great Warrior Skanderbeg). '55 Othello. '58 Rasskazi o Lenine (Stories About Lenin). '64 Lenin v Polshe (USSR-POL) (GB: Lenin in Poland). '69 Siuzhet Dlya Nebolshovo Rasskaza (USSR-FR) (Theme for a Short Story).

ZAMPA, Luigi

(b. 1905). Director/screenwriter. Born: Rome, Italy

Luigi Zampa studied scriptwriting and directing in Rome during the late Thirties and was drafted into the army during World War II to make training films. His first postwar film, *Un Americano in Vacanza*, exhibited a neorealist style which he developed in *Vivere in Pace*, a bleak condemnation of war, shot on location, which received critical acclaim. The bitter *Anni Difficili*, made in collaboration with writer Vitaliano Brancati, was an ironic comment on Italy's recent history, subject first to Fascism, then the Germans followed by the Allies. Since the mid-Fifties he has continued to write and direct many films, though his style gradually moved away from neo-realism towards a more popular, commercial approach.

Films include: 1933 Risveglio di una Città (doc). '41 L'Attore Scomparso. '42 Fra Diavolo. '45 Un Americano in Vacanza (GB: A Yank in Rome). '47 Vivere in Pace (GB: To Live in Peace); L'Onorevole Angelina (GB: Angelina). '48 Anni Difficili (USA: Difficult Years; GB: The Little Man). '52 Processo alla Città. '53 Anni Facili. '55 L'Arte di Arrangiarsi. '59 Il Magistrato (IT-

the musical Sweet Rosie O'Grady *(1943). Below: Mai Zetterling in the lifeboat drama* Seven Waves Away

SP). '67 *Le Dolci Signore* (USA: *Anyone Can Play*). '79 *Letti Selvaggi* (IT-SP).

ZANUCK, Darryl F.

(1902–1979). Producer. Born: Darryl Francis Zanuck; Wahoo, Nebraska, USA

A leading figure in Hollywood for over forty years, Zanuck was at Warner Brothers during the studio's formative years in the late Twenties and early Thirties, but is best known as the creative head in charge of 20th Century-Fox productions for most of the period from 1935 through 1970. After war service in France as a young man, he worked in a variety of jobs and tried his hand at writing. This led to employment as a gag writer at the tiny new Warner Brothers studio where he worked his way up to scriptwriter, producer and finally head of production by the late Twenties. He initiated the cycle of gangster movies and Busby Berkeley musicals before leaving to set up his own company, 20th Century Pictures, in 1933. Here his best known productions were *The House of Rothschild* and *Les Misérables* (1935), and he was the leading figure in the 1935 merger between 20th Century and the ailing Fox studio. As boss of the new 20th Century-Fox he revived the fortunes of the company, developing a new group of stars including Tyrone Power, Alice Faye, Don Ameche, Sonja Henie and later Betty Grable and Henry Fonda. Zanuck promoted the move into Technicolor during the early Forties – *The Return of Frank James* (1940), *Blood and Sand* (1941), *Wilson* (1944) – and toward location filming and socially conscious pictures later in the decade, winning the studio's first Best Picture Oscar for Elia Kazan's *Gentleman's Agreement* in 1947. He was the only producer to win the Irving Thalberg Award three times – in 1937, 1944 and 1950 – before the rules were changed limiting each producer to a single award.

Films include: 1928 *Noah's Ark*. '34 *The House of Rothschild*. '38 *Alexander's Ragtime Band*. '39 *Jesse James; Drums Along the Mohawk; Young Mr Lincoln*. '40 *The Grapes of Wrath*. '41 *How Green Was My Valley*. '50 *All About Eve*. '52 *Viva Zapata!* '56 *The Man in the Gray Flannel Suit*. '62 *The Longest Day*.

ZANUCK, Richard

(b. 1934). Producer. Born: Richard Darryl Zanuck; Los Angeles, California, USA

As the son of Darryl Zanuck young Richard grew up in Hollywood, played hide-and-seek on the Fox lot and was later educated at Stanford University. He joined the story department at 20th Century-Fox during the mid-Fifties and gained his first experience as a producer working for his father. During the Sixties he served as vice-president in charge of production after his father had been reappointed president of the studio. When both Zanucks were ousted from the company, he set up as an independent producer in partnership with David Brown. Their Zanuck-Brown Productions was responsible for two of the biggest hits of the Seventies, the Oscar-winning *The Sting* and *Jaws*.

Films include: 1959 *Compulsion*. '61 *Sanctuary*. '65 *The Sound of Music*. '69 *Butch Cassidy and the Sundance Kid*. '70 *M*A*S*H*. '73 *The Sting*. '74 *The Sugarland Express; The Black Windmill* (GB). '75 *The Eiger Sanction; Jaws*. '82 *The Verdict*.

ZANUSSI, Krzysztof

(b. 1939). Director/screenwriter. Born: Warsaw, Poland

A student of physics and philosophy before he turned to the cinema, Zanussi graduated from the Łódź film School in 1966. After completing a number of shorts he directed his first feature *The Structure of Crystals* in 1969, and developed into the leading Polish director of the Seventies. A thoughtful rather than instinctive director, who writes all his own scripts, he prefers intimate, small-scale subjects, exploring the relationship between a few characters, often within an academic setting. During recent years he has made a number of films in the West, including three pictures for German television and an Italian-Polish-British television movie about the life of Pope John Paul II. He won the Jury Prize at the Cannes Film Festival with *The Constant Factor* in 1980.

Films include: 1969 *Struktura Kryształu* (USA: *The Structure of Crystals*). '71 *Życie Rodzinne* (GB: *Family Life*); *Za Ściana* (GB: *Behind the Wall*). '73 *Iluminacja* (GB: *Illumination*). '74 *The Catamount Killing* (GER). '75 *Bilans Kwartalny* (USA: *A Woman's Decision*). '77 *Barwy Ochronne* (GB: *Camouflage*). '78 *Spirala* (GB: *The Spiral*). '80 *Kontrakt* (GB: *The Contract*); *Constans* (GB: *The Constant Factor*). '81 *Versuchung* (GER); *From a Far Country – Pope John Paul* (GB-IT-POL). '82 *Die Unerreichbare* (GER) (GB: *The Unapproachable*).

ZAVATTINI, Cesare

(b. 1902). Screenwriter. Born: Luzzara, Emilia, Italy

Gaining a variety of early experience as a journalist and writer for children's magazines with many stories and novels to his credit, Zavattini first turned to screenwriting during the mid-Thirties. During the Forties and especially during the postwar period he emerged as one of the leading theoreticians and scriptwriters of the Italian neo-realist movement. Most notable was his close collaboration with director Vittorio De Sica over a period of thirty years, from a first sensitive script about childhood, *The Children Are Watching Us* to his last, *A Brief Vacation*. A prolific writer, he was nominated for an Oscar for three of his most celebrated original scripts for De Sica – *Shoeshine* and *Bicycle Thieves*, both of which won special Oscars, and *Umberto D* – but never won the award himself.

Films include: 1943 *I Bambini ci Guardano* (co-sc) (GB: *The Children Are Watching Us*). '45 *La Freccia nel Fianco* (co-sc). '46 *Sciuscià* (USA/GB: *Shoeshine*). '47 *Un Giorno nella Vita* (co-sc). '48 *Ladri di Biciclette* (co-sc) (USA: *Bicycle Thief*; GB: *Bicycle Thieves*). '51 *Umberto D* (co-sc); *Miracolo a Milano* (co-sc) (USA/GB: *Miracle in Milan*). '56 *Il Tetto* (GB: *The Roof*). '61 *La Ciociara* (IT-FR) (GB: *Two Women*). '62 *Boccaccio '70 ep La Riffa* (IT-FR) (GB: *After the Fox*). '70 *I Girasoli* (IT-USSR) (co-sc) (USA/GB: *Sunflower*). '73 *Una Breva Vacanza* (IT-SP) (USA: *The Holiday*; GB: *A Brief Vacation*).

ZECCA, Ferdinand

(1864–1947). Director/producer. Born: Paris, France

Zecca's place in film history is secure. He was a café monologuist and musician, engaged by Charles Pathé to make gramophone records. Zecca conceived the notion of making small films to synchronize with the records, and *Le Muet Mélomane*, a talkie made in the last years of the nineteenth century, was the result. In 1900 Zecca ran Pathé's stand at the Paris Exposition, and more sound films were shown. This was a short-lived novelty, but Zecca was far from finished. He shortly became Pathé's head of production, directed many films himself, and supervised the work of others, such as Lucien Nonguet and Gaston Velle. Zecca took the 'chase' films so popular at that time to a high peak of lunatic yet precisely choreographed invention, and was thus the precursor of the Keystones and all the other action comedies. In sharp contrast, he was the first to see the possibilities of low-life and crime subjects, and his classic *Histoire d'un Crime*, which showed every detail from crime to execution, complete with death-cell dreams, was probably the first movie to fall foul of authority when the Paris Police banned the final horrors (now happily restored). And Zecca was the first to use intertitles.

Films include: 1898 *Mésaventures d'une Tête de Veau*. '99 *Le Muet Mélomane*. 1901 *Histoire d'un Crime; À la Conquête de l'Air*. '02 *Les Victimes de l'Alcoolisme; La Catastrophe de la Martinique*. '03 *La Vie d'un Joueur; La Grève*. '05 *Dix Femmes Pour un Mari; La Course à la Perruque; La Course aux Tonneaux*. '07 *L'Affaire Dreyfus*. '12–14 *Scènes de la Vie Cruelle* (series).

ZEFFIRELLI, Franco

(b. 1923). Director. Born: Florence, Italy

Zeffirelli began his career as an actor and as a set painter, serving his apprenticeship under Luchino Visconti first in the theatre and then in films. Further experience as a set and costume designer led to full director status in the theatre and he developed an international reputation during the late Fifties and Sixties. His highly developed visual sense meant that he was destined to follow Visconti into film-making. His first two features still remain his best-known works for the cinema – an adaptation of *The Taming of the Shrew* (1966), starring Elizabeth Taylor and Richard Burton, and a youthful, lively and visually stunning version of *Romeo and Juliet*, which turned out to be the most popular and commercially successful Shakespeare film ever produced. The film won Oscars for Costume Design and Cinematography and also received nominations for Best Picture and Director.

Films include: 1966 *Florence – Days of Destruction* (doc). '67 *The Taming of the Shrew* (USA-IT). '68 *Romeo and Juliet* (GB-IT). '72 *Fratello Sole, Sorella Luna* (IT-GB) (USA/GB: *Brother Sun, Sister Moon*). '77 *Jesus of Nazareth* (GB-IT) (orig. TV). '79 *The Champ* (USA). '81 *Endless Love* (USA).

ZETTERLING, Mai

(b. 1925). Actress/director. Born: Västerås, Sweden

An attractive blue-eyed blonde who first made her name as an actress in Sweden and Britain, Mai Zetterling subsequently developed in the Sixties into an intelligent writer-director of her own films, mainly dealing with modern feminist themes. After studying at the Royal Dramatic Theatre School in Stockholm she appeared on stage and in films and received acclaim for her provocative performance in *Frenzy*, directed by Alf Sjöberg from a script by Ingmar Bergman. She became well-known as an actress in British films during the period from 1947 to 1963, most notably as the star of *Frieda* and as the delightful foil for Peter Sellers in the comedy *Only Two Can Play*. As a director, too, she divided her time between Sweden and Britain, making her early shorts and *Vincent the Dutchman* (1972) for the BBC, while her first features, *Loving Couples*, strongly influenced by Bergman, and the rather more Felliniesque *Night Games* were filmed in Sweden. Most recently she has returned to Britain to direct *Scrubbers*.

Films include: 1941 *Lasse-Maja*. '44 *Hets* (USA: *Torment*; GB: *Frenzy*). '47 *Frieda* (GB). '48 *Quartet ep The Facts of Life* (GB). '49 *The Bad Lord Byron* (GB). '50 *Blackmailed* (GB). '53 *Desperate Moment* (GB). '54 *Knock on Wood* (USA). '57 *Seven Waves Away* (+co-prod) (GB) (USA: *Abandon Ship*). '61 *Only Two Can Play* (GB). '63 *The War Game* (short) (dir) (GB). '64 *Älskande Par* (dir) (USA/GB: *Loving Couples*). '65 *Lianbron*. '66 *Nattlek* (dir; +co-sc) (USA/GB: *Night Games*). '68 *Flickorna* (dir; +co-sc) (GB: *The Girls*). '82 *Scrubbers* (dir) (GB).

Above: a publicity shot of Efrem Zimbalist Jr. Right: Adolph Zukor celebrates his eightieth birthday with the help of Mary Pickford. Below: Fred Zinnemann on set for Julia

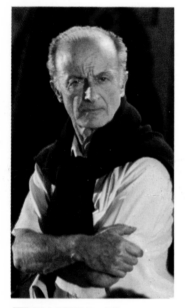

ZIMBALIST Jr, Efrem

(1923–1985). Actor. Born: New York City, USA

Educated at Yale University, Zimbalist turned to the theatre after distinguished war service. He gave up a promising career on the stage after the death of his first wife, but returned to acting during the late Fifties, branching out into television and films. Slim, dark and handsome, he is best known for his starring roles on television in *77 Sunset Strip* and *The FBI* series. He made his film debut as early as 1949, playing the younger son of Edward G. Robinson in *House of Strangers*, directed by Joseph Mankiewicz, but had his most interesting role as the sympathetic sex researcher who becomes involved with the young Jane Fonda in Cukor's *The Chapman Report*.

Films include: 1949 House of Strangers. '57 Bombers B52 (GB: No Sleep Till Dawn). '58 Too Much, Too Soon. '60 The Crowded Sky. '61 By Love Possessed. '62 The Chapman Report. '65 Harlow; The Reward. '67 Wait Until Dark. '74 Airport '75.

ZINNEMANN, Fred

(b. 1907). Director. Born: Vienna, Austria

After completing his law studies at the University of Vienna, Zinnemann became interested in the cinema. He worked as an assistant cameraman on a few films before emigrating to the USA where he was employed on a variety of features and documentaries, mainly as an assistant director. Signed by MGM in 1937 he spent the next five years directing shorts before graduating to features in 1942. His one MGM feature of note was *The Search*, starring Montgomery Clift as an American GI who befriends a refugee boy in postwar Europe. But Zinnemann's career as a director took off during the early Fifties in collaboration with producer Stanley Kramer and then at Columbia. After directing Marlon Brando's first feature, *The Men* (1950), he had his first big success with the dramatic Western *High Noon*, starring Gary Cooper. And in 1953 he had his biggest critical and commercial hit with *From Here to Eternity*, based on the James Jones novel set in Hawaii at the time of Pearl Harbor. It won eight Oscars including Best Picture and the Best Director award for Zinnemann. (He had previously been nominated for *The Search* and *High Noon* and had won his first Oscar for one of his MGM shorts in 1938.) Zinnemann was less successful with a number of his subsequent productions, solidly crafted pictures which had their dull patches and failed to attract audiences. But he made a major comeback in 1966 when he once again directed the top Oscar winner and won his own third Academy Award for a highly-acclaimed film version of the Robert Bolt play, *A Man for All Seasons*.

Films include: 1929 Menschen am Sonntag (GB: People on Sunday). '35 The Wave (doc) (MEX). '38 That Mothers Might Live (short). '48 The Search (USA-SWITZ). '52 High Noon. '53 From Here to Eternity. '55 Oklahoma! '59 The Nun's Story. '66 A Man for All Seasons (GB). '73 The Day of the Jackal (GB-FR). '77 Julia. '82 Five Days One Summer.

ZSIGMOND, Vilmos

(b. 1930). Cinematographer. Born: Hungary

Vilmos Zsigmond studied at the Academy of Film and Theatre Arts in Budapest (1951–55), graduating with fellow cameraman Laszlo Kovacs. They both fled after the 1956 uprising, and Zsigmond did odd jobs in New York and Los Angeles before gaining a reputation as a cameraman on television commercials. He worked on low-budget pictures for most of the Sixties; but Kovacs, who had shot Robert Altman's *That Cold Day in the Park* (1969), recommended his compatriot to Altman for *McCabe and Mrs Miller*. Zsigmond consolidated his reputation for fine location photography and sumptuous use of colour with two more films for Altman and *Deliverance* for John Boorman. He shared a Cinematography Oscar with Kovacs and others for *Close Encounters of the Third Kind*.

Films include: 1971 McCabe and Mrs Miller; Red Sky at Night; The Hired Hand. '72 Images (EIRE); Deliverance. '73 The Long Goodbye. '74 The Sugarland Express. '77 Close Encounters of the Third Kind (co-photo). '78 The Deer Hunter; The Last Waltz (add. photo. only). '80 Heaven's Gate.

ZUGSMITH, Albert

(b. 1910). Producer/director/screenwriter. Born: Atlantic City, New Jersey, USA

Even while a youngster, Albert Zugsmith showed entrepreneurial talent, organizing a booking agency for teenage bands on Atlantic City's famous seaside boardwalk. In 1935 he founded the Atlantic City *Daily World*, becoming its editor and publisher. He acted as consultant to newspapers and radio stations; and in 1947 he merged with Smith Davies of Cleveland, Ohio, to negotiate major sales and refinancings of newspapers throughout the USA. He moved into television and then, bitten by the film bug during a brief teenage Hollywood stint as a band publicist, he went back

there as a producer. His period of glory came in the late Fifties, when he produced films by Douglas Sirk and Orson Welles at Universal. Then he joined MGM's list of producers as head of his own company and soon began to direct as well as produce cheap and often prurient shockers, including the minor cult film *Confessions of an Opium Eater*, very loosely based on Thomas De Quincey's Victorian memoirs.

Films include: 1952 Invasion USA (co-prod. only). '56 Written on the Wind (prod. only). '57 The Incredible Shrinking Man (prod. only); The Tarnished Angels (prod. only); Touch of Evil (prod. only). '58 High School Confidential (prod. only). '59 The Beat Generation (prod. only). '62 Confessions of an Opium Eater (dir; +prod. only) (GB: Evils of Chinatown). '64 Fanny Hill: Memoirs of a Woman of Pleasure (prod. only) (GER). '69 Sappho Darling (sc. only). '70 Two Roses and a Golden Rod (dir; +sc. only).

ZUKOR, Adolph

(1873–1976). Executive. Born: Ricse, Hungary

A poor Hungarian immigrant who reached the United States in 1889, Zukor went into the fur trade and built up a prosperous business in New York and Chicago. Moving on to run penny-arcades, he was in time for the nickelodeon craze, and with Marcus Loew developed a major theatre and cinema chain. In 1912 he imported the French feature film, *La Reine Elisabeth*, with Sarah Bernhardt. It succeeded, and Zukor took the idea further by forming his Famous Players in Famous Plays company, with Broadway impresario Daniel Frohman to provide the players, and Edwin S. Porter to direct. Now Zukor rose rapidly to dominate the industry. Famous Players merged with the Jesse Lasky Company to become Famous Players–Lasky; the distribution chain Paramount was taken over, and Paramount eventually became the name of Zukor's whole concern. In the Twenties a huge chain of cinemas was added. Until 1936 Zukor was president of Paramount. After that he held the chairmanship, and was still chairman emeritus when he died at the age of 103. But by then his cherished company was a small part of the vast Gulf and Western complex. Zukor was not a film-maker. Except for a period in the Thirties when he went to Hollywood to pull the company out of financial difficulty, he stayed in New York (where until the Thirties Paramount also had studios), planning his deals and guarding his manifold interests. He was a reserved man who made friends with difficulty, but rivals and enemies felt his full ruthlessness. Samuel Goldwyn and Lewis Selznick were two whom Zukor worsted; Goldwyn recovered, Selznick and others did not. The long nocturnal walks which Zukor took through New York as he made his critical decisions became part of his legend; for his company those decisions invariably turned out well. He called his 1953 autobiography *The Public Is Never Wrong*. He might have said that of himself – almost certainly he thought it.